GENESIS

translated and interpreted by Hermann Gunkel

Mercer Library of Biblical Studies

Hermann Gunkel, *Genesis*
Translated by Mark E. Biddle. Foreword by Ernest W. Nicholson. 1997.

Forthcoming

Peter Stuhlmacher, *Vom Verstehen des Neuen Testament: Eine Hermeneutik* (^{2}1986)
Bernhard Duhm (1847–1928), *Das Buch Jesaia* (^{4}1922)
Hermann Gunkel (1862–1932), *Einleitung in die Psalmen* (1933)

GENESIS

translated and interpreted
by
HERMANN GUNKEL

translated by
MARK E. BIDDLE

foreword by
ERNEST W. NICHOLSON

MERCER UNIVERSITY PRESS · 1997 · MACON, GEORGIA

ISBN 0-86554-517-0   MUP/H400

The paper used in this publication meets the minimum requirements
of American National Standard for Information Sciences—
Permanence of Paper for Printed Library Materials, ANSI Z39.48-1984.

Library of Congress Cataloging-in-Publication Data

Bible.   O.T.   Genesis.   English.   Biddle.   1997.
Genesis / translated and interpreted by Hermann Gunkel ;
English translation (from the ninth German Impression, 1977
= the third edition, 1910) by Mark E. Biddle.
[12]+lxxxviii+478 pp. 7x10" (18x25.5 cm.)
Includes bibliographical references.
ISBN 0-86554-517-0
1. Bible. O.T. Genesis—Commentaries.
I. Gunkel, Hermann, 1862–1932.
II. Biddle, Mark E. III. Title.
BS1233.B53 1997
222'.11077—dc21   97-11506

CIP
r97

Contents

Foreword to the English Translation

by Ernest W. Nicholson

Hermann Gunkel as a Pioneer of Modern Old Testament Study

Hermann Gunkel was born in 1862 in the town of Springe near Hannover. He studied at Göttingen University and taught Old Testament at Halle University and then Berlin and was appointed professor at Giessen in 1907. He returned to a professorship at Halle in 1920 from which he retired in 1927. He died in 1932.

Gunkel was one of the most creative and influential scholars of the twentieth century. His main contribution was the introduction of new methods of research which transformed the face of Old Testament study and, indeed, indirectly of New Testament study also. In his commentary on Genesis (first edition 1901) he built upon the current results of Pentateuchal research but at the same time both in the methods he employed and in the results he achieved went significantly beyond them. The commentary was thus itself a pioneering work. To appreciate its achievement it is necessary to know something of the background in Pentateuchal research against which it was written as well as another major contribution by Gunkel published a few years earlier.

1

By the time Gunkel was beginning his professional career the so-called Documentary Theory of the Pentateuch, which was so brilliantly argued by Julius Wellhausen in the 1870s, had gained the support of most leading Old Testament scholars of the day. The focus of this theory was upon the composition of the Pentateuch as a literary corpus. The method employed was literary critical or source critical in the sense that the different sources (J, E, D, P) and the redactional material that now unites them were separated from each other on grounds of style, vocabulary, and the like, as well as the distinctive theological and religious outlook and interest that could be discerned in each source. The emphasis was accordingly upon the creativity of the separate authors or "schools" of authors who composed the original documents and upon the contributions of the various redactors who combined them.

As a result, little importance was credited to the precompositional stage in the development of the literature. That the authors of the various documents were frequently dependent upon inherited oral tradition was generally acknowledged. Now and again attention was drawn to the antiquity of the subject matter of a passage over against the relatively late literary expression of it by the authors of the Pentateuchal sources. But no serious attempt was made by Wellhausen and his followers to elevate the investigation of the precompositional stage in the emergence of the literature to a subject for research in its own right. Quite the contrary was the case. Wellhausen himself held a low estimate of the significance of the precompositional stage and spurned the task of investigating it as of no more than antiquarian interest and outside the scope proper of the theologian and exegete. The work of creative planning, arrangement, and composition of the diverse materials in the sources of the Pentateuch was held to be the accomplishment of the authors of these sources; it was they who gave order to, and wove connections between, whatever medley of disconnected oral materials they inherited.

In the closing years of the nineteenth century, however, there emerged a movement which rejected as inadequate the preoccupation of Wellhausen and his followers with the strictly compositional stage in the creation of the Pentateuch and whose members were confident that rich results were to be gained by just such a study of the precompositional stage in the history of Pentateuchal traditions and literature.

The movement in question was *Die religionsgeschichtliche Schule* (the History of Religions School). Its earliest members attributed its foundation to Albert Eichhorn (1856–1926), professor of church history at Halle from 1885, though perhaps it would be more accurate to say that a number of scholars were responsible for its emergence but on the basis of his ideas and inspiration.[1]

Within the field of biblical studies the emphasis of this movement, as its name indicates, was upon the historical development of religion, whether that of ancient Israel or of Judaism or of Christianity. Such an undertaking was not in itself new. What was new were the methods these scholars now brought to bear on the task, and the deeper dimensions they endeavored to uncover in the origin and historical development of biblical religion. Thus among a series of "theses" laid down by Albert Eichhorn in 1886 was: "Any interpretation of a myth which does not consider the origin and development of the myth is false."[2] Eichhorn regarded the preoccupation of scholars with a purely literary-critical handling of the biblical materials inadequate for a full investigation of the origin and development of biblical religion. It would not do simply to separate the sources from each other, arrange them chronologically, and then solely on this basis attempt to depict the history and development of the religion. One must focus attention upon the *substance* and *ideas* of the texts and seek to trace the origin, development, and transformation of these in the period before they found final expression in the relatively late literary documents in which they are now contained. In short, with Eichhorn "the attention of modern scholarship became directed to the period of tradition development."[3] Thus entered what has become known as the traditiohistorical method of inquiry into the biblical literature.

2

In Old Testament research it was Hermann Gunkel who pioneered these new ideas. His first major work, published in 1895, was *Creation and Chaos in the Beginning and*

---

[1]See Hugo Gressmann, *Albert Eichhorn und die Religionsgeschichtliche Schule* (Göttingen: Vandenhoeck & Ruprecht, 1924). Douglas A. Knight has offered a detailed description and discussion of traditiohistorical research in his book *Rediscovering the Traditions of Israel*, SBL Dissertation Series 9 (Missoula MT: Society of Biblical Literature, 1973).

[2]Cited in Gressmann, *Albert Eichhorn*, 8.

[3]Knight, *Rediscovering the Traditions of Israel*, 71.

at the End of Time. A Religiohistorical Investigation of Genesis 1 and Revelation 12,[4] which was dedicated to Albert Eichhorn and could be said to be a working out, with regard to the biblical creation myths from Genesis 1 to Revelation 12, of Eichhorn's "thesis" noted above.

Gunkel's preliminary remarks concerning his approach are directed specifically against Wellhausen's handling of Genesis 1. Wellhausen drew a sharp contrast between the nature of this chapter and that of the creation-paradise narrative which follows in Genesis 2–3. In the case of the latter "we are on the ground of marvel and myth"; the materials for this narrative come from "the many-colored traditions of the old world of Western Asia. Here we are in the enchanted garden of ideas of genuine antiquity; the fresh early smell of earth meets us in the breeze."[5] But Genesis 1, Wellhausen argued, is quite unlike this: "It would be vain to deny the exalted ease and the uniform greatness that give the narrative its character. The beginning especially is incomparable: 'The earth was without form and void, and darkness lay upon the deep, and the Spirit of God moved upon the water. Then God said: Let there be light, and there was light.' But chaos being given, all the rest is spun out of it: all that follows is reflection, systematic construction; we can easily follow the calculation from point to point."[6]

Certainly, Gunkel agreed, Genesis 1 as it lies before us is not to be considered ancient; in outlook and theology it "points us to the time when reasoned reflection has replaced the old poetic way of contemplating nature."[7] Nevertheless, he argued, this does not mean that Genesis 1 is nothing more than the invention of its author. In considering such a narrative "we must differentiate strictly between a narrative as it lies before us and its prehistory. In dealing with the narratives in Genesis it is the task of research, after the literary facts have been ascertained, to raise the question—often much more important—whether perhaps something can be stated concerning the earlier history of the narrative. By doing so it will not infrequently be seen that, though handed down to us in a later revised condition, there is here subject matter from a period in Israel long before that of the extant record of it."[8] By this he means: "It is the common fate of older narratives conserved in a younger form, that certain features, which once had good meaning in the earlier context, are transmitted in a new association to which they have in the meantime lost connection. Such old features—fragments of an earlier whole, without connection in the present account and hardly understandable in the intellectual situation of the narrator—betray to the researcher the existence as well as individual features of an earlier form of the present narrative."[9]

---

[4]*Schöpfung und Chaos in Urzeit und Endzeit. Eine religionsgeschichtliche Untersuchung über Gen 1 und Ap Joh 12* (Göttingen: Vandenhoeck & Ruprecht, 1895).

[5]*Prolegomena zur Geschichte Israels* (Berlin: George Reimer, 1883) 320. ET: *Prolegomena to the History of Ancient Israel* (Edinburgh: Adam & Charles Black, 1885; repr.: New York/Cleveland: Meridian Books, 1957) 304.

[6]Ibid., 298.

[7]*Schöpfung und Chaos*, 5.

[8]Ibid., 5-6.

[9]Ibid., 6.

This latter statement describes succinctly what lies at the heart of the traditiohistorical method, and Gunkel proceeds to draw attention to the sort of features he has in mind in considering the narrative in Genesis 1. Thus, for example, the notion of "chaos" itself, as Wellhausen conceded, was inherited by the author from much more ancient mythology. Other features point in the same direction, for example, the idea that in the beginning there was darkness and water. Such an idea was certainly not the invention of the Priestly author; it originated in an ancient myth. Or, again, the term *t^hom* ("deep") without the definite article betrays itself as having come down from a much more ancient myth. Similarly, an ancient mythological conception is echoed in the depiction of "the Spirit of God" "brooding" upon the face of the deep. Thus one after another Gunkel drew attention to features in this narrative which its author inherited from a more ancient source and on account of which Gunkel gave the second chapter of his book the title "Genesis 1 is not a free composition of the author."

Gunkel also ranged over other allusions to, or features of, ancient myths which are preserved in the Old Testament and which echo the same myth discernible behind Genesis 1 or variant forms of such a myth referring to the primeval sea monster Rahab, Leviathan, and so forth. His purpose was not merely to trace the origins of such mythical material; he was more concerned to investigate the ways in which such ancient material was adapted and transformed within the development of Israel's own religion. By such means something of the very distinctive differences between Israelite religion, most notably its monotheism, and that of other ancient Near Eastern religions are brought into relief.

3

Here then was an example of the results that could be achieved from a careful investigation of possible traditional elements preserved within literary documents of a much later period. But a further step remained to be taken. In *Creation and Chaos* Gunkel was predominantly concerned with tracing the history of tradition with, for the most part, only incidental attention to the literary forms whereby ancient traditional material was transmitted and developed in the course of Israelite history. With the publication of his commentary on Genesis Gunkel gave much more attention to the "types" (*Gattungen*) or "forms" of Hebrew literature; that is, he now concentrated not only on the history of traditions but on "literary history" (*Literturgeschichte*) about which he wrote, in addition to his introduction to the commentary on Genesis, many shorter contributions.[10]

By "literary history" Gunkel had in mind a history of Hebrew literature in a different sense from that which characterized the well-known genre of "Old Testament introduction," though much had been achieved by the latter. We have to remember, he argued, that

---

[10]"Fundamental Problems of Hebrew Literary History," in *What Remains of the Old Testament? and Other Essays* (London, 1928) 57-68, originally published as "Die Grundprobleme der israelitischen Literturgeschichte," *Deutsche Literaturzeitung* 27 (1906): 1797-1800, 1861-66, reprinted in *Reden und Aufsätze* (Göttingen, 1913) 29-38; "Literaturgeschichte," RGG, 2nd ed., vol. 3 (Tübingen, 1929) cols. 1677-80; "Sagen und Legenden II. In Israel," RGG, vol. 5 (1931) cols. 49-60; *Das Märchen im Alten Testament* (Tübingen, 1913), ET: *The Folktale in the Old Testament* (Sheffield, 1991).

in literature such as that of ancient Israel, the personalities of the individual authors are of far less importance than in literature of later ages. In antiquity the power of custom was far greater than it is in the modern world, and besides, like everything else connected with religion, religious literature is very conservative. Accordingly a history of Hebrew literature has comparitively little concern with the personality of the writers, but must primarily occupy itself with the literary "types" that lie deeper than any individual effort.

Many such types had already been incidentally identified by scholars: myths, folk-tales, popular stories, cultic legends, historical narratives, and, in poetic literature, dirges, love songs, taunt songs, thanksgiving psalms, psalms of praise, distinctive types of prophetic oracles, and so forth. It is the task of literary history to study them systematically in order to show the materials with which each type deals and the form it necessarily assumes. It will be found that each type originally belonged to a quite definite "setting in the life" (*Sitz im Leben*); that is, the particular literary form in which a subject matter found expression was itself dictated by the particular setting in life to which it was addressed. Thus in studying such literary types "we must in each case have the whole situation clearly before us and ask ourselves, Who is speaking? Who are the listeners? What is the *mise-en-scène* at the time? What effect is aimed at?"[11] Such a study will also reveal that with few exceptions such types were originally not written but oral compositions.

The importance of this method of "type criticism" or, as it was later to become more familiarly known, "form criticism" (*Formgeschichte*) in the study of a text such as Genesis is as follows. First, since different sorts of subject matter found expression in different literary types or forms, by isolating the original individual literary units the scholar is able to penetrate behind the present larger literary context of the material to an earlier stage in its formation and transmission. Type or form criticism thus reveals itself as an essential handmaid of the traditiohistorical quest; that is, an investigation of the form in which, and the process whereby, a particular subject matter has been transmitted illuminates the origin and development of what has been so transmitted. Second, however, the isolation of such original literary units enables the scholar to uncover the earlier stages in the history and growth of the literature itself. In this way, for example, the extent to which the Pentateuchal materials had already taken shape during the long period before the work of the Yahwist and Elohist writers would be illuminated.

When Gunkel applied this method of form criticism in his study of Genesis he found a great variety of such types: myths such as are found in Genesis 1–11; stories about individual patriarchs; ethnological legends explaining the origin of the relationship between different tribes or peoples; etiological stories explaining some custom or institution; cultic legends telling of the foundation of particular sanctuaries; etymological stories explaining how individuals or places acquired their names; and so forth.

Of the great antiquity of many of these Gunkel was in no doubt. They are much older than the Pentateuchal literary sources in which they are now found. He pointed out, for example, that the tribal and race names which many of them preserve are almost forgotten in other Old Testament literature: from the historical records of Israel we know nothing of Shem, Ham, and Japheth, of Abel and Cain, of Esau and Jacob, nothing of Hagar and scarcely anything of Ishmael. The great age of such stories is also indicated by, for

---

[11]*Reden und Aufsätze*, 33; "Fundamental Problems of Hebrew Literary History," 62.

example, "the earthiness of many elements that reveal to us a religion and morality of an ancient period. One need consider only the many mythological remnants such as the narrative of the angelic marriages (6:1ff.), of Jacob's struggle with the deity (32:35ff.), of the many stories of the patriarchs' lying and deception, and so forth."[12] It is also evident, Gunkel claimed, that not a little of this material was inherited by Israel from its ancient Near Eastern neighbors; the discussion of the origin of the creation myths in the Old Testament in his *Creation and Chaos* had already exemplified this. He argued that it is probable that most of the stories concerning the patriarchs were in circulation before Israel entered Canaan. In particular, the religion displayed in these legends, containing here and there as they do the names of pre-Yahwistic gods (El Olam, El Bethel, El Shaddai, etc.) points to their non-Israelite origin. He saw it as one of the most brilliant achievements of the Israelites that they were able to take over such ancient material and adapt it to their own national religion and ethos.

It is already clear from these observations that Gunkel believed the authors of the Pentateuchal sources to have been heirs of an already existing mass of much older material. In just what shape, however, did it come to them? Wellhausen had claimed that "Oral tradition among the people includes only individual stories which surely come from the same circle of thought yet which are not organized into a planned totality. The recorder [by this Wellhausen of course means the authors of J, E, etc.] of the individual narratives is the one who initiates the plan and the connections."[13]

Gunkel accepted that popular stories such as Genesis contains originally existed as independent units; even in their present form they provide clear evidence of this. The original unity of the separate stories is shown, for example, in the fact that they are in each case filled with a single harmonious sentiment: in the story of God's command to Abraham to sacrifice Jacob emotion is predominant; in that of Jacob's deception of Isaac, humor; in the story of Sodom, moral earnestness; in the story of Babel, the fear of Almighty God. He went on to argue, however, that in many instances such stories were already joined together at the oral stage of transmission and that it was not left to the authors of the Pentateuchal sources to initiate "the plan and the connections," as Wellhausen had argued. In other words, already at the oral stage individual stories concerning the same individual or dwelling upon a similar theme were attracted to each other and were thus combined to form "cycles of legends" (*Sagenkränze*).[14] According to Gunkel,

---

[12]See below, xlviii.

[13]Wellhausen, *Die Composition des Hexateuchs und der Historischen Bücher des Alten Testaments*, 3rd ed. (Berlin: George Reimer, 1899) 8.

"Die Composition des Hexateuchs," *Jahrbücher für Deutsche Theologie* 21 (1876): 393-450, 531-602, and 22 (1877): 407-79. The articles were subsequently reprinted as in his *Skizzen und Vorarbeiten* II (Berlin, 1885). A second edition with a supplement revising some earlier conclusions as well as further reflection on various Pentateuchal texts in the intervening years was published in *Die Composition des Hexateuchs und der Historischen Bücher des Alten Testaments* (Berlin: George Reimer, 1889); the 3rd ed. appeared in 1899 and the 4th ed. in 1963 (Berlin: Walter de Gruyter). References here are to the 3rd ed.

[14]Though not wholly satisfactory, the translation "legend" for the German *Sage* (plural *Sagen*)—as consistently below—is preferable to "saga," which connotes a more extensive narration (e.g., the Icelandic sagas) than the brief narratives in Genesis about the patriarchs.

one such "cycle," though here the original legends have been much more artistically and skillfully woven together, the story as a whole displaying a fully developed narrative art as against the much older briefly told legends, to the extent indeed that the Joseph narrative is more appropriately classified as a *novelle* than a "cycle" of legends.

4

The influence of the methods pioneered by Gunkel upon subsequent Old Testament study can scarcely be overestimated. To a large extent they set the agenda for research for decades to come. Indeed, it is no exaggeration to say that there has not been an area of Old Testament research in the twentieth century that has not been indebted directly or indirectly to Gunkel's work. Among his writings, none has proved more influential than his commentary on Genesis both for its contributiuon to the development of the new methods he introduced and also for its own insights into the diverse materials which that book comprises.

The translation of Gunkel's *Genesis* into English, thus making it available to a much wider readership, is long overdue. It is all the more welcome at a time when there is renewed debate about key issues with which it is concerned in the study of Genesis and of the Pentateuch as a whole.

Translator's Preface

Perhaps the greatest challenge to the translator of theological German, especially when the German original dates from the turn of the century, is the charge to faithfully render the original into readable contemporary English. These dual requirements often conflict with one another and must be balanced. For example, Gunkel preferred the "scholarly passive," characteristic of a certain German style. I have frequently chosen to tighten the syntax in English, replacing Gunkel's passives with active constructions. On the other hand, for example, I have not attempted to correct an earlier era's gender exclusive language for two unequal reasons. First, any such paraphrasing would have risked adulterating Gunkel with contemporary ideology—a practice to which he vigorously objected in biblical studies. Second, editing Gunkel to make him more gender inclusive would likely have lengthened an already substantial volume. I hope, at least, that determination and effort stand in some directly proportionate relationship to the reliability and readability of the final product.

Readers who wish to consult the original will find access facilitated by references to pagination that appear, as nearly as permitted by the peculiarities of German syntax, at the end of the section relating to the original page. For example, <1> marks the end of original page 1 and the beginning of original page 2.

The German original includes Gunkel's own translation of Genesis. To avoid the comedy of a translation once removed, since Gunkel's commentary itself calls attention to unique features of his translation, and for considerations of space, I have opted to omit the text of Genesis in this English edition. At any rate, Gunkel supports unusual translations in the discussion in the commentary.

I thank Mercer University Press Publisher Cecil P. Staton, Jr. for his recommending the project; and Senior Editor Edmon L. Rowell, Jr., who edited the translation, for his attention and care. I offer the translation in gratitude to my mentor Prof. Dr. Hans Heinrich Schmid.

April 1997   *Mark E. Biddle*

Foreword to the Third Edition

For the third edition I have carefully and thoroughly revised the whole work over the course of several years. Very few pages have not been modified to a greater or lesser degree and very many have been given an entirely new appearance. Indeed, only in rare cases have I offered the viewpoint I represented earlier. Instead, I have been satisfied, without comment on my former position, to include what I now consider correct. Extensive new material, especially folklore and history of legend, has been added. Thus, my Genesis has become a new book, although the spirit of the whole, I think, remains the same.

Certain very minor discrepancies, attributable to the long period of preparation for publication, may be excused. My final position on matters is expressed in the introduction, printed last.

My warmest thanks I owe to all my helpful colleagues and friends whose advice has so often assisted me, especially my old and trusted friends Professor Zimmern in Leipzig and Professor Greßmann in Berlin, and not least to the publishers, who have shown patience throughout the long years of slow progress toward publication.

Those who wish further information concerning my literary-historical investigations may refer to my popular work *Elias, Jahve, und Baal* (1906); to the essay concerning Ruth in the *Deutschen Rundschau* 32 (1905): 1ff.; further to "Israelitische Literatur" in *Kultur der Gegenwart* 1/7 (1906): 51ff.; and to various essays in *Religion in Geschichte und Gegenwart*. How long until Old Testament scholars finally understand what a mighty task literary-historical problems present them, \<v\> even in the realm of the narratives, and when will the testament of the great Herder finally be executed?

The informed reader will understand why I have not interacted with the hypotheses of Jensen (*Gilgamesch Epos in der Weltliteratur*, 1906) and Völter (*Ägypten und die Bibel*, 4th ed., 1909). I have also not cited the purported Masai primal narrative published by Mercker (*Die Masai*, 1904). It seems undeniable to me that the biblical narratives have had a marked effect, even in wording, on these Masai narratives. I have reported the textual emendations suggested by Sievers and others for "metrical" reasons only when they are also supported on substantively convincing grounds.

The book is dedicated to [Adolf Harnack] the man among all my theological teachers from whom, next to my father, I have learned most and whose cordial goodwill accompanied my decades of study.

Gießen, February 1910   *Hermann Gunkel*

Introduction

The Legends of Genesis

¶1. Genesis Is a Collection of Legends

Reuß, *Das Alte Testament* 3:57ff.; *Geschichte der heiligen Schriften A.T.* ¶¶130ff.; Sellin, *Biblische Urgeschichte*, 14ff.

1. Does Genesis (that is, the so-called "First Book of Moses") recount history or legend? This is no longer a question for the modern historian. But it is, nevertheless, worthwhile to make clear the reasons for the modern attitude.

Historiography is not an inborn ability of the human intellect. Instead, it arose in the course of human history at a certain point in development. Uncivilized peoples do not write history. Incapable of objectively interpreting their experiences, they have no interest in reliably transmitting the events of their time to posterity. Their experiences become discolored under their hand; experience and imagination intermingle. They are able to present historical events only in poetic form, in songs and legends. Only at a certain stage of culture does objectivity mature to the point and the drive to communicate one's own experiences to posterity becomes so great that historiography can arise. Such historiography deals with the great public events, the deeds of the leaders of the people, the kings, and especially the wars. Consequently, in order to develop, historiography requires a state organized in some way. In a later time, sometimes much later, the art of historiography the human race learned from the history of the state was applied to other realms of human life. Memoirs or family histories also developed then. Many groups of people, however, never attained strict historiography and remained at the legend (or its modern analogies) phase. Thus we find two different types of historical tradition in ancient civilized peoples: strict historiography alongside popular tradition that sometimes deals with the same material, but in a popular-poetic manner, and that sometimes refer to the earlier, prehistorical period. Historical memories can also be preserved in such popular traditions, although in a poetic treatment.

2. Historiography developed in Israel in precisely this fashion. In the time that gave us Genesis, Israel had long possessed <vii> a, by ancient standards, highly developed historiography, which, as usual, dealt with the deeds of kings and especially with wars. The accounts of the so-called 2 Samuel, especially, can be mentioned as a testimonial to this historiography.[1] At the same time, however, legend must also have had its place in such a poetically gifted people as Israel. Since, incomprehensibly, legend and falsehood have been confused with one another, there has been some hesitancy to accept the existence of legends in the OT. But the legend is not a lie. Instead it is a specific genre of literature.

---

[1]Cf. my article "Geschichtsschreibung im AT," in *RGG*.

Legend—the word is employed here in none other than the generally acknowledged sense—is a popular, long-transmitted, poetic account dealing with past persons or events. Now if the advanced spirit of OT religion made use of many types of literature, why not this one? Indeed, poetry and poetic narrative, too, were especially dear to Israelite religion, as to religion in general. Poetic narrative is much more capable than prose of communicating ideas, including religious ideas: "Legends are infinitely deeper, freer, and truer than chronicles and histories. How would we evaluate the longest and most reliable chronicles of all the Burgundian kings over against Siegfried and Chriemhild?"[2] Genesis is much more a book of religion than a book of kings. Legends are surely present in the OT. One need only think of Samson and Jonah. Therefore, the question of whether the accounts of Genesis are history or legend does not involve belief or unbelief, but simply better understanding. It has been objected that Jesus and the apostles apparently regarded these accounts as reality and not poetry. Certainly. But NT figures had no particular stance regarding such questions. Instead, they shared the opinions of their time. We may not, therefore, seek information in the NT concerning questions of the history of OT literature.

3. Since legend and history differ considerably in origin and by nature, many characteristics distinguish the two. A chief characteristic is that legend usually originated as an oral tradition, history in written form. Both are grounded in the nature of the two genres. Circles unaccustomed to writing transmit legend. Historiography, however, a type of scientific endeavor, presumes the practice of writing. At the same time, committing a tradition to writing serves to establish it. Oral tradition cannot remain pure over time, nor is it, consequently, a sufficient medium for history. Now Genesis clearly contains the final written record of oral tradition. The patriarchal narratives do not seem to suggest that they were written by the patriarchs themselves. Instead, at many points, the significant period of time lying between the fathers' time and the narrators' time <viii> is obvious ("until this day," 19:38; the kings of Edom until David are listed, 36:31ff.; the phrase "the Canaanites lived in the land at that time" [12:6; 13:7] must have been written at a time when this people had long since vanished). The overall style of the accounts, in particular, however, can only be understood on the presumption of their oral transmission—as will be shown below (¶3:4). This circumstance is especially apparent in the many variants treated below (¶4:4). If, however, Genesis contains oral tradition dealing with the far-distant past, then, according to the observations above, it contains legend.

4. A further distinguishing characteristic involves the circles in which legend and history circulate. The actual subject of history is great public events. Historians discuss private circumstances only if they have public significance. But legend discusses personal and private matters dear to the people and it loves to portray political situations and personalities so as to connect them to popular interests. History must recount how and why David was able to liberate Israel from the Philistines; legend prefers to recount how the boy David once killed a Philistine giant. How does the material in Genesis relate to this? It contains—with the exception of a single chapter (14)—nothing dealing with great political events. Its subject is not the history of kings and princes; instead it deals primarily with the history of a private family. We hear a multitude of details, credible or not, without value, for the most part, for proper (political) history: Abraham was pious and

---

[2]Paulsen, *Deutsche Schule* (1901), 139.

noble and he once rejected his concubine out of love for his wife; Jacob deceived his brother; Rachel and Leah were jealous. These are "insignificant anecdotes from country life—stories about wells and water disputes—and from the bedroom." Pleasant enough to read, they record anything other than historical events. The historiographer does not report such things, but popular legend tradition delights in such details. When Abraham placed his whole confidence in God, when Jacob buried foreign gods at Shechem, and other such events attracted no public attention.

5. Any report purporting to be a credible, historical reminiscence also requires a conceivable pathway leading from the eyewitness of the event reported to the reporter. The situation differs for legend, the creation of tradition and imagination. One need only apply this criterion to the first accounts of Genesis to recognize their character immediately. No human was present at creation. No human tradition reaches to the time of our race's origin, the primordial peoples, the primordial languages. In earlier times, before the decipherment of Egyptian and Babylonian documents, Israelite tradition may have been considered so ancient that it seemed possible to seek here <ix> such recollections of prehistoric circumstances. Now that the world has clearly revealed itself to us, however, so that we see that the Israelite people is one of the youngest in the neighborhood, such suppositions are totally disproved. Millennia elapse from the rise of the aboriginal peoples of the Near East to the appearance of the people of Israel. Therefore, Israelite historical traditions concerning the primordial times cannot be seriously discussed. Very significant doubts also arise, however, concerning the patriarchal narratives. According to the tradition, the 400 years of Israel's sojourn in Egypt followed the patriarchal period. Nothing is recounted from this period. Historical memory has apparently been completely erased here, except for a few genealogies. A multitude of insignificant details, however, are reported concerning the patriarchal period. How is it conceivable that a people can preserve the most minor details in the history of its ancestors? Oral tradition cannot preserve such details reliably in such freshness for such a long time. And now, let us consider the narratives in detail. In most cases, the question of how the reporter could know the things he recounts may not even be asked if one does not wish to occasion laughter. How does the narrator of the Flood Narrative know the height of the water? Is Noah supposed to have measured it? How did one learn what God in heaven said or thought to himself or in the heavenly council (cf. 1; 2:18; 6:3, 6-7; 11:6-7)?

6. The most obvious characteristic of legend is that it frequently reports extraordinary things incredible to us. The reality of this poetry differs from the reality pertinent to prosaic life and ancient Israel also considered many things possible that seem impossible to us. Thus, Genesis reports many things that contradict our advanced knowledge. We know that there are many more species of animals than could be accommodated in an ark; that Ararat is not the highest mountain on the earth; that the firmament of heaven, whose creation is recounted in Gen 1:6ff., is not a reality but an optical illusion; that the stars could not have come into being after the plants, as Genesis portrays it; that the earth's flowing water does not, as Gen 2:10-14 contends, come largely from four major streams; that the Euphrates and the Tigris do not share a common source; that the Dead Sea had long been present when people lived in Palestine and did not first develop, as Gen 14:3 assumes, in historical times; that a chronology that counts only 2,666 years from the creation to the Exodus from Egypt is entirely impossible, not only according to geological evi-

dence, but also according to the historical reports of the Babylonians and the Egyptians; and so forth. Most of the many etymologies of names in Genesis do not even merit consideration according to the state of our linguistic knowledge. Indeed, early names and even a word such as Babel are naively derived from the Hebrew on the assumption, obvious to ancient Israel but entirely impossible for us, that the language of earliest humanity was Hebrew. The theory underlying the patriarchal legends that all the peoples originated through the expansion of one family and one patriarch each is extremely childish (cf. below ¶2:4 <x> and in the commentary, 86-87). Following our modern historical worldview, truly not an imaginative construct but based on the observation of facts, we consider the other view entirely impossible. If the modern historian is still rather cautious regarding what he declares impossible, he will still certainly maintain that animals—snakes or donkeys—do not speak and have never spoken, that there is no tree whose fruits grant immortality or knowledge, that angels and humans cannot reproduce (6:1ff.), that one cannot defeat a world-class army with a force of 318 allies (14:14-15), and that no human can live for 969 years (5:27). It is especially remarkable, however, that the Hebrew account does not even perceive the great improbability of the things reported: the first woman is not amazed when the serpent begins to speak to her; the narrator does not even ask how Noah was able to bring the animals into the ark; etc. This feature clearly indicates to us that we would do injustice to this naiveté to incorporate it into sober reality. Since the accounts of Genesis are mostly religious in nature, they constantly speak of God. The way, however, the accounts speak of God provides one of the most certain criteria for whether they are meant historically or poetically. Here, too, the historian must be aware of worldview. We believe God works in the world as the quiet, hidden, basis of all things. Sometimes, his efficacy can almost be apprehended in particularly momentous and impressive events and persons. We sense his reign in the wondrous interrelationship of things. But he never appears to us as an active agent alongside others, but always as the ultimate cause of all. The situation differs significantly in many Genesis accounts. God walks in Paradise, forms people with his own hands, and closes the doors of the Ark (7:16). Indeed, he breathes something of his own breath into the man and he makes failed attempts with the animals (2:19-20). He smells Noah's sacrifice (8:21). He appears to Abraham and Lot in the form of a traveler (Gen 18-19), or the angel calls from heaven (22:11; etc.). God appears to Abraham once in his true form as a burning torch and a smoking firepot (15:17)! Characteristically of God's speeches in Genesis, he almost always speaks, not in the dark hours of a person's deepest emotion, in ecstasy, i.e., as the prophets heard God's voice, but quite simply as one person to another (12:1; etc.). We can understand such accounts as the naiveté of ancient people, but we hesitate to believe them.

7. These arguments can be even more forcefully strengthened by comparing these accounts, which we consider poetry for inherent reasons, with examples of Israelite historiography known to us. These conflicts with reality, indeed with possibility, do not occur throughout the OT but only in very specific passages of similar tone. In contrast, in other passages considered more or less strictly historical for other reasons, we do not observe these conflicts. One thinks <xi> primarily of the central passage of the book of 2 Samuel, the account of Absalom's rebellion, the precious jewel of ancient historiography in Israel. The world depicted here is well known to us. In this world, iron does not float on water, snakes do not speak, gods and angels do not appear like normal persons. Instead, everything happens in the customary manner. The difference, then, between legend and history

has not been imposed upon the OT. Rather, the attentive observer can discern it in the OT itself. Furthermore, one may consider the fact that individual accounts in Genesis not only resemble the legends of other peoples, but also relate to them in origin and nature. One cannot consider the Flood narrative of Genesis history and that of the Babylonians legend. Indeed, the OT. Flood account is a daughter recension of the Babylonian. Nor can one declare all the other accounts of the creation of the world fiction and Genesis 1 history. Instead, Genesis 1, as much as it differs in its religious spirit from the other accounts under consideration, relates very closely to them in terms of its literary character.

8. The major issue, however, is and will remain the poetic tone of these narratives. Historiography, which wants to instruct concerning actual events, is by nature prose. Legend, however, is by nature poetry. It seeks to gladden, elevate, inspire, touch. Thus, one who wants to do justice to such old accounts must have sufficient esthetic sensibility to hear an account as it is and as it wants to be. Here, too, it is not a question of reaching an unkind or even skeptical judgment, but rather lovingly to understand the nature of things. Whoever has the heart and the sensitivity must observe, for example, that the narrative of Isaac's sacrifice is not concerned with establishing certain historical facts. Instead, the hearer should feel the heartrending pain of the father who is to sacrifice his own child with his own hand and, then, his infinite thankfulness and joy when God's grace frees him from this heavy sacrifice. Whoever has recognized the unique poetical charm of these old legends becomes angry at the barbarian—there are also pious barbarians—who thinks that he can only value these accounts if he treats them as prose and history. The judgment that such an account is legend is not meant to diminish it. Instead, it is meant to express the evaluator's sense of something of its literary beauty and his belief that he has thereby understood it. Only ignorance can understand such a judgment as impious. Instead it is the judgment of piety and love. These poetical accounts are, indeed, the most beautiful produced by a people on its journey through history. Israel's legends, especially the legends of Genesis, may be the most beautiful and profound ever. To be sure, something will be destroyed for the child who cannot yet distinguish between reality and poetry if one tells him that his beautiful narratives are "not true." This attitude, however, would be unseemly for a modern theologian. The evangelical church and <xii> its commissioned representatives would do well not to be closed—as has so often been the case to this point—to this awareness that Genesis contains legends, but to recognize that only this awareness makes a historical understanding of Genesis possible. This awareness has already become common among the historically trained such that it cannot be suppressed. It will surely—it is inevitable—reach the people. We are concerned, however, that it be offered to them in the proper spirit.[3]

¶2. Types of Legends in Genesis

1. Two groups of material are clearly evident. (1) Legends concerning the origin of the world and the ancestors of humanity, the narratives to the Tower of Babylon. The

---

[3]I gladly cite Stöcker's words here: "Without a doubt, the primal history in the Bible has legends and legendary elements. It is futile to deny it and it is time to say this openly to believing Christianity" (*Literar. Beilage zur "Reformation"* 2/11 [Nov 1903]: 85).

arena of these accounts is the remote past, their sphere of interest the whole world. (2) Legends concerning Israel's fathers, Abraham, Isaac, and Jacob, and his sons. The arena here is Canaan and its environs and the interest concentrates on a family with the more-or-less background implication that the people of God descended from them. At the same time, a distinction in the God concept is also involved. The primal accounts have a more universalistic view: Yahweh, the creator of heaven and earth (2:4b), or at least of humans and animals (2:5ff.), and the Lord and Judge of humanity (as in the narratives of Paradise, of the angelic marriages, of the Flood, and of the Tower Construction). On the other hand, the god who appears in the patriarchal narratives—who visits Abraham and protects Jacob, who intervenes in the minor circumstances of an individual's life, who gives good fortune on the journey, and who grants house and home—appears more like a family god, associated, however, with the God of the people of Israel and the numen of sites in Canaan. There are additional distinctions in the God concept. A reserved, somber attitude dominates in the primal narratives. They recount frightful divine judgments and presume a deep cleft between humanity and deity which a human does not traverse unpunished, while in the patriarchal narratives a god appears whose inviolable grace rules over even children and grandchildren. Furthermore, the deity always appears in the patriarchal legends in secret, incognito, or by speaking only from heaven or even in a dream. In the primal legends, however, the God concept is more anthropomorphic: God walks intimately among people and no one is astonished. The Paradise legend presupposes that he was accustomed to coming to them every morning. He even closes the Ark for Noah and appears, attracted by Noah's sacrifice, in person. Indeed, he forms humans and animals with his own hands and even makes failed efforts in the process (p. 12). In the Flood account he regrets having created humanity and finally promises never again to impose such a horrible punishment. <xiii> In the account of the construction of the Tower, he seems for a moment almost afraid of the growing might of humanity, etc. Furthermore, the actual actors in the patriarchal legends are always people. The deity only appears as an exception. In the primal legends, however, the deity drives the action (as in Creation) or is at least significantly involved (Paradise, angel marriages, 6:1ff., Flood, Tower Construction). This distinction is only relative, for the deity appears in this way in a few patriarchal narratives, especially in the Hebron (Gen 18) and Sodom (Gen 19) legends, as well as in the Penuel narrative (32:25ff.). On the other hand, the Cain-Abel narrative as well as the legend of Canaan's curse (9:20ff.) are to be classified with the legends where people are the actors or chief actors. But, on the whole, this distinction characterizes the two groups. This emphasis on the deity's activity in the primal legends means that these legends have a stronger "mythical" character. They are weakened myths.[4]

2. "Myths"—one need not fear this word—are narratives about gods, in contrast to legends whose agents are humans. Now the mythical accounts of Genesis have come to us in faded colors. We recognize this from the accounts themselves since at a few points we are in a position to infer a form older than the one transmitted (cf. p. 120-21, etc.). Gen 6:1-4, in its present form, especially, is only a torso (cf. p. 59). We see the same phe-

---

[4]More on the distinction between primal myths and the patriarchal narratives in Haller, *Religion, Recht, und Sitte in den Genesissagen* (1905), 48ff. Concerning the historical basis for this distinction, see below ¶4:2.

nomenon when we compare the primal legends with the allusions to the myths we read in the OT poets and prophets and in the later apocalypticists (cf. the commentary, pp. 33ff., 122ff., and the material collected in *Schöpfung und Chaos* [1895]). The same conclusion results most clearly from a comparison of the primal narratives with Oriental myths, especially from a comparison of the biblical Creation and Flood narratives with the Babylonian recensions (cf. pp. 127ff., 67ff.). The immense scope, the unusually brilliant colors, originally characteristic of these myths, are blurred in the biblical primal legends. The equation of divine figures with natural objects or realms, battles among the gods, divine reproduction, etc. have fallen out of Genesis. One can perceive the peculiar character of Israelite religion in this. The characteristic feature of Yahwism does not favor myths. From the outset, this religion was inclined to monotheism. A divine story requires at least two gods. Consequently, actual, unaltered myths could not be tolerated in the Israel we come to know from the OT—at least not in prose, allusions to myths were permitted the poet. Remnants of an older viewpoint underlying our Genesis tradition are preserved, then, in the poetry. It was more accepting of myths. This quiet aversion to mythology dominates the primal legends preserved for us. Israel's monotheism wants to know only either of myths in which <xiv> God acts alone—as in the Creation narrative, then, however, there can be no actual "narrative," in which action and counteraction produce a new reality—or in which the story takes place between God and people. According to specifically Israel concepts, however, humans are too weak to be worthy counterparts for God, too weak for their struggle with God to become a significant interaction. As soon as God intervenes, everything is decided. If one wants to tell a "story" at all in such cases, humans must act first. This is the structure of the Paradise and Tower legends. The Flood legend, where God appears from the very beginning, differs. But, after his appearance, the account is unable to produce suspense for the hearer concerning the fate of humanity. Further, one may note that the legends transmitted with mythical echoes are much fewer in number than the patriarchal legends without mythical elements. One may also perceive this as an effect of the abhorrence for myth.

3. Since Genesis contains no actual, pure myths, it is not necessary to offer here an extensive discussion of the origin, nature, and original meaning of myth. We can be satisfied with the simple definition of myth as a "story of the gods." Only a few observations pertaining to Genesis will be offered here. A series of myths can be understood in terms of a natural event often or regularly occuring in the real world which provided the palette for an account of such an event in the primordium. Thus, the creation of the world is portrayed as a grand spring, and the frequently observed appearance of the rainbow after the rain gave occasion for the account of the rainbow's origin after the Flood. Many myths respond to questions and thus want to teach. This is also true of the primal legends of Genesis. The creation narrative asks, "What are the origins of heaven and earth?" and, "Why is the Sabbath holy?" The Paradise account asks, "What is the origin of human reason and mortality?" as well as "What is the origin of the human body and spirit? the origin of human language? the origin of sexual love (2:4)? How is it that the woman has so much pain in childbirth, that the man must cultivate the resistant field, that the serpent crawls on its belly? etc." The response to these questions comprises the proper content of the legends in the cases mentioned. The Flood legend differs. It seems to reflect a historical event (p. 77). But an "etiological" (basis-establishing) element stands at the end: "Why

will such a flood not recur (8:21f.; 9:8ff.)? What does the rainbow mean (9:12ff.)?" The natural conclusion of such an account is a clause with "therefore." "Therefore, man leaves father and mother and cleaves to his wife" (2:24; etc.). All these questions, however—characteristically for these myths in contrast to the legends—do not concern Israelite matters but those pertaining to the whole world. One knows that ancient Israel was generally not oriented toward speculation and that it always concerned itself mostly with immediate, Israelite matters. Here, however, the ancient people was able to deal with universally human problems, the most profound questions of the human race. In a unique fashion, this took place <xv> in the Creation and Paradise narratives. These are the beginnings of theology and philosophy. It is no wonder that special emphasis has been placed on these passages in postbiblical times and that, as long as Genesis has been read, every generation to this day has read its most profound ideas into these accounts. A certain class of etiological accounts, termed "cultural legends" by Greßmann,[5] asks about the origin of human civilization: "How old and what are the origins of the consumption of fruits and flesh, clothing with leaves and skins, animal husbandry, farming, the arts of the smith and musician, construction of cities and civic life?" The narratives of Paradise, of the Cainites, and of the construction of the Tower record answers to such questions.

4. The patriarchal legends follow the primal legends in Genesis. Characteristically, their heroes are tribal patriarchs, ancestors of the peoples, mostly of Israel. These legends are based on the viewpoint that each of the peoples, including Israel, originated from the ever-expanding family of one ancestor. Israel already expressed this view in its diction which, in many, although not all, cases designated a people or clan as "sons of PN."[6] This theory also lived among the Arabs and was known to the Greeks, at least in earlier times, while no trace of it can be found in Egypt and Babylonia.[7] As a result of this fundamental viewpoint, the genre of the genealogy illustrates the interrelationships among peoples.[8] Two nations are said to be descended from brothers, i.e., they are closely related and are equals. If one of them is richer, mightier, nobler, it is said that its ancestor was the first-born brother or that it descended from the better mother, the other's ancestor was the younger or it descended from the concubine. Israel's division into twelve tribes is conceived in terms of the ancestor Israel's twelve sons. If a few of the tribes constituted a closer union, one maintains that they descended from the same mother. More remote relationships exist between the uncle and nephew, Abraham and Lot, the ancestors of Israel and of Moab and Ammon, respectively. This theory reflects reality to the extent that the bond constituting the unity of the clan or the tribe in the simple circumstances of the desert tribes is not some political organization but the feeling of blood kinship,[9] furthermore, that many clans really descend from the man after whom they call themselves or are at least associated with him as their leader.[10] On the other hand, we know enough

---

[5]ZAW 30:25.

[6]Nöldeke, ZDMG 40:170-71.

[7]Ed. Meyer, *Israeliten*, 229-30.

[8]Stade, *Gesch. Isr.* 1:27ff.; Guthe, *Gesch. Isr.*, 1ff.

[9]Benzinger, "Government," in *Encycl. Bibl.*

[10]Nöldeke, ZDMG 40:158; Kittel, *Babyl. Ausgrabungen*³, 16-17. Cf., esp., the many tribal names that were originally personal names to which Meyer (*Israeliten*, 318, 341-42, 347), in particular,

about the origin of the peoples to say cconfidently that peoples and tribes also form in quite different ways, perhaps through the incorporation of foreign clans or through the <xvi> fusion of immigrants and natives, and that the purity of blood always maintained by Israel is only a figment of Israel's imagination.[11]

The theory, then, that the nations originated from a patriarch's family does not stem from the observation of the facts but results from mythical thought that seeks to understand everything, including the nations, as having originated through reproduction.[12] At any rate, a numerous tribe or even a whole people is chronologically too distant from the patriarch it claims for an oral report about him to be preserved.[13] The existence, in such cases, not only of the patriarch's genealogy but also of individual narratives about him, can be explained, first, as the application of the circumstances and experiences of the people, itself, to this primal figure. This situation quite clearly pertains to many cases. When a person named Shechem, the ancestor of the city of Shechem, is presented to us as an enamored youth killed by Simeon and Levi, the ancestors of the two tribes, everyone is prepared to see in this, not historical facts, but only the legendary incarnation of historical events. We do not reinterpret legends or legend fragments dealing with such national persons, then. Instead, we understand, in contrast, their actual, for us now attainable sense, by attempting to interpret the heroes they treat as peoples and tribes and the stories about them first as experiences of peoples. On the other hand, however, one must undertake this attempt with great caution, for we must account for the possibility that a few of these figures did not originally represent peoples, but only became ancestors secondarily in a later tradition. Furthermore, after the figures of the "patriarchs" were fixed as heroes of the accounts, other kinds of accounts that did not originate in the history of peoples may have become associated with them. We can confidently understand as personifications of peoples and tribes especially those figures whose names are otherwise known to us as names of peoples (cf. esp. Cain, Canaan, Ishmael, Ammon, Moab, the twelve tribes and their clans). The situation differs for figures such as Abraham, Isaac, and Jacob, the patriarchs of Israel; Lot, the patriarch of Ammon and Moab; Esau, the patriarch of Esau; and Laban "the Aramaean." These figures who do not bear the names of the peoples and tribes they represent, must, therefore, have originally had another significance, and must have come to represent their peoples only by the "decree" of the tradition.[14] It follows that details recounted concerning them may trace back to the fates of their peoples, but that everything may not simply be systematically understood in this fashion. One must proceed even more cautiously with figures such as Abel, as well as with the women and daughters Sarah, Hagar, Rebekah, Leah, Rachel, Dinah, and Tamar, since it <xvii> is not clear at all that they were ever supposed to have represented a tribe. It should also be remarked that Shem, Ham, and Japheth may have been three aboriginal peoples and that Jacob and Esau probably originally represented two classes of the popula-

---

and others have called attention.

[11]Küchler, *Hebräsche Volkskunde*, 26-27.

[12]Cf. p. 87 in the commentary and, esp., E. Meyer, *Gesch. des Altertums* 1/1², 34.

[13]Nöldeke, 158.

[14]Meyer, *Israeliten*, 231.

tion (p. 308). Some accounts that treat patriarchs—we may cautiously say—originally depicted experiences of the peoples.

Once in ancient times—presumably—disputes over wells took place between the citizens of Gerar and the surrounding Bedouins until there was finally a treaty in Beer-sheba. The legend depicts these things as a dispute and a treaty between Abimelech, king of Gerar, and the patriarchs Abraham or Isaac (21:22ff.; 26). According to the legend, Simeon and Levi secretly murdered the youth Shechem. But Jacob denied any association with the brothers (Gen 34). The story underlying this legend will have been that the Canaanite city Shechem was secretly attacked by the tribes Simeon and Levi. But the other tribes of Israel remained neutral in this battle (cf. p. 359). Similarly, a portion of the Tamar legend (Gen 38) depicts the earliest circumstances of the tribe of Judah. Judah united with Canaanites, in the legend, Hirah from Adullam and Judah's wife Bath-shua. A series of Judaeo-Canaanite clans (Er and Onan) disappeared early. Finally, two new clans (Perez and Zerah) arose (cf. pp. 396, 402). In a wider sense, history, more precisely cultural history, echoes in the Jacob-Esau legends. Here we hear how the shepherd, although the younger brother, overcomes the hunter through his superior cunning (cf. p. 308; the Cain-Abel legend is comparable, cf. pp. 48-49). Legends concerning the Judean clans Perez and Zerah (38:27ff.) and Ephraim and Mannaseh (48:13f.) assume a similar competition between brothers and should perhaps be understood as an echo of a historical event in the first case, and quite surely in the second. Reuben, the firstborn among the Israelite tribes, loses the birthright because of a crime (49:3-4). The tribe Reuben, foremost in earliest times, forfeited this status. Shem, Japheth, and Canaan were originally brothers. But now Japheth has a much broader territory than the others and Canaan must serve the other two (9:20ff.). Often we hear of migrations. Abraham migrates from the northeast to Canaan, then Rebekah to marry Isaac, and finally Jacob. Ur-Casdim, Haran (Nahor's city, 24:10), and the land of the "sons of the East" are mentioned as points of origin. The antiquity and historicity of these reports are disputed. Yet, there can surely be no objections to the latter detail (cf. pp. 167-68). The Joseph legend presumes a migration of Hebrew tribes to Egypt. The account of Abraham's trip to Egypt contains a similar motif (12:10ff.).

Now, inherent in the nature of the legend, we cannot perceive ancient circumstances in them clearly, but only as though through a mist. The legend poetically recast historical memories and concealed their contours. Popular tradition added all sorts of material. Thus, whole figures with other origins—as we have just seen—were joined to the patriarchs and interwoven into what seems at first a historically and poetically <xviii> unified fabric. Thus, for the most part, the time of the event cannot be determined from the legend itself. Sometimes the place is not evident either, and occasionally not even the acting subject. The legends forget where Jacob and Esau, Cain, Shem, and Japheth actually belong and what Jacob and Esau originally meant. Consequently, one may urgently warn the scholar who seeks to derive historical occasions from the legends not to proceed pedantically[15] and not to surrender to the belief that one can obtain historical facts from the patriarchal legends through a simple retroversion into political history without further support (see

---

[15]Cf. Luther, *ZAW* 21:46: "The consistent application of the methods employed by Wellhausen et al. would soon produce absurd results."

further p. xxiii).[16] Only a barbarian would disparage these legends because things of the past are more concealed than revealed in them. They are often more valuable than any prose reports about actual events. If, for example, we were to have good historical reports about Ishmael, they would be rather inconsequential to us because this "wild ass" hardly did anything for humanity. Now, however, that the hand of literature has touched him, he lives eternally. The character of the tribes or classes portrayed, however, are clear to us in these legends. Esau, the hunter from the steppe, lives unthinkingly from hand to mouth, forgetful, generous, brave. The shepherd Jacob is much more clever, accustomed to considering the future. His uncle Laban exemplifies the sheep rancher in the Far East, greedy and deceitful, but outwardly an extremely honorable man, never wanting for an excuse. Ishmael, the Bedouin, is a "wild ass" of a man. Cain wanders like a murderer far from Yahweh's blessed land. The attitudes toward the events are also clear to us in many cases. Indeed, we hear most clearly how the legend despises Canaan's immorality, how it derides Esau and Laban, how it rejoices that Lot's greed acquired the worse land, etc.

3. Because we have these accounts from two sources (J and E) from about the ninth and eighth centuries, it has often been believed that the legends themselves stemmed essentially from the time of the Israelite monarchy and that they provide no evidence concerning history prior to that period (cf., e.g., Wellhausen, *Prolegomena*, 319ff.; <xix> idem, *Israel. und Jüd. Gesch.*[4], 11; Holzinger, *Genesis*, 271). In reality, however, they are much older. The names they contain attest primarily to this conclusion. Even if we may consider them historical, almost all are obscure for us. We know nothing of Shem, Ham, and Japhet from Israel's historical tradition, hardly anything about Reuben, Simeon, and Levi, and very little about Ishmael and Cain from the oldest tradition. These names, then, predate historical Israel. They refer to peoples and tribes from an earlier period. The advanced age of the legends of Jacob and Esau is especially obvious, however. These figures, indeed, were secondarily equated with Israel and Edom. But these very dual names and some elements of the legend not suited to the historical peoples Edom and Israel, show us that the old account originally had quite different circumstances in mind. In the legend, Jacob timidly fears Esau, his brother; in history, Israel conquered Edom in war. In the legend Esau is stupid; in history Esau is famed for wisdom (cf. p. 308). We can derive other evidence for the age of such legends from the history of legend in Israel. In general, legends in the book of Judges no longer discuss the ancestors of the tribes or peoples (except for Judg 1). Instead they tell of the individual leaders of the tribes. The last, historically datable narrative in the old style is probably the legend of the attack on

---

[16]Cornill (*Geschichte des volkes Israel* [1898] 30ff.), Steuernagel (*Einwanderung der israelitischen Stämme* [1901]), and Procksch (*Nordhebräisches Sagenbuch* [1906], 331ff.) have attempted comprehensive interpretations of the patriarchal legends as reminiscences of historical events. It seems to me that such extensive interpretations of an entire legend cycle are very dubious. Individual events echo here and there in the legends. The notion, however, that the patriarchal legends would be in a position faithfully to preserve a whole chain of events stretched over many decades seems very unlikely from the outset. The great variety of these and similar attempts (collected in Luther, 36ff.) already demonstrates the uncertainty of all these hypotheses. For more concerning these hypotheses, cf. 315-16, 323-24; Meyer, *Israeliten*, 251n.1; and Eerdmans, *Alttest. Studien* 2:34ff.

Shechem, the Dinah legend in Genesis (34). In the earlier period of the judges, then, as far as we can tell, this narrative style disappeared. From then on, such accounts are only transmitted, but not newly formed.

6. We term these legends "historical" if they mirror historical events, "ethnographical" if they predominantly offer a depiction of the circumstances of the peoples. Thus, one will characterize the legends of the treaty at Beer-sheba, of the attack on Shechem, and of the demise of the older Judean tribes as "historical," and, contrariwise, the legends of Cain and of Ishmael as "ethnographical" legends.

7. In addition to such motifs[17] in the accounts of Genesis, there are the "etiological" legends, i.e., those with a goal, those which want to explain something. A multitude of questions occupy an ancient people. The child looks wide-eyed at the world and asks, "Why?" The answer it gives itself and which intially satisfies it may be very childish, very incorrect, and yet, if it is a spirited child, captivating and touching, even for adults. Ancient peoples also raise such questions and answer them as well as they can. These questions are also usually the same we ask ourselves and seek to answer in our scientific disciplines. What we find here, then, are the beginnings of human knowledge, of course only minor beginnings, but as beginnings still worthy of our respect. At the same time, however, they are especially touching and charming to us, for in these answers ancient Israel expressed its most intimate attitudes, clothing them in the colorful garment of poetry.[18] Such questions are: <xx>

(a) Ethnological. Questions are asked about the reasons for the status of peoples. Why is Canaan his brothers' servant? Why does Japheth have such an extensive territory (9:24ff.)? Why do Lot's sons live in the inhospitable East (cf. pp. 175-76)? How did Reuben loose its birthright (49:3-4)? Why must Cain wander about restlessly and transiently? Why will the one who kills Cain be avenged sevenfold? Why is Gilead the border against the "sons of the East" (31:52)? Why does Beer-sheba belong to us and not the Gerarites (21:22ff.; 26:25ff.)? Why does Joseph possess Shechem (48:22)? Why did Ishmael become a desert people with this dwelling place and this god (Gen 16)? How is it that the Egyptian farmers must pay the heavy 20% tax while the fields are free for the priests (47:13ff.)? The question of why Israel has this glorious land of Canaan is raised with particular frequency. The legends recount many ways the patriarchs obtained this particular land: God promised it to Abraham because of his obedience (12:7); when Lot chose the East at the parting at Bethel, the West became Abraham's property (Gen 13); Jacob obtained the blessing of the better land from Isaac by deceit (Gen 27); God promised it to Jacob at Bethel (28:13); etc. Such ethnological legends, which recount a fictional narrative in order to explain the status of the nations, and the historical legends, which still contain the remnant of a tradition of an actual event, are, of course, often difficult to distinguish in individual cases. Very often, ethnological and ethnographical features appear together in the same legend. The presumed circumstances are historical, but the explanation is poetic. The answer given to such questions always involves

---

[17]A "motif" in this sense is an elementary, self-contained portion of poetic material; cf. Scherer, *Poetik*, 212.

[18]Concerning such questions of primitive peoples, cf. von der Leyen, "Zur Entstehung des Märchens," *Archiv für das Studium d. neuern Sprachen u. Literaturen* 114:15.

explaining the current situation as the result of an act of the patriarchs. Our ancestor dug the well at Beer-sheba, therefore, it belongs to us, his heirs (26:25ff.). The ancestors established Gilead as the border (31:52). Cain's patriarch was cursed by God to eternal wandering, etc. There is a particular preference for finding such an explanation in a wonder-working word once spoken by God himself or a patriarch. The legend then recounts how this word came about once in antiquity (9:5ff.; 12:2-3; 15:18; 27:28ff.; etc.). And this explanation was considered sufficient enough that, later, there was a separate literary genre of "blessing" (cf. commentary on Gen 49). As childish as these explanations may seem to us, it was equally impossible for the ancients to find the real reasons for things. We nevertheless may not overlook the profundity speaking through these poetical legends. Current national situations—these accounts assume—are not accidents, but are based on events of the distant past; they are to a degree "predestined." In the ethnological legends, then, we have the beginning of a philosophy of history.

(b) Ethnological motifs, the beginnings of linguistics. Ancient Israel deliberated a great deal concerning the origin and true meaning of the names of peoples, mountains, wells, sanctuaries, and cities. Names were more significant to Israel than they are to us. Israel was convinced that names must have some relationship to the things named. The ancient people was entirely unable <xxi> to give the correct explanation in many cases. Both for other peoples and for Israel, names are the oldest material in the language. They stem from vanished peoples or from an earlier phase of one's own language. Many of our names, such as Rhein, Mosel, Neckar, Harz, Berlin, Ludwig, etc., are not clear to those untrained in linguistics. Because of this very oddity, these words will have attracted the attention of the ancient people. Of course, ancient Israel explains such names, unscientifically, in relation to its current language. It associated the old name with a modern, more or less phonetically similar word, and it recounted a brief narrative to establish why this word was spoken here and then remained as a name. We know such popular etymologies, too.[19] The Langobards used to be called Winiler. But once when the wives of the Winiler put on beards as a trick of war and Wodan saw this out his window early in the morning, he said, "What kind of long beards are these?" Since that time the Winiler have called themselves longbeards, i.e., Langobards (Grimm, *Deutsche Sagen*, no. 389). According to the legend, Wartburg bears that name because the landgrave, who was lost there on a hunt, said, "Wart', Berg, du sollst mir eine Burg werden (Wait, mountain, you will be my fortress)!" Such legends are very frequent in Genesis and later, as well.[20] The city of "Babel" got its name because there God "confused" (בָּלַל, 11:9) the languages; "Jacob" is explained as "heel-holder" because he held his brother, whom he begrudged the birth-right, by the heel at birth (25:26); Zoar means "trifle" because in prayer Lot said, "it is only a trifle" (19:20, 22); Beer-sheba, "well of seven," because there Abraham gave Abimelech seven lambs (21:28ff.); "Isaac" (Yiṣhaq) got his name because his mother laughed (צָחַק) when his birth was promised (18:12); and so forth. In order to recognize

---

[19]"'Ach Allm' stöhnt' einst ein Ritter; / Ihn traf des Mörders Stoß; / 'Allmächt'ger' wollt' er rufen; / Man hieß davon das Schloß" (Uhland, "Die Schlact bei Reutlingen").

[20]Benzinger (*Archäologie*², 100) offers examples of popular etymologies of names in the OT. Such etymologies in modern tribal legends are treated in Littmann, "Semit. Stammessagen der Gegenwart," in *Orient. Studien: Th. Nöldeke gewidmet*, 945, 952.

the great naiveté of most of these etymologies, one must consider that the Hebrew legend innocently explains the Babylonian word Babel from the Hebrew and that very crude assonances often satisfy: Cain is derived from קָנִיתִי, "I have acquired" (4:1); Reuben even from רָאָה בְעָנְיִי, "he saw my suffering" (29:32); etc. Scholars have not always sufficiently recognized this etymological naiveté. Consequently, even in most recent times, some have been misled into attempting to confirm some of these unsatisfactory etymologies by modern means. Many theologians are even wont to characterize one such (albeit very ingenious) explanation as "authentic etymology" (Yahweh = "I am who I am," Exod 3:14). But etymologies are not revealed. The etymological legends are especially valuable to us because they are especially clear examples of the category of etiological legends. <xxii>

(c) More important than these etymological motifs are the cultic legend motifs intended to explain the institutions of worship. Such cultic institutions play a great role in the life of the ancients. Already in the earliest time accessible to us, many of these practices were no longer, or at least not entirely, comprehensible to those who performed them. Practices are much more tenacious than concepts and the cult in particular is unusually conservative. In many cases, we too, whose worship withstood a powerful purification in the Reformation and again in Rationalism, do not, or only partially, understand the original meaning of what we see and hear in our churches. Ancient Israel considered the origin of many such cultic practices. Although adults, deadened by familiarity, no longer note the unusual and incomprehensible, they will be stirred from their rest by the children's questions. If children see their father performing all manner of unusual practices at the Passover feast, and—this is expressly indicated (cf. Exod 12:26; 13:14)—ask, "What does that mean?" one should tell them the Passover story. The same situation applies to the twelve stones at the Jordan (Josh 4:6) which the father should interpret to his children as a memorial of the crossing of the Jordan. In these examples, then, we clearly see how such a legend responds to a question. Similarly, one asks about the origin of circumcision, the Sabbath. Why do we not eat the sinew of the thigh (32:33)? Why does one anoint the holy stone at Bethel and offer the tithe there (28:18, 22)? Why do we sacrifice at "Yeru'el"—the name of the site of Isaac's sacrifice (22:1-19; cf. p. 238)—not a child, as Yahweh actually requires, but a goat? No Israelite could have cited the actual reason for all of these things. They were much too old for this. But in this need, the myth or a legend intervened. One told a narrative and explained thereby the sacred practice. Once long ago, an event occured that quite naturally gave rise to this practice. We perform the custom in memory and imitation of this event. This narrative, however, intended to explain the custom, usually takes place in the primordium. The ancient people thus reflects the quite correct impressions that the rites of worship trace back to time immemorial: the trees at Shechem (12;6) and Hebron (18:4) are older than Abraham! We practice circumcision for the sake of Moses whose firstborn was circumcised as a substitute for him whose blood God desired (Exod 4:24ff.). We rest on the seventh day because God rested from creating the world on the seventh day (2:2-3, a myth because God himself acts in it). The thigh sinew is sacred to us because Jacob smote God there or—as they say later—God smote Jacob (32:33; cf. p. 351). Jacob was the first to anoint the stone at Bethel because it was his pillow when the deity appeared to him (28;18). At "Yeru'el" God first required Abraham's child, but then was satisfied with the goat (Gen 22). And so forth.

Again and again on such occasions we hear of specific locales—of Bethel, Penuel, Shechem, Beer-sheba, Lahai-roi, Yeru'el, etc.—and of <xxiii> the trees, springs, and memorial stones at these sites. These are the most ancient sanctuaries of Israel's tribes and clans. The earliest period directly perceived something of the being of the deity in these natural landmarks. A later period, however, to which this association no longer seems evident or obvious, raised the question as to why precisely this place and this sacred sign are so particularly sacred? The consistent response was, "Because the deity appeared to the patriarch at this site. In memory of this fundamental revelation, we worship God at this place." The cultic legend stems, therefore—and this is of extraordinary significance for the history of religion—from a time in which religious sensibility no longer directly felt the divinity of the site and the natural landmark and no long understood the sacred practice. In the legend the immediate impression of the divinity of the sacred symbol has become a one-time experience of the patriarch and inner certainty has been objectified as an external procedure. The legend now must establish how the god and the patriarch met at precisely this place. In the heat of midday, Abraham sat under the tree when the men appeared to him. Consequently the tree is sacred (19:1ff.). The desert well of Lahai-roi became Ishmael's sanctuary because his mother, fleeing in the desert, met God who comforted her at this well (16:7ff.). By chance, Jacob spent the night at a certain site and rested with his head on the stone when he saw the heavenly ladder. Consequently the stone is our sanctuary (28:10ff.). Moses accidentally came with his flock to the sacred mountain and the thornbush (Exod 3:1ff.). Each of the more important sanctuaries of Israel will have had such a legend of its origins. We may imagine that such a sanctuary legend was originally recounted at sacred festivals at the same site, just as the Passover festival and the Exodus legend belong together, the Purim festival and the Esther legend, the Babylonian Easter festival and the Babylonian Creation hymn, and just as our Christmas and Easter would be inconceivable without their stories. The cultic legends are, therefore, so valuable to us because we become aware of Israel's sacred sites and practices, and, at the same time, because they place us, quite vitally, in the ancient religious sensibility. These cultic legends are our chief source for Israel's earliest religion. Genesis abounds with them; Only a few appear in later books. Almost every text where God appears at a specific site is based on such a legend. We have the beginnings of the history of religion in these legends.

(d) In addition, another series of other types of legend motifs may be distinguished. Only the geological motif will be mentioned here. Such geological motifs want to explain the origins of a locality. What is the origin of the Dead Sea with its horrible devastation? The region was cursed by God because of the horrible sin of its inhabitants (Gen 19). What is the origin of the salt pillar resembling a woman there? A woman transformed into salt, Lot's wife, was punished for glimpsing the mystery of the deity (19:26). But how were patches around <xxiv> Zoar excepted from the general destruction? Because Yahweh spared it as Lot's refuge (19:17ff.).

All of these etiological legend motifs thus are far removed from the current disciplines to which they correspond. We regard them with the same emotions one has when one thinks back on one's childhood. But they are also extremely valuable for our disciplines: by presuming or describing certain circumstances, they offer us the most important material concerning the knowledge of the ancient world.

8. The legends almost always unite various legend motifs and combine them in the most varied mixtures. The legend of Hagar's flight (Gen 16) can be described as ethnographic to the extent that it depicts Ishmael's lifestyle, and ethnological to the extent that it seeks to explain these circumstances. Part of it is cultic in nature: it justifies the sacredness of Lahai-roi. At the same time the account has etymological motifs for it interprets the names Ishmael and Lahai-roi. The Bethel narrative (28:10ff.) simultaneously explains the cult and the name of Bethel. The legends of Beer-sheba (21:22ff.; 26) have historical traces, in that they tell of a treaty between peoples made there, while they also contain cultic (they explain the sacredness of the site) and, finally, also etymological elements. The Penuel narrative (32:23ff.) explains the sacredness of the place, the names Penuel and Israel, and the fact that one does not consume the thigh sinew. The pattern continues. The etymological motifs, in particular, never appear independently in the older accounts in Genesis, but are only employed as secondary features. When they predominate or even consitute the whole account, they indicate later narrative fiction—such is the case in the narrative of the encounter between Jacob and Esau (p. 354) and especially in the narrative of the birth of Jacob's sons (p. 322).[21]

9. In many cases, these features also indicate the origin of the legends. It can be clearly shown for many of the etymological motifs that those parts of the legend that explain the names were devised for this very purpose. The notion that Abraham gave Abimelech "seven" lambs at Beer-sheba (21:28ff.) was certainly devised to explain the name, just as was the notion that Isaac's mother "laughed" (18:12ff.), etc. The accounts of the sons of Judah, 'Er, Onan, Shelah, Perez, and Zerah (Gen 38), is essentially the history of the Judean clans, just as the events of the attack on Shechem can be deduced with a great degree of certainty from the Shechem legend (Gen 34).

Now, several legends or legend fragments, however, do not contain such motifs which are transparent to a degree for us, such as large sections of the Joseph account (p. 384). Furthermore, the chief motif of the Jacob-Laban narrative, the account of the deceptions, cannot be understood either as a historical echo or etiologically. Jacob's meeting with Rachel at the well belongs in the same category, <xxv> as do many others. But even when we find in a legend motifs we can interpret, we still see rather frequently that the whole legend cannot be explained in this way, but that it also contains passages of lesser or greater scope which resist any such interpretation. Thus, the migration of Abraham or Isaac to Gerar or to Egypt will reflect some historical material, but the delivery and recovery of the wife must have some other origin (p. 172). The attack on the city of Shechem is historical, but not the fortunes of Dinah (p. 359). In the Tamar narrative, tribal history and unintelligible legend material dealing with Tamar's marriage of necessity are especially to be distinguished (p. 403 orig). To the extent that the Cain legend depicts Cain's current situation, it offers ethnographical information. But the fact that he killed a brother named Abel cannot be explained in this manner (pp. 48-49). It is especially remarkable, however, that the element we cannot interpret is always the actual basis of

---

[21]Eerdmans's (2:49) assessment that "most legends" originated from the names is superficial. As shown above, the legends have entirely different roots, as well. In the earliest legends such as those of Hebron, Sodom, Jacob, and Laban, especially, the etymological element is significantly diminished.

the account. In many cases, a legend-critical parallel (see ¶5:2, 4) shows us that the legend contains material from elsewhere: for example, the legend of Hebron (p. 199), of Sodom (p. 214), of Lot's daughters (p. 216), of Isaac's sacrifice (p. 239), of Jacob and Rachel at the well (pp. 318-19), of Jacob's struggle at Penu'el (p. 352), and especially of the adulterous Egyptian woman (p. 405), etc. One sees quite clearly in the narratives of Jacob and Esau (pp. 289-90, 307-308) and of Jacob's contracts with Laban (p. 341) that a secondary Israelite understanding reinforces the legends and that entities from Israel's history entered them: Jacob and Esau were equated with the historical peoples Israel and Edom and the treaties of Jacob and Laban were given a meaning related to the history of the peoples. But we can also imagine the reverse situation, that a legend, perhaps occasioned by history or in response to a question, was significantly expanded by the addition of all manner of diverse poetic motifs. This may be the case, for example, in the Dinah and Tamar narratives. If we combine all these observations—applicable, more or less, to every old legend—into one image, we come to the conclusion that legend material treated in the patriarchal legends is, on the whole, neither historical nor etiological in origin. Many narratives or much of the narrative material must have already existed before they received this new meaning on Israel's lips.[22] As beautiful stories, they must have long been in circulation and will have orignated as pure products of the imagination. In the commentary such incomprehensible passages are termed "novelistic" for want of a better expression. Some may prefer the expression "fairy-tale-like."[23] <xxvi>

¶3. The Artistry of the Legends in Genesis

1. The beauty of the legends in Genesis has always delighted sensitive readers. Not accidentally, painters have very often taken the material for their paintings from this book. Scholars have been touched by the beauty of these accounts much less often, probably because to them esthetic perspectives frequently do not seem consistent with serious scholarship. We do not share such a prejudice, however. We think that whoever overlooks the artistic form of these legends not only robs himself of a great pleasure, but cannot completely fulfill the scholarly task of understanding Genesis. Instead, it is totally appropriate for scholarship to seek the basis for the unusual beauty of these legends, a question whose response leads, at the same time, deeply into their content and also their religion.

2. The first question concerns whether the form of these accounts is prose or poetry. Until now, the general view has been that all the accounts in the OT are written in prose. In the meanwhile, however, this assumption has been disputed by Ed. Sievers, the Germanist who has broken new ground in Hebrew meter. In a great, and in many respects,

---

[22]This result, at which I arrived through repeated examination of the individual legends and to which Meyer (*Israeliten* [1906]; cf., e.g., 250-51) assisted me, I now find again in Wundt (*Völkerpsychologie* 2/3 [1909]: 360, 418) and in Greßmann (11ff., 18, 20, 23).

[23]Concerning "fairy-tale-like" material in Genesis, cf. ¶3:16 and the index at the conclusion of the commentary (s.v. "literary," cf. "stylistic"). Greßmann (12ff.) even calls these primitive accounts "fairy tales." Yet it should be noted that the characteristic fantasy of the fairy tale is generally absent in Genesis and, further, that the accounts of Genesis are very tightly composed in contrast to fairy tales.

admirable work (*Metrische Studien II: Hebräsche Genesis*, 1904, 1905), Sievers has published a Genesis arranged in verses.

First, what is the style of Genesis? Characteristically for the accounts of Genesis, as for all the accounts of the Old Testament, they do not have an elevated, rhythmic style, but refrain from any rhetorical embellishment. The narrators take pains to characterize matters clearly and plainly with the simplest expressions. Not even a metaphor, a rhetorical expression, an ornamental phrase, a poetic combination of clauses, or a detailed description is permitted here. Everything lofty and passionate is suppressed in the account proper and only becomes slightly more prominent in the speeches reported (as an example of poetic expression in speech, cf. 19:8). It is unusual that the hot-blooded Hebrews narrate so calmly. These narrators seem to belong to an entirely different class of people than the fiery prophets! Nor does one find in the legends the characteristic division of thought into two clauses, the so-called "parallelismus membrorum," the most characteristic trait of Hebrew poetic style. The modest beauty of the old narratives so attractive for us consists for the most part in this very calm and meagerness of narrative style. The "blessing of Jacob" (Gen 49) constitutes a clear exception to this style. It is not an account, however, but a poem, and, for this reason, it does not actually belong in Genesis. Furthermore, the diction rises to a rhythmic, poetic style in certain passages at the high point of the account, especially if the legend reports wonder-working words, just as the magical words in fairy tales tend to be poetry and just as "strophes summarizing the most import aspects, statements, and the moral of the account in the form of poetic mottoes" in the earlier Brahmanic and in Buddhist literature interrupt the epic <xxvii> prose.[24] A similar phenomenon appears in the modern tribal legends translated from Tigre by Littmann,[25] in the Scandinavian Skalden, and in the Irish poets.[26] These observations concerning style also pronounce the verdict concerning the rhythmic form of the accounts, however—if we are not mistaken. Accounts of this modesty cannot have a strict rhythmic structure. Here we find no trace indicating that the choice or position of words were in any way determined by a given rhythm to which they were more or less to conform, no interjections unnecessary for the sense but intended to fill out the metrical unit, nor any other lesser or greater divergences from natural diction demanded by the rhythm such as those found throughout the Medieval rhythmical chronicles to which Sievers (1:376) incorrectly appeals. Nothing other than Hebrew anapestic rhythm and the language's characteristic combination of two or three words with major accents into a logical unit produces the mistaken impression of meter. Admittedly, good Hebrew prose also has a nice rhythmic euphony which could surely be more precisely described. But these prose rhythms do not compare to consistent "blank" verse, but only to the freest "mixed meter" of poetry (Sievers 1:129ff.).[27] <xxviii>

---

[24]Cf. Geldner, "Gāthā," *RGG*.

[25]*Orient. Studien, Th. Nöldeke gewidmet*, 947, 953ff.

[26]Oldenberg, *Literatur des alten Indiens*, 45.

[27]Sievers's attempt to demonstrate the metrical structure of Genesis is not only of extreme significance because of the identity of the author, the prime metrist OT research possesses or has ever possessed. If this attempt had succeeded, we would have obtained a new and extraordinary aid for textual and especially source criticism. Sievers's positions, however, suffer from the following

weaknesses: (a) Sievers himself graciously admits "that the same sequence of words can often be accented differently" (2:168)—thus, according to Sievers, נֹחַ בְּנֵי or even הָאֱלֹהִים אֲשֶׁר אֵת (41:25) could have one or two accents (1:389; 2:127), and הָאֲדָמָה אֶת־כָּל־פְּנֵי (2:6; 1:383; 2:7), מִצְרַיִם אֶת־כָּל־הַרְטֻמֵּי (41:8; 1:387; 2:125), and מַזְכִּיר אֲנִי אֶת־חֲטָאַי (41:9; 1:387; 2:125) could have two or three accents, etc. (b) It is not difficult in a narrative text, even when the style is strict and tolerates nothing superfluous—especially for such an extraordinary philologist as Sievers—to strike one or more words as an addition or to assume a lacuna where the assumed meter requires. A catalogue of these "lacunae" and "insertions" appears in 2:217ff. Now without question such emendations of the transmitted text are occasionally necessary. It must also be acknowledged that Sievers often undertook them with great skill. But, it is still beyond question that this approach and the ambiguity mentioned under (a) concerning the proper accentuation significantly diminishes the certainty of results. (c) The following may be added. In Hebrew lyric, as is well known, sections indicated by the sense are very clear. Consequently, these logical divisions are to this point the only fully certain indication of metrical units and the given basis of all attempts at metrical analysis. These divisions are so clear in many cases that one can often surely recognize the rhythmic divisions even without knowledge of meter, guided only by the sense. This aid, however, abandons us in accounts where the logical divisions are not nearly so simple and permit multiple rhythmic interpretations. And now Sievers abandons this logical basis for rhythmical divisions by assuming that many Hebrew accounts exhibit a greater metrical freedom in which the caesura and the verse endings do not necessarily coincide with the logical divisions ("the concealment of the caesura by the sense" and "enjambment," 2:167). In this way, however, the door and gate are opened wide for caprice. In order to convince oneself that one can arrive at very different results by applying this means, one may compare Sievers's own, very different versifications of Gen 2:41 (1:382ff., 386ff.; 2:6ff., 124ff.) and may also consult the attempts of Erbt, based on essentially the same principles ("Urgeschichte der Bibel," *Mitteilungen der Vorderas. Ges.* [1904] no. 4). (d) In addition, Sievers assumes individual strands of various meters in the three generally recognized documentary sources, J, E, and P—in all fourteen different subsources—colorfully intermixed in the current text. Then, too, come the additions of redactors and interpolators. By all these means even the most stubborn text can be metrically tamed! A clause that resists being forced into the metrical scheme even by the aids mentioned can be excised and assigned to another source! These substrands, however, are hardly conceivable as literary units and, above all else, Sievers's assumption that later additions had a different meter than the text (2:216) is especially odd. It compares to the notion that the glossators of Homer prepared additions in iambic trimeter (cf. Meyer, *Israeliten*, vii). (e) The deciding factor concerning Sievers's whole metrical textual system, however, is to be sought in those very numerous passages where we are clearly able to recognize the source distinctions for substantive reasons. I—as I may assure the reader—took up Sievers's work with the greatest expectations and, fully prepared to learn from the great metricist here too, examined it. To my own surprise, however, the result was that Sievers's source distinctions, to the extent that they offer something new, can almost nowhere be sustained (cf. the "source analyses" at the beginning of the individual exegeses). In very many passages, Sievers separates material that belongs together or links unrelated materials. Thus, his whole system fails because of his impossible source analysis. Yet, it should be expressly added that in the details, especially in textual criticism, much can be learned from him and that the great service he has rendered to the study of Hebrew meter is in no wise diminished thereby. Procksch (210ff.) follows Sievers on the whole, differing only in details, and doubts Sievers's "subsources" in particular. The individual narratives would have frequently had different meters and sometimes even alternating meter, e.g., heptameter mixed with hexameter and trimeter. But such an assumption shakes the whole hypoth-

3. Since the legends were already very old when they were committed to writing (cf. ¶¶4, 5), the language of Genesis is by nature archaic. This archaism should be echoed in translation. We know biblical and extrabiblical variants of individual legends, especially of the Creation, Flood, and Paradise narratives, variants with strict rhythmic form and rhythmic, poetic style. Since these variants predate those transmitted in Genesis, one may postulate that other <xxix> legends also once had poetic form. The older genre in poetic style can be distinguished from the later, prosaic genre much as the German heroic song differs from the later "folk book." Yet, such an older, poetic form can only be postulated for the myths and perhaps also the sanctuary legends (¶3:5).

4. A second question concerns whether these literary works are popular tradition or the products of individual poets. Modern scholars have correctly answered this question in principle arguing that Genesis records oral popular tradition. We can ascertain how such "popular traditions" arise. Of course, in the final analysis, an individual always created such a work. Now, however, we characteristically never observe such popular traditions, such as language, in development, but when we hear of them, they appear as ancient material inherited from the past. A long period lies between the authors who first composed them and the time that transmitted them to us. In this interval, however, the legend has been recounted from generation to generation and has passed through many hands. However faithfully such legends are reproduced, they are nevertheless transformed on their way through the centuries (¶4). Thus, legend is ultimately a community product.[28] This transformation of legend occurred unconsciously, at least in the earlier phases. One may speak of the conscious transformation of the accounts only in their latest forms. Narrators and hearers considered the legends "true" stories. Our historical books in which narrators shift almost imperceptibly from legends to actual "historical" accounts which themselves mix legend and historical elements demonstrate that this understanding applies to OT legends. The legends, themselves, which earnestly provide the bases for actual current situations, also confirm this understanding. Because the woman was taken from the man's rib, the man longs for her companionship. This narrative was not a poetic embodiment of an idea for the narrator, but an actual event. This perspective inheres in the nature of the matter. Legend stems from times and circles which did not yet have the intellectual ability to distinguish between fiction and reality. It is, therefore, no minor error for modern scholars to treat the Paradise legend as an allegory with no interest in reality. Furthermore, and precisely because the whole people created legend, it is also an expression of the

---

esis. Procksch did not attempt the task incumbent upon him, to publish the whole text metrically arranged according to his principles. Instead, he limited himself to individual, supplemental indications. Will someone in the future succeed in discovering the free rhythms in which the accounts of Genesis move? At any rate, such an attempt will be all the more convincing if it makes measured use of textual criticism.

[28]A. l'Houet (*Zur Psychologie des Bauerntums* [1905], 34) impressively describes the history of such popular traditions "as a common effort of a whole tribe, of whole, long-gone, generations of the same tribe, on one and the same theme. There was no grandfather, no grandmother who did not already know it as a grandchild, who did not allow it to pass through their hands in the course of their lives, changing it, never much, but always a little, as a stream takes traces of all the banks through which it flows."

people's spirit. This observation is very significant for our evaluation of statements in <xxx> Genesis. We are justified in considering the preferences and attitudes Genesis presents us as the common property of large groups.

5. Accordingly, we must examine Genesis, first, in the form it had in oral tradition. If we want to understand the legends we must depict the situation in which they were told. We hear of such situations in Exod 12:26-27; 13:14-15; and Josh 4:6: when children ask about the reason for the sacred custom or the meaning of a sacred symbol, their father answers by telling the story. Thus, one may imagine how the Sodom narrative was told in respect to the Dead Sea and the Bethel legend to the heights of Bethel. We must imagine the normal situation, however, as follows. On a dreadful winter evening the whole family sits by the hearth. The adults and especially the children listen intently to the old, beautiful, often-heard and ever-popular stories from ancient times. We join them and listen along. Many of the legends have (cf. below) such a distinct, literary style that one can hardly understand them in this form as the products of the people, itself. Instead, we must assume that there were professional storytellers in Israel, as among the Arabs and many peoples past and present. Such folktellers, learned in the old songs and legends, moved about the countryside. They could be found at folk festivals.

We have seen previously (p. xxvi) that the current prose narrative style may have been preceded by a poetic style in at least a few legends. We may assume another situation for these songs. We may imagine, namely, on the analogy of the Babylonian creation poem, by form, a spring hymn to Marduk, that the cultic legends trace back to sanctuary songs sung by the priests at holy festivals at the sacred site (cf. p. xxi). However this may have been, our sanctuary legends are certainly no longer sung and, as their uniquely colorless mood demonstrates, also belong in their current form, not at the holy sites themselves, but in popular tradition.

6. A new question, again of fundamental character, concerns the identification of the basic unit for examination and appreciation by Genesis research. A series of different units could be considered. The most comprehensive unit is the whole Pentateuch, Genesis, then the individual book of legends that preceded it, then the individual legends comprising the book. Among these, independent legends such as the accounts of Hagar's flight (Gen 16) or of Isaac's sacrifice (Gen 22), and certain combinations of several legends into a "legend cycle," such as the legend cycle treating the fates of Abraham and Lot until the births of their sons, or the one combining the experiences of Jacob with Esau and Laban into one account, or the one whose hero is Joseph, are to be distinguished. We must consider all these units. But the primary question concerns which deserves primary consideration, <xxxi> that is, which of these various units is original in oral tradition? This question is repeated in many similar cases. Which unit is the standard, the song book, the individual collection in it, or the individual song? The Gospel, the speech, or the individual saying transmitted from Jesus? The whole apocalypse or the individual apocalyptic source document, or the individual vision? It is also of decisive significance for the understanding of Genesis that one consciously consider this question and correctly answer it. A popular legend exists by nature in the form of an individual legend.[29] Only later did collectors gather

---

[29]Reuß, *A.T.* 3:73: The patriarchal legends "originally arose individually, without context, inde-

several such legends or did authors form larger literary constructions from them. This process also applied to Hebrew popular legends. Even in their present form, the legends of Genesis give clear evidence of this process. Each individual legend preserved in its old form is a self-contained whole. It begins with a clear beginning, it concludes with an easily discernible conclusion.

One may compare individual cases. Abraham wants to obtain a wife for his son. Since he is too old himself, he sends his oldest servant. Thus the account begins (Gen 24). It is then reported how the servant identifies the appropriate maiden and brings her back. Meanwile, the old master has died. The young master takes the bride and "is comforted over his father." Anyone can see that the narrative has ended. God commissions Abraham to sacrifice his son. This "exposition" makes an entirely new beginning (Gen 22). Now it is reported how Abraham was determined to carry out the command and almost did so. But at the last moment God himself hinders the sacrifice. Abraham retains Isaac. "Then they returned together to Beer-sheba." Each time, then, the account begins in such a way that one notes a new beginning. And it clearly concludes when the knot has been happily untied. Then no one can say, "And what happened next?" Similarly, the fact that they manifest a consistent tone demonstrates the unity of the individual legends. Thus, emotion governs the narrative of Isaac's sacrifice (Gen 22), humor the narrative of Jacob's deceit of Isaac (Gen 27), moral sobriety the Sodom narrative (Gen 19), and reverence for the sovereign God the account of the construction of the Tower (Gen 11). Many accounts would be entirely ruined if followed immediately by another so that the reader would be forcefully carried from one mood to another. Instead, even now, any competent narrator makes a pause after telling one of these narratives so that the imagination will have time to recover, the hearer may once again reflect upon what has been heard, and the mood stimulated may subside. Whoever has actively followed the account of Isaac's sacrifice, for example, needs to rest and recover from the shock experienced at the end. Those accounts intended to establish a current situation (cf. pp. xiii-xiv, xvii-xxii), in particular, need a pause at the end so the hearer may compare the <xxxii> prediction expressed in the account and its existing fulfillment. One may recall the conclusion of the Paradise narrative, the Flood account, or perhaps the account of Noah's drunkenness. In a later time, one compiled larger units, legend cycles which more or less artfully combine individual legends. But even in these cases, one can, for the most part, extract the originally independent units from the combinations without difficulty. Thus the legend cycle concerning Abraham and Lot falls clearly into the following narratives: (1) the migration of Abraham and Lot to Canaan, (2) their separation in Bethel, (3) the epiphany in Hebron, (4) the destruction of Sodom, (5) the birth of Ammon and Moab, and (6) the birth of Isaac. The Jacob-Esau-Laban legend cycle consists of the legends of Jacob-Esau, of Jacob-Laban, of the origin of the twelve tribes, in addition to individually interpolated cultic legends. The accounts of Joseph's experiences with his brothers, of "Potiphar's wife," of the dream interpretation in prison, of Pharaoh's dreams, and of agricultural circumstances in Egypt (47:13ff.) are also clearly distinct from one another in the Joseph narrative.

---

pendently of one another." Wellhausen, *Composition*[3], 8: "The tradition in the mouth of the people knows only individual narratives" (cf. also *Prolegomena*[6], 294, 334).

The resulting consequence for interpretation is that every individual legend is always first to be interpreted on its own. The more independent an account, the more surely it is preserved in an old form. The "relationship," however, between the individual legends is, in many cases, of later origins,[30] if not simply the commentator's imposition. As an example of an ancient legend almost without precondition, one may take the account of Hagar's flight (Gen 16) concerning which we need to know only that there was a husband, Abraham, and a wife, Sarah. The legend itself says everything else. An example of a later account is the legend of the wooing of Rebekah (Gen 24). This legend presumes a whole series of individual elements from other narratives: Abraham's family and emigration, Yahweh's promise associated with the emigration, the fact that Isaac is the son of his old age and his only son, etc. Even in this passage, we must first consider the individual legend.

7. What is the scope of such an account? Many of the Genesis accounts hardly extend beyond ten verses: that is, the accounts of Noah's drunkenness, the Tower Construction, Abraham's trip to Egypt, Hagar's flight (Gen 16), Ishmael's expulsion (21:8ff.), Abraham's trial (Gen 22), and Jacob at Bethel (28:10ff.) and Penuel (32:25ff.). Alongside these very brief narratives, a series of others, the "extended" accounts, comprise roughly a chapter, namely, the Paradise narrative, the accounts of Cain's fratricide, the Flood, the appearance of the deity at Hebron (Gen 18), Rebekah's engagement (Gen 24), and Jacob's deception of Isaac (Gen 27). Only the later legend cycles exceed this dimension. This scope of the legends distinguish them markedly from our current products. Even the most complicated legend constructions in Genesis, such as the Joseph narrative, are, measured by current cri<xxxiii>terion, of rather modest scope; the older individual legends are, however, remarkably brief for modern tastes. This brief scope of the old legends, of course, indicates their character, at the same time. They concern very simple events which can be sufficiently depicted in a few words. And this scope simultaneously reflects both the narrator's skill and the hearer's comprehension. The earliest narrators would have been unable to shape more extensive literary works. Neither did they expect their hearers to be able to follow them for days, even weeks, with undiminished attention. Rather, the ancient period was satisfied with very minor creations which hardly fill a quarter hour. When the account has ended then, the imagination of the hearer is sated and his powers of comprehension are exhausted. At most, we may imagine that when the story ends, the hearers, like our children, may have wanted the same account once more.

At the same time, on the other hand, we see from our accounts that a later period was no longer satisfied with very brief legends. A more mature esthetic sensibility required larger room for expression. Thus, larger compositions came into being. The fact that the legends began to be committed to writing, especially, facilitated this expansion of the legends. Now written accounts are by nature more extensive than spoken accounts. The eye can comprehend larger units in reading than the ear in hearing. Accordingly, this, too, is a measure of the age of the legends which must be employed, however, with caution. The briefer the legend, the more likely it is preserved in an old form.

---

[30]Wellhausen, *Prolegomena*[6], 334: "The individuality of the individual account is the most essential and original, the context is a secondary matter only introduced by the collection and literary fixation of the accounts."

This brevity of the legends, as we have seen, indicates the poverty of this old art. But, at the same time, this very poverty is its special advantage. The limited scope within which the narrator must operate forced him to apply his whole artistic power to the most minor points. These creations are as concentrated and as effective as they are brief. The limited ability to comprehend attested by these small literary works leads simultaneously to the need to shape the accounts as clearly and transparently as possible.

8. In order to discern the latter, one must first note the structure. The accounts, not just the more extensive, but also the briefest, are arranged unusually distinctly in "scenes." We term those smaller portions of an account distinguishable from one another through the change of persons, of place, or of action, "scenes." Thus the story of Noah's drunkenness (9:20ff.) is arranged as follows. Exposition—Noah's Drunkenness. I. The Events. (1) Canaan's shamelessness, (2) the piety of Shem and Japheth. II. The Words. (1) concerning Canaan, (2) concerning Japheth and Shem. The Paradise narrative in chap. 3 has the following structure: I. The Sin. (1) the serpent seduces the woman, (2) woman and man sin, (3) the consequences: cessation of innocence; II. The Interrogation. III. The Penalty. (1) the curse on the serpent, (2) on the woman, (3) on the man; IV. Conclusion: the expulsion. <xxxiv>

Through such beautiful, clear structures, the accounts gain the impression of clarity, the precondition of any esthetic effect. Thus, the whole divides into sections and parts which, themselves, are very transparent and whose interrelationship is very clear. These arrangements are not laboriously contrived, instead they flow from the nature of the matter as though they were quite obvious. One may note, for example, how exquisitely the structure corresponds to the content in the Paradise narrative. In the Fall the sequence is serpent, woman, man. The interrogation begins with the final effect and follows the same course back. Here, then, the sequence is reversed: man, woman, serpent. The penalty applies, first, to the principle guilty parties, thus, the original sequence returns here: serpent, woman, man. It is, therefore, advisable for the modern reader to attend to arrangement since it also reveals the course of the action.

9. The legend narrator, furthermore, did not expect his hearers—as the modern novelist can—to attend to many persons simultaneously. The minimum number is two, of course, because at least two persons are necessary for a complication in the plot. Thus two persons appear in the account of the separation of Abraham and Lot (Gen 13), of Esau's sale of the birthright (25:29ff.), and in the narrative of Penuel (32:23ff.). Three persons appear in the narrative of the creation of the woman (God, man, woman), in Cain's fratricide (God, Cain, Abel), in the account of Lot in the cave (19:30ff.), in Isaac's sacrifice (Gen 22). Four appear in the Paradise narrative, in Abraham's trip to Egypt (12:10ff.), in Hagar's flight (Gen 16), in Jacob's deception of Isaac (Gen 27). Yet there are also accounts in which several persons appear as in the "extended" narrative of the wooing of Rebekah (Gen 24) and, especially, in the accounts of the twelve sons of Jacob. Here, too, however, the narrators cultivated simplicity and transparency. Thus, in many cases where a plurality appears, these many are treated as a unit: they think and want the same and one acts like the others. Humanity in the Flood and Tower accounts, the brothers Shem and Japheth (9:23), the three men at Hebron and Sodom (Gen 18–19, in the original form of the account), Lot's sons-in-law at Sodom (19:14), Pharaoh's courtiers (12:15), the citizens of Shechem and the brothers of Dinah (Gen 34), the citizens of Timna (38:21), and similarly in many other cases, are treated like one person. This corresponds to the

circumstances of that ancient period which did not distinguish the individual from the group as sharply as the present.

At the same time, however, the narrators' inability to conceptualize and portray differences among individuals occasions this combination of various person. The limits of the capacity of even an esthetically trained narrator to characterize several individuals at that time can be seen in the very clear example of the Joseph narrative. The account juxtaposes Joseph and the eleven. Joseph's full brother, the youngest, Benjamin, is distinct from the others. Among the remaining ten, Reuben (Judah) assumes a special place. This exhausts the narrator's powers of characterization, however. He is unable to conceive of the remaining nine <xxxv> as individuals. They are "the brothers." Further simplicity is attained through the structure which, as we have seen, ultimately divides the account into nothing but small scenes. Only rarely do all the persons of the account appear at the same time in these scenes. Instead, only a very few persons, often only two, always appear to us at once.[31] One may compare the scenes in the story of the wooing of Rebekah (Gen 24). The first scene shows Abraham and the servant, the second the servant alone on his journey and at the well, the third the servant and the maiden, the fourth the maiden and her family, the fifth (the major scene) the servant with the maiden at her home, the sixth the servant on the return journey with the maiden, and the last, these two with Isaac. In the story of Ishmael's expulsion (21:4ff.) we see the following in sequence: Sarah, as she hears Ishmael laughing and as she prevails upon Abraham; Abraham as he expels Hagar; further, Hagar alone with the child in the desert and finally delivered by the angel. The story of Jacob's deception (Gen 27) deals first with Isaac and Esau, then with Esau and Isaac, further with Jacob and Isaac, Esau and Isaac, Esau's hatred for Jacob, and finally with Rebekah's advice for Jacob. The narrator's particular task is to establish why this sequence of scenes took place. They saw no harm in occasionally dropping a person from the sequence, for example, the serpent after the temptation (after 3:5), Rebekah after Jacob's flight from Esau (after Gen 27). This arrangement makes for extreme clarity in the account. The hearer need not keep an eye on a confusing multitude of people. Instead they appear in sequence. Thus, the reader has time to consider and gain an impression of them at leisure. All the persons appear together only at the high points of the action, as in the final scene of the modern drama: as in the Paradise narrative (3:14ff.), in Noah's drunkenness (9:24ff.), and at the end of the Joseph narrative (46:29ff.). There, too, the narrators considered division necessary. They were unable to portray a dialogue among many persons. God did not confront all of the participants with their sins in a common address at the end of the Paradise narrative, but turned first to the serpent, then to the woman, and finally to the man. Elsewhere, too, the style resolves conversations into nothing but two-party dialogues.

10. The clear distinction between major and secondary persons further emphasizes the synopsis of the various persons. The hearer need not search long to determine which persons deserve particular attention. Instead, the narrator makes it very clear, indeed, simple,

---

[31]Olrik ("Epische Gesetze der Volksdichtung," *Zeitschr. für deutsches Altertum* 51:5) establishes as one of the "epic laws of folk literature" that two is the largest number of persons who may appear at once: "Only two people ever appear at once on the stage." This law also generally applies in Genesis.

by dealing chiefly with the most important person. Thus, the patriarchs themselves are the major figures in most of the patriarchal narratives. The following presents the figures in a few accounts in the order of their importance for the narrator. <xxxvi> Cain, Abel; Abraham, Sarah, Pharaoh (12:10ff.); Abraham, Lot (13:7ff.); Hagar, Sarah, Abraham (Gen 16); the servant and Rebekah are the chief persons in chap. 24; in chap. 27 the main figures are Jacob and Esau, their parents are secondary; in the Jacob-Laban narrative the main characters are Jacob and Laban, the wives are secondary. One should not confuse compassion or respect with interest. Cain is more important than Abel for the artistic interests of the narrator, Hagar more than Sarah. The servant is the main character in chap. 24, whereas Abraham, for example, only plays a secondary role. In many cases, the fortunes of only one major figure are followed, for example, especially clearly in the Joseph narratives.[32]

11. How are the persons who appear portrayed? First, the brief treatments of secondary figures is noteworthy. We are accustomed in modern works to portrayals of every person who appears, where possible, as an independent individual, if only with a few features. The ancient legend narrator operates quite differently. He fleshes out the persons secondary to him, in general or momentarily, very scantily or not at all. Obviously to ancient sensibilities one does not linger over slaves. Esau's (32:7) or Laban's (31:23ff.) companions only appear to depict the power of these men. The narratives did not consider it necessary to indicate more precisely the crimes of Pharaoh's two chamberlains (40:1) or Dinah's thoughts (Gen 34), nor those of Sarah on the journey to Egypt (12:10ff.). Hirah, Judah's friend (Gen 38), is not characterized. Er's sins (38:7) are not indicated. Nothing characteristic is reported about Judah's wife (Gen 38). Nor is anything reported concerning Joseph's chief of staff (43:16ff.), etc. But the portrayal of the main characters is also remarkably scanty in our terms. Very few traits are attributed to them, sometimes only one. Cain is jealous of his brother. Canaan is shameless; Shem and Japheth are chaste (9:20ff.). In the story of the separation of Lot and Abraham (13:2ff.), Lot is greedy, Abraham accommodating. In the Hebron narrative (Gen 18), Abraham is hospitable, in the emigration (Gen 12) obedient to God's command. In the Penuel narrative (32:25ff.), Jacob is strong and brave; in the Jacob-Esau narrative, clever; in the Joseph narrative, he loves Rachel's sons. In the already rather complicated depiction of the Fall story, the serpent is clever and evil, the man and woman are as inexperienced as children, the woman has a sweet tooth and is easily persuaded, the man follows his wife.

Each individual narrative also usually knows of only one divine trait. In most legends, God is the gracious helper; in others, as in the Paradise and Tower narratives, he is the lofty ruler who knows how to keep humans in their limits. This economy of the legends is remarkable to us. After all, we are accustomed to encountering skillfully portrayed characterizations consisting of many individual elements in modern literary works. This skill of the ancient narrators differs significantly. Of course, it depends on the actual circumstances of the ancient period since <xxxvii> people of that time were simpler than complicated people now. Yet, it would be an error to believe that the people of that time were as simple as they are depicted here in the legends. As evidence, one may compare the characterizations offered by a more mature art in the book of 2 Samuel. From this

---

[32]"There is always one formal main character" (Olrik, 10).

example one also discerns that more is involved here than the abbreviation of reality contained in any literary portrayal. Rather, Genesis expresses a particular folk psychology. This viewpoint was unable to comprehend and portray many, and certainly not all, of the aspects of a person. It was only capable of seeing a few features. It strove all the more, however, to conceptualize the essential features of the person and, consequently, formulated stereotypes. Thus, in the account of her flight (Gen 16), Hagar is the pampered slave, Sarah is the jealous wife, and Abraham is the right-thinking and accommodating husband. Rachel and Leah (29:31ff.) are types of the "beloved" and "despised." In the account of Abraham's trip to Egypt (12:10ff.) or in the Jacob narrative, Pharaoh acts like a Western king in the narrator's conception. His courtiers are typical courtiers. Abraham's servant (Gen 24) is an old, faithful servant. In the story of his deception (Gen 27), Isaac is a blind old man, and Rebekah is a partisan, cunning mother. In the emigration (Gen 12) and in Isaac's sacrifice (Gen 22) Abraham is the obedient and pious individual. A series of figures exemplify nations or classes of the population: the wrathful Cain, the shameless Canaan, the generous but not very deliberative Esau, the tricky Laban, the much more cunning Jacob (cf. above p. xvii).

Undoubtedly, the fact that the legends present us not so much with individual persons as types, once again indicates poverty of comprehension. But how the narrators made a virtue of necessity! Given their limitations, they accomplished extraordinary feats. They conceptualized types they observed with a clarity and certainty comparable to the Egyptian artists ability to paint ethnic types. For this reason, many of the old legends still captivate the current, even the uneducated, reader. They reflect many universally human circumstances, still directly observable today. To be sure, the enjoyment they give the connoisseur, to whom they offer the most intimate clues as to the circumstances and attitudes of antiquity in the most pleasing form, is all the greater. This simplicity of the characters depicted also suggests that the art of these popular legends is far from capable of showing a development in the characters, an improvement or a deterioration. Anything of this sort modern interpreters believe they have found in Genesis is imposed. Thus, Jacob's "impure" character did not change at all. Joseph's brothers were not "reformed" in the course of the account, but punished. The legend also attained this simple clarity by juxtaposing the two major actors: the clever-shepherd Jacob and the foolish-hunter Esau, the shameless Canaan and the pious Shem and Japheth, <xxxviii> the magnanimous Joseph and his jealous brothers, the shepherd Abel, beloved of God, and the unpleasant farmer Cain, the despised Leah and the beautiful Rachel, the hospitable Lot and the Sodomites who shamefully disregard the rights of the guest, etc.[33] Whereas the individual legends, then, know essentially only one trait of the acting persons, the legend cycles can offer more extensive descriptions, although in an unusual manner. The most important example of this is, of course, the characterization of the Joseph figure in the Joseph-legend cycle. There, each individual legend elucidates one or two aspects of his character. His father favored him, although his brothers despised him for it, and he had prefiguring dreams, one legend says (Gen 37); everything flourished under his hand, he was handsome and pious, says another (Gen 39); he knew how to interpret dreams, says a third (Gen 40);

---

[33]This is the "law of opposites" in epic popular literature (cf. Olrik, 6).

he was also clever, says a fourth (Gen 41); etc. The combination of all these individual elements constitutes a total picture.

Similarly, the narrators economize remarkably in their descriptions of the person's outward appearance. They reveal nothing to us about hair, skin tone, eyes, or clothing. In all of these, they assume the normal Hebrew type. When they depart from this rule of presentation, they do so for very specific reasons. Esau is red and hairy (25:25), apparently as a prototype of the people associated with him; Joseph wears a sleeved garment as a sign of his father's love (Gen 37); Leah's weak eyes are the reason Jacob despises her (29:17).

If we now ask about the fundamental principle underlying the narrators' emphasis on specific traits of their characters, it becomes clear that they usually totally subordinate characterization to action. Those personal traits portrayed are necessary for the course of the action. Everything else possible is omitted. The story of Jacob's deceptions (Gen 27) recounts how, on the advice of his mother, Jacob brings his father Isaac to bless, not Esau, but him. Thus, Jacob is clever, he deceives. Esau is stupid, he allows himself to be disadvantaged. Isaac is easy to deceive, blind. Rebekah is sly, she gives cunning advice, and, at the same time, she is biased in Jacob's favor. In an "extended" account, this is now linked with other elements: Jacob is a shepherd who remains at home with his mother; Esau is a hunter whose game his father loves to eat. The modern narrator would add a multitude of additional character features in order to shape the material colorfully and vitally. The old narrator scorns this. Thus, one can clearly discern the esthetic interest of the narrators. For them, action is primary; Characterization is only secondary.

12. By what means do the narrators present the characters of their heroes? The modern artist tries to illuminate the complicated thoughts and attitudes of his characters in extended presentations. If one regards Genesis from the perspective of such an account, one is <xxxix> astonished to find so few statements concerning the psychic life of the heroes. Very rarely are the thoughts of the actors explicitly explained to us: those of the woman when she desirously regarded the tree in Paradise (3:6), those of Noah when he released the birds "to see whether the water has receded from the earth" (8:8), those of Lot's sons-in-law who believed their father-in-law was joking (19:14), those of Isaac who fears the people of Gerar could kill him for his wife (26:7), or Jacob's clever ideas for averting the revenge of his brother Esau (32:9, 21), etc. But this, too, seems very brief and insufficient in relation to the psychological portrayals of our time. And such statements are by no means the rule in the legends of Genesis. Rather, the narrator often suffices with only a very brief allusion: "he was angry" (4:5; 30:2; 31:36; 34:7; 39:19; 40:2); "he was afraid" (26:7; 28:17; 32:8); "he was comforted" (24:67); "he came to love her" (24:67; 29:18; 34:3; 37:3); "she was jealous" (30:1); "he was horrified" (27:33); "she hated him" (37:4); etc. Very often we do not find the slightest statement concerning the thoughts and attitudes of the person involved, even at points where we note the absence of such a statement with a certain amazement. The narrator conceals from us why God prohibited the Paradise tree to the people (2:17), as well as the serpent's motivations for seducing the people. He does not state Abraham's mood when he left his homeland (Gen 12) or Noah's when he entered the ark (7:7). We do not hear that Noah was angry at Canaan's shamelessness (9:24), that Jacob was disappointed when Laban deceived him with Leah (29:25), that Hagar rejoiced when she received the promise that Ishmael would become

a people (21:18), indeed, not even that the mothers rejoice when they hold their firstborn sons in their arms (4:1; 21:6; 25:24ff.).

Particularly noteworthy is the example of the account of Isaac's sacrifice (Gen 22): what modern narrator would omit a description of Abraham's psychological state whose faithful obedience won the onerous victory over paternal love and whose sorrow was transformed into joy in the end? What is the reason for this peculiar phenomenon? One can discern this in an example such as 19:27-28. In view of Sodom, Abraham heard the remarkable words of the three men: they wanted to go down to Sodom, they said, to investigate the city's guilt (18:20-21). He thought about these words. On the next morning he got up and went to the same place. He wants to see whether anything happened to Sodom in the night. And actually he sees there below smoke—something has taken place there, but at the same time this smoke obscures the vicinity—he does not perceive what may have happened. This minor scene was apparently valuable for the narrator not as a historical fact, but because of the thoughts Abraham must have had at the time. Nevertheless, he does not portray these thoughts themselves. He indicates only the external circumstances to us. We must supply the key matter ourselves. This narrator, therefore, had insight into the psychic life of his hero. But he was unable to make these inner processes so clear that he could articulate them. Similar situations can often <xl> be observed in Genesis. On very many occasions when the modern narrator would offer a psychological explanation, the ancient narrator offers an action.[34] The psychic status of the people in Paradise and after the Fall is not unfolded, but one striking example is recounted in which it is manifest (2:25; 3:7). The narrator says nothing about Adam's thoughts when his wife offers him the forbidden fruit but only that he ate. He does not present the fact that Abraham had a hospitable personality; instead, he recounts how he received the three men (18:2ff.). He does not say that Shem and Japheth had pious and respectful attitudes; rather, he has them act piously and respectfully (9:23). It is not stated that Joseph was touched when he saw Benjamin again, but that he turned away to cry (42:24; 43:30). Nothing is said about Hagar, mistreated by Sarah, feeling profoundly offended in her maternal pride, but that she ran away from her mistress (16:6). Laban is not said to have been blinded by the foreigner's gold, but to have hurriedly issued an invitation (24:30f.). There is no account of obedience to God conquering paternal love in Abraham, but only of his immediate departure (22:3). Tamar is not said to have proven faithful to her husband even beyond the grave, but to have been able to obtain children from his seed (Gen 38). One sees where the narrator placed the chief emphasis. He did not have the modern attitude which finds human psychic life most interesting and a valuable object of art. Instead, his childish tastes prefer to linger over the externally conspicuous facts. In this, however, his accomplishments are outstanding. He is extraordinarily capable of choosing the very action most indicative of his hero's spiritual state. How could respectful modesty be better portrayed than in the legend of Shem and Japheth, or maternal love better than through Hagar's behavior—she gives her son to drink (21:10), nothing is said of her drinking herself. How could one better depict hospitality than through Abraham's behavior at Hebron (18:2ff.). And the simple manner in which

---

[34]Olrik (8) establishes this as a universally valid law of popular epic literature: "every characteristic of persons and things must be expressed in action; otherwise it is insignificant" (cf. also n. 1).

the innocence and "knowledge" of the first people are illustrated is downright brilliant (2:25; 3:7). These simple artists did not know how to reflect, but they were master observers. The admirable art of indirect description of humans through their actions is the primary feature that makes the legends so vivid.[35]

Although these ancients were poorly equipped to discuss psychic life, one still has the impression that they permit us insight into the depths of their heroes' hearts. These figures live before our eyes and thus the modern reader, enchanted by the lucid clarity of these old legends, may completely forget what they lack. Even when the narrator says nothing of the inner psychic life of his heroes, it is not entirely lost to the hearer. At this point we must <xli> remember that we have before us stories that were told orally. In addition to words, another link unites narrator and hearer. The tone of voice, the facial expression, or even a hand movement also play roles. In this way, without saying a word, he communicates to his hearers joy and pain, love, wrath, jealousy, hatred, compassion, and all the other emotions of his heroes, which the narrator also experienced. Our interpretation, however, incurs the task of reading between the lines the spiritual life the narrator did not explicitly portray. This is not always very easy. The moods of the ancient period and their expressions are remote to us in many respects. Why does Rebekah veil herself when she sees Isaac, for example, (24:65)? Why did Lot's daughters go to their father (19:32)? Why did Tamar desire descendants of Judah (Gen 38)? How were the growing shame and the sin of the first people related (3:7)? In such cases, earlier interpreters often erred by simply assuming modern motifs and attitudes. But even those interpreters who want to avoid modernizing, who consciously strive to rediscover the psychic life of Hebrew antiquity, easily make mistakes. Not unusually, in such cases it may be hardly possible to reach a firm decision.

13. A further means for expressing the spiritual life of persons is speech. Words are not as vivid as actions, but they are better able to reveal the inner life of persons. Ancient narrators understood extraordinarily well how to find the words corresponding to the attitude of the speaker. Thus, words express the evil of the sly serpent and the inexperience of the childish woman (3:1ff.), Sarah's jealousy of her slave (16:5) and Abraham's accommodating nature (16:6), the righteous indignation of Abimelech (20:9), the foresight of the clever Jacob (32:9), and the bitter complaints of those deceived by Jacob, Esau (27:36), and Laban (31:43). Particular masterpieces of characterization in words are the account of the temptation of the first humans (Gen 3) and the conversation between Abraham and Isaac on the way to the mountain (22:7-8). In contrast to German ballads, for example, Hebrew accounts always explicitly introduce speech. The rule of style is to avoid two speeches in sequence by the same person. Instead, they are separated by another's statement or by an action. Notably for our tastes, the persons of Genesis often do not speak where a modern narrator would surely have them speak, even when the nature of the matter seems to require a statement. We may imagine that Joseph complained vigorously when he was cast into the well (37:24) and taken to Egypt (37:28; cf. also 42:21), that an exchange of words preceded Cain's act of homicide (4:8), that the expelled Hagar left Abraham's house wailing and crying (21:14), and that Isaac plead touchingly for mercy when his father bound him on the pile of wood (22:9). But we hear nothing of all this!

---

[35]"The legend always climaxes in one or more key situations of graphic nature" (Olrik, 9).

The people do not respond at all when God curses their life. They did not even recriminate themselves (3:16ff.). Rebekah says nothing in Gerar (Gen 26); Noah says not a word in the Flood legend; Abraham says not a word in chap. 18 when he is <xlii> promised a son (18:10), or when he is commanded to sacrifice Isaac (Gen 22); Hagar is equally silent when she sees the child dying and then when God hears Ishmael's crying (Gen 21). Whoever follows these observations cannot easily believe that the persons of Genesis are meant to be portrayed as silent, even callous. To him, the only talkative character would seem to be—God.

What is the source of this unusual economy of words? First, it certainly reflects the fact that much less was said and much more briefly in that culture than in the talkative present when everyone feels the need to pour out one's heart and to reveal its wondrous secrets. The ancient period differed. Then, as is still the case among our peasants,[36] words did not pass the lips so quickly. At the same time, however, this economy of words in the book of Genesis is based in the style of the narrators. The narrators subjugated everything to the action. They did not take up speeches which did not further the action itself. In this interest, they especially avoided depicting the attitudes of the passive persons in speeches. Whether Joseph complained or remained silent when his brothers sold him changes nothing of his fate. The words Abraham or Noah speak when God commands them are insignificant. It is enough that they obey. God's curse decides the fate of the first people. No self-recrimination can help. What more will the exchange of words that preceded Cain's act of homicide tell us when we already know the reason he became a murderer? Naturally, it also seems that people do not respond to God's promises—as is quite common. What should one say when God has spoken? The reverse of this peculiar economy of words is that those speeches the narrators do find worthy of reporting are necessary in the context of the account. The conversation between serpent and woman (3:1ff.) is supposed to show how the consumption of the forbidden fruit came about. Cain pours out his guilt-laden heart before God. Therefore, God decides to mitigate his sentence (4:13ff.). Abraham bids his wife to pretend to be his sister. Thus it happened that she was taken into Pharaoh's harem (12:11ff.). Abraham gave Lot the freedom to move to the West or the East. Thus Lot chose the Jordan Valley (13:8ff.). At Sarah's request, Abraham took Hagar as a concubine and at her second request he returned her (Gen 16). These are not superfluous speeches, then. Instead, they are necessary in order to provide the inner reasons for the subsequent action. The curses and promises (3:14ff.; 4:11-12; 8:21-22; 9:25ff.; 12:2-3; 27; 28:13-14; etc.) are especially necessary. Indeed, they are the climax of the entire account, toward which all the preceding strives.

Thus God is understandably so often introduced speaking in Genesis (1; 2:16-17; 3:9ff.; 4:6ff.; 7:1ff.; 11:6-7; 12:1ff., 7; 13:14ff.; 15; 16:8ff.; and often). Speech is the chief means whereby God influences the action in the patriarchal legends. In a few passages, the narrators have even introduced soliloquies, the most abstract form of speech (2:18; 6:7; 8:21-22; 18:12, 17ff.; 26:7; etc.) when, according to the situation, no one was present to hear the person speak. This case is quite common in relation to God. <xliii> Whom should God tell his most secret plans? Yet, in a few cases, we can reconstruct an older

---

[36]Cf. A. l'Houet, *Psychologie des Bauerntums*, 111, 178.

form of the account in which God turned to his heavenly company (1:26; 3:22; 11:7). At any rate, there are, indeed, speeches in the brief legends intended either to characterize a person or to give the judgment of the narrator or serving some other purpose intended by the narrator, without being totally necessary in the context.

Many speeches in Genesis are unusually brief. One may recall the complaint of Hagar ("I flee from my mistress Sarah," 16:8), or statements of Lot's daughters (19:31), of Sarah (21:10), of Abraham ("I will swear," 21:24), of Rebekah (24:18-19), of Jacob ("swear to me today," 25:33), of Isaac ("she is my sister," 26:7), of the shepherds of Gerar ("the water belongs to us," 26:20), of Isaac's slaves ("we have found water," 26:32), of Laban ("indeed, you are my flesh and blood," 29:14), etc. In contrast, speech becomes more extensive in the solemn and impressive curses and blessings. Yet one may generally see the economy of words as a defining characteristic of a certain type in Genesis. Such words often do not indicate the true intentions of the actors and not infrequently disclose their psychic life only indirectly. Consequently, the words are often not entirely clear to us. Interpretation requires a special skill. The fact that God prohibited the Tree of Knowledge to the people is recounted, but the reason is not indicated. What were his thoughts when he threatened them with immediate death, a threat that is not subsequently fulfilled? Similarly, we hear how, in fact, the serpent wants to tempt the woman, but not why. And even such psychological masterpieces as the account of the temptation of the first people are only indirect descriptions of the psychic life.

14. Very many legends are equally sparse in the description of the accompanying circumstances. A deep chasm stands at this point, too, between old and contemporary narrative styles. In fact, the ancients obviously knew nothing of intimate sentiments for the land. We see no trace of a feeling for nature in Genesis. The fact that the Paradise narrative takes place under green trees, the Hagar legends in the barren wastes of the desert, and the Joseph narrative in the land of the Nile influences the course of the account in individual details, to be sure. The people clothe themselves with leaves; one loses one's way in the desert and there is no water there. But it does not determine the mood of the action in any way. But disregarding this life of nature concealed from the ancient, how easy it would have been to offer a description of Paradise. What modern poet would have passed over this opportunity. The old narrators, however, were satisfied to say that beautiful trees grow there and the source of mighty streams is there. Similarly, for example, the implement with which Cain killed Abel is not indicated (4:8). It is only stated that Noah planted grapevines and drank wine (9:20-21). The intervening act, that he pressed wine, is omitted. How Hagar's contempt was expressed (16:4) is no more recounted than the action whereby Sarah avenged herself. It is common to admire the wealth of "details" in the accounts, and rightly so. But this should by no means be <xliv> understood as though the legends brim with concrete, conspicuous details. In general, they do not offer a wide scope of concrete features. These few details, however, appear in such an extraordinary selection that we are justified in asking about the purpose of almost every element, even the most insignificant. Indeed, one will be unable to find anywhere in Genesis elements with the sole purpose of contributing to vivid portrayal. Even the fact that Rebekah carried the jar on her shoulder, as graphic as it is, has a specific function in the whole of the narrative (cf. p. 252).

This economy of "detail" is all the more remarkable since such barely indicated elements often stand alongside other extremely detailed features, especially in the "more extensive" accounts. For example, the meal Abraham set before the three men is described in great detail (18:6ff.) in contrast to Lot's meal which is only briefly mentioned (19:3). It is very fruitful for interpretation to consistently note brevity and breadth and always to inquire as to the narrator's interests. In general, the obvious rule is that the narrator describes the main action concretely, but only alludes to or omits events secondary to the main action. For example, the three days of the journey are passed over in the account of Isaac's sacrifice; By contrast, the brief walk to the site of the sacrifice is depicted in great detail (22:4ff.). The narrator very self-consciously controls the account according to his literary sense. Similarly, the experiences of Abraham's servant the day he made an offer for Rebekah are reported in great detail; but all the days of his journey to Nahor's city are treated in one clause (Gen 24).

This emphasis on the action is also evident in the nature of the conclusion. The legends end immediately when the intended point has been reached, not slowly fading, but abruptly halting. This observation is important for interpretation. The situation immediately prior to the end is the narrator's intended climax. There are two kinds of conclusions: the normal kind adds a brief clause after the climax so that the excited emotions may subside (prototypical example: Isaac's sacrifice, Gen 22); the rare, apparently therefore more impressive kind concludes with an emphatic speech (example: Noah's curse, 9:20ff.).[37]

15. The observations above suggest that the old legends subjugate everything to the action. Other literatures have accounts in which the action is only the framework or the link, but the key is the psychological portrait, the ingenious conversation, or the idea. These ancient Hebrew legends differ entirely. Above all else, the ancient required action from the narrator. He wants something to happen in the story to bring him joy. The first requirement he makes of such an action, however, is that <xlv> it be internally coherent. The narrator should offer a coherent chain of events in which one thing follows necessarily from the other.[38] The chief charm of such a legend consists in its ability to show how one thing results from the other. The more comprehensible, the more necessary this relationship seems to be, the more charming the account appears. A famine forces Abraham to go to Egypt (12:10ff.). He fears, however, that he will be killed there because of his beautiful wife. Consequently he pretends that his wife is his sister. Deceived, Pharaoh has Sarah brought to him and gives gifts to Abraham. Consequently God smites Pharaoh. As a result, he releases Sarah, but allows Abraham to keep the gifts. Sarah has no children, but she desires them (Gen 16). Consequently she gives Abraham her servant as a concubine. Hagar conceives by Abraham. As a result Hagar becomes presumptuous in relation to her mistress. This vexes the proud housewife most bitterly. Therefore, she has Abraham return Hagar to her and mistreats her. As a result, Hagar runs away from Sarah into the wilderness. Here, however, God has mercy on her and promises her a son.

---

[37]This "law of the conclusion" that the legend calms the excited emotions in one way or the other after the concluding event corresponds to the "law of introduction" that the legend does not begin with a moving action, but builds from calm to excitement. The rarer form discussed above also occurs, indeed as a new technique for achieving poetic effect, in Spanish romances. Cf. Olrik, 2-3.

[38]Concerning this unity as a law of epic folk literature, cf. Olrik, 10.

One notes how each subsequent element links with the preceding in such cases, how each preceding element seems to be the natural cause or at least the precondition of the following. We are accustomed to assessing this kind of account as childish style. This assessment, however, is only partially correct.

These accounts are very cohesive. The narrators are uninterested in digressions, "episodes" in which the accounts and epics of more developed literatures are so rich. Instead, they strive with all might and determination toward the goal. "Any incidental is suppressed and only the characteristic is emphasized concisely and effectively."[39] Consequently, as much as possible, there are no new beginnings in the same account. It is an uninterrupted whole. New preconditions are very rarely reported. Instead, the style involves giving as many preconditions as possible at the beginning. It is considered permissible to pass over such elements, internally necessary results of the preceding but not contributory to the main action, while, on the other hand, every necessary element of the main action must be expressly reported. This stage of Hebrew narrative does not practice the art of suggesting events in speeches, customary in German ballads (cf. Scherer, *Poetik*, 237). Nothing should be excessive or insufficient. Consequently, the old legend prefers not to resolve the entire action into various threads and weave them together. It "holds firmly to the only strand; it always has only one strand."[40] It almost always follows only one main motif and leaves everything else, as far as is possible, to one side.

Many legends love repeatedly to transform the same motif. One may consider how the Paradise narrative links everything to the nakedness and clothing of the people and how the relationship of "field" and <xlvi> "man of the field" (human being) runs throughout the whole legend, how the narrative of Joseph's abduction to Egypt (Gen 37) treats the sleeved garment and the dreams, or how the account of Jacob's last will (47:29ff.) consistently illuminates the actions of the dying man in an unusual manner in relation to the bed (47:31)—to bless he sits up in it (48:2), dying he stretches out on it (49:33), etc. As a rule, quite in contrast to our sense of style, the expression is repeated with the recurrence of the substance so that the same word often runs through the narrative like a red thread. Sometimes the narrator repeatedly employs a whole chain of words. Instructive examples are the two recensions of the account of Jacob's deception of Isaac (Gen 27; cf. pp. 298-99). Undoubtedly, this practice originally arose because of the poverty of the language. The narrators, however, whose narratives are available to us, adapt this style because they can thereby reproduce their impression of the account's unity. Precisely because of this inner coherence of the legend, it is possible at many points where there are lacunae or accretions in our tradition to discern the original. Often our task of source analysis must be guided by the keywords in the legend.[41] Source criticism has another order of certainty here than in the prophets, laws, and songs, which are not characterized by this conciseness. Certain accounts characteristically also often contain certain words found only or predominantly in them, so that one thinks of these narratives as soon as one hears these expressions. These are words like *nephilim* (giants), *tehom* (primal sea), "ark,"

---

[39]Olrik, 9.

[40]According to Olrik (8), who discovered the "single strand" as a law of epic folk literature.

[41]Many of Sievers's source distinctions falter because of insufficient attention to these keywords and interrelationships (cf. above ¶3:2).

"flood," "create," etc. Understandably, only the earliest and most beloved accounts produced such terms (cf. pp. 5, 59, 62, 67, 103-104, 121, 150-51, 211-12).

16. Furthermore, the course of the action should be likely, extremely credible, even necessary. The hearer should not be able to object at any point that events recounted are unlikely given the preceding or per se. Elevated too highly, Hagar must become arrogant (16:4). Sarah, however, could do nothing other than feel vexed (16:5). Admittedly, the plausibility sought by these old narrators differs from the one we discuss. Their knowledge of nature differs from ours. For example, they considered it very credible that all species of animals entered the ark. The manner in which they discuss God and his interventions is more naive than possible for us in the present. They considered it quite natural that the serpent spoke in the primal period, that Joseph become minister so quickly (41:37ff.) and that, in his high position, he saw to individual sales of grain himself (42:6), etc. We would term these elements "fairy-tale-like" but the ancient would have found them unobjectionable. Even the fact that Joseph in Egypt was unconcerned for his relatives at home was unobjectionable to them. The plausibility of the folk narrative—as <xlvii> Olrik[42] correctly emphasizes—"always" takes into consideration "only the central forces of the action." "External plausibility concerns it much less." The hearer, too, captivated by what Joseph experienced in Egypt, forgot his father and his brothers.

On the other hand, the events in a well-told legend may not be so simple that one can already guess its further course after the first words. Then, it would cease to interest the reader. No one likes to hear the obvious. Instead, the narrators depict a complicated situation (in their terms) whose final conclusion cannot be foreseen by the hearer. He will listen all the more intently. Jacob wrestles with a divine being. Which of the two will be victorious? Jacob and Laban are equally sly. Who will be able to outwit the other? The clever, but pacifistic, Jacob must encounter the stronger but less reflective Esau. What will he do (32:4ff.)? Abraham must go down to Egypt. What will happen to him there? All these narratives are enthralling to some degree. Breathlessly, the childish hearer listens and rejoices when the hero finally escapes all dangers. The account is, thus, always reported on the precondition that they are not yet known to the hearer. "Prefiguring motifs" (to use Goethe's expression), that is, those which prefigure the result of the process—such as are common, for example, in the Nibelungenlied—are not permitted here. The narrators love contrasts very much. The child expelled into the wilderness becomes a mighty people. A poor slave, languishing in prison, becomes the lord of wealthy Egypt. The narrators strive to press such contrasts to a point wherever possible. In Hagar's situation of total despair, God has mercy on her. When Abraham had already stretched out his hand to slay Isaac, God restrains him. Lot delays (19:15ff.) and Jacob holds fast to the deity (32:27) until daybreak is near. The next moment must be decisive. Where this tension is entirely lacking, however, without some complication, there is actually no "story." Thus, the Creation account in Gen 1 cannot be called a "narrative" (p. 118). This piece will once have been rich (cf. p. 121), but is by nature nothing more than a learned construction, although already from a rather ancient period. Similarly, actual complication is missing

---

[42]Olrik, 9.

in the many "comments" the narrators report from popular tradition and in the narratives they themselves formed from such traditions (cf. 4:4).

The legends, as we have seen (2), are not simply free creations of the narrator's imagination. Instead, the legend is based for the most part on adapted material and has also often taken up and reworked certain information resulting from contemplation and reflection. These backgrounds of the legend are treated above. Our task here is to observe the literary adaptation of the preexistent material in the legends. We have reached the proper midpoint of our investigations. <xlviii>

17. As shown above, many legends respond to specific questions. Thus, these legends are not the harmless play of a purposeless creator or of an imagination seeking only beauty. Instead, they have a specific purpose. They want to instruct. If these accounts are to fulfill their calling, they must clearly stress this point. Indeed, they do to a high degree, so much so that even we of a later generation can discern the original underlying question, far removed from us. To the sensitive reader who has sympathetically accompanied the unfortunate/fortunate Hagar on her way through the desert, no statement in the whole story will fall on the ear with as much impact as the statement ending all her distress: God heard (21:17). The narrator intends this impression, however, for he wants to build the explanation of the name Ishmael (God hears) on this statement. Or which clause in the legend of Isaac's sacrifice makes such an impression on the memory as the gripping statement by which Abraham, with a torn heart, appeases the question of his unsuspecting child: God will provide (22:8)! This statement, which God himself actualized, is so emphasized because it responds to the question concerning the origin of the name of the site *Yeruel* (God provides).

Other legends reflect historical events or situations. In these cases, the narrator's task was to make such allusions sufficiently obvious to his informed hearer. Thus in the legend of Hagar's flight, the actors are, first of all, individual persons whose fortunes we follow with sympathy. But, in the central passage concerning God's statements about Ishmael (16:11ff.), the narrator permits the fact that a people and its fate is involved to shine through.

Hebrew tastes especially prefer to allow the names of the main heroes and locales to sound even when an actual name etymology is not intended. Some legends abound with such allusions. The Flood narrative, for example, plays with the name "Noah" (8:4, 9, 21), the narrative of Isaac's sacrifice with "Yeruel" (22:8, 12, 13), the account of the reunion of Jacob and Esau with "Mahanaim" and "Penuel" (cf. pp. 343-45, etc. These legends are rich in all manner of allusions. They are transparent to a degree. Even one who reads them, quite innocently, simply as beautiful stories, enjoys them. But only one who holds them up to the light of their original understanding can perceive their brilliant colors. To him, they appear as small glittering and shimmering works of art. The peculiarity of Hebrew folk legends in relation to other legends consists, if we do not err, especially in this pointed brilliance. In fact, the talent and preference for the ingenious obviously characterizes the intellect and literature of Israel particularly—to this day.

The narrators' skill is especially manifest in their ability to avoid every appearance of intentionality despite the strong emphasis on the intended element. With wondrous elegance, with fascinating grace, they were able to reach the hidden goal. They tell a small story, so true to nature, so attractively, that we hear them quite unsuspectingly. And, all at once, without our foreseeing it, they have reached their goal. <xlix> For example, the account of Hagar's flight (Gen 16) intends to explain how Ishmael came to be born in the desert. To this purpose, it sketches an image of his father's household. Through a completely credible chain of events, it shows how Ishmael's mother, still pregnant, was brought to despair and so fled into the wilderness. As a result, Ishmael became a child of the desert.

In many cases, the narrator's task was rather complicated. The effort was to respond to a whole series of questions simultaneously or to incorporate a multitude of given preconditions. Thus, one variant of the Tower narrative asks how the many languages and the city of Babel came into existence, the other about the origin of the various dwelling places of the people and an old building. In many cases, the narrative material was given in the tradition (cf. 2:10). Thus an extant account of a hero's hospitality toward three deities was applied to Abraham in Israel. The narrators intend, however, not only to motivate the institution of the cult at Hebron through this account, but, at the same time, to explain the birth of Israel and to interpret his name. The task here, then, was to combine the various materials into a unit. The narrators demonstrate their skill particularly here. They adapt the guiding thread of the account from the main motif. From the secondary motifs they spin an individual scene and incorporate it with easy grace into the whole. Such secondary motifs are usually etymologies, for example. Thus, a scene incorporated into the account of the cult at Yeruel intends to explain the name of the place "God sees." This minor scene, the discussion between Abraham and Isaac (22:7-8), however, expresses the attitude of the whole account so well that we would not want to do without it, even though it has no particular purpose. Or, in other cases, the artists juxtaposed two main motifs and they devised an extremely simple and natural transition from one to the other. Thus, the first part of the Hebron legend discusses the hospitality toward the three men; The second part, intended to provide the background to Isaac's birth, connects very simply by recounting that the men conducted a conversation at table, and that they promised Isaac on this occasion. The most exciting task of the interpreter of Genesis is to investigate these matters, and thus not only to discern the earliest sense of the legends in Israel but at the same time to observe the nuances of the literary composition of these accounts. Admittedly, this fusion of various motifs did not always succeed. In the Tamar account, for example, the actual (traditional) Tamar novella and the narrative concerning the tribe of Judah, not entirely harmonious in style, stand alongside one another (p. 403). The Israelite interpretation of the Jacob-Esau-Laban narratives is rather superficial.

In all, even the earliest accounts of Genesis do not involve hastily conceived, naive, or even raw accounts. Instead, they manifest a mature, well-developed, highly energetic art. The narratives are highly "stylized."[43] <l>

---

[43]"Our [narrative] folk poetry is formulaically [i.e., in its forms] bound to a much higher degree than is usually thought" (Olrik, 11). Whoever compares Olrik's essay with the presentation above will note, to his own amazement, the accuracy of Olrik's contention (p. 1) that there are certain "epic laws" common to all folk literature based in the "common intellectual situation" of primitive peoples. Future work in Old Testament narratives must be oriented to recognize these universally valid laws. A later period may then emphasize elements peculiar to Israelite narrative art.

18. Finally, reference must also be made to the fact that the narrators seldom explicitly express an opinion concerning the characters or their actions. The narrative style of Genesis does not utilize consistent epithets for heroes as does Homer. This reticence of the narrators with respect to their own assessments differs markedly from later legends and historiography influenced by the prophets. Naturally, the legend narrators also had such opinions. They are by no means objective; instead, they were extremely subjective. Often, the proper understanding of the legend consists in our sharing the narrators' judgment. But they almost never expressed it. They were unable to reflect expressly concerning the processes of psychic life. Such a judgment becomes clearly evident only in speeches of the acting persons which illuminate what has already transpired (cf. especially the speeches of Abraham and Abimelech in chap. 20 or the final scene of the Jacob-Laban narrative, 31:26ff.). At the same time, however, this suppression of judgment clearly shows that narrators, at least the earlier narrators, were not primarily interested in expressing universal truths. To be sure, certain truths probably underlie the legends to a degree—such as a view concerning the value of belief underlying the story of the emigration, concerning the rewards of hospitality in the Hebron legend (Gen 18), and concerning the destruction of humanity because of immorality in the legend of Noah's curse. But one may not understand these accounts as though this were its real purpose. They are not tendentious. The situation differs for the myths which, at any rate, as shown above (pp. xiii-xiv), respond to questions of a more general nature, and for the later collectors "J" and "E,"[44] who wish to express certain ideas concerning Yahweh and Israel, concerning piety and morality (5:3), although they are very much hampered by the fixed style.

19. As we can discern from Genesis itself, the narrative art described in its essential features gave rise to another relatively closer to modern art. While a classical example of the first type is the account of Hagar's flight (Gen 16), the clearest example of the second is the Joseph narrative. A comparison of the two accounts shows the great difference between the two types. In the former, everything is unusually brief, forced; in the latter, similarly noteworthily, much is expanded.

The first difference to come to attention is the scope of the accounts. In the interim, narrators have learned to construct and come to prefer larger works of <li> art. The second distinction consists in the fact that they are no longer satisfied with recounting individual legends, but are now able to combine several legends into a whole. Here, then, the inherited style involving the "single strand" (3:15) is abandoned and a complicated action is created consisting of several strands. This is the case in the Joseph narrative as well as in the Jacob-Esau-Laban and Abraham-Lot legend cycles. Let us consider how these combinations came about. Related legends were combined. It seemed especially appropriate, for example, to combine legends that treated the same person into a small epic, as in the Joseph and Jacob narratives—the inner unity of the whole consists then in the "concentration around a central person."[45] Similarly, legends as varied as the one concerning Abraham in Hebron (Gen 18) and the one concerning Lot in Sodom (Gen 19) were joined to the end of these collections. Thus in "J" a Creation account and the

---

[44]Concerning the legend collections "J," "E," and "P," see ¶¶5 and 6.
[45]Olrik, 10.

Paradise narrative were fused (Gen 2, 3). Both deal with the beginning of humanity. In "P" the primal legends concerning the creation and the Flood originally formed a whole.

We observe many cases that share the same form of combination. The more important legend is divided into two parts, the less important is inserted into the middle. We term this form of composition, rather common in the history of literature—one recalls the *Thousand and One Nights*, the *Decameron, Gil Blas*, or the Hauffic legends—"framing accounts." Thus the Jacob-Esau narrative became the framework for the Jacob-Laban legend. Similarly, the Abraham-Hebron narrative joins the Lot-Sodom account. Now in order to evaluate the art of these compositions, one must primarily observe the boundaries of the original legends. The narrators usually find the transition from the one account to the other through very simple means. Above all else, the journey often constitutes this transition. When the first portion of the Jacob-Esau legend ends Jacob sets our for the "East" (27:42ff.). He undergoes a series of experiences in that land and then returns to Esau. In the Joseph narrative, Joseph's abduction to Egypt, then his brothers' journeys link the individual accounts. Similarly, the Abraham-Lot legend recounts how the three men first called on Abraham before going to Sodom (18:16). How are these various journeys explained? Everything previously recounted envisions Joseph's abduction to Egypt (Gen 37). His brothers' journey is occasioned by the same great famine which already played a decisive role in Joseph's elevation in Egypt (42:1). The brothers' experiences in Egypt presuppose this advancement (42:6). The Joseph narrative, therefore, has been exquisitely fused into a whole. The Jacob narrative is less unified. But here, too, the fact that Jacob goes to Laban is also given an inner justification. He flees from Esau. Otherwise, the original legends stand disjointedly alongside one another.[46] <lii> In contrast, the Abraham-Lot legend does not imply why the three men go straight from Abraham to Sodom. No inner dialogue between the various legends has been created, then. The narrator made greater efforts, therefore, to create artificial linking elements. Consequently he recounted that Abraham accompanied the men almost to Sodom (18:16), indeed, that he went back to the same place the next morning (19:27-28).

Here one has the most marked impression of a conscious art attempting to form a larger unit from originally diverse materials. We find closer connections than such "frameworks" in the Joseph accounts. Here a whole series of accounts are harmonized and interwoven. Pursuing the same link, the latest editors then arranged the traditional legend material into a whole: first the primal legends situated in the far East, then the patriarchal narratives localized in the East and South of Canaan, then the Joseph accounts, finally the stories of Moses and the Exodus. Migrations create the connection here: therefore Abraham must migrate from the East to Canaan,[47] and the immigration of Joseph's brothers to Egypt prepares for the Exodus of their descendants from there.

20. Another characteristic feature of the Joseph narrative is its expansiveness, quite distinct from the conciseness of the old accounts. We find a multitude of long speeches, of soliloquies, of expansive descriptions of situations, and of expositions of the thoughts of the acting persons. The narrator prefers repeating what has already been recounted once

---

[46]Both the "full concentration" and the "loose accumulation" of narratives also often appear elsewhere in epic folk literature (cf. Olrik, 10).

[47]Meyer, *Israeliten*, 249.

more in the form of a speech. How is this "epic breadth" to be evaluated? Not as a special
peculiarity of this one account only: we find the same characteristics, although less distinctly, in the narratives of the wooing of Rebekah (Gen 24) and of Abraham with
Abimelech (Gen 20), and in details of the Jacob narratives (especially in the legend of the
encounter of Jacob and Esau; Gen 32ff.). The account of Isaac's sacrifice and details in
the Abraham-Lot narrative also offer parallels. Apparently a particular narrative art, a
developing new taste, expresses itself here. This new art is not satisfied, as is the old
style, to recount the legend as briefly as possible and to disregard all secondary points as
much as possible. Instead, one strives to ornament them more richly and to develop their
beauties, even if they are only incidental. The desire is to hold situations perceived to be
charming and remarkable before the eyes of the hearer as long as possible. Thus, for
example, the fear of Joseph's brothers when they stood before their brother is treated in
great detail. One intentionally narrates as slowly as possible so that the hearer has time
to completely enjoy the charm of the situation. Thus, Joseph may not reveal himself
immediately during the first encounter so that the same scene may be repeated. He must
require that Benjamin be brought before him because Jacob will delay this command for
a long time, thereby delaying the decisive moment. The legend similarly retards the
account of Isaac's sacrifice immediately before God's intervention in the action (22:9-10)
in order to postpone the catastrophe and <liii> to sharpen the tension. "This delaying treatment is particularly capable of making an impression on the memory."[48] The means repeatedly utilized to extend the account involves recounting the same scene twice: twice
Joseph interprets dreams of prominent Egyptians (Gen 40ff.); twice Joseph's brothers must
meet with him in Egypt; twice he hides valuables in their sack to frighten them (42:25ff.;
44:1ff.); twice they discuss Joseph's cup, with the chief of staff and with Joseph himself
(Gen 43; 44); etc.[49] Usually the two variants differ from one another in some way. The
apparently older form in which the two actions agree almost entirely and are even
recounted in the same words, occurs in Genesis only in the account of Lot's daughters (p.
217).[50] Sometimes, although certainly rarely, the narrators may have devised new scenes
on the basis of the old motifs, for example, the final scene between Joseph and his
brothers (chap. 50). The inserted interlude depicting Abraham's negotiation with God concerning Sodom is quite unique (18:23ff.). (This can almost be termed didactic literature:
it is written to deal with a religious problem that moved the author's time and came to
his mind when considering the Sodom narrative [cf. pp. 202ff.]).

The same narrators have an extremely noteworthy preference for long speeches,
indeed, to such an extent that even the action is subordinated to the speeches. The most
indicative example is the meeting of Abimelech and Abraham (chap. 20). Here, in fact,

---

[48]Olrik, 9.

[49]This is the epic "law of repetition" mentioned by Olrik (3-4). Newer literature describes the
magnitude and significance of the matter by describing individual components. Folk poetry, which
lacks this vital fullness, would soon complete the description. In order to avoid this, it has only one
escape, repetition. The number three, characteristic of such repetitions according to Olrik and also
very common in the OT on such occasions, does not occur in Genesis. Instead, the dual repetition
is the stylistic rule here.

[50]Cf. Olrik, 8-9.

events are not recounted in the order of their occurrence—quite contrary to the rule always observed in the old style—but a series of events are omitted at the beginning so they may be "supplemented" in the following speeches. Thus the narrator attempted to construct more interesting speeches, even at the cost of the account of the facts. It is also very popular to give the speeches content by allowing the persons in the story to recount once more what has already been reported (42:13, 21, 30ff.; 43:3, 7, 20-21; 44:19ff.). The rule of style for such repeated speeches (in contrast to Homer) is to vary the second time slightly or to grant the second report some peculiarity through the introduction of a new element (cf. comments on 3:2-3). This preference for longer speeches is, as one clearly recognizes, a secondary phenomenon in Hebrew legend style, the sign of a later period. We see this in the fact that precisely those passages we recognize as the latest addenda to the legend or as insertions (13:14-17; 16:9-10; 18:17-19, 23-33) contain such extensive speeches. We can also identify this joy in <liv> expansion in the other genres of Hebrew literature. Thus the brief, forceful style of an Amos is followed by the expansive style of a Jeremiah. The concise laws of the Covenant Code and the long-winded explanations of Deuteronomy, the curt proverbs comprising the core of Proverbs and the extensive speeches secondarily prefixed to the book as its introduction, and the oldest folk songs, often only one line long, and the long poems of literary poetry relate to one another in a similar fashion.[51] We are not always sympathetic with this later period's tastes. For example, the Joseph narrative risks becoming sluggish because of excessive breadth. On the other hand, this verbosity simultaneously signifies a newly gained intellectual power. Whereas the old period can only express its inner life in brief, detached words, this generation has learned to observe itself more closely and to express itself more completely. At the same time, the attention given to the psychic life of the individual has increased significantly. Thus, a masterpiece of characterization was created in the account of Isaac's sacrifice. The narrator of the Joseph story manifests the skill to compose an image of a man from many small elements. The description of Joseph's inner vacillation when he sees Benjamin (43:30) and the psychological portrayal when Jacob hears that Joseph is alive (45:26ff), etc., are especially successful.

The distinction between the two descriptive genres is so great that it is advisable to distinguish between them with different names. It is advantageous to call only the first "legend," the second, in contrast, "novella." Naturally, the transition between the two is fluid. One can designate such transitional forms as the Laban-Jacob or the Rebekah accounts as "novelistically adorned legends" or as "novellas based on legend motifs."

21. Something can also be said, albeit with caution, about the age of this style. The art of narration learned from the legends was later applied to historiography where the same or similar observations can be made. We see that already the oldest historiography known to us follows the "more expansive" style.[52] Thus we may assume that this "more expansive" legend style, at any rate, must have already existed at the beginning of the monarchical period. The brief style must have already been in use for many centuries at

---

[51]Concerning this "distension" of units, cf. "Israelitische Literaturgeschichte," in *Kultur der Gegenwart* 1/7:54.

[52]Cf. my article "Geschichtsschreibung im AT," in *RGG*.

that time. This observation, however—one should note this—only determines the age of the narrative style, not the age of the accounts in this style preserved for us, themselves.

22. The very brief "comments" that occur occasionally in Genesis stand in starkest contrast to the expansive legends—for example, when it is stated, very briefly, that Jacob encountered the divine host in Mahaniam (32:2-3), that he bought a field in Shechem (33:18ff.), that Deborah died and was buried near Bethel (35:8, 14), that Rachel died near Ephratha when Benjamin was born <lv> (35:16ff.), or that Sarah was buried in the cave of Machpelah (p. 268). It is certainly no accident that many of these "comments" mention the place where the event occurred, indeed, that it is often the main point of the whole tradition. Consequently, we must see such information as local traditions adapted directly from oral tradition. Such brief local traditions can still be heard in the German countryside and read in legend books (cf. Grimm, *Deutsche Sagen* nos. 2, 6, 11, 12, 19, 21, 22, etc. and, e.g., also K. Bader, *Hessische Sagen* 1, nos. 8, 10, 11, 17, 19, 20, etc.). Later narrators sometimes constructed whole narratives from such "comments" (cf. 4:4).

¶4. The History of the Transmission of the Legends of Genesis in Oral Tradition

Guthe, *Geschichte des Volkes Israel*, 156ff., 161ff. (with further bibliography)

1. The legends were already very ancient and had already undergone a long history when they were committed to writing. This is the nature of the matter: the origin of legend is always remote from the perspective of the inquirer and goes back into prehistoric times. So it is in this case, too. The advanced age of the legends is evident, for example, in the fact that they often speak of peoples and tribes that later subsided or disappeared—namely, Shem, Ham, Japhet, Cain, Ishmael, Reuben, Simeon, and Levi (2:5). It is further evident in the earthiness of many elements that reveal to us a religion and morality of an ancient period. One need consider only the many mythological remnants such as the narrative of the angelic marriages (6:1ff.), of Jacob's struggle with the deity (32:35ff.), of the many stories of the patriarchs' lying and deception, and so forth.

2. Israel surely did not produce a very large segment of these legends, but received them from abroad. By nature, these stories wander from people to people, from land to land, and even from religion to religion. Many of our German legends and fairy tales have also come from abroad. Even now, modern civilized peoples exchange nothing of their intellectual treasures as easily and as often as their stories. One may consider the truly immense distribution of foreign novels in Germany. Now if we consider that Israel lived on soil fertilized by millennia of culture, that it by no means lived there alone but was surrounded by nations, some culturally superior, further that international commerce and trade of the ancient period was conducted from Babylonia to Egypt and from Arabia to the Mediterranean via Palestine itself, then we will even expect this status of Israel among the nations to be mirrored in its legends. Similarly, its language can be expected to be filled with loan words.[53]

---

[53]Cf. "Israelitische Literatur," 55.

These legends, themselves, bear particular testimony to the fact that they have come together from a wide variety of sources. They are extraordinarily <lvi> multicolored. A few take place in Babylon, others in Egypt, others to the East and South of Canaan, others in Canaan itself. A few of them envision the fathers and patriarchs as farmers (Paradise legend), others as shepherds. A few praise the cunning of the patriarchs (Jacob, Abraham, Noah). Another, however, considers the acquisition of knowledge to be a crime against God (Paradise legend). The God concept is equally varied in the legends.[54] The deity is bound to the night (Penuel and Sodom legends), but elsewhere appears by day as well (Hebron legend). The deity is revealed in dreams, but also walks visibly among people. The horror of mystery surrounds the deity, but the first people communicate with him quite intimately. He appears in fire and smoke (chap. 15) or entirely apart from such signs. He dwells in a tree, in the well, in the stone, and then seems to be little more than a local numen, or he travels with the shepherd as his patron deity. His residence is the fertile land (Canaan)—as in the Cain legend—but he also reveals himself to Abraham in the distant Haran. He also helps the patriarchs in Egypt, as well as in Gerar and in the city of Nahor. He becomes involved in the most minor matters of house and home, but also rules the whole world he formed and orders the affairs of humanity (primal legend). He sees the most secret matters (38:10). But another time he must go to the place in order to observe the matter personally (11:5; 18:21). He appears in person to act and speak, but also works secretly and mysteriously holds the strands of events in his hand (Joseph novella). He is gracious to the patriarch, but also violently attacks him by night (Penuel legend). God is unconditionally superior to humanity (11:6) and, occasionally, a god is even vanquished by a human (Penuel legend). In quiet resignation, a person submits to God's curse (Paradise narrative). But, in childish obedience, he also trusts his wisdom and goodness (Abraham's emigration) and worships him as the guardian of right (16:5; 26:22-23) and goodness (38:7). Almost always, at least in the extant recensions without exception, it is one God. But in certain passages, polytheism still echoes through (e.g., in the "we" of the Creation and Tower narrative, also, distantly, in the heavenly ladder at Bethel as in the "hosts" of Mahanaim; in the Hebron legend, three gods originally appear [p. 199]; in the Penuel legend Jacob even wrestled with a nocturnal, apparently subordinate, demon). All this cannot be based on one and the same God figure. Instead, the widest variety of concepts must come together here. Clearly, too, the name "Yahweh" was only secondarily imprinted on these legends. Genesis nowhere, apart from the secondary chap. 15, discusses the appearance in fire and smoke, earthquake, thunder and lightning, otherwise characteristic of Yahweh in the rest of the OT, and there is not a single tribal or personal name associated with Yahweh.[55] In contrast, we hear the name *el* in proper names such as Israel, <lvii> Ishmael, Penuel, originally perhaps also Jacob-el, Joseph-el and we also hear explicitly of the el-roi at Lahai-roi (16:13), of the el-olam at Beersheba (21:33), of the el-bethel at Bethel (31:13). This series also includes el-shaddai and el-elyon. Two of our legend collections (E and P) even avoid calling the god of the patriarchs "Yahweh" (5:2). One may see in this a final remnant of the awareness that

---

[54]This has been well established by Haller, who also offers an abundance of independent observations.

[55]Greßmann, 28.

these accounts actually have nothing to do with the God of the historical Israel, just as the book of Job, which clearly deals with foreign material, does not employ the name "Yahweh." But even in the third source (J), which speaks of "Yahweh," the name "Yahweh Sabaoth," at least, is missing. Although a few distinctions in the God concept indicated can be explained as inner-Israelite developments, the whole abundant variety can only be understood as the result of the fact that the legend material as a whole does not derive from Israel but is of extra-Israelite, or at least pre-Yahwistic, origins.

We may generally assume Babylonian influence for the primal legends. According to them, in fact, Babylonia itself was a primordial home for the human race and Babel was the oldest city in the world. Indeed, the Flood account mentions the land of Ararat and the Paradise narrative the streams of the East. We can demonstrate Babylonian origin for the Flood legend of which we possess Babylonian recensions. The Creation narrative agrees with the Babylonian in one, very significant, element, the division of the primal sea into two parts, the waters above and below. The ten patriarchs of humanity are, in the final analysis, identical with the ten primal kings of the Babylonians. The biblical figure of Enoch, in particular, traces back to the figure of the Babylonian Enmeduranki (p. 138). Nimrod, the king of the Babylonians and the founder of the Assyrian states, will have been derived from an Assyro-Babylonian legend figure. The legend of the Construction of the Tower deals with Babylonia and must have originated in that region. Iranian parallels to the Paradise legend show that it, too, came from the East, perhaps from Mesopotamia (pp. 37-38).

This origin of the primal legends explains their distinction in relation to the patriarchal legends established above (2:1): their universalistic attitude is to be understood against the broader perspective of cosmopolitan Babylonian culture, their stronger anthropomorphisms as well as their unusually somber fear of God as the final remnant of the pagan religion that once imprinted these materials. The influence of a higher culture also explains the fact that, whereas the patriarchs lived from animal husbandry according to the oldest patriarchal legends (cf. lin.59), the primal legends envision farmers (cf. also 8:22, "sowing and harvesting") and speak of viniculture (9:20), indeed, even of great structures, cities, towers, and ships.[56] Scholars' opinions are divided concerning the time and nature of the entry of these legends into Israel. It seems likely to us for inherent reasons that they had already come to Canaan in the second millennium, migrating from people to people, and were adopted by Israel when it was grafted into Canaanite culture. In addition to Babylonian influence, the material in Gen 1 also manifests <lviii> Canaanite influence (pp. 104, 131-32). The figure of Noah may be of Canaanito-Syrian origin (p. 80). The biblical Eve may be related to the Phoenician *Hwt* (p. 23) just as Esau may be related to the Phoenician *Usoos* (p. 290). We know from the Amarna correspondence that Canaan already felt Babylonian influence in this early period. A later period, however, in which Israel's self-consciousness had been awakened, would hardly have adopted such foreign myths (cf. pp. 73-74, 131-32).

Characteristically, we do not observe Egyptian influence in the primal legends.[57] In contrast, we suspect it, although we are unable to demonstrate it with certainty, in the

---

[56]Haller, 17-18, 48ff., 121ff.

[57]Meyer, *Israeliten*, 210.

Joseph novella which is set partially in Egypt and may be based on Egyptian legends (cf. pp. 385-86). This seems especially likely for the legend of Joseph's agricultural policy (47:13ff.).

The situation differs in particular for the legends of Abraham, Isaac, and Jacob and his sons other than Joseph. The Israelite origin of the narratives dealing with the latter is clear on the whole. They explicitly mention Israelite names—that is, in the legends of Dinah (Simeon and Levi, Gen 34), of Tamar (Judah, Gen 38), and of Reuben (35:22). These legends transmit reminiscences of the historical Israel which entered Canaan and are, thus, the latest in Genesis. It must be asked whether the legends of Abraham, Isaac, and Jacob preexisted Israel in Canaan or were brought there when Israel arrived. Now one notes that these accounts consistently play out not in Canaan proper but in the steppes east and south of the land. To be sure, the fathers also occasionally come into contact with Canaan. But it is extremely noteworthy that reports of them at Canaanite sites appear almost solely in "comments" (3:22) or later compositions, but not in actual legends—for example, of Abraham in Shechem and Bethel (12:6-7, 8; 13:5ff.; pp. 166-67, 176, resp.), of Jacob in Bethel, Succoth, and Shechem (28:10ff.; 33:17ff.; 35:1ff.; pp. 314, 356, 365-67) as well as in Ephratha (35:16ff.; p. 369). The most significant exception involves the localization of the account of the three men visiting Abraham in Hebron. It can still be clearly discerned that the legend did not originally belong here, however (p. 199). This observation leads to the conclusion that the patriarchal legends did not originate in Canaan, but were introduced there by Israel. One held fast to the memory that the fathers do not belong in Canaan proper, but in the East and South. As a rule one did not venture to localize the accounts concerning them in Canaan. Instead, one was satisfied with recounting "comments" associated with only a few Canaanite places despite the great value possibly given this early presence of the fathers as a justification for Israel later taking possession of Canaan. The patriarchal legends do not mention at all sites in Canaan as important as Jerusalem, Jericho, Dan, Shiloh, Ophrah, and many others.[58] The fact that the oldest accounts do not envision the patriarchs as farmers, but as nomads, specifically as sheep raisers, further indicates this origin of the patriarchal legends in the steppe.[59] Even

---

[58]Eerdmans, 2:30.

[59]The fact that the old legends conceive of the patriarchs Abraham, Isaac, and Jacob as nomads is obvious from the following: the steppes are their stopping place (20:1; 24:62); they dwell in tents, not only when they are migrating (12:8; 13:3, 12, 18; 31:25, 33) but normally (18:9; 24:67; 25:27; 26:17, 25), even when they are very near the city (18:1ff.; 33:18-19). They possess flocks, especially of small livestock, which are always mentioned first or exclusively (as with Laban; 30:43; 34:23). They measure wealth in terms of livestock, not farmland (12:16; 13:2; 24:35; 26:14; 30:43). Abraham presents his success to those far removed through camels. One could not have driven camels such a long distince so quickly (Gen 24). The patriarchs receive livestock as gifts, even from kings, not farmland (20:14). When Jacob works for Laban, he serves with the flocks, not as a fieldhand (30:29). When the grown sons go to the field, they can be found with the livestock, not in field work (34:5; 37:12). When the fathers must leave their homeland, they are sad for the things they cannot bring along, not for the cultivated land (45:20). They struggle with their neighbors over pastures and watering places (13:7; 21:25ff.; 26:20ff.). If Abraham and Lot had been farmers, they could have remained together (13:7). Occasionally, e.g., in famine, they move to the cultivated land or even into the city (12:10ff.; 20:1; 26:1) and then even dwell in a house (26:8, Lot in Sodom).

the Abel-Cain narrative was originally <lix> told by sheep raisers (p. 48) and the Cain genealogy contains many names from the East and South (p. 51). The occupation of sheep raiser, who is forced to be peaceful because of his animals' clumsiness, also agrees well with the unusually pliant and accommodating character of the patriarchs who constantly enter into treaties and whose chief trait is cleverness, even slyness. This character does not agree, however, with the militant spirit of later historical Israel.[60] The circumstances of the nomadic period are portrayed here with such fresh vividness that one can only assume that they represent an authentic, if modifed, memory of the circumstances of the ancestors' lives.[61]

Finally, it should be noted that the Canaanite divine name *Baal* never occurs in the patriarchal legends.[62] Greßmann's assumption,[63] however, that the El figure, found almost exclusively in the accounts of Israel's ancestors, was not adopted by Israel in Canaan (as in the commentary, pp. 186-87, 233, 279-80), but was the god of Israel's ancestors, seems extremely likely. Accordingly, the Hebrew tribes must have already known these legends before they entered Canaan.[64] Because of this origin <lx> the legends have moderately significant historical value. Thus, one of the most important questions of Genesis which has repeatedly occupied the deliberation of scholars can be very simply resolved. Why do the patriarchal legends assume the fathers' presence in Canaan prior to Israel's ultimate entry into Canaan? The response would be that to the extent that sites in the Negev and in the East are involved, historical information echoes in the legends. To the extent, however, that places in Canaan proper, such as Bethel and Shechem, are mentioned, no historical tradition is present. Rather, Israel localized its patriarchs brought from the steppe at a few, but not many, sites in the land only after it had entered Canaan. Thus, the opinion arose that Israel's ancestors must have already been in Canaan before Moses and Joshua. Only a series of late-developing legends then transposed events of Israel's historical period (after the entry) into that assumed ancient period (e.g., Gen 34; 38).

The broad strokes of the total picture of the transmission of legends in Israel is, then, as far as we can discern, the following: the primal legend is essentially of Babylonian ori-

---

But they never remain there (20:15; 34:21). Both Abimelech of Gerar and Hamor of Shechem (20:15; 34:10, 21) assume that their lifestyle forces them to move about (20:13). Significantly, wine does not occur in the Hebron narrative (18:8). They probably eat bread, however (18:6; 19:3; 25:34; 27:17; 37:25) and without bread, that they must obtain somehow, they probably could not live (42:1; 43:2ff.). A shepherd like Jacob may well have grown vegetables, too (25:30). In contrast, only the latest legends presume that the fathers farmed. The correct view of the patriarchs' life is given in Meyer, *Israeliten*, 132n.1, 305; Luther, *ZAW* 21:159; Greßmann, 25-26. Eerdmans (2:38ff.) differs somewhat. He does not distinguish between the information in the old legends and the secondary passages (cf. below 4:5) and thus comes to the conclusion that the patriarchs were "sedentary people."

[60]Meyer, *Israeliten*, 303; Greßmann, 26.
[61]Haller, 32.
[62]Greßmann, 28.
[63]Ibid.
[64]The same result is reached by Meyer (*Israeliten*, 83) and Greßmann (28-29), who attributes the legends set in the South to the tribe of Judah, those set in the East to Reuben. But such tribal names are not mentioned in the legends. Rather, they deal with much older circumstances.

gin; the patriarchal legends are essentially of ancient Hebrew origins with a few insertions from Israel's historical period; the Joseph legend is oriented toward Egypt. Canaan mediated the primal legend to Israel, but had no effect on the patriarchal legends on the whole. Israel was too proud to have adopted the ancestral figures of the Canaanites and it was too aware that it was not native to Canaan and that it was not ethnically Canaanite.

This analysis of the material as a whole, however, does not yet by any means exhaust the entire, complicated, history of the legends. Rather, it can be demonstrated in a few cases and suspected in very many, without diminishing the significance of these three main streams, that the individual accounts had a longer prehistory. This is likely for the Ishmael legend, which must have originated in Ishmael, just as the figure Lot must have been at home in Moab where Lot's cave was identified (19:30). The Sodom legend may have once been related to the lava fields of Arabia (p. 214). The Song of Lamech and the genealogy of Lamech must have stemmed from the wild, murderous, Arab Bedouins. The image becomes even more complicated if we consider the manifold legend parallels. First, some legends and legend motifs have parallels in Greek materials: the story of Abraham's reception of the three men is told of Hyrieus at Tanagra (p. 199); the story of "Potiphar's wife" has many parallels in Greek accounts (p. 406); there are also Greek parallels to Reuben's curse (p. 370) and to the struggle of the brothers Jacob and Esau (p. 288); the legend of Lot at Sodom recalls the legend of Philemon and Baucis (p. 213) and Isaac's sacrifice recalls that of Iphigenia (p. 239). Related material also occurs in the primal legends: the Greeks were also familiar with the contention that man and wife were originally one body (p. 13), the myth of the blessed time in the very beginning (pp. 114-15), <lxi> etc. Greeks and Hebrews were not in direct contact in the period under consideration here. The materials common to them will not have been the property of these two peoples alone, then, but must have come to them from a great store of traditions originating in the Orient. The discovery of related legends among these two peoples can be most simply explained by the fact that we are especially well informed concerning the accounts of these two peoples. Thus, from this perspective, we glimpse narrative material common to a much broader circle. We encounter this circle forcefully when we begin to collect parallels from the entirety of world literature. Here, however, we see at first an incomprehensibly multifaceted image. We find parallels to the legends and motifs of Genesis among the most distant peoples. Motifs that could have originated anywhere are not the only ones involved: the world is an egg (pp. 105-106) and heaven is a sea (p. 108); creation is based on the division of heaven and earth (p. 108); a ladder leads up to it (p. 309); brothers kill one another (p. 44); the dying one prophesies (p. 302); the hero is transfigured (p. 137); looking back is prohibited (p. 212); the water of life exists (p. 8); people are petrified (p. 212), etc., etc. In addition to these, however, enough complete accounts agree remarkably with the biblical accounts so that they must have had some historical relationship to them. Thus, the story of "Potiphar's wife" is known, not only to the Egyptians and Greeks, but also to the Indians, Persians, modern Arabs, and many other peoples (p. 406); the Sodom narrative belongs to a particularly widespread type of narrative (p. 213) and the Hebron legend belongs to a related, also very common type (pp. 192-93); the basic motif of the Joseph account, the mistreatment of the youngest, high-minded brother by the others is very common. Even details of the Joseph narrative recur (pp. 385-86); Similarly international are the basic motifs of the daughter who deceives her father and conceives a child by him (p. 217), of the faithful widow who conceives a son by her husband after his death (p. 403), even of the innocence and the fall of the first people (p. 37), and surely many others, as well. I have been satisfied in this realm—to the extent of my powers—to gather the materials and to refrain from drawing any further conclusions. May my work soon find the necessary supplementation! Then, however, it may be hoped, such international legend research will sharpen our sight for the treatment of the legends in general, will demonstrate the immense history of Israelite legend material throughout the world, and, not least, will open our eyes to the uniquely Israelite in the biblical legends.

Naturally, the foreign material in Israel has been thoroughly accommodated to the people and the religion. This accommodation can be most clearly seen in the Babylo-Hebrew Flood legend (cf. pp. 72-73). Polytheism has disappeared: the many gods have been omitted in favor of the One (Creation myth, cf. pp. 126ff.) or have been demoted to servants of this One (Hebron legend, cf. p. 199). The local Elim numina are equated with Yahweh, <lxii> and their names are regarded as epithets of Yahweh at these locales (16:13; 21:33; 31:13; cf. pp. 186-87). And although individual legends, such as, especially, the Penuel narrative, obstinately resist Israelitization, the appropriation of these legends and their infusion with the spirit of higher religion still remains one of the most brilliant deeds of the people of Israel. But even disregarding religion, a multitude of alterations have taken place during the adaptation of the legends. We can survey them only in part. The foreign figures are displaced by native figures: thus, the Hebrew Enoch (pp. 137-38) replaces the Babylonian priest-magician Enmeduranki; the perhaps Syro-Canaanite Noah replaces the Babylonian Flood hero. The Egyptian stories at the end of Genesis are applied to the Israelite figure Joseph. Thus, in very many cases, the narratives now narrated in relation to certain figures may not have originally referred to them. Or native figures were equated with foreign figures: thus the legendary figures Esau and Jacob were identified with the presumed ancestors of the peoples of Edom-Seir and Israel; thus Jacob was assigned the representatives of the Israelite tribes, Reuben, Simeon, Levi, Judah, etc., as sons and Abraham, Isaac, and Jacob became ancestors of the people of Israel. Or, the legends were localized at a specific site: thus the story of the three men, also known to the Greeks, was localized at Hebron; the legend of the destroyed cities, which does not yet mention the Salt Sea, was localized at the Dead Sea (cf. pp. 213ff.). Individual, specifically Israelite elements then found their way into the legends, for example, the predictions that Esau (Edom) will one day free himself from Jacob (Israel; 27:40), that Joseph would obtain Shechem (48:22), and that Manasseh would give way to Ephraim (48:13ff.). The motif of the border treaty at Gilead has been newly inserted into the Jacob-Laban legend, (31:52); The Sodom legend has been supplemented by a piece concerning the sparing of Zoar.

3. The exchange or fusion of various traditions introduced further transformations. We may imagine that such things took place very often through commerce, especially, perhaps, during the great pilgrimages to the tribal sanctuary, also through the activity of the professional traveling storyteller. Thus, the legends wandered from one place to another and are, consequently, told of various sites in our current tradition. The story of Sodom and Gomorrah was, according to another tradition, it seems, associated with Admah and Seboim (cf. p. 215). According to a third tradition, a similar account was told in Benjamin in relation to Gibeah (Judg 19). Ishmael's deliverance was localized both in

Lahai-roi (16:14) and in Beer-sheba (21:14). The encounter between Jacob and Esau upon Jacob's return was placed at Mahanaim and Penuel (32:4ff.), where it may not have originally belonged. Esau is, apparently after all, not originally at home here in the north, but in the south of Canaan (cf. pp. 343-44). The patriarchs' names are mentioned at the most widely varied sites. All are supposed to have been founded by them: Abraham especially in Beer-sheba, but later also in Hebron, etc.; Isaac not only in Beer-sheba (26:23ff.), but also in La<lxiii>hai-roi (25:11); Jacob in Beer-sheba, but also in Penuel, Mahanaim, later also in Bethel and Shechem (28:19; 32:31-32; cf. pp. 388, 391, 440). We will probably never be able to say confidently where the figures were originally situated. Nor can we know whether Abraham or Isaac was original in the Gerar narrative (Gen 20; 26). These transfromations are mostly too old for us to be able to identify the details. Various legends were also combined (see above pp. xxiv, xlv), such as the Paradise and Creation accounts of J, the Creation myth and the myth of the blessed time in P. Furthermore, various figures became fused. Thus the figure of Noah in Genesis consists of three originally distinct figures, the original Babylonian builder of the Ark, and the viniculturist and father of three peoples whose homeland is Syria or Canaan. The figure of Cain seems to have undergone the following history: (1) Cain, the ancestor of the Kenites, celebrated for his blood vengeance, cursed in the legend as a fratricide is (2) equated with the first smith Tubal and obtains Jabal = Abel as his brother, and is then (3) identified with Canaan and inserted in the first genealogy (p. 54). According to the Esau legend, Jacob is the sly shepherd who outwits the hunter. Related, but still different, is the Jacob of the Laban legend, where Jacob is the clever son-in-law who outwits his adroit father-in-law. In the Joseph legend, in contrast, Jacob represents the old father who tenderly loves the youngest son; nothing is said of his cunning. The strong Jacob struggling with the demon at Penuel differs entirely. The Jacob to whom the deity reveals himself at Bethel is different yet again. The genealogy of the patriarchs was then established when the legends were fused: Abraham became Isaac's father and Isaac became Jacob's father; Ishmael became Abraham's son and Lot his nephew, etc. The grounds for this transformation are also very obscure to us. The age of this genealogy cannot be stated. An inner harmonization of the legend materials with one another went hand in hand with these alterations. This harmonization was not completed. The legends are still a colorful world. But, on the other hand, one may imagine that the legends were once much more divergent and that the Israelite tradition mitigated these distinctions quite considerably. The fusion of the legends may have already been underway for the patriarchal accounts before the entry into Canaan. We may imagine that when, under the first kings, Israel began to cohere as a people, the process proceeded particularly quickly and thoroughly.

4. And, just as legends wander from place to place, they also wander through various times. In general, they are simply retold, often with a fidelity almost incredible to us, perhaps only half understood or having become completely unintelligible, and yet still further transmitted.[65] One can comprehend this fidelity if one remembers that the ancient

---

[65]Concerning the fidelity of "medieval" legend tradition, cf. l'Houet, 258-59: "As a boy, he was told the legends of the region; then he considered them his whole life long in his heart, not like a modern person, who believes, above all else, that innovations and improvements and, if possible,

people believed in the truth of these stories, <lxiv> and that, if the narrator should digress, the hearers, like our children, would censure every alteration as an error, but, especially, if one also considers that these ancients, quite in contrast to moderns, do not need to exercise their personalities by altering and innovating. One can also recognize how faithfully the legends were recounted by comparing the variants of the same account in the various legend collections. Despite minor variations, they often still agree in the overall structure, even sometimes in wording. One may compare, for example, the two variants of the Rebekah narrative. And yet, even these so faithfully recounted legends succumb to the common alteration. When a new generation arises, when the external circumstances have changed, or when human thought has evolved, even popular legend cannot remain the same. Slowly and haltingly, always at a certain distance, the legends follow the common course of change—one more, the other less. Here, then, legends offer us extraordinarily important material for understanding the evolution of the community. One can write an entire history of the religious, moral, and esthetics values of ancient Israel from Genesis.

If one wishes to become familiar with this history, one begins most appropriately with the variants. Characteristically, the legend exists in variants, as do all oral traditions.[66] Each one who retells the story, however faithfully, and especially every specific group and every new period, renders the transmitted story somewhat differently. The most important variants in Genesis are the two Ishmael narratives (Gen 16; 21:8ff.), then the legend of the danger of the patriarch's wife transmitted in three recensions (12:13ff.; 20; 26), and further the related legend of the treaty at Beer-sheba, also in three recensions. The variants of these accounts have been transmitted almost totally independently of one another. Additionally, in many cases the accounts, combined by the hand of a redactor, have been transmitted in the J and E variants (or by the various hands in J). The chief examples of this appear in the Jacob and Joseph narratives. Sometimes other biblical books transmit to us variants of whole legends or of individual legend motifs. Thus, the idyllic account of how Jacob met Rachel at the well (29:1ff.) is also reported of Moses and Zipporah (Exod 2:15ff.); Jacob discards the foreign gods under the oaks of Shechem (35:2ff.) as does Joshua (Josh 24); Joseph (Gen 41) and Daniel (Dan 2) interpret the dreams of foreign kings. Such twice-told <lxv> stories or multiply occurring motifs permit the scholar his first observations. When he has sharpened his eyes in this way and identified certain lines of development, he may also compare with one another the legends only reported once. Then he will begin to see the extraordinary multifaceted nature of these legends. We have the crudest and the most tender, the most objectionable and the most sublime, those that display a very archaic, semipolytheistic religion and others that express the most noble development of faith. Furthermore, the history of the legends can be recognized in the individual accounts themselves. There we see, if we look closely, reshapings in a new sense, whether slight or more comprehensive. Further, one sees the addition of new ideas the narrator missed in the old narrative (e.g., 13:14ff.; 18:17ff.; 23ff.; 19:17ff.; 21:11ff.; 22:15ff.; etc.). In individual, rare cases, we may even assume that

---

a complete renovation must be undertaken, but like a medieval, who may allow a minor, beautiful point to mature. And at his death, as an old man, he transmits the heritage further."

[66]Cf. here, as well, the nice description of modern popular traditions by l'Houet, 34ff.: "Like a circle of playmates, each piece of popular poetry exists in many similar forms."

later hands added a whole account to the tradition (chap. 15). One usually recognizes such additions by the fact that they are relatively abstract. The latest contributors were more interested in ideas than in narrative. Consequently, such additions often contain only speeches. Sometimes, brief narrative "comments," such as often exist among the people as local traditions (¶3:22), were tastefully extended by later narrators: the story of Abraham's emigration (p. 167), the legends of Rebekah's marriage (p. 246), of the covenant with Abimelech at Gerar (p. 298), of Jacob at Bethel (p. 314), and of Sarah's burial in P (p. 268) originated in this way. The story of the births of Jacob's sons developed similarly (pp. 321-22). The account of the separation of Lot and Abraham is also a graft on an old trunk (p. 176). The second part of E's Bethel narrative combines all manner of traditions concerning Shechem and Bethel and thus attempts to erect a new structure from transmitted "scraps" (pp. 365-66). Omissions intended to remove that which had become objectionable surely occurred much more often with the faithful narrators than such additions.

We observe lacunae in the legends every step of the way (in 9:22; after 12:17; after 16:14; cf. pp. 191-92; the second part of the Hebron legend is missing, cf. pp. 195, 198; etc.). Indeed, sometimes, so much has become offensive or has lost its interest for later narrators, that a few of the legends have become only a torso: that is, the legends concerning the angelic marriages (6:1ff.) and Reuben (35:22). In other cases, only the names of the legend figures have been transmitted to us without their legends: that is, the ancestors of humanity, Nahor, Yizkah, Milkah (11:29), Pichol, Ahuzzath (26:26), Kemuel, Bethuel (22:21f.), Keturah (?), Adah (4:19; 36:20), and Shaul, the son of the Canaanite woman (46:10). From the legend of the giant Nimrod, we have only the proverb, "A great hunter before Yahweh like Nimrod" (10:9); from the legend of the Horite Anah we have only a comment (36:24). From other examples we can see that individual narrative elements have lost their context and, consequently, can no longer be properly understood: the narrators do not know why the dove brought Noah an olive leaf (8:11), why Judah was afraid to give his youngest son to Tamar, too (38:11), why Isaac had only one blessing (27:38), and why he must eat good food before the blessing (27:4), etc. Therefore, something like a blue haze lies over very many legends, obscuring the colors of the landscape. <lxvi> We often have the feeling that we are, indeed, in a position to reproduce the attitudes of the old legends to a degree, but that the current narrators did not correctly perceive these attitudes. All observations should be investigated in order to discern the reasons leading to such reshapings and thus to describe the inner history of the legends. Only a brief sketch will be offered here.

5. The most important moment in the history of the legends is probably the later period when the external circumstances under which they originated have changed and, therefore, the accounts also have undergone certain changes. People forgot who the king of Gerar actually was (Gen 20; 26) and preferred to replace him with the king of Egypt (12:10ff.). Or, when the Philistines possessed Gerar, they inserted into the old Gerar legend a circumstance not yet known to the oldest recension of the narrative (21:22-23; 26). The figure of Hagar, a type of the headstrong Bedouin woman (Gen 16), lost this characteristic tone in the later tradition which was no longer familiar with the desert (Gen 21). Later redactors radically abbreviated the stories of Jacob's shepherd tricks on Laban (30:25ff.)—once the delight of knowledgeable hearers and therefore highly developed—for

readers uninterested in these matters (cf. pp. 330-31). Also, only fragments are preserved for us of the theories concerning the gradual development of human skills and abilities (4:17ff.). Quite significantly, the narrators had different lifestyles than the ancestors: the latter were shepherds, the former were farmers. Now, the legend did, in fact, faithfully maintain the general picture of the ancestors as shepherds (¶4:2). Nevertheless, a few, although not very many, features that presume farming have made their way into the legends (cf. pp. 295, 326, 390, 399, 441; cf. also the later blessings, 27:28; 49:11-12, 15, 20; so, too, the "house" of Isaac in 27:15 has probably been introduced into the old legend telling of the struggle of the shepherds and hunters; cf. also 15:3; 28:31; 33:17 and the tradition of Haran, possibly secondary everywhere it appears pp. 168, 246, 317). Quite often, a legend's characteristic features, far removed from its place of origin, are diminished or replaced by other elements. This is especially evident in the cultic legends discussed further below (pp. lix-lx). Many more legends will have been forgotten when they ceased to be interesting. In addition, the imagination powerfully excited by such accounts continued to work almost involuntarily.

6. The most significant material for us is the history of religion.[67] As we have seen (p. xlix), the God concept of Genesis manifests an extraordinary multifacetedness: we observe, in addition to the local numina and the god of the family, the much more sublime figure of the national god and even the Lord of all peoples. Precisely here, however, it is important to remember the extra- and pre-Israelite origins of these accounts <lxvii> and not simply to explain the basest view of God as the earliest belief of historical Israel in order to date the more noble God figure of the primal history to the very late period. Instead, Greßmann observes correctly that the religion of Genesis is not simply the religion of Israel. A God concept like that of the Penuel legend may not be taken into consideration for the oldest period of historical Israel, but for the extra- or pre-Israelite circles who devised this account.[68] Therefore, if we wish to understand the truly Israelite concept, we must pay attention not so much to the legend material itself, but to what Israel made of it, or to the history it underwent in Israel. The decisive observation is that Israel imprinted the whole variety of the god concepts transmitted in the legend materials with its "Yahweh" and thereby elevated it. The degree of the development of its concept of "Yahweh" can be discerned in its ability to subsume the Canaano-Babylonian gods of the primal narratives: Yahweh—earliest Israel could have maintained this—brought the Flood on the whole earth and dispersed all the nations in Babel. Universalistic ideas must, therefore, have already characterized Israel's earliest religion. In addition, however, the baser ideas of earlier stages of religions had not been entirely forgotten. Otherwise one would not have continued to transmit the old legends but would have destroyed them. Genesis shows us, however, how the higher ideas struggled with the baser materials and transformed them incrementally.

Thus we observe in very many legends a monotheistic tendency, an abhorrence of mythology already discussed (cf. pp. xxii, liv). This attitude continued to work in Israel. Thus a series of accounts were radically diluted. The history of this removal of the

---

[67]In addition to Haller, cf. E. Zurhellen (*Theologische Arbeiten aus dem Rheinischen wissenschaftlichen Predigerverein*, n.s. 10).

[68]Greßmann, ZAW 30:24-25.

mythological can still be traced for the Creation myth, for which we have poetic variants of an older viewpoint (cf. pp. 123-24). The Flood account is also rather bland already in the oldest Hebrew report (in J), for the same reason. The legend of the angelic marriages (6:1ff.), which must have been much richer in an older Israelite tradition, is now completely garbled (p. 59). We have nothing more than the name of the "Nephilim," the Hebrew "Titans," said once to have been very famous (6:4). Furthermore, we can observe how the older legends very naively discuss the deity's appearance on earth, but how the later period found this offensive and continued to refine divine revelation. We hear very rarely in the legends that the deity himself simply walked among people—so still in the Paradise and Flood legends. It is truly Israelite instead to clothe theophany in the veil of secrecy. The deity appeared unrecognized (Gen 18) or one adopted the old belief and recounted that he only appeared in the dark of night (Gen 19). Thus the deity was revealed and yet his being was not wholly disclosed. Even later recensions replace the deity with a subordinate divine being, whom J <lxviii> calls "Yahweh's messenger" and E "God's messenger." This reworking, however, did not take place throughout. Enough passages have remained that assume the appearance of Yahweh himself for the older recension to continue to shine through the younger (cf. p. 186). The same attitude led to the transformation of the appearance of God on earth into a dream revelation (e.g., 30:2) or to the contention that the messenger remained in heaven and spoke from there to the patriarch (e.g., 21:17). The secret of dreams veiled the self-revealing deity or one no longer saw the deity at all but only heard him. The final step in this development are those legends in which the deity no longer appears at a specific place but in which the deity guides the whole as the ultimate basis, as in the Rebekah and Joseph narratives. Thus, through many intermediate states, Genesis moves from a crass mythology to a belief in providence very attractive to us moderns. It is a true wonder that the Penuel legend (32:25ff.) is transmitted in such an ancient form. It was helpful that it remained unclear here which god actually attacked Jacob.

At the same time, the association of cultic sites and the deity was dissolved in this gradual refinement of revelation. The belief originally presumed in the cultic legends that the god belonged at this very site and can only act here, is not evident in a single legend in Genesis. Instead, the opinion of the legends in their Israelite form is that the sites were holy to the deity because the deity once appeared to the patriarch in antiquity here. Even the ancient Hebron legend, which permits the appearing deity to eat (18:8), no longer says that the deity came forth from the tree. In the story of Hagar's flight, the matriarch meets the god at the well (16:7). But the actual relationship of the god to the well is left in the dark. The age of this whole development can also be seen in the Bethel narrative. The oldest religion sought the god of the site in the stone itself, as the name of the sacred stone beth-el = "God's house" shows. But the one Israelite recension of the legend maintains that the deity dwells high above Bethel in heaven and only a ladder still mediates between God's actual dwelling and his symbol. This belief in the deity's heavenly house, however, as the originally mythological view of the heavenly ladder demonstrates, stems from a very ancient period (cf. p. 314). Many cultic legends come to us in very faded form. We hear nothing whatsoever in the Ishmael narrative (in both recensions, Gen 16; 21), nor in the legends of Hebron (Gen 18), Mahanaim (32:1ff.), Penuel (32:25ff.), etc. that these sites are places of worship. The legend of Isaac's sacrifice (Gen 22), once a cultic legend, no longer has an etiological intention in the recension transmitted, but is only a character portrayal. The anointing of the stone at Bethel (28;18), once a sacrificial act, seems now to be only a kind of dedication rite. The masseboth, once holy stones, symbols of the deity, are now only simple memorial or grave stones (cf. pp. 312, 341, 369). The Cave of Machpelah, previously probably the seat of a <lxix> goddess,[69] is now only the burial site of the matriarch in our account (cf. p. 269). There are other examples. From this bland attitude of the sanctuary legends one perceives that at the time the sanctuaries were receding from the foreground of religious interest for certain circles of the people. The bond between sanctuaries and religion had already been loosened for many when the passionate polemic of the prophets cut it entirely. Otherwise, how would the people of Judah have tolerated the "deuteronomic reform" which destroyed these sites except the royal temple in Jerusalem (2 Kgs 23)! Genesis also makes a multitude of statements concerning the deity's relationship to people. In individual legends preserved in particularly ancient forms, the idea of people's moral or religious behavior does not even come under consideration in relation to such acts of God. God reveals himself to Jacob at Bethel because Jacob comes to Bethel. Similarly, the deity also attacks Jacob at Penuel for no discernible reason. Abel's sacrifice pleased God because he loved the shepherd Abel. He rejoices at Hagar's unbending defiance (Gen 16). He protects Abraham in Egypt and arranges for the patriarch's lie to have a good outcome. Jacob receives Isaac's blessing through lie and deceit. In the patriarch's conflict with others, however, God takes the side of his darling, even when he is apparently in the wrong, like Abraham before Abimelech (20:7), or when he has acted rather dubiously, like Jacob with Laban (30:25ff.), etc.

In addition, some legends lie on a higher plane. According to them God makes his grace dependent on people's righteousness. He destroyed the evil Sodom, but spared Lot because of his hospitality. He killed Onan because of his unkindness (38:9-10). He drove Cain away because of his fratricide. Joseph, whom he helped, merited this help because of his piety and his nobility. He gave Abraham a son because of his cordiality toward strangers (Gen 18). Taken as a whole, these legends belong to a later, morally more sensitive period. In Israel, however, they are ancient. The belief that God looks with pleasure on the righteous but requites the evildoer according to his sin was surely well known to Israel's religion (cf., e.g., 1 Sam 24:20; 2 Sam 3:39). In a broader sense one may also include another group here which recounts how God has mercy on the suffering and despairing. He cares for the despised wife (29:31), he rewards the peaceful (13:14-15) and brings the innocent Joseph from the prison. Such a God concept is expressed especially grippingly in the legend of Hagar's expulsion (Gen 21). A third kind of legend strongly emphasizes what gains God's good will. God considers belief, obedience, unshakable confidence, to be righteousness. On God's command, Noah builds a ship on dry land (cf. p. 61). Abraham left the safe homeland and moved abroad following God's word. He trusted God's promise that he would become a people, although he did not have even one son (Gen 15)! The legend of the wooing of Rebekah (Gen 24) also shows how such an <lxx> absolute trust in God finds its reward. The legend of Isaac's sacrifice (Gen 22) sketches a wonderful character portrayal of how the true believer subjects himself to

---

[69]Greßmann, ZAW 20:6.

even the most difficult and frightful experience if God commands it. The famed prayer of Jacob (32:10-13) portrays the humble thankfulness of the pious individual who finds himself unworthy of divine grace. Accounts and passages which speak of faith in this way constitute a high point of religion in Genesis. They lend this book its primary value, even for current piety. Without a doubt, however, these are all later configurations. The accuracy of this judgment can also be demonstrated for most of them on other grounds. The Babylonian Flood recension knows nothing of a test of the hero's faith. Jacob's prayer is secondary in the context (cf. pp. 345-46). How remarkably this profoundly sensitive prayer differs from the behavior of the slippery Jacob otherwise, how markedly it differs from the accompanying legend of Jacob's fight with the deity! The story of Abraham's emigration is also a late extrapolation of an older "comment" (¶4:4) and the story of God's covenant (chap. 15) is a free composition not based on old tradition at all! Thus, we can see a development here from a crude to the highest idea of God: Genesis reflects the struggle higher religion fought for Israel's soul. At any rate, however, "in relation to morality, the native form of Yahwism in the patriarchal legends stands high above the attitudes of other religions which permit the gods crudely to struggle contrary to everything the ethic of the time requires of people."[70]

Furthermore, the patriarchal legends demonstrate the error of believing that ancient Israel knew only of God's relationship to Israel. Instead, the legends regularly discuss God's relationship to individuals. To be sure, these figures are sometimes types for peoples, but the legend understands them as persons and depicts God's relationship to them often as God was believed at the time to relate to individuals. One would rob some of these accounts of all their attraction if this were misperceived: the Hebron legend (Gen 18) was so gladly heard by its ancient audience because it recounts how God rewards hospitality (yours and mine, too!). The account of how God heard the voice of the crying boy Ishmael (21:8ff.) is so touching because God had mercy on a child: this God will also hear the cries of our children! We discern another line of development in the older narratives' naive mixture of profane and religious motifs, with no apparent sense of impropriety. Thus, the legend of Abraham in Egypt (12:10ff.) glorifies the patriarch's cunning, the matriarch's beauty, and God's faithfulness. The Flood legend not only praises Noah's piety, but also (in the interlude concerning the sending of the birds, cf. p. 64) his cleverness. The legend of Hagar's flight (Gen 16) tells very realistically of the circumstances in Abraham's house and then of God's assistance. These legends stem, then, from a time when temporal and spiritual were still intertwined, when the men of Israel fought simultaneously for God and the <lxxi> folk hero ("sword of Yahweh and of Gideon," Judg 7:20), when forceful humor was still compatible with piety. One thinks of the cheerful killer Samson, who is also God's nazir, and of the humor of the legend of Abraham in Egypt (cf. pp. 172-73). Now one sees in the variants, especially of the latter legend (in Gen 20 and 26; cf. pp. 223-24), that a later epoch could no longer tolerate this mixture of profane and religious motifs. It was at least offensive to them that one should simultaneously glorify God and the profane characteristics of people. This period formed narratives, then, that are "spiritual" in the proper sense—that is, that only treat God and

---

[70]Haller, 42.

piety and in which profane motifs recede—such as the legend of Abraham's emigration (Gen 12), of the covenant (Gen 15), of Isaac's sacrifice (Gen 22), etc. Here the former folk tale is in the process of becoming a "legend," that is, a "spiritual" account. The earlier period also knew patriarchal legends that were purely profane in nature such as the legend of the separation of Abraham and Lot (Gen 13) or of Jacob and Laban. But these worldly legends became much less prominent on the whole. And, a great deal of religious material also found its way into these, too, in later tradition. For example, offended by the fact that Canaan belonged to Abraham because Lot did not want it, the later tradents added the reference that God himself promised Abraham the land once again after Lot's departure (13:14-17). People had doubts about telling that Jacob ran away from Laban and, consequently, added the notion that God suggested this plan to him (31:3). If we compare the total impression of Genesis with other great folk legends, such as the Homeric poems or the *Nibelungenlied*, we clearly discern the unusual predominance of religious thought in Genesis.[71] Now, one may well doubt whether ancient Israel itself was ever so "spiritual." Instead, there will have been certain "spiritual" circles from whose hands we have received the folk legend (cf. ¶5:3).[72]

7. Furthermore, a whole history of morality can be read from the legends. Joy over the figures of the patriarchs dominate very many of the patriarchal legends. Much, therefore, that we find apparently offensive in these figures was not problematic to the period that first told these narratives. Instead, they were an occasion for enjoyment or enthusiasm (cf. also Sir 44:19, "Abraham brought no spot on his honor"). The ancient people enjoyed Benjamin's life by robbery (49:27), Hagar's defiant courage (cf. p. 191), the bravery of Tamar (cf. pp. 399ff.) and of Lot's daughters (cf. pp. 216-17) who took measures as they could, furthermore Abraham's clever lie in Egypt (cf. pp. 169-70), Joseph's sly presentation of his brothers to his king as sheep raisers (47:1ff.; cf. pp. 440-41), Rachel's trick by which she deceived her father so masterfully (31:34; cf. pp. 337-38), and especially the tricks and ruses of the archrogue Jacob <lxxii> (cf. pp. 292-93, 300-302, 303, 328, 354). One cannot overlook here the role trickery and deceit play in the patriarchal legends and how the earlier period enjoyed this and is characterized by it for us. Now we see in many examples how a later tradition took offense at these narratives, reinterpreted or reshaped them, and attempted to eradicate objectionable features as much as possible. This is most clear in the variants of the legend of the endangered ancestress. Here later narrators reshaped the whole narrative they found to be extremely objectionable. They transformed, for example, Abraham's lie into a mental reservation (20:12), reinterpreted the disgraceful gifts the patriarch received for Sarah as an apology (20:16), and finally derived his wealth from Yahweh's blessing (26:12ff.). Similarly, Abraham's deportation (12:20) has been transformed into its opposite (20:15; cf. p. 223), etc. So that God's mercy on her may not occasion offense, the defiant Hagar of chap. 16 is transformed into an unfortunate, suffering woman (cf. pp. 229-30). The attempt has been made to explain Abraham's behavior toward Hagar by adding that God commanded him

---

[71]Haller, 19, 158.

[72]Arthur Bonus ("Zur Biologie des Märchens," *Preuß. Jahrb.* 119 [1905]: 260-61) describes the "spiritualization" of old Indian accounts under Buddhist influence, whereby the whole narrative is finally "purified and moralized," and gives an example.

to expel her (21:11ff.). Particular effort has been made to absolve Jacob's behavior toward Laban of the accusation of dishonesty: in several long speeches, the narrator introduces evidence that no shadow lay upon Jacob. Jacob's wives and, finally, Laban himself must acknowledge that he is in the right (31:4ff., 36ff.). Here, too, things have been mitigated by attributing things people find objectionable to the rule of God: God caused the flocks to give birth consistently in Jacob's favor (31:7; cf. p. 332). The narrators intervened less forcefully in the Tamar narrative. But here, too, they tried mightily to cleanse Jacob: Judah went to the sacred prostitute, they emphasize, for example, only after his wife had died (cf. pp. 398ff.). The effort was also made to shape the story of Lot's daughters, which would have been very offensive to later narrators, favorably for Lot, at least. Lot was outwitted by his daughters (cf. pp. 217-18). The old period surely rejoiced over the fathers, but they did not consider them saints and quite naively reported all sorts of things about them that were not exactly model behaviors.

A few of the old accounts are thoroughly "crude." They describe the fathers as types of the old populace just as people are. We even hear a few things about Abraham, whose figure otherwise most embodies the ideal of faith, peacefulness, and righteousness, which are not ideal, to be sure, but are authentically human nonetheless. The story of Hagar's flight (Gen 16) depicts the people in Abraham's house as follows: Sarah as the jealous wife, Hagar as the defiant slave, and Abraham as the accommodating husband. Such characterizations would have been intolerable to the later, "spiritually" sensitive period. Rather, this period saw the fathers as the model of piety and, indeed, of the lofty, tender piety of this generation. In this way, however, an unusual dissonance has arisen in the image of the fathers. The same Abraham who cast his son Ishmael into suffering (21:14), who had no doubts about handing Sarah over to the foreign king and even accepted gifts in exchange for her (12:10ff.), is supposed to be the same man who is the high example of faith for all times! And the sly Jacob says the wonderful thanksgiving prayer (32:10ff.)! We can resolve this <lxxiii> dissonance and free these legends from the dreadful suspicion of falsehood by recognizing that the various tones derive from various times. The ancient period had no objections against occasionally simply admitting that the foreigner was in the right in relation to the fathers—that is, Pharaoh was just in relation to Abraham (12:18f.) and Esau in relation to Jacob (27:36). Indeed, a few of the fathers were simply abandoned: Simeon, Levi, and Reuben were even cursed by the patriarch (49:3-7)! Israelite patriotism was still sound enough at the time to find such things unobjectionable. But the later period with its arrogant, one-sided veneration of the "people of God" could not tolerate the notion that the fathers could have once been unjust. Thus one sees how one of the narrators takes pains to show that Abraham was not entirely in the wrong in relation to Abimelech (in the speech, 20:11-13 E; cf. p. 221).

For the same reason, in order to avoid disgraceful reports concerning the fathers, only a fragment of the story of Reuben's curse was transmitted (35:21f.) and several attempts were made to transform the legend of Simeon and Levi (Gen 34). First an excuse was sought for the brothers: indeed, they defended the honor of their sister (J). Finally they were even vindicated and their betrayal of Shechem was portrayed as a natural consequence. Here, too, God finally takes their side (E, cf. p. 361). Such transformations do not always please us. And sometimes it may seem to us as though they make the matter worse rather than better. For example, the lie of Abraham, who pretends that his wife is his sister (12:12f.), is a lie whose slyness was a source of joy for the ancient people, but still more tolerable than the mental reservation (20:12) that replaces it and which seems Jesuitical to us. Yet one must not loose sight of the joy over the gradual refinement of moral judgment we observe in Genesis.

8. The history of esthetics discernible from these legends has already been treated above (¶3). Here only a few additions will be offered. One takes a deep look into the heart of the ancient people by collecting the chief motifs which gladden the eye of the narrator. This will not be undertaken at this point.[73] Only briefly, once again, attention will be called to how little murder and war are discussed here (cf. above p. lii). In this, the legends of Genesis differ significantly from the old Germanic legends in which fighting and war fill human life and are the subjects of accounts. In marked contrast, Genesis treats peaceful activities and domestic things, especially reproduction. Eating and drinking also play a significant role. These narrators are very familiar with the life of shepherds and farmers and are, therefore, a major source for our "archaeology." They are inexperienced in political things. In this area, instead, they are rather naively folklorish. The joyful optimism that runs throughout the patriarchal legends is also characteristic. "Offensive situations are avoided if possible, all critical situations are resolved simply and quickly"[74] (12:17ff.; 16:7ff.; 21:17ff.; 22:11f.; 38:25ff.; 41:1ff.). Also, Yahweh <lxxiv> himself is predominantly the gracious protector and helper. Thus, the legend has an idyllic color, even those customarily called "patriarchal." The more serious aspect of the God concept resounds particularly in the primal narrative. Here, too, however, the ideas of the righteousness of divine judgment and God's grace which governs the righteous and still has mercy on the sinner mitigates the pagan-somber attitude. The older legends are often rather crude. One need only think of the legend of the defiant Hagar (Gen 16) or of how Jacob deceived his blind father to the enjoyment of the hearers (Gen 27), or even of the extraordinarily crude manner in which Laban's clever daughters duped their father (31:33ff.). It must have been a strong generation that took pleasure in such stories. Later accounts differ significantly. They overflow with tears (i.e., the legend of Hagar's expulsion [Gen 21], of Isaac's sacrifice [Gen 22], and, especially, the Joseph legends). A new generation that loves emotion and tears expresses itself here.

Another distinction between the older and the younger periods involves the fact that the former took pleasure in the familiar things of its nearest surroundings, while the latter sought to lend its accounts exotic attraction by setting the legend abroad and by interweaving foreign practices into the description (Joseph legend). One may compare the fact that the characters of the old legends act in realistic ways—any wife would be irritated by the insolence of a concubine (16:5) and any good brother would avenge the disgrace of his sister (34:7)—while a later art finds divergence from the norm noteworthy, for example, the manner in which Rebekah is sent for by her bridegroom against common practice (24:61ff.) or the manner in which the dying Jacob prays, not on the ground, but on his bed (47:31).

---

[73]A few remarks on this subject may be found in Holzinger (123ff.), but in the context of the description of the Yahwist.

[74]Haller, 39-40.

9. Accordingly, we have abundant criteria for assessing the age or youth of an account. Often we can portray an extensive prehistory of the legend in question, that is, in the Hagar legend of chap. 16 where the god who appeared was first an El, then Yahweh himself, then his messenger (cf. pp. 186-87). Sometimes, a series of different reasons point to the same conclusion concerning the age of a legend. Thus, for many reasons, the legend of Abraham in Egypt (Gen 12) is to be considered very ancient. It is very brief, bears an ancient local color, does not idealize the figures, etc. In contrast, many criteria suggest that the Joseph legend is to be considered very young. It has the latest, very expansive style, few etiological elements, contains the doctrine of providence, etc. Very often, however, the various considerations are intermingled: the legend has old and young elements colorfully intermixed. For example, the account of chap. 15, which has no plot complication, is relatively young, but the epiphany in fire and smoke is certainly an ancient concept. The individual developments were not strictly self-contained. Ancient concepts often survived for long periods. Therefore, one may not imagine this history of the legends as simple and linear, but as rather variegated and eventful.

If we review this whole history of transformations once again, we must say that we certainly surveyed only a minor portion of <lxxv> the whole process. These transformations will have already been long at work even in a time into which our sources permit us no insight. This may warn us against trying to establish the original meaning of the legend too hastily.

10. And if it is hardly possible for us to indicate the original sense of every individual legend from our sources, then we may also only approach the question of the original identity of the figures in the patriarchal legends with great caution. A few of them are actually names of peoples, tribes, and cities—that is, Cain, Shem, Ham, Japhet, Canaan, Ishmael, Ammon, Moab, Shechem, Hamor, and the tribes of Israel. Of course, Israel and Edom are also the names of peoples, but, notably, the ancient legend does not employ Jacob and Esau instead of these names. "Israel" and "Edom" are, thus, not original legend figures. An inscription of Thutmose II (ca. 1500) mentions a central Palestinian city or province named Y'qb'ar, which would correspond to a Hebrew Yaqob-el (Hebr. l = Eg. r). The name Yaqob-el would relate to Jacob as Yiphtah-el and Yabne-el relate to Yiphtah and Yaben. One may also compare the tribal or place names Israel, Ishmael, Jerahmeel, and Jezreel.[75] Yet the conclusion that the biblical figure of Jacob traces back to this very Canaanite Yaqob-el would be premature since similar forms with el very often appear among the West Semitic names from Hammurabi's time, since Yahqub-êl (Yaqubum) is specifically attested as a personal name,[76] and, furthermore, since the foundations of the Jacob legends in Genesis are not actually located in Canaan. A few scholars[77] equate Asher with the Syrian geographical name 'Y-s-rw found in the inscriptions of Seti I and Ramses II (ca. 1400). Similarly, Joseph is equated with the Canaanite city name Yŝp'r mentioned by Thutmose III.[78] Yet it should be noted that many other names, particularly

---

[75]Meyer, Israeliten, 281-82.

[76]Ranke in Greßmann, 6.

[77]W. Max Müller, Asien und Europa, 236ff.; Meyer, Israeliten, 540; in contrast Sethe, GGA (1904), 935ff.; Eerdmans 2:65ff.

[78]This equation is dubious, however (Meyer, Israeliten, 292).

such as those of Abraham, Isaac, and those of all the matriarchs, are not tribal names. Furthermore, to contend that a few of the figures bear the names of peoples is not to claim that most of the accounts concerning them or even just the total portrayal of their persons can be explained in relation to the fates of the nations. Very much reported about such a folk hero can have been secondarily applied to him, as is obviously the case for Joseph, for example (cf. above pp. xv-xvi, xxii). The understanding of the figures in Genesis as nations is, thus, by no means a general key to them.[79] The interpretation that they were formerly gods is no more successful. To be sure, a few figures among them could have originally been gods. Thus, as is known, Gad is the name of a god of good fortune, although it should be noted that the name also occurs as a personal name.[80] The name Obed-edom ("servant of Edom") also seems to point to a god Edom, who may also occur elsewhere (Meyer, 298n.1; Wellhausen, *Composition*³, 45n.1). Jeush, an Edomite clan name (36:5), is the <lxxvi> Arabic divine name *Yaghuth*. A Sabeean god *Cainân* is also attested (Meyer, *Israeliten*, 397).

The typical example of such a coincidence of the names of the god and the political unit would be "Asshur," simultaneously an ethnic and a divine name (cf. Meyer, *Israeliten*, 296ff.). Other divine names postulated are Shelah (cf. the name Methushelah = man of Shelah, p. 155), Reu (cf. the name Reuel, p. 155),[81] Nahor (the name has been rediscovered as the name of an Aramaic god Nahar, cf. pp. 155-56), Terah (perhaps = the northern Syrian god *Tarḫu*, p. 157), Haran (cf. the name Bethharan = temple of Haran, p. 159). "Sarah" and "Milkah" were, as we know, the names of the goddesses of Haran to which the biblical figures Sarah and Milkah could be related. Even Laban's name may be reminiscent of a god: Lebanah = moon (cf. p. 162). The question has also arisen as to whether Joseph may not been an ancient Canaanite god.[82] In earlier and more recent times, the attempt has been repeatedly made to explain the original figures of Abraham, Isaac, and Jacob as gods, too.[83] Now Isa 51:1-2; 63:16; 65:4; Jer 31:35 seem, indeed, to indicate an ancestral cult at the graves of the patriarchs Abraham, Israel, Sarah, and Rachel, as still exists in Hebron. But the Israelite figure may well have replaced a deity (p. 269).[84] Eerdmans (2:7) also correctly points out that historical persons are still venerated as saints at their graves in the Moslem Orient. The cultic name *Pahad-Yiṣhaq* (31:42 = "horror of Isaac"), however, does not evidence a god Isaac. The divine name, as the parallel "God of my father" clearly indicates, is not "Isaac," but "Horror of Isaac," that is, the God whom Isaac fears, just as "Holy one of Israel is the God whom Israel considers holy" (pp. 338-39).[85] In order to demonstrate a god Jacob, appeal has been made to a Hyksos king *Yʿpq-hr, Yʿqp-hr* = (the God) "Jacob is pleased." But the reading is uncertain.[86] Meyer

---

[79]Meyer, *Israeliten*, 250.

[80]Meyer, *Israeliten*, 533.

[81]According to Meyer, Reuel = "friend of God."

[82]Yet this theory seems to be very questionable.

[83]So, recently, Meyer, *Israeliten*.

[84]Greßmann, 6.

[85]With Eerdmans 2:10-11, and Greßmann, 7-8; contra Holzinger, 206 and Staerk, *Studien* 1:59ff., etc.

[86]Cf. Ranke in Greßmann, 7.

(*Israeliten*, 267ff.) follows Lagarde in equating Abraham with the Nabateean god Dusares and interpreting it as *Dû-šarâ*, that is, the spouse of a goddess *Šarâ*. But whether the second component of the name Dusares is really a goddess and not, perhaps, simply a region remains disputed.[87] Even if a few patriarchal figures were concealed gods, this explanation cannot be carried through with respect to the most significant, Abraham, Isaac, and Jacob. In addition, Babylonian materials attest the names Jacob and Abraham[88] as <lxxvii> common personal names. Therefore, they will probably have been nothing other than human beings. It is especially significant, however, that the legends are by no means full of mythical echoes. Instead, only a very few elements that could be so interpreted occur. Thus, Joseph's dream that the sun, moon, and eleven stars must bow to him (37:9) seems to have originated as an oracle referring to the lord of heaven before whom the highest powers in heaven bow. Yet this dream, it seems, only found its way secondarily into the Joseph narrative (cf. pp. 390-91) and nothing else suggests that Joseph was the highest heavenly ruler. Jacob's struggle with the deity has often been interpreted such that Jacob is envisioned as a semidivine giant (so also in the commentary, p. 349). But Greßmann[89] shows that stories can also be told of struggles between people and demons. Even the theory of Winckler,[90] previously often repeated by the author, that Abraham's 318 servants are actually the 318 days in a year in which the moon is visible, is extremely uncertain since the number 318 is not attested in this meaning in the Orient (cf. in the commentary, pp. 277-78).

The entire assumption that the partriachs are humanized deities must seem likely as long as one proceeds from the general presupposition that the legend developed from the myth. Now, however, that this theory has been shaken and scholars have begun to see the basic form of account in the "fairy tale,"[91] that focuses on people, one will also be inclined to recognize the patriarchs as nothing other than human beings. At any rate, we must demand a much greater precision of future mythological interpreters of the Genesis legends than we find among the current such interpreters. Furthermore, it will not be sufficient to explain only individual aspects of an account as mythic. Instead we require to be shown that whole legends bear striking similarities with preserved myths or that the legends can be understood very clearly as original myths. To this point, scholars have not yet succeeded in this demonstration.[92] And we must further require that <lxxviii> those

---

[87]Eerdmans 2:12-13; Greßmann, 5.

[88]For Abraham, cf. Meyer, *Israeliten*, 265f. and Greßmann, 1ff.; Abiram is also a personal name in Hebrew. Egyptian material (the list of Soshenk I) refers to a place *pa ḥqra 'brm* = "field (הקל) of Abraham," i.e., perhaps the field where the holy tree stood (Meyer, *Israeliten*, 266). For Jacob, cf. Greßmann, 6-7; cf. pp. lxv-lxvi.

[89]Greßmann, 20; cf. also Eerdmans 2:8.

[90]*Gesch. Isr.* 2:27.

[91]So, recently, Wundt, *Völkerpsychologie* 2/3.

[92]The older theory of Goldziher (*Mythos bei den Hebräers* [1876]), who essentially based his deductions on the etymologies of names, has already disappeared. Stucken (*Astralmythen I Abraham, II Lot, III Jacob, IV Esau*) bases his contentions on individual aspects of the legends for which he collects parallels from all over the world in a confusing quantity. But these parallels are often only very approximate. According to Stucken, just as Etana, born to heaven by an eagle according

scholars who want to acknowledge the presumed mythical bases of these legends first carefully examine the history of these legends clear to us from our sources.[93] Without the preceding esthetic analysis of the legends, this whole body of research swings in the air. If, however, we consider figures like Abraham, Isaac, and Jacob to be actual persons with no original mythic foundation,[94] that does not at all mean that they are historical figures, no more than Brunhilda and Siegfried, although their names are personal names, must be historical entities for this reason alone.[95] For even if, as may well be assumed, there was once a man called "Abraham," everyone who knows the history of legends is sure that the legend is in no position at the distance of so many centuries to preserve a picture of the personal piety of Abraham. The "religion of Abraham" is, in reality, the religion of the legend narrators which they attribute to Abraham. Greßmann (9ff.) has wonderfully portrayed the way in which one must conceive of the development of figures such as Abraham and Jacob.

---

to the Babylonian myth, looks down on the earth, so Abraham and Lot also look into the land from Bethel, so Abraham looks to heaven and on Sodom. But such analogies are too weak to stand the test. Winckler (2 [1900]), who builds on this uncertain foundation, depends particularly on the characteristic numbers: the four wives of Jacob are the four phases of the moon, the twelve sons the months; the seven children of Leah are the deities of the days of the week, the 300 pieces of silver the youngest, Benjamin, receives are the 30 days of the last month, the five garments of honor are the five leap days, Joseph's garment recalls the garment of Tamar and Ishtar (and every other garment!); the fact that he was cast into the cistern corresponds to the descent of Tammuz into the underworld; that his garment was dipped in blood and that his father believed he was consumed by an animal are an allusion to Eber's murder of Adonis; etc. Recently Winckler (*Altorient. Forschungen* 3:385ff.) and his students Erbt and A. Jeremias, operating on the assumption of "keywords" supposed to allude to mythical elements, have raised the structure to the giddy heights. Beside the preceding, the following objections can be levied against the whole system. (1) That the legends of Genesis, especially in their original form, do not display the hairsplitting clarity and the spirit of learning attributed to them, but that they are the fresh and natural products of a vigorously sensitive people. (2) That they originally existed, like all folk narratives, as individual stories so that one may not seek in them a comprehensive system. (3) That it is both undemonstrable and unlikely that the Hebrew narrators lived with astronomical thoughts of Babylonian origin. (4) That it is difficult to comprehend, indeed it is grotesquely one-sided, why one would seek the explanation of all myths in the calender, etc. Given the good sense of one's contemporaries, one may expect that the whole "system" will shortly break asunder as it deserves. Cf. against Winckler, recently, Meyer, *Israeliten*, 252-53; Luther, *ZAW* 21:146ff.; Eerdmans 2:14ff.; etc. Cf. also Meyer's judgment concerning the "Oriental world view" (*Gesch. des Altertums* 1/22:328-29, 529-30) and Wundt's judgment concerning astral mythology (2/3:49ff.) and concerning Stucken (2/3:516n.1).

[93]Stucken failed notoriously to do this. Here, not even the results of source criticism are always employed.

[94]Recently, Eerdmans (2:5ff.) and Greßmann (9) come to the same conclusion.

[95]On the "positive" side, the attempt has repeatedly been made, even in most recent times, to salvage the historicity of Abraham at least. Recently, Assyriology and Egyptology have been called upon to make contributions. The best refutation is the analysis of the legends. See the bibliography in "Abraham," *RGG*; in the commentary, cf. pp. 167-68, 282-83. Concerning the purported historicity of the Joseph figure, cf. in the commentary, pp. 383-85, 421.

There was—it must be assumed—an original account, perhaps the one concerning the three gods visiting an old man, that, in the fashion of such accounts (which did not differ from modern "fairy tales"), mentioned a name popular at the time. Other, appropriate materials were attributed to this "Abraham" figure. <lxxix> The decisive step toward our "Abraham," however, was taken when Israel appropriated the figure that had developed in this fashion as its ancestor. The original Jacob may have been the sly shepherd Jacob who deceived the hunter Esau. Another legend of the deception of the father-in-law by the son-in-law was all the more easy to add because both are shepherds. A third legend cycle concerning an old man who loved his youngest son was applied to this figure and this youngest was named Joseph at a time when Jacob was equated with Israel's assumed ancestor "Israel," etc. Thus, we conclude that the chief fathers are literary figures. The historical value of these figures consists in the historicity of the circumstances in their legends, their religioethical value in the ideas which these accounts express.

¶5. Yahwist, Elohist, Yehowist, the Older Collections

1. The collection of legends had already begun during oral transmission. It has already been described above (pp. xlv-xlvi) how individual stories first were attracted to one another and finally how larger groups of legends were formed. Collectors also created connecting pieces. A particular example is the story of the birth of Jacob's sons (29:31ff.) which is not a folk legend but was devised by old narrators and must have already existed prior to J and E (cf. pp. 321-22). When the legends were committed to writing, this process of collection continued and the whole tradition of the old accounts was collected. It is difficult to determine the extent to which the main groups our Genesis now contains already existed in oral tradition. It seems certain, however, that the fusion of these groups, that is, the primal narratives, the patriarchal legends, the Joseph narrative, and the following account of Israel's Exodus, was first the product of written collections. This documentation of popular traditions will have occured in a period generally inclined to write and when one may have feared that the oral tradition could die out if not documented. One may imagine that the guild of legend narrators may have ceased then for reasons we do not know. For its part, literary fixation will have contributed to the death of the other surviving remnants of oral tradition much as the written law ended the institution of the priestly torah and as the New Testament canon put an end to the early Christian charismatics.

The literary collection of legends was not accomplished by one hand or in one period, but by several or even many in a very long process. We distinguish two periods in this process: the earlier for which we thank the collections of the Yahwist (J) and the Elohist (E), then a later, comprehensive reworking by the so-called priestly codex (P). Consequently, essentially only the legends we know from J and E have been utilized above. All of these legend books contain not only these legends of the origins, but also recount the other stories. One can describe (with Wildeboer) "Israel's election as Yahweh's people" as their <lxxx> theme. In the following discussion, however, they will generally only be treated to the extent that they come under consideration for Genesis.

The distinction of these three "documentary sources" of Genesis is a common result of a century and a half of Old Testament scholarship. Since the awakening of modern Protestant biblical scholarship, the critical questions of Genesis have been treated with special preference. An amazing expenditure of industry, of discernment, of brilliant powers of comprehension has been applied to this work. The result is a product of which future generations may be proud. It is currently possible in many cases to determine the source documents to the verse, in a few cases to the word, although, of course, much will always remain uncertain. The final decisive turn in the history of Genesis criticism was the work of Wellhausen, who taught us in his masterpiece *Prolegomena zur Geschichte Israels* to determine the sources of Genesis chronologically and to locate them in the total course of the history of Israel's religion. The most recent period of criticism has recognized that the documentary sources J, E, and P, themselves, trace back to subsources. Budde's *Urgeschichte*,[96] especially, has demonstrated this for J. <lxxxi>

2. How is the literary character of the "sources" J and E and their subsources to be assessed? First, it must be generally admitted that these sources rest on oral tradition, that they are collections. But several different varieties of such "collections" are conceivable. Some collections were produced by literary personalities who have consciously striven to rework the diverse received material into a unity and to imprint upon it the stamp of their intellects. Some collections came together as though of themselves, with no evidence of such intentional personalities, in which the received pieces stand alongside one another loosely without displaying a strict unity. It stands to reason that the two types of collec-

---

[96]Admittedly, Eerdmans (1 [1908]) has recently sought to refute the so-called newer documentary hypothesis entirely. He disputes the notion that the alteration of יהוה and אלהים traces to various sources and thinks that many accounts in Genesis presuppose polytheism, wherein אלהים means a plurality of gods, but "Yahweh" means one of them. In the details, he attempts to demonstrate that many of the accounts divided by the critics on the basis of the alteration in the divine name are in reality completely unified and that a documentary source such as P never existed. But the tools with which Eerdmans works are not fine enough to do justice to the tender art of these accounts. In order to defend the unity of the accounts, he is often satisfied with discarded "apologetic" devices. He demonstrates only that the redactors who combined the various sources proceeded not wholly unskillfully although more insightful research notes breaks everywhere and recognizes, e.g., that 16:3, 15-16 are written in an entirely different style than their context and are radically distinguished by their dry, learned character from fresh folk legend. Eerdmans also dismisses the conspicuous distinctions in the diction of the sources with a few comments. His own source analyses, however, are to be thoroughly rejected as insufficient (cf., e.g., in the commentary, pp. 142, 386-87, etc.). He is even prepared to attribute such schematic passages as the genealogies (Gen 5; 11:10ff.; 36:1-14) to the same source as the vital accounts of Abraham in Egypt, of the separation of Abraham and Lot, of Jacob and Esau, and sections of the Joseph narrative (p. 87)! His religiohistorical assumptions are also very strange. According to him, the accounts of Genesis bear polytheistic character up to the Exile and even Amos 4:11 (cf. pp. 36, 71, 89) still presupposes polytheism, while monotheism is supposed to have been first represented by Deuteronomy and only later in the legends, and came to dominate especially since the Exile. Eerdmans built his basic understanding of the development of Genesis on this purported alternation of polytheism and monotheism in the legends. Thus, the multitude of other considerations that must be taken into account in the division into documentary sources are overlooked for the most part. On the whole, therefore, Eerdmans's attempt must be regarded as a failure, while the second part of his studies offer much that is superb. Concerning the details, cf. the source analyses at the head of the interpretations. We are thankful that Eerdmans writes in German, although his German admittedly still needs a few finishing touches.

tions must be treated very differently in interpretation. In the first instance the author must primarily be interpreted, in the second, the material adapted. How are the sources J and E and their subsources to be evaluated accordingly? Current research is generally more inclined to emphasize the personality of the author in these sources and subsources.[97] The attempt has been made to gain a unified image of the author from the variety of information in these documents[98] and the dominant emphasis has often been placed on the author in the examination of details and the character of their documents as collections relegated to secondary status. In contrast, it should be pointed out that (a) these documents do not display a strictly unified character, but rather contain extremely varied materials. J encompasses individual legends (e.g., Gen 16) and legend cycles (such as those concerning Abraham-Lot, Jacob-Esau-Laban, and Joseph), brief (Penuel legend) and extended (chap. 24) stories, crude (Gen 16) and tender (e.g., 37:35) materials, religiously and morally ancient (Jacob-Esau legend, Hebron legend) and young (12:1ff.; 15) materials, stories in vibrant, ancient colors and others which are very bland. E does not differ greatly. It contains, for example, the touching story of Isaac's sacrifice (Gen 22) and also a variant of the very ancient legend of Jacob's struggle (cf. pp. 347-48). This variety demonstrates that the legends of E, and even more so of J, do not bear the character of a specific period, let alone <lxxxii> of an individual personality, but that the collectors essentially took them as they found them.[99] (b) A consideration of the J and E variants points in the same direction. On the one hand, the two often agree with one another notably. Both follow, for example, the briefest style in the Penuel story, the most expansive in the Joseph narrative. Precisely because they are so similar, they could be combined by a later hand such that they often flow together imperceptibly for us. On the other hand, they often diverge from one another. J very often has the older form, but sometimes E does as well. Thus, the earthy Hagar narrative of J (Gen 16) is older than the tearful version of E (Gen 21). In the account of the birth of Jacob's children, J speaks quite innocently of the magical effect of the mandrake (30:14ff.), which is replaced by the effectuality of divine grace in E (30:17). In the Dinah legend, which describes Jacob's horror over his sons' deed, J is more just and ancient than E, where God himself must protect Jacob's sons (cf. p. 361). In the Joseph narrative, J's Ishmaelites, who disappeared in later times (37:25), are older than E's Midianites (v 28; cf. p. 393). In Jacob's testament, E, according to which Jacob wishes to be buried near his beloved (48:7), tells the tale more softly and

---

[97]Dillmann, *Kommentar zu Numeri*, 629; recently, esp., Meyer, *Israeliten* (see "Jahwist" in the index).

[98]Cf., e.g., Holzinger, 110ff., 191ff. Recently, Luther (in Meyer, *Israeliten*, 108ff.), esp., has attempted to portray the person of "J¹": He was a proponent of the "nomadic ideal," an opponent of everything cultic, and related to Amos(!). But which passages may we reasonably derive from "J¹"? May one really derive such character traits of J from his work? Procksch (207ff., 289ff) has also offered a characterization of the authors J and E, although much more cautiously. The usefulness of the book suffers from the lack of an index. Cf. in opposition to such attempts l'Houet, 259, 292, who portrays the "impersonal" nature of "Medieval" art.

[99]Conversely, Luther (in Meyer, *Israeliten*, 105ff.) considers J to be an author who worked freely with the tradition. But how much smoother the accounts must have been if J had really altered them accordingly to his preference!

tenderly than J, according to which he wants to rest in his own grave (47:29ff.; cf. pp. 446-47), etc. On the other hand, E does not yet know of Philistines in Gerar, as J does (21:32, 34; 26; cf. p. 388). Jacob's deceit (Gen 27) by means of the fur wrapping in E is more naive than the deceit by means of the smell of the clothing in J. The original concept of the stone at Bethel as the house of God can still be heard in E, but no longer in J (p. 314). Only in J, not yet in E, does a secondary Israelitization suddenly appear in the legend of the treaty at Gilead (31:52; cf. p. 341). In the Joseph legend, Reuben, who disappeared in the historical period, has the same status assumed by the later much more famous Judah in J. The diction of E, the avoidance of the name Yahweh in Genesis, rests, as shown above (p. l) on an older memory lacking in J. Yet, on the other hand, one cannot fail to notice that this consistent avoidance of the name Yahweh prior to Moses also manifests a theological reflection yet foreign to J's character.[100]

These observations, which can easily be multiplied, also demonstrate that there is no direct literary relationship between J and E. J neither copied from E nor E from J. That the two sometimes agree even in wording is to be explained by the close relationship between the traditions.[101] The main thing, however, is to discern from the <lxxxiii> way in which the legends in these books have come together that they are not unified works or even combinations of unified works. Instead they are collections that are not of one piece and could not have been completed in one operation but which arose through a process of development. This recognition can be gained primarily through a precise examination of the character of J since most of the material we have in Genesis is from J. We distinguish three sources in the primal history of J, two of which offer originally independent, sometimes parallel threads. It seems particularly obvious that J contained two parallel genealogies of humanity's earliest ancestors, in addition to the Cainite genealogy transmitted to us also a Sethite genealogy of which 5:29 is a remnant. A third source was also employed in the combination. The legend of Cain and Abel, which cannot have originally taken place in the primordial period, stems from this third source (cf. pp. 2-3). We can also perceive three hands in the Abraham narratives. In a legend cycle treating the fates of Abraham and Lot, other passages, probably from another legend book, such as the legends of Abraham in Egypt and of Hagar's flight (Gen 16), have been inserted. A third hand added details such as Abraham's intercession for Sodom (cf. pp. 159ff.). The composition of the Jacob narratives is even more complicated (cf. pp. 285ff.). The legend cycle of Jacob, Esau, and Laban has been supplemented by a few cultic legends. Finally, legends concerning the individual sons of Jacob have been added. We are indeed able to survey this process as a whole, but we are no longer in a position to distinguish individual hands here. While the individual primal narratives stand alongside one another loosely, a few of the Abraham narratives, and especially the Jacob-Esau-Laban legends, have been more tightly woven into a unit. The consolidation is even firmer in the Joseph legend (cf. pp. 380ff.). Here, the legends of Joseph's experiences in Egypt and with his brothers

---

[100]It should also be noted that E also frequently uses אלהים even after the revelation to Moses. Cf. Procksch (197-98) who sees—probably correctly—this as an expression of monotheism.

[101]Procksch (305ff.) and Carpenter (*Composition of the Hexateuch* [1902], 220n.a) reach the same conclusion. I find no confirmation in Genesis for the reverse conclusion (Meyer, *Israeliten*, 7, 8, 9, 14, 21, etc.) that E is dependent on J.

comprise a well-structured whole. The section concerning Joseph's agricultural policy (47:13ff.), which interrupts the context, demonstrates, however, that here too several hands have been at work. Furthermore, quite clearly the Tamar legend (Gen 38), which does not deal with Joseph, and the "blessing of Jacob" (Gen 49), which is not a legend but a poem, were inserted only later.

This survey suggests that J is neither a unified work itself nor does it trace back to older, self-contained, unified works. Rather, it was constituted by the combination of several, indeed of many hands. We see similar phenomena, although only in light traces in Genesis, in E, also: the two related Gerar legends (Gen 20; 2122ff.) are currently separated by the Ishmael narrative (21:8ff.; cf. p. 231) and one thread derived Beer-sheba from Abraham (21:22-23), the other from Isaac (cf. comments on 46:1-3). The history of the literary collection offers, then, a very colorful image. We may be certain that we can survey only a small portion of it. In the ancient period, there may have been a whole literature of such collections of which only the remnants are preserved for us, just as the three synoptics represent the remnant of a large evangelical literature. The P source offers evidence for the accuracy of this view. <lxxxiv> It is often related to J (thus P contains a primal history as does J), but it also occasionally agrees with E (as in the name "Paddan," in the designation of Laban as "the Aramaean"). In the details it also adds entirely new traditions (such as the comment that Abraham emigrated from Ur-Casdim, the account of the purchase of the Cave of Machpelah, etc.; cf. pp. 102-103, 257-58, 371, 465-66). The most important observation for this whole picture of the history of collection, however, is the one that introduced this discussion: the whole process had already begun in oral transmission. The first hands that documented legends may have already committed such related stories to writing. Others have added new legends. Thus, the whole material gradually grew. In this way, our collections J and E, along with others, developed. "J" and "E" are, thus, not individual authors, but narrative schools.[102] It is relatively insignificant what the individual hands contributed to the whole because they are very indistinct and can never by identified with certainty.

3. These collectors, therefore, are not masters but servants of their material. We may imagine them, filled with reverence for the beautiful, old accounts, striving to render them to the best of their ability. Their chief trait was fidelity. Consequently, they adopted much that they only partially understood and that was remote from their own sensibilities. They often preserved peculiarities of individual accounts. Thus, the account of the wooing of Rebekah does not call the city of Haran by name while other passages in J do (27:43; 28:10; 29:4; cf. p. 252). On the other hand, such collectors by no means reproduce the transmitted material totally without alteration. They infused the legends with their spirit. The unified diction of the collections clearly indicates that such a recasting of the legend material took place. We may, however, identify the spirit which fills them from the general impression they created. This impression reflects the—somewhat indefinite—idea they had in mind (cf. esp. the primal history, in the commentary, pp. 1, 161). For the later additions and redactions, the details suggest the attitude of the redactors. We may regard

---

[102]Budde, *Kommentar zum Richterbuche*, xiv; cf. also Stade, *Bibl. Theol.* 1:26; Carpenter, 192-93; and Kautzsch, *Hlg. Schrift des AT*³ 1:3.

the spiritualization of the legend material, observed in the preceding (pp. lviiff.), especially, as their work. We also gain an impression of their character by comparing Genesis with the traditions of other ancient peoples and recognizing their high religious and ethical superiority (cf. in the commentary p. 9). Thus we may imagine the collectors, towering above their people, with the intention of elevating them to their ideals through the collection of legends in a great work.

But they also made many other alterations: they combined various traditions (cf. pp. 450, 462), smoothed the contradictions among them (cf. p. 358), omitted much old material, lightly reworked others (cf. 8:7; p. 64), added much—for example, traditional <lxxxv> "comments"—but, especially, expanded motifs that pleased them particularly, composed a narrative of sorts by the combination of various traditions or elsewise (cf. pp. 365-67, 321-22), etc. They continued, therefore, the process of reshaping and harmonizing the legends that had been at work for such a long period. In the details, it is difficult, indeed, for the most part probably impossible, to distinguish what belongs to such alteration of oral tradition and what was produced by the collectors or even later. Some transformations discussed above were surely only undertaken in the documentary tradition. In general, one will be inclined to attribute an inner literary reshaping to oral tradition and a more external, which only omits or adds, to the collectors or redactors. At any rate, such a question does not elicit the most decisive interest. The main issue continues to be to understand the inner reasons for a transformation. A few larger passages could also have been omitted or obscured then. Thus, the Hebron legend, as the statement in 18:10 clearly shows, points to a continuation which told of a second visit of the three men with Abraham, but which is currently missing and was probably omitted by a collector (cf. p. 198). Or other larger passages were only added in the document: for example, genealogies that are not remnants of legends but only surveys of ethnographic circumstances (such as 22:20ff.; 25:1ff.); further, a passage such as Abraham's conversation with God outside Sodom (18:23ff.) which is, by nature, very late in origin (cf. pp. 202-203); etc. Even a large, ancient poem was secondarily added to the legends (chap. 49). We cannot survey the total picture of the changes produced by these collections. But, despite the collectors' fidelity in the details, we may imagine that the whole impression of the legends was significantly altered by the collection into large works and the repeated reworking. The rich colors of the individual legends, especially, may have been obscured: the original points of the legends become indistinct through combination with other accounts (p. 176); the various attitudes of the individual legends are harmonized now that they stand alongside one another. Anecdotal material, now associated with serious narratives (p. 173), is no longer perceived to be funny. The spirit of higher religion has suppressed the lower. Thus, the legends now make the impression of an old, originally colorful image, which was then darkened and significantly painted over by a later hand. Finally, it should be emphasized that the collectors' fidelity is especially evident in Genesis. In the later legends, which directly involve religious interests, especially in the legend of Moses, the redaction may have been more thorough.

4. The two schools of J and E are very closely related to one another. Judging from their overall attitudes, they must have belonged in essentially the same epoch. Among the materials they transmitted, the collectors will have primarily regarded the youngest material, that is, that nearest their time and sensibilities, with particular pleasure. Their distinction consists primarily <lxxxvi> in diction. The most significant example is the fact

that J uses Yahweh before Moses and E uses Elohim. There are also other examples: after his return to Canaan J calls the patriarch "Israel" and E, "Jacob"; J calls the maiden שִׁפְחָה, E, אָמָה; J calls the corn sack שַׂק, E, אַמְתַּחַת; etc.[103] This diction, however, should not be regarded, either here or elsewhere, as characteristic of an individual pen, but as characteristic of a circle, a region. In very many cases we cannot distinguish the two sources through the vocabulary. In these cases the distinguishing characteristic consists in the fact that the variants of the two sources offer unified accounts individually discrete in content—Jacob deceives Isaac through the smell of Esau's clothing in J, through the animal skin in E, a difference that governs a great portion of the two narratives (Gen 27)—or, in the fact that various accounts have certain thematic elements or words—Joseph is sold to an Egyptian husband by the Ishmaelites in J (39:1b), to the eunuch Potiphar by the Midianites in E (37:36; cf. above p. xl).

Often such characteristics are much less clear. In such cases, therefore, we can only offer conjectures concerning source analysis. When such distinctions abandon us, we are no longer able to distinguish between the two sources. In the primal narrative we are unable to discover the hand of E at all. It likely had no primal narrative, but began with father Abraham. Meyer (*Israeliten*, 238) also considers the fact that the table of nations and ethnographic lists, in general, are absent in E and hypothesizes that E "did not intend to integrate the Israelites into a general context of national and world history as does J." Often, but not always, the J tradition has an older form than E. J has the most vibrant, graphic accounts; in contrast, E has a series of touching, tearful stories such as the sacrifice of Isaac (Gen 22), the expulsion of Ishmael (21:8ff.), and Jacob's tenderness toward his grandchildren (48:10b). The difference in their concepts of God's revelation is especially conspicuous: the ancient divine epiphanies characterize J (e.g., Gen 16; 18; 19); in contrast, dreams (e.g., 21:3) and the call of the angel from heaven (e.g., 21:17), thus the most nonsensory types of revelation, characterize E. E, but not J, explicitly expresses the idea of divine providence, which turns sins to the good, in the Joseph narrative (50:20). Consequently, one has a right, as is now quite common, to consider J older than E on the whole. Since J replaces Reuben with Judah in the Joseph narrative, since it contains specifically Judahite tradition in the Tamar legend, and since it recounts so much about Abraham, who—it seems—was first located in the Negeb (south of Judah) and later in Hebron, one may seek it in Judah with many modern scholars.[104] It is common to assume, in contrast, that E stemmed from northern Israel.[105] This source actually speaks rather often <lxxxvii> of northern Israelite sites, but also of Beer-sheba (21:32; 46:1). Further, the Joseph legend of E (37:8) occasionaly even presumes Joseph's kingdom, although this, too, can stem from the tradition, etc. At any rate, there can be no discussion of an intentional partisanship of the two collections for the Northern or Southern kingdoms. They are too faithful for this.[106] Additional characteristics of the

---

[103]Summaries of the diction of the sources can be found in Holzinger, and Carpenter, 384ff.

[104]In contrast, Luther (in Meyer, *Israeliten*, 158), following others, considers him to be a Northern Israelite.

[105]Thus, recently, Procksch (175ff.), Meyer (*Israeliten*, 271), Carpenter (217), Cornill (*Einleitung*⁶, 48), and Kautzsch³ (1:3: "no doubt"!).

[106]Erbt ("Urgesch. der Bibel," in *Mitteilungen der Vorderas. Ges.* [1904/4]) detects political

collectors can hardly be gained from Genesis. Of course it would be easy to paint a colorful picture of J and E if one allowed oneself to attribute everything in their books to them. That is forbidden, however, by the character of these men as collectors.

5. The question of the age of J and E is extraordinarily difficult. Since we understand them here as the result of a process of recording old traditions, we must resolve this question into a series of subquestions. When did these legends originate? When did they become known in Israel? When did they receive essentially their current form? When were they committed to writing? Our task, here, then, is not to name a specific year, but to situate a long process chronologically.[107] This, however, is a very difficult task, for intellectual processes, in general, are very difficult to determine chronologically. In addition, we know too little about ancient Israel—a hindrance to us in reference to other such questions in the OT—to offer anything with certainty, here. Other datings of OT documents, to the extent that they result only from religiohistorical grounds, are not nearly as certain as often claimed today. Here, too, our criticism, if it is to remain sound, must take a great step backward.

The origin of many legends lies in a time preceding historical Israel. Israel must have already possessed the foundation of the legends of Abraham, Isaac, and Jacob before its entry into Canaan.[108] The genealogy of Jacob's twelve sons, which does not agree with the territories of the tribes in Canaan known to us, will also render older circumstances. The brief legend style is also most ancient. The accounts concerning the "judges" are already composed in the more expansive style. Other materials streamed in after the entry into Canaan. The Babylonian primal narratives were received from Canaanite hands. Materials in the Joseph accounts, probably mostly from Egypt, were added. Those legends, redactions, and "comments," which presume the possession of the land and knowledge of places in Canaan, clearly stem from Canaanite times. The youngest of the actual "legends" deal with <lxxxviii> Reuben's loss of significance (49:3-4), the origin of the clans of Judah (Gen 38), and the attack on Shechem (Gen 34), thus events from the earlier "period of the judges." No legends about the ancestors are preserved for us from the later "period of the judges," but legends about leaders of the tribes (cf. p. xvii). New ancestral legends were no longer composed then. Therefore, the period of the formation of patriarchal legends came to an end then (ca. 1200).[109] Other considerations demonstrate that this dating is correct: an addition to the Paradise narrative presumes that "Asshur" lies to the west of the Tigris (2:14). This idiom stems from a period when the great Assyrian cities in the East did not yet exist, thus before 1300. Even the reports available to P still contain memories of the pre-Israelite dominion of the Hittites over Canaan (cf. p. 268). The fact

---

tendencies in J and E. The books are "state documents," and the primal narrative, in particular, is a "diplomatic presentation" (38). Thus, the Paradise narrative of "J¹," e.g., is supposed to dispute Babel's claim to world dominion (7) in the interests of the Davidic empire (40), etc. Such fantasies rob the legends of the best they have, their clarity and innocence.

[107]"The dates offered for J and E fail to understand the complexity of the problem" (Stade, 1:27).

[108]Haller, 11.

[109]According to Greßmann (34), the period of the origination of the majority of the individual accounts falls around 1300–1100.

that Canaan was once a province of the Egyptian empire still echoes in the descent of Canaan from Ham. On the other hand, the sanctuary of Jerusalem, so famous in the monarchical period, does not appear in the patriarchal legends. Instead, cultic legend shifts the establishment of this sanctuary to the time of David (2 Sam 24). The years of battles with the Philistines, the kingdom of Saul, Saul's strife with David, the united monarchy under David and Solomon, the division and war of the two kingdoms—all this has no effect on the legends. Then no new patriarchal legends can have originated in that period. The effects of later history only become apparent in the selection. Among the tribal legends, those concerning two leading tribes, Joseph and Judah, receive special treatment.

The period of the transformation of legends follows the period of their formation. This period essentially coincides with the period of the early monarchy. At that time, when Israel merged into a unified nation out of a splintering into different tribes and regions, the various traditions grew together into a common folk legend. The great upswing Israel took under the first kings will have given it the inner strength to coat the older of the received accounts, to relate them to itself, and, in part, to localize them in Canaan. The Jacob-Esau legend (Gen 27) was then interpreted in relation to Israel and Edom. In the meanwhile, Israel had subjugated Edom. This took place under David, and Judah maintained possession until about 840. In the meanwhile, Ephraim overtook Manasseh (48:13ff.), perhaps at the beginning of the monarchical period. The Joseph legend contains an allusion to Joseph's monarchy (37:8, E) which only found its way into the legend secondarily. The Jacob-Laban legend does not yet mention the horrible wars with the Aramaeans, which begin around 900, but only occasional border attacks. The table of nations does not mention the city of Asshur, the royal residence until 1300, but Nineveh, the residence beginning around 1000 (10:11). Thus we may assume, with respect to the circumstances of the account, that the legends assumed essentially their current form by around 900. The only allusion to political events after 900 is the allusion to Edom's rebellion <lxxxix> (ca. 840). It is, however, clearly an addition to the legend (27:40b). There is no evidence as to what else may have been added: the mention of the Assyrian cities (10:11-12) does not imply that these comments belong in "Assyrian" times. Assyria had surely long been known to Israel. Nor may we base conclusions on the mention of Kelah. The city was rebuilt in 870, but had been a royal residence since around 1300. According to Lagarde (*Mitteilungen* 3:226ff.) and Spiegelberg (*Aufenthalt Israels in Ägypten*, 26), etc. the Egyptian names of Gen 41 point to the seventh century. This, too, is not a sure clue. The names, in that time very common, were already known in an earlier period (cf. comments on 41:45). If, however, no new political allusions found their way into the legends after ca. 900 and they have been essentially fixed since this time, they will still have undergone many additional inner transformations. We must assume a long period in which the religious and moral changes in the legends, treated above, were performed.

This period continued into the epoch of legend collection and is concluded by it. When were the legends committed to writing? This question is especially difficult. We have only internal criteria. We cannot establish these criteria, however, in any way other than by dating the sources. Unfortunately, then, we move here, as is true of many of our datings, in a circle and have no prospects of escaping. Scholars should consider this circumstance here and elsewhere before they propound overly optimistic claims. Further, one should note that even the collections were not finished in one operation, but developed in a process lasting for untold decades or centuries. The proper question in dating the sources concerns how the two related to "writing prophecy." Now, a great deal of material in Genesis has points of contact with prophecy. But the assumption of many modern scholars that this contact must be attributable to the influence of the writing prophets is rather dubious in many cases. We do not know the religion of Israel sufficiently to maintain that certain ideas and attitudes were first introduced by those prophets whose writings we have, that is, since Amos. The Flood narrative's serious discussion of universal sinfulness and the glorification of Abraham's faith are not specifically "prophetic." The collector's abhorrence toward the *masseboth* [pillar; memorial], which J overlooks, but which still appear in E (28:22, etc.), toward the "golden calf," which the legend in E (Exod 32) regards a sin, as well as toward the teraphim, which the Jacob-Laban legend humorously mocks (31:30ff.)—all this need not rest on the influence of the "prophets." Similar attitudes could have existed in Israel already long before the "prophets." Indeed, we must assume them in order to be able to understand the appearance of the "prophets." Admittedly E calls Abraham a נָבִיא (20:7) and therefore lives at a time when *prophet* and *man of God* were the same. But the ranks of the נְבִאִים flourished long before Amos; Hosea (12:14) even calls Moses a "prophet." Nothing stands <xc> in the way, then, of considering J and E essentially "preprophetic." A series of considerations supports this view: the prediction of Israel's demise, the struggle against foreign gods and against the sacred sites of Israel, and the rejection of sacrifice and worship practices characterize writing prophecy. These very characteristics of the "prophets" do not occur in the legends of J and E. J does not consider any other gods than Yahweh in Genesis, and Jacob's disposal of the foreign gods in preparation of a sacred act devoted to Yahweh (35:4 in E) does not sound "prophetic." The establishment of the many altars and sanctuaries by the fathers truly sounds quite different than the prophets' passionate struggle against worship at these very sites![110]

Whereas these collections do not contain authentically prophetic ideas, then, they do have much which must have been extremely offensive to the prophets. They adopt a particularly cordial attitude toward the sacred sites which the prophets so bitterly combatted. Their naiveté with respect to the old religion and morality is the exact opposite of the frightful accusations of the prophets. We know from the prophetic redaction of the historical books how the legitimate disciples of the prophets related to the ancient tradition. They certainly would not have cared for the folk legend, with such pagan content, but would have eradicated it! Accordingly, one must indeed decide that the collections essentially fall before the great writing prophets and that the points of contact with the spirit of this movement in J and E show how the ideas of the prophets were current in many respects already long before Amos. This also follows from a series of other considerations. The legend of Abraham's emigration (Gen 12), which glorifies his faith, presumes, on the other hand, Israel's flourishing prosperity which it does not expect to end. It surely stems, then, from the time before the great Assyrian crisis. Passages which, seen from the standpoint of the history of legend, are as late as chap. 15 or the narrative of the birth of Jacob's sons, still have very ancient religious motifs (cf. pp. 182-

---

[110]Contra Luther in Meyer, *Israeliten*, 138.

83, 321). This does not preclude the possibility, however, that a few of the latest sections in the collections are also "prophetic" in the proper sense. Thus, Abraham's conversation with God outside Sodom is in content a treatment of a theological problem, by form an imitation of the prophetic "dispute" with God. The prophetic threat of Israel's demise also stands in the background (cf. pp. 203-204). Joshua's farewell speech (Josh 24), with its unconcealed mistrust of Israel's fidelity, formally imitates the prophetic sermon. In the following books even more examples may occur, especially in E. In Genesis they are extremely isolated. Accordingly, we may still place both collections as a whole before the appearance of prophecy, J perhaps in the ninth, E perhaps in the first half of the eighth century. Yet, it should be emphasized that such numbers always remain very uncertain.[111]
<xci>

A redactor (R[JE]), whom we will call the "Yehowist" following Wellhausen's precedent, later combined the two collections. This combination of the two sources occurred before the addition of the later legend book P. We may place this collector in the final period of the state of Judah. R[JE] proceeded in Genesis with extraordinary care. He expended considerable discernment to preserve as much of the two sources as possible and to produce a good unit from them, although he also found it necessary, of course, to omit much incompatible with the adopted report. In general, he based the final product on the more extensive source, in the Abraham narrative J. He contributed very little in his own words to Genesis. We recognize his few contributions with certainty in a few brief additions intended to unify the variants of J and E. They are relatively few in number (16:9-10; 28:21b; further in 31:49ff.; 39:1; 41:50; 45:19; 46:1; 50:11, several in Gen 34). Most are trivialities. Furthermore, we may date certain additions, for the most part not very extensive, to this period and attribute them perhaps to this redactor or to his contemporaries. A few retrace the tender lines of the original text more darkly (18:17-19; 20:18; 22:15-18). A few are spiritual expansions of worldly accounts (13:14-17; 32:10-13). Most are divine speeches (13:14-17; 16:9,10; 18:17-19; 22:15-18; 26:3b-5, 24, 25a; 28:14; 46:3bβ; 32:10-13; 50:24γ) which, characteristically of these latest contributors—who want to offer ideas, not stories—are especially solemn promises for Israel: Israel will become a mighty people and take possession of "all these lands." Then all the nations Israel will conquer are listed (15:19-21; 10:16-18). These additions stem from times when the great world upheavals threaten Israel's existence and when faith clung to these promises, probably from the Chaldean period, then. Here and there "deuteronomistic" diction also appears (i.e., a diction that belongs in the period of "Deuteronomy," the law of the land under Josiah, 623; 18:17-19; 26:3b-5).

---

[111]Other recent datings: Carpenter, 199, 222: J 850–650, E before 750; Meinhold, *Urgeschichte*, 7, 16: J around 800–700, E around 750, JE around 600; Procksch, 178ff., 238-39, 286: E the first half of the 3rd century, younger sections in E in the 7th cent., J around 950; according to Stade (27) people wrote "in the manner of J" on into the 7th cent.; Cornill, 56, 49: J (older layer) arround 850, E around 750; Kautzsch[3] 1:3-4: the oldest layer of J "shortly before the middle of the 9th cent.," E around 750.

¶6. Priestly Codex and the Final Redactions

1. This source is so unusually distinct from the other sources in diction and spirit that it can be extracted almost to the precise word in almost all cases.[112] Like the older collections J and E, it, too, encompasses <xcii> more than Genesis. Instead, the primal and patriarchal narratives are only a brief preparation for the chief matter, here, Moses' giving of the law. The priestly codex is of particular significance for us since, in an earlier period of OT scholarship, the total perspective on the OT was based essentially on its information. It is to Wellhausen's undying credit that he recognized the proper character of this source (*Prolegomena*[6], 293ff.). Previously, it had usually been considered the oldest. In this way Wellhausen demonstrated the error of the former view of the OT as a whole and, thus, prepared the field for a vital, truly historical understanding of the history of Israel's religion.

2. The style of P is extremely peculiar, remarkably expansive, oriented toward juristic clarity and thoroughness, always with the same expressions and formulae, with precise definitions and monotone formulae, with consistent schemas with nothing superfluous, and with genealogies and superscriptions heading every chapter. It has the tone of prosaic learning, indeed, often the style of legal documents (e.g., 11:11; 23:17, 18), here and there, however, not without a degree of solemn dignity (especially in Gen 1, but also elsewhere: cf., e.g., the scene in 47:7-11). One must read the whole source in sequence in order to perceive the sobriety and monotony of this remarkable book. The author is apparently painfully precise and exemplarily orderly, but he, like many other scholars, was not gifted with a feeling for poetry.

3. The selection of material in whole and part is very characteristic. Of larger narratives, P offers only the accounts of the creation, the Flood, God's revelation to Abraham (Gen 17), and the purchase of the cave of Machpelah (Gen 23), otherwise only comments and genealogies. He was only able to employ individual observations from by far most accounts. One may compare the old colorful and poetic legends and the meager information P communicates from them in order to see what interests him. He does not want, as the ancients did, to narrate poetically, but to establish facts. Consequently, he could not employ the many individual elements contained in the old legends, but only adopted a very few facts from them. He abandoned the moods of the legends. He did not see the personal lives of the fathers: their once so concrete figures have become very

---

[112]Recently, Eerdmans (1) has disputed the assumption of a document "P." According to Eerdmans, such an assumption is contradicted by, e.g., the fact that the document is not completely preserved in Genesis (6–7). But it is understandable enough that the final redactor, even with the best intention, could not transmit all documentary sources but must occasionally omit portions. Further, Eerdmans finds it strange that the same document which treats the story of the patriarchs so briefly, becomes so intricate in chaps. 17 and 23 (7). He overlooks the fact that the Chronicles also begin with lists and continue with extensive accounts. He doubts the strict monotheism of an account such as chap. 23 since the cave of Machpelah is the seat of a "superstitious ancestor worship" (8). He does not note that chap. 24 [*sic?*] does not presume such ancestor worship with even a single syllable, but combats it, etc. It is almost incomprehensible, however, that the uniformity of the diction in this document made so little impression on him. Cf. also p. lxin.70.

bland to him. In ancient times, very many of these legends took place at specific locations and, thereby, had vitality and color. P only knows of two sites, the cave of Machpelah, where the fathers lived and lay buried (Gen 23), and Bethel, where God revealed himself to Jacob (35:61, 11ff.). <xciii> He omitted all other locations. In contrast, he had a great preference for genealogies which, as we have seen (¶5:3), were the last to be added to the legend tradition and which, by nature, are very abstract and prosaic. A very great portion of P in Genesis is nothing other than genealogy (Gen 5; 10; 11:10ff.; 25:12ff.; 36). Even accounts he gives extensive treatment display the same blandness. None of the accounts are proper "narratives." The account of the purchase of the Machpelah cave would have only been a comment for an earlier legend narrator. P developed it extensively, but he did not have the poetic capability to shape the account into a "narrative" (cf. pp. 268ff.). The "major and state undertakings" P offers in the place of the old narratives no longer recount but only report speeches and acts (Wellhausen, *Prolegomena*[6], 338). Even the accounts of the Creation, the Flood, and the Covenant with Abraham (Gen 17) are quite remote from the vibrancy of the old legend. They are clearly wanting in concrete narrative material. Instead, P offers something else that is, admittedly, far removed from the spirit of the old legend, namely, legal regulations in detailed scope (1:28ff.; 9:1ff.; 17:9ff.). P becomes more expansive later only with the lawgiving of Moses. Further characteristic is his pronounced sense for schemata. This order-loving man encased the colorful legends of the ancient period in his gray schemata. They lost all their poetic fragrance, however. One may read the genealogy of Adam (Gen 5) and Shem (11:10ff.). But he also confines the patriarchal narrative in a schema. Further, P adds an extensive chronology to the legends. It plays a great role for him, but it is hardly suitable for the simplicity of the legends. By nature, chronology belongs in history, not in legend. Where historiography and legends are vital genre, they are distinguished, even if unconsciously. This mixture of genres in P shows that in his time the natural feeling for legend and for narrative had been lost. Accordingly, it is no wonder that P's chronology consistently produces humorous peculiarities when incorporated into the old legends. According to it, the Egyptians desire Sarah, still a beautiful woman at 65 years of age (cf. p. 169), and Ishmael's mother carries the sixteen-year-old on her shoulder (cf. p. 228). Further, P superimposes a grand periodization of world history over the whole material. He distinguishes four periods, from the Creation to Noah, from Noah to Abraham, from Abraham to Moses, and from Moses onward.

Each of these periods begins with a great revelation of God. Twice, a new divine name is mentioned. At the Creation, he is called *Elohim*. He calls himself *El shaddai* to Abraham and *Yahweh* to Moses. Certain divine regulations are announced with each "covenant": first, that humans and animals are to eat only plants (1:29-30); then, after the Flood, that one may eat animals, but may not kill a human being (9:3ff.); then, to Abraham, that he and his descendants should be circumcised (17:9ff.); finally, the Mosaic law. Certain divine blessings or promises are added and signs of the covenant <xciv> are given. We perceive here the product of a world-encompassing intellect, the beginning of world history in grand style, just as a proper scientific sensibility can be observed elsewhere in P, as well. One need think only of the precision in the structure of the creations in Gen 1 and of his definitions there. But the material of the legends employed by this, in itself, extraordinary world history, is very oddly distinct from it. The "signs of the covenant" are rainbows, circumcision, and Sabbath—an extremely remarkable list! How far removed is this spirit of world history, which even attempts to calculate the duration of the world, from the spirit of the old legend which originally consisted only of an individual narrative and was never capable of elevating itself to such universal considerations. In J, for example, we hear nothing of the relationship between Abraham's religion and that of his fathers and compatriots. Nor may we fail to mention that this viewpoint of P—that Yahweh first revealed himself very generally as "God," then somewhat more specifically as *El shaddai*, and only at the end by his proper name—is still very childish. The actual history of religion does not begin with the general and develop toward the concrete, but, to the contrary, it begins with the most concrete and only slowly and gradually do people learn to comprehend the abstract.

4. The author's religion is characterized by the fact that he says almost nothing of the personal piety of the fathers. For him, only the objective aspects of religion are significant. For example, P says not a word concerning Abraham's faithful obedience. Indeed, he unashamedly reports that Abraham laughed at God's promise (17:17). The religion he knows consists of regulation of practices. It is important to him that one celebrate the Sabbath, that one observe circumcision, that one eat certain things and not others. In these things he is very particular. He does not recount, apparently intentionally, that the fathers sacrificed anywhere, surely because his time considered these sites pagan. Similarly, he does not distinguish between clean and unclean animals in the Flood narrative. In his opinion legitimate worship and the distinction of clean and unclean began with Moses. Here, however, we hear the priest from Jerusalem who maintains that worship at his sanctuary is the only valid continuation of Mosaic worship. The Israelite theocracy—in modern terms, the basic idea of his work—is the purpose of the world. God created the world so that God's statues and commandments may be performed in the Temple at Jerusalem. The divine epiphanies in P are peculiarly abstract. He only recounts that God appeared, made a speech, and left again (so, e.g., Gen 17). He omits everything else. He follows the style of the latest additions in JE here, which also contains such divine speeches without introductions. In this manner, P clearly expresses his religious aversion to entangling the supernatural God in the things of the world. It is as though he smelled the pagan origin of these theophanies, just as he consistently omits reference to the angel whose origin in polytheistic concepts he vaguely sensed (cf. p. 112). At the same time, <xcv> one learns here his positive interest: the content of the divine revelation is important to him, but not its "means." This is the spirit of an orthodoxy ambivalent toward history. Not accidentally he envisions these divine speeches as the establishment of covenants: this originally juristic form is apparently familiar to him. This combination of the priestly, academic, and especially juristic, perhaps remarkable to us at first, is in actuality quite natural: in many ancient peoples, the priesthood is the caretaker of learning and especially of the law as well. It surely was also in Israel where the priests were accustomed since ancient times to settling difficult transactions. P learned his style writing contracts—this is very clear in many passages. Particularly characteristic for P, however, is the fact that he says nothing more of the sacred symbols which once had such great significance for ancient religion, as the patriarchal legends themselves show.

Nothing more can be read here of the memorial stones, the trees and groves, or of the wells at which the deity appeared according to the old legends. P rejected all this material from the legend, apparently because he considered them pagan. The effects of the frightful prophetic polemic can clearly be seen here: the same spirit that desecrated the ancient holy site of Bethel as pagan in the "reform" of Josiah here expels everything from the old legends that reminds these descendants of paganism. Certainly, then, P's concept of God is higher, more developed than in the ancient legends. Nevertheless, P stands far below these ancients who, although they did not yet know the "ecclesiology" of Jerusalem, knew what piety is. The best aspect of P's style is shown in the famed and particularly characteristic account of the Creation (cf. pp. 117ff.): despite his prosaic definitions and classifications, P's style has a solemn dignity here. The supernaturalistic concept of God, classically expressed in this P account and so markedly distinct from all the other Creation myths, especially from the Babylonian, makes this chapter a milestone in the history of revelation. Like their religion, the morality of the patriarchs is also purified in P. Here, too, P seems to be the final word in a development we have already followed in J and E. The old patriarchal legends, an expression of the earliest folk life, certainly contained much which later generations, if completely honest, would actually have considered sin and shame. And yet the fathers, this period believed, must have been examples of piety and wisdom. What effort they must have taken to remove by necessity at least the most crudely offensive features! P made a clean sweep here: he simply omits the offensive material (e.g., the dispute of the shepherds of Abraham and Lot, Lot's greed, Ishmael's expulsion, Jacob's deceptions). He dares to maintain even the opposite of the tradition in certain cases. Ishmael and Isaac peacefully buried their father together (25:9), as did Jacob and Esau (35:29). Details he is unable to discard, he is able to give another basis. Thus, he explains Isaac's blessing on Jacob by Esau's sinful mixed marriage (26:34-35; 28:1ff.), and he shifts the blame for the crime against Joseph to the sons of Bilhah and Zilpah (37:2). <xcvi>

5. All of this suggests that P treated the tradition he received rather capriciously. He omitted old traditions or altered them according to his wishes. He extrapolated comments to whole narratives and from whole narratives he took only comments. He mixed motifs from different legends. He maintained, for example, that the blessing Jacob received from Isaac was the Abraham blessing, something the old narrators had not even considered (28:4; for other examples, see pp. 258, 267, 371). From the loosely connected narratives of the old traditions, he formed a continuous, self-contained account. This, too, is an indication of the latest period. He replaces the legends with his chapters and their regular superscriptions. This narrator knew nothing, therefore, of the fidelity of the ancients. He will have had the impression that one must mightily intervene here in order to erect a structure worthy of God. The old J and E were not actually "authors," but only collectors; P, however, is a proper "author." They only loosely heaped up the received building stones; P, however, erected a unified structure in accord with his tastes. Nevertheless, one would err in the belief that he even invented the information he offers in Genesis. The tradition was too strong to permit this, even for him. Instead, he only reworked the material, although forcefully enough. We can sometimes see in the details that he followed his source in the sequence of events when none of his interests were involved (pp. 116-17). One may not reject any information that occurs only in P for this reason. Instead, one must reckon with the possibility that he adapted it from his source. The source, however,

was—at least in Genesis—neither J nor E themselves, but was related to them (cf. pp. 102-103, 257-58, 371, 465-66).

6. The time of P is clear according to this depiction. In every respect, he stands at the conclusion of the whole history of the tradition, surely separated by a great temporal breach from J and E. The vital legend which was the raw material of the old collectors J and E must have died out by P's time if he was able to do violence to them in this manner for his historical construction. A massive spiritual revolution must have occurred in the meanwhile, a revolution that created something entirely new in the place of the old folk tradition recorded in the legends. P is the document of a time that consciously renounced those old traditions and believed it necessary to lay the foundations of religion differently than the fathers had done. The character of this innovation which came to dominate at that time is very clear to us from P. The spirit of the learned priest is expressed here. Furthermore, P's general character makes it clear to us that it does not involve the work of an individual with a particular orientation, but of a large circle whose convictions he expresses. P's document is practically an official declaration. P came from the ranks of the Jerusalemite priests. Consequently the name "priestly codex" is extremely fitting. Since Wellhausen, we know the time in which this spirit belongs. It is the epoch after the great catastrophe of the people and state of Judah when the people, horrified by the frightful impression of its immeasurable misfortune, recognized that its fathers had sinned and that a great religious <xcvii> reform was necessary. P, with his imposing lack of reverence for what had previously been the most sacred traditions of his people, can be understood only against this time period. We are also well aware that after all other authorities had been ruined or destroyed, only the priesthood of that time was still upright and capable of holding the people together. After its reconstruction, the community of Judah stood under the dominion of priests. The unusually developed historical learning of P also belongs in this period. The former era produced exquisite storytellers, but no trained historiographers. In the Exilic period, however, Judean historiography lost its naive innocence. Under the powerful influence of the superior Babylonian culture, Judaism also learned to appreciate precise citations of numbers and dimensions. It now becomes accustomed to great care in statistical information: one documented genealogies; one rummaged through the archives for reliable documents; one developed chronologies; one even devoted oneself to world history on the Babylonian model. The same emphasis on precise chronology also appears in Ezekiel, Haggai, and Zechariah, the same historical learning and especially the genealogies also in Ezra, Nehemiah, and in the Chronicles. Even the numeration of the months found in P arose in Judaism in this period. The progress presented by this learned intellect in contrast to the naiveté of previous periods is unmistakable, even though the products of this learning are often not very attractive to us. The fact that early grand historical constructions such as P offers work for the most part with mythic or legend material, that is, are insufficient, is probably a common case in the beginnings of "world history." One may compare P with [the Babylonian priest-historian] Berosus on this point. Even the emphasis P places on Sabbath, the prohibition against the consumption of blood, and circumcision is understandable in relation to this period. That era, when everything depended on the free will of the individual, emphasizes religious commandments that obligate the individual. Indeed, one can say that the piety of the patriarchs, who are always portrayed as *gerim* (foreigners) and who must always

make their way without sacrifice and cult, is a mirror image of the piety of the Babylonian Exile when, in a strange land, one had no temple or sacrifice. P's religious assessment of mixed marriage, especially with Canaanites, whereby one forfeits one's part in the blessing of Abraham (28:1-9), and the zeal with which he collected the genealogies of his people, also point to this time when Judaism, living dispersed among the pagans, knew no more zealous struggle than to keep pure its blood and religion. Even more certain than this evidence derived from Genesis, however, is other evidence that flows from the legal passages in the following books. Finally, the late origin of P's diction supplements these arguments.[113] Accordingly, the dating of P in the Exile belongs to the most assured results of criticism.

We need not be concerned at this point with the century in which P was written. Yet, it can be said that in the opinion of very many <xcviii> scholars, P is the law book of Ezra to which the community was obligated in 444 and which Ezra somehow helped to prepare. We may conceive of the completion of the book, therefore, in the period from ca. 500 to 444. P was not finished all at once, either, although this is not a consideration for Genesis.

7. The final redactor who combined the older works JE and P (R^{JEP}) probably belongs, therefore, in the period after Ezra, certainly before the schism of the "Samaritan" community which took along with it the Pentateuch. The necessity for such a combination of the old and the young collections shows us that the old legends had worked their way too deeply into the heart to be rooted out by the new spirit. Meanwhile, mighty historical storms had desecrated the old holy sites, their whole past seemed to these men to be sin. And yet, the old accounts that glorified these sites and mirrored the old period so innocently could not be destroyed. P's attempt to suppress the old failed. A respectful hand created a combination of JE and P. This final collection was accomplished with extraordinary fidelity, especially to P. Its author did not want to allow a seed of P to fall to the ground if at all possible. We cannot fault him for preferring P to JE. P dominated Judaism from the outset. The redaction employed the chronology of P in particular as the framework for the accounts of J and E. We are able to attribute only very little in Genesis to his hand with varying degrees of certainty: that is, a few harmonizing glosses or supplementations such as 10:24; 15:7, 8, 15; 27:46, in 35:13, 14; further, retouchings in 6:7; 7:7, 22, 23; further, 7:3a, 8, 9; then, the distinction between *Abram* and *Abraham*, *Sarai* and *Sarah* even in J and E, etc.

8. With this, the activity of the redactors in Genesis is largely concluded. But, work (διασκευῆς) on the text continues in the details for a long time. We see minor reworkings in chap. 34 and in the numbers of the genealogies where the Judean, Samaritan, and the text of the Greek translation differ from one another. Larger additions and reworkings also occurred in Gen 36 and 46:8-27. The final great insertion is the account of Abraham's' victory over the four kings—a "midrashic" legend from the latest period.

---

[113]Wellhausen, *Prolegomena*⁶, 385ff.; Ryssel, *De elohistae pentateuchici sermone* (1878); Giesebrecht, ZAW 1:177f.; Driver, *Journal of Philology* (1882): 201ff.

9. Thus, Genesis is the confluence of many sources. It remained in this final form. In this form, the old legends have exercised an immeasurable influence on all later generations. One may regret that the last great poetic genius who could have formed a true "Israelite national epic" from the individual stories did not appear. Israel produced great religious reformers who created a comprehensive unity in religious spirit from the dispersed traditions of their people. But it did not produce a Homer. This is fortunate for our scholarship at any rate. Precisely because there was no great poetic whole and the passages were left in an essentially unfused stated, we are able to discern the history of the whole process. Consequently, <xcix> legend scholars should conduct research in Genesis, quite unlike they have previously; And theologians should learn that without legend research, and especially without legend analysis, Genesis cannot be understood.

10. A word is in order concerning how Genesis came to have the undeserved honor of being considered a work of Moses. Since ancient times, Israel knew the tradition that the divine prescriptions concerning cult, law, and practice, as the priests proclaimed, derived from Moses. When these prescriptions, originally transmitted orally, were documented in smaller or larger works, they were naturally circulated under the name of Moses. Now our Pentateuch also consists, in addition to the legend collections, of such law books from various time periods and of very different spirits. It seemed very appropriate to combine both legends and laws into one book because the legends concerning the Exodus also dealt primarily with Moses. So Genesis became the first part of a work whose later portions tell chiefly of Moses and contain all manner of laws supposed to derive from him. Genesis, however, has nothing inherently to do with Moses. The fiery spirit of the mighty, wrathful titan that Moses must have been according to the tradition, and the spirit of these accounts where so much humor and tenderness can be found, are separated by a mighty cleft. No one who reads Genesis innocently would get the idea that it could have been authored by Moses.

11. In the canon of the Bible the whole work is called the "Torah," the "Pentateuch," divided into five books. The first is named for its first word *Bᵉreŝith*, that is, "in the beginning," in the Greek translation, the *Septuaginta*, by the first account "Genesis," that is, "the Creation of the World."[114]

12. In conclusion, if we survey the whole history deposited in this book, we perceive that it can almost be termed a compendium of the whole history of Israel's religion. But precisely because of this inner multiplicity, Genesis makes such an honorable impression. Only the greatest creations of the human spirit can be compared with it: perhaps the mighty domes, in whose form and ornamentation the spirit of many generations expresses itself, or the states which developed slowly over the centuries, or the "Faust," the expression of a very overpowering human life. All these very great creations are not inherently unified because they are more than the products of an hour. And yet, we sense in these creations an inner unity that unifies all the variety. After all, the same people who built the cathedral constitute the state. One will be unable, however, to prevent the pious observer who has reached this conclusion from recognizing this unity in the variety of the history of Israel's religion as the providence of God who once spoke childishly to children and then maturely to adults. <c>

---

[114]Concerning these names, cf. Holzinger, 1ff., and the introductions.

Abbreviations of Biblical Books, Journals, Monographs, and Authors' Names

A	Codex Alexandrinus (LXX)	Mal	Malachi
Act	Acta	Matt	Matthew
Am	Amos	ms(s)	manuscript(s)
ApBar	Apocalypse of Baruch	Nah	Nahum
Bar	Baruch	Neh	Nehemiah
Cant	Canticles	Num	Numbers
Chr	Chronicles	Obad	Obadiah
Col	Colossians	OrAsar	Prayer of Azariah
Cor	Corinthians	OrMan	Prayer of Manasseh
Dan	Daniel	OrSib	Sibylline Oracles
Deut	Deuteronomy	Pesh	Peshitta
En	Enoch	Pet	Peter
Eph	Ephesians	Prov	Proverbs
Esth	Esther	Psa	Psalms
EthEn	Ethiopian Enoch	PsSol	Psalms of Solomon
Exod	Exodus	Qoh	Qoheleth (Ecclesiastes)
Ezek	Ezekiel	R, red	redactor
Ezr	Ezra	Rev	Revelation (Apocalypse of John)
Gal	Galatians	Rom	Romans
Gen	Genesis	s.v.	*sub verbo* (under the word)
Hab	Habakkuk	Sam	Samaritan
Hag	Haggai	Sam	Samuel
Heb	Hebrews	SapSal	Wisdom of Solomon
Hos	Hosea	SlavEn	Slavic Enoch
Isa	Isaiah	Sus	Susanna
Jer	Jeremiah	Sym	Symmachus
Jon	Jonah	TargJon	Targum Jonathan
Josh	Joshua	TargOnq	Targum Onqelos
JSir	Jesus Sirach	Test XII Patr	Testament of the 12 Patriarchs
Jubil	Book of Jubilees	Theod	Theodotian
Judg	Judges	Thess	Thessalonians
Kgs	Kings	Tob	Tobit
Lam	Lamentations	VetLat	Old Latin version
Lev	Leviticus	Zech	Zechariah
Luc	Lucian's LXX recension	Zeph	Zephaniah
Mac	Maccabees		

ARW	*Archiv für Religionswissenschaft*
BA	*Beiträge zur Assyriologie*
DLz	*Deutsche Literaturzeitung*
GGA	*Göttinger Gelehrte Anzeigen*
HW	*Riehms Handwörterbuch des biblischen Altertums* (1884)
KAT³	*Keilinschriften und das A.T.*, 3rd ed. (1902)
KB	*Keilinschriftliche Bibliothek* (1899ff.)
MDOg	*Mitteilungen der Deutschen Orientgesellschaft*
OLz	*Orientalistische Litteratur-Zeitung*
RE	Herzog's *Realencyclopädie*
RGG	*Religion in Geschichte und Gegenwart* I (1909)
StGThK	*Studien zur Geschichte von Theologie und Kirche*
ThLbl	*Theologisches Literaturblatt*
ThLz	*Theologisches Literaturzeitung*
ThStKr	*Theologische Studien und Kritiken*
ThT	*Theologisch Tijdschrift*

ZA   *Zeitschrift für Assyriologie*
ZAW   *Zeitschrift für alttestamentliche Wissenschaft*
ZDMG   *Zeitschrift der Deutschen Morgenländischen Gesellschaft*
ZDPV   *Zeitschrift des Deutschen Palästina-Vereins*
ZNW   *Zeitschrift für neutestamentliche Wissenschaft*   <cii>

Ball   Ball, *Book of Genesis in Hebrew* (1896)
Benzinger[2]   Benzinger, *Hebräische Archäologie*, 2nd ed. (1907)
Budde   Budde, *Urgeschichte* (1883)
Cheyne   Cheyne, *Traditions and Beliefs of Ancient Israel* (1907)
Delitzsch   Delitzsch, *Neuer Commentar zur Genesis* (1887)
Dillmann   Dillman, *Genesis*, 6th ed. (1892)
Driver   Driver, *Book of Genesis*, 4th ed. (1903)
Eerdmans   Eerdmans, *A.T.liche Studien* I (1908)
Eerdmans II   Eerdmans, *A.T.liche Studien* II (1908)
Ehrlich   Ehrlich, *Randglossen zur hebräischen Bibel* I (1908)
Enc Bibl   *Encyclopaedia Biblica*
Enc Brit   *Encyclopaedia Britannica*
Frankel   Frankel, *Über den Einfluß der palästinensischen Exegese auf die alexandrin-
                    ische Hermeneutik* (Leipzig, 1851)
Gesenius[14]   Gesenius-Buhl, *Hebräisches Handwörterbuch*, 14th ed. (1905)
Greßmann   Greßmann, *Ursprung der israelitisch-jüdischen Eschatologie* (1905)
Guthes BW   Guthe, *Kurzes Bibelwörterbuch* (1903)
Haller   Haller, *Religion, Recht, und Sitte in den Genesissagen* (1905)
Holzinger   Holzinger, *Genesis* (1898)
Jeremias ATAO[2]   Alfred Jeremias, *Das A.T. im Lichte des alten Orients*, 2nd ed. (1906)
Kautzsch[3]   Kautzsch, *Heilige Schrift des A.T.* I, 3rd ed. (1909)
Kautzsch-Socin[2]   Kautzsch und Socin, *Genesis mit äußerer Unterscheidung der Quellenschriften*,
                    2nd ed. (1891)
Kittel   Kittel, *Biblia Hebraica* I (1905)
v.d. Leyen   Eugenie von der Leyen, *Zur Entstehung des Märchens im Archiv für das
                    Studium der neueren Sprachen und Literaturen* CXIII 249ff.; CXIV 1ff.; CXV
                    1ff., 272ff.; CXVI 1ff., 282ff.
Meinhold   Meinhold, *Biblische Urgeschichte* (1904)
Ed. Meyer I[2]   Ed. Meyer, *Geshichte des Altertums* I, 2nd ed. (1909)
Olshausen   Olshausen, *Beiträge zur Kritik des überlieferten Textes im Buche Genesis* (Mit-
                    teilungen der Berliner Akademie der Wissenschaften, June 1870)
Procksch   Procksch, *Nordhebräisches Sagenbuch* (1906)
Reuß   Reuß, *Das A.T.* III (1893)
Roscher, Lex.   Roscher, *Ausführliches Lexikon der griechischen und römischen Mythologie*
Seigfried-Stade   Siegfried und Stade, *Hebräisches Wörterbuch* (1893)
Sievers   Sievers, *Metrische Studien* I (1901) II (1904, 1905)
Spurrell   Spurrell, *Notes on the Text of Genesis* (1896)
Strack   Strack, *Genesis* (1897)

ET   English translation.
§   Refers to Gesenius-Kautzsch, *Hebräische Grammatik*, 27th ed. (1902)

<#> Locates in the English translation the end of page # of the German original. Here, for example,
    marks the end of page ciii of the original: <ciii>

Primeval History

The Primeval History according to J

1. The Paradise narrative (2:4b-3:24). 2. Cain and Abel (4:1-16). 3. Cain's genealogy (4:17-24). 4. Seth's genealogy (4:25-5:29). 5. Angelic marriages (6:1-4). 6. Flood (6:5-8:22). 7. Noah's vineyard, Canaan's curse (9:20-27). 8. Table of the Nations (10). 9. Tower of Babylon (11:1-9).

Modern scholars agree, almost to the verse, in attributing these verses to J. The only current literary issue in this section, therefore, concerns the composition of J.

The compiler responsible for transmitting these legends will have sought initially to arrange them according to chronological sequence: first an account of the origins, of human life in Paradise, and of the expulsion. Thereafter he may have intended to illustrate the gradual, frightful increase of human corruption after the Fall: The first sin was only a child's sin, the second, however, a fratricide. Humanity grows ever more wicked through the progress of culture, as evidenced by Lamech's cruel song of revenge, raging of murder and blood to the point that even the boundaries between deity and humanity threaten to fall. Thus God regrets having created humanity and old humanity is destroyed in the Flood. But a remnant is saved, and the history of humanity begins anew. Yet humans have not improved: Infamy exists even in the house of the pious. Titanic arrogance attracts God's judgment and produces the disruption of the original unity of humanity: Thus the peoples of the earth arise and spread themselves across the globe. Following this introduction it is now time to recount Abraham's genealogy and story.

Thus this Primeval History, as the final compiler of J may have intended, speaks of the sin of humanity—which after a brief period of innocence transgressed God's commandment and became entangled in the evil in which it still lies—and of the wrath of God—who cast the people from the Garden, limited their lifespan, eradicated old humanity through the Flood and dispersed new humanity at the Tower. Simultaneously, however, it speaks of the grace of the Highest, who did not allow the first pair to die immediately, who favored the pious Abel, who warned the fratricide and then showed even him mercy, who pardoned Noah when he found him just, and then established an eternal vow of his forbearance, who finally, when humanity was divided through his judgment, chose Abraham and founded a new people in him. This Primeval History of humanity is of such religious and ethical grandeur that other nations can offer nothing equivalent (see Sellin, *Biblische Urgeschichte*, 42-43).

Now, little investigation is required to demonstrate that this strand, intended by the final compiler, is not very prominent <1> in the narratives themselves. Almost without exception, the units themselves begin quite abruptly. They are reserved toward or even contradict one another: The account of Cain's fratricide presupposes that people already populated the whole earth at that time. According to 4:17 Cain built the first city named Enoch; According to 11:4 Babel was the first city, built much later; According to a third note, Nimrod had already ruled Babel (10:10). Cain's genealogy, concluding with the division of humanity into three professions, apparently seeks to explain, not the origins of the shepherds, musicians, and smiths of a long past primordium, but of contemporary humanity. It did not originally, therefore, take account of a continuation in which all humanity was destroyed in the Flood. Furthermore 6:1-4 did not originally introduce the Flood Legend. Also, the Noah of the Flood, the father of Shem, Ham, and Japheth differs from Noah the farmer, the father of Shem, Japheth, and Canaan. Finally, the Table of the Nations, according to which the nations divided through the growth of families, actually parallels 11:1-9, according to which they were separated by God's intervention (see a series of such observations in Wellhausen, *Composition des Hexateuchs*[3], 8-10).

All these and similar findings suggest, first, that the old Legends did not originally exist in the current combination, but each existed independently in oral tradition (see Wellhausen, *Prolegomena*[6], 334). It is thus not unusual—to the contrary it is the normal case both here and elsewhere in Genesis (see the introduction ¶3:6)—for two legends to be mutually independent. Each of the primeval legends—of paradise, of Cain and Abel, of the angelic marriages, of the Flood, of Noah's vineyard, of the Tower—stands on its own feet: None necessarily presumes another or points to another as its natural continuation. Only later were these legends placed in a certain relationship. Linking passages such as 4:25; 5:29; 6:6; 9:18-19 are, as can be seen, very few in number. The relationship among the primeval narratives is especially loose, looser than in the other legend collections in Genesis. This observation suggests in relation to source criticism that one may not search for original sources that would have been completely or even partially self-contained. Rather, these original collections will have consisted essentially of individual, only loosely interrelated legends. Many of the narratives contain isolated particulars concerning human inventions. It would be reasonable, then, to seek a thread in the legends that coherently recounts the story of these matters. But this expectation is also disappointed: Even though Gen 2–3 already portrays the people driven from Paradise as farmers, and thereafter such culture-historical notes are promiscuously intermixed (see on 4:17-24), it is not possible to discern a comprehensible structure. Exegesis must take this circumstance into account and explain each of these narratives in isolation. As a result, one would certainly not wish to overvalue an investigation of original collections! Such investigation can yield very little for the understanding of the narratives themselves.

Certainly, however, older collections form the basis for J's Primeval History. This circumstance can be clearly recognized in the Paradises and Tower of Babel legends, as well as in the Table of Nations, all of which consist of two sources. Several, at least three, strands can also be detected in the Cain narratives. The existence of several collections can be deduced with particular clarity, however, from the fact that we possess two parallel primeval genealogies, via Cain and via Seth. By nature, such genealogies are not old folk legends, but can only be conceived of as academic anthology. There must, then, have been at least two proto-collections (on this and what follows below, see the commentary). Wellhausen began the precise, very difficult investigation of these two sources (recently published in *Composition des Hexateuchs*[3], 7-9). It has been continued by Budde, *Urgeschichte*, and Stade, <2> *ZAW* 14, 250ff. (see the summaries in Holzinger, *Hexateuch*, 138ff. and *Genesis*, 120ff.), most recently by Meinhold (*Biblische Urgeschichte*, 129-30, 117), Erbt ("Urgeschichte der Bibel," *Mitteilungen der Vorderasiatischen Gesellschaft* [1904]), and Sievers ("Metrische Studien II: Hebräische Genesis," *Abhandlungen der*

Philol.-Hist. Klasse der Kgl. Sächs. Gesellschaft der Wissenschaften 23 [1905]). The
starting point is not so much the content of the legends—for in this respect each legend
ultimately stands alone—but indications pointing to a redaction. The redactional interpolation 9:18a, 19 is designed to lead from the Flood legend to the genealogy of Shem, Ham,
and Japheth. Thus the Flood legend and this genealogy belong to the same source. On the
other hand, the story of Noah's vineyard presupposed the other genealogy of Shem,
Japheth, and Canaan. Gen 5:29, originally a portion of the Sethite genealogy in J (see the
commentary), looks back to Yahweh's curse on the field (3:17, עִצָּבוֹן) and forward to
Noah's vineyard (9:20-27). Accordingly, a recension of the Paradise narrative originally
belonged with the Sethite genealogy and the account of Noah's vineyard. The two genealogies via Cain and via Seth are mutually exclusive. The account of the angelic marriages
may have preceded the account of the Flood as a motivation for the awful punishment.
One may assume, then, the following division of the parallel units. The first collection
will have contained (1) portions of the Paradise narrative, (2) Seth's genealogy, (3) Noah's
vineyard, (4) a Table of Nations (Shem, Japheth, Canaan), (5) the Legend of the city of
Babel. The second collection will have consisted of (1) portions of the Paradise narrative,
(2) Cain's genealogy, (3) angelic marriages, (4) Flood, (5) a Legend of the nations (Shem,
Ham, Japheth), (6) the Tower of Babel legend. The account of Cain's fratricide does not
seem to belong to either source, but seems to have only been included by the compiler
of the final form (more in the discussion of the individual units). For reasons discussed
below (p. 26 and concerning 4:25-26) the first collection will be termed "J^e," the second
"J^j." Units composed or inserted by the compiler of the final form will be termed "J^r."
     Others disagree. According to Wellhausen (*Composition*^{3}, 14) one may assume an
original core (2; 3; 4:16-24; 11:1-9) later expanded with supplements. The disunity of 2;
3; and 11:1-9 contradict this assumption. It is entirely a matter of the combination of two
sources, not of a "core" and "supplements." Budde (*Urgeschichte*) distinguishes two
sources: J^1 consists of 2:4b-9, 16-25; 3:1-19, 21; 6:3; 3:23 (Paradise narrative), 4:1, 2bβ,
16b, 17-24 (Cain's genealogy), 6:1, 2, 4; 10:9 (angelic marriages and Nimrod), 11:1-9
(Tower construction), 9:20-27 (Noah's vineyard). J^2 contains a creation account, a paradise
narrative, the Sethite genealogy, Flood legend, and Table of the Nations. According to
Budde, J^2 is a thorough reworking and reconfiguration of J^1, which, he believes, issued
"from a high place" and "represents a somewhat official, very conscious correction of
original folk tradition" (462). Budde has the great honor of having identified two sources
in J's Primeval History and having thereby shown research the way for a long time to
come. But the chief distinguishing characteristic of his two sources, namely the presence
or absence of the Flood account, is inadequate since all of these legends are very independent of one another and an allusion to the Flood account only occurs in 9:18. Budde
places the composition of his "J$^{2\text{“}}$" in the Assyrian period owing to the Babylonian material
contained therein, while he considers "J$^{1\text{”}}$" older. "J$^{1\text{”}}$" also contains eastern material, however: the accounts of Paradise account, the Tower, Nimrod. Stade (*ZAW* 14:274-283) distinguished three layers: (a) 2; 3; 11:1-19; (b) 4:25-26, 17-24; 9:20-27, perhaps also 10:9,
and 6:1,2; and (c) the Flood legend. The third was added after the first two had already
been combined. But these layers do not constitute in themselves clear units. All these
attempts, which have contributed a great deal in the particulars to the elucidation of the
narratives, share the effort to find the unifying thread in the stories themselves. They fall

aside as soon as one takes <3> seriously the fact that in oral tradition and even in the collections each legend is independent of the others.

Meinhold follows the source analysis offered in the commentary entirely, with the exception that he, too, considers the Flood legend a later addition. In response one can nevertheless point out that a compiler who wished to include the Flood legend will hardly have first offered the Cainite genealogy.

In more recent times the attempt has been made to employ meter, too, as a criterion for source analysis. But the question of whether these texts have any metrical structure whatsoever and what that structure might be in particular cases is yet unresolved (see Introduction ¶3:2). For example, the attempts of Erbt and Sievers differ markedly from one another in results and neither has come to a convincing source analysis. Erbt distinguishes J¹, J², and E: J¹ contains a paradise narrative, Cain's fratricide, angelic marriages, Nimrod, Tower construction and dispersion; J² another Paradise narrative, here, too, a legend of Cain's fratricide, Cain's genealogy, a Flood narrative, a Table of Nations, a legend of the establishment of Babel and the confusion of languages; E a third Paradise narrative, Seth's genealogy, a second Flood account, Canaan's curse, a second Table of Nations. J¹ is supposed to have written quadrameter, J² and E hexameter. Sievers differentiates (1) Ja, the "heptameter-text," containing a Paradise narrative, Cain and Abel, Noah's birth, Flood, Tower of Babel; (2) Jβ, heptameter alternating with a shortened verse, containing a Table of nations; (3) Jγ, the "hexameter-text," containing the Cainite genealogy, the song of Lamech, the Sethite genealogy (!), angelic marriages; (4) Jδ, hexameter alternating with a shortened verse, appearing in the Paradise narrative, angelic marriages, Cain's curse, a Table of Nations; and, (5) Jε, the "octameter-text," appearing in the Paradise narrative.

1. The Paradise Narrative 2:4b-3:24

Source: The following account begins again at the very beginning, in a time when nothing alive existed yet, and comes at the end to the current status of humanity. In relation to 1:1-2:4a, then, it rests on an independent tradition. The first part of the narrative offers an account of the origins that differs markedly in detail and tone from P (1:1-2:4a). The entire narrative can be clearly distinguished from P in attitude, especially in its antique earthiness (Wellhausen, *Prolegomena*⁶, 303)—e.g., in its anthropomorphisms, and in its diction (עָשָׂה or יָצַר, P בָּרָא; חַיַּת הַשָּׂדֶה, P חַיַּת הָאָרֶץ; הַפַּעַם 2:23; בַעֲבוּר 3:17; מַה־זֹּאת 3:13; עִצָּבוֹן 3:16, 17 only in J; "earth and heaven," 2:4b, P "the heaven and the earth," 2:4a)—and stems, thus, from another source. The divine name יהוה (אלהים) points with certainty to J. See further below, p. 25ff.

2:4b-25. *Account of the Origins.* The earth is originally dry, then water, man, trees, animals, and woman come into being. This sequence differs totally from that of P.

4b-7 *The Primal State, the Water, the Man.* This account, too, knows of a primal state. The sentence structure is probably: v 4b protasis, vv 5-6 parenthesis, and v 7 apodosis. The long parenthesis gives the sentence a somewhat sluggish character, suggesting that a redactor has been active here (for a conjecture concerning the reason for the insertion see below pp. 27-28). The points of departure for J and P differ greatly. There water is present at first, here dry land—the earth was originally a waterless desert. There water is the enemy, here the friend. Gen 2:5 indicates how the narrator envisions the current status of the world: everything depends on the rain, from which, nowadays, all fertility on earth <4> derives. These descriptions in P and J refer to very different climates: in the former the climate of a flooded alluvial land, here the climate of a land which groans in late summer under drought until the deity grants the fervently desired rain and thus creates the whole world anew. This is the climate of the Syro-Arabian desert, northern Mesopotamia, Syria, and Canaan.

4 בְּיוֹם *"in that day."* It is unlikely that J places any value on the contention that everything came into being on the same day, but, in contrast to P, he does not assume several days of creation. יהוה אלהים occurs in Genesis only in chapters 2 and 3 (LXX ὁ θεός differs from the Hebrew in 2:5, 7, 9, 19, 21). The juxtaposition of the two divine names may be explained according to the usual assumption of a later harmonization with P (so certainly in LXX of 7:1; 8:21; 9:12; LXX commonly diverges from the Hebr. text in usage of the divine names, see Eerdmans 1:79). Eerdmans (1:78ff.) explains it as the result of the application of a polytheistic legend to Yahweh (3:22). But it may be better considered the product of the combination of two sources of the Paradise legend, one employed יהוה, the other אלהים (compare Budde, 233-34; see further below, p. 24).

5 The primal state of creation is portrayed negatively, as is common in other creation narratives (see the two Babylonian narratives *Schöpfung und Chaos*, 401-402, 419; *KB* 6/1, 1, 39-40; and Winckler, *Keilinschriftl. Textbuch*[2], 98, 102; also the Egyptian portrayals, Erman, *Ägypt. Rel.*, 28, Hommel, *ThLbl* 32, 555, the late Jewish 4 Ezr 6:1ff., see also Prov 8:22ff., the old Nordic H. Gering, *Edda* 3 and in the Wessobrunner Prayer [Müllenhoff and Schere, *Denkmäler deutscher Poesie und Prosa*[3], 1], among others). This was apparently the style of creation myths, just as other "etiological" narratives (see Introduction ¶2:3,7) regularly begin with a negative portrayal. "Yahweh sends rain" like Ζεὺς ὕει. It is quite clear to the Israelites living in Canaan that Yahweh gives the rain: indeed, rain comes from heaven, "from Yahweh." Thus all life in Palestine depends on God's grace. On the other hand, it was also clear to the Palestinian farmer that he must also do something himself in order for the plants to grow: שִׂיחַ shrubs (especially in the desert, Gen 21:15; Job 30:4, 7) sprout solely because of God's rain; but in order for עֵשֶׂב (especially useful plants, food for people and cattle) to flourish humans must take action. Before rain and humans existed there was neither שִׂיח nor עשׂב. This reflection of human participation in God's creation seems most naive to us. According to most scholars the categorization of plants in P (Gen 1) is according to the nature of their seed. Characteristically, this text does not mention trees. There must have been few trees in the environment in which the myth originated. Regarding טֶרֶם with impf. see §107c.

6 According to LXX, Pesh, and others "spring," אֵד, may be related to Babylonian *edû*, "flood, high water" (compare Delitzsch, *Handwörterb.*, 22). In Job 36:27 it (apparently) designates the heavenly water container; In Targ it means "clouds." Recent translations offer "mist." The meaning "flood" is preferable. To be sure, mist moistens the earth, but it does not "water" it (Holzinger). The rare word, which may also have occurred in Isa 33:21 (אדיר corrupted form of אֵד יהוה?), a passage alluding to the Paradise stream (see "General Remarks" ¶6), will have been a technical term in this narrative of origins similar to תְהוֹם and תֹהוּ וָבֹהוּ in Gen 1. If the translation "spring, flood" is correct, the אֵד seems to have been conceived of as a spring bubbling forth on the plain. The concept of the origination of the *'ed* in the dry land parallels the concept of the birth of the sea in the lap of the earth (Job 38:8). On the tenses of יַעֲלֶה וְהִשְׁקָה see §112e. Notably, the text does not say that Yahweh created this *'ed*: Yahweh's "creations" are recounted beginning in v 7. The, surely very ancient, concept that the *'ed* does not proceed from Yahweh may be detected here. Further, this account of the *'ed* which watered the earth is notably distinct from that of v 5, according to which Yahweh's rain <5> makes it fertile. The Targum, which translates *'ed* with "clouds," harmonizes the two concepts. On the question of how the narrator came to combine the two concepts, see below p. 28.

7 The total context is as follows. Originally the earth was dry, then it was moistened; Then Yahweh created his creatures from moist earth; From moist earth he "formed"—with his own hand—the man (v 7) and the animals (v 19), just as the potter forms (יָצַר a potter's term) his creations from moist earth. Trees could only grow on moistened earth (v 8). The background of the concept of the formation of animals and humans from earth is probably the fact that the narrator's culture knew clay images of humans and animals, such as those found in great numbers in archeological digs in Palestine (cf. Benzinger, 2nd ed, 221f.). The human body is formed from יָפָר, "dust." This origin of the human body is frequently alluded to the in the OT (3:19,23; 18;27; Psa 90:3; 103:14, etc.). Similar concepts also occur in Babylonian (e.g. KB VI/1, 121, ll 34f., 287, l. 4ff.; Zimmern, KAT³, 506), Greek (Preller-Robert, *Griech. Mythologie* I⁴, 81-82), Egyptian, Indian, and Chinese (Jeremias, *ATAO²*, 167n.2) myths; Latin *homo* also derives from *humus*, as the ancients already knew (cf. Quintilian, *Inst. Or.* I/6, 34, *Hygin, fab.*, 220; cf. also A. Dieterich, *Mutter Erde*, 76n.2). This idea responds to the question, "Of what does the human body consist?" the ancients answer, "of earth." The earth, mother of all life, brought him forth like the plants and the other creatures. Thus humans become earth again in death (3:19). Here the notion has been monotheistically transformed: Yahweh creates the man from the earth (see Nöldeke, *ARW* 8:161-62)—a first attempt at organic chemistry. For the accusative יָפָר see §117hh. This dust is taken from אֲדָמָה. עָפָר and מִן־הָאֲדָמָה were probably originally variants; עָפָר is probably secondary (cf below, p. 26). The idea that the man was formed from אֲדָמָה also serves to explain the name of the man: His name is אָדָם because he originated from the אֲדָמָה. According to vv 5, 6, אֲדָמָה is the watered, cultivated land, the field. The life of the אָדָם is very closely related to this אֲדָמָה: he was created from the field, his profession is cultivating the field (v 5; 3:23), he lives on the field (3:23), and he returns to the field when he dies (3:19). Consequently, the myth derives even his name from the field. Thus the man is, and his name means, "man of the field." This etymology can only have arisen in an agricultural society. What follows explains the riddle of life in a childish fashion. The man contains something mysterious, life, that which he exhales through his nose, the נִשְׁמַת הַיִּים, "the breath of life." This juxtaposition or confusion of life and breath is very natural for ancient observers. As long as one has breath, one lives, but life leaves the body with the breath. Whence comes this wonder, this mystery? Only God can have given it. Now the myth explains in its childish way that God breathed into the man something of his own breath. This divine, wonder-working breath, however, became an independent being, or so the narrator probably intends: Thus the man became נֶפֶשׁ חַיָּה. As naive as this investiture is, it is an equally deep concept. The man is related to God, his breath an emanation of the divine. One may note the fine distinction between נֶפֶשׁ חַיָּה and נִשְׁמַת חַיִּים. The נְשָׁמָה—as we would put it—is the principle of life common to all.

The נֶפֶשׁ (the life produced) is unique in each one, the individual. At death God re-
claims the נְשָׁמָה (Job 34:14), but the נֶפֶשׁ goes to שְׁאוֹל (see Siegfr.-Stade, *Wb.*, 431).
The breath of life is blown into the nose because the man breathes through the nose (Isa
2:22). The soul also returns through the nose (2 Kgs 4:35) and the demon exits through
it (Josephus, *Ant* VIII.2.5). The notion that the man was created immortal or at least with
<6> the capacity for immortality, a notion deduced from the giving of the soul through
God's breath, is far removed from the narrative which seeks only to explain the fact of
life, and from Hebrew antiquity. The myth responds, then, to a series of questions concerning the human body, life, purpose, and name.

8-15 *The Garden in Eden.* **8** *Yahweh Plants a Park.* The ancient Hebrew, like his
neighbors, considered quite a number of trees, with their powerful life force and the
mysterious rustling in their branches, to be God's sanctuaries. Humans plant the fruit trees
in the field, but the cedars of Lebanon were planted by God. Oases or natural parks,
upward-sprouting wildernesses in the midst of infertile land, also seemed to him to be
God's plantings. This text speaks of such a particularly holy park. The garden is called
"the Garden of God" (Ezek 28:13; 31:8f.), the "Yahweh Garden" (Isa 51:3; Gen 13:10).
According to the original concept, Yahweh as *genius loci* is home here. Because of an
aversion to the mythological, this concept is no longer explicitly stated in chapter 2, but
it is still assumed in 3:8, where God strolls in the garden. LXX translates גַּן with
παράδεισος = פַּרְדֵּס = *pairidaeza*, a term from the Avesta, "walled enclosure, fenced
enclosure, circular wall." In Persian it must have had the further meaning "enclosed
space" (cf. Bötticher, *Arica* 24, no. 77, where the Greek passages are collected). Thence
our "Paradise." עֵדֶן, as a proper name always anarthrous, is by context a mythological
territory. The Hebrew heard his Hebrew עֵדֶן "bliss" in the term (LXX παράδεισος τῆς
τρυφῆς; cf. Mailand). Certainly, however, the author did not invent the name (contra
Dillmann) for one does not invent such names. Instead the names in the old legends are
always traditional. At any rate, עֵדֶן is unrelated to the territory of עֶדֶן on the
Euphrates, but may be related to the Babylonian *edinu* "steppe." Accordingly, גַּן עֵדֶן
will have originally meant "garden in the steppe, oasis," just as the opposite of the garden
of God in Isa 51:3 and Joel 2:3 is the desert. The notation that the garden was situated
in the far East corresponds quite well to this understanding: To the east of Canaan lay the
vast steppe of whose frightful dangers the Canaanite farmer told with horror. The location
of Paradise in the desert, of all places, can apparently be explained in terms of the impression of contrast: The garden of God seems all the more magnificent if located in the
horrible desert. At the same time, this situation explains why Paradise is inaccessible for
us. Other geographical data occur in vv 10-14 and 3:24. Notably, both here and in v 9
Yahweh creates only trees, but the creation of shrubbery and plants was announced in v
5. For the dynamics of this difficulty see below pp. 27-28.

V **9a** recounts once again the origin of Paradise. V 9a parallels v 8a. They are probably variants from separate sources. וַיַּצְמַח is less anthropomorphic than וַיִּטַּע (v 8). Regarding כָּל־עֵץ "all types of trees," see §127b. For נֶחְמָד "desirable," see §116e. Ezek
31:8f. describes the trees of the garden of God with great pathos as wonderful, broad-
branched, towering cedars, cypresses, and plane trees. In contrast, the description here is
childishly idyllic: impressive trees with tasty fruit.

9b The style of the clause, if not impossible, is nevertheless noteworthy: "and the tree of knowledge, etc." is awkward (compare Holzinger). Is one of the trees an insertion (Budde, 51-52; cf. p. 25)? Gen 3:22 explains the tree of life: Whoever eats of it lives eternally, i.e., its fruit bestows immortality. Hebrew proverbs often refer to this tree (Prov 3:18; 11:30; 13:12; 15:4). It must have been a well-known concept. The well of life, whose water renders immortal, is similar (Prov 10:11; 13:14; 14:27; 16:22; Psa 36:10). Such <7> things exist in the wonderful fairy tale world of myth. They are not unique to Israel, Babylonian tradition also speaks of the water of life, the plant of life, and the oil of life (Zimmern, KAT³, 523ff.) and probably also knows the tree of life just as the Egyptian speaks of the tree from which gods and the blessed live (Erman, *Äg. Rel.*, 93); Iranian and Indians also know the tree of life and the water of life (Windischmann, *Zor. Studien*, 165ff.; Spiegel, *Ar. Periode*, 168ff.; Bartholomae, *Altiran. Wb.*, 480, 1468-69, 1791 [with bibliography]). The Nordics tell of the apples of Idunn which bestow eternal youth. The Alexander novel, *1,001 Nights*, the German fairy tales, etc. tell of the water of life (compare Wünsche, *Sagen vom Lebensbaum und Lebenswasser*). The tree of knowledge can be similarly understood. It is also a miracle-tree whose fruit gives its consumer knowledge. The serpent states so in 3:5, but the narrators admits it in 3:7 and God, himself, does also in 3:22. EthEnoch 32:3 describes the tree, then, quite properly: τὸ δένδρον τῆς φρονήσεως οὖ (עֵץ) ἐσθίουσιν ἁγίου τοῦ καρποῦ αὐτοῦ καὶ ἐπίστανται φρόνησιν μεγάλην. According to P. Dhorme (*Revue biblique* 4:271ff.), the Sumerian Gudea inscriptions mention the "tree of truth" (*giš-zi-da*) and the "tree of life" (*giš-ti*), located at the eastern entrance to heaven. We should not be surprised to encounter both in the garden of God for they embody characteristically divine properties. According to the OT, immortality is a divine prerogative and according to 3:5,22 "knowledge" renders one like God. On the construction הַדַּעַת טוֹב וָרָע see §115d.

Vv **10-14** serve first to highlight the majesty of the garden with its powerful resources of water. Such irrigation can be conceived in terms of the river, like the Nile or the Tigris and Euphrates, flowing through the Garden in many canals and overflowing periodically. This aquatic wealth also characterizes the Garden (Gen 13:10; Ezek 31:7ff.). The narrator envisions the river springing up in Eden outside the Garden, then flowing through the Garden and dividing into four rivers. Since, in his opinion, these four rivers comprise all the earth's major streams, he believes that all the significant flowing water comes from Paradise. The four rivers can be explained by the fact that the ancient Orient speaks of the four corners of the world, of the four directions of the heavens, of the four parts of the earth (Babylonian, cf. Zimmern, KAT³, 631ff.; Egyptian, Erman, *Äg. Rel.*, 5). The intention here, then, is that every region of the world has a stream which brings its water. C. Fries (*Neue Jahrb. für das klass. Altertum I Abt.* 9, 689ff.) compares the four streams of Paradise with Greek traditions concerning the four streams of the underworld and the four sources of Ogygia, the fabulously beautiful island of Calypsos (*Od.* 5:70ff.). Modern pedagogical mnemonics still employs the notion of four rivers springing up alongside one another (cf. the four rivers of the Fichtel Mountains or of St. Gotthard). Now the narrator concerns himself with representing the location of the Garden on earth in relation to the four rivers proceeding from it. Apparently, he enumerates from East to West. He concludes with the Tigris (*Hiddeqel*, Bab. *Idiqlat*, old Persian *Tigrâ*) and the Euphrates (*Perath*, Bab. *Purattu*, old Persian *Ufrâtus*) in this order. The first two named are, accordingly, streams in the far East, of which he hard obscure knowledge (cf. Meyer, *Israeliten*, 210). Notably in this regard, the Nile is not considered here: the transmitted tradition is of Oriental origin (cf. Meyer, loc. cit.). The author wanted to establish geographically the course of the streams other than the Euphrates, which was well-known to his readers. His geography is, admittedly, very immature. The Tigris and <8> the Euphrates, in his view, come from the same primary stream. The author defines the other two streams, Pishon (> פוש, σκιρτᾶν, "to spring up") and Gihon (> גיח, "to gush forth," later identified with the Nile, Sir 24:27), in terms of the lands around which they flow in his opinion. *HaH'vila*, elsewhere and in the Samaritan Pentateuch here, too, without article, is located according to 10:29 in Arabia, according to 10:7 in Cush; Meyer (*Israeliten*, 325) compares it to the Χαυλοταῖοι of Eratosthenes (in Strabo, *Geographica* 16, p. 767) and seeks the land in the north Arabian desert on the Caravan route from Egypt to Babylon; According to others it is in southern Arabia (cf. Siegfried in Guthes *BW* and Gesenius[14] s.v. Cush = southern Arabia with the associated Nubia; cf. Winckler, *KAT*[3], 137, 144-45). According to Delitzsch (*Paradies*, 51ff., 72ff.), Meyer (*Israeliten*, 210), and others, it is the land of the Cossaeans or the Cissites. Since the narrator, himself, senses that no clear concept is associated with the name *Havila*, he includes information concerning the products of this land. This, too, is a rather immature method of geographical description. *Havila* has gold of the best quality—gold came to the Hebrews in various degrees of purity—*B'dolah* (βδέλλιον, an aromatic resin that, according to Pliny, comes from Arabia, Babylonia, Media, and India, more in Gesenius[14]) and the Sohamstone (an unknown gem-stone, cf. Gesenius[14]). These products of *Havila* are not reserved for use at home, but are exported to the West (Meyer, *Israeliten*, 326). Of interest is the comment that the Tigris flows "before," i.e., to the East of, Asshur. The statement has occasioned some difficulty since in later times all the major cities of the Assyrian empire lay to the East of the Tigris. But the oldest capital Asshur, the center of the oldest empire "Asshur" (residence until 1300, *KAT*[3], 35) lay to the west of the Tigris. This note must, therefore, be quite ancient. In the 8th century one would have certainly mentioned Nineveh instead of Asshur (Meyer, *Israeliten*, 210n.1). The geographical concepts behind these details are so immature that it is entirely improper to attempt to reconcile this system of rivers with actual geography: Paradise is located where the Euphrates and Tigris spring up from a mighty parent stream, also the source of two other great rivers of the world. The author's world view rests only partially in reality and partially in traditions whose origins cannot be sought, at any rate, in actual geographical circumstances. Even though it is impossible to locate Pishon and Gihon, it is possible to say where the tradition located Paradise. The starting point is the very significant circumstance, both for us and already for them, that the Euphrates and the Tigris originate there. Thus, they located Paradise in the upper course of these two rivers, in the mountains which border Mesopotamia in the North. We also know from the Flood legend that this mountain was considered the highest in the world. The world's four rivers, two of which were known, two sought in the distance, were thought to spring up on this mountain. Here imagination located the Garden of God. These mountains tower into heaven, neighbors of the deity. No foot touches them, no eye penetrates their secret. What might be up there? In the midst of the horrible desert lies a wonderful Garden, a gloriously irrigated land, for all water originates there. Regarding the same concept of Paradise on the mountain of God in Iranian sources and elsewhere in the OT, see below "General Remarks" ¶6. This tradition originates, then, in Mesopotamia. Literature concerning the location of Paradise may be found in the commentaries. The section concerning the four rivers (vv 10-14) distinguishes itself from its contexts through its somewhat dry, academic tone. The author also locates Paradise differently than מִקֶּדֶם in 2:8 and in 3:24 (see the commentary). If *'ed* (v 6) is to be translated "spring, flood," the river in 10-14 is a legend variant. In this case, the verses would be an old addition. The sources report three different versions of the irrigation of the earth: (1) by the rain, v 5, (2) by the *'ed*, v 6, <9> (3) by a river system, vv 10-14 (cf. Erbt, 3; Sievers 2:242) **12** Concerning וּזֶהַב see §10g. To טוֹב Samaritan adds מְאֹד. The spelling הוא for the feminine is an orthographic peculiarity of the Pentateuch text (§321).

V **15** reiterates 8b, but the verse is nevertheless too original to be a redactional parenthesis (from the same hand responsible for the insertion of vv 10-14). The two statements stem from two different variants of the Paradise narrative. Since גַן is masc., one should read לְעָבְדוֹ וּלְשָׁמְרוֹ (with Dillmann). The man should work and guard the Garden. The basis of this idea is not the modern Protestant notion of the value of profession and work, but the naive ideal of an ancient farmer that the first people were gardeners. The tree bears its fruit, year after year, almost without human work; the field, however, must be laboriously cultivated (3:17ff.). Thus the farmer's ideal is to be a gardener and to live effortlessly from the fruit of the tree: and now a gardener in Paradise! Even Paradise must be worked and guarded. This element indicates that the author conceives of Paradise not as an absolutely perfect place, but only as a beautiful locale. Against what must Paradise be "guarded"? Probably against beings at enmity with God, against demons. The man fulfills roughly the same role here as the Cherubim later (3:24). Is this motif a mythological residue (cf. Gressmann, *ARW* 10:361ff.)?

16-17 The commandment concerning food. God permits the consumption of all the fruits of the trees, entirely at will (this is the significance of the inf. abs.). The tradition that the first people fed on the fruit of trees also occurs among the Greeks (literature in Dillmann) and similarly, too, already in 1:29. Now the narrative turns to the key issue. **17** The man should not eat of the Tree of Knowledge, or he will surely (inf. abs.) die on the day (as soon as) he eats of it. The words can be understood as an indication that the fruits themselves are poisonous but also—somewhat removed from the letter, but nevertheless probably our narrator's intention—as an indication that God will punish transgression with death (see below "General Remarks" ¶5). This threat is not carried out later: they do not die immediately. This circumstance cannot be explained away (as, for example, does Dillmann: the toil and suffering are the beginning of death), but must simply be acknowledged. The difficulty modern commentators find in this non-fulfillment of the divine words will not have been so strongly felt by the ancient narrator. Instead, he would answer, "God is and will be the Lord of his words, later he 'regretted' the statement." Indeed, he would have seen it as an extraordinary example of divine mercy that he did not enforce the word. Gen 20:3, where God threatens to kill Abimelech yet allows him to live, is very similar. Nevertheless, it is still remarkable that God immediately punishes the serpent for lying (3:4) and that the narrator offers not a word in explanation of this whole situation (see further under "General Remarks" ¶5). The narrator does not say why God prohibits eating from this tree under threat of such horrible punishment, but presumes it to be self-evident. The narrator very often does not communicate motivations (see introduction ¶3:12, 13). We must discern them from the results. At any rate, the reasons were not communicated to the man. He should obey without justification, just as Abraham obeyed when he left Haran and when he offered Isaac: childish obedience. The fact that God's first commandment concerned eating is also childish. On the widespread motif of the violated prohibition, compare the comments on no.'s 3 and 46 in Grimm's *Kinder- und Haus-Märchen*; v.d. Leyen 113:262-63, Böklen, *Adam und Qain*, 80ff., 89-90 (with bibliography). How is the man familiar death that he has neither experienced nor seen? Such questions may not be asked of naive myth. Notably, God already <10> mentions the name of the Tree to the man and thereby reveals to him its secret power, of which the man otherwise first learns from the serpent (3:4-5). Undeniably, the point of the following story of seduction is thereby ruined, a circumstance which cannot be attributed to such a good storyteller. Consequently, Budde (49ff.) correctly suspects that like 3:3, 2:17 originally spoke only of "the tree in the midst of the Garden."

18-24 *The Man's Helper.* This unit is the conclusion of the account of origins. **18** As was true of the creation of humanity in 1:26, deliberation comes first. It is surely an ancient element. נעשׂה LXX Vulg, is a correction influenced by 1:26. God finds that the man, in his current state, is not yet complete. His life is too lonely, his work to hard. He must have assistance and companionship, "a pillar on which to lean" (Sir 36:29). On the inf. cstr. חֱיוֹת as the subject, see §114a. כְּנֶגְדּוֹ means "as over against him = corresponding to him, his counterpart."

19-20 Here the creation of animals follows that of the man. The sequence is inverted in P (1:20ff.,26ff.) The creation of the animals does not appear here as in P as an independent act of creation, but is incorporated in a narrative. It occurred once under quite specific circumstances and had a quite definite objective at the time. The myth is very well aware of where and when and why the animals were formed. The abundance of particulars comprises the myth's unique charm. In order to get a sense of this naive beauty, one may compare the counterpart in chap. 1, where this particularity is almost entirely absent.

19 Read עוֹד after אלוהים with LXX, Sam (Ball); further with Sam read אֶת־ before כָּל־חַיַּת־הַשָּׂדֶה (Ball). חַיַּת הַשָּׂדֶה includes domesticated animals expressly distinguished from other animals in v 20. Such approximate designations are common in popular usage. The learned precision of P represents a contrast. The narrator omits fish: after all, they cannot be the man's "helpers." He has not mentioned the sea previously either. The author, then, is far removed from the learned exhaustiveness of P. יִּקְרָא־לוֹ מָה means "what he would say about them, what he would call them." Through the names, the man establishes his relationship to the things—such is the clever presupposition. נֶפֶשׁ חַיָּה is syntactically impossible. It is difficult to say how it came to be in this text, perhaps from v 7 (Sievers 2:244)?

20 Hebr mss, Pesh, Vulg, Targ-Pseudojon, Ball, Kittell read וּלְכָל־עוֹף, perhaps only an assimilation. "But for a man (וּלְאָדָם, without article because it is employed qualitatively, Delitzsch) he found no suitable helper." "This expression does not fit the situation." It should not be explained as a textual corruption, however—the readings הָאָדָם or וִמְצָא have been suggested (cf. Holzinger)—but as evidence of the author's naiveté. The mention of death in v 17, as well as v 24, are similar cases. The scene of the creation of the animals contains: (1) an ancient view of names. The Hebrew did not perceive the name as incidental, but as a given essential. Things are really called by the names the man gave them. How can this be? The myth answers, "Because Yahweh determined it to be so." As Adam saw the lion, he named it "lion." Consequently, the lion was henceforth called "lion" according to Yahweh's will. Naturally, the presumption is that the first man spoke Hebrew. This represents a first reflection concerning the nature of language. It is instructive to observe that the first words of the man are namings: Naming is the beginning of all knowledge. (2) Further, <11> a naive view of the relationship between the man and the animals becomes apparent. They are related to him: like him formed from the earth. God considers it possible that one of them could be a "helper" for him. On the other hand, they are different from him. It is probably no accident that the author does not attribute to the animals a "breath of life," breathed into them by God. The man feels distant from them: they are not "helpers" for him. By giving them their names he demonstrates his superiority (cf. Wellhausen, *Prolegomena*⁶, 298, 306). Hebrew antiquity regarded animals sympathetically. They thought of them anthropomorphically (Job 38:41; 39:13; Prov 30:24-28) and they unabashedly admired some of them: Indeed, the donkey occasionally saw more than the prophet (Num 22). The most ancient period even found traces of the divine in some animals. In the myth under consideration, the man is certainly conscious of his superiority over the animals, yet he views himself as more closely related to them than moderns do. Gen 1, where the animals "are neutral beings over which he rules" (Wellhausen), is quite distinct. (3) Furthermore, the scene presupposes a naive view of God: he forms the animals, brings them before the man, and conducts a futile experiment (cf. Schwally, *ARW* 9:170). The Melaneisans also tell of several failed attempts during the creation of humanity (Waitz-Gerland, *Anthropologie der Naturvölker* 6, 665).

21-25 *Creation of the Woman.* **21** The fact that the man falls into a deep sleep is a particularly beautiful, highly vivid element: God's creation and activity always remains a secret. "The creature should not see how God works but receive what he has produced" (Herder). תַּרְדֵּמָה, more than שֵׁנָה (normal) sleep, is an especially deep, wondrous sleep, a divine sleep (1 Sam 26:12; Isa 29:10), deep stupefaction in ecstasy and vision (Job 4:13; 33:15; cf. Dan 8:18; 10:9; thus LXX ἔκστασις). The motif of magical sleep is common in legends and fairy tales. One thinks, for example, of the magical sleep of Kaiser Rotbart in the smokehouse, of Brunhilda, of Sleeping Beauty, and of Snow White (cf. v.d. Leyen 113:253 with bibliography). The man had rejected beings that, like himself, were formed from the Earth; now God forms a being for him from part of his own body: a wise idea! The man will certainly experience such a being as related! Why does God take a rib? The answer to this question can no longer be ascertained with certainty from our text. This element may have originally been explainable in terms of the sexual relations for which the woman was destined.

23 "Just as he was disappointed by the futile experiment with the animals, the man now delightedly exclaims the following words on seeing the woman" (Wellhausen, *Prolegomena*⁶, 298). It is an "exultant welcome" (Herder). The words have a stricter rhythmic form, as often at the climax of the account in legends and fairy tales (cf. the introduction ¶3:2). The strophes are a hexameter and paired trimeters. Both strophes place strong emphasis on זֹאת (cf. Sievers 1:385; 2:210; contra 2:9). Joyfully referring to the woman, the man thrice repeats זֹאת, "this one here." The first time זֹאת is intensified by הַפַּעַם "this one this time" = "this one, finally." Stade (*ZAW* 17:210ff.) stumbles unnecessarily over the doubled emphasis and translates זֹאת adverbially "now." <12> The man recognizes immediately how closely related to him the woman is. A direct feeling tells him that this being is related to him in a manner quite distinct from the animals, that she derives from his own body. The first emotion to overcome him when he sees her is delight: bridegroom's joy! Then he exercises the right to give names. Such a name may not be omitted at the origin of the new being (cf. comment on 1:5). He names her *'iššȧ*, because she belongs to *'iš*. The man speaks Hebrew. The assonance is even stronger in the reading מֵאִישָׁה "from her husband" (Sam, LXX, Targ-Onk, Ball). Concerning לֻקֳחָה see §10h.

24 The following words are not those of the first man. Such concluding remarks, introduced with "therefore," stem from the narrator (Meinhold, 77). One should note this "therefore." The myth answers the question, "Why? Whence comes this?" In response one first recounts the myth and then continues, "Therefore, thence it comes" (cf. 10:9; 26:33; 32:33). This is, then, the prototypical example of an etiological myth (cf. introduction ¶2:3). The question presumed here is, "How is it that man strives for union with woman?" The myth answers, "Man desires to become one flesh with woman because he was originally one flesh with her." In love that which was originally one is reunited. "He seeks his flesh" (Herder). The nature of the love he intends is very clear from the expressions he uses: it is sexual union. The myth discusses this quite openly and frankly. Man leaves father and mother for the sake of woman. So great is his yearning for woman that it breaks the strongest bonds. The saying is difficult, since according to Israelite marriage law, the wife must follow the husband. Such an ancient myth does not speak of purely spiritual abandonment (contra Holzinger). Does this text reflect an ancient matriarchal law under which the husband visits the wife in her home (Robertson Smith, *Kinship and Marriage in Early Arabia*, 176), or should we think of a marriage law under which the grown son leaves the household and control of the parents when he takes a wife and establishes his own household (Meyer, I/1², 31; Rauh, *Hebr. Familienrecht*, 34-35)? וְהָיוּ + שְׁנֵיהֶם (LXX, Pesh, Vulg, Targ-Pseudojon, Philo, cf. Sam, NT, Ball, Kittel) immediately alongside שְׁנֵיהֶם (v 25) would be ugly. The myth of the origin of woman (1) explains man's attraction for woman in relation to the nature of her origins: the two, originally one, strive to become one again. (2) It employs the expressions "Flesh of my flesh and bone of my bone" (i.e., originally blood relatives) and "to become one flesh" (i.e., to unite corporally) and understands them in the most literal sense. (3) At the same time, it explains the name *'iššȧ*. Childish reflection finds deep ideas in the words and idioms of the language. The myth is often misunderstood. It does not discuss "marriage." Nor does it seek to represent monogamy as the norm. Rather, God creates only one woman because he does nothing superfluous. One man and one woman can produce the whole of humanity. Nor does the myth mean that the woman was originally "coordinated" with the man, that she did not stand "under him" (Holzinger). Rather, the woman is only the man's "helper" and the man is "the man." The myth does not represent ideals (Dillmann), but seeks to explain data. The same ideas also occur in Plato (*Symp.*, 189ff.), here, too, with the goal of showing that love seeks to restore people to their old nature and to make of two one (p.191). This yearning and searching for the (original) whole is called love (p. 192). According to Grimm (*Deutsche Mythologie*⁴ 3:162), among the Greenlanders, woman originated from the thumb of man. Other parallels are listed in Cheyne, 74-75; Böklen, *Adam und Qain*, 26. P tells the story quite distinctly from J. According to P, humans were created from the very beginning as a pair. <13>

25 *The Primal State.* The narrator intends to present the state of the people before they ate from the Tree of Knowledge in terms of the fact that they were not ashamed in each other's presence (hithpa.). The counterpart is 3:7: When they had eaten, they recognized that they were naked, i.e., they were ashamed and tried to clothe themselves. The narrator was not in the position to describe explicitly the psychological state of the people before and after the transgression. But he makes these inner states apparent by mentioning a single, especially vivid example in which they manifest themselves. With regard to this indirect style of presentation, see the introduction ¶3:12. Accordingly, a comparison of 2:25 and 3:7 suggests how the narrator conceives of the knowledge of good and evil. He demonstrates that the first people lacked this knowledge in that they were not ashamed; The fact that they were ashamed shows that they possess it. The knowledge and ignorance treated here concern, then, in the first instance, the difference between the sexes. The model for these elements is clearly the state of children who are not yet ashamed—a state one can observe in every lane in the East, where the children go naked. This ignorance of male and female is not, however, the whole issue in the Paradise narrative, but only an especially prominent example. The narrator wants to illustrate the entire intellectual state of children in this one aspect. He understands "knowledge" as that which adults possess to a greater degree than children—insight, reason, including the knowledge of the difference between the sexes. The diction as it appears elsewhere demonstrates the accuracy of this explanation: Children "do not know about good and evil" (Deut 1:39), i.e., they do not know the difference between good and evil, they "do not know to choose good and avoid evil" (Isa 7:15-16). They reach, for example, into the fire, they fall into the water, they eat things which can do harm, they do not know how to behave, nor do they understand moral distinctions. The adult, however, "distinguishes, chooses, and sets right." The aged become childish again, they forget the distinction between good and evil: Good or poor food and drink tastes the same to them (2 Sam 19:36). Later the serpent indicates another side of this "knowledge of good and evil" (3:5): This knowledge makes one like God (cf. 3:22). For this reason, God proscribed it for the man under penalty of death (2:17). We have parallels for this concept, too: It is attributed to the good judge, who recognizes good and evil matters (1 Kgs 3:9); In the highest sense, only God (or the angel), who looks into the depths and from whom one can conceal nothing (2 Sam 14:17), possesses it. Accordingly, the word has a somewhat ambiguous sense, like our "reason": It encompasses higher and lower capacities (contra Gressmann, *ARW* 10:351ff., who wants to abandon any effort to understand the Paradise narrative because of this difficulty; see, further, below, p. 29).

The preceding discussion suggests that the people in Paradise did not yet engage in sexual relations—they had not even yet recognized their sexual differences—and that the "knowledge" is not solely the "conscience" (the capacity for moral distinctions; the usual interpretation), but includes it. Wellhausen's interpretation (*Prolegomena*[6], 299ff.)—that it was the knowledge of the secret of the world, through which one can see God's intentions, and that this knowledge is to be understood historically as human culture—is also incorrect. The myth does not speak of a knowledge of the magnitude spoken of in

Goethe's *Faust*, but of something much lesser: in fact, the narrator chooses the knowledge of the difference in the sexes as an example! This text does not actually treat human culture. The myth speaks not so much of the human arts and skills the child learns during upbringing, but more and more distinctly <14> of what the child acquires by nature as he grows toward sexual maturity—mature judgment, reason. In the context of the narrative the verse is a transition to what follows. How long was the man in Paradise? Owing to its nature, the myth cannot give such precise determinations. "No hour strikes in Paradise" (Herder). "I cannot judge the passage of time, for all measure of time was forgotten." In the background of the depiction stands a perspective on the history of human clothing (2:25; 3:7[21]). Greek tradition also maintains that the first people wore no clothes (Plato, *Protag.*, 321 C; Diodorus, *d.i. Hecataeus v. Abdera* 1.8.5) as suggested by the nature of the matter. Our scholarship today still compares (mutatis mutandis) the first humans with children.

Chapter 3. The Expulsion from Paradise, 1-7.

1-5 *The Seduction of the Woman.* **1** The narrative begins with the introduction of a new character and a description of its chief characteristic (1 Sam 25:2-3; Job 1:1). According to the clear wording of the verse, as well as to 3:14-15, the serpent is one of the animals. It is the most clever of the animals; it is even more clever than the still-childish people. According to v. 5 it has secret knowledge that, beside it, only God himself knows. It can also talk. Finally, it has animosity toward God whom it slanders to the people. How is this to be interpreted? It is not remarkable for animals to think and speak like humans in fairy tales, animal fables, and even in legends. Hebrew legends also know of the talking donkey (Num 22). "The wild animal experiences everything, speaks with everyone, and it is not a school exercise for him but truth" (Herder). On this most ancient level, the difference between human and animal is not yet perceived. Therefore the woman was not at all surprised when the serpent suddenly opened its mouth. There is nothing particularly remarkable about the fact that in Paradise the serpent had language. It was a time, the ancient would respond to us, when animals could still speak—the time of myth. Furthermore, the description of the serpent as especially sly and malicious can be explained as the result of its sinister impression. It is the image of cleverness elsewhere, too (Matt 10:16; cf. Bochart, *Hierozoicon rec. Rosenmüller* 3:246ff.). The fact, however, that it knows the secret of the Tree, which otherwise only God knows, in other words that it has supernatural knowledge, demonstrates that this text has a mythological background. Originally the "serpent" will have been an evil, serpentine demon, hostile toward God and humans, which was reduced to an animal in Israel. Serpentine gods or demons are common among peoples (among the Semites, cf. Baudissin, *Studien zur sem. Religionsgeschichte* 1:255-56; Nöldeke, *Zeitschr. für Völkerpsychologie* 1:412ff.; Robertson Smith, *Religion of the Semites*; Stade, *Bibl. Theol.*, 141; Wellhausen, *Skizzen und Vorarbeiten* 32, 152-53; Jacob, *Beduinenleben*[2], 24; Pietschmann, *Geschichte der Phön.*, 227; among the Egyptians, cf. Amélineau, *Revue de l'histoire des religions* 51:335ff., 52:1ff.; among the Indians, cf. von Schroeder, *Indiens Literatur u. Kultur*, 377f.; among the Iranians, cf. Spiegel, *Eranische Altertumskunde* 3:530ff.; among the Greeks, Marx, *Griechische Märchen von dankbaren Tieren*, 96ff.; also in Israel, cf. the veneration of the serpent image in Jerusalem, 2 Kgs 18:4; additional literature in Baudissin in Herzog, "Drache zu

Babel, Eherne Schlange," RE³). Comparison of the Paradise serpent with the Babylonian Tiamat (so also Zimmern, KAT³, 529) is inadequate. Indeed both are evil, but Tiamat is a frightfully powerful, world-ruling monster, whereas the serpent is cunning. They are (apparently) entirely separate figures. Later Jewish-Christian interpretation (WisdSol 2:24; John 8:44; Rev 12:9; 20:2) of the serpent as the devil is incorrect, but, as is very often true in similar cases, on the right track. The sub<15>sequent narrative has always excited the delight of sensitive readers through its mastery of psychological description. In the few words and actions with which he describes his characters, the narrator makes their inner lives clear. His masterpiece is the description of the woman. The serpent, bitterly evil and sly, wants to harm God and seduce the people. It turns to the woman. Why to the Woman? The woman is livelier, more appetitive, and awakens earlier than the man. A highly interesting, even piquant scene follows. In childish, trusting harmlessness, the young, inexperienced woman stands before it. She does not suspect how ruinous the words of the evil serpent are. The symbols of childishly dull innocence and of sly seduction stand alongside one another. "Did God really say?" The serpent possesses wondrous knowledge. It has heard—the narrator does not betray how—of God's prohibition to the people. Now it takes the position that it has only imprecise information and would like now to be precisely informed by the people themselves. It greatly exaggerates God's prohibition and acts as though it were astonished at such harshness: "harsh God, cruel commandment" (Herder). Thus, it ingratiates itself through pretended sympathy and sows mistrust and suspicion toward God in the heart of the unsuspecting wife. Regarding כל ‏. . . לא‎, "none at all," see §152b.

2-3 She is quick, however, to reject the ignominious suspicion and zealously emphasizes the permission. מִפְּרִי כָל־עֵץ (Pesh., Ball, Sievers 2:254; cf. also LXX) expresses the sense more sharply. While, according to this text, God gave the commandment to both, God's words in 2:16-17 are addressed only to the man. The solution to this difficulty may be found below (p. 28). Neither did God directly forbid the people to touch the fruit (2:17). This small difference may be a supplementation such as the narrators offer elsewhere in the second report of the same matter (cf. the introduction §3:20). The element is meant to portray the zealous nature of the young woman. The fact that the serpent and the woman say אלהים and not יהוה is usually explained in terms of the delicacy of the Israelite feeling for language that avoids this name in conversation with non-Yahwists. The same phenomenon also occurs, however, in 4:25, where such discretion is not at issue (cf. on this below, p. 25 and on 4:25-26). The expression "the tree that stands in the midst of the Garden" leads to the conclusion that the narrator knew of only one miracle-tree (contra 2:9). The narrator intentionally avoided placing the name of this tree on the lips of the woman. Budde (48ff.) concludes correctly that he thus assumes that the woman does not yet know the secret power nor, therefore, the name of this tree.

4-5 Thus the serpent brought the woman to the subject it wants to discuss. Now it dares to characterize God's word explicitly as false. God pronounced the prohibition, not in your, but in his own interest! "You will most certainly not die" (with an unusual, pointed placement of the negative, §113v). The sleeper and the blind keep their eyes closed. Whoever opens them, wakes, sees, observes. The eyes of the blind who become sighted open. The first people were as blind. Their eyes were "bound." They saw each other naked and still did not notice their gender. Now, the serpent assures her in secretive tones, they will suddenly perceive what was previously unseen. The expression occurs in a similar meaning of wondrous (pneumatic) experience in 21:19 and 2 Kgs 6:17, where vision suddenly perceives what the usual, weak eye is unable to see. This new knowledge is, according to the context, the knowledge of good and evil. What sort of inquisitive expression may the young woman have made when she heard of such a great secret, and how may it <16> have privately grieved her that this knowledge is forbidden her by God! Very subtly, the serpent does not explicitly invite her to eat. It understands the art of seduction. The facts that the serpent maintains are, in the narrator's opinion, largely accurate. It correctly indicates the secret power of the tree. Knowledge truly makes one like God (3:22). It is also true that the people do not die immediately after eating. At the same time, the serpent hints at an elucidation of these facts: God may be jealous so that he begrudges people the great good. φθονερὸν τὸ θεῖον is an ancient notion well known to us from the Greeks. The narrator does not expound his own assessment of this elucidation (cf. the introduction §3:18). Regarding the construction וְנִפְקְחוּ see §112oo.

6 *The Transgression.* The serpent has now done its work. For the time being, nothing more will be said of it. The quiescence of figures not necessary to the main story line characterizes legend style (cf. the introduction §A3:9; similarly, for example, the woman from Tekoa in 2 Sam 14:21ff.). The subsequent description is wonderful. The woman now inspects the tree more closely and notices, for the first time, that it bears very beautiful fruit. This charms her. For the refined serpent, the essential point about the fruit may be that they possess secret power, but in her childishness, the woman thinks how beautiful they look and how marvelously they must taste. With harmless and childish desire, she commits the most consequential act of her life. Parallels in German fairy tales are the Wolf's seduction of Little Red Riding Hood or the disguised Queen's seduction of Snow White. וְנֶחְמָד הָעֵץ לְהַשְׂכִּיל is usually interpreted "that the tree was desirable in order to become wise." The context suggests that it may be better to translate with LXX, Pesh, etc., "that the tree was delightful to look at." The clause is parallel to "that it was a delight for the eyes" and is probably only a scribal variant. Characteristically, the motivation of the woman to eat requires a long period, of the man only a short period. When woman seduces, man is unable to withstand. It is superbly noted that the two sin together: children like to sin (sneak a snack, for example) together (Holzinger). The woman's seduction of the man is a common motif: The harlot seduces Eabani (KB VI/1:126ff.), Isis Ra (Erman, *Äg. Rel.*, 154-55), Delilah Samson. Further, one thinks of "Potiphar's wife," Epimetheus, Phaidra, Eriphyle, Tannhäuser, etc. Read with MT, Pesh ויאכל Sam, LXX ויאכלו destroys the point that the man ate too (Ball). Sievers (2:245) reads the plural and strikes ותאכל so that the people eat together. But how much finer is the transmitted text!

7 The first result of eating is the one announced by the serpent. The narrator makes this very clear according to the rules of Hebrew style by employing the same expression: "their eyes were opened." And what sort of knowledge do they now acquire? They believed that they would gain the highest knowledge. Now they recognize nothing other than that they are naked! This is the clearest indication of the peculiar manner in which the concept of "knowledge of good and evil" fluctuates. With this example, the myth wants to say that, formerly unknowing children, they are now instantaneously adults. With the same example it previously portrayed their ignorance. This, too, very ingeniously conforms to the Hebrew sense of style. <17> As long as they were ignorant, they knew no shame and wore no clothes. As soon as they became knowledgeable "they recognized" that they were naked. They had not so much as considered this before. Where did they suddenly acquire this knowledge? The old myth answers with greatest clarity that the acquisition of knowledge is the magical effect of the Tree. The expression "their eyes were opened," that also refers elsewhere to wonderful, supernatural experiences (cf. above on v 5), also supports this interpretation. The sin they commit and the knowledge they acquire are not, then, directly, psychologically linked here. Nevertheless, one may say that the narrator already has a very vague notion, although he does not attain clarity regarding it in his presentation, namely that enlightenment, maturity can only be achieved through sin. One thinks of the way the first news of sexual matters reaches adolescent children. The first people now undergo the development from ignorance to knowledge which we all understand—albeit we in the course of years, they, by the power of the Tree, in a moment. It is customary to see a relationship between sin and shame here: "awakening shame" is "the nearest companion of sin," "the mandatory witness of injured innocence" (Dillmann, Holzinger, etc.). The relationship, however, does not appear at all in the narrative; rather, shame here is a perception superior to childhood. The text explicitly says "they recognized that they were naked." This knowledge proceeds not from the sin as such, but from eating of the Tree. The fact that the relationship asserted between guilt and (sexual) shame does not exist in reality is known to anyone who has observed children. Since antiquity theology has employed this passage as a source for the doctrine of sin. To be sure, in the narrator's opinion, a sin was committed here. He describes masterfully how it came to pass, "from the first stirrings of doubt, of desire, to the sinful deed" (Meinhold, 80), so masterfully that the sin portrayed here can be understood as an archetype of sin. But the myth is far removed from an interest in offering a doctrine of "Sin." Such principally theological considerations destroy the naive beauty of the old story. The first outward consequence of the eating is that the people cover themselves. Why fig leaves? Because of the shape of the leaves, perhaps? The fact that the narrator reports only the people covering themselves and nothing else demonstrates his delicate sensibilities. The old material may have been much cruder. This narrator is a quite different man than those who tell of the wiliness of Lots daughters, of Tamar, or even of Rachel!

8-13 *The Discovery.* The narrative does not report that Yahweh knew all, saw all, rather that, strolling in the Garden, he accidentally discovered the transgression. Yahweh's (absolute) omniscience, therefore, is not presupposed. This is consistently true in the oldest narratives (11:5; 18:21). The ancient Hebrew was incapable of conceiving of omniscience (in the absolute sense). Nevertheless, here too, Yahweh is immensely superior to humans in understanding and knowledge. He interrogates the man with the same certainty as a mother interrogating her child. He sees through him completely and soon brings him to confess.

8 *Yahweh Strolls in the Garden.* The old view that Yahweh dwelt in this Garden can still be heard here, if only dimly (cf. on 2:8): a childish view of God. Ra, too, strolled "every day" among humans in the primeval period, "for his heart wished to see what he had created" (Erman, *Ägypt. Rel.*, 154-55). לְרוּחַ הַיּוֹם is usually interpreted as the evening breeze. It does not begin, however, until "a few hours after sundown" <18> (Nowack, *Archäologie* 1:51) and thus can hardly be called the "wind of the day." It is better understood (so Jensen, KB VI/1:573) as the cool sea breeze which arises in the early morning (Nowack, *Archäologie* 1:51) and reaches the mountain heights, e.g., Jerusalem, around 2:00–3:00 (Hann, *Klimatologie* III²:102-103; cf. Cant 2:17; 4:6 according to which the lovers remain together [in the night] "until the day breathes and the shadows flee"; cf. Budde on this passage). The transgression occurred at night; The new day brings remorse. This interpretation seems especially likely because the account concerns sexual sin. In Babylonia an exquisite light breeze blows from the northwest before sunrise (Hann, *Klimatologie* III²:106). The notion that the deity strolls in the Garden in the early morning is originally a myth from this period: when the treetops rustle and sway in the "day wind, the beloved Lord walks through the wood." The assumption seems to be that his palace is in the Garden. An example of a gazebo located in a garden has now been found in Asshur (*Mitteil. der Deutsch. Or. Ges.* 33 [1907]). The people hear the sound (קוֹל) of his steps and hide. Otherwise, we may supply, the man had always presented himself when God came into the Garden; God had then enjoyed his favorite creation. The man, himself, gives the reason for hiding in v 10: "I was afraid." Just as the child who has transgressed its father's commandment flees his look, so the man did not dare to appear in God's sight.

9 When God does not find the man, he calls to him (with a loud voice): "Where are you?" This statement presumes he does not know where the man is.

10 The modern narrator would now describe how the man, every limb shaking, stepped partially out of the trees and remained at some distance from God. The ancient narrator has no sense for such secondary circumstances and pushes on to the essential matter, the words spoken on this occasion. The man's subsequent statement is an exceptionally realistic portrayal of a guilty conscience. The man is portrayed as an erring child, not as a hardened sinner (Meinhold, 83). He heard in the question the accusation that he did not voluntarily present himself and seeks to excuse himself: "Indeed, I heard your footsteps, but I was afraid to come forward." But he cannot bring himself to admit as well to Yahweh the full truth about the cause of his fear. Instead he adds a partial excuse: "I am naked." Naked people do not appear in public. "So I had to hide." With these words, however, the man gave himself away. He knows that he is naked!

11 Yahweh notices this and immediately thinks, "he did not know this before!" Immediately he also guesses the reason: "He has eaten of the Tree." Threateningly he snaps at him, "How do you know this? You haven't transgressed my prohibition, have you?"

12 The man dare not lie—"in this regard, too, like the innocent child" (Meinhold, 83)—but neither dare he confess. So he tacitly admits the transgression, but shifts the guilt to the woman. Shortly thereafter he admits his own transgression. He describes his own sin as quite natural, "Then I had to eat" (Meinhold, 83). Thus he tells God, unintentionally, how the matter developed. He even dares an implicit accusation against God himself: "Why did you give her to me?" The man is at the same time cowardly and defiant. The narrator <19> knows the human heart.

13 Now God ignores the man and turns to the woman who had accompanied him. Notably, the narrator, as is his manner, does not explicitly indicate this precondition. "Confess, what have you done?" A threatening question. The woman, no better than the man, cannot do so in her opinion (Meinhold, 84) and shifts the guilt further to the serpent. The serpent is not further interrogated: as a very wicked being, it can be believably credited with the seduction. Thus, the entire situation lies clearly before God's eyes: the man ate the fruit; the woman gate it to him; the serpent seduced her to do so. The Hebrew admires the wisdom of Yahweh who discovered the whole complicated affair with a few questions. He is unaware of his limited view of God's knowledge. The common folk enjoy such clever stories of perceptive examining magistrates (cf. the widely told story of Solomon's judgment, Gressmann, *Deutsche Rundschau* 33:175ff.; the history of Susannah and Daniel; similar stories also appear in *1,001 Nights*, and, especially, in India; cf. v.d. Leyen 94:20, 22; 96:8ff.).

14-21 *The Curses.* They are the narrator's main concern. The event is so important because it had consequences that last until today. Yahweh pronounced a curse that continues in effect until the present. Concerning the curses in this account, cf. the introduction §2:7a and the commentary on 9:25ff. where it is demonstrated that such curses are to be understood as responses to specific questions and that they form the objective and climax of the whole narrative. The curses have strict rhythmical form, as is appropriate for such wonder-working words (cf. the introduction §3:2). Concerning the elegance of the structure, cf. the introduction §3:8. The sin proceeds from the serpent, via the woman, to the man. The interrogation proceeds from the man, via the woman, to the serpent. The curse begins with the chief perpetrator, the serpent, and goes then to the woman and the man. Very beautifully the curse on the man occupies final position. This curse is the main point for the narrator, who narrates for men. The sequence of the curses involves an intensification that concludes disturbingly with the most frightening words.

14-15 *The Curse on the Serpent.* The meter, with which we begin best, in v 14 where the pathetic speech of the curses begins, is a heptameter and a hexameter. V 15a is difficult, probably to be read with Sievers (2:10-11) as a heptameter, V 15b as a pair of trimeters. The serpent does not walk on feet like other animals. It moves eerily on its belly. Its diet is equally unusual. It eats (in the opinion of the Hebrews) dust. What is the origin of this wretched lifestyle which distinguishes it from all cattle and wildlife? Our narrative answers this question, "Because it seduced the people, Yahweh cursed it." Naturally, the conclusion would be that formerly the serpent moved in another fashion and consumed another diet. Yet the narrator has hardly considered this implication. The myth considers the serpent's current state and finds in it a divine curse. It considers no further. The saying suggests <20> quite distinctly that, for the narrator, the serpent is an animal and nothing more. "The devil does not crawl on his belly and eat dust" (Reuss).

15 Extraordinarily and dreadfully, too, this animal is engaged in an eternal struggle with the woman and her descendants. Humans and serpents are in mortal combat. Each fights in his own way: the serpent strikes at the human's heels when it has opportunity; but the human, given the opportunity, smashes the serpent's head. (The opposites are noteworthy: heel, head. Hebrew poetry loves such diction.) Neither wishes to wound, but to kill. What is the origin of this bitter mortal combat? It is the dreadful effect of Yahweh's curse. One can fill in the rest as follows: because serpent and woman once allied against God, Yahweh has condemned them to eternal enmity. The diction in v 15b offers difficulties: שׁוף occurs elsewhere only in Psa 139:11, which is corrupt, and Job 9:17, where it probably means "to snap up, seize." A play on words seems to occur in our text. The simplest explanation is that the original *scriptio defectiva* was incorrectly resolved with ו instead of א. שׁאף has the necessary dual meanings (1) to snap, (2) to trample (so Gressmann in a personal correspondence). At any rate, the intention of the text is that human and serpent cannot accuse one another: what one does, so does the other. Nothing is said of an end to the struggle, of a victory: they will hate and kill each other as along as there are people and serpents. The serpent is very clearly an animal here, too. The "seed of the נָחָשׁ" are serpents just as the "seed of the woman" are humans. The myth belongs to the category of myths and fairy tales very common in antiquity and among primitive peoples which tell how certain animals came by their unusual characteristics, "why the flounder has its oblique mouth, the donkey its long ears, and the bear its stumpy tail" (cf. v.d. Leyen CXV:16, with bibliography). Characteristically, the Paradise narrative associates a motif as childish as the movement of the serpent on its belly with motifs as serious as those which deal with humans. It is also possible, of course, that a faded myth underlies this battle between human and serpent. A distant comparison may be made to the Greek myth in which a crab came to aid Hydra in a struggle with Hercules (*Apollodor bibliotheca* II/5:2:4, based on archaic depictions; cf. Furtwängler in Roscher's *Lex.* 1:2 col. 2198). The Christian, especially the Lutheran, church has interpreted this passage as a "Proto-evangelium" referring to the (dying) Christ's victory over the devil or, generally, to the victory of the human race over devil and sin. The allegorical interpretation continues to be influential even today.

16 *The Curse of the Woman.* The strophes are a heptameter and a quadraemter (cf. Sievers 2:210). Read וְאֶל־הָאִשָּׁה with Sam, LXX, Pesh (Vulg); cf. ולארם in v 17 (Ball, Kittel, Sievers 2:245). הֵרֹנֵךְ (Sam הֵרְיוֹנֵךְ) "your pregnancy" is certainly corrupt. Frequent pregnancies were a great blessing for ancient women, not a curse (LXX reads τὸν στεναγμόν σου). Suggested readings include הֲגוֹנֵךְ "your groaning" (Dillmann, Erbt) or יְגוֹנֵךְ "pain, suffering." One may compare Psa 13:3 where עַצְּבוֹת (according to the Pesh., cf. Cheyne, Psalms, 373) and יָגוֹן stand as parallels. The narrator thinks of the many dangers and pains that plague the woman in her sexual life, especially those associated with pregnancy and birth—labor pains are proverbial in ancient Israel—and seeks the reason for all this distress. At the same time, he wonders about the contradictory behavior of the woman who longs for the man who, after all (וְהוּא contrast) enslaves her. If, in the most ancient Israelite viewpoint, the wife was considered the husband's purchased property, <21> the woman desires her own slavery! The saying about the woman's desire seems to assume that the woman has a stronger libido than the man. Relatedly, she is considered a seductress. For תְּשׁוּקָתוֹ LXX has ἡ ἀποστροφή σου = תְּשׁוּבָתֵךְ as does apparently Targ-Onk (cf. 2 Sam 17:3 LXX; Nestle, "Marginalien 6," ZAW 24:312ff.). LXX also has ἡ ἐπιστροφὴ αὐτοῦ for Hebr תְּשׁוּקָתוֹ in Cant 7:11 (cf. also Targ.); LXX of Gen 4:7 has ἡ ἀποστροφὴ αὐτοῦ. The root שׁוק is not attested elsewhere in Hebr in the meaning "to long for, desire." Nevertheless, it seems hazardous to strike from the Hebrew lexicon the word that occurs twice in the transmitted text with the apparent meaning "carnal desire" (cf. also שׁקק = "to yearn"). What is the origin of the woman's misery? It is God's curse. This curse on the woman's sexual life—one may well conjecture this as the myth's intention—corresponds to her sin: she recognized her gender through a sin. Sexual intercourse will be the inevitable consequence and the woman will become pregnant. Thus her sexual life and childbirth are cursed. Just as one could not ask the myth regarding the former form of the serpent (v 14), so one may not burden the myth here with the question of the nature of the former relationship between man and woman: It has not thought so far. Nor is it correct that birth without the Fall is imagined as painless (Meinhold, 88); rather, without the enjoyment of the fruit, there would have been neither conception nor birth.

17-19 The curse on the man, as on the chief character, is the most extensive. Many parallels occur: בְעִצָּבוֹן תֹּאכֲלֶנָּה 17 ‖ בְזֵעַת אַפֶּיךָ תֹּאכַל 19aα; 19aβγ ‖ 19b. Holzinger removes v 18b as a gloss, thereby, however, disturbing the meter. It seems easier to regard vv 19aα and 19b as insertions from another source. A prose introduction precedes the poetry (as in v 14 and very often in the prophets). The poetry itself is best analyzed with Sievers 2:10-11. Vv 17b and 18 are heptameter, v 19 three quadrameters. Read וְלְאָדָם in v 17 and perhaps לְאָדָם in v 21 (yet cf. the commentary on 4:25). In order to impact the man, God curses the field from which the man is to support himself henceforth: now he will eat bread, no longer the splendid fruits of the Garden of God, indeed bread from the sweat of his brow! It is also possible to curse objects (not just persons): money that has been stolen (Judg 17:2), the fruit basket and the kneading trough that they remain empty, the herd that they miscarry (Deut 28:17ff., etc.); here the field, that it produce thorn and thistle (Jer 23:10; Isa 24:6f.). Work, itself, does not constitute the curse. Man is created for work (2:15). But the fact that his work is so bitter, that the field is so obstinate, seems to the Hebrew, whose land does not bear of itself, to be a heavy burden. Yahweh's curse produced this. The myth equates man and farmer here. The man takes his nourishment from the "plants of the field." The expression עִצָּבוֹן in v 17 is intentionally the same as in v 16. Regarding אָכַל אֶת־הָאֲדָמָה, cf. Isa 1:7; 36:16; Gen 31:15; like Ass. *akâlu* "to have usufruct of" (cf. Winckler, *Zur Genesis*, 390). It ends, however, with death. The myth asks here how death came into the world. Many pagan creation accounts maintain that death was not original, but came upon people through transgression of a commandment, through inattentivenss or misunderstanding of some <22> kind (H. F. Fielberg in a private correspondence). The man cannot complain about death, however: *reddenda est terra terrae* (Cicero), "everything that is from the earth, returns to the earth" (Sir 40:11). Thus death lies in his nature. It is the common view of Hebrew antiquity that mortality is an essential characteristic of human nature. Only very late Judaism under the influence of newer views of foreign origin inclined toward the belief that God destined humans to eternal life. It is not permissible to import this later belief into the old myth. Neither may one even ask at this point whether humans would have been immortal apart from the transgression. "You must return to the dust." This statement assumes the practice of burial, certainly very ancient in Hebrew culture. Babylonian also knows the idiom *târu ana ṭîṭi* = "to return to the earth" = "to die" (e.g. Sintflut, 134). The reference to the man as "dust" humiliated him to the utmost—he who had believed that he could become like God. The myth expresses an extremely pessimistic view of human life and specifically of farming. It opposes the opinion, surely common in its time, that farming was a gift of the deity, with the contention that the field is cursed—a note of pessimism from primitive times. Such gloomy viewpoints resound in a deeply moving manner in many portions of Job (7:14 etc.). The curse is very important lest one give in to the illusion that ancient Israel lived continually in the joy of the harvest thanksgiving festival.

20-24 The conclusion of the narrative is kept to the extreme minimum in accordance with the old, beautiful legend style. The sayings are not uniform. V **20**, where Ḥawwa is explained as a supreme honorific title for the woman, does not fit the context, especially since the interpretation of the name seems to presuppose that Eve has already born children. No name at all is expected here. "The man" has no proper name. J^e and J^j consistently (with the exception of 4:1; see the commentary) refer to the first woman as "the woman" (3:2ff.; cf. 2:23) or "his woman" (2:25; 3:8, 21; 4:25). The poem stems from another context and another source. At any rate, the name חַוָּה (Εὔα, *Eve*) is an old tradition, although not of Hebrew origins. Nöldeke (ZDMG 42:487), Gressmann (ARW 10:359-60) and others call attention to Aram. חֶוְיָא, "serpent." The belief that the serpent appears at the beginning of the human race is widespread. Among the Abyssinans, for example, the first king was named Arwê, "the serpent" ZDMG 1:9; 7:341). The name Hawwa may be identical with the Phoenician goddess Ḥwt whom Lidzbarski (*Ephemeris für semit. Epigraphik* 1:30) considers a serpentine chthonic goddess. The goddess of the underworld is regarded the first mother because people also originally stem from the underworld to which they return (cf. A. Dieterich, ARW 8:12, 20ff.). The Hebrew associates חַוָּה, naively enough, with the word חַיָּה "living being."

21 This poem, too, does not fit well here and probably belongs to the variant, traces of which have already been evident. The comment, very anthropomorphic, is surely very ancient. Ancient perspectives derive the arts and inventions from the gods (Benzinger[2], 160). The poem contains an old theory concerning the earliest human clothing. We hear the same from the Phoenicians (cf. *Eusebs Exzerpte aus Philo Byblius Fragm. hist. graec.*, ed. C. Müller, III.566; traditions of other peoples in Diodorus 1.43; 2.38.2; Lucian amores, 34, etc.). The fact that God clothes the people is understood here, in context, as a final meagre alm, as a preparation for suffering. Regarding לָאָדָם see the commentary on v 17. <23>

22-24 The expulsion is recounted twice. וַיְשַׁלְּחֵהוּ (v 23) ‖ וַיְגָרֶשׁ אֶת־הָאָדָם (v 24a). According to v 22 God decides to expel the man so that he may not access the Tree of Life. This decision is carried out in v 24a,bγ. These clauses, which belong together in terms of content, contribute the new motif of the Tree of Life to the preceding account. According to v 17, in contrast, God had already decided to expel the man to the field and executes this decision in v 23 so that the man may farm the field and taste the curse. According to this analysis, v 23 concludes the foregoing major source. Vv 22 and 24a,bγ, in contrast, are elements of a variant. For other reasons, too, v 22 does not suit the context of the chapter: after the curse only its fulfillment can come. The situation of God speaking to someone, and, especially, of God to a degree fearing the humans is very strange (cf. Budde, 57-58, 238ff.).

V **23** links to 2:5 and harmoniously rounds off the whole. The man cannot murmur about field work. He stems, after all, from the field.

22, 24 We are not told to whom the divine statement "like one of us" is spoken—originally certainly the heavenly "council" (cf. comments on 1:26). This ancient echo of polytheism is transmitted in an attenuated form. "The man has become like one of us" (אַחַד, st. cstr., see §130a) is not ironic, but a simple acknowledgment of the situation. Anyway, Yahweh does not say that the man has become like him personally. He is not like this one, particular God, but only like the essence of divine nature which characterizes Yahweh, too (similarly 1:26). The man has acquired a characteristic of divine being against God's will. The fear is, then, that he may also attain the second, immortality (וָחַי, §76i). Previously, when the man was still harmless and unwise, this was no concern. Now that he has become knowledgeable, it is an imminent concern. Then the man would be totally god-like and God does not want that. The man should not be equal to God (see further on this below, 32-33). Therefore God intervenes now, before it is too late, expels the man, and establishes a divine watch before Paradise to the East. Why to the East? Apparently because the humans are expelled to the East and later dwell in the East. According to this source, then, Paradise lies far to the West. Gen 4:16, according to which Cain dwelt east of Eden, agrees with this viewpoint. According to Jensen (KB 6/1:507, 576; *Gigamesch Epos* 1:33-34n.3), the land of the gods, where the Babylonian flood hero dwelt, also lay in the far West. LXX's καὶ κατῴκισεν αὐτὸν ἀπέναντι τοῦ παραδείσου τῆς τρυφῆς καὶ ἔταξεν τὰ χερουβιν = וישכן אתו מקדם לגן עדן וישם את הכרבים (Ball). But there is no reason to reject the Hebr text: שָׁכַן and הַשְׁכִּין are also used of the lying and resting of animals, and the cherubim are divine animals (a final reminiscence of the primitive worship of animals). "The cherubim" (cf. M. Dibelius, *Lade Jahves*, 72ff.) are introduced as well-known figures. These beings serve here as guardians of the divine, just as do the cherubim on the Ark in P (Exod 37:5-9) and those in Solomon's Temple (1 Kgs 6:23-27) who "shelter" the sanctuary with outspread wings. This function serves as the background of the title כְּרוּב הַסּוֹכֵךְ, the "sheltering cherub" (Ezek 28:16). Because of this significance of the cherubim as guardians, they are also employed elsewhere in the sanctuary, on the wings of the door (1 Kgs 6:32), on the walls (6:29), in the Tabernacle on the curtain (Exod 26:31), etc. According to another tradition, Yahweh sits (יֹשֵׁב הַכְּרֻבִים) or rides (Psa 18:11) on the cherubim. The <24> wondrous throne-chariot of Yahweh in Ezekiel 1 is a mythological representation of heaven and the four cherubim (Ezek 10:2) that bear the throne are the four great heaven bearers (cf. Gunkel, *Zum religionsgeschichtlichen Verständnis des N.T.*, 46). In form, the cherubim are chimeras with wings (of an eagle); according to Ezek 41:8, with two faces (of a man and a lion); according to Ezek 1:10, with four faces each (man, lion, bull, eagle). The description in Rev 4, according to which the four animals are each a (wondrous) lion/bull/man/eagle, is older than the complicated description of Ezek 1. The conceptions of such beings in Israel stem from foreign mythology. Divine beings as guardians of the holy occur among many peoples: Sphinxes lie before Egyptian temples. Images of chimeras appear on the entrance and terraces of Babylonian temples and palaces or on Babylonian and Persian representations on both sides of the holy tree (cf. Zimmern, KAT[3], 530). The dragon Ladon guards the golden apples of the Hesperides (Roscher, *Lex.* II/2, col 1786). Yahweh, himself, as a wall of fire, will guard the Jerusalem of the future (Zech 2:9). Dragons guard hordes of gold (cf. Dillmann, 84, with bibliography). At present nothing more can be said with precision concerning the origin and history of the cherubim, although it seems very likely that this particular concept found in Ezekiel is of Babylonian origins (cf. Zimmern, KAT[3], 632-33, and in Gesenius[14], s.v. כְּרוּב, according to which the bull colossus in Assyrian inscriptions from Susa are called *karibâti*, "the blessing ones"). The flame of the turning sword, depicted by painters in the cherub's hand, is really an independent being, a kind of demon. It is animate: in Hebrew idiom, it has a "spirit" (cf. the wheels of God's chariot in Ezek 1:21, Vulcan's hammer, or modern expressions such as "its sails are animate" or "And never erring in the shaking hand, the sword directs itself as though it were a living spirit" [Schiller]). The prophets also speak of Yahweh's sword as an independent demonic being (Isa 27:1; 34:5; Jer 47:6; Ezek 21:8ff.; cf. Gressmann, 79-80). Such a sword is all the more frightening since one cannot defend oneself against it. We hear of a wall of fire as protection for the sanctuary in Zech 2:9. Such magical guardians play a great role in legends and fairy tales (cf. in the Artus sages, the iron thresher that bars the entrance and permits not even the fastest bird entry [v.d. Leyen, 93:258n.3, with literature]; in the Skirnismal 8, Freyr's sword that swings on its own [Gering, Edda, 53], or the magic flame that surrounds Brunhilda). This concept of a sword of flame is mythological in nature and, like the Cherub, is of foreign origin. Thureau-Dangin (*Revue d'histoire et de litt. religieuses* 1:146ff.) associates the sword of flame with the bronze "lightning" Tiglath-Pileser I erected at the site of a destroyed city (cf. the inscription KB I/36-37, ll. 15ff.). Notably, two guards stand before Paradise. Furthermore, the expression וַיַּשְׁכֵּן applies only to the Cherubim, not to the sword of flame. This doublet can be explained by the two recensions of the myth. The purpose of the divine guard is to keep the people away from the Tree of Life. The myth seeks, then, to explain why people may never to return to Paradise. Only latest apocalyptic Judaism believes that individual righteous people may already enter Paradise and that it will one day be the heritage of all the pious. Christian theology has often read this hope into the old myth.

General Remarks concerning the Paradise Narrative

1. *Literary Criticism.* Budde (46ff.; cf. the brief review in Holzinger, *Hexateuch*, 156ff.) first pointed to two strands in the Paradise narrative. His results will be taken up and expanded here. The clearest traces of the existence of multiple sources are the following: The expulsion is recounted twice (3:23 ‖ 3:22, 24a). Two guards stand before Paradise (3:24bα ‖ bβ). The <25> clothing with animal skins (3:21) and the naming of Eve (3:20) do not fit the context. The curse on the people displays repetitions. The planting of Paradise and the placement of the man in it are recounted twice (2:8a ‖ 9; 2:8b ‖ 15). According to 2:8 Paradise lies in the far East, according to 3:24 in the far West, according to 2:10-14 in the North. According to 3:3 only one tree stands in the midst of the Garden, the Tree of Knowledge, whose name and power are still unknown to the people; In contrast, 3:22, 24bγ knows of two of God's Trees in the Garden. The syntax of 2:9, which also speaks of two trees in the midst of the Garden, suggests redaction. The double name יהוה אלהים can be explained, as suggested below (cf. commentary on 4:25, 26), in terms of two sources, one of which employed יהוה from the very beginning while the other employed אלהים for the oldest period and יהוה beginning with Enosh (cf. Budde, 232ff.). Both sources, referred to below as Jʲ and Jᵉ, are components of J.

Despite such signs of the compilation of sources, the foundation of the narrative bears the character of literary unity. Specifically, the seduction account in 3:1ff. is extremely self-contained. The narrative of chap. 2, although less coherent, is still unified, to a great degree, by the motifs of God, man, and field. A series of allusions unite the two chapters (3:1a alludes to 2:19; 3:1b-5, 1, 17 to 2:16-17; 3:7 to 2:25; 3:12 to 2:21ff.; 3:19, 23 to 2:7). It can be concluded, then, that the redactor essentially followed one source and that he utilized only fragments of the other. Judging from 3:1b-5 the main source is Jᵉ since this unit employs אלהים and is an integral component of the entire narrative. The variants and parallels that do not fit into the major strand of the narrative belong, then, to the secondary source. This secondary character is especially clear with respect to 3:21, 22, 24a. The main source Jᵉ characteristically knows of only one tree (3:1b-5) and (in accordance with the style of the beautiful old narratives, cf. the introduction §3:15) varies its treatment of the theme of the relationship of the man to the אֲדָמָה (3:17, 19aβγ, 23). The secondary source characteristically knows of two trees (3:22, 24bγ). Accordingly, passages in question may be divided as follows. Of the two variants 2:8 ‖ 2:9, 15, 2:8 belongs to the secondary, 2:9, 15 to the primary source (אֲדָמָה, 9a; cf. 3:6); accordingly, וְעֵץ הַחַיִּים is an addition from the harmonizing redactor. The original text of J^e probably read וּבְתוֹךְ הַגָּן עֵץ הַדַּעַת טוֹב וָרָע. All of chap. 3 belongs to the primary source. The secondary source may have included v 19aα (‖ "with toil you will eat of it," v 17, which belongs to J^e because of the allusion in 5:29—cf. the commentary on the passage), v 19b (‖ 19aβγ אֲדָמָה J^e), v 21 (the verse does not fit into the context), and v 22 (two Trees). Of the concluding poems, v 23, the continuation of vv 17, 18, 19aβγ, belongs to J^e. Because of the doubled guard, v 24 contains elements from both sources. Vv 24a (‖ 23) and bγ (Tree of Life) belong to J^j. Since 2:8, according to which Paradise lies in the East, was attributed to J^j above, 3:24bα, according to which it should be sought in the West, should be attributed to J^e, and bβ to J^j. Another characteristic of the secondary source J^j, according to this analysis, is its ignorance of the close relationship of the אָדָם to the אֲדָמָה (J^e). In places where J^e would use אֲדָמָה, it employs עָפָר (3:19b). אֲדָמָה does not appear in texts where J^e has it, in 2:8 in contrast to 2:9, in 3:24a in contrast to 3:23. The passage concerning the four streams (2:10-14), which locates Paradise in the North, belongs to neither of the two sources and is an ancient addition. The same is true of the naming of Eve in 3:20 (cf. commentary). The explicit naming of the tree in 2:17 stems from the redactor. עָפָר is an insertion in 2:7 under the influence of J^j. The reader should not fail to note the caution with which the present writer offers these conjectures.

2. *Characteristics of the Literary Style of the Narrative in Both Sources.* We have only a few fragments of J^j. Judging from the preserved elements, its account must have been rather similar to that of J^e. Here, too, the first people are in the wonderful Paradise that God himself planted (2:8). There, contrary to God's will, they acquired knowledge and became like God. Then, however, they were cursed to bitter field work and death (3:19aα,β) and ex<26>pelled (3:22, 24a). A divine guardian was place before Paradise (3:24bβγ). J^j also recounted the fact that the man received clothing after the expulsion (3:21; in a broad sense ‖ 3:7). Many traces show that the J^j account has a more mythological tone than J^e: "Yahweh planted" (2:8) in contrast to "He caused to sprout" (2:9); Yahweh clothes the people himself (3:21); "one of us" (3:22); the introduction of the mythological concept of the Tree of Life (3:22); the sword of fire demon (3:24) seems more mythological than the cherubim. Accordingly, we may conjecture that this recension predates that of J^e, but that the redactor employed only fragments of it precisely because of this mythological demeanor. Budde (244ff.) argues somewhat differently, not for two distinct narratives, but for two editions of the same narrative that were subsequently combined. Erbt and Sievers attempt other source analyses with the help of metrical analysis. Sievers assigns to J^a (heptameter text) 2:6, 9, 15-25; 3:1-7a, 8-18, 21, 24, to J^d (hexameter with a shortened line) 2:10; 3:7b, 22, 23, to J^e (octameter) 2:4b, 5; 3:19. He terms 2:11-14; 3:20 "remnants in J." But this "metrical" analysis divides thematic relationships. For example, לַעֲבֹד אֶת־הָאֲדָמָה in 2:5 is assigned to a different source than in 3:23. כִּי מִמֶּנָּה לֻקָּחְתָּ הָאֲדָמָה (3:19) is assigned to a different source than מִשָּׁם הָאֲדָמָה אֲשֶׁר לֻקָּה (3:23). The creation of the man is assigned to another source

than that of the animals and the woman. He removes the Tree of Life, which also charac-terizes a source according to Sievers, from 3:24, etc. The uncertainty of these metrical readings, however, can be recognized in the fact that Sievers himself (1:382ff.) has read 2:9ff. quite differently, and in that Erbt analyzes the meter of chap. 3 quite differently than Sievers.

The J^e recension we have reconstructed is, as far as we can see, completely preserved. The narrative is coherent and well-rounded. The conclusion (3:23) points back to the beginning (2:7). From an aesthetic viewpoint, the narrative, especially chap. 3, belongs to the most beautiful in Genesis (cf. the congenial explication in Wellhausen, *Prole-gomena*[6], 302ff., although contestable in details [cf. above on 2:25]; from an earlier period, cf. especially Herder's explication in the *Ältesten Urkunde des Menschenge-schlechts*, who revealed the true poetic understanding of this narrative). The breath of the mythical has not entirely dissipated, but everything foreign, barbarian is expelled. Chap. 3 is admirable for its (for the time) highly complicated psychological portrayal, for the art of rendering the most intimate states of mind in a straightforward statement or a simple action, for the beautiful consistency of the events, and for its ingenious arrangement (cf. the introduction §3:8). Also noteworthy is the tender modesty with which the sexual motif is treated as well as the great seriousness with which the narrator speaks of God and sin. In sum, it constitutes (for its time) the deepest thought concerning humanity and God, and in an extremely attractive form. It is wonderful mythological material refined to "noble simplicity." Gen 3 is the pearl of Genesis.

The narrator who gave us this recension must, accordingly, have been an especially gifted master. Nevertheless, one would err to assume that the narrative is essentially "a free creation of the narrator" (Nöldeke, *Alttestamentliche Literatur*, 9). Genesis does not consist of poetic creations of individuals but of traditions shaped by many generations until, finally, the last master has come. The applicability of this general analysis to this narrative is demonstrated by the comparison with J^j which agrees with J^e on the major points.

The J^e account did not have a uniform origin despite its present unity. It is—this observation seems to us more important than all source criticism—woven from two tradi-tions: (1) an account of Paradise and the expulsion and (2) a sort of creation narrative. The creation narrative and the introduction of the Paradise account are linked in 2:4ff. The Paradise narrative incorporates the description of Paradise into which the <27> people were placed, then God's prohibition against eating of the Tree, and finally the description of their innocence. All of this introduces the subsequent account in which they transgress the prohibition, loose their innocence, and then are expelled from Paradise. Everything else, however, constitutes an organic whole: the origin of the beings that belong to the field. The two bodies of material originally had nothing to do with one another. There are actually two quite distinct accounts, neither of which requires the other as prelude or con-tinuation. The two accounts were joined together because both deal with the primeval period. A thorough division of the sources and establishment of the wording is no longer possible, although a general separation of the bodies of material is. The Paradise account surely included vv 9, 15-17, 25; the Creation account (set in square brackets in Gunkel's translation), vv 7, 18-24, the formation of the man, the animals, and the woman. It is more difficult to separate sources in the introduction, whose sluggish style and inner contradictions (see above, pp. 4, 5-6) point to the combination of diverse material. One may best attribute vv 4b and 6 (אַך) to the Paradise account. V 6 may have once stood after v 9 (cf. Meinhold, 72). In contrast, v 5 obviously introduces a Creation account. Accordingly, the beginning of the Creation account must have spoken first of the dry original state, then of the rain, and finally of the man. Certain difficulties arose through the combination of the two bodies of material. While God actually formed the woman for sexual union with the man (vv 21-24), sexual union came to humanity, according to the Paradise account, only with "Knowledge." According to 2:5, the man is suited by nature for cultivating the field, while, according to the Paradise account, he is only cast out to the field by the curse (3:23). In the account of the origins, we miss the report of the origination of the rain, the bushes, and the herbs announced in 2:5. This infromation must have once been reported, but has fallen out in favor of the אַך and the Paradise Trees. Furthermore, the combination of the two bodies of material gave rise to the appearance that animals existed only in Paradise, for the account surely does not intend to suggest that they were expelled with the people. The two accounts also differ markedly in their views of the woman: One celebrates the finally successful creation, the other recounts that the woman's first act robbed the man of all joy. According to the Paradise account, the prohibition against eating from the tree was originally given to the man and the woman, as is still preserved in 3:1-3. This narrative will have spoken consistently of the human pair. When combined with the Creation account, however, the man alone was inserted everywhere prior to 2:22. The two bodies of material are also distinct in their structure: While the Paradise-Expulsion account is a very tightly coherent whole, the myth of the origins falls into individual, rather loosely connected segments.

3. *The Interpretation of the Myth.* This section will offer only an addendum concerning the narrative of the origins. Bibliography: especially Wellhausen, *Prolegomena*[6], 297ff.; see also Frankenberg, CGA (1901): 678; Schwally, ARW 9:160; concerning the anthropomorphisms, Haller, 50-51.

The unique character of the narrative can best be recognized through comparison with Gen 1. Gen 1 depicts the creative God who stands apart from the world and effects it through his almighty word. Gen 2-3 offers a much more immature concept according to which Yahweh "forms" his creatures with his own hand. Consequently, this narrative is full of naive anthropomorphizations of God. In Gen 1, the level of contemplation rises to the idea that once heaven and earth did not exist, that God created everything (as already the introduction to the Paradise narrative, 2:4b); Gen 2-3 represents, on the other hand, an ancient way of thinking satisfied to recount how rain, people, and animals came into being. But, with this account, it has also already reached its limit. The notion that the earth and even heaven were also created once, is still quite remote. Accordingly, Gen 2 does not speak of a "creation of the world" <28> in the proper sense. The horizon of the myth reaches no farther than that of the farmer. Its scope encompasses the field on which the plants sprout after the rain, in addition to the animals of the field and the birds, the farmer, himself, and his wife. He reflects on the origins of this life on the field. At the midpoint of his interest stands, naturally, himself and his wife. All other beings interest him only to the extent that they affect him. This interest explains the tone of childish astonishment at the wonders of the world, pensive meditations in a wonderfully graphic form. "It is no accident that natural science has not made any connection with Gen 2 and 3. But poetry in all times has held to the story of Paradise" (Wellhausen).

It remains only to interpret the Paradise narrative, in the first instance according to the J^e recension. One understands an "etiological" myth when one demonstrates (I) what it seeks to explain and (II) how the myth explains it (cf. the introduction § 2:3).

I. We discover the question the myth seeks to answer in its final words. It seeks to explain that which endures in the present as a result of the events reported. The fact that our myth concludes with a "therefore" as in 2:24 must mean: therefore man now has the knowledge of Good and Evil, to be sure, but he no longer dwells in Paradise and has much suffering and toil—the woman in the perils of her sex, the man on his cursed field. The myth, then, explains the weal and woe of humanity: its particular distinction, judgment, and its sorrowful fate, the toil of farming and the pains of birth.

(a) How does the myth view the knowledge of Good and Evil? We have already seen (cf. pp. 14-15) that the word can refer to higher or lower knowledge. The myth seems to take it in a medium sense. It recognizes that this knowledge is an advantage: The adult is superior to the child. Indeed, humans are like God in this respect. One may add, as antiquity understood it, that only humans have this knowledge. The animals do not. Now the modern would be likely to celebrate ardently the majesty of the human being. Judgment, the light of heaven, makes humans minor gods in the world. The myth speaks in an entirely different tone. It describes, with one example, what knowledge signifies. Formerly, humans went about naked like innocent children. Now they know better. To be sure—so we may interpret the thought of narrative—the adult has many advantages over the child, but he does not experience this superiority with enthusiasm. One does not speak of adolescence with fervor. One could object that, on the other hand, judgment makes one like God. Granted, but not like Yahweh. אלהים refers to many different powers; in ancient Israel even the ghosts of the dead are אלהים. The continuation of the narrative makes it clear enough that the myth does not mean that the humans have become totally like Yahweh: Yahweh remains superior. The man stands as a poor sinner before the penetrating gaze of God who can curse and expel him if he wills. Jewish interpreters have it quite right when they paraphrase 3:5 in their fashion: You will be "like angels." Consequently, we would do better to speak with the more precise expressions of our language concerning similarity to God and not God-likeness. Accordingly, it may be said, as the narrator of the seductive words of the serpent to the woman may have understood, that these words themselves are nevertheless true. But the serpent does not add that humans, become like God in this one respect, remain inferior to God in all others and that, if they err, they must fear God's harsh punishment. Thus, the serpent "deceives" the woman disgracefully by telling the truth, but, admittedly, only the partial truth. One must admit that this kind of deceit is narrated very ingeniously. <29>

(b) Furthermore, the myth considers the fate of the human race. It portrays the man as a farmer—it knows no other profession—the woman as childbearer. Now the myth considers the heavy toil of both: the toil of the childbearer, the toil of the farmer. Antiquity, too, feels this toil with deep pain. It describes the fate of humanity in the disturbing words of the curse: it is distress and suffering and finally death. This destiny is without hope: as long as there are people, women will bear in pain and men will eat from the sweat of their brow.

(c) The myth combined both observations. It has thus summarized human life and simultaneously offered the observation that these two aspects of human life belong together. In order to recognize its thought, we may pursue the example of the life of children which is clearly in view in one passage (our science, too, compares primitive peoples with children). How different is the life of children from that of adults! They do not yet know life's peril. One can see it. They play and laugh in the street. But, admittedly, neither do they yet have judgment. One can see it. They run around naked. When a person matures and becomes wise and puts on clothes, however, then the youth is sent to the field and the maiden to her room. Laughter is over. How does this come about? How can one explain the fact that judgment and life's perils are associated with one another?

II. The Myth answers this question. (a) It begins with its narrative of the primeval period when people did not yet know the toil of the present. This beginning stands in stark contrast to the end of the narrative (a frequently occurring narrative type, cf. the Sodom, Flood, and Joseph legends). Individuals and peoples dream a dream of happiness and peace and undisturbed enjoyment. The tradition transfers this image of longing into the primeval period or to the end of things. Or it imagines the wonderland far at the ends of the earth (e.g., the Garden of the Hesperides in the far West, the islands of the blessed, Elysium) or in Hades (a concept that often fuses with the far West) or high up in heaven (the islands of the blessed in the Egyptian conception; cf. Erman, *Äg. Rel.*, 93, Walhalla). On the Greek and Iranian concepts of the land of the gods, see Usener, *Sintfluthsagen*, 197ff.; on the "golden age," see Graf, "Ad Aureae Aetatis Fabulam Symbola, Leipziger Studien auf d. Geb. d. class. Phil." 8 (diss., Leipzig, 1885), 1ff. and Nikel, *Genesis und Keilschriftforschung*, 141ff. These ideal images have undergone manifold developments in the course of time. Every era reveals its chief characteristic in the manner in which it portrays the "golden age." How is Paradise described here? As a wonderful grove of majestic trees with delicious fruits. It had much, much water. There was good living and light work. The Hebrew farmer tells of this Paradise with joy and enthusiasm, just as the Arab is delighted to come to the richly watered, green plain of Damascus. Paradise was, however, the Garden of God himself—as the narrative hints. This element echoes the still-preserved ancient Oriental tradition of Paradise. The Israelite narrator himself, however, does not emphasize the fact that the man lived in those days in communion with God. Rather, the main point for him is that the man was as fortunate in those days "as the blessed gods" (cf. also the commentary on 5:29). On the other hand, however, the people were still children then, immature, "stupid." They went about naked and were unashamed. Thus one looks back on Paradise. The ancient thinks longingly of that beautiful time now irretrievably lost. At the same time, he feels superior to the men of those days.

(b) The myth recounts further how the people attained knowledge, but were expelled from the Garden and sentenced to a toilsome life. The modern may be inclined here <30> to introduce the historical perspective that people, having attained civilization, perceive the value of what they sacrificed in exchange (Wellhausen, *Prolegomena*[6], 301-302). But "knowledge" is not civilization (see above, pp. 14-15), is it? And clothing (the only thing in the myth, at any rate, one could call "civilization") is not something that makes people unhappy, is it? Or the modern would, somewhat more generally, portray it as though judgment itself were not a good, but a curse, as though restlessness, dissatisfaction, constant concern are givens along with better understanding. "The Tree of Knowledge is not the

Tree of Life" (Byron). "I am indeed more intelligent than all the dandies, doctors, tutors, scribes, and priests; I have also been robbed of all joy because of it" (Goethe). Ancient thought also strives, ultimately, for an inner connection between the two aspects of human life. Unaccustomed, however, to reflecting on psychological matters and viewing things, in ancient fashion, not subjectively, but objectively, it links the two only externally: the awakening to maturity takes place through a sin against Yahweh. The man stole it, against the will of Yahweh, who expressly prohibited him the tree. God, however, punished this crime by calling down on the people his curse of suffering. If one seeks an analogy true to the spirit of the myth that may have been in the narrator's mind, one thinks of the attitude in which adolescent children hear of sexual matters: it is a forbidden, and thus all the more exciting, knowledge that maturing children suspect and desire and that the adults deny them, as long as possible.

(c) Why, however, must acquiring judgment be a crime? Why did God not freely give the man judgment? This question is customarily answered as follows: this prohibition had only didactic significance. It was given in order to train the man to obey. God could not have seriously denied the man knowledge! No, instead, the purpose of this prohibition was none other than developing man for knowledge (Dillmann, 45, 47, 66). Such ideas may well suggest themselves to the modern Christian reader, but the old narrative does not express them in even a single word. Instead, the myth recounts that God prohibited the Tree to the man with harsh words and that he cursed him when he had eaten of it. The myth says as clearly as possible that God did not want the man to eat of the Tree and to acquire Knowledge. Now it lies in the very nature of old narratives that they do not expressly answer questions such as this one as to why God did not want it (cf. the introduction §3:12). Still both narrators dropped clues that were completely comprehensible to their contemporaries. Knowledge makes one like God, and God does not want humans to become like him (3:5, 22). This motif has become very foreign to us and seems to us even to be unworthy of God. It played a great role, however, in antiquity, even among the Hebrews. Once when the sons of God married the daughters of men and begot giants with them, God, in order to prevent the human race from becoming too great, shortened the life span of humans (6:1-4). When humans, working together, sought to build a tower reaching into the heavens, God broke their power by dispersing them (11:1-9). Similar ideas occur not infrequently in the prophets: God does not want anything else in the world to be high and glorious other than himself (Isa 2). Whoever desires something superhuman and wants to become like God in wealth, wisdom, or might, trespasses against God's majesty and is struck by lightning from the heights (Isa 10:13-14; 37:24; 14:12ff., etc.). For between deity and humanity stands a barrier God does not want humanity to cross. Thus God originally reserved knowledge for himself alone. But when the people acquired it against his will, he saw to it that the trees not grow into heaven and took Paradise from <31> them. Thus it is that people have judgment and, at the same time, such a harsh lot on earth.

4. *The Tone of the Myth Is Sorrowful.* When one calculates gain and loss, one cannot hesitate. The myth speaks dispassionately of reason, but with deep sorrow of the wretched fate of humanity. Human happiness is irretrievably lost. The cherub stands before the gates of Paradise. But the myth's sorrow over lost happiness does not yet have the full pathos of tragedy. Along with pain, resignation sounds clearly. A kind of resigned comfort is added to the announcement of death: "For you are dust and to dust you return."

Nothing unusual happens to man when he dies. "Fear not death, your fate; / Remember that the world before and after dies like you! / That is the lot of all flesh before God. / Why struggle against the statute of the Most High?" (Sir 41:3-4). Eternal life is a good which God has reserved for himself. Do not desire the impossible!

Another consideration points in the same direction. The tragedies that feel human misery most deeply would explain it as the result of massive guilt. They would depict how the man, in the arrogance of the Titans, rises against God and how the wrath of the offended God then flung him aside. But this myth treats the issue quite differently. The man did not commit an appalling crime with a full awareness of the significance of the matter. Instead, he was seduced, he committed a child's sin, he pilfered a snack, harmless. He had no idea of the frightful consequences of his deed. This is no tragedy, elevating humanity even as it crushes it. Rather, these are the piteous consequences of a foolish child's prank. Modern exegesis is incorrect, then, repeatedly to attribute to the man who reaches for the fruit a "titanic" defiance, an urge for freedom, which struggles against God. The man's sin is not arrogance, but childish disobedience.

It is particularly difficult to comprehend the religious tone of the narrative. We are so very accustomed to finding here the religious ideas that seem most profound to us that it will be very difficult for us to recognize accurately the ancient piety candidly expressed here. The characteristic of God that comes under consideration in the myth, in the first instance, is that he maintains the barrier between deity and humanity. This characteristic can, however, be discussed in rather distinct tones. One can see in it—as the Greeks did—the deity's jealousy and rebel, with open defiance or with secret murmuring, against this envious God who brought humanity to misery. In the dust, one can also worshipfully admire the same characteristic: The prophets celebrate in powerful descriptions the glorious, majestic God who throws the arrogant, who desire to be like him, back into the dust. Neither attitude appears in our myth. There is no trace of rebellion against God, nor of murmuring. Instead, the myth is convinced that God was right and the man wrong. It expressly asserts that the man was justifiably cursed. The sin the man committed is indeed portrayed, when its psychological origin is described, as a child's sin. But in the context of the curse, it is maintained with great gravity that it was a transgression: "I forbade you to eat from the Tree!" The man knew that he had acted contrary to God's commandment. And God had placed a death penalty on it. Indeed, God still allowed grace to govern and did not execute his original threat, like the loving father who does not punish the child as heavily as he had previously threatened. On the other side, however, the myth is also far removed from the thrilling enthusiasm of the prophets. How differently they portray the frightful outrage that can awaken the immense wrath of God. The tone of the myth, then, is to be sought between the two extremes. One may clarify it by <32> remembering the relationship of the Israelite farmer to his servants, a relationship very often compared to the religious relationship in ancient Israel. The farmer gives his servants sustenance and protection. In exchange, the servant must serve him. Between a good master and a good servant existed an amicable relationship. But there was also a difference between the two, and this difference is essential and should remain so. The master does not consider elevating the servant to his level and treating him as his equal (Luke 17:8). But if a servant is pampered by the foolish good nature of his master, he will eventually want to become his master's equal. And that he should not do! He should fear his master. The Hebrew imagines his relationship to God similarly. God is good and gracious, but he does not permit people to place themselves on an equal footing for humans should fear God. The Hebrew finds this attitude of the deity to be quite in order. The Hebrew, too, desires that everyone fear God. It annoys him when a person exceeds human limits. If, then, God in the myth wants to withhold knowledge from people, the narrator, himself, grants God the unrestricted right to do so; God had intended such good for the man and placed him in the majestic Paradise, only, admittedly, wishing to retain him under his hand. The narrator does not sanction the poisonous thoughts of the serpent who sees God's ill will in the prohibition. The serpent's statements were "deception," "seduction" (3:13). And if the man nevertheless misappropriated the tree and thereby became like God in one respect, God is entirely right to thoroughly punish him.

Finally, one may note the position in the whole structure of the narrative assumed by the sin committed. It is customary to call this narrative "the Fall." But by no means does the Fall occupy such a central position in the old narrative. Rather, the main point stands, as always in the old narratives, at the end. This main point is, then, the expulsion from Paradise (cf. Stade, *Bibl. Theol.*, 242). The sin committed is, accordingly, a secondary element intended to explain how people came to possess knowledge, to be sure, but lost Paradise.

These ideas and attitudes of the myth are admittedly deficient and inferior when compared to those available to us Christians. No historically educated individual will take offense at this claim: the many prophets and thinkers and poets who have lived since this ancient narrative have not lived in vain. Nevertheless, it is fitting "not to disdain small beginnings."

5. *Israelite Variants of the Paradise Narrative.* Job 15:7-8: "Were you born as the first of men and birthed before the hills? Did you listen in to the council of God and seize wisdom for yourself?" It has been shown in *Schöpfung und Chaos* (148) that these words allude to a recension of the Paradise narrative (similarly Dillmann in his Job commentary). Judging from the context, Eliphaz wants to say to Job in v 7a, "Are you really as supremely wise as you believe yourself to be?" Instead, he says scornfully, "Are you really the primal man?" This statement presupposes that the primal man was considered the model of all wisdom. Thus there must have been an account of the primal man that told of his wondrous wisdom. This narrative must have been well known to the poet's contemporaries. Then follows v 7b, "Were you born before the hills?" What does this question mean in this context and how can Eliphaz ask it of Job at all if the primal man was not said to have been "born before the hills"? It is similar to asking in German, "Are you Dr. Faust and have you made a covenant with the devil?" This interpretation seems much more likely than the usual understanding that the poet thinks of personified wisdom (Prov 8:22ff.) since wisdom is not explicitly mentioned while the primal man is. The <33> word תִּגְרַע "you seized for yourself, held back," in particular, demonstrates that v 8 also belongs to this presumed allusion. Job is compared to a being that, against God's will, invades his council and steals wisdom. How should the poet have come to this concept if such were not told of the primal man? The presumed myth reported, then, that the "first man," who was born before the world, listened in on the heavenly council and so stold wisdom. Accordingly, the first man, very much as in the Paradise account in Gen 2ff., committed a crime through which he usurped hidden divine wisdom. This interpretation is disputed by Budde (*Hiobkommentar*), Frankenberg (CGA [1901], 682), and

Meinhold (97-98) and accepted by Zimmern[3] (523), Cheyne (14), and Sellin (30). Cheyne cites the striking parallel of *Kalevala*, rune 3, according to which Youkahainen boasts, in order to demonstrate his wisdom, that, as the sixth of the wise and ancient heroes, as the seventh of the primal heroes, he was already present when the heavens were created.

Ezekiel 28:1-19 describes the fall of the king of Tyre. This portrayal contains many elements, however, that cannot be understood as the prophet's contrivances for the Tyrian king. The passage maintains, for example, that he dwelt in Eden, the Garden of God, but was cast down from the Mountain of God to the earth because of his crime. These strange elements are unfortunately concentrated in the corrupt section vv 12-19, but they can already be heard, even though less notably, in vv 1-10. The prophet has intermingled them with elements that clearly refer to the king of Tyre (e.g., allusions to the wealth and commerce of the city), but they stand quite apart from these more mundane references. If one takes them together one obtains a unified, cohesive, although naturally incomplete account. This very inner cohesion of individual elements is an important indication that they belong together apart from Ezekiel's use of them. The account so reconstructed is by nature a myth. It can be assumed, then, that Ezekiel has employed a myth here and applied it to the king of Tyre (see *Schöpfung und Chaos*, 148; regarding such "allegorized material," see *Schöpfung und Chaos*, 74). Ezekiel's book is replete with mythical material and the prophet's supplementary interpretation is always intermingled. The presumed myth echoing in vv 12-19 may have told of a wonderful and wise creature of God that was covered with the twelve (LXX) gems and that walked in Eden, the Garden of God, on the holy mountain, in the midst of fiery stones. It was without fault from the day of its creation until it was found guilty of a crime. Because of its brilliant beauty and despite its wisdom, its heart became arrogant. Then it was cast from the mountain of God, expelled by the Cherub from the fiery stones, and cast down to the earth. We obtain a few parallel elements from 28:1-10. A being, wise and glorious, became arrogant and wanted to equate itself with God: "I am a god; I dwell in God's dwelling!" Then, however, God shows him that he is a man and not God. He was desecrated, cast down, given over to death. The expulsion from Paradise recounted by this myth is so closely related to the Genesis narrative that one may consider it a variant. This understanding of Ezekiel 28 as a "richer and broader version" of the Paradise legend was first offered by Cornill. It is disputed by Frankenberg (CGA [1901], 682) and Meinhold (98-99) and accepted by Zimmern (KAT[3], 523), Bousset (*Rel. des Judentums*[2], 324), Sellin (21, 30), Cheyne (72), and on the whole by Gressman (116 and ARW 10:365-66). The problem does not change if one understands the king of Tyre, with Meinhold, as the patron deity of the city. In this case the question remains as to how Ezekiel came to conceive of the patron deity living in and being expelled from Eden.

Now, both variants differ markedly from the Genesis Paradise account both in <34> details and in overall tone. According to them, the first man was a kind of demigod who once dwelt with divine beings in God's dwelling and who could imagine himself a god. This dwelling, Paradise, lay on God's mountain. He walked among fiery stones, that is, originally, the stars of the heavens. Both recensions of the account are thus by far more mythological than that of Gen 2ff. Now, to be sure, the more mythological concept is not necessarily always the older in the history of religion. But since we often discern the process of the fading of the mythological in the history of Israel's religion, especially in Genesis (cf. the intro. §2:2; §4:2, 6), we may also regard the mythological traditions to be the older. Quite remarkably this figure of the heavenly primal man revives again in later syncretistic religions, especially in Parseeism and Judaism (cf. Bousset[2], 404ff., 557-58).

At the same time, Gen 2ff. itself also leaves the impression that it traces back to a much more mythological tradition. Glimmers of such older elements are the Garden of Eden, originally God's dwelling where there are magical trees with secret divine powers, further the serpent that may have originally been a demon, and the narrative's many anthropomorphisms which give it an especially ancient hue in relation to most of the legends in Genesis. Many questions that can hardly be answered from the present recension could find an answer in an older version. Why did God place the two Trees, which he did not intend to permit the man to enjoy, in Paradise at all? Of all things, why did he permit the evil serpent entry? These questions could be answered from a presumptive pagan recension as follows. The Trees belong by nature in the dwelling of the gods so that the gods may eat of them and have eternal life. Furthermore, the serpent, originally itself a god, dwells in Paradise just like the other gods. Even the peculiar circumstance that the serpent gives God's word the lie and thus apparently maintains justice may be explained, in the final analysis, only by the fact that in the oldest recension, the pertinent pagan god told a lie and the serpent told the truth. The deity, in order to keep the man at a distance, had claimed that the tree was poisonous, but the serpent informed him of the true nature of the Tree. In the older recension—we can well imagine—the sexual element, which the Hebrew chastely veils, is much more bluntly in evidence. In it the forbidden fruit, for example, would have had aphrodisiacal significance, just as in Oriental love poetry the plucking of the tasty fruit is a favorite image of sexual indulgence (cf. Jacob, *Hohes Lied*, 6ff,. esp. 7n.1).

6. *Variants of the Concept of Paradise* (cf. Greßmann, 215ff., 221ff.). While only a few allusions to the expulsion occur in the OT, references to the Garden of God in Eden appear all the more often. The Garden of Eden stands as an image of prosperity (Sir 40:17, 21), as the ideal of an exquisite, richly watered land (Gen 13:10) where the most majestic trees stand (Ezek 31:8), where joy and bliss rule (Isa 51:3). It is the strongest contrast to the desert (Ezek 36:35; Isa 51:3; Joel 2:3). It appears in a mythological description (Ezek 28) which locates the Garden of God on the sacred mountain of God, high above the earth (cf. above).

Notably, a few passages dealing with the eschaton speak of Paradise, according to the myth the original home of humanity. According to Ezek 36:35 devastated Canaan will become like the Garden of Yahweh, according to Isa 51:3 Zion's desert will. That this allusion is not an accidentally chosen image, but that it rests on a belief can be seen from the descriptions of Deut–Isa, according to which, in the end time, wondrous water will break forth and majestic trees will sprout up in the desert for Israel's joy and bliss when Yahweh reveals himself (Isa 41:18-19; 43:19; 49:10-11; 55:13 [Bar 5:8; PsSol 11:6-7]; cf. esp. Isa 35). We see, <35> then, the same belief in Paradise as an eschatological entity at work here that was often later expressed in the apocalypses (cf. EthEn 25:4-5; Rev 2:7; 22:2; 4 Ezr 8:52; TestLev 18, etc.). A concept from the primeval period is here transferred to the eschaton. For other examples of this remarkable religiohistorical process see *Schöpfung und Chaos*, esp. 87, 11, 367-71 and *Zum religionsgesch. Verständnis des N.T.*, 21ff.

We occasionally hear in these eschatological descriptions that Zion will be transfigured into Paradise (Isa 51:3 [EthEn 25:5; Rev 22:2]; cf. 4 Ezr 8:52; ApBar 4:6). Against this background it is possible to understand the prophetic prediction that in the end time water will flow forth from the sacred mountain (Ezek 47:1-12; Joel 4:18; Zech 14:8; Rev 22:1-2). These are "living," that is, first of all, naturally, "fresh-flowing" waters (Zech 14:8), which have the inherent power, however, to "heal" the waters of the Dead Sea so that animals can live in it ("Everything lives where the river flows," Ezek 47:9) and on its banks stand trees with never-failing fruits and never-withering foliage that serves as medicaments (Ezek 47:12). We learn the actual significance of this very unusual concept—that in no way whatsoever suits the actual water situation in Jerusalem and thus cannot derive from it—from Rev 22:1-2. According to this text, a stream of the Water of Life proceeds from the throne of God in the new Jerusalem and Trees of Life stand on either side. The prediction of a great flowing stream proceeding from the sanctuary rests, then, on the contention that Zion will one day become Paradise. The presumption is that Paradise is conceived of as the source of streams of the Water of Life (cf. Bertholet on Ezek 47:12). This idea also provides the background for the statement in the eschatological description in Psa 46:5: "A river, whose streams gladden the city of God, the most sacred of the dwellings of the Most High (עֶלְיוֹן)." This many-streamed river, which "gladdens" Zion, is the wonderful River of Paradise that pours forth life and joy. Isa 33:21 alludes to the same idea. Here Yahweh's protection over Zion in the end time is compared to mighty streams which spring up there (read מָקוֹר for מְקוֹם). The same is true of the description of Zion's glory in Psa 36:9-10: "They feast on the fat of your house, you give them to drink from the stream of your bliss; for with you is the source of life, in your light they see light." נַהַל עֲדָנֶיךָ is an ingenious allusion to the river of עדן (cf. Duhm on this passage).

A parallel to this belief is the prediction that in the end time Mt. Zion will become the highest mountain in the world (Isa 2:2; Mic 4:1; cf. Ezek 40:2; Zech 14:10; Rev 21:10). We can interpret this doctrine on the basis of Psa 48:3. This eschatological hymn refers to Zion as "the extreme North, the city of the great king." But "the extreme North" is the name of the mountain of God high above the divine stars where stands the throne of the "Most High" God (עֶלְיוֹן, Isa 14:13-14). (One may compare the Babylonian tradition that locates Anu at the North Pole—see Jensen, *Kosmologie der Babylonier*, 19ff., 23. Similar traditions appear among the Mandaeans—cf. Jensen, ibid.) Here, then, we hear of a mountain of the gods, the highest mountain in the world, the seat of the Most High God, and of the belief that one day Zion will become this mountain.

The prediction of Zion's future grandeur and of the waters that will one day flow from there appear together in Zech 14:8-10; Ezek 40:2; 47:1ff.; Rev 21:10; 22:1. From these texts we can reconstruct the whole image underlying these scattered allusions. Paradise is situated on the highest mountain in the world. From there its rivers go into all lands. Gen 2:10-14 points to the same concept. In its view the four major rivers of the world flow forth from Eden over the whole world. Eden must lie high above all the world (cf. above, p. 9). According to Ezek 28:13-14, too, the Garden of God lies on the mountain of God. The Iranian legends about the Garden of Jima, the ruler of the golden age, are very similar. This garden lay on the mountain Hukairya from which flowed the Water of Life, the basis for all fertility on earth. All manner <36> of magical trees, including the Tree of Life, grow there. From the Hara-berezaiti mountains, to which this mountain belongs, flow two major rivers and many other streams (cf. Spiegel, *Erânische Altertumskunde* 1:191ff., 462ff.; Bartholomae, *Altiran. Wb.*, 1300-1301). Even very late Judaism preserved the concept of the mountain of Paradise (EthEn 24ff., cf. also Jubil 4:26). Here the concept, which we can only infer from the prophets, is stated straightfor- wardly. This peculiar relationship between prophets and apocalypses can be substantiated in many other instances and can be explained by the fact that a foreign mythology had continued influence, that it was thoroughly amalgamated by the prophets, but that in a later time, when religion relaxed, it was swallowed whole (cf. "Zum religionsgesch. Verständnis des N.T.," 23ff.).

Judaism often locates Paradise in heaven. This, too, is not the capricious fantasy of a later generation. Isa 14:13f. and Ezek 28 already envision the mountain of God high above all things earthly, even above the stars. Its peak towers into the heavens. SlavEn 8 describes the River of Paradise as two sources which spring up in the heavenly Paradise, divide into four rivers, and flow down to the earthly Paradise. A variant of the River of Paradise is the river of fire which proceeds from God's throne (Dan 7:10; EthEn 14:19). Both concepts trace back to the same viewpoint: the heavenly river of fire flowing from the heights of heaven and dividing into four streams is the Milky Way with its four arms (cf. the star charts) which the Egyptians (Erman, *Äg. Rel.*, 93), Mandaeans (Brandt, *Mand. Rel.*, 186), Romans (*Plautus Trin.*, 940), Rabbis (Bousset, *Rel. des Judentums*[2], 371n.2), and even the Chinese (Wilhelm, *Zeitschr. für Missionskunde und Religionswissenschaft* 21:48) understood as rivers. This late Jewish concept may also be very old. Concerning Paradise in late Jewish tradition, cf. Bousset, *Rel. des Judentums*[2], 324ff., 556ff.; Volz, *Jüd. Eschatologie*, 374ff.

7. *Origins of the Account.* The myth is of extra-Israelite origins, as most scholars now agree. The many mythological elements it must have originally possessed and some it still manifests suggest this conclusion. The fact that the myth seeks the actual dwelling of God in the far distance, especially, supports it. The Iranian and Babylonian parallels to the Paradise concept also point to foreign origins (cf. above). Greco-Roman traditions also tell of the good fortune of humans in the golden era now past (bibliography, see above p. 30). One thinks especially of the garden with the golden apples beyond Oceanos guarded by the Hesperides and the dragons (cf. Roscher, *Lex.*, s.v. "Hesperiden"). The legends of Pro- metheus (Meinhold, 108) and Tantalus offer many parallels to the biblical account of the Fall, especially in the poetic recensions. A Persian legend tells of Meshia and Meshiane who lived at first only from fruits, but who, seduced by Ahriman, renounce the good God, loose their original purity, fell trees, kill animals, and learn to do every evil. Another sage reports how Jima, the king of the golden age, during which there was neither illness nor death, neither hunger nor thirst, gave himself over to arrogance and thus lost his kingdom to Dahâka. Furthermore, we hear that Jima still lives with his followers hidden away in a blessed garden and that one day at the end of the eras he will return once again with his faithful (cf. Spiegel, *Erânishe Altertumskunde* 1:473ff., 522ff.; additional bibliography in Dillmann, 48ff.). The conclusion that the Hebrew Paradise legend is, therefore, of Iranian origins, would, however, be far too premature. It would be much more likely that such traditions were the common material of the entire cultural realm. The suspicion that this protolegend, too, originated in Babylonia receives significant support from

the—admittedly not yet assured—references to the "Tree of Truth" and the "Tree of Life" in Sumerian inscriptions (cf. above, p. 8). Of course, the climate of Babylonia scarcely suits <37> the narrative of the origins (cf. above, p. 5). According to Babylonian tradition (cf. on Gen 1) the world is created, rather, from moisture. The fig tree (3:7) does not grow in Babylonia (cf. Herodotus I.193; further bibliography in Dillmann, 74). The fig (*tittu*, from *tintu = תְּאֵנָה) does, indeed, appear in the cuneiform texts. These texts may deal, however, with fruits imported from Mesopotamia or Syria (Zimmern in a private correspondence). The fig may even have been only secondarily incorporated in the Paradise legend.

Finally, there has been no success to date, despite certain points of contact in details, in reconstructing an analogy for the biblical Paradise legend in Babylonia (contra Stade, ZAW 23:174). Indeed, a Babylonian seal cylinder (Brit. Mus. no. 89:326), frequently reproduced recently, depicts two clothed, seated figures stretching out their hands toward a tree that stands between them. Behind one seems to be fixed a serpent. The other is horned, thus a god (cf. the figure, e.g., in Riehms, "Schlangen," ATAO² 203:1406). Whether this representation is related in any way whatsoever to the Paradise myth, as Delitzsch (*Babel und Bibel* 1:37) thinks, is entirely uncertain. Neither of the figures seems to be reaching for the fruits hanging at the bottom of the tree (cf. Jensen, *Christl. Welt* [1902], 488). In addition, the Babylonian Adapa myth should be mentioned at this point, whose text the reader will find translated by Zimmern in *Schöpfung und Chaos* and more completely by Jensen in KB VI/1:92ff., xviiff. Adapa, the supremely wise (*atrahasis*), the anointed, was the son of the god Ea. Ea granted him wisdom, but not eternal life. He performs the spiritual rituals in Ea's sanctuary in Eridu. Because of a violent act he committed, he is summoned before the throne of the god of heaven, Anu. There, on his father's advice, he succeeded in averting Anu's wrath. But when Anu graciously offered him the Bread and Water of Life, he rejected it because Ea had previously described them to him as the Water and Bread of Death. The point of the narrative is, then, that Adapa was once very close to becoming immortal, but that through excessive caution, misled by Ea's lie, he forfeited immortality. One is surprised by numerous similarities between this narrative and the biblical traditions, especially the poetic traditions mentioned above. Here, too, the hero originally had access to heaven. Here, too, he was very wise. Ea showed him the secrets of heaven and earth. Here, too, he was once near the food of heaven which bestows immortality, but a god begrudged it him and called the food of life poison. Even this last similarity resembles the Paradise narrative as we reconstructed it, etc. (cf. Zimmern, KAT³, 520ff.). On the other hand, the differences are so great that one can clearly recognize that they are not two different recensions of the same story, but two, basically quite different narratives, although related in details. Jastrow (*Am. Journ. of Sem. Lang.* 15:195ff.) wants to consider the rather crude legend woven into the Gilgamesh epic concerning the wild shepherd Eabani who lived with the wild animals until seduced by a heirodule and brought to people (KB VI/1:121ff.; Jensen, Gilgameŝ-Epos 1:4ff.) as the model for Gen 2ff. Yet, the two narratives are rather dissimilar to one another. Finally, the sacred cedar forest of the Gilgamesh epic (cf. Zimmern's review, KAT³, 571-72) has only a very remote similarity to Paradise. Both cases concern a sacred forest located on a mountain. Whether the sacred cedar of this forest is really, as Jensen (KB VI/1:441-42) thinks, a Tree of Life, is doubtful. Certainly the contention that Babylonia itself was originally the land of Paradise is incorrect. Paradise is not located in civilized land, but far from all people, in the inaccessible distance. At any rate, however, the biblical myth in the form we have stems from a farming people. Indeed, the myth equates man and farmer. If one may guess, one would <38> decide for Mesopotamia as the most likely origin of the tradition. The tradition would have gone out to the East and the West. The dry climate presupposed in the creation narrative of Gen 2 would also fit Mesopotamia.

8. *The Place of Gen 2ff. within the Tradition.* In Gen 2ff. the myth exists in a highly Hebraized form. It contains Hebrew-specific etymologies: *'iśśa* from *'iś* and *'adam* from *ᵃdama*. At the same time, the mythological element is strongly diminished (Wellhausen, *Prolegomena*[6], 303-304). The primal man, originally a demigod, is now only an ordinary man. The serpent-demon is now a serpent. Paradise, originally the dwelling of God himself, who allows the man to dwell with him there, is now created explicitly for the people (Meinhold, 73). The wondrous nature of the trees remains in J, but that of the water has disappeared. J avoids even the expression "Garden of God" or "Garden of Yahweh." This diminishment of the places and persons naturally produced a dampening of the entire narrative. Many obscurities arose in this process: the creation of the woman from the rib, the man as guardian of Paradise, the name Ḥawwa, etc. (cf. Greßmann, ARW 10:367). In addition, Israel will have added religious ideas and attitudes. Which and how they replaced the older ideas of the myth may not be demonstrated because of the shortage of material. But as soon as we know a well-preserved more-original form of the myth, it will certainly prove true, just as with Gen and the Flood legend, that Gen 2ff. is infinitely superior in terms of religion to related pagan myths.

9. *History of the Account in Israel.* The myth must have entered Israel in a very ancient time. It still bears extremely ancient elements. The assumption that it derived from a Babylonian original in the exilic or postexilic period (F. Delitzsch, *Wo lag das Paradies?*, 93-94) is totally impossible for internal reasons. No more tenable is Stade's opinion (*Geschichte Israels* 1:631-32, ZAW 23:178-79) that the narrative entered Israel in the period of Assyro-Babylonian influence under Manasseh. This supposition would have been completely understandable in the period before the discovery of the Tell-Amarna correspondence. Now, however, when we know from these very letters that the Babylonian influence in Canaan was already very strong in the pre-Israelite period and that Babylonian mythological texts reached even Egypt then, it has become much less likely. The advanced age of this account, which must belong to the very oldest in J, is attested not only by its archaic tone, but also by the comment in 2:14 that "Asshur" lies to the west of the Tigris (cf. the commentary), a comment which must be, in turn, younger than the foundation of the narrative. On the other hand, the myth, which equates man and farmer, cannot have been told in Israel before its entry into Canaan (cf. the assessment of the Flood legend below). Originally, the narrative will have had poetic form. The poetic recensions may be remnants of this original form. The myth must have been very beloved in Israel. We know four recensions of the narrative. We also have a great number of allusions to the Garden of God in Eden, to the great waters of Eden, to the Tree of Life, and to the creation of man from the dust. On the other hand, one should not overvalue the significance of the narrative for the ancient period. In those days, the myth was one old narrative alongside many others. The story of the Fall and the Expulsion are by no means the basis for OT piety, much less for that of the prophets or the psalmists. Ancient Israel

was much too practically oriented to allow theories concerning the origin of things to determine its behavior in any essential way. Only the belief in a returning Paradise had a certain significance (not to be underestimated) for the later prophets. The major point of the myth to us, the religious ideas of chap. 3, had, as far as we know, no influence whatsoever. Only in later Judaism, in a period when speculation had attained an entirely new significance in religion, <39> when these chapters stood at the beginning of Holy Scriptures and thus were read particularly often and with particular respect, and when, at the same time, speculation concerning the primal man intruded from outside once again—in this time a mighty accent fell on this old narrative. The Judeo-Christian dogmas of the primitive state, the Fall, and original sin grew in connection with this narrative and its interpretation. Christian theologians of all times have read the dominant anthropology of their times into Gen 2ff. The myth has not received significantly better treatment from the philosophers. One sees the same spectacle almost everywhere: repeatedly the apparently self-evident conviction that the myth must contain the "correct ideas" (Dillmann), and very rarely a historical exegesis that forgets itself and its time and, denying itself, seeks to understand the old narrative against the background of the ancient period. Thus the myth has experienced a history of interpretation, continuing down to today, that can hardly be overlooked. According to the doctrine of the church, this narrative recounts the most important event of human history until the redemption by Christ. The method of interpretation has, of course, been more or less the allegorical. This manner of interpretation, renounced in principle by contemporary scholarship, has been preserved here, in many remnants even among academic researchers, down to the present. But even when there has been a conscious break with traditional exegesis, the interpretation of the myth has often been rather unfortunate. Along with many truly historical interpretations, one finds all too many modernizing intrusions of which only a very small sample have been given above. In fact, modern exegetes (even the sensitive Reuß, 208) have even denied that which no one should have disputed, namely that our narrative intends to be a true story (like every myth and every legend!). Accordingly, the history of the exegesis of Gen 2ff. may be variously evaluated. Taken as historical data it is a hymn recounting the power this myth exercises over the human heart even today. "Precisely here is manifest the wonderful power and significance of such creative intuitions that have an unending power to excite new and more profound ideas in each new generation in an unending succession" (Paulsen, *Deutsche Schule* [1901], 138). The individual interpretations offered are often extremely ingenious and often of fundamental significance for the history of doctrine. Only one approach has been neglected and only in recent times come into its own—the major point of exegesis: the historical sense. For more on older exegetical literature, cf. Dillmann and Tuch[2], 43ff.

Source Criticism of Chapter 4

The source of chap. 4 is J. Evidence for this conclusion includes: יהוה v 3, etc., even v 26; לְבִלְתִּי v 15; אָרוּר v 11; יָלַד "to beget," v 18; הָיָה "to become something," vv 20, 21 (cf. Budde, 216ff.); a series of intimate relationship to the Paradise narrative appears in 4:1-16 (see the conclusion of the legend of Cain and Abel).

This statement does not yet solve the source problem of the chapter. Rather, a wealth of inner contradictions are conspicuous in this chapter, contradictions difficult to account for within a single source. Cain, who fears being murdered (v 14) and who will be avenged sevenfold (v 15), cannot be described in this passage as the son of the first man. The wandering Cain, driven from the field, is different from the city-founder Cain: City founders are sedentary. The shepherd Jabal—according to the context the first shepherd—conflicts with the shepherd Abel. If Jabal were the first to discover animal husbandry, the progenitor Cain cannot have built a city. The natural sequence is the reverse: first animal husbandry, then, many generations later, city building. It also <40> seems odd that after Cain's lineage has already progressed many generations, yet another lineage from Adam via Seth begins in vv 25ff. Furthermore, according to v 26, Enosh was the first to call on the name Yahweh, but the preceding material already unabashedly employs this name. Finally, one may call attention to the fact that the motivation for the name Abel is absent (v 2), while the name Cain is explained (v 1). Two hands also seem to have been involved here. One cannot attribute such confusion to one hand, nor to an initial collector. Even a collector would have kept to a better order.

The thread that leads out of this labyrinth is the observation that the lineage of Seth (vv 25ff.), which now breaks off with the third member, was originally conceived of as an independent genealogy. This sudden break occurred because P, following the same tradition, supplies a genealogy of Seth in chap. 5. This genealogy of Seth was originally completely independent of the genealogy of Cain and was only combined with it by a later hand. עוֹד and קַיִן הֲרָגוֹ כִּי הֶבֶל תַּחַת אַחֵר (v 25), which create a tolerable connection, stem from this redactor (cf. Budde, 155-56). The fact that two sources underlie this text does not surprise since we also found two primary sources in the Paradise narrative. Now the genealogy of Seth contains the important note that Enosh was the first to use the name Yahweh. Accordingly, the genealogy of Seth belongs to the source that uses "God" in the Paradise narrative (J^e) and, thus, the genealogy of Cain to the source J^j. All the difficulties are still not resolved, however. The account of Cain's fratricide does not conform to the genealogy of Cain. The former regards nomadic life as a curse, the latter as a natural profession. The Cain cursed and driven out by Yahweh is destined to become lost in the wide world and cannot become, among other things, the progenitor of humanity (cf. Stade, ZAW 14:254ff.). Cain as founder of a city conforms even less to the Cainite genealogy. The fact that the account of Cain's fratricide, which unabashedly calls God "Yahweh," does not derive from J^e is, itself, illuminating. Indeed, farmland, where according to J^e (3:23) the man was exiled, is regarded here (4:14) as the Yahweh's abode (Meinhold, 133). It follows that Cain's fratricide and city founding were added only secondarily, perhaps by the same collector who combined J^e and J^j. The results of this analysis are as follows: Sethite genealogy J^e (vv 25, 26); Cainite genealogy J^j (vv 17a, 18-24; v 1 may have been the beginning of this genealogy). Other traditions tell of Cain's fratricide (vv 2-16, Cain's birth will also have been reported here) and of the city Enoch (v 17b). The final collector (J^r) combined all of this into a tolerable unit by understanding Seth as Cain's substitute. Steuernagel (*Allg. Einl. in den Hexateuch*, 269n.1) offers another suggestion. He places 4:25, 26 after 4:1 and explains 4:19-24 as a later addition.

2. Cain and Abel 4:(1)2-16 J^r

1 Since elsewhere it is always "the man and his wife," the name חַוָּה has probably been inserted here from 3:20. ידע means "to know, to make acquaintance, to associate with," a euphemistic expression for sexual intercourse, often, but not solely in reference to the first occasion. Concerning analogies in other Semitic languages and the original sense of the idiom, cf. Gesenius[14], s.v. ידע 5 and Baumann, ZAW 28:30-31. In Paradise, when people did not yet know anything about male and female, there was no sexual intercourse. The words Eve speaks after delivery explain the child's name. Such interpretations of names are given for all the more important persons in Genesis (cf. the introduction §2:7b). The mother names the child, as almost always in J (exceptions in Eerdmans, 13ff.). In P, contrariwise, <41> the father gives the name. The difference is significant for cultural history. The one who has property rights gives names. We can discern, then, two periods in Israel's culture: one, still operative in J, in which the child belongs to the mother; the other, expressed in P, in which the child is the property of the father (cf. Nöldeke, ZDMG 40:150; Benzinger[2], 104). Eve's words are a cry of joy. Joy over the first-born is proverbial among the Hebrews (Jer 20:15). The woman rejoices particularly, however, when she gives life to "a man" (Job 3:3; cf. Hannah, 1 Sam 1; Sarah and Hagar, Gen 16; etc.). The name קַיִן is interpreted by the word קָנִיתִי she spoke. Concerning the scientific value of such folk etymologies, cf. the introduction §2:7b. אֶת־יְהוָה is very difficult. Older exegesis interpreted this passage as though Eve, in her first experience of maternal happiness, believed that she already had the promised redeemer concerning whose dual natures she had pronounced the correct doctrine (he is אִישׁ and יהוה at the same time). LXX διὰ τοῦ θεοῦ and Vulg per deum both read the transmitted text. The form "with Yahweh," i.e., "with his help," is unattested. The conjectural reading מֵאֵת (following Targ-Onk) is hardly correct. It seems to be a case of severe corruption. In LXX here and often ὁ θεός represents יהוה and, conversely, ὁ κύριος represents אלהים, elsewhere κύριος ὁ θεός. For statistics, see Eerdmans, 34-35, who is inclined to consider the LXX text more original and who also thinks that here the original legend employed Yahweh and Elohim together (p. 79).

2 The birth of Abel is recounted very briefly. No notice is given that Eve became pregnant again. Similar brevity characterizes Gen 38:5. Or are the two thought of as twins like Romulus and Remus so that the fratricide becomes particularly gruesome? It is peculiar that Abel is consistently called "Cain's brother" here, where it is obvious, and in the further course of the narrative. Correspondingly, Abel seems to have been the less known figure who bore the standing designation "Cain's brother." The Hebrew will have heard the nomen appell. הֶבֶל "breath, nothingness" in the name Hebel—a well-suited name for one who passed away early. This is, however, certainly not the original meaning of the name which the narrator will have no more invented than that of Cain. That Abel tended livestock does not entirely fit the Paradise narrative, according to which man is suited for farming and only for farming, an indication that this story was not originally intended as a continuation of the Paradise myth.

3, 4a It seems obvious to ancient Israel that the first people would have offered sacrifice to Yahweh. Where were there people without religion and religion without sacrifice? It seemed equally natural that one offers the deity the best one has: the farmer of the fruits of the field, the shepherd of the animals. Among the animals (as among people), the best is the firstborn, "the firstfruits of one's strength" (Gen 49:3). Thus, in accordance with ancient practice, it belongs to the deity (Exod 34:19). Among the various animal parts, the best, according to Hebrew taste, are the fatty portions. These sacrificial practices are imported here without reflection into the primitive period. One also notices that the sacrifice (and consumption) of animals is recounted quite harmlessly here (in contrast to P, cf. the commentary on 1:29ff.). Where did Cain and Abel sacrifice? They sacrifice, naturally, on an altar, where else? מִפְּרִי is a portion of the fruits, according to the context, naturally the best. חֶלְבֵהֶן should be more correctly pointed חֶלְבְּהֶן. Through the punctuation of the existing text, the Massorah avoids acknowledging the suffix הֶן with a singular (§91c). Sam, LXX, Pesh, and Vulg read וּמֵחֶלְבֵיהֶן. On וּמֵחֶלְבֵיהֶן "and from their fat" see §154n.1b. מִנְחָה means here (and regularly <42> in the ancient period) "sacrifice" in the general sense. In the official usage of the Jerusalem temple (Isa 1:13 and later in P) it is the "cereal offering." הֵבִיא is also a cultic term, "to bring in (to the holy area) = to offer." The nature of the offering is not described, but is presumed to be known. Genesis usually makes this assumption with the exception of abnormal cases in chap. 15 and 22.

4b, 5a שָׁעָה "to watch" (here "to regard with mercy") is an extremely significant expression: Whoever rejoices over a gift regards it; whoever does not like it, may not even look at it. Why did God regard Abel's sacrifice and scorn Cain's? This question has occasioned all manner of speculation since antiquity. The legend, which says nothing of Abel's greater piety, does not communicate the common opinion that God considered the attitude of the sacrificer (so already Hebr 11:4). Rather, it has so far only reported that Abel was a shepherd who sacrificed flesh, but that Cain was a farmer who offered fruits of the field. Yahweh, however—so it now continues—disdains Cain and his gifts and prefers Abel and his gifts. Thereby the narrative maintains that Yahweh loves the shepherd and animal sacrifice, but wants nothing to do with the farmer and fruit offerings. How did Cain recognize God's disfavor? Surely some sign during the inspection of the sacrifice, noted regularly in antiquity, must have originally been intended. But a good narrator cannot leave such an important element for the course of the plot to the reader's imagination, but must clearly portray it. Accordingly, something seems to be missing here.

5b "To become hot" means "to become angry." The ancient Israelite of the right sort is hot-blooded or temperamental. "To lower the countenance" means "to brood darkly." That jealousy over God's grace leads to rage and finally to murder is a realistic element. The legend knows the human heart.

6 The sudden appearance of Yahweh seems very strange. While the good old narrative (i.e., almost always J) always first reports the "where" and "how" associated with God's speeches (most clearly 3:8ff.; 16:7ff.; 18; 19; 15:17; 21:17; 22:11; 32:27; 2:16; 15:1; 20:3ff.; 28:13; 46:2), the style of later insertions and redactions (especially of P) is to introduce God speaking with a very bland introduction (17:1; 35:9) or with no introductory word whatsoever (6:13; 8:15; 9:1; 13:14). One recognizes in this characteristic difference the way in which the feeling for good, clear narration diminished with the passage of time. When such bland introductions already exist in J, one may usually deduce a lacuna or diminution, especially clearly in 6:3; 11:6 (1:26), probably also in 7:1, probably not in 12:1 (and 35:1 E). Thus, Yahweh's appearance seems to have fallen away here too. One may suspect that Yahweh originally appeared at the holy site where Cain now found himself. Yahweh's appearance at a sacrifice has also been omitted in 8:20-21, but preserved in 15:17 (cf. Haller, 79).

7 The Hebr. text reads literally: "Is it not true? If you desire good, rise (raise)." ("The countenance" is often supplied following Jer 3:12; Job 11:15, etc., but the inf. is extremely unbefitting. The translation "if you offer something good" is not much better.) "But if you do not wish to do good, sin lies in wait at the door"—but does a wild animal, to which sin is compared here, usually lie in wait at doors? At which door does sin lie in wait here? Furthermore, the idea is, "if you intend evil, sin lies in wait for you," idem per idem—and its desire is for you (but חַטָּאת is fem.) and you should rule over it" (v 7b parallels 3:16 verbatim). Hans Duhm's suggestion (*Die bösen Geister im AT*, 8-9) to strike הַטָּאת as a gloss and to understand רֹבֵץ as a demon's name, which is, admittedly, attested in Babylonian (cf. Zimmern, KAT³, 460) merits discussion. The demon may lie in wait at the house door. <43> The context does not mention a house, however. The entire passages remains difficult. The text is apparently severely corrupt (Olshausen, 380). The sense of vv 6ff. may have been, Yahweh, who knows hearts, recognizes what is taking place privately in Cain. He reads it in his countenance, just as he immediately suspected the first sin from Adam's words. He tells him to his face, as he told Adam earlier (3:11). One can see in your face what you are thinking. And, at the same time, he warns him paternally to repent, now before it is too late. For שׂאת one may read תִּשָּׂא, for לפח ח prob-ably תִּפֹל, for תמשׁל perhaps תָּשְׁלֵם. The rest seems entirely irremediable. The extreme corruption of the passage may be explained as follows: the text of this verse became un-readable and was restored, as well as possible, by a copyist in imitation of 3:16. Or has v 7b entered the text accidentally from 3:16 (Kittel)?

8 The continuation of the transmitted text "Cain said to Abel" seems to be lacking. Consequently, Sam, LXX, Pesh (cf. Vulg, Targ-Pseudojon) add נֵלְכָה הַשָּׂדֶה, "Let us go to the field." Yet it seems obvious to assume that these "content-barren" (Sievers 2:246; Frankel, 55) words were only secondarily expanded and that וַיַּמֶר (hif. impf. of מרה, "to quarrel, begin a fight") should be read for וַיֹּאמֶר. The conjectured word is constructed elsewhere with the acc. with בְּ, or עִם. Or perhaps וַיָּמַר > מרר, "he was bitter, angry," should be read. He struck him "in the field" (as in 2 Sam 14:6) where Abel had no helper and the murder no witness. He did not dare commit the murder at the cultic site, itself. אֶל should probably be read with Pesh and Vulg for the second occurrence of עַל and probably for the first, as well. The motif of fratricide occurs repeatedly in world literature: Osiris and Seth (Erman, *Äg. Rel.*, 34-35), the pair of brothers in 2 Sam 14:6, cf. also the enmity of the two Phoenician heroes, Hypsuranios and Usoos (*Philo Bybl. fragm. hist. graec.*, ed. C. Müller 3:566), Romulus and Remus, Eteocles and Polyneices. This legend motif excited the imagination: Those who should love another most become enraged in the most destructive struggle with one another.

9ff. *God's curse on the murderer.* The curse pronounced in the narrative is the story element which continued to have effect, thus the actual goal toward which the narrative strives, for us the point from which we look back and understand the narrative (cf. on 3:14ff.; 9:24-27). **9** The introduction of God occurs in this case as abruptly as in v 6. Originally the idea will have been that God, summoned by the voice of the blood, came to the murder scene. God's probing questions resemble those of 3:9, here because of their brevity extremely impressive. Cain lies audaciously and impudently. But no lie can stand before God. "Should I be my brother's keeper?" is a sarcastic joke on Abel's profession of keeping (sheep).

10 "What have you done?" (just as in 3:13), Yahweh forcefully asks the murderer. Regarding מֶה before a guttural, see §37d. "The voice of the blood of your brother which cries out to me." The Hebrew thinks of the spilled blood as a plurality (דָּמִים plur.). That blood speaks, that drops of blood respond, is also a common fairy tale motif (cf. v.d. Leyen CXIV, 8 n 4, with bibliography). According to the ancient Hebrew concept spilt blood raises the צְעָקָה (technical term, the victim's "cry" for help), it cries for vengeance on the murderer. If people cannot or will not avenge, it cries to Yahweh, and then Yahweh himself undertakes blood vengeance (cf. the story of Naboth, 1 Kgs 21). The belief demonstrates beautifully the Hebrew's profound sense of justice. The concept is more than an image. The Hebrew believes the blood of the murder victim, if covered with earth, becomes silent (Job 16:18; Ezek 24:7-8; Isa 26:21). The idea of the text is, then, that Yahweh learned of the murder <44> from this very cry of the blood. This statement about crying blood made a powerful, gruesome impression on the imagination of the ancient. From this point onward, the story rises steeply to its climax.

11-12 God's curse occurs in extraordinarily disturbing language, but not in a strictly rhythmic form. A curse takes the place of deserved death also in 3:11ff. **11** Cain offered the field the horrible drink of his brother's blood. Therefore he is now cursed "away from the field" (cf. 3:14). In another form the idea could be expressed as though the land that Cain polluted with his brother's blood (Num 35:33) spewed him out (Lev 18:25). The land is described as "the one who has opened its jaws," like a great animal. The same image refers to Sheol in Isa 5:14. In the context of J, the word means that, just as Adam was cursed out of the Garden to the field, so Cain is cursed further from the field to the desert (following Wellhausen, *Composition*³, 9). One may note the narrator's sensitive play with the word אֲדָמָה: Cain cultivated the field, offered the fruits of the field, gave the field his brother's blood to drink. But the blood cried out against him from the field, therefore the field refuses him its fruit and he is banned from it. The old art of narration loved such wordplay (cf. the introduction §3:15). The multiple occurrences of הָרַג in vv 8, 14, 15 offers another example.

12 Should Cain disregard the curse and attempt to cultivate the field, however, it will refuse him its "strength" (a poetic expression for "its produce," Job 31:39). If he remains there, he will starve. So he must go away. In this way he became "a wanderer and a fugitive." This restless life, to which he is now accursed, is not based on the guilty conscience of the murderer that will not let him rest, but, as the context shows, only his exile from the field. Whoever cultivates the soil rests peacefully at one place. The one, however, to whom the field denies its nourishing fruits must roam the wide world seeking his nourishment (Budde, 191). לֹא־תֹסֵף The jussive is usually accompanied by אַל, not לֹא (see §109c,d). It may be that תֹסִף (impf.) should be read. Regarding הוֹסִיף with an infinitive without ל see §114m. נע ונד is a horribly impressive alliteration.

13-14 Crushed by the frightful curse, Cain asks for mitigation. Cain's cry of pain, like the preceding speech of Yahweh in powerful poetic diction, makes a disturbing impression. **13** According to the context עָוֹן can mean "guilt," "crime," or "punishment." Guilt is portrayed as a heavy burden which the perpetrator must bear in toil and pain (Psa 38:5; Isa 24:20). A common translation in an earlier period was "My sin is too great to be forgiven." According to this translation, Cain is that type of sinner who cannot come to reconciliation because he considers forgiveness of sins impossible. This interpretation, however, does not agree with v 14 where Cain speaks only of his punishment, declaring it too harsh. Regarding מִנְּשֹׂא "away from bearing," "so that I cannot bear it," see §133c.

14 "I shall hide from your eyes." Yahweh has said nothing about this. It must be implied in Yahweh's words in v 12. The statement must assume, then, that whoever leaves the farmland also departs from Yahweh's presence (Wellhausen, *Composition*³, 9; Stade, *Bibl. Theol.*, 103). The general perspective underlying Cain's words, therefore, is that Yahweh dwells in the fertile land, where shepherd and farmer dwell. Outside, in the wide world, other powers rule. This association of Yahweh and the farmland corresponds to Israel's belief since it settled in Canaan. Yahweh dwells in Canaan. Whoever must <45> depart from Canaan departs Yahweh's realm and sets out for lands where other powers rule (1 Sam 26:19; Jon 1:3; cf. especially the account in 2 Kgs 5:17-18 and the ritual of the Day of Atonement which opposes Yahweh, the God of Canaan, and Azazel, the demon of the wilderness, Lev 16:7-10). The narrator accentuates the idea that Cain must now leave Yahweh by repeating it in v 16. Accordingly, it seems more than a casual phrase. We may articulate this element as follows: Cain solicited Yahweh's grace, indeed he slew his brother for it. He killed Yahweh's darling because he wanted to be God's darling himself. But now Yahweh punishes him by cutting the bond between himself and Cain. The criminal for religion is frightened by the idea of rejection by God. Thus Cain, who first appeared only as a paradigm, acquires a personality. "And anyone who finds me will kill me." Cain does not fear the avenger of blood, the relatives of the murder victim. Instead he fears everyone. The statement assumes that the sedentary farmer has the protection of his family, clan, tribe, state (cf. 2 Kgs 4:13), finally of Yahweh himself who protects these units. But out in the desert, everyone is the enemy of everyone else. There the farmer, forced to abandon the safe homeland, becomes as free as a bird. But who does Cain fear? Rapacious animals, responds Josephus. Adam's later sons, his as yet unborn brothers, say others. Still others have thought of pre-Adamites, naturally a total contradiction to chaps. 1–3. The only possible answer is that this legend does not think of Cain as the son of the first man at all. This Cain lived at a time when people already lived all over the earth.

15 At Cain's request Yahweh reduced the curse. Yahweh's leniency toward the fratricide comes rather quickly. The narrator may have thought his zeal for Yahweh was taken into account as a mitigating circumstance. The difficulty may be explained as follows. The tradition contained both—the fratricide and the mark of protection—and, consequently, the two must be combined, either well or poorly. The words seem to be a poem, a quadrameter. "Therefore," because of Cain's request, "whoever murders Cain will be avenged sevenfold." For לָכֵן (so also Sam, Targ-Onk, Aqu), LXX, Sym, Theod, Vulg, and Pesh have לֹא כֵן. On the casus pendens of the participle see §116w. The sense is that seven members of the murderer's family will die for the murder of the one Cain (Stade, ZAW 14:297). The statement presumes the ancient view of the solidarity and responsibility of the family, a view particularly effective in blood vengeance (cf. especially 2 Sam 21). In real life, the relatives of the murder victim executed such a "vengeance." Who is to undertake vengeance in case of Cain's murder is not clear from the narrative. Blood vengeance—duty and law among less civilized peoples, the only, although extremely effective protection of individual lives—is displaced with the development of the legal state, forbidden as taking the law into one's own hands, and is even labeled a crime. Israel's law presupposes blood vengeance but regulates it through the establishment of sanctuaries. The mark that Yahweh gives Cain was, naturally, on Cain's body. It belongs "to the realm of religious tattooing and stigmatization, which, widely dispersed, was also known to Semitic peoples" (Heitmüller, *Im Namen Jesu*, 174; Ezek 9:4; Isa 44:5; Lev 19:28; Deut 14:1f.; Rev 13:16f.; 14:9; Gal 6:17, etc.). According to the circumstances of the narrative, the mark of Cain was not, as the popular view maintains, a mark meant to designate Cain as a murderer (such as the haggard expression of the murderer) but a mark intended to protect him from murder (Dillmann). Whereof it consisted, the narrative <46> does not say. אוֹת does not have a suffix, see §117e. On the order object-subject see §115k.

16a With the protection from murder, Cain left field and Yahweh. **16b** The note concerning Cain settling probably still belongs to the Cain-Abel legend because of the assonance between נוֹד and נָד in v 14. The narrator will have interpreted נוֹד as "unsettled running around" and will have intentionally employed נָד in v 14 in preparation for the word. Nevertheless, the name is hardly the invention of the legend but tradition. The location of נוֹד cannot be ascertained. The expression יָשֶׁב is not unsuitable for the wandering Cain (contra Stade, ZAW 14:282). It can also mean "to sojourn." If the Cain-Abel legend does not originally belong after the Paradise narrative, "east of Eden" will be an addition. We conclude from this addition that at that time people had only a very obscure notion of the location of the land of Nod.

General Remarks

1. *The Original Sense of the Narrative.* Cain's fear of murder out in the world as well as the sevenfold vengeance which will come upon his murderer makes it clear that the legend in its original sense did not think of him as the son of the first man. Who, then, is this Cain? This Cain is the progenitor of a people. This follows, first, from the statement that Cain's murder will be avenged sevenfold. This statement makes no sense if Cain is nothing more than an individual farmer fleeing the land, whose relatives remaining on the farm cannot avenge him, but only if Cain has adherents who can avenge his death. The statement can only be properly understood if we take it as a poetic expression for the prosaic sense that every son of Cain will be avenged—by his brothers—sevenfold. Indeed, one can imagine that this statement was a folk rhyme in which the people of Cain menacingly and proudly boast of their heroic, gruesome blood vengeance (cf. Stade, ZAW 14:296ff.). That the legend understands peoples as individual persons has many parallels in the patriarchal legends of Genesis (cf. the introduction §2:4). It is also attested elsewhere that occasionally the poetic costume falls away and a statement like the one cited in which the patriarch is really the people, itself, sounds through (cf. 27:28-29, 39-40; 31:52; 48:22).

The fact that this Cain bears a mark on his body also supports this interpretation. We know of peoples who bear such marks: thus Israel bears the mark of circumcision, Kedar shorn sideburns, Ishmael golden earrings, etc. Such tribal markings are originally religious in nature. They mark the bearer as the property of the god and place him under his protection (Heitmüller, 175). This character resounds here, too: Yahweh gave Cain his mark. That such tribal markings indicating the individual as a member of his people simultaneously secure him against murder inheres in the nature of the matter (on the mark of Cain, cf. Stade, ZAW 14:299ff.; idem, *Bibl. Theol.*, 42, 146). Furthermore, the pair of brothers Abel and Cain with different professions, can be compared to the pair of brothers Esau, the hunter, and Jacob, the shepherd, as well as the sons of Lamech. In all these cases, the legend envisions tribes with different lifestyles.

Now our Cain legend reveals very clearly how it conceives of the current lifestyle of the people of Cain. As wanderers and fugitives they pursue their existence, far from the farmland that bears them no fruit, out there in the wilderness where everyone is everyone else's enemy. The life of Bedouins is described. The circles that first told this legend, however, consist of those who live on the fertile land, themselves, that is, semisedentary shepherds. They considered this profession well pleasing to God. The narratives of Abraham and Jacob also originated in these same circles. With horror—this attitude resounds clearly in the legend—they looked on the hideous and bloody tribes in the frightful desert, far from <47> Yahweh's presence. When they ask how Cain came to this horrible life, they answer, "he must have committed fratricide." Like a fratricide, accursed by Yahweh, he flees restlessly over the steppe. Meinhold (137) calls attention correctly to the legend circulating among Christian people that "the first king of the Gypsies ridiculed the Savior in Egypt and thus brought down on himself and his people the curse of being pursued from place to place." And yet many traces indicate that Cain was, nevertheless, held in high esteem. He, too, worships Yahweh, indeed, he has a particular zeal for his grace. Consequently, he, too, although far from Yahweh's land, bears his mark of protection. He is the older brother, an echo of reality: "The semisedentary state of the herdsmen and certainly the fully sedentary life of the farmer is younger than the Bedouin life" (Meyer, *Israeliten*, 395). Ishmael and Esau are also the older brothers.

Now, we also know of a desert tribe Cain in Israelite history. It seems obvious to equate it with the Cain of the Legend. This inference, expressed by Wellhausen, *Composition*[3], 9, ingeniously extrapolated by Stade, ZAW 14:250ff. (cf. also Zeydner, ZAW 18:120ff.; Driver, 71, etc.), and opposed in earlier editions of this commentary, has been represented particularly well in the interim by Meyer, *Israeliten*, 219, 394ff. This tribe Cain, although allied with Israel, held firm to its Bedouin lifestyle into historical times. The Rechabites in Jer 35 are a Kenite clan (1 Chron 2:55). Concerning its robber lifestyle, cf. its rocky refuges in Num 24:21. It lived together with the robber-folk Amalek on into the Saulide period (1 Sam 15:6). The act of Jael, who was a Kenite according to Judg 5:24, attests to the tribe's ferocity. Jehu took a Kenite to witness his bloody deeds (2 Kgs 10:15ff.). It is known that this tribe worshipped Yahweh, indeed displayed a particular zeal for him (2 Kgs 10:16; Jer 35).

Cain may have been a tribe of desert smiths. Admittedly, the legend itself does not say so, but it is nevertheless suggested by the etymology of the name (Cain = smith, cf. below) and perhaps also by the reference to the "hammer" (?) of the Kenites in Judg 5:26 (cf. Eerdmans, ThT 41: 492ff.). The desert smith, migrating, going where his trade took him, was despised by the Bedouin.

The legend of Cain transmitted to us offers historical data to the extent that it portrays the impression Cain made on his more-peaceful neighbors. The narrative the legend adds in order to explain his current state is poetic in nature and thus not to be considered an echo of historical circumstances. The motifs of this narrative have been transmitted from some other source. It is not historical, then, that Cain was once a farmer and was driven from the field (Meyer, *Israeliten*, 395). Nor are the fratricide and the figure of Abel historical. Only the fact that shepherds and farmers can live peaceably together in the countryside as brothers has been adapted from reality (Stade, ZAW 14: 290ff.).

A noteworthy parallel for Abel and Cain is the pair Jabal, the shepherd, and Tubal-Cain, the smith (4:20ff.). Was הֶבֶל originally identical with יָבָל (Wellhausen, *Composition*[3], 8; Greßmann, *Musik und Musikinstrumente im AT*, 2-3) and was he inserted into this narrative in a time when the progenitor of the Kenites was equated with Tubal?

Judeo-Christian Haggadah explains Cain's jealousy for Abel as the result of the love both had for their sister. Moser (*Nord und Süd* 104:54ff.) and Lepsius (*Reich Christi* 6:177ff.) want to alter the text of Gen 4 accordingly and thus gain a love story!

Cain was actually a moon hero and, thus, like Enosh, Abraham, and Isaac, identical with Yahweh (4:1). He was the son of Enosh and Ishah and took revenge on the serpent for the death of his father, killed before his birth. He is the serpent killer predicted in 3:15. Before the battle, in which he barely slayed the serpent, Yahweh advised him to rob the serpent—lying in waiting before the door, its hole—of its plunder <48> in its absence and then to overpower it (4:5b-7). After the fight, Yahweh benevolently made him aware that the serpent, as the dark face of the moon, is actually his brother, and advised, thus, that it be buried as quickly as possible (4:10f.). This is the content of a narrative incorporated in the Abel-Cain legend according to Böklen, *Adam und Qain*, 110ff. It is a characteristic example of the new lunar exegesis of the Bible which illuminates biblical accounts through mythological and late-Jewish parallels.

2. *The Current State of the Legend.* The narrative in its present state is very seriously obscured. The fact that Cain was actually a people is forgotten. Only because the original sense of the narrative was no longer understood was it possible to insert the narrative at this position. Many details have become unclear: how Cain recognized the rejection of his sacrifice; when, where, and how God spoke to him; what the mark of Cain was. All this is no longer clear to the narrator. The behavior of Yahweh, who rejected Cain's sacrifice and then, nevertheless, admonished him paternally, who cursed Cain and then without proper grounds pardoned him, can no longer be properly reconciled. Nor is it original that Cain's fear (he fears the murderers of the desert) and his flight (he flees from the farmland because it no longer bears fruit for him) are diversely motivated. Instead, the oldest recension will have indicated the same motive for both. Cain fears and flees blood vengeance. Other elements, in contrast, are well developed, especially the speeches, a sign of a later period (cf. the introduction §3:13, 20). The narrator understood how to depict with greatly disturbing gravity how God warned the sinner before the deed and punished him afterward—the voice of the conscience is God's voice!—and how he took vengeance on the murderer for spilt blood. Cain has become for all times the paradigm of the murderer pursued by divine vengeance. Thus the narrative depicts grand primal truths of the human race. The narrator from whom we have the legend in its present form seems to have known chap. 2 and 3 and, probably unconsciously, to have depended on them (cf. 4:11 ‖ 3:17; 4:9 ‖ 3:9; 4:10 ‖ 3:13). The similarity between 4:7 and 3:16 results from corruption. The saying concerning Cain's vengeance (4:15) occurs again in the Song of Lamech (4:24). Wellhausen's assumption (*Composition*[3], 9) that 4:15 arose as a misunderstanding of 4:24 is less likely. Rather, the saying bears marks of antiquity in the version in 4:15, too.

3. Cain's Genealogy (4:1, 17-24)

Cain's genealogy belongs to Jʲ according to the analysis above.

1. *Concerning the genealogy proper (vv 1, 17a, 18).* How should such a genealogy be evaluated? The legend originally existed as an independent narrative in which a few imaginative figures appear. Legends deal with father and son (Gen 22), mother and son (Gen 21), or other relationships. A later period then combined the individual legends into a legend cycle and related the various figures in a unified genealogy. The more legends flow together, the longer the genealogy becomes. One can compare the genealogy of the Heraclides, for example (cf. Meyer, *Israeliten*, 231). An extended genealogy such as the Cainite presupposed relatively many legends about individual figures. Later, however, the narratives themselves can be forgotten and nothing other than the framework can remain. So it is here, as if nothing else were transmitted to us of all the legends of Israel's fathers than the genealogy: Abraham, Isaac, Jacob, and his twelve sons! We do not have here the old legend itself, but the final echo of the legend. Collectors who wish to summarize the whole tradition known to them <49> take up such genealogies in order to bridge the intervals (cf. Wellhausen, *Prolegomena*⁶, 331). The names in these genealogies are not very recent inventions but rather ancient traditions. Since Bultmann (*Mythologus* 1:170-71) it has been known that we have these genealogies of the forefathers in a dual tradition: the names of Seth's genealogy communicated by P in chap. 5 are, in the final analysis, the same given by J in chap. 4.

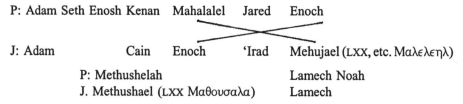

P: Adam Seth Enosh Kenan   Mahalalel   Jared   Enoch

J: Adam   Cain   Enoch   ʿIrad   Mehujael (LXX, etc. Μαλελεηλ)

P: Methushelah   Lamech Noah
J. Methushael (LXX Μαθουσαλα)   Lamech

Regarding the name forms in LXX, cf. Lagarde, *Abhandl. d. Gött. Ges. d. Wissenshaften* 26. P deviates from J in that he adds Seth and Enosh at the beginning, exchanges Mahalalel and Enoch in the middle, and adds Noah at the end. Further differences involve the forms of individual names. The two genealogies also agree in ending with three sons who become the ancestors of the three divisions of humanity (the genealogy of Shem ends similarly, 11:26). For more on the relationship of the two genealogies and their origin in the Babylonian King List, see the commentary on chap. 5. The names fluctuate a great deal in the tradition (cf. above): Hebr. has both Mehijael (LXX Μαιηλ) and Mehujael (LXX, Μαουιαηλ). The etymologies of certain of the names may be advanced: the Hebrew would associate חֲנוֹךְ with חָנַךְ, "to consecrate"; he would think of עֲדִי, "ornament," in relation to Adah, of צֵל "shadow" in relation to Zillah, and would derive Naamah from the root נעם, "to be lovely," etc. But the question concerns to what extent we have before us Hebrew, or much rather foreign and only Hebraized names (Dillmann). מְחוּשָׁאֵל would correspond to a Babylonian *mutu-ša-ili* (man of god; Lenormant, *Origines* 1:262-63). At any rate, such, mostly very dubious, etymologies do not yield very many conclusions, no more than one can reconstruct the Nibelungenlied from the etymologies of Siegfired

Hagen Kriemhild. A few of these names are appellatives like Adam and Enosh. Others such as Methushael are actual personal names; Naamah also occurs as a personal name, as does Cain, in Nabataean and Sinaitic inscriptions (Meyer, *Israeliten*, 397n.3). A few appear elsewhere as the names of tribes: Cain is the name of the nomadic people Cain; Seth is a poetic name for Moab (Num 24:17); Enoch is a clan in Reuben (Gen 46:9) and in Midian (Gen 25:4); Jared is a clan in Judah (1 Chron 4:18); Mahalalel is a clan in Judah (Neh 11:4); Adah is Esau's wife (Gen 36:2); Naamah occurs as the name of a city in Judah (Josh 15:41) and a tribe or place in the East (Hos 2:11). It is certainly no accident that all these tribal names lead us to the south and east of Palestine. Contrariwise, the name Tubal points to an entirely different corner of the world. Tubal refers to a people southeast of the Black Sea, the Tibarenes, the Tabal of the cuneiform inscriptions, famed for bronze work (Ezek 27:13). This genealogy contains, then, in addition to the Babylonian names, especially names from the southeast, probably reminiscences from Israel's earliest period. One may ask in respect to a few names whether they are not faded gods, as has been established in the Phoenician protogenealogy of Shamemrumos (Ὑψου- ράνιος = שמי מרו‎). One may raise this question especially of Enoch (cf. on 5:23-24). According to Hesychius Ἀδά is the name of the Babylonian Hera. Among the Phoenicians Naamah is the name of a goddess. Among the Sabaeans, קינ‎ is the name of a god (cf. Baethgen, *Beiträge*, 150, 152, and Mordtmann, ZDMG 31:86). The pair Tubal and Naamah may be compared with Hephaistos and Aphrodite (Dillmann).

2. The genealogy ends with an extensive presentation of the family of Lamech (vv 19-22). Lamech has two wives. This is not wrong according to Israelite notions. In fact, prophets attribute two wives to Yahweh himself in allegories (Jer 3:6ff.; Ezek 23). The three sons are paronomastically called Jabal, Jubal, and Tubal-Cain. The last, a double name, seems to derive from the identification of two figures. Because of consonance, the original in this passage seems to have been Tubal. Or <50> is Cain (following the Arab *qain* and Syr. *qainàyà*) in the meaning "smith" to be understood as Tubal's nickname (Wellhausen, *Composition*[3], 306)? In Hebr. קינ‎ means "lance." Nomadism, music, and smithery are traced to these three brothers. This comment belongs, in terms of content, with many others in the primeval history that are concerned with the invention of human arts: livelihood from fruit trees (2:15), aprons from leaves (3:7), coats from pelts (3:21), farming (3:23), city building (4:17), shepherds, smiths, and musicians (4:20-22), calling upon Yahweh (4:26), farming and vineyard keeping (9:20), the origination of the nations (10), brickmaking, city building, the origination of the nations and languages (11:1-9). One sees that Israelite antiquity also pondered the origin of human culture. Like every ancient civilization, Israel was convinced that all this originated in the long past primeval period. The contributions of the present are so minimal that they need not be considered. Antiquity reflects the quite proper impression of the inestimable age of human culture. Characteristically for Israel, all this is not attributed to Israelites but is placed in a time long before the formation of Israel. A historical impression is also operative here: Israel is a very young nation. Some have been troubled by the sequence of human accomplishments. We have an entire system of such a "cultural history" from Phoenician tradition, indeed, also in the form of a genealogy (in *Euseb. praep. ev.* 1:10 from *Philo Byblius*, cf. Dillmann, 6-7). Israel does not seem to have developed such a complete system. Gen 4:20-22 is the most extensive list comparatively speaking. Notably, the first use of fire,

which a wide variety of peoples from all over the world recount, is nowhere reported in Genesis (H. F. Feilberg in a personal correspondence). The first inventors are simultaneously considered progenitors of the circle in which the invention currently exists. This is a most ancient perspective: trade, craft, and profession are passed on in the family. "Tribal organization and blood union" governed every circumstance of life then (Meyer, *Israelitien*, 53). The three classes known by this tradition are nomads, musicians, and smiths. These are the three classes of the desert. "Even still the smiths of the Syrian desert and of Arabia comprise a caste" (Stade, ZAW 14:225). Accordingly, Lamech is the ancestor of the desert folk and his house is portrayed from the standpoint of the Bedouin. This desert population divides into three segments. First, the owners of herds, sons of the firstborn, the fully entitled members of the tribe; beside them, like Aoeden beside Homore, "separated from them by a wide chasm, and thence the descendants of a second wife, are the δημιοεργοί, of whom only the eldest, the χαλκεῖς are properly mentioned" (Meyer, *Israeliten*, 218). Tubal's sister Naamah does not belong in this context since no trade is attributed to her. She is an old legend figure who entered this context from somewhere else.

3. The Song of Lamech stands in no relationship to the discoveries made by Lamech's house. It is called Lamech's Sword Song as though it were occasioned by Tubal's discovery of metallurgy. "One must guard against interpreting this fragment by its [current] context" (cf. Wellhausen, *Composition*³, 307). The account of Tubal's discovery does not speak specifically of forging weapons nor does the Song of Lamech mention swords. The song speaks of fierce vengeance. There is no trace in the Song itself that such horrible blood vengeance was condemned. In contrast, Lamech boasts of this vengeance: He is a powerful, proud warrior who does not allow himself to be intimidated and who does not fear the enemy. This is a tone from Israel's beginnings, a proper desert song. Blood vengeance is, after all, at home in the desert. On ancient Arabic blood vengeance, which seeks to and does avenge one-hundredfold, see G. Jacob, *Altarabisches Beduinenleben*², 144ff., 220. Samson's humorous-violent victory song (Judg 15:16) is a similar song from the ancient period. A spiritually related scene occurs in the Gideon account (Judg 8:18ff.) where the princes of the Midianites proudly await death and Gideon's lad is to learn blood vengeance. The oldest period to <51> sing this Song of Lamech did not feel horror at the wild ferocity, but delight over the majestic strength of the hero. Of course, according to the most ancient Israelite religion, long effective in Israel, Yahweh, himself, is a powerful hero, who, zealously concerned for his honor, allows nothing to befall him, "gives his honor to no other," and takes horrible vengeance on his enemies. The juxtaposition of Cain with Lamech shows that Cain is not thought of as the ancestor of Lamech in the song. Such boasting over one's ancestor would have been entirely unthinkable to antiquity. Rather, Cain is a foreigner, a contemporary, perhaps a rival, at any rate a fierce warrior, whose blood vengeance is celebrated. We know nothing about the situation of the song. It is as though nothing from the entire story of Saul and David were preserved except the verse: "Saul has slain his thousands, but David his ten thousands." One should not deny that this Song of Lamech presupposes a definite situation (contra Wellhausen, *Composition*³, 307). We may assume that it was sung on return to the camp. One may imagine how the warrior, bespattered with blood, stands with head high before his wives and proudly announces to them what he has done. Whether

Lamech was once a tribe cannot be said. The Song only allows the conclusion that he was a warrior figure whose wild deeds were recounted (Meyer, *Israeliten*, 219, 395-96). The collector, however, who lived in a softer, more civilized time, will have placed the Song of Lamech at this position as a sign of the frightful decay of the human race, over which then comes the just punishment of the Flood. In terms of metrical form, the song consists of two four beat strophes (the introduction) and two paired trimeters (cf. Sievers 1:405, but see 2:13).

4. The units treated above—the genealogy, the family of Lamech, and the Song of Lamech—belong together in terms of context. All are reminiscences of the desert from Israel's beginnings, expanded with later material only in the genealogy and in the name Tubal. All of it could have been assembled by one hand. V 17b differs: Cain became a (the first) founder of a city and named the city after (Hebr mss, LXX, Pesh, Vulg בְּשֵׁם) his son Enoch. The basis is the tradition of an old city Enoch whose location is unknown to us and probably already to the collector (but see the comments on 5:21ff.). The man Enoch may have originally been the patron god of this city, as Asshur is the patron god of the city Asshur. We cannot say why it is said, not that Enoch himself, but his father Cain built this city. The building of a city is remarkable at this point because the construction of a city presumes the existence of many people and since livestock breeding only arises at the end of the genealogy. If we credit the collector of this unit (J') with good judgment, we must assume, with Holzing, 56, that this note was added secondarily.

Concerning v 1, see above, pp. 41-42.

17 The narrator does not say where Cain got his wife. If asked, he would have answered, in any case, that she was his sister. **18** On the construction וַיִּוָּלֵד אֶת, see §121b. **20** יָבָל (LXX Ἰωβέλ) may have originally read אוֹבָל. The corresponding word in Arab. means "the shepherd who herds the camels" (Gressmann, *Musik*, 3). "The one who dwells in tents and [with] herds." It is not necessary <52> to read אָהֳלֵי מִקְנֶה in analogy to 2 Chron 14:14 or to assume that a participle has fallen out before מִקְנֶה (see §117bb). The analogies "who use zither and shawm" (v 21) and "who forge bronze and iron" (v 22) support the transmitted text. **21** Gressmann (*Musik*, 3) interprets the name יובל as a form of יובל, "trombone," like Phoen. Κιννύρας = כִּנּוֹר. The hypostasized thing is the name of the inventor. Regarding these instruments, cf. Benzinger, *Archäologie²*, 238-41; Nowack 1:270ff.; Gressmann, 24, 28-29.

22 The text is in disorder. הוּא הָיָה אֲבִי is missing before כָּל־ (Ball). Conversely, Sievers (2:264) wants to move vv 20 and 21 behind v 22 and strike הוּא הָיָה אֲבִי in v 20 and הוּא הָיָה אֲבִי כָל־ in v 21. But כָּל־ in vv 22 and 21 attests, rather, that v 22 should be emended in light of v 21. חֹרֵשׁ and לֹטֵשׁ are probably variants of which the more unusual לֹטֵשׁ is the more original. Forced from the text, it was then reintroduced in the wrong position. The placement of bronze before iron may be a remnant of tradition. The "bronze era" precedes the "iron era" (Dillmann).

23a This is a solemn introduction such as Hebrew poetry loves (Gen 49:2; Isa 28:23; 32:9). "You wives of Lamech." With great pride the warrior calls himself by name here and in the following. On שְׁמַעַן, see §46f. **23b** On כִּי as the introduction of a speech, see §157b. הָרַגְתִּי should perhaps be understood as a reference to a one-time act that has just occurred. The enemy has only smitten him, but he has killed the offender. Perhaps, however, it should be understood, "I am in the habit of slaying" (§106k).

Whether the אִישׁ and the יֶלֶד are identical, or whether it should be understood that the vengeance will also meet the offender's child is unclear since we do not know the context of the statement. **24a** Regarding כִּי in the meaning "if," see §159bb. יֻקַּם (§29g) is probably better pointed יְקֹם (Budde, 133). **24b** A gigantic boast!

The whole story of the Cain figure seems, then, to be as follows: (1) Cain was originally the progenitor of the Kenites, cursed in the legend as a fratricide, famed for blood vengeance, and thus mentioned in the Song of Lamech as a wild warrior. (2) The name means "smith" or is at least so understood and thus came to be identified with the smith Tubal whereby Cain acquired the brother Hebel = Jabal. (3) Cain, variant Kenan, was introduced in the protogenealogy of humanity. Here he becomes Enoch's father and the founder of the city by the same name. (4) Later, when the Cain genealogy was interwoven with the Seth genealogy, the Cainites were understood as the godless, the Sethites as the pious. This was certainly not the original intention of the genealogies (cf. also the commentary on chap. 5), but perhaps already the opinion of their collector.

In the period before Mohammed a large Arabic tribe Cain inhabited SE Palestine and the Sinai peninsula. According to Nöldeke (*Enc Bibl* 1:130) this tribe may be associated with the Kenites, a conjecture Meyer (*Israeliten*, 399) finds unlikely because of the time span. <53>

4. The Genealogy of Seth 4:25, 26 . . . 5:29 J^e

The Seth genealogy, originally a variant of the genealogy of Cain, has been combined with it by the collector. This combination is accomplished by the words עוֹד, lacking in LXX, אַחֵר, rather awkward in association with the collective זֶרַע, and תַּחַת הֶבֶל כִּי הֲרָגוֹ קָיִן, words which, in this detail, are not very appropriate on the lips of the mother. According to this tradition, Seth was the first and only son of Adam (similarly in P, 5:3; cf. Budde, 154ff.; contra Eerdmans, 80). Only two fragments of J's genealogy of Seth are preserved. We may reconstruct the missing elements from P's genealogy of Seth (chap 5). This genealogy, like the genealogy of Cain, has also preserved a few comments in addition to the names. Three of them have been transmitted to us:

(1) The etymology of שֵׁת (4:25). The name Adam in v 25 causes difficulty since otherwise J has הָאָדָם (cf. also the comments on 2:17,21). Only P has "Adam" (5:1). Perhaps 4:25 also had הָאָדָם originally? Regarding Seth as a poetic name for Moab, see above, p. 51.

(2) A note concerning the beginning of Yahweh worship. This comment is related in content to those treating such beginnings (4:20-22; 9:20; 11:3, 4, etc.). There is no reason, therefore, to consider it the addition of a later scribe (contra Eerdmans, 81). The institution of religion belongs, in the ancient view, to most remote antiquity (the same idea in the Phoenician legend, *Euseb. praep. ev.* 1.10). This note is extremely interesting from a religiohistorical standpoint. It contradicts, at least in wording, the usual assertion (Exod 3:4; 6:12) that Moses was the first to employ the name Yahweh. We cannot state the reason for associating the name Yahweh with Enosh. We have here the oldest deliberation about the age of Yahweh worship, and the impression reflected in this note that the name Yahweh traces back to the primeval period and is older than Moses and the people Israel is assuredly correct. The names Azriyau from Yaudi in north Syria and Yaubi'di from Hamath are traces of extra-Israelite worship of Yahweh (cf. Zimmern, KAT^3, 465ff.;

Meyer, *Israeliten*, 247-48, 378). The incomprehensible age of the name Yahweh does not exclude the possibility that Moses was the first to reveal this God as Israel's national God. Furthermore, this theory is important for source criticism because, since this source employs אלהים prior to Enosh (cf. 3:1, 3; 4:25), the Cain-Abel Legend, which speaks of יהוה, cannot have stood in this source (cf. above, pp. 41-42). For אָז הוּחַל LXX reads זֶה הֵחֵל (הֹחֵל). It is unlikely that LXX concocted οὗτος from אָז because Vulg and Jubil read the same way (contra Eerdmans, 81). The "invocation of the name" of a god is a general term for the worship of a god (Zeph 3:9; Jer 10:25). Since in the most ancient viewpoint there are "many gods and many lords," the invocation of the name whereby one summons the pertinent god is the beginning of every prayer (cf. the beginnings of the Psalms Psa 3:2; 4:2; 5:2; 6:2; 7:2; etc.; this is still true of our prayers) and is an indispensable essential of sacrifice, thus a foundation of the cult. Consequently, the expression יהוה קָרָא בְשֵׁם is employed very frequently in association with the establishment of cultic sites (12:8; 13:4; 21:33; 26:25; 1 Kgs 18:24ff.). Literally it means "to call, invite in the name of Yahweh." Concerning name invocations, cf. Wellhausen, *Arab. Heidentum*[2], 213; Giesebrecht, *Gottesnamen*, 97; Heitmüller, 30; Stade, *Bibl. Theol.*, 150.

(3) An etymology of נֹחַ (5:29): He is called "Noah," because his father spoke <54> prophetically—יְנַחֲמֵנוּ "he will bring us comfort." How does Noah bring comfort? Surely the old narrator did not have the Flood in mind (Dillmann), which Noah indeed survived, but in which all humanity was destroyed. That would be unusual comfort! Rather, the narrator has Noah's vineyard keeping in mind. Yahweh cursed the field so that people must cultivate it with bitter toil. But now a youth is born who will provide the plagued farmer a comfort from this very same field. It is the wine that gladdens the human heart (Psa 104:15; Judg 9:13), that from the very beginning was meant for joy and becomes a water of life (Sir 34:27-28) so that the sufferer may drink and forget his pain (Prov 31:6-7). This is the ancient view of wine. It was, indeed, Israelite mourning practice to offer the grief stricken the cup of comfort in order to comfort him (לְנַחֲמוֹ) over the death (Jer 16:7; so Böhmer, *Das erste Buch der Thora*, 140-41, and Budde, 307ff.). LXX διαναπαύσει ἡμᾶς = יְנִיחֵנוּ (Ball, Kittel) = "he will give us rest" (cf. Exod 23:12) may be preferable. This statement concerning wine is valuable for understanding the Paradise narrative. Wine is the comfort for Yahweh's curse. This indicates that the narrator of the expulsion from Paradise did not think primarily of the religious aspect, alienation from God, but much more simply and realitiscally of the heavy burdens which the man suffers henceforth in the field (cf. p. 30). The word about Noah is also important for source criticism. In content and phraseology (עִצָּבוֹן, אֲדָמָה, אָרַר) it refers back to 3:17 J⁰ and must, then, belong to J⁰, itself. The result is that J⁰ contained (1) a Paradise narrative, (2) the genealogy of Seth, and (3) the story of Noah's vineyard. On the other hand, the author of 5:29 (see further immediately below) cannot have recounted the Flood. Noah brings comfort, not destruction. Correspondingly, the Flood narrative must belong to another source J^j (cf. p. 3). Possibly, indeed probably, the genealogy of Seth also possessed a comment concerning Enoch, analogous to that of P 5:24. Since J^j also speaks of Noah subsequently, this source must have also contained a transition from the progenitor (Cainite) genealogy to Noah which has now been omitted in preference for J⁰.

5. The Angel Marriages 6:1-6 Jʲ

Source criticism will be treated at the end.

1 וַיְהִי כִּי here means "it happened when" as in 26:8, etc. הָאָדָם is a collective, "humanity"; the individual man is בֶּן־אָדָם.

2 The apodosis is "They saw that they were beautiful." The construction is the same as in 1:4. On מִכֹּל אֲשֶׁר, in whatever forms, see §119w n.1. The statement makes clear that the sons of God in their superior might prevailed upon the daughters of men at will. בְּנֵי הָאֱלֹלהִים (or בְּנֵי אֱלֹהִים, בְּנֵי אֵלִים, even בְּנֵי עֶלְיוֹן) "the sons of God, the sons of the gods" is a term for divine beings which, according to OT belief, resemble Yahweh in essence and power but are subordinate to him. Such beings form his heavenly court; advise Yahweh concerning the affairs of his realm as his heavenly council סוֹד; praise and sing Yahweh's might and majesty; execute his missions and commands; etc. (cf. Job 1:6; 2;1 Psa 29:1; 89:7; Dan 3:25, 28). The "sons of God" parallel or appear in the same position as "stars" (Job 38:7; cf. Psa 82 with Isa 24:21 and Deut 32:8 LXX with Deut 4:19), "the host of heaven" (cf. 1 Kgs 22:19 with Job 1:6), "gods" (Psa 82:1,6), מַלְאָכִים, ἄγγελοι, "angels" (cf. Gen 28:12 with 35:7, cf. also <55> Dan 3:25,28; LXX of Psa 8:6; 97:7; 138:1 and Gen 6:2 LXX A), etc. These and other considerations indicate that Israel's angelology is to be understood as a remnant and aftereffect of older polytheistic religions. It should especially be noted that these beings are never called sons of Yahweh, but always only the sons of God or of the gods. Yahweh, himself, had neither wife nor child. This observation leads to the conclusion that belief in such beings originally had nothing to do with Yahwism but had its proper setting outside Israel. The phrase בְּנֵי אֱלֹהִים will have been understood in Hebrew usage as "beings belonging to the category of אלהים" (§128v). A older, polytheistic usage may stand in the background, however, which would have referred to sons of gods in the actual sense, i.e. beings begotten by gods, second rank gods (Meyer, *Israeliten*, 212n.1). Or is בני an addition of later tradition so that the narrative original told of אלהים-beings, themselves (Schwally, ZAW 18:145)? Narratives that deal with gods or sons of gods are by nature mythological and by origin probably extra-Israelite.

Also purely mythological, then, is **2**: the semigods take earthly maidens as wives, originally understood perhaps such that they were not permitted to marry in the world of the gods and thus took daughters of men (Meyer, *Israeliten*, 212). There are many parallels to this myth among the Greeks. A Phoenician account, similar to our narrative, comes to us from Philo (*Bybl.*, cf. *Fragm. hist. graec.*, ed. C. Müller 3:566). From Israel we have only this one fragment of the same narrative. The further development of religion in Israel suppressed mythology and left standing only a very minimal remnant like milestones of the way traveled. This consideration suggests the advanced age of this legend. The interpretation of this verse offered was already known to late Judaism. In this period of renewed intrusion of a mythological attitude and multiple mythological elements, stemming mostly from outside, Gen 6:1-6 attracted attention and was frequently treated (cf. EthEn 6ff., 19, 86; SlavEn 7, 18; Jubil 5; Judae 6; 2 Pet 2:4, etc.). An extensive narrative, independent of Gen 6, perhaps of Persian origin, seems to have also been incorporated in these treatments (cf. Bousset, *Rel. des Judentums*², 382, 560; with bibliography). The Judeo-Christian doctrine of the "Fall of the Angels" arose in this way. Gen 6 is so highly mythological that it has caused concern for many interpreters, ancient and modern, and has, thus, been subject to reinterpretation. The chief reinterpretations are the following: (1) Sons of God = sons of aristocrats who married maidens of lower class (so the old rabbinical interpretation); (2) sons of God = pious men, understood here specifically as the Sethites, who intermarried with Cainite maidens (so the church fathers, etc.). But "sons of God" never meant "aristocrats" or "pious," nor did בְּנֵי עֶלְיוֹן (Psa 82:6). Yahweh—this specific God—deemed Israel worthy of the honorific (adopted) "son" (Exod 4:22; Hos 11:1, etc.), individual Israelites or pious of the name "sons" (in the same sense; Deut 14:1; 32:5, etc.). But such statements occur only in particularly elevated diction, not in simple narrative. The expression "son of God" or "sons of God" for Israel or the Israelites is also avoided. Instead, בני אלהים means only "angels." Finally, since האדם (v 1) certainly means all humanity, the sense of the word in v 2 can be no other. Literature can be found in <56> Dillman, 120, and Franz Delitzsch, 146-47.

V 3 begins abruptly. Nothing is said of when, where, and to whom these words are spoken (Budde, 36). V 3 stands here, then, in a loose relationship to its context, a situation which shows us that this narrative appears here in a severely abbreviated form but which also complicates the interpretation of v 3 to a great degree. The sons of God, who, after all, are the primary sinners, are not punished. This omission is certainly not because the legend considers these beings as nature spirits with no moral responsibility. It is more likely because Yahweh might does not reach so far (Holzinger). Or is it perhaps because the excessively mythological has been expurgated? A sentence on humanity follows although humans bear no moral guilt: There is no mention of the women seducing the sons of God. But Yahweh intervenes against humanity with the same motivation as in 3:22 and 11:6-8. By interbreeding with the sons of God, humanity obtained a share of the divine nature. According to v 4 the children of these marriages were giants. The notion that the sons of God taught humanity all manner of arts (EthEn 8-9) is also ancient tradition. Thus, man acquired greater power than Yahweh's will permits. Consequently, Yahweh must devise means to mitigate this gain (Wellhausen, *Prolegomena*[6], 314-15; *Composition*[3], 308). Yahweh's sentence, like 3:14-19 and other curses and blessings, seems to have poetic form (a hexameter). The interpretation of the details is difficult. לֹא . . . לְעוֹלָם may mean either never again or not forever. The latter meaning occurs here. יָדוֹן is the impf. (§172r) or jussive (§109d) of the hapax legomenon דון (§72r) which may be understood (1) as a form of the root דין (a middle י form) "to judge," a meaning that does not suit the context, so that (2) Budde and others attribute the meaning "to rule," (3) Gesenius, Dillmann and others translate, "he shall lower himself," following the Arabic *dâna* (middle י), (4) Socin (ThStKr 1894: 211-12) translates, "he shall remain," following the Egypto-Arabic **dân, yidân*, and (5) Vollers (ZA 14:349ff.) suggests, "to be mighty," following the Assyrian *danânu*. The meanings mentioned in 2-5 cannot be identified in the OT although the name ידניה, also spelled ידוניה, "Jedoniah" occurs frequently in the newly discovered Judeo-Aramaic documents (cf. Sachau, *Drei aramäische Papyrus- urkunden aus Elephantine*, 18). It appears in Neh 3:7 in the abbreviated form ידון, "Yahweh abides," or the like. LXX (cf. Vulg, Targ-Onk, Pesh) translates καταμείν here. διαμενεῖ may also translate ידון in Psa 72:17 (Buhl). The Hebrew text has ינון. But this meaning also fails to render a clear sense. Is the divine spirit that will not abide in man forever the life spirit granted man by God? In this case, God's intention would seem to be—as indicted in v 3b, too—to shorten man's lifespan (Dillmann). Or is it the divine essence that Yahweh has in common with the sons of the gods and of which now humanity, too, against Yahweh's will, has obtained a portion? In this case, one would assume that Yahweh wants to destroy humanity with a catastrophe. V 3b would then be a "mistaken gloss" (Wellhausen, *Composition*[3], 308). The diction and continuation of the account seem to speak more for the first interpretation. The third strophe adds a reason to the first two (the decree). "Flesh" characterizes the feeble, mortal nature of man (and of animals) in contrast to the mighty, eternal "Spirit" of God (Isa 31:3; Psa 56:5; Job 10:4f.). In relation to v 3, "he is flesh" can mean nothing other than this: Because man is only flesh, i.e. an inferior, weak, earthly being, he does not deserve to live eternally (cf. the striking parallel in 3:19). בשׁגם (variously understood, cf. Budde, 14ff.). belongs, it seems, judging from the rhythm, to the following strophe. Syntactically, too, if taken with the preceding strophe, it would lag behind. Most mss and editions (cf. Kittel) point בְּשַׁגָּם (qal inf. > שׁגג with ב and a suffix), "in their error he is flesh." But the change of number is <57> intolerable. Furthermore, an error on the part of the daughters of men, not to mention of all of humanity, can hardly be discussed. Finally, the notion that man is flesh because he has sinned is hardly possible: Instead, conversely, man is inclined to sin because he is flesh. The reference of the suffix in בשׁגם to the angels does not give a satisfactory sense (cf. Dillmann, 122). As a result, the pronounciation בְּשַׁגָּם is preferable (so other mss and editions). בְּשַׁאגָּם = ב + שׁ relativum + גם "also." בְּשׁ = בַּאֲשֶׁר "while." The relative שׁ, common in later Hebrew, also already occurs in old songs (cf. Judg 5:7) and cannot be considered entirely implausible here. בְּשַׁגָּם would mean "while also" (LXX, Pesh, Targ-Onk, old Lat, Vulg "while"). "While he is also flesh." The sense may be that he, too—as noble as he is—is still only flesh, i.e., mortal, like the other earthly beings (Sievers 2:250). "So, then (as a consequence) their days will be 120 years." By context, the clause is to be understood only of the days of the individual human's life. Accordingly, 120 years is the maximum human lifespan, an assumption attested elsewhere in Oriental traditions, although not in the OT (cf. Herodotus 3.23). Since, however, this number does not agree with subsequent, sometimes much larger lifespans in P, the attempt has been made in ancient and modern times to argue that this passage concerns a period of grace lasting until the Flood—an unsystematic mixture of divergent, originally independent traditions. The manifold, undeniable difficulties of the verse lead Schwally (ZAW 18: 142ff.) to consider v 3a (up to לְעֹלָם) to have been redacted, v 3b to be secondary.

4a has been added to the preceding with no inner coherence, like a parenthetical note (cf. 12:6; 13:7). One would actually expect this remark after v 2. הַנְּפִלִים is a term like "giants" and "Titans." "The giants" are considered a well-known entity here. בֹּא אֶל is euphemistic (supply "into the rooms"). The author, anxiously concerned with mitigating the objectionable, tells only of the synchrony of the angelic marriages and the giants. But one must be very naive not to read between the lines here that, according to the original tradition, which the author shies away from reproducing, the giants were the angel's children. The expression "and afterwards," which sounds secondary and disturbs the context, is probably the addition of an anxious reader aware of the existence of giants in a later period, too, (cf. Num 13:33) who missed a reference to them here (Budde, 34). וְיָלְדוּ (pf. cons.) is the continuation of יָבֹאוּ (§112e). Note the change of subject. The unusually difficult syntax can be explained as the result of the author's predicament. He must say things which he would prefer to conceal. Gruppe (ZAW 19:145) and Holzinger try to help by emending the text.

4b intends to elucidate the expression נְפִלִים, archaic in the author's time, with the more usual, less mythological גִּבֹּרִים, "warriors." The reference to the military fame of these giants is very important to us. We have only fragments of giant legends in the OT. We hear of the נְפִלִים in Num 13:33, where they include the בְּנֵי עֲנָק, and in Ezek 32:27 which speaks of the "heroes" (גִבּוֹרִים), the Titans of the primeval period (נֹפְלִים מֵעוֹלָם, Cornill), "who descend to Sheol fully equipped, with their swords placed under their heads, with their bucklers (צִנּוֹתָם, Cornill) on their legs, for they were a horror to heroes in the land of the living." Here, too, the נְפִלִים appear as primordial warriors whose martial fame was known all over the world. Giant legends echo in Gen 29:10 and 32:23ff. Furthermore, remnants of the Nimrod Legend (Gen 10:8ff.), the names of the nations of giants אֵימִים בְּנֵי עֲנָק רְפָאִים who were also considered aborigines, a tradition of Og, king of Bashan whose coffin was displayed (Deut 3:11), and a few details in the Samson Legend (Judg 15:17; 16:3) have also been preserved. To later Judaism, which revived the giant legends, these primordial giants were considered an example of folly (*vis consilii expers*; Bar 3:26-28), of <58> arrogant crime against God (WisdSol 14:6; 3 Macc 2:4; Sir 16:7) and of sudden destruction. Another tradition concerning the "Nephilim" occurs in EthEn 15. Giant legends also occur among the Arabs, Phoenicians ("Philo Byblius," *Fragm. hist. graec.*, ed. C. Müller 3:566), the Greeks, and the Germans (Chantepies de la Saussaye, *Religionsgeshichte* 2², 501-502).

Tradition and Literary Criticism
of the Narrative of the Angel Marriages

The piece is a torso. It can hardly be called a story. The whole thing consists of three sentences (vv 1, 2, v 3, v 4) standing alongside each other in no precise relationship. The original narrative must have been much richer. It is difficult to imagine that there would ever have been a story about angelic marriages and giants if it recounted only these few details. The term Nephilim (on such terms in legends, see p. 67 and the introduction §3:15) and v 4b point, with particular clarity, to ancient material, already half-forgotten in the narrator's time. The present mutilation can be explained as the result of the highly mythological content of the tradition that gave the narrator offense. The pagans tell unashamedly of the time "when gods and goddesses loved." But Israel feels disgust for the interbreeding of divine and human. Thus, the narrator was able to communicate only very little of the whole legend and this only very cautiously (cf. v 4). There may have also been even later hands at work on the text (Dillmann).

These verses stem from J as evidenced by עַל־פְּנֵי הָאֲדָמָה הָאָדָם, יהוה (v 1), גִּבֹּר, הַנְּפִלִים (v 4), and the syntax of vv 2f. (cf. Budde, 6-9, 39n.1).

The piece currently introduces the Flood narrative in J. It has been placed before this narrative in order to illustrate by example the corruption of the human race presupposed in the Flood narrative. Originally, however, this tradition of angelic marriages and giants had nothing to do with the Flood narrative, just as the Babylonian Flood account knows nothing of it. Similarly, Gen 6:1-4 does not look forward to the Flood and the Flood legend begins only in 6:5ff. (so already Reuss). Which of the two collections contained in J, J^j or J^e, we can thank for this fragment is a question of very inferior value. The piece cannot have stood in J^e, in which the legend of Noah's viticulture must have followed immediately after the genealogy of Seth judging from 5:29. Contrariwise, it could well have introduced the Flood legend in J^j. The collector will have understood the נְפִלִים as beings in the predeluge period. It may also have been inserted only later.

6. Flood Legend in J^j
6:5-8 . . . 7:1, 2, 3b, 4, 5, 10, 7*, 16b, 12, 17b, 23aaa, 22, 23b; 8:6a, 2b, 3a . . . 6b, 7-12, 13b . . . 20-22

Regarding source criticism. The Flood Legend has been transmitted to us in J and P. The two reports have been combined very closely. The analysis given above of the components belonging to J depends on the work of an entire family of scholars. J is indicated by יהוה (6:5,8; 7:1,5,16b; 8:20, 21 2x's), יָצֶר (6:5; 8:21; it does not occur in P), הִתְעַצֵּב (6:6), and מָצָא הֵן (6:8, frequent in J). The narrative makes a very unified impression: Yahweh decides "to wipe men from the face of the earth" (6:7). He reports this decision verbatim to Noah (7:4) and executes it (7:23). Yahweh announces a forty-day rain, to begin in 7 days (7:4). This occurs (7:10, 12). The manner and chronology of the coming of the Flood corresponds, then, <59> to the manner (8:2b) and chronology of the disappearance of the water (cf. below, pp. 63-64). The clean animals, of which 7:2 speaks, are employed in the sacrifice (8:20). A speech of Yahweh begins the account, and a Yahweh speech concludes it. Both speeches refer to human sinfulness (6:5ff.; 8:21-22). The J text is currently only incompletely preserved. Furthermore, it is carved into small sections and repeatedly glossed. That it can be reconstructed at all results from its great unity and its quite striking difference to the P account. Within J, the Flood report belongs to J^j (cf. comments on 5:29). See further concerning source criticism in the discussion of P, where there is also a translation of the entire pericope.

6:5-7 *Yahweh's decision to destroy humanity.* This unit is not to be taken with 6:14 (Dillmann and Franz Delitzsch), but is the exposition to J's Flood account. Gen 6:5 is an especially lively beginning in medias res. Only the name of Noah, presumed in v 8, preceded this introductory unit, similar to 5:28ff. at the end of a genealogy. In contrast, the narrator certainly did not speak of Noah's righteousness because it will be portrayed subsequently with a characteristic example. The old narrator takes care not to anticipate his own point. Nor is a description of humanity's sin necessary in order to assume that it took place prior to Noah. It is enough that Yahweh sees this sin. What Yahweh sees certainly also exists, for Yahweh does not see erroneously.

5 A deeply pessimistic view of human sinfulness underlies this narrative. Humans contemplate nothing other than evil, evermore, so that Yahweh is truly sorry he created such beings at all! But people are still so (8:21), the narrator thinks; the Flood has not improved them. The prophets' polemic gives the impression that the people of their time were very self-satisfied. The old legend shows us, however, that complaints about the sins of the children of men we hear later in the prophets and psalmists were already made known in ancient times. The Egyptian and Babylonian narratives of extreme punishments the gods sent upon sinful humans (Erman, *Äg. Rel.*, 32-33; Zimmern, KAT³, 552-53) demonstrate that such an attitude can be attributed already to the ancient period and did not, as Smend (*Isr. Religionsgesch.*, 306) and Meinhold (141) see it, arise in Israel first under the influence of the prophets. The Egyptian god also says "by my life, my heart is weary of being with you" (Erman, 33), not to mention Hesiod's complaint about the "iron race" (*Op. et dies*, 174ff.). Characteristically, here, sinfulness is deeply felt, but not, as the legend otherwise prefers, presented through a clear example. Apparently, the old legend material did not contain such an example. It is also absent from the cuneiform narrative. Gen 6:1-4 has been placed in the breach by the collector. Human depravity is also the cause in many other Flood legends (cf. Winternitz, *Mitt. Anthrop. Ges. Wien* 31:315).

6 God feels regret and bitter pain: If he had known how evil people would become, he would have certainly not created them! How should we evaluate such anthropomorphisms? One need not be ashamed of them nor should one chide them or scoff at them. They demonstrate not only that the religion of the time was in its childhood, but also that it was vital and powerful. It had more life and power than a reflection, admittedly advanced in knowledge but simultaneously crippling and chilling. Even the most extreme anthropomorphisms in the OT are by far more gentle than, say, the manner in which the Babylonian speaks of his gods (cf. the cuneiform Flood legend). Our religion, too—although we realize quite clearly the insufficiency of such <60> modes of expression—will never transcend anthropomorphisms. Concerns were already expressed in the OT about Yahweh's "regret," in particular when God seems to be capricious (Num 23:19; 1 Sam 15:29). On the other hand, this idea is affirmed and plays a large role in the prophets where it signifies that God's rule is no iron fate, but that he remains the free Lord of his decisions (Jer 18:1-11). וינחם is probably an allusion to the name "Noah." The statement "He was offended deeply in his heart" is especially ancient.

7 The decision itself takes the form of Yahweh's soliloquy. It, too, is unspecific. In order to heighten tension, the narrator purposefully does not yet state the means Yahweh intends to use to annihilate humanity. Since v 7b repeats once again God's regret, we may conjecture that v 7 was originally the beginning of the legend material to which the Hebrew narrative added a moral foundation. This foundation is characteristically absent in the cuneiform recension (Haller, 58). But the Hebrew narrator, too, derives the Flood not from the "righteousness of God, who punishes the evil, but from God's regret over his creation" (Haller, 54). אֲשֶׁר־בָּרָאתִי is probably a gloss. J usually uses עָשָׂה. Another probable gloss is מֵאָדָם עַד־בְּהֵמָה עַד־רֶמֶשׂ וְעַד־עוֹף הַשָּׁמָיִם, a wonderful interpretation of הָאָדָם in the style of P (6:20; 7:14, 21, etc.). The pedantic glossator missed the animals that were also destroyed in the Flood (cf. Budde, 249ff.). Gen 7:1 is not the immediate continuation of 6:8. 7:1 already speaks of "the Ark." Yahweh's command to Noah to build the Ark and the construction of the Ark, itself, must have already been narrated in the intervening material. On the other hand, Yahweh cannot have said anything about the imminent Flood because it is clearly announced in 7:4 as something new. Accordingly, Budde (256n.1) has quite ingeniously restored the lacuna: J reported two appearances of Yahweh. When Yahweh appeared to Noah for the first time, he commanded him to build a massive ship without adding a word about the reason for this construction! This would have been a difficult obedience test for Noah: a ship on dry land (cf. Heb 11:7)?! But Noah passed this test and built the ship. Then Yahweh appeared to him a second time and rewarded his obedience: This ship that you have built, apparently against all reason, only in obedience to me, I now ordain to deliver you in the coming Flood! The upward trend from 6:8 to 7:1 can be explained in this way. Because Noah pleased Yahweh, he decided to put him to the test. When he passed it so exquisitely, Yahweh declared to him, "You have I (now) found to be (the only) righteous one in the race." The parallel passage in P (6:13-22) is structured very similarly: (1) God commands Noah to build the Ark (vv 14-16) and (2) only then speaks of its purpose and of the flood (vv 17-22). This peculiar arrangement, totally inconsistent with the nature of the matter, can only be explained by the assumption that P adopted the narrative sequence of his exemplar. This exemplar must, then, have been very closely related to J. Concerning the analogy in the Babylonian material, see below, pp. 71-72. Like P (vv 14-16), J will have also discussed the material and dimensions of the Ark.

7:1-5 *The second appearance of Yahweh.* 1 The appearance itself is not described (attenuation of the narrative as in 4:6). The expression "your whole house" shows the pleasing brevity of the good narrator in contrast to the wide-ranging lists of P (6:18; 7:13; 8:16, 18). This statement suggests that Noah's house, specifically his sons, are discussed before 6:5 (analogous to 5:22, P). The statement <61> assumes that God not only rewards the man, himself, for his piety, but also his family for his sake (cf. the commentary on 19:12). תֵּבָה is a technical term in the Flood Legend. Is it perhaps an Egyptian or Babylonian loanword (bibliography in Gesenius[14] s.v.). אֹתְךָ is in emphatic position in the meaning "you alone." רָאִיתִי finds a close analogy in עַתָּה יָעַדְתִּי in 22:12. Now God is clearly convinced. צַדִּיק was originally a legal term referring to one in a legal proceeding who is just and obtains justice. It then was applied more generally to one who was just on the whole with regard to all his affairs, the innocent, righteous, honest citizen. It was then transferred to the religious realm to refer to the one just in God's eyes (לְפָנַי), the pious. God recognizes in Noah's obedience that he is a truly pious individual. Elsewhere, too, the legends speak readily of such faithful obedience on the part of the fathers and of how God views and rewards such obedience (12; 15; 22; cf. further on 15:6). Ezek 14:14, 20 treats Noah's righteousness as an example.

2 Beside Noah and his family, God also wants to save animals from the Flood. God wants to preserve what he has created. טָהוֹר means clean, i.e., that which is acceptable in the cult because it corresponds to the fixed requirement prescribed by sacred usage. Of animals if refers to suitability for sacrifice and consumption. The antonym is טָמֵא, that which is not permitted in the cult. In reference to animals, it designates that which cannot be sacrificed or eaten. Such dietary prescriptions, in many ancient religions a survivor of the most ancient religious view of animals (Stade, *Bibl. Theol.*, 136-37), has always played a great role in Israel's life. The original significance of such practices was already unknown to the most ancient period in Israel accessible to us (Stade, *Bibl. Theol.*, 140-41). J presupposes that it was already self-evident in the primordium. He could not imagine that there were ever people who could not distinguish between clean and unclean. At any rate, this impression of the age of these ceremonies corresponds to the religiohistorical situation much better the P's theory that they derive first from Moses. Why so many more of the clean than of the unclean animals? Because man has much greater need of the clean, he uses fewer of the unclean. This is naive human egotism. Because of the addition אִישׁ וְאִשְׁתּוֹ, "seven of each" means seven pairs (Dillmann). Ball, following Sam, Pesh, LXX reads שְׁנַיִם שְׁנַיִם, "two of each."

3a is a gloss: זָכָר וּנְקֵבָה is the diction of P. The old concise narrator mentions only בְּהֵמָה (v 2), in which he includes the birds. This is not precise enough for the pedantic glossator who follows P's model (Budde, 257). LXX and Pesh amplify the expression even more. V **3b** joins very nicely to v 2 (cf. 19:32).

4 On מַמְטִיר, "I will rain," see §116p. Winckler (*Gesch. Isr.* 2:83-84; *Altor. Forschungen* 3:401) associates the forty days of the Flood with the forty days during which the Pleiades are not visible, mid-April until the end of May. In Canaan this is approximately the time of the "late rain." For Greek tradition concerning the forty days of the Pleiades, cf. Ilberg in Roscher, *Lex.*, s.v. Pleiades. The "forty days" or the number forty also occurs frequently among other nations (bibl. in Boeklen, ARW 6:56ff.). V **5** employs, once again, the most extreme brevity.

7-10 The basis of the account of Noah's entrance into the ark must belong to J, since P recounts the same in vv 11, 13-16a. These verses have been heavily glossed, however (Budde, 258ff.). The expansive lists of Noah's family (v 7, cf. 7:1) and the various <62> animals (v 8, cf. 6:7) do not correspond to the style of J, but of P. Characteristic of P are the pleonastic use of אִתּוֹ (v 7) in lists (cf. Holzinger, 341), further that two each of all animals enter the Ark (v 9), and the expressions זָכָר וּנְקֵבָה (v 9) and אלהים (v 9; Sam, Vulg, etc. have יהוה). A J text may underlie vv 8,9 which was significantly reshaped by R (Holzinger). The sections remaining for J are to be arranged in the sequence vv 10, 7* to which v 16b joins superbly. Yahweh set a period of seven day after which the Flood will come (v 4). Noah uses this period to bring his family and the animals into the Ark according to Yahweh's commandment. When this period is up, the Flood comes (v 10). Before it comes, Noah enters the Ark as the last to do so (v 7*), and Yahweh closes the door after him (v 16b; cf. Budde, 258). R^JP chopped J into very small sections and placed them in the P account. In so doing, he reversed vv 7 and 10 to bring together the two chronological comments about the beginning of the Flood. **10** מַבּוּל derives from Bab. *abûbu* "Deluge," or better, with Zimmern and others, from the root ובל (cf. Bab. *bubbulu*, *bibbulu* "flood").

16b Yahweh himself closes the door in his grace in order to shield Noah (a very ancient anthropomorphic element). V **12** describes the duration of the whole Flood in J and must then have originally stood behind v 16b (Kautzsch-Socin). R^JP placed it here at the beginning of the Flood because he harmonized: in the beginning of the Flood, it rained forty days and then—further. V **17b** connects with v 12, the duration of the Flood.

Vv **22, 23aα,b** portray the rising of the Flood and the demise of all beings, again in a loose interrelationship. J means that if it should rain heavily and uninterruptedly (גֶּשֶׁם, v 12 in contrast to the usual מָטָר for forty days the result must be such a fantastic Flood that all beings would perish. **22** The peculiar expression נִשְׁמַת־רוּחַ חַיִּים is a composite of נִשְׁמַת חַיִּים J (2:7) and רוּחַ חַיִּים P (7:15). Since the whole verse belongs to J because of מות (|| גוע P 7:21) and חָרָבָה (|| יָבְּשָׁה P 1:9), רוּחַ should be removed as a gloss (Budde, 265). The frightful catastrophe is reported with great composure. There is no expression of horror at the demise of all humanity. Human life has minimal value (Haller, 107). V **23aα** is J (cf. 6:7; 7:4). V **23b** belongs to J because of the brevity of expression. In contrast, the expansive and unnecessary specification in v 23aβ in the style of P has been added by R (cf. 6:7). The subject יהוה should be inserted following וַיִּמַח (qal) with Budde (265-66). In order to lighten the context, R struck יהוה and read וַיִּמַח

as a niphal. The text of J would become even smoother if one reversed v 23aα, which narrates the action, and v 22, which describes the resulting circumstance.

8:2b, 3a cannot be the immediate continuation of the preceding. The conjecture is very plausible that the temporal reference in 6a originally preceded 8:2b, 3a and that R then displaced it in order to unify the chronologies of P and J to some degree (Wellhausen, *Composition*[3], 4). V **3a** J parallels vv 3b, 5 P. On the construction of this clause, see §113u. The scene of the sending of the birds follows now in J. This scene presupposes, however, that the Ark no longer floats but is already grounded. Correspondingly, it must have been recounted that the Ark was grounded with the receding waters and the place—a mountain—will have also been mentioned. The landing on a mounting occurs in many other Flood legends (Winternitz, 320f.). מִקֶּדֶם (Gen 11:2) <63> suggests that a mountain to the East (of Babylonia) was mentioned here. This would suit Babylonian tradition (cf. below). Since the subsequent material has a remarkable number of words from the root שלח (vv 7, 8, 9, 10, 12), one could suspect that the name of the land may have been שֶׁלַח (son of Arpachshad, 11:12). The following, lovingly presented scene (6b-12, 13b) has the goal of portraying the exceedingly great wisdom of Noah. No one in the Ark knows where they are and how things look outside. No one dares open the door—great streams of water could surge in—or take off the roof—the rain could begin again. One can look out the window, but through it one sees only the heavens above. What shall one do? How shall one learn whether the earth is dry? In this difficult situation the clever Noah knows a means. If one cannot exit oneself, one can send the birds to reconnoiter. "It was an old nautical practice, indispensable in a time which did not know the compass, to bring birds along to be released on the high seas so that the direction to land could be determined by their flight" (Usener, *Sintfluthsagen*, 254; cf. also Plinius n.h. 6:83; Dahlmann, *Mahābhārata*, 179; Keller, *Thiere des class. Alterthums*, 446n.260; Winternitz, 325n.1). Cheyne ("Deluge," *Enc. Bibl.*, no. 19) differs. He calls attention to an Indian fairy tale according to which animals haul up something from the flooded earth so that it can be newly created. The subsequent context is perceptibly disturbed by the sending out of the raven (v 7; Wellhausen, *Composition*[3], 13). (1) According to vv 8ff., Noah sent out the dove three times. This involves a definite number and each time the same animal (the cuneiform text and the recension of Berosus also tell of sending out birds three times). (2) The narrator created a nice climax. The first time the dove returns immediately (vv 8, 9). The second time it returns home only in the evening with an olive branch (vv 10-11). The third time it does not return at all (v 12). (Similar climaxes in both Babylonian traditions, too.) The raven that flies to and fro does not fit into this schema. (3) The purpose of sending out the birds, "in order to see whether the waters had receded," is indicated first in v 8, that is after the sending of the raven. This raven element does not stem from our recension of the text, then. LXX M, where the verse is marked with an obelisk, gives documentary confirmation for this conclusion (cf. Dahse, ZAW 28:5-6). The verse must belong to another recension. A raven is also sent out in the cuneiform text. In this presumed recension, however, the raven that flies to and fro "until the water dried up from the earth" must have occupied final position, just as in the cuneiform text. Dahse finds traces of this recension in the LXX mss d (t) x d2 (new Cambridge edition) where v 8 has παρ' αὐτοῦ (from Noah) instead of the otherwise attested ὀπίσω αὐτοῦ (after the raven), v 10 omits ἑτέρας πάλιν, and v 12 omits πάλιν. From this evidence, Dahse infers an older text which spoke not of the dove in the second and third positions but of other birds. The history of the text, then, would have been as follows.

The original Hebrew recension spoke of three different birds, as did the Babylonian. Later the dove was inserted in all three positions. The statement concerning the raven is, then, a remnant of the old text. Since in J Noah "waits seven more days" (v 10) before sending out the dove for the second time, one may conclude that he must have waited seven days once before, after the grounding of the Ark. Some indication of this must have stood before v 6b and is presently displaced by v 6a (Dillmann). The seven days of the Ark's resting also occurs in the <64> Babylonian version. But אֲחֵרִים is missing in some mss of LXX (see above). **6b** J must have mentioned the window, and the roof (v 13), of the Ark previously in God's commandment to built the Ark. **7** "The raven" refers to the particular raven at hand (§126r). LXX καὶ ἀπέστειλεν τὸν κόρακα + τοῦ ἰδεῖν εἰ κεκόπακεν τὸ ὕδωρ has made its way into v 7 from v 8 (contra Kittel). LXX and Pesh have וְלֹא שָׁב. **9** From the fact that the dove returns immediately, Noah concludes that water still stands everywhere: what a disappointment for him! Note the elegant description of the way Noah retrieves the dove. מָנוֹחַ is probably an allusion to the name נֹחַ, as are נִיחֹחַ (v 21) and וַתָּנַח (8:4, P). **10** For וַיָּחֶל, v 12 reads וַיִּיָּחֶל; Sam reads ויחל in both instances; Olshausen reads וַיְיַחֶל both times. Indeed, the form ויחל can be understood as a piel of יחל (§69u) and pronounced *wayaḥēl*. Ball reads וַיָּחֶל, but the root חיל in this meaning is doubtful. Kittel reads וַיְחֶל. **11** At dusk, when birds usually fly to their nests, the dove returns: thus—sadly enough—it still does not feel at home outside. But when it comes, see there (the word beautifully portrays joyous astonishment), it has a fresh olive branch in its beak. So the trees are already projecting up above the water. The olive branch is fresh, newly broken, otherwise it would demonstrate nothing. This small, charming scene indirectly portrays Noah's mixed emotions. Why an olive branch, of all things? One may suspect that this dove with the olive branch in its beak originally signified more than is apparent from the text of J. It is probably the symbol of a god. Correspondingly, the relationship would have originally been that god gives his protegé a sign that he is near and that he cares for him. A dove (?) in flight with a leaf before it can be seen on a Cyprian coin in Peitschmann, *Gesch. der Phönizier*, 224. Among the Greeks, the olive tree was the symbol of peace. **12** Sent out for the third time, the dove does not return. Therefore, it must be dry outside. Then Noah dares to open the roof (v 13b J ‖ v 14 P) in order to look around, and see there! What joy! The earth is really dry! He guessed correctly! Indeed, who was as clever as Father Noah! The wisdom of the Flood Hero was also extolled in the Babylonian tradition.

There is no report of how Noah and all those with them exited the vessel. Then follows vv 20-22. The first thing Noah does now is to build an altar and sacrifice. This is ancient thought. The same element occurs in Babylonian, Greek, and Indian Flood legends. He sacrifices—as the continuation of the account demonstrates—because the God who so far has been so horribly angry with humans, is also mysterious to him for stilling the rest of his wrath. The fact that Noah also built an altar is an incidental element. Without altar one cannot sacrifice. Since there <65> were so few animals then, his sacrifice of every kind of animal is especially valuable. Naturally Noah sacrificed only clean animals. J presupposed Israelite sacrificial practices as self-evident, even for the primeval period. He sacrificed them as עֹלֹה, whole, he ate nothing himself. One offers such a whole sacrifice on very unusual occasions, for example, in cases of divine wrath (2 Sam 24:25). Now is not the time for the intimacy of the זֶבַח which God and human enjoy together. וּמִכֹּל הָעוֹף הַטָּהוֹר is probably "amplification" as in 7:3a.

21 To the following scene compare the conclusion of the Babylonian Flood legend (see below pp. 70-71). The text does not indicate where Yahweh spoke this statement. In any case it will have been when he appeared at the altar attracted by the sacrifice (Haller, 74; see above, p. 43). The description of Yahweh's "regret," his change of attitude, is envisioned in a most ancient fashion. So far—so we may portray the whole episode—he was frightfully angry and he annihilated all humanity. Now that he has discharged his wrath, he has become amenable to milder temperaments. Now, at the right time, "the aroma of appeasement" reaches his nose. Then his wrath subsides and he comes to consider grace: I will not do it again for it does not help. Humans are evil from their youth onward. He now decides to bear human depravity, which enflamed him to such a frightful punishment, as unalterable or at least not to punish with such frightful judgment. This passage is, thus, significant for an understanding of the old "sin offering." The fact that God smells the sacrifice is recounted only here in the OT, although it is presumed in 1 Sam 26:19; Amos 5:21; Lev 26:31. רֵיחַ הַנִּיחֹחַ continues to be a sacrificial term even in the latest period. "I will not curse the earth again" is a characteristic ancient expression. To curse means to do harm through an (effective, magical) statement. Yahweh called forth the flood through his word, he cursed the rain down upon the earth. The legend of Atrahsis (Zimmern, KAT³, 552-53) also contains the notion that humans do not improve despite all divine punishment. **21b** The mode of expression now becomes increasingly fuller and more poetic and, in v 22, contains clearly recognizable fixed rhythms. Thus, it is not unusual that v 21b, as Hebrew poetry prefers, parallels v 21a in expression. Holzinger's misgivings about the authenticity of v 21, formally a doublet of v 21b and materially a doublet of v 22, and about the expression קְלָל, "excessive" and "imprecise" (following Budde, ZAW 6:37), are, therefore, untenable. The author does not mean that Yahweh intended henceforth to be unconcerned about the sins of humanity. Instead, he means that a universal world judgment is not to be expected again and he allows Yahweh himself to pronounce this in the most solemn manner. This element of the legend is cited in Isa 54:9. This view of the world's course is specifically distinct from the prophetic (and later apocalyptic) eschatological expectation.

22 "All the days of the earth" means forever. עֹד with negation means "not a second time" in the parallel passage Gen 9:11, 15 and elsewhere. Here it is expressively placed in initial position. The reading עַד "until" (Ball, Holzinger, Sievers 2:255) offers no assistance. Winckler's conjecture עַד כְּלוֹת, "until completed," (Forschungen 3:401-402) is unnecessary. קַיִץ is high summer, חֹרֶף is late fall or winter. In solemn rhythms that can be scanned as four-beat and six-beat strophes, the legend fades wonderfully away. The legends are not usually in the habit of concluding on the heights <66> of sentiment, but in full calm and composure. Characteristic examples are 22:19; 21:22 and especially the conclusion of the Joseph narratives in chap. 50. Of the very same character, however, as this conclusion of the Flood sage are also 9:25-27; 14:22-24; 15:18. Such exceptions from the usual rule make all the greater impression on the hearer. A further conclusion after these words is not to be expected. Nothing supports Wellhausen's suggestion (*Prole-*

gomena⁶, 310-11) that J (like P 9:12ff.) now had the sign of the rainbow. The rainbow is also absent in the Babylonian tradition.

Concerning the Flood Legend in J

(1) The narrative in J has not been transmitted to us in ancient form. The appearance of Yahweh in 7:1 is very unspecific, as is the description of the depravity of humanity. The demise of all life, especially, is portrayed rather colorlessly. Noah stands, as the later legends prefer, as the ideal of a pious individual, here specifically as a hero of faith. But the scene of the release of the birds that extols his wisdom stands out singularly. The current tradition finds it difficult to combine the two, Noah's faithful obedience and his wisdom, into a total image. Further, the oldest tradition, as we may infer form 6:9, spoke of God's intimate acquaintance with Noah. This has entirely disappeared in J. Older tradition, furthermore, explained the Flood mythologically: The great deep and the windows of heaven opened (7:11). Contrariwise, J tells much more moderately of a forty-day downpour. On the other hand, J also has a few very ancient elements: Yahweh closes the Ark himself (7:16); Yahweh allows his mind to be changed by the lovely aroma of the sacrifice (8:21-22). The scene involving the release of the birds is also very old. It distinguishes itself from its context by its vivid graphic quality. It does fit well into the composition as a whole (the scene is, in relation to the others, far too long). It strikes another, much more worldly tone. The fact that the legend contains a few terms which belong specifically to this account also indicates a very ancient tradition: מַבּוּל, "Deluge" and תֵּבָה, "Ark." Examples of similar terms are תְהוֹם, "primal sea," תֹהוּ וָבֹהוּ, "chaos," בָּרָא, "to create," אֵד in 2:6, גַּן־עֵדֶן, and הָפַךְ of Sodom and Gomorrah (Gen 19:25), all in very ancient traditions. An actual prophetic spirit does not appear in the legend (cf. comments on 6:5; 8:21)

Accordingly we conclude: (a) that the tradition of the Flood in Israel is very ancient and (b) that the current form of the legend belongs in a relatively younger time. (c) We may, however, imagine, on the analogy of the scene involving the release of the birds, that this older tradition was more mundane. The two predicates of Noah, that he is clever and the darling of a god, will have found their unity in the god pleasure over Noah precisely because of his wisdom. The god's sudden change of attitude—he thinks quite differently in the beginning of the story than at the end—will also have been given a better foundation there. Since a flood legend can hardly be accounted for in Canaan's climate, and since, on the other hand, the tradition itself localizes the legend in the East (cf. on 8:4; 11:2), we may assume—even without any other witness—the Babylonian origin of the legend. The terms מַבּוּל and תֵּבָה, both of which are probably loan words, also point to the foreign origin of the narrative.

(2) The Babylonian tradition we know from Berosus (in *Eusebius Chronicon* 1, ed. Schoene, 19ff.; C. Müller, *Fragm. hist. graec.* 2, 501-502; cf. Usener, *Sintfluthsagen*, 13-14) and, now, the cuneiform account confirm these conclusions most conveniently.

Berosus recounts that Chronos appeared to the tenth Babylonian king Xisuthros in his sleep and announced to him that humanity would be destroyed on the fifteenth of Daesius (May–June) by a flood. He commanded him to commit all things, beginning, middle, and end, to writing and to deposit them in the city of the sun, Sipara (Sippara). Then he should build a ship (σκάφος) and board it with his relatives and nearest friends, <67>

stock it with food and drink, load it with animals, too, winged and four-footed, and, when he has made all ready, depart. If asked where he sails, he should say, "To the gods, to ask them to do good for humanity." He obeyed and built a ship five (a variant in the Armenian text, fifteen) stadia long, two stadia wide, assembled everything as he was commanded, and boarded with his wife, children, and nearest friends. When the Flood had come and as soon as it ceased, Xisuthros released some birds. They found, however, neither nourishment nor resting place and returned again to the ship. After a few days, Xisuthros released birds once again. These returned to the ship, but with slime on their feet. Sent out for the third time, they did not return to the vessel. From this, Xisuthros recognized that the land must have reappeared and he disassembled a few of the joints. Then he saw that the vehicle was stranded on a mountain, exited with his wife, daughter, and helmsman, kissed the earth, built an altar, sacrificed to the gods, and then disappeared along with the others who had exited with him. When he and his companions did not return, those who had remained behind in the vehicle also exited. They sought him and called him by name. Xisuthros did not show himself to them again, but a voice sounded out of the air commanding them that they must (in order to be delivered) worship the gods for, because of his piety, he too has received a dwelling with the gods and he goes there. His wife, his daughter, and the helmsman have received the same honor. He commanded them further to go back to Babylon. They are destined to retrieve the writings from Sipara and to deliver them to humanity. The land where they were was part of Armenia. When they heard this, they sacrificed to the gods and traveled by foot to Babylon. A portion of this vehicle, which came to rest in Armenia, is present on the Cordyaic mountains of Armenia (according to Jensen, *Gilgamesch-Epos* 1:43n.2 perhaps the Djudi mountains). Many gather asphalt from it which they scrape away and use as amulettes. They came to Babylon, dug up the writings in Sispara, founded many cities, renovated sanctuaries, and rebuilt Babylon.

In Abydenus, whose report is the basis for Berosus, the hero of the Flood is called Sisithros (*Fragm. hist. graec.* IV, 281; cf. Usener, 14-15).

The cuneiform text, stemming from Assurbanipal's library, was discovered by George Smith in 1872. It has been translated and interpreted by Haupt (in Schrader, KAT², 55ff.), Jensen (*Kosmologie der Babylonier*, 367ff., KB VI/1, 231ff., 481ff., and *Gilgamesch-Epos* 1:40ff.), Zimmern (*Schöpfung und Chaos*, 423ff. and KAT³, 544ff.), Winckler (*Keilinschr. Textbuch²*, 84ff.), Jastrow (*Religion of Babylonia and Assyria*, 493ff.), and Jeremias (ATA², 228ff.). The Flood legend is transmitted here as a loosely inserted episode of the Babylonian national epic of Gilgamesh, king of Uruk (Erech). Gilgamesh visits his ancestor Utnapishtim ("He saw life"), nicknamed Atrahasis (the "supremely wise," in the inverted form Hasisatra = Xisuthros in Berosus) who, transported to the gods, dwells at the mouth of the streams, apparently in order to ask him about death and life. In response to Gilgamesh's astonished question why he, the most ancient, looks so young, Utnapishtim tells him the Flood story: Once the gods of the city of Surippak (located close to the mouth of the Euphrates) decided to destroy the city in a flood. But Ea, who sat in their council, wanted to save his darling Utnapishtim. On the other hand, he feared the gods were he to reveal their secret to a man. Then "the Lord of wisdom" found a clever means: He appeared to him in the night while he slept in the reed hut and commanded—the reed hut to build a ship!

Reed hut, reed hut!	Wall, wall!
Reed hut, listen!	Wall, forget it not!
You man of Shurippak,	Son of Upar-Tutu,
construct (?) a house,	build a ship, <68>
leave your property,	think of your Life!
leave all possessions	and save your life!

He also says a word about the dimensions of the ship and commands that the seed of all kinds of life be brought aboard the ship. The man, however, worthy of his clever patron deity and himself "very intelligent," "understands him well." In response to his question, he obtains instructions concerning what he should say to his fellow citizens: He has become the enemy of Bel, the god of the earth, and, for this reason, he departs now to the ocean to dwell with Ea, his lord. And, horribly enough, he should add that rich blessing will then be poured out on them. In the morning he sets to work. The Ark will be 120 els high (?) and 120 els wide (?), divided into compartments and equipped with a rudder (?). He loads great quantities of bitumen (*kupru* = כֹּפֶר 6:14) and asphalt into the ship. During the construction he offers a great and solemn sacrifice, probably so that the gods do not disturb his work. On [the sixth?] day, the ship is ready. Then he loads all his property, silver and gold, and the seed of all living things, his entire family, animals of the field, and master workers. Shamash has established a moment when the Flood should begin. When this moment arrives, Utnapishtim boards the ship himself.

I boarded the ship,	barred the door.
To the helmsman of the ship,	Puzur-Bel, the sailor,
I delivered the Ark	together with everything in it.
As soon as first	light of morning appeared,
arose on the horizon	a black cloud.
Hadad thundered	in its midst,
Nebo and Marduk	striding ahead of it—
The Anunnaki	lift high their torches,
with their radiance	they illuminate the land.
Hadad's turbulence	reaches to heaven,
all brightness	changes into night.—

The South wind drives the water ashore. The waters, however,	
surge like a fatal storm	over the people.
One no longer	sees the other,
no longer recognized	by heaven (?) are the people.
The gods were afraid	of the Flood,
they fled, they climbed	to Anu's heaven.

Now follows a characteristic scene: the gods cower down like chained dogs. The "Lady of the gods" loudly laments the destruction of the people which she, herself, advised. And the Anunnaki mourn with her. When the storm had raged for six days and nights, the weather subsided.

When I looked at the sea,   calm ruled,
    for all people   had become earth again—
I opened a hatch,   the light fell on my cheek,
    I knelt down,   sat there crying,
        over my cheek   my tears flowed.

When Utnapishtim looked out now, land appeared after twelve (double-hours?). The mountain *Nisir* (on the left side of the lower Zab) held the ship firmly for six days.

When the seventh day arrived:
I took a dove out   and released it;
    the dove flew   to and fro,
    with no resting place   it returned.
Then I took out a swallow   and released it;
    the swallow flew   to and fro,
    with no resting place   it returned.
Then I took out a raven   and released it, <69>
    the raven flew,   saw the water receding (?),
    ate, waded (?), cawed   but did not return.

Then he let everything out and offered a sacrifice of strong smelling incense in order to attract the gods.

The gods smelled the aroma,
    the gods smelled   the sweet aroma,
        the gods gathered   like flies around the offerer.

The Lady of the gods comes, too, and declares that Bel the initiator of the Flood should enjoy nothing of the sacrifice. Finally Bel himself comes. He begins furiously:

who has gotten out with his life?
    there should have escaped   destruction not one man!

Ninib guessed correctly that Ea had effected this deliverance.

Then Ea opened   his mouth and spoke,
    he replied   to the Hero Bel:
Ah, you most clever   of the gods, you Hero!
    How overhasty you were   to cause a Flood!
On the sinner   lay his sins,
    On the evildoer   lay his evildoing;

but such punishment should not lead directly to the complete annihilation of the sinner. Instead of causing a Flood, he can send lions, wild dogs, hunger or pestilence and thin out the human race! But not immediately a Flood that destroys everything! Finally, Ea nearly confesses that he was not uninvolved in the deliverance:

> I did not reveal   the secret of the great gods,
>   I sent dreams to the supremely wise,   thus he heard of the gods' secret.

Thus Bel is appeased, and now he generously does an additional favor for the one delivered. He touches him and his wife on the hand and speaks the words of blessing by which he transforms both into gods and directs them to the dwelling at the "mouth of the streams" (according to Jensen, KB VI/1, 507, 575-76, *Gilgamesch-Epos* 1:33n.3, the Straits of Gibraltar are envisioned like the Elysium of the Greeks).

Beside this text, remnants of another, similar version are also preserved (KB VI/1, 255-56). Finally, an additional fragment has recently been published (KB VI/1, 288ff.) that stems, according to the colophon, from the time of Ammizaduga, a successor to Hammurabi (ca. 1950) and also deals with the Flood and Atrahasis as the Hero of the Flood. The fact that there was a third recension is very significant for assessing the tradition even though the fragmentary state of this text has not permitted, so far, the recovery of many details. Concerning the other Atrahasis myths, see Zimmern (ZA 14:227ff., and KAT^3, 552ff.) and Jensen (KB VI/1, 274ff. and *Gilgamesch-Epos* 1:68ff., 75ff.).

(3) The resemblance of the Babylonian narratives to the Hebrew is very great. The cuneiform legend agrees with that of J in respect to four aspects of the course of events. Divine wrath is the cause of the Flood. The deliverance of the deity's darling is effected by a divine revelation in which, at first, only the construction of a ship is commanded while nothing is said about the Flood, itself. The ship is constructed with decks (P). We hear of bitumen (P). The vessel has a door and a window. The family, cattle, and animals of the field board. The hero, himself, boards last. The door is closed. Then comes the Flood. The Ark floats. People die. The ship is stranded on a mountain. In a difficult situation, the Hero has an idea after seven days (J) and learns from the threefold release of birds that the earth has become dry. The scene also preserved in Berosus, in paricular, exhibits the very close relationship of the legends. (Then he removes the roof—<70>in both J and Berosus). Disembarked, the hero sacrifices to the gods. The gods "smell the aroma"—a literal agreement—and promise not to send another Flood. The tradition in Berosus also adds that Xisuthros, too, is the tenth in his line as is Noah in the Sethite genealogy and that the landing site is Armenia as in P, "Ararat." The comment in P that Noah "walked with God" (6:9) has its Babylonian parallel in the Atrahasis legends which recount the hero's intimate relationship with his god Ea (cf. Zimmern, KAT^3, 557, 552-53). Divergent details include, especially, the information concerning the dimensions of the Ark and the duration of the Flood.

Such a great degree of similarity is no accident. Adaptation of Hebrew tradition cannot be seriously discussed. Rather, the common course of events in the story suggests the opposite hypothesis. Above all, however, the local color of the legend points to lower Babylonia as its homeland. Such floods do not occur in Canaan, but in the alluvial region of the lower Euphrates and Tigris. In the most ancient period, when the land was not yet protected by canals and dams, such floods would have been all the more devastating. The name "Ararat" in P also places the event expressly in the Northeast. Certain elements of the Hebrew legend that only receive their proper light from the Babylonian also speak particularly clearly. Here the two predicates of the hero, who is very clever and simultaneously the darling of the god, are no longer in dissonance, but belong together for the god is the "Lord of wisdom" himself. He loves and protects the "supremely wise" just as Athene, the goddess of wisdom, loves and protects the clever Odysseus. The deity's strangely sudden change of attitude in J can be explained in the Babylonian as the result of Bel's impetuous character and of Ea's wise, appeasing presentation. The Babylonian myth, where a South wind drives the flood ashore and the Ark to the North, also explains the origin of the Flood much better than does the forty-day rain of J. One can discern from this that the Canaanites have no perspective on such floods.

On the other hand, the dissimilarity of the two legends is extraordinarily great. The polytheism that figures quite prominently in the Babylonian version has fallen out of the Israelite tradition entirely. "The gods of the Babylonian account are truly pagan in their lies and toleration of lies, in their hunger for the sacrifice, in their behavior, in the caprice with which they deal with people, and in the reversal of their moods. How far removed is the God who brings judgment on humanity according to his justice, with which humans must agree in conscience" (Holzinger) and who spares one because he has recognized his piety. The last point, in particular, is very significant. The Babylonian legend does not mention the gravity of the acknowledgment of sin in which the Hebrew bows before God's judgment. This gravity of the Hebrew narrative includes the fact that it expresses no sympathy for perishing humanity. It deserved death, after all. In contrast, the Babylonian hero, who bears some guilt for the death of so many because of his lie, cries bitterly afterward. Very characteristic, too, is the motivation of the element, appearing in both legends, that the god only commands the construction of the ship at first without revealing the impending Flood. In the Babylonian version this happens because the god is afraid to divulge directly the secret of the gods. But in the Hebrew, it occurs because the god wants to test the true obedience of the man in this way. How immeasurably grander stands the Hebrew legend than the Babylonian! Thus we perceive in this Babylonian parallel the unique majesty of the God concept in Israel which was able to refine and transform the most foreign and offensive elements in this manner. And we may also say that the Babylonian legend strikes us as barbaric to a great degree, while the Hebrew is by far much nearer to us in human terms. If, now, we must also demur that we are accustomed to the Hebrew legend from youth onward, still we learn from such an example that our entire <71> world view owes much more by far to these Hebrews than to those Babylonians. Admittedly, what the Hebrew legend gained in religious content it lost in form. The Babylonian legend breathes a wild, grotesque, but still fascinating poetry. The Hebrew abandoned the brilliant mythological hue, but thereby it became plainer, poorer, more prosaic. The two are also markedly distinct in style: The Babylonian is preserved for us in the form of literary poetry, merged with other legends into an epic, in rather strict rhythms; But the Hebrew is in the form of the folk legend, in the old fashion, independent, in Hebrew narrative prose. In comparison with the cuneiform text, the Hebrew text is also more reflective: Whereas in the Babylonian version at first only one city seems to be affected by the Flood, J and P make it much more clear that the Flood covers the whole world. As a consequence, the hero in the former saves primarily his own property, but in the latter, on the instruction of his god, he attends to the continued existence of the animal world. It is interesting that in the Babylonian recensions master workers also board the Ark. According to Berosus, writings were even saved which treat the "beginning, middle, and end of all things." Elsewhere in Babylonian literature we also hear frequently that "knowledge" goes back to the time *lam abûi* "before the Flood" (cf. Zimmern, KAT³, 555). The Oannes legend in Berosus and the material concerning En-me-dur-an-ki (Ευεδωραχος in Berosus = Enoch) identified by Zimmern (KAT³, 533f., 540) agree with this view. Quite characteristically, the Hebrew legend knows nothing of the Babylonian Flood legend's interest for the continued existence of culture and books. The Hebrew tradition shows itself to belong to an uncultivated folk.

(4) How is the transition from the Babylonian legend to the Israelite tradition to be imagined? Many researchers have been inclined to think of a direct adaptation of the Babylonian material by a Hebrew author (P. Haupt, *Sintfluthbericht* [1881], 20; Usener, *Sintfluthsagen*, 256; cf. also Stade, ZAW 15:160; but contrast Stade, *Bibl. Theol.*, 243, and ZAW 13:175) who "ruthlessly transformed" his exemplar (Budde, 457), and have even sought to name a definite political occasion on which the legend came to Israel. Because the preexilic prophets, who so frequently cite the similar Sodom account, do not mention the Flood legend, but exilic prophets are the first to do so (Ezek 14:14, 20 and Isa 54:9), it has been conjecture that it migrated to Israel only then or one to one-and-a-half centuries earlier during the period of Assyrian dominance. Thus F. Delitzsch (*Paradies*, 94) and P. Haupt (*Sintfluthbericht*, 20) think of the Exile, Budde (*Urgeschichte*, 515-16, with reservation) of the time of Ahaz, Kuenen (ThT 23:167ff.) and Stade (*Gesch. Israels* 1:631), of that of Manasseh, Kosters (ThT 19:325ff., 344) of Merodach-Baladan's embassy to Hezekiah, more generally Stade (*Bibl. Theol.*, 238ff.) of the seventh and eighth centuries, and Marti (*Religion des A.T.*, 56, 67) of the time of the older prophets. All these assertions resulting from one-sided literary critical considerations must be opposed on principle. First, in the history of the legend tradition, one may not only or primarily think of the authors who gave us the legends, but rather of the oral tradition from which the legend authors create (cf. *Schöpfung und Chaos*, 135). Legends travel from one people to another not so much on definite, datable political occasions, but in cultural epochs though trade and commerce. Furthermore, the argument *ex silentio*, so often applied in OT scholarship, which is supposed to demonstrate the youth of the Flood legend, is to be undertaken in the OT only with the greatest caution. In many spheres we know too little about ancient Israel to allow us in most cases to conclude anything from our ignorance. Accordingly—quite apart from the fact that many specific elements of the two traditions do not, in fact, agree—direct adoption and adaptation of the Babylonian legend by an Israelite author is very improbable. <72> An examination of the religious character of these authors demonstrates, however, the complete improbability of this hypothesis. If a man such as our narrator became acquainted with the Babylonian material, filled with the most crass mythology, he would have only felt disgust. Furthermore, a comparison of the Babylonian and the very different Israelite narratives teaches that a long history must lie between the two (cf. *Schöpfung und Chaos*, 143ff.). Finally, the preserved variants (in Babylonian, three cuneiform recensions and the legend of Berosus, in Hebrew the Vorlage of P) show that it is not a question of two authors but of related traditions. Thus, the assertion that the legend came to Israel only relatively late should be dismissed. All the other legend material that J contains in Genesis stems from very ancient times. The Flood legend, itself, has a few very ancient elements in J (cf. above, p. 67) suggesting that it

belongs, instead, to the narratives in the OT characterized by extraordinary antiquity. The fact that the literature preserved for us mentions the Flood legend so late demonstrates nothing at all. How much would we know about the primeval legend and the patriarchal legend without Genesis! We possess laws, a few songs, narratives, and prophetic writings from the old period: All these pieces are by nature far removed from the legends of Genesis. It is quite understandable, then, that we hear in them so few allusions to the legends. Nor does the possible absence of the legend in J^j and J^e permit the inference that it is young (Meinhold, 140): If we possess two collections treating essentially quite different materials, it seems quite reasonable to conclude that material absent from both can well have been present in the tradition. There is even less basis for objections against the assumption of a migration of the legend in ancient times since we now know from the Tell-Amarna correspondence that Canaan was already influenced by Babylonian culture around the middle of the second millennium (cf. Winckler, *Altorientalischen Forschungen* 1:140ff. and *Schöpfung und Chaos*, 150-51). This Babylonian influence is not limited, however, to Israel's most ancient period, but remained vital through the mediation of the Aramaeans and the Phoenicians. When the Israelites grew into Canaanite culture, they will have adopted these primal myths. Naturally, a more precise date cannot be given. Yet, nothing stands in the way of thinking of the period of the later "judges" and of the earlier kings of Israel (cf. also Zimmern, KAT[3], 560; Baentsch, *Monotheismus*, 99).

It has been suggested that the Jews became newly acquainted with the Babylonian legend in the Exile and that P utilized this new influx of material (Löhr, *Babel und die bibl. Urgesch.*, 16; cf. also Marti, *Religion des AT*, 67). It is not impossible that Judaism both then and later adopted other Babylonian materials, too (cf. the final comment of the Flood legend in P). Contrariwise, Löhr's assertion (15-16) that this story, not cited by the older prophets, existed only in priestly circles but not among the people is hardly tenable. The J narrative does not bear learned, least of all priestly, character.

(5) Geffcken (*Nachrichten der K. Ges. der Wissenschaften zu Göttingen Phil.-hit. Kl* [1900], 98ff.) and Bousset (ZNW 3:31; cf. also *Religion des Judentums*[2], 560ff., with additional bibliography) find, probably correctly, echoes of the Babylonian myth in Or. Sib. 1:242ff, where, in a Flood account, otherwise reproducing and extrapolating biblical material, the third bird released is the raven and Noah, looking out of the ship after the cessation of the rain, is overcome by strong emotion (1:233ff.). Both these elements mirror aspects of the cuneiform account. But whether, as Geffcken thinks, these poetic motifs stem from Berosus, whose account (reproduced above) is preserved for us only in excerpts, must at least remain questionable. In contrast, Jewish accounts in which one of the doves returns smeared (πεπηλωμένη) with filth (Josephus, *Ant.* I.3.5), Noah "departed" from his sons immediately after the Flood (EthEn 89:9), and, finally, Eve <73> commanded her children to document her biography and Adam's on clay and stone tablets since God will one day destroy the world with water and later with fire (*Vitae Adae* 49-50. in Kautzsch, *Apokryphen* 2:528; similarly also in Indian, cf. below, p. 76 and Persian, cf. Windischmann, *Zor. Stud.*, 205; Spiegel, *Er. Altertumskunde* 1:521) are strongly reminiscent of Berosus. Even Gilgamesh's journey to Utnapishtim echoes in Judeo-Christian tradition (treasure caves, an overview in Bezold, 33).

(6) Beside the Babylonian and Hebrew traditions, a few others preserved illustrate for us the path the Babylonian myth traveled. According to Lucian (*de dea Syria*, 12-13) the

legend said that the waters of the Flood receded into a rift in the earth beneath the temple of Derceto in the Syrian hierapolis (Bambyke). Once human depravity became so great that they must be annihilated. Then the fountains of the earth and the floodgates of heaven opened. The whole earth was covered with water and all humans drowned. Only Deucalion with his wife and children were saved in a great chest because of his piety. When he boarded, all sorts of four-footed animals, tame and wild, serpents and everything else that lived on the earth, came in pairs. He took them all in and none of them repaid him with unthankfulness, instead there was great friendship among them for God's sake. All of them drifted about in the one chest as long as the Flood lasted. After the water receded into the chasm mentioned above, however, Deucalion opened the trunk, built altars, and founded the holy temple of the goddess over the chasm (following Usener, *Sintfluthsagen*, 47). The narrator calls the hero of this story Deucalion τόν Σκυθέα, which Buttmann (*Mythologus* 1:192) has well corrected to τόν Σισυθέα. In Usener's judgment (47-48) only the name "Deucalion" is Hellenistic in this tradition. Otherwise, it is the Babylonian-Jewish legend, localized here at a Syrian sanctuary. The legend in this form resembles the recension of P in a few points (the fountains of the earth and the floodgates of heaven, two each of all the animals). Hierapolis is on the way from Babylonia to Canaan.

The city Apameia in Phrygia bears the nickname Κιβωτός, "Ark." Phrygians tell of the Flood that old king Nannakos brought upon his people so that they would pray for its prevention (*Zenob. prov.* 6:10; cf. Usener, 49f.). On coins from Apameia under Septimius Severus and others one sees portrayals of the departaure from the Ark. The Ark bears the name ΝΩΕ (reproductions in Riehm, "Noah," HW, and Usener, 48). It is difficult to accept the name "Noah" as really an old, native tradition here. The only question concerns whether the Flood legend, itself, was brought here by the Jews who were flooding all of Asia minor then, or whether the Jewish tradition supplemented a preexistent, native Phrygian tradition (cf. Usener, 50; Bousset, *Religion des Judentums*^{2}, 561n.1; Schürer, *Gesch. des jüd. Volkes* 3^3:14ff. and *Theol. Abhandlungen: C. v. Weizsäcker gewidment*, 53-54, where one also finds the material itself).

Another trail leads to Vetulonia in Etruria. There an "Ark of Noah" has been found in a grave supposed to stem to the seventh century B.C. It is a bronze ship with portrayals all kinds of standing animals. The ship is the product of Phoenician craftsmanship. A similar ship has also been found in Sardinia (cf. Usener, 248ff., with a reproduction and bibliography). These finds point to the Phoenician Flood tradition.

The Greek traditions are more difficult to evaluate (cf. Usener, 31ff., 244ff.). According to Apollodorus (1.7.2ff.) Zeus wanted to annihilate the iron race. But on the advice of Prometheus, his father, Deucalion constructed a chest (λάρναξ), loaded it with provisions, and climbed in with his wife Pyyrha. But Zeus destroyed all humans, except for a few who fled to the mountains, with a great gush of rain. Deucalion drifted nine days and nights on the sea and finally landed on the <74> Parnass. Then he climbed out an offered Zeus a sacrifice. When Zeus granted him a wish, he asked for people. He received them by throwing stones over his head that were transformed into people. Other traditions associate the Flood with the names Ogygos (Usener, 43ff.) and Dardanos (Usener, 45-46). Whether these traditions relate to the Babylonian must remain in question. The possibility should probably be held open since the stories are very similar in the whole sequence of events: One should note especially the "chest," the landing on a mountain, and the sacrifice after the deliverance (Winternitz, 329). On the other hand, individual points of striking agreement are lacking. The question would be decided if Plutarch's (*de sol. anim.*, 13) report that, as the myth tellers say, a dove released from the chest became a sign to Deucalion of the storm when it sought protection within and for clear weather when it flew away belonged to ancient Greek tradition. But this, too, is very doubtful (cf. Usener, 254ff.).

It is similar with Indian legends. Satapatha-Brahmana 1.8.1-10 (translated by A. Weber, *Indische Studien* 1:161ff. and by Pischel, *Sitzungsberichte der Berl. Akad. Phil.-hist. Cl.* [1905], 512-13) recounts that Manu, the first man, once saved a fish from mortal danger. In thanks it revealed to him that in a certain year the Flood would come. He should construct a ship if he wishes to save himself. This Manu did. When the Flood came he boarded the ship. The fish swam about him. He tied the ship's hawser to its fin. He landed on the northern mountain and climbed down from it gradually as the waters receded. Since, however, all creatures had died and Manu alone survived, a wife for him came miraculously into existence out of his sacrifice. With her Manu begot the human race. The same tradition, further developed, also occurs in the Mahabharata (cf. the translation of this episode by H. Jacobi in Usener, 29ff.; a review in Pischel, 514-15).

The following deviations are noteworthy. The Flood is called "the inundation of the world." In addition to Manu, "the seven seers" and seed of every kind are in the ship. The landing takes place on Himalaya. The fish finally discloses itself to be the god Brahman. Manu creates all beings through divine inspiration. Other Indian recensions are treated in Pischel (515ff.). Interestingly, in one of these recensions Manu must attend to the continued existence of the sciences and take the holy books with him on board (516). Here, too, the considerations that apply to the Greek tradition must be taken into account. Possibly, indeed perhaps probably, it was borrowed from the Babylonian (so most scholars, e.g., Oldenberg, *Religion des Veda*, 276n.3; Winternitz, 327-28). But no certain evidence can be produced for the present. Pischel (522) and others (bibliography 522n.9) argue against the assumption of Babylonian borrowing. In the broader sense the Persian Jima legend also belongs to the "Flood" accounts (Usener, 208ff.; Winternitz, 328-29, with bibliography).

Beside those already discussed, a multitude of Flood legends exist in many parts of the world (assembled by Andree, *Flutsagen*), especially in the volcanic oceans and on the earthquake plagued coasts of America. All this material is extremely pluriform (cf. the summary classification in Winternitz, 212ff.). The causes of the floods in these legends are many—rain, inundations of the sea, storms, earthquakes. This is natural since there have been many floods in many places, on islands, flat stretches of coast, and deep river valleys (E. Süss, *Antlitz der Erde* 1:28-29) at various times. Manifold, too, are the legends which recount such natural events, related essentially by the basic motif that a great water crisis killed many people, but that certain people, usually a hero or a couple, are saved. Among all these legends, those of the Babylonians, Hebrews, Indians, Persians, and Greeks, but especially those of the Babylonians and the Hebrews, are closely related (as Winternitz, 326, 329 demonstrates). The assumption, however, that all the Flood legends all over the world trace back to a great primal event or that the Flood tradition is even a reminiscence from a common primitive period of <75> humanity (Böklen, ARW 6:148, etc.) is not permissable. Leaving aside the question of whether a common origin of humanity can be demonstrated, it is very unlikely that any memories whatsoever could have been preserved from that primordial period many millennia before writing. On the other hand, many peoples, even entire large ethnic groups, know no Flood legend, e.g. the Egyptians, Arabs, Chinese, peoples in inner and northern Asia, Africa, etc. (cf. Andree, vii, 13, 125-26).

(7) The "Apologetic" perspective is wont to consider, pettily enough, only the question of whether the narrative is a "true story." This cannot be seriously discussed. Rather, the narrative in J (and P) is clearly a legend. In accordance with its development, atmospheric precipitation cannot exceed a certain volume and, in its most intense forms, is confined to a limited region (following E. Süss 1:127). A forty-day rain cannot produce a universal flood. The notion, further, that all animal species enter the Ark is childish. What technique did Noah employ to bring them in? The legendary character of the narrative is most clearly manifest in the manner it speaks of God. God appears and joins in the action, and the legend tells quite innocently of God's thoughts without indicating in any way the source of this knowledge. Accordingly, the question cannot be whether all this took place in this manner. Rather, it can only be asked whether a historical event underlies the legend. In order to search for this event, one must rely, not on the much later Hebrew, but on the cuneiform tradition. According to it, the Flood first impacted the city Surippak and its environs, in the lower river region in Babylonia, not far from the sea. What could have been the geological basis of such an inundation? The most characteristic element of the Babylonian account seems to be that the Ark, driven from the South inland against the current of the rivers, was stranded in the northern mountains. This element is so remarkable that it could only have been stimulated by a corresponding natural phenomenon. E. Süss (25ff.) suspects that a violent earthquake in the Persian Gulf may have been the cause. A powerful cyclone from the South, associated with voluminous rain and horrible darkness, drove the destructive waters far into the inhabited land. This event must have taken place in a very ancient time. The news of the terrible catastrophe was preserved through all times. This theory is certainly very plausible. In contrast, it is very improbable that the Gobi desert poured out the waters it formerly held (Schwarz, *Sintflut* [1894]). At any rate, Babylonia was not effected by this hypothesized flood (against this hypothesis, cf. Winternitz, 230-31). Even more unlikely is Riem's hypothesis (Sintflut [1906]) that the narrative refers to a mighty inundation of the whole earth through rainfall at the end of the tertiary period. According to a gracious communication from Prof. Penck in Berlin, this position is susceptible to the objection that "we find unambiguous evidence at numerous places on the earth's surface that for a long geological period no heavy rainfall has occurred. Very light and loose products of decomposition have been preserved in great quantities and have not floated away. One sees this at places in the southern Alps, and, especially, in the southern and eastern states of North America and southern China, where granite stones have been displaced entirely but not washed away. At other places on the earth's surface, on the other hand, one finds unambiguous evidence that desert circumstances have prevailed virtually indefinitely." Even more telling is the historian's objection, not refuted by Riem, that a catastrophe such as theorized by Riem must have occurred long before any historical documentation.

(8) Or, is it that the Flood narrative does not involve an, albeit very obscure, historical tradition, but that mythological material lies in the back <76> ground? According to the Babylonian traditions, the one saved is transported to the gods at the end of the account. Was this figure originally a god? Furthermore, the confident expectation, concluding both the Babylonian and the Hebrew legends and constituting a major point of the narrative (Isa 54:9), that such a Flood will not recur "all the days of the Earth," is difficult to understand if the flood is nothing more than a historical event. Whence the certainty that such an event will not be repeated? Speculation concerning world eras (on this cf. the comments on Gen 17:1-14) seems to stand in the background here like those attested to us in Greek (Usener, 39), Indian (Usener, 240; Pischel, 522), and Babylonian (from Berosus in Seneca, *Nat. quaest.*, 3.29) tradition, speculation that the great year of the world has its Summer (the world conflagration) and its Winter (the Flood). Our narrative would then be the myth of "the Flood." This supposition is supported by the fact that "the Flood" appears in the legend in P (Gen 6:17) as well as in Indian tradition (Usener, 240; cf. above p. 76) as an already known entity. This interpretation also explains the description of the Flood in 7:11 (P) as a kind of Chaos—the supra- and subterranean waters, united in Chaos and separated in the Creation, flow together again in the Flood—and the fact that P parallels the new order after the Flood with the Creation.

Interpretations of the Flood legend as a nature myth have already been offered in multiple combinations in both previous (bibliography in Franz Delitzsch, 156) and more recent times (Cheyne, "Deluge," *Enc Brit*, and "Deluge, 18," *Enc Bibl*; Usener, *Sintfluthsagen*, 234ff.; Zimmern[3], 55, 495n.1, and "Deluge, 8," *Enc Bibl*; further according to Stucken and Winckler also A. Jeremias, ATAO[2], 249ff.; Böklen, ARW 6:1ff., 97ff.; and Jensen, *Gilgamesch-Epos* 1:117ff.). These interpretations see the hero as the sun or light god who is finally transported to heaven or disappears as a star in the West. The Flood is the Ocean of Heaven which he travels, or Winter from which he saves himself, or a flood of light with which he overcomes his enemies. Böklen explains everything, recently also in the Paradise and Cain accounts, in relation to the moon: Noah and his Ark, its roof, decks and window, even the mud-covered feet of the dove, the fresh olive leaf, Noah's altar, the "bow," indeed even Noah's grapevine, drunkenness, and nakedness, anything one wishes. Winckler and his school find echoes of the doctrine of the seasons of the world. It may be objected against most of these astral interpretations that the chief motif of the legend, the annihilation of the people by a flood of water, resists any transferal of the narrative to heaven. If, however, this element is removed or displaced, the narrative slips completely through our hands. For arguments against this mythological understanding of the Flood legend, see Winternitz (331-32) and Nikel (*Genesis und Keilschriftforschung*, 181ff.) On the other hand, it must be admitted that individual mythological remnants may have found there way into the legend. Such elements include the fact that the hero may be a vitiated god, and, especially, that P portrays the Flood with shades of Chaos and that the theory of the world epochs regards it as the Winter of the world. The secondary parallelization of the Flood with primal Chaos can be explained in relation to the fact that the Flood legend and the Creation account report massive water and the subsequent origin of a new world. A similar view of nature underlies both narratives. They are clearly distinguished, however, primarily in that the Creation emphasizes the new world, the Flood the destruction of the old. The Flood legend agrees much more with the

Sodom story in the one, common chief motif of an individual delivered from a great catastrophe because of his piety (cf. "General Remarks on the Sodom-Lot Legend" ¶1).

Dähnhardt (*Natursagen* 1:257ff.) publishes all manner of expansions of the biblical Flood legend among modern peoples. <77>

7. Noah's Curse and Blessing, 9:18-27

Source criticism. The source is J (יהוה v 26). Vv 18a and 19 also belong to J (cf. the expressions נָפְצָה כָל־הָאָרֶץ with 11:9 and שְׁלֹשָׁה אֵלֶּה בְּנֵי נֹחַ with 10:29; 22:23; 25:4; cf. Budde 303). Vv 18 and 19 clearly conclude J's Flood narrative which so far has not recounted anything particular about the sons of Noah (while P has already mention their names several times: 5:32; 6:10; 7:13). At the same time, they introduce the genealogy of Shem, Ham, and Japheth in chap. 10. Furthermore, the expression "from them is humanity disseminated" (נָפְצָה) indicates that according to this genealogy the dissemination of humans across the earth is yet to be recounted (in 11:1-9). This, then, is the sequence of narratives in J^j. Contrariwise, the legend of Noah's drunkenness in vv 20-27 has other origins. Noah, "the farmer" and vintner who lies drunk in his tent, seems to be an entirely different figure than the righteous and pious Noah of the Flood legend (Dillmann). Whereas in the Flood narrative Noah's sons are married (they must have taken their wives with them into the Ark), here they are still so young that they live with their father in his tent. Canaan's behavior is not that of a grown man but exhibits "the common disposition of an undisciplined child" (Budde, 310). The difficulties, further, that Ham commits the sin while Canaan is cursed, that the evildoer is referred to as Noah's youngest son (v 24, while according to v 18 Ham is the second son), and finally that in the blessing Canaan is mention as the brother of Shem and Japheth can, only be resolved by assuming that this legend originally named the three brothers Shem, Japheth, and Canaan and that only a redactor (R^j) inserted וְחָם הוּא אֲבִי כְנָעַן in v 18 and חָם אֲבִי in v 22 to harmonize with the other tradition (Wellhausen, *Composition*³, 13). Accordingly, vv 20-27 belong to another tradition and also to another source in J (cf. Budde, 313). Thus, according to the analysis above (cf. p. 55 on 5:29) they belong to J^e. This source also continues in the subsequent accounts (cf. below). Eerdmans (77f) considers the proverb secondary: The legend which originally discussed Ham was employed in order to explain a proverb about Canaan, Ham's son. But legend and proverb belong together inseparably like guilt and punishment (introduction ¶3:8).

18 Concerning הַיֹּצְאִים, "who went out," see §116d. **19** Regarding שְׁלֹשָׁה אֵלֶּה without article, see §134k (cf. 22:23). נָפְצָה, with "omission of the reduplication," is from the root פצץ = פוּץ (see §67dd). LXX and Pesh have נָפְצוּ עַל כָּל־הָאָרֶץ. The expression belongs in the Tower legend (cf. comments on 11:9).

Vv **20, 21** are an exposition of Noah's vineyard and drunkenness. **20** By the expression "Noah, the farmer," the narrator means that Noah was the first farmer. This is presumed to be well known here (note the article הָאֲדָמָה): "Noah, the farmer" is a well-known figure. This source (J^e) will have also told of him in the preceding material. The tradition of "Noah, the farmer" is independent of the other in which the first man was already destined to farm the field and in which Cain was already a farmer. This Noah is also the first to plant vineyards—like Shin Nung, the first farmer and vintner in China (Ball on 9:20). The narrator includes with some interest a comment concerning the history of culture. For the construction, see §120d. Against the translation "Noah began to farm the land," newly suggested by Frankenberg (CGA [1901], 685), see Dillmann, 159, and Spurrell, 93. It would have <78> to read at least אִישׁ אֲדָמָה (without article). This figure of vintner Noah will have its home in Syria or Canaan. Syria was considered the wine cellar of the ancient Orient. The wine of Helbon was especially famous (Ezek 27:18; cf. Gesenius[14], s.v. חֶלְבּוֹן with bibliography; further KB 3/2:32-33; Strabo 15:735).

21 When he drank the wine he became drunk. One may not seek an excuse for intoxication in the spirit of an old narrative. So it goes in the world: whoever drinks easily becomes intoxicated (43:34; שָׁכַר = "to drink until satisfied" and thus "to become drunk"). The natural consequence is that he exposes himself. The Israelite, very modest by nature, perceives such a situation as extremely indecent. The additional comment that it happened in the tent, at least not in public, is meant to mitigate the offensiveness of the scene somewhat. The fact that the "farmer" lies in a "tent," not in a house, may only be the narrator's oversight. On the suffix in אָהֳלֹה see §91e.

22, 23 Part I. The behavior of the sons. According to 22 Canaan saw the shame of his father and communicated this (cf. §117f) to his brothers. Both are sins: He should not have looked (cf. the counterpart in v 23) and, at least, should not have spoken of it. This cannot be everything recounted about Canaan, here, for it is not so serious that Noah's frightful curse on him could be based on it. Further, since his brothers' chastity is portrayed in a concrete action, we expect that in contrast, Canaan's unchastity will be clearly in evidence in an act. In addition, v 24 presupposes that Canaan "did" something to him (not just said something about him). Thus Holzinger correctly finds a lacuna here. What may have stood there? Canaan's behavior, we may expect, will have been exactly opposed to his brothers' behavior. They cover their father with the garment, he will have taken it off and laid it aside. Thus we may explain the article, "the garment" (v 23), as an indication that Noah's garment had already been mentioned. Winckler (Forschungen 3:77) thinks of pederasty. This may well have been the case originally. At any rate, a later reader took such offense at the son's behavior toward his father reported here that he hesitated to transmit it. LXX reads וַיֵּצֵא וַיַּגֵּד. The motif of the child's unchastity in association with the father's drunkenness recurs, with a different twist, in the legend of Lot's daughters. It is well noted how the undisciplined boy "recounts" (with pleasure) his heroic deed, thus assuming that his brothers share his attitude (Meinhold, 126).

23 The narrator takes obvious pains to present the two brothers as chaste and pious in contrast to Canaan, thus the remarkable expansiveness of his depiction. The legend portrays ethnic types in this way: As these three brothers were, so now are their descendants. The sons of Shem and Japheth are chaste, but the Canaanites are shameless. The shamelessness of the Canaanites was, as we know, conspicuous to the Hebrews (cf. Gen 19; Lev 18:24-30; 1 Kgs 14:24). For וַיִּקַּח singular, see §146f. "שְׁכֶם does not form a plural" (Franz Delitzsch).

24-27 Part II. Noah's statements. In general the second part of the account corresponds to the first. Both exhibit extreme contrasts: shamelessness and chastity, curse and blessing. The blessing on Shem and Japheth, as reward for their virtue, is necessary and has not been secondarily added (contra Eerdmans, 77). In the patriarchal narratives such blessings and curses are very <79> frequent (Yahweh's blessing on Abraham, 12:2-3, and on Jacob, 28:13-14; Isaac's blessing on Jacob and curse on Esau, 27; Jacob's blessing, 49;

Moses', Deut 33; and Balaam's on Israel, Num 23-24, etc.). Ancient Israel regarded the blessing differently than we (cf. Stade, *Bibl. Theol.*, ¶76). For it, the blessing was not just a pious wish which may be fulfilled and may not be, as well. Rather, it was convinced that there are wondrous statements that do not fade away like an empty sound in the air but work and create. Just as the rain from heaven does not return without result, but creates fertility and bread, so Yahweh's word also works (Isa 55:10-11). Men of God are able to pronounce such words. The prophets were convinced that they could not only announce the future, but bring it about (1 Kgs 17:1; 18:36ff.; 2 Kgs 2:24; 13:14ff.; Jer 1:10; 3:12; Ezek 37:4ff., etc.). Fathers—this is the basis of the paternal blessing—could speak such words. This belief in the effectiveness of the paternal blessing seemed to be so natural that the blessing of the patriarch was frequently employed to explain all manner of questions. The legend explains current relationships between peoples, whose real basis was unknown, by deriving them from such words spoken once in antiquity. Why is Jacob mightier and richer than Esau? Why is Ephraim stronger than Manasseh? Why is Israel such a majestic, fortunate nation? One responds to such questions, "Because an ancient word was pronounced over them which promises them this." This understanding also implies that these blessings are not arbitrary, invented, but that they refer to quite specific circumstances. Furthermore, it suggests that they do not involve matters still in the narrator's future, but matters in his present. The goal of our exegesis of the blessing must be, then, to discern the historical situation the narrator has in view and to understand the blessings themselves as naive explanations of the circumstances of the time. In the composition of a narrative dealing with a blessing, the pronouncement of blessing is always the main point because it indicates what continues now as a result of this story. Everything reported in the narrative only has the purpose of indicating the cause and occasion of this word. Consequently, the blessing always occurs in a prominent position, indeed usually at the end of the account (cf. 3:14ff.; 4:15; 8:21ff.; 9:25ff.; 16:12; 27:27ff., 39f; 48:19ff.). The idea underlying the whole narrative is that the chastity of nations draws blessing upon them and unchastity, a curse (an incipient theology of history).

24 On the seghol in וַיִּקֶץ see §70a. On הַקָּטָן "the youngest," see §33g. The blessings have poetic form: The Hebrew sense of style requires it because they are conceived of as solemn, extraordinary, magical (the same was true of the old prophetic sayings, cf. 2 Kgs 13:17). The strophes are a hexameter, two paired trimeters (the first is metrically difficult), and a single trimeter (Sievers 1:405, otherwise in 2:27).

25 The curse on Canaan comes first and also follows each of the other sayings. It is, therefore, the main point. The saying assumes that slavery is the harshest curse on a people. "Servant of servants," means lowest servant like "son of songs, king of kings, heaven of heaven, holy of holies," etc. (see §133i).

26 Blessing on Shem. Notably, Shem himself is not blessed but his God. This may, however, be an intentional subtlety. The progenitor blesses (praises) the <80> god from whom all good things come to Shem. בָּרוּךְ יהוה is a common beginning of doxologies (Budde, 296). Budde (294-95) reads בָּרוּךְ יהוה שֵׁם, Graetz בָּרֵךְ יהוה אָהֳלֵי שֵׁם "Bless, Yahweh, Shem's tents." Meyer (*Israeliten*, 220n.1) defends the transmitted text. According to §103f n. 2, it can mean not only "to them" but also "to him." The latter is more appropriate here (Holzinger). Striking v 26b (Eerdmans, 77) destroys the parallelism.

27 *Blessing on Japheth.* יַפְתְּ is an ingenious allusion to יֶפֶת. Notably, the deity is called יהוה in v 26 and אלהים in v 27: Yahweh's name is only known to Shem, not to Japheth. "May he dwell in Shem's tents" is an intentionally secretive expression, as appropriate for the oracle, and cannot, as usually interpreted, refer to friendly relations with Shem (this would be perhaps יָגֻר "may he sojourn as a guest," or יִשְׁכֹּן would have a modifying "in peace," "together," or the like; cf. Psa 133:1). Instead, it must mean that Japheth drives Shem from his territory (cf. 1 Chr 5:10; Psa 78:55). This element of the blessing, as well as the statement that Japheth shall acquire a large territory, is not substantiated by the preceding narrative. Blessing and narrative do not entirely conform to one another. Poetic tradition is more conservative than prose. Consequently, one can conclude that the blessing is preserved in an older form than the narrative. It preserved elements lost to the narrative. The "messianic" interpretation of the passage (still represented by Franz Delitzsch and Driver), according to which it refers to a future adoption of the religion of Shem (Israel) by Japheth (the Christian church composed of Gentiles) is false: (1) because the context treats political and not religious circumstances, but especially (2) because, as shown above, the blessing by nature promises things that exist in the narrator's time.

The scientific interpretation of the blessing consists in the question, What current situation does the blessing presuppose?

(1) The legend views three nations, Shem, Japheth, and Canaan, as brothers. Canaan is subordinate to the other two nations, their most humble servant. (2) The legend expresses the same idea by calling Canaan the youngest of the brothers. (3) Shem is the firstborn. He worships Yahweh. He dwells in tents. Unquestionably, the narrator considers himself a Shemite. (4) Japheth rules over a broad land and dwells in Shem's tents. Significantly, however, Shem is not called Japheth's servant as Canaan is. Accordingly, Japheth has a very different relationship to his brothers: He has subjugated Canaan in his own land, he has driven Shem out of his territory.

When did these circumstances prevail? Modern scholars usually respond with Wellhausen, who understands the subjugation of Canaan as the one attested to us in the historical period of Israel and equates Shem with Israel and Japheth with the Phoenicians or Philistines (Wellhausen, *Composition*[3], 13; Stade, *Gesch. Isr.* 1:109; Budde, 315ff.; Meyer, *Gesch. d. Altert.* 1:214n.1; Holzinger, and recently again Meyer, *Israeliten*, 219ff.). Certainly, the ancient Israelite who heard this legend would also have understood the son whose god is Yahweh and who rules Canaan to be the progenitor of his people just as he interpreted the legend of Esau and Jacob in relation to Edom and Israel. It is open to question, however, whether the legend of the three sons referred to Israel and his neighbors from the very beginning. This interpretation is contradicted by the following. (1) The names Shem for Israel and Japheth for the Phoenicians or Philistines have not been transmitted to us as names for these peoples. The assumption that an otherwise unattested name for Israel occurs here is, indeed, difficult. We know this much for certain of Israel's history—we know its name. It is also rather improbable that Shem and Japheth are not proper names but <81> appellative designations, "secret names" (Budde, 328-29; 358ff.). They have been transmitted to us as actual names. (2) The interpretation of Japheth as the Phoenicians is especially difficult since they never forced Israel from its territory and Solomon's cession of the Cabul region to Hiram of Tyre (1 Kgs 9:11-3) is much too insignificant an event (with Dillmann contra Budde, 513-14, and Holzinger): *minima Noah non curat.* Furthermore, the Israelites knew full well that Phoenicians and Canaanites are the same people (10:15). Above all else, however, (3) how should one imagine that the name Japheth was later transferred from the Phoenicians to the peoples of the North with whom they certainly have nothing to do? This hypothesis most deserves discussion in the form given it by Meyer (*Israeliten*, 219ff.) according to which Japheth are the nations of the North "from whom proceeded the great invasion of Syria in the twelfth century in which the Philistines came to Syria." Correspondingly, it refers to the early monarchical period when the Canaanites were subject to the Israelite corveé, but not yet absorbed into Israel, and when David had created a demarcation between Israelites and Philistines. But in this interpretation, too, Shem must be a "fictional name" not found anywhere else in the old traditions. One can hardly read in v 27 that a certain agreement had been reached between Shem and Japheth. Thus the effort to relate these sayings to Israel's historical situation may be considered a failure. Now, Canaan was not subjugated for the first time by Israel. Instead, it had already stood under foreign domination many centuries before Israel. Babylonian, Egyptian, Hittite, and Northern rulers governed Canaan. But the legend itself, above all else, indicates that we may really search here for Israel's prehistorical situation. The father of these three brothers is Noah, the first farmer and wine grower. He is the same figure which another tradition equates with the very ancient hero of the Flood legend. The narrators, then, had the impression that Noah and his three sons represented incomprehensibly old relationships between peoples. Furthermore, the Table of Nations in Gen 10 places the three names Shem, Ham, and Japheth before all other nations. As will be shown below, J^e (the source that recounts Noah's drunkenness, see p. 79) probably also possessed a Table of Nations in which Shem, Japheth, and Canaan were the three groups of nations (cf. pp. 85-86). In any case, this source also subsequently reported the dispersion of the nations. We must regard this tradition that Shem, Japheth, and Canaan were primitive peoples correct, however, as long as the most decisive grounds do not contradict it. The accuracy of the narrator's impression of the great age of these nations results clearly from the fact that we know neither Shem nor Japheth from Israelite historical tradition. They are, accordingly (for Israel) primitive nations, no different then Ishmael, Jacob, Esau, etc. Given the imprecise concept we have of Canaanite and Syrian circumstances in the second millennium (cf. Winckler, *Gesch. Israels* 1:133), it is dangerous to advance hypotheses concerning the interpretation of this piece. Yet at least an attempt may be permitted here. We will be guided by what we really know or can surmise for good reason about the names in question.

Our sources employ Canaan in a dual sense as the name of a people and a region: Canaanite tribes settled originally in Gerar in southern Palestine (10:19), in the western and eastern Jordan region, in Coelesyria, on the seacoast, where we call them "Phoenicians," and far to the North. The name Canaan occurs on coins from Laodicea on the sea (cf. Meyer, I, ¶176). Some have argued that traces of Canaanites can be found in Cappadocia from the period around 1300 (Peiser in Schrader, KB 4:viii.). Winckler (*Gesch. Israels* 1:130) has suggested that the Hammurabi dynasty which ruled in Babylonia (ca 2100) was of "Canaanite" or West Semitic origins. At that time, Syria must have been in the possession of "Canaanite" tribes (cf. Winckler, *Gesch. Israels* 1:134; *Völker Vorderasiens*, 12-13 KAT³, 14; this view is rejected by Jensen, <82> for example, in CGA

[1900], 979; *Berl. Phil. Wochenschr.* [1901], 270; against him Zimmer, KAT³, 480f.). A tradition in J also speaks of Canaan in the broader sense when it calls Sidon and Heth (i.e., the Phoenicians and the originally non-Canaanite Hittites, who assimilated with the native culture) Canaan's sons. On the other hand, Canaan is also employed in a much narrower sense, as in the Egyptian sources. There *pa Kana'ana* means "the Canaan," southern Palestine (Meyer, *Israeliten*, 223). The same is true of *Kinaḫḫi* (= כנע) in the Tel-Amarna correspondence (cf. Winckler, KAT³, 181-82). J also describes the borders of Canaan (10:19): they stretch from Sidon to Gerar. Here only a portion of the original territory is assigned to Canaan. One must understand these disparate concepts of Canaan such that Canaan was suppressed or withdrew from an originally much larger territory to a remainder in the South. Since Japheth and Shem appear in Gen 10 as groups of peoples, we must first attempt to understand them in 9:20ff. in the same or at least a similar way. Accordingly, their brother Canaan must also have been a widely settled and widely dispersed people. One sees, then, how the reports we have about Canaan in the most widely scattered texts and this concept of Canaan to which the old legend forces us agree exquisitely. Shem, according to 10:21 "the father of all the sons of Eber," may, then, be interpreted with a degree of probability as the Aramaic-Hebrew ethnic group which established itself on originally Canaanite territory. They are still conceived of here as nomads. According to Winckler (*Gesch. Israels* 1:136) the great Aramaic migration took place in the second half of the second millennium (cf. also *Völker Vorderasiens*, 11). The legend presupposes that the name "Yahweh" was named among them. It has long been contended that this name was known, not just in Israel, but also among its relatives (cf. above, p. 48). Or did this divine name first enter this legend in Israelite tradition? Jensen (in Brandt, *Mandäische Schriften*, 44n.2) compares the name שם with the Babylonian *šumu*, "name," which also means "son," "oldest son" (who propagates the father's name). Meyer (*Israeliten*, 220 and n.2) thinks of *bᵉne šem* = אַנְשֵׁי הַשֵּׁם (6:4), that is, "people who have a name," a self-designation of Bedouins proud of their tribe. But who may Japheth have been? We have only the one, albeit very late (10:25), tradition that Japheth is a name for the peoples of the North and the sea. Hence Noah's blessing points us to a historical situation in which Canaan, i.e. the land from about Taurus to Egypt, was subjugated from the East by a nomadic "Semitic," "Hebrew" people. Simultaneously, the North sends its hordes into the whole world, over Canaan and the "Semites." May we think of the mass migration which included the Hittites and which encountered the Aramaic migration on Syrian soil (Winckler, *Völker Vorderasiens*, 22)? Or should we, following in Meyer's footsteps, think of the invasion of the Sea Peoples—although, admittedly, we place no value on his equation of Japheth with the Greek Titan Ἰάπετος or with the Egyptian name of the Sea Peoples *Kepht*? Or are the two migrations related, perhaps (Winckler, *Euphratländer und das Mittelmeer*, 15)? For the time being, it is difficult to say more. In any case, however, we still come to the second millennium for the required situation. We would have here the oldest report in the OT concerning relationships between nations, and, indeed, the legend itself makes the same claim. It has been preserved for so long because of its poetic sayings.

The history of the figure of Noah seems, then, to have been the following: He was originally a Syro-Canaanite figure, the first farmer and wine grower, progenitor of Syro-

Canaanite humanity, then of all humanity, for this reason he then made his way into the Babylonian Flood legend, which originally did not contain this name. <83>

8. The Table of Nations in Jᵉ and Jʲ 9:18, 19; 10:1b, 8-19, 21, 25-30

The separation of sources in this section between J and P has been definitively settled by Wellhausen (*Composition*³, 4ff.; despite B. Jacob, *Pentateuch*, 59ff.). Dual strands are indicated, especially, by the dual beginning of the family of Shem (v 21 ‖ v 22). Similarly, the whole table has a dual beginning (9:18a,19 ‖ 10:1a). Furthermore, dual sources are evident in the fact that Havilah and Sheba are derived from Cush in 10:7 and, contrarily, from Joktan in vv 28,29. In terms of its inner characteristics, the chapter also harbors very different elements: pedantic precision, dry lists (especially characteristic are vv 31, 32, 20, 5), and echoes of ancient legends (vv 8, 9). Scholars usually attribute vv 1a, 2-7, 20, 22, 23, 31, 32 to P. Distinguishing characteristics of P are the superscription in v 1a (like 2:4a; 6:9; 11:10), תּוֹלְדֹת (vv 1, 32), לְמִשְׁפְּחֹתָם (vv 5, 20, 31), the specifying בְּ (vv 5, 20, 32). P includes, as vv 20, 31, 32, 1a show, the introductory and concluding formulae אֵלֶּה בְנֵי־ and also the beginnings בְּנֵי יֶפֶת (v 2), וּבְנֵי גֹּמֶר (v 3 and the analogous cases in vv 4, 6, 7bis, 22, 23). The remaining sections are from other sources: v 1b ‖ v 1a P (Dillmann). The section in vv 8-12 tells of Nimrod, whom P does not mention among the sons of Cush in v 7a. The section also distinguishes itself significantly from P in tone.

V 21 parallels v 22 P. Eber, according to vv 21, 25ff. Shem's son, is his grandson in P (11:15ff.). The genealogy of Joktan (vv 26-30) gives different information concerning Havilah and Sheba than P. These sections have a different introductory formula than P: X "begot" יָלַד Y (vv 8, 26) or "Y was born to X" וַיִּוָּלְדוּ (v 1), יֻלַּד (vv 21, 25). Consequently, vv 13-14 (יָלַד v 13) and 15-19 (יָלַד) are also to be assigned to this source. This analysis is also supported by the expression נָפֹצוּ (v 18 and 9:19), for which P employs נִפְרְדוּ, and the descriptions of territory in v 19 and v 30.

That this source is J is demonstrated by יהוה (v 9bis), יָלַד "to beget," and בֹּאֲכָה (vv 19, 30). If one considers the result achieved, one sees that the redactor who combined the two sources preserved P completely (or nearly so) but incorporated only fragments of J: (1) the introduction (9:18, 10; 10:1b, 2), (2) notes concerning Nimrod (vv 8-12), (3) the genealogy of Mizraim (vv 13, 14), (4) the genealogy of Canaan (vv 15-19), (5) Shem's genealogy (vv 21, 25-30). V 24 has been inserted by Rᴾᴶ in order to be able include here J's genealogy of Eber. In P it follows later in 11:12ff.

An additional question concerns which of the two J strands are the source of these sections. Since the preserved introduction (9:18, 19; 10:1b) speaks of the Flood, it seems obvious to take these sections with the Flood recension (Jʲ). On the other hand, it can be expected a priori that the other recension (Jᵉ) will have also identitified Shem, Japheth, and Canaan, mentioned in 9:20-27, and the nations which derive from them. Gen 10:21, according to which Shem is "the older brother of Japheth," points to this source. This information only makes sense if the third brother, not mentioned here, is the youngest of the three. This leads to the conclusion that this source does not presume the age sequence Shem, Ham, Japheth—otherwise it would call Shem the older brother of Ham—but the sequence Shem, Japheth, and the third. This sequence, however, is the same we deduce from 9:20-27. The third, then, is—Canaan. At the same time, however, we can guess the order of the Table in J^e from this comment: Shem can only be called "the older brother of Japheth" here on the precondition that Japheth is treated immediately prior (Budde, 306). The arrangement, then, went, just as in P, from the younger to the older (cf. also 25:12ff.; 36:1ff.). They were: Canaan, Japheth, Shem. Canaan's genealogy in vv 15-19 provides additional evidence. Here is a dual use of the name Canaan.

V 19 speaks of Canaan in the more limited sense: He dwells from Sidon to Gerar. Contrariwise, v 19 speaks of Canaan in the broader sense: Heth also belongs to him (cf. above, p. 84). This unusual contradiction can easily be explained from the two genealogies of the sons of Noah in J. The broader sense of Canaan (v 15) agrees with the genealogy <84> of J^e in which Canaan stands alongside the great ethnic groups Shem and Japheth. Canaan in the more limited sense (v 19) belongs to the genealogy of J^j for whom this name designates not an ethnic group, but only an individual people. At the same time, notably, v 15 (Je) speaks of "Canaan," vv 18b, 19 (J^j) in contrast of "the Canaanites." This difference is, simultaneously, an inner distinction: V 15 presents "Canaan" as an individual; Vv 18b, 19, in contrast, drop this (archaic) concept. Now, the peculiar dissonance involving the discussion of individual persons in some sections (vv 8-12, 21-29) and peoples in others (vv 13, 14 [16-18]) also runs throughout the remaining portions of J's Table of the Nations. In terms of content this is, indeed, no distinction because the persons are for the most part nothing other than names of peoples, but is still a great difference in form. The same narrator who views the peoples as persons to such a degree that he can include among their names the very inappropriate name Nimrod, can hardly place names of peoples in the plural alongside these individual names. Consequently, we can easily assume here a source distinction and attribute the names of peoples to J^j and the personal names to J^e. Accordingly, one may take 9:18a, 19; 10:1b, 13, 14, 18b, 19 and probably 30 (because of its similarity to v 19) as J^j and 10:8, 10-12, 15, 21, 25-29 as J^e. Only fragments of both genealogies are preserved: of J^j the introduction, larger sections of the Hamite branch, the conclusion of the Shemite branch, the Jephtite branch is totally lacking; of J^e the beginning of the Canaanite branch (v 15) and the Shemite branch (vv 21, 25-29). The location of vv 8, 10-12 (Cush and Nimrod) in J^e cannot be determined. This source analysis, too, should be understood as only an attempt.

V 9 disturbs the relationship between vv 8 and 10 and stems neither from J^j nor J^e. Vv 16-18a are probably glosses (see below).

The current order of the sections of J stems from RJP who broke J, to the extent that he utilized it, into individual fragments and placed it into P. This procedure is very much the same as in the Flood pericope.

(2) How is the Table of Nations to be evaluated? The first impression on the modern, impartial reader must be extremely odd. It would be as if one were to say: "The sons of Germanus are Germany, England, Scandinavia. Germany begot Saxony, Swabia, Franken, Bavaria. Saxony begot Hannover, Braunschweig, and Hamburg." We understand what is being expressed, the relationship and classification of peoples. But the form in which this is said seems exceedingly peculiar to us. Peoples are viewed here as persons, relationships between peoples as familial relationships. Each people is attributed a progenitor from whose ever expanding family the people is to have arisen. Thus, the many peoples trace back to as many progenitors. If one, therefore, wants to describe the interrelationships of the peoples, one describes the relationship of their patriarchs. They are sons, grandsons, great-grandsons, etc. of the first progenitor, here Noah. Thus, J^e, J^j, and P have assembled

a genealogy of the nations in all seriousness, in good faith that the origins of the nations can be explained in this fashion.

This perspective seems strange to us moderns: (a) The names forwarded are the names of lands, peoples, and cities. A few (such as זידון = Fisher City; Kittim and Rodanim, v 4; cf. also the plurals in vv 13f.) bear these meanings *prima facie*. It seems naive to us almost beyond understanding that one could have ever considered such names the names of individuals. Guthe (*Gesch. Isr.*², 1ff.) thinks, as a result, that the author often did not want to speak of actual fathers and sons, but that the genealogy is only the medium of presentation intentionally employed in order to express ethnological relationships. (b) The theory underlying the whole system that all peoples arose from expanding families <85> is incorrect. We moderns are in a much better position to make statements concerning the origins of the nations than the ancients with their geographically and historically limited field of view. We observe repeatedly that peoples result from the fusion of older peoples (cf. Stade, *Gesch. Isr.* 1:28; Guthe, *Gesch. Isr.*², 1ff., 175ff.). As to how the primitive peoples in prehistoric times arose, however, there is no historical tradition—even Hebrew antiquity is separated from those beginnings by an immeasurable period of time—and hardly a historical theory. Everywhere humans appear, they are already members of a people. Nor does the family precede the people or the state. Instead, the family cannot exist without the larger union that protects it (cf. Meyer I²:8ff., 32-33). Particularly naive, however, is the idea that the peoples arose, not perhaps through the union of different families, but from one family, and that such isolation and inbreeding of one family was not perhaps the exception but the rule. Consequently, the current approach softens this childish theory by assuming that the servants and protégés united with the family as the foundation and thus the family grew into the people. But this modern assumption corresponds in no way to Genesis' view that the people consist of "sons" of the progenitor in the proper sense. (c) Finally, the claim of the Table of the Nations that it has named all the peoples is, in our terms, very naive. The "world" was much smaller then than now. Essentially, only the peoples of Syria, Canaan, Mesopotamia, Egypt, Arabia and their neighbors are mentioned here—only a very small portion of all humanity.

As a consequence, the Table of Nations is by no means, as was formerly believed, ancient tradition from the time of the origins of the nations, but rests on subsequent reflection.

(3) Origins of the Table of Nations. The conviction that the members of a people are sons of a progenitor occurs widely in the old legends and is apparently a very ancient concept on Hebrew soil. The theory did not result from observation, but is the product of mythical thought which "seeks to understand everything existent, social unions as well as the objects of the external world, as having originated through procreation" (Meyer I²:34; cf. also the introduction ¶2:4). Accordingly, the legend interprets kinship relations of the nations and tribes as family relationships (cf. introduction ¶2:4). When the legends then begin to coalesce, extended genealogies of nations arise. Such expansive genealogies are relatively late artificial products (cf. p. 50). Indeed the final products attempt to encompass the whole world of nations in a single genealogy! Such attempts are only conceivable at a time which was already long accustomed to such grand genealogies developed from many legends. The attempts of Hesiod systematically to order the Hellenes and the other nations known to him in genealogies offer parallels (Meyer, *Israeliten*, 231). The relatively

late age of these genealogies follows, further, from a consideration of the spirit of such a genealogy of the nations. It is the spirit of scholarship, a first attempt at ethnography. The men who speak here are no longer bound to the confined boundaries of their own people. Rather, their vision seeks to encompass and incorporate all the nations of the world. The perspectives they allowed to guide them will have been, especially, geographical, then also political, linguistic, ethnographic, perhaps even historical. The narrators acknowledge at this point, when they conclude the history of primitive humanity and turn to the ancestors of Israel, the schoarly requirement <86> to say something about the origins of the nations, the esthetic requirement to conclude the primal history distinctly, and not least, the religious requirement to make clear the election of Israel from the multitudes of nations. While we must locate such extended Tables of the Nations in the latest period of the legend tradition, they are, nevertheless, not to be placed in the very latest period. Ancient elements such as Jᵉ's report that Canaan has world significance suggest this dating. The genealogy of Jʲ seems to have replaced Canaan, meanwhile entirely forgotten as a world power, with Ham, better known at the time. Thus, this genealogy seems younger. At the time of Jʲ the world situation—it would seem—had shifted so that such a new arrangement seemed necessary: With the division Shem, Ham, Japheth, the author seems to have the Babylonian-"Semitic" world, Egypt, and the peoples of the North in view. Nimrod (Jʲ) points to the tenth or ninth century. חָם is also Egypt in Psa 78:51; 105:23, 27; 106:22 (חָם = "hot"?). The native name of Egypt *kêmet*, Coptic *kêmi, chêmi* = "Blackland" has nothing to do with חָם (cf. Gesenius[14], appendix 14). The usage of modern scholars who speak of Semites, Japhthites, etc., depends somehow on Genesis, but is principally distinct and should be distinguished from the diction of Genesis.

Bibliography on the Table of Nations can be found in Dillmann, Gesenius[14], A. Jeremias, ATAO², etc.

(4) The division of the world into three parts is very common elsewhere, too. Isa 19:24f. mentions Israel, Egypt, and Assyria. A hymn to the sun from the time of Amenophis IV mentions Syria, Ethiopia, and Egypt (Erman, *Äg. Rel.*, 68). The same phenomenon also appears in Iranian tradition according to J. Darmesteter (*Annales du Musée Guimet* 24: lviii-lvix; cf. also Justi, *Iranisches Namenbuch*, 289 and W. Geiger, *Ostiran. Kultur*, 99-100). The threefold division of lands and peoples is also preferred. One thinks of the Hellenes, Germans, Gauls, etc.

Concerning **9:18, 19** see above, p. 79. **10:8-12** Nimrod, the first גִּבּוֹר (v 8), ruled the Babylonian (v 10) and founded the Assyrian city-states (vv 11, 12). One notes the relationship between גְּבוּרָה and מַמְלָכָה, power and kingdom. According to ancient notions, the state was based entirely and solely on power. For this reason the Lord's Prayer begins "For thine is the kingdom and the power." Compare the expression הוּא הֵחֵל in v 8 to 4:26 and 9:20, all three passages from Jᵉ. Characteristically, this text which intends to mention the oldest states, refers to Babylonia, not Egypt (cf. also 11:1-9). Despite the proximity of Egypt, Canaan always gravitated more toward Babylonia in its cultural relations. The fact that the Babylonian states are mentioned before the Assyrian, and the latter are regarded as colonies of the former, is based on historical recollection. "In general, the inhabitants of both states consistently regarded themselves as closely related, for indeed the religion and customs, civic life and literature of the Assyrians stemmed from

Babylonia" (Meyer 1:326). The narrator wants to name the oldest and most important Babylonian cities in the following material. In his opinion, these cities, originally politically independent (cf. Winckler, *Geschichte Babyloniens und Assyriens*, 44), have always stood under the dominion of a king. They were unified in the most ancient period. Among the Babylonian cities, Babel was considered the first. Babel had preeminence in "Babylonia" since the displacement of the Elamites by Hammurabi (ca 2100) and since it was considered throughout the near East as the premier city of the world (cf. Meyer 1:170; Winckler, 62). Erech, Assyr. Uruk, 'Ορξόη, is today the ruin of Warka on the Euphrates, southeast of Babylon, one of the most ancient cities of Babylonia (cf. Winckler, 27). Accad is the native designation of the territory and the kingdom of Babylonia in the cuneiform literature. It occurs with particular frequency in the phrase "Sumer and Accad," that is, southern and northern Babylonia. Accad is also attested in the cuneiform literature as a city, <87> located in northern Babylonia and certainly identical with Agade, the residence of Sargon I (ca 2700; cf. Zimmern, KAT³, 422; Hommel *Grundriß der Geographie und Geschichte des alten Orients*, 400), located very near to Sippar (Abu Habba). The location and Babylonian equivalent of Calneh, LXX Ξαλαννή, are unknown. According to Jensen (ThLz [1895]: 510) it should perhaps be emended to כַּלְבָּה. Cullab, one of the more significant cities of Babylonia, appears frequently in inscriptions. For the location of Cullab, see Hommel (*Grundriß*, 390-91). According to Hilprecht (*Explorations in Bible Lands*, 410-11) and Hommel (348) Calneh may be the equivalent of Nippur (cf. A. Jeremias, ATAO², 270-71). Shinar, Babylonia, may be the Egyptian Sanger and the Shanhar in the Tel-Amarna correspondence, although Winckler (*Altorient. Forsch.* 2:107; KAT³, 238) places Sangar and Shanhar on the Taurus. Is the name שִׁנְעָר—Zimmern asks—related after all to the Gebel Singar west of Mosul, the "Singara" of the Greeks? The name could have migrated or adhered to this northern location (cf. also Hommel, 6, 300). A relationship between Shinar and cuneiform Sumer has often been suspected, although the latter signifies southern Babylonia and not the actual territory around Babel. Asshur here is the name of the land of Asshur on the middle Tigris to the lower Zab. According to legend, Nimrod "built" the Assyrian city, an expression avoided by the Babylonians. The narrator seems to proceed from the assumption that the Babylonian cities are older than Nimrod: a characteristic element. Nineveh, Assyr. *Ninua, Ninâ*, with an ancient Ishtar cult, perhaps the source of the name (Nineveh = city of Nina), opposite the modern Mosul, one of the oldest and most significant cities of the region, along with Kelah, the residence of the Assyrian kings at least since Assur-bel-kala (ca 1100) until Assurnasirpal (885–860), was finally elevated to the exclusive residence by Sennacherib (cf. A. Jeremias, "Ninive," in RE³, ed. Herzog, and ATAO², 271-72). The Assyr. equivalent and location of Rehoboth-ir ("city squares," "markets") is unknown. According to Delitzsch (*Paradies*, 261) it may be a Hebr. rendering of the Assyrian *rêbit* (רחב) *Ninâ*, the designation of the suburbs of Nineveh; According to Billerbeck it is at the location of the modern Mosul (cf. A. Jeremias, ATAO², 273). Calah, Assyr. *Kalḫu, Kalaḫ*, now Nimrud, seems to have been founded by Shalmanezer I (ca 1300) and remained, except for the occasional transfer to Nineveh mentioned, the residence until Sargon. Resen may be equivalent to Assyr. *rêsêni*, "springs." Since only two of the Assyrian cities named, Nineveh and Calah, are now known to us with some degree of certainty, it is currently impossible to indicate precisely the time in which this portrayal originated. Characteristically, however, the oldest Assyrian capital "Asshur" (residence until 1300; cf. Winckler, *Gesch. Babyl. u. Assyriens*, 144-45) is not mentioned.

Asshur is the modern Qal`at Shirgat. The very successful excavations of the Deutsch-en Orient-Gesellschaft have been conducted there since 1903. The statement "that is the great (greatest) city" usually refers to the four cities mentioned which formed a unity. But Schrader's (KAT², 99-100) contention that the entire city complex, including Calah, was regarded as one city called "Nineveh" since Sennacherib is without support in the inscriptions (Winckler, KAT³, 75-76n.4). It is also much more likely that הִוא הָעִיר הַגְּדֹלָה is a gloss which originally belonged with "Nineveh" in v 11 (cf. Jon 1:2; 3:2-3; 4:10; A. Jeremias, ATAO², 273n.3). The chronological situation of the Table of Nations based on Schrader's contention are, thus, invalidated. All these cities were attributed to "Nimrod." In later times, Nimrod was considered Asshur's hero. Asshur was called "Nimrod's land" (Mic 5:5). One may assume that this Nimrod, of whom only meager comments are preserved here, was a legend figure concerning whom the original tradition <88> contained narratives. It is easiest to assume that these Nimrod legends were originally native to Babylonia itself. It always seems most natural that the legends were originally recounted at the locales they treat. Meyer (ZAW 8:47-48; *Israeliten*, 448) suspects that the figure of the hunter Nimrod stemmed from wild animal rich Libya where the name Nmrt or Nmrq is very common. But the assumption of such a massive transformation in the tradition is very difficult. It seems much more likely, since we hear from Babylonian tradition of a Babylonian hero, a primeval king, Gilgamesh (written ideographically GIŜ.DU.BAR) with his seat in Erech, one of Nimrod's cities (cf. above, p. 68), to identify the figure of Nimrod with him. A second question must also be addressed, namely whether the name Nimrod is also of Babylonian origin or first arose on Hebrew or Aramaic soil. To this point, however, no "Namrudu" or the like has been attested in inscriptions as a second name for Gilgamesh (cf. further on v 9). It is particularly problematical that Nimrod descends from Cush (v 8). Otherwise Cush refers to Ethiopia and is associated with Egypt in this meaning in v 6 (cf. also comments on 2:13, p. 9). Could this be the redactor's erroneous confusion of Cush = Ethiopia (in P) with כוש = the cuneiform *Cassû* (in J) which ruled Babel form the seventeenth to the middle of the twelfth centuries (cf. Winckler, KAT³, 21ff.)?

V **9** disturbs the context (Dillmann) and constitutes an independent tradition. The one who inserted this comment will have known nothing more about the material than the proverb, "a mighty hunter before Yahweh like Nimrod." Here, too, then we have a scanty remnant of an entire tradition. It can be assumed from the outset that this tradition is Babylonian since it treats "Nimrod." Mythological hunting scenes appear on Babylonian illustrations, especially on numerous seal cylinders. The Gilgamesh epic also describes Gilgamesh and Eabani killing lions (KB VI/1:199 l. 5 and 225 l. 11). See also the colossal figure of the hero with the subdued wild animal (lion?) in his arms, probably correctly identified as Gilgamesh (A. Jeremias, ATAO², 266). Jensen (*Gilgamesch-Epos* 1:87n.1) thinks that Nimrod derives from a **Namurd, Namurtu* and that this is the proper pronunciation of the hunter god written "Nin-ib." Compare the Greek hunter-hero Orion and the German Hackelberend. לפני יהוה is difficult to interpret. Is it only a superlative expression like "Nineveh was a divinely large city" (Jon 3:3)? Or does the statement trace back to a narrative in which Nimrod hunted "before Yahweh"? Does it mean that Yahweh regarded Nimrod hunting and assisted him? The original legend of the hunter Nimrod would, naturally, have mentioned another god (probably a hunter god). "Yahweh," then, is due to the Israelitization of the material. We cannot say how the two Nimrod traditions related to each other originally. In terms of its character, we may associate the comment concerning the mighty hunter Nimrod with 6:1-4. But the conjecture that the verse also formed a literary unit with this piece is not demonstrable (contra Budde, 390ff.). The same is true of Dillmann's assumption that 10:8-12 once stood after 11:1-9. Later reports identify Nimrod with the constellation Orion who was also considered a mighty hunter among the Greeks (cf. Budde, 395ff.). Jensen (*Gilgamesch-Epos* 1:81ff.) suggests that "Nin-ib" (i.e., *Namurd*?) may have been incarnate in this constellation, specifically in Beteljeuse. **13,14** The seven sons <89> of Egypt. מִצְרַיִם is Egypt, specifically lower Egypt. Its etymology is uncertain. The ending is probably a locative. Ezek 30:5 and Jer 46:9 also mention לוּדִים alongside Egypt and Ethiopia. It is otherwise unknown. לְהָבִים is probably equivalent to לוּבִים, Libia. נַפְתֻּחִים, a scribal error for פתמחים according to Erman (ZAW 10:118-19), is the Egypt. *Ptomh* (*Pto-mhj*), or northern Egypt. According to Max Müller (OLz 5:475) פתנחים represents *p-to-(n)ehe*, the Farafra oasis. Speigelberg (OLz 9:276ff.) stays with פתנחים = *na-patûh*, "the people of the Delta," cuneiform *Nathû*, ναθῶ (Herodotus 2.165). פַּתְרוֹס פַּתְרֻסִים is Upper Egypt, Egypt. *Ptorês*, "land of the South." כַּפְתּוֹר is probably Crete, mentioned here as an Egyptian colony. According to others it is a territory in the Nile delta or southwestern Asia minor. Meyer (*Israeliten*, 221) associates "Caphtor" with the Kefti sea people and with יחם. Since Caphtor is otherwise considered the homeland of the Philistines (Amos 9:7), it may be assumed that the clause "from which the Philistines came" is a gloss which originally belonged with כַּפְתּׄרִים. Hypotheses concerning the יָמִים (LXX Αινεμετιειμ) and כַּסְלֻחִים (LXX Ξασμωνιειμ) may be found in Max Müller (OLz 5:475) and Spiegelberg (OLz 9:276ff.).

15-19 The sons of Canaan. **15** "Canaan" occurs here in the broader sense (cf. above, pp. 83-84). צִידֹן, the old Philistine capital, here as elsewhere, even after Sidon fell behind Tyre, refers to the Phoenicians in general. חֵת represents Egypt. Cheta, Assyr. *Ḫatti*. The Hittites came from Asia minor and ruled Syria and northern Palestine in the fourteenth and thirteenth centuries (cf. Winckler, *Völker Vorderasiens*, 21-22; KAT³, 183-84). The capital of the Hittite empire has been rediscovered by Winckler in Boghazkoi, a five-day journey east of Angora. Winckler's extraordinary discoveries there from the Amarna period in the Hittite and Babylonian languages demonstrate that Hittite culture was starkly dependent on Babylonian culture (cf. OLz 9:162ff.; MDOg [1907], no. 35). After its immigration, Israel had dealings with remnants of the Hittites in Canaan (Judg 1:26; Num 13:29, etc. and even still in Ezr 9:1). Their derivation from "Canaan" can be explained by the fact that they dwell in "Canaan" (in the narrator's time) and were probably Canaanized themselves. The Hittites were not Semitic. **16** יְבוּסִי is the Canaanite tribe in Jerusalem. אֱמֹרִי, *Amurri, Amurrûis*, according to the Omina tablets (reflecting the period around 3000), southern Syria and Palestine. Later in the Tel-Amarna correspondence it refers to the land of Lebanon in contrast to *Kinaḫḫi* (Canaan), southern Palestine. Egyptian Amara is northern Palestine. Later among the Assyrians it is the geographical designation for all of Palestine. In E it names the aboriginal population of Canaan (cf. Winckler, *Völker Vorderasiens*, 13; KAT³, 178ff.; Meyer, *Israeliten*, 478n.1). The documents discovered by Winckler in Boghazkoi indicate

that in the Tel-Amarna period and subsequent centuries, the region of Amurru was dependent alternatively on Egypt and *Ḫatti* (MDOg [1907]: 24-25, 41ff.) The home of the
גִּרְגָּשֵׁם is unknown.

17 According to Meyer (*Israeliten*, 335) the הִוִּי were at home in the mountains on
the northern border of Palestine (cf. 2 Sam 24:7; Judg 3:3; Josh 11:3). In his view (330ff.)
references to the Hivvites in Gen 34:2 and Josh 9:7 should be read with the LXX as references to the Horites. Knudtzon (*Beitr. zu Assyriol.* 4:298) associates them with the
Ammiya, Ambi of the Amarna correspondence. עַרְקִי inhabited ᾿Αρκη (Assyr. *Arqâ*,
in the Amarna correspondence *Irqata*, Caesarea Libani, today Tell ῾Arqa, north of Tripoli).
סִינִי were the inhabitants of Sini (mentioned by Jerome). According to F. Delitzsch
(*Paradies*, 282) it is the equivalent of Assyr. *Siânu, Ŝiana*, a northern Phoenician city and
should, thus, perhaps be read סִנִי.

18a אַרְוָדִי are the inhabitants of אַרְוָד (*Arwada* in the Amarna correspondence,
in the cuneiform literature *Armada, Aruada*; Aradus is the Phoenician island city north of
Tripoli, today Ruad). צְמָרִי were the inhabitants of Σίμυρα (south of Aradus, Eg.
ṣamar, ṣumur in the Amarna correspondence, Assyr. *ṣimirra*, modern Sumra). In contrast,
Winckler (MVAG 1:203) associates: (1) *ṣumur, ṣimirra* with Βότρυς and (2) Assyr.
Zimarra with Σίμυρα. חֲמָתִי were the inhabitants of חֲמָת (the metropolis on the
Orontes, Greek Epiphania, now <90> *ḥamât*). Vv 16-18a do not belong to J^j: the borders
indicated by J^j in v 19 are much smaller than the territories of the tribes mentioned in vv
16-18a. On the other hand, the tribal names do not seem to suit J^e, who treats the nations
as persons, either (see above). Consequently, these verses will be a gloss (cf. Wellhausen,
*Composition*³, 13). Such glosses are frequent and stem from "deuteronomists" (cf. the
comments on Gen 15:19ff.).

V **18b** can only be understood if one takes it with v 19. **19** גְּרָר is a city south of
Gaza (cf. comments on 20:1). Gaza is a well-known Philistine city. "Sodom and Gomorrah" are legendary cities, located according to legend on the site of the current Dead Sea
(cf. comments on chap. 19). "Admah and Zeboiim" are mentioned, it seems, in a variant
of the Sodom account (Hos 11:8; cf. "General Remarks on the Sodom Narrative" ¶5).
לֶשַׁע does not occur elsewhere. According to Jerome it is Calirrhoe east of the Dead
Sea. Wellhausen (*Composition*³, 13) suggests לֶשָׁה or לְשֵׁם (a locative form of לַיִשׁ).
Kittel suggests בָּלַע (14:2). In this manifold description of boundaries, a few seem to
have been added later. One may most easily remove עַד־עַזָּה and וְאַדְמָה וּצְבֹיִם
(Kautzsch-Socin).

21, 25-30 *Shem's genealogy.* **21** The modifier אֲבִי כָּל־בְּנֵי־עֵבֶר is meant to
make clear to the reader that Shem, obsolete by the time of the narrator, is to be identified
with יֶבֶר. Since v 21b is awkward it may be an addition, although a very old one. The
words "the older brother of Japheth" cannot stem from R^J according to Giesebrecht (DLz
22), since this redactor preferred the sequence Shem, Ham, and Japheth. The name עֵבֶר
is of particular significance since it is associated with the very frequent name עִבְרִים
"Hebrews," which was used by the Israelites of themselves in conversation with foreigners
or by foreigners. While עִבְרִים designates only Israel, עֵבֶר has a more comprehensive
sense here. The latter meaning will be the older. We hear elsewhere of the הַיַּרְדֵּן
עֵבֶר. the region East or West of the Jordan, depending on the standpoint of the speaker,
and of the עֵבֶר הַנָּהָר. the region West (or in a few passages East) of the Euphrates.

The latter (*ebir nâri*) was also the name for Syria and Palestine among the Assyrians and in the Persian Empire it was the Aramaic name for Syria (ᶜ*bar nahᵃra*). It may be asked which עֵבֶר is meant here and what is meant by the name עִבְרִים. Did the Canaanites call the Israelites the people from beyond the Jordan at first? Or was Israelite tradition correct to maintain that the patriarchs immigrated from ʾ*Eber hannāhār* (Josh 24:2-3)? Is this E? Or, since, in addition to the Hebrews proper, Arabic tribes are also derived from Eber, should we think of a third Eber in the Syrian desert? עבר is often equated with the Habiri known from the Amarna correspondence (originally by H. Zimmern, ZDPV 13:137; cf. also Winckler, KAT³, 196, and the bibliography in Gesenius¹⁴, s.v. עִבְרִי).

V **24** is the parenthetical remark of RPJ (cf. p. 85). **25** Hommel (*Aufs. u. Abh.*, 222), perhaps correctly, compares the region *el-aflaĝ* in central Arabia with Peleg. The name is interpreted here with a view to the following account of the Tower in reference to the "division" of the earth (= humanity, cf. 11:1). The lineage of Peleg is not continued here because the narrator will take it up later in order to derive Abraham's genealogy from it (Wellhausen, *Composition*³, 7). Abraham's family stems then from the firstborn son of the firstborn son of Noah. Israel's claim to be the "firstborn of the nations" becomes evident here. Regarding the construction of יֻלַּד see §121a,b. Joktan is the Jokshan of 25:2 (Meyer, *Israeliten*, 319). Vv 26-30 <91> deal with the sons of Joktan, tribes mostly in Yemen. According to Meyer (*Israeliten*, 244) Joktan originally belonged in the mountains east of Edom. With reference to the following, cf. especially Gesenius¹⁴, the source of most of the following citations. More precise information may be found in Dillmann, Holzinger, and the dictionaries. אַלְמוֹדָד is otherwise unknown. שֶׁלֶף is in Yemen, also according to the Arabic geographers. חֲצַרְמָוֶת is the modern *haḍramût* on the Indian Ocean. According to Glaser (*Skizze* 2:425) יֶרַח is *Mahra*, perhaps in southern Oman. For the location of הֲדוֹרָם see Glaser 2:426ff., 435. For אוּזָל Sam and LXX read איזל. According to the Arabs it is *sanʿâ*, the capital of Yemen; Glaser (2:434, 310, 427) locates it in the vicinity of Media. According to Glaser (MVAG [1897]: 438) דִּקְלָה, "Land of Palms" is the equivalent of Φοινικων (*Procop. Pers.* 1:19 and *Photius Bibl. cod.*, 3) or *Gôf*, the *Wadi Sirḥân* (cf. Winckler, *Altor. Forsch* 2:336; Hommel, *Aufs. u. Abh.*, 282-83). For the identification of עוֹבָל see Glaser 2:426. LXX and Lag read Γαιβαλ, Sam and 1 Chr 1:22 have עיבל. אֲבִימָאֵל is otherwise unknown (cf. Glaser 2:426). שְׁבָא is a well-known commercial people in Yemen (cf. Glaser 2:398ff.). אוֹפִר is Solomon's source of gold. Its location is disputed. According to Glaser (2:357ff., 368ff.) it lay on the east coast of Arabia. Beside the literature assembled in Gesenius¹⁴, see also Hüsing, OLz 7:87ff. חֲוִילָה is in central or northeast Arabia according to Glaser (2:323ff., 339-40). יוֹבָב may be the Ἰωβαρῖται (perhaps to be read Ἰωβαβῖται) on the Bay of Zallaq (cf. Glaser 2:302). The Hebr. text mentions thirteen nations descended from Joktan. It is probable, however, that the number twelve is intended here as elsewhere (cf. comments on 29:31ff.). Obal does not occur in LXX A (cf. Nestle, *Marginalien*, 10). Is מֵשָׁא the region of Mesene on the mouth of the Euphrates and Tigris? Or is it better to read with LXX Μασση̄ϵ, Μαση, מַשָּׂא (25:14; Prov 31:1) in northern Arabia (Dillmann; Meyer, *Israeliten*, 244n.2)? סְפָר is usually identified with Zaphar, the royal city of the Himyarites, in *Haḍramût* (contra Meyer, *Israeliten*, 244). "The eastern mountains" are not identifiable, perhaps the great spice mountains.

9. Tower Construction at Babel, 11:1-9, J^j and J^e

The Confusion of Languages at Babel:
The Construction of the Tower of Piṣ 11:1-9 J^j and J^e

Source criticism. The unit belongs to J: יהוה vv 5, 6, 8, 9bis. Various sources within this unit are indicated by the fact that Yahweh comes down to earth according to v 5 to inspect the tower and city so that Yahweh's subsequent speech (vv 6-7) is given on earth, whereas the statement "let us go down" in this speech (v 7) presupposes that Yahweh is still in heaven, not yet on the earth. Sievers (2:258; similarly Eerdmans, 76) harmonizes as follows: Yahweh first came down far enough to see, then came all the way down. But the text says nothing of this. Meinhold (115) suspects that in the polytheistic exemplar a divine emissary came down first in order to gather information. The Hebrew narrator, however, if one credits him with only a little competence, would have surely replaced him with the angel of Yahweh. Or, in order to eliminate the contradiction, some have assumed a lacuna in the text: After inspecting the city, Yahweh returned to heaven and spoke the words in question there (Stade, ZAW 15:158, 161-62, and *Bibl. Theol.*, 243; *Schöpfung und Chaos*, 149). One must assume, then, that God made several trips between heaven and <92> earth.

It seems easier than all these suggestions to theorize that two sources are present here. According to one Yahweh came down from heaven to orient himself concerning the efforts of humanity (v 5), according to the other, to frustrate their efforts (v 7). T. Naville already stated orally in Geneva in 1895/1896 that the Tower legend consists of two sources (cf. *Annales de Bibliogr. théol.* [1901] 160). The dual purpose of the structure further indicates two strands: (1) It should secure humanity a name, that is, fame. (2) It should help them not to become dispersed. These are different motives, difficult to integrate. The two statements in v 8 do not form a coherent context either: (1) "Yahweh dispersed them over the whole earth," (2) "they ceased building the city." That humanity, already dispersed over the whole earth, can no longer build the city is obvious. The same incongruity characterizes v 9ab (Yahweh confused there the languages) ‖ 9b (Yahweh dispersed humanity from there). Giesebrecht (DLz 22, 1863) attempts to alleviate these difficulties by explaining vv 4b, 8a, and 9b as glosses intended to harmonize the Tower narrative with the Table of Nations. But these clauses do not have the appearance of glosses. Further, the information concerning the construction material seems to be duplicated (v 3a ‖ v 3b). The two structures, city and tower—which could belong together quite naturally and need not point to two sources (Eerdmans, 76-77)—are also a doublet. All these observations can be most easily interpreted by assuming two recensions.

The unraveling of the whole web results best from the parallel between city and tower. The city recension includes vv 8b and 9a. The name of the city, "Babel," is explained in v 9a by the fact that Yahweh confused (בלל) languages here. V 7 (נִבְלָה) and v 6aa prepare for this element and v 1 presupposes it. The other recension, then, must include vv 9b (‖ v 9a), 8a (the counterpart of v 8b), 5 ("he came down," the counterpart to v 7 "let us go down"). Of the two statements of purpose in v 4, the clause "that we not be scattered," נָפוּץ, belongs to the Tower recension because of וַיָּפֶץ in v 8 and הֱפִיצָם in v 9. Consequently, the other purpose ("we will make us a name") belongs to the city source. V 2, a description of the original, single dwelling place of humanity, is the precondition of the Tower narrative which recounts the subsequent dispersion of humanity (just as v 1 gives the precondition of the city recension). The second mention of Yahweh (v 6aγ, b) may belong to the Tower recension since the first (v 6aα,β) is part of the city source. Because of הָבָה in v 7 (4), v 3a probably belongs to the City recension, v 3b to the Tower recension. The asphalt suits a tower better than a city whose stones are not so firmly joined.

The two accounts are very similar. The setting of both is Babylonia, the time is the primeval period when humanity was still unified with the same language and the same dwelling place. Both narratives intend to show the origins of current differences in language and dwelling place. The sequence of both narratives is also essentially the same. When it was still unified, humanity, emboldened by its communal strength, undertook a mighty work, namely, a structure made of bricks, a city or a tower. But Yahweh came down and destroyed human unity once and for all. Thus the structure was not completed.

At the same time, the narratives are characteristically distinct. The city recension recounts the confusion of languages; the tower story the dispersion of humanity over the earth. R^J ably fused the variants together. He left them essentially undamaged, producing only a few lacuna (in the city report between vv 7 and 8b, in the tower report between 8a and 9b), removing v 3b from its context (behind v 4b), and placing it with the related comment in v 3a. <93>

A difficult, although incidental, question concerns which of these two recensions belongs to J^e and which to J^j. After all, our legend stands quite independently and has no inner relationship to the Table of Nations, in particular. The expression נפוץ, characteristic of the Tower narrative, also occurs in 9:19 (10:18b) J^j. Accordingly, one could attribute the Tower recension to J^j. Gen 10:25 J^e (נפלג) could then be understood as an allusion to the account of the confusion of languages (also J^e). This analysis is not contradicted by the fact that J^e would then have narrated the origins of Babel twice (10:10; 11:4,9). Two different traditions are involved. A redactor could quite easily employ both. This assessment is, however, quite uncertain.

The source analysis offered here finds agreement with J. Boehmer (*Erste Buch Mose*, 137; Haller, 43, 122, 154; with reservations, Meinhold, 116-17; and Erbt, *Urgeschichte*, 22-23, 32ff., the latter assigns different sources). Cheyne (204ff.) also agrees in principle, although he assumes some corruption and secondary editing.

City Report, J^e (?). 1, 3a, 4aα, γ

Part I of the legend. The construction of the city. 1 שָׂפָה, "lip, language," is the whole; דְּבָרִים are the individual components. The two expressions are combined for the sake of emphasis. The implication may be that they are also unified in their plans (cf. Frankenberg, GGA [1901], 685). V **3a** links ingeniously to v 1. V 1 says generally that humanity has one language; v 3a concretely explicates what they said. Thus the legend recounts the discovery of brickmaking, albeit in an extremely naive manner. The people said, "Hey, let's mold bricks." According to the narrator, then, the word "brick" existed before the object. For the Babylonian tradition of the discovery of brickmaking see *Schöp-*

fung und Chaos, 419-20; KB 6/1:39-40; Winckler, *Keilinschriftl. Textbuch*[2], 98-99. For הָבָה > יהב "give" in the meaning "now then!" see §69o. The word characterizes the narrator (cf. vv 4, 7).

4aα,γ When the people have successfully made bricks, they get another idea. Now they want to build a city. The legend intends to recount the construction of the first city and is, thus, originally independent of 4:17. The people intend "to make themselves a name," that is, to gain eternal fame. This is an ancient motif: the ancients considered fame the greatest good fortune. The childless erected memorials (2 Sam 18:18) or placed a name plaque in the temple (Isa 56:5). The king built a mighty building from stones marked with his monogram or in which he places a plaque with his name. "He made this as his memorial" begins every dedicatory inscription of Egyptian temples since the earliest days (Erman, *Äg. Rel.* 56). The most powerful ruler, however, built an entire city to bring his name to the future (City of David, City of Sargon, Alexandria, Constantinople, etc.), for "children and cities preserve one's name" (Sir 40:19).

6aα,β, 7 . . . 8b *Part II: Yahweh's intervention.* When the people plan this (and are in the process of executing their plans), Yahweh intervenes. In accordance with the old legend style, his motive is not <94> indicated, but presumed: He does not want the people to have a name! God, the Eternal One, alone wants to have an eternal name. His name will be remembered from generation to generation. The human being, however, who came yesterday, shall be forgotten tomorrow! The ideas here are thus similar to those in Gen 3:22 and 6:3. Yahweh's speech is spoken in heaven according to v 7a ("Let us go down"). The statement presupposes (as does the variant "Yahweh came down" in v 5) that Yahweh dwells in heaven. Recent scholars (cf. Stade, ZAW 15:162ff.; *Bibl. Theol.*, 104; but see Greßmann, 99n.2, etc.) have maintained that ancient Israel did not know this doctrine, but one may compare Gen 28:12 (the ladder of heaven, see on the passage); Exod 19:11, 20 (J?); 34:5 (J? Yahweh comes down to the top of Mt. Sinai); Exod 24:10 (E? Yahweh reigns on Sapphir, i.e., originally the blue sky); 1 Kgs 18:33 (the fire of Yahweh, judging from the context, heavenly fire); Gen 19:24 (likewise, see on the passage); 1 Kgs 22:19 (Yahweh sits on his heavenly throne, the heavenly host stands to his right and left; I consider Schwally's [ZAW 12:159-60] misgivings concerning the authenticity and age of the passage to be erroneous); Isa 6:1 (Yahweh's palace in this passage is the heavenly, not the earthly temple; in the earthly temple there are no Seraphim but Cherubim over the Ark); 2 Kgs 2:11 (Elijah travels in the storm to heaven, to Yahweh). The fact that Yahweh was given the stars as servants (Judg 5:20) also agrees with this notion. This belief that the deity dwells in heaven occurs as a component or remnant of astral religion (or of meteorological religion) among peoples everywhere. It was a component of Canaanite religion certainly long before Israel. It would be extremely unusual if it were not known in ancient Israel. Yet it must be admitted that this concept was hindered in ancient time by the competing notion that Yahweh dwells in his sanctuaries on earth and that Yahweh's dwelling in heaven was more heavily emphasized only in later times under the influence of the prophetic impression of God's superiority over everything earthly and simultaneously under renewed foreign influence. Yahweh looks down on the earth from heaven and sees the city under construction. His divine insight recognizes immediately the basis of their strength: "Look (= הֵן referring to the imminent circumstance), they are one people. They speak the same language!" In his wisdom he immediately found the means

to subdue the arrogant. We will confuse their speech! On נִבְלָה (qal cohortative > בלל)
see §67dd. "Let us go down," Yahweh says in his "council" to his courtesans as in 1:26
and 3:22. This very ancient element points, in the final analysis, to polytheism. The oldest
recension of this legend must, therefore, have recounted that several divine beings
intervened in Babel. This element has fallen away out of aversion for polytheism. On
אֲשֶׁר in the meaning "so that," see §166b. שָׁמַע means "to understand" as in 42:23,
etc. Following Yahweh's speech a (brief) word is probably missing: he did what he had
decided to do.

9a *Conclusion.* עַל־כֵּן introduces here, as in 2:24, the motivation for the legend. קָרָא
should be restored הַקְרָא, "one calls" (§144d, e). The city is called בָּבֶל because there
Yahweh בָּלַל confused languages. From a literary viewpoint, this etymology is very
nice. Thus the name of the city, which was to have brought humanity fame and honor, became its disgrace and shame. Whenever one hears the name "Babel" one simultaneously
hears of the insolence and shame of ancient humanity. Seen philologically, the etymology
is childish since, naturally, "Babel" is not to be explained from the Hebrew. The cuneiform etymology of *Babil* as *Bab-il*, "God's gate," may also be only a Semitic-Babylonian
popular etymology of the word which may not even have originally been Semitic.

Tower Recension, J^j (?). 2, 4aβ, b, 3b

Part I. The Construction of the Tower. **2** Humanity came from the East. Or perhaps
it should be translated "they moved around in the East" (cf. comments on 13:11). נָסַע
means "to set out (and move on)." This notice may belong to the old legend and would
then be an independent tradition paralleling <95> 2:8 (J^j). It is also possible, however, that
the comment stems from a collector. The collector may have previously recounted that
Noah's Ark came down on an eastern mountain (J^j). This also seems to suggests that the
Tower recension is the work of J^j. בִּקְעָה is a broad plain in contrast to נַחַל. a ravine,
wadi. Shin'ar = Babylonia (cf. comments on 10:10) is a plain, indeed the broadest plain
in the then-known world, *the* בִּקְעָה.

4aβ, b The tower is to reach to heaven—ancient naiveté. Heaven is very high above
the earth so that it was a massive undertaking. But this undertaking was not impossible:
If one built high enough, one would finally reach heaven. The goal of the construction is
to keep humanity together. Why did they want to stay together? This becomes clear to us
from the context of the legend: because they are stronger with combined powers than if
they were to disperse. The notion that the Tower, whose top projects into heaven, is
visible on the whole earth is naive. V **3b** (suitably placed behind 4b) comments on the
construction materials. In Palestine one employed quarry stones אֶבֶן in the better buildings and joined them with clay; in inferior buildings bricks לְבֵנָה (probably a Babyl.
loanword) dried in an oven or the sun (cf. Benzinger², 91; Nowack 1:138-39; cf. esp. Isa
9:9). In contrast, quarries were unknown in Babylon and one had to be satisfied with
bricks joined (at least on the outside) with חֵמָר asphalt (cf. Herodotus I.179). Palestin-
ians were amazed that the Babylonians built the most glorious places and temples with
the most inferior material, bricks, and employed such a strong adhesive as asphalt.

5, 6aγ, b, 8a *Part II: Yahweh's Intervention.* **5** Yahweh comes down to investigate
the matter. One must assume that Yahweh had already heard about the construction. The
account of this may have been omitted. The notion that Yahweh sets out for the scene in

order to be better informed (so also 18:21) is archaic. God's omniscience and omnipresence (in the absolute sense) were entirely impossible concepts at the time (cf. above, p. 18). "He came down" is like "Let us go down" (v 7). Yahweh's speech in v 6aγ,b is similar to v 6aα. Yahweh, it is presumed, sees that the work of humans is very mighty, indeed dangerous for him. He thinks apprehensively of the future. This gigantic Tower is only the beginning. How will the matter continue? They will even be able to storm heaven (a very archaic manner of expression)! The assumption is that Yahweh does not want this. The deity does not want humanity to be able to do everything it plans. Instead, the deity wants to keep it within its limits. This recension, then, has the same basic view of Yahweh a priori as the City recension. One could almost say at this point that Yahweh was afraid. The narrator thinks no less of him, however. For a moment it almost seemed as though humanity could become almighty, but Yahweh showed that he is still mightier. הַחִלָּם is a hiph. inf. from חלל. For the patach see §67w. יָזְמוּ is from זמם (see §67dd).

8 Yahweh breaks their power by dispersing them over the whole earth. **9b** The legend's final clause, as in the City recension, communicated the name of the structure, the Tower here, and gave its etymology. This name has unfortunately fallen away. In contrast, the etymology has been preserved. The name is explained by the fact that Yahweh "scattered" them הֱפִיצָם (וְנָפוּץ v 4). The legend interpreted the name to mean "scattering." It must have been פִּיץ (or פּוּץ or something similar). The "Tower" of the legend can hardly have been anything other than a ziggurat such as those the Babylonians were accustomed to building in their temple complexes. Ruins of many such Towers are preserved. (Concerning such structures, see A. Jeremias, ATAO², 278ff.) In the event that the Tower of our legend was located in the city of Babel—which is admittedly uncertain given our source analysis—it can hardly have been <96> any other than the tower *E-temen-an-ki* which belonged to the Babylonian temple κατ' ἐξοχήν, the temple of Marduk, *Esagil*. This temple appears already under Hammurabi, ca. 2100 (cf. the repeated references in the introduction and conclusion of Codex Hammurabi), and under his third predecessor Sabum, and was surely in existence much earlier (*Beiträge zur Assyriologie* 4:349). According to most scholars, the temple lies buried under the ruins of Tell Amran, south of the hill *el-Qaṣr*, while Hommel (*Grundriß*, 326ff.) seeks it north of *el-Qaṣr* (see Baumstartk "Babylon," *Realencyclopädie*, ed. Pauly and Wissowa; F. Delitzsch, *Babylon*², 18; id., "Esagila," MDOg 7:2ff.; Weißbach, *Stadtbild von Babylon*, Alt. Orient V⁴; and especially Hommel, *Grundriß*, 298ff.). That it had fallen into disrepair in the legend's time is understandable. Apparently as a consequence of the unsolid brick materials and despite all the restorations of which we hear often enough, Babylonian temples were in a constant state of decay. That it was immense and seemed almost to reach to heaven, according to the legend, suits this particular tower superbly. Nabopolassar who rebuilt it once when it was "dilapidated and decayed," declares that he "grounded its foundation in the underworld and caused its pinnacle to reach heaven" as in the olden days (cf. KB 3/2:5-6). The last expression seems to have been particularly characteristic for Etemenanki. It also occurs in reference to the same temple in a document of Nebuchadnezzar (*Beiträge zur Assyriologie* 3:548) and in the Marduk hymn no. 12 (in Hehn, *Beiträge zur Assyriologie* 5:345-46; "he raised its pinnacle as high as heaven"; cf. also Zimmern, KAT³, 396, 616; Jeremias, ATAO², 277ff.). This temple and tower were the oldest and most famous structures in Babylon. The name of the temple and temple precincts in Babylonia are all

Sumerian, including the name *E-Sag-il* (towering house) and *E-temen-an-ki* (house of the foundation of heaven and earth). It is likely, however, that alongside these ancient, official names, strictly maintained in priestly circles, popular names in the Semitic-Babylonian language also existed. Such a popular name for the Marduk temple Esagil could have been, so H. Zimmern tells me, "the white house" *bîtu pisû* (> פצא "to be white"). A later text from the Arsacide period, in fact, characterizes Esagil as the "House of Day" in contrast to Ezida in Borsippa, the "House of Night" (cf. ZA 6:228). Similar epithets for temples, especially the Shamash temple, are attested, such as "brilliant, bright, radiant" temple. Others think of the tower of *Ê-zida*, the great temple of Nebo in Borsippa, now Birs Nimrud (bibliography in Cheyne, *Enc Bibl* s.v. "Babel" 7).

General Remarks Concerning the Legend of the Tower

I. *The original sense of the legend.* The legend answers several questions. The first recension explains the origin of the various languages and, at the same time, the origin and name of the city Babel. The second explains the dispersion of humans on earth and, at the same time, the origin and name of an ancient "tower" in Babylonia. The legend answers all these questions in its poetic manner. It is unable to give a scientifically sound explanation of the Babylonian names. It no longer knows about the origin of the city and the tower through historical reminiscence. It has even less historical tradition from the period in which the oldest languages and peoples of the near East arose, for human memory does not reach back to that time. This narrative should not be regarded a historical tradition, but a naive answer of the ancient period to certain questions it found important. The task of the legend scholar, however, is to recognize these questions and thus to untangle the various components of which the two recensions consist.

(1) The first question both recensions answer is general: <97> Whence come the differences between humans? The chief differences that separate people, however, are their various languages—still a major symptom of different nationalities for our science as well—and their various locations. How did this question arise? It arose from the contradictions between the old tradition which taught the unity of the human race (all people, the old legend maintained, descend from one pair) and experience which demonstrated the great differences among people. Once, one may assume, humanity must have been unified. Then, however, it disintegrated into various peoples. This division of the nations is conceived either as a natural consequence of reproduction and growth—as assumed by the Table of Nations—or as the result of God's forceful disruption of humanity—the opinion of our legend. But how does antiquity evaluate this dispersion? As a great misfortune, as a human catastrophe! For what could humanity have accomplished if it were one! It would have been capable of divine feats! "Nothing would have been impossible for it" And Yahweh, himself would have been unable to hinder it! Why, then, is humanity so severed? Because, otherwise, it would have become too mighty for the deity! The legend expresses these ideas in the form of a narrative. Once humanity had the same language and dwelt in the same place. Then, in sinful arrogance, it began a superhuman work. But Yahweh does not allow himself to be displaced from the throne. In order to break the power of humanity, he confused its language and dispersed it over the earth.

(2) The legend does not narrate so abstractly, however. Rather, it reports quite specifically. This specificity is its great poetic advantage over analogous constructions of

a later, more prosaic time. It knows quite precisely "where" and "how." The place was Babylonia according to both recensions. The oldest structure in the world was the city of Babel or, according to another tradition, the great Tower standing in Babel. "There Yahweh confused the language of all humanity and from there Yahweh scattered it over the whole earth." This information, to be sure, is not a historical tradition (cf. above), but neither was it grabbed out of the air. Babel was for Israel and its neighbors a very ancient city, the Tower surely a massive structure from time immemorial. In the view of all the peoples dependent on Babylonian cultural influence, the "wisdom" of Babylonia stemmed from the beginning of the human race.

It is no wonder that the original home of humanity was sought here and that the Israelites themselves claimed to have emigrated from this cultural center (cf. comments on 11:31). This Babel, however, is also the very place where the language of humanity was confused, for Babel was already in ancient times the market of the world, where the nations of the world flowed together (Isa 13:14; Jer 50:37; 51:44), and where the whole welter of human languages rang out together. Berosus narrates already in the Babylonian primeval history, in reference to Oannes, that a great multitude of ethnically distinct peoples populating Chaldea could be found together in Babylon (cf. C. Müller, *Fragm. hist. graec.* 2:496). The Hebrew associates Babel's multilingualism with the word בָּבֶל which he interprets to mean "confusion." He associates the name of the Tower with the word הֵפִיץ, "to scatter." At the same time, he emphasizes the might of earliest, still unified humanity in the imposing scope of the city Babel and in the mighty tower one sees in Babel. Still in the narrator's time, powerful Babylonian despots forced whole nations into servitude to erect structures intended to transmit the fame of the builder to the most distant future. Graphic representations of Assyrian construction sites with legions of workers beautifully illustrate Gen 11.

Thus, the legend reports the titanic undertakings of ancient humanity. The first humans, so it was recounted, wanted to build Babel, a city designed to be large enough to accommodate all of humanity, and they planned this ancient tower so tall that its <98> pinnacle reaches almost to heaven. Such mighty structures also made a gruesome impression on ancient humans. How many violent acts and how much blood must it have cost! "Memories of this impression continue to resonate in legend and fairy tale, custom, and belief." "Only demonic spirits, in German legends the devil, can complete them. Injustice, betrayal, and deceit are horribly related to their origins." "One remembers the Greek legend of the construction of Troy or the Nordic legend of the giant construction foreman" (cf. v. d. Leyen CXIV, 22f., with bibliography). Thus, the legend also considered these earliest human structures works of rebellious wickedness against the deity. These works are, however, incomplete. This element, too, is not capricious, but is surely drawn from the concept. It is an ever-recurring element in the history of our race that the greatest plans are conceived and begun, but not carried out. Just as almost all the medieval cathedrals have come to us incomplete, so will it have been in ancient times. The Tower was, it seemed to the foreign spectator at least, only half finished and the city incomplete. The Israelite legend understands this fate of all great plans of humans after its fashion. Such plans should not be executed, for humans should not have an eternal name and be almighty. Then humans would be like God! So, these structures stand there, memorials to human arrogance, but, at the same time, to divine judgment: incomplete! Earliest humanity was capable of mighty deeds, but Yahweh was mightier! Therefore, may the human race fear the gods!

II. *Origin of the Legend.* The legend clearly originated in Babylonia. It presupposes the perspective of Babylonian construction materials, of Babel, the world market, and the knowledge of the huge scope of the city and of the might tower at Babel. But the impression of city and tower the legend represents is that of the foreigner in Babylonia. The native knows what such a structure represents: it is no profane "tower," but a temple of the gods, not erected contrary to god, but for god by an ancient king. Only far from Babylonia can one seriously maintain that this tower was intended to reach to heaven itself. Furthermore, Babylonian tradition would not have called Babel the oldest city (Meyer, *Israeliten*, 211) and, least of all, would it have interpeted the name Babel as "confusion." To the Babylonian, his city is the site of divine revelation (cf. *Babil* = god's door), but to the foreigner the place of wickedness (cf. the prophetic name "impudence" for Babel in Jer 50:31) and of divine judgment. The legend arose, then, among barbarians who were not unfamiliar with Babylonia. Full of amazement and horror, these barbarians tell of the great Babel and its Tower—perhaps on the basis of adapted Babylonian legends—just as the Germans may have told of golden Rome and Engelsburg. These barbarians were probably Semites given the Semitic etymology of Babel which forms a major component of one recension. We may think of the Arameans, perhaps (Aram. בַּלְבֵּל "to confuse"). Wandering farther from land to land, the legend finally came to Israel.

III. *Current status of the tradition.* In its current form, the legend is intensely Hebraized. It manifests the Palestinian's amazement concerning the remarkable Babylonian construction material. It has been especially modified, however, through the omission of the polytheism still echoing lightly in one passage and the appearance of Yahweh alone in the place of the many gods. The two recensions distinguish themselves by a delightful conciseness. The first and last images stand in the sharpest contrast: the one language and the confusion, the one home and the dispersion. The intervening material leads on a direct path from one extreme to the other. In this, both recensions exhibit a narrative conciseness that <99> can hardly be surpassed. Thus, it is only recounted that humanity planned to build a city and to erect a tower, that they began to execute this plan is considered obvious and is not expressly reported, etc. This almost excessive conciseness may also partially result from omissions. The original legend surely must have made clear who the deity addresses in v 7 (originally the gods). The legends of the ancient period died out to a degree, some already when they were committed to writing. Some of that which was fortunately saved at that time subsequently fell victim to the religious misgivings of the copyists and redactors.

Of the two variants, the Tower recension seems to be the older. The concept of the Tower that reaches to heaven is more naive than that of the city large enough for all humanity. At any rate, the Tower is not as well known as world-famous Babel. The plural addressee in the city recension (v 7) is, however, an ancient element.

IV. *Citations.* In Judeo-Greek writings of the Hellenistic period, in a time when the primitive traditions of the various peoples were retrieved and compared, the Tower of Babel was also cited not infrequently (cf. E. Böhmer, *Erste Buch der Thora*, 189ff.; Gruppe, *Griech. Culte u. Mythen* 1:677ff.). Thus Eupollemos recounts (C. Müller, *Fragm. hist. Gr.* 3:211, 212) that the giants saved from the Flood built Babel and the Tower.

When they fall through divine intervention, the giants spread out over the whole earth. This account is nothing other than a combination of the narratives of the Nephilim and the Flood and the two recensions of the Tower story. Thus, the author had access to nothing more than our Genesis. The situation is similar in the interesting passage in Or Sib 3:97-155, whose author mixes Oriental and Greek traditions together in Hellenistic fashion: first the biblical Tower account (97-106) together with reminiscences from the Table of Nations (107) and Shem's genealogy (108-109), then suddenly the euhemeristically interpreted Greek myths of Chronos and of Zeus's birth (110-55). That Genesis also underlies the Tower account in these passages is demonstrated by the circumstance that here, too, the two Tower accounts are combined, indeed in the biblical association with the Flood (109) and with the explicit statement that the name Babel can be explained from the confusion of languages (104). The only addition is the Jewish Haggadah, also preserved in Jubil 10:19, 26, that the people wanted to climb to heaven (100) and that storms sent from the deity toppled the Tower (102). The fact that Alexander Polyhistor's prosaic paraphrase of this Sibylline passage (preserved in Josephus, *Ant.* I.4, by Eusebius in Synkellos, cf. *Euseb. Chronicon*, ed. Schöne I.23-24, etc.) quite probably spoke of the wrath of the gods on the Tower while our Sibylline text reads the singular here poses a particular problem. Geffcken's (*Nachrichten der Gött. Ges. der Wissenschaften Phil.-hist. Kl.* [1900] 88ff.) and Bousset's (ZNW 3:26-27; *Rel. des Judentums²*, 562-63) contention that this plural demonstrates the pagan, and specifically the Babylonian, origin of the Sibylline account is to be rejected since the remaining character of the passage, as just described, and especially the interpretation of the name "Babel" assures its origin in the Bible beyond all doubt. The plural—so seems the simplest assumption—was probably introduced by the pagan Alexander Polyhistor. Suppositions that the Sibylline passage stems from a Greek author or that the Sibylle affected pagan origins are more difficult. In no case, however, is the pagan or even the Babylonian origin of this tradition to be accepted (contra Stade, ZAW 15:161-62; *Bibl. Theol.*, 243). The contention that the Greek Sibylle employed an assumed Babylonian source falls away.

Traditions of the original monolinguality of humanity (but without <100> allusion to Babel and the Tower) occur in Greco-Roman tradition (*Hyginus fab.*, 143), further among the Persians, Indians, and Chinese (cf. Lüken, *Traditionen des Menschengeschlechtes²*, 314ff.). Narratives similar to the Tower legend occur among the Armenians, Mexicans, Africans, etc., but most are influenced by the biblical narrative (Lüken, 314ff.; Cheyne, *Enc Bibl*, s.v. Babel 3).

The Primeval History in P

1. Creation account (1:1–2:4a). 2. Sethite genealogy (5). 3. Flood legend (6:9–9:29). 4. Table of the Nations (10). 5. Shem's genealogy and 6. Terah's genealogy (11:10-32).

Budde (*Urgeschichte*, 464ff.) has theorized that P's Creation account may be dependent on one of the sources of J, namely Budde's J². This assumption is not confirmed by our analysis of the sources in J (cf. the overview of the two sources of J, p. 3). Rather, P does not entirely agree either with Jᵉ or Jʲ in the selection of material. Its exemplars here were, then, neither Jᵉ, Jʲ, nor the already combined "J," but another source, unknown to us but related to our tradition. A comparison of J and P in the Flood legend corroborates this (cf. below). Besides, this result is to be expected from the outset. It would be an un-usual case indeed, if P had access to a document which is also available to us. Of the en-tire rich literature of ancient Israel only scant fragments are transmitted to us.

10. Creation Account in P 2:4a; 1:1–2:3

2:4a *Superscription.* The statement is preserved as a the narrative's subscription. Sim-ilar statements appear elsewhere in P (5:1; 6:9; 10:1; 11:10) as superscriptions. Here, too, the clause will have also originally been a superscription—otherwise the statement would have clashed in P with the immediately following superscription 5:1—and will have been displaced by a redactor (Stade, *Bibl. Theol.*, 349) in order to begin the book with בְּרֵאשִׁית or for a smoother connection with the subsequent unit from J. P also placed the phrase אֵלֶּה תּוֹלְדוֹת—"these are the generations," descendants, genealogy, family history, elsewhere in P always a superscription, especially of genealogies—before the Creation account which, thus, he also understood as a genealogy. Just as generation follows generation in the genealogy, so God's creations follow one another here. LXX reads αὕτη ἡ βίβλος γενέσεως. בְּרָאָם contains the ה minusculum. Dillmann reads בְּרָאָם אלהים.

1:1-5 *Original state and first day.* **1** The verse can be best taken as a main clause "in the beginning God created heaven and earth"—a powerful statement! Simply and power-fully, the author first establishes the doctrine that God created the world. No statement in the cosmogonies of other peoples approaches this first statement in the Bible. Everything that follows has the goal, then, of illustrating <101> this clause. In another interpretation, v 1 is taken with what follows: "in the beginning, when God created heaven and earth." V 2 would then be a parenthetical clause and v 3 an apodosis. In the first case בְּרֵאשִׁית would be in the absolute state (cf. also the ancient transcription Βαρησήθ, Field Hexapla); In the second case, it would be taken with §130d as a construct state (one could also pronounce בְּרֹא as an infinitive). Both interpretations are possible, although the first understanding seems simpler. At any rate, the two are only grammatically, not semantically, distinct. In no case, however, is it permissible (because of the first construct) to understand הַשָּׁמַיִם וְהָאָרֶץ as a description of the primordial, still chaotic world and to maintain that v 1 refers to the creation of the world as Chaos (so Wellhausen, *Prolegomena*[6], 296; *Composition*[3], 105) so that v 2 then must describe the chaotic state of this first creation and only vv 3ff. describe the origination of the current ordered world.

This interpretation is contradicted by the following. (1) "Heaven and earth" is other-wise consistently the name of the current, organized world and cannot possibly be under-stood as the depiction of a chaotic primordial world. (2) The world as Chaos is not called "heaven and earth" but "the earth" (v 2). (3) The notion of a creation of Chaos is intrinsically contradictory and odd, for Chaos is the world before the Creation. The opposite of רֵאשִׁית is אַחֲרִית הַיָּמִים: primordium and eschaton (Stade, *Bibl. Theol.*, 349). בְּרֵאשִׁית בָּרָא is alliteration in this solemn passage. Here and elsewhere (Isa 42:5; 45:18, etc.) בָּרָא is a technical term for God's creativity. The expression, employed in Gen 1 alternately with עָשָׂה without semantic distinction, characterizes this particular narrative just as certain expressions characterize certain of the most ancient narratives (cf. מַבּוּל and תֵּבָה in the Flood legend, for example, p. 67). In use elsewhere, the word sig-nifies the peculiar activity of God that produces something wondrous, unheard of, new (Exod 34:10; Isa 48:7; Jer 31:22; Psa 51:12). Characteristically, it does not occur in reference to human production and is never associated with the accusative of the material as are other verbs of making. Since it is employed here as a special term in a narrative, it should be considered very ancient according to the criteria of legend criticism (cf. p. 67 and below). The fact that the expression is otherwise known to us only from later literature (Jer, Ezek, Deutero-Isa) does not contradict this understanding. The OT literature known to us is much too sparse to permit very much to be based on the more or less accidental occurrence or nonoccurrence of such an expression (contra Wellhausen, *Prolegomena*[6], 387; Stade, *Bibl. Theol.*, 92-93).

Nor may one maintain that the notion expressed by בָּרָא in the form we have just described would have been unattainable in Israel's ancient period (contra Wellhausen, *Prolegomena*[6], 304). Why should ancient Israel have been unable to think that it is God's business to produce the unheard of, the wondrous? "For what is too wondrous for God?" (Gen 18:14). While, therefore, nothing stands in the way of regarding the word בָּרָא in the sense described as very ancient, it should be emphasized, on the other hand, that only a later period can have given the word the profoundest sense present in Gen 1. This later period marked it as an expression of its developed supernaturalism according to which with the absolutely sovereign God has the world at his disposal and, standing above it, produces it from outside. Precisely because this supernaturalistic attitude could be expressed in these words, however, it was so favored in a later period. Concerning the history of אֱלֹהִים, originally a plural, "the (many) gods," later comprehended as a unity so that אֱלֹהִים became a singular term, cf. recently Meyer, *Israeliten*, 211n.1.

2 The continuation contrasts remarkably with this beginning. Whereas one may expect following this first clause that the world was only created by God and that before him nothing will have existed, the second clause describes the primordial state of the world preceding God's "Creation." The attempt has been made <102> to alleviate this contradiction by assuming that the world became תֹּהוּ וָבֹהוּ only subsequently (perhaps through the intervention of the Devil). Instead, it must be admitted that this intrinsic contradiction is to be understood historically: the material of v 2 belongs to the elements found by Judaism; v 1 was added by Judaism itself. That P could adopt such a depiction of Chaos demonstrates that he, too, did not yet clearly conceive of the notion of *creatio ex nihilo* (2 Macc 7:28; Hebr 11:3). The description of the chaotic primordial state is "a true mythological treasury" (Schwally, ARW 9:169).

תֹּהוּ וָבֹהוּ rhymes. Ancient diction loves such assonance (cf. נָע וָנָד 4:12, further 18:27: 21:23, etc.). Regarding the construction see §141e n.1[3]. תֹּהוּ "desert, wilderness, void" occurs elsewhere, too, as in Isa 45:18 in an allusion to the Creation narrative. בֹהוּ "void" occurs only in conjunction with תֹּהוּ, here and in Jer 4:23; Isa 34:11, in allusions to the Creation narrative which transfer the primordial chaos to the future (eschaton) (cf. *Schöpfung und Chaos*, 138-39). The expression תֹּהוּ וָבֹהוּ is apparently a term of the Creation narrative and consequently, in analogy to similar terms, is to be considered ancient (cf. below). That this term is known to us only from later literature is no contradiction (contra Wellhausen, *Prolegomena*[6], 387).

The expression "void and waste" points to a concept, similar to that in the Creation account of J, in which the earth was originally a desert (cf. p. 4). The LXX translation ἀόρατος καὶ ἀκατασκεύαστος is a very imprecise paraphrase. The Phoenicians, too, know Βάαυ, but as the wife of the wind κολπία they equate her with Νύξ and view her as the first mother of humanity. The Babylonians have a goddess Bau, wife of Ninib, the god of war. It is unclear whether the Hebrew concept was originally identical with the Phoenician and whether both were identical with the Babylonian (cf. Zimmern, KAT³, 410n.5, 509n.1). According to another view of the world's beginning, the world was originally darkness and water. תְּהוֹם, the primal ocean (fem.) is also a technical term. In the current world (יַבָּה) תְּהוֹם is the ocean under the earth (Gen 49:25; Amos 7:4, etc.). If, according to Gen 1, תְּהוֹם filled the whole world in the primordium, there must have been an intermediate notion that God drove back the primal תְּהוֹם and shut it up in the depths of the earth. This concept occurs most clearly in Or Man 3. The fact that the word תהום in the sing. is never employed in the determined state, and thus is treated as a proper name, implies that T*hom* was originally a mythological entity, that is, a goddess. The same is true of חֶבֶל, "arable land, earth." The Babylonian *Tiâmat* = Hebr. תְּהוֹם demonstrates the accuracy of this conclusion. *Tiâmat* is the primordial sea, represented as a goddess or feminine monster. The same concept of the primordial sea which gave rise to everything also occurs among the Egyptians, etc. An OT parallel is Psa 104:6 in which Tehom once covered the earth like a robe. The assumption of a watery or muddy primal element can apparently be explained as the result of a certain view of nature (cf., below, "General Remarks" 3).

The concept of darkness belongs with *Tehom*. In the Babylonian tradition, too, primordial sea and darkness appear together (as is especially clear in the Creation account of Berosus). We also find the doctrine that the world developed out of darkness among the Babylonians, Egyptians, Indians, Phoenicians, Greeks, Chinese (Welhelm, *Zeitschr. für Missionskunde u. Religionswissenschaft* 21:49), etc. The night is the first, the original, the light the beginning of the current world. The two concepts—that in the beginning "the earth was a desert and void" and that "darkness was upon the primordial sea"—were originally two distinct theories of the world's beginning. The subsequent case offers a third, once again probably originally allogenous, theory. The fact that these different views harmonize with one another quite well here results from the fact that they are greatly diluted and—as is the nature of the material—veiled in obscure, <103> dark secrecy. This description of the primordium is extraordinary and impressive precisely for its simplicity. "The Spirit of God brooded on the surface of the waters." The רוּחַ of God is usually (1) the divine power or the divine being which produces "demonic" phenomena in a person. Anything mighty and mysterious in human life that exceeds human strength and human scope, especially the mysterious experiences the prophet undergoes, is the effect of the רוּחַ.

(2) Related is the concept of the life-giving spirit or breath of God which produces in humans and in other creatures the wondrous secret of life (Psa 104:29-30). Here as a ἅπαξ λεγόμενον the רוּחַ is envisioned as the life-giving, shaping divine power that hovers over the formless and lifeless "waters" in the beginning. This concept also occurs in a Phoenician cosmogony (Phil. Byblius in Euseb. *Praep. ev.* 1.10) according to which, in addition to the murky, dark Chaos, the πνεῦμα (described as ἀὴρ ζοφώδης καὶ πνευματώδης) was present in the beginning. The word רחף occurs in Deut 32:11 in reference to the eagle that protects its young with extended wings (one may read with LXX יָעִיר "protects" for יָעִיר). We may well assume that the basic meaning of the word is related to the Syriac "to brood" and surmise that the ancient and widespread speculation

concerning the world egg echoes here (Dillmann, Delitzsch, etc.). We find this speculation among the Indians, Iranians, Orphics (Chantepie 2^2:324), in all three Phoenician cosmogonies, among the Polynesians (cf. Waitz-Gerland, *Anthropologie der Naturvölker* 6:234, 237, 241, 665; A. Bastian, *Heilige Sage der Polynesier* 12:229, 240-41), and elsewhere (cf. Dillman 4:20; Lukas, *Kosmogonien der alten Völker*, s.v. "Ei").

Speculation concerning the world egg emanates from the egg-shape of heaven (cf. the Chinese doctrine in Wilhelm, *Zeitschr. f. Missionskunde u. Religionswissenschaft* 21:44). The lower part of the earth or heaven beneath the earth is conceived as the other, invisible half of the egg (attested as the Iranian view in *Mînôkhired* 44:9; West, *Sacr. Books East* 24:85; cf. Windischmann, *Zor. St.*, 284). The origination of the organized world from the primordial waters is compared with the development of the young bird from the fluid in the egg. Thus, as we repeatedly hear explicitly stated, heaven and earth developed from the world egg (cf. Lukas, *Kosmogonien*, 89, 147, 194). Since it is attested as Phoenician doctrine (in Mochos of Damascius), this view is also to be considered the original intention of the Israelite cosmogony underlying this text. This view of the world egg, very naive in our terms, was extremely ingenious in antiquity.

The reference to the divine world principle as רוּחַ may also be very ancient. We will have to imagine this רוּחַ originally as a warm wind that incubated the egg. In any case, however, Gen 1 preserves only a scant remnant of the whole concept. The world egg is no longer discussed and the result of the Spirit's brooding is not stated. Instead, the continuation makes a new beginning in relation to v 2, with a new figure, the (personal) God (=Yahweh) and with a new principle of creation, the word of God. The creative God and the brooding Spirit are actually not intrinsically related to one another, but are mutually exclusive. The brooding Spirit is based on the concept that Chaos develops from within, the creative God imposes his will on the world from without. The reason this element is obscured is clear: supernaturalism forced the idea of evolution into the background (Wellhausen, *Prolegomena*[6], 296). The Jewish narrator, however, who does not call the first principle simply רוּחַ, but רוּחַ אֱלֹהִים, means אֱלֹהִים as a reference to the God of Israel. In his sense, the phrase should be translated "Spirit of God."

3 Everything that follows comes into being through God's word. This concept of creation through the word also occurs among many peoples. Marduk's word works wonders. The Egyptians know that Thot's instrument for creating the world was the word (Lange in Chantepie, de la <104> Saussaye 1^2:147). A similar idea occurs among the Indians (Lukas, *Kosmogonien*, 81, 82, 97) and even among the Quiches in Guatemala (Lukas, 261). Regarding the late Egyptian period, see Reitzenstein, *Poimandres*, 5n.3 (cf. pp. 63-64). This notion was not originally as sublime as it seems to us. As the Marduk myth shows with particular clarity, the spoken word that works wonders is actually the magical word. But, on the other hand, the concept of creation through the word is capable of higher spiritualization since the word can be understood as an expression of the will. The Jewish narrator took the concept in this sense and thus expressed his idea of God's relationship to the world: God acts on the world through his will. He does not enter the world and "form" with his hands (as in the older account, 2:7, 19, 22). Rather, he remains above it, outside, and commands what will be. He speaks and it happens (Psa 33:9). These brief clauses (v 3) are the classic expression of supernaturalism. Only a last breath of the mythological remains to them. Such clauses give our narrative permanent value. Command

and execution are closely associated here. The execution follows immediately and in precisely the same words as the command in order to indicate that it happened immediately and precisely as God had commanded. An esthetic assessment of the statements will be offered below.

Light is the first creation. Without light there can be no life and no order. Before light the world was dark, lifeless, chaotic. Darkness and Chaos are horrible. שְׁאוֹל, where there is no light, is also horrible. Light is good and beneficial. Similar notions of light as the first creation also occur among the Indians, the Greeks, the Phoenicians, etc. Herder (*Älteste Urkunde des Menschengeschlechts*) offers a lovely interpretation of the impression of darkness and light. Remarkably, in relation to the modern concept, light appears before bodies of light (vv 14ff.). This circumstance, frequently treated by modern "apologists," gave the ancient no difficulty. He envisions light as an independent thing, as a fine substance. He asks where light dwells (Job 38:19-20) and how heavy it is. Just as no earthly being can see sound, so also no human can weigh fire, only God (4 Ezr 4:5; 5:37). Therefore, it seems very plausible to the ancient that light is older than the stars. In pagan cosmogonies, light characterizes the higher gods.

4a "God found the light good." On the construction, see §177h. A similar statement recurs in the subsequent creations. Like the artist who evaluates his work critically when the ecstasy of creation has subsided, so God inspects each creation afterward, testing it. And he finds each good and beautiful. The work has succeeded. "God rejoices over his creations" (Psa 104:31). The narrator's assessment naturally corresponds to God's assessment of the world: the world is good. In the hymn of jubilation ancient Israel sang of the wisdom and goodness of the creator of the world. Later Judaism viewed the issue quite differently: the world lies in distress. One notes that the darkness is not called "good" and is actually not God's creation. Nevertheless, God subsequently separates the darkness and names it. Pursuing the notion we may say, then, that God takes possession of the darkness although it is not his creation and includes it in the order of his creations.

4b "God separated light and darkness," that is, he determined that they would no longer intermingle with one another, but would exist separately from now on. Stated concretely, he gave each of them a special place in the world (Job 38:19). Characteristically for the narrative, it speaks blandly and does not even indicate at all how the regular alternation between light and darkness, ordered by God, actually takes place. "Separation" also occurs in vv 6, 7, 14, 18. The statement actually assumes that prior to creation things were intermingled in a disorderly and chaotic fashion <105> and that they were separated in an orderly manner through God's creation. Yet this notion of "separation" is not consistently carried out in the entire account. Light, for example, is a new creation.

5a "Day" and "Night" are, in the author's view, the names of the times of day. They are "dark" and "light" by nature. "Darkness and light" are, thus, definitions of "day and night." Similarly, "firmament" is the definition of "heaven" (v 6), "dry" of "earth" and "gathering of the waters" of "world sea" (v 10). The fact that God also gives names seems very naive to us, but very natural to the ancient: things only have proper existence when they are named. A similar notion also appears in the introduction to the Babylonian creation myth. At the same time, naming is the privilege of the one with authority (Zapletal, *Schöpfungsbericht*, 15-16). By naming, God establishes the fact that he is Lord. The modern notion that name and thing have essentially nothing to do with one another, that the name is an accident of history, different among each people, would seem entirely impossible to ancient thought. Rather, the name seems to the ancient to be an obvious expression of the thing itself: things are called what they are. The natural assumption is that God speaks Hebrew. The Hebrew language is the real language. Other peoples do not actually "speak," they only stammer. This is the naive arrogance of this ancient people.

5b The period of a day is described here by its two segments (poetically solemn diction). Now the question arises whether the words "evening, morning" refer to the two beginnings or the ends of a day, that is, whether the new day begins with evening (so Neh 13:19; Dan 8:14) or morning in this system. Since, however, the light originated first and it then "became" evening, the latter is likely. A parallel would be as follows: the earth become green, the earth became white—a year passed. Babylonian tradition also has both systems (Jastrow, *Rel. Bab. u. Ass.* 1:67, 75). Notably, the regular alternation of day and night already began before the sun traversed the heavens. It seems reasonable, then, to suspect that the division into seven work days did not originally belong to the narrative material, but was added only secondarily (cf. below, pp. 111, 120). Naturally, the "days" are days and nothing else. The narrative intends to say that the regular alternation of night and day that we now see stems from the first day. Otherwise, the institution of the seventh day as the holy day would be entirely superfluous if one did not understand the "days" as days. The narrator will have regarded it as a particular glorification of God that he needed only a day each for such mighty works. God creates so effortlessly! The application of the days of creation to 1,000-year periods or the like is, thus, a very capricious corruption from entirely allogenous circles of thought. Regarding אֶחָד see §98a.

6-8 *Second day.* The dome of heaven—as we know only an optical illusion—is, in the viewpoint of antiquity, a firm structure based on columns (Job 26:11) with doors and windows (Gen 28:17; 2 Kgs 7:2). It is comparable to a tent, a house, or a city. Its substance is comparable to a mirror or to sapphire. Above the heaven, however, is an inexhaustible sea of heavenly water (Psa 148:4). Where would the rain come from otherwise? The rain is an outpouring of heavenly water supplies when God opens the floodgates of heaven (Gen 7:11; 2 Kgs 7:2, 19). The concept of a firm heavenly dome is universally distributed among primitive peoples (cf. Tylor, *Anfänge der Kultur* 2:71). Homer, too, expresses it in the epithets given heaven, <106> πολύξαλκος, ξάλκεος, and σιδήρεος. The heavenly sea is known among the Babylonians (cf. the well-known image of Shamash enthroned above the heavenly waters, reproduced, for example, in Guthes, BW, 67), Persians (Tiele, *Geshichte der Religion im Altertum* 2:290ff.), Egyptians (Erman, *Äg. Rel.*, 5ff.), Chinese (Wilhelm, *Zeitschr. für Missionskunde und Religionswissenschaft* 21:44), and primitive peoples (Waitz-Gerland, *Anthropologie* 6:269). This heavenly sea was originally heaven itself conceived as a mirror-clear water hanging wondrously above (the "glass sea," Rev 4:6, etc.). Another portion of the water, however, is here below, on earth (and below the earth).

Consequently, the world originated as follows. God separated the primordial waters into two parts, the waters above and the waters below, and he placed the firmament as a dividing wall between the two. Therefore, the firmament is God's work in the actual sense, just as light is. God arranged the world from the given materials (darkness and water) and from his own new creations (Meinhold, 38). The contention of Winckler (*Forschungen* 3:387-88) and his school (cf. Jeremias, ATAO², 164) that רָקִיעַ is the zodiac is totally unsupported by the text, indeed it is explicitly contradicted by v 8. רָקִיעַ is a definition of "heaven" (cf. comments on v 5a) and is, thus, not a part of heaven. Nor does the expression "firmament of heaven" (vv 14ff.) contradict the interpretation offered here. We, too, can speak of the "dome of heaven," such that the dome is nothing other than heaven itself.

The notion that above and below, heaven and earth, were once combined and that creation consists of a division of the two occurs frequently. Among the Phoenicians, the world egg divided into heaven and earth (Mochos of Damascius, 125; a similar notion also in Indian tradition, see Lukas, *Kosmogonien*, 89-90). Among the Egyptians, the god Shu lifted the goddess of heaven Nut, who lay on the earth god Keb, and thus separated heaven and earth (Erman, *Äg. Rel.*, 31-32). Melanippe of Euripides fr. 484 (*Trag. graec. fragm.*[2], ed. Nauck, 511; cf. A. Dieterich, *Mutter, Erde,* 42) also recounts the separation of heaven and earth, once a single structure. Especially closely related is the Babylonian tradition that Marduk divided the primordial sea *Tiâmat* into two segments. Regarding וַיְהִי מַבְדִּיל, see §266r. וַיְהִי־כֵן, in the Hebr text after v 7, is, if not a gloss, to be placed with LXX after the divine command in v 6. This formula appears in this placement in vv 11, 15, 24. After v 8a LXX reads וַיַּרְא אֹ' כִּי־טוֹב. Is it original (Schwally, ARW 9:162) or only a harmonizing addition of LXX (Fränkel, 60)? The author may have intentionally omitted the formula here because the waters below are still undifferentiated, not yet "good."

9-13 *Third day with two works, the separation of land and sea (vv 9,10) and the clothing of the earth with plants (vv 11,12).* **9, 10** The water that remained below comes together in one place (LXX has the better reading מִקְוֵה "gathering" for מָקוֹם; cf. v 10, Ball). Dry land appears as a result (on תֵּרָאֶה see §107n). Thus land and sea came into being. The precondition of the concept seems to be that previously water covered the face of earth (Psa 104:6). This concept does not entirely agree, it seems, with what has been presupposed so far, namely, that in the beginning the world consisted entirely of water. The author naturally meant that sea and earth then assumed their current form and shape. But he does not provide such details. He states only the general, not the particular (cf. below, p. 118). Thus we do not learn where the world sea (יַמִּים) was actually located. The ancient Hebrew (Babylonian) tradition maintains that the sea encircled the earth like a wreath and, at the same time, lay beneath the earth (Psa 139:9; 24:2). After v 9, LXX reads וַיִּקָּוּוּ הַמַּיִם מִתַּחַת הַשָּׁמַיִם אֶל־מִקְוֵיהֶם וַתֵּרָא הַיַּבָּשָׁה. The words, however, like other <107> LXX variants in Gen 1, will be a harmonizing expansion. "Consistent conformity is not the principle of the original text" (Wellhausen, *Composition*[3], 184).

11-13 *Creation of the plants.* God commands the earth to produce plants. The earth—in P's view—has the capability to do so by the power of this divine word (cf. comments on v 24). The basis is the natural observation of the fertility of the ground as it dries out in the Spring. The recension of the Babylonian creation account in Berosus also presumes that the earth is fertile (καρποφόρος) immediately after it arises from the waters. דֶּשֶׁא is the young, fresh greenery that sprouts just after the winter rain. From this דֶּשֶׁא grows everything else. The author, who loves precision, classifications, and definitions, divides the plants into (1) עֵשֶׂב "herbs" and (2) עֵץ "trees." The two are distinguished by the way they reproduce. The עֵשֶׂב produces (bare) "seeds"; the עֵץ,

"fruits" in which seeds are enclosed. Seen as the very beginning of botany, this classification is not bad.

The author's glance lingers on the manner of reproduction, as in vv 22, 28. The world is created such that, henceforth, it is self-perpetuating. This, too, is supernaturalism. The author returns to this classification of "tree" and "herb" in vv 29-30. The author places great value on the fact that God himself (here and subsequently) states the definition of the classes. He intends to make it clear that God established the classes and, thus determined the order of the world, himself. The classes are eternal. On the form of לְמִינֵהוּ (v 12), see §91d. The expression, characteristic of P, is a technical term in the priestly torah, common in lists of categories as an indication that the whole category, without exception, is intended: "after its (entire) kind," all subspecies included (e.g., Lev 11:14-16). One may read with Sam, LXX, Pesh, Vulg וְעֵץ in v 11 as in v 12 (Ball). Perhaps, פְּרִי should also be stricken with Ball. לְמִינוֹ (v 11), which belongs, as everywhere, to categorizations, in reference here to עֵץ, disturbs the connection of the relative clause and is probably a harmonizing addition. It is omitted in LXX, hex. Kittel.

14-19 *Fourth day, creation of the stars.* It is extremely remarkable, and not just for a modern view of nature, that the stars are created now, after the plants of the earth. For an interpretation of this arrangement, see below pp. 119-20. On the construction of יְהִי (v 14), see §145o. The author avoids the name "stars" (v 14), and "sun" and "moon" later (v 16). But he gives the definitions "lights," "the great light," and "the lesser light" (cf. comments on v 5a). With these more general designations he wants to indicate the nature of things. The expression מְאֹרֹת <108>—to be translated "lamps" not modernistically "luminaries"—is an echo of mythological views. The Egyptians call the sun god "the living lamp" (Erman, *Äg. Rel.*, 62-63). The (seven) stars were also represented as lamps in the Hebrew cult (cf. the seven-branched lamps in Zech 4 and the seven lamps in Rev 1:12). In P the poetry of this viewpoint has vanished. For him it is bare prose. The stars are lamps. The author's astronomical concepts are naturally nothing other than those of his time: God "placed" the stars "in heaven." They are considered only to the extent that they stand in relation to the earth. In contrast, these statements are of great significance for the history of religion.

Among the surrounding peoples and especially in the international Babylonian culture, the stars were considered gods. In Israel, too, sufficient traces occur from the most ancient to the most recent period to indicate that this belief was influential. Here, however, this viewpoint has been fully expelled. Yahwism was victorious over astral religion and the stars are only things, with no significance whatsoever for religion. With complete composure, the author can reflect on the purpose of the stars in the world. The fact that a purpose is communicated in relation to this creation (an initial step in this direction already in relation to the creation of heaven, v 6) is understandable because the geocentric viewpoint of this question of purpose does not force itself in relation to any other being in the whole world as it does in relation to the stars. The purpose is, however, to divide the times of day. When the sun rises, it is day. Their appearance and setting serve as signs (Jer 10:2) and times and days and years, that is, they herald the heavenly regions and the coming things (weather, plant and animal life, astrological matters), and from them humans calculate the calendar. They are the lamps that light the earth. The sun, however, rules the day and the moon the night.

A final trace of the notion that the stars were once animate and that they were heavenly rulers, gods, echoes only in this expression "rule" (cf. Job 38:33 for this expression) and in the "placement of the stars at the head of living beings" (Meinhold, 40; cf. below p. 120). Shamash and Sin are god-kings in Babylonian tradition. The Babylonian creation myth (5:12) says "he caused the moon to shine, placed the night under him" and in later Judaism, which discusses star-angels a great deal (cf. e.g. Eth En 82), the old belief was revived (Bousset, *Rel. des Judentums*[2], 370ff.). "The pagan myths are reduced [in Gen 1] to rhetorical metaphors, poetic images" (Franz Delitzsch). One can say that these reflections concerning the practical use of the stars are rather dispassionate. But this dispassion is surely infinitely superior in religious terms to the mythological perspective that regards them as gods and demigods. Modern natural science, which defines the essence of the stars better than Gen 1, would have been impossible if religion had not previously freed the spirits from their dependence on nature. The list of the ordinances of the stars (vv 14-15) is not particularly well arranged. It may be that the text was secondarily revised (Holzinger). Stade (ZAW 22:328) strikes the very disruptive לִמְאוֹרֹת. LXX has a harmonizing addition in v 14.

20-22 *Fifth day, creation of the fish and birds.* Fish and birds hardly belong together by nature. Here, too, it becomes apparent that the six-day work scheme does not suit the material very well. The author was forced to take two different undertakings together in order not to exceed the number six (a similar case on the third day, cf. below p. 119-20). Here, too, the author classifies. He differentiates by size. <109> (1) The great תַּנִּינִם: these are the largest aquatic animals of which the legends tell, originally mythological in nature. (2) All other aquatic animals. The author avoids calling them by their name דָּגִים "fish," but defines them as "all living beings that move, with which the water swarms." Similarly he avoids the name "birds," but defines them as עוֹף "flying animals," more precisely as עוֹף כָּנָף "flying animals with wings." LXX reads וִיהִי־כֵן after v 20, perhaps correctly (Schwally, ARW 9:162). On the construction כָּל־נֶפֶשׁ הַחַיָּה הָרֹמֶשֶׂת in v 21, see §126x. Since only the sing. of מִין occurs, the suffix in לְמִנֵהֶם (v 21) is to be considered a sing. suffix (§91c; but see §91k). Fish and birds acquire the capacity to reproduce through a divine blessing, as do people in v 28. The narrative responds thereby to the question of the source of the mysterious power of reproduction. It is the power of the divine word! All of Hebrew antiquity believed in such a wondrous efficacy of God's words. Here the narrative makes a characteristic distinction between the plants and animals. The plants were created such that they are able immediately to produce seed and fruit, but the birds and the fish receive a special blessing. The reason for this difference is probably that the fact that plants bear seed from which new plants develop seems more obvious, more natural, whereas the fact that the animals bear animals seems more wondrous, more remarkable.

24-31 *Sixth day, creation of the land animals (vv 24, 25) and people (vv 26-30).* **24, 25** The land animals are brought forth from the earth, as are the plants (v 11). Similar statements also occur in other cosmogonies. According to Egyptian doctrine, the mud of the Nile, heated by the rays of the sun, produced people, animals, and plants (Chantepie, de la Saussaye 1[2]:147). According to Phoenician tradition (from Philo Bybl. in Euseb. *praep. ev.* I.10) all the products of creation arose from the primordial mud Mot. In Ovid (*Met* I.416ff.) all the animals arise after the flood from the sun-warmed mud (cf. also A.

Dieterich, *Mutter Erde*, 36ff., esp. 42, 53, 67, etc.). This element probably points to a bearing "Mother Earth" as the world principle. It is combined, here, as well as possible, with supernaturalism. It is valuable to the author because he can also use it to demonstrate the difference between animal and human. God himself made humans (vv 26ff.). The land animals are characterized by nature as נֶפֶשׁ חַיָּה and classified as (1) בְּהֵמָה, tame cattle, herds, and beasts of burden; (2) רֶמֶשׂ, creeping animals such as snakes, lizards, frogs, etc.; and (3) חַיְתוֹ־אֶרֶץ, predators, wild animals. The author means, of course, that the animals were created as they now are. The tame animals were created as "tame" animals. חַיְתוֹ־אֶרֶץ (§90o) is an archaic expression and is employed, therefore, here in God's (solemn) speech. The prosaic expression חַיַּת הָאָרֶץ (v 25) appears in the narrative. The blessing is omitted, probably in order not to overload the sixth day's work which has already run long. Or has it perhaps only been omitted by a copyist (Zapletal, *Schöpfungsbericht*, 25)?

26-30 *Creation of humans.* The author strives to emphasize the great value of humans. <110> The human is God's last, highest creation and is treated with particular thoroughness. God himself made the human, in contrast to the other living beings. Therefore, the word of God (v 26) preceding the creation of the human has another form—not as in the other creations a command ("let it be" or "let the earth bring forth") but an announcement of a decision ("let us make people"). See the solemn introduction to the creation of people in the newly discovered section of the Babylonian creation epic (KAT[3], 586). The report that the human was created after God's image and that the human was given dominion over the animals explicitly expresses the special value of humanity.

The proper understanding of the plural, "let *us* make humans after our image and after our likeness," is a much-discussed question. The same idiom occurs in 11:7 (3:22) and Isa 6:8. (1) The earlier interpretation, that an allusion to the Trinity occurs here, can no longer be considered. (2) Neither is this plural to be understood as a *pluralis maiestaticus*. The practice of the ruler speaking of himself in the plural was introduced by the Persians (Ezr 4:18; 1 Mac 10:19), but Gen 11:7 and Isa 6:8 stem from a time well before the Persians. (3) Dillmann's interpretation that God "is the living personal combination of a multitude of powers and mights" or Zapletal's (*Schöpfungsbericht*, 28) reference to the occasional occurrences of the plural construct of אלהים (Josh 24:19; Gen 20:13—but see the commentary) do not justify the plural in the first person.

(4) Therefore, there can be no other interpretation than the natural, indeed obvious, explanation that God turns here to other אלהים-beings and includes himself with them in the "we" (so already Philo; recently, Budde, 484n.1; Stade, *Bibl. Theol.*, 349; Meinhold, 43, etc.). Such a concept, extremely foreign to modern Christian consciousness, was very common in ancient Israel. There are many אלהים or בני אלהים, a few of whom stand in God's (Yahweh's) service and together with whom he considers the affairs of his kingdom in the heavenly council סוֹד (1 Kgs 22:19-22; Job 1; Dan 4:14; 7:10; Psa 89:8; Rev 4, etc.). "Sons of God" are also witnesses of the creation in Job 38:7. The concept originates in polytheism, but is no longer polytheistic per se since it regards the one God (Yahweh) as the Lord, the sole determiner, but the other אלהים as greatly inferior, indeed his servants. Since P does not mention angels elsewhere, he will not have come to this plural on his own. We conclude, then, that he follows an old exemplar here. The question arises whether an ultimately polytheistic basis shines through here. Originally, this consultation

with the אלהים was recounted to honor humanity. This highest creation could only be created through the common activity of the entire divine council!

כִּדְמוּתֵנוּ בְּצַלְמֵנוּ, "in our image (בְ of the norm) and after our likeness," are two synonymous expressions in order to intensify the idea (cf. 5:3). צֶלֶם is originally more concrete, "painted image, statue," דְּמוּת is more abstract. Sam and LXX have וכדמותנו. The idea is not that the human is created in the image of the one God (Yahweh) ("in my image"), but in the image of the אלהים-beings ("in our image"; cf Psa 8:6). The human is "the minor god of the world." The same idea occurs in 3:5, 22 (cf. above, pp. 23-24, 29). P may have permitted the plural to stand for this very reason, that is, in order to prevent the almost blasphemous notion of similarity to Yahweh from arising (cf. Dillmann). Accordingly, Jewish tradition is not far from the truth when it maintains in its terms that the human is created in the image "of the angels" (citations in Dillmann). Although this notion is not to be overdrawn, the idea if אלהים-likeness is still quite powerful in the narrator's opinion. The value <111> he places on this can be seen in the repetition in v 27. These detailed, rhythmic words (three four-beat lines) sound like an echo, albeit weak, of a hymn to the majesty of humanity, a hymn such as the one in Psa 8. (Yet LXX omits בְּצַלְמוֹ in v 27; perhaps a later addition?)

What comprises the similarity to the divine? The author says nothing on this subject since he considers the matter self-evident. His thoughts on the matter are, however, very clear in 5:1-3, the continuation of the creation account in P: God created Adam in his image; Adam begot Seth in his image. The second statement is very clear: the son looks like the father; he resembles him in form and appearance. The first statement is to be interpreted accordingly: the first human resembles God in form and appearance. That P also understood godlikeness in this manner is evident from 9:6: Whoever slays a person injures God's likeness in the person. Therefore, this likeness relates first of all to the human body, although the spiritual aspect is not excluded. This notion of the human as the εἰκὼν θεοῦ also occurs in Greek and Roman tradition: the human is formed *in effigiem moderantum cuncta deorum* (Ovid, *Met* I.83). The same idea occurs in Babylonian tradition (cf. Jensen, KB 6/1:546; Zimmern, KAT³, 506).

The modern will object to this explanation that God has no form whatsoever, since he is a Spirit (John 4:24). The notion of God's incorporeality requires, however, a capacity for abstraction which would have been unfeasible in ancient Israel and which was first attained by Greek philosophy. Instead, the OT always speaks of God's form with great naiveté—of his ears, hands, and feet, of his tongue, his mouth, etc. God strolled in Paradise. Moses saw him, if only his back, from behind. He walked before Elijah, etc. God was envisioned, then, like a person, although much more powerful and frightening. Now we also notice another trend in Israel already in ancient times. The prophets perceive it as blasphemy to portray God in an image. Yahweh is much too powerful and majestic to be portrayed in an image which would resemble him (Isa 6). Already in the most ancient period it was thought that no one could see his countenance. Not even Elijah and Moses saw it. This aversion increased as the God concept in Judaism became more sublime through the influence of the prophets.

P especially avoids anthropomorphism as much as possible (Holzinger, *Hexateuch*, 380). P's era certainly did not produce the notion that humans bear God's image. Therefore P himself did not generate this concept but adopted it from his older exemplar. The ancient idea has already been reinterpreted in Psa 8:6ff., which associates godlikeness with humanity's dominion over the animals (likewise in Sir 17:2-4). But the text of Gen 1 contradicts such an equation. According to it dominion over the animals is promised humans in a special blessing. And Gen 5:3, especially, quite clearly involves simply the form. Christian dogmatists very often treat the topic of God's image. They usually associate it with the primal state which the text does not treat. Instead, according to 5:1, 3; 9:6, the image of God endures in humanity. The major difference between the OT and Christian dogmatics with respect to this point, however, consists in the fact that the topic plays a great role in dogmatics—the entire anthropology has been developed on the basis of this passage—whereas it has no particular significance in the OT. This notion does not occur at all in the prophets or the psalmists. One may read וּבְכָל־חַיַּת הָאָרֶץ with Pesh in v 26. Sievers (2:241) strikes וּבכל־הארץ.

"Male and female created he them" (v 27). J differs: the woman was not created together with the man, but was only formed secondarily <112> from his rib. The alternation between אֹתוֹ in v 27a and אֹתָם in v 27b, which Schwally (ARW 9:171ff.) finds objectionable and which Greßmann (ibid., 10:364n.2) wants to alleviate by reading אֹתָם both times, also occurs in 5:1-2. The expressions זָכָר וּנְקֵבָה are legal terms (cf. Aram. דְכַר וְנִקְבָּה in the Judeo-Aram. papyri from Asswan G 17). Other ancient cosmogonies also tell of a primal pair (so also 2:21ff.). This seems natural since all subsequent humans could stem from one pair (cf. above p. 13). The question of how to explain racial differences has not yet come into the author's view. In no way, however, does the concept of a primal pair imply the notion that all people are therefore equal before God (Dillmann). This is not an OT idea—instead the OT consistently emphasizes the special advantage of Israel—but one which appeared only in a later phase of development. Nor does this account of a primal pair intend to portray monogamy as original and therefore also the ideal (cf. commentary on 2:21ff, p. 13, and on 4:19, pp. 50-51).

28 Through a "blessing" the first pair were granted the power for such a mighty propagation that its descendants will fill the whole earth. Such a blessing is also given to the birds and fish (v 22), but not to the land animals (vv 24-25; cf. also the commentary on 12:2). The fact that the P narrative thinks of the propagation of humanity at this point distinguishes it markedly from the parallel account in J (2–3) according to which the people only discovered their sexuality through a sin (cf. above p. 14). At the same time, the people were promised dominion over the earth and all animals in harsh terms (כָּבַשׁ, רָדָה, "to subdue"). These are powerful words, the program for the whole history of the culture of the human race! Here, too—it seems—a hymn to humanity sounds through (cf. Psa 8:7-9). אלהים[2] is rather redundant. Is it an addition (Schwally, ARW 9:174n.2)? Pesh (LXX) reads וּבַבְּהֵמָה + וּבְיוֹף הַשָּׁמַיִם (cf. v 26). For חַיָּה, Sam reads הַחַיָּה.

29, 30 Humans and animals are given the plants for food: the animals, the "greenery of the herb," that is, grass and edible herbs; the people the seed-bearing plants, that is, especially grains and fruits of trees. The statement is to be understood in relation to 9:3 (P), according to which the consumption of meat is first permitted after the Flood. P follows the theory here, then, that the present era of the world was preceded by another in which human and animal were herbivorous. Of course, P did not devise this theory. The tradition of the Paradise account is similar (2:16; cf. above p. 10). Parallels from Persian and Greco-Roman traditions are treated in Dillmann, 36, and Usener, *Sintfluth-*

sagen, 202ff. It is, as Usener has shown, the image of the land of the gods where "the blessed gods lead their lives of joy every day," where eternal peace reigns, where even the animals abandon their enmity, an image the imagination of the peoples placed in the primordium. Isa 11:6-8 is an interesting counterpart. The prophet predicts that one day the wolf will live with the lamb and the leopard lie down with the kid. Cow and bear "will become friends," their young will graze together, and the lion will eat straw like an ox. What Gen 1 says of the primordium Isa 11 applies to the eschaton. Regarding this parallelism of primordium and eschaton, see above pp. 35-36 (cf. also Isa 65:25; Hos 2:20). There is a great difference between Gen 1 and Isa 11 in form. Gen 1 offers a prosaic dietary commandment in the precise form of the legal regulation (the perf. נָתַתִּי is juristic style, §106m); <113> Isa 11, in contrast, is a poetic depiction. The myth of the blessed primordium underwent many mutations among the nations, transformed according to the ideals of the people. The fact that peace appears as the chief issue in this context indicates that this particular expression is to be understood as a war-weary, aged people's desire for rest and peace. Earliest Israel, a young, aggressive people, will not have generated such weary attitudes. We know it in Israel from the period of the prophets, when the world rattled with weapons and Israel was exhausted from constant wars (Isa 11:6ff.; 19:23-25; 2:4; 9:5; Zech 9:10). In reality there was never such a state of peace. Whoever understands poetry knows, even without the objections of modern natural science, that this account of the golden era is a fiction, a beautiful dream of yearning hearts. P knew this tradition. As usual, he left the poetry aside and only adapted a "scientific theory" concerning the history of the diet of humans and animals. He is interested in the diet, however, as a priest. After all, in his religion, dietary commandments and prohibitions play a great role. Kraetzschmar (*Bundesvorstellung*, 193-94) notes correctly that this comment by P concerning the vegetarian diet of humans (v 29) does not fit well with their dominion over the animals (v 28). What does this dominion signify? Kraetzschmar deduces from this that vv 29, 30 are secondary in the text of P (cf. also Schwally, ARW 9:174n.2 who argues that v 29 is an addition to v 28 and v 30 is an addition to v 29). But 1:29 is assured through its relationship to 9:2-3: in 1:29 the people are given the herbs (‖ יֶרֶק עֵשֶׂב v 30) for food; Gen 9:3 adds that all the animals shall serve him as food—"like the green herb יֶרֶק עֵשֶׂב I give you everything." Instead, it can be deduced from the divergence observed by Kraetzschmar that a light trace here manifests something clearly evident to one familiar with the history of legends anyway, namely, that we see in this passage two, originally allogenous traditions combined by one author, P: (1) a creation account according to which humans rule over the animals (and eat them) and (2) a fragment of a tradition about the peace of the primordium according to which earliest humans lived only from vegetables (see further below, p. 121). It may be that פְּרִי־עֵץ in v 29 should be read with LXX (Vulg) more simply as פְּרִי. In v 30 נָתַתִּי should be inserted before the object (Olshausen; cf. 9:3).

31 *Conclusion of the sixth day's work.* The author intentionally states here, in the summary, that God found the world "very good." Concerning יוֹם הַשִּׁשִּׁי see §126w n.2.

2:1-3 *The seventh day.* The elaboration here is especially solemn, with many repetitions. **1** צָבָא is properly "army." It refers here poeticoarchaically to all classes of living beings. This usage indicates, as Zapletal (*Schöpfungsbericht*, 72ff.) in particular points out, the disposition of the entire unit toward realms and classes (cf. below, p. 119-20).

2a וַיְכַל "he completed" is difficult because it sounds as though God continued to work on the seventh day. Consequently Sam, LXX, and Pesh sought to smooth the text by reading בַּיּוֹם הַשִּׁשִּׁי although the statements concerning the sixth day were concluded in 1:31 and 2:1-3 deals with the seventh day. In addition, vv 2a and 2b are very similar (Wellhausen, *Composition*[3], 186). The two clauses are probably manuscript variants. The second reading וַיִּשְׁבֹּת, to which v 3 returns (שָׁבַת), is preferable. <114> וַיְכֻלּוּ (v 1) gave rise to וַיְכַל (Greßmann in a personal correspondence).

2b, 3 *Rest and institution of the Sabbath.* This is an etiological myth. This element answers the question, "Why is the Sabbath, that is, the seventh day, the sacred holiday? Why may one not do any daily work on this day?" The answer is, "Because after the six days of creation God himself rested on the seventh day from daily work (מְלָאכָה, a technical term, Exod 20:9, 10), and thus made the Sabbath a 'basic law of the world order' " (Hehn). At the same time, the myth explains the name שַׁבָּת as "rest day" from שׁבת "to take a holiday (cease working), rest." Yet one should note that the author, as is his custom, avoids stating the name *Sabbath.* God's "rest" on the seventh day is a marked anthropomorphism. Exod 31:17 is even moreso: "On the seventh day he observed Sabbath and recuperated" שָׁבַת וַיִּנָּפַשׁ (literally, "and caught his breath"). This notion is objectionable to modern religious consciousness and has, therefore, been reinterpreted (Dillmann and Franz Delitzsch). Isa 40:28 already denies the possibility that God may become weary. P usually avoids such anthropomorphisms. He would surely not have offered this element if it had not been useful to him because of the Sabbath. He values the fact that even God, himself, celebrated (v 2b) and thereby instituted (v 3) the Sabbath.

Wellhausen (*Composition*[3], 185-86) has sought to deduce from v 2b that the original text of P reported the creation as a seven-day effort with the creation of humanity as the seventh day. The arrangement in seven days, however, was intended by nature and from the outset to recount God's rest on the seventh day and to derive the Sabbath from this rest. Accordingly, God created nothing else on the seventh day, but only rested (Budde, 489-90). Dillmann takes לַעֲשׂוֹת with אֲשֶׁר: "the work that he finished creating." Schill (ZAW 23:147-48) places it with שָׁבַת: "He stopped finishing all his work." Both are difficult so Schwally (*Lit. Centralbl.* [1901] 1602) suspects textual corruption. The relative clause, also notable for the repetition of the subject, may be an addition.

3 The institution of the Sabbath through divine blessing and sanctification is recounted in particular detail. Blessing and sanctification are synonymous here. Through the blessing, that is, through the wondrously effective word, God sanctified this day, that is, appropriated it for himself, made it a sacred day. The notion is no longer quite comprehensible to the modern evangelical Christian because we no longer believe in the sacredness of the day. This is the source of the many reinterpretations in the commentaries. The ancient view, however, is the following. Just as God in his ineffable wisdom made distinctions among the children of man and blessed and elevated one, but debased and cursed the others, so also he differentiated the days. He blessed and sanctified one, the others he counted as regular days (Sir 36:7-13). The Sabbath is such a holy day. And the ancient regards this sanctity—speaking in our terms—as an essential, objective quality. It pertains to the day whether or not humans respect it. Thus the Sabbath is holy since the creation of the world. P does not say that humans should also observe it. It must be left open whether the historical sections of P mean that the Patriarchs already observed it (cf.

Exod 16). The Sabbath appears in the legal sections of P (Exod 31:12-17; 35:1ff.). Only a few comments can be offered here concerning the history of the Sabbath.

The name and institution of the Sabbath are apparently Babylonian in origin. Babylonian knows a *šapattu/šabattu* day—characterized as a "day for calming the heart (of the annoyed gods)," that is, as a day of atonement—and also a surely synonymous *šapatti* day, the 15th of the month or the full moon (if the full moon were to fall on the 14th or the 13th of the month, they, too, were <115> considered šapatti). In contrast, it is much less certain whether, as suggested by the 15th or 14th day of the month, the Babylonians also designated the 7th, 14th, 21st, and 28th days of the month—the days of the phases of the moon—and perhaps even the 19th day (as the 7x7th of the previous month) as *šabattu* days. It is only attested that they were considered *dies ater, ûmyu limnu*, on which the high priest, the king, and the physician were not to undertake certain actions. Etymologically, according to Zimmern, שַׁבָּת is, first, a loanword from the Assyro-Babylonian *šabattu* (*šapattu*), which, in turn, seems most likely to have come from *šabâtu, šapâtu* (= Hebr. שָׁבַת) "to judge," and thus to have represented *šabattu* and to have characterized the *šabattu* (full-moon day) as the "judgment" or "decision" day. Other etymologies of שַׁבָּת are offered by Meinhold (*Sabbat u. Woche*, 11ff.) and Hehn (*Siebenzahl und Sabbat bei den Babyloniern und im AT*, 91ff.; cf. Zimmern, KAT[3], 592ff., and ZDMG 58:199-200, 458ff.; Friedr. Delitzsch, *Babel u. Bibel* I5 [1905] 63ff.; Behrens, *Assyr.-babyl. Briefe kultischen Inhalts aus der Sargonidenzeit*, 107-108; Jeremias, ATAO[2], 182ff.).

In Israel, too, the Sabbath, always named along with the "new moon" חֹדֶשׁ in older texts, will have originally been the full moon, as Meinhold has recently proposed, which one celebrated as a joyous festival with sacrifices (Hos 2:13) and rested from daily work (Amos 8:5). Later, the seventh day was counted independently of the moon's phases, named the Sabbath, and sanctified by abstention from work. This Sabbath becomes especially prominent in the OT in the period after the state catastrophe when the forcibly cultless period required practices that would mark Jews as Jews (Wellhausen, *Prolegomena*[6], 340). This Sabbath is especially significant in Ezekiel 46:1. The age of this Sabbath in Israel is disputed. The earliest passages that offer it are Exod 20:9ff. and Deut 5:13ff., regulations concerning its observation in the Decalogue, and Exod 23:12 in the additions to the "Covenant Code." The concluding formula is omitted. It has already been stated that it was the seventh day. Concerning **4a** before **1:1** see above (p. 103).

General Remarks Concerning the Creation Account of P

(1) The source is generally assumed to be P. This is demonstrated by the diction: אֱלֹהִים, מִין (vv 11, 12, 21, 24, 25), מִקְוֶה (v 10), שֶׁרֶץ (v 20), שָׁרַץ (vv 20, 21), רֶמֶשׂ (primarily in P; vv 21, 26, 28, 30), the phrase פָּרָה וְרָבָה (vv 22, 28), חַיָּה (vv 24, 25, 30), רֶמֶשׂ (vv 24-26), דְּמוּת (v 26), זָכָר וּנְקֵבָה (v 27), כָּבַשׁ (v 28), and לְאָכְלָה (vv 29, 30). See Dillmann I and the index of P's diction in Holzinger, Hexateuch, 338ff.

Regarding the history and age of the words occurring in Gen 1, see Wellhausen, *Prolegomena*[6], 386ff.; Giesebrecht, ZAW 1:177ff.; Driver, *Journal of Philology* 11:201ff.; Zapletal, *Schöpfungsbericht*, 99ff.; and the commentaries.

(2) The entire manner of presentation is very characteristic of P (cf. Wellhausen's classic depiction, *Prolegomena*[6], 295ff.). The author—as can be seen on the first glance at his presentation—reported the individual day's efforts in a rather schematic manner. He begins with God's command, then, frequently "it was so." In this manner he recounts the execution of the creation with the same words as the command. Then come namings or blessings. Then God inspects the creation and finds it good. Each concludes with the statement: "thus were evening and morning, day X." This scheme is not carried out consistently. Command and execution do not always correspond precisely, individual elements of the scheme are occasionally omitted, etc. Regarding the differences which can been perceived through a closer examination, see below, pp. 120-21). Later reworkings continue down the same path (so LXX, cf. Wellhausen, *Composition*[3], 184). The scheme appears to be very characteristic of Gen 1. The same intellect was responsible for Gen 1 and Gen 5. On the other hand, content is missing. What an opportunity the author would have had here to describe the variety and manifold abundance of life and to praise the creator of the universe! It differs substantially from Psa 104, not to mention passages such as Job 38:4ff. The author disdained this <116> inexhaustible and wonderful material and chose only a few, simple major elements from the abundance. Similarly one notes in relation to the creation of the stars that the author has no perspective on the magnitude of his subject. It seems he was little impressed by the unearthly majesty of the starry sky that overwhelms the human heart and portends the eternal. One may compare in contrast Psa 8, 19. Or, with what a different tone he could have spoken of the dominion of humans in the world (Psa 8:7-9)! He had little understanding for the poetry of the golden era. And yet his limitation in communicating the material is not adverse for the esthetic impression in every respect. An extensive description could have become lost in the details. Only outlines, however, are given here that are all the more effective. P's usually pedantic style has a somewhat pithy quality, especially in the famous words "Let there be light!" The author speaks here through silence.

The author's contributions beyond the schema are primarily definitions. He is no poet able to conceptualize vitally and describe vividly, but a scientific man who wants to delve into the essence of things, who categorizes the abundance of phenomena in classes, and ponders the characteristics of these classes. Although these classifications seem very childish to us, this is nevertheless a true scientist. One could say that he is a rationalistic intellect. And if this intellect—for example in its treatment of the purpose of the stars—strikes us as prosaic, this phenomenon also accompanies many other scientific endeavors. One recognizes the same characteristic in the nature of the structure of the account. There is no development; there is no antagonist. The entire account consists simply of God's words and deeds one after the other. Now, inherent in the nature of the matter, such creations of God, individual acts in terms of their manner, could never be joined by a very tight arrangement. But, one can note in contrast the account of the origins in chap. 2 where the individual acts of creation, even though they do not quite grow organically into a unit, are still drawn along ingeniously on a single thread (cf. above pp. 25-26, 28-29). Contrariwise, seen from a poetic perspective, Gen 1 offers nothing more than the dry arrangement by days of creation.

While the order, viewed esthetically, is rather paltry, the unit contains—one would like to say—a scientifically exact structure that deserves full respect on its terms. First, the elements are created: the light, the heaven, the sea, and the earth covered with greenery. Then the individual beings that fill these elements are created: "Heaven and earth with their whole host." Thus, the path goes from disorder to order, from the elements to the individual beings, from the lower to the higher. The narrative, then, gives the impression of inclusiveness especially by means of its continual references to and continuations of what has already been said. The world is the creation of a wise God: "God's works are all good; They are sufficient for every purpose in its time" (Sir 39:16; 42:23). The manner of arrangement, then, also manifests a scientific sensibility. It is no accident that the science of our days does not interact with Gen 2, but with Gen 1, for here is an intellect after its intellect. In terms of form, this scientific sobriety intermingles, on the other hand, with a solemn tone. This tone is born by the many repetitions that give the whole a uniform dignity. The tone rises toward the end. The last creation is the highest, the human being.

The blessings of the last three days of creation sound ceremonial and the narrative dies away in dignity and solemnity with God's rest after the work. Both the dryness of the ideas and the dignity of the form combine into a coherent image. The "teacher" speaks in this manner. In ancient terms, the priest speaks so. Solemn dignity and didactic tone are the priest's manner. The interest in classes and definitions is priestly. This <117> interest has grown out of the priest's duty to distinguish that suitable for sacrifice and consumption from that prohibited (cf. comments on v 29-30, p. 115-16). Juridical precision is also priestly. Blessing is the priest's function. Interest in the Sabbath is priestly. Concerning the priestly aspects of P, cf. the introduction ¶6.6. It may be that one should guard against these characteristics of Gen 1. It would be understandable: everyone has, after all, become accustomed from early childhood to reading into this first page of the Bible what one can say about God and world. The artists, too, the giant Michaelangelo foremost, have illustrated Gen 1 such that we find it difficult to learn to read the text without seeing these images. It is the exegete's thankless but still necessary task to establish the fact that Gen 1 is not so "sublime" as it is usually found to be. The author, after all, did not shy away from placing extensive definitions in God's mouth. In sum, between the lines of Gen 1, one looks into the serious, clever, and somewhat dispassionate face of a dignified, ancient man.

(3) The description of Chaos and certain other elements which exhibit a poetic tone are to be excepted from this assessment. This material, however, is not attributable to the author P, but rather to his exemplar. But does Gen 1 trace to such a exemplar? Many modern scholars are inclined to regard Gen 1 as the creation of the author P, admitting the possibility only that P may have adapted details from other cosmogonies (so esp. Wellhausen, *Prolegomena*[6], 297; Giesebrecht, GCA [1895] 2:591; Löhr, *Babel und die bibl. Urgesch.*, 19; cf. also Nikel, *Genesis und Keilschriftforschung*, 61ff. etc.). Now it must be admitted at the outset that a very great portion of the account in its present state can be ascribed to P. Nevertheless, the question arises as to whether P may not have employed a transmitted account here just as he did not create his material elsewhere in Genesis, but transmitted reworked older traditions. In antiquity, one did not create cosmogonies.

That this is also true of the creation account in Gen 1 is evidenced especially by its arrangement. As has been seen since Ilgen (*Urkunden des Jerusalemischen Tempelarchivs* [1798], 433-34), it exhibits a formal arrangement according to six days of creation and a material arrangement according to eight creative acts. Of the suggested arrangements of the acts, the following seems the most natural.

1 Light	2 Heaven	3 Sea	4 Land (with plants)
5 Stars	6 Birds	7 Fish	8 Land animals and humans

Correspondingly, this arrangement is based on the idea that individual creations came to be in the same sequence as their elements: the stars are the beings of light and the birds the beings in the heavens; earth and plants belong together inseparably. This arrangement also accounts for the fact that the stars come into being only after the plants. The arrangement in six days, however, distributes as follows.

I Light	II Heaven	III Land and Sea
IV Stars	V Fish and Birds	VI Land animals and humans

One sees that land and sea, fish and birds are taken together here and that the fish are placed before the birds contrary to the original conception. Thus, however, the whole, beautifully conceived arrangement according to acts of creation is thoroughly disturbed. We may ascribe the arrangement in six days to P who wants to establish the sanctity of the Sabbath in this way (Budde, 491). It follows that he found a preexisting creation account whose original arrangement he either did not understand or observe, but which, in any case, he destroyed (Greßmann in a private correspondence; an earlier generation of scholars, cf. Budde, 491, and Dillmann, 14ff., the latter with bibliography).

The same conclusion results from an examination of the way God acts on the world, concerning which the narrative contains extraordinarily divergent material. Two major approaches may be distinguished. Either God appears as the sole actor—he says "Let it be" and it was; or he "creates" or "makes" things <118>—or he gives the element the command to produce things. These varied schemata are either internally consistent (1st, 2nd, 3rd days) or combined with one another—God says "Let it be" and it was, God creates it so (2nd and 4th days) or he gives the element the command and creates it so (5th and 6th days). Originally, these were three distinct concepts (cf. Schwally, ARW 9:162ff.). It follows, then, that different hands worked on this narrative (cf. Stade, *Bibl. Theol.*, 349).

Furthermore, one notes the following traces of an older exemplar (cf. *Schöpfung und Chaos*, 6ff.): (a) the description of Chaos, existent apart from God and before God's creation, with the ancient terms תְהוֹם and תֹהוּ וָבֹהוּ, with the concepts of the "wilderness and void," of the waters and darkness of the primordium, and the contention that God formed the current world from the Chaos; (b) the concept of the brooding Spirit, a portrayal of the world as originally an egg and the divine principle as a semi-impersonal movement and stirring; (c) the ancient notion that the darkness was not created nor found "good" by God (in Jewish belief, God is the creator of light and darkness, Isa 45:7); (d) the unsuitability of the earth producing plants and animals for the supernaturalism of the account which could trace back to an older concept in which Mother Earth produced the beings αὐτομάτως (this concept would suit the concept of the brooding Spirit exceptionally well); (e) the fact that the sun and moon were regarded living beings in the original arrangement (Dillmann et al.) and were appointed to "dominion" over night and day echoes a mythological perspective—an expression all the more remarkable since it occurs nowhere else in the OT (apart from Psa 136:8-9, a passage dependent on Gen 1; cf. also Job 38:33) and since P, himself, clearly considers the stars nothing other than things; (f) the "we" of the creation of humans, reminiscent of polytheism, is very old; (g) the notion that the human bears God's image, that is, God's form, is very archaic; (h) the notice concerning the diet of humans and animals in the primordium echoes an ancient myth, attested elsewhere as well, concerning the peace of the earliest period. These traces of an older account, although particularly evident in relation to Chaos and the creation of humans, can be found throughout the pericope. It follows from all this that P had access to an older account which already had a long prehistory at that time.

Now we are still in a position to offer a series of statements concerning this prehistory on the basis of Gen 1. The narrative has a few terms—וְבֹהוּ ,בָּרָא, תְהוֹם, תֹהוּ—native to it. In other words, whoever hears these words, thinks immediately of this account. Such standing expressions have already been mentioned in the preceding (cf. pp 5, 59, 67-68). Now, inherently, only very ancient, repeatedly recounted stories can form such characteristic words. We may, accordingly, count these legends among the most ancient in Genesis. This conclusion is thoroughly confirmed by the other characteristics of the legends considered here (Paradise, Flood, Angel marriage, Sodom, etc.)—disregarding for the moment the Creation account. (One may compare the German fairy tales "Frau Holle," "Knusperhäuschen," "Sleeping Beauty," etc.). One may also note that very few legends have produced such terms. According to this criterion, then, the creation myth belongs to the oldest stage of Israelite legend tradition.

Now since we have, furthermore, found a polytheistic echo in the myth ("we"), it seems appropriate to hypothesize that the narrative was once polytheistic (Stade, *Bibl. Theol.*, 349). This assumption would incorporate the further hypothesis that the myth came to Israel in an ancient period from outside. The description of Chaos and the first acts of creation point precisely in this direction. <119> The people who originated the myth conceived of Chaos and Creation in analogy to the seasons experienced in its land. It is therefore beyond doubt that, by describing the primordial state as water and darkness, the myth seeks to depict a world winter in which darkness reigns and water—rain or fog—abounds. The myth finds this state of the world before the creation horrible. The first creations of the good god are light and the division of the water. Such a viewpoint only fits a climate in which there is so much water in winter that it becomes onerous, even dangerous. This is not true of the Canaanite climate, where rain is always perceived to be God's benevolent act, but it is true of Babylonia. (Compare Sachau, *Am Euphrat und Tigris*: in January the ground is moistened by rain, a short while later there is standing water, pp. 45-46; fog in January, p. 53; bitter cold, pp. 53, 59, 75.) Gen 2, according to which the earth is originally dry and water must first come into being before humans can inhabit the earth, suits the Canaanite climate much better. The different Babylonian and Israelite New Years also support this understanding. In Israel the year originally began in the fall: the first creation of the new year is the winter rain. In Babylonia, however, the beginning of the year is in the spring when the rain is over (cf. *Schöpfung und Chaos*, 15-16; the annual inundation of Babylonia by the rivers reaches its height in May and June and, thus, does not come under consideration for an understanding of Chaos as Winter).

Thus we can establish the likelihood of a Babylonian origin for one element, indeed a chief element, of the myth. The statement concerning the "dominion" of the stars also fits well into this interpretation. The deification of the stars is, after all, a Babylonian phenomenon. To be sure, the Babylonian origin of the whole tradition in Gen 1 is not yet established. As shown above, it contains many elements and can, consequently, have been composed from the traditions of different peoples.

In Gen 1 this ancient creation myth appears in association with a fragment of the myth of primordial peace. Since an account of the origins and a Paradise narrative are also merged in Gen 2–3, one may well assume that P was not the first to combine the two myths we have in Gen 1.

Finally, concerning P's redaction of the text, it may be determined that P will have vigorously redacted his exemplar. This is demonstrated by the diction which conforms astonishingly to other passages in P. Part of the schema and the classifications, and probably also the arrangement in six days of creation, will also be his work. The entire tone portrayed above and especially the markedly prominent supernaturalistic element derive from him. He will have conserved the following elements of his exemplar: the remnants mentioned above; further (disregarding details); the sequence of the acts and many elements of the explication. More precise content and wording of the exemplar can no longer be determined.

The history we can elicit with greater or lesser probability from Gen 1 is as follows. An ancient myth, details of which point to Babylonian origins, came to Israel in the ancient period and persisted there for a long period. Originally polytheistic, it gradually became monotheistic. Another, also very ancient and foreign myth concerning the primordial peace was added to it. P encountered the material in this state, cast over it a new structure which explained the Sabbath and, through an energetically engaged redaction, stamped it with strict supernaturalistic Judaism and the priestly spirit.

(4) Allusions and variants in the OT confirm this portrayal of its history. Allusions to individual terms in the account include וָבֹהוּ תֹהוּ in Jer 4:23 (LXX οὐθεν = תֹהוּ without בֹהוּ?; cf. the commentaries), תֹהוּ in Isa 45:18; תְהוֹם as "primordial sea" in Psa 104:6, and בָּרָא in Jer 31:22; Isa 45:7, 18; 48:7; 65:17f.; Amos 4:13; Isa 4:5 (yet cf. LXX), sometimes in reference to eschatological creation. Deut-Isa frequently recalls the creation myth (45:7, 18; 44:24) as a <120> tradition from the primordium (Isa 40:21). We find the myth of primordial peace, in an eschatological application, in Isa 11:6-8; 65:25; Hos 2:20 (cf. also Ezek 34:25, 28; Greßmann, 193ff.). Exod 20:11 cites the creation Sabbath. The expressions עשׂה (not בּרא), נוּחַ (not שׁבת), and the triplet heaven, earth, and sea demonstrate that this passage is independent of Gen 1 (cf. Budde, 194-95). All the other allusions mentioned also certainly fall chronologically prior to P. It follows, then, that the material of Gen 1 (one should note, not Gen 1 in the current form) must have been present in the tradition prior to P.

Certain variants of the creation account further support this analysis, especially Psa 104:5-9. According to it, תְהוֹם and its floods once, in the primordium, covered the whole earth until Yahweh appeared, drove away the waters, and determined the boundaries that they may never again overstep. The narrative presupposed here agrees with Gen 1:2, 6f. in the characteristic element that תְהוֹם filled everything before Creation. It diverges very sharply in tone from the description in Gen 1. Whereas in its colorless supernaturalism

Gen 1:6-7 tells simply of God's command that the water gather together in one place, here we hear of God's mighty wrath which the waters fear: "They fled from your threat, driven away by the sound of your thunder" (v 7). This portrayal is, then, much more mythological and, thus, also much older. Such a portrayal cannot be understood as a simple explication and poetic restatement of the ideas in Gen 1:2, 6f. The allusions in Job 38:10f.; Prov 8:29; Jer 5:22; 31:35 (?); Psa 33:6f; 65:8; and especially Or Man 3 ("who bound the sea with his commanding word; who closed and barred the abyss with his frightful and majestic name") are more or less related. If one takes these allusions and Psa 104 together, the result is a very archaic recension still employed by poets in the latest period as a poetic ornament. According to this recension, a battle between Yahweh and תהום took place before creation. The sea stormed and tossed and held possession of the earth. But Yahweh intervened frightfully so that the waters fled. Then Yahweh bound the sea and shut the abyss. He established a boundary for the sea that it never again overstepped. The same mythical materials also appear in eschatological use and in allegories. What occurred once in the primordium before creation will recur in the end time: stormily and arrogantly the waters will flood. But, before the morning comes, Yahweh's voice will advance against them and banish them. The prophets and poets liken these waters to Israel's enemies (Psa 46; Isa 17:12-14; Hab 3:8ff.; cf. Nah 1:4; Psa 18:16). Finally, Isa 5:30 also employs the tradition. Here, the prophet concludes a mighty poem, encompassing all the plagues of the coming time and finally describing the incursion of the Assyrians, with a portrayal of a final, fearful roar like the sea-roar and darkness on earth and in heaven. Roaring sea and darkness are the last, that is, Chaos breaks in! Jer 4:23 is a very close parallel.

If we extrapolate this tradition of Yahweh's battle against the primordial sea another degree toward the mythological, we must conceive of the primordial sea personified, that is as a monster, as a dragon whom Yahweh conquered. We hear of such a battle between Yahweh and a dragon not infrequently. The dragon is called *Rahab* (Isa 51:9-10; Psa 89:10ff.; Job 26:12; 9:13; Sir 43:23; cf. Psa 87:4; Isa 30:7), *Leviathan* (Psa 74:12ff.; Isa 27:1; cf. Job 40:25ff.; Psa 104:26; Job 3:8), the *dragon* (Isa 27:1; 51:9; Job 7:12; Ezek 29:3ff.; 32:2ff.; PsSol 2:28ff.; cf. the *serpent*, Amos 9:2-3). This is not the place to assemble all the material and to demonstrate its prehistory and its interpretations and usages in Israel as was attempted in *Schöpfung und Chaos*, 29-90. For bibliography concerning these dragon traditions, cf. also Giesebrecht, GCA (1895), 587; Baudissin, "Drache zu Babel," in RE, ed. Herzog; Zapletal, *Schöpfungsbericht*, 85ff.; Cheyne, 4ff.; Cheyne, "Dragon," *Enc Bibl*; Nikel, *Genesis und Keilschriftforschung*, 85ff.; Hans Schmidt, *Jona*, 87ff.; etc. Here only that <121> which comes under consideration for the evaluation of Gen 1 will be discussed. Quite clearly, these dragon traditions combine a variety of materials. In particular, the various names, the dragon, and the great variety of the narratives about it (cf. the summary in *Schöpfung und Chaos*, 82ff.) support this notion.

The characters of these myths also differ widely in terms of their original significance. The dragon appears in a few passages as a personification of the sea and specifically of the primordial sea (especially in Isa 51:9-10; Psa 89:10ff.; Job 26:12; Psa 74:12-19; Isa 27:1; Psa 104:26; EthEn 60:7ff; 4Ezr 6:52; Job 7:12; Amos 9:3). In other passages it inhabits the Nile (especially in Ezek 29:3ff.; 32:2ff.; cf. *Schöpfung und Chaos*,

83, note also that Egypt is frequently called "Rahab," Isa 30:7; Psa 87:4). Elsewhere still it is the monster that detains the sun at night so that it cannot rise (Job 3:8; Schmidt, *Jona*, 89-90). In contrast, in Job 26:13 it may be the mythological monster that brings about the solar eclipse. Accordingly, the possibility must be kept in view (moreso than in *Schöpfung und Chaos*) that the mythology, not of one people (Babylonia, for example), but of several peoples and cultural realms may have been influential here, not just that of the Egyptians, from whose mythological treasury the myths employed in Ezek 29:3ff.; 32:2ff will have originated (cf. *Schöpfung und Chaos*, 90), but also that of the Phoenicians among whom a dragon myth was localized at Joppa (cf. the book of Jonah), and in later times also the Persians.

At this point, only those allusions that relate dragon and primordial sea to one another can be treated. An act of Yahweh is praised that occurred "in the days of the primordium," at the Creation, by virtue of which the world belongs to Yahweh. Then he dried up the waters of the great תְהוֹם and divided the sea. This idea is paralleled by statements that he conquered the great dragon at that time. This battle with the dragon, which parallels the drying up of the primordial sea, is clearly Yahweh's battle with the Chaos dragon. This battle is also applied to the eschaton (still so in EthEn 60:24-25; 4Ezr 6:52; ApBar 29:4) and then often interpreted in relation to the empire hostile to Israel (still so in Rev 12, 13, 17). A final reminiscence of God's battle against Rahab and Sea even occurs in the Rabbis (cf. Daiches, ZA 17:394ff.). The fact that this mythological dragon tradition, almost always transmitted in poetry form in the OT, is nevertheless ultimately identical with the tradition also employed in Gen 1:2, 6-7, despite the markedly different tone, may be concluded from the fact that the two agree in their view of the תְהוֹם. It dominated the world in the primordium but was overcome by Yahweh in Creation. The mediating position between the dragon myth and Gen 1 is represented by the poetic recensions mentioned first above (e.g., Psa 104) in which the dragon has disappeared but Yahweh's battle with the primordial sea still survives.

We conclude, then, that the tradition of Gen 1:2, 6-7 was once much more mythological and, in its current form, has been radically denatured. This assumption is all the more likely since we also observe such reduction of mythological elements in other traditions, the Paradise narrative, for example (see above pp. 35, 39). This suppression of the mythological is, then, a normal, regular process in Israel. Therefore, we have determined a long prehistory for one element of the creation account from the OT itself.

(5) *Age of the tradition in Israel*. From the allusions and variants identified we can trace a few aspects of the material in Gen 1 rather far back. The myth of the golden era already occurs in Isa 11:6ff. (and Hos 2:20); Yahweh's battle with the primordial sea in Isa 17:12-14 (cf. *Schöpfung und Chaos*, 100-101); the description of the final chaos, beside Jer 4:23, already in Isa 5:30. In addition, Isaiah already calls the Chaos animal *Rahab* (Isa 30:7b: "therefore I call this one [Egypt] רַהַב הֵם שָׁבֶת, the silenced Rahab," (i.e., Egypt may make a mighty noise like the Chaos monster, but it is still under Yahweh's might: God bound it). Now, to be sure, many influential scholars have recently declared almost all of these passages <122> to be inauthentic: Isa 11:6ff (Hackmann, *Zukunftserwartung des Jesaia*, 141ff.; Volz, *Vorexil. Jahveprophetie*, 61; Marti, *Jesaja*, 113), Hos 2:20 (Volz, 27; Marti, *Dodekapropheton*, 27-28; Nowack, *Kleine Propheten*[2], 23-24), Isa 17:12-14 (Stade, ZAW 3:16; Marti, *Jesaja*, 147), Isa 5:30 (Duhm, *Jesaia*[2], 40;

Marti, *Jesaja*, 62-63), Isa 30:7b (Duhm[2], 187; Cheyne, *Einleitung in das Buch Jesaja*, 256; Marti, *Jesaja*, 221).

This is not the place to treat extensively the questions raised. A few remarks are in order, however. At issue, primarily, as is often the case in modern criticism of the prophets, is the rather subjective impression the text makes on the critic. Admittedly, this argument is indispensable, but we must employ it rather cautiously. Many critics are inclined, for the sake of caution, to consider the passage in question as inauthentic rather than authentic. The effort to deny the predictions of salvation—most of the texts under consideration—to the older prophets is particularly prominent. In fact, many of these types of promises were secondarily inserted in the prophetic books. But, on the other hand, the "Shearjashub" of Isaiah stands firmly like a *rocher de bronze* as a witness to the prediction of salvation in earliest prophecy. The author is convinced that contemporary criticism has far exceeded the criterion of the demonstrable in its negations and that a sharp reaction must follow this period of criticism. This reversal, which the author has long expected, is poised to take place (cf. Greßmann, 238ff., and Staerk, *Assyrisches Weltreich* [1908]; the latter declares all of the passages name above, except for Isa 5:30, authentic once again; cf. pp. 43, 101, 93, 203, 199). The "oddity" of its depiction does not contradict the authenticity of Isa 11:6ff—after all, the prophet adapts foreign material here—nor does its unique status among the other Isaianic material—or do we know Isaiah so well that we are able to say that he could not have expressed something like this? The smoothness of the diction or the unspecific nature of the portrayal cannot be objected against Isa 17:12ff. Must Isaiah always make complex and concrete statements? Conversely, Hos 2:20 is proven authentic by the antiquity of the concept that Yahweh makes a covenant with the animals of the field. Isa 11:6ff and 17:12-14 are so extraordinary that it is truly difficult to attribute them to a "postexilic" glossator. Although not very well preserved, Isa 5:30, too, is the powerfully impressive conclusion of the whole poem and is shown to be Isaianic by the parallel in 8:22. Isa 30:7b, however, is assured with particular clarity by the immediately subsequent v 8. According to v 8, Isaiah receives the command to write publicly certain statements (apparently those mentioned immediately preceding) on a tablet. "One can write only a brief statement on a tablet" (Duhm). This tablet inscription can, then, be nothing other than רהב המשבת. The striking analogy in 8:1 demonstrates that the public exhibition of such a secretive inscription suits Isaiah's nature. One may believe that one understands the words רהב המשבת or one may consider them incomprehensible, but it is not permissible in any case to dispute their authenticity. One may also question the reading הַמְשֻׁבָּה, yet the main thing, the word בחר is thereby assured. Duhm's and Marti's suggestion to strike עָל־לֻיְח in v 8 in order to eliminate the tablet inscription is wholly dubious (cf. *Schöpfung und Chaos*, 39).

It has also been maintained that ancient Israel would have been unable to comprehend the notion of "Creation" and apply it to its God, Yahweh (Stade, ZAW 23:177f.; *Bibl. Theol.*, 93; Marti, *Rel. des AT*, 38; but cf. also Marti, *Gesch. der isr. Rel.* 5:161). It is certainly correct that the supernaturalistic understanding of the relationship between God and the world, as exhibited by Gen 1 in its current form, does not belong to Israel's ancient period. This earlier period was much more naive in its view of God and the world, as a comparison with the parallel account in J teaches. In J the existence of heaven and earth is presumed to be self-evident (cf. above, p. 28). Now we cannot attain an entirely clear view, to be sure, of how the material in Gen 1 may have sounded earlier. Nevertheless <123> we may assume that, from the outset, it contained the origination of the heaven and earth by God. Is such an idea impossible for ancient Israel? It will be difficult to maintain this. If there was an ancient narrative that asked where man and woman, animals and plants come from (so the Primeval history in J), then it is not impossible that one asked further how heaven and earth and sea and stars came to be. Indeed, Solomon's temple dedication song already states that Yahweh placed the sun in heaven (cf. 1Kgs 8:12; LXX; Wellhausen in Bleek, *Einleitung*[4], 236; the first semistich of the poem preserved in LXX is required by the versification, contra Stade, *Books of Kings*) and another source in J (2:4) speaks of the fact that Yahweh made heaven and earth.

Finally, however, one should remember that the surrounding civilizations, as far as we know, possessed creation myths which, as will be shown below, influenced Israel. Precisely because of this manifold influence Israel experienced from the earliest period, its religion and worldview were never entirely uniform. If, as shown above, we then encounter positive indications that the material of Gen 1 traces back to an earlier period, no objections may be raised from the perspective of religion history. One responds that the creation idea, which occurs rarely or never in the older prophets and which plays such a significant role in Deut-Isa, cannot be so ancient. But the early prophets discuss the near future of Israel and not cosmogony and ancient narratives. Only at a certain time did great political prophecy seize this notion, and only then did this dogma, formerly with no particular value for practical religion, acquire powerful significance (cf. *Schöpfung und Chaos*, 156ff.). The creation idea had its locus in an earlier period in accounts of the origination of the world—and we may add—in the ancient genre of hymns, just as a few of the hymns preserved in the Psalter contain many mythologizing allusions to cosmology and cosmogony (cf. Psa 19:2-7; 24:1-2; 104:21, 26ff.; etc.). We conclude from the preserved material, then, that the tradition of Gen 1, although in another form, must have existed already in a very ancient period. At the same time, it must be considered very likely that the same or a similar material also flowed into Israel once again in a later period.

(6) The observations and conclusions taken from Gen 1 are confirmed and extended through comparison with extra-Israelite creation accounts. Such creation myths exist among all peoples which have attained a certain height of culture. A rich body of material can be found collected in Lukas, *Kosmogonien der alten Völker* (cf. also Dillmann, 5ff.; A. Jeremias, ATAO[2], 129ff.; Zapletal, *Schöpfungsbericht*, 36ff.; Nikel, *Genesis u. Keilschriftforschung*, 117ff; etc.). For Gen 1, the cosmogonies of the peoples with whom Israel had cultural relations, the Phoenicians, Egyptians, and Babylonians, are of particular interest. These foreign creation myths recount not only the origins of the visible world, but, at the same time, of the gods. Gen 1, however, distinguishes itself radically from them all since there is no such theogony. This observation indicates the grandeur of Israel's religion. The surrounding nations believe in gods who came into being in a most ancient time. Israel's God, however, lives from eternity to eternity! Furthermore, all these creation accounts are mythological in nature. The effective powers and realms of visible creation also appear personified as gods or as horrible monsters and dragons. Thus, the Babylonian *Tiâmat* is the monster of the chaotic primal state, the Πνεῦμα or the Ἔρως of the Phoenicians and Greeks are gods, etc. In a mythological manner, the horrible im-

pression of gruesome Chaos is vividly portrayed by giving *Tiâmat* frightful monsters as allies. Or, relationships between natural powers are conceived mythologically as family relationships <124> in human fashion. The notion that Erebos and Nyx together produce Aither and Hemera is the mythological expression for the notion that light and day arise from darkness and night. It is even more crudely mythological to conceive of the chaotic world as a primal egg incubated by a divine being. Or the battle of light against darkness, which gives rise to the world, appears as the battle of the god of light against the beings of darkness. Thus, among the Babylonians, Marduk battles and conquers *Tiâmat* and then forms the organized world. Similarly, among the Egyptians, Re conquers the rebels and founds the order of the world. The mythological attitude characteristic of all of these creation myths distinguishes them once again very clearly from Gen 1. The pagan myths tell of gods whose relationships in reproduction and battle give rise to the world. Gen 1, however, knows of a sole God, not begotten and not begetting, at whose feet lies the world. There is no greater contrast, then, than between the colorful, fantastic mythology of these peoples and the intellectually clear, prosaic supernaturalism of Gen 1. Whereas, the first impression of such a comparison must be one of a mighty difference, a more precise examination teaches, however, that this great difference did not always exist. Certain mythological traces in Gen 1 demonstrate that the narrative must have originally been much more similar to the foreign myths (see above pp. 120-21). Still, in the present state, Gen 1 agrees with the pagan myths in the essentials of the description of the primal state. Thus, the result is that Israel did not, after all, posses its religious uniqueness, so characteristically expressed in Gen 1, in fully refined form from the beginning but only developed it in the course of history. The antimythological attitude of Gen 1 must have been preceded by a period in which the people thought mythologically.

The agreement of Gen 1 with foreign creation myths, namely, in the presentation of Chaos (cf. above, pp. 104-105), is now so great that it, too, occasions the hypothesis that the material of our narrative stems from outside Israel. It may be asked whether the presumed original home of the narrative can still be discerned.

The Phoenician creation myths (according to Philo Byblius purportedly from Sanchuniathon, in Euseb. *praep. ev.* 1, 10) recount that in the very beginning Πνεῦμα and dark Χάος existed. Through their union, called Πόθος, Μώτ, the primordial mud, replete with the germ of things, came into being. This Μώτ took the form of an egg which divided into heaven and earth. From it stream forth the stars which become rational beings. Their warmth and light illuminate and warm air, earth, and sea. Thus develop winds, clouds, rainfall, thunder, lightning, and finally, animate beings in earth and sea. Other portrayals (from Eudemus and Mochus) can be found in Damascius, *de primis principiis*, ed. J. Kopp, 125, 385. All of these myths speak of a primal egg, a point of contact with the material in Gen 1. Concerning the figure of Βάαυ, see above pp. 104-105. More on the Phoenician cosmogonies in Lukas, *Kosmogonien*, 139ff.; Baudissin, "Sanchuniathon," in RE3, ed. Herzog; A. Jeremias, ATAO[2], 141ff.

In the Egyptian traditions, too, the primordial water, Nun, plays a role (cf. Dillmann, 5-6; Lange in *Chantepie de la Saussaye* 1[2]:146ff.; Erman, *Äg. Rel.*, 28ff.). According to Prof. K. Sethe, it is questionable whether the egg that the god Chnum turns on the potter's wheel is the world-egg. The creation of the world through the word and the division of heaven and earth also occur among the Egyptians (cf. above pp. 106-107, 109).

Of particular significance are the Babylonian traditions, known from Damascius 125, 384 (cf. *Schöpfung und Chaos*, 17ff., as well as Zimmern, KAT³, 488ff.) and, since its discovery in 1873 by George Smith, from the cuneiform creation myth (so far only available in fragments, known by its beginning as "Enuma elish"). The Babylonian text in seven tablets has recently and most completely <125> been published in the original text, transcription, and English translation by L. W. King, *The Seven Tablets of Creation* (1902; cf. also the same edition of the original text in *Cuneiform Texts from Babyl. Tablets* 13 [1901]). The translation and transcription by Winckler in his *Keilinschriftl. Textbuch*², 102ff., is also based on this publication. The following earlier German translations and treatments of the then even less complete epic may be mentioned: Jensen, *Kosmologie der Babylonier*, 263ff. and KB 6/1:2ff.; Delitzsch, *Babylonisches Weltschöpfungsepos* (1896); Zimmern in *Schöpfung und Chaos*, 401ff., and KAT³, 490ff., 584ff.; A. Jeremias, ATAO³, 132ff.

According to Babylonian doctrine, too, the world stood at first in chaos: *Tiâmat* (= Ταυθέ in Damascius, θαμτέ [conjectured] in Berosus, Hebr תְּהוֹם) and *Apsû*, first mother and first father, saltwater flood and freshwater flood (Jensen, KB 6/1:559). From this pair proceed over a long course of time the first three generations of the gods. The subsequent section of the account now reports how strife arose between *Tiâmat* and the newly existent gods, her children, and how, after many failed attempts by the gods to vanquish *Tiâmat* and her horrible helpers, Marduk, one of the youngest, finally appeared. Marduk first elicited the promise that he will be given dominion over the universe. Then he equipped himself for battle and went out to engage *Tiâmat*. *Tiâmat*'s helpers fled, she faced him alone. Marduk reproached her for her crimes. Then the battle began. The god enclosed her with a net and released a storm wind against her. When *Tiâmat* opened her mouth to swallow him, Marduk directed the storm wind to blow into her mouth and force her mouth open. Then he threw his weapon into her open throat and pierced her insides. *Tiâmat*, who bore the "giant serpent" and other monsters, is probably portrayed, then, as a monster covered with scales who cannot be overcome from without. This view is not contradicted by the fact that Berossus calls her a "woman," for it is only natural that a female monster could later come to be seen as a woman (contra Jensen's lively polemic, e.g., *Gilgamesch-Epos* 1:60ff.). Then Marduk took her helpers captive and bound them.

After the battle, appeased by the gifts of the gods, the god had a clever idea. He cut the monster in two segments. From one half he made heaven, drew a boundary and established guards so that the water could not get out. The following material recounts the creation of the rest of the world, beginning with the stars. "He caused the moon to shine (?), subjected the night to him." Then follows a lacuna, unfortunately, so we are unable to indicate the sequence of the acts of creation with certainty. Then, on the sixth tablet, preserved only in fragments, probably as the final act, comes the creation of humans. Marduk said to Ea, "I will take blood, I will form (?) bone; establish people . . . ; I will create people who will inhabit [the earth]," whereupon follows the creation of people who, according to Berosus, too, are formed from earth and the blood of gods. The narrative concludes with a hymn glorifying Marduk as creator through numerous honorific titles.

The Babylonian myth is a poem in form and content, indeed a poem of great beauty, of thrilling power, and of vibrant color, although for our Greek-inspired sensibilities too garish and grotesque. Clearly the myth originated in the Babylonian countryside. The myth envisions the origin of the young world in analogy to the rebirth of the world each Spring. Just as water and darkness still reign in winter, so *Tiâmat*, the primal sea, once had control. The actual point of the myth is to describe the development of the current world from the primal sea: The god Marduk divided the primal waters into two parts, the water of heaven and the water on earth. The account itself makes it very clear that this is the myth's main point. <126> It accounts for the unusual manner in which *Tiâmat* is overcome by means of the god holding open her mouth with the hurricane and then cutting her up from the inside. Very characteristically, Berosus in his radically abbreviated summary, emphasizes precisely this point in the entire account of the encounter between the god and the primal woman: "Bel [= בעל, Marduk's nickname] went over there, sliced the woman down the middle and made from one half of her the earth and from the other heaven." This point of the myth can be fully explained, as Jensen (*Kosmologie*, 308) has shown, from the Babylonian climate. At the end of the rainy period, the spring sun breaks through and divides the gray masses of rain, clouds, and fog: thus the world was created. The notion of the daily battle between the sun god and the night may also have been influential. Winckler's school also thinks of astrological factors. *Tiâmat* is the water region of the zodiac which the sun transverses in the Winter until Marduk conquers the waters at equinox (cf. A. Jeremias, ATAO², 137). The myth attributed—this is a secondary notion—the creation of the world and the conquest of *Tiâmat* originally to the Bel of Nippur, in its preserved form, however, to Bel-Marduk, the city god of Babel. It seeks to say, then, that dominion over the world belongs to Babel: Babel's god created the world. In this form, the myth stems from the period of Babel's predominance since Hammurabi, that is, from the period ca. 2100. Yet one may suspect that the myth is much older in Babylonia (cf. Zimmern, KAT³, 491).

Concerning the relationship of the Babylonian myth "Enuma elish" to the Hebrew tradition see *Schöpfung und Chaos*, 3-170; the Catholic scholar Nikel, *Genesis und Keilschriftforschung*, 24-25; and Zapletal, *Schöpfungsbericht*, 61ff. Gen 1 agrees with this material in the following elements. (a) That the world originates through the division of the primal sea. Now, the idea of a division of the primal substance also occurs in other cosmogonies (cf. above, p. 109). Nevertheless, this agreement is of great significance because the divided original substance is conceived of as water in both traditions and especially since both traditions employ the same name (*t°hôm* = *tiâmat*). (b) Berosus also states that there was darkness at the beginning and this is a common concept elsewhere. (c) In the exemplar of P, the creation of the earth and the plants was counted as one act. Likewise in the Babylonian tradition according to Berosus, the earth surfaced from the flood bearing fruit (καρποφόρος) immediately.

Contrariwise, the Enuma Elish myth does *not* have certain elements that belong to the earliest form of Gen 1. The following are missing: (a) the element of the brooding spirit; (b) an equivalent for תֹהוּ וָבֹהוּ; (c) the ancient "we" in the creation of humans contrasts with an "I" in the Babylonian version; (d) the heavenly bodies are created in the Babylonian myth much earlier than in the Hebrew. Conversely, Gen 1 does not have the male-first principle corresponding to *Tiâmat*'s partner Apsû. Therefore, the final result is that the material of the two narratives diverge in many ways, but that they also agree in several elements, especially in those mentioned first. How is this complicated picture to be interpreted? There can be no discussion of a direct adoption of the Babylonian myth.

Instead, a partial influence of the Babylonian tradition on the Hebrew should be assumed. This is all the more likely since the major element on which both agree is difficult to explain from the Canaanite climate (cf. above p 121).

A much closer relationship exists between the Babylonian myth and the poetic recensions (mentioned under no. 4, pp. 122-23). These variants agree with it, first of all, in that they also have poetic, specifically hymnic, form. At the same time, they also agree in content. These variants also recount a battle between the creator god and $T^e hom$ in which Yahweh won dominion over the world, and some of them personify the primal sea as a horrible monster whose defiance Yahweh overcame before creating the <127> world. Not only the basic idea, but also details of the myth recur here. Thus the Hebrew tradition also speaks of "Rahab's helpers," who must grovel at Yahweh's feet (Job 9:13), and tells not only of Yahweh's might, but also of the ingenuity by which he overcame the monster (Job 26:12). Characteristically, too, god's scolding (נער) plays a great role in both traditions (cf. *Schöpfung und Chaos*, 111, 113). The major divergence of these poetic accounts from the Babylonian consists in the fact that they do not portray God's enemy as female. These narratives are much more mythological than Gen 1 (cf. above, pp. 123-24). On the other hand, the mythological element in them is much more prosaic than in the much baser Babylonian myth. They represent, then, a middle term between that ancient myth and Gen 1 and show us the way certain elements of the Babylonian narrative finally reached the author of Gen 1.

Now if, on the one hand, individual remnants of originally Babylonian material can be found assimilated in Gen 1, it cannot be excluded, given the great variety contained in Gen 1 (see above pp. 119-20), on the other hand, that other creation myths, perhaps from other nations, were also influential. This is especially likely for the concepts of the world-egg and the primal spirit which also occur in Phoenician tradition and may have originated there. Precisely because of this mixture of allogenous elements, we may also conclude that the Babylonian material, to the extent it is present in Gen 1 at all, did not come to Israel directly but through a wide range of intermediate steps (Driver, 31). If we were in a position to review the entire prehistory of this narrative, we would discern a colorful history of intricate influences.

Beside the Enuma Elish epic, we also possess a series of other Babylonian cosmogonic poems (cf. Zimmern, KAT[3], 497ff.) of which an oath that begins with a cosmogony deserve special mention (cf. Zimmern, *Schöpfung und Chaos*, 419-20; KAT[3], 498; Jensen, KB 6/1:39ff.; Winckler, *Keilinschr. Textbuch*[2], 98ff.; A. Jeremias, ATAO[2], 129ff.). Here, too, the world was originally a sea (*tâmtu* in an appellative meaning). The first creations, however, were the temples of the gods for whose service humans were created. Mention may also be made of the myth of the apparently serpentine and marine *LAB-bu*. Concerning him, people exclaim, "Futilely gods go out against him, until one succeeds in battle who thereby becomes king of the world" (cf. Zimmern, *Schöpfung und Chaos*, 417-18, and KAT[3], 498-99; Jensen, KB 6/1:45ff. and *Gilgamesch-Epos* 1:56ff.; A. Jeremias, ATAO[2], 138-39). This myth has a certain relationship with the material of the Enuma Elish epic and may have influenced the Hebrew poetic recensions. Portrayals of battles between a god and a monster occur very frequently (cf. Zimmern, KAT[3], 502-503; figures in A. Jeremias, ATAO[2], 133ff.).

The same can be said concerning the time when the indicated cosmogonic remnants came to the Hebrews that was previously said concerning the time of the arrival of the Flood legend (cf. pp. 73-74). To date, scholars entertain the most varied suggestions concerning this question. Hypotheses range from the Exile to antiquity when the Hebrews dwelt in Ur of the Chaldees (a summary can be found in *Schöpfung und Chaos*, 4). Many contemporary OT scholars are inclined to date such an adoption, if they accept it at all, as late as possible. One school, which tends to date the idea and the material in Israel according to the date of its first attestation in the writings of the OT, finds it natural that the account of the creation of the world, attested to us so late, also arrived in Israel not long prior to its attestation. This school makes every effort to guard against acknowledging that this account may be older, indeed much older, than its first attestation.

In contrast, one may warn OT scholars against overhasty application of literary-critical criteria to the <128> history of religion. It does not follow from our limited knowledge of ancient Israel and the fact that we know the creation account first in P—that is, in the period after the Exile—that the material became known in Israel only then or shortly before. Now, for internal reasons, the arrival of such cosmogonic myths in later times is very improbable. First of all, the assumption that P himself translated and reworked the Babylonian myth—disregarding substantial material variations (cf. above, pp. 129-30)—is already extraordinarily difficult on religiohistorical grounds. A man of such marked Jewish character, filled with Jewish abhorrence for pagan gods, would have hated and disdained such a narrative of the Babylonian gods, certainly such a grotesque and fantastic one. He would have never adapted it. It is equally unlikely that such myths will have made their way into Yahwism in the period of Assyrian domination over Judah when Babylonian culture flooded into Judah. Then the full consciousness of the peculiarity of Yahwism was already awakened in prophecy and prophecy conducted a passionate opposition to everything foreign. We may assume that the prophecy of the time would not have adopted the newly arrived accounts of foreign gods, whose foreign origins would have been obvious at first glance, but would have eradicated them root and branch. If such creation myths first became known then, they would certainly have experienced nothing different at the hand of the prophets than the Babylonian altars and the steeds of Shamash did.

We are directed to a much earlier time, then. We may consider the creation myths as a component of near Asian culture already known in Canaan before Israel. They came to be known in Israel as it gradually assimilated to the culture of Canaan. We may imagine, however, that an account which presumes such a great degree of reflection may not have actually been a popular tradition in the ancient period. Instead, it may have circulated only in "more educated" segments of society, perhaps among the priests. We also discern the antiquity of the Hebrew account when we compare the form it and the Babylonian myth gave sections where the two agree, especially the division of the water. The two recensions are so radically distinct that we must necessarily assume a long history and a great period of time in which the mythological disappeared to such an extent and the Babylonian material became so Israelized. In contrast, one may consider the mythological material so glaringly prominent in Zech 1ff. (cf. *Schöpfung und Chaos*, 122ff.). At the time, this material will not have been known for very long among Jews. But how clearly they preserved the fantastically mythological pallete! This assumption is wholly confirmed by the character of Gen 1 described above (pp. 117ff.). Gen 1, itself, is not all of one piece, but has an extremely peculiar mixture of older and younger elements which can only be explained by a long history of tradition. Finally, we also have a few allusions to the Babylonian creation myth, many chronologically remote from Gen 1 (cf. above pp. 123, 130-31). The oldest clear allusion is Isaiah's reference to Rahab (30:7).

(7) This produces the following historical portrayal. Certain portions of the ancient Babylonian myth of the world's creation came to Canaan along with many other elements of Babylonian culture in pre-Israelite times. Other foreign or native elements (world-egg, תֹהוּ וָבֹהוּ) were added. As Israel assimilated to Canaan's culture, it became acquainted with this account along with other ancient myths. We date this adoption of Babylonian myths about the time of the first kings of Israel (cf. Giesebrecht, GCA [1895], 600). Israel, however—and, for us, this is the most important aspect of the entire picture—adapted the myth very radically to itself and its religion. The mythological aspect, which its religion <129> resisted so strongly, was first dampened (as in the poetic variants) and finally expelled except for a very few relics. Finally P energetically reworked the material once again. The material, originally highly poetic, thus became ever more prosaic. But it was filled with Yahwistic ideas. Thus, this account, too, demonstrates the wondrous power of Yahwism to force the most foreign and objectionable material into its service and to mark it as its property. Such an account, however, in which the lofty and pure arises from inferior and modest beginnings, seems to us to be a wonderful and God-worthy spectacle. This is the nature of God's revelation: Gen 1 did not fall from heaven in final form, but it developed though a grand and impressive history. Alongside this main line of development we discern a few secondary strands: older recensions survive among the poets. The whole material undergoes an eschatological application. Here is not the place to trace these secondary lines.

(8) Beside Gen 1 another series of traditions in the OT, more or less extensively preserved, concerning the origin of the world can be instructively compared with Gen 1. The best-known parallel is the J account (2:4bff.) whose much more naive tone diverges quite radically from Gen 1 (cf. above pp. 28-29). Elsewhere, mythological components often echo in allusions to such traditions: Psa 90:2 recalls the time when the mountains were "born," when world and earth "were in labor." Or we hear how God laid the foundations of the earth as the morning stars rejoiced in unison (as at a celebration for laying a cornerstone), and all the sons of God exulted (Job 38:6-7). Or we hear how the sea broke out of the womb and God covered the newborn child with clouds as its diaper (Job 38:8ff). In Job 38:8-9 and Psa 90:2, mountains and sea are "born": the same view that the earth brought forth things on its own still echoes in Gen 1:11-12, 24. Or we hear of the great secret of creation, that God ordained that the earth be founded on the waters and yet not waver (Psa 24:2, etc.). Such allusions make it evident that, in addition to Gen 1, a series of creation traditions differed in manifold ways from Gen 1 in the selection of material and the manner of arrangement. This fact shows us that Gen 1 was by no means as unique in the ancient period as it may seem to us now. Among many cosmogonic theories, Gen 1 was only one, by no means determinative, theory. "There is no trace anywhere of a meticulous retelling of the details of Gen 1" (Dillmann).

(9) *The relationship between Gen 1 and natural science.* Older literature is catalogued in Dillmann, 12. Gen 1 contains, by its nature, two types of material: (1) the religious doctrine that God created the world through his word; (2) a scientific theory concerning

the sequence of the individual origins. It should never have been denied that the second, the cosmogonic theory, was also present in Gen 1, that the author was not merely interested in illustrating the religious idea, but that he wanted, at the same time, to recount the actual course of the origin of the world (cf. Wellhausen, *Prolegomena*[6], 296). This cosmogonic theory, however, if one wants to understand and evaluate it, should be situated in a conceptual history of natural science in the ancient Orient. This awareness determines the attitude of the historically oriented interpreter to the scientific content of Gen 1. The historian is not at all astonished that the scientific information in Gen 1 does not conform to the results of our modern natural science. Instead he assumes this divergence as self-evident. Natural science was still in its beginnings at the time. People still believed that the earth stood still, that heaven above was an actual dome in which God had placed the stars as lights, and that above the firmament of heaven was a mighty sea from which the rain streamed down on the earth. At that time, they did not yet know about the extremely <130> long epochs in which the current earth was formed and about the history the animal world has undergone. Then, seven days seemed quite sufficient for creation. The idea that the stars came into existence after the earth was still plausible. Gen 1 can even maintain that the plants of the earth existed before the stars! Despite the extreme difference between the religious spirit of Gen 1 and that of the cosmogonies of the surrounding peoples, Israel's knowledge of the world was no greater than that of its neighbors. To the contrary, the Babylonians and Egyptians will have known much more about the world than Israel's wise men.

If, then, the worldview presupposed in antiquity and our modern worldview differ so radically, the sequence of developments assumed by our science obviously cannot even be compared with the sequence Gen 1 maintains. Only a very unhistorical sensibility, therefore, can make the effort to harmonize Gen 1 and modern natural science, or, conversely, to set Darwin against "Moses." It is truly deplorable that so many theologians still do not want to acknowledge this actually self-evident truth so that when the uninformed or semi-informed first hear of the "natural history of creation" they can think that it refutes "the Bible"! The conflict "between theology and geology" is settled if both remain within their boundaries. Religion must leave it to natural science to make statements concerning the origin of the world and, also, of humanity, as well as it may. Natural science, however, will, if it observes its limits, neither deny nor confirm the doctrine of creation. It has roots other than scientific. It is (following Schleiermacher) the expression of faith in God's absolute power over the world.

11. Sethite Genealogy in P 5: From the Creation to the Flood

(1) *Source criticism.* The piece makes an entirely new beginning in relation to chap. 4 and thus stems from another source. This source is P. Evidence for P includes אֱלֹהִים (vv 1bis, 22, 24bis), תּוֹלְדֹת (v 1), בָּרָא (vv 1, 2), דְּמוּת (vv 1, 3), זָכָר וּנְקֵבָה (v 2), מְאַת שָׁנָה (וַיֹּלֶד J) הוֹלִיד (vv 3, 6, 18, among others, §134d), the sequence of ones, tens, and hundreds in the numbers (§134i), אֶת־הָאֱלֹהִים (vv 22, 24 as in 6:9), furthermore 5:1-3 which refers to 1:26-28, the naming by the father (cf. comments on 4:1), but especially by the entirely formulaic style. The whole passage deals almost exclusively with names and numbers. In P, 5:1ff. is the immediate continuation of 1:1–2:4a. V 29 (together with בֵּן) does not belong to P. These words do not conform to the schema of

P and distinguish themselves from P very clearly by their extremely ancient character. The word יהוה demonstrates that the verse belongs to J to whose Paradise narrative the words allude (see further p. 56). The genealogy of P begins with Adam, Seth, Enosh, and ends with Noah, so that it parallels 4:25, 26; and 5:28 (Jᵉ). R^{PJ} preserved P entirely because of its numbers, he left only the beginning of Jᵉ (because of the comments given there) and inserted the motivation of the name Noah from Jᵉ into P.

(2) *Origin of the tradition.* The tradition of the ten primeval kings of Babylonia relates very closely to the tradition of the ten patriarchs (cf. Hommel in *Proceed. of the Soc. of Bibl. Arch.* 15:243ff.; Zimmern, KAT³, 30ff.; 539ff.). The names of these kings according to Berosus (*Fragm. hist. graec.*, ed. C. Müller, 2:499-500) are Ἄλωρος, Ἀλάπαρος, Ἀμήλων, Ἀμμένων, Μεγάλαρος, Δάωνος, Εὐεδώραχος, Ἀμεμψι-νός, Ὠτιάρτης, Ξίσουθρος. The two lists agree on the following points: first in the period in which these men were supposed to have lived—from the Creation to the Flood; then in the number ten in these lists; further in the fact that an age, indeed a very advanced age is attributed to each of these persons; <131> finally in a series of striking details. In the third position stands the name "Man," Bab *amêlu* = Ἀμήλων, Hebr אֱנוֹשׁ. In the fourth position stands Ἀμμένων, perhaps Bab *âminânu, ummânu*, אָמָן "overseer," for which Hebr has קַיִן "smith" (cf. above p. 51). In the seventh position Hebr has חֲנוֹךְ. He lives "with God" and is transported to God. Εὐεδώραχος, too, is a famous man of god from the primeval period, initiated into the divine mysteries, into the "secret of heaven and earth," credited with the origin of the *barû*-priests, that is, the soothsayers, astrologers, haruspices (cf. Zimmern, KAT³, 533-34). In the eighth position stands Ἀμεμψινός = Bab *Amêl-Sin*, "man of Sin" (the moon god), probably identical with the *Amêl-Sin* mentioned in the cuneiform texts, also a wise man from the primeval period (cf. Zimmern, KAT³, 537). In Hebr מְתוּשֶׁלַח "man of (the god) שֶׁלַח ‖ מְתוּשָׁאֵל = "man of El" in Jⁱ. In the ninth position stands Ὠτιάρτης, to be read Ὠπάρτης, the father of Ξίσουθρος = the *Upar-Tutu* known from the Gilgamesh epic, the father of Atraḫasîs, the hero of the Flood (cf. above p. 68). In Hebr the Lamech named in the ninth position is the father of the Flood hero Noah. In the tenth position in both lists stands the hero of the Flood: Ξίσουθρος, נֹחַ.

This extensive agreement demonstrates that the two genealogies are related from a very early stage. According to the normal process of cultural history, the analogies of the Flood legend, as well as a few components of the creation account (cf. above pp. 71ff., 127-28), it may be assumed that the Hebrew tradition developed from the Babylonian. Indeed, this patriarchal genealogy will have been transferred together with the Flood narrative and a Creation account as a whole. The Babylonian names themselves are not preserved in the Hebrew. A thorough reworking either translated those names or replaced them with the names of Hebrew figures. The latter is especially true of Noah (cf. above, p. 83) and of Lamech, who, originally probably the father of Jabal, Jubal, and Tubal, has become the father of Noah here. Characteristically, the first Babylonian kings have become patriarchs in the Hebrew tradition. The Babylonian culture is so much older than the Hebrew that Babylonian tradition can speak of kings in a time in which the Hebrew cannot imagine kings but only private individuals. That P himself created the patriarchal list directly from the Babylonian source (Meinhold, 63ff.; Löhr, *Babel und die bibl. Urgesch.*, 11, 16) is already unlikely because sections of a list are preserved for us in the catalog of J^e—"Adam, Seth, Enosh . . . Noah"—that agrees with P against J^j and is certainly older than P. Such a learned genealogy will hardly ever have been popular (Löhr, 11). The question of the relationship of the Sethite table (J^e and P) to the genealogy of the Kenites (J^j 4:17-24), which was left open above (pp. 50-51) is to be determined from this. All fundamental divergences of the Cain table from the Seth genealogy are, at the same time, divergences from the Babylonian tradition: Enosh = Amelu is absent; Caanan = Ummanu does not occupy the fourth and Enoch ‖ Enmeduranki no longer the seventh position. Methushael ‖ Methushelah ‖ Amelsin is shifted from the eight to the sixth position. That which J^j had prior to P, the children of Lamech and the Song of Lamech, does not occur in the Babylonian tradition and will, thus, have been added to the Hebrew tradition from another source. The result is, then, that the Sethite genealogy stands closer to the Babylonian catalog than the Kenite table does. The Kenite table is tempered with characteristically Hebrew elements to a greater degree than the Sethite genealogy. How should we interpret this? Perhaps the Babylonian tradition came to Israel at different times and the Kenite table arose in an earlier time (so Zimmern, KAT³, 543).

Seven and ten patriarchs or primeval kings also occur very frequently among other peoples (bibliographies in Dillmann, 88; Lüken, *Traditionen des Menschengeschlechts²*, 146ff.).

(3) *The ages.* The Babylonian tradition, too, supplies the ages of the first names. <132> The appearance of such ages in P, too, should not be considered the creation of P (contra Holzinger). Instead, they rest on tradition. It must be remembered, of course, that P altered these ages somewhat according to the chronological system he followed. In the addition of such ages P agrees, then, with the Babylonian tradition against J^j and also, indeed, against J^e. The fact that these ages are so unusually large is also common to both traditions. The Babylonian ages are, indeed, much larger. Babylonian scholars, educated in astronomy, reckoned with much longer time periods than the Hebrew. Both are based on the assumption that the earliest humans were much more long-lived than contemporaries. P calculates the lifetimes of the fathers from Adam to Noah to be 700–1,000 years, from Noah to Abraham 200–600 years, for the patriarchs 100–200 years, and for the present 70–80 years. What mighty power—such were the thoughts that underlie such calculations—must the early fathers have had, they who could beget the whole of humanity! The older the world becomes, the weaker and more short-lived become the people (4 Ezr 5:50ff.). The more sin increases, the more lifespans diminish (Prov 10:27). As it was in the primordium, so it will be again in the eschaton (Isa 65:20; cf. Greßmann, *Eschatologie*, 205). Notably, P does not give a reason for death itself, and he sets the age at which the fathers become parents very late. In the eschaton, too, death remains—it is considered self-evident—and a 100-year-old is still a youth (Isa 65:20; cf. Meinhold, 61-62). The advanced ages can be further explained by the fact the some of those patriarchs may have originally been gods. Enoch's 365 years are to be so interpreted (cf. the following).

Finally one may also make mention of the fact that it was necessary to fill the great time periods of the primeval history with the few names in the tradition. Here, too, modern theology has no reason whatsoever to become enthusiastic for such ancient naive theories also found among other ancient peoples (Josephus *Ant.* 1/3.9; cf. Dillmann, 108). Here, too, the skills of "apologetics" have damaged more than served the true interests of religion (bibliography in Dillmann, 107-108). The Babylonian tradition indicates only the duration of the kings' reigns. The Hebrew tradition replaces them with the lifespans of the patriarchs. Since, however, these numbers are intended simultaneously to define the duration of the whole epoch and the lifespans were not suited to this purpose, the Hebrew tradition devised an unusual and yet extremely ingenious means. The ages of the patriarchs when they begot their eldest sons are totaled! Concerning the remarkable synchronisms which result from this accounting, see Nestle, ZAW 24: 130ff. The details of the numbers differ radically from one another in the Hebr, Sam, and LXX. A summary table can be found in Dillmann, 110; Budde, 92; Holzinger, 61. The entire sum from Creation to the Flood in Hebr is 1,656, in Sam 1,307, and in LXX 2,242 years. These differences are apparently not accidental but rest on chronological systems that calculate the whole duration of the world with an apocalyptic climax. According to Nöldeke (*Untersuchungen*, 11-12), Hebr calculates 2,666 years from the Creation to the Exodus or two-thirds of 4,000 years with 4,000, then, as the duration of the world. Klostermann (*Neue kirchl. Zeitschr.* 5:208ff.) thinks of a system of Jubilee weeks. According to Bousset (ZAW 10:136ff.) the starting point was the number 3,001 for the beginning of the construction of the temple. Riedel (in Zimmern, KAT[3], 541-42) demonstrates that the lifespans of the patriarchs, with the exceptions of Enoch (365) and Lamech (777), rest on unusual combinations of the month numbers 30 and 31. Thus Adam's age 930 equals $30^2 + 30$. Enosh and Mahalalel lived $905 + 895 = 1,800 = 2 \times 30^2$ years, etc. B. Jacob (*Pentateuch*, Leipzig [1905]; cf. the overview, pp. 46ff.) offers another chronological system. Additional literature is cited in Dillmann, 112-13. Of the varied systems, in the judgment of most moderns (since Bertheau, *Jahrb. f. deutsche Theol.* 23:657ff.), the Sam, with which the book of <133> Jubilees agrees, is the oldest. Notably, according to Sam not only Methushelah (so the Hebr), but also Jered and Lamech died in the year of the Flood. This will have been intended to mean that these three died in the Flood itself. Accordingly, the intention may have been that the first five patriarchs were good, the subsequent patriarchs (with the exception of Enoch who was raptured before the Flood) were evil. At the same time, Sam shows very clearly how lifespans diminished as sin increased. Thus, the religious belief that the people's sin is destruction stands in the background (cf. Budde, 100ff.). According to Bousset, the original system is preserved in Josephus, *Ant.* 8 and Hebr is better than Sam. Recently, B. Jacob has supported the latter position. In the Babylonian tradition, "the 10 primeval kings with their average reigns of 12 sars" apparently correspond "to the first 10 world months of a world year of 144 sars" (= 432,000 years; Zimmern, KAT[3], 541).

(4) The character of such a genealogy is treated above (p. 50). In the final analysis, it—and the Babylonian genealogy, too—will consist of legend figures who must have once lived. The current character of the chapter diverges radically from the simplicity of the old legend which, like all poetry, avoids precise numbers. In J[j] (and also, indeed, in J[e]), so far as we can conclude from the few remnants, the scholar borrowed from the learned Babylonian tradition and accommodated the material to the character of the old legend. In P erudition regains prominence. The suggestion that P fashioned his reports directly from J (Holzinger, 63) cannot be demonstrated here either and is hardly likely. Characteristic of P's style is, above all else, the schema he imposed on the whole: "When A was X years old, he begot B. After B was begotten, however, he lived yet Y years and

begot sons and daughters. Accordingly all the years of A were X+Y years. Then he died." This schema, executed with as little variation as possible, also demonstrates the lack of poetical sensibility and the scientific hyperprecision of the author. The same schema (excluding the final clause concerning the total lifespan) occurs once more in 11:10-26 P.

(5) *Divergences from the schema and details.* V **1a** is a superscription like 2:4a; 6:9; etc. סֵפֶר means not only our "book," but also smaller records (Jer 32:10; Isa 50:1; etc.). It is a loanword from Bab. *šipru, šipir* "sending, letter." Holzinger's (and Eerdmans') suggestion that the word סֵפֶר implies that this was the beginning of the whole P document is without foundation. Since סֵפֶר otherwise always signifies an independent writing (Eerdmans, 4) one may assume that P writes here as though he was copying from a preexistent document (cf. Neh 7:5).

Vv **1b, 2** "[resume] the thread broken off by the Sabbath" (Meinhold, 61) and repeat the most important information concerning the people from the previous material. The people God created on the sixth day bore God's image and were ordained to reproduce. As a supplement it is added that God gave the man his name (as in 1:5, 8, 10). Now the divine blessing ("be fruitful") is fulfilled and, at the same time, the name "man" and God's image are reproduced: Adam bore God's image. Seth, Adam's son, was Adam's image. Thus, Seth and his descendants also resembled God. It is syntactically noteworthy that, as in 1:27, אָדָם is constructed sometimes as a proper name with singular verbs and sometimes as an appellative with plural verbs. This can hardly be removed through conjecture. Instead, it seems to be motivated by the nature of this transitional passage. Since the whole section makes good sense in the context, one may not <134> consider it the addition of later hands (contra Holzinger).

3 וַיּוֹלֶד has no object. בֵּן may have fallen out (Olshausen). Hebr mss read כִּדְמוּתוֹ בְּצַלְמוֹ with the same prepositions as in 1:26. **5** חַי is a perfect as in 3:22. אֲשֶׁר־חַי refers to "all the days which Adam lived." This addition clearly distinguishes these days from the days mentioned in v **4** which passed after he begot his son (contrast 25:7; cf. König, ThStKr [1906], 136-37).

The statement concerning Enoch in vv **21-24** is unusual. It does not say that he died (וַיָּמֹת), but mysteriously and allusively that he suddenly disappeared (וְאֵינֶנּוּ; cf. Isa 17:14; etc.; more precisely, but still mysteriously, "God took him away," 2 Kgs 2:9). Where he took him, P intentionally does not say. The authentic Jewish aversion to the mythological prohibits P from speaking more clearly. The old tradition means, he was transported to God, to God's dwelling (cf. the specific description of the rapture of Utnapishtim, pp. 70-71). Israelite tradition also recounts such a rapture for Elijah, and probably also originally for Moses. There are parallels in Babylonian (of Utnaphistim-Xisuthros, where the same verb *leqû* = לקח is used of the rapture as is employed in the OT of Enoch and Elijah; cf. Zimmern, KAT³, 551) and Greco-Roman tradition (e.g., of Hercules, Ganymedes, Romulus, Empedocles). Such rapture legends can usually be explained by the fact that the raptured individual was originally a god demoted to a man, although it is still maintained that he finally became a god again (cf. above, p. 78). The duration of his life (365 years) seems to indicate that this situation also applies to Enoch. This number, the number of days in the solar year, is remarkably short among the other lifespans. <135>

Shamash, the sun god, is mentioned first among the gods who reveal to Enmeduranki, the Babylonian prototype of Enoch. Enmeduranki is also the king of Sippar the cult city of the sun god Shamash (cf. Zimmern, KAT³, 533-34, 540). The expression "he walked *with* God" (not *before* God or *after* God), as in 6:9 of Noah, is also significant and seems to be a final echo indicating Enoch's intimate communion with God. God appeared to him and revealed secrets to him. The name חֲנוֹךְ > חנך "to consecrate," τελειοῦν, may also point in this direction. We do not learn the nature of these secrets from the Hebrew tradition. The Babylonian tradition knows of a similar circumstance with respect to Enmeduranki. There Enmeduranki receives the art of the oracle, specifically of the *bârû* priesthood, as a revelation. We may assume that the characteristics of the Babylonian figure were transferred to the Hebrew name "Enoch" (Meyer, Israeliten, 318). Yet, there is no report of Enmeduanki's rapture.

Later Jewish tradition speaks of Enoch and attributes to him the knowledge of those secrets which were most highly prized at the time: Enoch, the great world traveler, saw all the mysteries of heaven and earth, knew all the secrets of the past and the future, especially astronomy (cf. Sir 44:16, אוֹת דַּעַת לְדוֹר וָדוֹר, παράδειγμα μεγανοίας [*sic*] ταῖς γενεαῖς and set all this down in books. We can see old Babylonian loan material in at least a portion of the account (Bousset, Rel. des Judentums2, 559). The title of heavenly scribe and the concept of the heavenly tablets Enoch is supposed to have read are especially reminiscent of the Babylonian tradition (Zimmern, KAT³, 405, 541). Thus the ancient Enoch tradition, already quite lost in P, revived in later Judaism. It is interesting to note for the history of the Israelite literary tradition how the figure of the great "apocalypticist" finally developed from the ancient oracle priest. In this manner the old wisdom poet Solomon, who spoke of plants and animals, became the poet of Proverbs and Qoheleth in the tradition. In this manner the singer-king David utlimately became David the liturgist and Psalmist. The tradition traced "wisdom" to Solomon, "songs" to David, and "mysteries" to Enoch. The more "wisdom," "songs," and "mysteries" changed, the more the figure of the heroes of these genres evolved. Some theologies have seen an early notion of the belief in immortality in Enoch's rapture. But the old tradition is far removed from such a belief. If men like Enoch and Elijah do not taste death, that means nothing for the common believer! We are not Enoch and Elijah.

Regarding the singular וַיְהִי vv 23, 31, see §145q. In both passages וַיִּהְיוּ should be read with Hebr mss and Sam, as in vv 5, 3, 11, etc. (cf. 9:29). וַיִּתְהַלֵּךְ אֶת־הָאֱלֹהִים in vv 22 and 24 does not fit the context. In the first instance, LXX and Luc have וַיְחִי after the phrase. The difficulty can probably be explained by the fact that P knew no way to better incorporate the comment he found in his exemplar into the schema. אלהים seems to indicate that the clause does not come from J°. 32 Noah's age when he first became a father is remarkable, <136> more than 300 years older than all the others. The age can be explained by the fact that Noah's sons must still be young when the Flood came. They have children only after the Flood. The three sons, begotten in the same year, are en-visioned as triplets (so, with reservations, Böklen, ARW 6:49).

12. Flood Legend in P (and J) 6:9–9:17, 28, 29

Flood legend in P 6:9-22; 7:6, 11, 13-16a, 17a, 18-21, 24; 8:1, 2a, 3b, 4, 5, 13a, 14-19; 9:1-17, 28, 29. (1) The distinction of the J and P sources is a masterpiece of modern criticism. The final gleanings may be found in Budde, 248ff. The two names of God יהוה and אלהים, employed alternately and with no perceptible difference in meaning (cf. 6:22 with 7:5), point to dual sources. One may note further a multitude of repetitions. It is narrated twice that God sees the evil of humanity (6:5 ‖ 11, 12), that God announces to Noah the destruction of humanity by a Flood (6:17 ‖ 7:4), that God commands him to enter into the Ark (6:8 ‖ 7:1) together with his whole household (6:18 ‖ 7:1) and a certain number of all the clean and unclean animals (6:19, 20 ‖ 7:2) in order to preserve them alive (6:19 ‖ 7:3). Then we hear twice that Noah enters the Ark (7:7 ‖ 13; together with all his family and animals, 7:7-9 ‖ 13-16), that the Flood comes (7:10 ‖ 1), that the waters rise and the Ark floats on the waters (7:17 ‖ 18), and that all living things die (7:21 ‖ 22). The cessation of the Flood is announced twice (8:2a ‖ 2b); Noah twice learns that he can leave the Ark (8:6-12, 13b ‖ 15, 16); Twice God promises not to send another Flood (8:20-22 ‖ 9:8-17).

There are also several contradictions and irregularities. According to 6:19, 20; 7:15, 16, Noah takes along are a pair of every animal; according to 7:2, seven each of all the clean and only two each of the unclean. Gen 7:11 explains the Flood, in a mythological echo, as the confluence once again of the upper and lower waters; according to the much simpler 7:12, it was only a great, forty-day rain. The way in which the Flood ceased differs similarly: Gen 8:2a belongs with 7:11; 8:2b belongs with 7:12. According to 8:6-12 Noah must exert his own reason to learn whether he may already exit the Ark; in 8:16 God simply commands him to do so. The two sources differ especially, however, in the manner they indicate times: The one has a very precise chronology indicating year, month, and day (7:6, 11, 13, 24; 8:3b, 4, 5, 13a, 14); it also gives precise figures for the measurement of the Ark (6:15), and the depth of the water (7:20); the other has only approximate figures (7:4, 10, 12; 8:6, 10, 12). The figures of the first are, at the same time, much greater than those of the other.

The beginner can learn the proper way to distinguish the sources from this pericope. One proceeds from the surest criterion of source analysis, namely, from the names of God, and determines next the individual passages, and then the contexts that contain אלהים and יהוה. Accordingly, J includes 6:5-8 (יהוה, 6:5, 6, 7, 8), 7:1-5 (יהוה at the beginning, v 1, and conclusion, v 5, of the passage), 7:16b (יהוה), 8:20-22 (יהוה vv 20, 21). P includes 6:9-22 (אלהים vv 9, 11, 12, 13, 22; in addition vv 9-12 ‖ vv 5-8 J and vv 17-22 ‖ 7:1-5 J), 7:16a (אלהים), 8:1 (אלהים twice), 8:15-19 (אלהים v 15, at the beginning of the passage), 9:1-7 (אלהים vv 1, 6), 9:8-17 (אלהים vv 8, 12, 16, 17; in addition 9:8-17 ‖ 8:20-22). The differentiation, therefore, succeeds immediately for the beginning (6:5–7:5) and the conclusion (8:15–9:17), but not yet for the middle, where the names of God do not occur in closed contexts. The task now is to draw conclusions concerning the yet unanalyzed section from certain characteristics of the passages already attributed to J and P. The animals of the Ark are a pair each according to 6:19-20 P, according to 7:2 J seven pairs of the clean and two each of the unclean (cf. this differentiation of clean and unclean also in 8:20 J). Accordingly, P also includes 7:15, 16a (concerning 7:8, 9, see above p. 64). According to 7:4 J, the chronology of J is as follows: after seven days comes a rain of forty days duration. J, then, also includes 7:10 <137> (seven), 12 (forty), 8:6-12 (seven, forty), and 13b (the end of the passage 8:6-12). The other chronology, much more precise and dealing with much larger numbers, stems, therefore, from P. Accordingly, P includes

7:6, 11, 13-16a (concerning vv 15, 16a, see above), 18-20 (a unit describing the rise of the Flood and linked with the figures in v 20), and 8:3b, 4, 5, 13a, 14. Now only a final supplement remains: 7:17b parallels v 18 P and is thus from J. The origin of the Flood in the rain (7:4, 12) belongs to J and, therefore, so does 8:2b; The other, more mythological description in 7:11 belongs to P, and therefore, so does 8:2a. In reference to the destruction of all flesh, J employs the expression מָחָה מֵעַל פְּנֵי הָאֲדָמָה (6:7). The same expression occurs with the object אֶת־כָּל־הַיְקוּם in 7:4. Consequently, 7:23a also belongs to J. P uses גָּוַע in 6:7. Accordingly, 7:21 stems from P and the parallel 7:22 (מות) from J. P describes the entry into the Ark in 7:13-16a. Therefore, v 7 is from J. (Concerning individual later additions in 6:7, 3a; 7:7, 8, 9, 23; 8:20, cf. above pp. 61-63; regarding 7:17a, cf. below, p. 145).

The result must be tested as to whether the sections attributed to J and P produce two coherent and characteristic accounts and whether they agree with the other sections attributed to J and P. Both are true to a great degree. The J report is not fully reproduced by the redactor. But what we have of it manifests a very clear unity (cf. above p. 59-60). The account has the character of a very old, popular, native legend (cf. 7:16b; 8:21-22; cf. above p. 67). The diction is that of J (cf. above pp. 59-60). The impression of unity is much clearer still in the P account. Here the dispassionate spirit of scholarship, apparent in the precise data and figures, characterizes the whole report. P reproduces the old legend "in the style of a legal document" (Holzinger; cf. the description of the character of the legend in P by Wellhausen, *Prolegomena*⁶, 309ff.). This spirit of classification and chronology clearly characterizes P and, simultaneously, sharply distinguishes it from the naive-poetic style of the legend in J. The individual elements, which give the legend its particular charm and which are already few in the Flood legend of J, have fallen completely aside in P (cf. the very characteristic difference between the two accounts in 8:16). The Noah of P is not a living figure, but only the bland stereotype of piety. The whole legend in P has a somewhat stiff and solemn character. Since it lacks any complication, it should actually not even be called a "narrative" (cf. Holzinger, 76). Other distinguishing characteristics of P are the superscription אֵלֶּה תּוֹלְדֹת נֹחַ (6:9 as in 2:4; 5:1; etc.); the remarkable breadth of the portrayal which, in its wondrous solemnity and at the same time its pedantic precision, cannot overdo its constant repetition of the same expansive formulae (cf. above p. 118); the proclamation of laws (9:1-6), including a dietary regulation (9:2-3); and certain favorite ideas such as the notion of God's בְּרִית (6:18; 9:9ff.), of the sign of the covenant (9:12ff.), and of humans in the image of God (9:6). It is further characteristic that Noah does not offer sacrifice in P (contra J 8:20) and that P does not distinguish between clean and unclean animals in the Flood legend (contra J). According to P legitimate sacrifice and the differentiation of clean and unclean were first revealed to Moses. Furthermore, 9:1ff alludes to and continues God's statement in 1:28ff. The diction points to P: דֹּרֹת, 6:9 (J singular 7:1); 9:12; הוֹלִיד, 6:10; כָּל־בָּשָׂר, 6:12, 13, 17, etc. (J שֶׁל־הַיְקוּם, 7:4, 23); הַשְׁחִית and שָׁחֵת, 6:13, 17; 9:11, 15 (J מָחָה, 6:7; 7:4, 23); גָּוַע, 6:17; 7:21 (J מות, 7:22); הֵקִים בְּרִית, 6:18; 9:9, 11, 17 and נָתַן בְּרִית, 9:12; אֹתוֹ in lists, 6:18; 7:13; 8:16; etc.; זָכָר וּנְקֵבָה, 6:19; 7:16 (J אִישׁ וְאִשְׁתּוֹ, 7:2); לְמִינֵהוּ, often in P (6:20; 7:14); רֶמֶשׂ and רָמַשׂ not in J, but very frequently in P (6:20; 7:14, 21; etc.); לְאָכְלָה, 6:21; 9:3; בְּרָשָׁנָה, 7:6; עֶצֶם הַיֹּום הַזֶּה, 7:13 (חַיָּה, "wild animal," 7:14, 21; 8:1; etc.); מְאֹד מְאֹד, 7:19; the specifying בְּ, 7:21; 8:17; 9:10, 15,

16; שֶׁרֶץ and שָׁרַץ, 7:21; 8:17; 9:7; פָּרָה וְרָבָה, 8:17; 9:1, 7; לְמִשְׁפְּחֹתֵיהֶם,
8:19; "you and your seed after you," 9:9; עוֹלָם in combined phrases, 9:12, 16. The expressions cited do not all occur in P only, of course, but in contrast to other sources are
most common in P and, at any rate, very characteristic in comparison to J (contra
Eerdmans, 30-31). <138>

(2) It is especially instructive to observe the work of the redactor in this piece. The
redactor took pains to preserve as much of both accounts as possible. A tolerable fusion
of the two was possible because they were fundamentally related and similar in narrative
sequence and arrangement. The redactor preserved P very faithfully and based his own
work on it. He supplemented the P account with passages from J. He did not preserve the
J report so well. Where J and P reported parallel material, he either omitted J or placed
the two variants alongside each other. He was willing to tolerate repetitions if they were
not too disruptive. The beginning of the account in both P and J contained three sections:
I. the corruption of the earth (6:5-8 J, 9-12 P); II. God's command to build the Ark (13-16
P; not preserved in J); III. the command concerning what should enter the Ark together
with the revelation concerning the Flood (6:17-22 P; 7:1-5 J). The redactor preserved P
completely (6:9-22) and placed it in the middle of the whole. He prefaced it with section
I from J (6:5-8) which now forms a tolerable unity with section I from P. He placed
section III J at the end, which now belongs with section III from P. The structure of the
whole then is (1) J I + P I, (2) P II, (3) P III + J III. This is a well-devised way to form
a unit from the two sources and to lose as little as possible in the process. The redactor's
procedure was somewhat different in the account of the boarding (vv 6-16). Here he took
components of P and J and formed a new construct. Here, too, P fared better than J. P is
preserved in more compact masses, J is dissolved into individual sections. The redactor
offers first a comment concerning Noah's age from P (7:6) as the introduction of this
passage. Then he found the following in both sources: I. a date for the beginning of the
flood along with a description of this beginning (7:10 J; 7:11 P); II. the account of the entrance into the Ark (7:7, 16b J; 7:13-16a, 17a P). Here he placed J before P, but, in order
to make the presentation smoother, he combined both chronological indications. The
sequence is, then, (1) J II, (2) J I + P I, (3) P II. Inserted in P from J are v 12, a comment
about the duration of the Flood which the redactor understood in a harmonizing fashion
as a reference to the beginning of the Flood, and the closing of the door in v 16b which
seemed suitable only here in the second definitive account of the entrance. The redactor
treats the rising of the waters in vv 17-20. The passage stems entirely from P whose expansive description pleased the redactor. He inserted the parallel fragment from J (v 17b)
in this context.

The death of all flesh (vv 21-23) is composed as follows. First v 21 from P, from
whom the immediately preceding stems, then the two parallel clauses from J (vv 22, 23a).
The two clauses are transposed in order to achieve a better connection to the foregoing.
J's comment concerning Noah's deliverance (v 23b) connected superbly to this, and, as
the conclusion of the whole, then came the maximum depth of the water (v 24) from P.
The following passage, concerning the cessation of the waters (8:1-5) stems once again
in its entirety from P. The redactor took pains to preserve as much of J as possible, too.
Consequently he inserted vv 2b, 3a from J alongside the parallel information from P. J's
chronological note, which was unfortunately not useful in this context, he preserved by

placing it before v 6. Contrariwise, he did not know how to incorporate the information from J concerning the grounding of the Ark and, therefore, was forced to omit it. From this point, his procedure becomes less complicated since he found passages in his sources that corresponded to one another less precisely. He read first in J a passage (vv 6-12, 13b) according to which Noah learned through his ingenuity that the waters had dried up and in P (vv 13a, 14-17) God's command to abandon the Ark. He combined both without difficulty by placing J before P. It was necessary, however, to insert the date from P (v 13a) before v 13b (J). The evaporation must first occur (v 13a P) before Noah can discern it (v 13b J). The redactor adopted the exit from the Ark from his chief source, P (vv 18, 19). He left out the parallel passage from J here. He placed the briefer of the two concluding passages (8:20-22 J and 9:1-17 P) first and allowed the more expansive to form the conclusion of the whole. One sees from all this the acu <139> men the redactor employed so that no grain, especially of P, should fall to the ground. He admired P very greatly. J had to pay the cost of the procedure. The stylistic consistency of the whole produced in this fashion is no small wonder.

The redactor's attitude toward P suggests that P was nearer the redactor then J was, thus that P is younger than J. The same relationship can be seen with great clarity in the whole nature of the two accounts: J offers the old folk legend, P a later learned version. This is by no means to say that every individual element of P must also be younger than the corresponding element in J.

Eerdmans (31-32) diverges from the rather universally accepted source analysis by attributing 6:5-8; 7:1-5, 10, 13, 16b, 12, 23; 8:20-22 to J, 6:9-22; 7:6-9, 17-22, 24; 8:1-19; 9:8-17 to P, and 7:11, 14-16a to a "postexilic redaction." In his view 7:13 belongs to J despite the style which differs completely from 7:1 (J) and despite its similarity to the known P passages 6:18, 8:16, 18. In 7:8 the distinction of clean and unclean not contained in God's command in 6:19 would come as a complete surprise if its belongs to P. Gen 7:11a, which Eerdmans removes from P, cannot be separated from the P passages 8:4, 5, 13, 14 because of its chronology. Gen 7:11b is demonstrated to belong to P by the allusion to it in 8:2. In reference to 7:17a he ignores that this partial verse parallels v 18 (likewise with respect to the parallelism of v 21 and v 22). His fails to note that the "rain" in 8:2b refers clearly back to the "rain" in 7:4, 12 and indicates J. He overlooks the fact that God's explicit direction (8:15ff.) makes Noah's exertion of his own wits (8:6-12) unnecessary. Eerdmans' is, thus, a remarkably imprecise source analysis such as we have not experienced in quite some time in Genesis. Eerdmans (30-31) regards the "so-called P recension" an older version from the preexilic period "which was enriched in the postexilic period by other components." His evidence for the preexilic composition of the P account is only the highly questionable observation that P calculates according to the solar year. In reality, however, the number "twenty-seven" (cf. especially LXX) suggests that P's recension originally meant lunar months and a lunar year (cf. below). He bases the later origin of the J passages, however, on the fact that (in their current form!) they appear incorporated into P (p. 82). He overlooks the marked differences in content between the two recensions. After what has been said above, it is unnecessary to refute these statements.

Flood Legend in P. 6:9-12 Noah (9-10) and the corruption of the earth (11-12). Introduction. **9** צַדִּיק בְּדֹרֹתָיו resembles צַדִּיק בַּדּוֹר הַזֶּה in 7:1 (J). This coincidence of expression demonstrates the fundamental kinship of the two recensions. Characteristically, J illustrates Noah's righteousness in the course of the narrative, indeed, very ingeniously (cf. p. 62). In P it is simply asserted at the beginning, without illustration. As a narrator, J is incomparably better than P. The distinction between the singular and plural is also significant (בְּדֹור הַזֶּה J; בְּדֹרֹתָיו P). Here, P improves the tradition. In his <140> chronology Noah saw very many (18) generations (cf. the summary overview by Nestle, ZAW 24:130ff.; B. Jacob, *Pentateuch*, 16). It is, therefore, necessary neither to understand דֹרֹת here in the otherwise unattested sense, "contemporary" with Wellhausen (*Prolgeomena*[6], 390-91) nor even to emend to בְּדְרָכָיו with Winckler (*Forschungen* 3:396). תָּמִים is a cultic expression referring to the unblemished sacrificial animal. Applied to people, it refers to the cultically and ethically blameless, innocent. Such expressions, of course, are not to be taken in the profound Christian sense. To the Jew these are surely lofty and rare predicates. There will have been few "righteous." There are some. "Noah walked with God." The same phrase occurs in P in reference to Enoch (5:22). In both cases it refers not to simple piety, but to intimate communion with the deity. As in the case of Enoch, it is a final echo of ancient Noah legends which recount his communion with the deity. Illustrations of this communion are God's revelations to Noah in the Flood legend. Later periods know of Noah apocalypses. The Babylonian Flood hero also recounts such intimate communion with the deity (Zimmern, KAT[3], 557, 552-53).

10 This comment concerning Noah's sons repeats 5:32 P, as P, concerned with the exhaustiveness of every section, loves to do (cf. 1:26-28; 5:1, 2). **11, 12** Schwally (*Lit. Centralbl.* [1901], 1603) wants to explain P's characteistic expansiveness in terms of the cooperation of various hands and the indeterminacy of the description. Gen 9:2ff. shows the specific sins the source available to P had in mind. Since P had no account of Paradise, of the Fall, and of the expulsion, he thought that the earth slipped gradually into sin. חָמָס is a term for criminal oppression of the unprotected by those mightier than they. "With the expression וְהִנֵּה נִשְׁחָתָה (v 12), the narrator may have alluded to טֹוב מְאֹד וְהִנֵּה (1:31), a contrast of what had come to be with what had originally been" (Franz Deltizsch). Regarding בָּשָׂר, cf. p. 58. The word may encompass humans and animals as it does here (cf. comments on 9:1ff.).

13-16, 17-22 *Two divine speeches (1) concerning the Ark and (2) concerning the Flood and deliverance.* Regarding the original reason for this arrangement, see pp. 61-62. Characteristically, P omitted the test of Noah's faith. P has no taste for personal piety. Only the objective elements of religion are dear to him. The same phenomenon is apparent in the account of Abraham's exodus (cf. comments on 12:5).

13-16 *First speech.* **13a** It is not said when, where, and how God appeared. This unspecific manner of divine revelation characterizes P (p. 43). P is a positivist. He is interested in facts; circumstances and poetry mean nothing to him. The expression, "the end has come before me," that is, "according to my decision" (Dillmann), is not simple. Winckler (*Forschungen* 3:396) thinks of the root קוץ: *taedet me generis humani*. This, too, is linguistically difficult. According to Schwally (*Lit. Centralbl.* 1602) מִפְּנֵיהֶם is a gloss. V **13b** is difficult. One may read וְהִנָּם מַשְׁחִיתָם "and they are about to ruin the earth," that is, "because of them the whole world order comes out of its groove." The clause is, <141> according to Schwally (ibid.), apparently a textual expansion. For the explanation of these clauses, see the comments on 9:1-7. Eerdmans (29) suggests, without foundation, a polytheistic וְנִגְנוּ מָשְׁחִתִים "let us ruin the earth."

14-16 *Description of the Ark.* Such descriptions are P's native element (cf. the description of the Tabernacle in Exod 25ff. P). The description is significantly improved by Winckler's (*Forschungen* 3:397-98) brilliant observation that the קִנִּים are disruptive in v 14 and belong before v 16b (Sievers 2:251 has also noted that vv 14ab and 16b belong together) and, further, that וְאֶל אַמָּה תְּכַלֶּנָּה interrupts the clear parallelism of the two components of v 16a (בְּצִדָּהּ ‖ מִלְמַעְלָה) and must have originally stood at the end of the dimensions in v 15. The arrangement of the whole would be as follows: (1) the material of the Ark, (2) the dimensions of the Ark, (3) roof and door, and (4) decks. **14** תֵּבָה (LXX κιβωτός, Vulg *arca*) is also a technical term for the Ark in J (7:1). גֹּפֶר, which occurs only here, is probably a conifer (cf. Gesenius14, s.v.). One may read קִנִּים קִנִּים "nothing but cabins" (§123d) following Philo (*quaest. in Gen* 2, 3; cf. Lagarde, *Onomastica Sacra*², 367). On the jussive תַּעֲשֶׂה see §75t; For the construction, see §117ii. The Babylonian tradition also speaks of כֹּפֶר *kupru* (cf. above, p. 69). The pitching of the ship is an ancient invention. According to Berosus (cf. above p. 68) there was asphalt on the Ark. Even in the oldest ships discovered in Egypt, seams and joints were filled with asphalt (*Tägl. Rundschau* 10/6 [1902]). For the article in בְּכֹפֶר, see §126m.

15 The dimensions are significantly smaller than the Babylonian (cf. above pp. 68, 69). **16** צֹהַר means "back, roof" (cf. Arabic and the Canaanite gloss ṣu'ru in the Amarna correspondence; cf. also Gesenius¹⁴). Winckler (*Forschungen* 3:398n.1) compares וְאֶל־אַמָּה תְּכַלֶּנָּה "you shall complete it to a cubit [Ger. *elle*] (better הָאַמָּה?)"—with the transposition of the clause to the end of v 16 (already Wellhausen, *Gesch. Israels* I [= *Prolegomena*¹], 335n.1)—to the phrase *ina ištên ammat* "to a cubit," that is, measured by the cubit, which always appears in Assyrian texts following dimensions. It is explicitly remarked that the Ark should have a door in its side because there is no door in a normal vessel (Küchler in an oral communication). The Ark had several compartments (in the Babylonian tradition, too; cf. above p. 69). The world also has three stories (Winckler, *Forschungen* 3:398n.3).

17-22 *Second speech, the Flood and deliverance.* **17** וַאֲנִי "but I" is in contrast to Noah. Such a word often stands at the beginning of a new section. הַמַּבּוּל is a technical term for the Flood as in J (7:7). It is very interesting that "the Flood" is introduced here as a known entity (similarly in the Indian tradition, cf. above pp. 75, 78). This can probably be explained by the fact that "the Flood" plays a role in speculation (of the world year; cf. above p. 78). "Water of the earth" is probably meant as the definition of the word הַמַּבּוּל, perceived by P as a foreign word. P loves such definitions (cf. above p. 118). It may be simpler, however, to explain מַיִם here and in 7:6 as interpolations. Conversely, Sievers (2:252) considers הַמַּבּוּל a gloss, although מַיִם in 7:6 depends on our passage. The reading מִיָּם "from the sea" is infeasible (Dillmann) because the comment concerning the origin of the Flood in 7:11 does not mention the sea.

18 בְּרִית is a word employed in multiple nuances. Two parties disinterested in or even at enmity with each other enter solemnly into an agreement. They promise to be mutual friends and to live in שָׁלוֹם. They place each other under obligation, the weaker assumes an obligation, or the stronger accepts one freely, etc. Accordingly בְּרִית can mean the solemn act of covenant making and the content of the covenant, the friendly relationship established, the <142> law imposed thereby, or the obligation assumed therein. Concerning the original meaning of בְּרִית, see Zimmern, KAT³, 606 (contra Seybold, *Orient. Studien, Th. Nöldeke gewidment* 2:757-58). The word was already applied to the relationship of the patron god to the community of his worshipers in the pre-Israelite period (cf. the אֵל בְּרִית or בַּעַל בְּרִית, that is, the "patron god" of the Shechemites in Judg 9:4, 46; cf. recently Meyer, *Israeliten*, 558). The image is especially favored among the followers of the prophets (Deut) because it makes clear the ideas that Yahweh's grace, sworn in a solemn covenant, will remain inviolably over Israel, but that, on the other hand, Yahweh's grace also places Israel under certain obligations. According to P's theory, a special revelation and בְּרִית of God introduces each new age (cf. comments on chap. 17). This revelation to Noah is such an inaugural revelation. The content of the בְּרִית here is that God promises Noah his protection in the universal destruction (v 17) and, in response, expects obedience to his directions. This בְּרִית of God, which relates specifically to Noah ("with you") and excludes him from the general destruction, is distinct from the בְּרִית in 9:9ff., which applies not only to Noah, but the whole world until today. P is not yet theologian enough to feel the need to seek a connnection between these covenants. The suffix בְּרִיתִי expresses the notion that God grants Noah this his covenant of his own free will, in free grace. The verb הֵקִים implies the same idea. P avoids the otherwise common כָּרַת (cf. Holzinger, *Hexateuch*, 341, 377). Concerning בְּרִית in P, cf. Stade, *Bibl. Theol.*, 345f. P repeats the expansive list, "you and your sons, and your wife and the wives of your sons," in 7:13; 8:16, 18; The counterpart in J can be found in 7:1.

19, 20 P takes great pains for the greatest precision in the list of animal types. It is, after all, a matter of great importance that all be actually mentioned here. The list recurs with minor variations in 7:14-16, 21; 8:19; 9:2-3, 10 (cf. 1:24, 26, 28, 30). P needs only one pair in the Ark. According to his theory humans and animals in the Ark live only from plants and there were no deaths (Meinhold, 147). Regarding לְמִינֵהוּ, cf. 1:12, 21, 24-25. Concerning הַחַי in v 19, see §35f (Sam, LXX הַחַיָּה). LXX and Pesh have שְׁנַיִם שְׁנַיִם in vv 19, 20. Ball reads וּמִכֹּל רֶמֶשׂ (v 20) following Sam and the versions. **21** P defines מַאֲכָל as that אֲשֶׁר יֵאָכֵל and determines the purpose of the מַאֲכָל; it should be לְאָכְלָה (early attempts at logic; cf. the definitions in 1; cf. above, pp. 107, 109, 110, 111, 118-19).

7:6, 11, 13-16a, 17a *The entrance into the Ark and the beginning of the* <143> *Flood.* V **6** is a calculation by the lifespans for the patriarchs in the absence of a fixed era as in chap. 5. On the syntax of the clauses, see §164a. **8** For וְכֹל read with Sam (LXX) and Pesh וּמִכֹּל (Ball; Sievers 2:253; Kittel). V **11a** employs the style of legal documents. Such diction is (according to Erman's oral communication) quite normal in Egyptian official style (cf., for example, *Zeitschr. f. äg. Sprache* 38:4, "in the fifth year, in the third summer month, on the sixteenth day, on this day.") (On the construction of שָׁנָה, cf. §134o.) V **11b** contrasts radically with this very prosaic dating. These words offer an ancient and very poetic concept of the primal ocean (shared with the Babylonians) situated in the depths under the earth (Gen 49:25; Psa 24:2) and the waters above heaven held back by floodgates. תְּהוֹם רַבָּה occurs otherwise only in poetry (Isa 51:10; Psa 36:7; Amos 7:4). In form, these words are poetry: a heptameter. Consequently, it can be assumed that these words are not from the author P, but stem from the tradition he utilized. The idea is, what God separated at Creation, the *waters* and *above* and *below*, rush together again now. A second Chaos fell in on the world. The old world was created from water. Through water it was destroyed (2 Pet 3:5-6). Concerning this parallel between Flood and Chaos, see above p. 78. **13** Regarding שְׁלֹשָׁה, see §97c. For אֹתָם, LXX and Pesh-Urm have אִתּוֹ (cf. 8:16, 18). The idea that all beings entered the Ark on the same day is amazingly unrealistic. In J, by contrast, Yahweh permits Noah seven days for this. P "is remarkably unconcerned about the possibility and probability of the proceedings" (Holzinger). **14** LXX mss omit כל צפור כל־כנף. It may be an addition. V **17a** reprises vv 6 and 11 and belongs, accordingly, to P (Budde, 263-64). "For forty days" is a gloss influenced by v 12 J.

18-21, 24 The rising Flood, the destruction of all Flesh. The solemn monotony of the description characterizes P. V **19b** intends to portray <144> the universality of the Flood. **20** Regarding the significance of the figure "fifteen cubits" in v 20, cf. the commentary on 8:3b, 4.

8:1, 2a, 3b-5, 13a, 14 The receding Flood is described as the counterpart to the rising waters. **1** The beautiful notion that God also mercifully remembers (the expression זָכַר is frequent in P in this sense) the animals expresses an amicable, naive view of God (cf. Jon 4:11) and will hardly stem from P, but probably from his exemplar. The Flood recedes when the standing waters are driven away by wind and the influx of new water is hindered. The first idea is not quite transparent. Whence could such deep waters be driven by wind? The transposition of vv 2a and 1b (Dillmann, 146) accomplishes nothing. The comment in v 1b may stem from the tradition underlying P in which the Flood was envisioned as much less deep. V **2a** corresponds precisely to the clause in 7:11b. These words also sound like poetry: a pentameter? Is a verb paralleling וַיִּסָּכְרוּ missing, perhaps (Sievers 2:254)? **3b** Strack recommends the reading מִקֵּץ הַחֲמִשִׁים.

4 The waters rose for 150 days (7:24) and finally stood fifteen cubits above the highest mountains (7:20). From this day, the seventeenth day of the seventh month, onward they receded. On this very same day, the Ark was grounded. Therefore, it was gliding precisely over the mountain at the water's high point and was grounded with the slightest fall of the water. Accordingly, it drew fifteen cubits of water. Since the Ark is thirty cubits tall—so the author imagined it—it was sunk halfway into the water. The whole unit is a thoroughly artificially conceived theory. וַתָּנַח is an allusion to נֹחַ (cf. p. 65) and probably stems from P's exemplar. אֲרָרָט (Isa 37:38; 2 Kgs 19:37; Jer 51:27) is an Armenian region between the Araxes and the Wan and Urmia Seas, the homeland of a mighty people called the Urartu by the Assyrians and the Alarodians by Herodotus. They called themselves the Chalder (bibliography in Dillmann, 146-47, and Gesenius[14]). Pesh and Targ translate *Ararat* with *Qardu* (= Cordyene, on the left bank of the upper Tigris to the upper Zab). *Šanda* (MVAG 7:30ff.) wants to equate the אֲרָרָט of the Flood narrative with the mountain *Ararti* (otherwise read *Arardi*) in Assurnasipal's Annals I:61 <145> (= KB 1:62-63) which he locates in the Cordyene mountains. It remains likely, however, that אֲרָרָט here as elsewhere in the OT is Urartu, Armenia. In the old tradition Noah disembarked and sacrificed at a very definite mountain and place, of course, a place sacred to those who lived in the vicinity. **13** LXX reads לְחַיֵּי נֹחַ (cf. 7:11; Frankel, 61; Ball; Kittel). The indication of the era belongs to the date.

Chronology of the Flood (following Dahse, ZAW 28:7ff.)

	Hebr.	LXX mss b d g p w d²		Jubil
Beginning of Flood	2/17	2/27	2/27	2/17(27)
Highpoint of Flood	7/17	7/27	7/27	--
Waters recede	1/1	1/1	--	1/1
Earth dry			2/17	2/17(16)
(Opening of Ark)	} 2/27	2/27	} 2/27	2/27
Exit			3/1	3/1

Given this significant divergence of figures, it is very difficult to discern the original calculation and the reasons for the divergences. Almost all texts say that the water receded on New Year's Day of the 601st year after Noah's birth. This date apparently has some special significance which was, therefore, recognized by the editors. With the receding of the waters on New Year's Day a new period begins. Up to that moment it had been "the old world" (2 Pet 2:5). Noah had lived 600 years to this point, that is, a Babylonian νῆρος. The reference to New Year's Day does not mean the old Hebrew fall New Year, but the beginning of the year in the Babylonian calendar on the first of Nisan. The waters have already receded by this point, but the earth is still moist. P also counts by the Babylonian calendar, which he elsewhere regards as instituted by Moses (Exod 12:2). Jubil 6:17 counts similarly (cf. Dahse, ZAW 28:8). Apparently one year was assigned for the course of the Flood (supported by EthEn 106:15). If this year is divided such that five months were assigned to the rising, five months for the receding of the waters, and two months for the drying of the earth, then one obtains, calculating from the 1/1 as a fixed date, 2/27 as the beginning, 7/27 as the highpoint, and 2/27 as the end of the whole matter, that is, the figures of LXX. Apparently, a lunar month is in view. It is a simple and natural calculation. The Hebrew text reckons with eleven days more for the whole matter which it accommodates in the <146> drying of the earth. This reckoning, however, must be understood as the result of an editor's desire to arrive at a solar year in the place of a lunar year by adding eleven days (Böklen, ARW 6:54-55). In order to highlight the receding water, an additional date, when the mountain tops became visible, is given: 10/1, in the majority of LXX mss 11/1. This chronology, however, involves the difficulty that the rising as well as the recession of the Flood lasted 150 days or five solar months although, calculated by calendar dates and the lunar year, the figure would total 147 (148) days. Here "150 days" may be a customary imprecise designation for five months. Dahse (ZAW 28:7ff.) disagrees. He depends on the LXX mss b d g p w d² and Jubilees and arrives at the following chronology: beginning of the Flood 2/17, highpoint 7/17, appearance of the peaks 10/1, the waters dry up 1/1, the earth is dry 2/17, opening of the Ark 2/27, exit from the Ark 3/1. According to Dahse, this chronology is based on a solar year. But given such an assumption, a reason for the unusual 17th and 27th dates can hardly be discerned and from 7/17 to 1/1 are more than "150 days." Whether the specifics of the LXX mss mentioned and of Jubilees involve traditions or whether they only represent Haggadah, I venture no decision.

15-19 *Exit from the Ark.* **16** It is very noteworthy that God here in P simply reveals what in J Noah learns (under the protection of his God) through his own extreme cunning.

In J the wonder is an exception, in the dogmatizing P its "power is prolonged." **17** Sam, LXX, Pesh read וכל־החיה as do Hebr mss, LXX, Pesh, and Sam in v 19. For הוצא read the Qere הַיְצֵא. "They shall be fruitful and multiply," the statement at creation is repeated here concerning the animals, as in 9:1 concerning the people, at the beginning of the new world. **19** MT separates the related words וְרֶמֶשׁ and רֶמֶשׂ (cf. 7:14, 17). LXX has καὶ πάντα τὰ κτήνη καὶ πᾶν πετεινὸν καὶ πᾶν ἑρπετὸν κινούμενον ἐπὶ τῆς γῆς = וכל־הבהמה וְכל־העוֹף וְכל הָרמשׂ הָרמשׂ עַל־האָרץ (Ball, Kittel). The notion that the animals left the ship arranged "by their kinds" is a good example of P's love of order. But it is certainly not poetic.

9:1-17 *Two speeches of God to Noah.* Significantly, the two speeches are addressed <147> to Noah and his sons, but not to the women. The woman has no place in official worship. **1-7** The new order of Creation: the old order is renewed (vv 1, 7) and altered. The memory of the creation (v 1) governs the whole piece (cf. above p. 78). That the people (just as the animals in 8:17) are now promised propagation and multiplication through a divine "blessing" can be well understood from the situation. How else can all of contemporary humanity have been produced by the few delivered from the Flood, how can Noah have become the "renewer" of the human race (Sir 44:17, תחליף, literally "second growth"), if God's special "blessing" had not granted him such tremendous increase? The more difficult question is why people are once again promised dominion over the animals. People—so it goes—now acquire the right to eat animals just as they do plants (v 3). Only the blood they may not eat (v 4). Whereas one may now kill animals, the killing of people is strictly forbidden for both human and animal (vv 5, 6). Clearly, the permissions and prohibitions are very closely related to the dietary regulation at Creation (1:29-30). The reason they ensue now, after the Flood, cannot be discerned from P. P must have adopted elements of his exemplar without their contexts (just as he did above, cf. pp. 62, 143). This context can be reconstructed, however. At Creation God allowed humans and animals to eat only plants (1:29f). But this state of peace was not preserved. "The earth become full of violence" (6:11); "All flesh (humans and animals) took evil paths" (6:12). That is, humans and animals fell upon one another: humans murdered humans and slayed animals; animals consumed humans and animals. God intervened in this general corruption and destroyed the whole race. In this tradition, the destruction of the animal world was also motivated for they, too, had committed evil. This understanding of the story is still preserved in Jubil 5:2. Now, however, after the Flood, God establishes a new order: the right to kill animals, that people had taken for themselves, is now permitted them subsequently. (Peace in the animal world is not reestablished either.) But explicitly prohibited are (1) the consumption of blood and (2) killing people. So the whole describes how the generations and eras have passed over the earth until the current world of strife and murder developed from the first ideal world of peace. This tradition is related to that of Hesiod ("Werke und Tage," 109ff.) in which the sequence recurs—first vegetarian diet, then flesh consumption.

If, then, we may assume with great certainty that this entire context in which Creation and Flood are set here is older than P, it is clear, on the other hand, that it does not belong to the most ancient tradition but was only added in the course of development. This is to be expected from the outset because the individual legend was always original and the context was added only secondarily (cf. introduction ¶3:6). This history of the tradition can still be discerned from the text of P. The tradition of the era of peace was added only later to the Creation account, as we have seen (cf. above pp. 115, 122). And here, at the conclusion of the Flood legend, the two speeches of God, vv 1-7 and vv 8-17, stand alongside each other without context. Only the second clearly belongs to the Flood legend itself, and even has a parallel in J (8:20-22). But the first, which refers back to the Creation account <148>, has no counterpart in either J or in the Babylonian recensions and, in terms of its essential content, is not an original component of the Flood account. P has no feeling for the poetry of this tradition of the periods of peace and strife. Of the whole context, he preserved only the two regulations (1:29-30; 9:2ff.). As a priest he was interested in them because they were dietary regulations. In this way P constructed a history of the human diet. First, only plants were allowed; then animals, too; and later from Moses on only the clean animals besides the plants.

4 P may have added the prohibition of the consumption of blood to the tradition. P emphasized this prohibition as much as possible through the position he gives it here. To him, this prohibition is the most important commandment in the law (next to the Sabbath, perhaps), the basis of all order and morality. It merits the death penalty (Lev 17). The consumption of blood appears on the same level as murder, idolatry, and harlotry in Ezek 33:25-26. Even Acts 15:29 associates it with murder! The abhorrence of blood is certainly very ancient in Israel (1 Sam 14:32ff.). It is the source of the practice of ritual slaughter. Mohammed prohibited the Arabs from consuming blood (Wellhausen, *Arab. Heidentum*[2], 118). In response to the question why one should not consume blood came the answer, "Because the blood is 'the soul' or 'the soul' is in the blood" (Lev 17:11, 14; Deut 12:23). The two statements are approximately synonymous for ancient thought. Whether this answer found by ancient deliberation was really the original reason for this abhorrence is another question. Concerning the prohibition against the consumption of blood, cf. Stade, *Bibl. Theol.*, 142; Benzinger, *Archäologie*[2], 408. דָּמוֹ is an explanatory gloss (Ball).

While God permits the spilling of animal blood, spilling human blood is most vigorously prohibited by him in vv **5, 6**. Concerning לְנַפְשֹׁתֵיכֶם, see §139f. מִיַּד אִישׁ אָחִיו means "by you among one another." אִישׁ אָחִיו is a fixed idiom for "one another" (Zech 7:10; Budde, 283ff.; cf. also §139c; Winckler, *Forschungen* 3:403 assumes textual corruption). The words שֹׁפֵךְ דַּם הָאָדָם בָּאָדָם דָּמוֹ יִשָּׁפֵךְ, which require the death of the murderer with such extreme gravity, are by form poetry (two trimeters). The words are extremely ingenious: each word in the first semistich is repeated in the second in order to show that the murderer experiences precisely what he did. At the same time, the words play, in the way the Hebrews loved so much, with the consonants ד and ם: דַּם הָאָדָם בָּאָדָם דָּמוֹ. (A parallel, for example, can be seen in Psa 122:6ff., which play with the consonants in שָׁלֵם [Jerusalem].) Since the saying differs radically in tone from P, it is thought to have been taken from a source. It breathes the serious spirit of the ancient period (cf. the story of Naboth) and may be an old verdict. P could utilize the saying here so well because it is so general. Only later—P will have thought—did God establish who among the people should have the right to kill the murderer. In the concluding clause (v 6b), P entirely abandoned the divine speech form—very characteristically, for him it is only a form. The prohibition against the consumption of blood in this passage and the later repetition of the same prohibition in P for Israel alone (Lev 17:10-14) are as compatible as the institution of the Sabbath in Gen 1 and the Sabbath commandment in the decalog. The later synagogue derived the so-called "Noachide" commandments, theoretically valid also for non-Jews, from this passage. Modern scholars have exchanged these <149> non-Jews (living in Canaan) with the "proselytes," that is, the σεβόμενοι τὸν θεόν (cf. Schürer, *Gesch. des jüdischen Volkes*[3] 3:128-29). But there is not even a trace present in the text that would show us that the verses have "proselyte discipline" in view. **7** The conclusion returns to the beginning. וּרְדוּ (as in 1:28) should be read for וּרְבוּ in order to avoid the repetition of the same word (so Ball and Kittel following Nestle).

8-17 *The second speech, the covenant.* **8-11** The content of the "covenant" is God's promise not to send a Flood. God gives this promise to all those who were impacted by the Flood, that is, humans and animals. This idea that God's covenant also applies to the animals sounds amazingly profane for P, who otherwise thinks of a "history of salvation" in relation to covenants, and is probably to be attributed to P's exemplar (Kraetzschmar, *Bundesvorstellung*, 195). Vv 8-11 parallel 8:21-22. For the sense of these verses, cf. above p. 78. **10** Regarding מִכֹּל, compare 6:2; 7:22. For the attributive article in הַחַיָּה, compare 1:21 and §126x, unless one should simply read חַיָּה with Schwally. Regarding the construction יֹצְאֵי הַתֵּבָה see §116h. לְכֹל חַיַּת הָאָרֶץ is absent in LXX and is a variant of בְּכֹל חַיַּת הָאָרֶץ (Holzinger omits).

12-17 P elaborates the sign of the covenant, the rainbow, with great solemnity: thus the repetitions (which Schwally would like to interpret here and in 6:11-12 as superfluous) and probably also the third person אלהים in v 16. אוֹת, "sign," is a thing, a process, an event by which one perceives, learns, or remembers something or discerns the credibility of a matter. Such signs of perception, confirmation, and remembrance play a great role in antiquity which desired to have everything visible and comprehensible. Examples of signs can be seen in 1 Sam 10; Luke 2:11-12; 1:18ff.; etc. One should probably, therefore, distinguish between a "sign" and a "wonder." A "sign" can simultaneously be a "wonder," but it can also be a quite normal thing. In a time when contracts were not yet written it was customary to establish a "sign" to accompany solemn vows, promises, and other "covenants" designed to remind the parties of the covenant at the proper moment and thus to guard against violations of the covenant. Examples of such covenant signs in profane life can be seen in Gen 21:30 (cf. 38:17). The reason the sign of the covenant here is the rainbow cannot be determined on the basis of the text of P alone. Here, too, then, P must have reproduced his source. This is also suggested by the way the bow is discussed as though it were an independent being and, further, by the anthropomorphism according to which the sign is also for Yahweh himself, so that he may not forget his promise, and by the archaic, poetic sound of the words in v 14, especially בְּעַנְנִי עָנָן (on the form, see §52d; on the syntax, §117r). The original significance of the sign can be deduced from the word קֶשֶׁת. קֶשֶׁת is the bow for shooting, not the arc inscribed by a compass. Yahweh has such a קֶשֶׁת (קַשְׁתִּי v 13). In Lam 2:4 and 3:12 Yahweh's immense warbow is the rainbow in heaven. According to this concept, then, Yahweh is a mighty warrior who carries bow and arrow. The view that lightning flashes are Yahweh's arrows (Psa 7:13-14; Hab 3:9-11) is related. These mythological ideas are surely most ancient. <150> The account of the origin and significance of the rainbow must also trace back to earliest prehistory. When Yahweh tires of shooting his arrows—so may one have originally put it—he puts his bow aside. Therefore the rainbow appears in heaven after a thunderstorm. The ancient rejoices over this phenomenon because he sees that now the wrath of his god has passed: "He removed the missile of wrath from the bow in the clouds and loosened the string of anger" (*Schatzhöhle*, ed. Bezold, 24). A similar notion occurs among the Indians, where the bow is Indra's war-bow which he sets aside after the battle against the demons, and among the Arabs (cf. Wellhausen, *Prolegomena*[6], 311n.1; *Arab. Heidentum*[2], 209). A similar element also occurs in the Babylonian creation epic where, it seems, Marduk's bow, carried as a weapon in the battle against *Tiâmat*, is placed in heaven as a bow of stars after *Tiâmat*'s defeat (cf. Delitzsch, *Babyl. Weltschöpf.*, 109; KB 6/1:33; Winckler, *Keilinschriftl. Textbuch*[2], 123). Böklen's contention (*Archiv für Religionswissenschaft* 6:124ff.) that Yahweh's קֶשֶׁת is the moon is refuted by Ezek 1:28; Sir 43:11f; 50:7. Concerning the rainbow in popular belief throughout the world, cf. Melusine 2:9ff. P's exemplar associated this etiological myth with the Flood legend. The old mythological tones will have already been diminished here (otherwise P would not have adopted it). The rainbow in heaven is a sign that God remembers his vow and that the rain will not grow to a Flood. This is certainly a wonderfully poetic concept and a glorious conclusion to the whole narrative. P retained this element because he sought three covenant signs (the rainbow, circumcision, and the Sabbath) for his paradigm of world history with its three covenants with Noah, Abraham, and Moses. This is certainly a wonderful compilation! Of course, the idea is that God only now created the rainbow (נָתַתִּי v 13): While God speaks—one should think—the bow appears for the first time. Regarding the construction of vv 14-15, see §159g.

15, 16 Regarding בְּכָל־בָּשָׂר "with all flesh," see §119i. It may be an addition in v 15 (Kittel). Eerdmans (29) wants to translate אלהים in v 16 as a plural and find in it the echo of a polytheistic recension. This cannot be demonstrated, however. **28, 29** Conclusion of the Noah narrative. It is chronology as in chap. 5. **29** Many mss read וַיִּהְיוּ (Ball, Kittel); others read וַיְהִי.

A few statements may be made concerning P's exemplar. Here and there, older elements shimmer though P's account, especially the poem concerning the origin of the Flood in 7:11 (and 8:2a), the saying in 9:6, the ancient myth concerning the rainbow, the tradition of the end of the era of peace and the new world order, and, further, the covenant which also applies to the animals (cf. above) and to which Deut-Isa 54:9 alludes (Kraetzschmar, 195). The exemplar is also responsible for the names (including *Ararat*), the terms תֵּבָה and מַבּוּל, and, further, the information that the Flood lasted a year. Since a point of contact with J occurs at a noteworthy point in the structure (cf. above, pp. 61-62) and the P account agrees generally with the order of J, it can be assumed that P followed his exemplar rather faithfully <151> in the sequence of events. Precisely because of this contact with J, we may imagine that this exemplar was rather similar to the J account. But, on the other hand, it is not identical with J. The older elements that glimmer through do not occur in J (contra Wellhausen, *Prolegomena*[6], 390; Budde, 467-68; Holzinger, 85-86; etc.). How did the two Israelite recensions, J and P's exemplar, arise? Is an inner-Israelite development involved or was the Babylonian legend adapted by Israel at different times? We hardly have the means to answer this question. It only seems improbable that P reworked the Babylonian tradition directly. Here, too, neither the cuneiform Flood account nor that of Berosus has the elements characteristic of P's exemplar mentioned above (contra Löhr, 16).

13. Table of Nations in P 10:1a, 2-7, 20, 22, 23, 31, 32

For source criticism, see above p. 85.

P follows a exemplar related to J^j here. As in J^j the Table of Nations follows the Flood account and is structured according to Shem, Ham, and Japheth. P will also have taken the sequence, beginning with the younger and ascending to the elder, from his exemplar. J^e also originally had the same sequence (cf. above p. 85).

Regarding the evaluation and origin of such a genealogy of the nations, cf. above pp. 86-88. Only a few comments will be made here concerning scholars' endless efforts to identify the names mentioned (bibliography, p. 88).

2-5 According to the following, Japheth encompasses the peoples to the north and the west. גֹּמֶר occurs in Assyr as a gentilic. The Gimirrai are the Greek Κιμμέριοι. Around 700 BC the Kimmerians (probably Iranians, from north of the Black Sea, "Crimea"?) migrated to Asia minor where they encountered Phrygians, Assyrians, and Lydians (cf. Meyer 1:516, 545ff., 556; Winckler, KAT^3, 101-102; Hommel, *Grundriß der Geogr. u. Gesch. des Alten Orients*, 210f.). Gomer includes the אַשְׁכְּנַז (mentioned in Jer 51:27 along with *Araraṭ* = Assyr *Urarṭu*, a region in Armenia, and Minni = Assyr *Mannai* in Armenia, and, therefore, probably to be found in Armenia; probably = *Aŝgûza, Iŝkûza* and, therefore, perhaps to be emended אַשְׁכּוּז; according to Winckler, KAT^3, 101-102 = Σκυθάι; yet Hommel, *Grundriß*, 212-13 holds firmly to the reading אשכנז and at the same time associates it with the Phrygian Ascaina, while E. Meyer, *Zeitschr. f. vergl. Sprachf.* 42:12 accepts only the latter equation). רִיפַת (1 Chron 1:6, דיפת; according to Josephus, Paphlogonians, not attested in the inscriptions) and תֹּגַרְמָה (a people who, according to Ezek 27:14, exported stallions, teams of horses, and mules to Tyre; according to Ezek 38:6 in the far North; LXX θεργαμα, θοργαμα, probably also to be found in the vicinity of Armenia; perhaps = Assyr *Tigarimmu*; cf. Friedr. Delitzsch, *Paradies*, 246). מָגוֹג, famed for the prediction of the coming of Magog and his king Gog in the eschaton (Ezek 38f). In the Jewish view in Ezekiel's time, it was a semimythical land in the farthest North (39:2). The suspicion that the name "Magog" in this passage <152> arose through corruption of the name of the king Gog (Ezek 38, 39) and made its way into the Ezekiel tradition, does violence to the tradition. Yet, there is a close relationship between the names Magog and Gog. The latter in the form *Gâg(aya)* is now attested as early as 1400 BC in the Amarna correspondence as a common designation for northerners, barbarians. מָדַי is the equivalent of the Assyr *Madai*, Medians. They are first mentioned in the OT in 2 Kgs 17:6. יָוָן is the Assyr *Yavanu*, Ionia, Greece. Since the eighth century the Greeks advanced toward the East (cf. Meyer 1:490ff.). יָוָן includes the אֱלִישָׁה (exporters of purple to Tyre, Ezek 27:7; meaning uncertain; according to Stade, *de. pop. Javan*, 8-9, and Meyer 1:341, Carthage, perhaps = *Alaŝia*, found in the Amarna correspondence and the Hittite documents, and exported copper; according to Winckler, MDOg [1907] nos. 35, 41 = Cyprus), תַּרְשִׁישׁ (usually, yet without convincing grounds, identified with the known Phoenician colony Tartesus in Spain; cf. P. Haupt in Stade and Schwally, *Books of Kings*, 117-18; *Verh. des 13. Or. Kongr.*, 232ff.), the כִּתִּים (usually interpreted as inhabitants of Κίτιον, Κίττιον on Cyprus, Cyprians; yet, perhaps here as elsewhere in the OT, of broader significance; according to Winckler, *Forschungen* 2:422, 565ff., southern Italy, specifically Sicily), and רֹדָנִים (with 1 Chron 1:7, Sam, and mss; probably with LXX the Rhodians; according to Winckler, *Forschungen* 2:422 perhaps to be read דֹּרָנִים, Doranim, Dorians; other suggestions in Gesenius14, s.v.). The remaining population of the shores of the Mediterranean Sea descended from these peoples. תֻּבַל (תֻּבַל, Ezek 27:13; Assyr *Tabal*) are the Tibarenes who inhabited Asia minor from south of the Black Sea to Cilicia. Whether this people Tubal is related to the Tubal-Cain of Gen 4:22 cannot be said with certainty (cf. above, p. 51). The Tibarenes were also famed for their bronze-work (cf. A. Jeremias, ATAO², 257). מֶשֶׁךְ (Sam מושׁוך [מושׁך], LXX Μοσοχ), often mentioned with Tubal, is the Assyr *Mušku, Musku*, Μόσχοι, who were located southeast of the Black Sea. Winckler (*Forschungen* 2:131ff; KAT³, 68) seeks Muski and מֶשֶׁךְ in Phrygia (cf. also A. Jeremias, ATAO², 258). תִּירָס may be the *Turuša* who attacked Egypt in the thirteenth century (Meyer 1:312) = the Τυρσηνοί a pirate people on the Aegean Sea. אֵלֶּה בְנֵי יֶפֶת has fallen out after הַגּוֹיִם (v 5; cf. vv 20, 31; Olshausen).

6, 7, 20 deal with Ham's sons, peoples of the South. According to Jensen (*Sunday School Times* 41/5:68) they are listed from South to North from the standpoint of the observer. According to Speigelberg (*Aegyptologische Randglossen zum AT*, 9-10) the viewpoint is political: Cush appears first as the dominant power which also claims sovereignty over Spain and Palestine. This interpretation would point to the period of the twenty-fifth Egyptian dynasty (around 707–664). כּוּשׁ (Assyr *Kušu*, Bab *Kûsu*, Eg *Kaš, Kiš, Keš*) is Nubia. Here, too, מִצְרַיִם, Egypt, appears together with Cush. On the other hand, Arabic tribes are also included under Cush in the following. For this and other reasons, Winckler (KAT³, 144-45; etc.) assumes a southern Arabian Cush thought to be associated with Cush. Against this Meyer (*Israeliten*, 315ff.) holds fast to the contention that Cush always indicates the Nubian kingdom. "We may not, however, assume that the Hebrews knew our atlases." According to v 7, Cush included סְבָא (according to Josephus, Meroe between the Nil and Atbara; or, perhaps, according to Dillmann a stretch of coast on the Red Sea; essentially identical with שְׁבָא? cf. Zimmern, in Gesenius¹⁴ s.v.), חֲוִילָה (according to 10:29 assigned to Yoktan), סַבְתָּה (= Sabota in *Ḥaḍramût* in southern Arabia? according to Glaser, *Skizze* 2:252-53, Σάφθα on the Persian Gulf), רַעְמָה (= the city רגמת in a Minaean inscription? cf. Hommel, *Aufs. u. Abh.*, 231; according to Dillmann = the Ραμμανῖται of Strabo), and סַבְתְּכָא (perhaps = Σαμυδάκη to the East of the Persian Gulf; cf. Glaser 2:252). From רַעְמָה <153> are descended שְׁבָא (the Sabaeans, assigned to Yoktan in 10:28, to Keturah in 25:3) and דְּדָן (also in the Minaean and Sabaean inscriptions; cf. Glaser, *Skizze* 2:397; Winckler, KAT³, 142 above; counted with Keturah in Gen 25:3). Winckler contends (*Forschungen* 1:24ff.; KAT³, 136ff.; MVAG 3:1ff.) that מצרים = *Musri* was also the name of northwestern Arabia. Küchler (*Stellung des Jesaja in der Politik seiner Zeit*, 8ff.) and Meyer (*Israeliten*, 455ff.) disagree (Winckler responds in *Die jüngsten Kämpfer wider den Panbabylonismus*, 31ff.). פּוּט, the Egyptian Punt, the coast of Somalia on the Red Sea (W. Max Müller, *Asien u. Europa*, 107ff.; Speigelberg, *Aegyptologische Randglossen zum AT*, 9), Bab *Pûta*, cuneiform old Persian *Putiyâ*, is first mentioned in the OT in Nah 3:9 along with the Libyans (bibliography, Gesenius¹⁴, s.v.). כְּנַעַן, Canaan, is mentioned here, probably because, as the archaeological digs have now shown, it was very Egyptian in character since ancient times and gives the impression of an Egyptian annex (cf. Steuernagel, *Isr. Stämme*, 119).

22, 23, 31 Shem's sons are listed, it seems, from E. to W., and at the same time, S. to N. עֵילָם is Assyr *Elamtu*, Elymais, the land of the Eulaeus and Choaspes rivers. The capital city is *Šušan*. The nation is not "Semitic," but belongs to the Babylonian cultural realm. The Elamites governed for a period around 2100 in Babylonia (cf. Meyer 1:157, 164ff.; A. Jeremias, "Elam," in RE³, ed. Herzog; and, especially, Weißbach, "Elymais," in Pauly-Wissowa, *Realencykl. der klass. Altertumswiss.*, and Hommel, *Grundriß*, 33ff.). אַשּׁוּר are the famed world conquerors. אַרְפַּכְשַׁד has not yet been confidently identified. Cheyne thinks (ZAW 17:190) that it is a corruption of אַרפך כשׂד. In this case, ארפך would be Ἀρραπαχῖτις on the upper Zab (hardly = Assyr *Arrapha* which, according to Andreas, "Arrapachitis," in Pauly-Wissowa, is to be sought instead in the vicinity of *Soleimânîye*, north of *Diyâlâ-Gyndes*) and כשׂד would be equatable with the כֶּשֶׂד in 22:22. The word is probably a name for the Babylonians proper, who would otherwise be very noticeably absent from the list. Jensen (ZA 15:256) thinks it reflects **Arbakišâdu, *Arbkišâdu, *Arpkišâdu*, "land of four banks," that is, land of the four banks of the Euphrates and the Tigris. Delitzsch (*Paradies*, 255-56) argues that it means the land of the four regions of the world like *kibrat arba'i* in the famed Babylonian royal title *šar kibrat arba'i* (king of the four regions of the world). לוּד is usually equated with Lydia (Assyr *Luddu*) whose inhabitants, however, are also not "Semites." According to Jensen (DLz [1899] no. 24, col. 936) it may, however, refer to the land of *Lubdu* (pronounce Luvd) mentioned in the cuneiform literature which can be found near the headwaters of the Tigris. אֲרָם is the well-known "Semitic" nation. The following descend from אֲרָם: עוּץ (included in Gen 22:21 among the Nahorites), probably identifiable in the cuneiform literature as *Uṣ* on the lower Orontes (cf. Friedr. Delitzsch, *Paradies*, 259, and in *Ztschr. f. Keilschriftforsch.* 2:87ff.). According to Josephus it is in Trachonitis and Damascus (cf. Meyer, *Israeliten*, 239). The same name also occurs among the Horites in Gen 36:28 and as a name for the land of Edom in Lam 4:21. חֻל and גֶתֶר are unknown. מַשׁ (Sam משׁא, 1 Chron 1:17 מֶשֶׁךְ, LXX Μοσοχ) may be, with Jensen (KB 6/1:576) the mountainous region of *Mâšu* mentioned in the Gilgamesh Epic. According to Jensen (*Gilgamesch-Epos* 1:24, 34ff.) it is the Lebanon-Antilebanon Mountains. **31** It may be that בְּגוּעהם should be read as in vv 5, 32 (Kittel). V **32** is the conclusion of the Table of Nations.

The Table of Nations seems to point to a relatively late period (cf., e.g., the name Gomer), but seems to be, on the other hand, older than the period of P (note the absence of the names פָּרָס which appears as early as Ezek 27:10; 38:5 and עֲרָב in Jer 25:24 for the first time in the OT; cf. Dillmann). P will have taken the list from his exemplar. <154>

According to Jewish tradition, the number of all the nations in the whole Table (P + J) is seventy, according to Christian tradition seventy-two (cf. Poznański, ZAW 14:301ff.; Krauß 24:301ff; Krauß 19:1ff.; 20:38ff.; 26:33ff; cf. also Nestle, ZAW 24:211ff.).

14. Genealogy of Shem in P 11:10-26

The source is P. The scheme of the passage is very similar to the first genealogy of P in chap. 5. In contrast to chap. 5 the lifespans are not given here—but they were not necessary for the chronology (cf. above, pp. 135-36)—nor is the concluding phrase "then he died." Sam contains both and LXX at least the latter. P seems, if the Masoretic text is correct, to indicate through this extreme brevity that he places less value on this genealogy than on the more extensive one in chap. 5. While to this point P has given an overview of all the descendants of Noah up though his children and grandchildren, he now follows a particular line, namely, the main line: those named are always the firstborn as in chap. 5; Israel, which descends from them, is the firstborn among the nations. The coexistence of the two lists which pursue different purposes does not speak against common authorship (contra Eerdmans, 4, 28); Yet two different traditions (cf. below) were utilized. Noteworthily, the Table contains only nine members while one would expect, judging from the usual rule, a fixed number, say, ten here. One may probably conclude from this that the genealogy is not completely preserved here in its original form. Originally—perhaps in P's exemplar—Noah may have been counted as the first in the series or Abraham as the tenth. LXX perceived the difficulty and inserted Canaan (5:12ff.) after Arpachshad and provided him with Shelah's numbers. The numbers of the Hebr text differ here too from Sam and LXX (summary tables in Dillmann and Holzinger). The total of the ages at which those named in the genealogy became fathers for the first time is 390 in Hebr, 1,040 in Sam, 1,270 in LXX (1,170 in LXX A). As in chap. 5 the actual principle of the different calculations is unknown. In Dillmann's judgment, the Hebr is the best of the three texts. The chronological introduction "two years after the Flood" in v 10b is probably valuable to the author because he can introduce a kind of era in this way. How P arrived at this number from 5:32; 7:6; 8;13; 11:10a is difficult to say. P's calculation can <155> have been only rather imprecise. He does not clearly distinguish between ages at first conception and ages at birth and he calculates the year as a fixed date without indicating the months. Consequently it is rather precarious to strike the information in v 10b, which does not fit well with the other numbers, as a gloss. The lifespans continually diminish. The author intends to say, "everything came forth well from God's hand, but became gradually worse because of people" (with Sellin, 13). The names are only partially transparent to us. אַרְפַּכְשַׁד is, according to 10:22, the name of a (not to be clearly identified) people. Cheyne (cf. above regarding Arpachshad in 10:22) wants to read כֶּשֶׂד here, which would conform to the information in 11:31 that Terah emigrated from Ur of the Chaldees. It is peculiar that "Arpachshad" in 10:22 is Shem's third son while here he, like all the others named, is considered the firstborn. This seems to reflect two different traditions not harmonized by P. שלח may be the name of a god (cf. Mez, *Gesch. der Stadt Ḥarrân*, 23): מְתוּשֶׁלַח 5:25ff. ‖ מְתוּשָׁאֵל 4:18 (cf. above p. 135). עֵבֶר is the name of a region (10:21; cf. above pp. 92-93). Regarding שְׂרוּג, see the comments on 10:25. רְעוּ may be the name of a god: רְעוּאֵל (cf. Mez, *harrân*, 23). שְׂרוּג is the region of Sarug near Harran. "Aramaic" tribes on the northern limits of the Syro-Arabian desert descend from נָחוֹר according to 22:20-24. Harran is considered "Nahor's city" in 27:43; 28:10; 29:4. Jensen (ZA 11:300) suspects that the name was originally the name of a god (cf. the Aram. proper name עבדנחר, probably a corruption of עבדנהר). Zimmern compares the divine name Ναχαρ, which appears among many other, partly Semitic and especially Aramaic gods on a Greek curse tablet found in Carthage (published by Molinier in the *Mémoires de la Société Nationale des Antiquaires de France* 58 [1899] and by Wünsch in the *Rhein. Museum N.F.* 55:248ff.): ὁρκίζω σε τὸν θεὸν τὸν παντὸς [βυ]θοῦ κυριεύοντα Ναχαρ (p. 250 l. 32). Aram. *Nahâr* would correspond to Hebr נָחוֹר. The Mesopotamian proper names *Na-ḫa-ra-a-u, Na-ḫa-ra-u, Nah-ḫi-ri-i, Na-ḫi-ri*, and the place name *Til-Naḥiri* may be related (cf. Zimmern, KAT³, 477-78). Meyer (*Israeliten*, 238) thinks of a corruption of נחר, the name of the Euphrates. Nahor is Abraham's grandfather according to v 24 P and a brother according to v 26 P and in J (22:20; 24:15; 29:5). A double tradition has been combined here in P, who therefore distinguishes two different "Nahors." Jensen (ZA 6:70; *Hittiter*, 153) sees in תֶּרַח the divine name *Tarḥ(u)*, Ταρκ(ο) attested in northern Syria. He also thinks (*Gilgamesch-Epos* 1:286; as did Friedr. Delitzsch, *Prolegomena*, 80) of Assyr *Truḥu*, ibex, Aram *tarāḥā*. The names point, to the extent that they are comprehensible, to Mesopotamia. Concerning Abram and Harran, cf. comments on v 27. J must also have possessed a Table similar to P's.

15. Genealogy of Terah in P 11:27-32

Source criticism. Vv 27, 31, 32 can be attributed to P with certainty. P is indicated for v 27 by the superscription and the expression הוֹלִיד (twice). V 27a repeats v 26 P just as 5:32 is repeated in 10:1a. V 32 contains the chronology of P. <156> The date of death concludes the section concerning Terah, just as 9:29 concludes the section concerning Noah in P. P is indicated for v 31 by its expansiveness, its similarity with 12:5, and the expression אֶרֶץ כְּנַעַן which is particularly frequent in P. The names of the cities Haran and, especially, Ur of the Chaldees are, it seems, characteristic of P here. The Abraham legends of J mention no name for Abraham's home city. The name Haran in J occurs only in the Jacob legend (27:43; 28:10; 29:4). In the Abraham legends of J, one strand knows nothing whatsoever of Abraham's home city but speaks only of his homeland (Aram-Naharaim, 24:10). The other strand knows of Abraham's home city, but does not mention it by name, calling it only the "city of Nahor" (24:10). This city of Nahor is, however, judging from interrelationship of the passages, the city from which Abraham emigrated. The distinction of two cities in the Abraham narrative, of Ur of the Chaldees and Haran, cannot be accommodated in any of the strands of J. Accordingly, it is very unlikely that J recounted anything about "Ur of the Chaldees." This name only appears in Genesis (11:28, 31; 15:7). Gen 11:31 belongs to P. Gen 15:7 stands in a J passage, but is probably an addition (cf. below). For these reasons, too, the name in 11:28 will not belong to J either. On the other hand, the book of J must have already traced the family of Abraham to Babylonia. This follows from the Tower legend narrated immediately prior to this passage (Meyer, 234f.). Concerning the historical character of this tradition and concerning "Abraham as a Babylonian," see "General Remarks Concerning the Migration legend" ¶¶2, 3. The entire Terah section in P may have consisted of the vv 27, 31, 32 mentioned. P does not characterize Bethuel and Laban as descendants of Nahor, but as "Arameans" (25:20; 28:2, 5), and therefore need not have had any further comment concerning Nahor here (Dillmann). The inner section, vv 28-30, seems to belong to J. This is indicated by the expressions אֶרֶץ מוֹלֶדֶת v 28 (not in P) and עֲקָרָה v 30 (not in P). The clause in 11:29 resembles that in 4:19 J (cf. also 10:25). In light of the discussion above, בְּאוּר כַּשְׂדִּים (v 28) will be a redactional addition.

27 Eerdmans (28) suspects that the superscription originally read ואלה תולדת אברם, in support of which the analogy of 25:19, where the first words of the Isaac narrative report Abram begetting him, can be adduced. Three sons occur here as for Lamech and Noah. Those begotten in the same year are triplets (Winckler, *Forschungen* 3:405). The same is true of Noah's sons in P (5:32). P speculates that אברם is his actual name and that he was renamed אברהם by God on the occasion of the covenant in chap. 17. J and E seem have been unaware of this distinction, but the redaction incorporated it into the texts of J and E. In the rest of the OT (with the exception of the quotations of Genesis in 1 Chron 1:27; Neh 9:7) he is called only "Abraham." The etymology given by P for אברהם (Gen 17:4) has only the value of an ingenious popular etymology. The two forms of the name are to be understood as dialectical variants. Hommel explains the ה as an orthographic peculiarity, as an expression of the length of the vowel in analogy to Minaean (cf. MVAG [1897] no. 3: 271; cf. also Winckler, *Gesch. Isr* 2, 25-26). The name Abram corresponds to the Babylonian, but probably originally the "Canaanite" or West Semitic *Abirâmu* (Zimmern, KAT³, 482) and probably stands on the same level as אֲחִירָם. אַבְרָם stands for אֲבִירָם just as אַבְנֵר stands for and alongside אֲבִינֵר (Meyer, *Israeliten*, 265). The name is, from the very beginning, a simple personal name and appears as such in the OT (אֲבִירָם Num 16; 1 Kgs 16:34). It is not, then, originally a divine name. The name Abram occurs in the list of the Palestinian localities conquered by Shoshenk I, a contemporary of Rehoboam: *pa hqra 'brm* = אברם חקל "the field of Abram." This may be the field with the tree of Abraham near Hebron (cf. Breasted, *Am. Journ. of Sem. Lang.* 21:22ff.; Speigelberg, *Aegyptol. Randglossen*, 14; Meyer, *Israeliten*, 266). <157> More concerning the origin of the figure of Abraham can be found in the introduction ¶4:10. The hypothesis that הָרָן is merely an alternate form of חָרָן (cf. Wellhausen, *Prolegomena*⁶, 313) is hardly correct. The place name בֵּית הָרָן (Num 32:36; in Moab) may point to a god Haran (Mez, *Gesch. der Stadt Harrân*, 23). לוֹט is considered the ancestor of Moab and Ammon (19:30-38; cf. Deut 2:9, 19; Psa 83:9). The name Lotan occurs among the Horite tribes (36:20, 22, 29). The name Lot may have originated there (Stade, *Gesch. Isr.* 1:119).

31 אוּר כַּשְׂדִּים. The added name "of the Chaldees" makes clear the location of this Ur in contrast to another city named "Ur." There must, then, have been several "Urs." We know of only one Ur, the old southern Babylonian *Uru* (not *Jugheir*, SE of Warka, on the right bank of the Euphrates). This Ur was named for the Chaldeeans when the Chaldeeans advancing from the "Sealand" (who are probably to be distinguished from the ancient Babylonians themselves) took possession of it. Later Jewish tradition also seeks Ur in Babylonia (Judith 5:6; Jubil 11; additional texts in Dillmann). The identification with this Ur in southern Babylonia seems to be contradicted by the fact that the names of Abraham's ancestors, to the extent that they are comprehensible, do not originate in Babylonia, but in Mesopotamia (e.g., Serug, Nahor, perhaps also Terah; cf. Dillmann). The כַּשְׂדִּים for whom Ur is named, could also be the Kasdim named in 22:22 among the Nahorides to be found on the northern limits of the Syro-Arabian desert (cf. also Job 1:17; 2 Kgs 24:2; cf. regarding these כַּשְׂדִּים Winckler, *Altoriental. Forschungen* 2:250-52). It may be objected to the latter location of Ur of the Chaldees, with good reason, however, that we know that the Babylonian Ur as well as Haran were the two seats of the moon cult and that, therefore, these two locales are inherently related. Later Jewish Haggadah interprets אוּר כַּשְׂדִּים as "the fire" of the Chaldeeans and speaks of Abraham's persecution by Nimrod (Beer, *Leben Abrahams*, 1ff.). But the hypothesis that the name arose from this legend is untenable (contra Staerk, *Studien* 1:74). The notion that the name made its way into the text from later learned conjecture is equally unfounded. חָרָן, Assyr *Harrânu*, Syr and Arab *Harrân*, Κάρραι in NW Mesopotamia, was once a significant

metropolis (cf. Mez, *Gesch. der Stadt Ḥarrân* [1892]; Winckler, KAT³, 29-30) שָׂרָי
stands alongside שָׂרָה just as אַבְרָם stands alongside אַבְרָהָם. שָׂרָי is probably
an archaic by-form with the Arabic feminine ending *ay* (pronounced *â*; Meyer, *Israeliten*,
265), also the older name in P's theory, subsequently changed to שָׂרָה by God (17:15).
For more concerning Sarah, see the comments on 11:29. For the difficult וַיֵּצְאוּ אִתָּם one
may read וַיֹּצֵא אֹתָם with Sam, LXX, VetLat, and Vulg. P does not indicate the reason
for Terah's departure just as he will not have motivated Abraham's departure. He is only
interested in the fact, not its motive, the trial of faith (cf. above p. 143). Later times
imagine, as it does for Abraham's departure, an expulsion by the idolatrous Chaldeans
(Judith 5:6-9; cf. also Jubil 12).

32 According to the Masoretic text Terah lived 205 years so that he lived another 60
years after Abraham's departure. In contrast, according to Sam, he lived a total of 145
years, so that Abraham emigrated only after Terah's death (so also Acts 7:4). The figure
in Sam is to be considered the original, as suggested by the wording of vv 31-32 (Budde,
429ff.). The figure was changed because 12:1 says: "Depart from your father's house."
<158>

The Patriarchal Legend

The patriarchal legend is by form the story of a family. The leading basic idea of this
story, as the collector understood it, is that God chose this family in order to raise up the
people Israel from it. Yahweh's providence over Israel's beginnings is the motto of this
story.

Abraham Narratives

The Abraham Legends of J and E
Composition and Character of the Abraham Narratives in J and E

(1) Abraham's genealogy, 11:28-30 Jᵃ. (2) Abraham's and Lot's migration from Haran
to Bethel, 12:1-8 Jᵃ. (3) Abraham's move to Egypt, 12:9-20 Jᵇ. (4) Abraham's and Lot's
parting at Bethel, 13 Jᵃ. (5) Yahweh's covenant with Abraham, 15 JᵇE. (6) Hagar's flight,
16 Jᵇ. (7) Yahweh with Abraham in Hebron, 18:1-16aa Jᵃ. (8) Abraham's intercession for
Sodom, 18:16ab-33 (essentially an extrapolation) Jʳ. (9) Lot's hospitality and deliverance,
Sodom's destruction, 19:1-28 Jᵃ. (10) Lot begets Moab and Ammon, 19:30-38 Jᵃ. (11)
Abraham in Gerar, 20 E (a variant of 12:9-20 Jᵇ). (12) Isaac's birth, 21:1-7 (notice) JᵇE
(in E, the introduction to 21:9-21). (13) Ishmael's rejection and his deliverance at
Beersheba, 21:9-21 E (a variant of 16 Jᵇ). (14) Abraham's contract with Gerar, 21:22-34
EJᵇ (the second Beersheba account in E, continuation of the account of Abraham in Gerar
in E). (15) Isaac's sacrifice, 22:1-19 E. (16) Nahor's sons, a genealogy, 22:20-24 Jʳ
(currently the introduction to 24 J). (17) Rebekah's betrothal, 24 Jᵃ and Jᵇ. (18) Abraham's
sons with Keturah, 25:1-6 Jʳ (genealogy, addendum).

The overview shows that in JE the Abraham narratives were rendered predominantly
following J. J is preserved especially well (as far as we can discern) in the first part of
the narratives (nos. 1-10 to the end of the Lot narrative), with the sole exception of chap.

15 where E was apparently also employed. Only in the second part of the narratives (nos. 11-18) are larger and coherent portions of E incorporated (as in nos. 11-15). E appears quite purely in nos. 11, 13, and 15.

An examination of the composition of the first portion, which stems from J, is particularly interesting. In their current form, a relationship between some individual legends becomes apparent. Nos. 2, 4, 7, 9, and 10 belong together. These passages comprise a legend cycle: Abraham and Lot migrated together from Haran and come to Bethel (no. 2). There, however, they parted: Lot moved to Sodom in the Jordan valley, Abraham remained in Canaan and dwelt in Hebron (no. 4). Now the narrative takes up the Abraham thread first: Abraham receives three men at Hebron who, in gratitude, foretell the birth of a son and promise to return in a year (no. 7). Now the narrator turns to Lot: in Sodom Lot cordially receives the men, but the people of Sodom want to violate them. So, the men save Lot, he finally flees with his daughters to the mountains. Sodom, however, is destroyed (no. 9). Hereby are given—so thinks the legend (cf. the interpretation)—the definitive homes of the fathers: Abraham dwells from now on in Hebron. But Lot had to abandon the Jordan Valley and dwell thereafter in the "mountains," that is, in the mountains of Moab. Now must follow the narrative concerning the births of the ancestors' sons from whom the current nations descend. The story of how Lot begot Moab and Ammon is preserved (no. 10). These narratives do not stem, then, <159> from another source (contra Kautzsch-Socin[2] n. 83; somewhat differently Kautzsch[3], 33) but are absolutely necessary as the conclusion of the Lot legend and as a counterpart for the story of Isaac's birth. The conclusion of the legend cycle is missing: how Isaac was born and how he received his name because his mother "laughed" (18:12), how the men reappeared (18:10), etc. (cf. the interpretation). These legends are held together especially by the common, clearly executed theme—concerning Abraham and Lot, their migrations, and final homes, and concerning their descendants.

This legend cycle, then, answers the question, "How did the peoples who name themselves after Abraham and Lot originate and come to these locales?" Furthermore, the legends point clearly to one another: no. 2, the migration to Bethel, is only provisional and requires no. 4 as its continuation. If no. 4, in contrast, brings Lot to the Jordan Valley, then the continuation is already envisioned that he moved later thence into the mountains where his descendants live now (at the end of no. 9). The first account already prepares explicitly in 13:13 for the second (Sodom's evil). The following passages of the legend-cycle (nos. 7 and 9) begin precisely where the thread left off. The men visit Abraham in Hebron and Lot in Sodom. From no. 7 onward the two threads are structured similarly—the same men visit Abraham and Lot—and woven artfully together—the Sodom-Lot legend (nos. 9 and 10) is inserted into the Abraham narratives (no. 7 and the unpreserved conclusion) so that the two portions of the Abraham narrative are related to the Sodom-Lot legend as "frames" (for the expression, cf. the introduction ¶3:19). In order to compile these complicated blocks into an organic unity, however, the first portion of the Abraham narrative (18:10) refers to the second portion. Furthermore, two small intermezzoes were created to combine firmly the Abraham and Lot legends. For this reason, the men go from Abraham to Lot—a very simple and almost obvious, but for this very reason, highly pleasing way to bind the two legends together. Not yet satisfactory, the threads were woven even more strongly together through the account of how Abraham accompanied the men up to the point when they inspected Sodom and spoke with them about Sodom (18:16aβ, b, 20-22a), indeed of how Abraham returned to the place on the following morning (19:27-28). In this second portion of the legend cycle, the work of the legend collection and the material employed can, therefore, be easily distinguished. The legends (1) of Abraham at Hebron, (2) of Lot at Sodom, and (3) of the birth of Ammon and Moab existed as independent legends. The combining thread will be the collector's addition. The fact that precisely these two accounts of Abraham at Hebron and of Lot at Sodom were attracted to one another is based on their similarity. In both legends divine beings are hosted by patriarchs. At the same time, however, the two accounts stand in beautiful contrast to one another. The wonderful hospitality of Abraham, which God rewards so gloriously, and the shameful behavior of the Sodomites toward the strangers, which God punishes so frightfully.

Finally, the two portions of the Sodom-Lot legend (nos. 9 and 10) are bound together through the appearance of Lot's daughters—major figures in no. 10—already in no. 9. The situation in which the narrator presents them in no. 9 is a variation of the motif of the legend in no. 10: in the legend they conceive by their father. The narrator adds that they are already engaged, but were still virgins and were in danger of rape. If one considers the difficulty such a legend compiler overcame in order to meld these legends, surely originally incompatible with one another in many elements, then one cannot praise the art of this poet of God's grace highly enough. While, then, in the second portion of the legend cycle the original legends and the additions of the collection are clearly distinct, the first portion (nos. 2 and 4) comprises in itself and with the second portion (nos. 7 and 9) such a coherent unit that the individual passages are hardly conceivable as independent narratives. Thus, the point of the Bethel narrative (no. 4) can <160> only be understood against the Sodom narrative (cf. the interpretation). One is hardly inclined to attribute such extensive melding of the legends to an individual artist for the compilers hardly dealt so freely and consciously with their materials in whose truth they believed. The hand of an individual narrator can be found most easily in the departure account (cf. the interpretation, p. 167). Accordingly, the nature of this first portion shows that the whole collection does not trace back to one author, but that it grew gradually in oral tradition, although an individual and extremely significant poet may have come upon it finally. Judging from its interest in Hebron, we may place this collection in Hebron itself. We may also attribute to this collection no. 1, the introduction to the Abraham narrative, and the one source in no. 17 that recounts Abraham's death and simultaneously provides the transition to the Isaac narrative.

Later, another hand inserted other Abraham legends into this legend cycle. These additions include not only no. 3, Abraham's move to Egypt, a passage that Wellhausen (*Composition*[3], 23) already recognized as a later addition, but also no. 5, Yahweh's covenant with Abraham, and no. 6, Hagar's flight. The latter two passages also interrupt the accounts of Abraham's and Lot's common fates and destroy the close relationship between nos. 4 and 7. These two passages, which stem from another, although related, source (and, just like no. 3, need not be younger than the legend-cycle simply because they were inserted in it later), seem to fit in this position. Before Isaac, the real heir, is announced (no. 7), a heritage must first be promised in general (no. 5) and the false heir, Ishmael, must be removed (no. 6). In no. 11, Isaac's birth, 21:6b, 7 do not belong, at any rate, to the legend-cycle. The continuation announced in 18:10, 12 is not preserved. Further, the additions probably also include the account of the contract in Beersheba in J (in no. 14)—according to the main strand, it seems, after immigrating Abraham remained in Hebron the rest of his life—and the second source of the Rebekah narrative (in no. 17).

No. 8, Abraham's intercession, an extrapolation from a later period, is of another origin than these additions which are all independent narratives (cf. the interpretation). Additions from a third hand to be attributed to J only in the broader sense are, furthermore, the two related genealogies (nos. 16 and 18). The information in no. 16 agrees with neither of the two sources of no. 17 (cf. the interpretation).

Therefore, four phases can be discerned: (a) the individual legends; (b) the Lot and Abraham legend-cycle, a first collection, "J^a"; (c) additional legends, "J^b"; and (d) expansions, omissions, further additions, "J^r." Thus we are able to examine the development of "J" here, too.

The passages taken from E currently form no organic unit. Originally the two Gerar legends belonged together: No. 14 is the natural continuation of no. 11. No. 13 (Ishmael's rejection) has been interposed because, like no. 14, it deals with Beersheba. No. 12 introduces no. 13. Two compilers can be distinguished for E at this point.

Notably, the passages from E are all variants of J^b, while J^a has no parallels in E. We may therefore assume that these passages of "J^b" were also adapted from a legend collection, although we can hardly speak of a legend cycle here where the passages stand rather independently of one another. Yet, almost all these passages share the notion of Abraham, not settled in Hebron at one place, but migrating in southern Palestine, in the Negeb and its environs (according to no. 3 from the Negeb to Egypt and back; in no. 6 not very far from Lahai-roi; according to no. 14 in Beersheba; cf. also <161> no. 17). The first portion of the passages (nos. 3, 5, 6, 12) deal with Sarah and the child she will bear. This source J^b is very closely related to E, whereas J^a assumes a more independent position in relation to both.

The (at any rate, not very important) question of how the two sources of the primeval history J^e and J^j may be related to the Abraham J sources J^a and J^b, I dare not answer. J^a is printed in the same font as J^e, J^b in the same font as J^j.

Sievers 2:263ff. offers another analysis of the J passages. Regarding "meter" in Genesis, see introduction ¶3:4.

The basic idea of the Abraham narratives as compiled in the Yahwistic book is Yahweh's grace and wisdom. He chooses the patriarch; leads, protects, and blesses him through life; gives him the desired son who continues the line; brings the son the proper life-partner; and blesses the patriarch himself with a beautiful end (Haller, 38). Abraham's deed, however, is unconditional obedience in which, confidently, he subjects himself to his God. Thus was Israel's original ancestor—so the book wants to say—and thus should you, his son, be, too! The narratives acquire a peculiar tone by means of the fact that Abraham, who would later become the father of such a great people, is now still an individual. It is all the more difficult for him to believe the promises, all the greater are the dangers, all the heavier the trials, until all turns to a good end. So God blesses those who truly trust in him.

16. From Abraham's Genealogy in J^a 11:28-30

For the source analysis, see above pp. 156-57. Only these concluding comments from Abraham's genealogy in J are preserved. J would have prefaced the Abraham narrative with them because they were necessary for understanding the subsequent narratives: we must know about Nahor and Milcah because of chap. 24, because Rebekah descended from them (cf. also 22:20ff.); Sarah's childlessness is the precondition for almost all the following narratives, even for the departure. Abraham's faith in God's promise that he will one day become a great people (12:2) is all the more astonishing since he did not even have one son at the time. The question of whether the passage belongs to J^a or J^b is of lesser significance for such a small passage. Both sources must have employed such introductory comments concerning Abraham. The passage is attributed to J^a above because it does not speak of the home city, but generally of Haran's land of birth (cf. comments on chap. 24).

Regarding the names Abram, Nahor, Haran, and Sarai, see above pp. 156-57. Haran is more precisely identified here as "father of Milcah and Iscah." Milcah and Iscah must, therefore, have been better known figures than Haran. The reference to Abel as "Cain's brother" (4:2) is a similar situation. All these names, now almost lost, will have once been well-known legend figures. Haran's "land of birth" is Aram-Naharaim (cf. above p. 156). One misses a comment concerning the ancestry of Sarah. This information was probably stricken later because of 20:12 (Meyer, *Israeliten*, 238-39). Significantly, the wife of the firstborn, the honored patriarch, is called merely שָׂרָה "princess," <162> and the wife of the second son, the Aramaean, is called מִלְכָּה "queen." This difficulty would disappear if one were to assume the Babylonian origin of the names. In Babylonian, *šarratu* means "queen" and *malkatu* "princess." *Šarratu* is the name of the goddess of Haran, the wife of the moon god Sin, the god of this city. *Malkatu* is the name of Ishtar, the daughter of the moon god, who also belongs to the pantheon of Haran. These may have been the original meanings of the names Sarah and Milcah. If this theory is correct, Abraham, Sarah's husband, would appear here in the place of the god of Haran. The name of Laban, who dwelt in Haran (Hebr. לְבָנָה = "moon" in poetry), could also be a reminiscence of the moon cult of Haran (cf. Jensen, ZA 11:298ff.; Zimmern, KAT^3, 364). In Israel—and this can be said with confidence—this original significance of the figures of Abraham and his associates would have been long forgotten in the current tradition. Nothing in the legends suggests to us the memory of these gods. Indeed, Meyer (*Israeliten*, 238n.4, 245n.3) vigorously disputes the origin of Abraham and his circle as Haranite deities. In rebuttal, he renews the contention that Sarah is the Arab *Šarâ*, the name of a locality, contained in the name of the Nabatean god *Dusares*, "Lord of *Šarâ*" (267ff.; cf. the introduction ¶4:10).

28 עַל־פְּנֵי *coram*: the father must see the death of his son. **29** Regarding וַיִּקַּח singular, see §146f. **30** וּלֵד here and in 2 Sam 6:23 is the Kethib Or; Sam reads יָלַד; וּלֵד is apparently a scribal error.

17. Abraham's Call and Migration to Canaan Jᵃ 12:1-4a . . . 6-8

Source criticism. The passage is J because of יהוה, מוֹלֶדֶת (v 1), קלֵּל (v 3), נִבְרְכוּ (v 3), הָאֲדָמָה (v 3). כֹּל מִשְׁפְּחֹת (v 3). Within "J" the passage belongs to Jᵃ, the legend cycle (see above pp. 158ff.). V 2b parallels v 3b, but such repetition of thought is understandable in such a solemn text. The location of the altar at Shechem and the altar at Bethel follow twice. But they are probably only manuscript variants or additions. V 6b, which prepares the way for the prediction in vv 7aβ, is a gloss like 13:7b. In the current state of the text a clause concerning the fact that Abraham came to Canaan in his migration is missing between vv 4 and 6. It was omitted by Rᴶᴾ who wanted to include P's comment on this subject.

Arrangement. The passage is arranged very lucidly: (1) the command to depart (vv 1-3) and (2) the departure (vv 4, 6-8). In the first part Yahweh promises to show Abraham a land (v 1), in the second he shows it to him (v 7).

1-3 *Abraham's call.* **1** *Yahweh speaks.* The manner of his appearance to Abraham is not recounted. This nonspecific style, radically divergent from the old narratives in J (cf. the counterpart in vv 18-19), is the sign of relatively late style. Concrete elements are missing generally in this legend. Regarding this unspecific narrative style, see above pp. 43-44. Yahweh demands of Abraham the most difficult thing of all: he should depart from homeland, clan, family. There is a similar emphasis on the strong, confrontive authority in the similar passage, 22:2. The ancient lives at home in the secure protection of large and small units (2 Kgs 4:13). Abroad, he is free as a bird. Expulsion is like death (2 Sam 14). Abraham's fatherland in Jᵃ is Aram-Naharaim (24:10). Ur of the Chaldees is not mentioned in J (cf. comments on 11:28). Characteristically, Abraham's home city is not discussed. This is probably no accident. Abraham's ancestors are not envisioned here as city dwellers (cf. comments on chap. 24 and above p. 156). In addition, Abraham should move to a land that God does not even name yet. God does not make it easy for him. God does not give a reason <163> (nor in 22:2). True belief (as understood by Hebrew antiquity) is manifest in not asking for God's reasons. Thus, God lays upon Abraham the most difficult test of faith. The narrator knows, of course, what Yahweh intends by this command: Yahweh wants to create a people Israel for himself, that "lives peculiarly," and lead that people to Canaan. The legend explains here, then, how Israel became an independent people in possession of Canaan. The legend mirrors the relationships between the nations: just as Abraham moves haphazardly into the wide world to obtain a new dwelling place, so the nations, whose situations at home have become unbearable, move far away in search of land. One may think, for example, of the migration of the Cymbians. The migrations of Rebekah and Jacob parallel Abraham's migration from Aram to Canaan. Concerning the possible historical background, see general remarks 2, 3 (pp. 167-68). The Israelite legend views early Israel as an individual. It recounts the motive of the departure not as hunger, oppression, or similar national circumstances, but as a personal motive. This motive, however, is—and this is the special religious majesty of the Israelite legend—a test of faith. This old legend knows nothing of later theological considerations (already known to Judaism; cf. above p. 158) that the departure was necessary in order to preserve Abraham's monotheistic religion from contamination from the increasingly deteriorating nations. Nor does J go on to portray Abraham's non-Israelite descendants as having once again fallen away from Yahweh and the true religion. The example here seems to be not that Abraham worshipped Yahweh but how he did so. In contrast, Josh 24:2 E offers an occasion for the later viewpoint. According to it, Abraham's ancestors worshipped other gods.

2, 3 The added promises, like all the patriarchal blessings, are not arbitrary creations, but concern quite specific current circumstances (cf. above p. 80). The word "blessing" recurs again and again. Yahweh showers Abraham with blessings. **2** The legend stands still in astonishment before the secret that one man produced an entire nation (cf. above p. 148). How can this be? The answer is: this wondrous multiplication is the product of a wonder-working word of God. "Look at Abraham, your father, for I called him as one man, but I blessed him and made him many" (Isa 51:2). This prediction, inherent in the nature of the matter, is the most common promise to the fathers (cf. 13:16; 15:5; 17:2, 6, 16; 18:18; 26:4, 24; 35:11; 46:3, etc.). In the narrator's opinion, it has now been fulfilled (Num 23:10). The subsequent promises also respond to contemporary questions: "Why is Israel such a famed, blessed people?" This promise refers not to Abraham alone, therefore, but simultaneously to his descendants: God still blesses Abraham in Israel. This is most evident in the bestowal of the land (12:7). "You will become a blessing," that is, your name will be used as a blessing, that is, people will say, "May you be blessed like Abraham" (on the wording, cf. Zech 8:13; Prov 10:7; Psa 21:7; on the sense, cf. v 3); or, more generally, "you will become an object of blessing" (cf. Psa 37:26; Isa 19:24). Since the imperative with the copula וֶהְיֵה after the cohortative expresses the expected consequence (§110i), the more concrete interpretation seems better: "so that you become a word of blessing." It may be best to read וְהָיָה with Giesebrecht (*Gottesname*, 15), as reflected in the translation above. Winckler (*Forschungen* 3:406) wants to read והיה אברכה and to understand it as a variant of the following ואברכה (v 3). In the narrator's opinion these promises are also fulfilled in the present: Israel is now a very great, widely famed people. This is also true of the subsequent promises.

3 וּמְקַלֶּלְךָ (with Hebr mss, Sam, LXX, Pesh, Vulg; cf. 27:29; Num 24:9; Ball; Kittel) is to be preferred <164> given the parallels. The word placement in v 3a is chiastic, solemn. God promises to treat all others, individuals and nations, just as they themselves relate to Abraham and Israel: their enemies are Yahweh's enemies; their friends, his friends. He will always take Israel's side. Examples include the way Yahweh smote Pharaoh and Abimelech for Abraham's sake, the way he helped Jacob against Laban, the way he blessed the house of the Egyptian for Joseph's sake, the way he brought a curse upon Moab, whose king wanted to curse Israel, by means of the very seer whom the king had summoned (Num 23–24). Here one hears the innocent expression of the popular attitude which later the prophets resisted so bitterly and yet were very rarely able to overcome themselves. The statement "by you shall all the nations bless themselves" recurs frequently (18:18; 22:18; 26:4; 28:14). "To bless oneself by someone or with someone's name" (niphal or hithpael) means "to mention someone's name when pronouncing a blessing," that is, if one wishes oneself something good, one could not wish for better than the fate of the one concerned (cf. Psa 72:17; Gen 48:20; Jer 4:2, and the contrary, Jer 29:6, 22; Isa 65:15-16; Zech 8:13; Psa 102:9; an example in Ruth 4:11-12). Antiquity expresses its admiration for a person's good fortune in this manner (Stade, *Bibl. Theol.*, 152). Later times understood the statement in a passive sense—"through you shall be blessed"—of the spiritual blessing which will come to all nations through Israel (so the versions, Sir 44:21 [LXX]; Gal 3:8; Acts 3:25; and still a few recent interpreters such as Driver; Procksch, 290n.1). But this passage does not involve matters still to come in the time of the narrator. Instead, they are fulfilled in his time (Judaism, which could not see the patriarchal promises as fulfilled in its miserable present, interprets it differently; cf. Zech 8:13). Furthermore, the notion that Yahwism is to be transmitted to all nations is, as far as we know, of much later origin (Isa 19). Finally, this universal, spiritual viewpoint (v 3b) would stand in stark contrast to the popular particularism (v 3a). Later time imported the contemporary apocalyptic views and speculations into many passages in Genesis, and especially into the promises (e.g., the "Protevangelium"). Later generations place dominion over the world in the place of Canaan, the land promised to Abraham (Rom 4:13). They read into Gen 15 the idea that God showed Abraham the end of the world (4 Ezr 3:14) and the heavenly Jerusalem (ApBar 4:4; cf. further Gal 3:16; Hebr 11:10, 13; etc.). The legend stems, in light of the above, from Israel's heyday. Israel considers itself to be very numerous, blessed and protected by God, very famous and praised among the nations. Fame-loving Israel often overvalued its reputation among the nations.

4a, 6-8 *Abraham's immigration and initial settlement in Canaan.* The tradition of Jacob is very similar. He also moved from Aram via Shechem to Bethel. **4a** The fact that Lot accompanied Abraham is recounted in preparation for the following accounts of Lot (13:5ff; 19). They stem from the same hand, therefore (cf. above, p. 159, and below). J must have already discussed Lot. We learn nothing from J about the nature of his relationship to Abraham because the genealogy of Abraham in J is only preserved for us fragmentarily. **6, 7** Abraham set out into an unknown, remote land (v 4a). He set foot on the soil of Canaan, not <165> knowing that this was the land that God meant (here the lacunae). He came as far as Shechem (v 6a). Now, however, God appears to him a second time and says to him (לו Sam, LXX, Pesh, Vulg, Ball, cf. Kittel), "to your seed I will give this land!" (cf. 7). A wonderful statement! "Abraham was an individual and he received the land as a possession" (Ezek 33:24). This promise of God—so the legend probably thinks—is more than the promise in v 1b for it did not yet discuss the notion that Abraham would one day posses a land. God rewards belief in his word in this way by giving something even more precious than he had promised. Compare the similar motif in the Noah account (7:1ff.) to this beautiful amplification. The promise of the land is an especially frequent element (13:15; 15:18; 26:3; 28:13; 17:8; 35:12). The legends answer the question of why Canaan belonged to Israel.

Shechem ("back," that is, the watershed), an old Canaanite city on the mountains of Ephraim between Ebal and Gerazim, appears often in ancient accounts (Gen 33:18ff.; 34; 35:4; 48:22; Josh 24:25-26, 32) and must, therefore, have had great importance in ancient times. Shechem is already mentioned in the context of a campaign of Sesostris III (Meyer, *Israeliten*, 413). According to the Amarna correspondence (185:10) it was probably the metropolis in central Canaan (Steuernagel, *Isr. Stämme*, 120-21). Under Gideon it was dependent on Israel; Abimelech conquered and destroyed it (Judg 9). It was rebuilt and became a center in Israel (1 Kgs 12:1, 25). Called Flavia Neapolis, it was the center of the "Samaritan" population under the Romans. It is now called *Nâbulus* (cf. Guthes, BW, s.v.). Concerning the cultic sites and the history of Shechem see Meyer, *Israeliten*, 413ff., 542ff. The precise information concerning the place is not an indifferent comment, but a major concern. Abraham receives the promise of the land in the most significant place in the land. Simultaneously, the narrator answers the question why the site (מָקוֹם = holy place as in 22:3f.; 28:11, 19; 2 Kgs 5:11; Jer 7:12, etc.; likewise ὁ τόπος, 3 Macc 1:9) is holy, or, specifically, why an altar stands under the tree at this place. The answer is, "Because Yahweh appeared to Abraham under this tree." Through this, Abraham perceived that Yahweh loves to appear here and, therefore, erected this altar to him. This Abraham altar is, therefore, the one standing there at the time, the altar well known to the legend. It was dedicated "to the Yahweh who appeared to him," thus not to Yahweh outright, but to this particular Yahweh. Regarding this insignificant sounding differentia-tion, see 16:13; 35:1. Interestingly, the legend considers the tree older than Abraham. So it seemed to the legend to be very ancient.

Concerning tree worship in Israel see Benzinger[2], 316; Stade, *Bibl. Theol.*, ¶53; Greßmann, 55. Regarding אֵלוֹן, perhaps a derivative of אֵל, "god," see Stade, *Bibl. Theol.*, 112n.2. The tree is called אֵלוֹן מוֹרֶה. A מוֹרֶה is an אִישׁ אֱלֹהִים, a man of god, who knows how to give oracles. The oracle-giving deity can also be so called (Isa 30:20). Such oracles were often required in ancient Israel in cases of private and public distress (examples: Gen 25:22f.; 1 Sam 9:6ff.; Num 5:11-12; Exod 22:8; Jon 1:7; etc.). There were many ways one could obtain an oracle from God. Therefore, we may interpret the tree's name as "oracle terebinth" and assume that one could elicit oracles from the tree. "Oracles and omina from sacred trees or at tree-cult sites are widespread among all peoples" (W. Robertson Smith, *Rel. der Semiten*, 149; Bötticher, *Baumkultus der Hellenen*, 11; one thinks of the oak of Dodona). The voice of the tree is perceived in the rustling of its branches and interpreted by the oracle or priest (cf. the prophetess Deborah under the palms of Bethel in Judg 4:4-5). We hear again of the אֵלוֹן מוֹרֶה (singular in LXX, Sam) in Deut 11:20. The Hebr has the plural in this passage: in later times, then, the tree propagated. According to Deut 11:30, it stood near the "Gilgal," that is, a "stone circle" (cf. Benzinger[2], 42). Gilgal is now *Ĝulêĝîl* (cf. Buhl, *Palästina*, 202-203). This tree is probably identical with the <166> אֵלוֹן מֻצָּב mentioned in Judg 9:6. According to this passage, a holy stone stood near the tree. מֻצָּב is a variant or an intentional corruption of מַצֵּבָה. The Israelite legend recounts that Joshua erected this one "in Yahweh's sanctuary" (Josh 24:26). According to another tradition, it stemmed from Jacob (Gen 33:20; cf. comments on the passage), who purchased the sacred precincts (33:19) and who is also supposed to have buried idol images beneath the tree (35:4). Joseph's grave was also located there (Josh 24:32). It should be distinguished from the אֵלוֹן מְעוֹנְנִים located at another place (Judg 9:37; Gall, *Kultstätten*, 115). Later periods prohibited sacred trees (Isa 1:29; Deut 12; etc.) as Canaanite sites, which was in fact originally the case. The legends that glorify these trees are, therefore, older than prophecy. On the other hand, they are younger in Israel than Israel's arrival in the land.

8 On the suffix in אׇהֳלֹה, see §91e. Why did Abraham not remain in Shechem, but move further? The legend offers no inner motivation for this. The external ground, however, which the legend was compelled to recount, was the fact that the tradition asso-ciated Abraham's name with several places. Therefore, the patriarch must have moved on from Shechem in order to found other sites, too. The legend conceives of Abraham here as a nomad (Abraham's nomadism is clear in J[b], cf. above p. 161). This is a final remnant of historical memory, for Israel was once such, specifically nomads who moved through the cultivated land. The Kenites moved around in Canaan in the historical period. The new site that he founded is, accordingly, located between the old Canaanite cities of Bethel and Ai, thus south of Shechem. Abraham continues migrating from the North southward. Concerning the location of Ai, see Buhl, *Palästina*, 177; Guthe, BW s.v. Ai. The sacred site of Bethel seems to have been located here between Bethel and Ai, i.e. outside the city of Bethel to the east. This site is a famed pilgrimage sanctuary. Abraham founded, then, during his first sojourn in the later Northern Kingdom, the two greatest sanctuaries of the ancient period. Another, much more specific tradition, attributes the sanctuary of Bethel to Jacob (28:10ff.; 35:1ff. JE). The two variants are mutually exclusive. Clearly, at any rate, Jacob was the first to discover the sanctity of the place. The more specific Jacob tradition seems to be the older. Abraham's name, therefore, may have been associated with Bethel only secondarily. For more concerning Bethel, see the comments on Gen 28:10ff. There "he called on the name of Yahweh." The word is a technical term for the worship of God (cf. the comments on 4:26). Abraham performs the cult himself, as also in other passages (15:9ff.; 21:27, 32; 22:9) and like the other patriarchs (4:3-4; 8:20; 31:54; 35:7). Priests do not yet appear in the patriarchal legends. The narratives maintain that these stories played out at a time before Israel possessed a proper priesthood (cf. Haller, 73-74).

General Remarks Concerning the Departure Legend

1. The account is not very specific and can hardly be called a "story." It is therefore to be considered young in this form. The narrator probably found only the "comments" that Abraham came from Aram-Naharaim and that he founded the altars at Shechem and Bethel. He extended these "comments" into an "account" of sorts which he placed before the Abraham narratives as a motto. So we should evaluate Abraham: he is the faithful, the obedient, and therefore the blessed one.

2. Since the cuneiform reports became known, special emphasis has fallen on the comment about Abraham's homeland and departure. Again and again the attempt has been made to find religiohistorical connections whether one imagines Abraham as dependent upon Babylonian religion, perhaps the lunar religion in Ur of the Chaldees and Harran, or at least on Babylonian culture, or whether one <167> conceives of Abraham's departure as a dissociation from the religion of Babylonia, as a kind of *Heĝira* (cf. Winckler, *Abraham als Babylonier*, 25-26; Baentsch, *Monotheismus*, 50, 58ff.; A. Jeremias, ATAO², 324ff.). Hardly anything concerning lunar religion occurs in these narratives (cf. the introduction ¶4:10) just as Abraham's religion bears no characteristically Babylonian elements whatsoever. The legend itself gives no occasion to regard Abraham as a Babylonian by language and rearing. Conversely, it manifests no protest against things Babylonian. The departure legend does not say even a word suggesting that Abraham has another religion than his relatives. Accordingly, the constructions of modern Assyriologists do not depend on the Abraham legend, itself, but upon late Jewish legends (cf. above, pp. 158, 164).

3. Recently Meyer (*Israeliten*, 235ff.) has called attention to the fact that old passages in E mention the land of the *b^{e}ne qedem*, that is, the great steppe east of Palestine, the original home of the Aramaeans, as the homeland of Israel's patriarchs (cf. esp. 29:1). Meyer is inclined to regard this tradition as historically correct (247). In contrast, J

assumed that the ancestors came to Canaan from the land where the majority of the Aramaean people were at his time, that is, from Aram-Naharaim. Thereby he "simultaneously gained the bridge to Babylonia he required for the total outline of his work" (249). By recounting that the ancestors came to Canaan from Babylonia via Haran he connected the primeval history which ends in Babylonia with the patriarchal legends (234) and, at the same time, gave his people greater distinction through association with the ancient cultural center Babylonia (211). According to this analysis, then, Abraham's origin in Babylonia would not be based on historical tradition at all. Now, the Jacob-Laban legends (which see) seem to have originally taken place, not in Haran, but in the eastern steppe. Yet, on the other hand, the association of names from Abraham's circle with Haranite divine names (cf. above p. 162), although disputed by Meyer, point to Haran. Perhaps, one should assume a dual tradition. The whole question is not yet ripe for discussion.

18. Abraham in Egypt in 12:9-13:4 J[b]

Literary criticism. The passage is J because of יהוה (v 17), כָּבֵד (of plagues, v 10), נָא (vv 11, 13), and מַה־זֹּאת (v 18). The account falls clearly into two portions: (1) the central passage, Abraham's experiences in Egypt (12:10-20; 13:1), and (2) the introduction and the conclusion (12:9; 13:2-4), according to which Abraham moved from Bethel to the Negeb and from the Negeb back to Bethel. The central passage is an old, very colorful legend. The framework, in contrast, is by nature of later origins. It offers (with the exception of 13:2, see below) no positive information whatsoever and has only the purpose of incorporating the account of Abraham in Egypt at this point. The fact that the account did not originally belong in this context in J (Wellhausen, *Composition*[3], 23) is demonstrated by the following. (1) J intends to narrate Abraham's journey from Haran to his home in Hebron. The way stations Shechem and Bethel are well chosen. They lie on the direct route. The journey to Egypt is, therefore, a disruptive excursus. If the original narrator had known it and wished to incorporate it, he would have placed it after the move to Hebron. (2) The following narrative recounts that in Bethel Abraham and Lot separated to the right and the left. Lot moved then to the Jordan valley, to the southeast (left), Abraham to Hebron in the northwest (right). The narrative presupposes, then, that their general route of march went from north to south. Accordingly, they could <168> not have been in Egypt immediately prior to this separation. (3) The core of the legend of Abraham in Egypt does not mention Lot (וְלוֹט עִמּוֹ in 13:1 is an addition), who moved with Abraham according to the preceding and the following J material. Accordingly, the account does not stem from the main strand of J (J[a]), but from a related source (J[b]) and was incorporated here by an RJ. The paragraph is, therefore, neither a later "excrescence" (Wellhausen)—instead it bears (cf. below) all the signs of a very ancient legend—nor is it "dislocated" in J (Dillmann, Holzinger)—nothing indicates that it once stood in another position in J. R[J] inserted the account in this position, before the Bethel legend, because through it he can explain Abraham's wealth presupposed by the Bethel legend. R[J] is responsible for 12:9; 13:3, 4. In contrast, judging from the variants set in the Negeb, 13:1 belongs to the old legend (Holzinger). Gen 13:2 is taken from the introduction to the following Bethel account.

The same legend is recounted once more of Abraham in Gerar (chap. 20 E) and of Isaac in Gerar (chap. 26 J[r]), and must, therefore, have been very popular.

V **9** is the redactor's transition. Regarding the construction, see §113u. The Negeb is the southernmost part of Canaan, south of the Judean mountains, a waterless high plain, mostly pasture land. **10-20** *The legend of Abraham in Egypt.* **10** The occasion of the move to Egypt is a famine. Narratives and legends tell of famines in Canaan, especially as the reason for emigration (26:1; 43:1; 47:4; Ruth 1:1; 2 Sam 21:1; 2 Kgs 4:38; 8:1). Egypt, the rich grain land, the land of pleasure and culture, is the desire of its barbarian neighbors. Thus, the Hyksos came to Egypt. Since their time, Egypt was flooded with Canaanite elements. Especially in times of famine, people sought grain or even refuge in Egypt whose fertility was dependent, not on rain as in Canaan, but solely on the Nile so that it can also have wealth in years when all Canaan groans under poor harvests. One may compare the migration of Jacob's sons to Egypt and the famous image of Benihassan (e.g., Riehm, HW 288/9) where thirty-seven Amu (Canaanites) seek refuge in Egypt (cf. Meyer, ¶¶43, 98, 109; Spiegelberg, *Aufenthalt Israels in Ägypten*, 24ff.; Heyes, *Bibel und Ägypten*, 1ff.). From Canaan's mountains one goes down (יָרַד) to Egypt, in the opposite direction one goes up (עָלָה). The narrators know precisely what they are doing in such matters in contrast to moderns who no longer travel on foot.

11-13 The following conversation takes place at the border, an interesting situation (cf. 31:52; Ruth 1:7ff.). Abraham is in a difficult position. Hunger forces him to go to Egypt. But here he is a גֵּר (alien) without protection and right. He must fear being killed for his beautiful wife. In this dilemma he finds an extremely simple and effective way out. His thought process is as follows. It is dangerous to have a beautiful wife in Egypt. Whoever wants her will have to kill her husband. But one can acquire a beautiful sister from her brother with goods. Then it may still "go well" for her brother. He can obtain abundant gifts for her. Therefore, he pretends that his wife is his sister. The legend glorifies the beauty of the matriarch in this way. The Israelite is convinced that Hebrew women are more beautiful than other women. The narrator presupposes that at the time Sarah was still a young woman whom the Egyptians would desire. According to P, Sarah was at least 65 years old. Simultaneously, the legend praises Sarah as a faithful woman who—as a good wife should—surrenders her own honor in order to protect the life of her lord. "Who may despise the people that has such women?" (Judith 10:19). But the legend particularly praises the cleverness of Abraham who foresaw the danger and who knew the proper means <169> to counter it. The old legends narrate such accounts of the fathers' ingenuity rather frequently (e.g., of the cleverness of Noah, 8:6ff.; of Jacob, who deceived Esau and Laban; of Joseph, 47:13ff.; 46:31ff.). Among the narratives of the later period, one may compare the cunning of David (1 Sam 21:3ff., 13ff.), Michal (1 Sam 19:13ff.), Absalom (2 Sam 13:23ff.), Amnon (2 Sam 13:1ff.), Job (2 Sam 14), etc. "It is not good to allow one man of them to survive, for if one allows them to survive they could deceive the whole world" (Judith 10:19). Ancient Israel regarded the lie much more mildly than we. If no particularly foul intention is associated with it, it was not considered dishonorable. Indeed, a prophet such as Jeremiah (38:24ff.) resorted to lying in times of distress and one can even say the Yahweh himself sends lying spirits (1 Kgs 22:19ff.). The fact that earliest Israel did not think badly of Abraham's lie of necessity is shown in the fact that Yahweh himself assists him in what follows. How should a poor גֵּר in a strange land get by without lies? Yet a later refinement of moral judgment may be detected (cf. the comments on 20:2). Besides, one may remember the demeanor of modern travelers in barbarian lands. The narrator rejoices quietly over the fact that Abraham lied so extraordinarily well and made a virtue of necessity. He recognizes himself with great joy in the clever tricks of his ancestor. It displeases us more than the lie of necessity that Abraham sacrifices his wife's honor. The ancient Israelite, who did not know the chivalrous duty to protect his wife or daughter to the death, perceived it differently (cf. Gen 19:8; Judg 19:25). This—in our view—lack of a sense of honor can be explained in terms of Israel's low estimation of woman. Woman is inferior to man. The life of a man is worth more than the honor of a woman. Finally, we are most displeased that Abraham even accepted gifts for his wife. Even ancient Israel later had greater sensitivity on this point (cf. comments on 20:26 and Abraham's high-mindedness according to Jewish legend, 14:22ff.). The customary exegesis imports the fundamentals of Christian morality into the interpretation of this naive legend.

12 The word order in v 12b is gracefully chiastic. Regarding אֲחֹתִי אַתְּ without conjunction see §157a. "For your sake," "on account of you"—Abraham explains to Sarah that she could do something for him for which he would be grateful to her. These are notions that the good wife cannot resist. **14-16** It takes place now entirely as Abraham had imagined. Therefore the statements are repeated. Indeed Pharaoh himself even sends for her. This element is meant to laud the beauty of the matriarch. Sarah, admired by the Egyptians, is not envisioned as being veiled (so also in 24:15ff. and often; Benzinger[2], 78). The description of Pharaoh's behavior is very true to nature. Oriental kings behaved in this way. The beautiful women of their land whom they could possess enter their harems. The courtiers play the role of procurers. The well-known Egyptian fairy tale of the two brothers recounts a similar story (cf. comments on 39:1ff.; Ebers, *Ägypten und die Bücher Mosis*, 262-63; Heyes, *Bibel und Ägypten*, 18-19). Pharaoh's gifts are intended in lieu of Sarah—a remnant of earlier wife purchase. Yet the word "to buy" in reference to the acquisition of a wife is avoided here as usual. Among the gifts are <170> no horses. This is not because the legend knows that the Egypt of the time did not possess horses (Ebers, 265-66; Heyes, 30-31), for in this case horses would never be mentioned among Pharaoh's property (24:35; 32:15-16; cf. Job 1:3; 42:12). The nomads of the time have no horses (G. Jacob, *Beduinenleben*[2], 73). The legend's limited knowledge of Egypt is clear from the fact that it assumes camels in Egypt (as in Exod 9:3)—which were indeed there in prehistoric times (cf. G. Möller, MDOg [1906] no. 30, 16-17)—but which no longer existed in the historical period until they were reintroduced by the Persians (contra Heyes, 26ff.). This legend then has only hazy ideas about Egypt. It knows neither the name of the Pharaoh nor that of his capital city. The list of slaves in the midst of the animals (also in 24:35; 30:43) would not be objectionable in itself, but would only demonstrate the ancient estimation of slaves as property, wherein Israel does not differ from other ancient peoples. But the words "menservants and maidservants" disrupt the related "asses and she-asses" and are, therefore, probably an addition (Olshausen; Sievers II, 265). The Sam reading עבדים ושפחות והמרים ואתנות (Ball) is probably a secondary improvement. פַּרְעֹה is an Egyptian royal title (= Eg. *per 'o* = "great house," like "the Sublime Porte"; cf., e.g., Steindorff, *Beiträge zur Assyriologie* 1:343). Meyer (*Israeliten*, 10, 20, 24-25) hypothesizes that the word originally characterized E and was inserted only secondarily in "J[1]." This hypothesis, if true, would also suggest that our section does not belong to the main strand of J (Meyer, *Israeliten*, 260n.3).

17-20 So far it has gone well for Abraham, but all the worse for Sarah. She is in the greatest danger of disappearing into Pharaoh's harem. This would be, however, a great disgrace for a "manned" Israelite woman (not for a virgin) who is to belong to no other man. The notion that the promise would thereby be placed in danger of remaining unfulfilled usually found here (so Franz Delitzsch) is not derived from the legend itself, but from the entire context of the Abraham narratives. It was, therefore, probably not the original intention. Yahweh then intervenes and assists Abraham in regaining his wife. The legend does not conceal Pharaoh's reproach of Abraham (vv 18-19). It naively presents Pharaoh's relative innocence (similarly in 26:10, even more distinctly in 20:9ff.). The naive portrayal of foreigners and enemies of the patriarchs, especially of Esau, is one of the patriarchal legends' great distinctions. On the other hand, it recounts that Pharaoh, actually innocent of adultery, is smitten by God and finally draws the shorter straw with Abraham. The variant in 20:7 tells the story in an even more offensive manner for our sensibilities. A popular religious attitude is expressed unabashedly here: Israel's opponents may be in the right or the wrong, it will go poorly for them in any case. For Yahweh is Israel's God. If they protest, the Israelite hearer takes up their words with scorn and derision (cf. 31:43; Haller, 114). Such legends show us how to understand the people's religious attitude so stringently combated by the prophets. Regarding Yahweh as the God who sends pestilence, see Greßmann, 85ff. וְאֶת־בֵּיתוֹ (v 17) is awkward and seems to be imported here from the variant in 20:17 (Kautzsch-Socin[2] n. 55; Kittel). Of course, Pharaoh discerns from the plagues that he has committed a sin. This is the standard conclusion in antiquity. But how did he learn that he committed this sin against Sarah and that Sarah is the wife, not the sister of Abraham? <171> The variants respond to this question: through a divine revelation (20:3ff.), by chance (26:8). Our variant must also have originally answered this question. Good, old narratives do not leave such important questions open. We have identified a lacuna here, therefore. Originally—or so we may surmise—Pharaoh will have asked his wise men and magicians (cf. the very similar cases in 1 Sam 6; Jon 1:7ff.; further, Gen 41:8; Exod 7:11, etc.). Earliest Israel naturally believed that the nations also have their gods and oracles. Later times, however, took offense at this. In the Pentateuch, the "scribes and wise men" of Egypt remained only in passages in which they know nothing (Gen 41:8) or could not compete with Yahweh's mouthpieces (as in the Exodus narrative). In contrast, they have been expurgated here where they proclaim the truth. Or has the lacuna arisen because it was explicitly stated in this passage that Sarah was not Abraham's sister, which would collide then with 20:12? LXX adds ἐναντίον σου (= לְפָנֶיךָ) after אִשְׁתְּךָ in v 19. The precondition for Pharaoh's statement is that the Egyptians also know that adultery is a sin. It is the universal conviction of all peoples who know patriarchal marriage. For the Egyptians, see the witnesses in Heyes, 38-39. "Take her, go," in v 19 is very brief. Pharaoh becomes gruff. Abraham rejoins not a word to Pharaoh's reproaches. The narrator states thereby that Pharaoh is actually in the right. At any rate, it is completely insignificant for the course of the narrative what Abraham may have said. The narrator does not present Abraham's thoughts on his "dismissal." This is the style of the ancient legend (cf. the introduction ¶3:12). The narrator, however, gives away what these thoughts were. That Pharaoh has Abraham taken across the border is by no means disgraceful in the legends' view but rather praises Abraham. Pharaoh learned how dangerous he is. Therefore he takes care that no further injustice occur to him (עָלָיו v 20, to protect him) and brings him with sack and pack across the border (cf. the request of the Gadareneans, Mark 5:17). Concerning safe conduct in the ancient and modern Orient cf. Heyes, 39-40. Pharaoh does not dare to take the gifts from Abraham. With the last words—"and all his belongings"—intentionally placed at the end and repeated in 13:1, the narrator has a grin all over his face.

13:1 The conclusion of the legend, as often, after all danger, reestablishes the original circumstance. Abraham returns to the Negeb. The legend presupposes that he came from there and that his permanent residence was there. Here one would actually expect a comment that the famine (12:10) also passed now. The legend, however, is not concerned with this. It employed the famine as the motive for the journey to Egypt; it has the motive explaining the return (12:19b). It leaves the matter at that. וְלֹוט עִמֹּו is a gloss. Here the redactor remembers Lot whom he had forgotten in the preceding.

2-4 *Transition to the following account.* Abraham's return to Bethel. The author (R^J) knows nothing more to report than what he took from 12:8. Only v 2 differs. It is the beginning of the account of the separation of Abraham and Lot. **2** Concerning the article in בְּמִקְנֶה, etc., see §126m.

General Remarks Concerning the Legend of Abraham in Egypt

The legend does not respond to a definite question, and is, therefore, not etiological <172> in nature, nor does it seem to mirror historical events, although, of course, the colors are borrowed from the situation at the Egyptian-Canaanite border. In a few broader elements, the legend agrees with the Exodus narrative: the move to Egypt because of a famine, distress in Egypt, fortunate deliverance wherein the Egyptians suffer "plagues" and Israel becomes wealthy (cf. Reuss, AT 3:236n.5 and Steuernagel, *Israelitische Stämme* [1901], 100). Yet it should not be assumed that the Abraham legend has the same historical events in view, for similar immigrations and emigrations will have taken place frequently in Egypt, nor that J fashioned the pertinent elements of the Exodus account after our legend (contra Luther in Meyer, *Israeliten*, 122ff.). For more concerning the historical background, see the comments on chap. 20. On the whole, the legend will be of "novelistic" origins in Hebrew tradition and will have been applied secondarily to the patriarchs.

The narrative glorifies the cleverness of the father, the beauty and self-sacrifice of the mother, and, especially, the faithful assistance of Yahweh. The narrator enjoyed recounting the matriarch's encounter with serious danger. But after he had properly frightened his hearers, he recounted joyfully further how Yahweh intervened at the right time and Abraham finally left Egypt, feared as a man of God, together with his wife and rich possessions.

The legend is characterized by the clear arrangement of events, each of which always follows from the preceding (cf. the introduction ¶3:15). At the same time, it is characterized by its brevity. It is not stated, but presumed as self-evident, that Sarah acted according to Abraham's wish and pretended to be his sister. There is no word at all about Sarah's feelings, nor about what Abraham thought upon his dismissal, etc.

Characteristically for the religious spirit of the account, the ancestors' merits and God's faithfulness are praised alongside each other. The two do not interfere with one another at all in the ancient view. The same phenomenon occurs in the Noah account

(8:6ff.) and especially in the Jacob legend. Indicative of the account's moral attitude, Abraham's lie is not perceived as unjust in any way. The old legend is not exactly sensitive in sexual matters either. To be sure it does not explicitly state what took place with Sarah in Pharaoh's harem—it would have seemed altogether too crude to state this in clear language—but we know what usually took place in the harem. In all of this, the narrative is the example of an ancient Hebrew legend. For more, see the comments on chap. 20.

The cheerful, even joking attitude that appears at the end of the legend is now severely dampened by association with the serious accounts, and especially with the pious departure legend.

19. The Separation of Abraham and Lot in 13:2, 5-18 J[a]

Source criticism. The narrative continues the legend of the migration of Abraham and Lot from Haran to Bethel (12:1-8) and, simultaneously, introduces the visit of the three to Abraham (18) and to Lot (19; cf. the "Composition of the Abraham Narratives," p. 159) and stems, therefore, from the Abraham-Lot legend cycle in J[a]. The characteristic indication of J is יהוה (vv 10, 13, 18). The LXX readings ὡς ὁ παράδεισος τοῦ θεοῖ (v 10) and ἐναντίον τοῦ θεοῦ do not alter the identification of the chap. as J assured by the context, especially not since both times the name of God appears in additions to the text. Concerning vv 14-17 see below.

Vv **2, 5, 7a** constitute a unit. As long as Abraham and Lot were not too <173> rich, their shepherds were able to get along easily. But when their wealth grew, there were conflicts between the shepherds over wells and pastures. In that hot land these are very precious things on which the life of human and livestock depends. The Hebrew legend likes to tell that the fathers were this rich (similarly elsewhere of Abraham, chap. 24; Isaac, chap. 26; and Jacob, 32:11). At the same time, relationships between peoples shine through, although in the form of family history. Multiplication of herds (and population) forces nomadic peoples to divide. "If Abraham and Lot had been only individuals with families and servants, there would have been room enough for both" (Reuß). Disputes, as envisioned in v 7a, play a great role in the lives of nomads. The same motif occurs in the story of Gerar (26:20ff; 21:25). Regarding the form אֹהָלִים see §93r. אֹהֶל means the tent together with its occupants just as בַּיִת means the house together with the inhabitants. Vv **3, 4** belong to J[r] (see the previous narrative).

V **6** is superfluous in the context of the narrative. The fact that the lack of room is the cause of the bickering can already be understood from vv 2, 5, 7 and is made entirely clear by vv 8, 9. Good narrative says nothing explicitly (contra Eerdmans, 11). Consequently, v 6 is to be attributed to P (cf. below on the passage). V 6bβ, "so they could not remain together," cannot belong to J either (with Kautzsch[3] against Kautzsch-Socin) since it anticipates v 7. The ancient narrator does not obviate his own point in this manner. V **7b**, like 12:6b, is probably a gloss and stands at the wrong place. One would expect it after v 5. "The Perizites," also mentioned with the Canaanites in 34:30 and Judg 1:4, seem to be the population of פְּרָזוֹת, open villages, in contrast to the citizens of the fortified cities. According to Budde on Judg 1:5 and Meyer (*Israeliten*, 331n.1) it should be pronounced פְּרִזי here, too.

8, 9 *Abraham's suggestion.* The German legend would recount here that the ancestors settled the matter with weapons in a duel. The legends of Genesis, however, portray the fathers for the most part as very unwarlike (cf. the introduction ¶4:2). Abraham was, so the legend recounts, very peace-loving and magnanimous. He finds it odious and unworthy that they, uncle and nephew, bicker about what is mine and yours. It is better to part peacefully. He is prepared to leave the decision entirely to Lot, although it would have been the place of Lot, the younger, to yield to the elder. If Lot then receives the worse portion in the end—the narrator thinks—it is his own fault. אַחִים (v 8) means "brothers" or relatives (14:16, etc.). "Separate yourself" מֵעָלָי "from on me." The expression is refined Hebrew. Now he is "on him," that is, he is a burden to him (cf. 25:6; Exod 10:28; 2 Sam 13:17; 19:10). Regarding the abbreviated conditional clauses in v 9b see §159dd. It may be that הַשְׂמְאִל and הֵימִן should be pointed as infinitive absolutes (Ball).

10, 11aαβ In contrast to Abraham, Lot is self-serving. He thinks nothing of begrudging Abraham the better portion. From Bethel, situated on a hill, both have a good view to the south. From there one can look westward to the brown mountains of Judah, eastward to the green Jordan region. The "Jordan region" is, in context, the Jordan valley to the east and south of Bethel, that is, "the valley from Jericho to Zoar" (Deut 34:3). At the time, this valley was—in the narrator's view—much more <174> majestic than at present. For then—this is clearly the narrator's presumption—there was not yet the Dead Sea that now covers the greater portion of the "Jordan region." The legend imagines the state of the Jordan region at the time to be as majestic as the landscapes near Jericho (cf. Buhl, *Palästina*, 39) and En-gedi, in its opinion the final remnants of the former Jordan region, were in its time. Thus Lot chooses the wonderful Jordan region. Abraham must be satisfied with the inferior land. Zoar is, from the perspective of Bethel, the farthest point of the Jordan region (in the South; cf. Buhl, *Palästina*, 271). בֹּאֲכָה צֹעַר (v 10) is, then, to be taken with כֻּלָּהּ. The many interposed modifiers are very remarkable. Furthermore, the reference to the subsequent destruction of Sodom and Gomorra, measured by the beautiful, old legend style, is artistically objectionable. At this point in the narrative, Lot does not yet know this future fate of the region and the hearer should not know it yet either (cf. Holzinger and below). This reference to Sodom's destruction was originally all the more unnecessary since this account was actually to follow shortly. It seems to have been necessary in later times, however, when the Bethel legend was separated from the Sodom account by the interposed material. Similarly, the combination of כְּאֶרֶץ מִצְרַיִם and כְּגַן־יהוה is unusual. One will probably have to consider the weaker כְּאֶרֶץ מִצְרַיִם as the older. The original author may, then, have written כִּי כֻלָּהּ מַשְׁקֶה כְּאֶרֶץ מִצְרַיִם בֹּאֲכָה צֹעַר. Others strike כְּאֶרֶץ מִצְרַיִם (so recently Kautzsch[3], 24; Pesh reads צֹעַן, cf. König, *Fünf neue arabische Landschafts-namen*, 29). For כֻלָּהּ Sam has כֻלּוֹ. The Canaanites considered Egypt the ideal of a richly watered, majestic landscape.

11aγ, 12bβ, 13, 18 *Parting and Final station of Abraham and Lot.* **11** לוֹט[2] is an explicitum. מִקֶּדֶם does not mean "to the east." It should either be read קֵדְמָה (with Stade, ZAW 14:276n.2) or translated "he moved around in the East" (as perhaps also in 11:2; נסע as in Jer 31:24). V **13** prepares for the subsequent Sodom narrative. This portrayal of Sodom's sin as well known to Yahweh from the outset differs somewhat from the one in chap. 19, according to which the deity first learns of it personally in Sodom itself. The old Sodom legend has a lower view of God than the one that appears in the legend cycle.

18 Hebron was originally the capital city of the Kenite tribe Caleb allied with Judah (Josh 14:14) and later of David as long as he was king of Judah only (2 Sam 2:1ff.; cf. "Hebron," in BW, ed. Guthe). J does not mention the city itself. The altar erected by Abraham according to the legend is, of course, "the altar at Hebron," standing there later, in the narrator's time. This is apparently the famed sanctuary at Hebron where Absalom's rebellion broke out (2 Sam 15:7ff.). Concerning the location of Mamre, see Buhl, *Palästina*, 160; "Mamre," in BW, ed. Guthe; and see the comments on chap. 23. Josephus (*Ant.* I/10.4; ἡ Ὠγύνη καλουμένη δρῦς; cf. also *Bell. jud.* IV/9.7) also mentions the tree at Hebron. It was still venerated in Eusebius' time (*Onom.*, 210) by the pagans along with "the angels hosted there by Abraham" until Constantine build a basilica on the site (Eusebius, *Vita Const.* III:52; cf. "Mamre," in BW, ed. Guthe; Meyer, *Israeliten*, 262-63). Chap. 18 is the direct continuation of v 18.

Vv 14-17 are an addition according to Wellhausen (*Composition*[3], 23-24). The words disrupt the context which treats the movements of Lot and Abraham together. One <175> can discern the later period of the words by the fact that a divine speech is communicated without a description of Yahweh's epiphany but only a statement of the fact (cf. above pp. 43-44). Later generations are no longer concerned with the narrative, but the ideas. The purpose of the insertion is better to motivate the possession of Canaan. According to the old account Canaan belongs to Abraham because Lot freely relinquished it. The pious glossator could not consider this profane motivation sufficient and therefore added that later Yahweh explicitly promised the land to Abraham. Similar additions are 26:3; 50:24; 15:7-8. The special emphasis on this idea that God himself gave Canaan to Abraham can be accounted for in a time when Israel's possession of the land began to be doubtful (cf. comments on chap. 15). Consequently, this idea plays a great role in later literature (cf. Staerk, *Studien* 1:38ff.).

V 15 repeats 12:7. 16 The image of the dust of the earth is comparable to "the sand of the sea" (22:17; 32:13) or "the stars in heaven" (15:5; 22:17, etc.). Regarding אֲשֶׁר (v 16) "so that," see §166b. Sievers (2:267) wants to improve the somewhat clumsy clause through the insertion of לְאִימֶנָה after אֲשֶׁר. It may be easier to strike אֶת־עֲפַר הָאָרֶץ as an inserted explicitum. 17 קוּם הִתְהַלֵּךְ is asyndetic (§120g). Abraham is to take possession of the land by wandering around it. This element does not occur in the old narrative. Instead it is a later theory. According to J[a] Abraham did not move haphazardly throughout Palestine, but on a direct path from his homeland via Shechem and Bethel to Hebron (Wellhausen, *Composition*[3], 24).

General Remarks Concerning the Legend
of the Separation of Abraham and Lot at Bethel

This legend cannot be understood without the continuation in chaps. 18 and 19, which must have originally followed immediately and which are already foreshadowed by 13:13. Lot, as the story goes to this point, has chosen the beautiful Jordan region. But now chap. 19 adds that Yahweh later destroyed "the whole Jordan region" (19:25). Thus, Lot's majestic land became water. He could not return to Canaan. He had forfeited it. Therefore he moved to the "mountains." His self-service has served him poorly enough. This is the point of the passage which has been largely overshadowed in its present form by the interposition of other legends. Accordingly, the original attitude of the legend is not just joy at the reliable, honorable ancestor—the major point of the whole account for later generations—but, also a little malicious glee over greedy Lot. The legend assumes that the mountains of Canaan are better than those of Moab. The legend clearly bears the local flavor of Hebron. Abraham continues to dwell in Hebron. His descendants reside there. Lot's sons, Ammon and Moab, live in the "East," whereas from the standpoint of northern Israel, they dwell in the South.

This account differs characteristically from old legends in that it does not stand alone but presupposes the Sodom narrative to such an extent that it cannot even be imagined without it. Even the point of the Lot legend, that his self-service serves him poorly, can only be understood in relation to the Sodom account. The narrative is, consequently, to be considered a later composition, a graft on an older branch (cf. the "Composition of the Abraham Narratives," pp. 160-61). On the other hand, the narrative is not to be set in the latest period of the tradition, either. Instead, one should note that, somewhat like 29:1-14, it was originally of purely profane nature. <176> It is also difficult to accept the notion that it is based on a historical event, at least not one that could refer to Israel, Ammon, and Moab. When Israel took possession of Canaan, it did not come from the North with Ammon and Moab, but after they had long occupied their residences, it conquered the land beginning with Jericho. Accordingly, the whole account seems to be of "novelistic" origin.

20. God's Oath to Abraham 15 J^bE

Source analysis. The disunity of the passage can be perceived from many traces. According to vv 12aα, 17, God appears in the evening just as the sun sets. Contrariwise, it is already night in v 5 and all the stars are in the heavens. Abraham's doubtful question (v 8) strikes one as odd after Abraham's faith has just been praised so highly (v 6). It is equally remarkable that Yahweh ceremoniously mentions his name once more in v 7 although he already presented himself to Abraham in v 2. God's speech in vv 13-16 comes too soon, for God himself first appears in v 17. The extensive oracle in vv 13-16 cannot well precede the very brief v 18b. The details of the source analysis are very difficult and therefore frequently treated. Bibliography can be found in Dillmann and Holzinger (cf. further Procksch, 7-8; Eerdmans, 36ff.; Kautzsch³, 26-27).

In the first section, vv 1-6, the following passages should apparently be attributed to J: v 1a (except for בַּמַּחֲזֶה: at this point in the narrative Abraham does not yet "see" anything, but only hears God's words; he sees Yahweh first in v 17), 1bγ (your reward is very great), 2a, 3b, 4, 6. The verses yield a tightly cohesive unit: the lament in v 2a ("give") responds to the promise in 1bγ ("reward"). Similarly, v 4 responds to v 3b (יָרַשׁ). The divine speech in v 4 is introduced in words similar to the one in v 1. יהוה (vv 1, 2, 4, 6) demonstrates that this context stems from J. (The analysis to this point essentially follows Budde, *Urgeschichte*, 416n.1).

In the second section, vv 9, 10, 12aα, b, 17, 18a, bα belong to J. These clauses also stand in a good relationship to the preceding and with one another. Yahweh has now seen Abraham's faith (v 6). So he decides to reward him with an additional, more glorious promise and to intensify this promise in a solemn covenant ceremony. "When you found his heart to be true (נֶאֱמָן cf. הֶאֱמִן Gen 15:6) before you, you made the covenant

(כָּרַת בְּרִית as in Gen 15:18) with him" according to the report on Gen 15 in Neh 9:8. The content of the two promises also agree. As the reward for Abraham's faith, he will obtain a biological heir. Now Yahweh promises him to give the land of Canaan to these descendants. Accordingly, vv 9-10 connect very well to v 6 while vv 12aα, b introduce v 17 (as 19:15 introduces 19:23). יהוה in v 18 demonstrates that this passage also stems from J. Within J this account does not belong to the legend cycle J^a where Abraham is promised the possession of the land in 12:7 and the birth of a son in chap. 18. Attempts (Wellhausen, *Composition*^{3}, 22 etc.) to incorporate this account somewhere in the legend cycle fail, therefore. Such rearrangements of whole passages in otherwise coherent sources are very rarely plausible in Genesis given the manner in which our sources came together.

Into this J account the following sections from E have been inserted: בַּמַּחֲזֶה (divine revelations in dream or vision characterize E, 21:22; 22:1; 46:2; the expression does not occur elsewhere in E), vv 1bα, β ("I will shield you" parallels "I will reward you" in v 1bγ J), v 3a (∥ v 2a), v 5 (according to which it is night, whereas in J the sun first sets in v 17; the promise in v 5 is the response to the complaint in v 3a; cf. the expression זֶרַע). In the second part v 11 belongs to vv 13-16. The sign in v 11 which first announces disaster, then well-being, is illustrated in vv 13-16 (cf. the interpretation). Such a sacrificial sign, however, bears such an ancient <177> character that the verse can hardly be traced to a redactor. On the other hand the oracle in vv 13-16 cannot appear in J in this position (before Yahweh's appearance in v 17). Some have sought to help by placing vv 13-16 after v 18 (so Holzinger) although the brief statement in v 18bα is much more impressive without the explication in vv 13-16. It seems more obvious to derive the verses from E. Abraham's sleep (v 12aβ) already suggests that E possessed a similar account. Abraham's sleep does not fit the scene in vv 17-18 where God actually appears and Abraham also actually sees him, not in a dream. At the same time, such a sleep in connection with the reception of revelation characterizes E. Furthermore, the verses in question employ the term הָאֱמֹרִי (v 16) which E usually applies to the pre-Israelite population of Canaan.

The redactor based this chap. on J, and, it seems, adopted it completely. Contrariwise, he was able only to employ fragments of E. The E account seems to have been similar to J's: as in J, first a divine promise, then Abraham's complaint and God's comfort, then a sacrifice offered by Abraham (v 11) and an additional divine promise.

Later these passages were glossed heavily. Glosses certainly include the descriptions of the land in vv 19-21 (Budde, 344ff.) and probably also v 18bβ, γ which do not correspond to one another very well. חֲשֵׁכָה גְדֹלָה (v 12) is a displaced explanation of the unusual expression עֲלָטָה (v 17; Chauvin, *Muséon* 5:103ff.). Further additions are אַרְבַּע מֵאוֹת שָׁנָה (v 13), which corresponds to the chronology of P (Exod 12:40) but contradicts v 16, then בִּרְכֻשׁ גָדוֹל (v 14), a P expression (e.g., 12:5), and v 15, which interrupts vv 14 and 16 is probably a gloss (cf. בְּשֵׂיבָה טוֹבָה, a P expression, e.g., 25:8 [Couard, ZAW 13:156-57]). Finally, vv 7 and 8 are also probably an addition. Because of their content, which contradicts v 6, they apparently cannot be from J (the presumption that Abraham's homeland was "Ur of the Chaldees" in v 7 disagrees with J; cf. p. 156 and לָרֶשֶׁת with the land as the object is deuteronomistic; Holzinger, *Hexateuch*, 287). But neither can they derive from E because of the name יהוה. A later hand, who overlooked the inner relationship between vv 6 and 9-10, inserted vv 7 and 8 in order to create a relationship external to the passage. The source analysis offered here, however, like many of the sort in similarly complicated cases, is to be regarded as only an attempt to master the difficulties of the chapter. J passages may be identified rather securely since the J account is coherent and complete. In contrast, the assignment of the remaining text to E and R is questionable.

Eerdmans (36ff.) suggests an apparently simpler solution: he considers vv 1, 2, 4-6 and 7-12, 17-18 to be two passages of different origins which were subsequently glossed. The following grounds speak against this analysis. Vv 1, 2, 4-6, a very brief passage containing only one speech, will have hardly ever been an independent account. It is unlikely that v 3 is a secondary explanation of v 2 since the verse contains the key word ירשׁ which recurs in v 4. Because of אוּר כַּשְׂדִּים, v 7 hardly stems from J. Vv 13-16 belong with v 11. Procksch (7-8) attributes vv 1bβ, 2, 5, 6, 12b, 13, 14a, 15a, 16 to E. But יהוה in vv 2 and 6 speak against this. The appeal to the ὁ θεός of the LXX in v 6 is unfounded for in precisely such fine distinctions the generally unreliable LXX does not faithfully transmit the text. Furthermore, the "deep sleep" in v 12 does not suit J (cf. above), although the "dismay" does, etc. The source analysis of Sievers (2:274ff.) is a step backward in relation to what has already been recognized. He divides the whole unit after the excision of a few additions as follows: I. vv 1aβ, b, 3-6, 18a, bα; II. vv 2, 8-17. Sievers separates the related vv 12 and 17. Yahweh's speech (vv 13-16) before his appearance (v 17) is impossible. The covenant ceremony (v 17) without the saying (v 18) misses the point, etc. <178>

I **1-7** *The promise of the biological heir J^bE.* **1** אַחַר הַדְּבָרִים הָאֵלֶּה is common in E, but it also occurs in J (22:20; 39:7). "The word of Yahweh comes to someone" is a technical term for prophetic revelation. The narrator, then, imagines Abraham as a נָבִיא as does E in 20:7. The concept is singular within J (only again in v 4) and points, at any rate, to a relatively late period in which man of God and prophet were identical (for more cf. on 20:7). According to v 5 "in a vision" refers to a night vision. According to ancient belief, the deity appears in a dream, semi-sleep, or ecstasy (cf. the descriptions in Job 4:12-16 and Num 24:3-4). Concerning dream revelation see the comments on 20:3. This manner of revelation is younger in the patriarchal legends than the naive view, recounted in Gen 2–3 and 18–19, that the deity appears corporeally on earth. "Do not fear, I, myself, will shield you." This statement from E presupposes a definite situation in which he needed a "shield" and could fear. This situation, which E must have described in the preceding material, will have been the departure from home. In a strange land, unprotected, Abraham "feared." The metaphor, "God is a shield for his righteous," is common in the songs (Psa 3:4; 18:3, 31; Deut 33:29, etc.) and will have originated in religious lyrics. Winckler (*Forschungen* 3:411) thinks of מָגֵן and translates, "I will give you your reward," which requires the reading מְמַגֵּן. But מָגֵן is not construed with the dative of the person. The parallel in J^b, "your reward is great" (according to which Abraham must have just done something special meriting reward), seems also to presuppose that Abraham's departure had been narrated just prior to this passage. Therefore J^b seems to have recounted the departure somewhat differently than J^a. In J^a God gives the grandest promises already with the first command to emigrate (12:1-3). In J^b he adds them only subsequently when Abraham had already obeyed. Correspondingly, one may also assume that the sections of J^b in chap. 15 originally stood before 12:10ff. in J^b. Sam reads the simplified אַרְבֶּה for הַרְבֵּה (§131q).

2a J breathes a very ancient spirit. Whoever departs (that is, dies, 25:32) without children bears such heavy sorrow that there can be no joy for him. What could God give him? The precondition of this and other Abraham legends (chaps. 16, 18) is that Abraham had no son for many years. The legends in chaps. 15, 16, and 18 relate to one another in the use of this motif. Abraham does not articulate a request for children. Reverence hinders him from requesting explicitly (cf. 2 Kgs 2:19; 4:1, 28, 40; 6:5, etc.). He can only complain. In addition, he considers it no longer impossible to have children. The presumption is that he is already old and already long married. With this complaint, however, he revealed his heart's wish which God now fulfills for him. וְאָנֹכִי "But I" indicates, as it often does, the contrary (cf. 18:13). V **2b** reads literally "and the son . . . of my house is Damascus Eliezer." מֶשֶׁק is a ἅπαξ λεγόμενον; its meaning is unknown. The clause is nonsensical. The versions or modern improvements of the text offer no help. Not even the approximate sense can be indicated. The consonants אליעזר are customarily understood as the name of Abraham's chief servant. Since, however, this name occurs only here, not even in chap. 24, this interpretation is questionable to an extreme degree. Therefore, nothing can be said concerning the source of this phrase. It is impermissible to strike the words הוּא הַמֶּשֶׁק as a gloss (so recently Kautzsch³). One may explain as a gloss only that which one understands.

3 The childless master will have as his heir the slave born in his house, not bought (14:14). But this is considered a great misfortune. The narrative does not think of Lot as an heir. It may be that it does not even know him <179> (Haller, 143). The slave has no father. He is not called "son of so and so," but "son of the house of so and so."

5 The stars in heaven are a beautiful and proud metaphor for Israel's infinite population. אִם־תּוּכַל is an indirect question (§150i). **6** וְהֶאֱמִן means "he believed repeatedly" (§112g, dd, ss). Abraham's faith must have already been discussed in the preceding (cf. comments on v 1). Abraham showed his faith the first time when he left his homeland on God's command. Now he has proven his faith. Ball's objections to this reading are, therefore, unjustified. The passage has received paramount significance because one of the greater minds has taken it up and read into it his deepest experience. Originally it did not have such great weight. הֶאֱמִין means "to trust the word, the promise of God." צְדָקָה is the quality of the one who is צַדִּיק (cf. comments on 7:1), that is, righteousness. In a religious context, then, it means the behavior of a good, pious, faithful servant of God. The clause in v 6 means, then, that this act of faith against all probability was in God's eyes a clear indication that Abraham is righteous. Therefore God considered him his faithful and pious servant. Paul (Rom 4) took the words πιστεύειν and δικαιοσύνη in the deepest sense and understood them as the opposite of all ἔργα, an interpretation far removed from Genesis. At any rate, the passage is also prominent in the OT. In all his unpretentiousness, this narrator knows the point of religion. And the importance of this knowledge to him can be seen in the fact that he shaped a narrative with the purpose of pronouncing the truth that God wants nothing more than a heart that trusts him. וַיַּחְשְׁבֶהָ is a feminine in the neuter sense (§122q).

II. **7-21** *The covenant ceremony JER.* **9, 10, 12aα, b, 17, 18a, bα** J. Concerning the relationship between parts I and II in J, see above. The fact that this extremely impressive sign of divine grace is only given now, when Abraham's faith has been proven, we may well understand as a religious profundity. The sign that strengthens faith is not given to the unbeliever or the doubter, but to the believer. Whoever believes most faithfully will also see the most. Judg 6:36ff. and 22 Kgs 20:8ff are not nearly so deep. This interpretation is on the (admittedly not entirely certain) condition that vv 7 and 8 are a later addition. Two elements coincide in such covenant ceremonies as in many other ceremonies: (1) the sacred act described precisely here and (2) the sacred, liturgical words which express the sense and meaning of the act, here in the form of an oath. The oath is a necessary component of the covenant ceremony. The act varies. Sometimes it is a common sacrificial meal (31:54) at a sacred site (cf. also Exod 24:11) including sprinkling with the same sacrificial blood (Exod 24:8), or sometimes a simple meal (Gen 26:30; 31:46; cf. 2 Sam 3:20), eating the other's bread (Josh 9:14) or salt (Num 18:19). Kraetzschmar's view (*Bundesvorstellung*, 43ff.) differs somewhat. According to him the meal did not actually belong to the בְּרִית and the בְּרִית (= covenant ceremony) always consisted of the rite described in Gen 15 and Jer 34. This cannot be demonstrated, however. The nature of the <180> covenant ceremony presupposed here in vv 9, 10 is, indeed, most solemn and terrible. Animals are slaughtered and cut into pieces. The two parties pass through the bloody lane between the pieces while saying the curse formula, "May the deity chop the covenant-breaker into pieces like these animals!" (Jer 34:17-20). The idea of the rite is that the oath taker who enters into the animal in this fashion thereby identifies with it and in the event of the breach of covenant swears upon himself the fate of the animal (Meyer, *Israeliten*, 560 and n. 1). Similar types of covenant ceremonies also occur among the Babylonians (cf. the extensive description of a covenant ceremony involving Ashur-nirari of Assyria and the northern Syrian prince Mati'ilu, MVAG [1898], 228ff.; Peiser), the Greeks (ὅρκον διδόναι ἐπὶ τομίων, cf. Meyer, *Israeliten*, 56; Usener, ARW 7:301), etc. This practice is the source of the idioms בּוֹא בַבְּרִית, עָבַר בַּבְּרִית, עָמַד בַּבְּרִית, ὅρκια τέμνειν, *foedus ferire*, and perhaps also כָּרַת בְּרִית (cf. Kraetzschmar, 44ff.). The detailed description of this rite here is, of course, not the creation of the narrator. Instead, he presumes the covenant sacrifice of his time here. Jer 34, where a calf is divided, knows it in a somewhat different form. The details of the sacrifice described here (why must it be precisely these animals? etc.), as so often in such cases, evade our interpretation. Such ceremonies usually stem from the most ancient prehistorical periods whose ideas are no longer known and no longer comprehensible to later historical periods. Israel, like every historical people, must have practiced many such incomprehensible ceremonies. This description of the covenant sacrifice, which surely gives only a portion and presumes another portion to be known (Haller, 67), also suggests that the opinion that the ancient Hebrew cult was extremely simple and that the earliest period placed little value on ritual is incorrect. גּוֹזָל is, judging from the context, a kind of dove. It seems that an instruction concerning what Abraham should do with these animals has fallen out after v 9.

10 אִישׁ־בִּתְרוֹ means "one of each, one piece of him" (§139b, c). Vv **12aα, b, 17** describe precisely the individual phases of the divine epiphany. The narrator has summoned all his art in order to paint the terrible impression of the theophany. Yahweh's presence is announced by mighty horrors which fall upon Abraham (cf. especially Job 4:14, as well as prophetic statements such as Isa 21:3, 4). This view characterizes the ancient god concept. The deity is terrible might. Whomever he nears is horrified. Yahweh himself comes only after sunset. As long as the sun is in heaven, he does not allow himself to be seen (a very ancient view, cf. comments on 19:15ff.). Immediately before he comes, there is (wonderful, gruesome) darkness (v 17). When he appears, he looks "like a smoking pot (figures of ovens in Benzinger², 65) and a fiery torch." Such a description of God's appearance is very naive and surely very ancient. Yet one should note how carefully the narrator speaks. He does not say directly that this epiphany is Yahweh, but merely gives that impression. Even Abraham did not see Yahweh's form itself (cf. Job 4:16). This manner of divine revelation is unique in Genesis.

In contrast, the characteristic Israelite narratives of Yahweh's appearance in the burning thorn bush (Exod 3:2), in the burning and smoking Sinai (Exod 19:9ff., 20, 18; Deut 4:11), and especially in the pillars of smoke and fire (Exod 13:21) offer analogies. The author seems to have taken these Moses legends as a pattern. Here, then, a concept foreign to the patriarchal legends has found its way into them. This manner of theophany, according to which <181> Yahweh is a fire demon "who allows his majesty to be seen in dark night," can be explained originally from the fact that, in Israel's earliest belief, Yahweh was the god of the Sinai volcano (cf. DLZ [1903], cols 3058-59; Meyer, *Israeliten*, 69-70). Not Abraham, only Yahweh himself passes between the pieces. Yahweh's "covenant" is his free decision, not a contract between two parties (Staerk, *Studien*, 36). Regarding the construction וַיְהִי לָבוֹא (v 12) "was about to set," see §114i. On the construction וַיְהִי . . . בָּאָה (v 17) see §111g. The masculine form הָיָה (v 17) after the feminine יָלְטָה is remarkable.

18 Yahweh's words are very brief in relation to the extensive preparation. But, for this very reason they make an extraordinary impression. The perfect נָתַתִּי, "hereby I give," is contract style (cf. 1:29; 9:3; 20:16; etc.). One should note the refinement that the words Yahweh spoke on this occasion are not actually (with ו cons. with impf.) recounted, but only their essential content is briefly communicated (therefore the perf. כָּרַת). The narrator is hesitant to say more. This reluctance is very understandable, for the words spoken in covenant ceremonies usually take the form of the self-deprecation, which one cannot recount of Yahweh.

11, 12aβ, 13a, 14a, 16 *The parallel account of E.* V **11** contains a sacrificial sign. It was the custom in Israel, also, to pay attention to all manner of signs in the sacred hour of the sacrifice when the deity is near (cf. comments on 4:5). The fact that the eagles (regarding the species, cf. §126t) tried to land on the sacrificial animals and seize the sacrifice signified gruesome, threatening misfortune in the narrator's opinion (parallels are the bird in the dream of the Egyptian baker which also signified misfortune, 40:17ff., and, especially, the harpies who steal the sacrifice, Virgil, *Aen.* 3:255ff.). The fact that Abraham shoos them away, however, means that the misfortune will transform into good fortune (following Dillmann). E further illustrates both in the following. **12aβ** Regarding תַּרְדֵּמָה "sleep of god" (LXX translates well ἔκστασις), see comments on 2:21 (further on v 1). **13a, 14a** Now, the future of his seed is revealed to Abraham in the style of prophecy, that is, in solemn (יָדֹעַ תֵּדַע) and mysterious (consequently the Egyptians are not mentioned by name) words. The prediction of Egyptian servitude does not occur elsewhere in the Abraham narratives. The later period, which knew greater goods than the possession of the land of Canaan, read into this passage that God then showed Abraham all eons, past and future, the heavenly Jerusalem and the end of the ages (ApBar 4:4; 4 Ezr 3:14; ApAbraham 9ff. [in StGThK I/1:20ff., where there is also an extensive haggadah on Gen 15]). Regarding בְּאֶרֶץ לֹא לָהֶם (v 13) see §155e. **14a** "With וְגַם begins the divine talio" (Franz Delitzsch). **16** The comment "the fourth generation" presupposes a genealogy, probably of Moses, according to which he depicts the fourth generation from Levi. Such a genealogy occurs in Exod 6:16ff.: Levi, Kehath, Amram, Moses. The statement in v 16b presupposes that God does not punish every sin immediately, but his manner is to wait until sin has fruitfully accumulated, in order then to destroy <182> the sinner suddenly and horribly. This allusion to the accursed destiny hanging over the Amorites also makes a terrible, sinister impression.

Redactional passages. **15a** For the diction, compare 25:8 P. **18bβ** The Euphrates was considered elsewhere, as well, as the (ideal) northern border of Israel (Deut 1:7; 11:24; 1 Kgs 5:1 etc.). In reality the territory Israel settled and controlled was much more modest. The Hebrew national sentiment, especially in later times, loves grand hyperboles in such matters which elicit our objections. The "stream" of Egypt is surely the Nile. This, too, is a grand hyperbole. Usually the נַחַל מִצְרַיִם, Assyr. *naḥal* (*mât Muṣri*, the "brook of Egypt" or the *Wâdi el 'Arîš* (contra Winckler, KAT³, 147-48) is considered the ideal southwestern border of Israel (Num 34:3; Josh 15:4, 47; 1 Kgs 8:65; etc.). For this reason, Lagarde (*Bildung der Nomina*, 140), Ball, and others want to insert נַחַל.

19-21 In the opinion of the one who inserted it, the list of the ten nations is impressive, although some of them are very small tribes. Both descriptions belong, it seems, to a time when the simple promise "of this land," that is, of the land of Canaan, is no longer sufficient and when it "was the dream of bold patriots to possess an empire equivalent to the two mighty world empires on the Nile and the Euphrates" (Kraetzschmar, 60). Similar lists of the peoples of Canaan are very common (10:16ff.; Exod 3:8, 17; 13:5; 23:23; etc.) and always secondary (Holzinger, *Hexateuch*, 483). Concerning Hittites, Amorites, Canaanites, Girgashites, and Jebusites see 10:15-16. Concerning Kenites see the comments on Cain (4:1ff., p. 48). Concerning the Perizzites see 13:7. Concerning the Rephaim see 14:5. The Kenizzites are a tribe (originally Edomite, Meyer, *Israeliten*, 346ff.) in southern Judah (Caleb is a Kenizzite, Num 32:12). The Qadmonites, "the easterners," or perhaps the inhabitants of Qedem (Meyer, *Israeliten*, 244) appear only here. Sam (LXX) adds וְאֶת־הַחִוִּי in the penultimate position (Ball, Kittel). Neh 9:8, which cites Gen 15 (cf. above), already had vv 19-21 in its exemplar.

Character and age of the passage. The passage is hardly to be called a "narrative." There is no development of plot. It bears, therefore, a similar character to chap. 1 and 12:1-4. One may well consider it a later composition. The inconcrete nature of the theophany in 15:1 (just as in 12:1) is also a sign of later origin while, on the other hand, the concrete theophany in v 17 seems strange within the patriarchal legend. Notably, the account is not localized. The understanding of Abraham as a prophet is also late (15:1). But especially the abstract representation in v 6 ("he believed") is a very significant sign of late style. An early narrator would have recounted an act at this point which would have portrayed Abraham's faith, as in 12:4; 22:3ff. In addition, one may note that only later passages in Genesis mention God's oath to Abraham or to the other patriarchs (22:16; 24:7; 26:3; 50:24). The ancient legends themselves were satisfied to speak simply of God's promise (cf. 12:7; 28:13). This agrees with the fact that outside Genesis, too, the older literature preserved for us does not discuss this oath (and covenant) of God, but Deut and the literature dependent on Deut very often do (cf. Kraetzschmar, 61ff.; Staerk, *Studien* 1:41ff.). One may conclude from all of this that Gen 15 does not belong among the older legends. The passage stems from a time when Israel's possession of the land began to become doubtful. In that time, the belief that the possession of Canaan was insured by God's most impressive pledge was comforting (cf. Mic 7:20; Psa 105:9; 2 Kgs 13:23; etc.; Staerk, 47).

On the other hand, the very ancient description of Yahweh's epiphany (vv 12, 17) and, especially the very marked anthropopathism in which Yahweh underwent the oath ceremony himself (cf. in contrast Exod 24) show that we must not date <183> such compositions too late (contra Staerk, 47; Sievers 2, 279). It is a sign of the great antiquity of the patriarchal legends that even the latest passages still contain a few very ancient elements.

The notion, however, that Abraham's faith "is [a] corrective to 17:17ff., where Abraham greeted the promise with unbelieving laughter " (Eerdmans, 39) is entirely untenable. How much more ancient is chap. 15 than chap. 17 on the whole!

In the event that our source analysis is correct, J^b and E are also fundamentally related here. The two are also similar in that both portray Abraham as a prophet.

21. Hagar's Flight 16, 25:18 J^b

Source criticism. In chap. 16, vv 1a, 3, 15, 16 belong to P (cf. below). The rest belongs essentially to J. Evidence for this identification includes: יהוה, vv 2, 5, 7, (9, 10,) 11, 13; שִׁפְחָה, vv 1, etc. (E אָמָה); נָא, v 2 twice. Since the main strand of J continues 13:18 immediately with chap. 18ff., chap. 16 (like 15) is an insertion in J^a from an old source, J^b. The relationship created in this manner by R^J is as follows: In chap. 15, Abraham is promised an heir. Ishmael is not this heir (chap. 16). But Isaac, whose birth is then predicted in chap. 18, is the true heir. This relationship is not, as can be clearly seen, intended in the legends themselves—it does not appear at all in chap. 16—but it was added secondarily. J^b may have already thought similarly.

E offers a variant to the account of Hagar's flight in chap. 16 in the narrative of Hagar's expulsion (21:8-21). In order to unite the two accounts, R^{JE} inserted 16:9 according to which the angel admonished the fugitive Hagar to return to Sarah. According to this construction, she was then expelled by Abraham in chap. 21. V 10, it seems, was then also inserted in order to mitigate the hard lot of Hagar, who should now return to slavery, with a promise. The verses are recognizable as redactional: (1) by the plodding style (the thrice repeated וַיֹּאמֶר לָהּ מַלְאַךְ יהוה, vv 9, 10, 11); (2) the command to subject herself to Sarah once again (v 9) contradicts the statement Yahweh heard of her humiliation (vv 11) and will comfort her for it; (3) the clause "I will make your seed great" (v 10) may not precede the promise "you shall bear a son" (v 11), but must follow it (cf. Wellhausen, *Composition*^{3}, 19-20); (4) in v 10, the deity speaks in the first person. In contrast, v 11 speaks of Yahweh in the third person. The one who inserted v 10 did not understand the delicate element of the ancient legend that Hagar did not recognize the god at first (cf. below). Contrariwise, v 8 belongs (with Dillmann against Wellhausen) to the ancient legend, not the insertion (cf. below).

The narrative's conclusion has been sharply abbreviated in favor of 21:20-21. The final clause of the narrative is, it seems, still preserved in 25:18. The final redactor (R[JE.P]) also removed the birth of Ishmael because he wanted to include P's version in 16:15.

1b, 2, 4-6 *Part I. Hagar's pregnancy and flight.* **1b** The beginning is missing a statement concerning Sarah's infertility which may be preserved in 11:30 (Sievers 2:279; Kautzsch[3], 22). According to Israelite legal practice, the parents of a young woman could give her a female slave to take into the marriage (24:59, 61) who was then her personal property (1 Sam 25:42) and was not, like the other female slaves, at the disposal of the husband (29:24, 29). Female slaves in Israelite households will have commonly been foreigners (1 Sam 30:13; 1 Chron 2:34-35; cf. Benzinger[2], 124). They came <184> to Canaan as prisoners of war or by purchase. Egyptian slaves, often mentioned (cf. the passages above and Heyes, *Bibel und Ägypten*, 44ff.), will have been valued because of their many skills.

2 The great secrets of begetting, conception, and birth are derived from the deity throughout antiquity (cf. comments on 24:2). In polytheistic religions a particular (usually feminine) deity is usually oversees love and reproduction. In Israel, this, too, like much else, is applied to Yahweh (Stade, *Bibl. Theol.*, 140) who thereby acquires many, somewhat widely varied predicates. According to Israelite legal practice, the wife can, if she is infertile, substitute another wife for herself and adopt her children (see also 30:3, 9). Gen 30:3 describes the form of this adoption. On the other hand, such a concubine remains, at the same time, the "maidservant" of her "mistress" (v 4). It is understandable enough that such ambiguous relationships result in difficulties. In Babylonian law, too, the wife can give her husband a maidservant as concubine (Hammurabi ¶144) who enjoys special status when she has borne children (cf. Kohler und Peiser, *Hammurabis Gesetz* 1:106). Of course, it costs Sarah self-control to give the slave, her personal property, to her husband. But she does it because she hopes to obtain children in this way. Childlessness is a great shame. But motherhood brings honor and status in the home (Gen 30; 1 Sam 1; Benzinger[2], 112-13). The slave is not asked, of course, about such partial transfers. It is a great honor to her to have intercourse with the master. On the pronunciation of אָבנֶה, see §51p. וְבְנֶה means "to acquire a family" here. According to Gesenius[14] it is a denominative of בֵן, but compare also Assyr *banû* "to build, create, procreate."

4 When Hagar notices that she is pregnant, she behaves, not surprisingly given human nature, insolently toward her infertile mistress. The slave who is given too much honor takes on airs (cf. the proverb in Prov 30:21ff.). The legend condemns this, however, in the strongest terms for it was disrespectful to the mistress. The slave should honor the mistress. "The mistress of the tent claims obedience in her realm. It is the husband's responsibility to secure it for her, otherwise she has the right to complain, in the absence of a higher temporal authority, to Yahweh" (Haller, 140). One sees how incorrect it is for contemporary scholars to maintain that there was no great difference in ancient Israel between wife and slave. Babylonian law also presumes that the maidservant who has born her master children may become insubordinate and decrees that such a maidservant may not be sold, but only reduced to servant status (Hammurabi ¶146). The case of Hagar must, therefore, have also been very common in Babylonia. On the accentuation of וַתֵּקַל qal see §67p.

5 Sarah does not punish this impudence immediately but appeals to Abraham. The presumption is that she no longer has full control over Hagar who is now Abraham's concubine and the mother of one of his children. She is all the more indignant about the "injustice," indignant also with Abraham who is responsible for the conduct of his concubine, so indignant that she even calls for Yahweh's judgment against her husband. She should have merited reward from him, not insult. חֲמָסִי means "the injustice done me" (§135m). The basis for the appeal to Yahweh <185> is the ancient belief—to Israel's honor—that Yahweh cares for the weak and oppressed who cannot help themselves (cf. the introduction ¶4:6). To judge "between me and you," that is, to be arbitrator, is a legal term (Isa 5:4; Deut 1:16, etc.) ביניך with a pointed (that is, declared invalid) second י is probably only a scribal error for בֵּינֶךָ (Sam; see §103o).

6 Abraham, fair and just as he is, sees that Sarah's complaint is grounded and now releases his concubine from his property and protection once again. The statement "she is in your hand" has juristic significance, therefore. Abraham's calm brevity contrasts with the feminine, passionate, verbosity. Sarah had allowed herself to be disdained previously; now, however, she turns the spit and lets Hagar feel that she is the mistress. What Sarah did to her is no more stated than it was stated previously how Hagar had insulted her mistress. The ancient narrator is very economical in such circumstances. She will not have been lenient with her, for an Israelite slave was accustomed to a sound beating (Sir 30:33ff.; Exod 21:20-21). With a few strokes, the portrayals of these three individuals are completely clear. Abraham is good-natured and just; "he obeys his wife." According to her will he takes Hagar as a concubine and according to her wish he releases her again. Sarah is the passionate wife, proud of her wife status in the household, cruel and very subjective in her passion. In order to obtain children herself, she gave Hagar away, but she took credit herself for this as a service to her husband. She comports herself in her passionate excitement over her injured respect—psychologically very accurate—as selfless in relation to Abraham. The Israelite husband, however, may well have sighed privately over his temperamental wife (Prov 25:24; 27:15; Sir 25:16ff.; 26:6-7). Finally, the slave's varying fate pleases and touches the hearer. She was first a slave, then the master's concubine and mother of the heir, and as such insolent toward the childless mistress, then severely mistreated and deeply injured in her maternal pride. These three, husband, wife, and maidservant, are apparently Israelite stereotypes. The naive legend finds it very natural that they behave as they do. From now on, Hagar is the key figure. Her defiance has not been broken. She can no longer tolerate life in Sarah's tent. So she decides to flee to her homeland, Egypt. She is a pregnant woman: better all the dangers of the desert path than humiliation in Sarah's tent! In the narrative's structure, the clause, "she fled from her," is a key point, the climax of the preceding and the precondition of what follows.

7, 8, 11, 12 *Part II. The revelation at the well.* God cares for the courageous woman himself, however. In v **7a** the angel of Yahweh meets her at a well in the desert. "The well" (with article) is a specific well. V 14 gives the name and situation. Hagar came to this well in her flight, perhaps in the evening. The path in the desert leads from water source to water source. **7b** "At the well on the way to Shur" parallels v 7aβ and anticipates v 14b. It is a gloss, therefore (cf. LXX, Luc). If the ancient legend spoke of the "way to Shur," it would have done so at the end of v 6 (Ball, Holzinger). שׁוּר "wall" was probably the original name of the Egyptian border fortification in the East (Meyer I, ¶240;

Israeliten, 101n.1) and then the stretch of the border in northeastern Egypt, perhaps corresponding to the current *Ĝifar* (Guthe, *Gesch. Isr.*, 163). The divine being is the מַלְאַךְ־יהוה. The same figure appears frequently in the ancient legends in J. E <186> has מַלְאַךְ אלהים. Like the king or the noble, the god also has a messenger, "herald," or "ambassador," who is known as such. The concept of the messenger of the gods, also attested among the Greeks and Babylonians (Zimmern, KAT³, 454), is very understandable in and of itself. Now it is remarkable, however, that the OT often speaks of this messenger of Yahweh or God as though it were Yahweh or God himself. Thus v 13 sates that Hagar calls the one who spoke with her Yahweh, whereas according to vv 7ff. only the messenger of Yahweh spoke with her. Similarly, the messenger of God who appears in 31:11 says, "I am the God of Bethel" (v 13). There are other similar passages. This difficulty is not to be alleviated by the acceptance of the unclear notion that the messenger is simultaneously a form of Yahweh himself (so, e.g., Marti, *Gesch. der isr. Rel.*⁵, 78-79; Kautzsch³, 27), but much more simply through a religiohistorical observation.

The earliest legends speak very unabashedly of appearances of God: Yahweh appears in person, one hears his footsteps, sees his form, and hears his voice. A later period, however, would perceive it as a profanation to report such human behavior of Yahweh himself. They recount that Yahweh himself did not appear, but a subordinate divine being, his "messenger." This law of development, that certain predicates of the deity become objectionable in progressive religion and are assigned to a lower divine being, also plays a great role elsewhere in Israel and beyond. According to an ancient viewpoint, Yahweh himself goes about in the night of the plagues (Exod 11-12); in a later view, his messenger (2 Kgs 19:35). Originally, Yahweh inspired the prophets. The later prophets are inspired by the angel. The earlier period says, "Yahweh bless you!" and "Yahweh accompany you on the way!" (Gen 48:15; 28:20). The later period says, "The angel bless you!" and "The angel accompany you!" (Gen 48:16; 24:7). In earlier times one recounted how Yahweh himself, but later the angel, led Israel through the wilderness (Exod 32:34; Num 20:16). Originally, Jacob fought with a god at Penuel. The later periods say that it was the angel (Hos 12:5). This change is particularly clear in Exod 4:24, where the Hebr still reads יהוה, but LXX has ἄγγελος κυρίου. Precisely because of this origin in reflection, the figure of the messenger of Yahweh has "always remained a shadowy phantom" (Meyer, *Israeliten*, 216). The figure of the angel so created is not extremely recent, however (Hos 12:5; cf. also Gen 24:7; 48:16), so that it is not feasible, at any rate, simply to remove מלאך as secondary from the texts in 16:7 and related passages (contra Sievers 2:282-83). Now when the messenger was inserted in our and similar narratives they were not entirely remodeled. It must be insisted, especially, that the "'el roi" is Yahweh himself. The result was that the messenger of Yahweh appears to Hagar (altered) and that she believed she had seen Yahweh (ancient). Later readers, who already found both together in their texts, will have accounted for the situation by assuming that a wondrous, mystic relationship existed between Yahweh and his messenger, perhaps that "Yahweh's name" was in the messenger of Yahweh (Exod 23:21; cf. Stade, *Bibl. Theol.* 1:96ff.). But we can go yet a step further. The god about whom the legend speaks was not originally Yahweh, otherwise the name of the child would be *Šemaʿya* or *Yišmaʿya*. Instead, this god was called אֵל, or more precisely אֵל רָאִי. Israelite tradition considers the name "'el roi" to be Yahweh's epithet at this site, just as Yahweh is called "'el

Bethel" at Bethel (31:13; 35:7) "'el olam" at Beersheba (21:33), and "'el, the God of Israel" at Shechem (33:20). These epithets were originally, we may confidently assume, the names of the local numina themselves. When it took over these sacred sites from the natives, Israel also received the names of the deities, understanding these names as epithets of Yahweh at these sites, however. It is very interesting to see that the religion Israel found in place called their gods "el." We discern three religious phases in the legend, then: the god that appears in it <187> was originally *el roi*, then became Yahweh, and finally the messenger of Yahweh. As his name suggests, this *el* originally had a close relationship to this well. He is the numen of the well. The old legend maintains this view by recounting that he appeared at the well. An even more ancient recension would have recounted that he came forth from there and also, perhaps, that it was the very time when he was accustomed to appearing. In Israel and the related nations, wells are often considered sacred. In the earliest periods, one saw the divine in the living, ever-bubbling, and, wherever it goes, life-giving water. The fact that the Hebrew legends recount so much about sacred wells can be explained by their significance for that dry land. Concerning sacred wells, see Stade, *Bibl. Theol.*, ¶52; Benzinger[2], 317 (with bibliography); German well legends in Grimm, *Deutsche Sagen*, nos. 103-105.

8, 11, 12 *God's conversation with Hagar.* Hagar—the conversation originally assumed—does not recognize the god at first. Such encounters and conversations with the unknown deity are very frequent in the ancient legends (cf. comments on 18:1). What follows shows, then, as is often the case in such theophanies, how the god gradually lifts the veil of divinity. In the moment when he is recognized he immediately disappears, however. **8** The god addresses her, not she him. She would not dare to do so because he looks "frightful" (Judg 13:6). "Hagar, Sarah's maidservant"—this man is remarkable. She does not know him, but he knows her name. "Is this," Hagar thinks, "a man of God, perhaps?" (Judg 13:6). "Where do you come from, where are you going?" still always the first question when one encounters a stranger in the wilderness (Merker, *Masai*, 106). Hagar answers, as though with clenched teeth—no moaning and complaining but only the fact—that she is fleeing. Her statement, "my mistress," ingeniously stands in close connection with the god's statement, "Sarah's maidservant." **11** He responds: "You are pregnant." Hagar's pregnancy—the statement presupposes—has been a secret to this point. The man even knows this most intimate secret! So she is inclined, therefore, to believe him when he now predicts the birth of a son. וְיָלַדְתְּ is a composite form of the participle וְיֹלֶדֶת and the perfect consecutive וְיָלַדְתְּ which are both presented here as options (§80d; similarly in Judg 13:5, 7). Following Isa 7:14, the part. is preferable (conversely Ball, Kittel). We frequently hear in the legends how a word of God is issued concerning the still unborn child (18:10ff.; 25:22-23; Judg 13; Luk 1). The ancient people enjoyed telling about the ominous status of pregnancy when the woman attends to every sign and goes to the oracle to learn something about the mysterious future (Gen 25:22). The legend likes to report, then, that what the man became later was already predicted to his mother before his birth. His later destiny is not an accident, then, but was determined from the beginning by God (Judg 13; Jer 1:5; Gal 1:15). Even his name is not based on the caprice of the parents, but was determined by God himself (Luke 1:13, 31). The boy shall be called *Yišma'el* "because Yahweh has heard (שָׁמַע) of your mistreatment" and, therefore, will care for you. (עָנְיֵךְ is intentionally the same word as וַתְּעַנֶּהָ in v 6).

But—Hagar must think—how in the world does this remarkable person know about this <188> mistreatment which she did not complain to him about? This is certainly a man of God. He has a right to speak in the name of God!

And now in v 12 she even hears from his mouth predictions about her son's fate. These words should—the narrator thinks—encourage Hagar to persevere in all afflictions and burdens, for there is a rich, indeed a superabundantly rich reward for the hardship. In the following, the legend depicts with unmistakable pleasure Ishmael's destiny as a Bedouin. Poetry appears here at the climax: two quadrameters and a trimeter. This fate is described with drastic diction: Ishmael shall become a wild ass of a man (constr. §128l). Job 39:5-8 gloriously describes the wild ass: an animal of unruly desires for freedom that laughs at cities and drivers. This is an impressive image for the Bedouins who share the wilderness with it. Concerning the wild asses of Arabia, see Jacob, *Beduinenleben*[2], 115-16. Further, he will be constantly at war with everyone, "not from aggressiveness, but from need: the wilderness does not sufficiently nourish its children and forces them to robbery and bloodshed" (Nöldeke, ZDMG 40:175; cf. the vivid description of the Bedouins in Meyer, *Israeliten*, 304). Consequently, Ishmael's life is nothing other than a struggle—a life, precious for heroic, belligerent men, but, admittedly, full of toil and danger. "And he will set his face against all his brothers." This situation will be more pleasant for him than for his brothers whose fields he plunders and whose herds he steals. This powerful description of Ishmael's fate can warn the modern, on analogy with chap. 21, not to take the preceding narrative too lightly. Instead, the legend means that this independent Ishmael is a son worthy of his defiant mother who did not want to take the yoke either and who cast off the secure life because it was a life in subjection. And just as she now, in the moment of blessing, stands before God defiant, with her whole world fallen to pieces, so shall her son be, unruly and at enmity with the whole world.

13, 14 . . . 25:18 *Part III. Conclusion.* The god has now disappeared. Hagar is alone once again. Now God (v 13) and well (v 13) receive their names. The names of the god, אֵל רֳאִי, and of the well, בְּאֵר לַחַי רֹאִי, are closely related. לַחַי רֹאִי seems to have been a locality for which the well and the god were named. The god is named after the place as are *'el Bethel* (31:13), *ba'al Ḥaṣor, ba'al Me'on, ba'al Ḥermon*, etc. In analogy to Judg 15:14ff., where a mountain peak is called לְחִי "jawbone," more precisely "jawbone of an ass," one may suspect that רֹאִי may have originally been the name of an animal (thus perhaps the "antelope"; cf. Wellhausen, *Prolegomena*[6], 323-24). The legend wants to explain this name which was already remarkable and incomprehensible in the ancient period. The text (literally, "have I not seen behind my seer here?") is nonsensical. Hagar did not gaze after the angel and the narrative does not emphasis the notion that the angel "saw" her. Sievers (2:283-84) suggests כִּי־גַם הֲלֹם אַחֲרֵי רָאִיתָ "for your eye followed me even here (in the wilderness)" or, better, הֲלֹא גַם־אַחֲרֵי רָאִיתָ "have you not also seen after me?" Eerdmans (42-43) reads הֲגַם הֲלֹם רָאִיתָ אַחֲרֵי רֹאִי <189> "have you also seen after me to this point, my seer?" But the intention of the old legend is surely not that the god has seen after Hagar, that is, that he followed her with his eyes from the "house of the mistress," but that he dwells at this well and met her here. Wellhausen's (*Prolegomena*[6], 323-24 and 324n.1) suggestion to read אֱלֹהִים for the text's הלם and to insert after רָאִיתִי an additional וָאֶחִי "I remained alive" ("have I seen the deity and remained alive after my seeing?") is not very satisfactory either. The word "at this place" הֲלֹם (strongly emphasized) cannot be conjectured out of existence. Instead, it is the main point. It explains why this very place is named for this word (cf. 11:8; 16:13; 21:17, 23; 22:14; 32:30). "Truly (הֲ §150e) I have seen in this place. . . . " The corruption is hidden in אַחֲרֵי רֹאִי. אַחֲרֵי seems to represent אַחֲרִית, "the (fortunate) end." The sense was probably "Here I have seen the end of my distress." הֲלֹם means "hither, here" (Judg 20:7; cf. הֵנָּה "hither, here," Gen 21:23 and שָׁמָּה "thither, there"; contra Sievers 2:283). The vocalization לַחַי רֹאִי (v 14) is hardly the ancient pronunciation of the name, but probably introduces a later interpretation of the incomprehensible word ("the living, who sees me"). אֵל רֳאִי (v 13) understands the punctuation as "god of seeing." Kadesh is *'Ain Ḳadîs* (cf. comments on 14:7). Bered (LXX Βαραδ, LXX, Luc, Philo, Jerome Βαρακ; cf. Nestle, ZAW 21:329) is unknown, to be sought west of Kadesh (Meyer, *Israeliten*, 323). Currently, the Arabs consider *Muweilih*, a stop on the caravan path northwest of Kadesh, once a populous place with a number of wells, to be Hagar's well (cf. Palmer, *Schauplatz der Wüstenwanderung Israels*, 272ff.).

The conclusion of the narrative is missing. One would expect to hear how Hagar remained at this well, how she bore and named Ishmael there, how Ishmael grew and became a people whose residence was at this well and whose god was this *'el*. The concluding clause of the whole narrative may be yet preserved in 25:18 (cf. Dillmann, Holzinger), to which Meyer (*Israeliten*, 323) would also prefix 25:11b: "Ishmael settled by the well Lahai roi and dwelt (LXX sing.) from Havilah to the wall of Egypt." Similar geographical descriptions can be found in J in 10:19, 30. Concerning Havilah see the comments on 2:11. The Asshur intended here is not Assyria on the Tigris, but probably the northern Arabian Bedouin tribe that also occurs in Gen 25:3 and that may also be intended in Num 24:22, 24; Psa 83:9 (Hommel, *Altisraelitische Überlieferung*, 240ff.; Glaser, *Skizze* 2:438-39; but see also König, *Fünf neue arabische Landschaftsnamen*, 12ff.; Meyer, *Israeliten*, 320ff.). Or is בֹּאֲכָה אַשּׁוּרָה a doublet of the preceding (so Wellhausen, *Composition*[3], 2n.1; Meyer, and others)? נָפַל, "to alight, settle down," also refers to Bedouins in Judg 7:12. The last clause repeats the prediction of 16:12. Thus the words of God are fulfilled. The one who wrote this final clause seems to have taken פְּנֵי־עַל to mean "eastward."

General Remarks Concerning the Legend of Hagar's Flight

1. *The original meaning of the legend.* The legend speaks (as does the variant in chap. 21) of Ishmael, the patriarch of the יִשְׁמְעֵאלִים. This was a nomadic people from the earliest times. According to chap. 16 it was centralized around Lahairoi; According to 21:21 E its homeland was the steppe of Paran, that is, the *et-Tih* wilderness in the northern Sinai peninsula. These data agree with one another very well. According to the legend it was a Bedouin people, freedom loving, quarrelsome, troublesome for its neighbors, and famed as marksmen (21:20) like the Suti of the Egyptians (Meyer, *Israeliten*, 324). In addition, they were traders like all Bedouins (Meyer, *Israeliten*, 324). Ishmaelite caravans bring spices from Gilead to Egypt (37:25ff.). In the historical period, this tribe of Ishmael disappeared. An "Ishmaelite" appears for the last time in 2 Sam <190> 17:25 (cf. 1 Chron 2:17) under David. "The Egyptians (of the Old Kingdom) do not yet know the Ishmaelites; in the Assyrian period, they have disappeared again. They belong, there-

fore, to the period from the 12th-9th centuries" (Meyer, *Israeliten*, 324). "The nomadic and seminomadic population varies in antiquity as today. Old tribes dissolve, move away, or are destroyed, new ones take their place" (Meyer I, ¶288; cf. idem, *Israeliten*, 324). Later, when the old tribe Ishmael no longer existed, the name Ishmael was extended to several northern Arabic tribes (so in P Gen 25:13; but also already in Judg 8:24 where Midian is counted to Ishmael). The final clause (25:18) describes the dwelling place of the Ishmaelites in this sense. The later tribal league Ishmael had some historical relationship to the old tribe Ishmael. We do not know what. For such name transfers, compare the history of the names Saxony or Prussia. The legend in chap. 16 speaks of Ishmael in both meanings. The foundation speaks of Ishmael in Lahairoi (in Paran). The final clause, from a later tradition, speaks of the Ishmael spread over northern Arabia (cf. Stade, *Gesch. Israels* 1:144-45). This old Ishmael is the son of Hagar. We may conclude, therefore, that there must have been an ancient people Hagar from which the people Ishmael descended. The same name occurs again then many centuries later for the people הַגְרִים or הַגְרִיאִים (1 Chron 5:10, 18ff.; 11:38; 27:31; Psa 83:7; also "sons of Hagar," Bar 3:23) mentioned in 1 Chron 5:19 along with Jetur, that is, the Itureans, according to Meyer (*Israeliten*, 328) may be sought east of Moab and Ammon. It may not be identical with the Αγραῖοι or Αγρέες of the Greeks. One should also see Winckler (MVAG [1898] no. 1: 51) according to whom הגר also occurs in the southern Arabic inscriptions as a tribal name. Do these הַגְרִים have anything to do with the ancient Hagar people or are the names only accidentally the same (Meyer, *Israeliten*, 328)? In contrast, the *Ḫagarânu* (var. *Ḫagrânu*) mentioned in Sah. 1:45 (cf. KB 2:84-85) are an Aramaic tribe to be found in very close proximity to Babylonia. Concerning the nations Ishmael and Hagar see Meyer, *Israeliten*, 322ff.

According to the legend, Hagar is an Egyptian. This is a constant element of the legend (16:3 P; 21:9 E; variant in 21:21, Ishmael had an Egyptian wife). Intermingling of Bedouin tribes with refugee Egyptians is attested (cf. Exod 12:38 and the story of Sinuhe in Erman and Krebs, *Aus den Papyrus der kgl. Museen*, 14ff.). Winckler (*Altorientalische Forschungen* 1:30ff.; idem, KAT³, 141ff.; cf. also MVAG [1898] 1:1ff; 4:1ff.) and following him Cheyne (266ff.) maintain that Hagar was not originally an "Egyptian," but a Musrite from the Arabic tribe מצר, *Muṣr*, whose residence was in Shur. But this claim of the existence and great significance of an Arabic land *Muṣr* has recently been vigorously disputed (cf. Küchler, *Stellung des Propheten Jesaja zur Politik seiner Zeit*, 8ff.; Meyer, *Israeliten*, 455ff.).

The legend treats the origin of the tribe Ishmael. The main question in both variants is, "How did Ishmael come to be a Bedouin?" The answer is, "His mother left the patriarchal household with him and wandered in the wilderness." The name Hagar (Arab. *haĝara* "to separate oneself, to go away") may have had some effect on this migration of Hagar (Dillmann). At any rate, the motif of the flight or the expulsion of the mother with her child is not uncommon elsewhere.

The legend also explains the name *Yišma''el*, "God hears." It tells of a severe difficulty which came upon the mother either before (16) or during (21) her wandering, but also of how God then heard.

Furthermore, the legend of chap. 16 also explains how Ishmael came to his present dwelling place in Lahai roi and to his god, El roi. In response to this question it recounts that the ancestress received the prediction of Ishmael's birth and fate in this very place from this very god. At the same time, the legend was able to explain the unusual names of the place and the god. <191>

Ishmael as the elder of Abraham's two sons parallels Esau, Jacob's elder brother. The Semitic peoples were originally Bedouins and the semisedentary or completely sedentary Semites are deposits of the desert tribes in the agricultural land. The tradition preserves this information by declaring the Bedouins to be the elder brothers (Meyer, *Israeliten*, 305).

Accordingly, the legend contains all manner of etiological material mixed with "novelistic" elements. Our attempt to distinguish between the two is, of course, as always in such cases, only an attempt. A question we cannot answer has to do with why Ishmael is Abraham's son and Isaac's brother. It seems unlikely that it originally dealt with two ancient fraternal peoples Ishmael and Isaac because the earliest recension (chap. 16; cf. chap. 21) does not mention Isaac in this relation at all. It is equally difficult to interpret the reference to Ishmael as a slave's son, the basis of a significant portion of the legend. The Israelites understood this element, in any case, to mean that they, themselves, and not Ishmael, are Abraham's legitimate descendants. But what may the original sense have been? Is the element perhaps merely of "novelistic" origins?

2. *Age and origin of the legend.* This legend of Ishmael must be very old. It presumes the current existence of the ancient people Ishmael of whom there is no historical report. The legend knows Ishmael's population center, its character, even its god and the name of the older people from which it derives. The characters of the persons portrayed are very ancient. Sarah is a passionate wife, "Hagar an insolent, defiant" woman, and her son is "at enmity with the whole world" (Reuß, 253n.2). Abraham, however, plays a somewhat unhappy role between these two stubborn women. The legend does not recount this, however, to the shame of the patriarch, nor with an unrelenting veracity, but because it thinks men are just this way. Neither does it take offense that God has mercy on Hagar. Instead—in the opinion of the earliest tradition—the god rejoices over the unbroken power of the courageous woman. An ancient view of God becomes apparent here, then, comparable perhaps to the Samson or Jacob narratives. Another very ancient element is the fact that the legend associates the child much more closely with the mother than with the father. The earliest situation, when the child knew the mother but not the father, may echo in this element.

The legend may very well have been of Ishmaelite origin in its earliest form. The portrayal of Ishmael's nomadism, not as later, sedentary Israel would have, as a curse, but with distinct joy over the glorious life of the Bedouin, points particularly in this direction. When the god wanted to comfort the matriarch, he foretold the fate of her son. Furthermore, that the god takes, not Sarah's, but Hagar's part in the conflict between the two women also supports this notion. A series of elements would easily conform to such an Ishmaelite origin: the defiant nature of the matriarch, the desert child born at a desert well, the ancestral god also the god of a well.

3. *Style and preservation of the legend.* The recension of chap. 16 is a wonderful example of ancient legend style. The first part of the legend, in particular, is distinguished by the multiplicity and verisimilitude of its images. At the same time, the legend stands out for the strict coherence of the action and, especially, for its amazing brevity. The

narrator goes to extremes to omit that which is not absolutely necessary by not stating even so much as when and how the divine being departed. Yet, one may suspect that an earlier recension may have had a clause here which the later period omitted as objectionable, perhaps to the effect that the god disappeared into the spring. The narrative is also obscure at several other points: it does not distinctly state that Hagar did not recognize the god at first; it does not report at which point in the action she gained this <192> knowledge (originally between vv 12 and 13); our recension no longer states that the spring was a sanctuary, although it may have originally done so in the omitted conclusion.

22. The Three Men Visit Abraham in Hebron 18:1-16aa J[a]

Source criticism. The narrative stems from J: יְהוָה vv 1, (13), 14; רוּץ לִקְרַאת v 2 (only in J). Among expressions which J prefers one can mention מָצָא חֵן (v 3), עַבְדְּךָ = "I" (vv 3, 5), further כִּי־עַל־כֵּן (v 5), לָמָּה זֶּה (v 13), and the recurrent נָא (vv 3-4). In terms of content, J is suggested by the naive tone employed in reference to God. The narrative is a major component in the Abraham-Lot cycle (see the "Composition of the Abraham narratives," pp. 158-60). In the legend cycle it is the immediate continuation of 13:18.

The structure is very clear: I. Abraham hosts the men (vv 1-8); II. The conversation over the meal (vv 9-15). The two parts are of equal size and of a similar aesthetic quality.

V **1a** is a superscription like 22:1a and 2 Kgs 2:1a. The clause does not belong to the old legend. The legend itself begins with v 1b (cf. also belong on vv 2b and 4). 1b The exposition is especially artful. The purpose of such an introduction is to show how the deity and the hero met at a certain place given in the tradition. Such expositions occur in 28:10ff.; 32:23ff.; Exod 3:1ff.; etc. Here the place is the tree at Hebron. It is now recounted, with extreme verisimilitude, how midday (when the way-weary traveler seeks shelter and the resident seeks shade) brought the man and the deity, who appears to him as a traveler, together under the shadow of the tree. There sits Abraham in his tent, at the entrance (פֶּתַח, accusative of location, §118g). The tent is mentioned already here because the narrative wants to use it in the following (cf. v 6 and esp. vv 9ff.).

2a Now when he looks out (by chance), behold, three men are standing before him (עָלָיו, because Abraham is sitting; cf. 1 Sam 22:6). The description portrays surprise: suddenly they are there. Divine beings always appear in surprising ways (21:9; 22:13; Exod 3:2; Josh 5:13; cf. also Zech 2:1, 5; 5:1; 6:1). They also disappear in equally mysterious ways (Judg 6:21; 13:20-21; Tob 12:21). This element of surprise expresses authentic religion in naive form—reverence before the secret of the deity. Human beings only know what the deity reveals to them. Most remains obscure. The narrator intentionally calls the three "men." They look like men, and Abraham considers them to be so (similarly אִישׁ, 32:25; Josh 5:13; Judg 13:10-11). But the narrator knows that they are divine beings. The notion that the deity can appear to people, unknown, in plain, human form and only later reveal himself also occurs in Judg 6; 13; Tob 5; etc. The motif that the incognito deity seeks hospitality and brings majestic reward also occurs particularly often. It occurs in the OT in Gen 19. Among the Greeks there must have been a series of such legends: "For even the blessed gods, in the image of wandering strangers, assuming any form, often traverse lands and cities so that they may see both the sin and the piety of mortals" (*Odysee* 17:485ff.). One recalls Philemon and Baucis (Ovid, *Met.*, 8:616ff.), the fable of Phaedrus (appendix 3) in which Mercury is the guest of two women, further Demeter's welcome in the house of Celeos at Eleusys (*Hymn. Hom.* 5:96ff.), Jupiter's stay in Lycaon (Ovid, *Met.*, 1:211ff.), <193> Hecate's in Thesus (Callimachos), Hercules' in Molorchos, and especially the fable of Dioscures (Herodotus 6:127; Pindar, *Nem* 10:91; Pausanius III/16.3). The German gods also wander through the world and seek lodging at night. The prophet also takes the place of the deity (so also Grimm, *Märchen*, no. 87) in the Hebrew legend (1 Kgs 17:8ff.; 2 Kgs 4:8ff.) as Christ and Peter or a dwarf does in the German Middle Ages (Grimm, *Deutsche Sagen*, no. 45). The deity learns the fate of people firsthand. Some shove the poor wanderer away at the door; others receive him cordially. Thus, the god can reward and punish: "He condescends to dwell here, experiences everything. Should he punish or spare, he must appear to men as a man" (Goethe, "Der Gott und die Bajadere"). In this belief, however, "lies the most sublime sanctification of hospitality: one will be hesitant to turn away a stranger who could be a heavenly god visiting in human form " (Grimm, *Deutsche Mythologie* I4, xxixff., III4, ix). The deity wants to test Abraham here in this fashion. Consequently, the men remain standing before the tent in the attitude of those who silently seek admission.

2b Every element in the following intends to depict how extravagantly hospitable Abraham was, how brilliantly, therefore, he stood the test. His decision to host them is made immediately and will be carried out immediately. To the best of his ability, then, he tactfully shortens the uncomfortable situation of asking for them. The householder acts in this manner when he wants to especially honor a guest. He bows deeply before the strangers as though they were princes (2 Sam 9:6; 14:4; 1 Kgs 1:47). הִשְׁתַּחֲוָה is a technical term for a certain bow: the knee on the ground, "the nose in the dust" (19:1). **3** With many and the most courteous words he requests the honor that they deign to enter his tent. Oriental courtesy is more prolix and submissive than ours. The inferior avoids saying "I" at first in addressing the superior in order not to be a nuisance, preferring instead the self-reference "your servant" (33:5; 42:11; 2 Sam 24:21; 2 Kgs 8:13; etc.). The rabbis want to read אֲדֹנָי as קְדֹשׁ, that is, an address to God: "Oh, Lord." This reading is incorrect. At this point, Abraham does not yet know that God is before him. Instead he believes he is speaking with "men." Abraham addresses the three men in the singular. This notable alternation between singular and plural continues through the entire narrative: v 2 plur.; v 3 sing. (Sam plur.); v 4 plur.; v 5 plur. (LXX v 5b sing.); v 8 plur.; v 9 plur. (LXX sing.); v 10 sing.; vv 13-15 (Yahweh v 13) sing.; and v 16 plur.

Formerly, this circumstance was usually explained by identifying one of three as the master and the other two servants: Yahweh and two angels. V 5b contradicts this understanding, however. In it all three agree to remain with Abraham. It would have been solely the master's prerogative to make this decision. It is equally remarkable that all three begin the mealtime conversation in v 9, but that then one continues it in v 10. The alternation between singular and plural follows no principle, then, but is entirely haphazard. Therefore, Kraetzschmar (ZAW 17:81-92) has attempted a source analysis in which the singular and the plural passages belong to different sources. Ball (comments on 18:1) makes a similar suggestion, as does Sievers (2:286ff.) who assigns vv 1-2a (up to עֵינָיו), 3b, 13-14a, 15 to the "Yahweh version" and the rest to the "three men version." This "universally recognized" (according to Kautzsch³, 30) hypothesis fails, however, because the legend in 18:1-16a clearly constitutes a unified, well-organized whole (cf. also Eerdmans, 72). Sievers' source analysis disrupts the cohesion of v 2 ("he lifted his eyes—and saw") and likewise of the section vv 12-15 (which is—as the quadruple repetition of the word צחק demonstrates—strictly coherent). One must conclude in favor of redaction. Fripp (ZAW 12:24) has suggested restoring the singular everywhere (cf. also Stade, *Bibl. Theol.*, 98n.1). Kautzsch (loc. cit.) also considers the singular source as the "more naive" to be the older of the two sources he assumes. But <194> the original form was surely the plural "three men" reminiscent of polytheism (cf. below). Later copyists and redactors, contrariwise, thought only of Yahweh who alone interested them and, consequently, inserted the singular several times and יהוה in v 13. The rabbis, following them, vocalized אדֹנָי (Cheyne, 294, judges the situation similarly). This reworking took place unsystematically, however, just as did the one which inserted the "messenger of Yahweh" for "Yahweh" in other passages (cf. comments on 16:7, 13). The plural can, therefore, be accepted as the earliest text of the legend: אֲדֹנָי, בְּעֵינֵיכֶם (Sam), תַעֲבֹרוּ (Sam), עַבְדְּכֶם v 3 (Sam), נָשׁוּב, וַיֹּאמְרוּ, אַחֲרֵיהֶם v 10, וַיֹּאמְרוּ v 13, נָשׁוּב v 14, and וַיֹּאמְרוּ v 16. In contrast, the legend collector, from whom v 1a stems, already understood the narrative as an "appearance of Yahweh" (yet cf. LXX ὁ θεός. Kautzsch[3] (30), who sometimes reads the plural and sometimes the singular with no guiding principle, considers the plural in v 9 impossible: "How shall the three have asked after Sarah simultaneously?!" But in reality, the narrators constantly allow a plurality to act and speak together (cf. 11:3, 4; 34:14ff., 31; 38:21; 40:8; 42:10, 13; etc.; cf. the introduction ¶3:9). Regarding אֹמְרָא in v 3, see §105[a,b]n.2.

4 The first thing the traveler does when he stops to rest is wash his dusty, burning feet (Luke 7:44). People wore sandals. Notably, Abraham mentions only one tree while 13:18; 18:1 (and 14:13) speak of several terebinths. LXX and Pesh have the singular in all these passages. Wellhausen (in Bleek, *Einleitung*[4], 643), Stade (*Bibl. Theol.*, 112n.1), and others consider the plural to be a later tendentious emendation intended to remove the character of singular holiness from the tree. Several trees standing together, however, could also be holy and this change can be explained much more simply by assuming that in the earliest period only one tree stood there (so the old legend), but in a later time several (so the collector of the legend cycle, 13:18; 18:1; and 14:13). Josephus (*Bell. Jud.* IV.9.7) knows once again of only one oak of Abraham. A similar change can be seen in Gen 12:6 and Deut 11:30. Concerning the story of the tree see the comments on 13:18 (p. 175). The Israelite farmer sits to eat (27:19; Judg 19:6; 1 Sam 20:5; 1 Kgs 13:20). In Amos' time, the Babylonian practice of eating semireclined on the κλίνη arose among the upper class (Amos 6:4). The practice presupposed here of lying down for a meal (one propped oneself on one's arm, thus הִשָּׁעֵן is indeed the ancient Bedouin fashion, therefore an extremely ancient element.

5 Abraham offers only very modest snacks: some water and a bite of bread, which one can accept from anyone (וְאַחַר Hebr mss, Sam, LXX, Targ-Jon). Indeed, he exerts mild pressure on them: "for you have come by your servant for this reason," that is, the occasion demands it and you must submit to it. כִּי־עַל־כֵּן means "because that's how it is" (§158b n. 1). It may be that סָרְהֶם אֶל should be preferred with LXX and Vulg. At this point, the men accept. It is a fine detail that the deity speaks so briefly in contrast to the verbose courtesy of Abraham. Such behavior corresponds to the dignity of the deity.

Similarly, the women's expansive speeches contrast with David's brief responses (1 Sam 25:24ff.; 2 Sam 14:5ff.; etc.).

Vv **6-8** describe now how Abraham prepares the meal. Two elements assume prominence: (1) Abraham does everything in great haste—it is not polite to allow guests to wait; and (2) it is a majestic and, especially, a very plentiful meal. Of course, the legend joyously recounts such beautiful matters just as Israelite legends in general speak of eating and drinking often and gladly. Hebrew antiquity did not prepare particularly tasty food in special cases. It honored the guest through the quantity set before him (43:34). The same was true in the German Middle Ages and in the countryside of today (cf. L'Houet, 54, 253-54). The details communicated are interesting for the history of culture. The wife prepares the bread—male egoism shoved the unpleasant work of cooking on the woman—the husband the meat (cf. <195> Benzinger², 70). Slaughter is a matter for the men among the Arabs, too, and in the whole Islamic Orient (Jacob, 88).

6 The legend—Lessing would be pleased at this—avoids description, but gives action. It does not say, "Sarah was in the tent," but, "He ran to her in the tent." In this way the narrator deftly communicates to us where Sarah was because he needs that information for the second part (vv 9ff.). One *se'a* is 12.148 liters (cf. Benzinger², 193-94). Three *se'a* for three men is a hefty portion! According to 1 Kgs 5:2 קֶמַח and סֹלֶת are two different types of grain. סֹלֶת is the finer sort. The earlier period knows only קֶמַח, even for sacrifice (Judg 6:19; 1 Sam 1:24). The later period employs סֹלֶת for sacrifice (so P and Chron; cf. Wellhausen, *Prolegomena⁶*, 62-63). Here סֹלֶת is a later correction of קֶמַח. A later, more presumptuous period objected to the idea that Abraham placed only קֶמַח before God. LXX and Vulg translates only סֹלֶת (Ball). A bit of the history of culture is mirrored in the text, here, then. עֻגּוֹת are thin, round flat cakes, baked here (in simple conditions) on hot stones or iron sheets (cf. Benzinger², 64). This could have been enough. But Abraham slaughters meat in addition. Meat was very rare in the ancient period for a private Israelite. **7** He chooses the animal himself so that there would also be a rather nice cut of meat. The cook must "prepare" it, that is, boil it in the ancient period. Later practice roasted meat (1 Sam 2:12ff.). **8a** To drink, he chooses two kinds of milk. The reason Abraham did not place any wine before his guests although the region of Hebron is, indeed, the classic locale for viticulture in Palestine (cf. the legend of the spies in Num 13) is a difficult question. One may explain this element through the fact that the legend imagines Abraham as a Bedouin. But the other possibility should also be mentioned that the legend did not originally belong to the wine region Hebron, but was only secondarily localized there (see further below, pp. 199-200).

8b Abraham himself does not partake of the meal; instead, with extreme courtesy and civility, stands before them to serve them. The whole description of the hospitality still corresponds completely to current practice (cf. Jacob, 85ff.; Löhr, "Gastfreundschaft im Lande der Bibel einst und jetzt," *Palästinajahrbuch* 2, ed. Dalman [1906], 52ff.; Benzinger², 131ff.). The narrative portrays a highly ethical culture. This period considered hospitality to be the virtue peculiar to the husband—a view which can be explained against the primitive lodging circumstances. As in earlier times it is still a virtue among the Arabs to exercise generosity to the point of impoverishing oneself (cf. Jacob, 86-87). Also noteworthy is the special emphasis on courtesy which the ancient Israelite did not consider a matter of external form, although desirable, but an indispensable expression of good character. The fact that the deity eats here is an extremely ancient element. Hebrew legend recounts a similar matter only in 19:3. Indeed, Judg 13:16 explicitly rejects the notion that the angel could have eaten human food. The older commentators, Jews and Christians, set aside this information, which they found highly objectionable, by claiming that God only seemed to eat (cf. already Tob 12:19).

9-15 *Part II. The table conversation.* Thus, the deity experienced Abraham's generosity. He passed the test admirably. This, too, then, <196> is, in the broadest sense, an account of a test of Abraham. Now the deity intends to reward him and give him a host's gift. God, himself, rewards hospitality which finds no reward otherwise. This gift, however, must of course be something especially nice, worthy of God. It is a son in old age! The deity gives Abraham a son by speaking an effective word on the force of which Sarah conceives and bears. The same motif—that the man of God, in thanksgiving for hospitality shown him, gives a childless wife whose husband is old a son through his word—is also the basic motif of the legend of Elisha and the Shunamite (2 Kgs 4:8ff.). The narrator's task in the following was to introduce such a word into the narrative as easily and unaffectedly as possible. This artistic task is resolved here in a wonderful way. Abraham's generosity is demonstrated when he invites the men to table. At the table (more precisely after the meal), however, it was customary to have a conversation. Correspondingly, the narrator shapes the second part of the legend as a conversation around the table.

9 In Hebrew terms, it would have been unsociable for the host to annoy the guest with questions. Instead, the guest begins the conversation (different, e.g., than in Homer). The letters ו, י, and א are pointed in אליו, that is, they are declared invalid. The reading לו seems to be intended. The conversation begins with a daring transition: "Where is Sarah, your wife?" The angel begins the conversation with Hagar in a similar fashion (16:8). The tone of the words is the same as in 16:8. Abraham had not yet mentioned the name of his wife to the men. Nevertheless, they still know it! What sort of remarkable men are these? It is noteworthy how the narrator envisions the knowledge of the deity. They come to test Abraham and they ask where Sarah is. They are not yet omniscient, then. But this is obvious to the legend. The wondrous thing about them is, however, that they know so much more than humans (regarding both points, see above p. 18). Their question about Sarah presumes that she does not show herself to the strangers. The Hebrew wife did not have the same freedom of movement as the virgin (cf. 24:15; 29:9). On the other hand, she did not live in the seclusion of the harem, either. Currently, one may never ask the Muslim about his wife.

10a These words are also extremely amazing. How do they know that he does not yet have a son with Sarah? And, especially, how do they come to this prediction? Was sort of men may these be (cf. the parallels 16:11)? "We will come again." Abraham will think that the men plan such a long journey that they will stop by him a year later on the return journey. Now since there is no account of the men visiting Abraham a second time, it can be inferred that the narrative originally had a continuation which reported that the men returned to Abraham (more below, p. 199). כָּעֵת חַיָּה means "at this time, when it comes to life again, that is, next year" (§118u). The same expression occurs in the legend variant (2 Kgs 4:16). The statement seems to be based on the originally mythological notion that "time" dies and comes to life again a year later (cf. the Adonis myth; L. Köhler, ZNW 9:77). LXX and Pesh apparently add לַמּוֹעֵד הַזֶּה (cf. v 14).

10b, 11 These two parenthetical clauses function to make the subsequent portion comprehensible. The ancient narrators are very economical with such interruptions of the narrative. **10b** That the wife listens when guests come, with whom she may not speak however—a harsh denial—is certainly comprehensible. But women are curious in general (27:5). In order to make the following understandable, it is explicitly stated that the tent door in which Sarah stands was behind the men. It may be that Sam (והיא) and LXX should be followed in the pointing וְהוּא (Sievers 2:288; Kittel). <197> **11** Ball and Kittel suggest כְּאֹרַח נָשִׁים (cf. 31:35). The sense of the (reserved) expression is that her "period" had ceased. She was, therefore, no longer in a state to conceive according to human notions. Isaac, then, is born contrary to all probability—a motif which often recurs in the legends (25:21; 30:22; 1 Sam 1; Luke 1). The legend makes it clear that the child was entirely a gift of the deity.

12 The narrator does not report what Abraham said in response to the extraordinary promise because it is not necessary for the continuation of the action. One must imagine Abraham as calm and in control of himself. At the same time, it is a religious subtlety that the laughter is attributed, not to Abraham, but to Sarah. One may not say of Abraham that he laughed about God's word. P 17:17 is less sensitive. Sarah considers the men's statement a joke like those old women are accustomed to hear. I, an old woman, will never again attend to the joys of love (עֶדְנָה) with my husband! Syntactically, she conceives of the matter as a fact (perf. הָיְתָה) and is amused by it. בָּלָה is a crude expression used, for example, of torn rags. Of course one may not speak of Sarah's "unbelief." She does not know, after all, who speaks. **13** But the men become nearly angry now. How can Sarah doubt our words? Now they demonstrate once again their wonderful knowledge. They know that Sarah has heard and laughed. They know Sarah's thoughts, without hearing (indeed, she laughed only "to herself" v 12) or seeing her (in fact, she stood behind them, v 10)! Abraham may think that these must certainly be men of God (cf. Judg 13:6)!

14a The statement "Is anything too wonderful for Yahweh?" (in form a proverb) is very characteristic for ancient religion. The pious does not doubt that Yahweh could do everything that he wants, even the most wondrous thing. He can cause the sun to stand still and iron to float on water. Of course, the statement has a different meaning here in the mouth of the ancient legend than in the mouths of modern philosophers of religion because antiquity had no, or a very unclear, idea of what we call laws of nature. The fact that the deity, incognito, speaks of Yahweh in the third person has analogies in 16:11; 19:13; Judg 13:5, 16; 6:12. LXX has אלהים, which Eerdmans (72) prefers. **14b** In a tone of serious conviction the men repeat their promise (LXX reads לַמּוֹעֵד, perhaps with the addition of הַזֶּה **15** so that Sarah, fearful, becomes intimidated and lies. But they are not fooled, "No, but (לֹא כִּי §163a) you did laugh." One notes the emphatic brevity. Now that Sarah, herself, has become involved in the conversation they speak to her directly. Previously (v 13) they spoke to Abraham about her, a well-considered intensification. This small scene of Sarah's laughter has the purpose in this context of demonstrating the surprising knowledge of the men—they know the most hidden thoughts—and, simultaneously, of portraying their wonderful grandeur—Sarah is afraid of them, they are "very terrible" (Judg 13:6). In the whole context, the word "laughter" is supposed to impress us. Therefore, it is repeated four times.

16aα "The men <198> arose from there" is the preliminary conclusion to the narrative. The next statement makes the transition to the Sodom narrative and stems, therefore, from the legend collector (J^a).

General Remarks Concerning the Hebron Legend

1. The most important preliminary question for understanding the narrative is "Did Abraham recognize the deity from the very beginning or in the course of the conversation?" This question has already been answered in the preceding to the effect that he did not recognize the deity. Additional evidence for this understanding includes the following. The legend intends to recount that God wanted to put Abraham to the test. He could only do this, however, incognito, for who would not be happy to exquisitely entertain a known god? Instead, it was precisely because he did not know him, and still entertained him so gloriously, that he proved himself so convincingly! We are supposed to think that Abraham received every unknown traveler in this fashion! The wondrous knowledge that the men then demonstrate signifies in this context the partial lifting of the veil of divinity. On the other hand, this unveiling was not yet such that it reveals the deity (contra Dillmann, Holzinger, etc.). This is demonstrated by the fact that (a) it is not expressly stated that Abraham now recognized the deity, an element which could hardly be omitted in the context (cf. Judg 6:22; 13:21), especially since such a recognition is horrible and disturbing (28:17; Judg 6:22f; 13:22; Tob 12:16). (b) One who demonstrates wondrous knowledge need not, therefore, be a god; instead, one would conclude first that he is a man of God (Judg 13:6; cf. also Judg 6). (c) The element of Sarah's lie is especially probative. The God who travels incognito in human form demonstrates his majesty in that Sarah dared not admit the truth to him. But if Sarah knew that he is Yahweh then this lie of hers would be a grievous sacrilege. (d) The word הָאֲנָשִׁים (v 16; cf. comments on v 2) seals the argument. With this word, the narrator says that they departed incognito, like they came. Later readers, who did not understand the spirit of the old legend and its subtleties, did not retain this original understanding of the narrative, however. It seemed entirely impossible to them that the patriarch should not have recognized Yahweh. Therefore they introduced יהוה in v 13. A similar process is repeated in the gloss in 16:10 (cf. also Judg 6).

2. Vv 10, 14 indicate a continuation of the legend which must have originally followed by necessity (cf. above pp. 159-60, 196-97). This continuation must have recounted how the promise was fulfilled, how Sarah bore a son, and how she named him Isaac in memory of the fact that she "laughed" (יִצְחָק from צָחַק), then how the men returned the following year, further how Abraham now recognized the deity (at this point, it must have been clearly stated who the three "men" really were), and finally, also, perhaps how he now erected an altar to this deity beneath the tree. This continuation is now missing. Gen 21:1a, according to which Yahweh himself was with Abraham, hardly stems from this continuation for this can hardly have been the meaning of the old legend according to no. 3 (see below). Nor can 21:6b, which gives another etymology for "Isaac," be a fragment of the older recension. Why was this continuation lost? It would have contained all manner of material which was objectionable to the later period.

3. Who are these three men? The ancient narrator responded to this question in the passage which reports the concluding revelation of the deity. We must unravel it from the context preserved for us. Assuredly, the legend did not think that Yahweh was equally present in all three (so Dillmann, Franz Delitzsch, Reuß, and others). According to ancient belief, Yahweh was conceived realistically as an extremely individual personality so that it would have been entirely impossible to divide him into three figures. Instead one may only ask whether Yahweh was one of them and the other two were angels or whether all three were Yahweh's messengers. The latter option is indicated with great certainty by the fact that legend speaks not of a master and two servants, but of "three men" and the fact that, in its <199> original form, as we may hypothesize it, it treated these three as equals (cf. esp. וַיֹּאמְרוּ, vv 5, 9). Gen 19:13, 16 (cf. also 19:22) points in precisely this direction. One may also ask whether the legend would have spoken so unabashedly of the men eating (or in the following narrative of the Sodomites attempted assassination of the men) if it thought that Yahweh was one of them. Now the legend bears such ancient elements (the deity appears in person, he eats bread and veal, they lie down at table, there is no wine) that it does not seem too bold to hypothesize that the narrative may stem from a pre-Yahwistic period in which these three men were not originally messengers of Yahweh, but three gods. Israel would then have later applied this legend, like others, to Yahweh (cf. esp. 16:13). The introduction of the singular into the account (cf. above on v 2) would then signify a progressive Yahwization of the narrative (cf. recently also Eerdmans, 72). This hypothesis is further supported by the fact that the legend (cf. comments on v 8 and "General Remarks concerning the Sodom-Lot Legend," no. 2) seems to have been localized in Hebron only secondarily. This hypothesis receives further confirmation in the fact that a very similar Greek narrative has been preserved for us. Zeus, Poseidon, and Hermas—according to others Zeus, Apollos, and Poseidon—are received by Hyrieus, an old Boeotian man. After the meal they invite him to wish for something. Since he is childless, he wishes for a son which he receives from them through a miracle. From the seed of the three gods, which they bury in the earth hidden in a steer skin, a son is born after ten months. It is Orion (cf. Roscher, Lex III/1 cols 1018, 1029-30). Apart from the repulsive manner of the child's origination based on a popular etymology ('Ωρίων [οὐρίων] from οὐρεῖν in the sense of *semen emittere*), this narrative agrees with the Hebron legend in all the major points. It can hardly be denied that it is essentially the same legend. One must, therefore, infer an ancient oriental narrative preserved for us in Hebrew and Greek manifestations. If our hypothesis concerning the history of the tradition is correct, the three gods are not indigenous to Hebron but were first transferred there by the legend. The "angels" which, according to Eusebius (*Onom.*, 21) were venerated in his time along with the oak by pagans in Hebron (cf. above p. 175), are not, therefore, ancient tree numina but nothing other than the angels known from Gen 18 (contra Meyer, *Israeliten*, 263-64).

4. *Meaning of the Legend (in its Hebrew form)*. This legend material came to Israel and was transferred to the tree of Hebron and to Isaac's birth. The coexistence of "tent" and "tree" at which the actions are portrayed in the style of Hebrew narrative (cf. the introduction ¶3:15) can also be explained by such a transferal. The tent belongs to the ancient legend; the tree was added later. In Hebrew tradition, the narrative will probably have been understood as a cult legend and will have sought to answer the question, "Why

do we have the right to set the table for the deity beneath the tree of Hebron?" The answer is, "Because the deity deigned to accept food and drink from Abraham's hand at this site." Thus, the notion that the "men" ate and drank here received special significance. It is the initiation of the still-enduring sacrifice which was understood in earliest times as the deity eating. In addition, the legend in the Hebrew tradition acquired an etymological element: it explains the name of Isaac from the fact that Sarah "laughed." The insertion of this motif of "laughter" into the context is superb. No one who did not already know would observe that the narrator has a definite objective in view from v 10b onward. This nice insertion of the motif is the old style's particular claim to fame.

5. *Relationship of the legend to the other Abraham legends.* The narrative reports how the deity promised Abraham a son. It is entirely impossible that this promise was already made to him. Thus, the legend excludes <200> chap. 15. The narrative wants to describe the sanctification of the sanctuary at Hebron. As a consequence no altar stood there at the time. Abraham only built it later. Therefore, 13:18 cannot have preceded chap. 15. The legend recounts that Abraham did not recognize the deity at first. One may compare the account in 1 Sam 3. When Yahweh called Samuel the first time, he believed he was hearing Eli's voice for he had not yet come to know Yahweh, he had not yet received a Yahweh revelation. Later, however, he recognized Yahweh's voice and perceived immediately every time that it was Yahweh! Since Abraham did not recognize Yahweh it follows that he had not yet experienced a revelation of God. This account is supposed to be the first—and (disregarding the related continuation) probably also the only—revelation to Abraham. The legend excludes, then, not only 13:14ff. and chap. 15, but also 12:1ff., 7, which belong to the legend cycle, that is, in the end, all the preceding material. Our legend is, accordingly, completely independent from all others, a narrative in and of itself. Here, then, is evidence for our hypothesis concerning all the old legends in the earliest form: every legend stands alone.

23. Transition from the Abraham-Hebron Legend to the Lot-Sodom Narrative 18:16ab-33

The passage consists of three parts.

I. 16aβ, b, 20-22a, 33b These verses are not by nature an independent legend, but an interlude. Their purpose is to make the transition from the Abraham legend to the Lot-Sodom legend. The verses stem, therefore, from J (cf. יהוה, v 20 and חִשְׁקִיף, v 16), and, in fact, from the hand of the collector of the legend cycle, J^a (cf. above, p. 160). This transition proves to be light and pleasant. The hospitable Abraham "accompanies" (31:27) his guests part of the way. They set out toward the east, until they come to the place where one has a view of Sodom (v 16). There, in sight of Sodom, they once again make remarkable statements. They had heard of Sodom's evil (v 20) and they were now going to confirm it (v 21). Then they departed (v 22a), but Abraham returned to Hebron (v 33b). The Lot-Sodom legend follows at this point in the legend cycle. Even now the three beings are still unknown (cf. הָאֲנָשִׁים in v 16 and esp. v 22). Once again the deity lifts his veil a little. But Abraham still does not recognize him. The narrator wisely reserved the disclosure for their second (unpreserved) visit. The singular (v 21) and יהוה (v 20) have been introduced into this passage, too. The original text will have read וַיֹּאמְרוּ (v 20), אֵלֵינוּ, וְנִרְאֶה נֵרְדָה, and נֵדְעָה (v 21). The revelation communicated to Abraham (v 20) is intended, at the same time, to glorify him as the confidant of the deity, from whom God does not withhold his secret plans. Magnificently, this scene takes place in sight of Sodom. According to Jerome (*Epist. CVIII ad Eustochium virg.*, 12), the point is Caphar Barucha (= *Kefr barîk*), now *Benî na'îm*, east of Hebron (cf. Buhl, *Palästina*, 158-59). In terms of the history of religion, vv 20-21 are <201> interesting. The deity is not conceived of as omniscient by nature (cf. comments on 3:8ff.; 18:9), but learns many things through his messengers and spies stationed all over the earth (cf. 28:12; 11:5; Zech 1:10-11; Job 1:6ff.; etc.). **20** זַעֲקָה (probably better written צעקה with Ball following Sam and v 21) is a technical term for the cry concerning an unjust event (cf. 4:10) The fact that Gomorra is also mentioned in this context is remarkable since we hear only of Sodom in 18:16, 22, 26; and 19:1 and only of a city in 18:24, 26, 28; 19:4, 12, 13, 14, 15. Outside of 19:29 (P) and 14:2, 8, 10, 11, Sodom and Gomorra appear in the legend only here, in 13:10 (gloss) and 19:24 (25), 28. Consequently, "and Gomorra" in J is to be considered a harmonization with another tradition (Sievers 2:288-89; Kautzsch[3], 30). Concerning כִּי (v 20) "indeed, certainly," see §148d. But it may be that בָּאָה אֵלַי (אֵלֵינוּ) should be inserted before this conjunction (with Kittel; cf. 19:13). **21** LXX, Targ-Onk, Arabs read הכצעקתם. הַבָּאָה, participle, is better than the text's הַבָּאָה (§138k); כָּלָה is better than כָּלָה (Wellhausen, *Composition*[3], 26n.1). Abraham does not respond at all to this statement by the men. How does Sodom's reputation concern these men? Why do they want to learn about Sodom's sin? Concerning Abraham's thoughts at this point cf. the introduction ¶3:12.

II. **17-19** *Yahweh's soliloquy, the motivation for the subsequent revelation to Abraham (v 20-21).* Abraham deserves to learn about the divine plan. After all, he is supposed to become a great, Yahweh-blessed people. Wellhausen (*Composition*[3], 26) recognized these verses as an addition. (1) The diction raises suspicion (cf. לְמַעַן אֲשֶׁר, v 19; cf. Holzinger, *Hexateuch*, 483). The diction breaks out into pious generalities (cf. Holzinger) and recalls deuteronomistic diction (cf. Duet 6:1-3; Fripp, ZAW 12:23). (2) According to v 17, Yahweh already knows what he will do, while according to v 21 he only wants to obtain information in Sodom and reserves the right to decide further (cf. Holzinger). The hand responsible for this insertion read the old text, then, rather cursorily. (3) It is inept to have Yahweh speak of himself in the third person in v 19 (in a soliloquy! in contrast to v 14). Here the editor forgot the form of Yahweh's soliloquy. One sees that this man is more concerned with communicating musings than narrating accounts. (4) He is also far removed from the spirit of the old legend when he subjects the promise to the condition that Abraham's sons keep justice and righteousness. Yahweh's promises to the fathers are always given without condition in the old legends. This understanding corresponds to ancient religion. The ancient period conceives the relationship between God and people not as a conditional, but as a natural matter. Yahweh is Israel's God, who blesses and assists Israel, whom the people may trust just as a wife expects only good from her husband and children from their father. The prophets bitterly resisted this popular belief: Yahweh is more than a national god. He wants, first of all, "justice and righteousness," and only if Israel keeps to this way of Yahweh will Yahweh fulfill his promises to Israel. The verses contain, therefore, notions from the prophetic or postprophetic period. (5) Finally, the secondary character of the verses is also clear in the allusion in v 18 to promises already made to Abraham (12:2, 3), as v 19b also explicitly states, whereas the old legend in 18:1-16 (as is true of the old narratives in general) is entirely free of such allusions to other accounts. And (6), the narrator presupposes that Yahweh speaks with Abraham, while according to the old legend in 18:1-16 the veil of the divine has not yet been finally lifted. Thus a nuance of the old narrative is effaced. The <202> editor may already have read the singular and the word יהוה (v 13) in a few passages in the text before him. The purpose of the insertion seems to be to make clear that God's subsequent communication to Abraham (vv 20-21) was a great honor for the patriarch. It represents, then, a thick retracing of the delicate lines of the original.

17 The perfect in וַיהוָה אָמָר interrupts the narrative. It refers, of course, to a soliloquy. Hebr mss, Sam, and Targ-Jon read אֶת־אֲשֶׁר. **19** ידע is used here of God who establishes a closer relationship with humans (Baumann, ZAW 28:32). "His house after him" refers to his descendants.

III. 22b-33a *Abraham's intercessory prayer for Sodom.* Wellhausen (*Composition*[3], 25-26) recognizes the passage as secondary. (1) If one assumes the unity of the text, the information concerning the "three men" would occasion insurmountable difficulties. According to v 22a, "the men," that is, according to the preceding, the three men, departed from Abraham. According to v 22b, however, Yahweh remained. The two parts of the verse, taken precisely, contradict one another. Equally difficult is the following. According to v 20 the three men originally intended to go to Sodom; according to our text, Yahweh himself intended to go. But according to 18:22b, 33a; 19:1, Yahweh himself did not do so, at first remaining with Abraham (v 22b) before departing (v 33a). According to 19:1 only the two angels were in Sodom. The attempt has been made to resolve the difficulty by suggesting that Yahweh was also present in the two in Sodom, just as in the three who appeared to Abraham, and in the one who remained standing before Abraham so that God simultaneously departed (in the two to Sodom) and remained (in the one; cf. Franz Delitzsch; Dillmann; similarly now Procksch, 292n.1). But such self-contradictory perspectives are entirely un-Israelite (cf. above, p. 198). Instead, one must admit that the vv 22b-33a together with vv 20-22a do not render a unified picture. Additional evidence for the secondary origin of the passages includes the fact that (2) according to vv 23ff Yahweh had already reached the decision to destroy Sodom, which Abraham sought to reverse if possible, while according to vv 20-21, this decision was by no means firm (cf. p. 201 II.2, 3). (3) Abraham knows Yahweh while according to vv 20-21, the deity is still incognito (cf. above II:6). (4) the god concept in vv 22b-32a is quite different from the one in the old legend (18:1-16)—here the men eat bread and veal; there, however, Yahweh is "the judge of the whole world" (v 25) before whom man is "dust and earth" (v 27; cf. Wellhausen). (5) Abraham's intercessory prayer for Sodom is also difficult to understand in the context of Israelite antiquity. It would have consistent with ancient practice for Abraham to put in a good word for his relative Lot. But it would have hardly been comprehensible for ancient Israel how a pious Israelite could pray for a godless people.

One discerns the nature of this account (1) from its placement in its context. This narrative is not, by nature, an independent account, but only an episode in a larger whole. It is only comprehensible on the condition that God's revelation to Abraham concerning Sodom has preceded it and that the account of Sodom's destruction should follow. It presumes, therefore, a passage that belongs, itself, not to an independent legend, but to an artificially constructed framework. (2) The account treats a religious problem: whether a righteous <203> minority may avert the destruction of a godless people. The passage does not recount events, then, as the old legends always do, but it portrays thoughts in the form of an extensive discussion. Long speech without any action always indicates later origins in the narratives (cf. the introduction ¶3:20). This episode is sharply distinguished by nature from the other sages. All this implies that the passage is not an old legend but a later extrapolation. Accordingly, the passage will not have entered here from a separate source, but it is an "excrescence" (Wellhausen).

The Problem. That death and destruction come upon an entire people to punish its sins is a notion which was entirely unobjectionable in Israel in the ancient period. We hear such verdicts very often, especially in the prophets. Thus, the old legend, too, recounts that the city must be destroyed because its citizens were evil (13:13). Such verdicts are comprehensible in the context of the social relations of the ancient period when individuals were (naturally not entirely, but relatively) insignificant in comparison to their communities. When God and humans treat the family, the clan, the community, the people as a unity, they are such in reality (2 Sam 21; 2 Kgs 9:25-26; Exod 20:5-6; etc.). The notion that individual citizens in the god-accursed Sodom were righteous will have seemed quite atrocious. How can that be possible! But in the later period, when maturing culture dissolved the ancient unions and differentiated the individual—the first great independent persons in Israel known to us are the prophets Amos, Hosea, and Jeremiah—when the struggle of religious parties, in which the individuals must take a position, was ignited, in that time another attitude arose in Israel. The individual felt independent and wished for a particular fate. He would have perceived it as injustice, indeed as nonsense, if he were only considered as member of the community, if God were simply to pass over him and his righteousness and go to the business of the day. We know such attitudes from the final period of the state of Judah (Deut 24:16; Ezek 18:2; [Jer 31:29]). The question of what would happen to the pious individual if his people were destroyed because of its sin, whether God would withdraw the catastrophe from the whole people on his account, will have lain on the hearts of the prophets' followers all the more because prophecy announced the destruction of its people. The inserted passage treats this problem. An ancient reader reads the Sodom account and asks, "But righteous individuals could still be in Sodom? Did Yahweh treat them just like the evildoers? Does Yahweh make no distinction between righteous and unrighteous?" And he responds, "Far be it! (v 25) Otherwise God would not be righteous! Otherwise all fear of God would be in vain!" Instead, in the name of the moral world order, he demands that Yahweh care for righteous individuals in Sodom, that Yahweh forgive the whole place on account of the righteous. On the other hand, he also admits that if there are too few righteous, they cannot be taken into consideration. He expressed these ideas by placing his concerns in the mouth of Abraham and allowing Yahweh to respond. In this way, these ideas retained the (ancient) form of a righteous person, a darling of the deity, making intercession with God for the righteous and their city. The stylistic prototype will have been discussions between God and humans as they could be read in the prophetic literature where the prophet makes intercession with God <204> or "disputes" with him (cf. Amos 7:1ff; Jer 12:1ff.; etc.; from later literature esp. 4 Ezr vis. I-III).

Significantly, however, Abraham's intercession takes the form of a negotiation. Even though in the whole city there were only 50, 45, 40, 30, or indeed even only 20 or finally

10, Yahweh would have spared the place. One clearly perceives in the scale the struggle of the author. He was satisfied with this final answer. It does not, however, appear to us to be a sufficient response. For, if the righteous were only five in number, they would all be treated as evildoers. Characteristically, the author does not arrive at the solution that these few righteous should be removed and delivered from the general destruction. His view is indeed fixed, on the one hand, on the righteousness of individuals, but, on the other hand, also on the state of the totality. This solution—the solution of Ezek 14:12ff.—would have been suggested by the Sodom-Lot narrative in which Lot and his household are, indeed, delivered because of his righteousness. One can also see that these ideas did not arise for the author from the legend itself, but that he imported them into the old legend from elsewhere. For this very reason, one may not see in Abraham's intercession for the foreign city a particular compassion (Franz Delitzsch). The author is not greatly concerned for the fate of Sodom. Instead he treats an abstract problem here, as his words (v 25) clearly indicate. We encounter a similar spirit of abstraction in Jer 18 and Ezek 14:12ff., 18. The author treated his material very well stylistically. Abraham's speeches present the problem he wanted to treat with full force. Simultaneously, however, the author perceived that these objections of Abraham could easily sound impious and, therefore, he has Abraham speak as reverently and humbly as possible in other passages. Abraham speaks in the tone of a faithful, old servant who may speak freely to his lord without giving offense. Yahweh's brief and decisive responses contrast nicely with the man's expansive and very subjective words. At the same time, God's patience is portrayed. God does not become impatient during all of this negotiation and truly reduces to the least conceivable minimum (the prophets, to be sure, speak even more harshly, Jer 5:1; Ezek 22:30, but only in the greatest pathos). That the author tried to write well can also be seen in the effort he took to vary expressions. Regarding the history of individualism in Israel cf. Löhre, *Sozialismus und Individualismus im AT* (1906) and Meyer, *Israeliten*, 508.

Sievers (2:287-88) proposes another analysis: vv 17, 20, 21, 22b-33—Ja, v 16—Jδ, v 22a—Jβ, vv 18, 19—an addition. But v 16 introduces a discussion outside Sodom and belongs, therefore, to vv 20-21, and this discussion concludes with v 22a. Similarly, Abraham's intercession (vv 22bff.) cannot be the original continuation of the revelation (vv 20-21; cf. above p. 202 III.2, 3). Here, too, Sievers' metrical analysis does not further source criticism in any way.

V **22b** is, according to rabbinic testimony, a תקון סופרים, a scribal correction. This testimony is not an ancient tradition, but a conclusion drawn from the current text (Spurrell). In essence, however, it is correct, because, judging from the context, the verse must have originally read "Yahweh remained standing before Abraham." The words <205> were altered as the result of religious aversion, in order to avoid excessive anthropomorphism, and because "to stand before someone" has the connotation of "to serve someone" (otherwise 19:27). An emendation for a similar motive may also occur in 1 Sam 19:20 (cf. Thenius-Löhr on this passage). The author responsible for this insertion took the phrase "the men" (v 22a) imprecisely in the sense of the men beside Yahweh, that is, the two angels.

23 See Job 9:22. **25** כְ means "just as . . . so also" (§161c). The words of the verse carry a deep pathos. The foundations of the earth would shake then! What should one expect from human judges if the highest judge does not care about justice! The words reveal a passionate desire to discern righteousness in God's rule. The same attitude is classically expressed in Job's speeches (Driver). **27** עָפָר וָאֵפֶר is a play on words. For the substance compare 2:7. **28** "Will you destroy the entire city for the sake of five?" is sophistry in our terms. Yahweh does not destroy the place because of the missing five, but because of the great sinful multitude. The narrator does not perceive the statement as sophistry, however, but as ingenuity. **30** The first two times Abraham only negotiates over five. From now on he becomes bolder and lowers the number by tens (Franz Delitzsch). One sees that the narrator writes deliberately. וַאֲדַבְּרָה is the cohortative following the jussive (§108d): Do not become angry "so that I can speak, thus I will speak." **32** The author stays with the number ten. **33a** "Yahweh went forth"; whither is unclear.

24. The Account of Sodom's Destruction and Lot's Deliverance 19:1-28 Jᵃ Jʳ

This account belongs to J. Linguistic evidence for this conclusion includes: יהוה, vv 13bis, 14, 16, 24bis, 27; הִנֵּה־נָא, vv 2, 8, 19, 29; the frequent נָא, vv 2, 7, 18, 20; לִקְרָאת, v 1; פָּצַר, vv 3, 9; כִּי עַל־כֵּן, v 8; עַבְדְּכֶם, vv 2, 19; לְבִלְתִּי, v 21; and הִשְׁקִיף, v 28. In J it is the second, larger legend of the Abraham-Lot legend cycle (Jᵃ), woven into a unit with the Abraham narrative through 18:16, 20-22a, 33b and 19:27-28.

The narrative experienced the same fate as chap. 18: it exists in an expanded and redacted form. (a) The notice concerning Lot's wife (v 26) occurs too late. The suffix in אִשְׁתּוֹ is without clear referent. This verse will be a secondary addition to the legend. The references to Lot's wife in vv 15 and 16 stem from the same hand. The Zoar intermezzo (vv 17-22) is also such an outgrowth on the trunk of the old legend. This passage comes too late after וַיְנֻהֵהוּ (v 16). It interrupts the cohesion of the clauses, "when dawn appeared," (v 5) and "when the sun rose" (v 23). Lot's expansive speech seriously disturbs the impression of extreme haste the old legend intends to make. Naturally, the earliest legend recounts Lot's escape to the place where his descendants live later, namely, into the mountains of Moab. This Zoar interlude includes the words וְלוֹט בָּא צֹעֲרָה (v 23b) and of what follows, v 30a. Here, the fact that the narrator found it difficult to motivate Lot's subsequent departure from Zoar is a new indication that this Zoar interlude is of later origin. Both outgrowths, of Lot's wife and of Zoar, are inherently related by the statement "do not look back" (v 17) and will have been inserted by the same hand, albeit in a very ancient period. (b) According to the original form of the legend three deities came incognito to Sodom. They are called, as in chap. 18 (cf. comments on 18:2a and p. 199), "the men" (vv 5, 8, 10, 12, 16). Lot hosts and protects them, but the Sodomites want to violate them. These two elements only make sense if both parties were unaware with whom they were dealing. The later tradition, however, did not comprehend this feature and consequently, as in chap. 18 (cf. comments on 18:3), inserted the singular in the conversation with Lot concerning Zoar (vv 17-22). But since the plural also appears occasionally here, indeed with no guiding principle, in vv 17 (LXX καὶ εἶπαν) and 18, it may be concluded that the plural was also originally employed throughout this passage.

<206>

In sum, the chronological sequence of the additions and redactions in chaps. 18 and 19 may be determined with a degree of probability. (a) The earliest addition is the intermezzo concerning Zoar and Lot's wife in which, still following the original text, the three "men," that is, angels, were in Sodom. (b) Later, the singular (= Yahweh) was inserted in many passages. (c) The larger insertions, 18:17-19 and 18:22b-33a, already presupposed this singular. (d) Still later the insertion in 18:22b-33a was taken into consideration and it was concluded that only two angels could have been in Sodom. Consequently, שְׁנֵי הַמַּלְאָכִים (v 1) and הַמַּלְאָכִים (v 15; in Sam also in v 12 and in LXX in v 16) were inserted.

Kraetzschmar (ZAW 17:81ff.) offers another attempt to master the difficulties of chaps. 18 and 19 and to distinguish the various hands therein. He distinguishes two sources in the two chapters, one containing the singular and a second, the plural. Kautzsch[3], 31, follows him. Here, too, as in 18:1-16a (cf. above, pp. 193-94), this differentiation disrupts the organic cohesion. Thus one cannot possibly remove 19:18 (plural) from the context with v 17 (וַיֹּאמֶר sing.) and vv 19ff. (sing.). Kraetzschmar's opinion that the plural must be younger than the singular corresponds to a viewpoint which is currently widespread, to be sure, but is very unlikely for religiohistorical reasons (cf. above pp. 199-200). Sievers (2:287) divides the text among his three "major strands" of J, although this often separates substantive relationships. Thus, vv 2a and 2b, which he attributes to different sources, is linked by the *Stichwort* לִין and v 9ba may not be removed from the context. V 15aα corresponds to v 23a. V 20b (מִצְעָר, אִמָּלְטָה) belongs to the context of vv 17-22. Vv 27-28 stems from the same hand as 18:16, etc.

The legend displays a beautiful, clear structure. I. Lot receives the men (vv 1-3) and II. the counterpart, the Sodomites attempted assassination (vv 4-11). III. Lot's deliverance (vv 12-16) and IV. the counterpart, the destruction of Sodom (vv 23-25).

1-3 I. *The three men with Lot.* The verses are originally the immediate continuation of 18:22a, 33b. **1a** שְׁנֵי הַמַּלְאָכִים is an explicitum inserted secondarily. Originally, הָאֲנָשִׁים (18:22a) was intended as the subject of וַיָּבֹאוּ. There was a great room in the gate (cf. the plan of an Aramaic gate in the *Mitteilungen aus den Oriental. Sammlungen der Kgl. Museen zu Berlin* 11:11). This is the place for public commerce and communication, judicial proceedings and contract making, also convivial conversation with natives and foreigners (Benzinger[2], 102, 130). There Lot sits in the evening, resting after a full day's work. One sits there on a stone bench, perhaps, or on a spread-out cloth. **1bff.** The following scene of invitation and hospitality closely resembles the one in chap. 18. The author demonstrated his art here by agreeably varying the motif. He strives to repeat as little as possible. Vv **1b, 2a** offer genuine elements like those contained in 18:2. They could not be omitted from any invitation. סוּר refers to turning aside from the main thoroughfare onto a side street. "In the morning, then, you may go on your way" indicates that they are supposed to stay with him for only one night. They could accept this offer.

Now **2b** brings a small variation. The men decline, at first, and Lot must entreat them. The entreaty apparently plays <207> a great role in ancient hospitality. It is polite for the guest to decline, at first, for the host to entreat a good deal (מְאֹד; cf. the account of entreaty in Judg 19:55; also 1 Kgs 13:14ff.). This element probably intended to depict the "mean" as poor, insignificant people for whom modesty is seemly (cf. Ezek 16:49, "they did not assist the poor and the insignificant," and Isa 1:10ff., where Sodom and

Gomorra are mentioned as examples of the oppression of the insignificant). **3** Lot's meal for his guests is apparently narrated with the greatest possible brevity in order not to weary the reader after 18:1-8. The narrator's sense of style differs somewhat, therefore, from later style (e.g., in the Joseph narratives) which delights in repetitions and varies much less (cf. the introduction ¶3:20). Anyway, the narrator can report Lot's hospitality with such brevity here because he has still other evidence of his generosity in petto (vv 6-8). מַצּוֹת are unleavened cakes baked when one does not have time to wait on the bread to rise (Benzinger², 64), here in order to be able to put something before the guest immediately. Neither Abraham nor Lot have something already prepared—very simple circumstances. Here, too, the "men" eat (cf. comments on 18:8). According to vv 2ff., Lot dwelt in a house in Sodom, whereas the legend collector envisions him as a tent-dweller (13:12). On this small point, then, the old legend and the collector differ from one another.

4-11 II. The shameful behavior of the Sodomites stands in sharpest contrast to Lot's cordial hospitality. At the same time, their shamefulness offers the opportunity to highlight Lot's hospitality once again. Contrast was the most preferred stylistic device in Hebrew literature in all periods. The coarse tastes of the passionate Hebrew tolerate the harshest contrasts. **4** אַנְשֵׁי סְדֹם is a gloss (Olshausen, etc.). They "encircle" the house which, therefore, is conceived of as freestanding—on the farm. The very marked emphasis on the fact that all the people of Sodom, without exception, were equally guilty is probably associated with the account of Abraham's intercession and is, therefore, probably an addition. מִקָּצֶה means "from the extremes, in toto" (Siegfried-Stade). **5** The old legend considers the vice of pederasty entirely heinous. Such a city deserved fire and brimstone! Israel considers such unnatural lechery תּוֹעֵבָה (Lev 18:22) and specifically Canaanite (Lev 20:13, 23). The "men" are portrayed as blooming youths whose fresh beauty excites the evil lust of the Sodomites. This presupposition is significant religiohistorically. In the earliest period many gods were thought of in this way; in the narrator's time the angels (cf. also Tob 5:4ff.; Mac 16:5ff); and later the transfigured blessed (ApPet, ed. Bouriant, pp. 19, 18). Ancient Israel did not conceive of Yahweh as a blooming, fresh youth, but as a mature man, a mighty warrior. These observations show that the original intention of the story was hardly that Yahweh was among the "men." The notion that the Sodomites attempted pederasty on Yahweh himself would have been too crass even for the earliest Hebrew legend.

6-8 But, now, Lot demonstrates his hospitality. Courageously he appears before the evildoers, coming out of his house. Cautiously he closes the door behind him so that the guests suffer no harm (v 6). Cordially (אַחַי) he asks them to do no injustice (v 7). Magnanimously, he would even prefer to surrender the honor of his own daughters (v 8). We are supposed to think, "This was an honorable man, who held sacred the right to hospitality! He deserved to be delivered!" To us <208> moderns, however, this surrender of his daughters appears in another light. The ancient Israelite considered it admirably magnanimous to surrender one's own daughters for the sake of foreign guests (cf. Judg 19:25 and comments on Gen 12:13). One can also see that Lot's offer is by no means a "sin" (contra Franz Delitzsch) by the fact that the "men" let it pass. They wait to see how far the Sodomites' evil and Lot's hospitality will go. **8** הָאֵל = הָאֵלֶּה (Sam). The expression "shadow of my roof" is remarkable since narrative style otherwise totally avoids such elevated poetic usages (cf. the introduction ¶3:2). It is also unrealistic: it is night. It is probably a formulaic, originally juristic, archaic idiom (Sir 23:18; 29:22). Whoever enters under "the shadow of the roof" is sacrosanct. The sacredness of the right to hospitality had great significance on this cultural level, as it still does in similar circumstances, for example, among the Arabs.

9a The Sodomites, however, are infuriated at the foreign judge of morality. Whoever enters our land should remember that he is only one (הָאֶחָד, "that one there") and should keep quiet and not presume to pass judgment! This portrayal is apparently very true to nature. בְּלוֹט is a gloss (Olshausen, etc.). וַיִּשְׁפֹּט refers to the "paradoxical consequence" (cf. §111m). Kautzsch³, 32, prefers וְיִשְׁפֹּט. שָׁפוֹט accentuates the contrast (§113r; cf. §113p). It is a stylistic rule that the narrators of the legend followed almost without exception never to allow a person to speak twice in a row (cf. the introduction ¶3:13). Consequently, the dual וַיֹּאמְרוּ is very remarkable. The first speech will be an amplifying addition. The same is true, apparently, of וַיִּגְּשׁוּ לִשְׁבֹּר הַדָּלֶת (v 9bβ) which disrupts vv 9bα and 10. **9b** Now the Sodomites' rage and lust have risen to the extreme. **10, 11** And if the "men" had not now assisted Lot with their wondrous power, Lot and they themselves would have fallen into the Sodomites' hands. The Hebrew speaks of demonic blindness elsewhere, as well (cf. 2 Kgs 6:18; Zech 12:4; Deut 28:28). The notion that one cannot find a door is an authentic fairy tale motive which v. d. Leyen (CXIII, 255-56), quite correctly, derives from dream experience.

Thus, the narrative reaches the turning point. The deity who came to test the Sodomites (18:20-21) has now learned, personally, that they are truly very evil. They sought to commit an appalling evil. The narrator's and the hearers' hair stands on end when they only think: pederasty with the deity! At the same time, however, the men saw Lot's noble disposition. Thus they decide to destroy Sodom and to deliver Lot. Quite characteristically, the narrator does not communicate this decision itself, the aim of all the preceding and the origin of all that follows. He reports, in the old style, actions and speeches, but not thoughts (cf. the introduction ¶3:12).

12-16 III. *Lot's deliverance.* **12** The text is difficult. It is probably simplest (with Ball, Kittel, and Kautzsch³, 32) to strike חָתָן as the beginning of a <209> gloss חֲתָנֶיךָ occasioned by v 14 and to read בָּנֶיךָ without ו. The religious background of the statement is that the deity does not deliver only the righteous one but his whole house, also, for his sake. The same situation pertains in the biblical and the Babylonian Flood account. Whether all those spared are pious and worthy to be spared is not even asked. The patriarch is the unlimited monarch of the house, as well as the one properly responsible for religion (as, e.g., in Deut). Consequently, the family is a cohesive unit seen from the outside (Rauh, *Hebr. Familienrecht*, 39). Only the most advanced individualism thinks otherwise (Ezek 14:15ff.). The deity asks who else (עֹד) he has in the city—"still others," that is, beside the two daughters who dwell in Lot's house (vv 8, 15) and with whom the "men" were already acquainted. (A later recension added Lot's wife whom we must assume was already dead according to the ancient legend). Besides them, he only has his two future sons-in-law in Sodom (v 14). If the men here, then, ask about Lot's other sons and daughters, they prove to be insufficiently informed (so also Ball). An Israelite narrator would not have recounted this, either, if he thought that Yahweh was one of the three.

13 The "men" now inform Lot to the extent necessary. They do not yet reveal their actual nature to him yet. The statement "Yahweh sent us" is essentially ambiguous. Yahweh can send either humans or sons of God. According to this statement, Lot will have considered them, however, men of God commissioned by Yahweh to destroy the city (cf. Jer 1:10). Had Lot known that he was in the presence of divine beings, he would not have failed to tell his sons-in-law (v 14) and he would not have lingered in such a fashion (v 16). At the same time, however, the words seem to express the narrator's opinion that they were three messengers of Yahweh (thus not Yahweh and two servants; cf. comments on vv 16, 22). צַעֲקָתָם and לְשַׁחֲתָהּ have different suffixes (Vulg לְשַׁחֲתָם; Kittel).

14-16 The following is extremely exquisite artistry. It is supposed to describe the impression such an announcement of a sudden catastrophe makes on people. Lot, himself, impressed by the uncanny manner of his guests, is inclined to believe them (v 14). But he cannot decide so quickly, either: He lingers (vv 15, 16). The ancient narrator certainly did not intend to reproach Lot because of "weak faith." After all, it is no small measure suddenly to abandon house and home on the word of strange men! But Lot's sons-in-law, who did not hear and see them, consider everything a bad joke (v 14). Concerning the motif of initial laughter at a word of God see 18:12. The narrators who devised this motif were very well acquainted with human nature. Mockery has always been the lot of the prophets in every period. But Lot's hesitation is employed artfully to sharpen the tension. The work of destruction must take place before the sun rises! If Lot lingers any longer, the destruction will also reach him (v 15)! Dawn is breaking! Thus, we are supposed to listen, breathlessly rapt, and to exhale relieved when we hear in v 16 that Lot is led forcefully from Sodom at the last moment. Now the destruction can begin; Lot is delivered. The narrators love very much to excite such tension. It seems to them to be very beautiful, if possible, to compress the entire tension of an account into a single moment (cf. comments on 22:10-11; 32:27; 38:25; also 27:30; 31:33-34; 44:12). The religious precondition is that the deity works at night, indeed, is linked with the night. In the ancient viewpoint, it corresponds both to the horrors of the <210> night, which the ancient felt very sharply and interpreted as the product of the wandering deity, as well as to the being of the deity, himself, who reveals himself only in the darkness of the night in order to guard his eternal secret (15:17; Exod 4:24; 12:29; Judg 6:38, 40; 2 Kgs 19:35; Isa 17:14). Germans speak similarly of a spirit's hour. The legends readily tell of an appearance of God immediately before dawn (32:25ff.; Exod 14:24—in the final night watch; Psa 46:6), as it does here. In German legends, too, the spirits' power ends with the stroke of one (Grimm, *Deutsche Sagen*, no. 175 and Goethe, "Thümer"), with the first rooster crow (Grimm, nos. 183, 188, 207), or at sunrise (cf. v. d. Leyen, *Märchen in der Edda*, p. 49 and n. 20; Hock, *Vampyrsagen*, 10n.1). This belief can explained originally in relation to dream life: "When the night is past and the morning sun shines, the dream also ends and the spirits of the dream lose their power" (v. d. Leyen CXIII, 257; cf. also Stade, *Bibl. Theol.*, 101n.3). In addition to this view that God reveals himself by night, there stands another according to which "light is the garment he wears," and the place where he dwells (Psa 104:2; 1 Tim 6:16). The two viewpoints can be traced to the influence of entirely different religions—the second to a light, or more precisely, a sun religion. This perspective is, it seems, the more recent in Israel which later became the ordinary viewpoint. The divine figures in the Sodom account—who appear in the evening and disappear at sunrise—differ significantly from those in the Hebron narrative—who appear in the light of day, at midday. This, too, is evidence that these figures were originally distinct and that the two legends did not originally belong together. This conclusion is, in fact, obvious for the legend scholar.

14 לְקֵחַ refers to the future (§116d). The men—we can assume—have already paid the bride-price, but they have not yet brought the brides home (Rauh, *Hebr. Familien-recht*, 16-17). **15** כְּמוֹ is a poetic form, "just as." It signifies the simultaneity of two processes (cf. König, *Syntax*, 557; §387e). הַמַּלְאָכִים is a gloss as in v 1. וְאֶת־אֶשְׁתְּךָ and וּבְרַד אֲשֶׁתּוֹ (v 16) are intended to prepare for v 26 and are additions (cf. p. 205). LXX reads וְיֵצֵא after הַנִּמְצָאֹת (so Kittel), but it is probably only an addition. **16** The words בְּחֶמְלַת יהוה עָלָיו can only be understood on the condition that the "men" are messengers who execute Yahweh's command. The words are probably an addition, however. וַיַּנִּחֻהוּ, "they left him there," implies that, here, outside the city, he is in safety and that they, themselves, turn back now. The immediate continuation of the verse are vv 23a, 24.

17-22 Zoar (LXX Σηγωρ), situated on the southeastern shore of the Dead Sea, not buried by the alluvium, once lay in a well-watered region with a tropical climate (cf. Dillmann and Buhl, *Palästina*, 271; bibliography in Blanckenhorn, ZDPV 19:54n.1). Israel is amazed that this bit of land was excepted from destruction and explains it as the result of Lot's request for this Zoar as a place of refuge. Yet, the legend still maintained that Lot must actually flee to the mountains (v 17), which he actually did according to the earliest tradition. The legend of Zoar is, thus, a geological legend. At the same time, it contains an etymological motif. The city is called Zoar "small," because in his request Lot said, "It is, indeed, only מִצְעָר a small matter." The many words Lot speaks are meant to show how pitiably he entreated <211> and to provide the motivation for the fact that the deity could not deny such an imploring request. Lot is portrayed here as a frail old man who can no longer climb the mountains so quickly. The fivefold הִמָּלֵט plays ingeniously with the name לוֹט (Ball). **17** On the alternation between singular and plural see above, p. 205. The plural is to be accepted throughout as the oldest reading: וַיֹּאמְרוּ (LXX, Pesh, Vulg) v 17, עַבְדְּכֶם בְּעֵינֵיכֶם הַסְדְּכֶם וַתַּגְדִּילוּ עֲשִׂיתֶם v 19, וַיֹּאמְרוּ נָשָׂאנוּ הֲפַכְנוּ v 21, and נוּכַל v 22. Regarding אַל־תַּבִּיט (impf. following אַל) see §107p. "The mountain" is the mountain to the east of the Sea. **20** The narrator intentionally repeats the word מִצְעָר. It is supposed to make an impression because the narrator wants to take it up again in v 22b (cf. comments on 18:12ff.). **22a** A statement like לֹא אוּכַל would hardly be suitable in Yahweh's mouth, but only in the those of the servants of God who have been commissioned to spare Lot in any case. This, too, demonstrates that the earliest recension of the text read the plural throughout these speeches. **22b** Regarding עַל־כֵּן compare 2:24; 11:9.

23-25 IV. *Sodom's destruction*. V **23b** takes vv 18-22 into consideration and also belongs, therefore, to the addition. According to the original report, the heavenly storm broke loose immediately after v 16. But here Lot receives enough time to go to Zoar! **23, 24** The events follow—the syntax indicates this (cf. §164b)—immediately one after another. Thus, the deity waited until the last possible moment! The Sam reading (יָצָא, as in 15:17) is preferable (Kittel). Notably, the "men" do not destroy the city, as they announced in v 13, but Yahweh himself does. The earlier recension will have also attributed this destruction to the "men," that is, originally the three gods who appeared (cf. comments on 18:1-16) for whom the Yahwistic recension substituted Yahweh (cf. also v 14). ועל־עמרה is an addition (Sievers 2:288-89; Kautzsch³, 32; cf. comments on 18:20). Blanckenhorn (ZDPV 191:58) interprets the catastrophe described here as a tectonic earthquake during which gases, hot springs, masses with petroleum and asphalt content rise from newly opened fissures. Thus, the air could be filled with flame and smoke could form (cf. also Greßmann, 32ff.). But, since it says that it rained fire and brimstone, it is more likely that one should think of a volcanic eruption associated with an earthquake (Ed. Meyer, *Sitzungsberichte der Berliner Akad. d. Wissensch.* [1905]: 641n.2; *Israeliten*, 71). Concerning the concept of Yahweh as a volcanic deity see the comments on chap. 15 (p. 181). מֵאֵת יהוה and מִן־הַשָּׁמָיִם are doublets. The first (also in Mic 5:6) is the ancient, mythopoeic expression, like ἐκ Διός. The second is the modern, conceptual-prosaic expression. The second will be a gloss from a later period (Olshausen). Since, however, the subject is יהוה, מֵאֵת יהוה can only be used here in a very diminished sense. The expression, already so faded here, presumes that people were accustomed since the earliest period to thinking of Yahweh in heaven and to deriving meteorological phenomena, especially the rain, from him (cf. comments on 11:7). **25** The narrator accentuates the total destruction of the whole region because of 13:10 (cf. the interpretation of that legend, pp. 175-76). הָפַךְ, "to overturn, overthrow," of an earthquake that "overturns" the land, is (along with derivatives) <212> a technical term for Sodom's destruction (cf. v 21; Deut 29:22; Isa 1:7; 13:19; Jer 49:18; 50:40; Amos 4:11; Lam 4:6; Nöldeke, *Untersuchungen*, 21n.1; regarding such terms, cf. above pp. 120-21). According to Sievers (2:288, 291) אֶת־הָעִיר should be read. It is probably simplest to strike וְאֵת כָּל־יֹשְׁבֵי הֶעָרִים as an amplifying addition (cf. above p. 201). Herewith the Sodom legend ends.

26 *Appendix: a geological legend which interprets a remarkable saltstone formation resembling a female figure as a petrified woman.* This stone column (or was it already a different one?) is mentioned again by Sap 10:7, Josephus, *Ant.* I.11.4, and others. It may have stood on *Ĝebel Usdum* southwest of the Sea, a ridge consisting of marl, limestone, and large salt layers, well weathered and completely covered with caves, fissures, peaks, and outcroppings (cf. Dillmann and Buhl, *Palästina*, 42). A forty-foot-high column currently standing there (figure in Stade, *Gesch. Israels* 1:119) is called "Lot's daughter" nowadays. The ancient people maintained that these columns were Lot's wife who became stone because of a sin. The transformation of people into stone is a very common legend motif. "If rocks in a certain region resemble people, the legend recounted that these rocks were originally people who were then petrified as rocks" (v. d. Leyen CXIV, 15). The Greeks tell of such petrifications of Nioe, Cadmos, and Harmonia. The same motif occurs in *1,001 Nights* in the "Story of the Petrified Prince" (translated by Weil, 3rd ed. 1:49ff.) and in the "Story of the two Jealous Sisters" (Weil 3:316ff.). German legends tell of Hans Heiling's rock (Grimm, *Deutsche Sagen*, no. 328) and of Frau Hütt near Innsbruck (Grimm, no. 233). Andree (*Ethnographische Parallelen* 1:97-98, 301) offers other examples from Germany (the monk and nun at Eienach), Persia ("today people still show foreign travelers such magical stones on the Iranian high plain in many places"), from Bulgaria, Dajak, southern Australia, Africa, India, New Mexico, and Lake Titicaca. Additional bibliography can be found in Tylor (*Anfänge der Kultur* 1:346n.2), Tobler (*Im*

Neuen Reich 2 [1873]: 165-66), E. Süss (*Antlitz der Erde* 1:56), and Bonus (Preuß. *Jahrb.* 119:287-88). Nordic legends often relate that the appearance of the sun transforms monsters and trolls into stone, as in the Alwislied of the Edda (H. Gering, *Edda*, 86; cf. also, ibid., 156). Petrification through a look also occurs in the legend of Perseus who shows the head of the Gorgon. It also occurs frequently that one becomes stone if one looks back contrary to command, as in the "Story of the two Jealous Sister" in *1,001 Nights* (Weil 3:316ff.). This element must have a very specific significance. What, precisely, remains to be examined. The Hebrew narrator also explains the sin of Lot's wife in this way. She looked back contrary to an explicit command and, thus, glimpsed the secret of the deity. God does not want to manifest himself wholly to people. Whoever has seen him, must die. The prohibition against looking back also recurs frequently in legends and customs: in the Orpheus legend, in *1,001 Nights* (Weil 1:316ff.), further in Greek tradition in association with chthonic sacrifices and the Babylonian spell priests in the purification of the ill (cf. Jastrow, *Rel. Bab. u. Ass.* 1:337), and "in the more recent popular belief in relation to seances, recovery of treasures, and similar magical practices which have developed from soul-cult concepts" (Stoll in *Lex.*, ed. Roscher, s.v. Eurydike; cf. Grimm, *Deutsche Sagen*, no. 175). Such a prohibition is especially difficult to observe because one unintentionally turns around if something happens behind one.

Vv **27, 28** stem from the poet of the Abraham-Lot legend cycle. The aesthetic purpose of the interlude has already been elucidated above (pp. 159-60); a psychological analysis of the exciting passage is given in the the introduction (¶3:12). One may best read בַּבֹּקֶר <213> + וַיֵּלֶךְ (Kittel). Hebr mss and Sam have ויל פני כל הארץ הככר, of which הארץ and הככר seem to be variants. Kittel prefers ועל פני כל־הככר. כִבְשָׁן is a smelting oven in contrast to תַּנּוּר, a cooking oven. Exod 19:18 compares the smoke of the כִבְשָׁן to the fumes of an erupting volcano. This smoke, therefore, should probably be conceived as thick black or yellow fumes. This smoke, so the narrator imagines, lies on the land henceforth and until now. Later generations maintain that such a smoke covers the Dead Sea (WisdSol 10:7). In reality, it is often only covered by haze or a veil of fog (Dillmann; see further, p. 214). The whole narrative of Abraham-Hebron and Lot-Sodom takes place according to the legend cycle in less than twenty-four hours. At midday the men come to Abraham. In the early afternoon they are his guests. In the late afternoon they go to Sodom where they arrive in the evening. At the break of day Lot is delivered. At sundown Sodom is destroyed. At dawn of the following day Abraham sees the traces of the divine deed from a distance. The narrator was able to compress dramatically the events into the briefest period and, thus also to establish a chronological unity between the two legends. This legend cycle, therefore, has succeeded in every aspect. V 27b takes the insertion in 18:22b-33a into consideration and is, thus, also an insertion.

General Remarks Concerning the Sodom-Lot Legend

1. *Legend type.* The legend of Sodom's destruction by divine judgment has many parallels (cf. Grimm, *Deutsche Mythologie* 14:481-82; Tobler, *Im Neuen Reich* 2 [1873]: 167; Cheyne, *New World* [June 1892]: 239ff.; idem, *Enc Bibl*, s.v. "Sodom and Gomorrha 4"; Driver, 203n.1; Winternitz in *Mitt. Anthrop. Ges. in Wien* 31:312-13; Ed. Hahn, *Zeitschr. f. Ethnologie* [1903]: 1015n.4, 1016n.1, with bibliography). In many places, people tell that a once-thriving site was destroyed by the deity (e.g., the German legend

in Grimm, nos. 11, 112, 113). And it is often added that this happened because of the evil of the inhabitants (e.g., Grimm, nos. 92, 96, 233, 235, 239). Further, it is said that one or a few pious individuals were spared (here one thinks, especially, of the Flood account, structurally related to the Sodom account, cf. above p. 78). People readily imagine that evil and righteousness were demonstrated in the reception afforded a traveler, in reality a god. This category of legends includes the Greek legends of Philemon and Baucis and of Lycaon. A narrative very similar to the Sodom-Lot legend can be found in P. Cassel, *Mišie Sindbad*, 7, concerning the city Holaolokia where a certain Arhat was cordially received by only one man, while others threw sand at him. Arhat announced to him the imminent destruction of the city and commanded him to save himself. The man went into the city and told his relatives, but they scoffed at the news. When the city was destroyed (by a shower of earth and sand), the man saved himself. The German legend Grimm no. 322 is also related. According to it Alt-Tesch was shaken by a rockslide because a farmwife hard-heartedly did not want to give a passerby, who was our Lord himself, any of her butter. Grimm no. 45 is particularly close: a wandering dwarf comes to a little village during a rainstorm, knocks on all the doors, but is received by only one pious couple. On the following morning, the entire village is shaken and only the hut of the two old people is spared. One may also compare the account of *Birket-râm* (Phiala Lake near Banias, a volcanic crater lake). A once-thriving city denied hospitality to a stranger and was, therefore, covered with water (cf. Baedeker, *Pal"stina und Syrien*[5], 293). The Sodom account belongs, therefore, to a very widely dispersed <214> legend type. The contention of A. Jeremias (ATAO[2], 360ff.) that the Sodom account is dressed with motifs of the (cosmic) flood of fire, that is, the change of the world summer, finds no support in the text.

2. *Location.* Such narratives are naturally localized at sites which occupy the imagination because of their desertion or peculiarity. Ours is localized at the Dead Sea.

Ancient Israel senses most vividly the eerie impression made by the Dead Sea—no fish in its waves, the water extremely salty, and the vegetation not productive, but deadly, "lonely silence, not a trace of human life or activity," salt stones in unusual forms in the vicinity (Benzinger[2], 17-18; Guthe, *Pal"stina*, 153ff.). No one lodges there and no one dwells there. Whoever passes by is horrified at all its plagues (according to Jer 42:17-18). The legend is concerned with the development of this horrible landscape. Whoever sees parcels of this land and the sufferings it must suffer from Yahweh—brimstone and salt, the whole land a conflagration, it is not sown and produces nothing—says, "Why did Yahweh do this to this land? Whence comes this awful wrath?" Then someone answers, "Because they sinned against Yahweh his wrath burned on this land. Yahweh overturned them in his wrath and rage!" (following Deut 29:21-28). Thus the Hebrew concludes from the horrible impression of the place, that a frightful sin and a terrible judgment of God must have once occurred here.

The legend reports this in very precise detail. There, where the horrible Sea now lies, was earlier a wonderful oasis, richly watered like Paradise (13:10). One recounts this former state gladly for the sake of the contrast (regarding this type of narrative, cf. the Paradise legend, p. 30). The land to the north and south of the Sea offers the occasion for the contrast. In earlier times, the city of Sodom lay in this oasis, once so rich, as the legend reports.

The legend also knows the sin of this old city very precisely. It was unnatural lechery, Canaan's sin. Because of this sin, which they wanted to commit even against the deity, the city was annihilated. Characteristically, Israelite-Jewish sensibility discusses the lechery with great sobriety. There is an uninterrupted series of examples of this from the earliest period to the letter to the Romans (1:26-27).

This much could well be understood as the result of the impression made by the Dead Sea. One could also entertain the notion of a historical event of which a last reminiscence echoes here. Albeit, the legend's notion that the "entire Jordan region" was previously a paradisiacal landscape (13:10; 19:25; according to which, it seems then, the Dead Sea is supposed not to have existed at all in this early period; cf. also 14:3) is an error. The geological evidence shows that in the historical period the Jordan has always poured its water into the Dead Sea (cf. Dillmann; Franz Delitzsch; Buhl, *Palästina*, 35). But one may hypothesize, perhaps, that the southern portion of the Dead Sea, which is very flat, only came into existence in later times through a natural event, as often occurs (so recently Blanckenhorn, ZDPV 19: 51ff.; Guthe, *Palästine*, 155).

Notably, however, the legend speaks of fire and earthquakes, but not of water, although the locale is now particularly characterized by the salt sea there. It is further characteristic that the legend seems to speak of a volcanic eruption (cf. comments on 19:24, p. 211) that cannot have taken place at the Dead Sea in the historical period (Blanckenhorn, 42; Guthe, *Palästina*, 30). Significantly, too, fog sometimes covers this Sea, but not the "smoke of a smelting oven." All this suggests that the Sodom legend did not originally refer to the site of the Dead Sea, but to some other locale and that it was only secondarily applied to the Dead Sea <215>. One may refer now to Meyer (*Sitzungsberichte der Berl. Akad.* [1905] and *Israeliten*, 71) who suggests that the legend may have originally explained the origin of one of the monstrous *Harras*, that is, the lava fields of Arabia (cf. the map at the end of the first volume of Doughty, *Travels in Arabia Deserts*) and, thus, will stem from a time when Israel's ancestors dwelt in that region, in "Midian." Such an assumption is unobjectionable. This legend would not be the only one to migrate from one people to another, from one site to another (cf. the Hebron legend, pp. 195, 199-200). Accordingly, the name of Lot, the patriarch of Moab and Ammon, or in an older tradition, a Horite clan (36:29) will not be original to the legend. When this legend was transferred to the Dead Sea, it was convenient to identify the righteous one delivered by the deity with Lot whose home in "the cave" (19:30) was in the vicinity. Or was the figure of Lot originally situated in the Sodom legend and only secondarily transformed into the patriarch of Moab and Ammon (Meyer, *Israeliten*, 261)? At any rate, the legend collector, although he still knew the older tradition of the "smelting smoke" (19:28), clearly conceived of the legend at the site of the Dead Sea since he offered in the subsequent section (19:30-38) the account of the birth of Ammon and Moab.

3. In its current state, the narrative bears novelistic trappings. Lot's cordial hospitality and the deity's nocturnal activity, in particular, are portrayed in many details. Lot's daughters are introduced in order to prepare for the following account (19:31-38) in which they play an independent role. But the narrator knows very well how to motivate their introduction in this early position (v 8). Lot's sons-in-law also appear. But these persons seem to be present only for artistic effect. A later hand also added Lot's wife as well as Zoar's deliverance. At the time of the addition, the legend established a firm footing at

the Dead Sea. Then local peculiarities like the remarkable salt columns and the oasis of Zoar were interpreted with elements of the Sodom-Lot legend. Later, the "Sodom apples" were also seen as a memorial of the divine wrath (WisdSol 10:7).

4. *Citations and imitations.* Prophetic literature very often cites the Sodom account: Sodom as the clearest example of horrible evil (Isa 1:10; Jer 23:14; Deut 32:32), specifically of public (social) evil (Isa 1:10), of shameless sin (Isa 3:9), and of horrible, complete, eternal destruction by God's wrath (Isa 1:7, 9; 13:19; Jer 49:18; Zeph 2:9; Deut 29:22; Amos 4:11) in an instant (Lam 4:6). Often (as in our account, Gen 19, cf. comments on 18:20) Sodom is mentioned alone (Isa 1:7; 3:9; Lam 4:6), as well as in association with Gomorra (as in the glosses, 13:10; 18:20; 19:24, 28; further 19:29 P and in chap. 14; further 10:19; Isa 1:9-10; 13:19; Jer 23:14; Amos 4:11; Zeph 2:9; Deut 32:32) and neighboring cities (Jer 49:18; 50:40; Ezek 16:46ff.). These references to "neighboring cities" seem to intend Adma and Zeboiim. Hos 11:8 speaks of the cities Adma and Zeboiim and their frightful destruction. They occur along with Sodom and Gomorra in Deut 29:22; Gen 14:2; 10:19. Therefore, Hosea probably knew a variant of the account. It may be that Adma and Zeboiim, too, did not originally lie on the Dead Sea.

Deut 29:22 and Ezek 16:49-50 are more extensive. Deut 29:22: the site is entirely brimstone, salt (cf. Zeph 2:9), burned, uncultivated; Ezek 16:49-50: "This was the Sodom's guilt: it lived majestically and in joy, had plenty of bread and prosperous comfort [cf. Gen 13:10] along with its daughters, but they did not care for the suffering and the poor [Ezekiel understood the treatment of the three travelers, then, as a typical case of unsociable behavior; cf. also Isa 1:10]; and they were arrogant and committed abominations before me [unnatural lechery, for which "abomination" is a technical term]; then I did away with it as soon as I saw this" (cf. Gen 18:21; but it may be better to read with Cornill, "as you [Jerusalem] have seen"). Ezekiel had before him the legend attested in Genesis which he interpreted in his fashion. Allusions to the Sodom legend or similar accounts can also be found in Psa 11:6; 140:11; Isa 34:9-10. An imitation of the Sodom-Lot <216> legend may be the account, preserved in two recensions, of the abomination at Gibeah (Judg 19). The central section of this account very closely resembles the Sodom legend. It agrees with it not only in the chief motifs, but even in many minor incidentals. The scene in Judg 19:22ff. is particularly similar and is even recounted in similar terms. The account also employed other individual elements from older legends (Judg 19:19 = Gen 24:25; Judg 19:29 = 1 Sam 11:7). This imitation also demonstrates the advanced age of the Sodom account.

Kraetzschmar (ZAW 17:87-88) has also called attention to the fact that the account is usually cited with the phrase כְּמַהְפֵּכַת אֱלֹהִים אֶת־סְדֹם יְאֵת עֲמֹרָה (Amos 4:11; Isa 13:19; Jer 50:40) which speaks not of יהוה but of אלהים. Kraetzschmar infers quite rightly from this observation that the account was not originally Yahwistic. Other observations suggest the same conclusion (cf. above). Non-Yahwistic origins are also very probable for many other legends. In contrast, Eerdmans' (36, 71) contention that the אלהים in this phrase should be translated "the gods" is to be rejected from the outset. Where does polytheism occur elsewhere in Amos?! Rather, it is noteworthy that the period which transformed the three men into messengers of Yahweh possessed a relatively universalistic God concept: Yahweh is the avenger even of Sodom's evil! This is incipient monotheism and it surely belongs in a very early period (cf. Kautzsch[3], 31).

25. Lot's Daughters 19:30-38 Jᵃ

1. *Source.* The legend stems from J (בְּכִירָה and צְעִירָה, vv 31, 33-35, 37-38; חִיָּה זָרֵי, vv 32, 34) and not from another context (contra Kautzsch³). It is a necessary component of the legend cycle of Abraham and Lot, the counterpart to the account of Isaac's birth which originally followed immediately. Furthermore, the repeated appearance of Lot's daughters in the Sodom account demonstrates that the narrator of this legend intended to report an account concerning Lot's daughters later. The clauses "he dwelt together with his two daughters in the mountains" and "he dwelt together with his two daughters in the cave" (v 30) could not have been written by the same author in sequence (Eerdmans, 12). The solution to the difficulty is very simple. Lot's migration from Zoar to the mountains (v 30a) belongs to the Zoar insertion (vv 17-22). Yet, the words "Lot went up" could have been the introduction to the ancient legend.

2. *The original and later meaning of the legend.* The legend is ethnological in nature. It deals with the origin of the peoples of Moab and Ammon, Lot's sons. At the same time, it explains the two names. It takes מוֹאָב in the sense of מֵאָב "from his own father." According to it, the patriarch of the בְנֵי עַמּוֹן was actually called בֶּן־עַמִּי "son of my father" (cf. comments on v 38). Accordingly, the legend recounts how Moab and Ammon were born as a result of the two daughters' intercourse with their own father. In later times, especially since it become customary to see Moab and Ammon as traditional enemies (Deut 23:4ff.), this parentage was assuredly seen as a particular disgrace. This understanding of the narrative can already be found in Deut 32:32, "for their vine stems from the vine of Sodom, from the fields of Gomorra." "They," that is, Israel's enemies (v 31), who scoff at Yahweh and Israel and see Israel's misfortune as evidence of Yahweh's weakness, are Ammon and Moab who, according to the early legend, stem from Sodom and Gomorra, the source of their poisonous character (concerning Moab's wine, cf. Isa 16:7ff.; Jer 48:11., 32ff.; concerning Moab's mockery and arrogance, Isa 16:6; Jer 48:26-27, 29-30; Ezek 25:8). The prophetic poet would certainly not have recalled Moab's parentage at this point if the original legend had not recounted something evil, sodomite of Lot. Accordingly, recent scholars have understood the account as a creation of Jewish folk humor with no connection to ancient tradition. The namelessness of Lot's daughters is cited as evidence for this understanding (cf. Stade, *Gesch. Israels* 1:118). However, the fact that Lot's two <217> daughters are nameless does not indicate that they must have always been so. Instead, later tradition normally forgets such names. That they were once legend figures, however, is suggested by the Lot-Sodom account where they already appear and play a certain role. Now, the age of the account is indicated by the fact that it is localized. Lot dwells "in the cave." "The cave" of Lot is a specific cave, like "the cave" of Elijah (and of Moses) on Horeb (1 Kgs 19:9; Exod 33:2) and "the spring" of Hagar (16:7). This element cannot have been first devised in Israel. One must, rather, have pointed to a cave in Moab named for Lot. Consequently, we must ask whether the entire legend may not be of Ammonite-Moabite origins, just as we have assumed that the legend of Ishmael's birth at Lahairoi stems from Ishmael itself (cf. above, p. 191). On the lips of the Moabites and Ammonites, of course, the account would not have been recounted in derision, but very seriously, even in praise of the matriarchs (cf. also Haller, 138). The fact that Lot's daughters were in no way ashamed of their children's parentage but,

instead, publicly proclaim it and establish it for all times in the names of their sons points to this interpretation. Further support of this understanding lies in the fact that the narrator of the Abraham-Lot legend cycle cannot possibly narrate an account concerning Lot at this point, after he has just praised Lot's nobility, which he would have understood as a malicious account of shame. Accordingly, the legend's earliest intention should be regarded as follows: a great catastrophe destroyed all humanity. Only Lot and his daughters remain. Thus, as things normally go, the maidens would have been condemned to infertility. In such cases, however, in the face of childlessness, the ancient Hebrew woman is capable of heroic, even desperate decisions (16:2; 30:1ff., 18) and she acquires male seed where she can find it (cf. especially the Tamar legend, chap. 38). The narrator, himself, twice expressly states that this is the thinking of Lot's daughters and that they did not simply commit lechery, "we want to preserve the family" (vv 32, 34; cf. the same statement in the Flood account, 7:3). The sons, however, born from such a bed, are by no means ashamed of this parentage. Instead, they proudly proclaim the heroism of their mother (cf. the Tamar account) and the purity of their blood. They were not begotten by strange seed, but by father and daughter, purest thoroughbred! This Moabite-Ammonite tribal legend seems still to be understood without malice in the legend cycle. Yet, the early period already offers a certain criticism of the account through the fact that, as in the corresponding context in the Tamar legend (chap. 38), Yahweh's name is avoided (cf. Haller, 20). At any rate, the later period did not understand the heroically proud sense of the legend, but heard in it only incest.

A variety of the motif of the daughter bearing her own father's child also occurs in the account of Smyrna or Myrrha who, enflamed to illicit love for her father Theias by the enraged Aphrodite, deceives him for twelve nights during which Adonis is conceived. It is also recounted how Myrrha got her father drunk (cf. Roscher, Lex 1, 69ff.). The same motif, although diluted of the father-in-law and the daughter-in-law, occurs in the Tamar novella. The old German Wölsungen legend (chap. 7) also knows of heroic incest.

3. The style of the account is extremely unusual. The two consummations are recounted in almost the same words (vv 33, 35), as are the two summons (vv 32, 34b). In a broader sense, the summons and the consummations also correspond to one another, as do, finally, the two births. These parallels are no accident, but intention. The second summons (v 34) would not have been necessary for the continuation of the action and is only present because of its counterpart. The account is, therefore, especially artful. Additional examples of such "epic" style are Judg 9:8ff.; Job 1:6-12; 2:1-7; 1:13-19.

31 "Our father is old." The implication is that if it is to be done at all, it must be done soon. <218> "There is no man on earth." The legend seems to presuppose that all men were impacted by the catastrophe which was, therefore, originally envisioned like the Flood. The legend here is, like the Flood account, in the process of transforming an originally local into a universal catastrophe. עָלֵינוּ would be better read אֵלֵינוּ (Vulg, Ball). The expression כְּדֶרֶךְ כָּל־הָאָרֶץ is discrete. As crude as things may be. the narrator clearly strives to report them as cautiously as possible. The Tamar legend is very similar. **32** For לְהָ Sam has the better reading לְכִי (Ball; Kittel). They must intoxicate their father because he would never knowingly and willingly agree to their wishes. A similar motif occurs in the Tamar legend (cf. comments on 38:13-14; cf. also the legend of Noah and Canaan). The legend assumes that, if the existence of the family is in question, the woman is more passionate and reckless than the man. This element of prefatory intoxication is rather repugnant to us. For the earliest Hebrew sensibility, it is only a particularly successful stratagem. **33** The narrator emphasizes that Lot noticed nothing. He wants to exonerate Lot (cf. the similar exoneration of Judah in 38:16ff.). It seems very unlikely to us that he would not notice anything. The ancients were more gullible. Other incredible elements occur in 19:26; 25:26; 38:28ff.; etc. For בַּלַּיְלָה הוּא (regarding the construction, cf. 24:8; Mesha 3) Sam and Kittel have הַהוּא as does v 35. One of the passages is to be emended. **35** For וַתָּקָם LXX, Pesh, and Vulg have וַתָּבֹא, a harmonization with v 33.

37 The attentive hearer has noticed that the word אָב (eight times) and especially the phrases מֵאָבִיהֶן מֵאָבִינוּ (three times) have occurred frequently in the foregoing. This prepares a point. Now in v 27 the elucidation follows. The goal was the word מוֹאָב. This is ingenious by the narrator's tastes. We should be pleased. One must remember the main issue when considering this etymology. The other etymologies in Genesis are not much better, however (4:24; 29:32, 34; 30:23, 24). It would be a basic error to attempt to bring scientific sobriety to this naive name interpretation. **38** The author did not take בֶּן־עַמִּי as "son of my people" which would not express the characteristic aspect of this child. Instead, in order to be able to derive Bene-Ammon <219> in a manner similar to the derivation of Moab, he understood עַם "relative" in the sense of "father" ("father's brother") which also occurs in Arabic (Krenkel, ZAW 8:283-84; Wellhausen, GGN [1893], 480n.2; Nestle, ZAW 16: 322-23). LXX (followed by Ball) adds λέγουσα· ἐκ τοῦ πατρός μου after v 37a. But this motivation is entirely superfluous after the many preceding allusions. In v 38, LXX reads καὶ ἐκάλεσεν τὸ ὄνομα αὐτοῦ Αμμαν, ὁ υἱὸς τοῦ γένους μου. Ball emends accordingly, but destroys thereby a subtlety of the original text which refers to Moab, the father of the people of Moab and Ben-Ammi, the father of the people Bene-Ammon (so the customary usage). Thus the Lot narrative is concluded. In the legend cycle the birth of Isaac and the second visit of the men with Abraham originally follow now.

26. Abraham with Abimelech in Gerar 20 E

Source. The passage uses אלהים. P does not contain such colorful and for him highly objectionable narratives. Also, Abraham dwells only in Mamre according to P, not in Beersheba or Gerar. Consequently, the passage is from E. Other indications of E include revelation in a dream (vv 3, 6) and the diction—אָמָה, maiden (v 17; J uses שִׁפְחָה), לְבָב (v 5; J uses לֵב), and the rarer expressions נִקָּיוֹן (v 5), אָמַר אֶל, "to say something about someone" (v 2), נָתַן with accusative and infinitive with לְ, "to permit someone to do something" (v 6), etc. (cf. Dillmann and Holzinger).

Originally, the legend followed closely upon the legend of Abraham's immigration to Canaan. His wife is still young and desirable and he does not yet have a child (cf. Meyer, *Israeliten*, 237n.3). R^JE could find no better position for the account than this. Yet it does not fit well after 18:11-12 according to which Sarah is already an old woman. There is also no room for the event of chap. 20 between the promise in 18:10 that she will become pregnant and the arrival of the pregnancy in 21:1-2.

1 According to the following legends Gerar lies in the vicinity of Rehoboth (*Reḥêbe*), 26:22, and Beersheba (*Bîr es-Seba ʿ*), 21:22ff.; 26:23ff. Chap. 26 presumes, more precisely, that it lies closer to Rehoboth than to Beersheba. In order to avoid conflicts with the Gerarites, Isaac moves from Rehoboth to Beersheba. Now since Beersheba is situated farther to the north than Rehoboth, we will seek Gerar in the South where the name *Wâdi Ĝerûr* is preserved west of Kadesh. The information in 2 Chron 14:12-13 (Gerar on the highway from Canaan to Egypt) and in Gen 20:1ab ("between" Kadesh, 14:7; 16:14, and Shur, 16:7) agrees with this identification. The contrasting statements in 21:32, 34; 26:1, 8, 14, 15, 18 (but not in chap. 20) that Gerar was in the possession of the Philistines at that time result from a later confusion with another Gerar, the current *Umm Ĝarrâr* SSE of Gaza. Accordingly, v 1aβ belongs to the older tradition of our legend. In contrast, the Negeb (v 1aα; 12:9) lies much farther to the north than the Gerar of the old legend. Yet, this phrase could belong to E. One would have to assume a lacuna which, as in the parallel recensions, would narrate that Abraham, driven by famine (12:10; 26:1ff.) moved from the Negeb (12:9-10) to Gerar (26:1; Holzinger). This comment could have been omitted in order to avoid excessive repetitions of chaps. 12 and 26. וַיָּגָר בִּגְרָר is a play on words (Holzinger). The old legends are strewn with such allusions to names.

2 "Abraham pretends that his wife is his sister and Abimelech takes her from him. Both of these are stated very briefly" (Dillmann). Accordingly, as in v 1, a redactional abbreviation seems to have <220> been introduced (Holzinger). One may note, however, the following. The fact that the king has not approached Sarah too closely is apparently stated for the first time in v 4 and cannot have been narrated yet in the preceding. V 6 then adds that God hindered him from approaching her. How this took place, however, we learn only from the final word of the legend, וַיֵּלֵדוּ (v 17). It was a sexual illness. Similarly, the motives of Abraham and Abimelech, passed over in v 2, are laid out in detail in the subsequent speeches. Here we apparently do not have "clumsy" presentation (Dillmann) but, rather, a narration which differs radically from the usual style. Whereas the usual style recounts things in their natural sequence, this more refined narrative intentionally leaves a lacuna at the beginning in order to fill it in gradually in the course of the account. One may compare the book of Jonah where several such "supplements" occur. We do not learn the content of the message the prophet is supposed to deliver in 1:2 or 3:2, but first in 3:4. We do not hear the reason for his flight in 1:3 but only in 4:2 (a similar case involves 1:1). This narrative style is chosen by authors who wish to narrate somewhat more artfully and, at the same time, to heighten the tension through such lacunae. This "supplementary" style may be compared, for example, with the exposition of modern dramas which allow the background to be deduced gradually through allusions. It is probably not accidental that Sarah's experiences in Abimelech's harem are semi-concealed, semirevealed in this fashion. The sensitivity of the narrator will also have caused him to choose this style here. Accordingly, nothing essential need have been omitted in v 2. LXX sought to fill in the apparent lacuna from 26:7: ἐφοβήθη γὰρ εἰπεῖν ὅτι γυνή μού ἐστιν, μήποτε ἀποκτείνωσιν αὐτὸν οἱ ἄνδρες τῆς πόλεως δι αὐτήν. וַיִּקַּח. With or without לְאִשָּׁה, לקח means "to take to wife, to marry" like the Bab *ahâzu* (Winckler, *Forschungen* 3:414). The continuation proceeds in two discussions: (1) God's with Abimelech, vv 3-7 (v 8 is an appendix) and (2) Abimelech's with Abraham, vv 9-13. Then follows (3) the result, the king's appeasement of Abraham and Sarah, vv 14-16 (v 17, conclusion). The narrator apparently prefers to transmit extended speeches. Indeed, in their favor, he abbreviated the account proper (v 2). A similar phenomenon occurs in E in chap. 31 (cf. comments on 31:2).

   3-7 God's conversation with Abimelech. 3 Belief in the revelatory power of dreams belongs to the earliest stage of religion and continues, too, in the historical religions (Tylor, *Anfänge der Kultur* 1:44), a more developed epoch adapts this ancient, popular belief in order to be able to express a more spiritualized concept of God. The dream is the form of revelation which least involves the deity with the earthly. This manner of revelation characterizes E (cf. the introduction ¶4:6). The value the narrator places on this can be seen from the repetition of the word בַחֲלֹם (v 6). Regarding הִנְּךָ מֵת, "now you must die," see §116p. Abimelech will have understood the statement to mean that God intends to kill him immediately, right there in bed. Appearances of God, a spirit, or the devil who threaten people with immediate death are common in the legends (cf. Exod 4:24; Gen 32:25ff., and perhaps also "The Story of the Fisher with the Spirit," in *1,001 Nights*; trans. Weil[2] 1:30-31). Afterward, God "regrets" the death threat, very much as in 2:17. The legend presumes that the nations, too, know or at least could know that the adulterer deserved death and that it is a sin against God himself. There is, even in the early period, a certain international morality protected by religion (cf. also v 9 <221> and 39:9). Ball and Kittel prefer Sam's reading אוֹדֹת + עַל (cf. 21:11, 15).

   V **4a** is "supplementary" in order to explain Abimelech's clear conscience. The narrator hesitates to say more about this. **4b, 5** Abimelech, in great distress, fearing his immediate death, protests his innocence: "גַם, ὅμως: a nation equally just" (Franz Delitzsch). גּוֹי has given commentators difficulty. It is translated "people" (2 Kgs 6:18; etc.) or even by a few "pagans" (Eerdmans, 41). According to Geiger (Urschrift, 365) it is an addition, according to Ball and Kittel, dittography of גַם. The interpretation that Abimelech considers it obvious that the God's wrath will come upon, not only the person of the king, but the whole people is much simpler (cf. vv 7, 8, 9). The clause in v 4b assumes that God does not kill righteous people but evildoers. V **5** is "supplementary": Sarah, too, had said that she was his sister. "Heart" and "hand" refers to thought and deed. כַף is the palm made impure by sin. **6-7** Now God relents. He "regrets" his threat. But Abimelech should undo the injustice he has inadvertently done. Now the narrator raises the veil far enough to say that God, himself, restrained Abimelech. We still do not learn how, however. חֲטוֹ is an unusual orthography for חֲטֹא. Abraham is, God says, a נָבִיא. In this passage the word designates a "man of God" whose property is under God's protection, whom God represents, whose word God hears (cf. Psa 105:15). The Elijah and Elisha narratives (2 Kgs 1:9ff; 2:23f; 6:15ff.) portray the divine protection the נָבִיא enjoys. Originally, as the earliest descriptions clearly show (1 Sam 10:5-6; 19:18ff.), the Israelite נָבִיא was an ecstatic who felt the effect of the Spirit of God in mighty convulsions of body and soul. The use of the word in this passage in such a depleted sense is only conceivable in a period when the characteristic, extraordinary aspects of prophecy have already diminished considerably and when one was accustomed to referring to every man of God with the term. הִתְפַּלֵּל was (originally) the technical term for the intercession of the man of God (Deut 9:20; 1 Sam 7:5; 12:19, 23; Jer 7:16, etc.). Concerning the intercession of the men of God see Stade, *Bibl. Theol.*, 203. The command to procure intercession for oneself also occurs in Job 42:8. The moral viewpoints prominent in the chap. are unusual. Although God knows Abimelech's innocence, he wanted to kill him at first because he regards the deed and not primarily the attitude. While this is intended in ancient fashion, a modern perspective is also apparent here: God finally takes Abimelech's innocence into consideration. In an entirely ancient manner, however, Abraham must make intercession for the innocent Abimelech. **8** The point of the verse is the statement "they became very afraid," an element the narrator values a great deal because through it he can portray God's protection for Abraham. The structure of the account strongly accentuate this element. It stands between the two discussions. Abimelech's fear is the consequence of all that precedes and the precondition of all that follows. <222>

9-16 *Abimelech's discussion with Abraham.* Vv **9-13** serve the purpose of providing the basis for an evaluation of the extremely complicated (in the narrator's opinion) transaction. On the one hand, he firmly maintains that Abimelech is actually in the right. Abraham is unable to respond to his harsh reproaches (v 9). The narrator thinks nothing can be said in response (similarly in the variants 12:18-19; 26:9-10). To this point, then, he follows the old tradition. On the other hand, however, he also wants to avoid charging Abraham with injustice and presents the matter once again from Abraham's perspective (vv 10-13). This paragraph has been added by the narrator (thus the new beginning, "Abimelech said to Abraham"; a similar case in 27:36). Winckler's explanation (*Forschungen* 3:414) that v 10 is a secondary reading for v 9 is more superficial. The narrator believes that he has vindicated Abraham to a degree. It really is true that pagans are usually godless (v 11). And the lie was not even a real lie (v 12). The narrator waivers in his assessment. The major point for him, however, is that Abimelech, whether or not in the right, must finally come to understand that he must give Abraham significant gifts. God stands on the side of his darling even if he does not seem to be in the right. The narrator seems to have been a man whose morality did not keep step with his religion. His religion does not obligate one to unconditional truthfulness. Yet one may not forget that he did not freely devise this narrative, but only purified it leaving many objectionable elements.

9 Pesh reads מֶה עָשִׂיתִי לָךְ which seems better to suit what follows (Ball, Kittel). **10** ראה means "to see, experience, learn" (cf. Genesius14 s.v. ראה 3b; and esp. Bacher, ZAW 19:345ff., according to whom ראה was employed in this sense in interrogatory clauses by the jargon of biblical exegesis in the old Palestinian school). Vv **11-13** is once again "supplementary." **11** כִּי אָמַרְתִּי means "(I did this) because I said. . . . " רַק means "at any rate, surely." At any rate, such an idea, stated blatantly as self-evident to the foreigner, is going a bit far! Israel's disdain for pagans becomes crudely evident here. The statement presumes that the law knows no obligation to the foreigner, but surely religion does. **12** The narrator took offense at Abraham's simple lie, narrated in the variants in chaps. 12 and 26, and attempted to clear Abraham. His substitute at this point, a mental reservation, demonstrates that his sense of the truth still leaves something to be desired. The narrator apparently devised the comment that Sarah was Abraham's half-sister ad hoc. The earliest tradition (11:29) knows nothing of this. Nevertheless, this excuse does not stem from very recent times because marriage between half-siblings, although not unheard of in ancient Israel (as in other nations; cf. Spurrell; 2 Sam 13:13), was prohibited in later times (Deut 27:22; Ezek 22:11; Lev 18:9,11; 20:17). V **13** is also supposed to be an excuse. Abraham did not behave this way on this occasion only; it was his standard practice. This, too, the narrator, who here seeks as many excuses <223> as possible, has invented. Accordingly, E also told of Abraham's emigration—as is self-evident. The plural construction of אלהים (הִתְעוּ) occurs elsewhere in E, so it is said (cf. 35:7; §145i). It is entirely impossible that the plural is intended polytheistically here (contra Eerdmans, 41). The same plural understood as a singular also occurs in the Amarna correspondence (Knudtzon, nos. 192, 198, 213, etc.): *ilaniya* = "my gods," in the sense of "my god" in reference to the Egyptian king. But is it possible that התעו here, נגלו in 35:7, as well as יִשְׁתַּחֲווּ in Isa 2:8 are not plurals at all, but archaic singular forms of ל"ו verbs? The expression shows that E must have recounted that Abraham crisscrossed Palestine (as did J^b, in contrast to J^a and P).

14-16 *Abimelech appeases Abraham and Sarah.* **14** The gifts are supposed to make restitution for the injustice and to obtain Abraham's friendship so that he will pray for him. וַעֲבָדִים וּשְׁפָחֹת is a gloss as in 12:16. E normally uses אמהות (Dillmann). V **15** is the opposite of 12:19-20. **16** "Eye-covering" is a naive legal term. It refers to appeasement which hinders one from seeing the harm done one (Job 9:24). Instead of "to all those who are with you," it may be better to read, "in regard (לְ) to everything which has befallen you" (אֹתָךְ from אָתָה, "to come upon" with accusative, Job 3:25; a solemn expression the sense of which is equivalent to the more prosaic בוֹא). Eerdmans (40-41) translates "for everything with you" and interprets it in relation to the possible pregnancy of Sarah. This interpretation is, however, completely excluded by the current recension of the narrative. This would also be a peculiar expression for pregnancy. The final clause should probably be read וְאֵת כָּל וְנֹכָחַת, "but you are vindicated in its totality (that is, in all this)" (נֹכָחַת is a part.; on the construction, cf. §§116k, 118mff.). Other translations and attempts can be found in Dillmann and Holzinger. The 1,000 (shekels) of silver (the obvious unit of measure "shekel" is omitted; §134n)—a very considerable sum (according to the Phoenician value, 291 marks, according to Babylonian, 281.20 marks)—are not, of course, the monetary value of the fourteen animals given, but a separate gift. The herdsman Abimelech reckons in animals and money, like the farmer Hosea reckons in grain and money (Hosea 3:2). This mixture of barter and monetary economies is important data for the history of economic conditions. At the same time, the verse is interesting for the legal status of woman. One can harm her and reestablish her honor. The husband, however, receives the propitiation because the woman cannot acquire property. The narrator emphasizes this explicit declaration of Sarah's honor in order to remove the last objectionable element from the situation. Abimelech expressly says "your brother." He acknowledges, then, that Abraham has stated the truth (contrast "your wife" in 12:19).

17 *Conclusion.* Through the statement "he healed" we finally learn what the narrator has already insinuated in v 6-7, namely, that Abimelech was ill. But only the final statement, "they begot children," suggests that the illness inhibited sexual intercourse. The narrator employed the "supplementary" style throughout, then. Concerning Yahweh as a god of plagues see Greßmann, *Israeltisch-jüdische Eschatologie*, 85ff. V **18** is the addition of a later hand for whom this last insinuation was too subtle and who, in addition, misunderstood the text. The reason no children were born lay, according to the <224> preceding, not only in the woman. Linguistically, the addition can be recognized by the יהוה (Sam אלהים).

Comparison of the Variants 12:9ff.; 20; 26:6ff.

These three narratives are closely related in content and also share much vocabulary: אֲחֹתִי הִוא (12:19; 20:5; 26:7), מַה־זֹּאת עָשִׂיתָ לִּי (12:18; 20:9; 26:10), גּוּר (12:10; 20:1; 26:3), etc. (cf. Kuenen, *Einleitung* ¶13 n. 11). Scholars are of various opinions concerning the age of the variants. Wellhausen (*Prolegomena*[6], 317n.1), Keunen (loc. cit.), Holzinger (176), Frankenberg (CGA [1901], 692), and Proksch (297-98) consider chap. 26 older than chaps. 20 and 12. Conversely, Dillmann (324) considers chap. 20 older than chap. 26. The true art of such a comparison consists in beginning, not with arbitrary individual points, but with those points which characterize the total structure of the narrative.

1. The chief difference between the three accounts consists in the fact that chap. 12 naively recounts things that must have seemed extremely objectionable to later sensibilities, while chap. 20 and especially chap. 26 take pains to mitigate these dubious elements. All the essential diferrences in content of the legends are to be understood from this perspective.

a. According to chap. 12 Pharaoh took Sarah to wife. What he did with her is not explicitly stated, however. But we may imagine. In contrast, chap. 20 certifies several times that nothing offensive took place. God himself hindered it. Chap. 20 attempts, therefore, to remove the objectionable elements from the account. Chap. 26 proceeds even more energetically. It omits the entire ticklish situation and only envisions the possibility that someone might have desired the ancestress. According to chap. 12, then, adultery was committed, according to chap. 20 it was averted at the last moment by God, and according to chap. 26 it theoretically could have taken place.

b. Similarly, the plagues are discussed in various manners. In chap. 12 they are intended to make Pharaoh aware of the sin which has taken place. In chap. 20, they are supposed to protect Abimelech from committing the sin. In chap. 26 they are not necessary because nothing evil has taken place yet. On the other hand, the narrator of chap. 26 did not want to omit the chief objective of the account, the portrayal of the protection under which the patriarch stands. Thus, he reports the king's command, "Whoever touches this man shall die." But why is the statement so forceful? After all, no one had considered harming Isaac. The narrator had other recensions in view where such harm has, indeed, taken place.

c. Similarly, the information concerning the ancestor's wealth differs. According to chap. 12, he receives gifts for his alleged sister. Contrariwise, according to chap. 20 he acquires them only subsequently as propitiation and to declare Sarah's honor. According to chap. 26, too, Isaac becomes very rich, but because Yahweh blessed his fields. The somewhat disgraceful gifts of chap. 12 become extremely honorable in chap. 20 and, finally, in chap. 26, in order to mitigate them completely, gifts from Yahweh.

d. The treatment of the patriarch also varies. According to chap. 12, he was escorted to the border. This element, too, was later perceived as compromising and was consequently altered in the other recensions. According to chap. 20, in contrast, he was even permitted to remain in the land "wherever you please." Now, since the preceding does not discuss the fact that he could be expelled, this element can only be understood as a tacit contrast to the older recensions. Chap. 26 addresses the problem differently. Here Isaac is finally "sent away" (26:27), but because of jealousy since he has become too rich for his hosts.

e. Abraham's lie in chap. 12 mutates into a mental reservation in chap. 20. Chap. 26 agrees with chap. 12 on this point.

All of this suggests the character of the accounts. In ancient naiveté, chap. 12 recounts things that must have seemed extremely objectionable to later sensibilities. Chap 20 preserves the facts in general and goes to extremes to remove the objectionable elements and to vindicate Abraham. These concerns account for the peculiarly <225> confused attitude of vv 9ff. Chap 26 energetically intercedes and excises the offensive material. The fact that later times were more refined in such moral matters is also evident in other legends (cf. the introduction ¶4:4).

2. The character of the narratives agrees with this assessment in other areas as well, beginning with their religious character. Chap. 12 offers a peculiar mixture of worldly and religious motifs. The legend celebrates the clever ancestor, the beautiful ancestress, and the ever-faithful God. In addition, it feels a certain malicious glee over the misfortune of the mighty Pharaoh. Later periods could no longer tolerate this mixture of worldly and spiritual. They made the account into either a worldly or a spiritual narrative. Thus, chap. 20 is a "legend." It glorifies only God and his assistance. Profane attitudes are entirely eliminated. Nothing is said concerning Abraham's cleverness or Sarah's beauty. Chap. 26 differs. Here, God's intervention in the encounter between Abimelech and Rebekah is omitted. Abimelech learns that she is Isaac's wife by accident. Thus, the account has become a profane adventure in which the idea of God's protection only stands in the background (cf. 26:3a). The aesthetic attitudes of the narratives also vary widely. Gen 12 is an old legend in brief, beautiful style of the ancient period. Gen 20 exhibits the later style which prefers extensive speeches and even narrates in a refined "supplementary" style. Gen 26 is esthetically insignificant. The shift of motifs and situations has resulted in the disintegration of the legend into two narratives. It has lost its "complication," since the danger to the ancestress is only hypothetical, and has ceased to be a true "story."

Consequently, the chronological sequence of the variants is Gen 12, 20, 26.

This does not suggest, however, that every individual element in chap. 20 is younger than those in chap. 12 or that those in chap. 26 are younger than those in chap. 20. Instead, one sees that the lie of necessity, already eliminated in chap. 20, resurfaces in chap. 26. Chaps. 20 and 26 both narrate the account concerning Abimelech of Gerar. This man is an old legend figure concerning whom our legend books preserve another account (21:22ff.; 26:19ff.). His memory was lost, it seems, to the later period. One can assume, therefore, that the legend originally dealt with Abimelech but that later, when Abimelech's identity was no longer known, it was transferred to Pharaoh. This exchange, however, is not "the chief issue" in the total structure of the account, but only a secondary issue, and is no reason to seek the "original form" of the account in chap. 26 (contra Proksch, 297n.1). According to Winckler (*Forschungen* 1:32-33, and KAT[3], 141ff.), as in the Hagar account, there is a confusion here of northern Arabic מצר, *Muṣr* with מצרים, Egypt. This suggestion, however, has received harsh criticism (cf. above p. 190). If, as is likely, a certain memory of historical situations stands in the background here, one will have to assume an old, temporary migration to Gerar. Abimelech is attested as a Philistine name, and in the cuneiform inscriptions in the form Abi-milki, as a Phoenician name (cf.

Zimmern, KAT³, 482). Whether the legend originally associated the migration to Gerar with the name Isaac or the name Abraham will be difficult to ascertain. Since, however, Isaac is less known in later times than Abraham, one may, nevertheless, consider Isaac the more original here.

27. Isaac's Birth and Ishmael's Rejection 21:1-21 EJ^b

Source criticism. The account of Ishmael's rejection (vv 8-21) belongs to E (evidence: אֱלֹהִים, vv 12, 17[x4], 19, 20; אָמָה, vv 10bis, 12, 13; שִׂים לְנוֹי, vv 13, 18 [J עָשָׂה, 12:2], and rare expressions such as חֵמֶת, "bottle skin," vv 14, 15, 19; etc.). In terms of content, characteristic E elements are God's revelation by night (vv 12f.), the voice of the angel from heaven (v 17), etc. J has a variant of this narrative in chap. 16. <226> According to P Ishmael remained in his father's household (25:9). Similarly, Ishmael's age speaks against P (cf. comments on v 14a). E prefaced this account with a brief "note" concerning Isaac's birth and naming. While this Ishmael account is an old legend, the note only represents a transition. V 6a stems from E (אלהים). These two passages currently disrupt the Abimelech accounts which originally belonged together in E (20; 21:22ff.). R^JE recognized the opportunity to insert a few remarks concerning Isaac's birth and naming from J. They followed 19:38 in J. Vv 1a, 2a, 6b, and 7 belong to J (evidence: יהוה, v 1a; v 6b offers a different interpretation of the name Isaac than v 6a and seems to belong together with v 7). This brief J passage does not belong to the Abraham-Lot legend cycle, however (cf. above, pp. 161, 198), and will, therefore, stem from J^b. Sievers (2:294-95) dissects the account of Ishmael's rejection into two sources (vv 8-11, 14b-16, 19ba, 21a—Eα and vv 12-14a, 17-19a, bβ, 20, 21b—Eδ) but destroys the context unified very tightly by the delivery (v 14a), emptying (v 15), and refilling (v 19b) of the bottle skin, by the carrying (v 14a), casting down (v 15), and taking up, once again (v 18) of the child, by the sitting (v 16, twice) and standing of the mother (v 18), as well as by the crying of the boy (v 16) which God hears (v 17, twice). Similarly, v 11 (וַיֵּרַע בְּעֵינֵי) is not to be separated from v 12 (אַל־יֵרַע בְּעֵינֶיךָ).

1a, 2a, 7, 6b J; 6a E *Isaac's birth.* **1a** Is this section from J^r? **2a** The phrase "in his old age" (as in v 7) emphasizes the divine miracle that happened to Abraham and Sarah. Therefore, it is not a superfluous addition. V **7** is, in its current wording, still pointless. Originally, v **6b**, which contains a point suitable for v 7, may have stood after v 7 (Budde, *Urgeschichte*, 224n.1) or even better after v 7a (Sievers 2:295). The difference in the two recension's explanation of the name Isaac is unusual. In J (vv 6b, 7) it is entirely profane. The old woman is ashamed to have become a mother at her age. In E it is pious. The late mother thanks God for this joy (=laughter, Psa 126:2). Sarah's profane attitude in J agrees entirely in tone with 18:12 and is a sign of the advanced age of this passage. The motivation of the name, itself, is different from the one intended in 18:12, however. In form, vv 6b, 7 are poetry, two double trimeters. מָלַל is an Aramaic word. It occurs in Hebr only in poetry. Regarding the construction see §106p. The message, your wife nurses a child (בָנִים, plural of the category, §124o) is brought to the husband from the delivery room—as we would put it (cf. Jer 20:15). Concerning יִצְחָק (v 6b) see §10g.

8-21 E *Ishmael's rejection.* **8-13** *Part I. The events in Abraham's tent.* The introduction of the legend, vv 8-10, is especially exciting. The legend explains how Ishmael's rejection came about in elements that are exquisitely true to nature. Sarah's love for her son is responsible. A mother's love can become frightfully <227> horrendous when someone tries to encroach upon and harm the beloved child. **8** In order to make this clear, the legend places us on the day of Isaac's weaning (וַיִּגָּמַל in pause, §51m). Weaning took place very late in ancient Israel after the child had already become "large" (v 8), that is, after three years (1 Sam 1:23-24; 2 Macc 7:27). This day is still celebrated in the East as a family festival. On this day the mother rejoices over her child after the dangerous years of infancy. If ever, she regards it with tenderness and pride on this day. To this point, she lived in the joy and concerns of the moment. The first stage, now attained, directs her view to the future. **9** On this day, Sarah (accidentally) sees Ishmael playing with her son. Concerning מְצַחֵק see Baer ¶52n. Concerning the expression see Zech 8:5. LXX and Vulg add אֶת־יִצְחָק בְּנָהּ (Ball, etc.), which, as the context shows, is necessary for the sense (Holzinger). The element is woven from the name יִצְחָק and is an ingenious allusion to it. Later tradition found this motivation for Sarah's horrible jealousy insufficient and maintained that Ishmael "persecuted" Isaac (Gal 4:29) or even that Ishmael practiced idolatry. In the style of the old legend, Sarah's thoughts when she saw the children playing are not conveyed. We must infer them from the circumstances. The mother thinks—what else would she have done on this day?—of her child's future and is already preparing for it—for a mother's love makes one farsighted. When she sees the children playing together, she realizes that one day they will share the inheritance as men. The precondition is that the children of the wife and of the concubine have equal rights of inheritance (Benzinger², 297). According to Babylonian inheritance law, too, the father can recognize the sons of the maidservant and give them part in the estate (Hammurabi ¶170). **10** Thus, she passionately demands a horrible thing of Abraham, that he reject Hagar and even his own son. This was possible according to Israelite law, therefore. Babylonian law is much more humane. According to it, the concubine may not be released if she has children without support for the rearing of the children (Hammurabi ¶¶137, 139). Sarah's passion forms the counterweight in the narrative to the touching tone of the following. Sarah does not mention Hagar by name, but disdainfully as "that slave there" (cf. 2 Sam 13:17; differently in 16:2, 5, "my maidservant"; cf. also 16:6). The difference between the two recensions is even clearer in 21:12, "your maidservant" or Abraham's maidservant. Accordingly, in E Hagar is Abraham's maidservant and, at the same time—in accord with ancient Hebrew practice—Abraham's concubine. According to E Hagar had no further relationship with Sarah. This state of affairs explains Sarah's jealousy for Hagar's child—Sarah has no interest in the child (according to J, she will have adopted it!)—and the fact that, according to what follows, Abraham and not Sarah has authority over the slave. עִם־יִצְחָק is unnecessary and probably an addition.

11-13 The old tradition now recounted that Abraham, accommodating as he was, obeyed his wife, with a heavy heart, of course. But—so we may make the situation clear for ourselves—"she cornered him with her words" and "tormented him so that he was despondent to the point of death" (Judg 16:16; 14:17). <228> The older legend, very familiar with human nature, surely considered Abraham's tractability understandable. The later period, which would like to see in Abraham a moral ideal, found it very objectionable that he rejected his own child in this fashion. Consequently, our narrator inserts vv 11-13 which assert that Abraham took extreme offense at these matters, at any rate. But God appeared to Abraham, commanded him to reject Ishmael, and at the same time reassured him concerning the fate of his son. The passage betrays its late origins (1) in content. If the old legend knew anything about this command of God, it would have reported it in the beginning of the account and built the whole account on it alone (as in 22:2). A command of God is a fully sufficient reason for the pious and tolerates no other in addition. On the other hand, if the old legend shows itself to be so concerned with portraying Sarah's jealousy, it does so in an effort to explain fully Ishmael's rejection on this basis alone. (2) In form. The abstract quality of the discussion of God's revelation (only v 14 indicates that it involves a night vision; similarly 22:3; nothing is said of the location of this revelation) betrays a late period (an omission, 22:3 or addition, 26:24). (3) God's promise to Abraham that Ishmael will become a great people (v 13) interferes with the subsequent promise to Hagar (v 18). The glorious promise to the thirsting Hagar (v 18), given to encourage her and to comfort her in her heavy sorrow, is significantly diminished in its effect if the reader has already heard that God has decided this and has even already communicated it to Abraham. (4) The variant in 16:6 reports a similar act of Abraham explained simply as the result of his tractability, without religious motive. Characteristically for ancient sensibility, Abraham regrets only his son—he surrenders the maidservant easily; after all, she is only a maidservant (וְעַל־אֲמָתֶךָ, v 12, is missing in v 11, probably an expansion). Furthermore, he is comforted by the idea that Ishmael, however, will not continue his name, "Your seed will be named only for Isaac," that is, only the sons of Isaac, not of Ishmael, are supposed to preserve Abraham's name as that of their ancestor. This statement is a reflection from the narrator's time. The name Abraham was unknown outside Israel in his time. 13 The statement, "I will also make the son of the maidservant (Sam הָאָמָה הַזֹּאת) a people," presupposes that this prediction concerning Abraham's "seed" was already pronounced by God on another occasion. Such a reference to an earlier account betrays the later origin of the element. Sam, LXX, Pesh, and Vulg add גָּדוֹל after לְגוֹי (v 14; cf. v 18).

14-16 *Part II.* With deep compassion, the legend recounts further Hagar's rejection and distress. **14a** They receive only a bottle skin (of goat skin, Benzinger², 70) with water and a loaf of bread. What will happen to her when this sparse provision is exhausted? Will she find the way in the pathless land? וְחֵמַת is in construct state with the accent on the first syllable (cf. §95l). שָׂם עַל שכמה ואת־הילד is poor Hebrew and should be rearranged וְאֶת־הַיֶּלֶד שָׂם עַל־שִׁכְמָה. The text arose through the introduction of the P chronology, according to which Ishmael was sixteen or seventeen years old at the time (16:16; 21:5). But here Ishmael is a small boy carried on the shoulder whom his mother casts down in despair (v 15) and who then begins to cry. An early reader <229> harmonized the contradictions to a degree by rearranging v 14 and altering the gender in v 16. LXX reads וַיִּשָּׂא [הַיֶּלֶד] אֶת־קוֹלוֹ וַיֵּבְךְּ (Kautzsch-Socin). In contrast, he inconsistently left the phrase "she cast the boy down" in v 15 (Wellhausen, *Composition*³, 15). **14b** "She lost her way in the desert of Beersheba." Abraham's dwelling place in this account is not far from Beersheba, but not in Beersheba itself (cf. comments on v 19a). This does not agree with 20:1aβff., according to which Abraham dwells in Gerar between Kadesh and Shur. Our narrative did not originally continue chap. 20 (cf. above, p. 161).

15-16 Now mother and child enter the most horrible, mortal distress. The way is lost; the water exhausted; now they will die. The account approaches the climax and, consequently, becomes especially detailed (cf. 22:4-10). The situation is described precisely. Indeed, an exception is even made here to the general rule that thoughts are not explicitly indicated (v 16). She cast the boy down (in despair) under the first good bush, probably a Genista bush (רֹתֶם, Job 30:4; 1 Kgs 19:4), for protection from sunburn. **16a** "She, herself, sat down (לָהּ as in 12:1) opposite, as far away as a bow shot (כְּמְטַחֲוֵי, pal'el part., §75kk; a bow shot is a common unit of distance among the ancient Arabs; Jacob, 256), for she said, 'Let me not (אַל־אֶרְאֶה, cohortative, §108b) see the death of the child (רָאָה בְ, "to regard with compassion")'." Of course, the boy will be exhausted before his mother. He will die before her. But the mother's eye cannot view his death throes. So she goes away some distance, and yet—oh dear, inconsistent mother's heart—not too far. **16b** Once again the touching scene is depicted (as in 22:6, 8) to engrave itself deeply into our hearts. There sits the mother waiting on the death of her child. And there lies the boy, thirsting for water and crying (text following LXX; cf. comments on v 14a). We must imagine a pause here.

17-19 *Part II. The turning-point: Ishmael's deliverance.* **17** "Then God heard the voice of the boy." This statement, which brings all suffering to an end, still resounds in the hearts of its hearers. "God hears." He is a merciful God. "God hears" even the voice of crying children. The statement "God heard" is heavily emphasized here, then. So that it may make a lasting impression, it is repeated once again in v 17b. At the same time, the narrator has made a point in the most wonderful manner. Apparently he also wants to explain Ishmael's name ("God hears"). The legend will, thus, have reported after v 19 that she then named the boy "Ishmael," for she said, "God heard the cries of the boy." This is also the reason the child is not mentioned by name earlier. This naming is then omitted by R^JE because Ishmael's name has already been mentioned in 16:11. The angel of God occurs in the Pentateuch only in E (22:11; 31:11; in the plural, 28:12; 32:2). E speaks reverently of the angel of God, as J does of the angel of Yahweh, in passages where the earlier recensions mentioned Yahweh or God himself (cf. comments on 16:7). "God has heard" parallels the variant in 16:11, "Yahweh has heard." He calls from heaven as in 22:11. This refinement of the revelation characterizes E. The angel's words begin with a question, "Hagar, what troubles you?" just as in the variant in 16:8. While 16:8 involves an actual question, however, which is also answered then, the question in E is an exclamation of kind sympathy. "God has heard the crying of the boy, even there where he lies" (בַּאֲשֶׁר, §138e). The place is a specific place, a place where God hears, that is, a sacred site. The narrator intends to say that in their most extreme distress, when Hagar cast down the boy in despair, she found the very place where God is near and hears. When her distress was at its greatest, God's assistance was also nearest. At this point stands a bush, which was, therefore, a sanctuary <230> (cf. Moses' thorn bush, Exod 3:2, Elijah's bush, 1 Kgs 19:4). Here we hear, then, of a second sanctuary in Beersheba which was "a bowshot" from the spring. The legend was able to explain in an extremely exciting way why the two were located so far apart.

18 So hold the boy firmly; Do not cast him down again as though he were dedicated for death. He is destined for greatness. He will—an extravagantly lofty prediction (cf. comments on 12:2)—not only live and one day beget children, he will even become a great nation. Thus, the angel gives Hagar new courage. **19a** Simultaneously, he opens her eyes (cf. 3:5, 7). That is, she suddenly sees what she had not previously noticed. A well is a deep (rock-lined) hole in the earth into which water flows from below, sometimes hidden to view by a slight elevation of the ground and often not easy to recognize from a distance (Benzinger[2], 207). Whether the well was already there, or only now came into existence through God's word, we do not learn (as in 22:13). The tender legend spreads a chaste veil over this. According to the original recension, this well is surely a sacred well. God appears and "hears" at this site (v 17). V 14 suggests that it was the well-known well at בְּאֵר שֶׁבַע. בָּאֲשֶׁר הוּא שָׁם seems to be a play on the name בְּאֵר שֶׁבַע. Originally, Hagar will have not only named Ishmael, but also the well, after v 19 (as in the variant 16:14). One may further hypothesize that the legend will have originally asso-ciated שְׁבִי with שָׁוַע (= שַׁוְעָה, "cry for help). The narrative would suit this very well since the fact that the boy called out and cried occupies a pointed position. E omits this name because in the immediately following he wants to recount another origin for the well from another tradition. **19b** A touching feature is the fact that there is no account of Hagar drinking. This is mother's love. The narrator is primarily concerned with Ishmael's fate here.

20-21 *Conclusion. Ishmael's future fate.* His maturation (the maturing of a boy in the midst of the dangers and distresses of the desert is a miracle of God); profession (read רֹבֶה קַשָּׁת or רֹמֵה קַ, Olshausen; the bow is the weapon of the Bedouins, Isa 21:17); dwelling (Paran, the desert plateau between Canaan and Egypt); and wife (an Egyptian; originally a variant of the comment that Hagar herself was from Egypt; parents choose a wife for their son, 34:4; 38:6; Judg 14:2). "He dwelt in the desert" (v 20) and "he dwelt in the desert of Paran" (v 21) are manuscript variants.

Comparison of the Two Hagar Legends 21:8-21 and 16:1-14

The two variants agree in structure and in many details. The actors are the same: jealous Sarah, accommodating Abraham, the Egyptian slave Hagar who, before her mis-tress had a child, bore to Abraham Ishmael, the ancestor of the Ishmaelites in Paran. Both variants respond to the same questions (cf. above on chap. 16). How did Ishmael become a Bedouin? How did he get the name Ishmael? How did he come to the sacred well at which the people Ishmael later dwelt? The responses to these questions are also very similar in both. First, both variants recount a scene in Abraham's tent in which Sarah, jealous and <231> cruel, tries to persuade Abraham, and Abraham acquiesces, and on their decision Hagar leaves Abraham's tent and goes into the wilderness. Both variants recount Hagar's great distress. But now God intervenes, he reveals himself at the well, for "God has heard" and attended to the suffering. Thus the child and the well receive their names. Ishmael grows up in the wilderness and becomes a people. Even details agree, for example, that the god begins his speech with a question to Hagar.

On the other hand, the two variants differ markedly from one another in many details and, especially, in attitude. Whereas in chap. 21 moving and tender elements assume the foreground, the tone of the legend in chap. 16 is much more earthy and forceful. This very significant distinction is especially apparent in the characterization of the Hagar figure. The narrator of chap. 16 rejoices at the unbroken strength of the courageous woman. But the legend in chap. 21 laments Hagar with many tears as a rejected slave. Accordingly, the destinies of Hagar in the two variants are also very distinct. In Gen 16, she shares the guilt for her fate and has fled defiantly. But in Gen 21 she is entirely innocent and has been expelled against her will. In Gen 16, her distress consists in the mistreatment which her mother's pride will not tolerate. This mistreatment applies to her person alone. In Gen 21, however, the distress consists of rejection itself: mother and child come to mortal distress in the wilderness. Consequently, the author of Gen 21 places all emphasis on the depiction of the distress of mother and child in the wilderness. But Gen 16 does not mention the dangers of the wilderness at all. In Gen 16 Sarah is jealous of the arrogant slave elevated to concubine; in Gen 21 she is jealous of the slave's child who is not supposed to inherit with her son. In 16 Hagar knows her way around the wilderness; but in 21 she loses her way in the wilderness. Only when God opens her eyes does she find the well. In 16 God hears the mistreatment of Hagar; in 21, the crying of the child. All these differences result from the one major difference that Hagar is depicted in Gen 16 with powerful colors in robust local hues as an authentic, defiant, headstrong Bedouin matriarch, whereas in Gen 21 the local hues are faded and Hagar has become the purely human figure of a poor, rejected mother with her thirsting child.

Accordingly, the J recension is undoubtedly much older than the E. The later period, which no longer knew Hagar as a people, forgot her true identity and only preserved the notion that she was an unfortunate woman. The wilderness lay far in the narrator's past—he was a farmer or a city dweller himself—and seems to him only a land full of dangers, without paths and water. Simultaneously, however, the time had become more tender and took more pleasure in tearful than powerful stories. This later origin of chap. 21 is especially apparent in the fact that, according to Gen 16, Ishmael receives his name, it seems, at his birth, whereas, according to Gen 21, he is named only when he is already several years old. The religious concepts of 16 are also older than those of 21. In 16 the angel appears corporeally on earth; in 21 Hagar only hears his voice from heaven. The fact that the well is a cultic site is significantly obscured in both variants. Yet J preserved the ancient epithet of Yahweh at this site. The name of the sanctuary in J, Lahairoi, which occurs only here, is also more original than the frequently mentioned Beersheba of E. In contrast, the fact that E also knows of the bush in addition to the well is an ancient feature. The angel's question to Hagar is transmitted in J in context, whereas the context has been omitted in E. A greater moral sensibility inspired God's command to Abraham to obey Sarah, a later addition to the legend in E. The addition is still missing in J. A series of later features may trace back to the collector of E. He will have essentially found the account already in this form. Nevertheless, his recension is not slavishly dependent <232> on J. Instead, it is saturated with a genuine artistic spirit and is at least on equal standing with the original.

28. Abraham's Covenant with Abimelech 21:22-34 EJ[b]

Sources. The fact that the report is not a unit is indicated primarily by the doubled וַיִּכְרְתוּ בְרִית (vv 27b, 32), the dual gift (vv 27a, 28-30), the unusual imbalance of the account in which vv 25, 26 suddenly interrupt the cohesion of vv 22-24, 27, the double explanation of the name Beersheba as the well of the oath (vv 23, 24, 31) and the well of seven (vv 28, 29, 30), and, finally, the alternation between אלהים, vv 22, 23, and יהוה, v 33 (cf. Kautzsch-Socin[2] n. 92; whereas Eerdmans, 44-45, defends the unity of the passage!). The foundation of the account employs אלהים (vv 22, 23). P is ruled out by חֶסֶד (v 23), הִנֵּה (adverbially, v 23), כָּרַת בְּרִית (v 27), בַּעֲבוּר (v 30). E is suggested especially by the relationship to chap. 20, as well as phrases such as the rare נִין וָנֶכֶד (v 23), etc. Vv 22-24, 27, 31, which form a coherent unit, clearly belong to

E. Abimelech invites Abraham to an oath because he has recognized his close relationship to God (vv 22, 23). This account, therefore, originally continued Gen 20 which describes the relationship of the two men and, at the end, shows how Abimelech recognized and treated Abraham as a "נָבִיא." The two accounts also belong together in Gen 26 (J[r]). In E, the narratives are currently separated by the Ishmael legend which originally had no relationship to the Abimelech accounts and was inserted by R[E] because it also dealt with Beersheba. A comment concerning the fact that Abraham has meanwhile left Gerar and now dwells at another place must have fallen out before 21:22 (cf. "here," v 23 and "this place," v 31). Abraham acquiesces (v 24) to Abimelech's request that he swear eternal friendship to him. Thus, the two conclude the covenant (v 27). Therefore, the place is named "well of the oath" for their oath (v 31).

A variant has been intermingled into this account. Characteristics of the variant are (1) יהוה (v 33). (2) Vv 28-30 explain the name Beersheba as "well of seven," because Abraham gave Abimelech seven lambs there as a witness that this well belongs to him. (3) Accordingly, the two sources depict the covenant differently. E values the friendly relationship between Gerar and Abraham. But the variant emphasizes that this well belongs to Abraham by contract and not to Gerar (Kautzsch-Socin[2], n. 92). (4) Whereas, then, vv 28-30 discuss the well which is Abraham's property, vv 25, 26 discuss, in contrast, other wells that continue to be disputed. Therefore these verses, too, belong to the variant. (5) Vv 28-30 parallel v 27a (Abraham's gift to Abimelech). (6) V 27b parallels v 32a (covenant-making). V 27b ("both of them" as in v 31) belongs to E. V 32a, which comes after the E account has clearly ended in v 31, belongs, therefore, to the variant. (7) The same is true of v 33 (יהוי). Here Beersheba is a sanctuary. E has not yet said anything about this. (8) Finally, one may note that in the sections to be attributed with certainty to E, especially in Gen 20, Gerar is never associated with the Philistines (Wellhausen, *Composition*[3], 18). We do not even hear about this association in 21:23, where it would have been very easy to mention this name. The later confusion of the old legend site Gerar with the Philistine city of the same name (cf. comments on 20:1) has not yet taken place in E. Accordingly, v 32b will also belong to the variant. Vv 25, 26, 28-30, 32, 33 stem from it, then. The reconstruction of the whole source from these fragments follows below.

Since the word יהוה occurs in these verses (v 33), one must attribute them to J. This conclusion is not contradicted by the fact that J attributes the establishment of Beersheba to Isaac in Gen 26 (Kautzsch-Socin[2], nn. 92, 93, etc.). J is, after all, woven together from several strands. The question concerning to which of the various strands of J this passage may belong is <233> rather inconsequential. Since the "legend cycle" J[a] thinks of Abraham as settled in Hebron, the section may derive from J[b]. Kraetzschmar (*Bundesvorstellung*, 13ff.) offers a similar analysis attributing vv 25-31 to a parallel recension of J. Gall (*Kultstätten*, 46-47) distinguishes (a) vv 22-24, 27 (31); (b) vv 25, 26, 28-30 (31a) (the verses listed under [a] and [b] could be from E according to Gall); (c) vv 32, 34 from R; and (d) vv 33 from J, displaced from Gen 26. Procksch (20-21) follows the source analysis forwarded in this commentary. Kautzsch[3] attributes both reports to E. Sievers (2:296) wants to improve the whole unit by a very unfortunate rearrangement of vv 25, 26 before v 23.

22 Pichol also appears in v 32 and in 26:26. It may be an expansion here (Procksch, 11; Kautzsch[3], 35m). **23** "Here" is not an insignificant addition. Abimelech presses for undelayed fulfillment (Franz Delitzsch; cf. Judg 20:7 and the expression "on the spot"). This element is valuable for the narrator because he wants subsequently to explain the name of the place with the oath made there. Abimelech demonstrated "friendship" to Abraham by receiving him in his territory (20:1, 15) and acknowledging his rights, even giving him bountiful gifts (20:14). The legend permits a glimpse of the fact that Abraham is currently the weaker party, dependent on the cordiality and protection of the people of Gerar. Later, however, this relationship could be reversed. Then Abraham's descendants should thankfully reflect on the old times and requite the Gerarites for hospitality toward their ancestor. The old narrator presumes, then, that his people is currently superior to Gerar, but remembers the earlier period when the reverse was the case. He shows how this eternal covenant, that still exists between "us" and Gerar, came to be. **24** Abraham is thankful enough to enter into the alliance. I, for my part, am ready. The patriarch, negotiating as an equal with a king, appears here, no longer as a private citizen, but as the chieftain of a tribe (cf. 23:6, "prince of God," and chap. 14).

25-26 *The disputed wells.* There must have been several as evidenced by the following. (1) Abraham calls Abimelech to account several times (יְהוֹכַח §112g; Sam ויכיח). But Abimelech declares (each time) that Abraham never spoke with him about the matter before. Accordingly, a different well must have been involved each time. (2) Even the glosses in 26:15, 18, which attempt to harmonize our account with the narrative in Gen 26, presuppose that Abraham dug several wells. They are the same ones Isaac finds according to Gen 26. Accordingly, v 25 should be read בְּאֵרֹת (or בְּאֵרֹת) following LXX. These wells must have been discussed previously (note the article בְּאֵרֹת הַמַּיִם, as in 26:32 because 26:25 preceded). The glossator of 26:15, 18 must have still read about these wells in his text. Later the passage was omitted because it seemed to conflict with chap. 26 despite the glosses in 26:15, 18. Then the singular בְּאֵר was inserted in the Hebrew text of v 25 on the assumption that the disputed well was Beersheba. The original beginning in J[b] was, therefore, Abraham's servants dug certain wells, but the people of Gerar took them away. And (vv 25-26) whenever Abraham complained, Abimelech did not want (impf. with ו consecutive, §112dd) to hear about it. In other words, he did not give the wells back. Abimelech's speech is verbose. He knows nothing! This subterfuge is portrayed realistically (cf. the report of <234> Wen-Amon, *Ztschr. für äg. Sprache* 38:5). But Abraham—accommodation is one of his chief traits—repeatedly acquiesces. **27** E. It is customary to give gifts at the conclusion of a covenant (1 Kgs 15:19). The gift here is supposed to represent Abraham's willingness to enter into the covenant, but, at the same time, that he was (still at that time) the weaker party in need of protection.

28-30 J[b]. There is a gaping lacuna between vv 26 and 28 in J[b]. In it J[b] must have told of "the seven lambs" (v 28; one notes the article and the אֶת, §117a; Kautzsch-Socin), mentioned "this well" (Beersheba, v 30), and, further, in preparation for v 32a ("they made a covenant in Beersheba") have recounted how this treaty came about. J[b] will have recounted, therefore, the following. Later Abraham's servants dug a new well, the current Beersheba. At about the same time, Abimelech came to Abraham. They decided to cooperate and to maintain cordiality toward one another henceforth. Abraham brought the necessary animals for a solemn transaction. But he ordered that seven lambs be set to one side. According to the significant information in v 30, these seven lambs were not for the covenant meal (26:30), but were an extra gift for Abimelech intended to establish

Abraham's legal claim to Beersheba. The practice of giving and receiving such guarantees with contracts is surely very old. In a later time, contracts were committed to writing so that the document was the testimony (cf. Jer 32). From this point onward, vv 28-30, 32-34 are, it seems, the uninterrupted continuation. **28** Concerning לְבַדְּהֶן see §91c; concerning לְבַדָּנָה (**29**) see §91f. **29** Sam reads הכבשות as does v **30** (Ball). Yet see §126x. תִּהְיֶה (v **30**) means "it should be," §122q.

31 Beersheba was still a famous oath site in the time of Amos (8:14). Originally, the name meant "seven wells," as J[b] (v **28**ff.) sill knows. Concerning the number seven, especially common in circumstances associated with worship, see F. v. Andrian (in *Mitteil. d. Anthropol. Ges. in Wien* 31:225ff.), Hehn (*Siebenzahl u. Sabbat*, 34ff.), and Meinhold (*Sabbat*, 20). The question of the origin of the number's holiness—from the seven planets, the seven days of the week, or, more likely, the peculiar character of the number itself—is not yet determined. Seven wells also occur elsewhere among the Mandaeans, Syrians, and in the Algiers (Nöldeke, ARW 7:340ff.), among the Greeks, Persians, and Indians (Roscher, *Abh. der Sächs. Ges. der Wissensch., Phi.-hist. Kl.* 21, no. 4, p. 3) and even in Germany (Andrian, *Mitteil. d. Anthropol. Ges. in Wien*, 253-54). The word "seven wells" probably has superlative significance as does *Negenborn* (Wellhausen, ARW 8:155-56; as does Enneakrunos in Athens, Dieterich, ARW 8:156). Currently Beersheba has three wells (cf. Guthe, BW, s.v.). V **33** offers as a supplement very reliable, old information concerning Beersheba. A sacred tree stood there, a tamarisk (*tamarix syriaca*). Regarding holy trees, see comments on 12:6. According to the legend Abraham planted this tree. Yet, אֶשֶׁל may be a correction for אֲשֵׁרָה (Cheyne, *Enc. Bibl.* s. v. "Tamarisk Tree"; Stade, *Bibl. Theol.*, 112; Meyer, *Israeliten*, 257n.4). The site is a Yahweh sanctuary for Israel. The legend asks "Why?" and responds, "Because Abraham founded the <235> cult there." Concerning the expression "to call on Yahweh's name," see comments on 4:26. The cultic name there was *Yahweh 'el 'olam*. This ancient comment is to be interpreted in reference to 16:13. The pre-Yahwistic name of the numen there was *'el 'olam* (cf. Χρόνος ἀγήρατος in Damascius *princ.* 123, 381-82, Kopp). Yahwistic Israel, which took over the site and the cult, also retained the god's name but interpreted it as an epithet for Yahweh at this site. Since **32** J[b] does not assign Beersheba to Philistine territory, but E knows nothing whatsoever of Philistines in Gerar, **34** can stem from neither of the two sources and must be a redactor's concluding addition (Kautzsch-Socin2). A discussion of the whole account and its variants can be found at the end of Gen 26 where there is also additional information concerning Beersheba.

29. The Sacrifice of Isaac 22:1-19 E

Source criticism. The bulk of this passage stems from E (אלהים; revelation by night, vv 1, 2; the introduction of the discussion, vv 1, 11; the angel calls from heaven, v 11). Vv 15-18 are an addition (cf. below).

1a נִסָּה means "to see what condition someone or something is in"; in a religious sense, "whether someone will obey God's command or not" (Exod 16:4; Deut 8:2; 13:4). The use of this concept in reference to God implies an anthropomorphism because, strictly taken, it excludes omniscience. The narrator himself is unaware of this, however. E values establishing from the outset that God's command to sacrifice Isaac was a trial of Abraham because he can explain this strange command in this way and because he wants to reprise these notions at the end (v 12). Such accounts of trials are beloved in religious literature. The saint's unusual piety is demonstrated by the fact that he is subjected to a particularly difficult situation in which a normal person would stumble. The OT reports temptation accounts of Noah (cf. above, p. 61), often of Abraham (12:1; 15; 18), and of Job. The NT reports them of Jesus. Other literatures report temptations of Buddha (Windisch, "Mara und Buddha," *Abh. d. Sächs. Ges. Wissenschaften* [1895]; Oldenberg, *Aus Indien und Iran*, 104ff.), Zoroaster (*Avesta* V:19:1ff.; cf. Bartholomae, *Altiran. Wörterbuch*, 1673-74; Jackson, *Zoroaster*, 51ff.; Geldner, *Religionsgeschichtl. Lesebuch*, 347-48), and of St. Antony. The motif also occurs in fairy tales. The clause "God tested" is probably parenthetical. וַיֹּאמֶר continues וַיְהִי. Revelation occurred by night according to v 3 (cf. 21:12-13). **1b** Such a brief conversation has the purpose of assuring the speaker of the addressee's attention. The idea expressed by הִנֵּנִי is "Speak, I am listening" (1 Sam 3:9). Conversation between people begins similarly in E (v 7). Therefore, E imagines divine revelation entirely in the forms of a human conversation. He does not discuss the abnormal, uncommon elements of prophecy.

2 The words "your only, beloved" make clear the weight of the self-denial (cf. 12:1). "It is as though God added that he knows well what he asks" (Steinthal, *Zu Bibel und Religionsphilosophie*, 13). The case of Jephthah's daughter (Judg 11:34) is similar. She was his only child! The context of the Abraham narratives also contributes an awareness that Isaac's death would invalidate all of God's promises. "Isaac" is an addition as in 21:10. <236> Such a command presupposes that God can require anything of a person and that the person, if God commands, must obey. הַמֹּרִיָּה occurs only here and in 2 Chron 3:1. According to the latter text it is the name of the threshing floor of the Jebusite Ornan, that is, the name of the site of Solomon's Temple in Jerusalem (2 Sam 24:18ff.). But, disregarding the late attestation of the name *ham-Moriyya*, only the name of a region can have stood here judging from the clear circumstances of the passage (Wellhausen). God would reserve mentioning the name of the specific site. Accordingly, הַמֹּרִיָּה is a later, Jerusalemite emendation (cf. further on v 14). Pesh reads הָאֱמֹרִי (so Dillmann; Procksch, 13n.1, etc.). Holzinger mentions other untenable suggestions. The child sacrifice is of course an עֹלָה, that is, a sacrifice God receives whole. **3** Abraham's reaction to this command of God is not recounted (cf. the introduction ¶3:13). In contrast, the external situation is painted vividly. The narrator's compassion is not evident in the words, but the hearer notes it in the intonation of his voice. Abraham takes two slaves with him. An aristocrat travels abroad in this fashion. The splitting of the wood is in the wrong place (Holzinger) and is probably an addition from another hand who missed a preparation for v 6 ("he took the wood for the whole offering") here. אֲשֶׁר־אָמַר־לוֹ הָאֱלֹהִים (cf. also vv 4 and 9) presume that the place, not yet named in v 2, is more precisely characterized in the meanwhile. A lacuna can be assumed here, then. This lacuna may be explained most simply by the assumption that later readers omitted the description of the site because it did not fit the place with which they identify the site of Gen 22. It seems easiest to place the lacuna behind v 2. It may have read as follows: "Abraham responded that he was ready. Then God told him the place." הַמָּקוֹם is the cult site (cf. comments on 12:6). Vv 4-8 are portrayed with particular skill. The narrator indirectly depicts the characters through speeches. **4** From a distance Abraham sees the site. It was elevated, therefore. **5** He leaves—the delicate narrator reports—the slaves behind. They should not witness the horrible scene. Nor may Abraham tell them what he plans to do. The slaves seem to have been introduced solely to depict Abraham's tenderness. He placed great value on this feature, therefore. A pretext must suffice for the slaves. It was customary to make a small excursion or detour in order to worship at a sacred site—an interesting archeological note. One may also note that, correspondingly, the site was already sacred before Abraham. **6** The boy carries the heavy burden, the father the dangerous—knife and fire (that is, the basin of coals)—so that Isaac may not cut or burn himself. This caution of the father, who must, after all, slaughter his son, is an especially beautiful element.

Vv **7, 8** are a masterpiece of psychological depiction: the childishly inquisitive, unsuspecting boy alongside his father, who says nothing about what he plans to do (the latter element also occurs in Judg 11:35). Thus <237> the legend narrates with profound compassion. The narrator has tears in his eyes. At the same time, however, he wants to say, "Look, this is obedience to God!" The statement assumes that the usual animal for a whole offering is a sheep. Isaac is envisioned as a clever child. The child's cleverness is manifest in good questions. Isaac's question makes no mention of the knife. The good narrator avoids boring thoroughness. In his response, Abraham evades the lie of necessity (Haller, 114). The statement, pronounced in most bitter agony and yet in unchanging obedience, "God will provide for himself," is supposed to effect us deeply. Especially impressive is the repetition, "so the two walked together." The words briefly bring the whole, touching scene once more into view. Elijah's final walk with Elisha is similar (2 Kgs 2:1-8). Vv **9, 10** are an extremely detailed depiction. The tempo is intentionally ritardando in order to sharpen the tension. We are supposed to listen with baited breath. The rite of the עוֹלָה is described in the following (cf. v 2). "The altar" still stands there. ערך is a "sacrificial term for the layering of the wood on the altar" (Siegfried-Stade). שׁחט "to slaughter" is a term for slaughtering by severing the jugular so that the blood flows out. The angel does not prohibit Abraham from taking the knife, but from the hand movement with which he intends to slaughter (v 12). Therefore, "and he grasped the knife" will be an addition.

11 Thus, Abraham demonstrated his obedience. Now, finally, the resolution: God intervenes. God's intervention occurs here as in 16:7 and 21:17 at the highpoint of the narrative when everything has come to extremes. It is fitting for God not to appear at a lesser point, but at the moment of decision. This is a beautiful and profound feature of the legends which speak, in their fashion, of the eternal comfort of all pious souls. God may be long silent, but in the final distress he will speak. V 11 also stems from E (the angel calls from heaven as in 21:17; introduction of the conversation as in 22:1, 11). Accordingly, יהוה has replaced האלהים (Pesh). The reason will be shown later. The repetition of "Abraham, Abraham" depicts the urgency of the cry. Abraham should hear as quickly as possible, otherwise it will be too late in a moment and the child's throat will be cut. **12** That the angel speaks as though he were God himself points to an older recension in which, not an angel, but God himself spoke (cf. comments on 16:7b). Indeed, this suits vv 1f. even better. Since God himself gave the command, he must also rescind it himself. The redaction left the God who appears by night (vv 1-2) but replaced the God who appears by day with the messenger. Instead of אֶל־הַנַּעַר, Sam, LXX, and Vulg read עַל. V **12b** refers back to v 1. God wanted to test Abraham as to whether he is god fearing. This has now been determined. The performance of the sacrifice is, then, unnecessary: God does not want the procedure itself, but the attitude resolved to perform the procedure—an advanced concept of spirituality. The narrative thus returns at the conclusion to the beginning and rounds off the whole nicely.

13 וַיַּרְא וְהִנֵּה portrays the surprise. <238> Suddenly he saw a goat. Everything God sends appears in such a surprising fashion (cf. 18:2; 21:19). Is אַחַר better read אֶחָד (any one), following Hebr mss, Sam, LXX, Pesh, etc. (Olshausen), or even better אַחֲרָיו (Kittel)? The animal was caught in such a remarkable manner that it was easy to capture. Abraham sees this as a divine sign that he should offer it as a sacrifice. A sacrifice is necessary here in the ancient view. The sacred procedure begun must be completed. A young stag, sent suddenly to the altar by a god, also appears in the *Iliad* (8:248ff.). נֶאֱחַז (pf.) can be better pointed נֶאֱחָז (participle, after הִנֵּה) with LXX, Pesh, Olshausen. The mss offer both. Concerning animal sacrifice as a substitute for human sacrifice see Frazer (The *Golden Bough*[2] 2; 2:37, 38n.2), Zimmern (KAT[3], 596-97), A. Jeremias (ATAO[2], 368-69), W. Robertson-Smith (*Rel. der Semiten*, 276ff.).

14 The naming surely belongs to the old legend just as every legend which treats a cult site gives the site its name. Very often the naming comes at the conclusion (16:14; 21:31; 28:19; 32:31; etc.). The text has been reworked. As in v 11, יהוה has been substituted for אלהים. The final words, "on the mountain (בְּהַר construct state; on the construction cf.§130d) Yahweh appears," make no sense in the context. Other translations are equally unsatisfying (see Dillmann). The context does not require a proverb or the like here. Accordingly, the text is corrupt and has been misunderstood. One should read, "so Abraham named this place ' . . . '." The name of the place must have stood at this point. Currently, the interpretation of the name has been substituted. Originally, it was given subsequently, "for (אֲשֶׁר as in 31:49) he said (אָמַר), 'Today, on this mountain (בָּהָר, the article with demonstrative force) God revealed himself (and reveals himself repeatedly—יֵרָאֶה)!" Abraham gratefully remembers the words he spoke in extreme duress to his son (v 8): "God will see to it." These words, then only an expression, have now become truth. God has truly provided himself a sacrifice according to his will. And it was not Isaac! Thinking of this, Abraham joyfully exclaims, "Here, at this site, I have learned that God provides for himself what he wants!" Thus the site received its name. Regarding the emphasis on the place (on this mountain, here) in Abraham's exclamation, compare 11:8; 16:13; 21:17, 23; 32:30 (cf. also Josh 5:9). **19** The return is actually a given. The ancient narrator reports it so that the excited emotions of the hearer may gradually calm (cf. the slow fading of the Joseph narrative). Abraham also dwells in Beersheba according to 21:22ff.

15-18 With the naming and Abraham's return, the narrative is, by nature, ended. Vv 15-18, a second angelic revelation, clearly betrays itself as a supplement (Wellhausen; Dillmann). According to the old legend, Abraham's reward was the fact that he could keep Isaac—a fully sufficient reward for the paternal heart! A later editor, to whom this reward seemed insufficient, added a great promise. He took pains to have the angel speak as solemnly and impressively as possible: God's oath (cf. above, p. 183), the ancient and mysterious phrase נְאֻם־יְהוָה ("utterance of Yahweh," originally the characteristic word for the inspiration of the man of God, employed here on the lips of the angel in an entirely denatured sense), <239> and the solemn particles יַעַן אֲשֶׁר (v 16) and עֵקֶב אֲשֶׁר (v 18). The author could offer nothing new, however, in terms of content ("bless" as in 12:2; "many descendants," 12:2; 16:10; "like the stars in heaven, " 15:5; "like the sand," 32:13; "conquer the gate of your enemies," 24:60; "all the nations will bless you," 12:3). The author attempts, as one sees, to be effective by concentrating language. The addition is printed [in Gunkel's translation] in the font usually used to indicate additions in J. **16, 17** כִּי (v 16, after וְאָם־יְהוָה) depends on נִשְׁבַּעְתִּי and is resumed through the כִּי at the beginning of v 17. After אֶת־יְחִידְךָ (v 16) one may add מִמֶּנִּי (cf. Sam, LXX, Pesh, Vulg, Kittel, etc.; cf. v 12).

General Remarks Concerning the Sacrifice of Isaac

I. The current narrative in the context of E intends to depict Abraham's fear of God. He will offer his only son if it pleases God (James 2:21). The author wants to portray a religious ideal through Abraham. The narrative is a characterization—the trial of the righteous. In order to illuminate Abraham's faith the narrator employs the motif of child sacrifice. It is the most severe test God can lay on a father. At the same time, the legend speaks of the mercy of God who does not permit Abraham actually to kill his son. "In order for the trial to end, he makes it possible for you to bear it" (cf. the Hagar narrative in E, chap. 21, which is similar in this respect). The narrative's charm consists in its tenderness and depth. It derives from a inwardly perceptive, tender soul. It contrasts with the Jephthah narrative which deals with a similar motif. Isaac is "redeemed," but Jephthah's daughter is sacrificed. Isaac is an unsuspecting child, but Jephthah's daughter is a brave maiden who goes to death willingly. The vengeance Yahweh granted her father sweetens her bitter death for her. Accordingly, the Jephthah narrative is harsher and more ancient, Gen 22 softer and more modern. Indeed, the narrator knows that, in the final analysis, God does not desire this sacrifice. But the legend still reckons with the possibility that God could require it. Polemic against child sacrifice (so yet Kautzsch[3], 36) is, accordingly, quite remote here. Wrath and abhorrence toward this dark practice is not under discussion here. One may not even attribute the intention to pronounce a doctrine concerning child sacrifice to the legend; consequently, the account is also very difficult to teach now. Instead, it only presents the heart-rending pain of the father who is supposed to carry out this severe sacrifice. Yet, the final redactors, who stand near the prophets, may have read a condemnation of child sacrifice in the narrative.

II. *The original meaning of the legend.* Although the narrative is only a character portrayal in its current form, it still seems appropriate to ask whether, like other legends dealing with sacred places, it may not have originally had a more concrete meaning. The analogy of the Jephthah narrative points in this direction. Admittedly, in its present form, it is only a historical legend. However, in a brief addition (Judg 11:40) it refers to a lament festival celebrated in memorial of this story. This lament festival recalls the lament festival of Adonis or Tammuz (Ezek 8:14) or that of Hadadrimmon at Megiddo (Zech 12:11). Clearly, the narrative of Jephthah's vow was originally an etiological myth.

1. *The place of the sacrifice.* The legend places the sacrifice at a specific location. The name has become illegible in the present text through corruption (cf. comments on v 14). Later tradition contended that this place was the site were Solomon's Temple stood later, *ham-Moriyya*. Following the legend (rather capriciously), הַמֹּרִיָּה was interpreted as יְהוָה יִרְאֶה and, as a result, the name יהוה was inserted in vv 11 and 14 (Wellhausen). For this reason, the naming originally given in v 14 seems to have been suppressed. These

readings are not, however, those of the original text. הַמֹּרִיָּה in v 2 is clearly an insertion. It is also very unlikely <240> that E, who otherwise employs only אלהים, would
have, in this narrative, explained a name with the assistance of יהוה. But this localization
of the legend is especially contradicted by the fact that the description of the place, which
originally stood after v 2, is omitted (cf. above) apparently because it did not suit *ham-
Moriyya*. Rather, אלהים must have originally stood in vv 11 and 14. The name originally
intended, however, explained as אלהים יראה, must have consisted of two elements. One of
them, in analogy with other ancient names in Genesis, will have been אֵל; but the other
was a word which one could interpret as יִרְאֶה. This hypothesis is confirmed by two
additional allusions to this name. Legends love repeatedly to echo the characteristic names
in ingenious allusions (cf. the introduction ¶3:17). Thus, v 12 says that God recognized
that Abraham is god fearing, יְרֵא אֱלֹהִים. Furthermore, Abraham sees a goat (v 13),
אַיִל [וְהִנֵּה] וַיַּרְא. אַיִל is an allusion to אֵל just as קוֹץ alludes to קֵץ in Amos 8:1-
2. Of these three allusions to the name we seek the last (v 13) indicates unequivocally that
the divine name must have been אֵל. The two final allusions (vv 12 and 13) demonstrate
that this name stood in second position. In the constitutive explanation (vv 8 and 14), this
position is altered because the (very ingenious and profound) interpretation offered there
emphasized אלהים: "God himself provides." The three allusions—יְרֵא אֵל, יִרְאֶה אֵל־,
and יְרֵא אַיִל point with great certainty to the names יְרִיאֵל or יְרוּאֵל. Linguistically,
the two forms could alternate like פְּנוּאֵל and פְּנִיאֵל (Gen 32:31, 32; cf. יְרִיאֵל in 1
Chron 7:2, LXX , Luc Ἰαρουηλ; יְרוּאֵל in 2 Chron 20:16, LXX Ἰεριηλ; cf. §90o). The
name Jeriel is attested as a name of a family in Issachar (1 Chron 7:2). Jeruel is a
wilderness in Judah (2 Chron 20:16). The first does not come into consideration because
of its location. In contrast, the latter is very possible. According to 2 Chron 20:16, 20 it
lay between Engedi and Jerusalem in the vicinity of Tekoa. Now it is only explicitly
attested that a wilderness was named Jeruel. Yet we may assume that in the vicinity of
this wilderness there was a site Jeruel for which the wilderness was named. The
information in v 4 that the site was at a distance of three days' journey from Beersheba
suits this Jeruel very well. This hypothesis is not contradicted, at any rate, by the fact that
Jeruel is not mentioned anywhere as a cult site. What would we know about the sanctuaries at Lahairoi, Mahanaim, Mamre, or the Machpela cave without Genesis? Accordingly,
one may suppose with great certainty that the name of the site in Gen 22 was Jeruel or
Jeriel and with a degree of likelihood that this Jeruel refers to the one near Tekoa. Later,
specifically Jerusalemite tradition, painfully aware of the absence of the supremely revered
sanctuary in Genesis (Jerusalem only occurs in Gen 14), relocated the legend in Jerusalem
and probably found the basis for doing so in the fact that the name Jeriel sounds like the
name of the ancient temple site אֲרִיאֵל (Isa 29:1, 2, 7). It is known that י and א
alternate very frequently in initial position in ancient and recent times. When the name
Ariel fell into disuse in Jerusalem and the name *ham-Moriyya* arose, it was imported into
the text. These corrections severely corrupted the text of v 14. Wellhausen (*Composition*³,
19) wants to read הַמֹּרִים for הַמֹּרִיָּה (v 2) and to identify the place (following the very
late, Samaritan tradition) with Shechem. Stade (*Bibl. Theol.*, 245; v. Gall, *Altisraelitische
Kultstätten*, 112ff.), and Procksch (12) think of the אֵלוֹן מוֹרֶה near Shechem (12:6), but
it is much farther from Beersheba than a three-days journey.

2. *Gen 22 is the cult legend of Jeruel.* This legend treats child sacrifice. Child sacrifices were well known in ancient Israel as well as among its neighbors (cf. Marti, *Gesch. d. isr. Rel.*[5], 45ff.; Smend, *Alttest. Religionsgesch.*, 128-29; Stade, *Bibl. Theol.*, 170-71, 244ff.; Benzinger[2], 364; concerning child sacrifice among the Semites, see Robertson Smith, *Rel. d. Semiten*, 276ff.): the Moabites (2 Kgs 3:27), Ammonites (Lev 18:21; 20:2ff.), Arabs (cf. Wellhausen, *Arab. Heidentum*[2], 115-16), Aramaeans (2 Kgs 17:31), Phoenicians, in whose history they played a significant role (cf. Pietschmann, *Gesch. der Phönizier*, <241> 168.), and many other peoples. Canaanite child sacrifice is confirmed, it seems, by the archaeological discovery of a multitude of children's corpses (Hugues Vincent, *Canaan*, 188ff.; regarding the reference to child sacrifices, specifically, the burning of children among the Assyrians, cf. Zimmern, KAT[3], 434 and n. 3, 599). In Israel too, especially in times of distress, people offered this most difficult sacrifice in order to still the wrath of the deity (cf. 2 Kgs 3:27; Mic 6:7, where child sacrifice is a propritiatory sacrifice; 2 Kgs 16:3; 21:6). Yet it does not seem to have been common practice in the earliest, historical period of Israel attainable to us, the law in Exod 22:28 notwithstanding (cf. Wellhausen, *Prolegomena*[4], 88). In contrast, it occured, usually under the influence of neighboring peoples, often and in many places, whether in particular distress, private or public, one resorted to this means to expiate Yahweh's wrath (cf. Mic 6:7; 2 Kgs 16:3; 21:6 [3:27]) or whether this sacrifice was the rule, or at least common, at a certain site. Thus, it is sacred practice in Jerusalem, although not in the Temple (thus not on Ariel) but at the Topeth in the Valley of Hinnom (2 Kgs 23:10; Jer 32:35) where it was offered to Melech (Jer 7:31; Ezek 20:25-26) who was identified with Yahweh. But even where the old requirement to offer all firstborn to Yahweh was observed, the milder practice had already arisen of "redeeming" (פדה) human firstborn (Exod 13:2, 12ff.). As is common in the history of religion, outdated practices have been replaced with a "substitute," while the old theory was still valid. The prophets and prophetic laws battled against child sacrifice as a horrible, pagan abomination (Jer 7:31; Ezek 16:20; 20:26; Deut 12:31; Lev 18:21; 20:2ff.).

Gen 22 was originally the legend of child sacrifice at Jeruel. It narrates how at this site the deity actually wanted the firstborn son as a sacrifice, but how the deity accepted a goat as a substitute for the boy—this feature may also be understood as etiological. The current cultic status presumed by the legend is probably that one offered a goat at Jeruel. But the legend still knows that it should actually be a child. We may conclude that originally it was a child. The legend maintains its distance from polemic against this sacrifice. It is, therefore, preprophetic. Instead, it maintains the attitude which had already abolished the sacrifice long before the legend. The time had become softer. Then it was impossible for the tender father to offer child sacrifice.

An interesting counterpart, and perhaps the prototype of our legend, is the Phoenician cult legend according to which El himself instituted this cult by offering his "only born son" as a burnt offering to his father Uranos in a time of distress on an altar erected for the purpose (Philo, *Fr.* 2:24, *Fr.* 5, ed. Müller, *Fragm. hist. graec* 3:569, 571). The son is called Ἰεδούδ = ידוד, Hebr יָדִיד "darling," or Ἰεούδ = Hebr יָחִיד, the "only (son)," according to Philo, the Phoenician name of the only son, thus quite like Gen 22:2 "the only" or "the beloved son." A very precise parallel is the account of Agamenon's sacrifice of Iphigenia for whom Artemis substituted a doe. This narrative, too, is originally an etiological account of the replacement of human sacrifice (cf. Roscher, *Lex.* s.v. "Iphigeneia"). <242>

30. Nahor's Genealogy 22:20-24 J

This genealogy of Nahor will be very old. In all there are twelve sons, as with Israel, Ishmael (25:13-14), and Esau (36:15-19). The tribes are divided, as are the Israelites, into the legitimate and the illegitimate. The former stem from the wife, the other from the פִּילֶגֶשׁ or the foreigner "who as a result was not considered an equal, nor were her children, even though she was superior to the slave" (Rauh, *Hebr. Familienrecht*, 29-30). Among the full tribes, the two oldest have a special relationship, Uz and "his brother Buz" (like Cain and "his brother Abel," 4:2 and like "Simeon and Levi, the brothers," 49:5, etc.). In order to bring this sparse comment to life a bit, the narrator wanted at least to give it the form of a narrative and, consequently, suitably chose the form of Abraham receiving the report of their births. Yet from v 23b onward it falls back into the usual style of the genealogy. Later additions are אֲבִי אֲרָם (v 21) and וּבְתוּאֵל יָלַד אֶת־רִבְקָה (v 23a). Both disturb the cohesion significantly. At this point, when Abraham receives the report for the first time that Kemuel and Bethuel have been born, it is premature to speak of their children. Further, the number twelve is destroyed by these additions. Finally, v 23b refers back via v 23a to vv 21, 22. All or almost all the names of the original genealogy do not designate actual legend figures but are the names of old tribes artificially combined into a genealogy.

The passage does not belong to P, who offers other genealogical information concerning Aram and Uz (10:22-23). It has been placed here to introduce the subsequent narrative from J dealing with the Nahorides. In terms of diction, too, the passage belongs to the "Yahwist": גַם הוּא (vv 20, 24; Cf. Budde, 220ff.). The phrase וַיְהִי אַחֲרֵי הַדְּבָרִים הָאֵלֶּה does not indicate E since it also occurs in J (39:7). On closer examination, this passage belongs, however, neither to J^a nor J^b. It knows nothing of Laban, who plays a major role in both recensions in chap. 24, and originally nothing of Rebekah, either. Besides, J^a certainly does not presume in chap. 24 (24:24, 29), and J^b probably does not either (24:15; a comment concerning Laban from J^b will have fallen out before v 30), that such a genealogy of Nahor has already been communicated. The genealogy of Rebekah, however, which J^a and J^b contain themselves, did not originally call her the daughter of Bethuel, but of Nahor (cf. comments on 24:15; cf. also Mez, *Ḥarrân*, 21, who attributes the passage to "J^2," and Cornill, *Einleitung*^{6}, 55). This genealogy, originally of entirely allogenous origins, has, therefore, been inserted into these Abraham narratives in J by a very late hand and associated in makeshift fashion with the subsequent material by the addition of v 23a (cf. Meyer, *Israeliten*, 241-42). The genealogy of Keturah in 25:1-4 is to be similarly evaluated.

Concerning the tribal names see Dillmann, Gesenius-Buhl^{14} and Meyer (*Israeliten*, 239ff.). Regarding Milcah see 11:29. Uz is according to 10:23 P an Aramaic tribe; in Job 1:1-3 in the region of the Bene-qedem East of Palestine; according to Delitzsch (*Paradies*, 259) in the Obelisk inscription of Shalmaneser II on the lower Orontes; according to Gen 36:28 a Horite tribe; and in Lam 4:21 the land of Edom. Buz, mentioned in Jer 25:23 along with Dedan and Tema (cf. also Job 32:2) is, therefore, to be found in northern Arabia. In Assyrian the name is *Bâzu* (Delitzsch, *Paradies*, 306-307). Kemuel, the father of Aram, is not, according to Meyer (239) a tribal name, but a legend figure, the patriarch of the Aramaeans. Chesed is the presumptive ancestor of the Chasdim. These "Chasdim," not to be confused with the Babylonian Chasdim, the Chaldeeans, with whom they will be closely related, however, are an Aramaic Bedouin tribe. They are mentioned along with the Sabaeans in Job 1:17 (cf. Winckler, *Forschungen* 2:250-52; cf. above on 11:31, p. 157). Hazo, Assyr *Ḥazû*, is mentioned by Asarhaddon along with *Bâzu* (cf. above; Delitzsch, *Paradies*, 306-307). Regarding Pildash, compare the name פֻּנְדָּשׁ attested on a Sinaite inscription (in Lidzbarski, *Handb. d. nordsemit. Epigraphik*, 352). According to Meyer (24), Bethuel may be a patriarch like Kemuel. Is this figure perhaps nothing other than the personified sacred stone בֵּיתְאֵל (Baudissin, R[E] 12:136), which would then be equivalent to the Phoenician god Βαίτυλος (Philo, *Fr.* 2:14 in Müller, *Fragm. his. graec.* <243> 3:567) and the "western" god *Bait-ili* discussed by Zimmern (KAT[3], 437)? Tebah (in 2 Sam 8:8 miswritten בֶּטַח), in 1 Chron 18:8 Tibhat, is a city in *Aram-Ṣoba*, probably the *Tubiḫi* in the Amarna correspondence (Winckler, no. 127). In Egyptian it is *Tbchu* (cf. Meyer, *Israeliten*, 240; W. Max Müller, *Asien und Europa*, 173, 396). Winckler (in *Mitt. d. Vorderas. Ges.* [1896]: 207) identifies תַּחַשׁ with the Egypt. *Teḥisi* which W. Max Müller (*Asien und Europa*, 251, 258) locates north of Kadesh. Maacah is an Aramaic region near Hermon (2 Sam 10:6, 8). The other names are unknown.

To the extent that we know these tribes, we are directed to the northern border of the Syro-Arabian desert. According to Meyer (241) the legitimate sons are regions and tribes of the Syro-northern Arabian desert—thus we obtain information here concerning the nearly lost homeland of the Aramaic tribes—but the illegitimate sons are districts and regions of the Syrian farmland. Accordingly, the background is an account in which some of these tribes who originally dwelt in the desert migrated to the fertile land. Characteristically, the name of the people Aram, who played such an important role in the history of Syria and Israel (cf. also the position of the place of the name Aram in P, 10:23), was only secondarily inserted into Nahor's genealogy so that a series of later Aramaic tribes and regions, such as *Ṣoba, Geŝur, Ṭob*, and especially Damascus are missing, and so that Nahor is considered the brother of the (prehistorical) Abraham in the Hebrew legend. Therefore, we will have to regard the people named for Nahor to be a (for Israel) prehistorical people and we will find in this people the predecessors of the later historical Aramaeans. After the demise of the people "Nahor" individual tribes continued to exist as "Aramaeans." **24** Pesh reads שְׁמָה (Kittel).

31. The Wooing of Rebekah 24 J[a,b]

Source criticism. 1. Until now, the unity of the account has been accepted for the most part. A substantial series of inner contradictions, difficulties, or doublets, however, point to dual strands. Rebekah receives several maidservants (v 61); she only takes the nurse along (v 59). Rebekah's relatives do not know how to respond to the offer of marriage (neither yes nor no; v 50b); They accept the offer immediately, for Yahweh has already made the decision (vv 50ab, 51). In such an uncertain matter, they ask the maiden herself (vv 57-58; in the current context, this question refers to whether the maiden wants to go along immediately; the phrasing of the question refers, however, to whether she is willing to go at all). According to vv 50ab, 51, in contrast, they decide for the maiden without even asking her (Winckler, *Forschungen* 3:418 wants to eliminate this difficulty by rearranging vv 50, 57, 58-56, 51). Then, Rebekah sets out twice, v 61a ‖ v61b (cf. also Kautzsch-Socin[2], n. 110: "V 61a does not tolerate v 61b"). We hear twice where Isaac has taken up residence v 61 ‖ 25:11b. Laban runs to the man at the well twice, v 30 ‖ v 29 (since Ilgen, *Urkunden*, 149, interpreters have sought to eliminate this repetition by rearranging v 30a after v 29a; so recently once again Winckler, *Forschungen* 3:418; Eerdmans, 73; Kautzsch[3]; etc.). The servant gives Rebekah the bride gift (to be distinguished from the מֹהַר, the gift to one's relatives) twice, v 22 (cf. vv 30, 47b) ‖ v 53, once before the betrothal (v 22) and once after the betrothal. (The first gift, v 22, does not serve only as a greeting nor is it given in thankfulness for the service performed; it is much too large for this [contra Eerdmans, 73 n 1; Kautzsch3]. Sievers [2:303] wants to resolve the problem by striking v 22b.) It is especially remarkable that this first gift is given in v 22, before the servant knows Rebekah's parentage; in v 47, in contrast, after he has learned of it. This is all the more remarkable since a very valuable piece of jewelry is involved and we may imagine that the narrator would treat so much gold somewhat more cautiously <244>. Such an oversight can be readily attributed to a redactor, but not to a narrator. The slave puts two questions to Rebekah (vv 23a, 23b) and she answers twice (v 24 to v 23a, v 25 to v 23b; one also notes the doubled beginning, וַתֹּאמֶר, vv 24, 25, which rarely occurs in an old, unified account). Then, in the reprise, the second question is omitted (v 47). (Ball and Winckler, *Forschungen* 3:418, acknowledge these difficulties with vv 22-25, but want to eliminate them by rearranging vv 23a, 24, 23b, 25. Ball also wants to shift vv 22aβγ, b after v 25). Abraham considers the possibility that the journey will be unsuccessful and gives instructions for this case (vv 5, 6, 8; in the repetition, vv 39, 41). On the other hand, Abraham is convinced that Yahweh will give the journey success (v 7b; in the repetition, v 40). At this point in the reprise the combination of sources is especially evident. V 39 ("and if the woman does not want to come?") finds its direct continuation in v 41 ("then you are free of the oath!") and the interposed v 40 disturbs this coherence quite perceptibly (Kauthzsch-Socin[2] n. 107, perceived this difficulty; Sievers 2:303 suggests striking v 41aα). More minor difficulties permeate the entire chapter. The repeated אברהם at the beginning (vv 1,2) is disturbing. The destination of the servant's journey is stated twice (v 10). Similarly, the time is stated twice (v 11b). In v 14b the general second clause seems strange after the first very specific clause. We hear twice of Rebekah's parentage, the first time from the narrator (v 15), the second time from her, herself (v 24, for which reason Sievers 2:302 wants to strike the pertinent statement in v 15). In v 16a "a virgin" parallels "who had not yet known a man." V 21b (from לָדַעַת onward) is very noteworthy. At this point of the account, after the sign has been very precisely fulfilled, the servant already knows "that Yahweh his given his journey success." The release of Rebekah in v 29 seems to parallel the blessing in v 60. V 67 is also overloaded and hardly in order (cf. Kautzsch-Socin[2] n. 113). One notes, for example, the remarkable explicative אֶת־רִבְקָה after וַיְבִאֶהָ. "Isaac brought her into the tent" parallels "he took Rebekah as his wife." "He came to love her" probably parallels "Isaac was comforted."

    A series of the observations above have already been made. The hypothesis that two sources are involved here has also already been expressed (Knobel1, 185-86, and Reuß, AT 3:258n.4, 260n.3).

2. Source analysis can probably best proceed from the observation that in one recension everything (to the extent it is possible according to Hebrew marriage practice) depends on the maiden's willingness. She settles matters in the decisive moment (v 58) and then "follows the man" (v 61a). She, herself, is asked by her relatives (vv 57, 58) because they do not know what to say in such an uncertain matter (v 50b). Now, in accordance with the beautiful unity which these old narrators love, the first conversation between Abraham and his servant already treats the question of whether the maiden will be willing. The servant asks "and what if she does not want to come?" (v 5). Abraham responds, "Then you are free of your oath; only do not take Isaac back there" (vv 6, 8; cf. the servant's account in vv 39, 41). In this context the expressions הָלַךְ אַחֲרֵי (vv 5, 8, 39, 61) or הָלַךְ עִם (v 58) occur frequently. Similarly, the sign requested by the servant also depends entirely on the free, good will of the maiden. The whole episode, then, in which the maiden offers so endearingly to water the camels, belongs to this recension, that is, (on the whole) vv 13-20 and the reprise, vv 43-46. Consequently, it is also fitting that in this recension the maiden receives her gift first (even before her relatives). Therefore, vv 22 (and the reprise in 47b) and with it, also, the continuation in vv 30,31 are to be attributed to this account (concerning v 31, see the interpretation). V 31, however, suggests that Laban knows the question of v 23b. The response in v 25, then, belongs to v 23b. Compare also the expression "room" in vv 31, 23b. The unity of the passages assembled in this manner is demonstrated also by the role which the camels play in them. Indeed, the narrators love to reuse and vary such a motif at other points if they need to do so for any reason <245>. The sign by which the bride will be recognized is the cordiality with which she waters the camels (vv 13-20, 43-46). When they have drunk their fill, the servant gives her the gift (v 22) and asks about lodging (v 23b). She also considers the animals in her response (v 25). Her brother runs to the man who still stands near them (v 30) and offers lodging, for them, too (v 31). On the return journey they serve as mounts for Rebekah and her maidens (v 61a). Consequently, this recension also includes v 10 (the servant takes along ten camels), v 11a (he rests them outside the city), vv 32a, bα (Laban cares for them), v 35b (Abraham's wealth in animals, also in camels), and vv 63-65 (Isaac sees the camels coming from afar; Rebekah jumps from the camel). We preliminarily term this recension "Recension II."

Passages which parallel those extracted to this point are to be included in Recension I: v 7 (entirely; ‖ vv 5, 6, 8), v 23a (‖ v 23b), v 24 (response to v 23a; ‖ v 25), and the related vv 26, 27 (the servant praises God for what he has heard in v 24), v 29b (‖ v 30), v 40 (cf. v 7; ‖ vv 39, 41), v 47a (cf. vv 23a, 24), v 48 (cf. vv 26, 27), vv 50a, 51 (‖ vv 50b, 57, 58). Vv 52-56 are also from Recension I. Since v 57 connects directly to v 50b in Recension II, the interposed material must be from Recension I. These verses produce a clear unit: v 51—the decision, v 52—thanks to God, v—53 the gifts to the bride and her relatives (the former ‖ v 22), v 54a—the meal (consequently, vv 3 also belongs to I), vv 54b, 55, 56—the attempt to retain him and the request that he be dismissed. The continuation is v 59, the dismissal (שָׁלַח, v 59 and vv 54, 56) together with the nurse (v 60, the parallel to v 59 will, then, belong to II), and v 61b (‖ v 61a).

Characteristic for this Recension I are the expressions יהוה אֱלֹהֵי הַשָּׁמַיִם (v 7) and יהוה אֱלֹהֵי אֲדֹנִי אַבְרָהָם (vv 27, 48), יִשְׁלַח מַלְאָכוֹ לְפָנֶיךָ (vv 7b, 40), הִצְלִיחַ (vv 7b, 40; cf. 48), עָשָׂה חֶסֶד וֶאֱמֶת (v 49; cf. v 27), לָקַח אִשָּׁה לִבְנִי

דַּרְכֶּךְ (vv 40, 56), קַח וָלֵךְ (v 51; cf. וַיֵּלֶךְ . . . וַיִּקַּח, v 61), עֶבֶד אַבְרָהָם (vv 52, 59), "the servant" (vv 53, 61b; in contrast הָאִישׁ is common in II, vv 21, 22, 30bis, 32, 58, 61a; but this usage is not constant: II הָעֶבֶד, vv 10aα, 65bis [where אִישׁ = Isaac], contrariwise I הָאִישׁ vv 26,29, where the nuance that Rebekah wonders about "the man," that is, the unknown, is expressed), וַשְׁתַּחֲוֶה לַיהוה (vv 26, 48, 52), and "the men" (vv 54, 49). Consequently, I also includes v 3 (יהוה אֱלֹהֵי הַשָּׁמַיִם וֵאלֹהֵי הָאָרֶץ) and יהוה אֱלֹהֵי אֲדֹנִי (לָקַח אִשָּׁה לִבְנִי), v 12 and vv 4, 37, 38 (לָקַח אִשָּׁה לִבְנִי), v 21 (from לָדַעַת אַבְרָהָם and (עָשָׂה חֶסֶד עִם), v 14bβ (עָשָׂה חֶסֶד עמע), v 21 (from onward; the context suggests that the clause does not belong to II [cf. above] and the diction suggests that it belongs to I [cf. הִצְלִיחַ יהוה דַּרְכּוֹ; the main clause may be v 17a, cf. (הָעֶבֶד), v 32bβγ (הָאֲנָשִׁים), v 42 (אַבְרָהָם), v 49 (עָשָׂה חֶסֶד וֶאֱמֶת) and אִם־יֶשְׁכֶם as in v 42). V 67aβ (לְאִשָּׁה), v 49 (דַּרְכִּי אֱלֹנִי יהוה and . . . וַיִּקַּח) probably belongs to I and the parallel v 67aα to II.

This recension (I) is also coherent. Characteristically, the maiden does not appear here in an active role. Her relatives decide for her without asking her (v 51). They want to delay the servant and they then send him, the maiden, and the nurse (this, too, is a distinguishing characteristic) away (vv 54-56, 59). But the servant "takes" her and goes (v 61b). Accordingly, the sign by which the servant recognized the bride indicated by God will have been one that emphasized the activity of the maiden less. This sign is currently no longer clearly preserved. We may conclude, however, that he may have wished that the first maiden to come to the well would be the desired bride from his lord's relatives. Consequently, when a maiden comes, he runs toward her (v 17a), eager to learn whether Yahweh had granted him good fortune (v 21b) and asks here about her parentage (v 23a). And when he hears that she is truly closely related to his lord (v 24), he falls to the ground (v 26) and thanks Yahweh for his great mercy (v 27).

Furthermore, the passage where the gifts are given characterizes both sources. In II, where the servant has arranged with Yahweh a complicated sign and now sees all this fulfilled to his great, joyous amazement (v 21a up to מַחֲרִישׁ), he immediately gives the maiden a rich gift. He knows for certain that she is the bride God decreed and she will be willing. Recension I differs. Here the sign does not yet determine anything. The relatives have not yet been asked. Perhaps <246> they will say no (49b). Only when they have spoken (v 51) does the servant open his bag (v 53). In both cases, however, the gold is given the moment the servant is sure of the matter. The old man is much too experienced in the ways of the world to give it earlier.

At the beginning of the account, Abraham is still alive. At the end, when the servant returns to Isaac, he must be dead. The account must, then, have reported Abraham's death. A redactor who wanted to recount Abraham's death in a subsequent passage removed this report from Gen 24. At the same time אַחֲרֵי אִמּוֹ (v 67) replaced the original אָבִיו אַחֲרֵי and שָׂרָה אִמּוֹ was added to הָאֹהֱלָה (where it is syntactically intolerable; cf. Wellhausen, *Composition*[3], 27f.). There is some question as to where the two recensions recounted Abraham's death. Now recension I clearly speaks of Abraham as alive until v 61. "Abraham's servant" (v 52) calls on God and people to demonstrate love (vv 12, 42, 49) for "his lord" (vv 12 twice, 14, 27, 37, 42, 49). He calls Isaac "the son of his lord" (vv 44b, 51). But clearest are vv 54, 56, where he requests to be sent to his lord. In this recension, Abraham's death must, then, have been recounted after v 61. When the servant comes to Isaac, Isaac tells him that his father has died in the interim. V 66 may have been adjoined at this point. For his part, the servant tells him what he has experienced in the meantime. At any rate, the concluding clause, "Isaac was comforted over his father," belongs to this recension (I) and, accordingly, וַיֶּאֱהָבֶהָ to II. In contrast, recension II differs. Here, after v 8, Abraham is not assumed to be alive in any clear passage. Characteristic, rather, is the prayer (v 14ba) "whom you have chosen for your servant Isaac" (II) in comparison with "the son of my master" (I). It may be hypothesized, then, that in II Abraham's death is recounted before the servant's journey. That this beginning of the account is transmitted in fragments has already been long deduced from v 36, "he gave him all his goods" (cf. Hupfeld, *Quellen der Genesis*, 145-46). This statement is currently located in 25:5, recounted in relation to Abraham's death. It may have originally stood after 24:1 (Kautzsch-Socin[2], n. 115) and have been displaced like 25:11b. Now, by nature, the transferal of one's means only takes place if death stands as an immediate prospect. One does not disrobe until one goes to bed. The oath the servant must take also only makes complete and good sense if Abraham believes that he must shortly die. If he expected to live he would not require an oath, he would give a command. But Abraham's instructions (vv 5, 6, 8), in particular, presume his imminent death. They are final instructions. Accordingly, it may be theorized that II recounted the death of Abraham before the servant sets out, I recounted it upon his return. Therefore, 25:5; 24:36b, and also v 36a, which fits well in the context, are also to be attributed to II. Both recensions must have had a statement such as v 34, attributed to I above. The fact that vv 35, 36 (entirely) belong to II is confirmed by another consideration. The servant's speech does not simply have the object of recounting what has transpired. Instead, he reports those elements of his master's life which may bring his efforts success. Consequently, this speech varies in correlation to the different concepts of Laban's character. According to II, Laban is quite inclined to consider the money (vv 30-31), therefore the servant explains to him what a good match Isaac would be (vv 35, 36b). According to I, contrariwise, where Laban values relationship a great deal (vv 27, 28f.), it is not necessary to speak of Abraham's wealth. Instead, the servant is satisfied with recounting Abraham's wish.

Only a few details are yet to be treated. The information concerning Rebekah's parents in vv 24, 27 belongs, as shown above (p. 244), to I. The servant is (cf. above p. 244) joyfully astonished when he hears these names (vv 26-27). Consequently, we may confidently assume that the sensitive narrator has not already mentioned these names previously. Otherwise, he would have ruined the reader's surprise. Accordingly, the parallel information in v 15 (and v 45) is a passage from II (cf. also the usage <247> כִלָּה לְ, vv 15, 45 as in v 19 [twice], 22). Furthermore, since, according to I, the servant cannot wonder enough about the fact that he come directly to relatives of his master (v 26), we must imagine that he had no prior concept of how near he had already approached Nahor's house. In contrast, we find an entirely different concept in v 10 (at the end) according to which the servant has (consciously) traveled to Nahor's city. Accordingly, II includes אֶל־עִיר נָחוֹר (v 10) and, furthermore, all references to "the city" (vv 11a, ba, 13; concerning the expression, "I stand here at the water source," cf. vv 30, 43a). "To Aram Naharaim" in v 10 and "at the time when the water drawers come out" in 11bβ (‖ 11ba and, at the same time ‖ 13b) are to be assigned to I. One must, therefore, assume that I conceives of Nahor as a nomad. Of the two statements concerning Isaac's dwelling, v 62 can be very easily seen as the introduction to vv 63-65, while 25:11b represents the conclusion of the account equally well. Accordingly, one may include v 62 in II and 25:11b in I. Sections from both recensions seem to have been fused in v 7. The beginning and end assert that Yahweh himself will give the journey good fortune (I). In contrast, the relative clauses seem to want to establish that it would be a serious sin to take Isaac back (Yahweh himself promised this land to Abraham's seed; therefore he must remain in this land). They probably belong, therefore, to II (cf. the expression הצֵּאת הָאָרֶץ, vv 7, 5). The relative form of the clauses may stem from the redactor. In the exposition, those sections which emphasize Abraham's wealth, such as vv 35, 36b, belong to II (vv 1b; 25:5; and הַמֹּשֵׁל בְּכָל־אֲשֶׁר־לוֹ, v 2ab; cf. the repeated כָּל־אֲשֶׁר־לוֹ, also in v 36b; cf. further regarding the "blessing," which consists of money and goods, vv 1b, 35, and esp. 31). The rest (vv 1a, 2aa) would, therefore, be from I. Thus we obtain here, too, two somewhat distinct images. In I Abraham makes provision so that his son Isaac may acquire the correct wife, in II he thinks simultaneously of seeing to it that his belongings, that God has promised to multiply even more later (v 7), come one day into the right hands. V 2b seems to parallel וְאַשְׁבִּיעֲךָ in v 3 and to be, therefore, from II. In the same manner, v 9a (II) parallels v 9b (I). One should not misunderstand these lists. The distinction of the major contours of the sources is, I think, simple and reliable. The details, as often with such closely related sources, can only lay claim to a greater or lesser degree of likelihood. The sources may have been woven together even more tightly in the details. I thank my friend Lic. Hans Schmidt for essential assistance in working out this source analysis.

3. *Original meaning and stylistic character of the account.* The relationship of the variants to one another. The core of the legend is the migration of Rebekah from the North to Canaan and her marriage to Isaac. The migration legends of Abraham and, especially, of Jacob are parallels, the latter for the following specific reasons: Isaac's relationship to Rebekah is the same as Jacob's to his Aramaic wives Rachel and Leah. The fact that the male partner (Isaac, Jacob) has already settled in Canaan before the female is repeated in both legends. Insofar as one is interested in finding historical reminiscences here, one will think of the same or similar events or circumstances as they echo in the legends of Abraham and Jacob.

In both variants, the account is better termed a "novella" than a legend (cf. the introduction ¶3:19-20). In both, the presumably original ethnohistorical sense is significantly diminished, the "novelistic" treatment, in contrast, enhanced. The account is lovingly detailed. The content of the events is so limited that it would not be sufficient for an old "legend." Nor is there any actual "complication." The narrators will, therefore, have had access to little more than a "notice" (introduction ¶3:22) concerning Isaac's marriage which they lovingly expanded. In terms of their esthetic character, the account can be termed an "idyll," then. Consequently, we are unable to indicate assuredly who "Rebekah" originally was. Whether there was really once an Aramaic tribe named "Rebekah," or whether she was originally a mythical or <248> cultic figure, one may ask, but not answer (Meyer, *Israeliten*, 258). Scholars who otherwise overlook the artistic manner of the patriarchal sages are accustomed to saying a word concerning the style of this narrative. The contention usually proposed that this account especially characterizes the style of J, however, is distorted. The account, indeed in both variants, is characteristic of the later "more expansive" style. This narrative also manifests its later nature in that (in both variants) it presupposes other legends: Abraham's family relations and his emigration, Yahweh's promise and blessing on him, Isaac as the son of his old age, Laban's greed, etc. The narrators, then, have taken the features with which they have adorned this legend from other legends. The position the deity assumes in this accounts also shows its later character. The deity does not appear here, as in the older legends, as one agent alongside others (cf. as a contrast, for example, Gen 16, 18, 19), but remains, as in the stylistically related Joseph narrative, in the background of things (cf. introduction ¶4:6).

Otherwise the similarity in the overall structure and even in the details between the two variants is quite significant. Such an example (to which one may add from accounts of characteristically brief style perhaps the two variants of the Penuel and the Tower narratives) shows that the narratives must have been more or less firmly fixed in the tradition and that the narrators have faithfully maintained the total structure despite occasional departures in the details (cf. introduction ¶4:4).

Each of the two variants exhibits some signs of more advanced age in relation to the other. Recension II is recounted in a particularly fresh and vivid manner (the maiden's loveliness, Laban's greed as in Gen 29, also the concluding scene, vv 62-65), whereas Recension I is less colorful (the character of the maid is hardly described; Laban is, following later style—cf., e.g., comments on 26:1-16—idealized) and lovingly portrays especially the piety of the acting persons. Twice the old servant falls thankfully to the ground before Yahweh, and Rebekah obediently accedes to Yahweh command. The great role the camels play in II is also an ancient feature. It transports us to the naive attitudes of the ancient period. Finally, the servant's oath, shortly before Abraham's death, is also better motivated than in I. On the other hand, recension II, according to which the maiden also voices an opinion in reference to such a remote marriage, assumes a later marriage custom than I, where she is not even asked. The simpler sign in I seems older than the complicated one in II. The composition of I is tighter than II. The motif that Yahweh gives the journey success unifies all sections (vv 7b, 12, 14b, 21b, 26-27, 42, 48, 51, 56). Furthermore, the reprisal of the facts in the servant's account is better motivated in I, where the decision follows the reprise, than in II, where the whole repetition is rather purposeless. Accordingly, neither of the variants simply traces to the other. The relationship is rather—as is usually the case in oral tradition—a complicated one.

4. To which of the sources do the variants belong? Both variants clearly stem from J. This evidenced for I by the following: יהוה (vv 3, 7, 12, 21b, 26, 27bis, 42, 44b, 48bis, 50a, 51, 56), בְּנוֹת הַכְּנַעֲנִי (vv 3, 37; Holzinger, *Hexateuch*, 94, 107), אֲרָם נַהֲרַיִם (v 10; P פַּדַּן אֲרָם), יָדַע in the sexual sense (v 16; cf. comments on the passage), רוֹץ לִקְרַאת (v 17), הִצְלִיחַ (v 21), etc. Evidence for J as the source for II includes: יהוה (vv 1b, 31, 35), הִקְרָה (v 12ag; perhaps the phrase should be assigned to II), טֹבַת מַרְאֶה (v 16; cf. comments on the passage), and דִּבֶּר אֶל־לִבּוֹ (v 45). Since we have found two different strands in the preceding Abraham narratives—(1) the legend cycle which we have termed Jᵃ and (2) a second series of accounts which we have termed Jᵇ—the question arises as to which of the two variants is to be attributed to Jᵃ and which to Jᵇ. Yet, the significance of this question should not be overestimated. Since, ultimately, the legends are more or less inde <249> pendent of one another, the answer to such questions usually offers little to the comprehension of the text, itself. A wholly certain

response cannot be given for Gen 24 either because the points of contact are not very clear and, in addition, usually pertain to passages in Gen 24 whose attribution is not beyond doubt. Yet one may nevertheless assume that recension II belongs to J[b] (a list similar to the one in v 35 occurs in 12:16 J[b]; Yahweh's oath in v 7 like 15:18 J[b]; the expression כָּל־אֲשֶׁר־לוֹ in 25:5; 24:2, 36 as in 12:20 J[b]; the account of Isaac's birth in v 35 as in 21:1, 7 J[b]; and אוּלַי vv 5, 39 as in 16:2 J[b]) and recension I to J[a] (the motif of Laban's hospitality like Abraham's hospitality in Gen 18 and Lot's in Gen 19; the foot washing in v 32b as in 18:4 and 19:2; the dual question in v 49 as in 18:21; "to the right or to the left," in v 49 as in 13:9; "old, advanced in days," in v 1 as in 18:11; רוּץ לִקְרַאת in v 17a as in 18:2 [cf. 19:1]; וַיִּשְׁתַּחוּ אַרְצָה in vv 52, 26, 48 as in 18:2; 19:1). It should also be noted that the migration legend in Gen 12 (J[a]) knows nothing of Abraham's home city, nor does recension I here, whereas recension II speaks of a "city of Nahor." In contrast, one may not argue on the basis of the reference to Abraham's migration in v 7a—both sources must have recounted this—nor from the citation in v 7 ("to your seed I will give this land") which can derive from 12:7 (J[a]) or 15:18 (J[b]).

5. Sievers and Procksch attempt other source analyses. Sievers (II, 206-207, 300-301) attributes all but vv 53-55a, 60-67 (J[b]) to J[a], although he thereby destroys the unit linked by the motif of sending: שַׁלְּחוּנִי (vv 54, 56), וַיְּשַׁלְּחוּ (v 59); cf. also קַח וָלֵךְ (v 51) and וַיִּקַּח וַיֵּלַךְ (v 61). According to Procksch the following—his own text citations are often imprecise—belong to E: vv 1a, 2a, 4b-6, 8, 10b*, 11*, 13, 14a,bα, 45a*, 15b, 16bα, 45b*, 46aβ,γ, 20a, 22aβ,γ,β, 23b, 25, 28a, 29a, 30, 32b, 38, 5a, 41, 42a, 43, 44, 45aβ,b, 46aβ,γ,b, 47b, 50b, 54-56a, 57-59, 61b, 62, 64a, 65a, 67aβ. Everything else belongs to J. His contention, however, that "two complete strands" emerge in this manner, is not accurate. Beside the many lacuna in E already noted by Procksch himself the oath is missing in Abraham's speech (vv 4bff.), as is a reference to the camels taken along (v 10b), to the well (v 11), and to the appeal (vv 13, 43). Furthermore, this source analysis disrupts the following interrelationships: the expression לָקַח אִשָּׁה לִבְנִי links v 4b with vv 7b and 40. Vv 14, 16b, 20a, 43-45 belong together with vv 17, 18, 46. Laban's address to the "blessed of Yahweh" in v 31a can only be understood against v 30 (cf. the interpretation) and must, therefore, have stood in the same report, just as v 31b (מָקוֹם) refers back to v 25b. Vv 39, 61a belong together with vv 5a, 8a (הָלַךְ אַחֲרֵי). The "eating and drinking" in v 54 can only be properly understood against v 33, where the servant does not want to eat. V 63 is the precondition for the scene in vv 64ff.

1-9 *The commission.* 2 The chapter gives interesting information concerning the status of the slave in ancient times. Such a slave, born into the household, has great devotion to the household of his master. Tested in long service, he finally becomes administrator and executor of his master's will. He enjoys the greatest confidence with father and son. The legend considers him worthy to be placed at the center of a narrative. In the life of modern farmers, servant and maid, if they are aged and have, perhaps, been in the household for a long time, also have a substantial right to object and advise (A. l'Houet, *Psychologie des Bauerntums*, 41). On the other hand, the narrator considers it unnecessary to mention the slave's name: slaves usually do not have names in the legend, that is, they are not actually considered persons. The oath by the reproductive member, which also occurs in 47:29, is attested elsewhere (cf. Dillmann and Spurrell) and may also be contained in Babylonian legal expressions—"the one takes the front of the other" or "one smites the other's front" = one vouches for the other (cf. Meißner, *Mitteil. d. Vorderas. Gesellsch.* [1905]: 307ff.). It presumes the unusual sacredness of this member. The view which led to this practice in the earliest period <250> regarded the reproductive member as the divine aspect of humans and, therefore, saw the essence of deity in generation and fertility. The same view is expressed in the symbol of the phallus, whose form the Babylonian "boundary stones" may have born (cf. Roscher, *Lex.* 3:66), and certainly the Assyrian *Ziqqâti* did (cf. MDOg 22:26, 28; 26:22 and fig. 5; etc.). Contrariwise, as far as we can say at the moment, the Hebrew massebahs did not (Greßmann, ZAW 29:116ff.). This view is also expressed in the institution of religious prostitution and perhaps also in circumcision, etc. Here, in Gen 24, this viewpoint itself has long since been obscured. The period has become so modest that it may only refer to this practice from a distance. But the practice itself endured—as often happens. The oath before death also occurs in 47:29ff.

3 One administers an oath to another (הִשְׁבִּיעַ) by pronouncing against him the curse formula (אָלָה, v 41), that is, a wish for disaster, whereupon the other responds with an oath (שְׁבוּעָה), that is, a conditional self-deprecation (cf. Siegfried-Stade, s.v. אָלָה; Stade, *Bibl. Theol.*, 153). From our perspective, Abraham notably does not leave the choice of the bride to his son. In the view of ancient Israel, however, as a serious matter, this is the father's responsibility, not the youth's (cf. Benzinger[2], 106; Rauh, *Hebr. Familienrecht*, 14; but cf., e.g. also Judg 14:1-5). The same view occurs among many peoples at the same cultural stage and still in modern peasantry (l'Houet, 63). Wooing by a third party, who must be an older man, is also common and is still common practice among the Jews. Ancient Israel, like every prudent people, places great value of the purity of heritage (Judg 14:3). The particular aversion against union with Canaanites can be explained in relation to the fact that Canaan was the oppressed, disdained people in Israel's monarchical period. Reality was, however, quite different (cf. comments on 38:2). In a later period, when Israel was convinced of the absolute uniqueness of its religion and it recognized the dangers of intermarriage for religious purity, connubium with Canaan seemed a religious error (Deut 7:3-4; Exod 34:16). Yahweh's epithet, "God of heaven (LXX + τῆς γῆς)" in v 7 and, more extensively, "God of heaven and God of earth" in v 3 does not occur elsewhere in Genesis nor, indeed, in the whole preexilic literature. Contrariwise, the title "God of heaven" is very common in the Jewish literature from the Persian period and later (cf. Ezr 1:2; 5:12; 6:9-10; 7:12, 21, 23; 2 Chron 36:23; Neh 1:4-5; 2:4, 20; Psa 136:26; Jon 1:9; Tob 5:17; 10:12; Dan 2:18, 19, 37, 44; 4:34; "God of heaven and earth," Ezr 5:11). Jews employed these names when they wanted to make the character of their God comprehensible to foreigners (especially clearly in Ezr 5:11-12; Neh 2:20; Jon 1:9; Dan 2:37, 44; 5:23 [מָרֵא שְׁמַיָּא]) and, consequently, also occur in the responses of the Persian kings to the Jews (Ezr 6:9-10; 7:12, 21, 23 [1:2; Dan 4:34]). The same phenomena appears in the newly discovered Judeo-Aramaic documents (cf. Sachau, *Drei aramäische Papyrusurkunden aus Elephantine* 1:2, 15, 28; 3:3f.). No doubt the Jews chose these epithets with a view to their Persian masters (cf. Bertheau-Ryssel, *Esra, Nech. u. Ester*[2], 133; Lidzbarski, *Ephemeris für semit. Epigraphik* 1:250-51; Meyer 3:170-71). As Prof. Bartholomae has communicated to me, the Jews will have imitated Ahuramazda's title, "who created that heaven, who created this earth," often employed by Darius, Xerxes, and later kings in the old Persian cuneiform documents (cf. Weißbach and

Band, *Altpers. Keilinschriften*, 35, 37, 39, 41, etc.). Since, however, the Jewish epithet is not a translation of the Persian, they probably preferred an earlier Israelite epithet already in occasional use and employed it as the preferred title under the altered religiopolitical circumstances. This characterization is also confirmed by the fact that there are similar titles in the religions which <251> influenced Israel in the earlier period. In Babylonian "King of heaven and earth" is an epithet for Bel and Marduk (cf. Zimmern, KAT³, 357). The north Semitic peoples knew, and not just in later times (Lidzbarski, *Ephemeris* 1:243ff.), the "Baal of Heaven" (Zimmern, KAT³, 357; Lidzbarski, *Ephemeris* 2:122; Pognon, *Inscriptions sémitiques de la Syrie*, 159ff.) which may have been the model for the Israelite "God of Heaven." Sievers' hypoethesis (2:301) that the title is a later addition in our text is, therefore, probably to be rejected, especially since such predicates are quite well suited to this solemn passage (cf. Westphal, *Jahves Wohnstätten*, 227-28). Concerning אֲשֶׁר see §165b.

4 לְיִצְחָק is a gloss. The glossator is probably thinking of the fact that Ishmael is also Abraham's son. This culture places supreme value on the fact that the wife be a relative (Benzinger², 107; Rauh, *Hebr. Familienrecht*, 12-13; concerning endogamy among the ancient Arabs, cf. Wellhausen, *Nachrichten d. Gött. Ges. d. Wissenschaften* [1893], 437-38). The modern farmer says, "Buy your neighbor's cow, marry your neighbor's child" (l'Houet, 63). **7** Even as he dies, Abraham manifests his faith and obedience (similar situations in Tob 14:3ff.; Luke 2:29ff., and in the Jewish "Testaments). Thus the motif of the following is established, for the subsequent narrative recounts how God brings the fulfillment of this belief. An earlier period believed that Yahweh himself accompanied his devotees on journeys (28:15; 46:4). A later period, which had pious misgivings about this excessive intervention of God in worldly matters, prefers to say that Yahweh commissioned his messenger to this task (further, cf. comments on 16:7). The same motif occurs in Exod 23:20; 32:34; Psa 91:11; Tob 5:14, 22. "Who swore to me" refers to Gen 15. Similar references occur in 26:3 and 50:24, both are secondary. It is an addition here, also (Dillmann; Kraetzschmar, *Bundesvorstellung*, 62; Sievers 2:302). **8** Regarding נְקִיתָ see §75x. For זאת see §126y. For לֹא תָשֵׁב see §109d. Jᵇ recounted Abraham's death after v **9**.

10-32 *The scene at the well.* I. **10-14** *The servant alone.* **10** וַיֵּלֶךְ¹ (om LXX; cf. Kautzsch-Socin², n. 103) is a scribal error. For כָּל־ "all sorts of" (2:9), LXX, Pesh, and Vulg read וּמִכָּל־ (Ball, Kittel, Kautzsch³). נַהֲרַיִם (not with a dual ending, but the plural of the locative; or, following §88c "extension" of the ending ם־), in the Amarna correspondence Na'rima, Egyptian Nhrina, is the river land, that is, the region of the middle Euphrates (cf. Meyer, ZAW 3:307-308, and Gesenius-Buhl¹⁴). The city of Nahor is not mentioned by name here. In 27:43; 28:10; 29:4 it is identified with Haran. Our narrator, however, seems not to know this name. In such elements almost every significant narrative has its peculiarities. No local features from the great city of Haran are perceptible here <252> nor in the Jacob-Laban legend. This absence points to the fact that Abraham's relatives were located there only secondarily. Originally they were not, as Jᵃ (cf. comments on vv 12-14) and E (29:1) still maintains, city dwellers, but nomads (cf. Meyer, *Israeliten*, 242, and "The Jacob-Laban Legend" below). **11** The following scene is related to the one in 29:2ff. Both times preparations for the marriage of the ancestor with his Aramaic cousin are made at the well. That this site is "the well outside the gate," is surely an element of verisimilitude. The maidens come there in the evening to draw water (1 Sam 9:11; still common practice in the Orient; cf. Dillmann and Driver). The young men will probably have also come there. There the matchmaker has the best opportunity to see the beauties of the city passing in review. "He let the camels rest"—The source speaks neither here nor elsewhere of the servant's companions, although he must, of course, have had some (cf. לָנוּ, v 23b). This silence is probably an intentional refinement. The endearing service the young maiden shows the old man by watering his camels would seem excessive, even foolish, if a host of capable men stood beside him.

12-14 *The prayer.* Looking for a bride is a difficult matter—doubly difficult if one is supposed to choose a bride for another, but superhumanly difficult if the servant is seeking her for his young master. In such cases, when the ancient feels acutely the impotence of his own knowledge and ability, he turns confidently to the deity. The deity is to designate the bride through a sign. Concerning signs in Yahwism see Stade (*Bibl. Theol.*, 101-102). The servant chooses a sign, however, by which he recognizes the quite unusual courteous loveliness of the maiden. He wants such a friendly maiden as his master's wife and as his mistress in his old age. Thus, childish confidence in God and worldly-wise calculation are intermixed here most gracefully. This is consistent with the character of J[b]. At the same time, one notes the position the camels have here. They are a precious possession and are also dear to the one who deals with them daily. The narrator does not consider them unworthy to be the focal point of a motif and the old slave can observe in the maiden's handling of the animals whether she is suited to be a housewife. The Arabs also treasure the camel highly. "No subject is treated more extensively in the songs than dromedaries." "His cattle are more precious to the nomad than to the farmer" (G. Jacob, *Beduinenleben*[2], 61-62). J[a] seems to have portrayed the matter somewhat differently than J[b]. Here, Abraham's relatives are, it seems, nomads who are very difficult to find. The servant arrives in their country and comes at random to a well. Here, however, he asks Yahweh to relieve him from the continued very tiresome and uncertain search for Abraham's family and immediately to send him a maiden from the family.

12 "Yahweh, God of my lord Abraham" (also in vv 27, 42, 48). It is common practice to add predicates of God to the invocation which establish the supplicant's right to be heard (cf. comments on 32:10ff.). The servant appeals to Abraham's close relationship to Yahweh. He himself—it is presumed—has no personal relationship with Yahweh (Haller, 74; Benzinger[2], 103; Eerdmans, 73). **13** The request for a sign begins with a clause with הִנֵּה אָנֹכִי (as in Judg 6:37 and with הִנֵּה אֲנַחְנוּ, 1 Sam 14:8). Of course the supplicant's situation is indicated first. **14** Concerning the construction see §167c. The <253> servant thinks that he will make this request of several maidens. The one who responds, "I will also water your camels," should be the bride. The thirsty traveler asking the native for a drink of water and the resulting discussion and acquaintance are motifs from daily life (1 Kgs 17:10; John 4:7). The service the servant requests is minor, a drink of water, the kindness to be demonstrated through it, however, is very great: how many times must she run back and forth until the thirsty animals have been watered. Thus, her friendly attitude and her indefatigable industry will become apparent over and over. One sees how the Hebrew values the maiden's industry in the selection of a bride (Ruth 2:4). The modern farmer thinks similarly (l'Houet, 61). נַעַר in

the Pentateuch also means "virgin" (§122g, 17c; Qere Sam הַנַּעֲרָה). V 14bβ is from
Jᵃ. Thereby (בָהּ §135p) he will discern whether his lord's belief (v 7b) is true.

15, 16, 17b, 18-21a, 22, 23b, 25 The servant and the maiden according to Jᵇ. **15**
Rebekah comes even before he finishes the prayer. This rapid fulfillment of his prayer is
a clear indication that it was no accident but a gracious dispensation of Yahweh. For
כִלָה after טֶרֶם Kautzsch (§107c) suggests the impf. as in v 45. The genealogy of
Rebekah given here and in vv 24, 47 is remarkably confused. The indication of the
grandparents in vv 24, 47 is unnecessary since she has only been asked about her parents.
In addition, the servant rejoices that he has found the daughter of his master's brother
(אֲחִי singular in v 27 as in v 48) and Laban is not the son of Bethuel but of Nahor
according to 29:5. All this suggests that Bethuel has been secondarily inserted in 24:15,
24, 47 and that Rebekah was originally the daughter of Nahor and Milcah. This insertion
took place in order to harmonize the tradition of Gen 24 with 22:20-24 and with P 25:20;
28:2, 5 (cf. Mez, *Harrâ*, 19ff.; Dillmann; Kautzsch³, 39, etc.). Here the original text read
אֲשֶׁר יָלְדָה מִלְכָּה (Dillmann; freely translated in Gunkel's translation). The words
אֲחִי אַבְרָהָם, the major concern here, correctly do not appear in the parallel v 24. The
narrator, but not the maiden, knows that her kinship with Abraham is significant. "The jar
on her shoulder" (21:14; Exod 12:34; Josh 4:5) does not have solely picturesque
significance (as the modern would understand it), but is present to amplify the tension at
the same time. The old man mentioned a jar. Drinking from the jar is to play the decisive
role. He had hardly spoken these words when a maiden approached with her jar on her
shoulder. The servant's eyes and our eyes fasten on this maiden and her jar.

16 "A virgin" parallels "she had known no man." The latter phrase is probably to be
assigned to Jᵃ because of 19:8, the other, then, to Jᵇ. The maiden's beautify is discussed
in a characteristic manner. The servant did not take her beauty, but her charm as a sign.
Her beauty is an added gift of God's kindness: a serious view of marriage. Presumably
the maiden did not veil her face (Benzinger², 78). בְּאֵר is the whole well structure: a
hole in the ground, protected outwardly by large stones, walled internally and provided
with steps leading down to the well proper <254> (עַיִן), alongside it a stone trough (cf.
Benzinger², 207). From **16b** onward is intentionally narrated in great detail. The servant
and we with him observe every individual action of the virgin with great excitement. Will
she be the one? The pace slows immediately before the decisive moment as in 22:5-10
and 44:12. Thus she does not say the resolving word immediately after his request (v **17**),
but only when he has drunk his fill (v **19**). The further account (v **20**) that she also
immediately watered all the camels serves, then, to establish the sign as sure and certain.
The whole scene must be discussed slowly and with full significance. Vv 19aβ and 20b
bear the main accent. The maiden's haste (וַתְּמַהֵר, vv 18,20) here and subsequently
demonstrates her charm. Such haste is, simultaneously, a simple and much favored means
for the narrators to bind the context more tightly together. We should imagine that the
subsequent action followed the preceding without a gap (cf. vv 15, 17, 22, 28, 30, 33, 52).
While to this point the servant was amazed (v **21a**; משׁתָּאֵה miswritten from מִשׁתָּעֶה? so
Ball; construct state before the prep. §130a) now the maiden is (v 22) for now "the man"
gives her a gift, so stupendously large (worth about 472 Marks; Benzinger², 201) that it
does not correspond in any way to the kindness she has shown him. What is it supposed
to mean? Concerning nose rings see Benzinger², 83; Concerning nose and ear rings among

the Arabs see Jacob, 48. One should read with Sam וַיָּשֶׂם עַל־אַפָּהּ after מִשְׁקָלוֹ (cf. 47). שֶׁקֶל is implied after עֲשָׂרָה (§134n). **23b** The servant is much too observant of custom and etiquette to speak here at the well of his intentions toward the maiden. This subject should be treated at home with her relatives. Consequently, he now asks about lodging. בֵּית־אָבִיךְ is the accusative of location (§118g). **25** She is once again so cordial (and now, at the same time, so clever) as to offer him straw and feed, as well. The hospitable host praises his lodgings (Jacob, 86). <255> Between vv 25 and 30 a brief comment is missing in J^b (‖ vv 28-29). She runs quickly home. She wants to report the man's request to lodge overnight with them and she is burning to show her gifts.

30, 31, 32a,b,α *The servant and Laban at the well according to J^b*. The legend now humorously recounts Laban's selfishness. Gold catches his eye. Whoever shows so much gold is welcome with him a thousand times. He is extremely excited and stumbles over himself in courtesies in order not to lose the valuable visit (Sam כִּרְאוֹתוֹ, v 30; Spurrell, Ball). The figure of Laban is drawn here following the prototype of the doubtlessly older Jacob-Laban legend (Haller, 116). "Yahweh's blessed" (v 31) must refer to him because he has a great deal of gold. This is a naive, drastic way to determine God's grace. This is not only Laban's theology, however, but also the opinion of the narrator (vv 1b, 35). The fact that Laban also speaks of "Yahweh" is probably only the legend's naiveté. **31** LXX, Pesh, Vulg, Kittel add לוֹ after וַיֹּאמֶר. **32a** One may read וַיָּבָא אֶת־ with Olshausen following Vulg.

17a, 21b, 23, 24, 26, 27 *The servant and the maiden according to J^a*. The beginning is only preserved in a phrase in v 16. The context is explained above. **24** The original text read בַּת־מִלְכָּה אָנֹכִי אֲשֶׁר יָלְדָה לְנָחוֹר. Rebekah names herself after her mother first. The background is that her father is dead. Therefore she runs (v 28) to "her mother's house" and therefore her brother is the head of the family (vv 50, 53, 55, 60). This is true in both variants. **26-27** The servant is most joyfully surprised (וַיִּשְׁתַּחוּ, in a similar situation in Judg 7:15). He wanted to find any relative of his master's. Now Yahweh has brought him the nearest relative! The cousin is considered the most appropriate wife (29:19). Concerning the preposed אָנֹכִי see §135e. For אֲחֵי (v 27) one may read with LXX, Pesh, Vulg and v 48 אֲחִי (cf. comments on v 15). The presumption is that the servant knows his master's genealogy by heart.

28, 29 . . . 32bβγ *The servant and Laban according to J^a*. The maiden's motive for running home differs here from J^b. Extremely astonished at the question which has caught her off guard (v 23a), and even more so at the "man's" thanksgiving prayer (vv 26-27) in which he finally reveals himself as her uncle's servant, she runs as quickly as possible to her mother in order to unburden her heart. This is a very true-to-life conceptualization.

33-49 The servant's account is supposed to invoke Yahweh's authority for the proposal. Later narrator's took pleasure in such reprises. The rule of style called for avoiding literal repetitions. Instead small variations were introduced (cf. introduction ¶3:20). LXX, with no sensitivity for the style, repeatedly altered the second report in favor of the first. V 33 portrays the conscientiousness of the faithful servant who values his task above eating and drinking (cf. vv 55f.). Qere, Sam <256> read וַיּוּשַׂם hophal. Kautzsch (¶¶73-74) explains the kethib וַיִּישֶׂם (with reservations) as a qal passive. **36** Sievers (2:295) prefers זִקְנָתָהּ; in contrast, Sam, LXX (cf. 21:2, 7), Kittel, and Kautzsch³ read זִקְנָתוֹ. **40** "Before whom I walk" may have been changed from the original "who walks before me" as in 18:22. The God who has cleared the way until now will also give this journey good fortune. הִתְהַלֵּךְ "to travel back and forth" refers to several migrations. **41** Concerning אֵלֹהֵי see §95f. **42** Concerning אִם with a nominal clause and נָא see §159v. Regarding the construction compare the similar prayer in Judg 6:36ff. **45** The servant's prayer was spoken softly (אֶל־לִבִּי). One does not speak aloud of an offer of marriage one intends to make. The rule is to pray aloud, "to cry," קְרָא (Heitmüller, 30n.3). Regarding אֲנִי see §135a. V **46** is significantly more concise than vv 18-20. **47** בְּתוּאֵל בֶּן is an insertion (cf. comments on v 15). The offer, that is, the request of the relatives that they "give" him the maiden (cf. v 41), must have come after v 47b in J^b. The words have been omitted in favor of v 49 J^a. **49** "If you truly are." To this point they have shown him kindness as their relative's servant. Now, however, their faithfulness is put to the test. "So that I may turn aside to the right or to the left (עַל <257> miswritten from אֶל, Siegfried-Stade, s.v. פנה, 4) probably means, "so that I may then go in this or that direction."

50-60 *The acceptance of the Offer and the Release of Rebekah.* **50a** וּבְתוּאֵל is remarkable since, according to vv 29, 58, 55 Rebekah has only one brother (Laban), while, according to the glossator in vv 15, 24, 47, Bethuel is Rebekah's father, although he is mentioned here after his son Laban. The difficulty probably can be resolved most easily by considering Bethuel here, too, as a very ill-advised addition (Dillmann, Ball, etc.). וּמִלְכָּה may have originally stood here (cf. v 55; Holzinger; Sievers 2:304). Brother and mother make decisions concerning the maiden since the father is dead. **50b** They do not know how to say either good nor ill, that is, anything (31:24, 29; Num 24:13; etc.): not "No," because of Isaac's great wealth; not "Yes" because of the immense distance they would be sending the maiden. The redactor understood the statement in this sense, "We can say nothing to this because Yahweh has already spoken." **51** Yahweh has "spoken" through the sign. **53** It is common practice for the family of the bridegroom to give gifts to the bride and the family of the bride (cf. Benzinger[2], 106). The gifts to the relatives are a remnant of an earlier "bride purchase," but are hardly still perceived as such here. The same practice also occurs among the Arabs, who also know of a gift to the bride alongside the purchase price (Jacob, 57) and among whom the original significance of the bride purchase was already diminished in early times (cf. Nowack, *Archäol.* 1:155). A gift to the bride is also mentioned in 34:12 and in Codex Hammurabi ¶¶159-60 (Jastrow, *Religion Babyloniens und Assyriens* 1:59; Benzinger[2], 106). J^b in our text does not mention gifts to the relatives at all. Why have the many camels been brought along, however, if not to transport the מֹהַר (bride-price)? And a greedy man like Laban will not let his sister go without significant remuneration. This account has probably been omitted because it was already treated in the variant (v 53). One certainly may not maintain that the betrothal in this account was only a business transaction concluded with "hard sobriety" (Holzinger). An actual purchase is not discussed here, but gifts. The account thinks that a true marriage in which the man receives the correct wife whom he can love (v 67) is made in heaven. After all possible dogmatic and ethical subtleties were found in the OT in earlier times, a few scholars, in an effort to avoid anachronism, are beginning now to portray ancient Israel in its native state.

55-56 The fact that the servant, just arrived, presses to set out once again so soon is very remarkable, especially for Oriental customs (Frankberg, CGA [1901], 694). The servant presses for this in order to find his lord yet alive (also in v 33). It <258> is a pleasant feature that mother and brother cannot part so quickly from the maiden. The narrator introduces this motif because it lengthens the action. The same motif appears in Tob 8:19. The number is missing with יָמִים. For this reason, Olshausen, Ball, and Kautzsch[3] suggest, following Sam and Pesh, that חֹדֶשׁ (29:14; or יֶרַח, Deut 21:13) has fallen out of the text. It is easier, with Sievers (2:304) and Cheyne (348-49) to read יֹמַיִם "two days" (Hos 6:2). **57** The fusion of the two variants has been particularly successful here. J[b] provides interesting information concerning marriage customs. Usually the maiden is not asked, at least not officially. The offer is made in her absence. But in such a difficult matter, when she is to be married so far away, she is permitted, as an exception, to make the decision. **59** "Their sister" is consistent with "our sister" (v 60) and "your daughter" (34:8). As a trousseau the young woman receives her nurse. This is an amiable practice. The woman who from childhood on has been her most beloved and trusted companion, next to her mother, accompanies her now to the strange household, as well. E names the nurse Deborah (35:8). **60** The blessing at betrothal also occurs in Ruth 4:11-12; Tob 7:12. The blessing in verse (two "quadrameters") should perhaps be conceived as a bridal song. רְבָבָה is a wordplay on רִבְקָה (cf. the similar passage 49:8). The statements are very general. The narrator knows only that Rebekah was a matriarch of Israel. The original significance of the figure was unknown to him. The wish for the newly betrothed that she have many children seems altogether to crude for the overtender modern race. It seemed very natural to the ancient. The young woman in those days preferred to hear nothing more than this.

61-67 *Departure and arrival at Isaac's home.* **61** An indication of the destination is missing after וַיֵּלֶךְ (cf. v 10), probably Hebron. There the servant hears from Isaac that Abraham has died in the meanwhile (J[a]). The continuation is in v **66**. **62** Isaac had moved on (in the meantime, while the servant was on his journey). מִבּוֹא hardly makes sense. It is simplest, but uncertain, to read מִדְבַּר, or following Sam (LXX) בְּמִדְבַּר with Dillmann, Kittel, etc. A further difficulty involves the contradiction between vv 62a and 62b. According to Num 13:17, 22 (contra Josh 15:23 P), the Negeb lies farther north than Beerlahairoi (Meyer, *Israeliten*, 253). May one assume that v 62a is a correction influenced by 25:11b? Contrariwise, Meyer (*Israeliten*, 253, 323n.4) relates v 62a to Ishmael (cf. above, p. 189). **63ff.** The significance of לָשׂוּחַ in this passage is uncertain—to mourn, to contemplate, to pray? Pesh has לָשׂוּט, "to take a stroll." The Hebrew perceives the following scene as an interesting divergence from the normal manner of bringing someone home. **64ff.** Here, too, the emphasis is placed once more on Rebekah's initiative. **64** She jumps from the camel, a courteous greeting for one's superior (1 Sam 25:23; 2 Kgs 5:21; <259> Josh 15:18; and still today, cf. Dillmann). **65** Concerning הַלְוֶה see §34f. The woman observes the details of customs at all times, and especially marriage customs, even in such an unusual case. Only veiled does she wish to meet her bridegroom. Concerning the practice of veiling the bride (29:25) compare Dillmann; G. Jacob, *Hohes Lied*, 20n.3; Benzinger[2], 28. There is an image of the veiled Ishtar in Jeremias, ATAO[2], 109. According to our text, Rebekah jumped from the camel even before she had recognized Isaac. Winckler's (*Forschungen* 3:419f.) suggestion to place v 64b behind v 65 deserves mention. The continuation of this passage is v **67aα**. The conclusion in v 67 expressly states that Isaac acknowledged the measures the servant had taken. הָאֹהֱלָה (with article) is intolerable before שָׂרָה אִמּוֹ. The latter two words are an insertion (cf. above, p. 244). "He grew to love her" (naturally, one must love a maiden who treats old people and animals so cordially and who is so beautiful) and "he was comforted over his father." Thus the lovely account comes to a charming conclusion.

32. Keturah's Sons 25:1-6, 11b Jʳ

The passage does not belong in any case to P, who offers a different genealogy for Sheba and Dedan (10:7) and who knows only of Isaac and Ishmael (25:9). It contains parts of the preceding narrative: 25:5 is from Jᵇ, originally positioned after 24:1; v 11b is from Jᵃ, originally after 24:67. The diction also shows that the piece belongs to "J": כָּל־אֵלֶּה בְּנֵי (v 4; cf. 10:29; 9:19). On the other hand, it does not agree with either of the two recensions of Gen 24. It still speaks of Abraham's marriage and children, while Abraham is already near death in both recensions in Gen 24, has only one son, and finally died. The piece will stem, therefore, from the later hand in J (cf. p. 161). The later hand in J intends to introduce Keturah's children at this point (vv 1-4). At the same time, however, the editor was also interested in showing that only Isaac, not these children of a concubine, was Abraham's heir (vv 5,6). In order to introduce these additions, he took individual clauses from Gen 24. Abraham's death must have been recounted at the end of v 6, a comment which was later displaced by the parallel in P. In terms of character and literary status, the piece is related to 22:20-24. It is a "geographic-ethnological table in genealogical form" (Meyer). The figure of Keturah is "devised <260> solely to give the tribes in the southeast, whom one wanted to link with Abraham, a mother" and is, therefore, hardly a tribal name (Meyer). Contrariwise, the names of the tribes descended from her are, of course, based on tradition. There is another tradition concerning the origin of Sheba in 10:28 J.

Like 22:20-24, this piece also has been glossed. V 3b offers the names of peoples in the plural which are still absent in 1 Chron 1:32-33, whereas the other names appear in the singular (cf. above, p. 86). If one removes these plural names, eleven nations result. Originally, the number twelve will have been intended. "To the East" and "in the land of the East" are manuscript variants.

Of the peoples mentioned, we are familiar with the Midianites (originally east of the Elanite Bay [Gulf of Aqabah] in the vicinity of the "Sinai," in the "period of the judges" they immigrated into Canaan from the Transjordan), the Sabaeans (a famed commercial people in southern Arabia), and the Dedanites (also traders, mentioned alongside the Sabaeans, probably originally located in the vicinity of Edom). זִמְרָן is from זֶמֶר, a species of deer or goat (Deut 14:5). Meyer (318n.2) disputes the equation with Zabram (?), a city near Mecca, since we probably should not go so far South. Is Jokshan a variant for Joktan (10:25ff.)? Friedr. Delitzsch (Zeitschr. f. Keilschriftforschung 2:92) associates Ishbak with the land of Yasbuq, somewhere in northern Syria, mentioned in the monolith inscription of Shalmanezer II (1:54 = KB 1:158/159). Shuah (Job 2:11) is the Assyrian Sûhu on the Euphrates near Carchemesh (cf. Friedr. Delitzsch, Paradies, 297. but also Hiob, 139). The Asshurim, not to be confused with the Assyrians, are located at Ishmael's border according to Gen 25:18. This Asshur may also be intended in Num 24:22, 24 and Psa 83:9 (cf. Hommel, Altisr. Überl., 238ff.; Aufs. u. Abh., 277ff.; Winckler, KAT³, 151). עֵיפָה (Isa 60:6 alongside Midian) is the Assyrian Ḥayapa. Hanoch is also the name of the patriarch and his city as well as a clan in Reuben (cf. above, p. 50). Abida is a personal name and is attested in Minaic. Here, then, a tribe is named for its head. The same circumstance probably applies to Eldaah (Meyer, 308, 318). This genealogy treats tribes, therefore, which we would call "Arabs." Concerning these and the other names compare Dillmann, Gesenius-Buhl[14], and Meyer (*Israeliten*, 307-308, 312ff.).

The Abraham Narrative in P

The Abraham narrative in P contains the following sections.

1. Comments concerning the migration to Canaan (12:4b, 5) and the parting (13:6, 11b, 12a,bα) of Abraham and Lot, Lot's deliverance (19:29a,bα), and Ishmael's birth (16:1a, 3, 15, 16). There is no superscription at the beginning. Yet Eerdmans (22) hypothesizes that 11:27, 31, 32 (Abraham's family and their emigration from Ur of the Chaldees) belong to the Abraham passage and carried the superscription "this is the Genealogy of Abram" (cf. above, pp. 156-57). Information concerning Lot's sons is probably missing after 19:29. P's comments correspond generally to the J tradition, specifically to J^a (migration, separation, Lot's deliverance) and J^b (Ishmael). The placement of the narratives is generally the same as in J. Characteristically, the legend of Lot's parting also follows immediately upon the emigration legend. One sees that even the sequence of legends was generally fixed in the tradition. Yet, the Sodom legend, which follows the Ishmael legend in J, seems to have preceded it in P's exemplar.

2. A larger piece concerning God's covenant with Abraham (17:1-14) and the promise of Isaac (vv 15-22). Comments concerning Ishmael's circumcision <261> (17:23-27) and Isaac's birth and circumcision (21:1b, 2b, 3, 4, 5) follow. The first section corresponds for the most part to the Gen 15 account in J^b (and E), where the two motifs, covenant and promise of a son, are also linked. Yet the placement of the two motifs in P is the reverse of Gen 15. It can be compared with the placement of these motifs in the context of J^a where Abraham is first promised that he will become a great people (12:2 J^a), and that his seed will possess the land (12:7 J^a), and only secondarily that he will have a son (18:10 J^a). P will not have devised this remarkable sequence, but will have adopted it from his exemplar. In P's exemplar, the two divine speeches (1) concerning the covenant and (2) concerning Isaac's birth will have been two different narratives which P combined into one. Furthermore, 17:17, 21 (the promise of Isaac) also presupposes an account which must have resembled that of J^a in 18:12, 14. P probably also read of the renaming of Abraham and Sarah (but probably not of the institution of circumcision) in his exemplar, which would, therefore, hardly be identical with J^a. P intermixed other material from another legend: Gen 17:20 alludes to the Ishmael legend, a legend we know from J^b (Gen 16) and E (Gen 21). The wording of the clause concerning Isaac's birth (21:1b) is very closely related to that of J^b (J^r?) in 21:1a.

3. The second larger P section, the acquisition of the cave of Machpela and Sarah's burial in Gen 23, has no parallel in the other documentary sources. The passage is (quite like the covenant in Gen 17, in which there is no action, only speech) actually not a "narrative" and, thus, as it stands, not to be considered an old legend. According to the ancient legend style, such a passage can only be part of a legend or, if it stands alone, a "comment" (cf. the comment concerning Jacob's acquisition of the field near Shechem,

33:19-20). P will have found in his source a reference to the acquisition of the cave and the names as such a comment and will have then extrapolated his detailed account.

4, Abraham's death and burial (25:7-11a), a comment such as must have stood at the end of any Abraham narrative, amplified by P.

5. Ishmael's genealogy (25:12-17) is without parallel in the other sources (to the extent that they are preserved). The names of the twelve tribes are surely traditional and preexisted P. The result is that P's exemplar is not identical with any of our sources. It most closely resembles our "J^a," although P also has elements which we know from J^b and E. Otherwise, there must be traditions not attested to us. P intervened here even more energetically than in the Primeval History. He was only able to employ comments from most of the legends. He only offers extensive treatments of the divine revelation in Gen 17 and the purchase of the cave in Gen 23. Both are (indeed Gen 23 more so than Gen 17) free compositions of P, although on the basis of the information in his source.

33. Abraham's Migration to Canaan, Separation from Lot, and Ishmael's Birth
12:4b, 5; 13:6, 11b, 12a,bα; 19:29a,bα; 16:1a, 3, 15, 16 P

I. **12:4b, 5** *Abraham's migration.* P is indicated by the chronology (v 4b), the expressions רְכוּשׁ and רְכָשׁ (v 5), and וַיִּקַּח (v 5) in the account of the migration as in 11:31, etc. P seems to have said nothing <262> concerning the motivation for the migration. This churchman places little value on "purely subjective" piety. Instead he offers the chronology of the objective fact of the migration—which is much more important to him. P does not seem to have recounted a theophany here. He combined everything he had to say about the revelation to Abraham in Gen 17. Whereas according to J Abraham set out for an uncertain destination and only learns in Canaan that he has arrived at his goal (cf. above, p. 165), according to P Canaan was Abraham's, indeed even Terah's (11:31), destination from the outset. Here, too, J is much more ingenious than P. 5 Holzinger and Sievers (2:263) correctly miss in the very precise P the name חָרָן before אָחִיו. נֶפֶשׁ "souls" means, in this context, "slaves" (36:6; Spurrell; Gesenius-Buhl[14] 4c). אֶרֶץ כְּנַעַן is the regular designation for the land of in contrast to the people of Canaan in all prose sources, and does not, therefore, characterize P (contra Dillmann, 217 and Holzinger, *Hexateuch*, 340; with Sievers 2:266-67).

II. **13:6, 11b, 12a,bα; 19:29a,bα** *Separation and Deliverance of Lot.* P is indicated for 13:6 by רְכוּשׁ and by the analogy with 36:7. The final clause "they could not remain together" does not belong to J either (cf. above, p. 173). Gen 13:11b comes too late following v 11a (J) and must, therefore, belong to P. V 12a, which can be dispensed with in J more easily than in P, and v 12bα (עָרֵי הַכִּכָּר, also 19:29 ‖ J כִּכַּר הַיַּרְדֵּן, 13:11a) also probably stem from P. The clauses attributed to P comprise a good unit. Here, too, P took only bare facts from the legend. Everything concrete, especially the dispute of the shepherd's and Lot's greed, but also Abraham's peace-loving nature, are omitted. And there is no hint of the connotations of the legend, its malicious glee (cf. above, p. 176). **13:6** Read וְנָשָׂאה with Sam, Ball, Sievers (2:266), and Kittel. V **19:29a,bα**, a comment concerning Lot's deliverance, follows immediately upon 13:12bα. The clause does not belong to J (it comes much too late), but to P: שִׁחֵת, אלהים,

עָרֵי הַכִּכָּר, and זָכַר (as in 8:1). The heavy repetition makes it likely that bβ,γ is a variant of aα (cf. Eerdmans, 11). P does not recount, but assumes, the legend of the destruction of the cities. The legend may not have interested P since it does not deal with Abraham and the seed of the promise. It must have seriously offended him because it recounts an attempted abomination against the deity. The presupposed account will be essentially the one we know from 19:1-25. P, too, employs the term הֲפֵכָה (and הָפַךְ; cf. the comments above on 19:25). Differences from J are that the cities are not mentioned by name, that several cities are mentioned in which Lot lived, and that P thinks that God spared Lot (not because of his righteousness, but) for Abraham's sake. The latter feature must be P's justification for the legend. The other elements may have been extant in the tradition. In P, a comment concerning Lot's sons probably followed here. <263>

III. **16:1a, 3, 15, 16** *Ishmael's birth.* V 3 is superfluous after v 2a (J); It comes too late following v 2b; It breaks the relationship between vv 2 and 4 in J. Sarah's statement in v 2 בֹּא־נָא receives a response in v 4 וַיָּבֹא, v 3 would only disrupt the connection. Eerdmans (12) misses the legal conveyance of the slave in J. But this conveyance is expressed by בֹּא־נָא, just as the return is expressed by הִנֵּה שִׁפְחָתֵךְ בְּיָדֵךְ in v 6. The same relationship exists between 30:3 and 4. Furthermore, Abraham naming his son (v 15) contradicts the explicit information in the legend (v 11) that Hagar named him. This difference is all the more distinctive since, according to the J legend, Hagar had already left Abraham's house before Ishmael's birth and since in P the father always gives names (cf. above, p. 42). The dates (vv 3, 16) as well as the painstaking precision with which the procedure is described also indicate that the verses belong to P. P records the whole action like a registrar. One may also attribute v 1a to P because of the pedantically precise addition "Sarai, wife of Abram." The clauses extracted and assigned to P constitute a coherent unit. Here, too, there is no further discussion of Sarah's jealousy and Hagar's defiance (J) or misfortune (E). Instead, everything transpires in peace and order, and Ishmael remains in Abraham's household (25:9). P transformed the old legend, then, to Abraham's honor. Notably, P took no offense at Abraham's relationship with Hagar. But may one say that P has also altered the account slightly here and transformed a concubinage into a marriage? P's exemplar recounted that Hagar was Sarah's slave who left her to go to Abraham. It contained the legend in a form related to J[b], therefore. E reports differently that Hagar is Abraham's slave (cf. comments above on 21:10, 12).

34. God's Covenant with Abraham, Ishmael's Circumcision, and Isaac's Birth and Circumcision 17; 21:1b, 2b . . . 3 . . . 5 P

Source analysis. The piece belongs to P: אלהים, vv 3 (7, 8, 19), 9, 15, 18, 19, 22, 23; אֵל שַׁדַּי, v 1 (concerning יהוה in v 1, see comments on the passage); נָתַן בְּרִית, v 2; בִּמְאֹד מְאֹד, vv 2, 6, 20; הֵקִים בָּית, vv 7, 19, 21; "you and your seed after you," vv 7, 8, 9, 10, 19; לְדֹרֹתָם, vv 7, 9, 12; עוֹלָם in phrases, vv 7, 8, 13, 19; מְגֻרִים, v 8; אֲחֻזָּה, v 8; כָּל־זָכָר, vv 10, 12, 23; מִקְנָה, vv 12, 13, 23, 27; בֶּן־נֵכָר, vv 12, 27; נְשִׂיאִם, vv 10, 12, 23; נִכְרְתָה הַנֶּפֶשׁ הַהִיא מֵעַמֶּיהָ, v 14; פָּרָה וְרָבָה, v 20; הוֹלִיד, v 20; נְשִׂיאִם, v 20; and בְּעֶצֶם הַיּוֹם הַזֶּה, vv 23, 26. Further characteristic of P are the datings (vv 1, 17, 24, 25), the great formality, and favorite concepts such as covenant and covenant sign (cf. 9:8ff.). P cites the passage (21:1b, 2b, 4; 28:4; 35:12; Exod 2:24; 6:3-4, 8; cf.

Lev 12:3; 26:42). God's revelation to Jacob in P is closely related (35:9-10, 11-13a). The broad presentation in Gen 17 and in Gen 23 is markedly distinct from P's other brief comments in the Abraham account (Eerdmans, 7). But, in a similar fashion, genealogies and narratives appear together in the Chronicler. Sievers (2:284-85) does not improve the account at all by attributing vv 1a, 2a 6, 8, 13, 14, 16b, 17, 22, 23bβ (from בְּעֶצֶם) to other hands from P's school because of the many repetitions. V 2a, the theme of the whole, may not be omitted; v 4a does not parallel it but explicates it; v 6 is the absolutely necessary explanation of v 5; the grant of the land (v 8) may not be omitted, either; the determination of punishment in v 14 also suits the context well.

1-22 *Two divine speeches.* **1-14** *The covenant with Abraham.* P divides his whole history into four epochs. At the beginning of each stands a divine speech: to Adam, Noah, Abraham, and finally Moses. This attempt <264> to encompass and categorize the whole history of humanity deserves great appreciation. It is the beginning of a Jewish "history of the world." The fact that there are four world periods is very significant. A remarkable parallel to these four world periods are the four world empires of Daniel (Dan 7) symbolized by four mighty animals. These animals are apparently mythical in nature (cf. *Schöpfung und Chaos*, 327ff.; Marti, *Danielkomm.*, 48-49; Bertholet, *Daniel*, 48ff.). Dan 2 and especially 8:22, where the same tradition occurs, although in two other manifestations, show that this tradition predates the document "Daniel," as does Zech 2:1ff., where four horns represent the four world empires, and especially as does the circumstance that the number four can only with difficulty be accommodated with the world empires known to the author and is, thus, older than this concept itself. The mythological aspects of Daniel's animals raise the possibility that the tradition of the four world epochs of is pagan origins. This hypothesis is supported by Hesiod's *Works and Days*, 109ff., which atttests a tradition of four world eras, the golden, silver, bronze, and iron ages of the world. The comparison of biblical speculation, especially as contained in P, and old Greek speculation concerning the ages of the world seems all the more appropriate since there is an additional parallel between P (Gen 1) and Hesiod's doctrine of the golden age (cf. above, pp. 114-15, 148). The tradition of Dan 2:31ff., where the four metals—gold, silver, bronze, and iron (and clay)—also symbolize the four world empires, is very closely related to Hesiod's tradition. Finally, the doctrine that the history of the world falls into four periods (of 3,000 years each) also occurs among the Persians (cf. Stave, *Parsismus*, 145ff.; Boussset, *Rel. des Judentums*[2], 578n.1). Concerning additional traditions of the eastern peoples, see the bibliography in Behrmann, *Danielkomm.*, 15, and Böklen, *Verwandtschaft der jüd.-christlichen mit der parsischen Eschatologie*, 85-86.

The contemporaneous occurrence of the same speculation among the Hebrews, Persians, and Greeks suggests the hypothesis that a common ancient oriental, probably originally Babylonian, doctrine is involved which came to the three peoples on the periphery of the near Asian cultural world and which acquired a characteristic form among each of them. In addition to the four world periods (cf. also 4 Ezr 12:11; ApBaru 39), other texts speak of twelve (4 Ezr 14:11; ApBar 53; in ApBar 27; EthEn 90:17 this is the number of periods which immediately precede the end; the same is true of the number four in EthEn 89ff.; cf. Schürer, *Gesch. des jüdischen Volkes*[3] 3:199-200, and Rev 6:1-8—four animals and four riders; Rev 8:6-13—four throws from heaven). The number twelve also occurs among the Persians, who assume the 12,000 year duration of the world.

The numbers seven (SlavEn 33; Bousset, *Rel. des Judentums²*, 284) and seventy (to be precise 72) are also attested as the number of periods (cf. EthEn 89:59ff; 93; Jer 25:11; Dan 9). The whole speculation seems to have started from the concept of the total course of the world as a great year, a cosmic year, divided into four cosmic seasons and twelve cosmic months, and seems to have been of Babylonian origins. Now, however, no clear information concerning a cosmic year has yet been derived from the cuneiform evidence. That, in fact, this theory was already present among the Babylonians themselves, however, is implied with great probability in the scheme of world history in Berosus whose other information regularly proves to be authentically Babylonian. The ten antediluvial kings of Berosus with their reigns of ten times twelve sars seem to point to a cosmic year of twelve times twelve sars, that is, of twelve cosmic months of twelve sars each (Zimmern, KAT³, 538). In later times, such ideas may have come anew to the Jews through the mediation of the Persians. For us, this speculation is only significant here to the extent that it figures in P's <265> presentation.

In P we find only the following points of the entire complex. (1) That there are four periods in the history of the world. The Jewish tradition divides according to its own arrangement.

(2) Characteristically, a divine speech introduces each of these epochs. This feature, too, has a prehistory. The ethnic theory will have maintained that each of these world epochs were inaugurated and governed by a new god. Indeed, these gods may have been the stars at the "four corners" of the heavens and which, therefore, also govern the grand year in an astrological theory of the seasons (Zimmern, KAT³, 633). In the cosmic year of Berosus, a divine revelation to Oannes and his successors introduce the beginnings of the four world seasons (under the first, fourth, seventh, and tenth primordial king). We may see the prototype of P's fourfold divine revelation in this (Zimmern, KAT³, 535-36, 542ff.). (In the final analysis, the four animals of Dan 7 are to be interpreted against this theory. The fourth of these is the animal of the cosmic winter, the chaos animal. EthEn 89, where "seventy shepherds," that is, angels, originally gods, have dominion in the seventy periods, is a very close parallel. The Babylonian tradition will have been that each of these four astral gods corresponded to a metal, parallel to the association of the planet gods with metals and their colors which traces back to the Babylonians. This will then also have then been the source for the theory of the golden, silver, etc. ages.) P's Jewish tradition completely stripped away the astrological and polytheistic features of the whole, but maintained that there were four great revelations, each at the beginning of a world era. These revelations are, however, revelations of the same, one God.

(3) Judaism interpreted the details of the four revelations in its own terms by inserting elements of its own, Jewish tradition. Moses and Abraham are, at any rate, Jewish. The first two epochs—creation and the Flood—differ, however. Both accounts currently stand in a setting which seems to be older than P (cf. above, p. 148). It may be that these accounts came to Israel already linked as components of the whole speculation of the four world ages.

(4) Further, P's use of new divine names in association with the grand epochs of Abraham and Moses may be regarded as a remnant of the adapted theory. The names themselves—אלהים for the creation, אֵל שַׁדַּי for Abraham, Isaac, and Jacob (28:3; 35:11; 48:3; Exod 6:3), and יהוה for Moses—have been added in Israel. Concerning the

cosmic year and cosmic periods which are often associated with the "precession" of the sun, see J. A. Bengel, *Cyclus oder Betrachtung über das große Weltjahr zum Wachstum prophetischer und astronomischer Kentnisse* (1773); Marcus v. Niebuhr, *Geschichte Assurs und Babels* (1857), 237ff., 245ff.; Bunsen, *Die Plejaden und der Tierkreis* (1878); Trieber, *Hermes* 27: 321ff.; H. Winckler, *Gesch. Isr.* 2, 275ff.; idem, *Weltanschauung des alten Orients*, 32ff.; idem, KAT³, 317-18, 332ff.; Zimmern, KAT³, 538, 541ff., 635; Böklen, *Verwandtschaft der jüd.-christlichen mit der parsischen Eschatologie*, 81ff.; Bousset, *Rel. des Judentums²*, 572ff.; Gunkel, *Zum religionsgeschichtlichen Verständnis des NT*, 53; Greßmann, *Ursprung der israel.-jüd. Eschatologie*, 160ff.; A. Jeremias, ATAO², 62ff.; 223-24; idem, *Babylonisches im NT*, 8ff., etc.; Volz, *Jüdische Eschatologie*, 168-69; Cumont, ARW 9:330; etc. Concerning the divine names, P's theory that the primal period did not yet know the name Yahweh is based on the historical information that Yahweh and Moses belong together and simultaneously a reticence to call the God of the patriarchs "Yahweh." We may see this reticence as the final remnant of the impression that these early legends are of pre-Yahwistic origins. Whereas P already has a predecessor in E (and Jᵉ), the association of Abraham and שַׁדָּי אֵל occurs only in P. One may ask whether the two names were already associated with one another in ancient tradition. Subsequent materials evidence no comprehensible relationship between this divine name and the particular content of the revelation to Abraham. <266> P gives no etymology of the name and probably hardly considered it. שַׁדָּי אֵל is not etymologically transparent. Isa 13:6 and Joel 1:15 associate the word with שֹׁד "violent act, destruction" > שׁדד "to destroy," according to which it would mean "the violent, the destructive." From a religiohistorical perspective, this etymology is certainly possible. Modern scholars suspect that the pronunciation שַׁדַּי is artificial (= שַׁ + דַּי = ὁ ἱκανός Aquila, Symm., Theod.) and suggest שְׂדִי "my lord," Assyr *šêdu* "steer god," the Babylonian divine name, associated especially with Enlil, *šadû* "mountain," שׂרה "to be moist," or שׂדא "to cast," etc. (bibliography in Gesenius-Buhl¹⁴, s.v.; Stade, *Bibl. Theol.*, 76; Zimmern, KAT³, 358; Eerdmans, 16ff.). The name is surely very old, as such divine names always are. It belongs with 'el `olam, 'el beth-'el, 'el `elyon, etc., all belonging to the pre-Yahwistic period. The advanced age of the name is abundantly evidenced by Gen 49:24, as well as Num 24:4, 16 and, furthermore, by the fact that the word only occurs in archaistic poetic style or in solemn passages, never in simple narrative. Even P only employs שַׁדָּי אֵל in speeches, otherwise, even after Gen 17, אלהים. The impression P gives here that the name belongs in the "patriarchal period" is, therefore—as is usually true in such cases—quite right. Originally the name will have been linked with some location or symbol and then identified by Israel with its Yahweh. P may have been the first to employ the name, of whose great antiquity he was still aware, here where he needed an ancient divine name.

1a According to P, this is God's first and only revelation to Abraham. For P it is (cf. above) of significance for world history. This is the source of the multiple allusions to this narrative P offers in the further course of his book (cf. above). Because of this covenant, God led Israel out of Egypt and gave it Canaan (Exod 2:24-25; 6:2ff.). God remembers this covenant—so exilic Judaism comforted itself—even now in our distress (Lev 26:42ff.). "His presentation, too, is born along on the awareness of the significance of this procedure" (Dillmann). Notably, the theophany is, indeed, dated (characteristically for P), but not described at all, indeed not even localized. The latter is also true of Gen 15, therefore already true of P's source. What follows is even less a "narrative" than Gen 15. The author is not concerned with narrative, but with establishing facts and propounding ideas. P's other theophanies also have this bland form (35:9; Exod 6:3). יהוה is remarkable and was introduced into the text by a redactor, probably to harmonize it with Gen 16 and 18-19. **1b** The first word of the divine revelation mentions God's name (similarly 15:7 "I am Yahweh"; cf. 35:11; 46:3; 28:13; Exod 3:6, 14; 6:2, 29). This beginning is the style of revelatory speech. The legends recount that God appeared speaking first the most important word, that he named his name so that one may know who he is and by what name to call upon him henceforth. Significantly from a religiohistorical perspective, many speeches in the Gospel of John also have this beginning. The incarnate Λόγος, who wants to reveal himself, first gives his name: "I am the bread of life" (John 6:35ff.); "I am the light of the world" (8:12ff.); "I am the door" (10:7ff.); "I am the Good Shepherd" (10:11ff.); "I am the true Vine" (15:1ff.). In any case, this manner of speaking is very ancient, for it stems from a period which believed in "many lords and many gods." The "I am Yahweh" in legal and prophetic speech as well as the Babylonian "I am the Ishtar of the city of Arbela" are also comparable (Jastrow, *Rel. Bab. u. Ass.* 2:159, 161, 163, etc.). This divine self-identification is followed next by God's call to the person, "Walk before me," that is, be pious (Isa 38:3). This divine call, heavily emphasized primarily by its placement, is—as one may paraphrase P—the basic precondition for the covenant. וֶהְיֵה תָמִים means "thus you will be perfect" (§110f).

2 Concerning the meaning of בְּרִית see above pp. 144-45. P also emphasizes here that God grants <267> (נָתַן) the covenant in free grace. Thus the covenant is called בְּרִיתִי (v 2; cf. comments on 6:18) and the possessive is accentuated through אֲנִי (v 4; §135f). While v 2 reports God's decision to grant a covenant and the chief benefit of this covenant, the wondrous multiplication of the tribal patriarch, the subsequent vv 4ff. offer the elucidation of the decision. First come the promises in vv **4-8**: Abraham shall become an "Abraham," i.e. the father of a multitude of nations (vv 4-6). God will be his God and the God of his descendants and will grant him Canaan (vv 7, 8). **4-6** The notion that the patriarch has become a people on the force of the divine word is common in the patriarchal legends (cf. comments on 12:2). The fact that God speaks this word by changing the name of the ancestor is ingenious. Jacob's name change to "Israel" is similar (32:29). The element probably stems from P's source, then. Concerning renamings, a practice widely distributed across the whole world, compare Andree (*Ethnographische Parallelen* 1:173ff.), Giesebrecht (*Gottesname*, 10), Heitmüller (161-62): "Name changes are not merely symbolic in nature. They have very real value. The name is the bearer's source of power and fate. When one's name changes, so does one's character and destiny." It is also common for the name to be changed on the birth of the first son so that the man is called thenceforth "father of so and so." The etymology אברהם = אַב הֲמוֹן (namely of גּוֹיִם) is entirely impossible according to modern philological concepts. But the idea that P did not intend to offer an etymology but only a wordplay or the attempt to improve such an etymology by modern means are fundamentally in error. The unusual form אַב and the word המון are chosen because of their similarity to אברהם. P found both name forms, originally dialectical variants, and combined them so that the patriarch was called Abram before the covenant and Abraham afterward. The same process applies to Sarai and Sarah (cf. above p. 157). P also speaks elsewhere (vv 5, 16; 28:3; 35:11; 48:4) of a multitude of nations descended from the patriarch because he also thinks of Ishmael and Esau in the statement concerning Abraham and because in his national pride he thinks of Israel alone as a whole "community of peoples." J and E differ. They always think of only one people (Israel) in such promises. Some Sam mss read אֶת־שִׁמְךָ, v 5, without אֶת־ (cf. 35:10; Kittel). מְלָכִים (v 6) is emphasized with some emotion. The counterpart is Ishmael's נְשִׂיאִם (v 20). The prediction recurs in 35:11. The fact that P places such value on this element can probably be explained as the result of the attitudes of the later kingless period for which it was a powerful notion that kings once sprouted from Abraham's seed.

7, 8 P associates the notion that God will be the (patron-)god of Abraham and his seed and the notion that he will give him the land. The land is God's (characteristic) gift to his people. This is an ancient Israelite, actually a Canaanite belief. Both predictions also occur elsewhere in the patriarchal legends. The second is particularly frequent (cf. above, p. 164). The promise of the land seems to be nuanced in a peculiar fashion here by the idea that Abraham will one day receive the land, where he now resides as a poor, unprotected גֵּר, as "an eternal possession." A similar promise appears in the old legend in 28:13, the same idea in P in 28:4a; Exod 6:4.

9-14 God adds to the promises a statute Abraham is to keep. The new section is indicated by the new beginning וַיֹּאמֶר אֱלֹהִים אֶל־אַבְרָהָם and by the וְאַתָּה (in contrast to the אֲנִי, v 4). P includes the statute, to which God subjects <268> Abraham, in the בְּרִית, itself (v 10). But, as the accompanying clause (v 11) explains, it should also be a "sign" of the covenant (cf. Exod 31:13, 16). Additional questions concerning the relationship of this statute to the בְּרִית have little purpose. In such cases, modern scholars often import into the old text a precision of thought which would have been entirely unattainable. Circumcision is a very ancient religious folk practice in Israel. It is also attested among numerous other peoples—Egyptians, Edomites, Ammonites, Moabites, Arabs (cf. Jer 9:25), Phoenicians, and furthermore among many peoples in Africa, South America, and Polynesia, "according to a hasty estimation" about 200 million people (concerning circumcision in general, cf. Andree, *Ethnographische Parallelen* 2:166-67, 204; Ploss, *Das Kind* I², 342ff.; Lippert, *Kulturgeschichte* 1:390ff.; Stade, ZAW 6:136ff.; among the Egyptians, Reitzenstein, *Zwei religionsgeschichtliche Fragen*, 1ff.; Wilcken, Gunkel, and P. Wendland in *Archiv für Papyrusforschung* 2:4ff.; Heyes, *Bibel und Ägypten*, 48ff.; Meyer, *Israeliten*, 449). Such a practice cannot be evaluated any differently "than the manifold bodily disfigurations which can be found among unnumbered barbaric and wild peoples" (Stade, *Gesch. Israels* 1:423). Such signs are simultaneously tribal and cultic signs. The uncircumcised is foreign and, at the same time, unclean (Isa 52:1). The origin of such a custom lies in the most ancient past. It stems from a time when men went about naked (Stade, *Bibl. Theo.*, 147). Even Israel's tradition maintains that this practice stems from antiquity, according to Exod 4:24-25 J dating back to the Midianite Zipporah, according to Josh 5:2-3 E from Joshua, here, according to P, from Abraham. Furthermore, Gen 34, as well as ancient Israel's opposition to the "uncircumcised" Philistines, attests to the fact that the practice was well known in Israel's earliest period. In the historical period, circumcision was a vestige whose original significance had long since been forgotten. In fact, as far as we know, ancient Israel reflected very little concerning the significance of this ceremony. According to the very sketchy and obscure account in Exod 4:24-25 its purpose was to appease Yahweh's wrath. It is, therefore, an atonement ceremony of which there is no other trace. Was it originally undertaken in Israel, as among many other peoples, at the beginning of puberty to signify the acceptance of the young man into the community and the cult (so Wellhausen, *Prolegomena*[6], 339; Stade, ZAW 6: 135ff.; Marti, *Gesch. der isr. Rel.*[5], 51-52; Baentsch on Exod 4:24ff.; disputed by Meyer, *Israeliten*, 59n.2)? Was it, as Herodotus (II.104) had already heard and as Josh 5:2-3, 9 seems to suggest, adopted from the Egyptians (Meyer, *Israeliten*, 449)? Israel's prophets duly assigned it, like all vestiges, little value (Jer 9:25; *Archiv für Papyrusforschung* 2:15-16) and required a circumcision of the heart (Jer 4:4; Deut 10:16; 30:6). In Judaism, however, when the ancient pagan elements in the religion revived and when, in the distress of the Diaspora, special emphasis fell on those commandments which obligated the individual, circumcision gained extreme significance. For P it is one of the most important commandments of the law. Whoever is uncircumcised should be eradicated! For this reason, as the fundamental law of the covenant people, it is attributed to Abraham. Circumcision was discontinued only in the NT period—a true spectacle that the most powerful apostle must employ his gigantic power in order to topple a ceremony so worthless and senseless for higher religion! Characteristically for P's narrative style, this religious practice is not grounded in the account (cf. the counterparts Exod 4:25-26; Gen 32:23), as is usually the case in the old legends, but is simply established by statute without any human occasion, indeed without even an indication of a reason (cf. Wellhausen, *Prolegomena*[6], 339).

In the tradition of J and E we read nothing of circumcision as the <269> "sign of the covenant." P will have added this element to the Abraham tradition himself. This is all the more likely since this idea does not appear in the deuteronomistic tradition either (cf. Kraetzschmar, *Bundesvorstellung*, 204) From v **10** onward the author slips into the style of the "law." This explains the plural address forms which alternate with the singular (מִזַּרְעֶךָ v 12 and in v 13). This singular, however, hardly refers to Abraham, but in the common legal style, to the head of the Israelite household who is concerned with the Torah. Here, then, P has allowed the form of divine speech to Abraham to fall aside entirely. The first phrase, הִמּוֹל לָכֶם כָּל־זָכָר, is also stylistically interesting. The brevity of this phrase, the law proper, sharply contrasts with the verbosity of the following procedural regulations. This brevity characterizes the earliest Torah style. The syntax involving the infinitive absolute expressing the unshakable divine will (§113aa; regarding the construction §113gg) also belongs to the style of the old Torah (cf. Exod 20:8; Deut 1:16; 5:12). Thus, a picture of the history of the Torah style can be discerned from this section. The earliest Torah spoke in the briefest clauses, later times added additional, sometimes long-winded refinements, motivations, and the like. Later, the composite style which originated in this fashion became standard diction. One discerns the same history of style in the decalogs, etc. וּבֵין זַרְעֲךָ אַחֲרֶיךָ (v 10) is probably a gloss (Kautzsch-Socin[2]; Kittel).

11 Regarding the form of וּנְמַלְתֶּם see §67dd; regarding the construction with אֵת see §121d; regarding the perfect consecutive with ו see §112aa. V **12a** is repeated in Lev 12:3. V **12b** belongs with 13. The slave is not a person, not even in religion. Obviously, he will practice his master's religion (Benzinger[2], 125). Yet, the requirement that the slaves be circumcised, too, seems to be P's innovation. Ezek 44:7ff. still presupposes uncircumcised temple slaves (Kautzsch[3]). **14** Sam, LXX, Ball, Kittel add עָרְלָתוֹ to בַּיּוֹם הַשְּׁמִינִי, but it may only be an expansion. The idiom וְנִכְרְתָה הַהִיא מֵעַמֶּיהָ (frequent in P, Lev 17:9; 23:29; Num 9:13; etc.) is "one of P's solemn archaisms" (Holzinger). עַמִּים are the relatives in the earliest sense of the term (cf. Krenkel, ZAW 8:280ff.). It is disputed whether this refers only to excommunication or to the death penalty. Undoubtedly, however, men like P wished for the death of such a sinner (regarding this sense of the phrase, cf., e.g., Exod 31:14) and, if the pagan authorities were to have permitted it, would also surely have carried out the wish. In Lev 17:9-10; 20:3, 6 one may read between the lines, however, that the execution of religious criminals was not permitted by the authorities and that it was necessary, therefore, to limit oneself to believing that God will eradicate such sinners. Thus the concept of "venal sin" evolved. Originally, it was a sin to be punished by the people or the authorities, but then a sin which, in the belief of the pious, God will certainly avenge with death. אֶת־בְּרִיתִי הֵפַר. The addition of such very brief clauses, which powerfully expresses the abhorrence of sin at the conclusion, belongs to legal style (cf. Lev 18:23; 19:8; 20:9, 11, 12, 13, 16, 17, 19, 27; etc.). הֵפַר is the pausal form of הֵפֵר.

15-21 *The promise of Isaac.* Like the first, this second divine speech contains <270> first of all a blessing in the form of a renaming. Sarai will be called Sarah, "princess," because kings—consequently the prediction in v 6 is repeated in v 16—will come from her. **17** P took the "laughter" צחק associated with this promise from his exemplar. It stems from an old legend tradition and was originally intended to motivate the name יצחק (a feature which no longer figures prominently in P). This element was so firmly fixed in the tradition that even P could not remove it. Comparison with the parallel passage 18:12 illuminates the character of our passage: whereas there only the secondary character Sarah laughs, here the laughter is attributed to Abraham himself; whereas there Sarah can laugh only because she does not know the "men," Abraham laughs here in the presence of the revealed God! To exonerate P, one may assume that he took this element from his source. At any rate, P adds on his own that Abraham fell on his face before God (as was common). The result is that he falls before God and laughs at his promise! This combination offers a deep insight into the heart of this churchman and trained theologian who surely held these old narrators in high regard and who, nevertheless, stands so far beneath them in matters of religion! Regarding וְאִם see §150h. The ages at which Abraham's ancestors became fathers are generally less than 100 in Hebr. In contrast, in Sam and LXX (until Terah) they are much greater. This passage suggests that the great ages of Sam and LXX may have been shortened by the redactor in Hebr. **18** "May he live before you," that is, may you take him under your protection so that he continues to live (cf. Hos 6:2). Abraham places all his hope in Ishmael. He cannot believe in a son of Sarah. **19a** The words resemble 16:11 and will trace to P's source. **19b** הֵקִים בְּרִית here and elsewhere means "to maintain the (old) covenant," in other passages such as 6:18; 9:9, 11, 17 "to establish the (new) covenant." In profane usage, too, הֵקִים means "to (newly) establish and maintain." But one may not make too much of such distinctions, very fine distinctions for Hebrew thought which the Hebrew language cannot support. לְזַרְעוֹ does not link well with the preceding. After v 7 לִהְיוֹת לוֹ לֵאלֹהִים should perhaps be supplied and וּלְזַרְעוֹ be read with mss Sam, LXX, Pesh, Vulg (Ball, Holzinger, etc.) **20** Regarding

לִישמעאל see 19:21; 42:9. שְׁמַעְתִּיךָ—the word שמע is a necessary component of the Ishmael legend, since it explains Ishmael's name (also in 16:11; 21:17). Here, this original etymological relationship hardly appears. The promise that Ishmael will become a people also originates in the Ishmael legend (cf. 21:18). P takes the fact that "twelve princes" will come from Ishmael from the Ishmael legend to which he has access and which he transmits in the following material (25:13ff.). Characteristically for P's writing style, he fuses elements of various legends which always existed separately in the ancient period. The contention in v **21a** that the blessing of Abraham does not apply to Ishmael but only to Isaac also manifests a fusion of varied materials. Actually, the legend of the blessing of Abraham has no relationship at all <271> to the Ishmael legend. The same is true of 28:4, where the Abrahamic blessing is transferred from Isaac to Jacob. **21b** The emphasis on this specific date hardly makes any sense in this situation and can only be understood as a remnant of the exemplar which will have recounted something similar to 18:14. On the force of the word of God just pronounced, Sarah conceives the next night and bears a son a year later. One notes that even the expression לַמּוֹעֵד is repeated in both passages. **22** וַיַּעַל (as in 35:13)—P imagines that God has come from heaven to speak with Abraham and now returns. Nothing like this occurs in the old legends.

23-27 *First appendix: the circumcision of the house of Abraham, the fulfillment of the command.* The author executes this passage with pointed expansiveness precisely according to God's statements in vv 10-14 so that one may know that everything was faithfully carried out and that, at that time—this is, for the author, an event of historical significance for the whole world, so he provides a dual dating—circumcision was truly and faithfully introduced! P made the error of having Ishmael circumcised, as well. He is even the chief figure as the first example of the son of the household, although, on the other hand, he is supposed to be expressly excluded from the covenant the sign of which is circumcision (Holzinger). **25** The date of Ishmael's circumcision (in his thirteenth year) may be no accident. This date for circumcision may have been common among the Ishmaelite peoples. It was among the ancient Arabs (Origen, *Genesis* 1:16; cf. *Euseb. praep. ev.* VI.392b.; additional examples in Dillmann, 264) and Egyptians (Philo, *quaest in Genesim* III.47; Aucher, 217-18; cf. P. Wendland, *Archiv für Papyrusforschung* 2:23ff.). The remaining ages (16:16; 17:1, 2, 24) were established in relation to this data and the firm age in 21:5 (Abraham was 100 years old at Isaac's birth). **26** Concerning נמול see §72ee.

21:1b, 2b . . . 3, 4, 5 *Second appendix: Isaac's birth, the fulfillment of the promise. Source analysis.* Vv 3-5 clearly belong to P: the naming by the father and the precision (v 3), the allusion to 17:12 in v 4 and אלהים, the dating and מְאַת שָׁנָה in v 5. V 2b also belongs to P: לַמּוֹעֵד (17:21) and אלהים. V 1b (‖ v 1a), where יהוה must have replaced an original אלהים, probably also belongs to P. A clause concerning Isaac's birth is missing after v 2b. הַנּוֹלַד־לוֹ, more than superfluous in v 3, may have originally belonged in v 4 after בְּנוֹ (Winckler, *Forschungen* 3:415). <272>

35. Sarah's Burial in the Cave of Machpela 23 P

Source analysis. P is indicated by the juristic precision (cf. esp. vv 17-18), the many repetitions of the account, the dating (v 1), the names "sons of Heth," "Machpela," and קִרְיַת אַרְבַּע (v 2), and further by the expressions תּוֹשָׁב (v 4), אֲחֻזָּה (vv 4, 9, 20), נָשִׂיא (v 6), שָׁמַע אֶל (v 16), קוּם, "to become legally one's own" (vv 17, 20), מִקְנָה

(v 18), and the allusions back to this narrative in 25:9; 49:30; 50:13 (cf. Dillmann and Holzinger). Eerdman's polemic (20f.) against this analysis is very superficial.

The locality. P agrees with J³ in naming only Hebron as Abraham's dwelling. He diverges from J³ in failing to mention the tree at Mamre (probably because he considers it pagan). But he speaks of the cave of Machpela which the other sources, as far as they are preserved for us, do not mention. The place names contained in P are קִרְיַת אַרְבַּע and קִרְיַת הָאַרְבַּע (35:27), an older name of Hebron (Josh 14:15; Judg 1:10). It may have been called "four city" because four roads meet there. Later Arba is understood as the name of the patriarch of the Enakites (Josh 15:13) who were supposed to have lived here before Israel (Josh 15:14; Judg 1:10, 20). In the vicinity of Hebron lay Mamre, Abraham's dwelling place according to J³ (13:18) and probably also in P's opinion. "East of Mamre" (v 19) and thus not far distant—Abraham wishes in Gen 23 to have his dead in the vicinity—lies the "Cave of Machpela." This cave was situated at the end of a field in the "Machpela" (vv 17, 19; 25:9; 49:30; 50:13). Accordingly, "Machpela" will have been the name of the field. Currently, *Ḥaram râmet el-ḥalîl* three km north of Hebron is considered the site of the Abraham Oak at Mamre, while the cave is sought in the famed sanctuary *el-Ḥaram* east of Hebron (cf. Buhl, *Palästina*, 159ff.; Guthe, "Mamre, Hebron," BW). This does not agree with the information in the OT, however. The inhabitants of Hebron driven out by Israel were Enakites according to Judg 1:10, 20 and Josh 15:14. According to Gen 23, the sons of Heth possessed the land (vv 7, 12f.), city (v 10) and cave (v 11; cf. 25:10; 49:32). The same situation is presumed in 26:34-35 P. From their centers in Asia minor, the Hittites possessed in the second millennium, before the appearance of Israel in history, a large empire in Mesopotamia, Syria, and Babylonia, and fought with the Egyptians over Syria and Canaan (Meyer 1/2², see index). Whether they settled in southern Canaan, however, as is presumed here, is more than questionable. If the information given in Genesis 23 that they dwelt in Hebron is not entirely correct, then a final reminiscence of the once-so-powerful Hittite Empire has come to us here and in parallel reports (Num 13:29; Josh 1:4; Ezek 16:3, 45). P will have employed their name here as a conscious archaism just as he avoids the name Hebron in the patriarchal narrative and employed Kiriath-arba instead (cf. v 2). In Israelite times, Hebron was in Caleb's possession (Judg 1:20). After Saul's death it was David's residence (2 Sam 2:1-3). In the Maccabeean period is was a major Idumean city (1 Mac 5:65).

Meaning of the account. The comment that P took from his source will have said that Abraham purchased the Cave Machpela as Sarah's (and his own) burial site together with the field of Ephron for a certain sum (cf. above, pp. 257-58). This information from the exemplar is to be interpreted in the same way as the quite parallel passage (33:19-20) concerning Jacob's purchase of the field near Shechem. Both cases involve a field the patriarch is supposed to have acquired from foreigners. Characteristically, the purchase price is explicitly mentioned both times. The intention is to indicate that the property was acquired through an honorable purchase and, therefore, belonged legally to the ancestor. What interest, however, did the legend have in the possession of this field and this cave? The usual answer is, "Abraham acquired a right to the possession of the whole land through this purchase" (so recently Kautzsch³). One cannot take this explanation very seriously. If one acquires a plot of ground in the land, one does not thereby receive a right to the whole land! Rather, the legend itself demonstrates quite clearly the reason one placed such high value of the possession of this cave. It was there that <273> one could find the grave of the matriarch. Parallels are the accounts of the legal purchase of the mountain of Samaria, where Omri would be buried (1 Kgs 16:24, 28) and of the threshing floor of Arauna, the later temple site (2 Sam 24). In the field near Shechem, too, there was a grave, namely, that of Joseph (Josh 24:32). The ancient placed very great value on the fact that his sanctuary and also the place where he buries his dead are indisputably and without a doubt his property. Outstanding people, who value honor, do not bury their dead in loaned or donated graves, but on their own property (Benzinger[2], 128). In this interest, P, too, placed the highest value on our account which he executes in such detail and to which he repeatedly alludes (cf. above), whereas he passed over most of the other Abraham legends or took only a few comments from them. He values it almost as highly as the narrative of the covenant in Gen 17. P takes the greatest pains imaginable to demonstrate that the cave and field—this is the order in the chapter—was not yielded to Abraham for his use (vv 5, 6), nor given to him (v 11), but acquired by him for the full purchase price in fully legal fashion (vv 16-18). The great value P placed on this point can be explained as an expression of a sense of propriety and custom. It would have been extremely improper for the patriarch not to have purchased the grave. On the other hand, it may have seemed appropriate in this special case to be satisfied with a loaned or donated grave since Abraham was, indeed, only a "foreigner and sojourner" in Hebron. P devotes even greater effort to show that Abraham overcame all difficulties and legally acquired a plot of ground for burial. At the same time, the account casts an interesting, even though unclear, light on the religiohistorical circumstances. We may assume that Israel took over this site, like all others, from the Canaanites. The population, however, from whom Israel took over the site, will have seen the cave as a sanctuary. Their opinion may have been that the numen resided here in the depths or that a god or a hero lay interred here. One thinks of the grave of Zeus in Crete, of the "Silenos grave in the land of the Hebrews" (Pausanias, *Eliaea* 2:24), and of the grave of Dyonisius' nurse (Plin. *h. n.* 5:18). Concerning sacred graves and grave sanctuaries see W. Robertson-Smith (*Rel. der Semiten*, 150ff.) and Wellhausen (*Arab. Heidentum*[2], 103). Sarah (and later Abraham, himself) would then have replaced this hero or god in Israelite tradition. Cult at caves and graves is also expressly attested to us from the period of P (Isa 65:4). An allusion to the belief in Israel's descent from the Sarah housed in the cave is present, according to Duhm (see commentary) and Meyer, (*Israeliten*, 265, 284), in Isa 51:1. Isa 63:16 may also reject a cult of the ancestral spirits, specifically of Abraham. The cave el-Ḥaram near Hebron is still a sanctuary. In contrast, P characteristically declares the cave an ancestral grave and nothing else. As easily as the name of God otherwise comes to his pen, in this account he altogether avoids any mention of God and religion. The cave is a profane cave and the account of its acquisition is a profane narrative. The Jewish author could only adapt Machpela on the condition this it was consecrated to the memory of the fathers, but in no way to God. Previously, Canaan was rich in such sites that recalled the fathers. P eliminated all these sites from the patriarchal legend, apparently because he suspected their pagan origins. Only Machpela and Bethel were left in his work. We perceive thereby the special significance these sites must have once possessed if they could withstand even the energetically revisionist P. The former significance of Hebron, the center of Judah before Jerusalem, casts its shadow, therefore, even in P. <274>

1, 2 *Sarah's Death and Burial. Introduction.* **1** The chronological information, without significance for P's system of dating, demonstrates P's enchantment with numbers. Concerning the syntax of the numbers see §134h. "The years of Sarah's life" in v 1b (om LXX Vulg) is a manuscript variant and is preferable to the first reading (25:7; 47:9, 28; Ball; Kittel). הוא חֶבְרוֹן here and in v 19, as well as in 35:27, is probably a gloss (cf. 35:6, 19; 36:8; Ball; Eerdmans, 20). **2** P does not intend to depict Abraham's pain through the reference to "crying and mourning." P is not concerned with such personal emotions. Instead, the mourning ceremonies prescribed by custom are intended. Abraham fulfilled all righteousness in relation to Sarah so that now only the burial itself remains. וַיָּבֹא refers to entering the room where the corpse lies to mourn for the dead.

3-16 The negotiation with the Hittites is aimed, particularly, at portraying Abraham's great efforts to acquire the grave. The expansiveness of this whole negotiation is not unusual for the Oriental, who has more time than we do, but is quite natural. In addition, the P account manifests the comfort of this priest-jurist who can let himself go here in an area with which he is well acquainted. **3** All laments—laments for the dead (2 Sam 13:31; Ezek 26:16 [EpJer 32]), laments in communal distress (Isa 3:26; 29:4; 47:1; Jer 3:25; 14:2; Psa 44:26; 137:1; Neh 1:4; Lam 2:10), laments for the sick (2 Sam 12:16; Job 2:8,13; Psa 119:25), and laments for the gods (Ezek 8:14)—take place seated or lying on the ground. The same is true among the pagans (EpJer 31), the Babylonians (cf. Böllenrücher, *Hymnen u. Gebete an Nergal*, 37: "I sit and lament") and the Egyptians (cf. Erman, *Ägypten*, 432-33). "He stood up" means, then, "he ended the lament" (2 Sam 16:20). מֵת also refers to the corpse of one's wife (§122f). **4** In the following negotiation Abraham is very humble. He emphasizes that he is only a "foreigner" (an immigrant) and a "sojourner" (client) without rights and property and, therefore, entirely dependent on the people's good will, indeed he repeatedly falls to the ground before them (vv 7, 12). Such humility of the ancestor before "the people of the land" is remarkable in this very nationalistic narrator. P probably thinks that Abraham had no other means whatsoever to come into possession of the cave than this humility. Judaism, itself, can be characterized in this fashion: in certain situations one can be very deferential to the pagan whom one fundamentally despises (cf. 26:34-35). Concerning גֵר and תּוֹשָׁב see Bertholet, *Stellung der Israeliten und der Juden zu den Fremden*, 159-60, and Meyer, *Entstehung des Judentums*, 230. **5, 6** The Hittites treat Abraham with great kindness, even with deference. They are eager to fulfill his desire to bury his dead, but they consider a purchase entirely unnecessary. Anyone would lend or give a grave to such an honored man! Their courtesy conceals their inclination against a sale. They do not want Abraham to acquire property or rights in Hebron, but to remain a "sojourner" dependent on the good will of the citizens. For this very reason Abraham repeatedly emphasizes in this account that he only wants to acquire the cave for no other purpose than as a burial site (vv 4, 9, 13, 20). If he had desired more, the Hittites would have denied him. One may read לֹא שְׁמָעֵנוּ (cf. v 13). This formula stands here and below (cf. vv 8, 11, 13, 15) in cases when one, as courteously as possible, offers the other a better suggestion (אֲדֹנִי, vv 6, 11, 15). אֲדֹנִי, the singular "my lord," also in 42:10; 44:7, 9, alongside the <275> plurals can be explained in terms of the fact that if a group speaks, the speaker employs either "I" for himself or "we" inclusively. This is not an example of the personification of a community. The observation is important for the interpretation of the "I" of the Psalms in certain passages (cf. Psa 44:5, 7, 16; 74:12; Joel 1:6f.). נְשִׂיא אלהים "prince of God, spiritual prince" probably characterizes Abraham in P's perspective. He is a prince whose extraordinary dignity consists in his relationship to God, comparable to a high-ranking priest. The statement intends to honor Abraham. The offer to loan him the grave of his choice has the same intent. אִישׁ לֹא means "no one at all" §152c. Concerning יִכְלֶה see §75qq. Regarding the construction קְבֹר see §119x. 7 וַיָּקָם refers to the fact that they negotiate seated (cf. יֹשֵׁב v 10). All legal matters are handled while sitting (Ruth 4:1, 2, 4).

8, 9 Abraham does not agree to the Hittites' proposal but holds firm to his intention. He wants the cave as his own. But his rejection also has a very courteous form. It is supposed to seem that he heard only the positive aspect of their words, that they want to permit the burial. Now he permits himself to mention the plot of ground he has chosen. The cave corresponds to the practice common in Canaan (Benzinger[2], 128, 205; Greßmann, RGG 1, col. 1005ff.). The precision of the information "at the end of his field" is P's exact style. P emphasizes "for good money" (v 9) and later "current coin" (v 16) since he is concerned with the legality of the acquisition. For the same reason, he places great value on the witnesses to the purchase (בְּתוֹכְכֶם, v 9, בְּאָזְנֵי בְנֵי־חֵת, v 10, and especially לְעֵינֵי בְנֵי־חֵת, v 18; cf. vv 11, 12, 13, 16). **10** Concerning לְכֹל see §143e. It means "as concerns all" or perhaps "truly, entirely." בָּאֵי שַׁעַר (for the syntax see §116h) is a legal term like יֹצְאֵי שַׁעַר (34:24), a citizen with voting rights. All public gatherings occur in the gate (Benzinger[2], 102). In Babylonian legal documents, too, "gate" virtually means "court" (Jastrow, *Rel. Bab. u. Ass.* 1:173). The Judeo-Aramaic documents from Assuan use בְּעֵל קִרְיָה (A 9; E 10; H 10). **11** לוֹ should be read for לֹא following vv 5-6, 13, 14-15. (Kautzsch-Socin[2], n. 102). Ephron does not reject Abraham's request, but accepts it formally, omitting only the one point, that Abraham will pay for it. The author thus characterizes Ephron's <276> behavior as extremely courteous. In the matter which concerns Abraham Ephron does not say no. He is not inclined to sell the cave. This practice of offering an object as a gift if one does not want to sell it for some reason or if one wants to charge a great deal for it can still be observed today in the Orient (cf. Benzinger[2], 133). One notes that Abraham at first only wanted "the cave at the end of the field" (v 9), that Ephron offered him not only the cave but also the whole field as a gift (v 11) which Abraham then acquired (v 17). This escalation seems intentional.

12, 13 Abraham, however, insists on his wish with the well-known Jewish tenacity. **13** אַךְ אִם־אַתָּה לוּ שְׁמָעֵנִי—the anacolouthon illuminates the courteous dilemma of the one who does not wish to accept the excessive gift nor insult the generous giver. **14, 15** Finally, now, Ephron gives in and is prepared to sell. This way of allowing the subject of the purchase price to enter the conversation without asking in any way is Oriental courtesy. One should read לוּ אֲדֹנִי שְׁמָעֵנִי (cf. vv 5-6, 11). אֶרֶץ, om LXX mss, has probably arisen from אַרְבַּע. The property was, but the price is not of great consequence between the two (Ball; Sievers 2:300; Kautzsch[3]). **16** Concerning the weighing of the money (in ancient times not yet minted under state control) see Benzinger[2], 198. The author emphasizes that Abraham paid the full asking price in the common commercial shekel (cf. Benzinger[2], 198) in the presence of witnesses. Abraham does not attempt to bargain. He must be satisfied that he was permitted to make the purchase at all. Four hundred shekels of silver are ca. 1,000 Marks in the older system; in the later, Persian system about 400 Marks (Benzinger[2], 201).

17-20 *Summary of the results.* Vv **17, 18** are in the style of a bill of sale: the precise information concerning the location, the appurtenances (the trees standing on the property, mentioned explicitly, on whose legal possession P places great value, will probably have been once sacred trees), and the witnesses. P, accustomed to writing such bills of sale, falls here into the familiar style. Babylonian bills of sale (KB 4:7, 33), which list trees along with property (KB 4:101, 161, 165), and the Judeo-Aramaic documents which never omit information concerning the witnesses and, in real estate transactions, the precise description of the property, have a similar form. The Hebrews learned to draw up such contracts from Babylonian and Egyptian culture. In modern Palestine one must also explicitly purchase the olive trees standing on property in addition to the property itself (Guthe, *Palästina*, 97f.). **19** הוּא חֶבְרוֹן is a gloss (cf. comments on v 2). Mamre is hardly identical with Hebron, but is in the vicinity. According to the tradition, the patriarch resides outside the city like Jacob outside Shechem (22:18).

36. Abraham's Death and Burial 25:7-11a P

Source criticism. P is indicated by the chronological information, יְמֵי שְׁנֵי חַיֵּי (v **7**), בְּשֵׂיבָה טוֹבָה, גָּוַע, and נֶאֱסַף אֶל-עַמָּיו (v **8**), the <277> allusion to the Machpela narrative (vv 9-10), אֱלֹהִים (v 11a), and especially the expansiveness of the whole piece. The Isaac narrative in P concludes very similarly (35:28f.). **8** Mss Sam, LXX, and Pesh read וּשְׁבַע יָמִים (as in 35:29; Ball; Kittel; Kautzsch³). The phrase, נֶאֱסַף אֶל-עַמָּיו "to be gathered to his people," was probably originally understood in reference to the family grave (Stade, *Bibl. Theol.*, 184-85), then in reference to שְׁאוֹל where the relatives lie together, to the extent that a specific viewpoint is associated with such phrases (Holzinger). **9** The information that Isaac and Ishamel buried Abraham diverges radically from the other tradition that Hagar fled with Ishmael (Gen 16 J), or was even expelled (Gen 21 E), from Abraham's house. We may assume that P also read something similar in his source (cf. 17:20 where P betrays a knowledge of the Ishmael legend; cf. pp. 266-67), but that he consciously corrected the tradition because he did not want to believe that such repugnant things, quarreling and mistreatment, could have occurred in the family of the pious Abraham. **11a** The author means that God's promise (17:21) was fulfilled in this manner. P does not contain any other covenant with or divine revelation to Isaac, although it would have been appropriate for his overall view of history (Lev 26:42; Exod 2:24; 6:3, etc.), apparently because he did not have access to such a narrative in his source. P's very brief treatment of Isaac agrees with JE. Even at this point, despite all the energy of his intervention, he was led by the tradition. Concerning **11b** see pp. 289-90.

37. Ishmael's Genealogy 25:12-17 P

P is indicated by וְאֵלֶּה תֹּלְדֹת and the precision in v 12 (cf. 16:3, 15), בִּשְׁמֹתָם לְתוֹלְדֹתָם, וְאֵלֶּה שְׁמוֹת in v 13, and the formulae in v 16. Regarding v 17, see the comments on vv 7f. **13** The new superscription after v 12 is noteworthy (Eerdmans, 22). בִּשְׁמֹתָם after וְאֵלֶּה שְׁמוֹת is also redundant. Both, however, are still to be attributed to P (cf. to the second case 36:40). Bibliography concerning the names can be found in Gesenius-Buhl¹⁴, Dillmann, etc. נְבָיֹת, also mentioned along with Qedar in Isa 60:7, is the Assyr *Nabayâti*. The usual equation with the Nabateeans (נבט), who dominated the Syro-Arabian desert in the Greek and Roman period until Trajan, is uncertain. אֹדָר, Assyr *Qidri, Qadri*, often mentioned, are Arabs in the Syro-Arabian desert. אַדְבְּאֵל, Assyr *Idiba'il*, is on the Egyptian border. מִבְשָׂם is unknown.

14 מִשְׁמָע is only attested as the name of a mountain (in the Syrian desert and elsewhere; cf. the Arabian tribe *Isammê'a* mentioned by Assurbanipal; Delitzsch, *Paradies*, 298). דּוּמָה, now *el-Ĝôf*, is in northern Arabia, north of Teima. מַשָּׂא is probably Assyr *Mas'u*, often mentioned along with Qedar and the *Nabayâti*. **15** חֲדַד is unknown (Sam הֲדַד). תֵּימָא is Assyr *Têma*, today <278> Teima, in northern Arabia, southeast of the northern tip of the Elanite Bay [Gulf of Aqabah]. יְטוּר, according to 1 Chron 5:19 in the Transjordan, are the predecessors of the Ἰτουραῖοι near the Anti-Lebanon mountains. נָפִישׁ is mentioned in 1 Chron 5:19 along with Jetur. קֵדְמָה is unknown. These are mostly northern Arabian tribes. **16** According to Dillmann חָצֵר is the permanent village in contrast טִירָה the mobile Bedouin camp. The number twelve in association with tribes appears frequently (cf. comments on 29:31-30:24). Characteristically, the number of princes is mentioned. Accordingly, the Ishmaelite tribes (אֻמֹּת) must have been under נְשִׂיאָם. The people and the number of tribes becomes important when the twelve "princes" assemble in council. A similar understanding (see comments on the passages in question) may also be presupposed for Esau (36:15ff., 40ff.) and the Horites (36:29-30). Concerning v 18 see above, p. 189.

38. Abraham's Victory over the Four Kings 14

1-16 *Abraham's act of war.* **1-12** *The war up until Abraham's intervention.* **1-3** *Exposition: the four kings against the five.* **1** The beginning בִּימֵי וַיְהִי is historical style (cf. Isa 7:1; 2 Kgs 15:29; Ruth 1:1; Esth 1:1; 2 Sam 21:1). Similar lists of kings occur in Josh 10:3, 5, 23. The names of foreign kings mentioned in v 1 are surely not the author's inventions, but rest on tradition. The first part of the name כְּדָרְלָעֹמֶר (Kudur probably means "servant" or something similar) is a component of many Elamite royal names. The second is the name of an Elamite deity (Lagamar). The whole name, although in good Elamite form, is not yet attested as the name of an Elamite king (Zimmern, KAT³, 485-86; Jensen, *Gilgamesch-Epos* 1:326). אַמְרָפֶל of Shinar (i.e., Babylonia 10:10) is often identified, following Schrader (*Sitzungsber. d. Berliner Akad.* [1887], 600ff.), with Hammurabi king of Babel, who liberated Babylonia from the yoke of the Elamites ca 2100. This equation has been vigorously disputed by others, however, (e.g., Bezold, *Bab.-assyr. Keilinschriften*, 24ff.; cf. Jensen, *Gilgamesch-Epos*, 327). Winckler (*Abraham als Babylonier*, 23ff.; cf. above p. 167) builds a complete, imaginative construction on this questionable identification. In order to explain the ל in אַמְרָפֶל, which does not conform to this equation, Hüsing (in A. Jeremias, *Im Kampf um Babel u. Bibel⁴*, 13) reads לְמֶלֶךְ and translates, "It happened in the days of Hammurabi when 'Aryoch, king of 'Ellasar was king over Shinar, that they went to battle, etc." This is impossible Hebrew (cf. Beer, DLZg [1904], col. 359; Jensen, *Gilgamesch-Epos*, 328n.1). אֶלָּסָר is probably the old Babylonian city Larsa, now Senkereh, southeast of Uruk-Erech. אַרְיוֹךְ (the name also appears in Dan 2:14ff. as the name of a Babylonian courtier) is often explained as the Sumerian form Eri-Aku of the Semit.-Bab. name Rim-Sin of a king of Larsa and contemporary of Hammurabi. This derivation is very uncertain (Bezold, *Bab.-assyr. Keilin-*

schriften, 56; Jensen, *Gilgamesch-Epos*, 328). Yet, recently several Elamite royal names from the earlier period have become known which exhibit either the element Iri in the first position or the element Agun in the second so that Aryoch may also trace back to a good Elamite **Iri-agun* which is, however, not yet attested (cf. Scheil, *Délégation en Perse 5*, xii). תִּדְעָל may be attested as *Tudhul* in the texts mentioned below (p. 284). גּוֹיִם is the name of a people here, in any case, perhaps miswritten (Pesh גליא = Hebr. גלים, Ball), perhaps to be equated with the *Gutî* (between Babylonia and Media). Among those mentioned, according to vv 4, 5, 9, 17 Chedorlaomer is the chief, <279> although quite unusually this is not apparent in the (seemingly) strictly alphabetical list. The passage presumes then that kings of Elam ruled over Babylonia at the time—a situation known to us from the Babylonian tradition for the period around 2300 (cf. Meyer 1/2², 550ff.). It further presumes these Elamite-Babylonian kings possessed a world empire which stretched as far as Syria—this, too, is not to be considered impossible (Meyer 1/2², 552). An account which can report such ancient names and circumstances initially makes the impression of greatest antiquity. Almost all the subsequent names are also very ancient—names of peoples and cities that had long disappeared in Israel's time and regarding which the author must inform many of his contemporaries with parenthetical explanations.

2 The connection of this clause with the preceding is careless. The author seems to have forgotten during the long list of royal names that these names stand in the "genitive." The names of the "Pentapolis" near the Dead Sea only occur in legends and, indeed, the old tradition speaks either of Sodom and Gomorra or of Admah and Zeboiim. The association of all four will trace to the later harmonization of the various traditions (cf. above pp. 214-15]). The mention of these cities at this point excites strong objections to the historicity of the account. Zoar is mentioned otherwise only in Gen 19:17-22. Each of the cities has its own king in Canaanite fashion. The names of the kings of the four cities defy interpretation. The fact that they are not inventions is indicated by the namelessness of the fifth. LXX has Βαλλα for בֶּרַע and Σεννααρ for שִׁנְאָב. Regarding שִׁנְאָב and שְׁמֵאֶבֶר (Sam שמאבד) see Sellin, *Neue kirchl. Ztschr.* 16:932. **3** Already here the author mentions prematurely and not very adeptly the site of the decisive battle to be recounted in detail in vv 8ff. The notion that where the Salt Sea now lies was once a valley is the view of the Israelite legend (cf. 13:10; 19:25). The geological evidence shows, however, that this notion is erroneous. The Jordan has poured its water into this basin since distant prehistoric times (cf. above, p. 214). The "apologetic" information that the cities mentioned were located in the southern parts of the Sea, only later inundated (so, once again, Sellin, 933), is clearly not the opinion of the author of this passage. Instead, he equates the Siddim Valley and the (current) Salt Sea. Accordingly, we will have very grave doubts concerning this author's whole account of the battle in this fabled valley. The name "Siddim Valley" will be legend tradition. It may be that one should read שֵׁדִים "Demon valley" (Renan, *Histoire du peuple d'Israel* 1:116n.4, etc.).

4-7 *The events before the decisive battle.* The precise datings (regarding the temporal accusative, v 4b, cf. §118i; Sam, Kittel, and Kautzsch³ read וּבִשְׁלֹשׁ) arouse, one again, the appearance of extreme credibility. The naive folk legend does not narrate in this style, but strict history does. The perfect after the year also characterizes historical style (cf., e.g., 2 Kgs 25:1). The sequence vassalage (i.e., payment of tribute), rebellion (i.e., withholding tribute), punitive campaign also occurs in 2 Kgs 24:1ff.; 18:7, 9. Such a sequence was surely the rule in accounts of the punishment of rebellious vassals (cf. the similar style in the reports of the Assyrian royal inscriptions in reference to campaigns against seditious vassal states, e.g., KB 2:214-15, ll. 82ff., and idem, *Anm.*, ll. 87ff., and perhaps elsewhere). The peoples mentioned subsequently are all supposed to be aboriginal peoples. In reality הָרְפָאִים (with Sam, LXX, Kittel, Kautzsch[3]) are actually "spirits of the dead," corresponding, then, to the <280> Greek heroes, conceived as a giant people from the ancient period who lived especially in the Transjordan (Deut 3:11; Josh 12:4). The זוּזִים (perhaps = the זַמְזֻמִּים or merely a misspelling of it?) and the אֵימִים are distinguished from them here. According to an "antiquarian commentary" in Deut 2:20, 10-11, Zamzummim and Emim are local names of the Rephaim in Ammon and Moab. Whether these names have historical value is more than questionable (Meyer, *Israeliten*, 312, 477; cf. Schwally, ZAW 18:127ff.). In contrast, the חֹרִי are historically attested (according to Deut 2:12, 22 they were eradicated by Esau, thus in the area of the later Edom; Eg. Charu, cf. comments on 36:20ff.), as are the עֲמָלֵקִי (the "first of the nations," Num 24:20, here conceived of as southwest of the Dead Sea; cf. Num 13:29; concerning Amalek, cf. comments on 36:12; Meyer, *Israeliten*, see index) and the אֱמֹרִי (a once mighty people who ruled even over Babylonia from their home in Syria; Israel fought with their remnants in Palestine, cf. Meyer, $1/2^2$, see index; here—a final, surely very obscure residue of tradition—envisioned to the West of the Dead Sea; cf. also comments on 10:10). The battle site. עַשְׁתְּרֹת קַרְנַיִם is, according to Buhl (*Palästina*, 248ff.), the name of two cities in Bashan. The reference is probably to the current *el-Muzêrib* on the highway from Damascus to the Transjordan. The city is mentioned under the names "Ashtaroth" (according to Deut 1:4, the capital city of king Og) and "Qarnaim" (alluded to in Amos 6:13; 1 Macc 5:43; 2 Macc 12:21). We can now explain the names with certainty in terms of the new discovery that Astarte was portrayed with two horns (cf., e.g., Benzinger[2], 221 fig. 130). The transferal of a divine name to a city is a common process, interesting for the history of religion and politics. The name of the god is applied first to its symbol, then the whole sanctuary, and finally the human population which gathers around the sanctuary. Parallel cases are בַּעַל גָּד, בַּעַל חָצוֹר, and נְבוֹ, in German St. Peter, etc. (cf. Meyer, *Israeliten*, 296). Nothing further is known of חָם. קִרְיָתַיִם is a Moabite city, now *Krêyât*, west of *Mâdebâ*. The "plain" of Kiryathaim is the high plain north of the Arnon. שֵׂעִיר in v 6 is either to be stricken as a gloss or to be read with Sam, LXX, Pesh, Vulg, Kittel, and Kautzsch[3] as בְּהַרְרֵי שֵׂעִיר "on the mountains of Seir." אֵיל פָּארָן is to equated with the well-known harbor city on the Elanite Bay [Gulf of Aqabah] אֵילַה (or אֵילוֹת). The city seems to have its name from a large palm grove in the vicinity (אַיִל = "large tree"). The "desert" is the desert Paran between Canaan and Egypt (21:21). עֵין מִשְׁפָּט "spring of justice," that is, a spring at which the oracle pronounced judgment in the name of the numen of the spring (= the מֵי מְרִיבָה, "water of trial," known from the Moses narrative in Num 20:13; 27:14). מֵי מְרִיבָה was the name of the large spring at Kadesh (Num 20:1; 27:14; Meyer, *Israeliten*, 54-55). The site has been relocated in *'Ain Ḳudês* (*Ḳadîs*) in the *Wâdi Ḳadîs* (cf. Trumbull, *Kadesh-Barnea* [1884] and Guthe, ZDPV 8:182ff.). According to 2 Chron 20:2 הַצְצוֹן תָּמָר is עֵין גֶּדִי, currently *'Ain Ĝidî* on the western shore of the Dead Sea, rich in palms (cf. Buhl, *Palästina*, 164-65). The five kings come, as Babylonian armies which march on Palestine always do, via Syria. They march from the North, to the east of the "Siddim Valley" to the Dead Sea. Then the kings "turn" to the north until they come to the west of the "Siddim Valley." They make a large arc around this valley. Such a march through these deserted steppes sounds rather unlikely in these circumstances. One does not understand why after the conquest of Kiryathaim the kings did not turn directly to the "Siddim Valley" where, according to v 2, their actual enemies were. They subject themselves to very great danger <281> by moving to the south and leaving their enemies at their backs. If one wishes to salvage the historicity of such a campaign, one must assume that the actual goal was the conquest of the significant commercial center Elath or, with Sellin (*Neue kirchl. Ztschr.*, 933) explain the campaign as the result of a rebellion of the eastern and southern neighbors. One must, therefore, reject at least the precision of the reporting. But the suspicion arises that the account of this whole campaign had no other purpose than the narrator's wish to portray the importance of the final battle through this campaign while at the same time demonstrating his knowledge of prehistorical circumstances (cf. Nöldeke, *Untersuchungen*, 163).

8-12 The narrator expressively introduces the battle in the Siddim Valley with a repeat list of the opponents (**8, 9**). This repetition also manifests his joy in the multitude (cf. already the כָּל־אֵלֶּה, v 3) of the old and extraordinary names. He expresses the impression of the spectacular at the end, "four kings against five," that is, mighty and equally ranked opponents! This conflict shows us, however, how little the author understood the real circumstances. How can one compare the minor city kings of the Siddim Valley with the powerful world conquerors! The author's confusion can only be understood as the result of Judeo-Palestinian local patriotism which becomes even more crudely apparent in the portrayal of Abraham. Otherwise, it should actually read "five kings against four." Is this an oversight or an intentional chiasm? Notably, the sequence of the four kings in v 9 is different than in v 1. No reason for this can be given. **10** The Siddim Valley consisted solely of asphalt pits (on the construction §§123e, 130e). The sea currently spews asphalt. Those fleeing the battlefield fell into these pits. Judging from the context, one must relate this statement to the king of Sodom and the king of Gomorra (Sam, LXX, Pesh ומלך עמרה). Subsequently, however, the king of Sodom is still alive (vv 17ff.). Consequently, careless narration is to be assumed (similar to 2 Kgs 19:35). The mountains are those of Moab.

11 *Plundering of Sodom and Gomorra.* Notably, only these cities are plundered. What happened to the others? Furthermore, the enemies withdraw so quickly that Abraham, who pursues them, can only overtake them at the northernmost border of Canaan. Conceivably, the enemy troops would withdraw after a certain period given the situations of such world empires. But it is very wondrous that they depart so quickly. According to v 4 it is not a mere raid, but a conquest. Now, however, it may be hypothesized how the author may have come to this account. Because of the account which follows, he was only interested in the cities of Lot. He utilized the enemies' swift departure to portray the magnanimity and decisevness of Abraham who set out after them for Lot's sake. **12** Seen from a historical perspective the reference to Lot, a private citizen, in such a context of world proportions is also very strange. It was necessary for the author, however, because he is able in this way to make the transition to Abraham. Abraham intervenes because his nephew Lot is involved (v 14). Otherwise—one is to think—as accommodating as he is, he would not have concerned himself with the whole war of the pagan kings which does not concern him. <282> The double וַיֵּלְכוּ (vv 11, 12) is unattractive. Since Abraham is newly introduced in v 13, בֶּן־אֲחִי אַבְרָם, which also stands inappropriately in the clause after וְאֶת־רְכֻשׁוֹ, is probably a gloss (Dillmann, Kittel, Kautzsch[3]). The same is true also for the awkward וְהוּא יֹשֵׁב בִּסְדֹם. According to vv 16, 21, people were also taken away from the cities along with the things mentioned in v 11. The presentation is incorrect here, too.

13-16 Abraham's intervention is introduced effectively enough nevertheless. He decides quickly to plunge into the war because of his relative and wins a brilliant victory over opponents who conquered a multitude of peoples and even five kings (concerning the emotion this statement carries in Judaism, cf. comments on 17:6)! **13** Concerning הַפָּלִיט see §126r. Abraham's name and dwelling place are introduced once again here. Foreigners call Israelites הָעִבְרִי. The report will, therefore, be of foreign origin. It is no accident that our account assigns Abraham a dwelling "under the Terebinths of Mamre." The Abraham-Lot tradition the author utilizes locates Lot in Sodom and Abraham in Mamre (13:12, 18). For this reason, too, our account was placed after Gen 13. This is the only place it could have in Genesis. The narrator created the names of Abraham's allies from place names. מַמְרֵא in J is the name of the site of the holy grove. אֶשְׁכֹּל is taken from the name of the נַחַל אֶשְׁכֹּל, the "brook of grapes" near Hebron (Num 13:23f.). "Here one quite unmistakably has eponymic heroes" (Nöldeke, 166). עָנֵר will have a similar origin. These men are the בַּעֲלֵי בְרִית אַבְרָם (con-cerning the expression, cf. Neh 6:18), that is, according to the context of the chapter (cf. esp. v 24) not Abraham's patrons (contra Kraetzschmar, *Bundesvorstellung*, 24; Sellin, *Neue kirchl. Ztschr.*, 936) but his allies, "who have Abraham's solemn promise." The patriarchal narratives recount other such contracts (21:22ff.; 26:28ff.; 38:1).

14 Now the narrator turns to the main point: Abraham's intervention. אָחִיו means his cousin, relative. וַיָּרֶק means "he emptied, poured out," like arrows from the quiver or the sword from the sheath (Dillmann). But the word, employed in this metaphorical manner, would have an extremely poetic tone and would not suit the narrative style. Consequently, Sam וַיָּדֶק > דוק, "he mustered," LXX ἠρίθμησε is preferable, or per-haps even better with Winckler (*Forschungen* 1:102n.2), one should read וַיָּרֶק from דקה (= Assyr *dikû* "to summon troops"? admittedly, according to Zimmern's report, *dikû* is consistently spelled with *k* not with *k*). חָנִיךְ, a hapax legomenon, means "initiated, proven warrior" (a poetic term?). Sellin's (*Neue kirchl. Ztschr.*, 937) recourse to a presumed Assyr *ḫannaku* (KB 3/1:206-207, etc.) is erroneous according to Zimmern (private correspondence). "His house born" (thus especially trustworthy slaves in contrast to those purchased) sounds like a prosaic explanation of the hapax. It is important to the author that it was precisely 318 men because he can glorify Abraham for defeating such a mighty army with only 318 men! What should one think of a narrator who reports such victories! "If this is possible, nothing is impossible" (Nöldeke). The reference to Abraham's three allies does not improve the matter (as Sellin, *Neue kirchl. Ztschr.*, 934, maintains once again), for, even if we assume that these local dignitaries had large forces, it still not possible to arrive at a sufficient number. But how did the narrator arrive at the number 318? Such precise information would surely not rest on pure fantasy, would it? Midrash knows that the numeric value of the name אליעזר, the name of Abraham's chief slave according to 15:2, is 318. Has the number been derived in this way? Winckler

(*Gesch. Israels* 2:27) maintains that 318 is an astronomical number. The moon is visible for 318 days in a year. According to this interpretation, a myth could portray the moon god as a hero followed by 318 "consecrated" <283> servants in his battles. This interpretation, however, is mere conjecture. As H. Zimmern tells me, the number does not occur in Babylonia or elsewhere in the Orient. Nor is it in any way self-evident that the Babylonians calculated that the moon was visible for 318 days. The number 318 (more precisely 317+1) occurs once in Egyptian material (Erman, *Äg. Rel.*, 65), but it is probably only an accident. According to v 24 Abraham's allies accompanied him on the campaign. They should actually already be mentioned here, another example of awkward narration. The name "Dan" here, where only prehistoric names are involved, is an error. Before Israel the city was called Laish.

15 וַיֵּחָלֵק "he divided up" means he divided his people (is it corrupt?). The same maneuver occurs in Judg 7:16; 1 Sam 11:11; 13:17-18; Job 1:17. חוֹבָה lies 20 hours north of Damascus. Other locations are discussed in Gesenius-Buhl[14], s.v. Abraham follows the defeated forces for an immense distance. Abraham's victory is entirely fabulous and, since it is the conscious point of all the preceding, makes the chapter's whole account of the campaign of the Babylonian-Elamite kings extremely incredible. In an effort to remove the incredible elements from the report, it has been assumed that Abraham did not defeat the whole army of these kings, but that he only retrieved a portion of the plunder from the rearguard of the homeward bound army. The eastern kings themselves were not present (Dillmann; Kittel, *Geschichte der Hebräer* 1:161; Sellin, *Neue kirchl. Ztschr.*, 934). This is an entirely capricious interpretation. Instead, the account explicitly states that Abraham "struck Chedorlaomer and the kings with him" (v 17) and illustrates the magnitude of Abraham's victory by means of the magnitude of the distance of the pursuit. If he had only attached the rearguard he would have withdrawn rapidly after he had successfully retrieved the plunder and would have carefully guarded against coming too near the main army. And will the plunder have been found with the rearguard whose purpose is to protect the main army and not with the main army itself? 16 Thus Abraham obtained the plunder from the enemy. According to the following material, it was only (besides Lot and his property) the plunder from Sodom. The narrator also intentionally mentioned spoils of war only (v 11) in reference to Sodom (and Gomorra). Here, too, the literary purpose is clear. Abraham is supposed to be magnified because he did not retain any of the plunder, but returned everything to the king of Sodom. Consequently, only the spoil from Sodom is mentioned. But it is unusual that Abraham is supposed to have retrieved only this plunder from these four kings who came from so far away and who defeated so many kings in the meantime.

17-28 *Two concluding scenes: Abraham's meeting with Melchizedek and the king of Sodom.* These two scenes, although linked by the divine name אֵל עֶלְיוֹן (vv 19, 20, 22) and perhaps, also by the allusion הֶעֱשַׁרְתִּי (v 23)–מַעֲשֵׂר (v 20), do not fit together well. The payment of the tithe (20) is especially strange given Abraham's assurance (v 23) that he claims nothing of the plunder for himself. The two episodes are variants in the broader sense. Both speak of Abraham's encounter with princes of Canaan to whom he demonstrates his unselfishness in relation to the plunder. He tithes of it to one, he returns the stolen property to the other. Of the two pieces, the encounter with the king of Sodom is firmly anchored in the preceding. The fact that the foreign kings removed the means of transportation from Sodom and Gomorra (v 11), but that Abraham retrieved them (v 18) prepares for vv 21-24. The involvement of the allies, only to be surmised from v 13, is supplied in v 24. Accordingly, vv 1, 21-24 can in no case be an addition (contra Sellin, *Neue kirchl. Ztschr.*, 939-40). In contrast, the Melchizedek <284> episode has a less firm relationship to the whole, separates the appearance of the king of Sodom (v 17) from Abraham's negotiation with him (vv 21-24), and may, therefore, be a secondary addition inserted here from oral tradition or another source (Winckler, *Gesch. Isr.* 2:29; Baudissin, *Einleitung*, 85, etc.).

17 Where did the king of Sodom come from? He probably came from Sodom where he had previously gone. Sodom's destruction (contra Sellin, *Neue kirchl. Ztschr.*, 940) has not yet been recounted. The following episode takes place in the valley שָׁוֵה or the "King's Valley" near שָׁלֵם (v 18). Since שָׁוֵה also means "valley," Hommel (*Altisr. Überlieferung*, 151n.1) and Winckler (*Gesch. Isr.* 2:28) think (correctly?) of a corruption from the Babylonian *šarre* (= "kings") and, thus, "King's Valley." In the opinion of the author, שָׁלֵם is an old name like Sodom, Siddim, Rephaim, Emim, and all the other names. Given the emphasis on the king of this place in the following discussion, this name probably conceals a very famous place. According to Psa 76:3 שָׁלֵם is a poetic, and therefore probably archaic, name for Jerusalem. Consequently, שָׁלֵם should also be regarded as Jerusalem here. This interpretation is also supported by the fact that Melchizedek, in Gen 14 the king of Shalem, is compared to the kings of Zion in Psa 110:4. Furthermore, Gen 14 recounts that Abraham acknowledged Melchizedek's god as his own and tithed to Shalem. All of this gains particular significance if this text involves Jerusalem (so already Josephus, *Ant.*, I.10.2 and the Targums). According to Josephus (*Ant.* VII.10.3) the "King's Valley" lay in the vicinity of Jerusalem. A relationship with the historically insignificant location σαλείμ (John 3:23) southwest of Scythopolis is to be rejected, therefore. On the other hand, the reference to Jerusalem in the patriarchal legend is very remarkable. No other account in Genesis treats Jerusalem (concerning "ham-Moriyya," cf. comments on 22:2)—a circumstance which can be entirely explained by Israel's late acquisition of Jerusalem. Characteristically, according to Gen 14 the sanctuary at Shalem was not in Abraham's hands while all other sanctuaries mentioned in Genesis belong to the patriarchs. This image mirrors the fact that Jerusalem did not belong to Israel in the ancient period.

18-20 *The scene with Melchizedek.* The name מַלְכִּי־צֶדֶק is formed like אֲדֹנִי־צֶדֶק, King of Jerusalem (Josh 10:1; LXX and Judg 1:5-7, אֲדֹנִי־בֶזֶק). The name is good Canaanite (cf. the Phoenician name צדק־מלך; Lidzbarski, *Handbuch*, 357) and may mean "my king is Ṣidiq" (cf. Baudissin, *Studien* 1:15; regarding the divine name Ṣidiq or Ṣedeq, cf. Zimmern, KAT³, 473-74; Hebr 7:2 βασιλεὺς δικαιοσύνης). This king is a priest of *'el 'elyon*. In the narrator's opinion, *'el 'elyon* is also an ancient name. The author is quite right. The name is analogous to the ancient names *'el šadday, 'el 'olam, 'el beth-'el*, etc. and is attested as ancient in Israel by Num 24:16. Israelite tradition adopted such ancient names and interpreted them as epithets of Yahweh (Psa 78:35; 7:18; 57:3; etc.; cf. above, pp. 186, 234). In later and latest times, the name was often employed, especially for propaganda purposes (Westphal, *Wohnstätten Jahwes*, 258ff.). According to Lidzbarski (*Ephemeris für semit. Epigraphik* 1:252n.1), the Phoenician divine name Ἐλιοῦν, ὁ ὕψιστος mentioned by Philo (*Bybl. fr.* 2:12-13, in Müller,

Fragm. hist. graec. 3:567) is a relatively recent figure who came to the Phoenicians via the Jews. The narrator wants to depict Melchizedek as a worshipper of the true God. But, on the other hand, he wants to avoid the name "Yahweh" here where a non-Israelite is involved. Consequently, he chose a name which one could understand as a reference to Yahweh, on the one hand, and which was easily conceivable for a Canaanite, on the other. Finally, it would even be possible, but in no way demonstrable, that he still knew of a tradition in which the God of Jerusalem in pre-Yahwistic times was called *'el 'elyon*. The author also perceived the predicate, קֹנֵה שָׁמַיִם וָאָרֶץ, as most ancient—very conceivably. Concerning the age <285> of the doctrine of "Creation," in Israel, too, see above pp. 125-26. The similar phrase עֹשֵׂה שׁ' וא' occurs frequently in the Psalms. Melchizedek is simultaneously king and priest. As king he greets Abraham as he passes through with bread and wine. Regarding the practice of offering allies, caravans, messengers, etc. "food and drink" as they pass through, Sellin (938) calls attention to KB 5:50 l. 23; 207 l. 16; 209 ll. 12ff.; 242 l. 16 etc. As priest Melchizedek blesses Abraham. Blessing is the privilege of the priest. The blessing, as often, is in poetical form—a "heptameter" and a "doubled trimeter," צָרֶיךָ and מִגֵּן are poetical words. The words of blessing sound formulaic. Psa 110 also presumes the priestly monarchy of Melchizedek. It is not impossible that there were really such Canaanite priest-kings in pre-Israelite times. Josephus (*Contra Ap.* 1.18) mentions a Phoenician priest-king. Abraham acknowledges Melchizedek's God (v 22), sanctuary, and priestly office by tithing to him (v 20). (Concerning tithing see the comments on 28:22.) These elements are very remarkable in Genesis. No other passage values the notion that the pagan also has the true God. It is difficult to avoid the conclusion that the account regards the sanctuary and the priest-king of Shalem as the legitimate predecessors of the later Yahweh temple and priest-king of Jerusalem and that it thereby "assures the Jerusalem sanctuary the greatest age among all Israelite sanctuaries" (Westphal, 260). It has Abraham pay the tithe to Shalem to declare the extreme antiquity of the institution of the Jerusalemite practice of tithing (Deut 12:11; 14:22ff.). Accordingly, the tendency of this narrative is undeniable. When the later, kingless period considered the figure of Melchizedek, it will surely have seen in him the predecessor of the high priests whom the community honored like the kings and to whom the tithes were owed (Num 18:21ff.; Neh 10:38f.; Tob 1:7-8; cf. Wellhausen, *Prolegomena*[6], 142ff.). Accordingly, the hypothesis seems likely that even the figure of Melchizedek himself is nothing other than an artificial construction, a projection of the postexilic high priesthood in Abraham's time (Wellhausen, *Composition*[3], 313).

This hypothesis is contradicted, however, by the following observations. (1) It is very unlikely that the later community, opposed to everything pagan, especially Canaanite, will have sought the pattern for the high-priesthood in a Canaanite. Furthermore, one had the figure of Aaron, why one would need Melchizedek? Instead, it is likely that the understanding of Melchizedek as the predecessor of Israelite institutions is much older and stems from a time still naive enough to equate Canaanite and Israelite. (2) This is also supported by the mention of Melchizedek in Psa 110. Now many scholars date the psalm to the Maccabean period. But the acrostic on the name שִׁמְעוֹן uncovered by Bickell is not convincing. The pertinent letters appear at different positions in the verses. The force and momentum of the poem speaks against Maccabean origins. The poetry of the Maccabean period, concerning which we can form a clear picture from Sir, PsaSol, and the lyric passages scattered in the book of 1 Macc, was very epigonic. Furthermore, the dating of the Psalm to the Maccabeean period is contradicted by the fact that the poet still dares to announce a divine oracle in the fashion of the earliest poetry. Such vital prophecy, in which the person of the prophet is significant, however, was, as we know (1 Macc 4:46; 9:27; 14:41) long since quieted in the Maccabeean period. There is no reason, however, not to attribute this song <286> or the other royal songs to Israel's monarchical period. The idea of the Psalm, that the king of Zion is also Yahweh's priest (emphasized in the context of the poem because the priest stands under particular divine protection), does not contradict this dating. Why would it have been impossible to say this in ancient Israel? Such an idea would not be remarkable in Egypt, Phoenicia, or Babylonia. Jethro was simultaneously prince and priest. Israel's kings also occasionally functioned as priests (cf. esp. 2 Sam 6:14). We may assume, therefore, that Jerusalemite courtly tradition valued the fact that the king of Jerusalem was Melchizedek's successor. Such dynastic claims are very common. The "Roman" Kaisers of German nationality regarded themselves as successors of the Caesars. The Caesars appeared in Egypt as successors of the Pharaohs, etc. Such claims are intended to demonstrate the legitimacy of the new kingdom by portraying them as the continuation of the old. Thus one must conclude that Jerusalem was already the seat of a significant kingdom in pre-Israelite times and that Melchizedek was considered its main representative.

This conclusion is strengthened by the conquest tradition. There the king of Jerusalem appears as the head of an alliance of Canaanite cities (Josh 10). The Amarna correspondence also seems to suggest that the king of Jerusalem occupied the dominant position in southern Canaan at the time (cf. Steuernagel, *Isr. Stämme*, 120). The later Judean monarchy linked to this Jerusalemite tradition. David may have already been influenced by such ideas when he chose this very city as his residence, comparable to Charlemagne who renewed the empire in Rome. We will be inclined, accordingly, to consider Melchizedek as a traditional figure and perhaps as a historical person. The scene of Abraham's encounter with Melchizedek is not without poetic charm. The two entities which later form such a deep connection, the holy people and the holy city, come into contact for the first time here. Here for the first time Israel receives the blessing from its sanctuary. It is possible that we have a local Jerusalemite tradition in this scene which could be compared with the legend of Abraham's treaty with Gerar.

21-24 *Abraham's conversation with the king of Sodom.* The conclusion of the account is supposed to magnify Abraham's generosity. The account concludes "with an upraised arm" (v 22), with a speech (cf. comments above on 8:22). This speech acquires extreme generosity through is position. The narrator wants to express the fact that Abraham's generosity is more important to him that all his martial fame. Abraham had a right to keep everything, people and property, and the king of Sodom dared only to ask for the people. But with solemn oaths Abraham declines to take even the least portion for himself. The author effectively contrasts the behavior of the slaves and the allies with this sublime attitude. They are of lesser natures. The slaves ate from the plunder and the allies want their part. Abraham, however, is generous enough to care even for these insignificant persons. **21** נֶפֶשׁ means people (12:5). **22** The raising of the hand (to heaven) is an oath gesture (Deut 32:40; Dan 12:7) as it is in the Parsi religion (Edv. Lehmann in Chantepie de la Saussaye 22, 194). The Arabs also pray (as do many other peoples) with raised hands (G. Jacob, *Altarab. Parallelen zum AT*, 8). The assumption is that the dwelling place of the deity <287> is in heaven (Westphal, *Jahwes Wohnstätten*, 251-52) Abraham's speech intentionally repeats the divine name (v 19) so that one may clearly see that Abraham's God is also Melchizedek's God. LXX, Luc, A, and Pesh omit יהוה. Sam reads יהוה האלהים. יהוה is probably a later addition. Or does Abraham intend to rectify Melchizedek's confession of faith (Sellin, *Neue kirchl. Ztschr.*, 939). **23** אִם is an oath particle here §149). The apodosis is usually only implied in an oath or, more commonly, is entirely omitted. It must have contained a self-deprecation which the ancient Israelite avoided pronouncing because "one should not paint the devil on the wall." The idiom "from thread (חוט) to sandal thong" can be compared with [מן] חם עד חוט "from remnant (?) to thread," that is, everything, even the most insignificant, in the Judeo-Aramaic papyri from Assuan (G 25). Abraham refers to himself by name as an expression of his pride (cf. 4:23). Esther 9:10, 15, 16 attributes the same lack of greed to all Jews who do not reach out their hands for the property of their enemies. It is very unusual that this passage maintains that Abraham had cordial relations with Sodom which is discussed elsewhere only with disgust. This is only one of the chapter's many difficult puzzles.

General Remarks concerning Abraham's Victory over the Four Kings

Bibliography in Dillmann; Franz Delitzsch; A. Jeremias, ATAO², 343-44; and Sellin, *Neue kirchliche Zeitschrift* 16:930nn.1-2.

1. *Source criticism.* The passage is commonly assumed to belong to none of our documentary sources. In tone it differs radically from the legends in J and E (cf. below, no. 4). It agrees with P in its learned attitude and in a few expressions (רְכֻשׁ vv 11, 12, 16, 21; יְלִידֵי בֵית v 14; נֶפֶשׁ v 21), but diverges from it in style and in the reference to Jerusalem. Since Abraham is introduced anew in v 13, one can probably assume the chapter was not conceived as part of a larger whole, but from the outset as an independent piece.

2. *Historical character of the account.* The account contains very ancient information to be considered historical. This information includes, above all, the names of the four kings and probably also the historical framework of the whole episode, the domination of Elamito-Babylonian kings reaching to Palestine. The figure of Melchizedek can also be historical. Understandably, this chapter was formerly—and sometimes still is—thought to support the historicity of the person of Abraham (Hommel, *Altisr. Überlieferung*, 147ff.; Sellin, 929ff.). On the other hand, the account contains inherently impossible information (cf. Nöldeke, *Untersuchungen*, 156ff.). Abraham's attack—318 men defeat the army of the world conquerors—is especially inconceivable. The narrator's assumption that the Dead Sea was once an inhabited valley is also surely false. These arguments have not been invalidated by Sellin. In shrill contrast, then, the account contains very credible and entirely impossible information.

3. *The origin of the information in the passage is equally varied.* The author can only have the tradition of the four Babylonian kings (directly or indirectly) from Babylonian tradition, itself. It is unlikely that he created this passage from Canaanite (Dillmann), specifically from ancient Jerusalemite tradition (Hommel, 153). The account of Abraham's

victory, which glorifies Israel's patriarch in such a grotesque manner, surely does not stem from a Canaanite source. Instead, this will have only been recounted in Israel, although the author seems to want to maintain the foreign origin of this tradition through the phrase "the Hebrew" (v 13). The Babylonianisms, which Sellin (937ff.) sees as confirmation of the ancient Canaanite origin of the chap., are also very problematic in nature in Zimmern's judgment. The original names of the places and peoples and also the name of Melchizedek are Canaanite tradition. The account fuses, then, Babylonian, Canaanite-Israelite, and purely Israelite material. If one should think such a mixture <288> of motifs of extremely varied origins impossible (cf. Frankenberg, CGA [1901], 697), one may read the legend of Karl Ynach (Grimm, *Deutsche Sagen* no. 533) where medieval German and classical Roman heroes appear alongside one another.

4. *The style of this piece is similarly unusual.* The account does not appear to be a poetic, naive legend and clearly distinguishes itself thereby in tone from J and E. Instead, precise chronological information (e.g., v 4) characterizes historiography, whose tone the author consciously imitates (cf. comments on v 4). The author is learned. He presents his knowledge concerning temporally and sometimes also geographically distant matters. "Antiquarian comments" characterize him (Wellhausen). On the other hand, despite his archaeological knowledge, he manifests a remarkable ignorance of the actual course of such military campaigns. He wants to transmit history, but he transmits a legend whose chief point, Abraham's victory, is inherently totally impossible. Characteristic of his literary style, he uncritically intermingles ancient history and legend, the credible and the most recent inventions. This is the style of an incipient historical scholarship.

5. The purpose of the piece is obviously to glorify Abraham. The whole is effectively structured for this purpose. Only the second act introduces Abraham, the decisive character, for this reason. The book of Judith, where a mighty world war also provides the pedestal for Judith's deed, is very similar. The author wants to make it clear to us that Abraham is the greatest war hero in the world and more—an extremely noble man. He defeats kings. A king blesses him. He will not accept even a sandal-thong from a king! This view of Abraham, however, stands in clear contrast to the old legends where he never displays an aggressive streak nor shies away from occasionally allowing himself to be "enriched" by less honorable gifts of foreign kings (cf. the ancient legend in 12:16). These elements also show that the piece does not belong to the old legends, but is the product of an entirely different spirit.

6. *The spirit and time of the piece can now be discerned.* It is (in its present form) a legend from the period of Judaism. In the account of such a fabulous victory of Israel, it agrees characteristically with other Jewish works of legend (Chron, Judith, Test, Jubil). The Judaism of that time admired military fame all the more since it was incapable of conducting war, itself. Since it unfortunately found no occasion for boasting of its own acts of war, it loved to recount the mighty acts of its predecessors. Such accounts, however, grew in its imagination to monstrous proportions. After all, they were extremely inexperienced in political matters in the absence of a civic life and considered virtually anything possible. Thus, this piece belongs in a time when, despite a certain historical learning, the historical sense of Judaism had virtually disappeared. The unusual value on proud self-sufficiency may also characterize this Judaism, downtrodden, only all too consigned to humility in the misery of real life, and dubious of its advantage. One values the

virtue most which one does not possess. But it is especially remarkable that the narrator knows and values Babylonian matters. Other books from this period also manifest interest in the world empires (Esther, Daniel, Judith). The Jews are accustomed to looking beyond the borders of their nation and especially to inquiring about the history of the dominant nations. It is a period of extreme mixture of peoples in the Orient—the circumstances with which we in the Occident become acquainted in the period of the Roman Empire must have already existed many centuries earlier in the Orient—a period when peoples exchange cultures and historical reports (cf. Meyer III, 168; one thinks of Berosus, Manetho, and Josephus in a somewhat later period). In such a time, Judaism, too, did not wish <289> to stand back, but strived to claim its place in the history of the world empires. "Abraham, the Hebrew" was, one maintained, a contemporary of Chedorlaomer. At the same time, an element of Jewish national vanity was also involved. Jewish people who appear in such narratives of world events usually assume a very important position in the world empires (Daniel, Tobith and Achiacharos, Mordecai and Esther). Thus Judith depicts a campaign of a world power which a lone Jewish woman repels. According to Gen 14, Abraham vanquishes Chedorlaomer himself! One may certainly not consider it impossible that such ancient historical reminiscences were not yet extinguished in such a later period. One thinks of the historical knowledge of a Berosus. Furthermore, a popular legend tradition in Babylonian, attested to us from the Achemenide period, may tell of precisely these ancient kings (cf. the translation of the texts discovered by Pinches in Hommel, *Überlieferung*, 180ff.). From the (not yet published) narrative papyri from Elephantine we know that Judaism in the Persian Empire participated in world literature and was influenced by it. And just as fragments of the Ahiqar romance and (it seems) a Persian chronicle in Aramaic were found in Elephantine, just as the author of Dan 11 must have had access to a chronicle of the Seleucids and the Ptolemies, probably in Aramaic, so the author of Gen 14 will have had a tradition from the old Babylonian period. But the author "described" the situation in Palestine in "Abraham's" time "as he imagined them to have been in the early period: the Dead Sea did not yet exist, and the kings of Sodom and Gomorra and the primordial nations of the legends appear in person" (Meyer I/22, 551).

7. *The extent to which the piece already had a pre-history in Jewish tradition, and the extent to which the narrator's construction traces to it can hardly be determined.* The many names in the description of the military campaign have the strong flavor of the study, but the rest can hardly be popular tradition either. It is learned invention. "It may be a narrative told by the priests at Jerusalem" (Eerdmans, 92). The account is frequently not well told (cf. the commentary). Nevertheless, we find no trace of a composition from several sources, except perhaps in the Melchizedek episode. Sievers (2:267ff.) undertakes, although only provisionally, a "radical cure" of the text by suggesting several very harsh glosses and striking all "not entirely tolerable proper names," including Chedorlaomer and Melchizedek, even Melchizedek's priesthood. He also includes vv 22b, 23 in the Melchizedek insertion. The worldly king of Shalem offers Abraham the tithe (v 20) which he solemnly declines (vv 22b, 23). But וַיִּתֶּן־לוֹ can hardly mean this (v 20). Erbt (*Hebräer*, 62ff.) intervenes even more aggressively. Among other things, he makes Melchizedek into an Amorite priest dwelling at Shechem. <290>

The Jacob Narratives

The Jacob Narratives of JE

An Overview of the Composition of the Jacob Narratives of JE

1. The Jacob-Esau Narratives. Part I. With Isaac.
    a. The birth and maturation of Jacob and Esau—25:21-28 J(E), comments, introduction to 1d.
    b. Jacob purchases the birthright from Esau—25:29-34 E, an old legend.
    [c. Here the narrative of Isaac in Gerar has been inserted by a later hand—26 J, an old legend.]
    d. Jacob obtains Isaac's blessing by deceit and flees—27 JE, an old legend.
2. The Jacob-Laban narratives.
    a. The Bethel legend—28:10-22 JE, extended note, joined here to Jacob's migration to Laban and intended to be continued (4b).
    b. Jacob's arrival at Laban's—29:1-14 J.
    c. Jacob's marriage to Leah and Rachel—29:15-30 E(J).
    d. Birth of Jacob's children—29:31-30:24 JE, comments.
    e. Jacob serves Laban for flocks—30:25-43 J(E), continuation of 3c.
    f. Jacob's flight from Laban and the treaty of Gilead—31:31–32:1 EJ.
    b-f with the exception of d. old legends, performed in very novelistic fashion and woven together as a unit.
3. The Jacob-Esau narratives. Part II. Jacob's return, the continuation of 2f, and, at the same time, of 1d.
    a. The Mahanaim legends.
        α.The cultic legend—32:2-3 E, an old comment.
        β. Jacob's preparations for receiving Esau—32:4-22 JE, the introduction to 3bβ, novelisticly expanded utilizing other elements.
    b. The Penuel legends.
        α. The cultic legend—32:23-33 JE, an old legend, loosely inserted in the context.
        β. Jacob's encounter with Esau—33:1-17 JE, the continuation of 3ab, novelisticly expanded.
4. Jacob in Canaan.
    a. The Shechem narratives.
        α. The cultic legend—33:18-20 E, a comment with no discernible context.
        β. The Dinah narrative—34 JE, an old legend with no relationship to the preceding.
    b. The Bethel legend, part II—35:1-8,14 E, the continuation of 2a and 4ab, at the same time comments concerning the oak of Shechem and Deborah's death: a variety of materials loosely combined.
    c. Benjamin's birth—35:16-20 E, a few old comments.
    d. Reuben's' crime—35:21-22 J, a remnant of an old legend.
    [e. Esau's genealogy—36:9-14 and princes—15-19, genealogy and princes of the Horites—20-28, 29-30, as well as Edom's kings—31-39, probably stem from an independent source.]

In terms of content, the legends fall into the following groups:
    I. The Jacob-Esau narratives.
    II. The Jacob-Laban narratives.
    III. Legends concerning cultic sites Jacob established.
    IV. Narratives concerning Jacob's children, their birth and later fates. <291>

This varied material has been woven into a relatively good unit in its current state. The way the legends grew together can still be discerned in the close or loose interrelationship they now have. The Jacob-Esau accounts have been most firmly fused with those of Jacob and Laban. A "framework" has been formed from the Jacob-Esau legends into which the Jacob-Laban narratives have been inserted. This "legend cycle" has been woven together in the following manner. The end of the first part of the Jacob-Esau narrative recounts Jacob's flight from Esau. But he flees to Laban. Now, the entire Laban narrative follows. At the end of the Laban narrative Jacob flees from Jacob and returns then to Esau. Then follows a second part of the Jacob-Esau narrative. Accordingly, this Jacob-Esau-Laban legend cycle is not a loose combination from the hand of a redactor but an artful composition. A series of allusions (forward and backward) in 27:36, 45; 28:15, 20ff.; 29:12ff.; 30:25, 29-30; 32:5, 11, and especially the conclusion that returns to the beginning, bind the whole together as a unit. The same (originally humorous, then under the influence of more advanced religion more reserved) tone lies over the whole. Most of the narratives are also executed in the same novelistic fashion. The editorial work has not been so thorough, however, as to completely harmonize the narratives with one another. A few rough places have been left around the edges. At first, neither Jacob (31:1ff.) nor Laban (31:43-44) seems to have known that Jacob must necessarily come into Esau's territory when he flees Laban. Only when Laban has left does this new danger dawn on Jacob (32:4ff.). That is, the narrators were concerned with Laban to this point and only now remember Esau. Seen as a whole, this legend cycle is, however, a successful composition accomplished by simple means. This legend cycle must have come into existence in a very ancient period. It was already accessible to J and E in oral or literary tradition. Even apparent connecting passages such as 29:13-14; 32:29 bear the character of advanced age. We probably have an indication that this legend cycle existed in recensions other than the one transmitted to us in 27:45 (Rebekah wants to summon Jacob from Laban when Esau's wrath burns out). This reference seems to indicate a continuation of the account which does not appear subsequently (cf. 31:1ff.). Accordingly, 27:45 probably stems from another, similar legend cycle.

Furthermore, a few cultic legends concerning Bethel, Mahanaim, Penuel, and Shechem have been inserted in this legend cycle. These legends, which treat specific sites, are arranged along the path of Jacob's migrations. The Bethel narrative has a particularly close connection to the whole. The comment is inserted in J as in E into Jacob's migration to Laban, on which Jacob could well have visited Bethel, and both are supplied with new elements from the context. The two agree even in wording. In analogy with the arrangement of the Jacob-Esau narrative, E also offers a continuation of the Bethel narrative. After returning, Jacob visited Bethel a second time and only now actually established it. This continuation makes a modern impression in comparison with the old Bethel legend and will, consequently, be essentially a free composition with the esthetic purpose of strengthening the framework. The other cultic legends concerning Mahanaim, Penuel, and Shechem are included in relation to Jacob's return. As the overview shows, these cultic legends are inserted in the context in such a way that each cultic legend precedes an account of what happened there. A principle becomes apparent here. The Penuel narrative, which originated as an entirely independent narrative, must have stood, nevertheless, as the very old statement in 32:29 J indicates, in such a context already in a very early time.

Finally, narratives concerning Jacob's children were added. The account of their birth (29:31ff.) and the addendum (35:16ff.) are not an ancient legend grown from its own roots, but comments, by nature, unable to stand <292> alone. Instead, they can only be told in another context. But the context into which these birth narratives were inserted in both J and E is the Jacob-Laban narrative (30:25-26). The connection these comments have with the whole is rather close. Subsequently, even in the encounter with Esau, both J and E refer to Jacob's children (31:16, 17, 28, 43; 32:23; 33:1, 2, 5, 6, 13, 14). Now these comments bear several traces of quite advanced age. Accordingly, the whole legend cycle into which they were inserted must trace back to a very old time. On the other hand, the birth narratives point, at the same time, to a continuation. In themselves they are insignificant and first gain significance when specific narratives concerning Jacob's sons are recounted subsequently. It follows that even the accounts of Jacob's sons, that is, narratives such as the ones concerning Dinah, Reuben, Joseph, and Judah were already joined to the legend cycle in the ancient period. The details can no longer be determined. No relationship in content with the Esau-Laban cycle becomes apparent.

Therefore, we can trace the gradual growth of these narratives. First the Jacob-Esau legends were combined, then, also very closely, the Jacob-Laban narratives. Then the two were woven together into a unit through artful composition. The Bethel narrative has a close relationship to this legend cycle, the Penuel narrative a looser relationship. Finally, legends concerning individual sons of Jacob may have also been added. Their birth narrative was itself inserted into the legend cycle. These combinations were certainly not completed in one effort and may have existed in several variations. Gen 27:45 is probably a trace of these variants.

Such combinations must have already been accessible to J and E. Given this complicated development of the whole, there is no purpose in attempting to distinguish the specific hands of individual redactors. It will be very difficult to determine what features of the combinations trace to oral or written tradition.

At any rate, the beginnings of the process reach back to the earliest time accessible to us. The whole was already rather complete in a very ancient period.

The narrative of Isaac in Gerar, which does not fit into the context, and the genealogies of Esau will have been added only very late.

The Jacob narratives have essentially undergone a different fate than those of Abraham. Whereas the Abraham narratives, although also partially arranged in an artful order, remained essentially untouched and retained the form of the individual legend, the Jacob legends were arranged in a specific order in a very early period and were novelisticly shaped to a degree.

For later generations, the main point in the whole Jacob account was Yahweh's grace which guarded him on all his journeys, protected him in all danger, and brought him home from abroad, richly blessed, with two hosts (32:11; Haller, 38).

39. Birth and Maturity of Jacob and Esau 25:21-26a, 27, 28 J (E)

Source criticism. The account, an introduction to the subsequent Jacob-Esau narratives, falls into three parts: (1) the oracle (vv 21-23), (2) the birth (vv 24-26a), and (3) the different vocations of the two (vv 27, 28). The account of the oracle, which constitutes a self-contained unit, belongs to J: יהוה vv 21 twice, 22, 23; עָתַר v 21; and צָעִיר v 23.

Both sources must have recounted the birth. Since this passage (vv 24-26) has a very precise parallel in 38:27-30 J (v 24b parallels 38:27b verbatim), it will belong to J in the essentials. Yet the statement concerning Esau's hairiness should be attributed to E because of 27:11 (אִישׁ שָׂעִר). אַדְמוֹנִי belongs to J, therefore. This analysis is confirmed by the fact that E offers another etymology of Jacob in 27:36 (cf. comments on the text). <293> The comment concerning the vocation of the brothers must also have been recounted in both J and E. יֹדֵעַ צַיִד is a doublet of אִישׁ שָׂדֶה, and אִישׁ תָּם of יֹשֵׁב אֹהָלִים. One may well attribute אִישׁ שָׂדֶה to E because of the immediately following מִן־הַשָּׂדֶה in v 29 (E). On the other hand, J frequently employs the word צַיִד in the subsequent material (cf. 27:3, 5, 7, 19, 25, 30, 31, 33; Procksch, 19). Accordingly, one will also attribute 25:28 to J because of צַיִד and, in analogy with the preceding, assume that R^JE followed J on the whole.

I. 21-23 *Rebekah's pregnancy and the oracle.* **21** A long infertility of the mother before the birth of the child is a favored legend motif. How passionately the child is desired! This child is a gift of God from the very beginning. It is no wonder that so much becomes of him later (cf. above on 18:11). The word לְנֹכַח "in relation to" can be explained according to Frankenberg (CGA [1901], 697) by a practice, also attested in Arabic, of referring at the sanctuary to the one for whom or concerning whom one prays (cf. also Isa 37:14ff.). Concerning וַיֵּעָתֶר לוֹ see §121f. **22** But the children (a less specific expression than תוֹמִם in v 24) already struggled in the womb. The idea is that it was so much the nature of these two to fight that they could not even keep the peace in the womb! Apollodorus (*Biblioth.* 2.2.1) recounts similarly of Acrisios and Proitos. Sons of Aba, king of Argos, twins, they struggled already in the womb. הִתְרֹצֵץ > רצץ "to beat each other" is a strong expression. LXX ἐσκίρτω (Luk 1:41) seems to have though of the root רוץ. Rebekah, horrified at the unusual proceedings, goes (as ancient women usually did in such cases) to the oracle. Sievers (2:300-301) wants to place v 24b ("there were twins in her womb") before v 22, but would ruin the coherence of the passage in this way. The narrator prefigures the reason for the unusual movements, but Rebekah does not yet know it and is all the more amazed. If she had known it, she would not have inquired of the oracle. Our text is further supported by the parallel in 38:37. דָּרַשׁ is a technical term for inquiring of the oracle. The site of the oracle is not mentioned. The narrator from whom this passage is taken will have previously mentioned the name of a famed oracle site in the vicinity of Isaac's dwelling at the time (probably Beerlahairoi, 25:11b, or Beersheba, 28:10). We do not discover, unfortunately, the manner in which the oracle was obtained. Nowhere else do the patriarchal legends presume a regular service at a Yahweh sanctuary. It is a harsh anachronism here, therefore (Haller, 77). Rebekah's statement "If so, why then I?" hardly makes any sense. Ball, Kitttel, Sievers (2:307), and Kautzsch³ read with Pesh לָמָה חַיָּה אָנֹכִי "Why do I live?" Frankenberg (CGA [1901], 697) reads לָמָּה זֶה אֶחְיֶה "Why then should I live?" (cf. 27:46). It suits the context much better to read אָנָה לִי (has befallen me) for אנכי. She perceives a "prefiguration" of things to come in this event and asks what may be foretold. The belief that coming great events are announced ahead of time in horrible or remarkable "signs" can be found through all antiquity. Concerning prefigurations in the OT see Stade, *Bibl. Theol.*, 101-102. The legends like to report such signs. Hints of coming great and mighty things can be found in the small and insignificant (cf. comments on 37:5-11; 38:27-30).

23 On the oracle concerning the yet unborn see comments on 16:11f. <294> God responds, of course, in elevated language, in verse. The first is a "heptameter" or, if one strikes וּשְׁנֵי (or with Kittel יִפָּרֵדוּ), a "double trimeter," the second a "double trimeter." The oracle always has poetic form in Israel. The peculiar sign signifies something peculiar: two peoples are about to come into existence. And these peoples, although brothers (and thus, one would expect, similar to one another and at peace with one another) will "separate" (become divided, different, cf. v 27). It is especially remarkable, however, that the older will serve the younger (anarthrous רַב and צָעִיר in poetic style, §126h). In the earliest Israelite legal practice, the oldest brother inherits from his father and thus becomes his brother's lord. Details concerning this are given in the comments on vv 29-34. The reverse takes place with Jacob and Esau. The younger became the lord. The same or similar notion is also a favored legend and fairy-tale motif elsewhere, not just in J (contra Luther in Meyer, *Israeliten*, 128; cf. the stories of Joseph, David, 1 Sam 16, etc.; in German, e.g., in the legend of the four children of Haymon; a Polynesian parallel in Cheyne, 356). The legends repeatedly bring up the theme of the source of this remarkable situation in relation to Jacob and Esau. J responds to this question (25:21-23), "The divine oracle decreed it concerning the still unborn." E responds (25:29-34), "Jacob bought Esau's birthright." JE responds (27), "Jacob appropriated the preferred blessing by deceit." These three accounts are variants in the final analysis, then. The legend of the oracle concerning the still unborn understands the two difficult children as the ancestors of the two constantly struggling "peoples," Israel and Edom. Therefore, since Jacob and Esau originally have another meaning, it does not belong, at least not in this form, to the foundation of the Jacob-Esau legends (cf. comments on 27). Hos 12:4 may presume an older variant of the legend (cf. p. 290).

II. **24-26a** Wondrous things mirroring the future also occur at their birth. **24** For תוֹמִם Sam reads תאֹמִם (cf. 38:27). **25** Our text no longer offers an explanation of the name עֵשָׂו which will originally have stood there. Instead there are two allusions: (1) to אֱדוֹם and (2) to שֵׂעִיר. Edom is the name of the well-known people south of the Dead Sea (concerning Edom, see Buhl, *Gesch. der Edomiter* [1893]; Baudissin, RE³ 5:162ff.; Nöldeke, *Enc. Bibl.*, s.v. "Edom"; Meyer, *Israeliten*, 337ff.). Egyptian sources from ca. 1230 first mention Edom. According to later tradition Seir is the name of its land and mountain (36:8-9; Deut 2:12, 22; Josh 24:4; Ezek 35:2ff.), according to older comments the name of an aboriginal people which, according to Gen 36:20ff., where its tribes and clans are listed, was the oldest population of the land. They were Horites (Deut 2:12, 22), also mentioned in the Amarna correspondence (Winckler) 181:26 and in Egyptian sources from ca. 1180 (Meyer, *Israeliten*, 337). The legends consider Esau, a figure of unknown origins, the patriarch of the people Edom related to them in the way the figure Jacob is related to the people of Israel (cf. comments concerning him at the conclusion of chap. 27). The legends, then, identify three originally distinct figures: the fictive ancestor of the peoples of Edom and Seir and the legend figure Esau. Esau is Edom (36:8, 19); Esau is the father of Edom (36:9), Esau alternates with Edom or is employed for Edom in elevated, archaic sounding language (Jer 49:8, 10; cf. vv 17, 22; Obad 6, 8, 9, 18, 19, 20; cf. vv. 1, 8; Mal 1:2, 3; cf. v 4); Or the Edomites are called "sons of Esau" (Deut 2:4ff.; 1 Macc 5:3, 65); The genealogies consider the tribes and clans of Edom Esau's descendants (36:4ff.). Similarly, Seir is employed as an archaic, <295> poetic name for Edom

(Num 24:18; 2 Chron 25:11; cf. v 19; 2 Kgs 14:7). The most precise usage is that of 36:9: Esau, father of Edom, on the mountains of Seir. For more on this subject, see chap. 27.

The legend offers humorous glosses for the names Edom and Seir. The reddish-brown skin of the Edomites was amusing. The people who recount these legends will have been yellowish themselves (cf. the color of the Canaanites on the Egyptian images, Rehms, HW 288-89). אְדֹם is reddish-brown, a brownish-bronze (1 Sam 16:12; cf. P. Haupt, *Biblische Liebeslieder*, 57-58, 123). And, even more mischievously, people were amused that a real Seirite felt like a fur coat. He is as hairy as a goat (27:16, 22). These physical advantages of the beloved brother were used with great pleasure to explain his name. These are neighborly kindnesses. The humorous hues of the narrative have been disputed. Amazing! How can one overlook the facetious hyperbole of a statement such as that an infant boy looked like a fur coat? It cannot yet be determined with certainty whether, as has often been hypothesized (so recently, Meyer, *Israeliten*, 278), there is a relationship between the names and legends of עֵשָׂו and the hero Οὔσωος of the Phoenician legend (in Philo, *Bybl. fr.* 2:7-8. in Müller, *Fragm. hist. graec.* 3:566), who appears as a hunter and an estranged brother of [Σα]μημροῦμος or Ὑψουράνιος. The hypothesis of Prášek (*Forschungen zur Gesch. d. Altertums* 2:32ff.) and Cheyne (*Encl. Bibl.*, s.v. "Esau") that Usoos is the eponym of Palatiryos = *Usû* near Tyre is disputed by Meyer (*Israeliten*, 278n.2) since this assumption would not completely explain the information about him given in Philo. **26** The explanation of the name Jacob from עָקֵב, "heel," is delightfully blunt. When he appeared in the light of day, he held his brother's heel in his hand. He begrudged him the status of firstborn! This fittingly prefigures what is to come. E's similar legend motif appears in 38:27-30. Concerning the name יעקב see the introduction ¶4:10. The alteration of the number in ויקרא (v 26) and ויקראו (v 25) is noteworthy. LXX, Pesh, read singular, Sam plural. Hos 12:4—he had already deceived עָקַב his brother in the womb—assumes a tradition which recounted the birth narrative somewhat more crudely. It may have narrated how Jacob cunningly pressed ahead at birth (cf. 38:2ff.). Jer 9:3 contains an allusion to this or the other Jacob narratives (cf. Staerk, *Studien* 2:12).

III. **27-28** *The vocations of the two.* The oracle "they will separate" (v 23) begins to be fulfilled. The following material describes the characters of two different professions. But it cannot be said whether two different peoples were originally intended—Esau a hunting people, and Jacob a shepherd people—whether the legend may have had two different classes of the same people in view, such as the Targi divide into a hunting, fighting, and raiding nobility and a less significant shepherd class (Fritz Ohle, "Aus dem Lande der Sahara," *Zeitgeist* 18/1 [1904]), or whether the figures of Jacob and Esau are of an entirely different origin and may have originally been semidivine heroes. Of course the Israelite legend thinks here of the peoples Israel and Edom. Surely the following comments that Israel preferred Esau and Rebekah preferred Isaac are not to be interpreted ethnographically, but purely novelisticly. Concerning ידע, "to understand something," see Baumann, ZAW 28:27. שָׂדֶה is the free open land where the wild animals, the wild plants, and the hunter are at home, in contrast to the inhabited regions (cf. Gesenius-Buhl[14]). שָׂדֶה refers to Esau's home in v 29; 27:3,5; to the territory of Edom in 32:4; Judg 5:4. The legend gives a <296> naive reason for Isaac's preference for Esau. Ball and Kittel cautiously prefer לְפִיו. Subsequent material repeatedly assumes Jacob's special relationship to his mother and her family. One detects the maternal blood in the clever practices of the archrogue. In common OT usage, which presumes an elevated piety, אִישׁ תָּם would signify the ideal of the "morally and ethically blameless man." An older, profane ideal underlies this ancient legend. The shepherd praises the tranquil man who remains steadfastly and duly with his tents and flocks as "blameless" and looks with distaste on the restless hunter out there. In the same manner, the Israelite farmer later looks down on the "worthless fellows" אֲנָשִׁים רֵיקִים, who abandon house and home (Judg 9:4; 11:3), the אַנְשֵׁי דָמִים (opposite of תָּם; Prov 29:10). Of the two vv 27 and 28, v 28 introduces the narrative of Isaac's deceit. The account of the purchase of the birthright (vv 29-34) has been interposed.

40. Jacob Purchases Esau's Birthright 25:29-34 E

The source is E since 27:36 (E) is cited.

The legend asks how Esau's birthright was transferred to Jacob and responds, "Jacob bought it from Esau for a trifle." The legend was, therefore, originally an independent narrative. The motif of the purchase occupies the same position as the motif of deceit in chap. 27. Purchase and deceit are not so different to the old narrators. Whoever has a desire to trade has a desire to deceive. In order to make this unequal trade comprehensible, the legend employs as a motif the characteristic difference of two types—the hunter and the shepherd. The hunter lives from hand to mouth. He slays the animal he finds. He often returns home exhausted and without prey and must then go hungry. Today, however, he has something to eat, so he does not think of tomorrow (cf. Holzinger, 179). One may compare the description of the hunter and raider class of the Targi in the Sahara: "The Targi does not worry about what may happen tomorrow. He lives only for today. He never gathers reserves. A bad year is enough to throw the whole land into the most horrible famine." (Fr. Ohle, *Zeitgeist* 18/1 [1904].) The old Arabs also considered the professional hunter for the most part to be "a poor wretch who must take up the bow because he has no herds. If he is not able to skin fresh game for his sons, they will hunger" (Jacob, 114-15). The shepherd, however, is wiser: He does not slaughter animals, but raises them. Occasionally he also farms a little, has bread and vegetables. Therefore, he always has something to eat. He is accustomed to thinking not only of today but also of tomorrow and the day after tomorrow. Therefore, the shepherd Jacob is superior to the hunter Esau.

V **30** portrays the hungry Esau with drastic humor. He wants to "gulp down" "the red stuff, the red stuff there" (more precisely "the brown stuff, the brown stuff"). Why does he not name the lintel soup by name? He probably does not know that they are lintels. (Or did he forget the name in his hunger? Or should one read הָאָדֹם = Arab. *idâmun*, a condiment with bread, LXX ἕψημα—it consists of cucumbers, melons, leeks, onions, and garlic [Num 11:15]?). The mischievous legend alludes to the name of the people Edom and perceives in it a reference to the greed and stupidity of its ancestor. But the explicit statement עַל־כֵּן קָרָא־שְׁמוֹ אֱדוֹם, which states nothing more that any perceptive reader would understand, will be a gloss. The name Edom appears outside the gloss in 32:4 only in the genealogies of Gen 36 (Sievers 2:308; Meyer, *Israeliten*, 328n.3). "The figure of the hunter, who falls tired and hungry into <297> the tent and reaches for the first food he can find to satisfy his burning hunger is appealing to Germanic sensibilities, odious to the Hebrew" (Haller, 103; an ethnographically significant observation).

31 Jacob takes advantage of the situation. The narrator has no impression of ignobility or selfishness (Dillmann), but of cleverness and farsightedness. Jacob already thinks of the day when his father will die and is able to gain by skill the advantage nature denied him. According to Hos 12:4 (cf. comments on Gen 25:26) Jacob had already cheated his brother out of the status of firstborn. Concerning מְכֹרָה see §48i. בַּיּוֹם means "now, immediately." **32** "I go to die," that is "I must, after all (finally) die." "This was also a favorite excuse for committing a folly among the ancient Arabs" (G. Jacob, *Altarab. Parallelen zum A.T.*, 6). The element portrays Esau's imprudence. **33** But the cautious Jacob (who as a worldly man does not trust people) makes him swear first. The narrator, normally very sparing with words, adds explicitly that he sold Jacob the birthright. He wants to emphasize that with this the trade was concluded. Thus Esau forfeited the birthright once and for all. **34** Only now do we learn what this dish Esau desired so much actually was. It was—lentils! And for this the birthright! וַיֵּשְׁתְּ is probably an addition. "When the original only has one eating, one of the editors will surely be compassionate enough to give him something to drink as well" (cf. Wellhausen, *Text der Bücher Samuelis*, 25). The final words, "he ate, stood up, went away, and did not think about the birthright again," is supposed to portray Esau's imprudence once again. Now he is well-fed once again. Therefore, he was unconcerned for the future.

The most important question for understanding the Jacob-Esau legends, but especially this legend, is what the "primogeniture" may have meant. "Primogeniture" is a legal term, specifically of inheritance law. According to the ancient Israelite viewpoint, the firstborn was considered the best and the most competent among his brothers (49:3; Deut 21:17). This view is the source of the cultic practice of offering the firstborn, the best, to the deity. Metaphorically, Israel is called Yahweh's firstborn, that is, the people most noble, most majestic, most beloved by Yahweh (Exod 4:22; Jer 31:9). The earliest Israelite law to be deduced from the legends advantages the firstborn. The property remains undivided within the family. But the firstborn replaces the father and becomes "his brother's lord" (27:29). "The sons of his mother" and "his fathers fall down before him" (27:29; 49:8). This pattern of inheritance, which still often exists among German farmers (l'Houet, 65) while Babylonian law (Hammurabi ¶167) already prescribes the division of the estate among the brothers, was still valid in Israel in the historical period in the monarchy. The firstborn son succeeds his father and the brother becomes his servant. Later, then, it seems, it became practice that, at his death, the father determined the sole heir. The legend in Gen 27 already presumes this practice (cf. also 48:13ff.; 1 Kgs 1:30). Then inheritance law called for the firstborn to receive two-thirds of the total estate (Deut 2:15-17; cf. Rauh, *Hebr. Familienrecht*, 37, 40-41). When the old legend speaks of Esau's lost birthright, then, it means that he was actually due prominence above his brother but that he forfeited it. The sense in which it understood this prominence is not clear to us. The image of the birthright was then applied to relationships between the nations (cf. 2 Sam 19:44 where <298> "Israel" claims the birthright in relation to Judah). This motif sounds again in the legends of Perez and Zerah (38:28-30), of Manasseh and Ephraim (48:13-19), and in the blessing of Jacob (49). The birthright of a people always signifies the same thing, namely, that it has become mightier and richer than its brothers. The Jacob-Esau legends have been understood in this sense when they have been interpreted in relation to Israel and Edom. The birthright has been transferred from Esau to Jacob. This means that, although Esau-Edom is the older people, it is now far inferior to its brother Jacob-Israel in might and wealth. In this case, however, the narrators count Jacob as one of themselves and joyously report their own prominence. This situation is the source of the earthy, powerful humor which sounds through these narratives. The legend ridicules the stupid Esau who sold his entire future for a lintel dish and rejoices over the clever Jacob in whom the narrators recognize their own image. The legends belong, then, to the earliest, "earthy" type (cf. introduction ¶4:7). It is no wonder the concepts of right and wrong in these most ancient narratives differ from ours. One should simply accept this and not transform the cunning Jacob into a Christian. Nor should one measure and judge him by Christian standards or take offense at the fact that these narratives are full of humor.

Interpreters have often failed to understand the old legend by introducing spiritual ideas into it. The "birthright" for which Jacob outwitted Esau was the blessing of Abraham understood as the right to the promised salvation (Dillmann, Franz Delitzsch). But the old legend knows nothing of this. Only the latest redaction equates the blessing of Isaac and the blessing of Abraham (28:4 P), while these two blessings had nothing to do with one another in the old legends. The mixture of a later insertion which speaks of spiritual benefits and the ancient narrative which very naively speaks of wit and deceit creates a shrill dissonance. But the old legend is not guilty. For more concerning the humor in the Jacob narratives see the commentary on chap. 27.

41. Isaac and the People of Gerar 26:1-33 J^r

Source and composition. The source says יהוה (vv 2, 12, 22, 28, 29) and is, therefore, J. Additional linguistic evidences for J are טוֹבַת מַרְאֶה (v 7; cf. 24:16), הִשְׁקִיף (v 8), הֶעְתִּיק (v 22; cf. 12:8), קָרָא בְּשֵׁם יהוה (v 25), נָא (v 28), and בְּרוּךְ יהוה (v 29; cf. 24:31). E has the same account in reference to Abraham in 21:22ff. J recounts the same event once more in 12:10ff. and in 21:25ff. Since 12:10ff. and probably also 21:25ff. stem from J^b, the source of 26 could be J^a. Consideration of the context in which the account in 26 now stands in J, however, shows that it cannot belong to the dominant strand of J. It disrupts the Jacob-Esau narrative. In 26 Rebekah is still a young woman and Jacob and Esau have not yet been born, let alone grown up. In order to eliminate these difficulties, it has been assumed that the account in 26 was originally before 25:22-23 in J and was only secondarily displaced here by a redactor (cf. Wellhausen, *Composition*³, 28). It is more likely that 26 was inserted here from another, related, book of legends. The passage is printed above in the font employed for J^a.

In its current state, the chapter makes the impression of a mosaic (Franz Delitzsch). This character results not only from a few additions (cf. below) because even after their removal the chapter remains rather motley. It contains five parts: (1) Isaac's move to Gerar because of a divine revelation (vv 1-6); (2) Rebekah's adventure in Gerar (vv 7-11); (3) Isaac's wealth and his move from Gerar (vv 12-17a); (4) well disputes (vv 17b-22); (5) the treaty in Beersheba (vv 23-33). The variants (mentioned above), which form a tighter unity, demonstrate that originally nos. 2 and 3, the events in <299> Gerar, and likewise nos. 4 and 5, narratives concerning wells in the vicinity of Gerar, belong together. Our narrator separated nos. 2 and 3, originally a coherent narrative, for reasons presented in the discussion of Gen 20 (pp. 223-25). Nos. 4 and 5 are still interrelated. No. 4 speaks of strife with Gerar, no. 5 of the treaty which brought the strife to an end. The narrator felt that the various narratives did not form a proper unit and, therefore, provided a binding thread. Consequently, he prefixed a divine revelation (lacking in the variants) in no. 1. God appears to Isaac, asks him to remain in Gerar, and promises to protect and bless him. The subsequent material then shows how this promise was fulfilled. The endangered honor of the wife is preserved. Yahweh blesses his field so that he becomes wealthy. He allows him to find wells everywhere so that the people of Gerar must finally enter into a treaty with him. This strand is, admittedly, rather thin. In the account of the danger of the ancestress, the notion of Yahweh's protection is not explicitly apparent. The passage has not, therefore, become a completely cohesive composition.

Sievers (2:308ff.), who attributes the chap. from v 23 on to other sources, has, however, overlooked the relationship at hand. The covenant follows the dispute; the wells which belong undoubtedly to Isaac came after those in dispute. In addition, Abimelech's speech (vv 28-29) makes explicit reference to the preceding. Isaac is and remains Yahweh's blessed (vv 3, 12, 29; יהוה עִמְּךָ v 23 ‖ וְאֶהְיֶה יִמְּךָ v 3). Isaac accuses (v 27) the Gerarites of driving away his servants (vv 16, 19-21) and they attempt to gloss over the events (v 29).

I. **1-6** *Isaac moves to Gerar.* V **1a**α belongs, as the variant in 12:10 demonstrates, to the following legend as its introduction (contra Dillmann, who attributes to clause to E). V 1aβ,γ refers back to 12:10 J^b, and stems, therefore, from R^J. **1b** Isaac will have previously resided in southern Canaan, perhaps in Beerlahairoi (25:11). Vv **2-5** have been extensively expanded by a later hand (Dillmann, etc.). Evidence for this conclusion includes the following: "All of these lands" (vv 3b, 4) in reference to the regions of Canaan is later (hyperbolic) diction (1 Chron 13:2; 2 Chron 11:23). Furthermore, according to the context, God promises the possession of Gerar, specifically, with the statement, "I will give you all of these lands." The old legend, however, is not at all of the opinion in the subsequent material that Gerar later belonged to Israel. Instead, Gerar is an allied, but independent city. The addition is further discernible in that it refers back to the Abraham narrative (vv 3, 5). הִתְבָּרֵךְ in v 4 (22:18, J וְנִבְרְכוּ) is characteristic. In v 5 the expression שָׁמַר מִשְׁמֶרֶת, originally a technical term for the service of the priests in the sanctuary, further points to a later period. The list "commandments, statutes, and laws" is deuteronomistic. The idea that Abraham fulfilled so many commandments does not suit the spirit of the old legend, but manifests later (legal) piety. The final indication of the late origin of this addition is עֵקֶב אֲשֶׁר (as in 22:18). Only vv 2aα, 3a are the property of the original narrator. Yahweh appears to Isaac and commands him to remain in Gerar. Then Yahweh will be with him and <300> bless him. The continuation in vv 12, 28, 29 indicates that this promise (vv 3ab) also belongs to J.

2b "Take up residence in the land of which I will tell you," presumes Isaac has not yet arrived in his new homeland and is, therefore "incompatible with vv 3a and 1b" (Dillmann) The statement recalls in form 22:2b E. It could be, then, a fragment from J. In this case, it would probably have been spoken in Beersheba where, according to 46:1-4, E recounted an appearance of God to Isaac. V 2aβ, "do not go to Egypt," may also belong to E (Dillmann). A later editor could not let pass God's promise to Isaac to bless him—a promise which in the original context refered only to the blessing in farming and discovering water sources—without inserting the much more precious blessing he knew from the Abraham narratives (15:5; 22:16ff.; 12:3). For הָאֵל in vv 3, 4, Sam reads הָאֵלֶּה.

II. **7-11** *Rebekah's adventure.* The account is compared with its variants, 12:10ff. J^b and 20 E, above (pp. 223-24). There, too, the character of the version at hand is established. It attempts to eliminate the objectionable features of the original account and to turn everything to the glory of the ancestor. Remarkably, the narrator regarded adultery as objectionable, but not Isaac's lie (Haller, 113). **7** שָׁאַל לְ means "to ask about something" (32:20). Sam, LXX, and Pesh add היא after אִשְׁתִּי (Ball, Kittel). Characteristically for this recension, too, only "the men of the city" ask about the patriarch's wife, while in the other recension the king himself desires her. This element is a little more respectable and surely secondary.

8 The—very idyllic—scene is probably to be envisioned as follows. Isaac and Abimelech live across from each other on a narrow alley where one can see from the window of one house into the other (cf. the similar scene in 2 Sam 11:2). This motif is the only concrete element in the otherwise very bland recension and is not a bad device. וְהִנֵּה וַיִּרְא portrays the surprise. The element מְצַחֵק is derived from the name Isaac. One is to imagine that they caressed in such a way that the marital relationship of the two was unmistakable. Regarding the expression צָחַק see 39:14, 17. Modesty accounts for the fact that the couple are said to have caressed inside the house (cf. comments on 9:21, following Haller, 100). **10** The statement assumes that touching a married woman is a serious crime. Contact with a virgin is not so bad. If necessary, one can work it out later with her relatives. Concerning כִּמְעַט שָׁכַב see §106p. Concerning וְהֵבֵאתָ see §112h.

III. **12-17a** *Isaac's wealth and departure from Gerar.* **12-14a** This narrator explains Isaac's wealth, a feature necessary to the legend, differently than the variants. It is acquired by farming and Yahweh's blessing. Farming, <301> rarely explicitly attributed to the patriarchs in Genesis (30:14; 37:7), appears here as a particular exception, but is also occasionally undertaken by nomads (analogies in Dillmann). Therefore, it does not exactly depart from the image of the patriarchs, especially since the "city" Gerar would not have been possible if fields had not been in the vicinity. Here the element, however, is only a means for the narrator to avoid a dilemma: he must explain Isaac's wealth somehow. Concerning Bedouin life and the patriarchs' farming compare the introduction ¶4:2, 5. "Hundredfold" harvest is an immense exaggeration. Today, on the fertile Plain of Sharon, wheat produces eightfold on average and barley fifteenfold (Benzinger², 142). Regarding the participle in הָלוֹךְ וְגָדֵל see §113u. Yet one could also read וְגָדֵל with Ball. **14b-17a** Isaac's departure from Gerar is motivated here by the envy of the Philistines. Vv 15 and 18 stem from R^J. The verses are intended to harmonize the Abraham narrative, according to which Abraham dug these wells, and the subsequent Isaac narrative, which attributes them to Isaac. The editor must, therefore, have read in his text about the same wells in the Abraham narrative (cf. comments on 21:25). The insertion has a similar purpose, then, to that of vv 1aβ,γ and probably stems from the same hand, R^J. The means he devised is not unskillful since the context already reported the envy of the Philistines. The insertion betrays itself through (1) its reference to an earlier narrative and (2) the fact that in the subsequent account that wells are not redug, but simply newly dug (cf. Wellhausen, *Composition*³, 20-21). **18** Hebr reads בִּימֵי while Sam, LXX, and Vulg read עבדי (Ball, Kittel).

IV. **17b-22** *Disputes over wells.* The narrator takes the names of the disputed wells, Esek, Sitnah, Rehoboth, from the old legend. **17b** The valley of Gerar in the old legend is the *Wâdi Ĝerûr*. Esek (not yet rediscovered) lies in this *wâdi*. Thence, Isaac moves farther away from Gerar northward to Sitnah (according to Palmer, *Wüstenwanderung Israels*, 297, the *wâdi esh-Schutein*, northeast of *er-Ruhêbe*, but better sought south of *er-Ruhêbe*), then to Rehoboth (equated with *er-Ruhêbe*). An etymological legend has been developed from the names of the wells: "quarrel," "enmity," "open spaces." A dispute over a well is easily comprehensible given the circumstances of the steppe. Water is very precious, for on it depends the life of the plants, animals, and people. Especially when "the spring pasture withers and the pools of rainwater have dried up, the tribe must stop in the vicinity of a well from which it watered its flocks" (Jacob, 41). Consequently, disputes about wells will have been very common in the accounts of the nomads. Such an account of a dispute over water can be found in Stumme, *Märchen der Berbern*, 62. <302> Whoever finds a well, and especially a well with living (i.e., spring) water, perceives it as a special divine mercy. Characteristically, Isaac acquiesces every time. He is as accommodating as Abraham (13:8ff.) and avoids a struggle like Jacob (27:43; 31:20ff.; 33:1-2) **21** LXX reads וַיַּחְפֹּר יִצְחָק מִשָּׁם וַיַּעְתֵּק (cf. Ball). **22** Regarding the accentuation of רְבוּ see §72l.

V. **23-33** *Treaty of Beersheba*. **23** Now Isaac moves, once again in a northerly direction, to Beersheba. *Bîr es-Seba'* (equated with Beersheba) lies at an altitude 85m lower than *er-Ruhêbe* (=Rehoboth; cf. the map by Fischer and Guthe). The narrator assumes that Beersheba lies at a higher altitude (עָלָה). But since he also confuses Gerar with the Philistine city of Gerar (cf. above pp. 218-19), an error can be attributed to him here, too. **24, 25a** In Beersheba Yahweh appears to him, promises to bless him, and Isaac builds him an altar there. This passage is an insertion: the altar cannot be set up before the tent; the natural sequence is, rather, the reverse. The legend of Beersheba in its original form bases the sacredness of the site on the fact that the ancestor took an oath there. The appearance of Yahweh (vv 24, 25a) has the same purpose and, therefore, disrupts what follows. The editor betrays his later time by recalling the Abraham narrative (as in the insertion in vv 3b-5) and understanding the blessing, not like the old legend in reference to the discovery of water, but in reference to something broader, higher. The editor, probably the same as the editor of vv 3b-5, imitates especially 26:3a in the blessing (v 24) and 12:8 in the account (v 25a). The removal of the insertion greatly improves the coherence of the passage. V **25b** prepares for v 32. According to the context, Abimelech and Isaac did not know about this new well.

26-31 The covenant with Abimelech. To this point, Abimelech has not permitted Isaac very many privileges and has driven him from his legal property. But this did not harm Isaac. Yahweh let him find new wells again and again. Thus Abimelech recognizes that Isaac is "blessed by Yahweh." This notion that Yahweh's blessing can be shown especial-ly in finding wells bears the color of the place (the steppe) and the time (antiquity). Thus Abimelech takes pains to establish a good relationship with such a blessed one. Here, too, as in E (21:23), the notion that Isaac's descendants will one day be much mightier and will then be bound by this oath can be heard. **26** אֲחֻזַּת is a form like נְלָיָה (Dillmann). מֵרֵעַ "friend" (for the etymology, cf. Gesenius-Buhl[14]) is the title of the trusted coun-selor of the kings (2 Sam 15:37; 16:16; 1 Kgs 4:5; 1 Chron 27:33), as also later among the Persians, under <303> Alexander the Great, among the Seleucids and Lagides (cf. W. Grimm in *Kurzgef. exeget. Handbuch zu den Apokryphen* [1853] on 1 Macc 2:18), and perhaps already among the Egyptians (where *rḫ śtn* seems to mean "acquaintance of the king"), and in the Amarna correspondence (Winckler 181:11; Knidtzon 288:11, where *ruḫi šarri* has this sense and could be formed on the analogy of the Egyptian title), and is thus a title attested throughout Near Eastern high civilization. **28** LXX, Pesh, and Vulg have only one of the words בֵּינֵינוּ and בֵּינוֹתֵינוּ (Ball, Kittel). According to Sievers (2:311) בֵּינֵי is used of entities understood collectively, בֵּינוֹת of two parties considered separately and, therefore, בֵּינֵינוּ וּבֵינֶךָ is a gloss on בֵּינוֹתֵינוּ. **29** Concerning תַעֲשֶׂה with *sere* see §75hh. According to **30, 31** the covenant ceremony consisted of two parts: (1) a common meal in the evening and (2) the oath on the following morning. These two elements occur in the reverse order in 31:53-54. Unfortunately we hear nothing of the rituals executed. They are assumed to be known. Vv **32, 33** are intended to explain the name Beer-sheba as "oath well" and, at the same time, to show why this well remained to Isaac. Now, when there exists a treaty with Gerar, the people of Gerar do not dare to touch Isaac's property. If the text is correct, it should certainly be pronounced שְׁבָעָה. The narrator thinks that *šebu'a* later became *šeba'* (Reuß). But it may be that one should read שֶׁבַע and understand it in the same sense. The rabbis, with no sense for the context of the legend, read *šib'a* "seven" following 21:28ff.

General Remarks concerning the Account of the Treat at Beersheba

1. *Variants.* The account is preserved in three variants: in E 21:22-24, 27, 31; in Jᵇ 21:25, 26, 28, 29, 30, 32, 33; and as a supplement in J ("Jʳ") 26:17b, 19-23, 25b-33. A fourth variant is presumed by E (46:1ff.; cf. comments on the passage). The variants agree on the major point that a treaty was made between the ancestor and Gerar at Beersheba and in many details. There is also agreement in diction: אֱלֹהִים עִמְּךָ (21:22 E) and יהוה עִמְּךָ (26:28 Jʳ); the clauses in 21:23 E and in 26:29 Jʳ; עַל-אֹדוֹת הַבְּאֵר אֲשֶׁר (26:32 Jʳ) and עַל-אֹדוֹת בְּאֵר]וֹת[הַמַּיִם אֲשֶׁר (21:25 Jᵇ). The variants have a complicated interrelationship. Now they differ from one another; now they agree; each of the variants has its peculiarities. E offers (as far as we can see) only a poor conclusion to the narrative. He omitted the other wells which may have lost interest for the later period. In contrast, he preserved an old element by not calling Abimelech a Philistine (Wellhausen, *Composition*³, 18). On the other hand, he agrees with Jʳ in explaining Beersheba as "oath well" and in linking this account with the other concerning the ancestor's stay in Gerar. Finally, he also has an element in common with Jᵇ: Both call the ancestor Abraham, not Isaac. In contrast, the second variant of E, presumed in 46:1ff., derived the site from Isaac, as does Jʳ. Jʳ and Jᵇ were very similar in overall structure: after several wells continue to be disputed, they finally made the treaty in Beersheba; according to both, Gerar is a Philistine city; both emphasize that Beersheba belongs to the ancestor, not to Gerar. On the other hand, they differ in details: Jʳ oath well, <304> Jᵇ seven well; Jʳ Isaac, Jᵇ Abraham; Jʳ associates both narratives with Gerar, Jᵇ separates them and recounts the first in relation to Pharaoh. We may see this transfer to Pharaoh as a young element in Jᵇ (cf. above p. 224). On the other hand, the fact the he still clearly knows that Beersheba is a sacred site is an old element in Jᵇ. He even knows the tamarisk and the name of the local numen *'el 'olam*. But Jʳ, too, has preserved a characteristic element in the name of the "friend" Ahuzzath. It can be inferred from this state of affairs that the E variant is generally younger than those of Jʳ and Jᵇ. At the same time, this passage also makes it

clear that the points of contact between the three sources cannot be explained, as often assumed, by literary dependence, but by the relationship between the traditions.

2. *Original form of the legend.* The legend is very colorless even in the earlier variants J^r and J^b. Either it was originally much richer—then it must have also known something concrete about Pichol and Ahuzzath; or—as seems more likely—it was only a somewhat embellished "comment" (cf. introduction ¶3:22), a local tradition from Beersheba—then the figures Pichol and Ahuzzath must have had there proper setting in other legends.

3. *Original meaning.* The two legends of Gerar mirror, it seems, historical circumstances. The second legend of the treaty at Beersheba especially seems to contain historical material. The following is involved. The legends treat the relationships of the sons of "Abraham" or "Isaac" with Gerar. The former are understood as nomads, the latter dwell in a city and have an organized state with a king and his "friends" and field commander. The former were originally the weaker and in the early period were once guests in Gerar and its environs. There were misunderstandings and finally an eternal covenant. The descendants of the fathers are—the legend wants to make this clear—bound to this covenant even now that they have become much stronger than Gerar. Several wells in the vicinity are in dispute between the two parties. Beersheba, however, as two of the variants emphasize, does not belong to Gerar but to "us." At any rate, these political circumstances belong in a very early period, in the period when Israel's ancestors dwelt in tents in the steppe between Canaan and Egypt. This ancient origin of the tradition also explains the fact that it is so poorly preserved. Nothing more is left of Pichol and Ahuzzath than their names and "Gerar" has been confused with the Philistine Gerar not far from the coast. At the same time, the account interprets the names of the wells as "dispute," "quarrel," and "broad place," "oath" or "seven well" in terms of the ancient events, and still explains the holiness of the site Beersheba. According to the patriarchal legends Beersheba was a very ancient holy site. It was still in bloom in Amos' time (Amos 5:5; 8:14) and was a famed pilgrimage and oath site (cf. also 1 Kgs 19:3). According to the legends, the sacred symbol beside the well there was a tamarisk or asherah (cf. above p. 233). Not far distant was a bush (cf. above p. 228). The cultic name was *'el 'olam* (p. 233).

42. Jacob Deceives Isaac for the Blessing 27 JE

Source analysis. It is likely from the outset that the chapter is a composite of J and E because both sources presume this account in subsequent material (32:4-22; 33:1-16; 35:3, 7). A chain of variants evident in the chapter confirms this analysis (Wellhausen, *Composition*^{3}, 32ff.) despite Eerdman's (46ff.) incomprehensible objection. The starting point is the chief distinguishing characteristic that according to v 16 Jacob wraps himself in goatskins in order to deceive Isaac, while according to v 15 he clothes himself in Esau's clothing to the same purpose. Corresponding to the first mode of deceit Isaac makes a test by feeling Jacob's arm because he recognizes Jacob's voice but believes <305> that he feels Esau's arm (vv 21-23). Rebekah's ruse is a literary device (vv 11-13). Another test by Isaac corresponds to the second manner of deceit (with the clothing). He smells Jacob when they embrace and he smells Esau's clothing (vv 26, 27). Accordingly the manner in which the deceit is discovered also differs. In the first recension Isaac knows immediately that Jacob was the deceiver since he heard his voice (v 35). Vv 36 and 37 presume likewise. In the other recension, however, he does not know who may have deceived him (v 33).

Now the second recension belongs to J because of יהוה (v 27), the other, therefore, to E. Accordingly, vv 15, 26, 27, and 33 stem from J. Key terms are בְּגָדִים (vv 15, 27), נשׁק (vv 26, 27), "smell" and "to smell" (v 27, four times). E includes vv 11-13, 16, 21-23, 35-37. Characteristic words in this account are שָׂעִיר (vv 11, 23), חָלָק (v 11), הֲלֵקָה (v 16), משׁשׁ (vv 12, 21, 22; like 31:34, 37; Exod 10:21 E), קְלָלָה (vv 12, 13), יָדַיִם (vv 16, 22bis, 23bis), לָקַח בְּכֹרָה (vv 35, 36). Regarding מִרְמָה (v 35) compare 34:13 E. Regarding הֲכִי (v 36) compare 29:15 E. Regarding אָצַל compare Num 11:17, 25 E. So much for the, I think, reliable foundation of the source analysis. Vv 21-23 E conclude with the statement "thus he blessed him then," whereupon we expect the words of the blessing itself. Vv 21-23, therefore, parallel vv 24-27a which conclude similarly. Therefore, vv 24, 25 also belong to J. Likewise Isaac's negotiation with Esau (vv 33, 34) with the conclusion "bless me, too, my father" and the loud lament of Esau parallel vv 35-38 with the same conclusion. Since of these parallel passages v 33 stems from J and vv 35-37 from E, the related vv 34 and 38 are to be attributed to J and E, respectively. Regarding צְעָקָה גְדֹלָה עַד־מְאֹד (v 34), compare צְעָקָה גְדֹלָה (Exod 11:6; 12:30; Gen 19:13 J), and especially צְעָקָה גְדֹלָה עַד־מְאֹד (v 33). The blessing on Jacob can also be divided accordingly. V 28 belongs to E because of הָאֱלֹהִים, v 28b because of v 37 (דָגָן וְתִירֹשׁ), v 29aγ,δ because of v 37 (גְּבִיר "brothers"); v 27b to J (cf. above), vv 29aα,β (∥v 29aγ,δ E), v 29b because of 12:3 J. The curse on Esau stems from E: v 39 is the counterpart of v 28 E; v 40 is probably its continuation and can be understood against v 37 E. Because of יהוה (cf. also מַה־זֶּה and הִקְרָה 24:12 J), v 20 should also be attributed to J. The introduction of the discussion in vv 1bβ,γ and in v 18 is the usual one in E.

Additional distinguishing characteristics of the source, some of them seen first by Procksch, are: one consistently employs the expression צַיִד "game, hunt," especially in the phrases "to eat game" and "to hunt game." Judging from vv 25, 33, this recension is J so that vv 3, 5b, 7aα, 19b, 30b, 31 should also be attributed to J. The other, that is E, uses מַטְעַמִּים, especially in combination with עָשָׂה and the modifier כַּאֲשֶׁר אָהֵב (vv 4a, 7aβ, 9, 14, 17, 31a). This phrase does not specify the ingredients of the "delicacy." J says "so that the soul may bless" in v 25, which is followed in vv 4b, 19, 31b. The other source, that is E, says more simply "so that he (I) may bless" (vv 10, 7b). Judging from 45:28 בְּטֶרֶם אָמוּת in v 4 belongs to J. Judging from 50:16 and Deut 33:1, לִפְנֵי מוֹתִי in vv 7, 10 belongs to E. The perspectives of the two are somewhat distinct. In E Isaac's death is imminent, in J it is still distant so that v 2 also belongs to J. Expressions of the J recension are "her older (younger) son" in v 15 (elsewhere also in E), thus v 42 also, and "sit up and eat" in vv 19b and 31b. E expressions are גְּדָיֵי עִזִּים in vv 9, 16, שָׁמַע בְּקוֹל, common in E (21:12; 30:6; Exod 18:19; etc.), here in v 13 so that vv 8 and 43 should also be attributed to E. ברח in v 43 of Jacob's "flight" (also in 35:1, 7) points to E. Question and response in vv 18bβ, 19a correspond precisely to the question and response in v 32 and probably belong to E. Both are implausible in E, at least (cf. v 24) superfluous in J. Instead of בְּכֹר this J text says "the older son" (cf. above). Of the two variants v 30aα ∥ β, the first belongs to J (כִּלָּה with infinitive is frequent in J), the second, then, to E. The concluding section recounts Esau's animosity toward Jacob twice (v 41a ‖ v 41b). Because of שָׂטַם (50:15), v 41a belongs to E. V 4ab, where Isaac's death is not expected immediately (cf. above), belongs to J. Regarding אֵבֶל see 50:10 J. Regarding אָמַר בְלִבּוֹ see 8:21; 24:45 (6:6) J. The "words of Esau" in v 42 refer to what Esau "said" in v 41b. For this reason as well as because of the expressions "her older (younger) son" (cf. above) and הָרַג (as in v 41), v 42 belongs to J. חָרָן (v 43; 28:10; 29:4) characterizes J (cf. comments on 29:1). V 44b parallels v 45aα. Esau's forgetfulness in the latter fits well with 25:29-34 E (Procksch). Both recensions could have possessed clauses such as vv 1a, 5a, 6, 45aβ,b. Of course, both sources have not been preserved without lacunae—how otherwise would it have been possible to combine the two?—yet the accounts which the two must have contained can be easily discerned. <306> Procksch divides somewhat differently. He attributes vv 1aβ, b, 4a, 5a, 6, 7aβ, b, 8-14, 16-18, 21-23, 28, 29aα, β, 30aβ, 31a, 35, 37aβ*, 38aα, 39, 41a, 42, 43a, 45 to E. Sievers (2:312ff.) assigns vv 2-4, 6-10, 15, 17, 18aα, 19b, 20, 24-28, 29aγ, δ, b, 30aα, b, 31-34, 37-41a, 45 to Jα. He assigns the rest to Eδ, but thereby often disrupts sections which belong together. Here, too, Sievers's metrical system confuses more than it assists source analysis.

In order to understand the following narrative, the chief question concerns how Jacob's deceit is to be evaluated. Older and more recent theologians have felt obligated to justify religiously and ethically the standpoint from which this narrative is recounted (see recently Franz Delitzsch; Dillmann; cf. also Kautzsch, *Abriß*, 153). In an equally unhistorical manner, modern "anti-Semites" are accustomed to deriving the true character of the people of Israel, indeed of the Bible, from this and similar narratives. The voice of the truth-loving historian has been heard rarely enough in this battle which overanxious piety and malicious impiety wage against one another. (1) Many theologians have futilely sought to mold the narrative into a moral tale. Reference has been made to Jacob's many struggles, fears, and distresses and they have been seen as the proper punishments for sins and, simultaneously, the means of correction through which his impure intentions could be expunged (Dillmann). This, however, is not the perspective of the old legends which know nothing of Jacob's regret and according to which Jacob did not abandon his artifice and tricks. Instead, the older he got, the better he learned them. He surpassed the old fox Laban and his subtle tricks and, when he returned from this academy of deceit, he first deceived his brother rather masterfullly (cf. comments on 33:12-17). One may not, therefore, speak of Jacob's "proper punishment and correction," but rather of all manner of dangers and distresses which he escapes victoriously through his cunning and God's help. Nor may one, as the theological perspective prefers to do, construe Esau's guilt as "shortsighted imprudence" (25:29-34), for example (so already Hebr 12:16-17). But Gen 27 did not even originally presuppose this account (cf. comments on 25:23 and 27:36). The content of this narrative is and remains, therefore, that a deceit finally comes to a fortunate end. The rascal Jacob truly gains the blessing, Esau draws the short end, with no moral guilt, and the hearers are the fortunate heirs of the deceiver. This narrative is not, therefore, a "moral tale."

(2) At the same time it is truly difficult to mistake the fact that these legends of Jacob's deceit, especially the one under consideration, are recounted with humor (cf. already the comments on 25:29-34). How else could it be meant other than crudely humorously that Jacob imitates Esau's hairy skin by wrapping himself in the skin of

goats! No one can be serious with such an outrageous hyperbole! Furthermore, this legend quite clearly intends to depict types and, indeed, in Israelite understanding, national types. In the figure of Jacob, hearers and narrators of this legend discern themselves. The name of the people "Jacob" by which Israel refers to itself is explained from this event. It is entirely impossible, however, that the successors or sons of Jacob wanted here to recount something shameful of their hero or ancestor and thus brand themselves with an odious characteristic as their chief trait. Rather, all these narratives were surely originally recounted in praise of the hero and his successors. One cannot have seen sin and shame in these deceits, but only amusing, successful pranks. One should also understand that precisely the humor of these narratives mitigates the immoral elements in them.

(3) On the other hand, however, the modern must also be permitted to express without reservation his own attitude toward these narratives. For our sensibilities, this prank of Jacob's, particularly, is too immoral to be amusing. To deceive one's own blind, dying father seems to us to be simply loathsome. The role religion plays in these narratives is especially offensive to us, however. A divine blessing <307> is acquired through deceit! The deceiver Jacob is simultaneously supposed to be a recipient of the divine revelation! After he had just deceived his blind father, Yahweh appears to him and promises to be with him (28:23ff.). Indeed, God himself is supposed to have occasionally helped Jacob with his dubious pranks (cf. 31:10ff.)! The exegete should not allow his moral sensibilities to be confused by these narratives. On the other hand, however, he should also have enough respect for antiquity not to paint over these old legends with modern colors.

(4) One achieves the proper attitude if one considers these matters historically. There was a period in Israel, too, in which morality and religion were not yet closely linked in the way we now consider self-evident. The god originally discussed in these legends is not the majestic Yahweh, the law-giver of the ten commandments, but a much more primitive figure, a god who protects his darling and his tribe in all his doings, even the devious ones. This god concept was no more offensive to the earliest period than was the Greek legend that the prankster Odysseus owed his wiliness to the pleasure of the clever goddess Athene. To be sure, one may also see in the ancient Hebrew's glee over cunning and trickery, which also allows him to take no offense at deceit and lies, a characteristic feature of his disposition which—as everyone knows—has been passed on as an extremely questionable heritage even to his most recent descendants. On the other hand we should not forget that the emphasis on morality in religion is a heritage we owe to none other than ancient Israel and its prophets. The unusual prominence of trickery and deceit in this shepherd narrative is apparently based on the ancient observation that shepherds, in particular, are inclined to deceit, indeed they live from deceit (Haller, 116).

(5) The fact that even J and E have included these amusing narratives from the earliest period of Israel in their legend collections shows how beloved they must have been. They cannot be eradicated. On the other had, they will have attempted to recount them in the most gentle manner possible (v 12). They are—it seems—not without sympathy for the two deceived, especially for Esau (vv 30ff.). But it is only the "sympathy of the victor" (Meyer, *Israeliten*, 387). They were unwilling and unable to alter the fortunate end of the deceit.

(6) Remarkably, the humorous narrative of deceit and the account of the divine revelation to Jacob stand alongside each other very closely. One may well assume that the two

materials were originally of distinct origins and that, in the final analysis, distinct figures
are involved here. The religious element was only secondarily incorporated in the narrative
of Jacob's outwitting Laban (cf. comments on Gen 31).

1-5 *Isaac and Esau.* The narrative originally continued the exposition in 25:27-28.
The situation described in this narrative—the blind father on his deathbed, pronouncing
his blessing on his descendants—is repeated in Jacob's blessing on Ephraim and Manasseh
(48:10ff.) and is, therefore, a favorite legend motif. The last will appears elsewhere, too,
as a poetic situation: Abraham's (24:1ff.), Joseph's (50:24-25), Moses's (Deut 33),
Joshua's (Josh 23), David's (2 Sam 23:1-7; 1 Kgs 2:1-9), Elisha's (2 Kgs 13:14-19),
Mattathiah's (1 Macc 2:49ff.), Tobith's (Tob 14:3ff.), but especially later in the literature
of the "Testaments." If such final words contain predictions, the assumption is that the
piercing vision of the dying penetrates to the future. This is an old, often recurring belief
which must be associated with the death oracle. Hector and Patrocles prophesy in this
manner in the final moments of their lives in Homer (*Iliad* 22.358ff.; 16.850ff.). The same
motif is common in Egyptian (Meyer, *Israeliten*, 451-52), in old Germanic (Richard M.
Meyer, *Altgerm. Poesie*, 51; id., *Zeitschr. f. deutsche Philologie* 31:325), as well as in
Indian tradition, where widows sacrificing themselves prophesy (cf. Zachariae, *Zeitschf.
für Volkskunde* 18:177ff.), was still known in the Middle Ages and later (*Archiv für das
Stud. der neueren Sprachen* 95:95), and is still <308> employed by Schiller in *Wilhelm
Tell* 4:333ff. It is also not unusual for the blind to possess the gift of prophecy. One thinks
of the blind seer Tiresias and the blind prophet Ahijah (1 Kgs 14:4). Here the motif of the
prophecy of the dying, blind father is so nuanced that Isaac has the authority to speak yet
one effective blessing before his death (v 37-38). Originally this was understood in terms
of his determining his heir (cf. comments on 25:29-34).

1 Isaac's blindness, the precondition of the subsequent deceit, is communicated
immediately here. The narrators love to indicate elements to be employed in the course
of the account at the very beginning in order not to interrupt the subsequent account (so
already in 25:27-28; further 2:25; 22:1; 26:3; 29:2-3). On the other hand, the fact that
Rebekah overhears is not communicated at the beginning. The narrator avoids overloading
the exposition and wisely reserves this element for use as the transition from the first to
the second scene. The site of this legend is Beersheba according to 28:10. Concerning
וַתִּכְהֶיןָ in a dependent clause see §111q. Concerning מֵרְאֹת see §119y. "I do not
know the day of my death." J assumes (cf. above) that the blessing must actually be
pronounced on the day of death. This is a feature of the blessing "style." But Isaac, afraid
that death could surprise him, would prefer to pronounce the blessing today. E differs (cf.
above p. 299). The composure with which one views death is a characteristic quality of
antiquity and still of contemporary farmers (l'Houet, 10-11, 268). **3** Bow and arrow are
the weapons of the hunter (Isa 7:24). Kethib צֵידָה is the *nomina unitatis* of צַיִד; Qere
is צַיִד as elsewhere in Gen 27. **4** The presupposition of the statement, that Isaac must
first eat something good before he can bless, seems not a little strange to us. The fact that
the gods in the Babylonian creation epic feast before they determine fate (III:133ff.; KB
4:20-21) is a parallel. It is not easy to explain either of these texts. A sacrificial meal
seems originally to have been involved here at which the deity is cited. לִפְנֵי יהוה (v 7)
probably refers to this meal. Balaam also sacrifices before he curses (Num 23:1). The
current recension, at any rate, involves only a normal (especially tasty) meal. "So that my

soul may bless you" is a heightened poetic expression as in Psa 103:1 ‖ כָּל־קְרָבַי. "The soul blesses" means to bless from deep within one's whole heart. **5** שָׁמַעַת means "she overheard." The woman listening is an element of verisimilitude (18:10). Franken-berg (CGA [1901], 698) and Kautzsch[3] read לאביו for לְהָבִיא following LXX.

6-17 II. *Rebekah and Jacob.* (1) **6-13** *The discussion.* (2) **14-17** *The preparations for the deceit.* Characteristically, Rebekah (in both recensions) suggests the trick. She is the clever son's worthy mother. Wiliness and cunning are traits from her family (29:14). She teaches "her son" the best tricks. The Israelite does not hold it against her that she wants to appropriate the blessing for her Jacob. Isaac prefers "his son" with equal partisanship (v 5). Besides, the hearers are sons of Jacob for whom the blessing brings benefit. At any rate, one may not explain her preference for Jacob from 25:23. The two narratives are not to be merged <309> (cf. comments on v 13). **7** Concerning לִפְנֵי יהוה see comments on v 4. The word need not necessarily presume that there was an image of Yahweh in Isaac's house (Stade, ZAW 11:182n.1; Kautzsch[3]). **3** Concerning לַאֲשֶׁר see §119u. **9** On גְּדָיֵי see §93x. Regarding עָשָׂה with a dual accusative see §117ii. Two goats are a sumptuous meal for a dying old man (but cf. 18:6ff.; 43:34). It can be inferred from 18:7 that it was customary in Hebron for the man to provide the meat. Here the woman also knows how to do so. It is interesting for culinary history that Rebekah knows how to treat goats as "false" game. According to old tradition, the mode of preparation was, at any rate, boiling the meat (cf. comments on 18:7). **10** יְבָרֶכְךָ—in German terms "you" would be emphatically accented here (*you*; not Esau as he wants). The Hebrew accents much less emphatically than we (cf. Wellhausen, *Text der Bücher Samuelis*, 24-25). **11** Esau is "hairy," Jacob smooth. This is a stereotypical depiction (25:25). שָׂעִר as in v 23 like שֵׂעָר in 25:25 is an allusion to the name Seir. Since שָׂעִיר also means "goat" it can be assumed that this element of Rebekah using goats also developed from this name. The old legend finds high mischief in the name of Seir as an allusion to his hairiness and to the animal to whom he owes the loss of the birthright. The hearers surely rejoice over this impressive joke. The allusions to the name Isaac are formally comparable. In the current recension, these verbal jokes have been semiforgotten. The old narrator said שָׂעִיר and שָׂעִיר, the current narrator says עֵשָׂו and גְּדִי. **12** We are supposed to rejoice at the wit of son and mother. Jacob is clever enough to foresee correctly that his father will touch him. But the mother is even more clever to know a means to deceive him nevertheless. This dual usage of the goat is an ingenious device. Stucken (*Astralmythen*, 342ff.) lists more or less similar stories of deceit. Jacob fears becoming a "mocker," that is, one who mocks the holy (2 Chron 36:16) because the blessing is a religious matter ("before Yahweh," v 7). Such "mockery" is, of course, much worse than simple deceit. Jacob does not, however, fear the sin itself, but only its consequences and is immediately calmed when Rebekah takes these consequences. It is incorrect, therefore, that the words contain "a harsh condemnation of his actions" (contra Kautzsch[3]).

13 "On me be thy curse." In antiquity one believed it possible to divert the curse through such statements. The transferal of curse or guilt is "common in Germanic law, not unknown to Judaism [cf. Weber, *Jüd. Theol.*[2], 328-29], made imminently significant for Christian dogmatics by Anselm" (Haller, 109). Dillmann's comment that Rebekah will have already known from the oracle (25:23) that Jacob must and will have the blessing is fundamentally reversed. It intermixes two originally independent narratives and even destroys the point of the clause. **15** In the preceding, <310> Rebekah's advice and preparation of the food has been omitted from J. The good clothes are the festival clothes. Esau would have put them on before he entered for the blessing since the blessing is a religious procedure. The presumption is that the good clothes are in the custody of the mother, and that, therefore, Esau is still unmarried (contra 26:34-35). One may supply בִּגְדֵי before הַחֲמֻדֹת. **16** For חֶלְקַת LXX reads τὰ γυμνά = חלקת, feminine plural of חָלָק (Ball). **17** Bread is not mentioned either previously or subsequently. It will be an addition as is the wine in v 25b (cf. 25:34). The addition is not an improvement, for, if Esau lives from the hunt, where did he get bread and wine?

18-29 III. *Isaac and Jacob*. In both recensions Isaac does not eat and bless immediately. Instead he is suspicious and investigates. The tension is heightened in this way. We are supposed to think, "Will he discover it?" The scene is precisely realized in this interest, especially in J. Quite innocently, without calling his name, Jacob appears before the old man. Isaac notices that his son has returned very quickly. But Jacob is able to explain this (v 20). Yet, Isaac's suspicion has been excited, therefore he does not ask directly whether he is Esau. Now Jacob lies outright (v 24). Isaac seems calmed and eats. But, before he blesses, he smells Jacob and smells—the fragrance of Esau's clothing (vv 25-27a). And only now does he bless. The process is simpler in E: Jacob enters with a naked lie that he is Esau (v 19), whereupon Isaac—this is now omitted—eats. But, suspicious, because he hears Jacob's voice, he touches him before he blesses him (vv 21-23). Deception through the skin wrapper is more childish than deception through the clothing. Here, then, E has the earlier recension. **18** LXX, Pesh, and Vulg have וַיֵּבֵא as in vv 4, 5, 7, 10, 31, 33 (but cf. also בָּא v 35, תָּבוֹא v 33 and the counterpart יָצָא v 30). **20** Jacob lies while employing God's name. This could sound almost blasphemous to us. The old legend, however, does not hold it against him, but thinks, "That is a well-done lie." The presumption is that God sends the hunter prey if he wishes him well. This and similar examples (cf. Smend, *At.liche Religionsgeschichte*, 100ff.) should show modern theologians that, in the opinion of ancient Israel, God not only reveals himself in the life of the people Israel, but also in the lives of individuals. **21** Concerning הַאַתָּה see §100m.

22 Now Isaac is close to discovery. We are supposed to listen with baited breath. The words in v 22b (a "double trimeter," at the climax of the account a poem, as is occasionally the case in German fairy tales) <311> are splendidly conceived. It is a semiaudible soliloquy, such as held by the blind, whose psychic life is private. Isaac is to be imagined with shaking hands and a shaking voice. The content of the words, the first clause doubting, the second confidently affirming, is supposed to amuse us. So close to the truth and still deceived! If one wants to understand the old legend, sympathy with the poor blind man is not appropriate here. Yet E may have felt differently. **24a** Regarding the question see §150a. **25** For מְצֵיד בְּנִי (as in v 31) LXX and Vulg have מְצֵידְךָ. Concerning v 25bb see comments on v 17.

26 Even the old Isaac has ulterior motives. He says he wants to kiss. In reality he wants to smell. Concerning וּשְׁקָה see §10g. The notion that Esau has a particular smell, which one can even smell in his good clothes, is extremely crude by our tastes. This feature also portrays a stereotype. There are racial and national odors such as the *foetor iudaicus* and the smell of Negroes, as well as equally peculiar regional smells (cf. Andree,

Ethnographische Parallelen 2:213ff.).[1] Winckler (*Forschungen* 3:426) thinks of a flowery perfume without suggesting where the rough hunter gets his *eau de mille fleurs*. This element of the smell is employed dually here in an ingenious manner: Isaac believes he recognizes Esau by the smell; simultaneously, however, the aroma brings inspiration—in the aroma he smells the future of his son (**27a**).

From v **27b** onward is poetry, as always in blessings. There are a "double trimeter," along with a "trimeter" (v 27), a "hexameter" along with a "trimeter" (v 28), a "quadrameter," a "double trimeter," and a "quadrameter" (cf. Sievers, *Metrische Studien* 1:405, 577; contra Sievers 2:211, 78-79). שְׂדֵה מָלֵא, the reading of Sam, LXX, and Vulg, is probably preferable. V **28** is extraordinary: heaven and earth are supposed to give him their best. Rich dew in water-poor Palestine is a chief condition of a good harvest (cf. Benzinger, *Archäologie*[2], 22). מִשְׁמַנֵּי ‖ מִטַּל is, as in v 39, to be derived from שְׁמָנִים, singular שָׁמָן. מִ = מִן (§20m). In **29a** the ethnohistorical, specifically Israelite, features become most prominent. This Jacob, whom nations serve, is none other than the people Israel, before whom Edom, Ammon, and Moab bow. E abandons here the legend form and speaks of Jacob's "brothers." And the land, whose possession is promised in v 28, is none other than Canaan, Israel's property, although the name, surely by intention, is avoided. הֱוֵה is poetic. גְּבִיר only occurs here and in v 37. <312> For וְיִשְׁתַּחוּ, Qere and Sam read וְיִשְׁתַּחֲווּ. **29b** Concerning the idea see 12:3; On the construction (the singular אֹרְרֶיךָ is distributive) see §145l. Here the high point of the account has been attained. The blessing which is the objective of all the preceding is pronounced. Now it must be further recounted how the deception was discovered (vv 30-40). Whereas such conclusions are usually very brief, this scene is extensively elaborated. The reason for this breadth is that this scene is supposed to serve as the foil for the preceding. The curse on Esau, which would not have been absolutely necessarily in the context, is supposed to emphasize the blessing on Jacob. To the same end, Isaac's horror and, especially, Esau's pain over the loss is portrayed extensively. This portrayal is supposed to make it clear to us the magnitude of the blessing Jacob has received. The modern reader pities Esau here, as did already J and E but not the old narrators from whom the narrative stems. One who was previously amused at the way the poor blind man was deceived feels no sympathy here, either. Instead he laughs privately, as a true son of Jacob, at the successful trick.

30-40 IV. *Isaac and Esau.* **30** Esau comes as soon as Jacob has left (כַּאֲשֶׁר "as soon as," cf. Siegfried-Stade, *Hebr. Wb.*, אֲשֶׁר 3:7). The narrators love such rapid scene changes as a means of heightening the tension. If he had appeared a moment sooner, everything would have been different (cf. 19:23-24; 32:32). Vv **31-32** are intentionally structured much like the preceding. **33** This time, Isaac makes no test because he is convinced that the right one now stands before him. For מִכֹּל Kautzsch-Socin[2], Kittel, and Kautzsch[3] read אָכַל with good reason. "Thus he will also remain blessed." This is also the presumption in E (vv 37ff.). The word of blessing once spoken is irrevocable. Even

---

[1][*Translator's note.* Ironically, after Gunkel's reproach against pietists and anti-Semites for their lack of historical sensitivity to ancient Israelite literature (p. 300), he makes a statement here that is objectionable to contemporary sensibilities, even offensive to me. Rather than omit, correct, or apologize, however, I have simply translated Gunkel's statement and would encourage readers to interpret Gunkel with the same historical consciousness he called for above.]

the one blessing has no more power over it (cf. שְׂמָתִיו v 37). Concerning the magical effectiveness of the blessing see the comments on 9:24ff. (cf. Stade, *Bibl. Theol.*, 152-53; Haller, 81). **34** כִּשְׁמֹעַ should be read without וַיְהִי (so Sam, LXX) as in 34:7. An emendation of בָּרוּךְ יִהְיֶה: (v 33) into בָּרוּךְ: וַיְהִי (Ball) is unnecessary. Concerning גַּם־אָנִי see §135e. V 34 in J may be followed by an unpreserved "blessing" ‖ vv 39-40, if the phrase following v 38b in LXX and Luc (Lagarde), κατανυχθέντος δὲ Ἰσαακ = וַיִּדֹּם יִצְחָק (Ball, Kittel), does not stem from J. At any rate, the way Esau discovered that Jacob was the deceiver must have been portrayed. Perhaps he observed the clothing later. **36** Concerning הֲכִי see §150e. In pain and wrath Esau finds—an etymology for "Jacob"! This rare procedure for us was very familiar to the Hebrew. The prophets also make their wordplays in extreme wrath. The old Israelite hearer perceives this etymology that the name of his people means "deceiver" with pleasure (cf. above). This reminder of the narrative <313> in 25:29-34 surely does not belong to the original account. Originally the two accounts were variants. "Blessing" and "birthright" are actually identical (cf. 25:23). The same conclusion is suggested by the dual ויאמר in v 36a and b (Holzinger). בְּלֹרָתִי and בְּרָכָתִי are a play on words. It may be observed in other wordplays, the Hebrew hears the consonants more distinctly than the vowels. One may note the fine chiastic word placement.

Concerning **38** see above on v 34. **39, 40a** The blessing on Esau, the high point of this scene, is in verse as is the blessing on Jacob. It is (after הִנֵּה) a "heptameter" along with a "quadrameter" (cf. Sievers 1:405; contra 2:211, 78-79). Moved by love and compassion, Isaac would like to bless. But the world has been given away. Nothing remains for Esau other than—curse. Ingeniously, the narrative contrasts this curse with the blessing on Jacob by employing the same words both times but in a contrasting sense: הָאָרֶץ מִשְׁמַנֵּי "from the fat of the earth" (v 28), "far from the fat of the earth" (v 39), similarly מִטַּל הַשָּׁמַיִם. A similar ingenious play on words occurs in 40:13, 19. Esau's land was considered, then, to be very infertile, a view which is, however, seen objectively, not absolutely correct for the land of Edom (Palmer, *Wüstenwanderung Israels*, 334-35). "To live by the sword," that is, to live as a robber, from murder and theft, is the fate of the younger brother who does not want to submit to the elder, of the illegitimate son rejected by his relatives, of refugees who leave the safety of home and seek their bread out on the steppe with all manner of suspicious riffraff. Such a life does not appear here to be a criminal, but a sorrowful fate. Thus, because its land cannot nourish it, Edom as a people lives from robbing the caravans passing through its territory. "The desert does not sufficiently nourish its children and forces them to robbery and bloodshed" (Nöldeke, ZDMG 40:175). "And you must serve your brother." Edom was subjugated by David and remained subject to Judah until king Joram (2 Kgs 8:20ff.). Procksch (289) thinks of the temporary liberation of Edom under Hadad (1 Kgs 11:14ff.). V **40b** is clearly prose in attitude and is, therefore, an addition from a period when Edom had obtained its freedom from Judah, thus after ca. 840. תָּרִיד > רוּד, is much discussed. In Arab. it refers to the beast that has broken free and runs loose (cf. Baethgen on Psa 55:3). In Hebrew it means "to break free, to proclaim freedom" (qal Jer 2:31; Hos 12:1b; hiph. here; cf. comments on Gen 38:1). Textual emendation is unnecessary. The draught animal placed in the yoke is a common image for a "subjugated" people.

41-45 V. The final scene is simultaneously a transition to the following narrative. Jacob flees from Esau's traps. The presumption is that Esau is a crude killer (הָרַג is a crude expression, vv 41, 42) who wants to make up for his lack of cunning with his fists. Jacob is more clever, but inferior to him in strength. The same presumption <314> underlies Jacob's return (Gen 32ff.). Jacob, however, outwits him once more. This time, also—one notes the beautiful unity of the account—he is led by his mother to make his way to safety at the right time. **41b** יִקְרְבוּ is a conditional clause according to German linguistic sensibilities (§159c,e). **43** The reference to Haran is from J (11:31; 29:4). E knows nothing of Haran (29:1; cf. Mez, *Gesch. der Stadt Ḥarrân*, 15ff.; Meyer, *Israeliten*, 237). **44a** "A few days"—lovingly and soothingly, the mother intentionally presents the time as very short. **44b, 45a** A new character trait of Esau in this legend, also presupposed in the continuation and already in 25:29-34, is that he is a man of the moment. After a time, his wrath will burn out when he has forgotten the whole incident. Jacob and Rebekah differ, however. They think far ahead (25:31). Concerning וְשָׁכַח see §114r. "Then I will send for you." This does not happen subsequently. This probably indicates a variant to 31:1-3, 13 in which Jacob departs from Laban at God's command. Or is it only supposed to be a maternal comfort? **45b** Both children are taken from the mother because the fratricide is killed (by the relatives; cf. 2 Sam 14:7). גַּם־שְׁנֵיכֶם means "both of you at once" (§154[a] n. 1c.).

V **46** offers a new and much less innocent motive for Jacob's journey to Laban. Gen 26:34 P already alludes to this motive and 28:1ff. P elaborates it. The intention of the author of these verses was, then, to recall the motive obscured by the interposed account in 27:1-45 and, thus, to make the transition to the following account. The verse stems, then, from a redactor (Dillmann). It vexes Rebekah to see the foreign customs the whole day and to have to endure them. The assumption is that the daughters-in-law dwell in the tent with her (Haller, 94). Gen **28:10** constitutes the conclusion of the account. Jacob did as Rebekah advised him.

Hebrew tradition equates the characters of the legend, Jacob and Esau (Seir), with the Hebrew names Israel and Edom (cf. above on 25:25). Hebrew poetry consequently employs not only the prosaic-modern names Israel and Edom, but also the poetic-archaic Jacob and Esau, as, for example, our poets say "Franks" or "Gauls" for "French." The fact that originally different characters are involved here is demonstrated already by the fact that for the same character two, indeed three, names are transmitted. This conclusion is strengthened by 36:9ff., 20ff, where, along with Esau's genealogy, that is, the genealogy of the people Edom, the genealogy of the Horite Seir is communicated. Accordingly, Seir was originally the name of an aboriginal people in the land before Edom subjugated by it and partially fused with it. But—as the genealogies indicate—it still survived in remnants for a long period (Meyer, *Israeliten*, 336). Some narrative must, therefore, lead from Jacob to Israel, from Esau to Edom. Now characteristically, the legends which treat the relationship of the two <315> brothers employ, not the names Israel and Edom, but always Esau (Seir) and Jacob, whereas, in contrast, the historical accounts never say Jacob and Esau, but always only Israel and Edom. This means that the legends of Jacob and Esau are of non-Israelite origin. They did not even originally treat Israel and Edom, but were only secondarily applied to them. This can also be clearly discerned from the narratives themselves. The legends do not suit Israel and Edom properly. In the legend Jacob is not very brave and war-like. He also seeks his well-being by fleeing his brother. His-torically, however, Israel conquered Edom in war. In the legend, Esau's chief characteris-tic is his stupidity. Historically, however, Edom's great wisdom is famed (Jer 49:7; Bar 3:22-23). Eliphaz from Teman (Job 2:11; Gen 36:10-11) and perhaps even Job from Uz (Job 1:1; Gen 36:28; Lam 4:21) are Edomites (cf. now also Eerdmans 2:30ff.). What then were the figures of Jacob and Esau? We may only say that they are figures from very old legends and that they represent the types of the shepherd and the hunter. It remains completely obscure, however, how these two figures were originally further understood, where they actually originated, whether they were once gods or semidivine heroes, per-haps (cf. comments on 25:25), and what right one had to relate them to historical peoples. The assumption that Esau and Jacob were the names of early peoples is as undemonstra-ble as the analogous assumptions for Abraham and Isaac.

The proper interpretation of the sense of the legend depends, then, to the extent that it is possible, on distinguishing the original and the added Israelite components. The former lie in the foundation of the account, the latter very clearly in the blessings. The fact that blessing and account do not entirely agree is indicated by the following. (1) The blessing speaks of many brothers (vv 29, 37 E), but the legend only of two. 2) According to the legend, Esau and Jacob are hunter and shepherd, but the blessing treats an agricul-tural and viticultural land in v 28 (37) E (contrariwise, J may have preserved the old material in שָׂדֶה, v 27). The blessings are not, therefore, as one may assume from the outset, very old but, at least in this form, relatively young (likewise 25:23). Accordingly one may understand the old legend as follows: It varies the theme of hunter and shepherd as in 25:28-34. The two brothers struggle for precedence. The animal of the hunter tastes better, but the shepherd has easier access to his. The hunter is more warlike, but the shepherd is more clever. The hunter is the firstborn. He has little regard for the husband-man (the same is true among the Masai, Abyssinians, Somali, etc.; Merker, *Masai*, 312n.1). But the cunning of the shepherd finally wins the "blessing." He acquires the better field and even power over this brother. Along with these interpretable elements, the legend contains not a few others purely novelistic in nature. Israel interpreted this struggle of the unequal brothers in terms of its relationship to Edom. Edom the older people (Gen 36:31ff.) is Israel's firstborn brother. And yet, Israel had the better land, Canaan, full of corn and wine, and it subjugated Edom. This reinterpretation of the legend will have taken place in Judah, Edom's neighbor, in the period from ca. 980 (Edom's subjugation) unto ca. 840 (Edom's liberation). The legend, itself, however, must have stemmed from a much earlier period.

43. The Bethel Legend 28:11-22 EJ

Source analysis. The dual divine names point to dual strands: יהוה vv 13bis, 16; אלהים vv 12, 17, 20, 22. According to one recension, the "angels of God" appear on the heaven-ly ladder (v 12); according to the other, it is Yahweh alone (v 13a). Jacob recognizes the holiness of the site twice, because Yahweh resides there (v 16), and because the gate to heaven is there (v 17). In the broader sense, Yahweh's promise (vv 13-15) <316> parallels Jacob's vow (vv 20-22). It would have been inconceivable for the pious to combine the two. God's promise would only be called into question by a human vow ("if" v 20). One can successfully expose two rather well-preserved reports. E includes vv 11, 12, 17, 18,

20, 21a, 22. Characteristics of E are אֱלֹהִים, פָּנַע בְּ (v 11), the dream (v 12; but cf. also comments on v 16), the *Massebah* [sacred pillar, memorial stone] (vv 18, 22), and the tithe (v 22). Only Jacob's awakening (before v 17) and the naming of Bethel—which, as 31:13 and 35:3 show, E must have contained here and which must have stood after v 22—are lacking. This source analysis is supported by 31:13 (the anointing of the Massebah, the vow) and 35:1, 3 (cf. 28:20), 7 where E returns once again to the Bethel narrative. The exposition is missing in J, then follows vv 13, 15, 16, 19. Characteristics of J are: יהוה v 13bis, 16; נִצָּב עַל v 13. J has many parallels to vv 13-16: 13aβ ‖ 26:24; 13b ‖ 13:15; 12:7; 14aα ‖ 13:16; the list of the directions; 14b ‖ 12:3; 18:18. Concerning vv 14, 19b, 21b see the interpretation. Modern scholars are in full agreement concerning this source analysis.

11 The exposition seeks to establish how Jacob found the holy site (cf. comments on 18:1). At sundown he came by chance to a certain site, by chance he chose to overnight there (for the Hebrew goes to sleep at sundown), and by chance he takes one of the many stones lying around there then and now (cf. Driver; concerning מֵאַבְנֵי see §119w n.1) as a pillow (מְרַאֲשֹׁתָיו, Stade, *Gramm.*, §313b, 322c). He had, however, found precisely "the place" (הַמָּקוֹם = the holy place; cf. comments on 12:6) and the later holy stone of Bethel. The point of the account consists, then, in the fact that Jacob found the sacred by chance. There the holiness of the place was revealed to him through an epiphany. The stone is to be imagined as immensely large (cf., e.g., the figure of the stone in Benzinger², 319). Accordingly, Jacob was originally imagined as a giant here (cf. comments on 29:10; 32:26). Incubation may have been practiced in Bethel (Stade, *Bibl. Theol.*, 130).

12 הִנֵּה (twice) depicts astonishment at the epiphany. The word belongs to the style of the dream account (37:7, 9; 40:9, 16; 41:1, 2, 3, 5, 6, 17ff.; Judg 7:13; cf. Dan 2:31; 4:7, 10). The ladder (steps) leading from earth to heaven is not merely an image or a symbol, but it really stands in Bethel. The place is holy for this reason (v 17). This is an extremely ancient, originally mythological conception. God sends a messenger from heaven—where he dwells—to earth. In order to come from heaven and back again, however, these beings use a ladder. This ladder stands in Bethel. We hear elsewhere of such heavenly ladders. An obvious belief of the peoples, occasionally suggested by views of the rainbow, is that the heavenly beings come to earth or, sometimes also, that the transfigured reach heaven on such a ladder, stairway, or bridge (so among the South Sea islanders, the Scandinavians, in German fairy tales; Tylor, *Anfänge der Cultur* 1:294). In Egyptian tradition, too, the spirit of the dead climbs to heaven on a ladder (Erman, *Ägyptische Religion*, 98, 156, 189; H. O. Lange in Chantepie de la Saussaye I², 138). A ladder consisting of eight gates stacked on top of each other connecting the earth and the eight heavens occurs in the Mithra mysteries (cf. Cumont, "Mithras," in Roscher, *Lexikon* 2:3057; idem, *Mysterien des Mithra*, 105). Without a doubt, Babylonian influence is apparent in this motif (Zimmern, KAT³, 619, with bibl.). Similarly, Solomon's throne which stands on six steps (1 Kgs 10:18ff.) also seems to be the execution of a Babylonian idea and a representation of the heavenly throne above the six spheres (Böklen, *Verwandtschaft der jüd.-christl. mid d. pars. Eschatologie*, 35n.2; idem, *Ausgewählte Psalmen*, 90, 2103.) <317> But whether the much simpler vision of Jacob already depends on Babylonian influence (Winckler, *Religionsgeschichtler*, 60; A. Jeremias, ATAO², 375) is at least undemonstrable. The ladder on a stone appears not infrequently on oriental seals and coins. According to G. Hoffmann (*Zeitschr. für Assyriologie* 11:289ff.) it symbolizes the phases of the moon.

One notes that the angels are not portrayed with wings. The wings of divine beings are originally—as we moderns have forgotten—parts of the body of an animal (the eagle) and occur in the OT in chimeras (cf. Isa 6; Ezek 1). The concept of the מלאכי אלהים, the angels of God, has arisen from a dual root. It seems to more developed religion, not only in Israel, that it many cases it is more fitting for God, especially the highest God, not to appear himself, but to send a messenger. Now just as the wealthy and prominent have a messenger, but the great king has a number of people who stand ready for such service, the deity, too, has a divine messenger, in simpler circumstances, or many angels on hand when the image of a larger kingdom is in view. The image of the highest king of heaven is specifically in view here—an image which belongs to mythology and which Israel applied to Yahweh. Now whereas the (one) "angel of Yahweh" or "of God" alone stems from reflection, divine beings of the earliest faith come to life again in the (many) "angels of God." At a higher stage of religion, they have been demoted to servants and messengers of the highest God. Concerning the "angel of Yahweh" see p. 186; Concerning "the angels" see p. 56. According to E Jacob does not receive another revelation. It was not necessary. Rather, the revelation in E only signifies that this place is holy (Wellhausen, *Composition*[3], 30). The holiness of the place is understood here, as elsewhere, as something objectively present. The place was already holy and the ladder stood there before humans knew anything about it. The modern perspective, in contrast, is that nothing is in and of itself holy. "Thought makes it holy." There is no inherent "relationship" between this vision and the other Jacob narratives and the notion is falsely introduced by Dillmann.

13-15 The Bethel revelation according to J knows nothing of the ladder or of the angels, but only of an appearance of Yahweh himself. While in E the main point of the revelation is the holiness of the place, J places the emphasis on the words spoken by Yahweh. JE was able only combine the two loosely. **13** עליו "before him" (18:2, etc.) means "before Jacob" in the text of J. Yahweh appears on earth before Jacob. In the current context in JE, one is inclined to translate "on it," that is, on the ladder (so LXX, Pesh, Vulg) as in the artistic portrayals of the biblical scene. The self-revealing God first mentions his name (cf. p. 263). The same sacral first person style occurs in Egyptian (A. Dieterich, *Mithrasliturgie*, 194-95), further in Egypto-Hellenistic inscriptions, and elsewhere (similarly on ancient Oriental royal inscriptions; cf. especially Dießmann, *Licht vom Osten*, 90ff. and 90n.3). At the same time, he designates himself as the God of Jacob's fathers (cf. 26:24; 31:42). J and E express their understanding of this narrative in this way. The God who chose the patriarch blesses for his sake the son, the grandson, and us, his descendants. The following promises concern (1) the fate of Jacob's descendants (vv 13, 14; for the interpretation, cf. the parallels mentioned above); (2) Jacob's personal fate (v 15a); and (3) v 15b summarizes both. The motif is similar to the one in 12:7. On a journey in a foreign land, Jacob accidentally visited Palestinian ground. There Yahweh appeared to him and announced to the foreign, lonely, shelterless one, how his fate will improve gloriously. This ground will one day belong to his descendants! **14** This prediction distinguishes itself from the concrete words in vv 13, 15 through its bland attitude and <318> is probably an addition. Similar additions are 13:14ff.; 22:15ff.; 26:24; 31:23 (where 28:14 is cited); 46:3bb. וּבְזַרְעֶךָ does not occur in 12:3; 18:18 and is awkward. It is probably a gloss (Wellhausen, *Composition*³, 31; and others).

16 Jacob "awakens." The revelation came to him in his sleep, then, in both J and in E (cf. also הִנֵּה v 13). From the revelation imparted to him, he learns what he had not previously known, that Yahweh was present, that is, at home, in this place. The fact that the deity revealing himself in this way was not originally the almighty Yahweh, but a local numen, the "God of Bethel" (31:13; 35:7) still shines through the words. The attitude of Jacob's words is, however, as the concluding clause clearly demonstrates, not joyous thankfulness for such great promises, but (as always in such cases) terror before the deity. It weighs heavily on him that, unknowingly, he treated this extremely holy site as profane. He is "like one who unknowingly slept at the edge of an abyss" (E. Zurhellen-Pfleiderer, *Theol. Arbeiten aus dem rhein. wissenschaftl. Prediger-Verein*, ns 10:46). The presumption is that it is a serious sin even unknowingly to profane the holy.

17 The same impression characterizes the revelation in E. This place is—like everything divine—frightful (concerning the impression of the divine, cf. above p. 198). The relationship is as follows: Jacob saw the ladder of heaven. From this he concludes that God's dwelling and the gate of heaven is here. "The gate of heaven" (with article) is considered a well-known concept here (also in Psa 78:23) and is attested to us often in other religions (for Mithra worship see above on v 12; for Egyptian, cf. Erman, *Ägyptische Religion*, 98, 100; for Babylonian and Jewish, cf. Zimmern, KAT³, 619, 630, etc.). Naturally, "the gate of heaven" was originally conceived of as being in heaven. Since heaven is conceived as a firm structure, it seems obvious that it must have gates for the gods, stars, and wind (cf. comments on 1:6ff.). The "house of God," mentioned together with the gate of heaven, can, therefore, have originally been nothing other than the deity's palace in heaven (Isa 6). The earliest view considered heaven itself a house. Later, it was maintained that a divine palace, invisible to human eyes, stood in heaven. An older understanding of this narrative will have located God's palace and the gate of heaven in heaven over the earthly sanctuary of Bethel. The wording of our passages shows, however, that the E narrator, slightly mitigating the mythological elements, understood the earthly site as God's dwelling and as the gate to heaven. The popular etymology of Bab-il = gate of the gods (cf. above p. 97) is comparable. The words אֵין זֶה כִּי אִם־בֵּית אֱלֹהִים were originally understood as the etymology of בֵּית־אֵל. Concerning the concept of God's dwelling or of the gods in heaven see the comments on 11:7.

18 Jacob now treats the stone base of the heavenly ladder as a holy stone. He erects it as a Massebah and anoints it with oil. According to our text, this stone is the actual sanctuary of Bethel. Veneration of stones (cf. Stade, *Geschichte Israels* 1:456ff.; idem, *Bibl. Theol.* ¶55; Driver, 267; Robertson Smith, *Rel. der Semiten*, 152ff.; Marti, *Gesch. der isr. Rel.*⁵, 33-34; Baudissin, RE, s.v. "Malsteine"; Benzinger², 314-15; Greßmann, ZAW 29:116ff.; idem, *Altorientalische Texte und Bilder* 2:4ff.; Tylor, <319> *Anfänge der Cultur* 2:161ff.) is native in the Orient among the Phoenicians, Babylonians, Syrians, Arabs (Kaaba), Egyptians (obelisks), and even among the Greeks since the most ancient period, and is even well known in earliest Israel. Holy stones or rocks stand in Mizpah (31:45, 49), in Ebenezer (1 Sam 7:12; 4:1), at Sinai (Exod 24:4), and in Gilgal (Josh 4). There was a holy rock in Ophrah (Judg 6:21) and in Jerusalem, where it is still present, etc. *Massebahs*, that is, more or less artificially hewn blocks of stone "erected" upright (by nature they lie down), which we call by the Cetlic expression "Menhirs" (= long stones) because they are particularly frequent in Brittany, stemmed from prehistorical religion in Canaan and probably stood in every well-appointed sanctuary. The earliest view of them was that the stone is possessed by a deity (cf. the λίθοι ἔμψυχοι in Philo, *Byblios fr.* 2:19; Müller, *Fragm. hist. graec.* 3:568). This view is also attested for Israel in the name of the stone ביֿת־אֵל, "house of God." The Greeks refer to these stones with the Semitic loanword βαίτυλοι, Latin *baetuli* (cf. also the western God *Bait-ili* in cuneiform witnesses, Zimmern, KAT[3], 437-38, and the Phoenician god Βαίτυλος in Philo, *Byblios fr.* 2:14; Müller, *Fragm. hist. graec.* 3:567).

Ancient religion often naively identified the symbol and the god. "Rock of Israel," צור ישראל (the name of the god of Jerusalem, and therefore in the pilgrim song alluded to in Isa 30:29), can be explained as an example of this phenomenon. According to the testimony of the OT, such massebahs were also erected in Israel as victory memorials (1 Sam 7:12; 15:12), as gravestones (cf. also Gen 35:14), as boundary stones (cf. comments on 31:45), as well as entrance stones (1 Kgs 7:21; 2 Kgs 12:10; LXX 23:8; Greßmann). Isa 19:19 should be understood in relation to the latter practice. The custom of anointing the stones characteristic of stone veneration—so that they are called λίθοι λιπαροί or ἀληλιμμένοι, *lapides uncti, lubricati*, or *unguine delibuti* (a similar practice also among the Arabs, Wellhausen, *Arab. Heidentum*[2], 114, and Assyrians, cf. KB 1:45, 47; 2:113, 151, 235, and still in the region of Sidon, Pietwschmann, *Gesch. der Phönizier*, 207), originally understood as feeding the god resident in the stone, is also attested in the Bethel narrative. In a later, more developed era, the notion of Yahweh's residence in this stone was gradually forgotten. In the prophets, "Rock of Israel" is only an archaic expression. Already the old legend no longer understands the originally close relationship of stone and god and motivates it by a narrative to the effect that the stone was erected as a memorial of a divine revelation or some other event (31:34; Josh 4:9, 20; 24:26f.). Prophecy condemned the stones as Canaanite idolatry (Hos 10:1-2; Mic 5:12; Exod 23:24; 34:13; Deut 7:5; 12:3; 16:22; 1 Kgs 14:23; 17:10; Lev 26:1). Egyptian Jews still regarded the massebahs innocently, as Isa 19:19 and perhaps also the sanctuary of Elephantine indicate.

The relationship between stone and god has also been loosened in the Bethel narrative of E (cf. further below). It is proper to offer a gift to the revealed God or the known symbol of God or to venerate them in some other way. Consequently Jacob anoints the stone with oil (which he carries with him). Such anointings will have been common practice in Bethel. The legend also probably intentionally recounts the fact that the sacred rite occurs first thing in the morning. Morning is the time of sacrifice and later of prayer (Lev 6:5; 2 Kgs 16:15; Psa 5:4). The E recension preserved for us will probably no longer have understood the anointing as a sacrifice offered to the numen of the stone, but only as a rite of sanctification such as in Exod 30:30. Concerning anointing in the cult of Israel see Weinel, ZAW 18:48ff.; Stade, *Bibl. Theologie*, 169-70; Greßmann, *Urspr. der isr.-jüd. Eschatologie*, 258-59. V **19a** is J. E must have also had the naming (cf. 31:13; 35:3), but probably only after v 22. V **19b** is probably a gloss. At the time of this narrative there was no "city" here yet. Luz, distinct from Bethel and in the vicinity of Bethel according to Josh 16:2, was later overshadowed from the rising younger Bethel and was then considered the older name of Bethel (35:6; 48:3; Judg 1:23; Josh 18:13).

Vv **20-22** <320> are entirely from E. *Jacob's vow.* Jacob has now learned that he is at a place where the deity is near and hears. He uses the opportunity to present his wishes and makes a vow. The vow, an ancient, naive form of prayer, is a conditional promise: One promises the deity that, if that one of the wishes of one's heart is fulfilled, one will bring a specific gift. This form is naive because one hopes to gain the deity's favor through the prospect of a welcome gift (cf. Stade, *Bibl. Theol.*, ¶77). The vow falls by nature into two parts: (1) the condition (vv 20, 21a) and (2) the promise (vv 21b, 22). Vv **20, 21a** agree in content and wording with vv 15-16. J: (1) God with Jacob, (2) protection (שׁמר) on the way, and (3) return home. The two recensions of J and E reveal themselves to be fundamentally related. Common to both, above all else, is the natural assumption for the ancient that the emigrating Jacob knows no greater wish than one day to return. He has no intention, whatsoever, of staying away permanently—the ancient feeling for home. The fact that the deity accompanies one on the way seems to be an extraordinary grace (cf. comments on 46:4). **21b** A final clause, is an addition of R[JE], who found the subsequent material insufficient since it speaks only of the stone and not of God, himself. The legend thinks otherwise (in the form transmitted by E). It is self-evident to the legend that Jacob knows and worships "God" (cf. v 20). The new element added here is that he immediately considers this stone as God's seat.

22 The second etymology of בית־אל in E. Jacob vows to make the stone into the בית־ אל, that is, to venerate it henceforth as a sanctuary of God. Here, the stone itself is the "house of God." E may have simultaneously alluded to the temple which later stood here (cf. below). Concerning such ingenious plays with names see p. 238. According to v 22b, the tithe is practiced in the cult at Bethel. According to the legend Jacob instituted it. Tithing (of natural goods) as a tax to the king occurs in 1 Sam 8:15, 17, as a contribution to the sanctuary here as well as in 14:20 and Amos 4:4. According to Deut 12:17 and 14:23 tithes were used for sacrificial meals. According to P they were given to holy persons (cf. Stade, *Bibl. Theol.* see index; Guthes, BW, s.v. "Zehnten"). The continuation of the account and the payment of the vow follows.

General Remarks concerning the Bethel Legend

In its original intention, the legend recounts the origin of the sanctuary at Bethel. Bethel (now Betin) is a particularly famous sanctuary, already an oracle site (Judg 20:18, 26f.) and a pilgrimage site (1 Sam 10:3) in premonarchical times. At the time of the kings, there was a royal temple there (Amos 7:13), royally appointed by Jeroboam I with a Yahweh image, a golden bull (1 Kgs 12:28-29). The site was as significant in Israel as Cologne and Fulda in Catholic Germany. Bethel is frequently discussed and combated even by the earlier prophets (Amos 4:4; Hos 10:5, etc.). King Josiah desecrated the ancient site (2 Kgs 23:15ff.). The legend in Gen 28:10-22 originally extolled the site as a Yahweh sanctuary. It therefore stems from preprophetic times. Other elements of the legend, such as the anointing of the stone and the heavenly ladder, also speak for its advanced age. The account also reflects the powerful significance of Bethel. In Bethel stands the ladder of heaven. Thus, if the heavenly beings wish to come down and return, they must pass through Bethel. The ancient goes to the cultic site in order to "seek" the deity there. Do you want <321> to know a place where you can surely meet the deity, where it will hear your prayers and accept your sacrifices? Go to Bethel. There they will always make it through.

In its original form, the piece can hardly be called a "narrative" since there is no development. Instead, it is based on nothing more than a brief comment such as those we often encounter as a local tradition, not just in Israel (cf. introduction ¶3:22). The comment concerning Mahanaim is an especially close parallel (32:2-3 [some EVV =32:1-2]). The old comment explained the sanctity of the stone at Bethel, the origin of the site's name, and the origin of anointing and tithing. This comment was then inserted in the account of Jacob and further amplified in this context: Jacob encountered this stone on his flight from Esau and heard a promise here or made a vow which referred to his migration and the hope of return. The old tradition (the dream vision) and the supplementary material (the vow) can be distinguished with particular clarity in E.

Each of the two recensions has its ancient elements. Jacob's vow in E is more ancient than Yahweh's promise in J. Further characteristic is the fact that Jacob's words in E relate only to his individual condition, while J adds the promise, "I will give you this land." The account in E is, therefore, purely "novelistic" at this point. J, however, views Jacob simultaneously as Israel's ancestor. Elsewhere, too, simple novelistic accounts and recensions are often older than those which refer to Israel (cf. p. 315). Historical Israel comforted itself in difficult times with such words of Yahweh (cf. p. 182). The comparison of the two recensions in terms of their evaluation of Bethel is inappropriate since J is not transmitted whole (is there no mention of the stone whatsoever in J?) and since the most varied assessments occur alongside one another in E. Certainly, the earliest period understood the stone, itself, as "God's house" and that the appearing deity was originally the numen of this stone, the אֵל of Bethel (31:13; 35:7). A later development then relaxed the relationship between stone and deity. The whole site was called "Bethel" or one conceived of the deity dwelling in heaven and linked with the earthly sanctuary by a ladder. But the latter notion is by no means a witness to late Israelite reflection (contra Stade, *Bibl. Theol.*, 104), but stems, as the naive mythological concept of the ladder demonstrates, from a very early period. The original view of the stone as the house of God still sounds through in E in Jacob's words (v 22), while E's account of the vision presumes the (relatively) younger idea of the heavenly house of God and Jacob's words in E (v 17) mitigate the mythological aspects of this idea even further. The fact that one Yahweh, who has directly replaced the local numen here, appears in J sounds more ancient than E's vision based on the concept of the god of heaven. But the fact that J (as far as we can see) knows no association between Yahweh and the stone but only knows that Yahweh resides "at this site" is late. We gain insight here, then, into a complicated history which suggests one conclusion with full certainty, namely that E is not literarily dependent on J.

For E the Bethel account constitutes the midpoint of the Jacob narrative, as 31:13 and chap. 35 demonstrate.

Hos 12:5 mentions the Bethel legend. "In Bethel he (Jacob) met him (i.e., the angel); there he spoke 'with him'" (עִמּוֹ). The tradition presumed in Hosea, it seems, recounted the Bethel legend after the Penuel narrative (Gall, *Altisr. Kultstätten*, 97).

A. Smythe Palmer, *Jacob at Bethel*, Studies on Biblical Subjects 2 (London, 1899) with a great deal of folklore material (discussed in *Folklore* 11: 196ff.) is not available to me. <322>

The Jacob-Laban Legend

The Jacon-Laban legend bears similarity at certain points with the legend of Abraham's migration to Canaan and with the Rebekah legend. Like Jacob, Abraham also migrates from Mesopotamia to Shechem and Bethel and Rebekah also moves from Haran to Canaan. Jacob's wives have their counterpart in Isaac's wife who, according to the legend, stems from the same family. Laban also plays a role in the Rebekah legend. There are also a few less significant parallels. The Jacob and the Rebekah legends both recount a well scene associated with the initial acquaintance with the later wife of the patriarch. On the other hand, however, the parallel accounts are very different in many other elements so that they can hardly be termed "variants" in the limited sense. They remain distinct accounts with similarities in only a few points. It will also be difficult to forward a hypothesis concerning which of the legends may have priority. A hypothesis such as the notion that Rebekah and Rachel were originally identical figures (Steurnagel, *Isr. Stämme*, 40) will be difficult to demonstrate.

To what extent is the legend based on historical material? The current form of the tradition does not discuss Jacob and Laban as peoples. Instead, Jacob and Laban are private persons. National history only becomes prominent at the conclusion, where, in one recension, there is a sort of peace and border treaty (31:52). Here, it seems, the border between two peoples, Aramaeans and "Hebrews," is established. Now this national history appears in such an unmediated fashion that the conjecture that it was only secondarily added at least suggests itself. One may accordingly well assume that this national historical reference was also only secondarily introduced into this legend. On the other hand, the legend, even in its earliest form, seems nevertheless to have been based on certain ethnographic, for Israel prehistoric, circumstances. "Hebrew" and "Eastern" nomad tribes must have once lived together in that region and felt related to one another in order for such a legend to take shape. This contention can be demonstrated by the recently discovered Aramaic inscriptions—"the older the Aramaic, the more it resembles the Hebrew," (cf. Sachau, *Mitteilungen aus dem Orientalischen Sammlungen des Berliner Museum* 11:83)—and seems not unlikely from the historical standpoint either. The site where the earliest reports localize this narrative is, as Meyer (*Israeliten*, 235ff.) has recently shown us, the great desert in northeastern Palestine (cf. comments on Gen 29). There, in the "East," will have been the homeland of the "Hebrews" as well as of the "Aramaeans." We may also see historical echoes in Jacob's marriage with an easterner and his emigration from her land. Intermingling of the tribes as well as migrations from the East to the southwest will have taken place. We hear of similar situations in the parallel Abraham and Rebekah legends. Whether the same process in different forms echoes in these related narratives, however, or whether different events are involved can no longer be decided.

Recently Steuernagel (*Einwanderung der israel. Stämme* [1901]) has attempted to interpret the entire Jacob narrative historically. In the process he has constructed an entire system from the most varied sources with much sagacity and a remarkable gift for synthesis. His method is the much beloved explanation of not only all the figures of the legend together with their wives as earlier peoples or tribes but "in a unilateral exaggeration of a totally correct and fertile concept within its bounds . . . also the transformation, through a pair of very simple, essentially purely rationalistic devices, of everything recounted concerning them into genuine and purely authentic narratives concerning these very peoples." Thus he interprets Jacob's struggle with the God at Penuel in relation to a victorious war of the tribe Jacob against the <323> inhabitants of Gilead (61), his purchase of property at Shechem in relation to a tribute payment of the Rachel tribe settled near Shechem (90), even Joseph's colorful coat in relation to the superior clothing of many Josephites which incited the hatred of the other tribes (66-67), as well as Joseph's deportation to Egypt in relation to a struggle among the tribes in which individual Josephites were captured and sold (67). Meyer, whose words were just cited, correctly warns against such exaggerations (*Israeliten*, 251n.1). Other objections against Steuernagel's constructions can be found in this commentary, pp. 279-80.

The name "Laban" may have originally been a divine name (cf. above p. 163). Yet, very little mythological material can be discovered in the legend (cf., however, introduction ¶4:10).

Seen esthetically, we have the accounts of Jacob and Laban in an intensely novelistic form. The individual legends have been woven together into a unit. The content of this Jacob-Laban novella is the alternation of trick and countertrick between the clever Laban and the much more clever Jacob. First, Laban deceives Jacob and forces him to serve fourteen years for his daughters. But then during an additional service of six years Jacob outwits Laban and gains a great portion of his property from him. Thus the sly deceiver is himself deceived. Jacob, who came to him as an individual, without home and property, now has four wives, eleven children, cattle, donkeys, sheep, and slaves. He crossed the Jordan on foot, and now he has authority over two camps (32:11)! In the end he successfully escapes Laban with all this property. He obtained this success through patience, cunning, and especially God's blessing. It seems that the earlier tradition recounted this narrative, too, in a crudely humorous tone (cf. especially 31:33ff.). The later tradition took pains to shape the narrative as favorably as possible for Jacob and to demonstrate that, in relation to Laban, he was completely in the right (so E 31). The whole novella falls then into three parts: (1) Laban deceives Jacob (29:15-20); (2) Jacob outwits Laban (30:25-43); and (3) Jacob escapes Laban (31:1-32:1). A small novelistic interlude has been prefixed to the whole: Jacob's arrival at Laban (29:1-14). This small idyll has no perceptible etiological or historical reference and seems to be purely novelistic in nature. Later, after a close relationship between two persons has been established, it is a great pleasure to determine how the initial, still innocuous acquaintance was made. Thus the legend recounts here with joy how Jacob became acquainted with the woman whom he later came so to love. She was the first of the family he saw (as in Tob 7:1). The legend gladly details how the strong and clever Jacob utilized the opportunity to secure a cordial reception.

44. Jacob's Arrival at Laban 29:1-14 J (E)

Source analysis. Since Dillmann, v 1 (where the destination is the land of the sons of Qedem, while J mentions Haran [27:43; 28:10; 29:4], and P mentions Paddan-aram

[28:2]) has been attributed to E. In contrast, because of the expressions לַאֲשֶׁר (v 9 as in 40:5), רוּץ לִקְרַאת (v 13 as in 18:2; 24:17), and עַצְמִי וּבְשָׂרִי (v 14 as in 2:23) it has been attributed to J. The content of the passage hardly characterizes J. Sievers (2:320) and Eerdmans (59-60) also take v 1 with the following, an analysis made impossible by the mutually exclusive geographical information.

1-3 *The scene.* **1** קֶדֶם "the East" is a geographical term of, it seems, rather indefinite or varying character. According to the earliest report (ca. 1900) contained in the biography of the Egyptian Sinuha, one comes <324> to the "land of Qedem" via Byblos (Ranke in Greßmann, *Altorient. Texte und Bilder zum A.T.* 1:212) so that the desert region east of Damascus bears this name (Meyer, *Gesch. d. Altertums* I/2², 260). The East is to be sought further to the South if the sons of Keturah dwell there (25:6) and if, according to Ezek 25:4, 10, the "sons of the East" are enemies and probably also neighbors of Moab and Ammon (cf. Winckler, *Gesch. Isr.* 2:51ff.; Meyer, *Israeliten*, 243-44). According to the OT, Arabic tribes, and according to the earliest information, Aramaic tribes, too, dwell in the "East" (regarding the latter, cf. our passage and Num 23:7). According to E Laban lives here. Hos 12:13 ("Aram's fields") agrees, while J locates Laban's dwelling much farther away in Haran (cf. also the comments on 31:21, 23). Remarkably, local color of the great city Haran is totally lacking in the legends themselves. Gen 29:13 only parenthetically mentions Laban's "house." Gen 30:14, which mentions the "wheat harvest," is also entirely secondary. Otherwise, this legend treats shepherds whose focal point is the well (29:2) and who graze their flocks "on free plains which extend for miles" (30:36). Consequently, Meyer (*Israeliten*, 242-43) correctly assumes that E has preserved the old material here. Nahor's genealogy (22:20-24), it seems, also points to this conclusion. The account of Abraham's emigration (cf. comments on 12:1) as well as a recension of the Rebekah narrative still maintain that Abraham's relatives were not city-dwellers, but nomads (cf. comments on 24:10). These narratives were probably transferred to Haran when the Aramaeans migrated from the Syrian-northern Arabic steppe into Mesopotamia and Syria (cf. above, pp. 167-68; contra Eerdmans 2:85-86). "*The* stone" (with article) refers to the stone which, as everyone knows, lies on such wells in order to protect them from trespassers (Benzinger², 207). Sam, Targ-Onk, LXX, Ball, and Kittel read וְאֶבֶן.

3 This well belongs to several owners and is secured with such a heavy stone that it can only be opened when all the shepherds have assembled to use it under common control. The perfects with ו are the continuation of יֻשְׁקְ (§112e). The first clause (וְנֶאֶסְפוּ) would be a temporal clause in German (§164b 4). The description in vv 2b, 3 prepares for vv 8 and 10. The narrators love to offer such preparations at the beginning (cf. comments on 27:1). Later, more extensive style also preferred such repetitions. It is, therefore, not advisable to strike v 3 with Holzinger although the account would thereby become more interesting.

4-8 *Jacob and the shepherds.* **4** Thus, Jacob, too, has arrived very near to his destination through a benevolent providence (similarly to Gen 24). **5** Laban is called the son of Nahor here; in contrast to the son of Bethuel, the son of Nahor in 24:15, etc. בֶּן is not to be taken in the broader sense of "grandson" here. Instead, according to the original tradition of J, even in Gen 24, Laban is Nahor's son. He became Bethuel's son only secondarily (cf. above p. 252). **6** The fact that Rachel comes immediately after she has been mentioned is a convenient meeting such as the narrators love. The fact that she is seen before she appears is a gracious way of unifying the scene. **7** Jacob, himself a <325> shepherd, recognizes with an expert eye that the shepherds act impractically. They are losing time they could well use for grazing. The narrator reports this so the shepherds may explain to Jacob (v 8) and so he may gain the opportunity to serve (v 10). The account is, therefore, an exemplary unity. **8** The shepherds explain to Jacob why they cannot yet water their flocks. They are still waiting on the others. But they do not tell him why they are at the well so early. This is considered obvious—they go in order at the well. First come, first watered.

9-12 *Jacob and Rachel.* **9** בָּאָה is perfect. The maidens help the men with the work and are, therefore, relatively independent. They move freely and appear innocently before strange men (cf. Benzinger², 107). The married women differ (Gen 18:9ff.). **10** Jacob recognizes the situation immediately (כַּאֲשֶׁר "as soon as" 27:30). He sees a good opportunity to do his uncle a favor and to show how valuable he is as a worker. He immediately takes this opportunity because he knows that henceforth he will depend on his uncle's good will. The narrator makes it clear that he does so because of his uncle (and not merely because of Rachel's beautiful eyes) with the threefold לָבָן אֲחִי אִמּוֹ. At the same time, the narrator praises Jacob's physical strength. The fact that Jacob was originally a giant echoes through (cf. comments on 28:11; 32:26; Dillmann). **11** The kiss was the usual greeting among relatives (cf. Benzinger², 132). Jacob's crying immediately after his show of strength seems strange to us. There are parallels in Homer. The ancients unabashedly give their feelings free course. Jacob cries from joyous emotion at having found relatives in a foreign land. The Hebrew's strong (in our terms often sentimental) ties to the family, already expressed in the old legends (also 33:4; 45:14; 46:29) and later in the touching family novellas (Tobit and 4 Ezr 9:38ff.), still characterize Jewish family life today. "The deceiver Jacob, not very concerned with family ties, is suddenly very sentimental" (Haller, 6; cf. comments on vv 13, 14). **12** "Brother" means relative (v 15; 13:8).

13, 14 *Jacob and Laban.* As do Jacob's, Laban's characteristic and less noble qualities also seem to recede here. He very tenderly receives the favored son of his sister from whom he may not have heard for twenty years and the account gives no indication that he does so for calculated reasons. One can conclude that this small novella did not originally relate to Laban and Jacob and that it is not thoroughly fused into the context of the whole Jacob-Laban narrative. Otherwise, a <326> recension of Gen 24 (J) also seems to presume Laban's particular love for his relatives (cf. above p. 245). Laban's love for his daughters is comparable (31:28, 43, 50). **14** Laban is convinced by Jacob's words that he is really a relative, not an imposter, and he assures him of his protection. יָמִים is in apposition to חֹדֶשׁ (§131d).

The account bears a great similarity to the account in Exod 2:15-21. Moses, too, is in flight, in a strange land, at the well. Maidens come to water the flocks. Other shepherds are also present. Moses helps the maidens and waters the flocks. They come home. Moses is summoned, remains with their father, and marries one of his daughters. Such minor accounts have no master and transfer easily from one person to the other. Yet, the account is characteristically shaped in both cases. The assistance the hero offers the maidens differs in character. Moses cannot tolerate injustice and helps the maidens because they are pushed away by the shepherds. But Jacob offers assistance in order to secure a good reception with Laban. The well scene of Gen 24 is distantly related to both accounts. It is more closely related to the material reported by E. Littmann (*Arabische Beduinenerzählungen* 2, 41), especially with the Moses legend.

45. Jacob's Marriage to Leah and Rachel: Laban Deceives Jacob 29:15-30 E (J)

Source criticism. It is clear from v 16, where Rachel is introduced anew, that a new source begins here. Since the preceding probably belongs to J, this passage may stem from E (Dillmann; cf. מַשְׂכֹּרֶת v 15; 31:7, 41; J—שָׂכָר). Because of צְעִירָה and בְּכִירָה (19:31ff.), v 26 stems from J (E גִּלְדָּה and קְטַנָּה vv 16, 18). Procksch wants to attribute vv 27a, ba, 28, 30a to J, which, however, hardly improves the context. V 30a refers back to v 23b. "The week" (vv 27, 28) is the one begun in vv 22, 23, 25. And vv 19, 21 already speak of the "giving" of the bride (v 27).

The evaluation of the following narrative depends especially on the perception of Laban's character. The point of the following account is that Laban substitutes Leah for Rachel and thus "deceives" Jacob (v 25). His chief characteristic in this narrative is, then, that he is a deceiver. The same is also true later (31:7). On the other hand, he characteristically has an exquisite excuse (v 26) when he is called to account for his deceit. He regularly employs excuses and lies (31:27). Laban is described here as a selfish deceiver who loves to clothe his sly tricks in a cloak of honesty. It is obvious, therefore, that the narrator is amused at this contrast although, on the other hand, he is not in a position to explicitly comment on his hero (cf. introduction ¶3:12). He can only portray this contrast by juxtaposing the deceitful acts and the upright words and clue in the hearer with a mischievous glance, with a smile. An "ethical viewpoint" has even been sought in this humorous narrative. Laban avenges Jacob's deception of Esau and Isaac in this way. Jacob is being taught to "cling to his God" in this way (Dillmann). But the old narrator thinks differently. He recounts this narrative with humor because he knows that Jacob will repay the old deceiver his deceit with interest. A religious viewpoint comes into consideration in the narrative only to the extent that the (unexpressed) precondition is that Yahweh's blessing rests on Jacob (Holzinger).

15-20 *The agreement.* **15** The presupposition is that meanwhile Jacob has helped with the <327> work, that Laban has watched him closely, and that Laban has recognized that he is extremely useful. Yahweh is, after all, with Jacob (30:27; 28:15). So he wishes to keep him and decides to offer him wages. But, of course, he does not tell him how useful he finds him. Otherwise Jacob would demand a high price. Instead he chooses the mask of pleasant selflessness. He cannot tolerate his young nephew serving him for nothing! הֲכִי means "yes, indeed" (27:36; §150e). Regarding "and should you serve?" see §112cc. **17** The ancient Hebrew loves maidens with especially brilliant eyes. Dull eyes are a severe beauty blemish. **18** Such a suggestion will not have gone unheard (cf. Wellhausen, *Gött. Gel. Nachr.* [1893], 434). The lover serves the father of the beloved for her in the Mahrian-Walachian fairy tales, too, specifically by guarding the sheep (Wenzig, *Westslav. Märchenschatz*, 1). At any rate, seven years of service is considered here as a high purchase price. The enamored Jacob will certainly have valued the beautiful maiden highly and the greedy father will just as certainly not let her go cheaply. **19** Laban, who does not easily give away money and monetary value (30:31), gladly agrees to this suggestion which will allow him to save wages for seven years. But, of course, he has a splendid reason. One really does prefer to marry one's daughter within the family, especially to her cousin. Thus the property stays together and the blood stays pure (cf. Benzinger², 107). The same is still true in Iraq, for example (cf. Meißner, *Beiträge zur Assyriologie* 5:5). Significantly, too, Laban's daughter is consulted neither now nor in relation to the deceit (Haller, 101, 116). V **20** is a lovely element. A modern sentimental lover would think the opposite and, in his desire, find the time long. It is short for Jacob who feels more strongly. He would do anything gladly for Rachel. He is sure of her, after all.

21-30 *The deceit*. Laban wants to take this opportunity to get the ugly Leah a husband. He counts on Jacob being unable to discern the deceit in time because the bride is led veiled into the bridal chamber (24:65). But once the marriage has been consummated he will not do his uncle the injury of refusing the wife and disturbing the splendid feast. But then Laban already has a suggestion for making good *in petto*. He wants to obligate him for an additional seven years. If everything succeeds he will have killed two flies with one blow. **21** Jacob says "my wife" because now that he has paid the מֹהַר she legally belongs to him. **22** In this special case and contrary to the normal custom, the marriage takes place in the house of the father-in-law (Judg 14:10; Tob 8:18; Benzinger², 109). V **25a** depicts Jacob's surprise. The matter is indeed very vexing for Jacob. But the narrator cannot refrain from laughing: therefore, let whoever enters into eternal bonds beware! Deception in the acquisition of a wife is a common motif (cf. Grimm's *Märchen* no. 89; cf. no. 13; H. Gering, *Edda*, 18ff.; and Herodotus 3.1) and also plays a role in today's popular <328> custom in Hessen (cf. Hepding, *Hess. Bl. f. Volksk.* 5:161ff.). **25** Jacob is naturally indignant and he accuses Laban. רִמִּיתָנִי is probably an allusion to אֲרָם. **26** But Jacob wraps himself in his unassailable respectability and has an imposing reason for his action: My dear cousin, it is obvious that you are not a native. This is the local custom. The reason has been well chosen, at any rate, for such is often the custom in reality (cf. Lane, *Sitten u. Gebräuche der heutigen Egypter* 1:169). He should have told him sooner, however! **27** "Keep the week" refers to the fact that the marriage lasts a week (Judg 14:12; Tob 11:17; cf. 3 Macc 4:8; similarly among the old Arabs, Wellhausen, *Nachrichten der Gött. Ges. der Wissenschaften* [1893], 442). It is still considered very unrespectable for the young husband to disturb these festivities (cf. Wetzstein, "Syrische Dreschtafel" in *Bastians Zeitschr. für Ethnologie* [1873]: 291). "We" means "I and my relatives." Sam, LXX, Pesh, and Vulg read וְאֶתֵּן. Kittel suggests וְאֶתְנָה (?). In order to encourage him to agree to the transaction, Jacob will receive Rachel immediately, *praenumerando*. Bigamy must have been very common in ancient Israel (Benzinger², 105). Marriage to two sisters was prohibited by later law (Lev 18:18), but must have been considered entirely unobjectionable in the ancient period, otherwise one would not have recounted such of Jacob. Besides, Yahweh (of course only metaphorically) was said (Jer 3:6ff.; Ezek 23) to have two sisters as wives, Israel and Judah. Of course, simultaneous marriage to two women is considered an exception here (similarly in the *Arabischen Beduinenerzählungen* 2:29, published by E. Littmann). **30** גַּם² is senseless and should be stricken following LXX and Vulg (Dillmann). Thus, Jacob must serve for the unattractive

Leah as long as does for the beautiful Rachel. How furious he must have been and how he must have sworn revenge! Hos 12:13 mentions Jacob's "service" for his wives.

46. Jacob's Children 29:31–30:24 JE

1. *Arrangement.* The passage, distinctly segmented, falls into four sections: (1) Leah's children (29:31-35); (2) Rachel's adoptive children (30:1-8); (3) Leah's adoptive children (30:9-13); and (4) the mandrake and the children born thereafter (30:14-24).

2. *Source criticism.* Part I (29:31-35) belongs to J (יהוה vv 31, 32, 33, 35). Concerning v 32bγ see the interpretation. Part II (30:1-8) stems essentially from E: v 2 because of אלהים (cf. also 50:19 E); v 3a because of אָמָה (cf. pp. 218-19 on Gen 20); v 4b continues בֹּא אֵלֶיהָ in v 3b; v 6 because of אלהים; v 8 because of אלהים; v 2 responds to v 1b; v 1ab makes a new beginning and is still to be attributed to E; קִנֵּא ב (37:11) is E. The following belongs to J: v 1a (cf. the same beginning of the first and third sections in J 29:31; 30:9) and the phrase in v 3bβ (the same phrase in J in 16:2; the parallel clause in v 3bα belongs, therefore, to E; cf. 50:23 I). שִׁפְחָה in v 7 points to J, but the clause stands in an E context and the list of the individual sons seems (according to Procksch, 24) to characterize E whereas J only offers to total number (29:34). Accordingly, בִּלְהָה שִׁפְחַת רָחֵל will be an expansion. P includes v 4a and later v 9b (cf. the <329> very similar clause in 16:3). The redactor has reproduced E in its entirety here, then, and interspersed only two phrases from J. Later a little P was added. It is insignificant which source is the origin for clauses such as vv 5, 10. All three sources must have had more or less similar clauses. III (9-13) is entirely from J: v 9a (the beginning resembles 29:31; 30:1; עָמַד מִלֶּדֶת as in 29:35), v 10 (שִׁפְחָה), and v 12a (שִׁפְחָה). V 12b (the list of individual) as well as כִּי אִשְּׁרוּנִי בָּנֹות (v 13, the second etymology of אָשֵׁר are probably to be attributed to E. IV (14-24) falls into two parts. The first reports the dudaim (vv 14-16) and the second the birth of the youngest children (vv 17-24). The second stems entirely from E: אלהים (vv 17, 18, 20aα, β, 22bα, 23) and the list of the individuals (vv 17, 19). Only v 20aγ belongs to J with certainty (the second etymology of Zebulon ‖ v 20aβ E; cf. also הַפַּעַם 29:34-35; 2:23 and elsewhere in J and the very similar clause in 29:34 as well as the total number of sons) and v 24b (the second etymology of Joseph; v 24b יהוה ‖ v 23b אלהים), as well as v 22bβ (cf. 29:31 J). The first part of this section, the dudaim episode (vv 14-16), stems from J. Evidence for this conclusion follows: E motivated the birth and name of Issachar through God's intervention (vv 17, 18); but the story of the mandrakes (vv 14-16) offers another explanation for both. Both J and E must have possessed comments such as vv 20b and 21 (v 21 prepares for Gen 34). The clause "so that I gave my husband my maidservant" (v 18aγ) cannot belong to E because of שִׁפְחָתִי. It is therefore a gloss. Only v 22a (אלהים, זָכַר cf. 8:1) in section IV can be attributed to P.

3. This account is not properly a "narrative." The treatment is too superficial. The same motif, that a childless wife adopted the children of her maidservant, which is only employed to develop the legend of Hagar's flight, comprises almost the whole account here. Consequently, the passage cannot be regarded an old popular legend either, but an artificial construction, an imitation of an old legend. The narrators consider it necessary to report here the birth of Jacob's sons, concerning whom they want to reproduce tradi-

tional legends in the further course of the narrative. But they surely do not want to settle for a dry list of births. Instead they want to clothe the genealogy in the tasteful form of narrative (similarly in Nahor's genealogy, 22:20-24). In this account, however, the children's names must be explained above all. Further, it must be shown why Jacob's sons include the children of slaves among the legitimate children. The task of devising an account on the basis of such data may well have excited clever narrators. It is no wonder, however, that their narrative proves to be somewhat mediocre. They chose the relationship between two sisters, wives of the same man, as the motif for the account. Of course they are jealous of one another and want to excel each other in children so that, finally, they even give their slaves to their husband. The narrators sought interpretations for the names of the individual children which would suit this context to some degree. The passage is interesting for the history of legends because it shows us how narratives devised by the narrators themselves look. At the same time, we can discern the advanced age of the patriarchal legends. It belongs, in terms of its origins, to the latest passages in the tradition. On the other hand, it contains a very ancient element—the magical effect of the mandrake—which was objectionable to a later period and was consequently altered in E. This very young account, from the perspective of the history of legend, belongs, therefore, in an ancient period from the perspective of the history of religion. A similar conclusion can be drawn from Gen 15 (pp. 182-83). Finally, this passage shows how closely J and E, which both possess this account not based on old legend tradition, must have been to one another. J and E must have been very similar both in overall structure and in wording. Otherwise R^JE would have been unable to compose a tolerable unity from the two (Wellhausen, *Composition*³, 37).

4. The narrators found the names and, to great degree, probably also the arrangement in which the names stand in the tradition. The names differ widely in character: A few were originally animal names (such as לֵאָה, which, according to Nöldeke [ZDMG 90:167] may mean "wild cow," <330> רָחֵל "mother sheep," שִׁמְעוֹן may be cognate to Arab. *sim'u*, the hybrid offspring of a hyena and a jackal [Robertson-Smith, *Journal of Philology* 9:80, 96). Stade (*Gesch. Isr.* 1:152, 408) interprets them in relation to a totem which would have been prehistoric in Israel at any rate, while Meyer (*Israeliten*, 308ff.) interprets such animal names as derogatory and honorific names derived from the circumstances of life for the desert tribes and vividly contradicts the whole theory of the totemism for those tribes. Zebulon is, it seems, a patronymic of Zebul (Judg 9:28ff.), a tribe named for a person, probably its chief (Meyer, *Israeliten*, 538). According to Meyer (*Israeliten*, 539) it is an ethnicon (from the land of?) Naphtal. Thus, לֵוִי and לֵאָה may also belong together (Wellhausen, *Prolegomena*⁶, 138). Concerning the "Levites" in the northern Arabic oasis el 'Ola in ca. sixth or fifth century BCE, see Meyer, *Israeliten*, 88-89. Issachar = אִישׁ שָׂכָר = day laborer (49:14-15) named so by its Canaanite masters (Meyer, *Israeliten*, 536). גַּד is an Aramao-Phoenician divine name (Zimmern, KAT³, 479), the name of the god of fate, still known in Isa 65:11. The name Asher appears in the form *Asaru* in inscriptions of Seti I and Ramses II (ca 1400, thus in pre-Israelite times) as the name of a northern Canaanite tribe (cf. W. Max Müller, *Asien und Europa*, 236ff.). The Israelite tribe would have been named for the region where it dwelt (Meyer, *Israeliten*, 540; but cf. also Eerdmans 2:65ff.). Joseph, which may be associated with the Canaanite city name *Išpr* mentioned in Egyptian sources, may be a divine name (cf. introduction

¶4:10). There is also certainly much ancient in the order of the names: Reuben, here the firstborn (as also in the old poem in 49:3-4), becomes historically insignificant. Simeon and Levi, who stand after Reuben here (as in 49:5-7), in the ancient period, therefore, of great importance (cf. the old legend in Gen 34), disappeared in the historical period. Joseph is considered a tribe here, while Ephraim and Manasseh appeared later as independent tribes. Furthermore, the geographic circumstances of the tribes in Canaan do not agree very well with their classification. The division of the Israelite tribes into sons of Leah and Rachel is different from the later division into the kingdoms of Israel and Judah. All of this suggests that this genealogy does not reflect the circumstances of Israel's monarchical period, but those of an earlier period (so recently also Eerdmans 2:51 and Kautzsch[3]). Very characteristically, the royal tribe Joseph stands all the way at the end of the list and the tradition separates Benjamin from the other tribes. Benjamin was not born abroad but only when they returned to Canaan. A historical tradition may echo here to the effect that the tribe Benjamin only arose after Israel's immigration into Canaan. On the other hand, the age of the genealogy at hand should not be overestimated either: the Song of Deborah still knows Machir and Gilead, omitted here, among the ten tribes it lists. Individual variations in the number and order of the tribes continued to appear for a long period of time. Thus, Zebulon and Dinah were only inserted secondarily in their current position in J. Even Gen 49 and Deut 33 differ in the details. The youngest elements in our genealogy include the name Issachar (cf. above) as well as the association of Dan with Naphtali which assumes Dan's later residence in the North. Whether one may attribute the whole division of Israel into tribes only to the period after arrival in Canaan (with Meyer) seems very questionable to me. The division of the tribes into legitimate, born to the wife, and illegitimate, born to the concubine, also occurs in the genealogies of Nahor (22:20-24) and Esau (36:9-14). Luther (ZAW 21:36ff.) offers an overview of the use of the genealogy and the genealogical legends for the history of Israel by Wellhausen (*Isr. und Jüd. Gesch.*, 12ff., 18; *Prolegomena*[6], 316ff.), Stade (ZAW 1:112ff., 347ff.; *Gesch. Isr.* 1:145-46; *Akad. Reden und Abhandlungen*, 97ff.), Guthe (*Gesch. Isr.*, 40ff.), and Cornill (*Gesch. Isr.*, 30ff). The list may be expanded to included Kuenen (*Theol. Tijdschr.* [1871]: 281ff.), Steuernagel (cf. above pp. 315-16), and recently especially Meyer (*Israeliten*, 292, 444ff., 506ff.). The theories of interpretation are extremely varied and at present offer <331> very little which is certain. The tradition that Israel divides into twelve tribes is very old. This number was always only a theory in Israel's historical period. We observe twelve tribes also in relation to Joktan (10:26-27), Nahor (22:20-24), Keturah (25:1-4), Ishmael (25:13-14), and Esau (36:15-19, 40-43). It must therefore have been custom for these desert tribes at the edge of Near Eastern-Babylonian culture to number twelve tribes. Much farther away, the number twelve also occurs not only in reference to Aiolos's children (*Od.* 10:5), but, according to Szanto (*Sitzungsber. der Wiener Akad. Phil.-hist. Kl.* 154 [1901] V Abhandlung, 40ff), in the Delphic amphictiony, and city amphictionies of the Ionians in Asia minor, the Ionian Achaeans, as well in the Etrurean alliance, etc. Szanto interprets this in terms of the rotation of the care for the common sanctuary among the communities with each serving for one month just as Solomon's new division of Israel into twelve districts served the monthly provision of the court (1 Kgs 4:7; cf. Luther in Meyer, *Israeliten*, 148n.1). This is certainly very plausible. There would have been a central sanctuary in Israel's earliest period then!

5. The passage is instructive concerning the circumstances of the Israelite home. The Israelite man often had two wives. The two—passionate as Israelite women are (30:1)—make life difficult for him through their jealousy (30:2). And he is not inclined to fairness himself. No one can love two women, he would say. He "loves" one and "hates" the other. One perceives how common such relationships were in this account itself. Naturally it does not intend to recount evil of Jacob's home. Instead it reports only those things which—as everyone knows—occur throughout Israel (cf. also 1 Sam 1:5). Popular law also assumes the same situation: אֲהוּבָה and שְׂנוּאָה are legal terms (Deut 21:15)! Because of deplorable states of affairs such as those presumed here in Jacob's house, the later law decrees that the man may not have two sisters as wives (Lev 18:18). The constant reason for the wives' dispute is the number of their children. To have many sons is the greatest source of pride for the fertile, the most passionate desire of the infertile. The infertile must suffer scorn and disdain wherever she goes, at home and on the street (Luke 1:25). Infertility is a shame (30:23). In order to have children, the wife is even prepared to give her slave to her husband in order to adopt her children (concerning this legal practice, cf. comments on 16:2). She then expects God's reward for such self-denial (30:18). If one of the wives offered such a sacrifice and actually obtained children in this fashion, then the other will not stand back and she does the same. Now, in order to make things even more complicated and to see to a just balance, the legend gladly recounts how the preferred, to whom the husband often "went in," was infertile, but the disfavored had many children in her "suffering" (29:32). The same situation occurs in the account of Samuel's childhood (1 Sam 1). Finally, the religious aspect is not entirely absent, either. God gives children (30:2), opens and shuts the womb (29:31; 30:2). The infertile wife prays to him (30:6, 17). The mother thanks him (29:35). Regarding the basic ancient view that pregnancy and birth comes from God see 16:2. And if prayer does not help, then the dudaim may do so (30:14ff.).

I. **29:31-35 J** *Leah's children.* **31** That Yahweh cares for the despised is a comforting belief: Yahweh helps the poor, the despised, the despairing, the fugitive slave (16:7ff.), the rejected child and his unfortunate mother (21:17ff.), the shamefully sold and slandered (39:2, 21ff.). **32** The fact that etymologies concentrated in the following materials, as ingenious as they may be, may not be measured according <332> to the criterion of our learning is obvious. Nevertheless, modern scholars have not even wanted to acknowledge these name derivations as such. Thus the etymology רָאָה בְעָנְיִי = רְאוּבֵן is perilous in modern philological terms. The narrator, however, wanted to give not only an "allusion" (Dillmann), but an actual etymology of the name. In other cases, the interpreters, and even Kautzsch[3], have attempted to come to the assistance of the interpreters and create semitolerable etymologies for these words (cf. comments on v 33). Pesh, LXX mss read ראובל (perhaps cognate to Arab. *ri'bâl* "lion, wolf"). A second etymology of "Reuben" may be hidden in יאהבֵנִי (§60d; Ball). Then one must attribute this clause to the second recension (E). It seems plausible to assume that a word may have originally stood here that also contained the ר of "Reuben" and that was replaced by the more common אהב (Aram. אירב, "to be large"; אורב "to praise"; רַבִּי Dan 2:48 "to raise"). **33** The idea is not that the etymology of שִׁמְעוֹן is "[God is] a hearer" (Kautzsch[3]), but that the child was called שִׁמְעוֹן because Leah said שָׁמַע. So it is subsequently. **34** For קרא Sam, LXX, Pesh, and Vulg have קָרְאָה (cf. v 35; Ball, Kittel, Kautzsch[3]).

II. **30:1-3, 4b-8 E(J)** *Rachel's adoptive children.* **1, 2** The minor scene between Jacob and Rachel is supposed to make it apparent that Rachel finally reached the point she gave her slave girl to her husband. It was a difficult decision only comprehensible as the result of the excitement of a passionate moment! **2** Rachel was so passionate that even Jacob became angry with his beloved. **3** The form of adoption presumed here is that the slave gave birth "on the knees" of the wife so that children of the slave appear to be children of her own womb. This type of adoption is a barbaric, but very vivid symbolization of the adoption of one woman's children by another woman. The same ceremony may also be presumed for the man who adopts the child of his son (50:23). In this case the ceremony is much more difficult to interpret. This ceremony seems, then, to have originally been practiced by the woman and then to have become the form by which the man adopts, too (contra Stade, ZAW 6:143-56). Concerning אֲבָנֶה see 16:2. **6** It was very common for the ancient to understand a dispute with another as a legal matter. The same situation is common in the Psalms (cf. Psa 43:1; 9:5, etc.) as well as in Babylonian material (cf. *Ausgewählte Psalmen*², 97). <333> Concerning דָּנַנִּי see §26g. **8** נִפְתַּל properly refers to the wrestling match. The rare word is chosen because of the etymology. "God's fight," a divine struggle, probably refers here to a struggle for offspring, for divine blessing. But with whom did Rachel struggle? The text says "with my sister." But she has not vanquished her, since she herself has only two, whereas her sister already has four sons. Thus, there is no other option than to strike עִם־אֲחֹתִי with Sievers (2:322). The original meaning, then, was that Rachel fought with God and wrested from him the sons denied her to this point. This was later found objectionable.

III. **9a . . . 10-13 J (E)** *Leah's adoptive children.* **11** For the Kethib בָּגָד (in pause), LXX has ἐν τύχῃ and Qere and Pesh have the artificial בָּא גָד "good fortune has come." This phrase בְּגָד will have originally meant "with Gad's assistance" (on the syntax, cf. בְּךָ in Psa 18:30; Ball). The current narrator, however, does not have a god in mind. Instead, he understands the word as an appellative. The shift in meaning from a divine name to an appellative is common in the history of religion (cf. ″Αιδης, תְּחוֹם, אֲבַדּוֹן, etc.). **13** בְּאָשְׁרִי means "with my good fortune." Regarding the perfect אִשְּׁרוּנִי see §106n. בָּנוֹת is poetic (Cant 6:9; 2:2). One may concretely imagine such praise of women. They are the women who visit the woman about to give birth and who begin bragging about the mother with many children. The Israelite woman is very vulnerable to approval or reproach, fame or shame "among the women" (cf. 30:23; Luke 1:25, etc.). The idea of "shame" also plays a great role with the Psalmists (cf. *Ausgewählte Psalmen*² index s.v. "Hohn").

IV. **14-24 JE** *The mandrake and the children born afterward.* The recension preserved in J has exhausted the theme of the slave children and their adoption. The narrator comes now to a new theme, the biological children born subsequently, and employs a new motif for this reason. He took pains to shape this new motif realistically. It involves the dudaim (the sweet-smelling, golden yellow fruit of the mandrake, i.e., the *Atropa mandagora* or *Mandragora vernalis*) whose fruits and root were thought to effect one's fertility (cf. Tuch-Arnold² on the passage and Guthe, BW, s.v. "dudaim," with figure and bibliography). Hertz (*Gesamm. Abhandl.*, 273ff.; with a comprehensive bibliography) doubts that the dudaim are the fruits of the mandrake (cf., however, P. Haupt, *Bibl. Liebeslieder*, 64-65, 98). That the previously infertile wife conceives as the result of the consumption of a food, especially of apples, is a well-known legend motif (cf. Stumme, *Märchen der Berbern*, 93; G. Jacob, *Hohes Lied*, 7n.1; v.d. Leyen, CXV, 12). The dudaim are ripe in the days of the wheat harvest (in May). Then the children followed the gleaners in the field (2 Kgs 4:18). The reference to the wheat harvest is surprising in the context of this story which consistently portrays Jacob as a nomad. This, too, is a sign of the late origin of this episode (cf. ¶4:2, 5). On this occasion <334> Reuben finds the rare fruit. Reuben is the oldest (he is only about five or six years old). The others are not wise enough yet. He brings the fruits, however—this is a particularly well-devised element—home to his mother. Thus a dispute arises between the sister as to who should have the mandrakes. They rightfully belong to Leah. But Rachel would also like to have them. Characteristically, nothing is said about what Rachel plans to do with them. The narrator is hesitant to be explicit here. Similar reticence characterizes the legends of Lot's daughters and of Tamar. Finally, the two agree that Leah will give Rachel some of the dudaim, but that in exchange Rachel will grant Leah their husband for this night. The presupposition is that Jacob customarily spends the night with Rachel. He is, therefore, very unfair to the unloved Leah and withholds even the marital duty from her. This is also the presupposition of הַפַּעַם יִזְבְּלֵנִי (v 20). Civil law prohibits husbands from behaving in this manner (Exod 21:10). The behavior seems repulsive to us. The narrator, however, less sensitive, finds it unobjectionable. The whole scene is introduced here because it has consequences. Thus Leah and Rachel conceive at the same time: Leah because she has "hired" her husband, Rachel through the effects of the dudaim. Thus Issachar and Joseph were born at the same time. Issachar receives his name because of this very "hiring." The words שָׂכֹר שְׂכַרְתִּיךָ (v 16) are intended to prepare for the naming just as 22:8 prepares for the naming in 22:14 and 21:17 the naming of Ishmael, etc. שָׂכַר is not to be translated "to buy," which it never means, but "to hire," "to engage." She has "hired" her husband for a time for a price (following Wellhausen, *Composition*³, 36-37). The dudaim episode is developed from this name and from the comment in the tradition that Issachar and Joseph are the two youngest children. This whole context is already "obscured" in the report of J. J does not attribute Rachel's conception to the magical effects of the mandrakes, as was the original meaning, but to Yahweh who opened her womb (v 22). Between the two, originally related births of Issachar and Joseph, Zebulon (and Dinah) were inserted, at least in the current text. One can see from such examples that even such late passages were not devised by the author "J" before us, but are only reproduced by him. E reported nothing about the dudaim. Instead it reports, "God heard her." One may assume that he took offense at the magic and consequently omitted it. **15** וְלָקַחַת is an infinitive construct. But the perfect וְלָקַחַתְּ (§65g) seems more appropriate. For the construction see Num 16:9-10. **16** אֵלַי is emphatic. The presumption is that each of the women had her own tent (31:33). **17** According to this, E like J, recounted the birth of Reuben, Simeon, Levi, and Judah in the preceding (Procksch, 25n.1). **18** Leah's statement, "God gave me my wage," was also quite clear in the context of E, even without further explanation, because in E the fact that Leah had ceded her maidservant to Jacob was recounted immediately prior to it. R^IE, however, who had inserted the section vv 14-16 from J in between, had to add an explanation (v 18aγ) <335> יששכר has a Qere perpetuum יִשָּׂכָר. יששכר = שָׂכָר אִישׁ שָׂכָר (Wellhausen, *Text der Bücher Sam*, v-vi, 95-96). The narrators usually thought neither of a composition with אִישׁ

(Wellhausen, *Composition*[3], 37; Kautzsch[3]) nor with שֵׁי (Dillmann), but have simply dis-
regarded the ʾ in the name. **21** Among Jacob's children, Dinah holds a unique place. She
is the only girl among brothers, while 37:35 J assumes that Jacob also had other
daughters. She seems to have been inserted only secondarily into this context (in order to
prepare for the account in Gen 34). This is indicated by the fact that there is no etymology for her name. Gen 34 associates her with Simeon and Levi, apparently following
an earlier legend tradition. She does not appear in other legends or historical tradition. The
usual assumption that Dinah was also a Hebrew tribe is at least undemonstrable. The same
situation pertains to Sarah and Rebekah (Meyer, *Israeliten*, 423). **23, 24** The genealogy
also expresses Joseph's special position. Passionately desired and joyfully greeted, he is
born to the favored wife after a long infertility.

47. Jacob Serves Laban for Flocks 30:25-43 JE

Source criticism. Elements of both sources are fused in vv 25-31. Twice Jacob asks
to be dismissed (וְאֵלְכָה v 25 ‖ v 26a); twice Laban begins speaking (וַיֹּאמֶר v 27 ‖
v 28); twice Laban asks what he should "give" (vv 28 ‖ v 31); even the two clauses in
v 26b and 29a, so similar in form and yet so different in meaning (v 26b emphasizes the
conditions, v 29a the value of the service performed), could not be from the same pen.
J is certainly the origin of v 27 (יהוה; אִם־נָא מָצָאתִי חֵן בְּעֵינֶיךָ) and בְּגִלַל also
point to J; cf. Holzinger, *Hexateuch*, 97, 109; concerning נִחֵשׁ cf. 44:5, 15 J), v 30 (יהוה;
פָּרַץ is also common in J; concerning v 30a cf. 32:11 J). Vv 29 and 31 are related to
v 30. Accordingly E contributed v 28 (וַיֹּאמַר ‖ v 27 J; וְאֶתְּנָה ‖ v 31; שְׂכָרֶךָ
occurs in the same situation in E in 31:8) and v 26 (v 26b ‖ v 29 J). V 25 (וְאֵלְכָה
‖ v 26a E), therefore, should also be attributed to J. The subsequent section (vv 32ff.) is
thoroughly confused in the current text: according to v 31 Jacob at first wants nothing,
but in v 32 he suggests that he be given certain animals as a wage "today." According to
v 33, everything נָקֹד וְטָלוּא should belong to him from "tomorrow" onward, but according to v 35 Laban took these from Jacob and gave them to his own sons to pasture. In
addition, the verbs אֶעֱבֹר and הָסֵר in v 32 do not agree very well with one another
and there are too many objects. The text is nonorganic and redundant. These difficulties
can only be explained as the result of a combination of sources. Two entirely different
suggestions of Jacob's have been fused here (following Wellhausen, *Composition*[3], 38-39).
According to one recension, Jacob himself (אֶעֱבֹר v 32) takes the speckled animals from
the flock today. They are to be his payment. "Tomorrow" Laban is to inspect the flocks
to see for himself that Jacob only took the speckled animals (v 33). In exchange Jacob
will pasture Laban's (whole) herd. The other recension reads quite differently. According
to it Jacob will have nothing at all for the moment. Instead, he demands only a future condition. What should Laban "do" (v 31)? <336> He should "separate" the speckled animals
(הָסֵר מִשָּׁם כָּל־שֶׂה נָקֹד וְשָׁלוּא v 32; cf. וַיָּסַר v 35). The continuation, the determination of the future payment, has now fallen out: judging from the context of vv 37ff., it
would have been that the speckled young born to the remaining nonspeckled animals
would belong to Jacob. In order to prevent Jacob from gaining access to the speckled
animals and using them for breeding, Laban then sent the speckled herds three days'
journey away (v 36). This second report belongs to J because of its ties to v 31 (J). The
first, contrariwise, to E because of the reference of v 32, וְהָיָה שְׂכָרִי, to v 28 (E).

Accordingly, vv 32-34 are to be attributed to E, vv 32ab, 35, 36 to J. This analysis is also supported by the special emphasis on Jacob's honor often repeated in E (cf. the speeches in 31:6ff., 36f.). Linguistic observations confirm the division. The passages from E speak of "the speckled among the goats," בְּעִזִּים. In contrast the J passages speak of "the speckled sheep," שֶׂה נָקֹד. The word שָׂכָר (vv 32, 33) occurs in the same context in E (v 28; 31:8). Laban's response (v 34) is necessary in E. In contrast it is superfluous in J because וַיָּסַר (v 35) contains the answer. In this passage E is transmitted without omission. In J the point of Jacob's suggestion is missing. The subsequent vv 37-43 will stem essentially from J, as indicated especially by the concluding verse 43 (שְׁפָחוֹת; פָּרַץ is common in J; parallels in J in 26:13; 12:16; 24:35; 32:6). The doublets inserted in the J text will stem from E: וְלוּז וְעַרְמוֹן (v 37) is probably a variant of לִבְנֶה. The humorous allusion to the name לָבָן contained in the word לִבְנֶה is destroyed if joined by other names for trees. מַחְשֹׂף הַלָּבָן אֲשֶׁר עַל־הַמַּקְלוֹת (v 37) is by form poorly positioned in the clause and in content a doublet for the preceding. With Wellhausen (*Composition*[3], 39n.1), one may remove תָּבֹאןָ הַצֹּאן לִשְׁתּוֹת בְּקַתוֹת הַמַּיִם אֲשֶׁר (they are a doublet for בְּרָחֲטִים and separate it from לְנֹכַח הַצֹּאן), further v 39a (a doublet to the preceding clause v 38bb), and, from v 40, וַיִּתֵּן פְּנֵי הַצֹּאן אֶל־עָקֹד [וְכָל־חוּם] בְּצֹאן לָבָן (this clause separates the beginning and ending of the verse, which belong inherently together, and presumes that the colorful animals are in the vicinity of the white ones, a presumption which does not suit J according to vv 35-36). The remainder is a unity in form and content: פִּצֵּל (vv 37 and 38), variant מַחְשֹׂף (v 37); רְהָטִים (vv 38 and 41), variant שִׁקֲתוֹת מַיִם (v 39; cf. 24:20 J). The "black among the lambs" (vv 32, 33, 35, 40) suits (cf. below) neither J nor E and seems to have been added by someone who wanted to supply Jacob with sheep in addition to the goats. Eerdmans (53ff.) believes the unity of the whole can be salvaged with a few emendations. But how far removed this passage is from a uniformly composed, smoothly flowing account! Conversely, Sievers (2:323ff.) distinguishes six sources in 30:25ff.; 31.

The account of how Jacob obtained Laban's flocks is the turning point of the Jacob-Laban narrative. To this point things have gone poorly enough for Jacob. Laban has detained him for fourteen years through his deceit and Jacob still has nothing of his own. Now, however, that the difficult fourteen years are over, Laban must agree to a new contract, and this time Jacob successfully pulls the wool over the old deceiver's eyes. The old legends recount Jacob's revenge with a thousand joys. Jacob's trick is all the more successful because—in the opinion of the old narrators—he did not deceive or steal, but was able to maintain every appearance of righteousness. The narrators, especially E, emphasize Jacob's "honor." To be sure, we would not grant Jacob's "honor" and would indeed describe Jacob's actions as "deceit" (Kautzsch-Socin[2] n. 141), but the narrators are less sensitive than a modern Christian. They would answer us, "How else, then, should Jacob act toward the old fox? If he had not helped himself, he surely would have had to leave empty-handed!" (31:42). In the opinion of the ancient, Jacob is truly "righteous" in relation to Laban! Narrator and hearer are delighted that he acted with such extraordinary cunning and fleeced Laban so thoroughly. So the ancient legends tell the tale. <337> E already differs. It seems to have taken a degree of offense at Jacob's tricks (cf. comments on 31:8). In order to recreate the charm of this narrative, one must think that these shepherd stories were originally told in shepherd circles. There everyone is an expert and delights in stories about his own profession. These legends bear most clearly of all the legends in Genesis the color of a specific circle.

I **25-36** *The new contract JE.* The presentation in J is as follows: Jacob now has the upper hand on Laban. He has a good and urgent reason to leave Laban now for he longs for home. On the other hand, Laban must vigorously wish to retain Jacob for God's blessing obviously follows Jacob step for step. Jacob rightly suggests this to Laban, too (vv 29, 30). Therefore, Laban is entirely speechless when he hears that Jacob wants to return home. In horror, he can only stammer and does not even dare ask him to remain (v 27). Thus, he must agree to the contract Jacob offers him. Jacob has meanwhile hatched an extremely refined plan. At first, he wants nothing at all from Laban (v 31). This is the bait in the trap, for naturally the greedy Laban will gladly agree to these terms. Jacob only asks that Laban separate the speckled animals (it seems that only goats are involved here, not sheep too) and then the young born to the remaining solid colored animals (sheep are white, Cant 4:2; 6:6; Isa 1:18; Psa 147:16; Dan 7:9; goats are brown and white, Cant 4:1) will belong to Jacob. Laban gladly agrees to this suggestion because (presumably) not very many animals are speckled in the first place and monochrome animals surely would not produce multicolored young. Laban will have privately smirked and thought that Jacob is even stupider that he believed. The knowledgeable hearer is now intrigued. What does Jacob have in mind? The fact that Laban sends the colorful animals three days' journey away because he does not trust Jacob is also a nice feature (v 36)—so cautious and still outwitted! At the same time, the narrator prepares a point. This very caution later causes Laban considerable trouble (31:19a). E tells the story somewhat differently here. The fine psychological motivation is missing. Jacob simply makes a suggestion and Laban accepts it. The agreement, itself, is also very simple at first. As his wage, Jacob will take all the colorful animals (there are not many—a modest request; here, too, only goats seem to be intended) "today." As the fragments of E in vv 37ff. demonstrate, the idea is that this contract should be valid from now on. Everything speckled will belong to Jacob. The J recension is based on a wordplay: לְבָן gets everything white לָבָן (v 35). An earlier recension may have also alluded to the name Jacob (cf. the Arab. 'uqâb "striped and speckled clothing"; Ball).

26 The presupposition is that to this point all together have formed one family, the background for Laban's statement in 31:43 also. וְאֶת־יְלָדַי is an addition (Kautzsch³): Jacob did not serve for the children. עֲבֹדָה may refer to the period of service (Kautzsch-Socin², n. 137). **27** The anacolouthon in v 27a resembles the one in 23:13. נִחֵשׁ means "to perceive an omen, to learn through magic" (44:15; Stade, *Bibl. Theol.*, 102). By means of some sort of magic, Laban learned that the blessing resting on his flocks has come from Yahweh because of Jacob. <338> Regarding the syntax of וַיְבָרֲכֵנִי see §111h n. 1: "I have observed and come to the conclusion, etc." **29** Regarding עֲבַדְתִּיךָ אֵת אֲשֶׁר, "the circumstance as I, etc.," see §157c. **30** לְרַגְלִי (Isa 41:2) is the opposite of לְפָנַי as in Hab 3:5 (Ball). **31** אֶשְׁמֹר is a variant of אֶרְעֶה. **32** הָסֵר is intended as an imperative in J. The redactor may have understood it as an infinitive absolute (such as in 21:16). וְהָיָה refers to the immediately preceding. Nothing is missing. **33** "Then my righteousness will bear testimony for me," that is, then you will clearly see (what you have otherwise probably doubted) that I am an honest man. **35** The subject of וַיָּסַר is Laban (cf. בָּנָיו). J has עֲקֻדִּים here. In vv 32, 35 J has נָקֹד, in v 39 נְקֻדִּים and עֲקֻדִּים alongside one another. It should probably be assumed that the original text of J only mentioned נְקֻדִּי.

II 37-43 *Jacob's artifice and wealth.* Jacob only made this remarkably modest, indeed apparently foolish suggestion, because he had a fine plan *in petto*. He peels white (לְבָנוֹת, cf. מַחְשֹׂף הַלָּבָן in E) stripes in branches—they were branches of the לִבְנֶה: hearers laugh at this joke—and lays them before the sheep in the troughs. The presumption is that the animals mate when they drink. Now if the mating animals see the speckled branches, they conceive and later give birth to speckled young! Such breeding methods were known in antiquity (cf. Tuch-Arnold[2] on this passage). Thus Laban's flocks suddenly have only speckled animals and all the young now belong to Jacob! The account of this artifice was apparently extremely entertaining for the earliest hearers. The narrator therefore extended the matter even further. Jacob gathered the speckled animals so that stock, so precious to him, would not be lost again, and thus built his own flock. Indeed, the narrative is even more refined: Jacob only placed the staves before the strong animals, not the weak, so that Jacob received the strong young and Laban the weak! Hearers are delighted. Thus Jacob became a rich man. The richer Jacob became, the poorer Laban. It should happen to every Laban! The process is much more complicated in E. According to E, the matter was repeated "ten times" (31:7, 41). Again and again, Jacob offered a new contract, but each time, the flocks bore to Jacob's <339> advantage. E treated the same theme as J, therefore, and thoroughly exhausted it in several variations. A later time with no understanding of such shepherd stories radically reduced these variationss. Only the larger remnants of the first and smaller remnants of a subsequent variation are preserved for us. The first time all the speckled and spotted goats should be Jacob's wage. But Jacob peeled almond and plane-tree branches, laid them in the drinking troughs, and was able to gain speckled and spotted young in this way. This time, then, quite similar to J. When Laban then saw Jacob's wage, he permitted him only the striped, a very rare deviant. But Jacob arranged it so that the sheep (when grazing and also when mating) saw the ringed sticks and so bore young with these colors (v 40). Then he decided to offer him the speckled. Jacob repeated his artifice. And so on over and over again. Poor Laban was in a quandary and could not escape no matter how exasperated he was (31:8). The result, then, is the same as in J. Indeed, Jacob finally had brought Laban's whole herd to his side according to E (31:9)!

37 מָקֵל is a collective term (§123b). The meaning of לִבְנֶה is uncertain. **38** Concerning the form of וַיֶּחֱמְנָה see §95f. The word also occurs in 24:20 J. Concerning the form of וַיֵּחַמְנָה see §47k (cf. also Sievers 2:325-26). **39** For וַיֶּחֱמוּ one expects וַיֵּחַמוּ (§69f.) **40** Targ. Jon and Targ. Onq have כָּל־עָקֹד; LXX, Pesh, and Ball have לִפְנֵי (cf. Eerdmans, 54): "He put all the striped animals at the front of the flock." V. Chauvin (*Nouv. Revue de Théologie* 1:140-41) suggests: "And Jacob separated the old animals (והישנים), but the young (בְּנֵי הַצֹּאן), (namely) all (כל) the striped and black, he made into a separate herd (לבד)." With a distinction of sources, no conjectural emendation is necessary. **41** The strong animals go into estrus in the summer, the weaker in the fall (cf. Dillmann). LXX (Pesh) and Targ. Onq read בְּכָל־יַחֵם; Targ. Jon reads בכל עֵת יחם (cf. 31:10). וְשָׂם refers to a repeated action (§112dd,ee). לְיַחֵמְנָה is a piel infinitive with an irregular suffix (§91f).

48. Jacob Flees from Laban; Treaty at Gilead-Mizpah 31, 32:1 EJ

I **1-16** *The reason for the flight. Source analysis.* Jacob's long discussion with his wives (vv 4-16) is unified (cf. e.g. הַצִּיל in both vv 9 and 16) <340> and belongs to E. Reasons for this assignation are אֱלֹהִים (vv 7, 9, 11, 16bis), the revelation in the dream (vv 10, 11), the beginning of the discussion (v 11), the reminder of the anointing of the massebah and of the vow at Bethel (v 13; cf. 28:18, 20-22 E), and the expressions מַשְׂכֹּרֶת (vv 7, 41) and מֹנִים (vv 7, 41). The introduction (vv 1-3) is a composite of both sources: v 2 prepares for v 5 and is therefore from E; v 1 motivates Jacob's flight differently than v 2 and belongs, therefore, to J; the "wealth" of Jacob presumed in v 1 was just described by J in 30:43 and Laban's sons were discussed in 30:35; v 3 belongs to J because of יהוה and is cited by J in 32:10.

1-3 Both sources offer a profane and a religious motive for Jacob's flight. Jacob hears Laban's sons murmuring about his wealth since Jacob's "luck" diminishes their inheritance (v 1 J). He sees in Laban's expression that his attitude has turned against him (v 2 E). Then God appears to him and commands him to return home (v 3 J, v 13 E). The two motives contradict one another. The pious individual is motivated to act simply because God commands it. Any other consideration is, therefore, unnecessary (cf. comments on 21:11-13). And the clever Jacob, accustomed to foreseeing dangers and avoiding them (cf. 32:4ff. [27:11ff., 42ff.]), needs no divine command in the situation described. He can see for himself that Laban, whose greed he knows, will attempt to rob him of his wealth and that his only option is sudden flight. Earlier recensions will have grounded Jacob's flight in a profane manner and will have recounted this, too, to praise Jacob's cunning. God's command was added when the accounts became more learned. E, it seems, did not yet report God's revelation at this point in order to recount it in "supplementary" fashion in the following speech. See the comments on 20:2 concerning this stylistic device which abbreviates the speeches in favor of the account.

4-16 Jacob's discussion with his wives would not be necessary in the context of the narrative. In fact, J does not seem to have contained anything of it. J recounts here, as throughout the whole chap., in a "concise," E in a "detailed" style favoring long speeches reprising what has already happened (cf. introduction §3:20). This scene simultaneously provides E with a desired and very well devised opportunity to present his own assessment of the transaction which he cannot explicitly express (cf. introduction ¶3:18) and to demonstrate Jacob's legal claims in relation to Laban. To this purpose, Jacob must once more make a report concerning the whole matter and prove himself to be righteous. Simultaneously, the opinion of the two wives, the obvious judges, is invoked: if these two resolutely declare themselves to be against their own father then—the narrator thinks—very clearly right is really on Jacob's side. The whole episode is, therefore, of relatively late origin and does not belong to the old legend. V **5b** does not fit here as well as after v **7a** (cf. also Winckler, *Forschungen* 3:433). **6** In contrast to his father-in-law's ill will (v 5b), Jacob appeals emphatically to the judgment of the women. Concerning וְאַתֵּנָה see §32i. It is certainly an unusual "service with one's best effort" in which the servant finally takes away the master's whole estate! The narrator has no eyes for this side of the matter. As a son of Jacob, he stands <341> wholly on the side of his ancestor. **7a** Concerning הֵחֶל see §67w. מֹנִים occurs only here and in v 41. **5b, 7b, 8** Nothing is said here of the

artificial measures Jacob employed. God, E thinks, gives fertility to the flocks and caused
Laban's animals consistently to bear to Jacob's favor. This does not indicate, however,
that E did not recount Jacob's schemes in the preceding (this is the dominant opinion,
even Kautzsch[3]), but only that they do not seem entirely tidy, and that here, where he
wants to demonstrate Jacob's righteousness, he would rather appeal to God—we would
say to good luck. On the other hand, the suppression of the schemes is by no means a
"conscious lie" on E's part. Still today, many interpreters find such silences quite in order.
"Fundamentally, it was not his cunning, but God's control" (Franz Delitzsch). E's attempt
to excuse Abraham's behavior in Gerar is very similar (cf. above p. 221). Gen 21:11-13
can also be compared. Such unclear excuse attempts appear in ancient and modern times
everywhere piety feels bound to material which originates in morally or religiously unde-
veloped times. נְקֻדִּים עֲקֻדִּים is a play on words. The clauses are also similarly
constructed. Jacob wants to say, "Laban 'whined' around but every time it was to my
advantage." Concerning the singular יִהְיֶה see §145u. Regarding the whole sentence see
§159r,s. **9** Regarding אֲבִיכֶם for אֲבִיכֶן see §135o.

10-12 Jacob now tells how God helped him in his struggle with Laban by a
revelation. He saw in a dream that the mating rams all had a certain color. In the further
course of this revelation God commanded him to leave Laban (v 13). Now vv 10 and 12,
however, give rise to significant doubts. V 13 is not the natural continuation of vv 10-12.
The narrative begun in vv 10-12 is not yet finished. Rather, the following must indicate
the extent to which this revelation concerning the struggle between Jacob and Laban came
to pass. On the other hand, God's command to Jacob to return home (v 13) cannot have
been issued then, but only later when the flocks had born young. Furthermore, "how could
two so thoroughly dissimilar revelations have been coupled in this manner" (Wellhausen)?
The revelation of God's name (v 13) also stands, by nature, at the beginning of a divine
speech (cf. comments on 17:1). The explicit naming of God, in particular, shows,
however, that he has not appeared to Jacob since the Bethel revelation. Finally, the oracle
(vv 10, 12) cannot be incorporated into the J context any better than in that of E. Theses
verses will, therefore, have to be considered an addition (cf. Wellhausen, *Composition*[3],
38), rather poorly incorporated, stemming from a person who, continuing in E's tracks (vv
5-9), wanted to attribute Jacob's wealth not to his tricks, but to dear God's protection. It
is not clear which this glossator thought. Did he think the deity revealed to Jacob the color
of the mating rams and thus also of the future offspring—what a "revelation"!—so that
Jacob could make a new, profitable contract, or is God supposed to have meant to show
Jacob that he would come to his assistance in a contract already made? Frankenberg
(CGA [1901], <342> 700) argues the latter. בָּרֹד means "black and white, speckled"
(Arab. *arbad*, the color of the male ostrich; Jacob, 21).

V **10** introduces v 13 according to the preceding. **13** Regarding הָאֵל בֵּיתְאֵל see
§127f. The name appears in the form אֵל בֵּיתְאֵל in 35:7. Targ. Onq and Targ. Jon (cf.
LXX) read הָאֵל הַנִּרְאֶה אֵלֶיךָ בְּבֵיתְאֵל (Kittel). God "remembers" Jacob's pious
deed that obligated God and that Jacob made a vow to him if he "would lead him home
in peace to his father's house" (28:21). Now that the time has come for this, God intervenes and fulfills his worshipper's wish. Motivating God to intervene at the proper
moment is the very purpose of such a vow. The narrator, who wants to recount God's
protection for Jacob in the following material, has very appropriately incorporated a motif

from the Bethel narrative into the Jacob-Laban narrative. In this way, the whole Jacob composition gains coherence. The fact that the insertion of this Bethel motive is not very recent can be seen in the old name *'el beth-'el* (35:7), the local name of the deity of Bethel, which the E recension of the Bethel legend (28:11-12) strangely does not contain. A very old tradition is preserved here in a relatively young passage, then. Contrariwise, "the angel of God" has appeared in the place of the ancient local numen in the account (v 11; cf. above p. 186). **14-16** The wives' response places them wholly on Jacob's side. Their father treats them like "strangers," perhaps like slaves. What he gained through the marriage (Jacob's service) he consumed himself. The presumption is, therefore, that a decent father gives his daughter the מֹהַר or a least a portion of it to take with her into the marriage (Benzinger[2], 106; the same practice among the old Arabs, Wellhausen, *Nachr. d. Königl. Ges. d. Wiss. zu Göttingen* [1893], 434-35). To act otherwise is to "sell" one's daughter. We should not consider the ancient Israelite views of marriage too barbarous. Obtaining a wife is not a "purchase." The word מכר is intentionally employed here "to disparage Laban's mercenary attitude" (Rauh, *Familienrecht*, 15). In contrast, ancient Israel knows of no inheritance for daughters and their children (as long as there are other heirs; Benzinger[2], 266). The many head of livestock, then, that Jacob obtained with God's help belong by right to them and their children. This is a new reason Jacob is in the right! The very quantity of reasons the narrator gathers together arouses the suspicion, however, that he, himself, did not find the whole matter quite in order. The situation of the same narrator in Gen 20 is similar. There, too, he purifies an ancient, naive narrative as best he can. The phrase in **14b** stems from poetic vocabulary (2 Sam 20:1).

II **17-25** *Jacob's flight and encounter with Laban. Source criticism.* Vv 18aβ,γ,δ,b belong to P. All the rest belongs to E as indicated by אלהים (v 24), the dream vision, further the similarity in expression between v 24a and 20:3 (E), as well as the allusions to this revelation in the subsequent E passages (v 29, 42, 53b). The distance from Haran, where J locates this narrative (27:48; 28:10; 29:4; cf. above p. 317), to the mountains of Gilead is much too large for Jacob to have made his way in ten days. According to Kautzsch[3] this distance would require <343> something more like forty days. Consequently (cf. Meyer, *Israeliten*, 236-37), one must attribute the two related times of three and seven days (vv 22, 23) to E which must have located Laban's home in the "East" not too far from the Transjordan. "Laban, the Aramaean" (as in v 24) indicates that v 20 derives from E, as does גְנֵב לֵב (as in v 26). A few doublets point to the fact that J also participates in the passage: It is recounted twice that Jacob flees with all his property (vv 17, 18aa ‖ 21aa). Twice "he sets out" (וַיִּקֶּם v 17 ‖ וַיָּקָם v 21). Twice Laban overtakes him (v 23b ‖ v 25a). The fact that Laban does not notice Jacob's flight is, it seems, explained twice—by chance Laban was not present (v 19a) ‖ Jacob communicated nothing to him (v 20). Jacob's crossing the Euphrates, in particular, points to J (v 21) according to which Laban's home is to be imagined in Haran. The description of the situation (v 25) presupposed by J in the border treaty (vv 51, 52) also points to J. The notion that Laban must go far away to shear his flocks (v 19a) seems to belong with 30:36 J according to which he had cautiously sent his flocks three days' journey away. Accordingly, one may attribute vv 19a, 21, 25 to J and, in contrast, vv 17, 18aa (‖ v 21aa J; to נהג cf. v 26 E; regarding מִקְנֶה cf. v 9 E) to E. E further recounts Rachel's theft of the teraphim below (vv 30ff.). Also, teraphim do not occur elsewhere in J. Now, however, Meyer (*Israeliten*,

235) correctly points to the fact that the two clauses "Rachel stole her father's teraphim" (v 19b) and "Jacob stole Laban's heart" (v 20) are difficult to tolerate in immediate proximity to one another. Meyer wants therefore to attribute v 20 along with other clauses to an "E². " But v 19b may only be the addition of a later hand who did not understand the "supplement" in v 32. E is fully preserved in this passage. A few elements of J are missing, especially Laban's pursuit. The source analyses in the 1st and 2nd editions of this commentary differ somewhat (vv 19a, 21-23, 25b were attributed to J).

17-21 *Jacob's flight.* E explains simply how Jacob could flee from Laban: He deceived Laban. It is even finer in J: Laban was gone to shear sheep (where the presence of the master is necessary, 38:13). His sheep pasture, however—his excessive caution wanted it so—three days' journey away (30:36). Jacob used Laban's absence to flee and thus gained a head start of several days. How Laban must have been annoyed at his excessive cunning later! E (v 22) also knows of a three days' head start. **19b** The fact that the daughter thinks nothing of taking the best piece from her father's household effects for her own household is very true to life. Indeed it still takes place today. "Teraphim" are idol images, according to v 34 and 1 Sam 19:13ff. about the size of a person, probably also in the form of a person. Here, as in 1 Sam 19:13, 16, a single image is probably envisioned (Meyer, *Israeliten*, 211n.1), but not of Yahweh. The context suggests a household god. Such teraphim help the votary in house and home, blessing his family and his flocks. Rachel believes that by stealing this image she will take the good fortune of the house with her. Laban would rather permit another to have anything other than his house fetish he inherited from his father (cf. Bousset, *Wesen der Religion*, 37, 39). Teraphim must have been very common in ancient Israel. Yet one should note that our narrator does not associate Jacob (nor David in 1 Sam 19:13ff.) with the image. Foreigners like Laban have such images—this is known. One may overlook such behavior <344> on the part of the wife (Rachel and Michal, 1 Sam 19:13ff.). But it is not proper—in the opinion of these legends—for an Israelite man. Judg 17ff. differs somewhat. There, the teraphim in Michah's house is—it seems—condemned. This account (as is 1 Sam 19:13ff.), then, is entirely free of (prophetic) polemic against the teraphim (1 Sam 15:23; 2 Kgs 23:24), but it is full of derision concerning such a miserable god (cf. comments on vv 32ff.). Already in the ancient period, pious Israelites felt very superior to such a "god" which may be understood as a pixie, poltergeist, or a familiar spirit (according to Stade, *Bibl. Theol.*, 121; Schwally, *Leben nach dem Tode*, 35ff.; Westphal, *Jahwes Wohnstätten*, 1153, as an ancestral spirit). First Sam 19:13ff. is also a story satirizing the teraphim. The teraphim narrative in Judg 17, 18, where the teraphim is also stolen and a scene very similar to that in Gen 31:32ff. takes place, seems, as often assumed, written to disparage and mock. Concerning teraphim see Stade (*Bibl. Theol.*, ¶58:4) and Benzinger² (328).

The role the "theft" plays in this narrative is unusual. The narrator took every effort to distance Jacob from the deceit and lightheartedly abandoned Rachel, the less significant person, although a matriarch of Israel. This story does not involve chivalrous, proud people who would feel the word "theft" as a great insult, but circles in which a great deal of dishonesty takes place and where it would be quite extraordinary for one to say, "I have not stolen!" One may explain such circumstances from the temperament of the people who told these narratives, but especially from the fact that the legend is set among shepherds where the temptation to steal (on a lonely pasture, in the absence of the master; the animals difficult to distinguish; the accusations many, cf. v 39) is very great. On the other hand, significantly, even the old accounts only excuse the cunning acquisition of others' property, but, in contrast, apparently abhor violence and robbery. This, too, is significant for Israel's character and is distinct from many old legends and fairy tales of other peoples which glorify the thief and the robber (v. d. Leyen, 114, 22). Meyer (235) observes well that an earlier form of the account portrays the theft of the teraphim but a later, weakened recension the theft of Laban's heart. Scholars are inclined to attribute these portrayals to an "E¹" and an "E²." In E¹ Laban is angry about the theft, but Jacob is justified by Rachel's trick, whereas in E² Laban's feelings are hurt by the secret escape, but the deity forces him to be satisfied with reproaches. But both sequences are organically linked to one another by v 30.

19 Concerning the triliteral root of לְגֵז see §67cc. **20** Why is Laban called "the Aramaean" here and in v 24? It cannot be in order to motivate the subsequent border treaty which does not appear in the same source (E). A play on words with אֲרָם may have originally been given in this passage (as in 29:25). Or is the word simply an insertion from P (25:20; 28:5) by a later hand (so Budde, *Urgeschichte*, 422n.1)? **21** The name Gilead, which the source first explains later in v 48, is employed prematurely here for lack of another name. The same is true of "Beer-sheba" in 26:23. **23** אַחִים here means "clansfellow." "Just as the Greek brotherhood, the *mishpahah* will have developed from blood kinship" (Luther, ZAW 21:10). According to vv 32, 37, 54 the narrator seems to assume that Jacob also had "brothers" with him. The sudden appearance of these "brothers" of Jacob causes great difficulty here, however. Even Steuernagel's (pp. 38, 111) contention that Jacob's "brothers" are the brother tribes <345> of the Transjordan does not eliminate the difficulty. If the narrator had meant that Jacob had met brothers in the Transjordan, he would have been obligated to have explicitly said so. Everything becomes simple, however, if we assume that the account only speaks of Laban's "brothers," which Jacob emphatically designates as his brothers, too (vv 32, 37; he is, after all, related to them by marriage and has every reason in his situation to value this kinship), and further, that Laban was originally the subject in vv 46 and 56 (cf. Ball on v 46). **24** "Watch yourself," God warns Laban. This element was derived from the divine name "Terror of Isaac" (vv 42, 53). God forbids Laban to say a word. The narrator thinks of a word, not to mention an act, whereby Laban would encroach on Jacob's property or hinder him from returning home (cf. v 29). The subsequent impotent reproaches are gladly permitted. This element prepares for Laban's acquiescence at the end of the scene. מִטּוֹב עַד־רָע means neither good nor evil, that is, nothing at all (cf. 24:50; 14:23; 2 Sam 13:23). The translations by Procksch "evil instead of good" or by Winckler (*Forschungen* 3:436) "without good all the way to evil" are impossible judging by the analogies. **25b** The name of the mountain where Jacob camped is missing. The mountain was situated south or southwest of "Gilead." It can hardly have been Mizpah, of which E recounts but not J (v 49). Or is v 25bβ simply an addition perhaps (Sievers 2:328)? The mountain "Gilead" (in the more limited sense) is not the *Ğebel Ğil'âd* south of the lower *Zerkâ* (Yabbok) where the old geographical name is preserved. Instead, since the mountain formed Aram's border with Israel according to vv 51-52—the mountain itself belongs to Aram—and, according to the following context, lies north of Yabbok, it is to be sought farther to the north. The verb and object in תָּקַע אֶת־אֶחָיו (v 25) do not go together. One of the two is to be emended.

III. 26-43 *Jacob's negotiation with Laban. Source analysis.* The piece is comparable in many respects to the conversations between Jacob and his wives (vv 4-16 E). As in it, there is, among other things, a retrospective on what has transpired intended to portray Jacob's righteousness. There is a verbal parallel between the two passages in vv 41 and 7. Accordingly, one may hypothesize first of all that vv 26-43 also stem from E. Their origin in E is very clear in verses 29, 42 which are related with respect to content (אלהים) and which refer back to v 24 (E). Further indications of E are: the teraphim (vv 30, 32-37; cf. 19b) of which E speaks in the following (35:2, 4), further the expressions לֵבָב (v 26), כֹּה (v 37), and מֹנִים (v 41 as in v 7). Insertions from J are vv 27, 31, 36a, 38-40. Evidence for this analysis is as follows: v 31 does not belong in the context of E for v 32 answers the question of v 30 without regard to v 31. For its part, however, v 31 responds to v 27 (to גזל v 31, cf. 21:25 J). In addition v 27 parallels v 26 (E; וַתִּגְנֹב אֶת־לְבָבִי v 26 ‖ וַתִּגְנֹב אֹתִי v 27). Therefore, v 27 is from J. In E Laban reproaches Jacob for abducting his daughters (v 26), in J for secretly fleeing (v 27). It should be noted, however, that v 27, which we have assigned to J, agrees with E (vv 20, 22) in the combination of הִגִּיד and בָּרַח. Yet this agreement can be the result of the fundamental relationship of the recensions. V 36a and v 36bα are clearly a doublet. It may be hypothesized from this that J passages are also hidden in Jacob's speech. Vv 38-40 begin as do vv 41, 42. The final paragraph clearly belongs to E (cf. above). Accordingly one may attribute vv 38-40 to J. The report of E is completely preserved. Nothing of J seems to be missing either, except for the accusation of theft (after v 31), an accusation which infuriates Jacob (vv 36a, 38-40).

The passage has the purpose of explaining Laban's change of attitude. Extremely angry at the beginning, he is prepared to acquiesce at the end. Laban is overcome in J <346> by an angry speech of Jacob which so energetically presents Jacob's case that even Laban is unable to oppose him. In order to sufficiently explain this whole crisis, E has brought together a series of motifs. In addition to a parallel to Jacob's speech, he also has the teraphim narrative which clearly emphasizes Jacob's righteousness. He has also added a third, religious motif to these two profane motifs. God himself intervenes and restrains Laban. In this passage, too, the religious motivation was clearly only added secondarily (as in vv 13, 3, 10-12). J's recension is relatively short here, too. E, in contrast, displays a more expansive style here, too. The hearer's interest is now very heightened. How will Jacob succeed in escaping from Laban? When Jacob has behaved completely righteously and Laban has diminished in stature, the enthusiasm of the ancient public reaches its climax. This is the reason for Jacob's long passionate speech to which we are supposed to respond Yes and Amen with all our hearts.

26, 28 E Laban is not only insulted personally, but also in the name of his daughters whom Jacob has abducted "like prisoners of war," and whom, together with his grandchildren, Laban would like to have kissed good-bye. This is not a lie. It shows a new side of Laban. He is also a tender father. The narrator wisely introduces this motif here because he wants to use it later in the moment of crisis (v 43). Laban's two traits, greed and fatherly love, fit well together. The narration does not depict a fatherly love which includes the purse (v 15), but one that costs nothing: kissing is free. That one person can have several traits which motivate actions does not occur in the "concise" style, but is natural in the more extensive style where a wide variety of different elements have flowed together in the same account. **27** These words of Laban differ in J. They are an infamous lie, entirely in accord with the mask of this cad (cf. comments on 29:15ff.). It is interesting for the history of literature that one dismisses the departee with songs of joy. There must have been a genre of songs of farewell, then, joyous in content, which dealt with God's blessing, with a fortunate journey, and a joyous return home. Tambourines are depicted in Benzinger[2], 243. Concerning נֶחְבָּא with ל and infinitive see §114m. וָאֲשַׁלֵּחֲךָ means "so that I could have sent you away" (§111m). Concerning עֲשׂוֹ in v 28 see §75n (cf. 48:11; 50:20 in E). The infinitive functions here as the accusative of the object (§114c). **29** For עִמְּכֶם and אֲבִיכֶם one should read עִמְּךָ and אָבִיךָ with LXX and Sam. יֶשׁ-לְאֵל יָדִי means "it is (possible) for the numen of my hand," that is, I am able to do it. Brockelmann (ZAW 26:29ff.) suggests as the original sense of the idiom "that even the Hebrews once believed in a special 'spirit' of the hand to whom one owed thanks for the capacity to perform this and that" (literature on this and similar beliefs in Brockelmann, cf. also *Test XII, Test Reuben* 25, and Origenes *c. Cels.*, 8.58). Laban has the power because of the size of his company.

30, 32-25 *The stolen teraphim.* This <347> episode, apparently very ancient, is full of crude mirth. One is amused at Laban, who avoids everything God prohibited him from saying and places all his emphasis on this one point, in which he apparently is right, and who must draw the short end of this matter. At the same time one rejoices over his clever daughter, blood of his blood, who, through her crude trick, causes her father to make a large arc around her and to search everywhere except where the stolen object lies. Finally, the secondary motif of the poor household idol enhances the narrative's humor. The scene in v 35, where Rachel sits on the beloved idol and pretends to be in a state of extreme impurity (Lev 15:19ff.) in which a woman may not approach a god too closely, let alone sit on him (Lev 15:20 !) causes even the grumpiest to laugh. Poor Laban and poor idol! **32** The promise to punish the thief in life and limb is supposed to demonstrate Jacob's honor. Usually, one does not punish a thief so severely. The narrator reports this promise in order to heighten the tension. The same motif recurs in 44:9. In our terms the death penalty is too serious for this droll narrative. The narrator has more rugged sensibilities, however, and the father would not have killed his daughter anyway. Regarding the "unheard of" construction עִם אֲשֶׁר see §138f. The clause, "the one with whom you find your god shall not live," corresponds totally to the structure of 44:9a, "the one of your servants with whom it (the cup) is found will die." This is legal style. The reading of LXX, הכר מה לך עמדי, may be preferable (Ball). The plural suffix of גְּנָבְתַם, which refers to תְּרָפִים (also in v 34), does not indicate that תְּרָפִים should be translated as a plural (§124h, §145i). **33** LXX (cf. Sam) reads וַיָּבֹא לָבָן + וַיְחַפֵּשׂ (Kautzsch-Socin, Kittel). Here at the climax the account becomes ritardando (cf. comments on 22:9-10). Gen 44:12 is especially similar. The search proceeds according to age. The presumption is that each of Jacob's wives has her own tent—an interesting observation for the history of marriage. וּבְאֹהֶל שְׁתֵּי הָאֲמָהֹת is, as וַיֵּצֵא מֵאֹהֶל לֵאָה shows, the addition of a pedant. **34** The כַּר should not be understand as a saddle, but as a "palanquin" (a sedan chair, a long basket; cf. the depictions in Riehm, "Kameel," in HW; Jacob, pp. 28-29 [cf. 68]; Littmann, *Arab. Beduinenerzählungen* 2, 14 fig. 4). **35** The childishly respectful tone of

Rachel's address to her father is delightful. It is the duty of youth to stand before their elders (Lev 19:32). The expression explaining her supposed state is discreet (cf. 18:11; 19:31).

36-42 *Jacob's speech.* "Thus Laban stood there with a long face." But Jacob now turns the tables and takes advantage of the situation so favorable to him. The hearer, who has seen Jacob in misfortune for a long time, rejoices over this great moment. Jacob took Laban's whole flock. He is taking Laban's daughters and children away with him. Laban has even lost the teraphim. And in all of this, Jacob is completely in the right and can even give a great speech! Here, for the first time, something approaching passion appears in Jacob (Haller, 120). The narrator takes Jacob's words very seriously. We, <348> however, who do not take sides so impartially, find them a bit unusual while the great flocks which Jacob took from Laban so honorably (!) stand behind him. The pathos of these words is evident in the often rhythmic language (vv 36, 38, 39). Vv **36-40** give a great deal of information concerning the legal sphere. Whoever wants to prove the charge of theft is obligated to find the stolen object in the house of the thief (44:12) and to testify before witnesses. The accused must permit this handling of his household effects (idols belong to one's "household effects") and offers in his zeal an extreme punishment (44:9). But if the evidence is not discovered in the search of the household, the innocently accused becomes "angry." Witnesses and judges are the "brothers." For more on the duties of the shepherd see Benzinger², 139. He was to see that the sheep did not miscarry. He may not eat rams (who were otherwise slaughtered, v 38). A stingy master even requires compensation for the sheep torn by wild animals (lions, bears, wolves; for the stolen sheep, too; v 39). A decent master, however, permits the shepherd to produce evidence that the piece was really torn and does not charge him for it then (Exod 22:12; cf. 1 Sam 17:35). A cordial master considered theft by night differently than theft by day when one should be paying attention. Accordingly, the shepherd's life is no idyll. The shepherd lives day and night under an open sky, exposed to harsh variations of temperature (cf. Benzinger², 21) and may not even sleep at night but must be on guard against animals and thieves. For Babylonian shepherd law see Hammurabi ¶¶261-67.

39 אֲחַטֶּנָּה is from חטא according to the ל,ה paradigm (§75oo). Concerning the imperfect (of iterative action) see §107e. גְנֻבְתִי is in construct state. Regarding the form see §90l; For the construction see §116k. **40** Regarding the syntax of הָיִיתִי see §143a n. 1. **42** אֱלֹהֵי אַבְרָהָם is an addition. The name is very bland alongside the very concrete continuation. The divine name פַּחַד יִצְחָק, that is, the numen before whom Isaac is terrified (like Greek σέβας), is comparable to קְדוֹשׁ יִשְׂרָאֵל and תְּהִלַּת יִשְׂרָאֵל (Psa 22:4, LXX), the God whom Israel considers holy, whom Israel praises (cf. Isa 8:13). פַּחַד may also be a divine name in the phrase פַּחַד לָיְלָה (Psa 91:5) where it could signify the demons of the night (cf. *Ausgewählte Psalmen*², 166-67). The name "Terror of Isaac" is cleverly introduced into the account. This God appeared to Jacob as the God of the Fathers (v 29) and severely threatened Laban (v 24). The name is mentioned here to prepare for his appearance in v 53. This name only appears in this narrative; it has a very ancient sound; it was certainly the name of a local numen originally, perhaps even here in Mizpah or better in Beer-sheba (the latter option is supported by Staerk, *Studien* 1:61; Luther, ZAW 21:73-74; Meyer, *Israeliten*, 254). The assumption that this name originally <349> meant "the terror of (the God of) Isaac" is hardly likely. The two divine names *'el beth-'el* and *paḥad yiṣḥaq* stand immediately next to one another. The old concise legends have a much stricter unity. The clause, "if God had not been there for me, then . . . " occurs in Psa 124:1ff. as the beginning of a song of thanksgiving (cf. the German, "what would I have been without you"). Regarding the syntax see §158l, x. **43** Laban is unable to reply. The fox is in the trap. He must give up everything—wives, children, the livestock—although everything belongs to him. These words, which absolutely delight the hearers, are not an "ostentatious attack" (Holzinger), but, given the continuation, which shows Laban to be in a gentle mood, a mournful lament (cf. 27:34, where the deceived one also breaks out into bitter tears at the end). Laban's excitement is evident in the fourfold "my." He is especially sad about the idea that he must now commit his daughters and their children into the hand of the strange man and he does not know how he will treat them. "What could I yet do for my daughters today (tomorrow it would be too late)?" Here the narrative takes up the motif prepared in v 28 in order to explicate it in what follows. The usual understanding "How could I cause my own daughter's sorrow?" makes the transition to what follows difficult. לְ עָשָׂה then, does not have the negative sense, as it is usually interpreted, but the positive.

IV **44-45** *The treaty at Gilead-Mizpah.* The source analysis is particularly difficult since with a few additions the redactor has woven the two recensions into a whole. Dual strands are indicated by the following circumstances: two agreements are sworn, one more private in nature that Jacob will not treat Laban's daughters poorly (v 50), and one international in character that Jacob and Laban will regard the place as the border (v 52). Two different sacred symbols are involved, the massebah (v 45) and the pile of stones (v 46), two different places, Mizpah (v 49) and Gilead (vv 47, 48), two sacrificial meals (v 54 ‖ v 46b), two invocations of God (vv 49-50 ‖ vv 51-52), two divine names, the "Terror of Isaac" (v 53b) and "the God of Abraham and the God of Nahor" (v 53a).

The difficult question is how these varied parallel passages are to be arranged in two parallel strands. Here, the starting point is the observation that clever allusions to the place names occur in the passage. The words מַצֵּבָה (v 45) and יָצֶף (v 49) play with the name מִצְפָּה. The invocation in v 49, however, introduces the private agreement (v 50). In contrast, the name גִּלְעָד echoes in passages which speak of the גַּל (pile of stones) which is to be an עֵד (witness), that is, vv 44b, 46. Vv 51, 52 (the establishment of the border) also belong here: גַּל and עֵד belong together. Since the meal in v 46b is held at the גַּל, the parallel in v 54 belongs to the massebah. The invocation of the god common to both parties (v 53a) is to be attributed to the source in which both parties assume an obligation, that is, to the source which recounts the treaty between nations. In contrast, v 53b, according to which Jacob swears by the God of his fathers, belongs to the recension in which Jacob alone makes a promise, namely, to treat his wives well. V 44a best suits the report in which both ("me and you") assume a promise. Since וְהָיָה in v 44 cannot refer to בְּרִית (fem.), a clause must be missing before v 44b, perhaps, "I will pile up a heap" (Olshausen). According to v 51, Laban set up the pile of stones. A later hand attributed it to Jacob in v 46, probably because it was offensive that this Israelite sanctuary was established by a foreigner. Similarly, and for the same reason, v 45 was also altered. The presumption associated with Laban's explanation of the meaning of the massebah (v 49-50) is that he made it <350> and therefore knows what he wants with it (Wellhausen, *Composition*[3], 40-41). V 48 hardly belongs to the redactor since a naming which explains previous allusions customarily follow such reports. But one expects this naming at the end of the account and the words of v 48 would fit there exceptionally well. Laban offered Jacob a treaty, "This pile here will be a witness" (vv 51-52). Jacob accepts the treaty by repeating Laban's words verbatim, "This pile here will be a witness." Therefore, he names it Gilead. Accordingly, v 48 will have originally stood after v 53a and Jacob is to be understood as the subject of the clause. Conversely, Laban is probably the subject of v 54 (cf. above on v 23).

Red^JE contributed the harmonizing additions וְהִנֵּה הַמַּצֵּבָה (v 51), וְעֵדָה הַמַּצֵּבָה, and וְאֶת־הַמַּצֵּבָה הַזֹּאת (v 52). He will have also been responsible for וְהַמִּצְפָּה אֲשֶׁר אָמַר (v 49). The redactor will have read of the naming of מִצְפָּה at the end of the "Mizpah recension" and will have included it here, with limited success. V 47 also stems from a later hand. It anticipates v 48. The presupposition that Laban speaks a different language than Jacob is foreign to the rest of the context. Jegar-sahadutha is the literal translation of Galeed, and is therefore the Hebrew popular etymology of Gilead. The Aramaic words are not an actual Aramaic name, then, but are only a learned invention. The verse is the addition of a reader who let his Aramaic light shine here (Wellhausen, *Composition*[3], 41).

Of the two recensions, the Mizpah narrative belongs to E to whose account it is related at the beginning and the end. Laban, who must now surrender his daughters and their children to the foreigner, considers what he can still do for them today, that is, a good deed he can leave with them (v 43 E). As a benefit he leaves them with Jacob's promise to treat his wives well. In the morning, however, he kisses his grandchildren and daughters, blesses them, and departs (32:1 E). The divine name "Terror of Isaac" (v 53b) also indicates E as the source. E has already employed this name (v 42) and prepared for it in the preceding (cf vv 24, 29). Masseboth occur frequently in E, but not in J. Besides the recension employs אלהים (v 50). These arguments are so strong that one does not hesitate to regard יהוה (v 49) as a scribal error. Besides, LXX has ὁ θεός. The Gilead recension belongs, therefore, to J. The resulting analysis essentially agrees with that of Holzinger. Conversely, Procksch attributes the Mizpah recension to J, the other to E. Eerdmans (57ff.) believes that he can also salvage the unity of the text here (after striking vv 47, 48b, 49).

44, 46, 51-53a, 48 *The Gilead recension J.* Disarmed by Jacob's eloquent presentation (vv 37-40 J), Laban now declares himself ready for an amicable agreement. Both parties, he suggests, should henceforth do no harm. In order to understand the content of the בְּרִית, one should recall the external situation J described in the preceding (v 25b). The two patriarchs have camped on two opposed mountains, the extreme points of Israel and Aram; they met in the valley separating the two mountains—so we may imagine; there, where the road from Israel to Aram lead across the valley, the pile of stones was now heaped up "between the two" (v 51) and the border was established. Henceforth, neither may cross to do the other "evil." The pile of stones is to witness this agreement. Elements of national history, hardly an individual historical event, but probably a historical situation, shine through here. The establishment of the border would be unexplainable in relation to the private relations between Laban and Jacob. Instead—this is the silent presumption—it should also be observed by the peoples of Aram and Israel (cf. concerning such legends of the בְּרִית of the ancestors, 21:22-34; 26:26-33). For the dating of this element of the <351> legend it is significant that the legend does not yet presuppose the invasion of the Aramaeans which mangled Israel so horribly in the century from ca. 860 to ca. 770. There is no discussion of national hatred for the hereditary foe or of the gruesome battles which took place in Gilead itself (contra Wellhausen, *Prolegomena*[6], 321, etc.). Therefore, this element of the legend is older than ca. 860. Now, however, it is important to note that matters of national history do not occur in the rest of the Jacob-Laban legend and that the reference to national matters appears here quite abruptly. An element has made its way into the legend which refers to Israel and Aram only in this one point, the treaty, and only in J. The whole Jacob-Laban legend will, consequently, be much older and will have originally not even treated the historical peoples Israel and Aram. The situation with the narratives of Jacob and Esau (cf. 27:40), of Joseph, and of Tamar is similar. "Piles of stone" stand in Palestine, especially in the Transjordan, often as the remnants of prehistorical culture (Benzinger[2], 42-43; Stade, *Bibl. Theol.*, 116). The legend recounts how the patriarchs heaped up the גַּל. Such symbols could have very different meanings and are reinterpreted in each new era. In earlier Israel they were holy places where one eats the sacrificial meal (v 46) and calls on the deity (v 53). Such a גַּל stands here at the border. Piles of stone are still frequently border markers in modern Palestine according to Greßmann's oral communication. Holy stone heaps are known among the Arabs (cf. Wellhausen, *Arab. Heidentum*, 102; Goldziher, *Muhammed. Studien* 1:233-34). Concerning stone heaps all over the world, including border markers or vow sites, see Haberland, *Zeitschr. für Völkerpsychologie* 12:289ff. Since the stone heap is called upon as a witness here and the deity is called upon as judge (v 53a) an older concept will have been that the deity dwells in the stone heap and will thus see the evildoer who passes by and intrudes into the neighbor's territory. The appeal to the deity (v 53a), which occurs "remarkably late" (Haller, 41), is, therefore, a late improvement on the earlier concept that the stone heap, itself, witnesses to the treaty (Westphal, *Jahwes Wohnstätten*, 103). An even older opinion could have been that the fathers heaped up the mountain of Gilead, itself. They would have been portrayed as giants (cf. Judg 15:17).

46 For וַיִּקְחוּ LXX reads וַיִּלְקְטוּ. A common (holy) meal is associated with concluding the covenant as in vv 53-54 and 26:30-31. Such a covenant meal is the diluted form of an original sacrifice offered to the numen of the stone heap in which the blood ran over the stones (Robertson-Smith, *Rel. der Semiten*, 153; Haller, 65-66, 70). **48** The name is not *Gal'ed*—this is the interpretation—but *Gil'ad*. This etymology is, of course, no more significant linguistically than most of the popular etymologies. The article in הַגִּלְעָד already shows this (v 21). **51-52** Regarding the anacolouthon see §167b. Regarding the oath formula see §149c. **53a** Each one swears by the god of his ancestor. An addition, אֱלֹהֵי אֲבִיהֶם (lacking in Hebr mss, LXX) makes the two gods <352> one (Wellhausen, *Composition*[3], 41; et al.).

45, 49, 50, 53b, 54 *Mizpah recension E.* On parting, Laban would like to do something else nice for his family. He thinks of the possibility that Jacob could take other wives who could then displace his now aged daughters in Jacob's love and honor and whose new children could overshadow his grandchildren. Thus, he places his son-in-law under the solemn vow not to marry again. Such a vow, required of the son-in-law by the concerned parents of the bride, will certainly not have been uncommon in real life. A similar phenomenon appears in Babylonian marriage contracts (cf. KB 4:186-87 no. 11).

At the same time, Laban erects a memorial stone. This stone "on the mountain" (v 54) "set up high" (v 45; וַיְרִימֶהָ perhaps an allusion to הָאָרֵמִי v 20, with Ball, or to *Ramath ham-Miṣpe* with Procksch, 28), sees far across the land. Thus, God sees what Jacob does far from Laban with no human witness to bring Laban a report! Here, too, the belief that God himself dwells in the stone stands in the background (cf. p. 312). The memorial stone as witness of the covenant also appears in Josh 24:25ff. and Exod 24:4. The practice of placing border stones as border guardians also occurs among the Babylonians, Greeks, and elsewhere (Greßmann, ZAW 29:120-21). Jacob makes an oath with a sacrifice and a solemn meal. Spending the night at holy sites (v 54) also seems to have belonged to the sacred act. Mizpah (Judg 10:17; 11:11, 34), according to 31:23 on the mountain of Gilead, probably identical with Mizpah (Judg 11:29; perhaps also with Ramath-Mizpeh, Josh 13:26; Ramoth-Gilead, 1 Kgs 3:13; 22:3ff., etc., the Israelite city on the border with Aram), is north of the Yabbok (= *ez-Zerḳâ*) according to the context of the Jacob narratives, and is thus to be sought neither in *es-Salṭ* nor in the ruins of *el-Gal'ûd* (both south of *ez-Zerḳâ*). Instead it must have lain much farther north (cf. Smend, ZAW 22:155ff. who thinks of the current *er-Remthe*, southwest of *Der'a*; or is Mizpah the current *Masfâ* northwest of Gerasa? cf. Guthe, BW s.v. "Mizpa"). Concerning Ramath-Gilead see the recent article by J. Boehmer (ZAW 29:129ff.). The legend at hand is the cult legend of Mizpah. The Jephthah legend and perhaps also Hos 5:1 deal with this place. Since it is mentioned in a legend variant parallel to Mizpah, Gilead will not have been far away. According to Judg 10:17 it was situated opposite. Hos 6:8 and 12:12 mention it as a holy site. In Mizpah the sanctuary was a massebah, in Gilead a stone heap. The two cities and their sanctuaries are, therefore, not identical. **49** אֲשֶׁר means "because" (30:18). For וְהַמַּצֵּבָה (v 49) Sam has מִצְפָּה. For the name הַמִּצְפָּה LXX usually has the pronunciation Μασσηφα, leading Wellhausen (*Composition*[3], 43n.1) to suggest that the place was originally called הַמַּצֵּבָה but that the name was altered for very dubious reasons into הַמִּצְפָּה.

32:1 [some EVV =31:55] *Laban's departure, from E*. "He set out in the morning" continues 31:54. Laban is tender toward "grandchildren and daughters" as in 31:28, 43, 49f. He kisses them, that is, he does what he wished to do (cf. 31:28). <353>

49. Legend of Mahanaim 32:2, 3 E

This little piece stems from E: אלהים (vv 2, 3). The starting point for interpretation is the peculiar incoherence of the passage. Angels appear without saying or doing anything. In an effort to explain this brevity, the first and second editions of this commentary stated the conjecture repeated frequently by others that the passage is a fragment. The actual point of the original account—perhaps Jacob's struggle with the "wild hosts" of angels—was omitted by later readers because it offended them (cf. 6:1-4; 35:21-22). In contrast, Meyer (*Israeliten*, 275n.2) maintains that the piece is not the fragment of a once more extensive cultic legend, but was nothing more than a brief comment from the very beginning whose purpose was to give the etymology of "Mahanaim." Analogies in 33:17, 18-20; Exod 15:22ff., 27; Josh 5:13-15 (cf. also the Bethel legend, p. 314) support this explanation. They are nothing more than brief "comments" as would have been told at certain places to explain the name or some other characteristic of the place. In Germany, too, there are many such very brief local legends (cf. introduction ¶3:22). Thus, in Mahanaim the name was explained by the account of Jacob seeing a "camp" of God's angels there. That God's angels encounter a human or a hero must, then, have been a legend motif known at the time from other traditions. What was the meaning of this motif? "Angels of God," that is, originally divine or demonic beings (cf. above pp. 56, 310), appear here as a (originally infinite, 1 Chron 12:22) divine host. Such a belief in hosts of gods and spirits is widespread: "Indeed, the concept of a heavenly host which rushes into the night sky is not foreign to any of our European peoples" (Usener, *Götternamen*, 42; cf. in Germany the "wild hosts"). It is also certainly very old in Israel and plays a definite role in Yahwism (Judg 5:20; Josh 5:14, the "host of heaven," the "host of Yahweh," יהוה צְבָאוֹת, etc.; cf. Westphal, *Jahwes Wohnstätten*, 234ff.). A wide variety of influences may have merged in the concept. The host of stars was understood as the "host of heaven." But meteorological phenomena such as storms, rain, thunder, and the phenomena of the volcano may also have been derived from such a "raging host." Yahweh, who appears in the fire of Sinai, is accompanied by all the "holy ones" (Deut 33:3). Here, where the divine host appears on earth, the idea of the starry host lies far in the distance. Such spirit hosts—as is presumed here—roam through the land from a "camp." Of course, they are normally invisible to the mortal eye. But they can accidentally—פגע, "to encounter by accident" (28:11; Exod 23:4; 1 Sam 10:5)—encounter a person. But when Jacob perceives them, he concludes that their camp cannot be far away. The German legends of an appearance of the "wild host" (Grimm, *Deutsche Mythologie*[4], 768ff.) are comparable. It cannot be assumed that the "angels" said or did anything. It is enough that Jacob saw them. The situation is similar with the "wild host" which also usually permit themselves only to be seen or heard (by a traveler) in German traditions. The text does not support the usual explanation that the angelic revelation is supposed to assure Jacob of God's protective presence (cf. 2 Kgs 6:17). Such pieces which appear suddenly may not, at any rate, be interpreted in terms of their original meaning according to their current context. Yet, E may have already interpreted the passage in this way. Mahanaim (not a dual, §88c) was one of the chief sites in the Transjordan, the residence of Ishbaal (2 Sam 2:8, 12, 29), David's seat during Absalom's rebellion (2 Sam 17:24ff.), and the capital <354> city of one of Solomon's districts (1 Kgs 4:14). According to the Jacob narrative, the city lay north of the Jabbok, not too far from the Jordan (v 11; cf. also 2 Sam 2:29), south or southwest of Mizpah and Gilead, across from Penuel. The equation with *Mahne*, a ruin on the *Wâdi el-Himâr*, is therefore impossible.

The Second Part of the Jacob-Esau Narrative
32:4-22 33:1-16

is significantly distinct from the first part of this legend (25:21-34; 27). While an original, although for us difficult to understand, sense of events often appears in the first part, very little of this sense can be perceived here. Only the general structure of the second part—according to which Jacob is indeed inferior to his brother in outward power, but far exceeds him in cunning so that he maintains his advantage over him—agrees with the first part. This agreement can be understood as the result of the basic significance of the figures. While, furthermore, the legends of the first part are hardly localized, the second part is associated with specific places, Mahanaim and Penuel. But the reference to these places, however great their significance for the narrator (cf. below), does not very well suit the nations of Edom and Israel identified with Esau and Jacob. The territory of the historical Edom is far removed from Mahanaim and Penuel. It is hard to say how to eliminate these difficulties. If "Esau" is really native to the land of the later Edom, the legend would have been only secondarily localized in Mahanaim. But if the legend is actually at home in Mahanaim, then one should conclude that Esau did not originally dwell in Edom, but much farther to the north. The current legend addresses the difficulty by recounting that Esau moved from his dwelling place in the South to meet Jacob in Penuel. But this is only a stopgap since one hardly travels so far to meet one returning home. Meyer (*Israeliten*, 387n.1) thinks of Edom's former power far to the north—but all the way to the Jabbok?

The account is executed in novelistic fashion. Jacob now comes into urgent danger. His brother, who was once deceived by him and who then swore to kill him, now approaches. He cannot consider resistance since Esau brings four hundred men with him. Nor can he consider flight for the flocks are about to bear. How will the agile Jacob succeed in escaping this danger? The narrators gain the answer to this question from the names of the places where this meeting occurred. They interpret Mahanaim as "two camps" (dual) or "several camps" (plural). One recounts that Jacob divided his flocks and people into two camps. If Esau smites one, the other can escape (32:8-9). A second variation of the same theme is that Jacob divided his family into three parts—at the front the maidens with their children, then Leah together with their children, finally Rachel with Joseph. If Esau falls upon them, he will meet the maids with their children, Jacob's less-favored, perhaps even overtake Leah and her children, if only Rachel and Joseph can save themselves (33:1-2). Although the word "camp" does not occur in the current recension in this context, this division is so similar to the first that one may consider the two variants. A third variation (32:14-22) tells of another division. According to it, Jacob sends ahead one part of the flock as a "gift." He, himself, remained behind in the "camp." This element contains a play on words between מַחֲנֶה "camp" (32:22) and מִנְחָה "gift" (32:14, 19, 21, 22; 33:10). Since, however, it goes on to say that this "gift," too, in order to be more conspicuous, was further divided into five parts, the interpretation of Mahanaim as "several camps" also <355> echoes here. At the same time, although less intensively, the name Penuel is also influential. Looking at Esau's face, Jacob flatteringly assures him, is like seeing the face of a god, פְּנֵי אֱלֹהִים (33:10). The words פָנָיו אוּלַי in 32:21 also allude to "Penuel." Further, it is noteworthy how frequently the word עָבַר occurs throughout the piece (32:11, 17, 22, 23, 24bis, 32; 33:3, 14), thus in all nine times indeed, not just in contexts such as 32:11, 23, 24, where it was necessary. The narrators play with these words because the course of the action involves a passage עבר over a ford מַעֲבָר (32:23). The phrases עָבַר לִפְנֵי (32:17; 33:3, 14) and עָבַר עַל־פְּנֵי (32:22) occur frequently (to which עָבַר אֶת־פְּנוּאֵל in 32:32 alludes). This, too, will be no accident, but a creation on the basis of a phrase such as מַעֲבַר־פְּנוּאֵל.

From this or a similar name, the narrators derived the notion that at the "ford of Penuel" someone or something went on ahead. Who went ahead of whom finds many different treatments. The "gift" went ahead of Jacob's camp (32:17, 22). Jacob, himself, preceded his wives (33:3). Finally, Esau preceded—Jacob was clever enough to influence this—Jacob (33:14). The notion that Jacob sends messengers to Esau probably arose in a similar way—they precede him (32:4ff.)—as did the notion that Jacob remained on the other side of the ford (32:25)—the camp preceded him. The latter two cases do not employ the phrase עָבַר לִפְנֵי, however. Consequently, a very significant portion of the whole legend results from imaginative interpretation of the names. Such etymological interpretations are also very frequent in other old legends, although they are usually only employed as secondary elements (cf. introduction ¶2:8). The predominance of etymologies in this passage means, then, that this account is not an ancient tradition, but was extrapolated by the narrators on the basis of a few bits of information. The fact that the whole narrative consequently became blander than the old authentic legends usually are is not surprising.

The places establish the inner structure of the account. Mahanaim and Penuel lie opposite one another on either side of the Jabbok with the ford between. At Mahanaim Jacob made preparations to receive Esau. At Penuel he met him. In between was the fording of the river.

50. Jacob's Preparations to Receive Esau 32:4-22 JE

Source criticism. The passage divides into two parts. I. Jacob learns from messengers that Esau is approaching. In fear, he divides the camp into two parts and prays to Yahweh for deliverance. In the night he remains alone (vv 4-14a). II. Jacob sends ahead a gift of several flocks. In the night he remains in the camp (vv 14b-22). The first section reaches the point in v 14a which the second only attains in v 22. The two parts parallel each other in content, too. The second passage (cf. בַּמַּחֲנֶה v 22) knows nothing of the division into two parts in vv 8, 9. Therefore, vv 4-14a parallel vv 14b-22. Vv 4-14a stem from J as indicated by יהוה (v 10), "God of my father Abraham" (v 10 as in 28:13), שִׁפְחָה (v 6), מָצָא חֵן בְּעֵינֵי (v 6), and the list in v 6 (as in 30:43). Furthermore, vv 10, 13a look back on 31:3 (J), v 13b on 28:14 (Jᵉ). Accordingly, vv 14b-22 belongs to E. Jacob's prayer in vv 10-13 differ markedly from its surroundings in tone. First, while the narrative is otherwise entirely profane and only glorifies Jacob's cunning, a deep religious sensibility suddenly intrudes here. Jacob, slippery as an eel, feels—unworthy of all God's grace! In order to sense how "modern" this prayer is, one may compare it with the ancient Penuel narrative. Two different worlds come together here in the framework of one chapter. Second, the prayer also interprets the division into "two camps" somewhat differently than the preceding (vv 8,9). While, to this point, the division <356> had the purpose of permitting at least a partial flight from Esau, the camps are employed here to portray the magnitude of God's grace which made Jacob so wealthy. Third, the reference to the Jordan in v 11 is also remarkable. The old legend speaks of the crossing of the Jabbok here (Kautzsch-Socin² n. 155). Allusions to Yahweh's statements in earlier narratives (vv 10, 13), indeed to statements which are, themselves, secondary in their settings (cf. comments on 28:14; 31:3 [22:17; 16:10]), also indicate that the prayer is secondary. The passage employs motifs and expressions from vv 4-9 (the "two camps" in v 11 as in v 8; יָרֵא in v 12 as in v 8; יָבוֹא וְהִכַּנִי in v 12 as in v 9) and belongs to J judging from its diction. It stems, therefore, from Jᵉ.

I **4-14a** *The sending of the messengers, the division of the camp, the prayer J.* **4-7** The sending of the messengers whereby Jacob announces himself is supposed to demonstrate his deference to Esau. Jacob takes pains to appear as humble as possible to Esau (thus the courteous expressions "my lord," vv 5, 9; 33:8, 13, 14bis, 15; "your servant," vv 5, 19, 21; 33:5; "to find grace in your eyes," v 6; 33:8, 10, 15) in the hope he can be won over by the many compliments and speeches dripping with deference. All this, especially the sevenfold bowing (33:3), far exceeds the courtesy the younger brother owes the elder (contra Frankenberg, CGA [1901], pp. 701-702). The key to everything is 32:21 where the narrator expressly says that Jacob has a guilty conscience and therefore strives to appease Esau. This manner of helping oneself in distress through humility certainly corresponds to the common style of the narrators and hearers who apparently enjoyed Jacob's great skill in flattery. **4** שְׂדֵה אֱדוֹם is a gloss on אַרְצָה שֵׂעִיר. שָׂדֶה is "the broad, open space" (cf. Meyer, *Israeliten*, 329). **5** אַחַר is an apocopated form of אַאַחַר (§64h). **6** שׁוֹר וַחֲמוֹר is employed collectively like עֶבֶד וְשִׁפְחָה (§ 123b). שׁוֹר וַחֲמוֹר is a common rhyme. The same combination occurs in Isa 1:3. Sam, LXX, Vulg, and Pesh add וְצֹאן (Kittel, Kautzsch³). Concerning וָאֶשְׁלְחָה see §49e. **7** The idea is that, before Jacob's messengers reached him, Esau had already learned of Jacob's approach and set out immediately to overtake him (contra Sievers 2:329). His intention remains purposefully obscure in order to create tension. It is only said that he is in a great hurry and brings a large number of men with him. We are supposed to ask apprehensively with Jacob, "For what purpose? Is he still angry? Will he slaughter Jacob and his family and steal his flocks? Or does he come to greet his returning brother amicably and accompany him home?" The account does not establish how Esau comes to have four hundred men.

8, 9 *The division of the camp.* **8** שְׁנֵי מַחֲנוֹת is an etymology of מחנים which the knowledgeable will understand (contra Eerdmans 1:60). **9** The feminine הָאַחַת is impossible here. Sam has הָאֶחָד (Ball, Kittel). **10-13** Jacob's prayer begins with the "appeal" (v 10; cf. comments on 4:26), the naming of the God <357> expanded by a modifier (cf. comments on 24:12), here a participle (הָאֹמֵר). Hebrew prayers are more naive than ours. The added modifier contains a strong appeal to God. He commanded the return home himself and added promises. Thereby, Jacob has come into such great danger. Can God now allow him to fall? A thanksgiving follows the appeal (v 11; cf. *Ausgewählte Psalmen*², 206), even before the request. This corresponds to the fear one feels before God. Before one dares come to him with requests, one should praise and thank him. This thanksgiving also contains a comfort at the same time. The God who has so often helped will not abandon his worshipper now either. Only then comes the actual body of the prayer, the request (v 12). Yet another motif is added by which God may be persuaded—one hopes (v 13). The total structure of Jacob's prayer makes it the model, especially for prose prayers (cf. Isa 37:16ff.; Jer 32:16ff.; 1 Kgs 8:23ff.; Dan 9:4ff.; 1 Macc 4:30ff.; 3 Macc 2; 6; Tob 3:2ff., 11ff.; OrMan; OrAsar.; Psa 9; 16; 41; 44; etc.). **11** Jacob's thanksgiving prayer is the classical expression of human humility, a feeling of unworthiness of God's benefits. Joyfully Jacob compares his poverty on leaving with his wealth on returning. This is a natural element. When one returns to the same place it is natural to compare one's status then and now. The converse occurs with Naomi who left wealthy and returned poor (Ruth 1:21). The idea of sin often introduced here from the "context" of the Jacob legend is quite foreign (Driver). The author of this prayer has in mind a ford of the Jordan not far from Mahanaim and Penuel. One usually thinks of the one at ed-Dâmiye. **12** אֵם עַל־בָּנִים (Hos 10:14) is a colloquialism. A comment seems to have stood after **14a** in J to the effect that the place took its name, Mahanaim, from the division of the camp. This is the origin of the שָׁם (Dillmann).

II **14b-22** *Jacob sends ahead several flocks as a gift E.* It is common to give a gift when one meets with a superior whom one wishes to honor (43:11; 1 Sam 17:18; 2 Kgs 5:18; 8:9), especially if one has reason to fear him (1 Sam 25:27; Gen 43:11). The scene assumes that Esau heard of Jacob's approach and moves to meet him. The same is also true of J and was consequently omitted here. **14b** מִן־הַבָּא בְּיָדוֹ refers to that which came in his hand, that is, with him (35:4; Dillmann). **15, 16** The thorough description of the flocks—a similar list in Job 1:3—characterizes the style of this legend. We are supposed to hear this list with some expertise and think, "a clever man, this Jacob who makes such extraordinarily large gifts—Esau will surely be unable to resist him!" **16** Concerning וַעְיָרִם see §28b; Kittel prefers וַעְיָרִם. **17** The fact that the flocks are to move separately in different camps (עֵדֶר עֵדֶר לְבַדּוֹ, §123d) is derived from the name "Mahanaim." The narrator provides a very good explanation for this element. In this way they look <358> even larger. **18** One asks this question of everyone one meets in the desert (cf. comments on 16:8). **19** Jacob's instructions are delightful. The leaders of the flocks are to report to Esau that Jacob himself is coming "after them." Thus, when the following flock comes, Esau will expect to have Jacob before him now. But then comes—what a surprise!—not Jacob but a new gift. This, the main point of all the instructions, is repeated in v 21. This is an extremely refined way to present a gift! **18** Concerning יִפְגָשְׁךָ see §60b and Spurrell. **20** Concerning מֹצַאֲכֶם for מָצָאֲכֶם see §74h. V **21**, which probably contains a wordplay on "Penuel" (cf. above), is not superfluous here and cannot belong to J where Jacob does not yet think of a gift at this point (cf. comments on 33:8-11; contra Dillmann). Sam, LXX, Targ. Onq, Targ. Jon, Ball, and Sievers (2:330) read בָּא + יעקב. "To cover the face" means "to reconcile" (Stade, *Bibl. Theol.*, 167).

51. Jacob's Struggle with the Deity 32:23-33 JE

Source analysis. The crossing of the river is reported twice: v 23 ‖ v 24 (cf. וַיִּקַּח v 23 ‖ וַיָּקָם v 24). V 23 belongs to J because of שִׁפְחָה and "Jabbok," to which J alludes in v 25, 26b. V 24 belongs to E (cf. Dillmann). J (v 23) expressly states that Jacob himself crossed the river, but E (v 24) does not. Consequently, v 25 "he remained behind alone," is to be attributed to E (Dillmann). According to E, Jacob only crosses at the end of the Penuel narrative (v 32a). In the opinion of most, vv 25-32 belong to J, in Dillmann's opinion to E. Holzinger correctly finds indications for both. In many aspects, a dual recension becomes apparent. According to v 26a, Jacob's hip was dislocated by a blow, according to v 26b, in contrast, accidentally while wrestling. The naming of Israel is already a type of blessing (vv 28-29) and, therefore, conflicts with the words "he blessed him then" (v 30). The result of the struggle is also evaluated variously: according to v 29 Jacob was victorious; according to v 31 he barely escaped with his life. Furthermore, the fact that in v 25 the narrator, in v 27 God, reports that morning has broken also seem to be variants. The fact that in v 28 God asks Jacob his name, while in v 30 Jacob asks God will also be two variations of the same motif. The division into sources cannot proceed from the usage of the divine name since אלהים has an appellative sense and v 31 intentionally avoids the name Yahweh. Nor can it proceed from the name "Israel" which

J admittedly employs from 35:21 onward, but which E also knows (33:20). One may begin best with the renaming of Jacob (vv 28, 29) according to which Jacob "overcame" the deity. Overcame? How? He smote the deity during the struggle (v 26, cf. the interpretation) and held on until he forced him to bless him by this renaming (v 27). Thus we obtain a coherent unit in vv 26a, 27, 28, 29. At first, it seemed that Jacob would not be the victor (לֹא יָכֹל v 26a), then he was, after all (וַתּוּכָל v 29). Because of the impressive parallel between v 29 and 30:8, this recension, however, belongs <359> to E. Its beginning is (cf. above) vv 24, 25a; Its conclusion, very effective after the poignant words in v 29, is v 32a. The recension is preserved almost completely. Only the attack by an unknown figure is missing at the beginning. It was displaced by v 25b. The remaining material (except for v 33, on which see the explanation) belongs to J: vv 25a, 26b, 30, 31, 32b. This recension, too, forms a unit (cf. the interpretation). It is recounted very concisely, but nothing of significance seems to be missing. The two recensions are very similar. Place, time, essential course of the narrative, and the whole, unusual, nocturnal attitude are common to both. In addition, there are a series of individual features in common: both contain a question about the name; both conclude with a naming. Expressions also agree: עָלָה הַשָּׁחַר (vv 25, 27) and כַּף־יָרֵךְ (vv 26a, b, 33). The recensions are, therefore, very closely related. Holzinger attributes vv 27-29 to J, vv 30-32 to E. He recognizes the same relationships, therefore, but categorizes them differently. The same is true of Luther (ZAW 21:66) who assigns vv 25, 26a, 27-29 to J and vv 25a, 26a, 27 to J. In the first and second editions of this commentary, vv 26a, 27, 30, 31, 33 were assigned to E and vv 25b, 26b, 28, 29, 32 to J. But vv 28, 29 do not cohere well with v 26b nor does v 27 with v 30. Meyer (*Israeliten*, 57-58) attributes vv 25, 26a, 27, 30, 32aα to J and the rest to E, in essential agreement with Luther. But Jacob's two speeches (vv 27b, 30) cannot well stand alongside one another. Furthermore, vv 29 (Jacob victor) and v 31 (Jacob only fortunately escaped) are contradictory. Conversely, vv 25b, 26b ("wrestling") cannot be separated from one another. Procksch superbly attributes vv 24a, 25a, 26a, 27b, 28, 29, 32, and 33 to E. Yet, v 27a cannot be separated from v 27b. The many attempts demonstrate the difficulty of the task.

23 Concerning בַּלַּיְלָה הוּא see 19:33. Sam has ההוא (vv 14, 22). Jabbok, long equated with the current *Wâdi Zerkâ* (Smend, ZAW 22:137ff.) is, at points, a rather turbulent river in a deep ravine (נַחַל, v 24). Crossing a river by night is not without difficulty for flocks. Both sources recount this crossing without, however, adding an express motivation. The reason may well have been that Jacob does not want to be surprised by Esau during this difficult passage. **24** Sam, LXX, Pesh, Vulg, Ball, Kittel, and Kautzsch[3] read אֵת־כָּל־אֲשֶׁר־לוֹ. **25** Jacob remains as the last at the back of the column as is the master's duty. The idea probably is (cf. above) that he is still on the northern side of the river. Here he is entirely alone, far from any assistance, dependent on his own strength. J recounts less well that Jacob had already crossed the river (v 23). There an unknown being (J אִישׁ; cf. comments on 18:2) attacks him. E, too, spreads the veil of secrecy over the matter of who it may have actually been. The hearer may suspect the deity. Jacob, however, does not yet know at first. In the nocturnal darkness, he only knows that he has a strong, frightening opponent before him. He only learns that it is the deity in the further course of the narrative, in E through the request in v 27 and the agreement in v 29, in J through the avoidance of the name (v 30). This being "wrestles" with Jacob J. E, too, presumes something similar. What is the nature of this struggle? According to the well-known reinterpretation which takes offense at an actual struggle between God and Jacob, it is a prayer struggle. But one's hip does not become disjointed in a prayer struggle. All of the "spiritual truths" concerning Jacob's struggle for God's grace in fear of his sin against Esau as the conclusion of his purifications, which even Dillmann and Driver find here, have no support in the text. Exod 4:24-26, where Yahweh attacks Moses with the intention of killing him, is an instructive parallel. This is also God's intention here. The fact that the deity is usually on Jacob's side does not contradict this understanding, but only indicates that this legend is completely unique in the Jacob narrative, <360> just as the account in Exod 4:24-26 stands out in its context. See further on this issue at v 28. The deity appears by night, dreadfully, mysteriously (cf. comments on 19:14ff.). יֵאָבֵק occurs only here and in v 26. It is an allusion to and originally probably an attempted explanation of the name יַבֹּק. All these elements, that the deity attacks a person at night, unknown, and wrestles with him, breathe the same spirit and demonstrate the very advanced age of the account. Furthermore, the fact that they do not fight with weapons, but by wrestling, body against body, also points to a very ancient period. This is the character of fights in the earliest myths, for example, Hercules against Antaios, Hercules and Samson against lions. The fact that the god and man fight with one another, at first indecisively, and thus with roughly equal strength, indeed, that the man finally defeats the god (v 29), is also a sign of the earliest period. At that time, god and human were not as distinct from one another as Israel's classical period imagined. Jacob is conceived as especially powerful, perhaps even as a giant (29:10; 31:46ff.).

26a E. The absence of proper nouns and the change of subject is authentically Hebrew, but causes difficulties for our exegesis. Who smote the other on the hip? A later understanding, recorded in v 33b, thinks that God smote the man: this seemed to a later period the only worthy option. But the coherence of the passage is much tighter if we assume the reverse (with W. Max Müller, *Asien u. Europa*, 163n.1; Luther, ZAW 21:66; Meyer, *Israeliten*, 57; etc.). When Jacob sees that he is not superior in bodily strength to the other, he employs—as is extremely fitting to his character in general—a wrestler's trick (similar to Odysseus, *Il.* 23.725ff.) and smites the opponent on the hip socket, that is, the joint of the thighbone. Thus, severely injured and incapable of further resistance, the god resorts to pleading (27), "Let me go!" All of this is extremely ancient. The portrayal in Hos 12:5a [EVV 12:4a] is even more crude. He struggled with the angel and overcame him (וַיָּכֹל). He cried and pled for grace. (The subject of the send clause is the angel. The vanquished must plead for grace. The context of the verse in Hosea is very obscure for which reason, however, the very archaic clause is not to be explained as an addition.) The reason for the plea is that morning dawns. The statement presumes an extremely ancient viewpoint. The deity must disappear at sunrise. Jupiter's request (in Plautus, *Amphitr.* 1/3.34-35) offers a good parallel: "Cur me tenes? Tempus est; exire ex urbe, priusquam lucescat, volo." The statement has the esthetic purpose of escalating the tension (cf. comments on 19:15). The deadline expires in the next moment. What would happen if the sun were to rise? Would the sun reveal the figure of the god? The god dreads the dawn which seems to bring some unnamed and unnamable danger (E. Zurhellen-Pfleiderer, *Theol. Arbeiten aus dem rheinischen wissenschaftl. Prediger-Verein*, ns 10:43). But Jacob discerns from this request that he is in the presence of a god. While the account to this point glorifies Jacob's strength and presence of mind—his soul does not fail in any terror—the following praises his cunning. In Israelite thinking, cunning does not sully the hero. Jacob now notices who his opponent is and thinks, "Whoever has the deity should hold on." Therefore, he demands a "blessing." The statement, "I will not let you go unless you bless me," wondrous in tone for every Christian reader, originally had an entirely differently meaning. "To let go" is intended physically in the old account and even the "blessing" had no spiritual content here. "To bless" (cf. comments on 9:24ff.) means to speak an effective word such as only the deity can speak. Concerning אֲשַׁלֵּחֲךָ see §60f. <361> **28** Thus held in Jacob's strong fists and with the fearful morning light before his eyes, the god decides to pronounce the blessing. In homage to the brave champion, he first asks him his name, "Say, what is your name? You mighty man!" The statement presumes that he does not yet know Jacob! Accordingly, this account originally had no relationship to those Jacob narratives which recount divine epiphanies. The question, as in Exod 4:2, has the purpose "of directing the attention of the addressees to the current state of the matter in order to markedly emphasize the coming change" (Ehrlich). Why, however, did the god attack Jacob whom he did not know? Here we are apparently in an ancient religion far inferior to genuine Old Testament religion. There the deity bears many horrible features later transferred to the devil (cf. 2 Sam 24:1; 1 Chron 21:1). Thus the deity lurks like a predator by the way (Hos 13:7; cf. also Isa 8:14-15) and attacks the passerby. Such concepts, stemming from the most ancient period, were overcome by the later ethical religion and were pursued by prophets, who love the gruesome, only as metaphors. **29** And now the deity pronounces the desired "blessing" by changing Jacob's name to Israel. Concerning name changes, which do not have merely symbolic meaning but are also able to change the fate of the bearer, see above, p. 263. יִשְׂרָאֵל, which in analogy to ירדמאל, יִשְׁמָעֵאל, and יורעאל means "El struggles" (Meyer, *Israeliten*, 297), is interpreted here as "Struggler with God" (a similar popular etymology in Judg 6:32: Jerubbaal = "Fighter against Baal"). The expression שׂרה, only here and in the parallel Hos 12:4-5, is chosen because of the etymology. The name Israel occurs in the Egyptian form "Isir'r" first in the Merenptah inscription from ca. 1230 (cf. Meyer, *Israeliten*, 22-23; H. Ranke in Greßmann, *Altorientalische Texte und Bilder* 1:195). וַתּוּכָל is a qal imperfect; the perfect is יָכֹל (§69f). Ancient Israel thus interprets its name with proud arrogance to mean "victorious fighter against God and people," "unconquerable," "victorious," for whomever the deity could not compel, him will no enemy control! In the context of the legend, the deity acknowledged defeat. J recounts the story in a less ancient manner (26b, 30). Jacob, not the deity, went away injured. He displaced his hip in the struggle. This was a serious and extremely painful injury, but—one should remember—a mild outcome for Jacob, however, who at least saved his life in the frightful fight (cf. v 31). Now—so we may imagine the scene—the combatants release each other. Jacob asks the strong wrestler, acknowledging his might, about his name. But he does not tell it. Jacob concludes he is dealing with a god (v 31). The fact that the deity evades the question concerning his name has a parallel in Judg 13:17-18 and may be explained by the ancient belief, widespread among many peoples, that the knowledge of the name gives power over the bearer, even a god or demon. Whoever "knows" a god's name can henceforth "summon" him (Andree, *Ethnographische Parallelen*, 179ff.; Giesebrecht, *Gottesname*, 23, 45, 100; Heitmüller, 162ff.; v. d. Leyen, 114:11n.34; Meyer, *Israeliten*, 58;

Westphal, *Jahwes Wohnstätten*, 192-93; Roscher, *Ephialtes*, 42; etc.). This avoidance of the name is extremely suitable in the twilight of the legend. The presupposition is that the name was not "Yahweh," for which reason this name was not mentioned by J in v 31, either. In Hos 12:5 the deity who appears is "the messenger." Our recensions leave the question of who this god <362> was unanswered. It is possible, but not demonstrable, that, according to the more original recension, the god mentioned his name and Jacob thus obtained power over him. "He blessed him then." The clause is to be interpreted in context as follows: The god does not want to declare his name. But he wants to do something for the brave opponent, so he pronounces an effectual word over him. One should note the "there" (cf. 16:13; 21:17, 23). A special site is consecrated by this very blessing. This source does not report the content of the blessing. The legend seems to be significantly weakened in this respect.

31-33 *Concluding clauses.* **31** J The naming of the site (הַמָּקוֹם a "cultic site" here too? cf. comments on 12:6) is a very frequent conclusion of local legends. For פְּנִיאֵל Sam, Pesh, Symm, and Vulg have פְּנוּאֵל as in v 32 Hebr. Concerning the interchange of *i* and *u* (originally case endings) see §90o. This is also the name of a Phoenician foothill (θεοῦ πρόσωπον, Strabo 16/2:15-16). One may well assume that it was originally a mountain peak, similar in profile to a monstrous face, interpreted here, as there, in the earliest stage of religion as "god's face" (Meyer, *Gesch. d. Altertums* I¹, 247; E. Zurhellen-Pfleiderer, *Arbeiten aus dem rheinischen wissenschaftl. Prediger-Verein*, ns 10:33n.1). וַתִּנָּצֵל means "and yet escaped" (§111e). The general idea underlying this clause is the frequent notion in ancient Israel that whoever saw the deity must die (Judg 6:22; 13:22; Exod 33:20; cf. also the Greek legend of Semele) for so the deity guards his secret. He may well permit a human eye to see his face, but he does not allow the human mouth to revel his secret. Consequently, whoever has seen God's face and remained alive experiences particular good fortune (cf. Judg 6:23; 13:23; Deut 34:10; Tob 12:16-17). The relationship to the preceding is as follows: Jacob is happy to have just escaped destruction, although limping (**32b**), still alive! V **32a** is the conclusion of the account in E. The blessing is hardly spoken (v 29, the god disappeared) and Jacob has just crossed the river at Penuel when the sun rises. It was, therefore, high time for the god. Otherwise, the sun would have surprised him (similarly in 19:23). כַּאֲשֶׁר means "as soon as" as in 27:30. **33** The sinew of the hip is holy because "he"—here too the secret is kept—struck Jacob on it. The verse alludes to v 26a E, but means in contrast to the original sense of this clause, that the god struck Jacob. Consequently, at least the motivation in v 33b, but perhaps the whole verse, is an addition. גִּיד הַנָּשֶׁה is the *nervus ischiadicus*, which lies on the hip socket. This (almost finger thick) sinew will have come to the attention of the ancient Israelite because of its size and white color and was not eaten according to our comment, that is, it was excised and discarded during the slaughter. The fact that one did not eat certain portions of the animal for reasons of religious aversion also occurs frequently elsewhere (Frazer in *Anthropological Essays: Presented to E. B. Tylor* [1907], 136ff.; v. d. Leyen 114:13). The special sacredness of the hip sinew or the thigh is also attested elsewhere (Frazer, ibid., and *Golden Bough* II², 419-20; Robertson Smith, *Rel. d. Semiten*, 293n.667). בְּגִיד הַנָּשֶׁה parallels בְּכַף־יֶרֶךְ יַעֲקֹב. The second expression is the more precise and is therefore a gloss.

General Remarks concerning Jacob's Wrestling Match with the Deity

1. *The site of Penuel* lay south of the Jabbok according to v 23 J, directly beside the river according to v 32 E. The place is also mentioned in Judg 8:8-9, 17, and 1 Kgs 12:25. In Egyptian it is *Penau'aru* (Max Müller, *Asien und Europa*, 168). <363>

2. *Character of the god.* The character of the god at Penuel is quite peculiar. It is—if we may generalize the account—a being at enmity with humans who "lurks like a panther by the way" (Hos 13:7), here at the ford of the Jabbok, who attacks unsuspecting travelers and wrestles with them to the death. We may imagine that he is the numen of the river who is angry with Jacob because one crosses his ford. The belief that whoever traverses a river or a ford must appease the numen is also attested elsewhere (cf. Frazer in *Anthropological Essays*, 136ff.). We must envision this god's strength as greater than the normal human being's. The strong Jacob is not superior to him (v 26 J), but the difference is not all that great. He is subdued by Jacob's mighty blow (v 26 J). He is not one of the high gods, therefore. His fear of light suits his wild bloodthirstiness. He must disappear with the night. His name is not mentioned in either source. This god is not Yahweh, at any rate. After all, Yahweh is the god who loves and helps Jacob. This divine figure contributes significantly to our knowledge of the pre-Israelite religion displaced by Yahwism (cf. E. Zurhellen-Pfleiderer, 43-44).

3. *Legend parallels.* The motif of nocturnal battle with demons, monsters, phantoms, or the devil is attested quite frequently. Beowulf fights with Grendel by night. The same motif occurs in the Icelandic legends of Grettir and of Ormr Storolfsson. Roscher (*Ephialtes* [= *Abh. d. phil.-hist. Cl. der Kgl. Sächs. Gesellsch. der Wissenschaften* 20:2], 40-41) treats nocturnal wrestling with ghosts, phantoms, etc. in German, Vendic, and Lithuanian fairy tales. Roscher explains this fairy-tale motif, and the Penuel narrative itself, in relation to the possible influence of the nightmare phenomenon. Wrestling with an unknown figure was a dream well known even to the ancients (Artemidor 1:60 [Hercher, 56]). Yet Roscher comes dangerously close to the rationalistic-naturalistic interpretation which has long understood the Penuel as a dream experience (bibliography in Dillmann) when he interprets the whole Penuel narrative as a nightmare and explains Jacob's limp, for example, as rheumatism occasioned by sleeping on the moist river lowlands. The Penuel narrative is more closely related to those legends and fairy tales that tell of a god compelled by a human through deceit or force to leave behind his secret knowledge or something else divine. Thus, according to Homer, Menelaos held the old man of the sea, Proteus, until he revealed to him his knowledge (*Od.* 10.384ff.). Midas captured Silenos and coaxed his knowledge from him (Roscher, *Lex.* s.v. "Midas"). King Numa captured Faunus and Martius Picus and thereby learned the rites and sacrifices through which one could entice Jupiter to come down to earth (*Valerius Antias Annales* 2.6 [Peter, *Hist. Rom. Fragm.*, 153]). Meyer (*Israeliten*, 51ff.) explains even Deut 33:8 as Yahweh's fight with Moses in which he obtained the secret of the oracle, the Urim and the Thummim, and compares Exod 4:24ff., where Yahweh attacked Moses and Zipporah discovered circumcision as the means of atonement. Numerous ancient and more recent times report that a human steals the demon's cap and thereby obtains power over him (Roscher, *Ephialtes*, 44). The scholia on Lycophron (Scheer) 41, according to which at

the establishment of the Olympic Agone, Hercules challenged anyone who wanted to a wrestling match, are comparable. Since no one dared, Zeus came in human form and wrestled evenly with him for a long time until he revealed himself to his son. The material could be significantly multiplied. It cannot be discerned whether this legend—as maintained in the first and second editions of this commentary—was originally a cultic legend supposed to signify the banishment of the god at this site, whereby the "blessing" would be the characteristic act of the god at the holy site (Exod 20:24) and the <364> "limping" would also refer, perhaps, to the customary cultic dance (cf. 1 Kgs 18:26 "to limp").

3. *Age of the legend.* At any rate, the god-figure of the legend points to a very early period. This is also indicated by the peculiar tone of the legend which conceals the terror of the deity in the twilight of mystery and portrays a scene worthy of the brush of Rembrandt.

4. The Israelite tradition of the legend explains the names Penuel, Jabbok, and Israel. Thus etymological elements have been added. Of the two preserved recensions, the E recension almost in its entirety is more ancient than that of J. The injury of the god (v 26a) is older than that of Jacob (v 26b); Jacob's victory (v 29) is older that the mere escape (v 31); the name change (v 29) is much more ingenious and, simultaneously, much more magical than the simple blessing (v 30). In contrast, the question concerning Jacob's name in E (v 28) may be younger than the question about the name of the god in J (v 30). Originally, the legend was entirely independent and had nothing to do with the Jacob-Esau narrative. The courageous god-vanquisher and the Jacob who trembles before Esau are actually quite different figures. Even in the current tradition, the Penuel legend is only loosely tied to the preceding and following materials. Thus, the fact that Jacob has suffered a severe injury does not become apparent in the accounts which follow (cf. 33:3). In fact, the Penuel account actually disrupts the two Esau narratives between which it stands. The legend refers back (v 29 J) to fights Jacob had already survived. To this point he has only fought with "people." In this, his last and most difficult fight, he even vanquished the deity. To the extent that the legend includes Esau and Laban among these "people," then, it presumes narratives in a fundamentally different form and, at any rate, a renewed meeting with Esau cannot have followed immediately. The legend was located at this point in the current composition already prior to J and E because of the geographical situation of Penuel.

If one forsakes the impression this ancient makes on the historically educated reader and instead holds to the allegorical explanation by which the Christian church has appropriated it and which is dear to all our hearts, then one cannot sufficiently admire the power of religion to appropriate foreign material, to reshape ancient material in a new sense, and to transform dross into gold.

52. Jacob's Encounter with Esau 33:1-16 JE

Source criticism. The passage as a whole seems to stem from J: the four hundred men (v 1 as in 32:7 J), וַיַּחַץ (v 1 as in 32:8 J), שִׁפְחָה (vv 1, 2, 6), רוּץ לִקְרַאת (v 4), מָצָא חֵן בְּעֵינֵי (vv 8, 10, 15). Still, a few details from E have been incorporated: v 5b because of אלהים and because of the similarity with 48:9 (E); v 10b not so much because of (the appellative) אלהים, but because the statement continues 32:21 (E); v 11aβ because of אלהים and because of חֵן (as in v 5b). One may also include v 11aα (∥ v 10aγ). V 4 is redundant. וַיְחַבְּקֵהוּ and וַיִּשָּׁקֵהוּ are probably from E (cf. 45:14-15; 46:29). Vv 5aα,β probably belong to J (וַיִּשָּׂא אֶת־עֵינָיו וַיַּרְא as in v 1 J). These clauses speak of the wives and children. The response in v 5b (E) treats only the children. The question in v 5aγ, quite parallel to the question in v 8, probably belongs to J. Whether E may not also be involved in vv 12ff. must remain in question.

1-7 *The encounter.* **1** "Esau approaches and Jacob makes extreme preparations" (Franz Delitzsch). **2** For <365> אַחֲרֹנִים[1] Pesh has אַחֲרֵיהֶם (cf. LXX). For our sensibilities it is remarkable that the partisan love expressed in this arrangement is so transparently obvious. The narrators, however, do not take the slightest offense at this but find such preference for the favored person quite normal. Concerning this unusual lack of a sense of fairness, still observable in Jewish family life, see the comments on 30:16. In contrast we are pleased that Jacob (v **3**) precedes his family and exposes himself to the greatest danger. Otherwise—presumably—Jacob brings up the rear (32:25). Jacob's seven obeisances are a very excessive demonstration of respect. The vassal falls seven times before the king! One may compare the formula in the Amarna correspondence: "At the feet of my lord, my sun, I fall seven times and seven times!" One bow is usually sufficient, even in the presence of superiors of the highest order (18:2; 19:1; Exod 18:7; 1 Sam 20:41; 2 Sam 9:6). Jacob hopes to win his brother by such excessive demonstrations of respect. The hearers, however, are amused at the ancestor's cunning. **4** The main question for understanding the whole passage concerns Esau's behavior. The old, native legend, which recounts so much of Jacob's gifts, obeisances, and smooth words and seems to rejoice in them, cannot have simultaneously glorified Esau's "touching nobility" (Kautzsch[3]). The unity of tone in the narrative is destroyed in this way and Jacob's clever tricks loose their point, for, if Esau is really well disposed toward his brother from the beginning, then Jacob only breaks down open doors with all his preparations. Instead, the old legend will have portrayed Esau as a good-natured buffoon who can be won over by beautiful speeches and gifts. This concept of Esau appears somewhat more clearly in the second part of the passage (vv 12ff.). Yet, the later narrators may have already understood the narrative more nobly. וַיְחַבְּקֵהוּ is a joking allusion to "Jabbok." For the qere צַוָּארָיו, the kethib is צַוָּארוֹ (Kittel). וַיִּשָּׁקֵהוּ is suprapunctuated, that is, declared invalid. The plural "they cried" does not suit the situation in which Jacob has entirely different ideas. One may read וַיֵּבְךְּ following 45:14; 46:29 and with Ball and Kittel. Crying when meeting relatives also occurs in 29:11; 45:14-15; 46:29. The kiss to welcome relatives and friends occurs in 29:11, 13; 45:14; Exod 4:27; 18:7; 2 Sam 20:9. **5** Esau's question and Jacob's answer are intended, it seems, to portray Esau's astonishment at Jacob's abundance of children. מִי־אֵלֶּה לָּךְ "What is your relationship to these?" (Est 8:1; Ehrlich; similar to v 8). חָנַן, repeated in v 11, is probably another allusion to מַחֲנָיִם. Concerning the syntax of חָנַן with a dual accusative see §117ff. **6, 7** Full of tension and fear, the individual groups approach to demonstrate their respect for Esau, all thinking that as soon as he gives any indication that he will fall upon them they will run away as quickly as possible. This is an interesting situation for the narrator, so he describes it in detail. **6** הֵנָּה is a personal pronoun "she and her children" as in 13:1; 14:15.

8-11 *The gift.* Jacob divided his property into two camps so that in crisis one could escape (32:8, 9). <366> Against expectations Esau did not prove to be bloodthirsty. Now, however, when Esau asks what Jacob's relationship is to the first camp, Jacob offers him this "camp" as a gift! We are supposed to rejoice at Jacob's presence of mind which permits to him to make use of the altered situation immediately. The gift is very large, but it is better to lose a large portion of one's property than to lose all. At the same time, a play on words stands in the background. The מַחֲנֶה sent ahead (v 8) becomes a מִנְחָה (v 10). The subtlety of this account has been obscured by the combination of the J text with E, according to which Jacob sent a gift ahead at the very beginning. One should note Jacob's humble speeches here, too. He only hints at the offer of the gift (v 8b). In fact, he compares Esau with the deity himself, whose face one sees only with horror and fear (v 11; ancient Israelites were accustomed to the inferior making flattering comparison between the superior and God; 2 Sam 14:17). One must imagine a deep bow accompanying each word. Esau does not respond in such humble courtesy: אָחִי (v 9). Why does Jacob place such great value on Esau's acceptance of his gifts? Because only this assures him that Esau will not do anything to him. **8** For מִי one should probably read מָה (Ehrlich; cf. 2 Sam 16:2 = "What do you want with it?"). **10** כִּי־עַל־כֵּן occurs elsewhere in J. **11** בְּרָכָה is a greeting gift. On the ending of הֻבָאת see §74g. Sam, LXX, Pesh, and Vulg read הֻבֵאתִי.

12-17 *Esau is now appeased.* Now the task is to part with him in good graces. This, too, is recounted with powerful humor. **12-14** Esau, innocent as he is, now assumes that his brother will travel on with him (לְנֶגֶד). But Jacob's sole concern is how he can quit his dangerous company and he devises a plausible reason to get him to go on ahead. **13** Sam, LXX, and Pesh read וּדְפָקְתִּים (Kautzsch[3]). Concerning the syntax of the perfect with ו in the protasis and apodosis see §159g. **15, 16** Esau, still unsuspecting, wants at least to leave a guard behind for his brother. But such "protection" was suspect to Jacob. Thus, Esau finally departs. Jacob has no intention to keep his promise and follow Esau. Instead, he took an entirely different path happy to have escaped the danger intact. The current narrator, who seems not to have understood the humor of the scene, does not clearly emphasize the concluding point. Meyer (*Israeliten*, 275-76) hypothesizes that in J Jacob did not travel immediately to the Cis-Jordan, but went to Hebron by way of the Dead Sea. The account of Jacob and Esau may have actually concluded with Jacob following his brother (in hopes of not <367> encountering him again), however not to Hebron, which would have been too great a detour. The hand in J which combined the Jacob and Joseph legends surely brought Jacob from Mahanaim straight to the west since the Joseph narratives are related to the Dinah narrative situated at Shechem. In the recension of this account in J, however, Simeon and Levi must have been cursed. This curse is precisely the presumption of the Joseph account in J where neither of these two nor Reuben (35:21-22), but Judah leads the brothers (cf. Dinah legend no. 1). **15** One employs the idiom "May I find only grace before my lord," among others, when one does not dare to tell a superior "No" (similar expressions in 30:27; 23:13).

Jacob in Canaan 33:17–35:22

53. Jacob at Succoth and Shechem 33:17-20 JE

These two "comments" are currently the conclusion of the Jacob-Esau narrative. After Esau left him, Jacob does not, as he promised, follow Esau, but "safe and sound" (happy to have escaped the danger) goes to Succoth or Shechem. At the same time, the passage introduces the subsequent Dinah legend dealing with Shechem. The tradition of the Shechem site employed here was originally independent of the subsequent Dinah legend, however. It speaks of the "sons of Hamor" (v 19) so that Hamor is the name of a tribe, whereas in the Dinah legend Hamor is the name of a person, Shechem's father. אֲבִי שְׁכֶם, added by a later hand, is supposed to harmonize the two.

Source criticism. Vv 18-20 belong to E (Wellhausen, *Composition*[3], 317n.1): E cites v 19 in Josh 24:32; E presumes the sojourn in Shechem in 35:4; the massebah (v 20; cf. below) also speaks for E. In contrast, the comment concerning Succoth cannot derive from E: v 18 (שָׁלֵם) links directly to the Jacob-Esau legend; a lengthier (בְּיַת) sojourn in Succoth can have stood in between. The comment concerning Succoth therefore parallels the one concerning Shechem and belongs to J.

17 The author is only concerned here with telling about the סֻכּוֹת. Why does he mention Jacob's "house"? Because he thinks, "A man who builds huts for his livestock (out of twigs and bushes, Benzinger[2], 90) will have first erected a house for himself." Succoth, east of the Jordan (Judg 8:4-5), lying in the valley west of Penuel (Judg 8:8), in "the valley of Succoth," mentioned in Psa 60:8; 108:8 alongside Shechem, is to be sought in the vicinity of the ford *ed-Dâmiye* on the road from *es-Salt* to *Nâbulus* (Shechem; Dillmann). **18** שָׁלֵם can hardly be understood as a place name (LXX, Pesh, Vulg). V **18a** contains elements from P. Yet the word שָׁלֵם shows that E is also involved. It may be that one should read בְּשָׁלֵם with Ball following Sam שלום (28:21). **19** The account of Jacob's purchase of property is not intended to demonstrate Israel's right to possess all of Canaan (in accord with the usual interpretation), but can only intend to establish Jacob's legal possession of this field. The value of this field consists in the fact that a famed sanctuary stood there in the narrator's time (v 20) and Joseph's grave was located there <368> (Josh 24:32). The tendency of the Machpelah legend is very similar (cf. above pp. 268-69). The reference is probably to the same site attributed to Abraham in Gen 12:6-7 (cf. comments there). Bene-Hamor is also the name of the tribe at Shechem in Judg 9:28. קְשִׂיטָה is probably a unit of weight and money. Its meaning is also unknown in (Josh 24:32) Job 42:11. LXX, Pesh, Vulg, and Targ. Onq have "lamb." **20** מִזְבֵּחַ does not suit the verb וַיַּצֵּב well, but מַצֵּבָה does (35:14, 20). According to Josh 24:26 a "great stone" stood there. One should therefore read מַצֵּבָה and לֹה following Wellhausen (*Composition*[3], 48n.1) and others. The same exchange of the memorial stone, later considered pagan, for the innocent altar occurs in 2 Kgs 12:10. The comment that this memorial stone is called "el, God of Israel" is very interesting. The stone and the god are naively equated (cf. comments on 28:18 and Meyer, *Israeliten*, 295). The name "el, God of Israel" will have been the cultic name employed at this site. The comment that Joshua consecrated an altar at Ebal (east of Shechem) to "Yahweh, the God of Israel" (Josh 8:20) agrees with this comment. Concerning the sanctuary at Shechem, see Westphal, *Jahwes Wohnstätten*, 100-101; Meyer, *Israeliten*, 542-43.

54. Dinah Legend 34 JE

Source criticism. A series of doublets and difficulties give evidence (contra Eerdmans, 62-63, who struggles here, too—although as the only recent scholar—against source analysis) of two strands of the account. V 2b is very verbose. "He lay with her" probably parallels "he violated her." The remarkable lack of cohesion (usually the ornament of the simple, tightly composed accounts) in the subsequent material points to two sources. The account deals with Shechem (v 4), then Jacob (v 5), then Hamor (v 6), then Jacob's sons (v 7), then with Hamor (vv 8-10) and Shechem again (vv 11-12) with no perceptible relationship between them. Shechem speaks (vv 11-12) and he is answered (vv 13ff.), while according to vv 6 and 8 not he, but his father is present for the discussion. The suit for Dinah occurs twice. In one presentation Shechem's father (vv 4, 6, 8-10) proposed the marriage, according to the other Shechem himself (vv 11, 12). Hamor simultaneously suggested a general connubium (vv 9, 10), but Shechem only asked for the one, Dinah, as wife (vv 11, 12). The decision given the suitors also manifests two somewhat distinct strands. According to one recension the brothers declined the offer because Shechem was uncircumcised (v 14). According to the other they agreed to the connubium if the people would be circumcised (vv 15-17). The diction also demonstrates that these are different reports: בְּתֻנוּ (v 17) and בְּתְכֶם (v 8), in contrast to אֹחֹתֵנוּ (v 14). According to one recension, then, only Shechem's circumcision is required (v 14), according to the other that of all his compatriots (vv 15-17). This also accords with the following: according to one report Shechem did so without delay (v 19); according to the other Hamor, who was pleased with the matter (v 18a), convinced the people of his city to be circumcised (vv 20-24). One can clearly discern in וַיֵּצְאוּ (v 26) that two sources have also been combined in the subsequent account of the attack on the city and Shechem: if Jacob's sons have already left (the city) at the end of v 26, they cannot fall upon the people in the city and plunder its goods in vv 27-29. Nor may one respond that after Simeon and Levi attack first (vv 25f.) the other sons came to their brothers' assistance (vv 27-29) for Jacob scolds only Simeon and Levi in vv 30-31. Thus, on the whole, vv 25, 26 parallel vv 27-29. The attackers, according to vv 25, 26, are Simeon and Levi; according to vv 27-29, in contrast, they are all "the sons of Jacob." Those attacked and plundered by the sons of Jacob in vv 27-29 are the people of <369> Shechem. Vv 25, 26 differ, of course, for how could two men, such as Simeon and Levi, attack a whole city? Indeed, וַיֵּצְאוּ (v 26, a word which corresponds to וַיָּבֹאוּ in v 25) emphasizes that the two escaped luckily. Therefore, they exacted their revenge only on Shechem and wisely left the other inhabitants of the city in peace. This suggests that the phrase וַיַּהַרְגוּ כָּל-זָכָר (v 25b) did not originally belong to the context of v 25, but to vv 27-29 where it must have preceded כָּל-זָכָר. וַיָּבֹאוּ refers back to vv 15, 22, 24. הַחֹלִים, "the wounded," should be read for הַחֲלָלִים, which makes no sense. Accordingly, בְּהְיוֹתָם כֹּאֲבִים (v 25) belongs to the other recension.

The other verses can for the most part be separated according to this criterion: vv 30, 31 reproach Simeon and Levi specifically and thus comprise the continuation of vv 25, 26. The semiverse 13a, according to which (all) the sons of Jacob plan the attack, belongs, contrariwise, to the other recension. וַיֹּאמְרוּ אֲלֵיהֶם in v 14 is parallel. V 7 (the brothers' great wrath concerning Dinah's shame) agrees in tone with v 31. The precondition for the brother's coming in from the field is in v 5 (the brothers were still in the field). וַיִּשְׁכַּב אֹתָהּ (v 2) also belongs to this recension because of לִשְׁכַּב אֶת־ (v 7). וַיְעַנֶּהָ (v 2) should probably be attributed to the other recension.

Consequently, two continuous, self-contained accounts may be discerned.

I. *The Hamor variant.* Shechem, Hamor's son, rapes Dinah, but did not keep the maiden ("we will take our daughter and move away," v 17). Because he likes her—this is the necessary precondition here, too—he asks his father to woo her for him. Hamor goes to Jacob and speaks with him. He asks for Dinah and simultaneously offers a general connubium. Jacob's sons appear to agree to this offer, perfidiously making the circumcision of all Shechemites a condition. Hamor agrees. Likewise, the people of his city accept the proposal. But when they are recovering, Jacob's sons (not just Simeon and Levi) attack the city, murder, and plunder it. In terms of its content, Gen 35:(1)5 is the conclusion. (God, himself, commands Jacob to leave Shechem.) A divine terror falls on the surrounding cities so that they do not pursue Jacob's sons.

II. *The Shechem recension.* Shechem abducted Dinah. The maiden is currently in his house (cf. v 26; consequently, וַיִּקַּח אֹתָהּ, "he kidnapped, abducted her" in v 2b is to be included in this recension, Dillmann). But because he has come to love Dinah, he reassures her and promises to marry her. Jacob has been inactive, meanwhile, because he can undertake nothing without his sons who are in the field. When they come home, they are enraged. Now Shechem comes to them and in an effusive speech offers them a marriage present and gift. The brothers, although semipersuaded by the prospect of the beautiful gifts, still say no at first. They could not give their sister to an uncircumcised. But the enamored Shechem agrees to this condition immediately and is circumcised (together with his household). Now, the narrator thinks, the brothers will not have continued to deny Shechem's request. Then Simeon and Levi intervene, however. They are "Dinah's brothers" (v 25) in a special sense, thus her full brothers. They are more concerned for Dinah's honor than the others and are of the opinion that their sister's honor can only be cleansed with blood. (The Amnon narrative in 2 Sam 13 offers a parallel.) Thus they decide to kill Shechem. No valid agreement which would obligate them has yet been reached. They were admitted to Shechem's city as nearest relatives. They were able to overpower him (and his household) all the more easily because he was recovering. They kill him and take Dinah from his house. Their father, however, is extremely dissatisfied with them. He fears that the Canaanites will combine forces to attack him. The account cannot end in this manner, however. It is inconceivable, per se, and totally without analogy that an account should conclude with fear (v 30) and a question (v 31). We must yet hear whether Jacob's fear was realized. Consequently, Wellhausen (*Composition*[3], 320), Guthe (*Gesch. des Volkes Israel*, 48), and others (including the first and second editions of this commentary) have assumed <370> an account here that the Canaanites avenged Shechem's murder and killed Simeon and Levi. In contrast, Meyer (*Israeliten*, 419) has correctly pointed out that the narrator would have struck an entirely different tone if Jacob's concerns had been fulfilled, but especially that Simeon and Levi later move to Egypt and there become the ancestors of independent tribes in J and E, and, further, that a primal history of Israel which allowed these two tribes to expire already during the lifetime of the patriarchs is totally unthinkable. Consequently, the conclusion here, too, cannot have been much different than in the other recension. The Canaanites did not unite to avenge, and the deed of Simeon and Levi stood without the feared consequences. The concluding passage of one recension was omitted precisely because the redactor did not want to repeat the account. Yet Jacob probably cursed Simeon and Levi, like Reuben (35:21,22a), since they do not lead the brothers in J's Joseph narrative (cf. below).

Gen 49:5-7 preserves an allusion to yet a third variant of this narrative. There, too, it involves a malicious attack of the "brothers" Simeon and Levi and there, too, the patriarch disapproves of their excessive wrath and curses them in the end. In punishment, they will one day be scattered "in Israel." According to this variant, this demise of Simeon and Levi did not, however, as is usually assumed, transpire already in the ancient period, but is predicted by Jacob for the future. The "dissolution of the tribes which is transpiring or has transpired in the author's time is the revenge the descendants suffer for their ancestors' guilt" (Meyer, *Israeliten*, 422). According to Gen 49, the sin of Simeon and Levi consists in the fact that they "murdered the man, maimed the bull." The "man" is Shechem and perhaps his servants. This variant must have also reported something about maiming a bull. The Hamor recension also recounts something about Shechem's cattle (v 28). It can, therefore, be surmised that in their rage they maimed the bulls because in their haste they could not take them along. The words are intended to say, then, that in a blind rage Simeon and Levi wreaked fearful havoc in the attacked city.

2. The significance of a series of details for tribal history is especially clear. The persons of the legend are the fraternal tribes Simeon and Levi, as well as Shechem, the eponymous heroes of the famed Canaanite city Shechem. Hamor, Shechem's father, is the name of the Canaanite (more precisely Hivvite, v 2) tribe dwelling in Shechem (cf. Judg 9:28; "The eponym of the city is the son of the tribe which dwelt here," Meyer, *Israeliten*, 418). The "sons of Jacob" live as nomads according to the legend (vv 5, 7, 10, 21) while Shechem and Hamor dwell in houses (vv 26, 29) in a city (vv 20, 24, 25, 27, 28). Abraham and Isaac have a similar relationship to the Gerarites in Gen 20, 26. Remarkably, the Israelite tribes are envisioned as individuals but the inhabitants of the land are not. Their eponyms must have evolved into chiefs with numerous peoples in the same way "this took place throughout the Greek genealogical poems and histories" (Meyer, *Israeliten*, 421). The account about these legend figures may echo an event from Israelite prehistory. The fraternal tribes of Simeon and Levi attacked Shechem unsuspectedly, but the city remained in the hands of the Canaanites and the other tribes of Israel were neutral in this conflict (cf. Wellhausen, *Composition*[3], 320-21; Stade, *Gesch. Israels* 1:146, 152ff.; Guthe, *Gesch. Isr.*, 48; Steuernagel, *Isr. Stämme*, 82; Kautzsch[3], 56; etc.). Dinah and her experiences in the legend are also usually interpreted historically (so recently Kautzsch[3]): Dinah was an Israelite tribe related to Simeon and Levi, overpowered by Shechem and forced to join it, but avenged by the fraternal tribes. This historical interpretation of Dinah must be regarded quite skeptically, however. It is much more likely that the narrative, as far as Dinah is concerned, extends an allogenous legend motif in ancient tradition that was only secondarily related to historical <371> events. The same process transpired in the Tamar legend. The presumptive narrative material closely resembles the Greek account of the Dioscure who retrieved their abducted sister Helena (Stucken, *Astralmythen* 75n.2, 144n.2).

3. *Time of the event.* These things transpired when the tribes still dwelt in the land as nomads and related to the Canaanite cities in war and peace. The Canaanite alliance feared by Jacob (v 30) is one such as occurs in Josh 10; 11; Judg 5:19. That this event must have taken place in a relatively early period is indicated by the other reports we have concerning Simeon and Levi. While these tribes must have played a significant role in the earliest period—Moses and Aaron are Levites; next to Reuben, which also disappeared later, the tribe was considered the firstborn tribe in Israel—they no longer existed in later times. They are missing in the Song of Deborah and in the later narratives concerning the "Judges." At that time there were only individual clans and families of Levi, and the remnants of Simeon, last mentioned in Judg 1, were absorbed into Judah (cf. Stade 1:154; Meyer, *Israeliten*, 409ff.). The catastrophe that destroyed them and that was understood as a just retribution for their crimes at Shechem (49:5-7) must, therefore, have taken place in a very ancient period, not very long after the entry into the land. On the other hand, in Genesis we are almost always concerned with much older circumstances. Consequently, this legend does not properly belong in Genesis. Instead, in terms of its material, it would belong much better in the book of Judges, as would the Tamar and Reuben legends. These legends are placed here, however, because they speak of tribes as persons, a viewpoint and manner of speaking which, disregarding Judg 1; 10:3-4, is no longer customary in the narratives of the book of Judges. At the same time, however, this tribal narrative refers most clearly of all those in Genesis to the historical Israel. Meyer (*Israeliten*, 416, 421ff.) considers the account "in the main" as a reflection of the Abimelech narrative, according to which, after initial peaceful community, Shechem was attacked and eradicated by the Israelites. The legend does not, however, involve the destruction, but only a passing attack on the city and Shechem's enemies here are not Abimelech's tribe Manasseh, but Simeon and Levi. Accordingly, it seems more appropriate to assume another event from a somewhat earlier period. The city Shechem, metropolis of central Canaan, had surely experienced a great deal with the Israelites, both good and bad, before it fell to Abimelech (cf. Wellhausen, *Composition*[3], 320ff. and further under no. 4 [below]). The exceptional character of the Dinah legend is also manifest in the fact that it speaks of a violent act of the patriarchs who are otherwise depicted as very peaceful. The martial, passionate nature of ancient Israel becomes apparent here.

4. *Parallels.* In certain major features, the Dinah narrative relates to the legend of Abraham's (Isaac's) fortunes in Gerar (Egypt). Both times involve one of the patriarch's women who has come into the hands of a foreign (originally Canaanite) city dweller, but who is freed. Both times, a trick plays a role. The outcome differs, however: Abraham (Isaac) departs peacefully from the foreigner. In the Dinah narrative it comes to conflict. Both accounts treat related material in the broader sense. Gen 48:22, according to which Jacob conquered Shechem "with sword and bow" and granted it to Joseph, differs. This statement probably alludes to a historical situation which diverges, however, from the events presupposed in the Dinah legend in all the chief points. In the Dinah account, Jacob himself did not attack Shechem (instead, both variants agree that the father kept back). Further, Jacob's sons did not remain in Shechem, but (according to both variants) left it again. Finally, Joseph, Rachel's son, has no place in the Dinah legend. The expression in 48:22, "[I have] taken [Shechem] from the hand of the Amorites with sword and bow (in long-range and hand-to-hand <372> combat)" points more to battle on the

open field than to the sneak attack of Gen 34. Accordingly, the legend presupposed in
48:22 is not a variant of Gen 34 but probably a reflex of Judg 9 where Abimelech, a man
from Joseph, violently captured Shechem (cf. Wellhausen's suggestion in *Composition*[3],
318; contra Meyer, *Israeliten*, 414-15).

5. *Comparison and age of the variants*. (a) The character of the variants is determined
especially by the manner in which they evaluate the attack on Shechem. The Hamor
variant approves of this attack. It is the just punishment for the serious crime of rape.
Consequently, the matter comes to a fortunate conclusion and God himself sides with
Jacob's sons (35:5). Thus, the legend thinks, every pagan city in which a daughter of
Jacob is violated should be destroyed (the same assessment in later Judaism, Judith 9:2ff.).
Gen 49:5ff. contains the opposite judgment: the ancestor himself curses the passion and
trickery of the brothers and rejects any community with them. Their later demise is the
just punishment for their deeds! The Shechem variant assumes a complicated middle position between the two judgments. On one hand, the narrator emphasizes that Shechem's
crime must enrage the sons of Jacob and especially Dinah's full brothers (vv 7, 31). On
the other hand, he portrays how Shechem was ready to make atonement, how the other
brothers were almost persuaded, and how Jacob then feared the consequences of their
passionate deed. The narrator recorded this varying judgment in the conversation between
Jacob and the two brothers. Jacob says, "Consider the consequences!" But they respond,
"You consider our honor!" We are in the position to arrange these three different
assessments of essentially the same process in a history of the tradition. We know,
especially in analogy with the other Jacob narratives, that in the earliest period the
patriarchs were not portrayed exactly as ethical ideals (cf. pp. 191, 226-27, 301, 328) and
that at the time foreigners were evaluated favorably. A later time, contrariwise, as we
observe (cf. p. 224) especially in the example of the narrative of Abraham (Isaac) in Gerar
(Egypt), saw the patriarchs as examples of morality and judged the "pagans" even more
harshly. Thus, a few of the old patriarchal narratives which became offensive to a later
period were first lightly then much more vigorously reworked. Accordingly, the legend
to which Gen 49:5ff. alludes in which the Israelite patriarchs were cursed because of a
crime against foreigners belongs to a very ancient period. One can discern a slight
transformation of the ancient legend in the Shechem recension. The narrator maintained
indeed that the two patriarchs were reproached because of their passionate deed, but he
recounted the narrative as favorably as possible for them. They wanted to avenge their
sister's honor. The attack on Shechem is not portrayed as horribly. There is no reference
to the maiming of the bulls. But this portrayal, too, was intolerable to a later period:
Israelite patriarchs reproached because of a tricky deed! A later narrator responsible for
the Hamor variant was guided by this sensibility. Here the patriarchs are cleared of all
injustice. Their behavior with the pagans is quite in order in his opinion. Accordingly, the
Shechem recension is much older than the Hamor recension.

   (b) The same judgment results from an esthetic examination. The Shechem recension
is much more colorful and, at the same time, more concise. It portrays a multitude of
people in very few words: the enamored Shechem, the cautiously reticent father, the
offended but then appeased half-brothers, the extremely enraged full brothers. The Hamor
variant, in contrast, uses many words but is unable to depict a person vitally. The concrete
information of the Shechem recension that "the brothers" Simeon and Levi attacked

Shechem is surely older than the weakened statement that it was all of Jacob's sons. In addition, the old song in 49:5-6 confirms this concrete comment.

(c) An additional distinguishing characteristic is the fact that in the Hamor narrative elements of <373> national history figure more prominently: It speaks of official agreements between the city dwellers and the Bedouins, while in the Shechem variant Shechem appears simply as an enamored young man. Here, too, the Shechem variant seems to contain the older perspective. It contains the basic material in a purer, the Hamor variant in a more markedly ethnohistorical form (cf. the similar case, p. 341, where one variant has also preserved original narrative material more purely than the other). Because of this relationship between the recensions, Wellhausen's (*Composition*[3], 47 differently 320) and Procksch's suggestion that the Shechem variant said nothing of circumcision is unlikely, not to mention v 14, v 19, and בִּהְיוֹתָם כֹּאֲבִים (v 25). The Hamor recension would not have transmitted this extremely tricky element if it had not found it in existing tradition.

6. *Redactor*. The redactor who combined the two variants based the composition, as usual, on the later of the two sources, which was closer to his tastes, and interspersed the Shechem recension which he had in an essentially complete tradition. Through a series of small additions and alterations he produced a passable unity: אֹתָם (v 8) for אֹתוֹ; אֶת־שְׁכֶם וְ (v 13); אָבִיו (v 13); אֲלֵיהֶם for אֵלָיו (v 11); אֶל־אָבִיהָ וְ 14); וּבְעֵינֵי שְׁכֶם בֶּן־חֲמוֹר (v 18b); וּשְׁכֶם בְּנוֹ (v 20); עִירָם (v 20bis) for עִירוֹ (cf. v 24bis); וְאֶל־שְׁכֶם בְּנוֹ (v 24); וְאֶת־חֲמֹר and בְּנוֹ (v 26); in addition, וַיַּהַרְגוּ כָּל־זָכָר is transposed from v 26 to v 25 (cf. above). The phrase אֵת טִמֵּא אֲשֶׁר דִּינָה אֲחֹתָם (v 13), which occupies a syntactically intolerable position, is a gloss which has intruded into the text. The same is true of אֲשֶׁר טִמְּאוּ אֲחוֹתָם (v 27) which disrupts the description of the plundering of Shechem. כִּי טִמֵּא אֶת־דִּינָה בִתּוֹ (v 5) must stem from the same hand. The word טִמֵּא is frequent in P (cf. Holzinger, 214). The glossator emphasizes Shechem's sin in order better to motivate the subsequent punishment. Thus, this is another attempt to clear the patriarchs. Still other additions may be present, but cannot be identified with certainty.

7. *Sources*. The Shechem recension belongs to J according to an almost general agreement. Evidence for this is as follows: הִתְעַצֵּב (v 7; in the Hexateuch only J employs forms of the root עצב; Holzinger, cf. also *Hexateuch*, 103); נַעַר as a feminine (vv 3, 12; in J and D) and as a masculine (v 19; common in J, cf. Holzinger, *Hexateuch*, 185); דָּבַק (v 3; in J and very often in D); כֵן לֹא יֵעָשֶׂה (v 7; cf. 29:26). J "prefers" the term מָצָא חֵן בְּעֵינֵי (cf. Holzinger, *Hexateuch*, 98). The Hamor recension has many expression that otherwise characterize P: נָשִׂיא (v 2), נֹאחַז (v 10), הִמֹּל לָכֶם כָּל־זָכָר (vv 15, 22), כָּל־זָכָר (v 24), and קִנְיָן (v 23; Dillmann, 369; Holzinger, 213). This does not imply, however, that it stems from P (P certainly would never have appropriated such an objectionable narrative), but at most that the chapter was reworked by a later hand (Wellhausen, *Composition*[3], 319; other cases of reworking of an older account are Josh 22 and Judg 19ff.). Yet one should consider the possibility that these expressions shared with P (almost all are legal terms) were mostly dictated by the subject matter. This is the explanation of the fact that 34:9 (the suggestion of connubium) agrees in wording with the law in Deut 7:3. If, therefore, the source of this recension can be neither J nor P, only E remains. E is suggested by 35:(1)5, the conclusion of the account which stands in the

middle of a report from E. The introduction is 33:19, also from E. Cornill (ZAW 11:3ff.) has proposed the linguistic evidence: יַלְדָּה (v 4; יֶלֶד is common in E; J uses נַעַר; cf. Holzinger, *Hexateuch*, 184-85), אָחַר (vv 10, 21 as in 42:34 E), בְּמִרְמָה (v 13 as in 27:35; cf. 29:25), הֲלוֹא לָנוּ הֵם (v 23 like לָנוּ הוּא 31:16 E). Meyer (*Israeliten*, 413ff.) vigorously objects to the attribution of the two recensions to J and E, pointing out many peculiarities in this narrative. For explanations of these peculiarities see comments on 34:1, 25; 37:14. Sievers (2:332ff.) assumes two E versions, one with a peaceful outcome. He strikes vv 27-29, etc. Meyer (*Israeliten*, 415n.2) responds.

1-5 *Exposition.* Vv **1, 2** could belong to either source in terms of content. <374> The wording of v 1a corresponds exactly to 21:9 E. Consequently v 1 should to attributed to E. The fact that Dinah goes out to visit the daughters of the land is meant to explain how she left the protection of her father and thus came under Shechem's power. It is comprehensible enough that the young maiden went to others of her kind. Dinah is a grown young woman. One can hardly wonder how this chronological datum was deduced (cf. 30:21; 31:41). Nor is one to ask how Jacob's sons, still "tender children" in 33:13, are already fighting men (Kautzsch[3]). Different traditions have been combined. In v 2a, the mention of Hamor points to E. Meyer (331) thinks that חִוִּי is an intentional alteration of חֹרִי "Horites" (cf. LXX Χορραῖος here and in Josh 9:7; cf. comments on 10:17). The reference to Hamor as נְשִׂיא הָאָרֶץ is meant to explain why an incident in his family could result in the circumcision of the whole city. The substantive parallel in J, then, is v 19b: Shechem was highly regarded by his whole family. וַיִּשְׁכַּב אֹתָהּ—J usually employs עִמָּהּ (Cornill). The fact that Dinah is also abducted in the Hamor variant depends only on the assessment of וַיְעַנֶּהָ. Yet this circumstance can hardly be dispensed with in the total structure of the account in E (contra Kautzsch[3], who himself admits that doublets are apparently present in v 2b). "Jacob's daughter" in **3** points to J (cf. vv 7, 19) as does דָּבַק בְּ (cf. 2:24). V 3a seems to parallel v 3b. But here, too, נַעַר speaks for J (cf. above). Concerning נַעַר as a feminine see 24:14. "He spoke to her heart," that is, he comforted her (50:21; Ruth 2:13; Isa 40:1-2). He said, "Be comforted" (2 Chron 32:6-7). In effect, he promised to marry her. **4** Such *ex post facto* legitimation through marriage is also occasionally attested among the old Arabs (Wellhausen, *Nachr. d. Kgl. Ges. d. Wissenschaften zu Göttingen* [1893], 436). **5** שָׁמַע was originally without object as in v 7 and 35:22. Should וַיֶּחֱרַשׁ be read (Kittel)?

6-12 *The courtship.* In E the father of the young man seeks the hand of the maiden from her father. In J, contrariwise, the young man himself seeks her hand probably because his father is dead. He approaches the brothers who already have authority over their sister during the lifetime of their father (perhaps according to an ancient practice; cf. 24:50; Cant 8:8; Judg 21:22). Or does the father wisely stay back in such a difficult matter? The situation is not entirely clear in J, therefore, probably because the complete text has not been preserved. E has replaced the extraordinary with the normal form of proposing marriage. **7a** כְּשָׁמְעָם belongs with the following (cf. §111b). V **7b** is not the judgment of the narrator—the narrators never explicitly state their opinion of things (cf. introduction ¶3:18)—but that of the brothers, although the narrator approves, to be sure. "He has committed an abomination in Israel." The narrator employed the phrase especially common in his time for sexual crimes (cf. Deut 22:21; Judg 20:6, 10; Jer 29:23; and especially 2 Sam 13:12) and has thus committed a serious anachronism. **8** "Your daughter" resembles "your sister" in 24:59. Hamor cleverly avoids mentioning <375> Dinah's abduction, as does Shechem in vv 11-12. **9** Instead of אֹתָנוּ, Ball and Kittel prefer אִתָּנוּ (cf. Deut 7:3). The narrator wants to represent Shechem's love in his many words (11, 12). He does not even shy away from circumcision! The hearer gladly learns that the Canaanite took such pains for an Israelite maiden. **12** מֹהַר is the gift to the relatives, מַתָּן the gift to the bride. They are mentioned together as in 24:53. The size of these gifts is negotiated as part of the marriage proposal.

13-17 *The decision.* That the custom of circumcision is already presumed here has caused difficulty for some since it is supposed to stem from Moses or Joshua according to J and E (Exod 4:25; Josh 5:2ff.; cf. recently, Meyer, *Israeliten*, 416ff.). We can learn from such passages, however, that there was no universally recognized tradition concerning the origin of this custom and that the older legend sources were much too faithful to effect a secondary balance between such varied traditions. It is equally impossible to maintain that circumcision as a condition for acceptance into the community was only discussed since the exile (Kuenen, *Th. T.* 14:276). It is the ever-recurring error of one-sided literary critical method to consider things to be as old as their attestation. In reality, circumcision as a distinguishing characteristic of cultic and national community belongs to the very earliest period (1 Sam 18:25ff.; 31:4). Furthermore, one should note that the religious aspect of circumcision is completely missing here in J and E. It appears simply as a popular custom (cf. Meyer, *Israeliten*, 416-17). The transgression of the popular custom is disgraceful. The "uncircumcised" is the object of disdain (Josh 5:9). Marriage with him would be a disgrace for an Israelite maiden. Concerning circumcision see above on Gen 17 (pp. 264-65). The legend presumes that the Shechemites did not practice circumcision. This is a valuable, probably reliable archaeological comment.

13 The contention of Meyer (*Israeliten*, 417) that the "sons of Jacob" in this recension are not the ancestors of the tribes, but "the actual people of Israel" is incorrect. They are envisioned here as individuals just as are Shechem and Hamor. One should read either וַיְדַבְּרוּ בְמִרְמָה with Pesh (Dillmann, Kittel) or וַיְדַבְּרוּ with v 14 J. **14** לַעֲשׂוֹת הַדָּבָר הַזֶּה recalls לַעֲשׂוֹת הַדָּבָר (v 19; cf. 19:22). One may note that these words neither settle nor even promise the marriage. To the sensitive narrator this point is important because it mitigates the betrayal of Simeon and Levi (cf. above). Wellhausen (*Composition*[3], 320; *Prolegomena*[6], 339) theorizes regarding this passage that according to the earliest custom the young men were circumcised before the wedding ("bloody bridegroom," Exod 4:25-26; but cf. Meyer, *Israeliten*, 59n.2). It is possible, but by no means certain, that the legend originally had this practice in mind. The existing J recension no longer knows about this, however. <376> **15, 16** E recounts these agreements, supposed to have legal validity, with great precision. The sons of Jacob repeat Hamor's words, Hamor repeats theirs to his people (vv 21-23). **15** נֵאוֹת is a niphal imperfect (§72v) or a qal imperfect of a middle waw verb (§72r).

18-24 *The circumcision of Shechem and the people of Hamor.* **19** Concerning אֵחַר see §64d. "He was regarded very highly in his family" therefore he could initiate this new practice in his household without difficulty (Holzinger). **20** The "city" is intentionally unnamed since it is actually Shechem itself. **21-23** In the official negotiations the matter is presented somewhat differently. The personal reason is not mentioned. The narrators presume such cunning as self-evident. **21** Sam, LXX, and Pesh read אִתָּנוּ יֵשְׁבוּ (cf. vv

10, 23; Ball, Procksch, Kittel). **23** The prospect of possessing Jacob's flocks is meant to commend Hamor's suggestion. With a knowledge of human nature, he appeals to the greed of his compatriots. **24** The expansiveness can be explained by the fact that it is an official occasion. Yet v 24bβ, for which LXX has τὴν σάρκα τῆς ἀκροβυστίας αὐτῶν, is probably an addition (Procksch, cf. Ball). A clause from the Shechem recension may have also been fused into this section (Sievers 2:338). כָּל־יֹצְאֵי שַׁעַר may mean the "warriors" in analogy to Amos 5:3 (Ehrlich).

25-29 *The attack on Shechem and the city.* **25** In terms of content, וַיְהִי בַיּוֹם הַשְּׁלִישִׁי can belong to either source. Because of the syntax (with a subsequent perfect, בָּאוּ, v 27), may be attributed to E. Concerning the syntax see §111f,g. J may have only had וַיְהִי. Simeon and Levi are Dinah's full brothers here. According to the genealogy of the sons of Jacob in Gen 29-30, Reuben, Judah, Issachar, and Zebulon are also Leah's sons and Dinah's full brothers. The Dinah legend, therefore, must have had a different genealogy in view, the same to which 49:5 also alludes. בֶּטַח means carelessly, boldly, confidently (§118q). For עַל־הָעִיר one should read אֶל־הָעִיר. **26** לְפִי־חֶרֶב "according to the law of the sword," "according to the custom of war," see <377> Klostermann (Sam., 57). **27** Sam, LXX, and Pesh read וּבְנֵי. According to E, too, Jacob himself is not involved in the attack: a remnant of tradition. הַחֲלָלִים, usually translated "slain" (more correctly "desecrated," that is, the corpses lying on the battlefield, unburied; cf. *Schöpfung und Chaos*, 33n.3; Greßmann, *Ursprung des isr.-jüd. Eschatologie*, 81) makes no sense here. If the Shechemites were already "slain" or "desecrated" why do the brothers want to attack them? One should read הַחֹלִים, the "sick, weak" (‖ כֹּאֲבִים, v 25 J; cf. recently also Procksch, Kautzsch³). The חַלְלֵהֶם in Num 31:8 in the otherwise related passage Num 31:7-9 differs (contra Sievers 2:338). **28-29** The theft of the livestock and the goods of Shechem, not an absolutely necessary part of the account, has a basis in the tradition (49:6; cf. above) and, at any rate, is reported by the narrator with pleasure. **29b** For וְאֶת one should read אֵת as do Sam and Pesh and following Ball, Procksch, Kittel, Kautzsch³, and Sievers 2:338. Is בַּבָּיִת to be understood collectively as "in the houses"? Or is Shechem's house intended so that the clause should be transposed to the J text after v 26a with Procksch, Kautzsch³? This is even more likely since E has already discussed the plundering (וַיָּבֹזּוּ) in v 27. Pesh (בָּעִיר) evades the problem. LXX and VetLat have both readings side by side.

Vv 30-31 were originally an interlude in J. The conclusion is missing (cf. above). **30** בַּכְּנַעֲנִי וּבַפְּרִזִּי is awkward and is probably a gloss (Sievers 2:338; Meyer, *Israeliten*, 418). Significantly, Jacob's reproaches are not ethical in nature, but only refer to the disastrous consequences (Meyer, *Israeliten*, 418). The ancient Hebrew loves pleasant aromas, unpleasant odors are extremely repugnant to him. He compares the good name with anointing oil and unpopularity with stench. **31** A proud word (Meyer, *Israeliten*, 419)! יַעֲשֶׂה "May he treat?" (§107t).

55. Bethel Legend Part II. 35:1-5, 6b-8, 14 E

Source criticism. The passage belongs to E as evidenced by the following: אלהים (vv 1, 5, 7); אֶל בֵּית־אֵל (v 7 [3]) as in 31:13; the massebah (v 14). The account cites the E version of the Bethel legend (cf. וַיְהִי עִמָּדִי בַּדֶּרֶךְ אֲשֶׁר הָלָכְתִּי v 3, with 28:20). אֲשֶׁר אָנֹכִי הוֹלֵךְ אִם־יִהְיֶה אֱלֹהִים עִמָּדִי וּשְׁמָרַנִי בַּדֶּרֶךְ הַזֶּה 28:20). At the same time, the passage presupposes the E version of the Dinah legend (cf. בְּנֵי יַעֲקֹב v 5, with 34:13, 27). J does not employ the name Deborah (24:50).

Character of the piece. The passage is not a coherent account, but a loosely piled "heap," and, therefore, not an old legend but a redactional product. The piece contains (1) the conclusion of the Dinah narrative. An earlier recension of this conclusion may have recounted that the sons of Jacob were successful in escaping Shechem's neighboring cities that moved against them because of their infidelity (cf. 34:30 J). Later tradition, seeking to put a good face on the narrative, recounts that God himself <378> intervened and sent such a terror on the cities that the sons of Jacob were able to depart unharmed (v 5). But E took offense even at this and sought an honorable reason the ancestors found it necessary to leave the vicinity of Shechem. He found it by (2) linking their departure from this region with the second part of the Bethel narrative. God himself commanded Jacob to depart. Jacob did not hastily flee in fright, instead he left Shechem on God's command for a religious purpose and after the usual devotional preparations. The rather late character of this passage can be clearly seen in this fusion of motifs from two very different legends. The old legends are always completely independent of one another (cf. introduction ¶3:6). At the same time the late origin of the passage becomes evident in the bland tones of the Bethel narrative here. Nothing is said of the heavenly ladder, the holy stone, or the tithe. In place of the many divine beings who appeared to Jacob at Bethel, the one God appears in vv 1, 3. In place of the vow there is a new command of God. An older recension may have recounted here that on his return Jacob paid the vow, i.e. the tithe, and thus venerated the stone as the house of God (28:22; 31:13). This account originally had the purpose of strengthening the framework of the whole Jacob-Esau-Laban composition (cf. above p. 286). This accounts for the explicit reference to Jacob's flight from Esau (vv 1, 7) which connects the conclusion of the whole with the beginning. (3) Furthermore, the author probably found an existing comment that idol images are buried under the oaks of Shechem. He also incorporated this comment into the context by maintaining that Jacob buried strange gods there before moving to Bethel. E will have thought first of the "teraphim" of Rachel treated in the account in 31:19, 30, 32-35. E wove the comments discussed under (1)–(3) into a passable unit. In v 7 he repeated the words of v 1 and thus tied the whole together. Jacob executed God's command and erected an altar to the God who appeared to him during his flight from Esau. Because of this clear conclusion of the E version of the Bethel narrative, E probably did not later report an appearance of God at Bethel (contra Procksch, 38ff.). (4) Finally, another comment is added concerning the death of Deborah, Rebekah's nurse, and concerning her burial not far from Bethel. This comment is placed here, where it does not belong by nature, because it treats a place in the vicinity. The final redactor associated v 14, the erection of a massebah, with Bethel. This comment certainly does not stem from P, who considers such memorial stones pagan. But J, too, avoided the massebahs and also kept silent about the stone at Bethel (28:13ff.), as far as we can tell. The J version of the Bethel narrative gives no indication that such a continuation of the account can be expected to follow in J. E already tells of the Bethel massebah in 28:11-12 and cannot repeat himself here (contra Procksch, 39-40). Therefore, the only possible conclusion seems to be to consider v 15 the continuation of v 8 (with Cornill, ZAW 11:15ff.). Jacob erects the massebah on Deborah's grave. This understanding of the passage is all the more likely since E also speaks of another memorial on the grave of a matriarch in the material that immediately follows (v 20). The redactor transformed the Deborah memorial into a massebah of God because it received a gift, but, in contrast, left the Rachel memorial standing because no gift is mentioned. For Sievers's metrical source analysis (2:169-70), the passage 35:1-8, 14 is of fundamental significance. He relates v 14 to the massebah of Bethel, sees it as parallel to v 7, and finds two elohistic parallel texts of different sizes. One of these sources knows only the altar, the other only the massebah. But the relationship of v 14 to the Bethel massebah is at least uncertain, and in 33:20 the massebah stands peacefully alongside the altar in a unified E text, according to Sievers's contention. This can hardly be an "oversight." <379> This is truly a very uncertain foundation for an entire system of source analysis!

1 "Go up." Shechem lies 570 meters above sea level, Bethel 881 meters. The narrators are very knowledgeable concerning such things. **2** Whoever intends to appear before God at a holy site must undertake certain lustrations, for example, washings, in order to be טָהֹר, culticly pure. A multitude of rules on this subject preserve very ancient religious material (Stade, *Bibl. Theol.*, ¶¶70, 74). It is also necessary to wash or change one's clothes (27:15; Exod 19:10, 14; 2 Kings 10:22; Ezek 44:17ff.; Wellhausen, *Reste arab. Heidentums*[2], 55-56, 110). The original basic ideas are that one would desecrate the holy site in dirty work clothes and, at the same time, that the clothes worn in the sanctuary become taboo and become the property of the sanctuary (Robertson Smith, *Rel. d. Sem.*, 116ff.). Strict Yahwism also prohibits bringing foreign idols along on the pilgrimage. The religion is so sensitive on this matter that it does not even tolerate earrings! Yahweh demands that one serve him uprightly and faithfully (Josh 24:14) and he is a jealous God (Josh 24:19). Earrings were originally decorated with images of gods and amulettes (Syriac *qedâshâ* = earring; cf. Benzinger[2], 82). Such pieces of jewelry, therefore, were employed in the cult in the earliest religious practice (Hos 2:15; Exod 11:2, the Egyptian "vessels"). In Israel, too, images of foreign gods were not always and everywhere regarded as unfavorably as here. But the writing prophets were not the first to create this enmity. It is interesting to see here that one trend rejected earrings but took no offense at the massebahs. For depictions of ancient Israelite earrings see Benzinger[2], 83. The "purification" in this context is a secondary matter, the disposition of the gods the major point according to v 4b. **3** "Who hear me on the day of my distress" is psalm style (cf. Psa 77:3; 86:7; 20:2).

4 Concerning the terebinth at Shechem see comments on 12:6. The contention that images of foreign gods lie buried under the terebinths at Shechem parallels the other that the bones of Joseph rest there (Josh 24:32). Legends concerning buried treasures are frequent elsewhere, too (cf. e.g. Alaric's grave, Grimm, *Deutsche Sagen*, no. 372). Prof. Greßmann has called my attention (in a personal communication) to Olympiodor, *Fr.* 27 (in C. Müller, *Fragm. hist. graec.* 4:63) according to which in late Greek tradition, buried statues directed toward the land of the enemies repel the enemy attack. When they are exhumed, the enemies break in. Here, too, the burial of the idol images could have originally been intended to repel the attack of the Canaanites. In this case, the element would have belonged to the Dinah narrative and must have later been reinterpreted. Yet, the following speaks against this understanding. Notably, Joshua's last speech (Josh 24) delivered at the same site under the tree at Shechem (v 26), also treats the same theme

in the same words. One should dispose of the foreign gods (הָסִ֛רוּ אֶת־אֱלֹהֵ֥י הַנֵּכָ֖ר
Josh 24:23 = Gen 35:2). This speech is also based on the tradition that foreign gods were
once discarded at Shechem. This Joshua-Shechem narrative is, therefore, a variant of the
Jacob-Shechem legend in the broad sense. Guthe (*Gesch. Isr.*, 53-54) and Steuernagel
<380> (*Isr. Stämme*, 90-91) consider this obligation of the people in Shechem to
monolatry to be a historical tradition. Luther (in Meyer, *Israeliten*, 551) envisions an
annual festival in Shechem when Israel entered into covenant with Yahweh. **5** A "divine
terror" (Exod 23:27) is a mysterious, wondrous ("panicky") terror such as the prophets
often describe (cf. Amos 2:14ff.; Isa 19:13-14; Ezek 24:22-23). **7** The fact that the site
bears the name "el" is not unusual in the ancient period (cf. comments on Ashteroth-
Qarnaim above p. 275, and Meyer, *Israeliten*, 295). Concerning נִגְל֣וּ see the comments
on 20:13. Or is the form a plural after all refering to the "angels" in 28:12?

8 Since the tradition knows the name of Rebekah's nurse, one should think that it also
knew a narrative concerning this figure. The same is true of Pichol (21:22) and Ahuzzath
(26:26; p. 298). Concerning ancestral graves see Stade, *Bibl. Theol.*, ¶51. It is still
customary among us for a tree to stand at the grave (1 Sam 31:13). According to the
earliest viewpoint, still preserved in fairy tales and legends, the soul of the deceased
dwells in such a tree (cf. v. d. Leyen, 114:14 with bibliography). Even today in Palestine
there are not a few holy trees at the graves of saints (Greßmann, *Palästinas Erdgeruch*,
85). This Deborah tree is probably the same as the "Deborah palm between Ramah and
Bethel," which later tradition, misled by the shared name, associated with the prophetess
Deborah (Judg 4:4-5). **14** The massebah at the grave (as in v 20) is surely nothing other
than a simple gravestone in E as were certainly common in Israel as well as among the
Phoenicians and elsewhere. Originally, however, the grave of Deborah will have been a
holy site comparable to the grave of Dionysios's nurse at Scythopolis (cf. Plinius, *h.n.*
5.18 [16]). The drink (of water or wine) poured out on the grave is supposed to be for the
dead according to the earliest understanding. Such a practice also occurs elsewhere
(Bousset, *Wesen der Religion*, 49; among the Egyptians, cf. Erman, *Aegypten*, 415; *Äg.
Rel.*, 122; Ranke in Greßmann, *Altorient. Texte u. Bilder* 1:203, 206, 229; among the Babylonians, cf. Zimmern, KAT³, 638, 640; Köhler and Peiser, *Hammurabi's Gesetz* 1:103 [col
17.35, 40], among the Greeks, cf. Stengel, "Griechische Sakralaltertümer," in J. v. Müller,
Handb. d. klass. Altertumswissenschaft 5/3, 99ff.; among the Indians, cf. Oldenberg, *Rel.
des Veda*, 548ff.; among the ancient Arabs, cf. Wellhausen, *Reste arab. Heidentums²*, 182-
83; Jacob, 142-43; additional bibliography in <381> Torge, *Seelenglaube*, 128ff.). It is not
unlikely that there were such rites in Israel, too, since the practice of placing bread for the
dead on the grave is attested to us in Israel (Tob 4:18; Sir 30:18; Deut 26:14). Thus in
Palestine, jars and pots were also placed in the grave and on the dolmen—apparently
graves—included bowls as water containers for the dead (Greßmann, ZAW 29:115-16).
E considered such offerings to be innocent, and therefore not sacrifices offered to a deity.
אֲשֶׁר־דִּבֶּ֥ר אִתּֽוֹ is an addition from the final redactor who harmonizes the passage with
P's report. וַיִּצֹ֤ק עָלֶ֙יהָ֙ שֶׁ֔מֶן may also be an addition influenced by 28:18 (Cornill),
although the anointing of the gravestone also occurs among the Greeks (cf. Stengel,
Griech. Sakralaltertümer, 99).

56. Benjamin's Birth, Rachel's Death 35:16-20 E

Source criticism. The passage belongs to E (Ball). This is indicated by the massebah (v 20) on the grave (cf. v 14). E mentions the account of Rachel's death near Ephratha in 48:7 which repeats the wording of v 16a and v 19. One may also note וַיִּסְעוּ in v 16 as in v 5 (E), while J has the singular וַיִּסַּע (v 21). One may ask whether v 17, the first part of which seems to parallel v 16 and the second part seems to allude to 30:24b (J), does not derive from J (Holzinger). Since, however, no etymology of "Benjamin" appears in the wording of v 17, and since the verse makes good sense in the context of E (cf. especially the parallel 1 Sam 4:19ff.), one may leave it to E.

The passage continues no developed account, and is, therefore, not a "legend" proper, but only a pair of old "comments": one concerning Rachel's burial site and gravestone near Ephratha and another concerning the death of Rachel at Benjamin's birth. The narrative added an ingeniously devised etymology of "Benjamin."

16a שִׂבְרַת־הָאָרֶץ is a unit of weight of unknown value. The precise location of אֶפְרָתָה is unknown. The equation with Bethlehem (which comes too late to be taken seriously) in v 19 rests on a confusion of this Ephrathah with the clan Ephrathah situated in Bethlehem (in Judah, two hours south of Jerusalem; Micah 5:1; Ruth 1:2; 1 Chron 4:4; Josh 15:59 LXX). Rachel's grave, however, surely did not originally lie in Judah, but in the territory of the Rachel tribes. We can also clearly infer from Jer 31:15 and 1 Sam 10:2 that Rachel's grave was located near Ramah (*er-Râm*) on the way from Ramah to Gibeah, not too far from Bethel, on the border of Benjamin and Ephraim. Currently the grave of Rachel is said to be one and one-half km north of Bethlehem (cf. Buhl, *Palästina*, 159; Guthe, BW, s.v. "Rahel's Grave"). Vv **16-18** have the purpose of explaining Benjamin's name. Rachel lies in severe labor pains and must die. Futilely the midwife, who sees the gender of the child, comforts her (38:28), "This one, too, will be a son for you," But she does not want to be comforted and with her last breath names him "Ben-onim." The father, however, does not want to leave his child with such an unfortunate name and names him "Ben-jamin," that is, the son of good fortune (actually "of my right hand"). בֶּן־אוֹנִי is interpreted as "son of my misfortune" (from אָוֶן). The word, however, does not suit the specific situation particularly well nor does it contain a clear allusion to "Benjamin." It is consequently better to read בֶּן־אוֹנִים (plur. of אֳנֶה), "son of lament, sign." א in initial position is pronounced like י. Cheyne (420) correctly compares Kalevala 40:429-30 <382> (trans. by H. Paul) to this renaming, "His mother named him little bloom, strangers called him child of misfortune." For מֵתָה (perfect) it is better to read מֵתָה (participle) with LXX, Pesh, and Targ. Onq (Kittel). The beautiful poem in Jer 31:15 (two "hexameters" according to Erbt, *Jeremia*, 289) probably contains an allusion to this narrative, "A voice in Ramah, / A sigh resounds, / Bitter crying, / Rachel cries. / She will not be comforted for her sons / for 'they are' no more." Just as Rachel cried and sighed and would not be comforted when Benjamin was born, so it is now once again since she is robbed of her children. The eponymous name "Benjamin" is derived from the older designation יְמִינִי. בְּנֵי יְמִינִי is the tribe to the right, to the south, namely of Ephraim (cf. Meyer, *Israeliten*, 311, 522; Stade, *Gesch. Isr.* 1:161; etc.). Modern scholars interpret the fact that Benjamin is born in Palestine in contrast to his brothers as a memory that this tribe formed as the last, only after the entry into Canaan (cf. Stade, *Gesch. Isr.* 1:160;

Guthe, *Gesch. Isr.*, 41, 55-56; contra Meyer, 291n.3, according to whom Benjamin's birth at this point derives only from the fact "that Rachel, whose grave was in Yeminite territory, was said to have died giving birth"). Remarkably, very little is said concerning Jacob's feelings on this occasion when simultaneously his favorite wife died and his favored son was born. It is quite a contrast to the reprise in 48:7 where Jacob's love for the unforgotten Rachel becomes so beautifully apparent. Here, however, Jacob is a secondary figure for the narrator. He is only concerned with the touching scene of the young mother realizing her deepest wish and yet unable to rejoice because she must die. A very similar scene occurs in 1 Sam 4:19-22. There, too a mother who cannot rejoice when she hears that she has born a son and who gives the child a name of unfortunate meaning as she dies. Such motifs, apparently very attractive in antiquity, are easily transferred from one person to another (cf. above p. 319). **20** Concerning the gravestone see comments on v 14.

57. Reuben's Infamy 35:21, 22a J

The passage is indispensable for J in which neither Reuben nor Simeon and Levi (cf. above p. 359) lead the brothers in the following Joseph narrative. E, in contrast, where Reuben is the spokesman for the brothers and is portrayed honorably, cannot have possessed this account (Meyer, *Israeliten*, 276). J is also indicated by יִשְׂרָאֵל which is consistently employed by this source henceforth (37:3, 13; 42:5; etc.). How J explained this name change is no longer apparent. The passage is currently very brief, but the account must once have been more extensive. Now it breaks off in the midst of the narrative with the main point still to come. The copyist who has come so far is horrified by what he reads further and thinks, "God preserve me from copying such horrible things!" We know what the continuation must have been from the allusion to the legend in 49:3-4, Reuben's curse and loss of the birthright. The legend of Reuben's curse will have originally had significance for tribal history. The legend wants to establish why Reuben, who once had the birthright, has lost his status. This fall is grounded in ancient fashion (cf. comments on 9:24ff.) <383> in the father's curse. But this curse (as in 9:22ff.) is based on an infamous act against him. Whether the information that Reuben had forbidden relations with his father's concubine Bilhah (regarding פִּלֶגֶשׁ 22:24; 25:6, cf. above p. 240), ever had some meaning concerning the history of the tribe is, however, very doubtful. Dillmann (380), Stade (*Gesch. Isr.* 1:151), and Ulmer (*Sem. Eigennamen*, 16) theorize that the legend can be explained by an extremely ancient marital practice (polyandry or the like) perpetuated in this tribe. Wellhausen (*Prolegomena*[6], 321), Guthe (*Gesch. Isr.*, 25), and Holzinger and Steuernagel (*Isr. Stämme*, 16, 94) think of a historical event, perhaps the violation of a Bilhah tribe by Reuben. Notably, however, Homer also has a very similar account, the curse of a man by his father whose concubine he had seduced (*Il.* 9.447ff.). Accordingly, this narrative in Israel traces to adopted material and is not to be explained as tribal history. At any rate, the legend is very old, for in the historical period Reuben's birthright, still known to the legend, has long since passed. Nor does this account suit the residence of the tribes in the land. Reuben does not dwell in the vicinity of the Bilhah tribes, Dan and Naphtali. Why this event is localized at *Migdal-'eder* is very unclear. Even if we include Gen 49:3, we learn only a few points from this legend. We may theorize, however, that the account was once much richer. **21** *Midgal-'eder* means "tower of the flocks," that is, a tower erected to enhance protection of the flocks (Benzinger[2], 139). According to Micah 4:8 there was a *Midgal-'eder* in or near Jerusalem, which would suit the context of Jacob's journey very well. V 22a has a dual accentuation. יִשְׂרָאֵל has both the athnah and the silluq, that is, v 22a is considered either a half verse or a whole verse (cf. Franz Delitzsch). Reuben's infamy cannot be termed "incest," for there is no actual relationship between the son and the concubine of his father. Instead, it is considered a wanton incursion on the father's rights (Nöldeke, ZDMG 40:150).

58. Esau's Genealogy 36:10-14 and Princes 15-19, Genealogy and Princes of the Horites 20-28, 29-30, Edom's Kings 31-39

probably stem from an independent source. See no. 60.

Reports concerning Isaac, Jacob, and Esau in P

59. Account of Isaac (Jacob) in P 25:19 . . . 20 . . . 26b . . . 26:34, 35; 28:1-9; 35:6a, 11-13a, 15 . . . 29:24, 28b, 29 . . . 30:4a . . . 9b . . . 22a . . . 35:22b-26 . . . 31:18aβ,γ,δ,b . . . 33:18aβ; 35:9, 10, 27-29

A colorful image! Red.[JE,P] primarily adhered to JE in the Jacob narratives. On the other hand, he wanted to preserve as much of P as possible. Consequently, he separated P's report into small and extremely small portions and inserted them at suitable points in the accounts of JE. This procedure can only be explained on the precondition that P's information <384> concerning Jacob was very scanty. The old daring Jacob narrative could only excite offense in him. Consequently, he was satisfied with only a brief excerpt. Despite the many lacunae, however, we still have an idea of the content of his account. No longer passages will be missing. P transmitted only comments here, the framework of the account from JE, and a few speeches. Now the details show that P knew almost all the narratives transmitted to us in JE, indeed in the transmitted sequence. Several features of the tradition accessible to P agree with J: the divine speech at Bethel which promises Jacob that he would become the patriarch of a people and receive this land and the expression שִׁפְחָה "maiden." J will have also referred to Rebekah as Bethuel's daughter, although in its latest phase. On the other hand, P follows the E tradition in assigning Laban the epithet "Aramaean" (yet cf. above, p. 335), in the name "Paddan" (cf. 48:7), in the renaming of Jacob to Israel through God's word. Independent P traditions can be seen in the name of Esau's wives. All the other divergences of P from JE are, as far as we can see, abbreviations and tendentious alterations.

Strangely, P recounts essentially the Jacob narratives under the superscription "genealogy of Isaac" and then the Joseph legend under the superscription "genealogy of Jacob." This amazing shift has occurred because P had nothing to say concerning Isaac, but felt obligation, on the other hand, to include and to fill in a rubric for Isaac. This is made possible by the fact that P calculated that Isaac lived until Jacob returned from Laban, although this is entirely contradictory to the spirit of the old legend.

I. 25:19 . . . 20 *Superscription. Isaac's marriage.* The evidence that the superscription belongs to P is הוֹלִיד (v 19), the dating, its extreme precision, and "Paddan-aram" (v 20). Isaac's marriage is recounted between vv 19 and 20 (a remnant of the tradition of Gen 24), which is then fixed chronologically in v 20 (cf. 16:16; 17:24; 21:5). Paddan-aram only occurs in P. Hos 12:13 [EVV 12:12] has שְׂדֵה אֲרָם. According to the Arabic geographers it is *tell Feddân* in the vicinity of Haran. Assyrian *padanu* means "way," a synonym for *ḫarrânu*. Is Paddan, then, equivalent to Haran (Zimmern in Gesenius[14] s.v. פַּדָּן; cf. also Jensen, *Gilg.-Epos* 1:225n.2, 326n.5 and concerning this and other explanations of the name cf. Streck in Klio [*Beiträge zur Alten Gesch.*] 6:190-91)? P, which consistently refers to Bethuel and Laban as "Aramaeans," and thus considers them descendants of "Aram" (10:22), does not seem to regard them as Nahorides. Is this tendentious (cf. Budde, *Urgesch*, 425)?

II. . . . 25, 26b *Birth of Jacob and Esau.* Only the chronological comment is preserved. The fact that P treats the birth of two boys together indicates that P also considers them to be twins. Therefore, P knew the legend of their birth.

III. 26:34, 35; 28:1-9 *Esau's marriages. Jacob's blessing and journey to Laban.* P is indicated by the dating (26:34), בְּנוֹת כְּנַעַן (28:1, 6, 8), Paddan-aram (28:2, 5, 6, 7), El shaddai (v 3), פָּרָה וּרְבֵה (v 3), קְהַל עַמִּים (v 3; cf. 17:5-6; 35:11; 48:4), אֶרֶץ מְגֻרִים (v 4), אלהים (v 4), the verbosity of v 5, the repetition of vv 6-7, שָׁמַע אֶל (v 7), and especially the spirit of the passage. <385> We hear nothing here of that which so amused the earlier period and which must have been very offensive to the later, more morally sensitive generation. The blessing Jacob receives from Isaac and his journey to Laban remain but are justified quite differently. The author took the motif for both from the circumstances of his period when mixed marriages threatened the purity of the religious community, when opportunists made marriages with the daughters of the nations with whom they lived and interacted according to the criteria of status, wealth, and reputation, and when the first requirement of piety was to marry a daughter of Israel. Now P read in his exemplar—according to Meyer (*Israeliten*, 353n.1) he freely devised this himself—that Esau's wives were Hittites and an Ishmaelite, but that Jacob married Laban's daughters. Esau's marriages—so he imagined—displeased Isaac greatly. Through these marriages, however—this he adds to the tradition—Esau forfeited the opportunity to become the heir to Abraham's blessing. Consequently, the blessing was transferred to Jacob, but it was accompanied by the command to get his wives from his mother's family. Seen esthetically, this device is rather poor. None of the persons involved is a lively figure. Esau is portrayed most concretely. In the end he comprehends his error and wants to make good, but cannot find the right means. But this characteristic of Esau, who "skulks to one side like a scolded child," also shows how extensively P "deformed the figures of this legend" (Holzinger). The late composition of this section is also suggested by the fact that it intermingles motifs of quite different origins: a comment concerning Esau's wives, Jacob's blessing by Isaac, further the blessing of Abraham equated with the blessing of Isaac (which the old legends never do), and finally Jacob's marriage with Laban's daughters which, in the old legends, is the result, but not the intention, of Jacob's journey to Laban. P may also have derived the idea that marriage with Canaanites was not permitted the patriarchs from the Rebekah legend (24:3 J). The wording of 24:3-4 seems to echo in 28:1, 2.

26:34 According to 25:26b Jacob's fortieth year is Isaac's 100th. All that follows, even Jacob's move to Laban, occurred in this year—this is probably P's intention. In Isaac's 180th year—so P probably thinks—Jacob returned and Isaac died (35:27-28). Jacob was in Aram eighty years. According to JE it was only twenty years.

28:2 Concerning פַּדֶּנָה see §90i. **5** Ehrlich reads וַיִּשְׁלַח. **6** Should it read וישלח (Spurrell, Ball, Kittel)? According to Eerdmans (1:24) the certainly <386> very awkward בְּבָרְכוֹ אֹתוֹ is an insertion. **7** וְאֶל־אִמּוֹ is probably a harmonizing gloss which looks back to 27:43-44. **9** Ishmael was still alive then according to the P chronology (16:16; 17:24-25; 25:17, 26; 26:43) and was 114 years old.

IV. **35:6a, 11-13a, 15** *The Revelation at Bethel.* These clauses are currently located in a passage from E. The following features are evidence for P: אלהים (vv 11, 13a), the superfluous, precise location אֲשֶׁר בְּאֶרֶץ כְּנַעַן (v 6a; cf. 23:2, 19; 33:18; 49:30), the name לוּז (v 6a) and the mention of Bethel (v 15) whereas E has already said "Bethel" (vv 1, 3), El-shaddai (v 11), פָּרָה וּרְבֵה (v 11), קְהַל גּוֹיִם (v 11), the solemn "kings" (v 11 as in 17:16), the echo of the Abraham blessing (v 12 as in 28:4), the verbosity of v 12, "you and your seed after you" (v 12), and "God went up from him" (v 13a as in 17:22). This revelation at Bethel is currently linked to the renaming of Jacob as Israel in P (35:9, 10), thus with an echo of the Penuel legend. Here, then, remnants of two different legends have been united. That this inorganic linkage does not derive from P can be seen in the fact that 48:3-4, where P cites the Bethel revelation, says nothing about Jacob's re-naming, further in the dual beginning וַיֹּאמֶר לוֹ אֱלֹהִים (vv 10, 11) and in the fact that the revelation of God's name (v 11) is apparently the beginning of a divine speech and thus does not accommodate the preceding v 10. If one compares the two divine speeches in v 10 and vv 11, 12, one sees that the Bethel revelation must have originally preceded the first speech since it begins with the revelation of the name of God. Even the current text (עוֹד, v 9) characterizes it as a second speech. Accordingly, it can be theorized that the Bethel revelation in P originally occurred in association with Jacob's journey to Aram, not with his return. The analogy of the old legends further confirm this. This hypothesis is confirmed by the statement "be fruitful and multiply," which only makes sense if Jacob does not yet have children. Therefore, P placed this statement before the subsequent account of Jacob's marriages and children. On the force of this statement—so he thinks—Jacob had many children. The redactor of the whole (R^JE,P) was the first to place P's Bethel revelation at this position and to fuse it with the Penuel revelation in order to be able to retain both. This lack of relationship between vv 10 and 11 has been explained to this point by considering v 10 an insertion in P (Kautzsch-Socin², n. 171; Kraetzschmar, *Bundesvorstellung*, 190-91; Staerk, *Studien* 1:8n.11). The meaning of the Bethel revelation in P is that God himself now renews the blessing that God granted to Abraham (17:2-8), that Isaac inherited from Abraham (17:21), and that he in turn transmitted to Jacob (28:3, 4). Therefore, God confirmed Isaac's words. V 12b is very verbose. Is אֶתֵּן אֶת־הָאָרֶץ an addition perhaps (Holzinger, Kautzsch³)? V 13b is also probably an addition, a dittography from v 14.

V. . . . **29:24, 28b, 29** Jacob's arrival with Laban (currently missing). Jacob marries Leah (also missing). Leah receives Zilpah. Then he marries Rachel who receives Bilhah. The juristic precision and aridity of the passage points to P (cf. 46:18, 25).

29:24 לְלֵאָה בִתּוֹ is conspicuous following לָהּ. They are transposed in LXX. <387> Ball and Sievers (2:321) omit לָהּ. Sam, Targ. Onq, and Targ. Jon read לְשִׁפְחָה (Ball, Holzinger, Kittel; cf. v 29).

VI. . . . **30:4a** . . . **9b** . . . **22a** *Jacob's wives give their maidservants to Jacob as wives.* Vv 4a and 9b belong to P because of their similarity to 16:3. The legal transfer of the maidservant has already taken place in E through the statement in 30:3. The same case appears in 16:2-3 (contra Eerdmans, 12). Concerning v 22a see comments on 8:1. Whether P only tells of Jacob's marriage to the maidservants at this point (which he will have motivated in the same way J and E did so), or whether he also gave a detailed report of the birth of the individual children as did J and E, must remain open to question. P's opinion is that the maidservants became Jacob's "wives" (the same is true of Hagar in 16:3). This is hardly the intention of the old legends.

VII. **35:22b-26** *Jacob's children.* This passage belongs to P: Paddan-aram (v 26). In contrast to the old tradition, P has even Benjamin born in Paddan-aram. P is led to this divergence from the tradition by his love for order. R^JE,P placed the passage after Benjamin's birth. Because of v 26b, it originally belonged in P after Jacob's departure from Paddan-aram (cf. Wellhausen, *Prolegomena*[6], 237; etc.). The children are arranged by their mothers. The appearance of Bilhah's children before those of Zilpah is a remnant of tradition. **24** Sam (LXX), Pesh, Ball, Sievers (2:340), and Kittel read ובני. **26** Concerning יֻלַּד, singular, see §121b; Sam reads יֻלְּדוּ (Kittel).

VIII. . . . **31:18aβ,γ,δ,b** . . . **33:18aβ; 35:9, 10** *Jacob departs from Paddan-aram.* A comment concerning his stay in Shechem. Then there is a new (עוֹד) revelation (the first was at Bethel), perhaps localized at Shechem in P, a remnant of the Penuel revelation (‖ 32:29 J). P is indicated: in 31:18 by קִנְיָן, רְכֻשׁ, רְכֻשׁ, Paddan-aram, the presumption that Isaac still lives, and the similarity to 36:6 and 46:6; in 33:18aβ by the precise location by אֲשֶׁר בְּאֶרֶץ כְּנַעַן (cf. comments on 35:6a) and Paddan-aram; in 35:9 by Paddan-aram and "God appeared to Jacob" as in 17:1. Regarding 35:10 compare the sense and wording of the renaming of Abraham in 17:5, 15. P will not have recounted how Jacob obtained his wealth, nor will he have motivated Jacob's departure from Paddan-aram. Nor did he need to establish why Jacob is now to bear the name Israel according to God's will. He maintains the facts, but the original reasons were extremely offensive to him. In **31:18** Eerdmans (24) strikes מִקְנֵה קִנְיָנוֹ אֲשֶׁר רָכָשׁ on the basis of LXX and Pesh. Sievers's (2:327) omission of אֲשֶׁר רָכָשׁ[1] is better. Why the patriarch is not called Israel but Jacob in the following P texts, despite 35:10, is difficult to say. In a similar way, we do not known why he is <388> called "Israel" in the corresponding J accounts. This seems to be a sign that the text has been reworked.

IX. **35:27-29** *Jacob's return. Isaac's death and burial.* Characteristic of P, Isaac still lives. Further characteristic are the names Mamre and Kiriath-arba (v 27) and the chronology (v 28). Concerning the sense and wording of v 29 see comments on 25:8, 9. הוא חברון (v 27) is a gloss (cf. comments on 23:2). Particularly characteristic of P is the contention that Jacob and Esau as good brothers buried their father together (as once Isaac and Ishmael buried Abraham, 25:9). He passed over Jacob's dispute with Esau just as he did the dispute with Laban. According to 49:31 P, Isaac was also buried in the cave of Machpelah. This can be inferred from v 27, but it is not explicitly stated. It is not clear why.

60. Esau's Genealogy 36:1–37:1

The chapter comprises the following pieces.

    I. Esau's wives and children in the land of Canaan (vv 1-5).
   II. Esau's migration to Seir (vv 6-8).
  III. The Genealogy of Esau's sons in the mountains of Seir (vv 9-14).
  IV. List of the princes of Esau (vv 15-19).
   V. Genealogy of the Horites of Seir (vv 20-28),
       the princes of the Horites (vv 29, 30).
  VI. List of the kings of Edom (vv 31-39).
 VII. List of the princes of Esau (vv 40-43).

Source criticism. In this chapter all the available reports concerning Edom and the Horite people which preceded and fused with it have been combined, apparently by different hands and from different sources. In terms of content and form, the individual sections divide into two classes. (1) The genealogy of Esau's sons (III), the list of his princes (IV), and the corresponding reports concerning the Horites (V) as well as the list of Edom's kings (VI) contain old tradition, as recently demonstrated by Meyer (*Israeliten*, 328ff.) in particular. "A later time had neither the intensive interest in these matters nor the means to acquire such rich and apparently reliable reports." These sections, however, do not agree in style with P. Thus the comment concerning Anah in v 24b "has no counterpart in the whole book of the four covenants." The list of the kings of Edom (VI) with its reference to the Israelite monarchical period does not suit the "archaistic standpoint" of P either (Wellhausen, *Composition*[3], 49). The tradition concerning Esau (III, IV) like the one concerning the Horites (V) is preserved in a dual form. The two genealogies and the two lists of princes may derive from the same hand.

    (2) In contrast, the other sections (I, II, VII) exhibit P's style. One recognizes P's hand with particular clarity in II: v 6 compares to the similar passages in 12:5; 31:18; v 7 compares to 13:6. In addition one should note the expressions רְכָשׁ, קִנְיָן, נֶפֶשׁ, רְכוּשׁ, and אֶרֶץ מְגוּרִים. The following features of VII recall P: אֵלֶּה שְׁמוֹת, אֲחֻזָּה, "by their clans, their places, and their names," and the concluding formula in v 43b. P is indicated in I by the beginning וְאֵלֶּה תֹלְדוֹת (v 10). To v 2a one may compare 28:1, 6, 8; To v 5b one may compare 35:26b. At the same time, however, these sections differ from the first in content: as Meyer (*Israeliten*, 353) has established, they do not contain independent tradition (cf. the commentary). Remarkably, however, Esau's wives mentioned in I differ from those in P (26:37; 28:9). P calls them Judith, Basemath, <389> and Mahalath; Here they are called Adah, Basemath, and Oholibamah. It is therefore necessary to assume that a redactor suppressed information concerning Esau in favor of earlier traditions (Wellhausen, *Composition*[3], 49-50). In II, which exhibits P's style very clearly, as well as in VII, which contains information quite different from II and IV, P is preserved most purely. In the text above, the older traditions are printed in the font otherwise reserved for "J[r]," which is not meant as a judgment concerning its relationship to J, but only indicates that it is close to J in age.

The great detail of these reports about Esau can be explained by the fact that Israel considered Edom its nearest relative and especially by the fact the Edom was for Judah the most important of the neighboring nations. The tradition transmitted to us in the OT has been selected from a Judean standpoint. Most of the names are not otherwise known. Some recur in 1 Chron 1:35-54. Literature concerning the names can be found in Dillmann, Gesenius-Buhl, Holzinger, and especially, Meyer, *Israeliten*, 238ff., which is the source of the following comments.

The sections that come first, I, II, III, form a unit: (1) Esau's children born in Canaan (I), then (2) Esau's move from Canaan to Seir (II), and finally (3) Esau's grandchildren born in Seir (III). The scheme may stem from P.

Esau is the legendary patriarch of the people Edom, as Jacob is of Israel (cf. above, p. 289). The following genealogy of the "sons" and "grandchildren" of Esau contains, thus, the historical tribal groups and tribes of Edom. Edom divides accordingly into three groups: (1) Eliphaz from the legendary matriarch Adah, (2) Reuel from the matriarch Basemath, and (3) the sons of Oholibamah. The tribes, more precisely "thousands" of Edom are the "sons" of Eliphaz and Reuel along with the sons of Esau by Oholibamah.

I **1-5** *Esau's wives and children.* The elaboration of this passage is based on the historical comments transmitted in 36:10-14. At the same time, however, other material has been included. **1** הוּא אֱדוֹם is a gloss (also in vv 8, 19; cf. 25:30). **2** עָדָה is the mother of an Edomite tribe according to v 10. The same name appears in 4:19 as Lamech's wife. Her father אֵילוֹן is not transmitted in v 10 and probably stems from 26:34 where he is the father of Basemath. אָהֳלִיבָמָה is the mother of an Edomite tribe according to v 14. Names composed with אֹהֶל are not attested. עֲנָה is a Horite according to vv 20ff. חִוִּי is a scribal error for חֹרִי (Dillmann, etc.). The tribes derived from Oholibamah are considered to be of mixed Edomite-Horite ancestry. בַּת־צִבְעוֹן is the "gloss of a careless reader of v 25" (Holzinger) or simply a miswritten form of בֶּן־צִבְעוֹן (Sam, LXX, and Pesh; see Ball, Kittel, Kautzsch[3]; cf. v 27). The same phenomenon occurs in v 14. **3** בָּשְׂמַת is the mother of an Edomite tribe according to v 10 ("the one who smells of balsam," from בֶּשֶׂם, "balsam"?). The name also occurs in 26:34 P, but with a different father there. Ishmael's daughter, Nebaioth's sister, is Mahalath according to 28:9 (P). The name Basemath also occurs in 1 Kgs 4:15. **4** The names of Esau's children stem from the list in 36:10-14. אֱלִיפָז is a personal name (Meyer, *Israeliten*, 347). This is the name of one of Job's friends. רְעוּאֵל means "friend of God." Moses' father-in-law, a Midianite, has the same name (Exod 2:18 [Num 10:29]). **5** Oholibamah's sons are יְעוּשׁ (v 18; since Robertson Smith, *Rel. d. Semiten*, 29n.13, associated with the Arabic divine name *Yaghûth*; Meyer, *Israeliten*, 351-52), יַעְלָם (from יָעֵל "mountain goat"), and קֹרַח (the name of Levite clan known from the Psalter: the Edomite clan converted to Judaism and is counted among the Levites; Meyer, *Israeliten*, 352). <390>

II. **6-8** *Esau's migration to Seir.* In this passage, P seems to have been well preserved (cf. above). **6** The name of a region is missing after אֶל־אָרֶץ. Pesh has שֵׂעִיר (Ball, Kittel, Kautzsch[3]). Seir is the mountainous territory stretching from the Dead Sea to the Elanite Bay [Gulf of Aqabah] (details in Buhl, *Gesch. der Edomiter*, 28ff.). מִפְּנֵי יַעֲקֹב means in order to make room for him (cf. Exod 23:30; 34:24; etc.; Ehrlich). Here, too, P has everything taking place in peace and quiet. The brothers part company because the land has become too small for them. P borrowed this motif from the Abraham-Lot narrative (13:6), just as he borrowed the motif for Jacob's journey to Laban from the Rebekah legend. This mixture of legends also demonstrates P's late date.

III. **9-14** *Genealogy of Esau.* **9** This superscription belongs to the scheme that unifies I, II, and III and may originally have read, "This is the genealogy of the sons of Esau." **10** The ancient and very valuable genealogy of the Edomite people follows. There are twelve tribes in all if one omits the bastard Amalek (v 12). **11** תֵּימָן is also considered a tribe of Esau in vv 34, 32. It is known elsewhere. It is famed for its wisdom (Jer 49:7). According to Ezek 25:13 it is in the north of Edom. According to Meyer (*Israeliten*, 347) the name is a gentilic from Arab. *taim* = "worshiper." The tribe is named for its chief. קְנַז recurs in v 42. The Kenizite clans Caleb and Othniel have joined Judah. They are thus to be sought in northern Edom. The other sons of Eliphaz are unknown. **12** תִּמְנָע is Amalek's mother, according to v 22 a Horite. The tribe is considered to be of mixed ancestry (Edomite and Horite). Amalek is well known to us from Israel's history. It dwells north of Kadesh at the edge of the Negeb (cf. Nöldeke, *Enc. Bibl.*, s.v. "Amalek"; Meyer, *Israeliten*, 389ff.). **13** According to the pointing נַחַת זֶרַח שַׁמָּה וּמִזָּה should be translated "to go up and down, here and there" (Kautzsch-Socin[2], n. 178). Accordingly, these names seem to be artificial. But the vocalization is secondary. Concerning נַחַת see מְנַחַת (v 23). Regarding שַׁמָּה see the gentilic שַׁמַּי in the genealogy of Jerahmeel and Caleb (1 Chron 2:28, 32, 44-45). זֶרַח is attested in v 33 and is apparently identical with Ezrah from which Ethan the Ezrahite stems (1 Kgs 5:11). It may also be identical with the Judaean clan Zerah so that it would be necessary to assume that this clan also joined Judah (Meyer, *Israeliten*, 350).

IV. **15-19** *List of Esau's princes.* This list contains the same tradition as the preceding genealogy, only in a different form. Here, too, Amalek (v 16) is to be excised, as well as Korah in v 16 which is still absent in Sam and is preserved at the proper place in v 18. אַלּוּף or leader of the אֶלֶף, the thousand, is the native expression for the princes of Edom (cf. Exod 15:15) and the Horites (vv 29-30). Regarding such <391> lists of princes see the comments on 25:16. Siegfried-Stade (s.v. אַלּוּף) and Meyer (*Israeliten*, 329-30) think that there has been a confusion with אֶלֶף. But 25:16 speaks of "princes" נְשִׂיאִם of Ishmael in the same context. Concerning "thousands" see Meyer, *Israeliten*, 330, 500ff.

V. **20-30** These two Horite lists are also very ancient tradition. חֹרִי has previously been derived from חוֹר, "cave" and understood to mean "cave dwellers." This derivation is incorrect. The name appears on Egyptian memorials in the form *Ḫaru* as a geographic designation for Palestine (cf. Meyer, ZAW 3:308; Max Müller, *Asien und Europa*, 137, 149-56, 240; Jensen, ZA [1895]: 332f., 346-47; Schwally, ZAW 18:126; Meyer, *Israeliten*, 330). According to Deut 2:12, 22 the Horites in Seir were subjugated and eradicated by the "sons of Esau." The lists of Horites transmitted in Gen 36 show that Horite tribes must have existed for a long period. According to Meyer (*Israeliten*, 328ff.; *Gesch. des Altertums* I/22, ¶467) the Horites formerly populated all of Palestine, "probably a Semitic (Canaanite) desert tribe which entered Palestine from the South in the Hyksos period" and which survived in a later period only in the mountains of Seir among the Edomite tribes which immigrated later. Meyer finds reminiscences of an original Horite population of Canaan in the names Shobal, Manahath, Onam, Ebal, and Aran. The Horites are not related to the name Charri which seems to designate the Aryian elements in Mitani (cf.

Meyer, *Gesch. des Altertums* I/22, ¶¶455A, 467A). **20** לוֹטָן is probably related to לוֹט, Abraham's nephew. שׁוֹבָל (1 Chron 2:50ff.) is the name of a Calebite clan. צִבְעוֹן may be related to the Arab. for hyena (Nöldeke, ZDMG 40:168). עֲנָה and **21a** דִּשׁוֹן are listed here and in 1 Chron 1:28 among the sons of Seir, in vv 29-30 among the princes of the Horites. They appear once again in vv 24-25 among Zibeon. There were different lists, then. One considered them to be either an independent tribe or clans of Zibeon (vv 24-25). Since, however, two classifications cannot appear in this same genealogy, they must have been inserted in vv 20-21 from vv 29-30 (cf. Meyer, *Israeliten*, 343n.2). Concerning אֵצֶר see the literature in Meyer (343-44). דִּישָׁן is conspicuous alongside דִּשׁוֹן. LXX has Ρεισων ρισων. V **21b** is probably a gloss (Holzinger). **22** חֹרִי, the name of a people in v 20, is here the first clan of the first tribe. הֵימָם is הוֹמָם in 1 Chron 1:39. תִּמְנָע, according to v 12 a concubine of Eliphaz, has been introduced much like Oholibamah in v 25, in order to give Esau and Eliphaz Horite wives and thus to express the mixture of the Edomite and Horite populations (Meyer, 339). **23** עַלְוָן is עַלְיָן in 1 Chron 1:40. One may compare the region Μουνυχιάτις west of Petra to מָנַחַת. According to 1 Chron 2:52, the half of Manahath which dwells in Zorah belongs to the Calebite clan Shobal: "Thus a Horite clan survived in Zorah on the northwestern slope of the Judaean mountains" (Meyer, 340). עֵיבָל "is probably related to the mountains by this name near Shechem" (Meyer, 340). שְׁפוֹ is שְׁפִי in 1 Chron 1:40. אוֹנָם reappears as Jerahmeel's son in 1 Chron 2:26, 28 (cf. also the Judaean clan אוֹנָם). <392> **24** Sam, LXX, Pesh, and Vulg read אַיָּה. In Hebrew it means "goshawk." It appears as an Israelite personal name in 2 Sam 3:7; 21:8. Regarding עֲנָה see v 20. A remnant of a legend concerning Anah is preserved here. There is a similar legend-like motif in 1 Sam 9. It cannot be said what יֵמִם means (hot water? or is it simply an error for הַמַּיִם and thus a well legend like Judg 1:15?). **25** דִּשֹׁן is דִּישׁוֹן in 1 Chron 1:41. In Deut 14:5 it is a species of antelope. It appears as the personal name דחן in the *Safâ* inscriptions (Meyer, 341). Concerning אָהֳלִיבָמָה see the comments on v 2. Pesh omits בַּת־עֲנָה. It may be a gloss (Holzinger). **26a** Instead of דִּישָׁן, one should read דִּישׁוֹן with 1 Chron 1:41 and Sam. **26b** חֶמְדָּן is represented by חַמְרָן in 1 Chron 1:41 (from חמר, "to be red"?). אֶשְׁבָּן is the name of a color in Arab. (Dillmann). יִתְרָן is unknown. Personal names based on יתר are common. Ithran is a derivative of the personal name Jeter. The tribe is named for its chief (Meyer, 341ff.). For כְּרָן LXX has Χαρραν. **27** Is בִּלְהָן derived from בִּלְהָה, the name of Jacob's concubine (cf. Stade, *Gesch. Isr.* 1:146n.1; disputed by Luther, ZAW 21:55). For זַעֲוָן Sam has עָקָן; LXX and 1 Chron 1:42 read יַעֲקָן. According to Deut 10:6, the Bene-jaakan dwell south of Kadesh, in the western Arabah (Meyer, 343). **28** עוץ is reckoned to Aram in 10:23 P. Thus, the Horite clans seem also to have joined Aram. אֲרָן may be identical with אֹרֶן, a son of Jerahmeel (1 Chron 2:25; Meyer, 344).

29, 30 *The tribal princes of Seir.* With the exceptions of Anah and Dishon (cf. above concerning vv 20-21), the names are identical with the sons of Seir. Judging from LXX ἐν ταῖς ἡγεμονίαις αὐτῶν, לְאַלֻּפֵיהֶן (v 30) should be pronounced לְאַלֻּפֵיהֶם.

31-39 *The kings of Edom,* a very old and valuable list, the final remnant of what may have once been a much more comprehensive historical tradition from Edom, in form similar to the "epitome" of the Israelite book of Kings. It is "one of the most important witnesses of ancient Syrian civilization," which "the Bedouins advancing on the developed regions seized as quickly as the Arabs did later" (Meyer, *Israeliten*, 383-84; cf. 355ff.,

370ff.). V **31b** can be understood, "before there was a king in Israel," that is, before Saul, or "before an Israelite king ruled over Edom," that is, before David. The latter is the more likely: the Edomite king list naturally ends with the time of David when Edom was subjugated by Israel (Dillmann). The residence changes with each king. With the possible exception of the last, none of them is his predecessor's son. One may therefore surmise that the Edomites did not have a stable monarchy, but that these "kings" are comparable to Israel's "judges" (cf. Winckler, *Gesch. Isr.* 1:192). "Now one, now the other chief gains dominion in battle, whether against external enemies or against the king at the time, and holds his position as long as he can" (Meyer, 372). The place names, to the extent we can locate them, show "that Edom's population was concentrated in the mountains east of the Arabah" (Meyer, 376). The list seems to portray circumstances from about 1160 onward, shortly after Ramses II (Meyer, 382-83). **32** The name Bela, son of Beor, is remarkably similar to Balaam, son of Beor in Num 22ff. so that Meyer (376ff.) regards the two as originally identical. The name דִּנְהָבָה is attested often elsewhere, but not in Edom. **33** "Son of Zerah" means from the clan of Zerah which must have dwelt near Bosrah <393> (Meyer, 372). בָּצְרָה is also mentioned elsewhere (Amos 1:12; Jer 49:13; etc.) as a major Edomite city. It was located at the site of the current *el-Buṣêra*, 2¾ hours south of *et-Ṭafîle*. **34** Concerning תֵּימָן see the comments on v 11 above. **35** הֲדַד is the divine name attested throughout Syria. It also occurs as a personal name (Zimmern, KAT³, 443ff.). עֲוִית is associated with a series of hills on the eastern side of Moab. An act of king Hadad is reported, his victory over Midian in the "field," that is, the open steppe (Meyer, 329) of Moab. Edom must have exercised power this far to the north at that time, then. Meyer (381) associates this battle with the raids of Midian known from the Gideon narrative (Judg 6ff.) and places the events around 1080. Hadad probably "marched against" the Midianites "when they returned from their raids to the north" (Meyer, 382). **36** מַשְׂרֵקָה—We hear of an Edomite Μασρηκά (in the vicinity of Gebalene, southeast of the Dead Sea). **37** רְחֹבוֹת means "plaza, market," a common place name. Euseb. *Onom.*, 286, identifies it with a military post in Gebalene. The "river" is probably one of the brooks "which flow into the Dea Sea from the southeastern mountains of the Arabah" (Meyer, 373). **38** בַּעַל חָנָן is a construction like אֶלְחָנָן. The name gives evidence of the Baal cult in Edom. It will have gained popularity with the beginning of sedentary culture (Meyer, 382). Concerning עַכְבּוֹר compare עַכְבָּר "mouse."

39 For הֲדַר Hebr mss, Sam mss, and 1 Chron 1:50 read הֲדַד. This Hadad II was defeated by David (2 Sam 8:13-14; Meyer, 355ff., 371). For פָּעוּ LXX has Φογωρ = פְּעוֹר, a mountain at the edge of the Jordan plain. The city בֵּית פְּעוֹר is there. But it is difficult to imagine that Edom reached so far (Meyer, 374). מְהֵיטַבְאֵל means "El does beneficent deeds." Marquart (*Fundamente israel. u. jüd. Gesch.*, 10) translates the next passage as follows: "Daughter of Matred from Me-zahab (מִן מֵי זָהָב), gold water." The same place name may occur in the corrupt form די זהב in Deut 1:1. Characteristically, the name of this king's wife is probably indicated because he based his claims on her.

VII 40-43 *Princes of Esau.* The list, repeated in 1 Chron 1:51ff. is, according to Meyer (*Israeliten*, 353n.1), for the most part cobbled together from elements of the preceding and has nothing of the slightest historical value. In fact, the names of the matriarchs are considered names of tribes. Sections IV and VII have only קְנַז and תֵּימָן in common (v 42). תִּמְנָע (v 40) is Eliphaz' concubine in section III (v 12) and is considered a Horite in section V (v 22). אָהֳלִיבָמָה (v 41) is Esau's third wife in sections I, III, and IV, a Horite and the mother of several tribes. עַלְוָה (v 40) is probably identical with the Horite clan עַלְוָן (v 23). יְתֵת (v 40) is an error for יֶתֶר. LXX mss have Ἰεθερ (= Yithran, v 26; Meyer). The other names do not occur in the other lists. אֵלָה (v 41) is the harbor city Elath. פִּינֹן (= פּוּנֹן, Num 33:42-43) lies between Zoar and Petra. Copper mines were there. The site is now known as *Phenân* on the eastern edge of the Arabah. מִבְצָר (fortification) is Μαβσαρά, associated with Petra. The other names are unknown. LXX also has אַלּוּף צְפוֹ (as in sections III and IV) so that the full complement of twelve is obtained (cf. Nestle, *Marginalien*, 12). 43 הוּא עֵשָׂו אֲבִי אֱדוֹם is probably a misplaced gloss on אֱדוֹם (cf. Ulmer, *Semit. Eigennamen*, 24n.2). <394>

37:1 P *The conclusion of the Isaac-Jacob narrative in P.* In content, it continues 36:8.

Joseph Narratives

The Joseph Narratives in J and E

Composition, Character, Origin, and Source Analysis of the Joseph Narratives in J and E

The Joseph narrative consists of the following accounts.

1. Joseph is taken to Egypt, 37 JE.
2. Tamar's marriage of necessity, 38 Jb.
3. The adulterous Egyptian woman, 39:1-20a J (E).
4. Joseph's dream interpretation in prison, 39:20b–40 EJ (prelude to no. 5).
5. Pharaoh's dream and Joseph's elevation, 41 EJ.
6. The brother's first encounter with Joseph in Egypt, 42 EJ.
7. The brother's second encounter with Joseph in Egypt, 43, 44 JE.
8. Joseph reveals himself to his brothers, 45:1-24 EJ.
9. Jacob journeys to Egypt and takes up residence in Goshen, 45:25-28; 46:1-5, 28-34; 47:1-5a, 6b, 12, 27a JE.
10. Joseph makes Egypt pay taxes to Pharaoh, 47:13-26 J (?).
11. Jacob's final testament, 47:29-31; 48:7-22 JE.
12. Jacob's blessing, 49:1-27 Jb.
13. Jacob's burial; Joseph's death, 50:2-11, 15-26 JE.

I. Of these passages, nos. 2 and 12 stand completely outside the framework of the Joseph narrative. No. 2 has a distinctive theme: it deals with Judah and Tamar. No. 12 has a distinctive style: it is a poem, not an account. The details also demonstrate that the two pieces did not originally belong here. According to Gen 38, Judah parted from his brothers; according to J's other Joseph accounts, however, he is with them. In Gen 49, the many tribes of Jacob are blessed; in Gen 48, on the other hand, Jacob blesses only Joseph and his sons, and this blessing, the narrator thinks, is the foundation for their special advantage. See further on this chapter in the interpretation. Accordingly, these sections were inserted (into J) by a later hand. The other sections comprise an artistically arranged composition (in J and E). The main theme is Joseph and his fate. No. 1 is the introduction: Joseph, preferred by his father, envied by his brothers, falls into the misery of slavery through their crime and comes to Egypt. The following narrative intends then to show how all the sins of human beings were nevertheless incapable of impeding God's decision—how Joseph comes to high honors in Egypt, how he punishes the crime of his brothers, and how, finally, he accepts them again in grace. In the course of this narrative, the legend drops the strand concerning Joseph's relationship with his brothers at first and treats Joseph's lone fate in Egypt. At first in great distress, he becomes lord of Egypt because of <395> his wise dream interpretation and assumes charge of Egypt's grain trade in the time of famine (nos. 3, 4, 5). Thus, the narrator reached the point where he can once again very skillfully interweave the main thread. This same famine Joseph had foreseen and which made him second only to Pharaoh forces his brothers to journey to Egypt. Thus they come under Joseph's control. Now he has an opportunity to discipline them in the manner they deserve. Here, the narrators' esthetic interests become prominent. They delight in telling of striking changes in the fate of human beings. The slave is now prince and his one-time oppressors are now in his hand. But the ethical notion sounds through even more clearly: the brothers must now pay for what they once did to Joseph (nos. 6, 7). The legend reaches the high point in the account of how Joseph, finally touched by his brothers' fear, discloses himself to them and pardons them (no. 8). From this point, the account slowly diminishes: Jacob, invited by Joseph, moves to Egypt and comes under Joseph's care (no. 9). The account concludes idyllically. Dying, Jacob blesses the beloved son (no. 11). Joseph reverently fulfills his fathers last wish and dies at peace with his brothers (no. 13). Between Jacob's journey to Egypt (no. 9) and his death (no. 11), two pieces by nature intimately related, another section treating Joseph's relations with Egypt (no. 10) has been placed disrupting the beauty of the composition. In terms of content, then, it belongs to sections 3, 4, and 5, more precisely at the conclusion of no. 5.

II. The Joseph narrative is a "legend cycle." It distinguishes itself, however, as this overview demonstrates, from the other legend cycles through its particularly coherent composition. While elsewhere the individual legends of a cycle—as in the primordial legends and the Abraham narratives—stand alongside one another like a row of pearls and the binding thread is very inconspicuous, the Joseph account is a well-organized whole. While in the other legend cycles the individual legends underlying the whole can always be sharply differentiated from one another, one can only discern marked delineations in a few passages: as at the beginning of the "Egyptian" thread (in no. 3) and in the resumption of the main thread (in no. 6). For the most part, each passage directly continues the preceding. Here and there, the boundaries of the passages are quite fluid (especially in nos. 7-9) so that one finds it difficult to determine the limits of the passages. This indicates, then, that the individual legends which must be the components of the Joseph narrative have been firmly interwoven in the current state of the text. The unity of the whole conception is particularly clear in E who even dared to pronounce the basic idea of the whole (42:21-22 and 45:5-7; 50:20). Thus the Joseph account represents the height of composition in Genesis. Such a highly developed ability to unite blocks of material is not the beginning, however, but the end of narrative art. We may imagine that many centuries lie between the development of this style and, at the other extreme, the origination of that early genre that appears in the Penuel and Tower of Babel legends (cf. introduction ¶3.21).

At the same time, the Joseph accounts are far removed from the concise style of the ancient genre. They are the characteristic example of the detailed style. The chief means the narrators repeatedly apply for extending the account is to recount the same motif twice and to repeat reports in speeches (cf. introduction ¶3:20).

The characterization of Joseph also shows how much Hebrew narrative art learned over time. While the old legends were satisfied with two or only one major characteristic for the hero, a colorful portrayal is developed here. He is clever, handsome, beloved of God, "demonic" and lucky, son of the favored wife and preferred by his father, God-fearing, shy, honorable, devoted to his father and brother, etc. The narrators, however, employ their most developed art (in terms of their era) <396> to describe how he vacillates inwardly when he encounters his brothers. There are no other parallels in Genesis for such a complicated, one could say "modern," psychic state. It is also interesting to see that Joseph is depicted as an ideal in the narrator's opinion. Older art did not portray ideals but types (cf. the variants of the narrative of Abraham in Egypt, chaps. 12, 20, 26, and the introduction ¶4:7).

This inner complexity of the Joseph narrative includes the narrators' ability to awaken a number of different responses simultaneously in the hearer: concern for Joseph, indignation at his brothers, abhorrence for the scheming Egyptian woman, joy at Joseph's elevation, compassion for the aged Jacob, fear for his brothers' lives, "until the final reconciliation and the stirring reunion between father and son touch the reader deeply" (Luther in Meyer, *Israeliten*, 142-43). How different from the old legends which excite very few emotions in the hearer.

All this suggests that we may no longer call this account a legend. Instead, we must term it a novella. It is very important to note that J and E reported the Joseph accounts in essentially the same manner. Neither E nor J invented this new narrative art.

Furthermore, the characteristic features of the "novella" can be seen in the diminished prominence of the relationship to places while the old patriarchal legends are almost all linked to specific sites. The Hebron narrative originated in Hebron, the Penuel narrative in Penuel. But these Joseph legends, which envision Jacob very generally as dwelling "in the land of Canaan" (42:29; 45:25; Meyer, *Israeliten*, 271n.1) and which, in fact, play out, for the most part, abroad, can have been told all over Israel. Only the beginning (37:12-17) mentions a specific place, Shechem and its environs, and presumes that the hearer knows of it. Joseph's grave was also located there later (Josh 24:32; cf. also Gen 48:22). Consequently, we may surmise that the Joseph account in its oldest form originated at Shechem. Beside Shechem, Beer-sheba is also mentioned (46:1-5). But divine revelation there is clearly not an old cultic legend, but only the imitation of such. Toward the end, J and E mention the name of Jacob's burial site (50:10-11). But the narrators are unable to say anything specific about this site.

These accounts also characteristically omit the theophanies, once of such great significance, apart from this Beer-sheba episode. The narrator lives in another religious world. In it the gods no longer appear bodily, but the deeper insight recognizes the hand of the ruling God in natural events. Belief in providence has taken the place of belief in theophanies (45:5, 7; 50:20; cf. comments on Gen 24, p. 247, and the introduction ¶4:6).

Only dreams, the least sensory form of revelation, still indicate the deity's will. But even in them the deity no longer appears to speak (exceptions 46:2ff.; cf. Haller, 64, 79).

Furthermore, one may note the manner in which foreigners are portrayed. The old legend portrayed foreigners not much differently than the Israelites in terms of customs and nature. They considered it obvious that everyone speaks Hebrew. Abraham can speak with Pharaoh—so it was naively recounted (12:18-19). The narrators of the Joseph narratives, however, account for the fact that the hearers will surely distinguish Egyptian and Israelite. They know that Canaanites could only converse with Egyptians through a translator (42:23). They report foreign customs gladly and extensively, even when the continuation of the account did not require it (43:32). They thereby lend their narratives a unique, foreign charm. The legends are therefore to be associated with ancient and modern accounts which play out abroad and describe foreign matters. <397>

Finally, one may note the peculiar, tender, and touching tone that echoes throughout these narratives. The accounts are rich in tears although they maintain balance in this, too, and avoid, for example, portraying Joseph's pain or his brothers' regret (Luther in Meyer, *Israeliten*, 154) and may, therefore, seem to be the pearls of Genesis to more feminine tastes. The older legends of Genesis, however, have a much more powerful tone. One thinks of the Construction of the Tower, the Penuel legend, the Sodom legend, the Paradise narrative, etc. We can also trace elsewhere how the later accounts in Genesis begin to sound tender and softhearted tones (cf. esp. the two Hagar narratives, p. 230).

III. The very late form of the Joseph accounts also explains why only very little historical information echoes in them. Primarily, the names of the heroes stem from historical tradition. They are the old tribal names of Israel. In addition, the following details also stem from historical tradition. (1) Joseph's preferred status among the brothers. This legend motif may be very ancient: Joseph, in the historical period the northern kingdom's royal tribe (to which 37:8 probably alludes), already had a leading role during the entry into the land (Judg 1:22ff.). (2) Ephraim's advantage over Manasseh is historical (48:13ff.). The name of the northern kingdom was "Ephraim," not Manasseh. In contrast, Manasseh is still named before Ephraim in Judg 1:27ff. Gideon and Abimelech stem from Manasseh. (3) It is also historical that Joseph possesses the city Shechem taken from the Amorites in war (48:22), further (4) that Joseph was closely related to Benjamin, the second son of Rachel, and that (5) Benjamin was considered the youngest tribe in Israel. (6) Reuben's primacy and leadership (in E) is also historical. Since Reuben disappeared entirely in the historical period, we may conclude that the Joseph legend is very ancient in Israel. Later, the better known Judah replaced Reuben. Here, then, J represents a younger phase of the tradition. (7) The main question is whether the migration of the Joseph tribe to Egypt is based on historical information. The question is related to another, whether the Exodus legend traces back to historical events. This is not the place to treat this question in detail. Yet the author may well state his conviction that the Exodus is assured to be historical, especially by the old song in Exod 15:1, 21, in addition to other sources. The immigration of Canaanite or Hebrew clans and tribes to Egypt will not have occurred once, but many times (cf. comments on 12:10, p. 169). The legend also correctly maintains the motive that drove the Israelite tribes to Egypt: hunger. Abraham's migration to Egypt is a variant (12:10ff.). Steuernagel (*Isr. Stämme*, 54, 65ff., 93-94) interprets a whole series of other elements of the Joseph legend historically. But all these relationships seem very dubious. Even whether one can at least infer from the legend that the Joseph tribe was in Egypt first or alone (cf. Wellhausen, *Composition*[3], 344-45), cannot be demonstrated or considered likely (Meyer, *Israeliten*, 49n.1). Nothing the account says about Egypt is historical in the proper sense, either. The narrators do not portray Egyptian customs in order to depict the ancient past. Instead, they employ the colors of the Egypt of their day. It should also be noted that these portrayals, although somewhat bland, are not bad, especially in E, according to the testimony of the Egyptologists. They may be based on oral reports, perhaps of traders or soldiers, or even on the personal experience of the narrators (cf. Spiegelberg, *Aufenthalt Israels in Ägypten*, 26). Marquart's idea (*Philologus* VII. Suppl.-Bd. [1900], 677ff.), adopted by Winckler ("Abraham als Baby-lonier," 31) that Joseph was a historical person identical with *Janhamu*, the general of Amenophis IV to whom the minor princes of Palestine came for grain according to the Amarna correspondence, is quite "adventuresome" (contra Marquart; cf. Meyer, *Israeliten*, 287n.2; Heyes, *Bibel u. Äg.*, 233-34). Naturally, the "Joseph" figure is not historical, but the circumstances of Egypt portrayed <398> in the narrative are mostly the historical cir-cumstances of a specific epoch, namely, of the "New Kingdom" (cf. comments on 37:36; 40:1ff.; 41:38-39; cf. also A. Jeremias, ATAO[2], 390ff.). Eerdman's (2:67ff.) suggestion that Joseph may be the Semitic prince *'Irsw* who, according to Merenptah, exacted tribute from Egypt in the "years of shortage" is no better. Joseph was not a foreign ruler but a minister of Pharaoh.

Now if one compares the truly historical elements contained in the legend with the legend itself, one must say that the historical elements are not very prominent in the total concept. Very large and significant sections have neither historical nor etiological foun-dations. This is particularly true of Joseph's lot in Egypt where he is merely an individual and any notion that he represents a tribe would be entirely impossible. The high position Joseph assumes in Egypt concerns one Hebrew, but in no wise and in no sense the tribe Joseph. Similarly, the description of Benjamin, the tender youngest child, agrees remarkably little with the characterization of the tribe of Benjamin as a ravaging wolf (49:27; Meyer, *Israeliten*, 522). It is also especially unusual that the historical references apparent a few times in the Joseph narratives either do not conform to the other legends at all (such as the grant of Shechem in 48:22; cf. comments on the passage) or have a very loose relationship to the entire composition (such as the advancement of Ephraim before Manasseh in 48:13ff. and the comments concerning their births in 41:50-52). One may also call attention to the fact that the Jacob of the Joseph narratives is actually quite different from the hero of the Jacob accounts. There he is only a dying old man who loves Rachel's children. But we hear nothing more of his special gift of cunning and trickery which played such a large role in the earlier narratives. Accordingly we come to a hypothesis analogous to those expressed above for many other legends in Genesis that these accounts originally did not treat Joseph and his brothers but were only secondarily applied to the tribes of Israel and alloyed with Israelite material (cf. above pp. 172-73, 246, 308, 319, 341, 359-60).

Thus the question arises as to how one is to imagine the original form of these legends later interpreted in relation to Joseph and his brothers. The general assumption from which we proceed is that the legend cycle at hand was woven together out of a series of accounts originally independent of one another. The task, then, is to resolve the whole into presumably original components once again. We will have to conceive of these original accounts as "fairy tales," however. The Joseph account has even now, indeed, a strong relationship to fairy tales so that it is no accident that the material, in free paraphrases of the Bible, still recurs in modern fairy tale collections (cf. L. Gonzenbach, *Sizilianische Märchen* no. 91; Prym and Socin, *Der nue-aramäische Dialekt von Ṭûr 'Abdîn* 1:xix, 2:26ff.). The task formulated in this fashion lies in the realm of folklore. It is one which the author of this commentary can begin but not complete.

As we have seen, the whole is woven together from two chief motifs. (1) The account of Joseph's fortunes with his brothers comprise the framework. The glorification of the youngest, who will finally become the lord and deliverer of his brothers, is very common in legends and fairy tales (cf. Judg 6:15; 2 Sam 16; Rev 12; cf. v 17). The "contrast between the elder, dishonest and treacherous, and yet unsuccessful brother and the youngest, mistreated, noble, and successful brother" can often be observed. Indeed, it is the "basic motif of many accounts" (cf. v. d. Leyen, 115:13). The element of the brothers casting the youngest in a well from which, however, he is delivered so that he can expose the betrayers, similar to an element in the Joseph narrative, occurs very often (cf. Reinhold Köhler, *Kleinere Schriften* 1:292ff., 537ff., 543ff.; additional literature in Reinhold Köhler's notes to L. Gonzenbach's *Sicilianischen Märchen* 2:238, and *Zeitschrift* <399> *des Vereins für Volkskunde* 6:163-64; cf. also the *Märchen aus Tripolis* [95] collected by Stumme in which eleven brothers, jealous of the youngest, cast him into a well). The fact that traders draw him out of the well also recurs in modern fairy tales (in Köhler 1:538; Littmann, *Arab. Beduinenerzählungen* 2:32). A similar basic motif also occurs in Littmann, ibid. 2:19-20, 27-28, where the brothers want to kill the son of their father's second wife who threatens to become the father's successor and their lord but who then, on the advice of their youngest brother, leave him in the wilderness to die so that they do not commit the sin of murder. In the end, however, the abandoned one returns, forgives the brothers, and rewards the youngest. Finally, the fairy tale of "the orphan in the eyrie" (Wenzig, *Westslavischer Märchenschatz*, 26ff.) is also related. In it a boy exposed in a cave by his uncle escapes and is later adopted by a rich man. He becomes his heir and, then, when his uncle, impoverished, comes to him, reveals himself and forgives (according to Greßmann's report). In E, the motif of the stolen and later rediscovered child plays a corollary role.

2. Joseph's Egyptian adventures are inserted into this framework. The most important of these for the whole composition are Joseph's interpretation of Pharaoh's dreams and his elevation to the highest honor. Dan 2 is a variant. We also find the motif that whoever fulfills the task, solves the riddle, is rewarded with the highest honor, for example, in 3 Ezra [=1 Esdras] 3-4, in the case of Oedipus, or in the "Turandot." The account in the Genesis recension contains many Egyptian details and may have been originally narrated in Egypt by an Egyptian wise man.

Other narrative material has been added. These additions include:

3. The fulfilled dreams. Dreams predict the brilliant fate of the youngest son and his future dominion over his brothers and parents. Humans attempt to thwart the prediction, but they are finally fulfilled anyway. The modern Berbers still tell a similar story (cf. Stumme, *Märchen der Berbern*, 52-53) about Elkhatef. The same basic motif occurs in Grimm's legend no. 482 and often (cf. comments on 37:5ff., 20).

4. The slanderous adulteress. The wife wants to seduce the youth. When he resists her, she falsely accuses him of adultery to her husband. Thus the youth finds himself in great danger. The motif, played out in Egypt and with an Egyptian parallel, could be of Egyptian origin in this form. It is very common elsewhere, too, however (cf. the interpretation).

5. The account of Joseph's agricultural policy both continues and concludes the narrative of the dream interpretation. The account is etiological in nature in contrast to almost all the other Joseph narratives and may be based on an Egyptian legend.

6. Fear before the magician. A man, considered a great magician, utilizes knowledge he gained in an entirely natural manner in order to frighten people (cf. similar Indian motifs; v. d. Leyen, 116, 15-16). This legend, too, suits Egypt, the land of magicians.

A multitude of lesser motifs supplement these larger legend materials. The old man's love for the sons of his favored wife, the spoiled youngest child, the jealousy of the half brothers, the love of the full brothers, the bloody, deceptive evidence, the figure of the grand dream interpreter, the seven years of hunger, the treasure in the grain sack, the concern of the foreigner who has gained status for this relatives, the final will of the dying, the burial with the fathers, etc.

The total image of the prehistory of the material would, therefore, be as follows. A whole series of individual legends, most, perhaps, of foreign origin or international in character, were applied to the Israelite figure Joseph, interfused with some Israelite <400> material, and skillfully woven into a unity. They have come to us in J and E in a later, more detailed form as the Joseph novella (cf. also Meyer, *Israeliten*, 49, 145ff., 287-88).

Given these origins of the Joseph novella, it is extremely poor method to trace the whole account to a mythological basis without substantial evidence and to interpret Joseph as a form of the sun god, for example, or even of Tammuz (cf. Winckler, *Gesch. Isr.* 2, 62-63, 67ff.; A. Jeremias, ATAO^2, 383ff.). Instead, the question of whether mythological concepts underlie the novella may only be raised in reference to the constitutive details of the narrative material on a case by case basis. The mythical elements Winckler and Jeremias think they have uncovered here, however (e.g., Joseph in the cistern and in prison as an image of Tammuz in the underworld; Jacob's lament over the one presumably ravaged by a wild animal corresponds to the lament over the Adonis killed by Eber; Joseph's marriage with the daughter of the sun priest resembles "the marriage of Tammuz with the daughter of the sun," etc.) are all too bland to demonstrate anything. Individual mythical echoes may be heard (cf. comments on 37:5ff.). It is more than unlikely, however, that the whole is to be interpreted in this way and that this interpretation was still known to the narrators (cf. Luther in Meyer, *Israeliten*, 146ff.).

IV. Whereas source analysis of the Joseph narratives has previously relied on the alternation between יהוה and אלהים, along with other indicators, Eerdmans (65ff.) has recently disputed the allocation of the יהוה and אלהים passages to different sources and has attempted his own source analysis proceeding from the (of course long noted) interchange between "Jacob" and "Israel" and also considering a few other observations. He attributes 37:3-24, 28a, 29-33, 36; 43; 44; 45:28; 46:1, 2a, 28-34; 47:1-5, 13-27, 29-31; 48:1, 2b, 8-22; 50:1-11, 14-26 to the "Israel recension," 37:2, 25-27, 28b, 34, 35; 40; 41; 42; 45:1-27; 46:2b-7; 47:6-12, 28; 49:1a, 29-33; 50:12-13, to the "Jacob recension." All else was added later. In order to see the superficiality of this analysis, it is sufficient to note that the eldest brother is Judah in 37:26; 48:3,8; 44:14, (16), 18; 48:9, and, in contrast, Reuben in 37:(21), 22, 29; 42:22, 37 (cf. also the verses which speak of Simeon, the second eldest next to Reuben, which belong with the Reuben passages; 42:24, 36; 43:23). This distinction surely derives from the difference in sources. It is difficult to understand how Eerdmans could overlook such a universally recognized observation. Concerning the details of this source analysis see the interpretation.

61. Joseph Comes to Egypt 37:3-36 JE

Source criticism. A composite of both recensions. The chapter is full of doublets and repetitions. According to vv 25, 27, 28aγ; 39:1, Ishmaelites bring Joseph to Egypt; according to vv 28aα, 36, in contrast, Midianites. The Ishmaelites bought Joseph (vv 27, 28aγ); in contrast, the Midianites abducted him (v 27aα,β). The brothers are jealous of Joseph (1) because his father prefers him and gives him a sleeved garment (vv 3, 4) or (2) because he has dreams predicting his future dominion over his brothers (vv 5-11). (V 2 offers a third motivation for the jealousy: Joseph tattled on his brothers. This motivation probably stems from P according to Holzinger.) Joseph's sleeved garment is further discussed in vv 23, 31, 32, 33; his oracular dreams in vv 19, 20. The father is called Israel (vv 3, 13) or Jacob (v 34). The elder brother who intercedes for Joseph is called Reuben (vv 22 [21], 29-30) or Judah (v 26). Jacob twice gives Joseph the task of going to his brothers (vv 12, 13a, 14b ‖ 13b, 14a). Twice the brothers decide to kill him (vv 18b ‖ 19, 20). One brother contradicts them twice—vv 21 (where "Reuben" has been substituted for "Judah") ‖ 22. According to v 20, the brothers plan to say that a wild animal ravaged him. But according to v 33, their father makes this statement. This confusion <401> traces to the redactor. Jacob's sorrow over Joseph is also reported twice: We first hear that he cried at the conclusion of the passage, while it should have been stated at the very beginning: vv 34b, 35a (אָבֵל, הִתְאַבֵּל) ‖ 34a, 35b.

If one compares these doublets with one another, the result is two coherent, well-composed, and characteristically distinct variants. The motif of Joseph's dreams dominates one variant: Joseph had dreams which seemed to predict he would one day become his brothers' lord. Thus, they become jealous (vv 5-110). When they see him coming they say, "See, there comes the dreamer" (v 19) and they decide to kill him and throw him in the cistern. "Then we will see what becomes of his dreams" (v 20). Thus they attempt to thwart the oracle. But it is fulfilled despite human actions. Indeed, it is fulfilled through them, for "The oracles see and it comes true. The truthful praise the outcome" ("Braut von Messina," 2379ff.). Reuben's remonstrances convince them at least not to spill blood, but to throw Joseph into the cistern alive to languish there. But Midianites come along, pull him out, and sell him as a slave in Egypt. The continuation then recounts how Joseph's brothers finally had to bow in the dust before him after all (42:6, 9). The dreams, the cistern, and the thieving Midianites characterize this account, then. Just as the dream motif dominates this variant, the garment motif dominates the other variant. Israel gave Joseph a sleeved garment as a sign of his special love. The brothers envy him because of it, probably fearing that their father will favor him in the future division of the inheritance (vv 3, 4; a similar motif in the legends of Ishmael, 21:10, and of Jacob and Esau, 25:21ff.; 27). When Joseph eventually came under their control, then, they ripped the hated garment from his body (v 23). Meanwhile, the Ishmaelites arrive. They sell him to them on

Judah's encouragement (vv 25-27, 28aγ). They gain nothing by his death. They can also gain their objective of removing their brother from the excessively partisan love of their father by selling him abroad. When the Ishmaelites depart with Joseph, the garment remains in the hands of his brothers. They dip it in blood and deceive their poor father with it (vv 32-33). The garment and the sale to the Ishmaelites characterize this account, then.

Despite these characteristic differences, both accounts agree in overall outline. Joseph is preferred above his brothers. But this awakens the others' jealousy. When they are alone with him in the field, they want to kill him. But one brother averts their worst intentions for him. Thus a passing caravan takes Joseph to Egypt as a slave. In both recensions, this account in Gen 37 is the beginning of the whole Joseph narrative. Both go on to report how Joseph's fortunes changed in Egypt. Thus both variants rejoice at how good fortune became misfortune, but then misfortune became good fortune through God's intervention. It is especially ingenious that the very love of his father and the wonderful dream at first work to Joseph's disadvantage.

Of the two variants, the dream variant belongs to E, the garment variant to J. J is indicated by Israel, Judah, the expressions בְּזְקֻנִים (v 3; cf. 21:2; 44:20), וַיִּשְׂאוּ עֵינֵיהֶם וַיִּרְאוּ (v 25; cf. 18:2; 33:1), and הַכֶּר־נָא (v 32; cf. 38:25), the dual question (v 32; cf. 18:21; 24:21), and the fact that J cites the statement טָרֹף טֹרַף (v 33) in 44:28. Jacob, Reuben, the significance of dreams, and the beginning of the conversation, "He said to him, 'Here I am' " (v 13; cf. 22:1, 7, 11; 27:1; 31:11) point to E.

As for the details—vv 12, 13a belong together in terms of content (רְעֶה בִשְׁכֶם). Because of "Israel" v 13a belongs to J. V 14 b follows directly ("I will send you," v 13; "He sent him," v 14; "in Shechem, " v 13; "to Shechem," v 14). Vv 13b, 14a are parallel and thus from E. The beginning, "Jacob said to his son, 'Joseph!' " was removed. Vv 15-17 (Joseph comes <402> to Dothan) are probably best attributed to J since E seems to locate the event in the south (as indicated by the fact that later Jacob sets out for Egypt from Beer-sheba [46:5] and it conforms with "the cistern in the steppe," 37:22; cf. Meyer, *Israeliten*, 288n.2). Vv 19, 20 ("dreamer," "dreams") belong to E. The parallel in v 18bβ belongs, then, to J. V 18bα ("before he came near them") is probably the apodosis of v 18bβ and thus stems from J. The two settings for the action, "before he came near them (v 18bα) and "as soon as he had arrived" (v 23), resemble the two "when the sun was about to set" and "but when the sun had set" (15:12, 17, J). Accordingly, v 18a belongs with vv 19, 20 E, with which it fits very well. V 22 stems from E because of the cistern (cf. v 20). V 21 parallels v 22 (E) and belongs therefore to J. "He snatched him from their hand" (v 21) presumes that they had already captured him. This statement properly belongs, then, after v 23. When Joseph came near them, they fell upon him, removed the garment, and who knows what else would have happened! But Judah snatched him from their hand. The redactor did not want to utilize this statement here because he wanted to continue with וַיִּקָּחֻהוּ (v 24) and therefore moved it. The statement, "his garment, the sleeved garment that he wore" (v 23), is notably verbose. Yet this is no variant. Only one account spoke of Jacob's garment (contra Dillmann, Kautzsch-Socin, etc.). Instead, "the sleeved garment that he wore," is probably a (correct) explanatory gloss.

V 24 continues v 22. "The cistern" (v 24) is the one mentioned by Reuben (v 22). "They sat down to eat bread" (v 25) belongs to J. J employs such a minor interlude to allow the Ishmaelites time to arrive. They are not yet present previously for in their presence the brothers would have been afraid to murder their brother. According to this, the brothers remained in place. E imagines things differently. According to E, the brothers moved on, only Reuben "turned back" (v 29). Vv 25-27 are from J. V 28aα,β (through מְדָֽהַבּֽוֹר) are from E. וַיִּמְשְׁכוּ וַיַּעֲלוּ (v 28) are not variants (contra Kautzsch-Socin, Kautzsch³) for only one account spoke of the cistern. Instead, the words are to be taken together to mean "they went up" following §120d (Holzinger). V 28aγ (Ishmaelites) is J. V 28b, "they brought Joseph to Egypt," parallels 39:1 (J) and thus stems from E. The verb הֵבִיא also suggests this. J says הוֹרִיד (v 25; 39:1). Vv 29, 30 (Reuben) are E. The way Jacob learns of Joseph's supposed death is recounted twice. According to the declaration in v 20 E, the brothers simply told him "a wild animal devoured him." This statement recurs in v 33ab and will, therefore, have originally been the brothers' words, not Jacob's, here, too. According to the J report, the brothers "sent over" Joseph's garment dipped in blood (vv 31, 32). They did not come to him themselves, then, and did not directly report Joseph's death to him (so E), but stayed in the field (because they were averse to seeing their father's face) and only indirectly suggested to him (so that no suspicion would fall on them) the conclusion that Joseph was dead. Accordingly, here, too, only one variant spoke of Joseph's garment (contra Dillmann; Kautzsch-Socin; Sievers 2:344, etc.). וַיָּבִיאוּ (v 32) causes difficulties since the brothers did not come along themselves. One may read וַיָּבִיאוּ and attribute v 32aβ through וַיֹּאמְרוּ to E. Of the parallel vv 34b, 35a and 34a, 35b (Dillmann), the latter belongs to E because of "Jacob." "His father" in v 35b contrasts with the "Midianites" in v 36.

Secondarily, later hands contributed a few additions. "Then they hated him even more" (v 5b; absent in LXX mss). "They hated him even more because of his dreams [but nothing has yet been said about a dream] and because of his speech [the reference is to the one in v 2, P]" (v 8). These additions are intended to unify the various motives for the brothers' jealousy. The clause "he told this to his father and his brothers" in v 10 conflicts with the statement "he told this to his brothers" in v 9a. The clause in v 10a, in v 9 in LXX, is probably only a variant reading misplaced in the text.

The fact that two well-rounded and almost completely preserved parallel reports appear confirms these results. This source analysis <403> depends largely on Wellhausen, Dillmann, Kautzsch-Socin, and Holzinger, but goes beyond them in overall concept and in details. Eerdmans (65ff., 70-71) attends in this chapter to two criteria: (1) that "Jacob" alternates with "Israel" and (2) that Joseph was found by the Midianites according to one source and according to the other was sold to the Ishmaelites by his brothers. He attributes vv 3-24, 28a, 29-33, 36 to the "Israel recension" and the rest to the "Jacob recension." In a remarkable esthetic insensitivity, he disregards all the account's minor infelicities and even considers possible the coexistence in the same source of the two chief motifs of the dreams and the sleeved garment, which would have been mutually exclusive for any good, ancient narrator. How much more perceptive in contrast is Sievers's analysis (2:342ff.). In distinction to his predecessors, however, he wants to distinguish two strands in E based on the purported triplet, vv 21, 22, and 25—an unlikely hypothesis, however, given the cohesion of the E recension of this account.

Concerning **1** see pp. 380-81. Concerning **2** see the Joseph narrative in P. **3, 4** *The sleeved garment* J. V **3** begins the Joseph narrative in J. The verse makes a new beginning. That a father loves one son more than the others seems to us a grievous injustice against the others. The ancient Israelite, however, is more subjective than we and less inclined to pay attention to fairness. He would say, "No one can love two children equally" (cf. above pp. 324, 326, 354). Jacob most loves the son of his old age—a pleasant, amiably observed element, common in fairy tales. Both variants presume that Joseph is much younger than the others (E in v 30). Joseph also appears in the birth narrative (30:22ff.)—disregarding the younger, but then still very small Benjamin—as Jacob's youngest son. Admittedly, Jacob is not yet "old" then, and the difference in age between Joseph and the other brothers does not seem very great. One cannot demand strict precision in chronology from the legends. וְעָשָׂה means "he had him one made repeatedly" (according to §112h) as did Hannah (2 Sam 2:19; Ball; Kautzsch³; וַיַּעַשׂ). כְּתֹנֶת פַּסִּים is a shirt that reaches to the פַּסִּים, that is, probably to the extremities (Aqu. χιτῶν ἀστραγάλω, "ankle-length robe"; אֲפָסִים, "ankles"; cf. Franz Delitzsch), thus a long coat with sleeves worn by those who need not work. He treats him like a prince (2 Sam 13:18f.). Normal people wear a short coat with sleeves. Characteristically for the simple circumstances presumed here, a garment with sleeves alone can lead to murder and homicide. **4** For מִכָּל־אֶחָיו Sam and LXX read מִכָּל־בָּנָיו (Ball, Kittel, Kautzsch³). The construction of דַּבְּרוֹ (דִּבֶּר with the personal accusative) is not clearly attested otherwise. One may read דְּבָרוֹ "they could not bear the matter with him [like "the matter with the donkeys," 1 Sam 10:2, or "the matter of Uriah," 1 Kgs 15:5] in peace." Kittel suggests לְדַבֵּר לוֹ.

5-11 *Joseph's dreams* E. The Joseph narrative in E is full of dreams foreshadowing the future. Both of Joseph's dreams mean the same thing. The narrator may have had the brothers two trips to Egypt in mind in narrating two dreams. The first dream of gathering the sheaves is probably also supposed to contain a secretive allusion to the occasion of the grain transaction in Egypt on which the brothers will have to bow before Joseph. This dream seems to presume that Jacob also farmed. The same assumption also underlies 38:12 and probably also 46:31ff. In the other legends, the fathers do not farm, with the exception of the late reports <404> in 26:12 and 30:14. Concerning the fathers' Bedouin lifestyle and farming, see the introduction ¶4.2, 5. In the second dream, the eleven stars mentioned along with the sun and the moon are the constellations of the zodiac which characteristically number twelve according to Babylonian tradition. The twelfth star corresponds to Joseph himself. This is not contradicted by the fact that they are called כּוֹכָבִים which can mean both "star" and "constellation" (cf. ἀστέρων δώδεκα, Rev 12:1). As far as we know, Hebrew had no special word for "constellation." The notion that the sun, the moon, and the stars of the horizon bow down was originally a mythological image. The honor due the highest lord of heaven requires the mightiest beings of the world to bow to him (Psa 148:3; Job 38:7; Rev 4:8-11). In the proper sense, then, this would be the dream which would announce dominion over heaven to a divine child. Many Western and Eastern traditions, in and outside the Bible, transmit a myth recounting the birth of a god. A divine oracle proclaims the child's destiny, enemies seek to thwart the prediction and kill the child, but it is finally fulfilled nevertheless (cf. Rev 12). Often this account is applied to human heroes (cf. Matt 2; cf. "Zum religionsgesch. Verständnis des N.T.," 69f.; Meyer, *Israeliten*, 46-47). Thus it is also to be assumed here that elements of this myth have made their way into the Joseph account. It can also be discerned that this dream vision was not devised for this Joseph narrative, but only reinterpreted in relation to him, from the fact that only one mother is mentioned here, an element which does not fit well in the Joseph narrative. **7** Concerning הִנֵּה see comments on 28:12. **8** In the statement "Will you become our king?" the narrator sees an ominous presentiment concerning the later monarchy of the Joseph tribe. The statement may be poetry (a dual trimeter; Procksch). **10-11** His father scolds him, construing this dream as arrogance. The narrator, however, is not of this opinion. Instead, God gave Joseph these dreams. They were also fulfilled. Rather, the narrator wants to say, "What God had in mind for Joseph was so incredible that even his father could not believe it. Nevertheless, the father remembered the dream with the quiet presentiment that it might still be fulfilled" (Luke 2:19, 51). How did Jacob know about this dream since, according to v 9, Joseph only told his brothers? The narrators are not excessively concerned with such minor details. The minor discrepancy was already noted in the ancient period producing the reading preserved in v 10a (cf. above) which LXX found in the text (v 9a).

12, 13a, 14b J; 13b, 14a E. *Jacob sends Joseph to his brothers.* **12** אֶת־ is unpointed, that is, suppressed by the rabbis. **14** Where, according to this <405> narrative, is Jacob's dwelling place? According to E it is in Beer-sheba (cf. above p. 388). The information in J causes difficulties, however. V 14 expressly mentions Hebron. This agrees with the fact that in J, Jacob has most recently gone to Midgaleder (near Jerusalem?; 35:21-22), just as P also envisions Jacob as dwelling in Hebron (35:27; 49:29ff.; 50:13). Nevertheless, it is very unlikely that a loving, concerned father would send a young boy all alone on a journey as long as the one from Hebron to Shechem. The man who meets Joseph in the field also knows Joseph and his brothers. The result is that the legend transmitted by J imagines Jacob's dwelling in the vicinity of Shechem. מֵעֵמֶק חֶבְרוֹן (v 14) must therefore be an addition, either from the hand of a collector in J who harmonizes the various traditions, or a final redactor who referred to P (cf. Steuernagel, *Isr. Stämme*, 36; Sievers 2:343; Meyer, *Israeliten*, 161n.3). It is also a contradiction within J that Jacob's sons, if they dwelt in the vicinity of Shechem, live, after all, in peace with the citizens of the city, while according to the Dinah legend they had a dispute with them. This, too, points to various, not entirely harmonized traditions. **15-17** J. Joseph receives information from "a man" and follows his brothers to Dothan. Why did the narrator not report from the outset that Joseph's brothers' camped in Dothan? For what purpose did he recount this whole encounter with the man? The narrators report here so superbly, however, that we are justified in seeking the purpose of even the small elements, not to mention of such a significant section. The narrator wants to establish with this interlude how Joseph went so far from his father and fell into his brothers' hands. His father sent him nearby, to Shechem. Now, however, he is lured into following them to Dothan. At Shechem, so near their father, they would certainly have done him no harm. Farther away in Dothan, however, they had power over Joseph. This intermezzo also shows that Jacob must have dwelt not too far from Dothan in J. If he had gone such a long way as that from Hebron to Shechem with Jacob's will and knowledge, it would make no sense to emphasize so strongly that he continued on the much shorter distance to Dothan. Dothan is the current *Tel Dôtân*, twelve km north of Shechem, in the vicinity (southwest) of *Ĝenîn* (cf. Buhl, *Palästina*, 102). שמעיה אמרים would mean, "I heard someone say." Sam, LXX, and Vulg have the better reading שמעתים (Kittel, Kautzsch³; cf. §117f).

18a, 19, 20 E; **18b** J. When the brothers see him, they want to kill Joseph. **18b** On the syntax of הִתְנַכֵּל with the accusative see §117w. The word occurs three times more, only in younger documents. Yet it would be hasty to conclude from this limited material that J could not have written the word (contra Dillmann and Kuenen). **19** "The lord of dreams there" is mocking. Concerning הַלָּזֶה see 24:65. **20** They want to throw the corpse into a cistern so that the murder will <406> not be discovered. "Then we will see what becomes of his dreams" is derisive. When he is dead and his corpse rots in the cistern, his lofty dreams fall away (Franz Delitzsch). The motif of people attempting to thwart an oracle which, nevertheless, is later fulfilled, is dispersed extraordinarily broadly (cf. above pp. 385, 387, 391; further 1 Kgs 22; in Egyptian, Erman, *Äg. Rel.*, 82; in old German, v. d. Leyen, *Märchen in der Edda*, 21; in German, *Grimms Märchen*, no. 29; cf. also Kuhn, *Byzantinische Zeitschr.* 4:241ff.). **21** The redactor has altered "Judah" to "Reuben." **22, 24** E Reuben persuades them not to throw him "into this cistern here in the wilderness" (quite nearby) only after he is dead but immediately, while he still lives (cf. Jer 38:6) in order to deliver him in this way (v 22). And so it is (v 24). The narrators introduced one brother's intercession for Joseph here and in vv 26-27, 29-30 in order to complicate the account and, at the same time, in order to demonstrate through the contrast of one, merciful brother, the magnitude of the others' sin. Reuben's lie of necessity, with such a good objective, is completely permissible for the narrator. What else should Reuben have done? Characteristically, however, all the patriarchs lie occasionally. The reason Reuben offers is horror before spilt blood, especially the blood of a brother (cf. 4:11)! Killing without spilling blood seemed less severe to the ancient. Reuben suggests throwing Joseph into a specific cistern, whereas the brothers previously spoke only unspecifically of "one of the cisterns" (v 20). This element is one of the subtleties of the account. V 24b betrays Reuben's reason: the cistern to which Reuben refers was empty. Reuben sees to it, therefore, that Joseph does not find himself in a cistern where he would drown. A specific cistern is certainly involved here, whose location was known to the narrator (v 22), the Joseph cistern at Dothan. The notion that one does away with a person by putting him in a cistern, alive or dead, through a trick or force, occurs frequently in fairy tales (cf. the literature cited above, pp. 385-86, no. 1; further, perhaps, also Littmann, *Arab. Beduinenerzählungen* 2:25-26, 31-32, and Gonzenbach, *Sicilianische Märchen* 1:252; 2:121-22). Such things still occur today (cf. the report in the *Tägl. Rundschau* (14 July 1909) no. 323, concerning a crime committed a few days earlier in the vicinity of Athens where an apparently dying person thrown into an empty well by the murderer was pulled out by shepherds). It is easy to explain why such things are so common: no one can see into a well and no one can get out without help. There is even less reason, then, to explain the Joseph well as an image for the underworld (contra A. Jeremias, ATAO², 384). **21, 23** J has been edited several times in its current form (cf. above) and may have originally read, "When Judah heard this, he said to them, 'Let us not kill him!' When Joseph, however, came to his brothers, they removed his garment. But he snatched it from their hand." The usual explanation that they removed his garment with the intention of using it later is incorrect. The narrator thinks much more subtly. They ripped the garment from his body without premeditation, in rage over the hated coat. Only later, when Joseph has been sold, and they deliberate how best to <407> inform their father about his disappearance, they note the garment in their hand and decide to employ it for this purpose. On the construction נָכֶּנּוּ נָפֶשׁ see §117ll. LXX mss do not reproduce אֶת־כְּתָנְתּוֹ.

25-27, 28aγ J. Then they sell him, on Judah's advice, to Ishmaelites. **28aα,β,b, 29, 30** E. Midianites steal him from the cistern and take him to Egypt. Reuben, on returning, finds him no longer there. R^JE has unified the two variants by giving the J account (the purchase) preference and by linking it with the E account (Franz Delitzsch). The redactor understood the interlude of eating as a sign of the brothers' hardheartedness (2 Kgs 9:34). J presumes that a caravan highway passed by Dothan. This highway goes from the East (Gilead, v 25) via Bashan through the central Palestinian mountains to the coast and then southward via Lydda to Egypt. It is still a major caravan route (cf. Buhl, *Palästina*, 127; Guthe, ZDPV 8:217-18). E thinks of the highway from Hebron via Beer-sheba to Egypt (Guthe, BE, 713). In such geographical assumptions and information, the old narrators are uncommonly reliable. They know these things from their own lives (cf. 13:10; 18:16). The appearance of Ishmaelites and Midianites in the Joseph legend is a severe anachronism. According to the genealogy, they were the sons of Ishmael or Midian—Joseph's uncles! The legend narrators did not take the genealogy into account here and they envisioned the relationships between the peoples of Palestine as they existed in their own times (similarly in 40:15). **25** The narrator precisely indicates the caravan's homeland and cargo. The Ishmaelites are new figures introduced into the story and he strives to make this new introduction seem as likely as possible. The caravan brings spices from Gilead such as those employed in great quantities and highly valued in Egypt as medicaments, as private and cultic incense, as perfume or breath mints, and for embalming the dead. They originated in Syria and Arabia (cf. Heyes, *Bibel und Ägypten*, 80ff.) There is נְכֹאת—probably tragacanth, the gum of the *Astragalus gummifer* and other *astragalus* varieties "employed for medicinal purposes and as a cohesive, for example, for fixing mummy bindings"; צְרִי (with ו = וּצְרִי)—probably mastic, the resin of the mastic tree, the *Pistacia lentiscus* native to the Cis- and Transjordan and employed as salve (Jer 8:22; 46:11) as well as incense; and לֹט—labdanum, the resin of the *Cistus creicus* (cf. Riehm, HW; Dillmann and Heyes, 86-87)—thus only precious spices obtained in Gilead and exported to Egypt. The legend presumes that Canaan was a passageway for Egypt's international trade in the earliest period. Egyptian reports thoroughly confirm this information (cf. Meyer I[1], ¶238; Heyes, 52ff., 73ff.). Camels are the beasts of burden of Oriental caravan commerce, especially in Arabia. Specifically, "all trade in aromata is conducted by means of camels" (Keller, *Thiere des classischen Alterthums*, 30). **26, 27** Now Judah intervenes for Joseph for the third time. At this point, directly prior to the final decision, he gives an extensive speech. The murderer covers the blood with earth so it cannot "cry out" (4:10; Ezek 24:7; Isa 26:21; Job 16:10). **27** בְּשָׂרֵנוּ is a gloss (Sievers 2:344). Sam, LXX, Pesh, Vulg <408> read וּבְשָׂרֵנוּ (Ball, Kittel, Kautzsch[3]). The alternation between Ishmaelites and Midianites in the variants (and the equation of the two in R^JE) can be explained by the fact that in a certain (and probably rather ancient) period, the Midianites were considered part of the Ishmaelites (Judg 8:24). The E tradition seems to be the later here (concerning Midian, see Meyer, *Israeliten*, 314ff.). Such passing caravans occasionally steal children, the narrator thinks (similar claims are made now of the gypsies). For וַיִּמְשְׁכוּ E has "the Midianites." In contrast, R^JE understands the brothers as the subjects. The price of twenty shekels, that is, ca. fifty marks, is the average price for a half-grown youth (Lev 27:4-5).

30 In pain, Reuben now betrays his original intention. They may as well know now what he wanted. **31, 32aα,γ,b** (cf. above) **33aα,b** J; **32aβ** ("They came to their father and said") **33aβ** E. The brothers inform Jacob of Joseph's death. Here J is more artful than E who recounted a simple report, "Joseph is dead." E is not preserved entirely. The suffix in אֲכָלָתְהוּ has no referent. In J the frequent repetition of the same object, "Joseph's garment, the garment (v 31), the sleeved garment (v 32)," derives from secondary expansion. The sending of a sign such as a bloody garment or the like, whereby the murder which did not really occur is supposed to be falsely proven, is a frequent fairy-tale motif known from Snow White and Genovefa (cf. also Grimm, *Deutsche Sagen*, 437, 534). Regarding הַכָּתֹּנֶת (v 32) see §100l. Jacob's brief and therefore very gripping words are heartrending. They impress the reader indelibly, as do **34a, 35b** E, **34b, 35a** J. *Jacob's sorrow*. The wonderful scene also plays a role in German literature. It is cited in Schiller's, *Räubern* 2:2, where the bloody, deceptive, evidence also appears. This scene is supposed to bring the hearers to full awareness of the magnitude of the crime the brothers have committed! How hard-hearted they must be to cause their old father such pain! One may observe that the emotions of the poor, young Joseph are not portrayed. No modern narrator would have passed over his laments and entreaties. But the ancient narrators have the acting persons primarily in view in the interests of the plot and therefore often pass over the attitudes of the passive figures (cf. introduction ¶3.13). **34** Tearing the clothing is an Israelite mourning practice. Thus passion, sorrow, despair, and horror are expressed (v 29; 44:13; Num 14:6; Josh 7:6; cf. Torge, *Seelenglaube*, 192ff.). Donning sackcloth, that is, a hair loincloth (Schwally, *Vorstellungen vom Leben nach dem Tode*, 11) is a mourning practice, according to Schwally <409> (11ff.) the remnant of a cult of the dead. In contrast, Torge (192ff.) considers it an expression of pain. הִתְאַבֵּל and אָבֵל refer to mourning and performing the mourning ceremonies, thus donning sackcloth, refraining from anointing oneself, sitting in ashes (2 Sam 14:2; Isa 61:3), and undertaking the other rites that express pain (cf. Schwally, 9ff). Jacob does not want "to be comforted" (technical term, see 38:12), but to continue the mourning ceremonies until he dies. This is powerfully expressed. He wants to go to Sheol with ashes still on his head and sackcloth on his loins. This statement presumes that, in the underworld, everyone remains in the state one was in at death (cf. Schwally, 63-64; Stade, *Bibl. Theol.*, 183-84). And thus, in mourning garments, he wants to come to Joseph in Sheol. It is painful comfort to the survivor that there is after all a place of reunion (2 Sam 12:23). It is, however, bleak Sheol! Then Joseph may see, to the extent that the dead can still see, how faithfully his father mourned for him. "All of his sons and daughters" presumes that Jacob had many daughters. The other transmitted traditions know only the one, Dinah. Here, too, then, the Joseph legend follows its own tradition. Quite beautifully this touching description of Jacob's pain is followed (in both sources) by a very straightforward clause: his father cries for him. The comfort of his eyes has been torn from him. The foreigners sell him. To them, he is only a slave. **36** E. One should read מְדָנִים with the versions and above in v 28. Concerning the importing of Asiatic slaves to Egypt see Heyes, *Bibel u. Äg.*, 77, 31ff. פּוֹטִיפַר (variant פּוֹטִי פֶרַע, 41:45; 46:20; LXX Πετεφρης Πευτεφρης. cf. Lagarde, *Genesis graece Vorwort*, 20) is the Egyptian *Petepre* (in a later form), "that which Ra gives." The י is, for the moment, however, unexplainable according to Professor Erman's oral communication. Concerning סָרִיס, "eunuch," see comments on 39:1.

שַׂר הַטַּבָּחִים is probably, in analogy to the "chief baker" and the "chief cupbearer" (40:2), the "chief butcher." The state prison is in the house of this man according to 40:3. This is one of the specifically Egyptian elements that fill the Joseph legend. Since the New Kingdom the principal state offices were in the hands of the Pharaoh's personal slaves (cf. Erman, *Ägypten*, 156). An Egyptian fairy tale, as Professor Erman tells me, has one such lord high steward who is also a butcher. The title רַב טַבָּחִים also occurs in 1 Kgs 25:8ff.; Jer 39:9ff; 52:12ff; and Dan 2:14 in reference to a high-ranking military officer among the Chaldeeans, the "chief bodyguard" (?) in charge of all manner of executions. These different meanings of the title may be explained by the fact that the king's bodyguard was also responsible for slaughtering the animals and for executions. It would thus be understandable that the prison is in the home of the "chief butcher." The fact that this official is called "eunuch" does not seem suitable for the Egyptian situation where even the overseers of the harem are married (cf. Erman, *Ägypten*, 114n.7; contra Heyes, *Bibel und Äg.*, 117ff.).

62. Tamar's Marriage of Necessity 38 J[b]

Source: J. The passage employs יהוה (vv 7bis, 10). Favored Yahwistic expressions are לְבִלְתִּי (v 9), נָא (vv 16, 25), הָבָה "now then" (v 16), and כִּי־עַל־כֵּן (v 26). The account does not belong to the main thread of J which treats the Joseph narrative, but was inserted here only secondarily. This is also clear from the fact that Judah remains with his brothers in the Joseph narratives although according to chap. 38 he has separated from them (once and for all). One may also note that the legend (as in 48:22?) does not presuppose the migration to Egypt, but associates "the settlement of Palestine directly with the ancestors of the tribes and their sons" (38:5; Meyer, *Israeliten*, 422; Luther, idem, 204). The placement of the narrative at <410> this point is not awkward, however. In the Joseph legend a period follows chap. 37 where we hear nothing of the brothers. In the interlude—the hand responsible for the insertion thought—the story in chap. 38 will have taken place. This Judah account is, by nature, related to the other accounts which deal with individual tribes, that is, with the Dinah (Gen 34) and Reuben (35:21-22) legends. Whereas the other legends, to the extent that they mirror historical events, refer mostly to prehistorical circumstances, the Tamar legend as well as the Dinah account reflect events after the entry into Canaan and thus transmit clearly Israelite-specific reminiscences. It is interesting to see that these legends, originally foreign to the others, do not belong as a whole to the main thread of the legends even viewed literarily.

I. **1-11** *Exposition, recounted as briefly as possible.* The following account contains the tribal legend of Judah. It tells of ancient events in this tribe by treating it and its clans as persons in ancient fashion. This original sense of the account was still clear to a degree to the latest period (cf. Num 26:19-22). It has been expounded especially by Stade (*Geschichte Israels* 1:157-58) and discussed by Steuernagel (*Isr. Stämme*, 79), Luther (ZAW 21:56-57, and in Meyer, *Israeliten*, 202ff.), as well as Meyer, 433ff. One must, Meyer emphasizes correctly here too, guard against overpedantically translating every element of the legend directly into history.

1-5 *Judah's separation, marriage, and children.* **1a** Judah parts from his brothers, an element, which, especially for the ancients, is a striking exception (Haller, 94). Stated historically, the tribe of Judah abandoned the other tribes of Israel. This historical event also echoes in the more historically shaped account in Judges 1. According to this account Judah left the common camp and then conquered its later tribal territory. וַיֵּרֶד, "he went down"—The places mentioned subsequently lie on the western slope of the Judaean mountains. Or should וַיָּרֶד (> רוד, "he separated," Gen 27:40) be read? This word seems to be the technical term in the Judah legend. The very difficult passage, Hos 12:1b [EVV 11:12b], seems to refer to the same event with the same expression: "Judah has once again (as already in the ancient period) separated (רָד) from (מֵעִם) God, but he is faithful to the Qedeshim (קְדֵשִׁים)" (Cornill, ZAW 7:287). The second part of the semi-verse 12:1a probably alludes to an account which will have been similar to the second part of Gen 38 with the exception that Judah does not escape as leniently there as here. **1b** Hirah is already introduced here to make the subsequent account comprehensible. Judah sends him to Tamar (vv 12, 20-23). The figure of Hirah cannot have been devised for this purpose, however, for a servant would have been sufficient. It follows that Hirah was originally a legend figure known elsewhere, like Pichol and Ahuzzath in Gerar (chaps. 21, 26; cf. above p. 298) and Deborah, Rebekah's nurse (35:8; cf. above p. 368; Meyer, *Israeliten*, 433n.2; Luther in Meyer, *Israeliten*, 180). The hypothesis that the figure is to be interpreted genealogically is not likely given the nature of the account (Meyer, 434; Luther, 205). Yet, the information is based on the historical memory that the tribe of Judah became involved with Canaanites. Adullam is an ancient Canaanite royal city (Josh 12:15). It is probably *'Id el-Mîye* northeast of Eleutheropolis (cf. Buh., *Pal.*, 193; Guthe, BW, s.v.). Why is the patriarch's dwelling sought here to the west of the later tribal territory? Meyer (*Israeliten*, 435-36) speculates about this.

2 In Adullam he marries the daughter of the Canaanite Shua. The name of this man may have been merely created from Bath-shua, the transmitted name of Judah's wife. בַּת־שׁוּעַ is בַּת־שֶׁבַע in 1 Chron 3:5. In similar fashion <411> יְהוֹשׁוּעַ corresponds to אֱלִישֶׁבַע to אֱלִישׁוּעַ, יְהוֹשֶׁבַע. Is שֶׁבַע/שׁוּעַ the name of a god, perhaps? The legend betrays its advanced age through its innocent discussion of the connubium and commerce of Israelite tribes with Canaanites (differently already in 24:3 J). On the other hand, it is far removed from the events to which it refers. This is evidenced by (1) the whole legend form—Judah is no longer a tribe here, but a person; (2) the fact that the legend has forgotten Judah's military campaign and preserved only the (later) cordial relationship with the Canaanites; and (3) the fact that Simeon, who joined in Judah's military campaign according to Judg 1:3, is no longer mentioned here.

3-5 *The birth of Judah's children, historically, the origin of the clans of Judah.* Reliable tradition is the origination of the three clans of Judah, Er, Onan, and Shelah, from a mixture of Israelite and Canaanite elements in which, however, the Israelite elements were dominant. Concerning Er compare Eri, son of Gad (46:16; Num 26:16); To Onan compare Onam, a Horite clan (36:23; 1 Chron 1:40). For וַיִּקְרָא (v 3), read וַתִּקְרָא with Hebr mss, Sam, Vulg, and Targ. Jon and following v 4-5 (Ball; Spurrell; Sievers 2:345; Kittel; Kautzsch³). When Bathshua bore Shelah (LXX Σηλώμ; cf. the patronymic שֵׁלָנִי) she was living (LXX αὔτη δὲ ἦν = והיא; Dillmann, Ball, Spurrell, Kittel, Kautzsch³) in Kezib (probably = אַכְזִיב, Josh 15:44; Mic 1:14 near Adullam; Guthe, BW, s.v. compares *'Ain el-kezbe* on the *Wadi es sant*). The narrator thinks Shelah continued to live where he was born. The same legend motif appears in 16:11-12; 21:20. The comment that Kezib was Shelah's population center will also be historical.

6, 7 *Er's marriage and death*. The legend tells the tale extremely briefly here. It passes over the boy's growth and Tamar's home and clan. Tamar is a Canaanite, at any rate. According to vv 13, 24 (וַיֵּרֶד), and especially according to v 25—Judah is not present at the execution—she stems not from Adullam, Judah's dwelling place, but according to v 14 and, especially clearly, to v 21 (מֵעֵינַיִם) from Enaim. Wellhausen (*Composition*[2], 355n.1) and Steuernagel (*Isr. Stämme*, 79) associate Tamar with the city of the same name in the Negeb. But Enaim, Tamar's home according to v 21, is far removed from this city. The name "Tamar" (palm) also occurs elsewhere, especially in Judah, as a personal name (2 Sam 13:1; 14:27). Among the Israelites (Cant 7:8-9) and the old Arabic poets "palm" was a favored image for the beloved (G. Jacob, *Altarab. Beduinenleben*, 53), and thus a very suitable feminine name. The Egyptians also call the beautiful woman "a palm of love" (Heyer, *Bibel u. Äg.*, 135). Hardly a single element in the following account points to the fact that the Tamar figure originated genealogically. The figure will therefore be of a different origin (cf. Luther, ZAW 21:57; idem in Meyer, *Israeliten*, 205; Meyer, 434). Er's sin is also suppressed. The narrator reports only the absolutely necessary elements here. A similar, very brief exposition occurs in the book of Ruth (1:1-6). V 7 is based on the general principle that an early death is a great calamity and Yahweh's punishment (Prov 10:27; etc.). People who die too soon must, then, have committed some sin against Yahweh.

8-10 Onan neglects the levirate duties and dies. וְהָיָה וְשִׁחֵת (v 9) describes a repeated act (§112ee). Concerning אִם־בָּא see §159c. The legend presumes the practice that the surviving brother is obligated to father children with his sister-in-law. The firstborn is then considered the child of the deceased brother. This is "levirate marriage" (Lat. *levir* = brother-in-law; <412> Deut 25:5ff.). This very widely dispersed practice is explained variously: either as a remnant of polyandry, in which a group of brothers had a common wife and the children belonged to them in common (Robertson Smith, *Kinship and Marriage in Early Arabia*, 137), or from the wish to obtain a cult for the deceased which only his sons could perform (Stade, *Gesch. Isr.* 1:393-94; *Bibl. Theol.*, 188; Schwally, *Leben nach dem Tode*, 28; Marti, *Gesch. der isr. Rel.*[5], 57-58), or, most simply, from the fact that "wives are valuable objects retained in the family and the tribe if at all possible" and thus were passed on as an inheritance to the survivors (H. Schurz, *Altersklassen und Männerbünde*, 181; cf. Wellhausen, *Nachrichten der Kgl. Ges. der Wissenschaften zu Göttingen* [1893], 455-56, 461). Additional bibliography: Winer, *Bibl. Realwb.*, s.v. "Leivratsehe"; Spiegel, *Erânische Alterthumskunde* 3:678; G. Jacob, *Altarab. Parallelen zum AT*, 14, 24; Rauh, *Hebr. Familienrecht*, 39-40. The OT sources make clear to us the notions which the Israel historically accessible to us associated with this practice. There we find no trace that the practice was explained as veneration of the dead. Nothing in the Tamar narrative points to this cult. In contrast, the notion that Yahweh, himself, protects this obligation indicates that the legend, itself, knows nothing of the cult of the dead. Yahweh would not protect a cult which was not dedicated to him, would he? Instead, the ancient Israelite, if asked about the purpose of levirate marriage, would surely have maintained that this practice was carried out in love for the deceased so that his name may be preserved and so that his property may be passed on to heirs of his name (Deut 25:6; Ruth 4:10). Onan does not publicly neglect fulfilling this fraternal duty. It must, therefore, have been a very well-established practice. But he thwarts the matter by trickery. His motive is selfishness. He wants to beget his own children, not another man's. He wants to preserve his own name and have his brother's inheritance himself. His sin, therefore, is lack of love for his deceased brother, not the sexual aberration named for him. Consequently Yahweh kills him. One may note the view of God underlying this account. Yahweh's eyes see even the deepest secrets which no human eye sees. He protects the one who cannot help himself, the deceased whose rights are neglected (the mistreated slave, Gen 16; the crying child, Gen 12; the foreigner without rights, Gen 12:10ff.; etc.). The historical tradition presumed in vv 6-10 is that Er and Onan were lost as independent clans very early (Meyer, *Israeliten*, 434). Later Er was included in Shelah (1 Chron 4:21) and Onan in Jerahmeel (1 Chron 2:26).

11 *Tamar's return.* According to the law, Shelah must take his brother's place. But Judah did not want this because he fears for the life of his youngest son. He believes, then, that Tamar was somehow guilty of her husbands' deaths. A superstition lies in the background here, in any case, also very common elsewhere, according to which the first marital intercourse is or can be dangerous. This belief produced the narrative motif of the beautiful maiden whose embrace brings death (cf. Tob 3:7ff. and Wilh. Hertz, "Sage von Giftmädchen," in the *Gesammelten Abhandlungen* [1905], 156ff., with an extensive bibliography). Such a superstition existed in Israel in all periods. It is literarily attested, however, usually only <413> in later epochs. Further removed is the notion that Ishtar brings death to her lovers (Stucken, *Astralmythen*, 16; A. Jeremias, ATAO², 110, 381) since this does not occur through an embrace. Judah sends Tamar home on a pretext: Shelah is still too young. He wants to be rid of the burdensome, persistent woman who repeatedly reminds him of her rights and the rights of her husband. This becomes particularly evident in the fact that Tamar's father does not live nearby. It is apparently standard practice for the childless widow to return to the household of her father (Lev 22:13; Ruth 1:8ff; one should probably read שְׁבִי and וַתֵּשֶׁב in light of Lev 22:13 despite Isa 47:8 and with Ball). Concerning Tamar's legal status upon her return see Rauh, *Hebr. Familienrecht*, 18: the childless widow can choose to return under her father's roof (as in *Od.* 2:114-15). Notably, the narrator, in rare fashion, explicitly reports Judah's thoughts. We are supposed to know that it was indeed a serious injustice to the dead son and the daughter-in-law. But it would also be excusable since it was inspired by paternal love for the final survivor! The narrator does not state Tamar's attitude when she returns to her father's household although they are the lever for all that follows. They seem obvious to the narrator. At any rate, they can be discerned from Tamar's subsequent actions. The Israelite woman considers bearing children the purpose of her life. Her honor at home and among the people depends upon children. Childlessness is a disgrace. A woman's worst fate is to be returned as a childless widow to her father's house where she may be driven by mockery into a corner to lament. Thus, finally, the complicated exposition is complete. Now the narrator comes to the chief matter and, therefore, becomes even more thorough.

II. 12-26 *Tamar obtains the seed denied her through trickery.* **12-19** *The meeting with Judah.* **12** The death of Judah's wife interrupts the Tamar narrative and would not be necessary for the account and thus must be significant given the narrator's brevity to this point. The emphasis is on the fact that Judah only went to the *Qedeše* after his wife died. The narrator wants to excuse Judah, then. This element is significant because it demonstrates that it was already considered at least unpleasant in ancient times for a husband to visit a whore. In zeal to distinguish the periods and not to import modern concepts into antiquity, modern scholars have occasionally portrayed Israelite antiquity too crudely and maintained that adultery was only prohibited in ancient practice for the wife; but the husband was fully free to engage in sexual intercourse (cf., e.g., Benzinger^2, 105; Nöldeke, ZDMG 40:155). This is also surely the oldest legal state in Israel. Our passage shows, however, that a finer moral sensibility already existed in ancient Israel. וַיְנַחֶם is a technical term for certain rites intended to comfort mourners during the funeral celebrations. The narrator wants to say that Judah previously related to his wife very righteously. Then Judah went to the sheepshearing. At the sheepshearing where the result of a whole year's labor comes in, the lord himself sees after his flocks (31:19) and makes a "good day" for his servants, comparable to the harvest feasts (1 Sam 25:2ff.). גזז means "sheepshearing" in 1 Sam 25:7 and 2 Sam 13:23-24. Should it be pronounced גֹּזְזִים (Ehrlich)? עַל would suit this pronunciation (1 Sam 25:8). Judah's flocks graze up in the mountains (וַיַּעַל) near Timnah (= the ruin site Tibneh northeast of Adullam). Judah himself dwells below in Adullam, where—as the legend may assume—he farms. Enaim (probably = הָעֵינַיִם Josh 15:34; §88c; location unknown), where Tamar dwells, is on the way (v 14). Hirah goes with Judah, perhaps as his guest at the feast (2 Sam 13:23ff.). This accompaniment is <414> necessary for the narrator because Judah later sends Hirah from Timnah to Enaim (v 20).

13, 14 Tamar uses this good opportunity when her father-in-law passes through her home. In the old style, her thoughts are not indicated (cf. introduction ¶3.12), but at least her observations are. She knows now that she was sent home on a pretext. The family of her husband heaps disgrace on the head of their own, her dead husband! Then the brave woman decides to obtain her right, when she cannot demand it of the son, from the father, brought to her by chance. How does the legend judge this intercourse with her father-in-law? Not as is the rule in such cases (contra Benzinger^2, 288, and Nowack 1:345, who speak of the father-in-law's duty). Judah would have never freely agreed to this intercourse (v 16), just as, later, he did not approach his daughter-in-law too closely (v 26). Instead, the brave and wily Tamar does something here which totally contradicts custom. But, on the other hand, this is not criminal "incest" (contra Reuß, 286n.3; Wellhausen, *Composition*^{3}, 48, etc.), not to mention the fact that according to ancient Hebrew thought, no true kinship exists between a man and his daughter-in-law (Nöldeke, ZDMG 40:150). Judah, himself, says (v 26) that Tamar is in the right. This is no more incest in the ancient view than we would consider killing in war to be murder or that we would scold someone for indecency who publicly disrobed in order to save someone from drowning. Instead, Tamar's bravery consists in the fact that she surmounts common prejudice and takes her right to man's seed from her husband's family where she can get it. In order to acquire this right, however, the energetic woman does the most extreme thing an honorable woman can do. She becomes like the despised harlot. She undertakes something which, in normal circumstances, would be subject to the vilest and most horrible death penalty. She courageously risks life and honor. But, simultaneously, as a genuine matriarch of Judah, she arranges everything so cleverly that the dangerous path finally leads to the fortunate destination. Thus, the old legend rejoices over the energetic and clever woman. Tamar's fame has not yet been forgotten in Ruth 4:12. According to v 14, the widow wears mourning clothes her life long (Judg 8:5; 10:3; 2 Sam 14:2, "marital duty endures beyond the death of the spouse," Rauh, *Hebr. Familienrecht*, 17). According to vv 14, 15, the קְדֵשָׁה is also easily recognizable (cf. Prov 7:10): Her face covered with a veil, she sits by the way (the latter notion in Jer 3:2; Ezek 16:25; also Babylonian practice, EpJer 43). Those who have intercourse with her do not learn her identity. What may have been the origin of the practice of veiling the *Qedešim*? It may be associated with the veiling of the bride (G. Jacob, *Hoheslied*, 36) and both may be associated with the veil worn by Ishtar (A. Jeremias, ATAO[2], 110n.1, 381; Benzinger[2], 78). Yet, in ancient Israel, along with the veiled, there were also generally known whores, for example, those who also ran a sort of inn for travelers (Josh 2:1; this is the source for the comparison of the commercial city with the whore house in Isa 23:15ff.; Nah 3:4; Rev 18:3). וַתְּכַס (v 14), "She made herself a covering, she covered herself," as in Deut 22:12 (Jon 3:6) is like וַיְגַלַּח in 41:14, "he made himself a shearing, he sheared himself." Sam reads וַתְּתְכַּס (Kittel).

15-18 Judah enters the trap laid for him. The veil causes him to consider her a "whore." **15** The *Qedeše* is, therefore, and because of v 21, a type of whore (contra Luther in Meyer, <415> *Israeliten*, 179-80). At the same time, the veil—as the narrator expressly states in v **16**—prevents him from recognizing her. If he had recognized her he surely would not have touched her. אֶל־הַדֶּרֶךְ (v 16) is probably better read with v 21 עַל־הַדֶּרֶךְ (Ball). LXX reads ו אֵת ὁδόν. Kittel prefers אֵת־. Tamar asks for the "harlot's gift" (אֶתְנַן זוֹנָה Mic 1:7; Hos 2:14; 9:1). Judah promises her a goat **17**. Samson also presents himself to a woman with a goat (Judg 15:1). The practice of giving a goat on such occasions will stem from the fact that it is holy to the goddess of love and the sacrificial animal of her courtesans. This is attested in Greek tradition (cf. Dillmann and Roscher, *Lex.* I, cols. 395, 419). The clever Tamar wants a pledge, however. נָתַן עַד means "to give (to hold) until" (cf. 1 Sam 1:11), לָקַח means "to receive and keep" (v 23), שׁוּב means "to return home and remain" (v 11). In fact, **18** she wants his seal ring, chain, and staff. "Every Babylonian carries a seal ring and an artfully caved staff (מַטֶּה in contrast to מַקֵּל, a natural stick; 30:37; 32:11) and every staff bears an emblem of an apple, a rose, a lilly, an eagle, or something. For no one may carry a staff without a distinctive symbol" (Herodotus I.195). The ancient Egyptians also know such seal rings as well as such deluxe staves (cf. Erman, *Ägypten*, 314-15). According to Gen 38, it was considered obvious in ancient Israel that every important man, even when he journeys, brings seal and staff along with him. One wears the seal ring on the right hand (41:42; Jer 22:24) or on a cord around the neck (Cant 8:6). The latter practice also occurs among the Babylonians (Friedrich, BA 5:456). Egyptians wear seal stones around the neck and, since the New Kingdom, also seal rings on the finger (cf. Newberry, *Scarabs* [1906]). Yet the פְּתִיל (v 18; פְּתִילִים v 25) seems to have been a separate pendant (perhaps with an amulet). Such cords with amulets appear among the ancient Egyptians (cf. Erman, *Äg. Re.*, 144, 161) and Arabs (cf. Wellhausen, *Arab. Heidentum*[2], 164ff.). One employs the seal (on which the name of the owner, the image or symbol of his god, and the like are engraved, Friedrich, BA 5:457) especially to sign contracts. No contract is valid in Babylonia without a seal. Similarly, envelopes, doors, trunks, jars, and cargo shipments were sealed against slaves or thieves (Heyes, *Bibel u. Ägypten*, 236-37). A seal is, therefore, an almost indispensable thing (Friedrich, BA 5:456-57). Written contracts must have also been a common practice in Israel in this period when every leading person carries a seal. According to Barth (ZDMG 44:685-86) חוֹתָם is an Egyptian loan word. "The Egyptian seal stone (the 'scarab') was the prototype of the seal for the whole world at the time" (Erman, ZDMG 46:117). Representations of ancient Israelite seals can be seen in Benzinger², 82, 225; Greßmann, *Altorient. Texte u. Bilder* 2:101ff. The clever Tamar chooses a pledge, then, capable of demonstrating Judah's paternity beyond all doubt. The fact that Judah gives away such important objects (Hag 2:23) shows his lust.

20-23 Judah sends Hirah (from Timnah) with <416> the goat. A man such as Judah cannot himself require his pledge of the harlot. As is the case of intercourse with the harlot, this is something a leading man does, to be sure, but he does not publicly discuss. In this context the passage is intended to establish that the pledge remained in Tamar's hands. It is much more extensive, however, than would be necessary to make this point. The discussion between Judah and Hirah (vv 22-23), especially, could easily be omitted. But the narrator values the fact that Judah is entirely innocent in this matter, פֶּן נִהְיֶה לָבוּז, so that no slanderous suspicion may arise that such a wealthy man would fail to pay a poor harlot her wages! It is further noteworthy that Judah does not want to search further for the *Qedeše*, apparently because he does not want to publicize his intercourse with her. One sees in these examples that the narrator took pains to recount the objectionable story as wholesomely and gently as possible. The same is true of 19:33. Remarkably, *Qedešim* are discussed very innocently here (without abhorrence or anger). Such people exist, as everyone knows. It is another question, however, as to who becomes involved in this practice and who goes to her. Religious prostitution (קְדֵשָׁה, Assyr. *qadištu*, > קָדַשׁ, "to be holy") plays a great role since antiquity among the peoples of the Near East (a rich bibliography in W. Hertz, *Gesammelte Abhandlungen*, 216n.2) and was, as can be seen from this passage among others, also well known in ancient Israel. Israel may have learned these things from the Canaanites (Tamar is a Canaanite, after all). They were only finally eradicated from Israel through the prophets' polemic (cf. Stade, *Geschichte Israels* 1:480; *Bibl. Theol.* ¶66; Benzinger², 360). Luther (in Meyer, *Israeliten*, 177ff.) sees the *Qedešim* as virgins of whom, as in Babylonia and Cyprus (Herodotus I.199), Israelite custom also required a onetime public offering. This cannot be demonstrated, however, from Hos 4:13-14. For מְקֹמָה (v 21), Sam, LXX, and Pesh have הַמָּקוֹם as in v 22 (so Ball; Sievers 2:345; Kittel; Kautzsch³). The first reading is preferable, however, since it makes the situation clearer. The narrator presumes here that Tamar stems from Enaim, which later redactors no longer understood.

24-26 After three months, Tamar's pregnancy is apparent and Judah is informed. For כְּמִשְׁלֹשׁ (v 24) Sam reads כְּמִשְׁלֹשֶׁת (Ball; Kittel; Sievers 2:346; §97c) which represents "about (כְּ) after (מִן §119y n.1) three months." הָרָה לִזְנוּנִים (v 24) means "to become pregnant through harlotry," like "pregnant by a man" (v 25; see §121f). The results of immorality make the crime more serious. Judah commands that she be burned. The assumptions are (1) adultery by the wife is punished by burning in Israel (the same penalty in Lev 21:9 for harlotry by a priest's daughter and among the Egyptians, Herodotus 2.111; Ranke in Greßmann, *Altorient. Texte u. Bilder* 1:218). According to another (later) practice the adulteress must suffer death by stoning (Deut 22:23-24; Ezek 16:40; John 8:5). The execution of this penalty was especially disgraceful for the woman. She is stripped naked before her lover (Ezek 16:27, 28; Hos 2:5,12 is to be understood in this way). The whole population looks on in disgust <417> and derision (Ezek

16:38ff.). This is the precondition for the following. Very noteworthy is the extreme severity with which adultery was regarded and which diverges very remarkably from the religious prostitution practiced in the same period. One sees in this example that ancient people who knew the institution of *Qedešim* could be very strict in marital life. Characteristically for ancient perspectives, the fundamental distinction in the judgment of immorality depends on whether the husband or the wife commits it (cf. however, above on v 12). (2) Tamar is considered a wife. She is legally Er's wife to whom she is still obligated, or—the effect would be the same—Shelah's betrothed. Consequently, she is under the jurisdiction of her father-in-law, not of her own father. The patriarch has the right of life and death over his whole household (cf. 31;32).

25 Regarding the syntax of the clause, "She had already been brought out when she sent," see §116u,v and §142e. "To bring out" is a technical term as in Deut 22:21, 24; Judg 6:30; 1 Kgs 21:10; Sir 23:24; SusLXX 42, 62; SusTheod 43. "Out" means outside the door of her father's household (Deut 22:21; to the city gate, Deut 22:24; outside the city, 1 Kgs 21:13, or outside the "camp," Lev 24:14; Num 15:35-36). Why did Tamar not reveal herself to Judah immediately after their intercourse? She could have avoided the extreme shame of the procedure at the death site. She did not do so because she wanted to force her father-in-law to publicly legitimize her offspring. The courageous and clever woman accepts even the most extreme injury. The narrator, however, is glad to introduce this scene in order to utilize the tension to the last moment (cf. the account of Isaac's sacrifice). For לְאִישׁ one should read לְאִישׁ with LXX (Holzinger, Kautzsch[3]). The form הַחֹתֶמֶת (חֹתָם v 18) and the plural פְּתִילִים (v 18 singular, as is this passage in Sam, LXX, and Vulg) are noteworthy. 26 Judah confesses. "She is more just than I." This is also the narrator's opinion. She did the only thing left to her in her extreme need. צָדֵק מִן also occurs in Job 4:17. כִּי־עַל־כֵּן (18:5; 19:8; 33:10; 38:26; Num 10:31; 14:42), "for to this purpose or end" (Franz Delitzsch), appears in discourse when one secondarily imputes to another or to oneself a purpose one had not previously intended. How Tamar was lead away from the judgment site, how she now gained life and honor instead of disgrace and death, highly praised among women, the pride of her father's house and of her whole village, the glory of her descendants to the present day (cf. Ruth 4:12)—all of this the narrator omits. The style requires that the account be concluded as soon as possible when the climax of the story has been reached. One sees all the more the fact that the narrator considers it important to emphasize that Judah had no further relations with her. He takes offense, after all, at this intercourse with the daughter-in-law.

III. 27-30 *A briefly recounted conclusion, the birth of Perez and Zerah.* The fact that Tamar bears twins is—so the old legend probably thinks—a just reward for her heroism. Yahweh blessed her womb. Here, too, historical events seem to be mirrored. The Judaean clans Perez and Zerah formed after the demise of the older clans Er and Onan. Zerah appears as the name of an Edomite clan in 36:13, 33. The legend of the birth of these two is a variant of the legend of Jacob and <418> Esau (25:24-26; 38:27 parallels verbatim 25:24). Is this element "to be understood [merely] novelistically as an effort to illustrate that the firstborn was almost not the firstborn" (Luther in Meyer, *Israeliten*, 203; Meyer, *Israeliten*, 435), or are historical realities echoed here, too: that for a period Zerah seems the firstborn, that is, the mightier, then, however, it was Perez (from which David stems, 1 Chron 2; Stade, *Gesch. Isr.* 1:158-59)? At the same time, the legend explains the names:

Perez means "tear" because the child broke forcefully in front of his brother. It is said of Zerah that the midwife tied a red (scarlet) thread on him. This element is surely supposed to mean something, indeed, to motivate the name clearly. In west Aram. crimson is called זְחוֹרִי, in Syr זְחוֹרִיתָא, in Bab *zahuritu*. וַיִּתֶּן (v 28) implies that "one of them" reached out (§144d). For כְּמֵשִׁיב (v 29) one should read כְּמוֹ הֵשִׁיב with Ball (19:15) or כְּהָשִׁיבוֹ with Spurell and Kittel. מָה is a reproachful question. עָלֶיךָ means "for you" (20:3). Hebr mss, Sam, Pesh, Targ. Jon, Holzinger, and Kautzsch[3] read וַתִּקְרָא.

General Remarks concerning Tamar's Marriage of Necessity

The material in this chapter consists of two allogenous elements: (1) the account of the origin of the clans of Judah at the beginning and end of the whole unit and (2) the Tamar legend proper comprising the central passage. One can still clearly see from the style that the two materials differ. The first is arranged briefly, in the manner of a notice; the second is a beautiful, extensive narrative. The first material mostly echoes a tribal narrative; the second, however, contains legend material of a different nature. Thus, the Israelite element seems to have been added secondarily in this legend, too (cf. also Luther, ZAW 21:57; idem, in Meyer, *Israeliten*, 177ff.).

The central section, the Tamar account proper, is woven together from three motifs. (1) The account of the widow who maintains fidelity to her husband after his death and is finally rewarded with the decedant's child. The same motif, but in a much more delicate form, appears in the Ruth novella, whose narrator also expressly recalls Tamar as a example from the early period. In both cases, the means whereby the widow gets children secondarily is "levirate marriage." That the account did not simply grow out of this institution is evident, however, in the fact that both recensions emphasize that they would never have gotten children in the regular way. The relatives do not want the marriage at first. The same motif also occurs without levirate marriage in the Egyptian myth of Isis who also conceives a child by her deceased spouse, namely, after she has resurrected the deceased through magic (Erman, *Äg. Re.*, 34ff.). (2) The other motif, that the daughter conceives a child with the father—here with the father-in-law, against his will—is combined in the Tamar legend with the motif of the widow's rewarded fidelity. We know this motif from the much cruder legend of Lot's daughters (and another similar legend from Smyrna, cf. above p. 217). The Judith legend is more remotely related. It, too, shows the bravery and cunning of a woman who risks her honor for a higher purpose. (3) A variation of the motif of a woman found guilty of adultery and already "brought out" whose innocence is demonstrated in the last moment occurs in the "Story of Susannah." The narrator has artfully spun a whole from these different motifs (cf. Luther in Meyer, *Israeliten*, 200). The account obviously sides <419> with Tamar and is able lovingly to portray this pious, clever, and effective figure. In contrast, the "opponent" of Tamar, Judah, is not an as equally sharply defined, realistic personality. The narrator has, indeed, brought together many details about him, but no clear image comes into being from all of these details. The reason for the phenomenon is that the narrator seems intent on excusing Judah as much as possible. The apologetic secondary intention hindered him from depicting the figure of the patriarch concretely.

One gains the impression, then, that the narrative will have earlier been much more earthy. In this presumed earlier recension some chief characteristic of Judah's which motivated his actions must have been vitally portrayed. This will have been his sensuality, his intercourse with *Qedeŝim*, known to his daughter-in-law, which became the basis for her plan. It seems that such a recension is presumed in Hos 12:1, "But he was faithful to *Qedeŝim*." But the current recension still bears many features of extreme age. It is one of the "most earthy" legends and, in terms of its central subject matter, is thoroughly profane in character. The "didactic undertone" found in it (Dillmann, Driver)—that it intends to inculcate the duty of levirate marriage—is in reality quite remote. Instead it employs this practice as a novelistic motif.

63. The Adulterous Egyptian Woman 39:1-20a J (E)

Source, unity, and origin of the account. The passage falls into two sections: I. Joseph's favor in the house of the Egyptian who finally conveys upon him the office of majordomo (vv 1-6); II. the love and hatred of the Egyptian woman whereby Joseph ends up in prison (vv 7-20a).

Both sections stem essentially from J. According to E, Joseph was bought by the chief butcher Potiphar immediately after he was brought to Egypt (37:26) and, since Potiphar was also prison warden (40:3), he became a prison guard through his special favor (40:4). With this, Joseph's fortunes already begin to rise, for by means of an acquaintance he made in prison he is ultimately elevated to lord of Egypt. The low point of Joseph's suffering in E lies in the fact that he was sold as a slave. J differs. J lowered the depths to which Joseph was brought by construing Joseph's prison life as a special misfortune. Thus he recounts that Joseph came first to an unnamed Egyptian man. Soon highly regarded and even majordomo, he came under suspicion of a severe crime and was therefore thrown into prison. Here the low point of his fate consisted not so much in the fact that he became a slave, but in that something even worse happened to him: as a slave he was also thrown into prison. Thus, the contrast to his subsequent brilliant rise becomes even sharper. At the same time, his lot becomes even more colorful and varied. First he was his father's favorite child, then he was sold into Egypt. Here he first held a position of honor, then he found himself again in suffering and now in deepest distress, in disgrace in jail. Finally, however, he was elevated and become the second most powerful man in the land of Egypt. The narrator alternately frightens and gladdens his hearers in order finally to remove all our concerns for Joseph. The redactor (R^{JE}) inserted this interlude from J into the plot of E by equating "the Egyptian" of J and the "Potiphar" of E through the interpolation פּוֹטִיפַר סְרִיס פַּרְעֹה שַׂר הַטַּבָּחִים (39:1). This produced the difficulty, however, that "the Egyptian" who has a wife (J) is also a "eunuch" (from which many exegetes have concluded that eunuchs could also be married or that סָרִיס does not mean "eunuch" here as it normally does), and further, that the same man who, deeply offended, throws him into prison, honors him with his special trust in this same prison (40:4 E).

The fact that Gen 39 derives in toto from J is also indicated by the following: the Ishmaelites in v 1 (E Midianites; <420> cf. comments on Gen 37), 39:1 ‖ 37:28b, 36 (E), יהוה (vv 2, 3bis, 5bis), הִצְלִיחַ (vv 3, 23; cf. 24:21, etc.), בִּגְלַל (v 5; cf. 30:27), and הוֹרִד and הוּרַד (v 1; cf. comments on 37:28). The formula וַיְהִי אַחַר הַדְּבָרִים הָאֵלֶּה (v 7), common in E, also occurs in 22:20 in J.

E cannot have possessed the second of the two parts. This is excluded by the course of the action in E (cf. above). In contrast, one misses between 37:26 and 40:1 a statement concerning how Joseph came to be so highly regarded by the prison warden that he conveyed upon him the status of prison trustee (40:4). One expects a description similar to the one in 39:1-6. This passage itself, however, it so extensive that it seems reasonable to assume that clauses from E have been incorporated into it. One may well designate the following as such interpolations (following Dillmann, etc.): וַיְהִי אִישׁ מַצְלִיחַ (v 2; הַצְלִיחַ means "to have good fortune," while it is used in vv 3, 23 [J] of Yahweh and means "to give good fortune"), further וַיְשָׁרֶת אֹתוֹ (in v 4a; cf. 40:4; Exod 33:11, according to which Joseph becomes a personal servant while in v 4b and in the following account he became, rather, administrator of the household). If one also includes "Joseph found grace in his eyes" (v 4aα; the expression מָצָא חֵן is common in J, but also occurs elsewhere; cf. Holzinger, Hexateuch, 97-98), then one obtains a passable unit.

The J account is relatively broad in the following sections. With many repetitions, even in wording, the account progresses slowly and tranquilly. One must warn modern interpreters, however, against seeking to improve this style by omitting the "unnecessary" (contra Holzinger). There may be additions here and there, but they cannot be identified in most cases in such narrative styles. Kautzsch[3] attributes v 6a to E and overlooks the fact that this statement clearly prepares for v 8 (J in his view, too). Similarly, v 6b, Joseph's beauty, is a necessary precondition for the following account and must also be attributed to J (contra Holzinger). Procksch's attempt to separate vv 7-10 from what follows and attribute them to E is a sin against esthetics. In this way, the first portion of the account would be without consequence and the second without exposition. Regarding אלהים (v 9) see the commentary. The two parts are needlessly related through שָׁכְבָה עִמִּי (vv 7, 12; cf. 10, 14). Eerdmans (66-67) considers Gen 39 an independent account, inserted here secondarily as the result of a misunderstanding of 40:15 and 41:14. But 40:15 clearly refers back explicitly to this account.

In terms of the material's origin, both parts clearly diverge from one another. The first part was already given with the Joseph legend. A similar brief report in E (cf. above) is a parallel as is the immediately following account in which Joseph, in prison, found grace and trust once again as Yahweh's blessed (vv 21-23). Here, then, J gives the same motif two variations. For further examples of the same phenomenon see below. The narrative of the adulteress is an account of its own. This account, with no perceptible etiological or historical reference, to be termed a "novella" given its detailed narrative style, has been inserted here by the narrator for the esthetic reasons shown above. Since this novella offers little enough characteristic of Joseph, it seems particularly appropriate to assume that it is foreign material only secondarily applied to Joseph. An Egyptian fairy tale deals with a similar motif. The account occurs in the Papyrus d'Orbiney and has been published in German by Erman (Ägypten, 505ff.) and by Ranke (in Greßmann, Altoriental. Texten u. Bildern 1:223ff., etc.). Two brothers live very intimately in the same house. Once when the elder was not at home and the younger entered the house by chance, the wife of the elder attempted to seduce the younger. Yet he indignantly refused her and hurried back to the field. But when the elder brother came home toward evening, the wife presented herself as though she had been violently mistreated and accused the younger brother. Then the elder brother became as savage as a panther and wanted to kill the other. The continuation explicates other fairy tale motifs. Analyses of it can be found in Mannhardt, *Zeit-schrift für deutsche Mythologie* 4:232ff.; v. d. Leyen <421> 115:6ff; and A. Lang, *Myth, Ritual, and Religion: New Impressions* 2:318ff.

The motif of the wife who first pursues the young man dwelling in the same house with her and related to her in kinship or other bonds of fidelity, and then, scorned, accuses him of seduction and thus brings him to ruin, is frequent among the Greeks. The legend of Hippolytos and Phaedra is especially well known. Similarly "the wife of an Anagyrasian who had invited the wrath of the hero Anagyros falsely accuses her stepson as a result of scorned love." "The son of Cycnos, Tennes, seeks to ruin his repudiated stepmother Philonome; Phrixos his stepmother Demodike. Anteia or Sthenoboia behaves similarly for the same reason toward Bellerophontes, the vassal of her husband; the wife of Akastos toward his guest Peleus; Ochna, a Tanagreean maiden, toward Eunostos" (J. Ilberg, "Phaedra," in Roscher, *Lex.* 3:2224-25, who lists further usages of this motif in Greek literature and collects a series of related Oriental accounts [following Puntoni, *Studi di mitologia* 1:109ff.], including the widely dispersed, originally Indian framework account of the seven wise masters [the Syriac version in Fr. Baethgen, *Sindban und die sieben weisen Meister*, 13ff.] and the account of Combabos transmitted from the Syrian Hierapolis [Ps.-Lucia, *de dea Syria*, 23]). The following Indian accounts are to be considered: the account of Sundaraka, who rejects the offer of love made by her husband's teacher whereupon he tore his outer garment and showed it to her husband, "See, Sundaraka pounced on me and tore my garment" (*Somadeva Bhaṭṭa*, 20:140ff.; in Brockhaus, *Sammlung orientalischer Märchen* I/2:59); further, the account of Prince Kumala, who resists the love of his stepmother who has him blinded through a falsified command of his father Aśoka (*Divyavadana*, 405ff.; cf. Oldenberg, *Buddha*[4], 341-42; Kern-Jacobi, *Buddhismus* 2:394ff.); finally, an account in Katha saritlegendra is also similar (translated by C. H. Tawney 2:80-81). The Persian legend of Sijavush is famous. He scorned Sudhabe, his father's wife. She then lacerated her face and shredded her garment and told the king that his son desired her (in *Firdausis Shahname*, translated by Grafen Schack, 2:84ff.). A similar story was told about Constantine's son Crispus and his stepmother Fausta (Zonoras, *Epitome* 13.2 [Dindorf 2:179]; for a modern Arabic variant see Littmann, *Arabische Beduinenerzählungen* 2:30-31). German legend also knows the motif (cf. Grimm, *Deutsche Sagen* nos. 473, 474; Panzer, *Hilde-Gudrun*, 256). The roles of man and wife are exchanged in the story of Susanna as well as in the Genovefa narrative no. 532 (cf. also no. 437). A very widely dispersed motif is involved here, then. The assumption that the Israelite recension depends particularly on the Egyptian would only be demonstrated, then, if one could show the particularly close relationship of these two specific stories. This does not seem to be the case, however. Of the recensions known to me, the biblical recension seems most closely related to the Indian of Sundaraka and the Persian of Sijavush which agree with the biblical story in the use of the garment.

I. **1-6** *Joseph, sold to an Egyptian (v 1) advances to majordomo in his service (vv 2-6).* This is the effect of Yahweh's blessing which rests on him and accompanies him in everything he does. First Yahweh helps him to remain in the house of his lord (and not to go to the field or to the flocks) so that his lord always has him in view (vv 2aα, b). Then, when he sees the blessing of Yahweh in all his undertakings, he places him in charge of his household wishing to make use of this blessing for himself (vv 3, 4b). A similar legend motif occurs in the Jacob-Laban narrative (30:27ff.; cf. also the Isaac legend, 26:28). This foresight pays off: the whole household <422> is blessed (v 5). Then Joseph advances even farther. The master leaves everything to him. J reported this gradual increase in Joseph's influence with particular ease. He values this description because he wants to utilize Joseph's position of trust in the following narrative (vv 8, 9), but especially because of the contrast indicated above. He likes to portray how Yahweh's blessing and the father's love (Gen 37) are twice defeated in the struggle with the plots of evil people, but finally gain the victory in the end. V **1** is a repetition of 37:36 in the redactor's view. He considered it dispensable because Gen 38 intervenes (Holzinger). וְיוֹסֵף הוּרַד, not וַיּוּרַד, is a new beginning. The anonymity of the "Egyptian" is unusual in Genesis where all the other significant persons have names or are at least defined by status (39:22; 40:1). This is probably fairy tale in contrast to legend style. **2b** וַיְהִי] means "he remained" as in v 20b. This translation explains the position of v 2b after v **2a**. Winckler (*Forschungen* 3:452) strikes ויהי[3] (cf. Pesh.). **4** For בְּעֵינָיו Sam and LXX read בְּעֵינֵי אֲדֹנָיו (Ball). Concerning כָּל־יֶשׁ־לוֹ with no relative see §155n. Hebr mss and Sam have כל אֲשֶׁר יֶשׁ לוֹ (Ball, Kittel). Such majordomos (Eg. *mer per*) appear often in Egyptian pictures, sometimes with the staff or the papyrus scroll in their hand. **5b** Concerning וַיְהִי as the verb with בִּרְכַּת־יְ see §145q. **6** יָדַע means "to be concerned with something" (Baumann, ZAW 28:27). Concerning the use of אֵת compare עִם in Psa 73:25 (Ehrlich).

    II. **7-20a** *The love and hatred of the Egyptian woman.* **7-10** *The first temptation.* The notion that the wife wants to seduce the young man is also frequent in Hebrew and Egyptian proverbs (cf. Prov 2:16ff.; 5:3ff., 15ff.; 6:24ff.; 7:5ff. and Ranke in Greßmann, *Altorient. Texte und Bilder* 1:203). In simpler circumstances it is the young man who "persuades" the maiden (Exod 22:15). In more refined circumstances, the wife's excited but unsatisfied sensuality desires the fresh beauty of the young man. The narrator reproduces here, it seems, popular circumstances. With national pride, he juxtaposes the concupiscence of the Egyptian woman (of which Egyptian fairy tales also speak, Heyes, *Bibel u. Äg.*, 142) and the chastity of the Israelite youth. At the same time he praises Joseph's beauty which an Egyptian woman may well desire. Joseph rejects her demands as a malicious breech of confidence (vv 8-9), an element that recurs in all variants of the account. It always involves a youth associated very closely with the husband who therefore finds the strength to resist. Joseph's verbosity is supposed to portray his gravity and zeal. At the same time the narrator utilizes the opportunity to let Joseph repeat what has taken place previously. Such repetitive speeches, which later narrative art preferred, usually follow very closely the wording of the account. At the same time, however, the narrators take care, in order to avoid boredom, to introduce minor variations <423> (cf. the introduction ¶3.20). The new element here is v 9a. **8** מַה־בַּבָּיִת means "what is in the house" (§137c). Sam reads מְאוּמָה בְּבֵיתוֹ (cf. v 6 and LXX). Pesh and Vulg read בביתו (Kautzsch³). **9a** אֵינֶנּוּ means "he is not" not "it is not." V **9b** is interesting for the history of morality. Israel's morality, as such passages show, did not address solely Israelite interrelationships and permit everything in relation to foreigners, but considered adultery, even with an Egyptian, a serious sin against God who protects the sanctity of marriage. As among all people of higher morality, so also in Israel, and here with special emphasis, the demands of the law and of morality are exalted in the name of the deity.

The "fear of God" specifically hinders those sins humans could not or would not avenge, for example, those that occur in secret (cf. above p. 398). Egyptian morality also considered adultery a "malicious sin" (cf. W. Max Müller, *Liebespoesie der alten Ägypter*, 7). Concerning וְחָטָאתִי see §112p. אֱלֹהִים, not יהוה, is not a reason here to deny the verse to J, nor does it invalidate our source analysis based on the alternation of the two divine names (contra Eerdmans, 65-66). J employs "Yahweh" in the account (cf. v 3), but in speech concerning or to foreigners who know nothing of Yahweh he uses "God" (cf. 43:29; 44:16; Holzinger, *Hexateuch*, 93). **10** The fact that this occurs several times is recounted to make clear Joseph's resolution and, at the same time, to lengthen the situation. Concerning יוֹם יוֹם see §123c. Concerning the syntax of וַיְהִי . . . וְלֹא־שָׁמַע see §111f. לִהְיוֹת עִמָּה is supposed to replace the usually expression לִשְׁכַּב אֶצְלָה (Kautzsch³).

11-20 *The second temptation and its consequences.* The narrator depicted two encounters between Joseph and the Egyptian woman more extensively and thus distinguished them from one another in that the first time they only spoke, the second time they also acted. The second temptation is, of course, the more serious and is followed by consequences. In the old style, the two were combined into one. **11, 12** *The temptation.* The narrator presumes that Egyptian women (in contrast to the harem women of leading men; Heyes, *Bibel u. Äg.*, 133, 137) do not live in the strict segregation of the modern harem, but that, on the other hand, they are usually at home. He will have correctly portrayed conditions in Egypt (cf. Ebers, 305ff.). One should not overlook how reticently and chastely this offensive situation is recounted. וַיְהִי כְּהַיּוֹם הַזֶּה is probably a new beginning (contrast §114r).

13ff. *The consequences.* The woman was convinced that Joseph would never accede to her wishes. Thus her scorned love suddenly changes into hatred (as in the Amon-Tamar narrative in 2 Sam 13:15). At the same time—one may probably extrapolate—she suddenly sees how dangerous the situation will be if Joseph reveals what has taken place. So she decides to seize the initiative and ruin Joseph. The narrator does not communicate <424> these inward events so he narrates the external events all the more extensively (cf. introduction ¶3.12). Here, too, the narrative is bifurcated: the woman accuses Joseph (1) to the people in the household (vv 13-15) or (2) to her husband (vv 16-18). This prolongation of the narrative gives the narrator the opportunity to repeat previous events extensively twice (indeed, v 19 offers yet a third, very brief repetition). This would not have been necessary for the development of the matter, but is employed very skillfully for the action. The first lie, which takes place immediately and through which the woman is able to acquire witnesses, makes the second seem more probable. **13-16** *Before the household.* The woman calls her husband "him." This characterizes her impudence. She feigns aversion to Joseph in order to forestall suspicions to the contrary. She attempts to excite this aversion in the people, too, who were surely not well disposed toward the preferred and conscientious majordomo (Franz Delitzsch). Just as he took every liberty with her, he will not be afraid of them (with whom she deigns to associate herself; בָּנוּ לָנוּ, v 14). And she is a bit anti-Semitic. Egyptians look down on Canaanites (43:32; cf. 46:34). She leaves the facts as they occurred and only changes the motives and the sequence. She can appeal quite plausibly to her cry, that they heard, indeed, and to the garment she displays (רְאוּ, v 14). This web of lies has been conceived by a great artist. Rembrandt also portrayed this woman as a masterful liar. The alteration of the phrase "in her hand" (v 12) to "with me" (v 15) is especially subtle. This very insignificant alteration transforms the matter into its opposite. The garment she ripped from him he is supposed to have thrown off voluntarily (one can easily imagine why)! If a sign of true art is the ablity to obtain great effect through small means, one must admire such narrative art. **14** Regarding the anachronism "Hebrew" see comments on 40:15.

17, 18 *Before the master of the house.* Given the wording and the parallel (v 14), לְצָחֶק בִּי (v 17) belongs with הֵבֵאת. She feigns passionate anger, also directed (although cautiously, only parenthetically; cf. 3:12) at her husband as the final cause of her disgrace. Thus accused, her husband will surely not consider accusing her.

19, 20 *Conclusion of the account.* It is not necessary to state with whom the master becomes angry, because what follows immediately makes it quite clear: with Joseph, not with his wife. All the preceding (vv 13-18) is intended to show that the man could do nothing other than believe his wife (contra Dillmann; Franz <425> Delitzsch; and Heyes, *Bibel u. Äg.*, 169-70). There are analogies in all the variants. Characteristically, it is not recounted that Joseph defended himself. He has nothing else to say. The "prisoner" is a characteristically Egyptian element since Israel does not know the penalty of imprisonment (concerning the Egyptian prison, cf. Spiegelberg, *Studien u. Materialien zum Rechtswesen des Pharaonenreiches der Dynast.*, 18-21, 64-66, 84). It is hardly conceivable, however, that in reality a slave would be imprisoned for attempted rape of his mistress. He would certainly have been most severely disciplined, perhaps castrated (Diodor, *Bibl. hist.* 1:78), perhaps put to most heavy service or sold, but hardly put into prison where his labor would have been lost. This very tolerant treatment of Joseph is all the more remarkable since in the parallel accounts the presumably injured spouse brings about or wants the death of the youth (which is apparently, at least for ancient thought, most appropriate), and since no trace in the biblical version points to the notion that Joseph's master regarded his purported guilt less seriously for any reason whatsoever. Anything of the sort can only be supplied from outside the text. Such improprieties easily arise, however, in passages where two bodies of legend material, originally independent in origin, have been secondarily fused. The narrator who leaves the story of the adulteress and enters into the Joseph narrative proper must tell of the prison here since the Joseph account has Joseph in prison at the point where the author wishes to take it up. If one discerns the difficulties inherent in the matter, then one will judge that, given the circumstances, the narrator proceeded skillfully indeed. It will also be possible to dispense with the exposure of the liar and the justification of the youth which is actually necessary at the conclusion of the motif and which is rarely omitted in the other variants. The narrator of the biblical version is no longer interested in the woman and can do without Joseph's justification since he wants to report a brilliant rise. The fact that Joseph found himself in the prison where the royal prisoners, that is, the state criminals, lie, as unlikely as that may be for the foreign slave of a private citizen, was absolutely unavoidable. The statement "at the place where the prisoners of the king were," is not a later addition, therefore (contra Kautzsch-Socin; Ball; Sievers 2:346; Kautzsch³), but is necessary in the context. בֵּית הַסֹּהַר (v 20) only occurs in this account in J. J also uses בּוֹר (40:15; 41:14). E uses מִשְׁמָר (40:3, etc.). Concerning מְקוֹם אֲשֶׁר see §130c. Kethib is אסוֹדי. It is better to read Qere אֲסִירֵי with Ball and Kittel (also in v 22).

The Elevation of Joseph 39:20b-23; 40; 41

Composition. I. A prelude 39:20b-23; 40. In prison, Joseph interprets the dreams of two of Pharaoh's high officials, the cupbearer and the baker, whose service is entrusted to him. Both dreams are fulfilled. Nothing happens for Joseph at first, however. He remains in prison. This strand is dropped for the time being.

II. The main action 41. Pharaoh has two dreams that no one can interpret (vv 1-8). Now the narrator takes up the first thread again. The cupbearer remembers his experiences in prison and calls the dream interpreter Joseph to Pharaoh's attention (vv 9-13). Now Joseph is called, interprets the dream visions in relation to seven fat and seven lean years (vv 14-32), and adds the advice to gather grain while there is time (vv 33-36). In order to carry out this advice, Pharaoh places him in charge of Egypt (vv 37-46). On his commission, he gathers grain (vv 47-52) and sells it in the years of famine (vv 53-57).

The whole is a rather complicated construct. The analogy of the other legends in Genesis demonstrates, however, that such larger constructions developed from original legends of smaller scope. Accordingly, the task here, too, is to identify the smaller, <426> more original elements of the larger composition. (1) The whole falls clearly into two sections, the prelude and the main action. There is a marked caesura between the two. The main action makes a new beginning. (2) The prelude is very similar to the main action: both times eminent Egyptians have two dreams which correspond to one another. No one is able to interpret these dreams (וּפֹתֵר אֵין אֹתוֹ 40:8 ‖ וְאֵין־פֹּתֵר אוֹתָם 41:8). Joseph appears and correctly interprets the dreams in relation to the near future. They believe him. The subsequent period fulfills his words. (3) The main action could be understood independently even without the prelude. Consequently, one may imagine the development of the whole as follows: The original legend is the account of Gen 41. A later period, which took pleasure in more artful products, prefaced this legend with an additional piece which varies the same motif once more (Gen 40). The artist who formed a whole from tradition and his own composition shows a fine taste for circumstances. He was able to distinguish both parts of his composition gracefully from one another. The accent lies on the action, which has consequences, thus on the second piece. The first piece remains without consequence at first. Furthermore, the main action involves the Pharaoh himself, the prelude involves only two of his officials. The main action is also much more extensively described than the prelude. The artist found a simple way to conclude the first piece (40:23) and thus to find space for a new beginning (41:1). The means by which he takes up the dropped thread is equally natural and simple (41:9-13). Such a combination of two variations of the same motif is present when first the angel, then Yahweh himself appears to Elijah in the Horeb narrative (1 Kgs 19:5ff.), when he encounters first the minister, then the king himself (1 Kgs 18:7ff.), and when first Gehazi, then Elisha cares for the dead boy (2 Kgs 4:31ff.). In each case the first scene is spun from the second and exceeded by it (cf. *Elias, Jahve, und Baal*, 13-14). The elegant ease with which these compositions are created is truly amazing.

64. I. The Prelude.
Joseph's Dream Interpretation in Prison 39:20b-23; 40 EJ

Source criticism. The piece falls into two parts: I. Joseph's favor in the house of the prison warden (39:20b-23); II. Joseph's dream interpretation in the prison (40). The first piece introduces the second. As the favored servant of the prison warden, Joseph obtains a position of trust in the prison and thus makes the acquaintance of the cupbearer and baker, whose dreams he interprets. The first part continues the preceding piece and, like it, belongs to J. In content it parallels the clauses taken from E in 39:1-6a. J is indicated by יהוה (vv 21, 23bis) and הִצְלִיחַ of Yahweh (v 23). The second part (40), largely of one piece, stems essentially from E. Joseph is not in prison as a prisoner (as in J 39:20-23); Instead, his master, the chief butcher, in whose home the prison is, has employed him there (vv 4, 7). He was not bought from his homeland (as in J 37:27), but stolen (v 15a). Both agree with E's portrayal in 37:28 and 37:36. In the prison, Joseph serves the two high officials (v 4), while according to J he is, instead, the overseer of all the prisoners (39:22). Linguistic evidences for E are: וַיְהִי אַחַר הַדְּבָרִים הָאֵלֶּה (v 1), a particularly frequent phrase in E; שַׂר הַטַּבָּחִים (vv 3, 4 as in 37:36 [E]), and the similar phrases שַׂר הָאוֹפִים and שַׂר הַמַּשְׁקִים (vv 2, 9, 16, 20, 21, 22, 23; J employs שַׂר בֵּית־הַסֹּהַר for the first; cf. 39:21, 22, 23); מִשְׁמָר "prison" (vv 3, 4, 7; J says בֵּית־הַסֹּהַר 39:20, 21, 22bis, 23); compare also סְרִיסֵי פַרְעֹה (v[v 7,] 2; 37:36). Yet, a few traces of J are also present in the chapter: the words הֵפֵאוּ to מִצְרַיִם in v 1 which are "superfluous before v 2," the expressions מַשְׁקֶה and אֹפֶה, as well as the remarkable exchange, which only occurs here in Genesis, of מֶלֶךְ מִצְרַיִם (also in 39:20) and פַּרְעֹה (Meyer, *Israeliten*, 24-25); furthermore v 15b, according to which Joseph, himself, is a prisoner, and probably also וְהוֹצֵאתַנִי מִן־הַבַּיִת הַזֶּה in v 14. <427> These fragments of J indicate that J also possessed a similar account. A different situation is presented by the words אֶל־בֵּית הַסֹּהַר to אָסוּר שָׁם in v 3, which could not derive from E because of בֵּית הַסֹּהַר and because according to it, Joseph himself was in prison; furthermore, v 5b, which is "entirely superfluous" in the context of E with the expressions מַשְׁקֶה, אֹפֶה, מֶלֶךְ מִצְרַיִם, and בֵּית־הַסֹּהַר, which are characteristic of J; finally the extraordinarily awkward אֶת־סְרִיסֵי פַרְעֹה to בֵּית־אֲדֹנָי (v 7), according to which Joseph also seems to be a prisoner. All these are additions intended to harmonize E with J.

39:20b-23 J. Joseph's favor with the prison warden. This description parallels vv 2-6a in content and also in wording: וַיְהִי בְּבֵית אֲדֹנָיו v 20 like וַיְהִי־שָׁם בְּבֵית הַסֹּהַר v 2; וַיְהִי יהוה אֶת־יוֹסֵף v 21 verbatim also in v 2; וַיִּתֵּן בְּיַד יוֹסֵף v 22 like נָתַן בְּיָדוֹ v 2; אֵין רֹאֶה אֶת־כָּל־מְאוּמָה v 23 like וְלֹא יָדַע אִתּוֹ מְאוּמָה v 6; וְכֹל אֲשֶׁר הוּא עֹשֶׂה יהוה מַצְלִיחַ v 23 like כִּי יהוה אִתּוֹ וַאֲשֶׁר־הוּא עֹשֶׂה יהוה מַצְלִיחַ v 3. It is the second variation of the same motif. **21** וַיֵּט אֵלָיו חָסֶד means "he granted him favor, that is, he was favorable to him." In the context of the passage, however, וַיֵּט is to be read as a hiphil, "he let him gain favor" (Ezra 7:28; 9:9; cf. Ehrlich). **22** Concerning עֹשִׂים without subject see §116s. **23** Winckler (*Forschungen* 3:455) places בְּיָדוֹ at the end of v 22.

40 *Joseph interprets dreams in prison* E (J). **1-4** *Exposition.* Cupbearer and baker appear here to be high officials of Pharaoh. This element corresponds to Egyptian circumstances in the "New Kingdom" (since ca. 1300). The Pharaohs of that period based their power, as did the Roman Caesars and the Egyptians Sultans in the Middle Ages, on the slaves of their household who were simultaneously responsible for the personal service of the Pharaoh and for the matters of the kingdom (cf. Erman, *Ägypten*, 155ff.). The title of royal "bar scribe" is also attested in Egyptian (Erman, 265; cf. also Heyes, *Bibel u. Äg.*, 170ff.). Erman (269) has a depiction of a royal bakery. **2** E does not give a reason for the royal anger or, later, the verdict, nor is it necessary (despotism). **3** E does not regard the imprisonment of these officials as punishment, but as a period of investigation. Joseph's imprisonment is regarded differently in J (39:20). בְּמִשְׁמָר is in the absolute state (Ball; Sievers 2:347; Kittel; Kautzsch³; also in v 7; 41:10).

5-19 *The dreams and their fulfillment.* The situation is as follows: in a while the fate of both must be decided when Pharaoh pronounces his verdict. But this verdict is completely uncertain. The mood of the despot can mean life or death. In such a fateful time, the ancient heeds omens: the deity may announce his fate to him. In this case, the deity gives an oracle <428> through dreams. This belief in the divine origin of dreams, very widespread in antiquity (and even now), also well known in ancient Israel, especially frequent in Genesis in E (cf. above p. 220), is a characteristic Egyptian element at the same time. Dream interpretation is a feature of "Egyptian wisdom" (Ebers, 321-22; Heyes, *Bibel u. Äg.*, 175ff.). Along with dream interpretation itself, the tradition that this art stemmed from Egypt is also preserved until today. Even today one can buy "Egyptian dream books" in our bookstores. **5** אִישׁ חֲלֹמוֹ and אִישׁ כְּפִתְרוֹן חֲלֹמוֹ are probably variants (Winckler, *Forschungen* 3:455; cf. Sievers 2:347).

6-8 One should note the artfully thrilling, "supplementary" (introduction ¶3.20) narrative style. We first learn that they are depressed in v 6, why this is so only in v 8, their dreams, themselves, only in vv 9ff. In the regular narrative fashion, all this should have been told before Joseph's entrance. They are, in the narrator's opinion, justifiably sorrowful. The revelations they wanted, they have received. But, with no interpreter, they do not know what to make of them. "If they had been free, they would have been able to find an interpreter in Egypt" (Reuß). **7** The addition is a secondary extrapolation of an original אֹתָם. **8** Regarding the position of וּפֹתֵר אֵין see §152o. The courtiers and Joseph express two different views of dream interpretation. They think dream interpretation is a science that must be learned. Only a פֹתֵר—in Egypt a priest (Lange in de la Saussaye, *Religionsgesch.* 1²:151, 154)—will know how to do this (one can become familiar with the nature of this science and its methods from Artemidor's book of dreams; cf. Friedlaender, *Sittengeschichte Roms*⁶ 3:570-71, or from our books of dreams). Therefore, they think Joseph, who is not a trained dream interpreter, cannot interpret dreams. This is presumably the Egyptian view. Joseph thinks, however, that dream interpretation is God's matter, that is, it depends on God's inspiration and is, therefore, not linked with status and tradition. Instead, anyone to whom God reveals it can interpret dreams. "Why not me, then, also, if it please God? This is the opinion that would have been held in Israel, perhaps in prophetic circles. LXX reads פֹתְרָם.

9-19 The dreams and their interpretations are artfully composed. In accordance with the character of dreams, they are a mixture of realistic and fantastic elements. The rapid growth of the vine, for example, is fantastic, as is the fact that Pharaoh drinks the juice pressed from grapes. This element, which has occasioned all manner of remarkable perspectives (cf. recently Heyes, 188) can be explained in terms of the fact that Pharaoh would do such a thing only in a dream. In reality, of course, he drinks wine. At the same time, the dream combines the comprehensible and the incomprehensible. The art of interpretation consists in extracting the comprehensible and determining its meaning. This meaning, however, is sometimes indicated prima facie, sometimes only to be obtained through allegorical interpretation. When, for example, the birds eat the baker's bread in the dream, it means allegorically that they will eat his flesh in reality, etc. The art consists, then, in interpreting certain elements of the dream imagery as metaphors of future events (cf. "Allegorie im A.T. und Judentum," RGG 1:354-55). The purpose of the piece in context is to prepare for the fact that the cupbearer can later call Joseph to Pharaoh's attention (41:9-13). To this end, only one correct dream interpretation would have been necessary at this point. The narrator, however, offers two dreams <429> with interpretations. Thus the fact that Joseph can interpret dreams is demonstrated with certainty. In this effort, the author demonstrates his skill by ingeniously presenting the dreams in a similar fashion and, at the same time, differently. They are similar in that each dreams of his office and of his head; in both cases the number three plays a role. This similarity is also immediately apparent to the baker (אַף־אֲנִי בַחֲלוֹמִי v 16). Any normal man would have interpreted these very similar dreams similarly. Joseph, however, demonstrates his great skill by discerning their quite opposite meanings. The difference in the dreams consists, however, in the fact that the cupbearer dreams that he executed his office. The baker only wished to perform it, but is then prevented from doing so. Similarity and difference are (as in 27:39) skillfully summarized in the wordplay in the interpretation. יִשָּׂא אֶת־רֹאשֶׁךָ means "he will lift your head," by making you happy and free (v 13; 2 Kgs 25:27), by having you hung high on the stake (v 19). The sequence of the dreams is also considered. The favorable comes first, otherwise Joseph would not be asked a second time. The fact that the baker's expectation that he, too, would receive an encouraging interpretation is so harshly disappointed is an element the narrator is pleased to include. The hearer enjoys it when an ingenious narrator gives the narrative an unexpected outcome. The same motif of ingenious dream interpretation occurs in the "Entertaining Accounts" of Bar-Hegraeus (ZDMG 40:415-16).

9 Concerning וְהִנֵּה see §143d. הִנֵּה is the characteristic word in accounts of dreams and visions (cf. above p. 309). Since the interpretation speaks of lifting the head (v 13), the same must also occur here, in the dream, as it did in the other dream (v 16). One reads here, therefore, in analogy to עַל־רֹאשִׁי (v 16), עַל־פָּנַי "over my countenance." **10** There is no sure example of the construction כְּפֹרַחַת (§164g). One should read מָפְרַחַת (Ball) or כְּפָרְחָה (Kittel; Ehrlich). LXX reads θάλλουσα. נֵצָהּ is usually understood as the equivalent of נִצָּהּ, although the examples of this form are "for the most part uncertain" (§91e). One should read נִצָּה without mappiq, with Ball, "he (the vine) was covered in blooms" as in Isa 5:6, etc. The asyndetic perfects indicate the rapid sequence of events. **14** כִּי אִם־זְכַרְתַּנִי is a "perfect. confidentiae" according to §106n n.2: "Only, may you remember me." Wellhausen and others emend כי to אַך: "Only, will you then be sure to think of me?" (Holzinger following §106n) or "Nevertheless, when you think of me, then . . . " (Kautzsch[3], cautiously). Ball and Sievers (2:347) wonder whether וְעָתָה אָל תִּשְׁכְחֵנִי has fallen out. The addition of נָא in וְעָשִׂיתָ-נָּא is singular (§105b n. 2). **14-15** It is permissible in antiquity for the oracle giver to receive a reward for his efforts, just as seers and prophets are also accustomed to receiving such (Num 22:7; 1 Sam 9:7-8; 1 Kgs 14:3). Joseph <430> asks in return for his favorable judgment that the cupbearer remember him cordially to the Pharaoh so that he may be freed from the slavery he has fallen into unjustly. According to the J variant, in contrast, Joseph asked to be liberated from this house, that is, from prison, where he is unjustly. "From the land of the Hebrews" (v 15; cf. 39:14,17; 41:12) is a naive anachronism like 34:7. E surely knows nothing of the *Ḥabiri* of the Amarna correspondence (contra A. Jeremias, ATSO², 387). Cisterns are often employed in Canaan as prisons. Consequently, the word בּוֹר also means "prison." There is no wonder that J here and in 41:14 has another expression for "prison" instead of בֵית-הַסֹּהַר above (cf. p. 411). Individual accounts frequently have such minor peculiarities.

    16-19 *The dream of the baker.* **16** Regarding the construction of אַף-אֲנִי בְחֲלוֹמִי see §135f. **16-17** The baker dreams that he is once again in office and that, as is his usual duty, he brings baked goods in three baskets to the royal table (חֹרִי is, thus, the finest bread, common at court). In the upper basket is that which will be set before Pharaoh himself, in the other two, the food for the court. He carries the baskets on his head. According to memorials, this is Egyptian practice (cf. Ebers, 332; Riehm, "Egypten," HWB; Heyes, 195; and the figure in Erman, 269). But birds (innumerable in Egypt; Erman 321) eat the baked goods—this is the unusual point which will be interpreted allegorically. A similar omen occurs in 15:11. In reality, one would, of course, shoo the birds away, in a dream, one does not have the power to do so. **17** Is מַעֲשֵׂה אֹפֶה a gloss on חֹרִי¹ (v 16)? **19** מֵעָלֶיךָ¹, absent in Hebr mss and Vulg, destroys the play on words with vv 13, 20. It has been introduced here from v 19b (Ball; Sievers 2:347; Ehrlich). The intention, therefore, is not the penalty of decapitation, but, as v 22 also demonstrates, only that of impalement. This punishment was known to the Egyptians (Heyes, 201). There is an Assyrian depiction of an impaled person in Riehms, HW, 480. According to ancient conceptions, which were particularly well developed and very influential among the ancient Egyptians (cf. Erman, 413ff.), but were also understood in ancient Israel, the fate of the soul after death is tied to the care of the corpse. Consequently, desecration of the corpse is an especially horrible penalty.

    20-22 *The fulfillment.* **20** The narrator intentionally employs the same words here as in the interpretation. It happened exactly as Joseph had said! That Egyptian kings celebrate their birthdays with court festivities and also with amnesties is first attested from Ptolemaic times (cf. Ebers, 335-36). Regarding the form הֻלֶּדֶת see §69w, with the accusative as in Ezek 16:5. <431>

    23 It is psychologically very realistic that the fortunate eminent individual forgets the poor slave who announced his elevation to him. The hope of the hearers, who, fully sympathetic, wished that Joseph's fortunes would now turn, are disappointed. And yet, this whole account cannot remain without consequences. So we ask expectantly, "How will it turn out?"

65. II. The Main Action.
Pharaoh's Dreams and Joseph's Elevation 41 EJ

Source criticism. The account immediately continues the preceding. Consequently, one may expect the same sources E and J here as there. The chapter falls, with reference to the mixture of sources, into two parts: Pharaoh's dreams seem to be taken predominantly from one source. Judging from vv 9-13, the only clearly discernible section, this source will be E. E is indicated in vv 9-13 by שַׂר הַמַּשְׁקִים (v 9); שַׂר הַטַּבָּחִים (v 10); שַׂר הָאֹפִים (v 10); Pharaoh rages, קצף, in v 10 as in 40:2; מִשְׁמָר (v 10); v 11 compares to 40:5; Joseph is the servant of the chief butcher and servant of the imprisoned courtiers as in 40:4, etc. In the other sections, the following indicate E: וְאֵין־פּוֹתֵר אוֹתָם (v 8), similarly in v 15 (cf. 40:8). Yet there are also traces of J: חָטָאִי (v 9b) recalls חָטְאוּ (40:1 J); the clause "they brought him from the pit" בּוֹר (v 14) is comparable to 40:15b (J). The second account of the dreams does not entirely agree with the first. There are minor variations in expression (e.g., for יְפוֹת מַרְאֶה in vv 2, 4, יְפֹת תֹּאַר in v 18, etc.), as well as a few "supple mentations" (vv 19, 21). Now such repetitions are not usually precise, even in the same author. Instead authors (writing in the "expansive" style) love to incorporate minor variations and supplementations (cf. introduction ¶3.20). Yet the text seems to be overdone at a few points (vv 19, 23). Consequently, one may assume that J, too, whose account will have been very similar, has participated although the details cannot be discerned with anything approaching certainty. In the second part of the piece, many excesses and variants indicate greater use of both sources. The dream interpretation in vv 25-32 is very expansive. One may assume that this passage arose through the fusion of two passages from both sources. V 30a "then the plenty will be forgotten" parallels vv 30b, 31 "then it will no longer be noticed." The repetition of the dream is interpreted twice (vv 32bα ‖ v 32bβ). According to v 33, Pharaoh should appoint a man who, according to v 34b (וְחִמֵּשׁ sing.) should take one-fifth. In contrast, according to v 34a, they are officials (plur.), who, according to v 35a, should gather in all the grain. V 36a (פִּקָּדוֹן; cf. פָּקִיד v 34a) also belongs to the latter variant. The expression also changes conspicuously: קָבַץ אֹכֶל (v 35a; אֹכֶל vv 35bβ, 36a) for צָבַר בָּר (v 35ba). The same alternation occurs in vv 48 and 49. The prediction parallels the fulfillment: vv 54b and 55ff. contain a very conspicuous contradiction. Whereas according to v 54b, the famine effects all lands, but thanks to Joseph's wise preparations not Egypt itself, vv 55ff. describes how famine ruled in Egypt. The second variant includes those clauses in the preceding which speak specifically of (plenty and) famine in Egypt (vv 29, 30a, 36a). The first variant predicts a famine over the whole world (vv 30b, 31), where הָאָרֶץ should probably be translated "the earth." The two variants seems to have differed in one major point, then. Both proceeded from the dream interpretation, as is the nature of the account, and must finally result in a famine that forces Jacob's sons to journey to Egypt. They obtain this purpose, however, in different ways. The second variant speaks first exclusively of famine in Egypt and adds only subsequently that it also dominated the rest of the world (v 57; concerning v 56a see the comments on the passage). Contrariwise, the first speaks from the outset, it seems, of a general famine. The first links this legend tightly with the following, the second more loosely. J presumes v 57, which belongs to the second, in 42:5.

The following source analysis results: v 25-28 (entirely parallel to vv 29, 30a) E; vv 29, 30a (famine in Egypt) J; vv 30b, 31 (∥ v 30a famine <432> in the whole world) E. V 32 is unclear. Vv 34a (regarding הִפְקִיד compare 39:4,5 J), 35a,bβ, 36a is a unit (united by the plurality of officials, פָּקִיד and פְּקִדֹן, אֹכֶל) J (because of v 36a: famine in Egypt; this is also indicated by the expression אֹכֶל in the meaning grain, employed very frequently, perhaps exclusively, by J in this whole narrative; see 42:7; 43:2, 4, 22; 44:1, 25 and probably also 42:10). In the same manner, vv 33, 34b, 35bα (∥ v 35a; the singular is to be substituted in v 35bα), 36b (∥ v 36a) is also a unit, E (because of בָּר in v 35; cf. 42:3, 25; 45:23). In the subsequent section, v 48 is from J (אֹכֶל and קָבַץ as in v 35, and elsewhere; all the grain is collected; the good time effects Egypt, especially the "cities" as in v 35bb). V 49a is from E (צָבַר בָּר as in v 35bα). V 49aβ may be from J judging from the diction (cf. 32:13 and 15:1). V 49b (∥ aβ) is from E. V 47 (roughly parallel to v 48 in content) may belong to E. In the concluding section, vv 53, 54a, 55-57 are from J, v 54b is from E.

The central passage (vv 37ff.) is not unified either. Pharaoh twice acknowledges Joseph's unique wisdom (v 38 ∥ v 39). He twice makes him second in the kingdom (v 40 ∥ v 41). Two Egyptian statements are made concerning Joseph (v 43 ∥ v 45). Joseph's investiture is probably redundant (vv 42-43). V 46b, Joseph's exit, immediately continues v 43 where Joseph climbs into the wagon. In between he cannot have hastily taken a wife. V 50b is rather awkward and seems to be an addition. V 50a seems unaware of Joseph's marriage to a noble. "Manasseh" is explained twice in v 51. Source analysis must proceed from אלהים (vv 51, 52 E). Furthermore, נָבוֹן יְחָכָם (v 39) points to E (cf. v 33). Finally, פּוֹטִי פֶרַע (v 45) is a variant of פּוֹטִיפָר (37:36). Both are high officials of Pharaoh. Since 37:36 stems from E, 41:45 will belong to J. And since vv 44, 45 interrupt the coherence of vv 43, 46b, the latter verses are to be attributed to E. Consequently, we obtain the following result: E contributes vv 37 (cf. 45:16b), 39 (cf. v 33), 40 (∥ v 44 J), 41 (cf. vv 33b, 43b), 42b (the golden chain does not fit well here because if Joseph stands on the wagon it would not be visible), 43, 46b, 47 (cf. above), 49aα,b (cf. above), 50a, 51a,bα, 52. The following stem from J: vv 38 (39), 42a (וַיָּסַר as in 38:19 J), 44, 45a, 48 (cf. above), 49aβ. This source analysis is supported by the fact that it results in two unified texts. In the division of vv 33-36 and 48, 49 it agrees essentially with Leander (ZAW 18:195-96). Procksch differs, especially, in that he attributes vv 21a, 29-31, 34, 35bα, 36b and, in the concluding section, vv 47, 49, 53-54, 56a, 57 to J. This is erroneous since the variants v 30a ∥ vv 30b, 31 as well as the alteration of sing. and plur. in vv 33-35 are overlooked and no clear distinguishing principle is apparent in the concluding passage. It it still worth considering whether vv 41 and 43b may not be better attributed to J with Procksch. Indeed, it is not unknown to the author of this commentary how uncertain every source analysis remains, here and in many other cases. Kautzsch[3] acknowledges the insertion of individual passages from J. As usual, Eerdmans (67) disregards the difficulties which can only be solved by assuming various sources. Sievers (2:347ff.) divides vv 41ff. among four different sources, two strands each of J and E, which are supposed only to be preserved, however, in mostly fragmentary pieces.

1-7 *Pharaoh's dreams.* Dream revelations of the king, concerning the fate of the king-dom, also occur in Egyptian sources (cf. Erman, *Ägypten*, 710). This notion, to be under-stood originally in terms of the king's close relationship with the deity, is also known in Israel (cf. *Ausgewählte Psalmen*², 13) and in later Judaism (cf. Dan 2; 4; 5). **1-4** *The first dream.* V **1** makes a new beginning. Such new beginnings rarely occur within the old legends themselves. Instead, the rule is to link the individual scenes as closely as possible (12:11; 18:9; 21:14-15; 27:5). They are not rare, however, in the legend cycles (42:1; 47:13, 29) and they tend to appear at points where another legend or part of another legend originally began. So it is here. If the narrative seems to drop the thread of the Joseph account, it is in order to heighten tension. We are supposed to ask, "How will <433> Pharaoh's dreams lead to Joseph?" The passage of two years (considering the construction see 29:14) in which nothing happens is a retardant motif such as "expansive" accounts love. The repetitive וְהִנֵּה (vv 1ff.) depicts surprise. יְאֹר is usually considered an Egyptian loan word (Eg. *aur*; Heyes, *Bibel u. Äg.*, 202). **2** Cows rising out of the water and cows eating one another (v 4) are fantastic elements such as are natural in dreams (40:10-11). The first element is not interpreted subsequently. The cow coming forth from the Nile, the source of fertility, a symbol of the fat years, will be a specifically Egyptian concept (Heyes, 214ff.). Cow and harvest are related since one plows and threshes with cows. Seven holy cows are frequently mentioned in Egypt (Heyes, 214, 216). The whole account of Pharaoh's dream and its interpretation is conceivably an originally Egyptian narrative which an Egyptian wise man would have recounted in Egypt and which was applied to Joseph in Israel. We have a variant to this account in Dan 2. The narrator of Dan 2 imitated Gen 41, but is much less capable. אָחוּ "marsh grass" is an Egyptian loan word. **3** For דְּקוֹת (vv 3-4) Hebr mss and Sam read רַקּוֹת (cf. vv 19, 20, 27). רַקּוֹת may be preferable because of the alliteration with רְעוֹת (Ball; Kittel). Vv 6, 7, 23, 24 would suggest otherwise. **4** He wakes up from surprise—a remarkable dream!

5-7 The second dream is recounted somewhat more briefly because the first has already consumed our interest. This dream is constructed as much like the first as possible because it is supposed to have the same meaning. Consequently, not only אַחֲרֵיהֶן (vv 3, 6; necessary for the interpretation) is repeated, but also עֹלוֹת (vv 2, 5), etc. **6** The קָדִים (regarding the construction see §116l), "east wind," is feared in Palestine as in Egypt. It is more precisely the southeast wind here (Erman, 23; Heyes, 218). **7** "Behold, it was a dream" is a nice touch. His dream was so lifelike that it seemed real to him. One of the two dreams, so similar to one another, must have priority. That will be the first, for it can at least be imagined that cows would eat one another, but not that ears of corn would devour one another.

8-32 *The interpretation.* **8-13** The scene before Joseph appears. The purpose of this scene is to lead back to the main theme. At the same time, Joseph is to be introduced in a dramatic fashion. Will Joseph succeed where the magicians failed? **8** The narrator finds it only natural that Pharaoh is disturbed (40:7) for the dream surely means something. In such a situation the ancient turns to "wise men." The narrator knows that there are many of them in Egypt. The fact that Pharaoh calls all the wise (not so easily or quickly done in reality) is fairy-tale style (cf. comments on vv 37ff.; e.g., Baethgen, *Sindban oder die sieben weisen Meister*, 33). <434> All of them must be here so that Joseph's skill may be demonstrated all the more later. The account glorifies Joseph, then, who surpasses the

Egyptian magicians, as does Moses in the Exodus narrative, and as Daniel surpasses the Babylonian magicians. The wisemen and the magicians play a great role in Egypt and were certainly also famous abroad (Heyes, 219ff.) The etymology and precise meaning of חַרְטֹם is unknown, just as ancient magic (which was always secret) is very obscure for the most part. חֲלֹמוֹ and אֹתָם are mutually exclusive. LXX, Dillmann, Ball, and Kittel read אֹתוֹ (cf. v 15). Kautzsch[3] reads חֲלֹמֹתָיו. **9-13** The account of the cupbearer, a (very abbreviated) report of the events in Gen 40. **9a** Hebr mss, Sam, LXX, Dillmann, Kittel, and others read אֶל־פַּרְעֹה. V **9b** is a courtesan's apology. **10** Regarding בְּמִשְׁמַר see 40:3. For אֹתִי[1] Sam has אֹתָם (Dillmann, Kittel, etc.). **11** Concerning וַנַּחַלְמָה see §49e. **12** On the syntax of אִישׁ see §139c.

14 *Joseph is called.* The Egyptians valued purity very much. The upper class wore soft, white robes, wore their hair short, and were clean shaven. The common people cannot enjoy this luxury, of course (Heyes, 222ff.). The fact that Joseph gets a haircut is, therefore, specifically Egyptian. The fact that he does not appear before the king in everyday clothing would be understandable anywhere, but especially among the neat Egyptians (Heyes, 225). Concerning וַיְגַלַּח see the comments on 38:14. An emendation to the niphal (Kittel, Kautzsch[3]) is unfeasible since it does not occur.

15, 16 *The first introductory discussion.* **15** Naturally the king begins the conversation. Hebrew (וַאֲנִי) emphasizes here (as also often elsewhere) the person where we would emphasize the verb. Pharaoh believes, as do his officials (40:8), that dream interpretation is a skill certain men possess. **16** Joseph, however, rejects the fame for such a skill and attributes everything to God. This is also the narrator's opinion. Joseph is no professional dream interpreter, but an inspired individual, a "demonic" (v 38). תִּשְׁמַע חֲלוֹם—It is, therefore, obviously necessary that the dream first be told to the interpreter. Dan 2 differs. Here the king demands of the wise that they know the dream without being told—psychologically, a very unrealistic augmentation by an inferior narrator. "You know how to interpret dreams" (Ehrlich). Concerning בִּלְעָדָי see 14:24. Ball understands the clause differently. "God will reveal good things." Joseph does not forget to pay Pharaoh proper respect. עָנָה is the term for the oracle's response. <435>

17-24 *A very expansive repetition of the dreams.* This verbosity, characteristic of the style of the Joseph narratives, is based here on the special importance of the matter upon which all which follows depends. **21** Regarding the suffix in קִרְבֶּנָה see §91f. מַרְאֵיהֶן is singular (§93ss). **23** Hebr mss, Sam, LXX, and Pesh read וּשְׁדֻפוֹת as in v 27 (Ball, Kittel). Hebr mss, Sam, and Targ-Onk read אַחֲרֵיהֶן (Ball).

25-32 *Joseph's dream interpretation.* Joseph recognizes immediately that the dreams refer to the future and that they mean the same thing. He had explained the two so similar dreams of chapter 40 quite differently, but these two he explains as synonymous. Both prove correct when they are fulfilled. That—the narrator thinks—is the proper art of dream interpretation! **26** For פָּרֹת LXX and Sam have הַפָּרוֹת (cf. v 27, Ball, Kittel; but cf. also §126x). Time periods of seven days, years, etc. are very common everywhere (cf. v. Andrian, *Mitteil. d. Anthropol. Ges. in Wien* 31:225ff.). Seven years occur in the OT in 1 Kgs 6:38; 2 Kgs 11:4 (cf. also the week of years in Dan 9:24 and the Sabbath year in Exod 23:10-11; Deut 15:1ff.; Meinhold, *Sabbat*, 22-23). In the Ptolemaic period, the *Hnum* priests of Elephantine told of a seven-year famine under king Zoser (2800) which was fortunately ended on the advice of an Egyptian wise man (Heyes, 280ff.; Ranke in

Greßmann, *Altorient. Texte u. Bilder* 1:233). Ovid speaks of a nine-year Egyptian famine (*Ars Amat* I.647-48). **27** הָרֵקוֹת is the opposite of הַמְּלֵאוֹת (vv 7, 22), if one should not read הַדַּקּוֹת with Sam, Pesh, Dillmann (cautiously), Ball, and Kittel. V **28** refers back to v 25b. **30** Concerning וְקָמוּ see §112t. The fact that the earlier abundance will be "forgotten," "no longer noticed, perceived" (וְלֹא־יִוָּדַע v 31) is not idle imagination, but the interpretation of the element וְלֹא נוֹדַע (v 21). The expression וְכִלָּה, "devoured" (v 30), is also intentionally chosen, an interpretation of the devouring in vv 20, 24. <436>

33-36 Therefore Joseph suggests a wise measure to avert the impending disaster, a measure he himself is called upon to carry out. This is an easy transition from the dream interpretation to his advancement. Such a mediating interlude is lacking, much to the detriment of the account, in Dan 2. **33** Concerning יֵרֶא see §75p. **34** For the sense of יַעֲשֶׂה see 1 Kgs 8:32. The fifth measure (E) suggested by Joseph here is to be for one time only. According to 47:34 J, in contrast, Joseph introduces it as a permanent, standing institution. An Egyptian institution stands in the background. Of the two variants, J's is more realistic, E's more poetic. The poetic perspective of the legend is accustomed to understanding enduring circumstances as onetime events elsewhere, too. In contrast, the J variant (35) is more naive in that all grain is supposed to be collected. How are the Egyptians supposed to sustain themselves for so long? State granaries were an Egyptian cultural institution and "a characteristic of ancient Egypt" (Heyes, 279) which surely excited great astonishment and amazement at the "wisdom of the Egyptians" among the Israelites whose civic life was much less developed. The legend gladly tells of such great cunning and reports with joy that our Joseph taught this to the Egyptians. Concerning Egyptian granaries see Erman, 576-77; concerning royal granaries see 129-30, 133, 142, 159; for the maintenance of officials, soldiers, and family see 159; concerning years of famine see 567 and n.1; concerning provision for the poor and for Egyptian vassal states with grain see Erman, 140, and Heyes, 282-83. If the source analysis is correct וְיִצְבֹּר (singular) should be read with Leander and וְיִתְּנוּ should be inserted before אֹכֶל² following v 48 (Ball, Kittel). In the other case, one should perhaps strike בָר or אֹכֶל (Eerdmans, 67; Ehrlich). **36** לָאָרֶץ is "land" in contrast to the cities (v 35).

37-46 *Joseph's' elevation.* **38, 39** Joseph did not announce his advice explicitly in God's name. But Pharaoh, extremely astonished at the superhuman wisdom spoken by Joseph, acknowledges that God must have revealed this to him, that "God's spirit" is in him. This is the narrator's opinion. No human could have come to such wondrously wise advice on his own. The "spirit" is the divine power which produces wonders and mighty things in people. One may determine that God's spirit is in a person if one is struck by the mighty and mysterious impression certain phenomena produce. One does well to obey such a divinely endowed person, and, if possible, to use him to one's own advantage. Pharaoh acts in this manner here. For the narrator, this is understandable enough. In reality, such a swift elevation to primacy after the king will not have taken place quite so easily. It is, however, a much favored fairy-tale motif. Contrariwise, the fact that Canaanite slaves could obtain leading positions in Egypt is reality. The Pharaoh's of the New Kingdom chose their ministers (as did the Roman Caesars) from their household slaves <437> (cf. comments on 40:1) who were often foreigners (cf. Erman, 156-57, 683-84; Speigelberg, *Aufenthalt Israels in Ägypten*, 21, 25; Heyes, *Bibel u. Äg.*, 126). One may take *Janhamu*, an eminent official under Ameophis IV, who was a Semite judging from his name, as an example of a foreigner who rose to the highest ranks (cf. above p. 383). Characteristically for ancient Israelite religion, it is not recounted that Joseph converted Pharaoh to Yahweh, as Nebuchadnezzar did in the related account in Dan 2. The ancient narrators do not yet know the claim that even the foreign nations should serve Yahweh. They also know circumstances abroad well enough to know that such things do not occur.

40 *The decision (imperf.) and* **41** *the execution (perf.).* The verses are not necessarily mutually exclusive, therefore. The translation "it should kiss your mouth" for עַל־פִּיךָ יִשַּׁק is linguistically possible, but conceptually inconceivable. Newer translations follow LXX ὑπακούσεται, "it should follow your command," and read יִשַּׁק > נֹשֵׁק or יֵשַׁק > ppשׁ or > שׁוק. All are difficult. Concerning the accusative הַכִּסֵּא see §118h. נָתַתִּי means "I hereby give" (see §106m). One may not ask the legend mixed with fairy-tale elements which particular Egyptian offices Joseph may have assumed (contra Heyes, 226-27). Judging from what is said, the most likely would be the Egyptian *ḏ,* "at" or Vizier (Erman, 106; Heyes, 230-31). **42a** State documents are marked with the royal seal. Transferals of office in Egypt involve the transfer of the official seal. The vizier carries the royal seal (Heyes, 237-38). Similar practices are assumed in Esth 3:10: 8:2; 1 Macc 6:15. Concerning Egyptian seal rings see Erman, 313; Heyes, 235ff.; and above p. 400.

42b, 43 This investiture is specifically Egyptian. The glorious robes of שֵׁשׁ (שֵׁשׁ, "fine linen," is an Egyptian fabric and is also exported from Egypt, Ezek 27:7; the word is an Egyptian loan word *šes*; the transferal of robes as a distinction is also attested in Egypt; Erman, 317; Heyes, 242), the golden chain (as a gift from the king; cf. Erman, 159, 174ff., 317; Heyes, 248ff.; here it seems to be the king's own necklace; for such a gold chain on a king, see Erman, 114, figure), the state wagon (to be envisioned in the form of a "troika," decorated with emblems; concerning deluxe Egyptian chariots, see Erman, 650-51; Heyes, 252-53), as well as criers running before him (this practice still appears in the Orient; it is known in Egypt since ancient times; Heyes, 253-54; cf. also Esth 6:9,11). The legend recounts all of this with great interest in things foreign and, especially, with childish glee over the high honors to which our Joseph rises. The meaning of אַבְרֵךְ has long been disputed (bibliography in Spiegelberg, *Ägyptologische Randglossen zum AT*, 14ff., and Heyes, 254ff.). According to Spiegelberg it is the equivalent of Eg. *'brek'* "your heart to you" = "pay attention." Regarding the construction of וְנָתוֹן see §113z.

45a It is natural for the Canaanite slave, come to high honors in Egypt, to assume an eminent Egyptian name (cf. Erman, 157, 683). צָפְנַת פַּעְנֵחַ is probably equivalent to the Egyptian *depnute-ef-ônch,* "The god says, 'He lives'," according to Steindorff (*Zeitschr. f. äg. Spr.* 27:41ff.; 30:50ff.). Similar names <438> occur frequently beginning in the ninth century, but become common only in the seventh century (bibliography in Heyes, 258ff.). אָסְנַת corresponds to the Egyptian *ns-nt* "belonging to the goddess Neit," or, according to Spiegelberg (*Ägyptologische Randglossen zum AT*, 18-19) following LXX Ασενεθ, Ασεννεθ, it corresponds to *'ws-n-nt* "she belongs to Neit" (bibliography in Heyes, 261ff.). אוֹן is Heliopollis, Egyptian *Anu*, with a famed solar temple, north of Memphis, the chief seat of religious literature such as the Book of the Dead (Heyes, 265ff.). The high priest of On is one of the most eminent priests in the (New) Kingdom. The priest played a very significant role in civic life at that time (cf. Erman, 154-55; Heyes, 270ff.). Thus, Joseph married into one of the most eminent families in the land. One may observe that the legends report neither Joseph's conversion nor does it explicitly maintain that he remained faithful to his ancestral faith. In reality it was understood that a high official of foreign origins would at least publicly worship the Egyptian gods. Yet it should be noted that Joseph's new Egyptian name contains no divine name. According to Prof. Meyer (orally), this is the narrator's intention. Baentsch (*Monotheismus*, 49-50) sees in Joseph's marriage with the daughter of the priest of On a vital consciousness that the "fathers" were familiar with the religious ideas alive at that sanctuary—that is, according to Baentsch, 82, monotheism. But this element is apparently intended here only to show the high honor Joseph had gained, and nothing indicates that he shared certain religious endeavors with the priesthood of On. The narrator takes no offense at the marriage with a pagan. **45b** וַיֵּצֵא עַל is linguistically difficult. The clause may be nothing other than a variant of v 46b (Dillmann). Others offer conjectures. **46b** The ceremonious exit in which he presents himself to the land as its new lord. Inspection journeys are Egyptian practice (Heyes, 272-73; Erman, 106).

47-49 *The good years.* **48** Sam and LXX read הַשָּׁנִים אֲשֶׁר הָיָה הַשֹּׂבַע (Dillmann, Ball, etc.). **49** "Until he ceased counting" is in fairy-tale style.

50-52 *Joseph's sons.* The piece is inserted here because something will later be told about the sons (48:8ff.). **51** The rare form (piel, otherwise hiphil) and pronunciation נַשַּׁנִי is chosen because of its assonance with Menaŝŝe. It may seem strange to us that Joseph has completely forgotten his father's household, but it seemed quite natural to the ancient. Accordingly, if one were to ask the narrator why Joseph never once in all the long years sent a message to his father, he would answer, "He forgot his father's household." Similar elements often occur in Chinese dramas as "an unusual precondition for the effective surprises of later acts" (Gottschall, *Theater u. Drama der Chinese*, 206). **52** הִפְרַנִי, "he made me <439> fruitful," does not stand in good contrast to "in the land of my suffering." Instead, we expect a form of פאר (cf. Psa 149:4, יְפָאֵר עֲנָוִים בִּישׁוּעָה, "he glorifies the suffering with salvation," cf. Isa 61:3), thus הִפְאֲרַנִי or, since the hiphil does not occur, פֵּאֲרַנִי. LXX reads ὕψωσεν, ηὔξησεν. According to Meyer, (*Israeliten*, 15) Manasseh, Bab. *Mannaŝu*, is a personal name, the name of the chief for whom the tribe is named. Also according to him, Ephraim is the name of a region (514). It should not be assumed that both tribes are of partial Egyptian heritage (contra Rieß, *Preuß. Jahrb.* 74 [1893]:440).

53-57 *The famine years.* J already has 47:13ff. in view when he describes the famine years in Egypt.

V **56a** interrupts the coherence and is probably an addition. **56b** אֶת־כָּל־אֲשֶׁר בָּהֶם seems to be corrupt; LXX, Vulg, Pesh (Targ-Onk) read "granary." Lagarde (*Symmicta* 1:57) suggests a word such as the Talmudic אִשְׁבוֹרָא, sirus. Kittel wants to insert בָּר with Sam or to read (with LXX Pesh?) בָּל־אוֹצְרוֹת בָּר. בָּר also characterizes the diction of E (cf. above, p. 416). For וַיִּשְׁבֹּר one should read וַיִּשְׁבֵּר following 42:6 (Dillmann, Ball, etc.). Thus, the legends have accompanied Joseph from sorrow to honor and majesty. He now has the power to harm or benefit his brothers if they come to Egypt. Now the narrators take up the main thread of the Joseph account once again and report what happened when Joseph and his brothers saw one another in Egypt once again.

The Brothers' Encounters with Joseph

The accounts of Joseph's encounters with his brothers constitute the second part of the narrative of Joseph's experiences with his brothers. The famine drives the brothers to Egypt. But here they are in Joseph's power: he is the lord of Egypt. Thus—this is the esthetic attraction of the following scenes—the situation is totally reversed. Before, he was in their power; now they are in his. He also has the upper hand in that he recognizes them but they do not recognize him. The legend now recounts how Joseph made full use of this situation. He thoroughly punishes and torments them. They go from one fear and distress to another, just as they deserve in relation to him. The narrators' sense of justice is expressed here. After punishing them sufficiently, he pardons them and becomes their benefactor. Thus the legend glorifies Joseph's nobility. Similar situations occur in Chinese drama, especially the drama "Su-thsin," where "Su-thsin, the philosopher clothed in rags, shivering in the cold, whose own father chased from his house, humiliated by his own stepbrother, suddenly returns home with embroidered robes, the golden seal on his belt, and like Joseph in Egypt, sees those who committed crimes against him bowing before him in the dust and after a harsh censure forgives them" (Gottschall, *Theater u. Drama der Chinesen*, 54). "The sympathy elicited by the unexpected suffering of the fortunate and the surprise <440> elicited by the sudden good fortune of the unfortunate are always the intended effects" ([Gottschall], 54; cf. also p. 105, where the exile suddenly reappears as a high state official: "Father and mother, wife and mother-in-law, even his stepbrothers come to bow before him." "He hesitates at first to receive his relatives," "but he hears their requests and finally pardons them." "These relatives have transgressed against family duties. The hero can only restore the disturbed moral equilibrium through extraordinary forgiveness").

The two encounters between Joseph and his brothers closely resemble one another. Not only do they deal with the same situation, but the accounts have the same structure. Details also agree. Both times Joseph allows them to think of him as a magician (42:25ff.; 43:33; 44:5, 15); both times, in order to frighten them, he employs the technique of hiding valuable objects in the grain sack (42:25ff.; 44:1ff.); the first time he kept Simeon, the second time he wants to retain Benjamin. This implies that an earlier form of the legend knew of only one encounter, which would also have been completely sufficient for the course of the narrative: the brothers come to Egypt, Joseph recognizes them and torments them fittingly; he treats them as spies or thieves, throws them into prison, etc.; finally, he reveals himself to them and has them bring his father to Egypt. This one encounter has been separated into two scenes in accordance with later stylistic sensibilities. The two scenes are distinct in that Benjamin is not present the first time, but is brought along the second time on Joseph's express instructions and plays, then, the main role. The turning point of the whole, the revelation, can ensue, of course, only at the conclusion of the second scene. This expansion of the narrative is—in our terms—perhaps not to the advantage of the esthetic impression. Among other things, the repetition of the motif of the hidden money brought with it the unfortunate circumstance that this motif cannot be fully utilized the first time. The brothers fear they we will be treated as thieves because of this money (43:12, 18-22), but they are reassured that nothing will befall them because of it (43:23). This is per se very astonishing. But it can be explained by the fact that the same narrators want to recount the matter once more and this time seriously (44:1ff.). This expansion of the material occurs both in J and in E. It occurred, therefore, in a phase of the tradition prior to both works.

66. The First Encounter of the Brothers with Joseph without Benjamin 42 EJ

Source analysis. The chapter stems essentially from E. The following indicate E: the reminder of Joseph's dreams (v 9; cf. 37:55f. E); Reuben's status among the brothers (22, 37 [24]) and the allusion to his intercession for Joseph (37:22, 29f. E); the names אלהים (v 28b) and Jacob (vv 1 twice, 4, 29, 36), and the expressions מִשְׁמָר (vv 17, 19), בַּר (vv 3, 25), בְּזֹאת (v 15 as in 34:15), and סָהַר (v 34 as in 34:10, 21; 37:28). Sections from J have also been inserted. This is indicated by יִשְׂרָאֵל (v 5), as well as the dual account of the way the money is found in the sack—(1) on the journey (vv 27-28), (2) only after they arrived at Jacob (v 35)—even the second time this discovery is recounted as new and surprising. The expressions also interchange: אַמְתַּחַת (v 27-28) J, otherwise the chapter employs שָׂק; בַּר (vv 3, 25) E and אֹכֶל (vv 7, 10) J. The following details belong to J: vv 2 (with a new beginning וַיֹּאמֶר as in v 1b; v2a ‖ v 1a; "that we may live and not die" as in 43:8; 47:19 J), 4b (קְרָא אָסוֹן, v 38; 44:29 J), 5 ("Israel"; "among those coming" refers to 41:57 J; "you have come to see where the land is open," וַיָּבֹאוּ v 5 ‖ וַיָּבֹאוּ v 6b; consequently v 6b stems from E), 7 ("he recognized them and acted like a stranger," v 7 ‖ "he recognized them, they did not recognize him," v 8; אֹכֶל J; in contrast, the clause "he spoke harshly to them," belongs to E because of v 30), 9bβ ("you have come to see where the land is open" ‖ "you are spies," 9bα; the latter belongs to E because of vv 30, 31, 34), 10 (response to the accusation of v 9bβ), 11a (‖ 13a = 32 E), 12 (once again the same accusation as in 9bβ; according to E, this question concerns who the brothers are; in contrast, according to J, it concerns why they have come; this distinction is confirmed by אֹכֶל in v 10), <441> 27 (where אֶחָד־שָׂקוֹ must trace a redactor's emendation), 28 (up to לֵאמֹר), and 38 (קְרָא אָסוֹן, repeated in 44:29 J). The text of E has been preserved almost without interruption. Yet וַיְדַבֵּר אִתָּם קָשֹׁת (v 7) originally stood after v 9a in E (Dillmann) and v 28bγ (beginning with לֵאמֹר) after v 35 (Kautzsch-Socin). Procksch attributes vv 1a, 2a,bα, 7a,bβ, 10a, 11a,bα, 12, 15a, 16a,bα, 17, 18, 19, 21-24, 25aβ,γ, 29, 30a, 31a, 33, 34aγ, b, 35, 28bβ, 36, 37 to E. But this analysis is unfortunate where it differs from the analysis offered above. The analysis of vv 29-37 is particularly erroneous. The assurance that they are harmless people (vv 30a, 33 34aγ) responds to the suspicion that they are spies (vv 30b, 31b, 34aβ). Thus, the two belong together. Furthermore, vv 36-37 presuppose the demand that Benjamin be produced (v 34aα). Accordingly, the whole section (vv 29-37) is a unit and stems entirely from E. Thus, the expression מְרַגְּלִים (vv 30, 32, 34) belongs to E, as do the clauses in vv 9bα, 11b, 14, 16bβ. Furthermore, the question (v 7), the accusation (vv 9, 12), the excuse (v 10), and the account (v 5) are all linked by the word בוֹא (usually with ל and an inf. constr.). In a similar fashion, לִשְׁבָּר־אֹכֶל link vv 7b and 10b and אֵינֶנּוּ link vv 13, 32, 36. The reminder of the dreams (v 9a) has the obeisance as a necessary precondition, etc. Eerdmans (67ff.) also considers Gen 42 to be unified and considers only vv 27-28 as redactional.

1-4 *The brothers journey to Egypt.* V **1** makes a new beginning (cf. comments on 41:1). שֶׁבֶר is grain offered for sale (Dillmann). Jacob's statement, "What are you looking at (What are you waiting on)?" is an energetic beginning. For תִּתְרָאוּ Sam reads תתיראו (Ehrlich). Kittel (following LXX and VetLat) suggests תְּאָחֲרוּ, "Do you wait?" as a possibility. **2** Concerning וְלֹא in a purpose clause see §109g. **3** "Ten of Joseph's brothers go to the Nile Valley, so many in order to obtain more and to be able to bring more back" (Franz Delitzsch). **4** Jacob does not permit Benjamin to go along because of his special concern and because the way is so dangerous. As the only son of the beloved Rachel left to him and as his youngest son, he loves him more than all his other sons (44:20ff.). The preference of the father for one (which seems quite natural to the ancient narrators; cf. comments on 30:16; 33:2) is the precondition for all that follows.

5-17 *The brothers' first discussion with Joseph.* **5** "In the midst of those coming," that is, those who, according to 41:57, come to Joseph from all over the world to buy grain. **6** That the brothers meet Joseph while purchasing grain is obvious in J according to 41:57. The verse stems, therefore, from E. שַׁלִּיט, a late word in Hebrew, may have been inserted by a later hand (cf. Kuenen, *Einleitung* ¶16 n. 12, etc.). The notion that the kingdom's highest official sells grain in person is a fairy-tale element. Such elements also occur in 41:8, 38ff., 49; 44:4. Concerning הַמַּשְׁבִּיר see §126k. **7** It is natural enough that the <442> brothers do not recognize him. In the meanwhile, the boy Joseph has become a man. Additionally, he now bears an authentic Egyptian name and appears in the clothing of an eminent foreigner. E adds that they think him long since dead (v 22). וַיַּכִּרֵם וַיִּתְנַכֵּר is assonant. A similar scene, although perhaps in imitation of the biblical account, appears in Wenzig (*Westslav. Märchenschatz,* 29-30). Why does Joseph treat his brothers so poorly here and in the following scene? It has been said that he wanted to "test" or even "reform" them and that he acts as the "tool of providence," "under the impulse of a higher necessity," contrary to his natural inclinations (so Dillmann; even more complicated and modern according to Franz Delitzsch). The ancient narrator thinks much more simply: Joseph wants to punish his brothers. This is not—in the understanding of antiquity—base "revenge" because they deserve punishment indeed. Nor is Joseph a Christian who simply forgives injustice done him according to the Lord's commandment. One should not import Christian ideas here. קָשׁוֹת is employed in a neutral sense (§122q). **9** One of the most significant elements in the account: thus, the dreams the brothers strove to hinder have been fulfilled nevertheless! The suspicion that they are spies can be explained by circumstances on the Egyptian border. Egypt feared the greed of its neighbors, especially to the East. The border to the East was fortified and zealously guarded (cf. Erman, 692, 708). **10** Concerning וַעֲבָדֶיךָ see §163a. It may be, however, that the ו should be stricken following Sam, LXX, and Pesh (Ball, Kautzsch[3]).

11ff. The suspicion that they are spies seems to be strengthened by the fact that they are so many (the assumption is that—then as now—it is rare and unlikely from the outset that a man would have ten sons). Consequently, the brothers assure him that "they all" are the sons of one man, brothers (vv 11a, 13a) and they have not come together for a hostile purpose. So far the two sources agree. E continues, then, that, in order to demonstrate this contention, they detail their family situation more precisely (v 13b). In the J continuation, omitted here but reconstructable from 43:37-7; 44:19-23, Joseph interrogated them further about his father and his brother. The two recensions were, thus, very similar to one another. **11** נִחְנוּ is a rare form (§32d). Sam reads אֲנַחְנוּ. **13a** Despite the accents, a new section begins after עֲבָדֶיךָ (Dillmann, Holzinger, Kittel). Others strike אֲנַחְנוּ (Olshausen). **13b** "The one (who is yet missing) is no more." The expression "is not" is intentionally euphemistic. They could not say what they did to him. If the account were more refined, Joseph would have inquired further at this point. **14** "As a man of high status, Joseph wants to behave properly toward them" (Dillmann). The expression resembles 41:28, suggesting that הַדָּבָר should be inserted (Ball; Sievers 2:351; etc.). **15-16** Why does he demand that they bring Benjamin and why does he keep them in prison for so long? First, he wants to punish them (on a likely charge). Furthermore, he would <443> like to have Benjamin, his full brother, with him. The oath "by the life of the king" is Egyptian practice (Driver). The pronunciation חֵי in the oath by God, חֵי in the oath by humans is only rabbinical finesse. **16** Concerning הֵאָסְרוּ, "you must remain in prison," see §110c. For כִּי in the nominal clause of an oath see 1 Sam 20:3; 26:16; 29:6 (Ehrlich). **17** So he allows them to sit there for three days. They deserve nothing else from him. Oriental officials behave in this way. The significant role played by the prison in these Joseph accounts is remarkable (39:20ff.; 40:1ff.; 42:19ff.). The Egyptian prison must have been a well-known stop for Hebrew men.

18-24 *The second conversation.* The material per se does not require this division into two conversations. But the narrator wants to do this in order to take up more space. The two conversations differ in that Joseph is more harsh the first time, the second time (after considering the matter for three days) he proceeds more leniently. Only one of the brothers should remain in prison. **18** Concerning עֲשׂוּ וִהְיוּ see §110f. "I fear the deity" refers to the fact that God punishes the upperclass individual who treats the unprotected foreigner as guilty merely on the basis of suspicion (cf. above, p. 397). This notion will have also been the real reason, in the legend's opinion, that Joseph refrains from chastising his brothers too harshly. One should not overlook the fact that the narrator presumes a certain international religious morality here. The deity protects—even foreigners know this—the unprotected homeless (cf. comments on 20:3; 39:9). **19** Concerning אֲחִיכֶם אֶחָד see §134d. **20** They will "die" if Joseph gives them no grain. וַיַּעֲשׂוּ־כֵן seems to be a variant of וַיַּעַשׂ לָהֶם כֵּן (v 25; Kautzsch-Socin; Ball; etc.). **21-23** In the fear of their heart, the brothers recognize in this distress (צָרָה) the just retribution for the distress (צָרָה) to which they once subjected their brother Joseph without heeding his pleas. The same expression, צָרָה, is employed intentionally. That which they once did is now done to them. No one heeds their words now. The basis is the universal principle that the sinner is punished in a manner appropriate to his sin. This account is particularly beautiful in that the brothers already recognize why this happens to them even before they suspect the relationship. Thus they express a fundamental notion of this narrative. The description of Joseph's fear does not occur in the account in Gen 37. It is "supplied" here. The brothers' words contain, in ancient Hebrew terms, a very complex psychological portrayal: <444> they remember what they thought when Joseph was in anguish. **22** Reuben's words are an approximate citation of 37:22. **23** This element, that Joseph speaks Egyptian and converses with his brothers through "the" (usual) translator, is particularly demonstrative of a very advanced, one could almost say refined, narrative art. In the older, more naive accounts, the difference in languages was over-looked. All the pagans who appear in them simply speak Hebrew with one another (cf. above, p. 383). בֵּינֹתָם refers to two distinct parties, בֵּינֵיהֶם does not (cf. above p. 297). **24** Joseph cries. Tears also play a significant role in the rest of the Joseph narrative. He cries because he remembers his own pain and because he sympathizes with his brothers. Despite this compassion, however, he does not refrain from fully executing his plan. Indeed, he prepares a new horror for his brothers (v 25). They must be punished, and they have not yet been sufficiently punished. This element, Joseph's compassion, unnecessary in the immediate context, is employed at this point with skillful wisdom. We are supposed to know already that Joseph is not only angry, but also capable of com-passion. Thus, the subsequent total reversal in Joseph's attitude is anticipated. The whole psychological portrayal of Joseph, in whom two attitudes struggle with one another, is the most complicated and complete characterization in all of Genesis. Joseph chooses one of the brothers to cast, bound, into prison. He is to pay for the sins of all. Joseph does this also in order to use him as a hostage to maintain power over the others. He binds him "before their eyes." They are to see that matters are serious. The one chosen is Simeon, the eldest after Reuben of whose friendliness toward him Joseph has just learned. If the brothers consider, they must also be astonished and touched by this twist of fate that the eldest of those guilty is now punished. **25** "They filled their sacks with grain." The coordi-nation of the finite verb with the infinitive is unusual. The clause is probably an addition. It is also obvious. Or should לְמַלֵּא be read (Ball; Kittel)? He gives them provisions for the journey to assure them of his grace. They will seem all the more guilty later when the theft of the money is discovered—once again an almost refined element (the same motif occurs in 44:1). וַיַּעַשׂ is probably an error for וַיַּעֲשׂוּ (Dillmann, etc.; cf. Pesh, Vulg). The money in the grain sack is comparable to the royal crowns hidden in a sack of barley in an Egyptian fairy tale (cf. Ranke, in Greßmann, *Altorient. Texte u. Bilder* 1:22-23) as well as to the gold in the pot of olives in the story of Ali Hodyah, merchant of Baghdad in *1001 Nacht* (Weill 3:243ff.).

26-38 *The journey home and arrival.* **27, 28** Insertion from J. The J account is abbreviated in order to avoid repetition of E. According to 43:21, all the brothers found their money in their sacks. This element will have stood after v 28bβ. מָלוֹן is not properly "inn," but a barn- or shed-like building erected <445> on the wilderness route (Franz Delitzsch). The money is on the top in the sack so that it is found as soon as the sacks are opened. E differs. The money is found only when the sacks are emptied so that it is deeper in the sack (v 35). When they see the money, they are terrified. They fear that when they return—as they must for Simeon's sake—they will be treated like thieves. At the same time they are concerned about the way the money may have gotten into their sacks. They believe—a fairy-tale element—that God must have miraculously put the money in their sacks in order to punish them. This fear was precisely what Joseph wanted to cause. הָאֶחָד (v 27) means "the first" (§134k). LXX and Vulg (Ball) add לְ after הוּשָׁב (v 28). Concerning חָרַד אֶל see §119gg.

29-34 In the manner of the "extensive style" the preceding events are repeated in a detailed speech (cf. introduction ¶3.20). **29** Concerning הַקֹּרֹת see §122q. **30** According to LXX, בְּמִשְׁמָר should be inserted after אֹתָנוּ (Ball; Holzinger; Driver; etc.; cf. 40:3). **32** Sam, LXX, and Pesh (Ball) read אֲנַחְנוּ אַחִים. שֶׁבֶר should be read after וְאֶת

following LXX, Targ. Onq, and Pesh (with Dillmann; Ball; etc.; cf. v 19). 34b LXX, Pesh, and Vulg (Ball; Kittel) read וְאֶת־אֲחִיכֶם. The fact that they must then pass through the land is a "supplementation" common in such repetitions. סחר means "to move around," here of a traveling trader. V 35 apparently interrupts the dialogue, but is eminently fitting to the context. The discovery occurs precisely at the point when the new journey to Egypt is advised. The element heightens the conflict, then. וַיִּרְאוּ וַיִּירָאוּ is a case of assonance. 36 Jacob's brief, passionate statements are impressively distinct from the brothers' long speeches. Here and in similar passages in the Joseph narrative (such as 37:33ff.; 44:27ff) the narrators find touching, even heartrending tones, well known to any Bible reader. Because of them, this narrative seems to the modern the most beautiful narrative in Genesis. Jacob complains, "You speak well. It makes no difference to you. My children, not yours, are involved" (Dillmann). Consequently, Reuben (37), here, too, very nobly offers his own sons as a pledge. It should be noted that by resisting a new trip to Egypt for the brothers Jacob will actually leave Simeon in prison. Thus, he places little value on his fate. According to the tradition presumed here Reuben has two sons. According to 46:9 he has four. Jacob could no longer resist Reuben's words and gave his permission <446> (also in the J parallel, 43:9-11). The unpreserved continuation in E will thus have recounted that the brothers returned to Egypt immediately upon their arrival in Canaan. They are compelled by the thought of Simeon's fate. J differs. According to J Joseph retained no pledge. Instead, he trusted that the famine would bring them back to him sooner or later. According to J, then, a longer period transpires between arrival and departure (43:10). Only when the famine compelled him did the father give consent (43:1ff.). Accordingly, J is more slowly paced and expansive. Consequently, the redactor, who always prefers the more detailed report, took up the J report in the following section. 38 J (‖ v 36), Israel's response to the brothers' declaration that they cannot return to Egypt without Benjamin. Concerning the original placement of this statement see the comments on 43:1, 2. Concerning Jacob's statement about שְׁאוֹל see the comments on 37:35. Sad is the fate of the old man who may not depart comforted by a joyful look at his blossoming children, but must go to the underworld in misery and distress over his children. This statement constitutes a deeply felt contrast to Jacob's eventual beautiful death. Regarding the syntax see §159g.

67. The Brothers' Second Encounter with Joseph 43, 44 JE

As the account approaches the climax its pace slows. Consequently, the individual scenes are separated from one another such that they approximate whole narratives in scope: (1) the decision to travel (43:1-14); (2) the encounter in Joseph's house (43:15-34); (3) the hidden cup (44).

Source criticism of Gen 43–44. The pieces stem from J (cf. Wellhausen, *Composition*[3], 56ff. and Dillmann): Judah speaks for the brothers (43:3ff., 8ff.; 44:16, 18); the father is called Israel (43:6, 8, 11); the first encounter with Joseph is described somewhat differently than in E (42)—the chief distinctions are that Joseph asked the brothers about their father and brother (43:7; 44:19) and that the money is discovered immediately in the first night watch (43:21). J is further indicated by the expressions אָכַל (43:2, 4, 20, 22; 41:1, 25), מָלוֹן (43:21), מִסְפּוֹא (43:24), אַמְתַּחַת (43:12, 18, 21-23; 44:1, 2, 8, 11, 12), הִתְמַהְמָהּ (43:10), מְעַט in the constr. state (43:2, 11; 44:25), and קָרָא אָסוֹן

(44:29). אֱלֹהִים in conversation with pagans (43:29; 44:16) is no argument against J (cf. comments on 39:9). Yet, clauses have also been adapted from E. This is clearly true of 43:14a and 23b which assume Simeon's imprisonment (cf. comments on Gen 42). Procksch also attributes vv 12a, 13, 14b, 15aβ,b, 16aα to E. But J (v 22) also presumes the כֶּסֶף מִשְׁנֶה (v 12 [v 15]). J must also have reported the fact that Benjamin also makes the journey (vv 13, 15). Concerning v 14b see the comments. J must have also reported that Joseph had seen the brothers (vv 15bβ, 16aα) prior to v 16aβ. Only the fact that he also sees Benjamin seems to conflict with v 29. But see the comments on the passage.

I. The Decision to Travel 43:1-14 JE

1ff. Wellhausen's brilliant insight (*Composition*[3], 57) has illuminated the whole context. Notably, 43:28 speaks of a journey which the brothers plan (אֲשֶׁר תֵּלְכוּ־בָהּ). This statement cannot be made, then, at the end of the first, but at the beginning of the second journey. It belongs then in the context of 43:1ff. The repetition in 44:24ff. points in the same direction. Accordingly, the whole context of J <447> can now be reconstructed. When the supplies were exhausted, the father commissioned his sons to travel to Egypt (43:1, 2 [44:25]). But they answer, "We cannot do so without Benjamin" (44:26). Then he responds, "Benjamin will not go with you. If something were to happen to him, I would die in distress" (42:38 [44:27-29]). Here follows 43:3ff: Judah explains to him why it would be impossible to appear again before the man without Benjamin. Judah's statement presupposes that Israel has not already heard of Joseph's demand. Accordingly, the report the brothers gave their father at the end of the first journey (44:24) cannot have mentioned it. The narrator will have based this silence on the fact that the brothers did not dare say anything about it at first and only mentioned it when they can no longer avoid doing so. As a wise artist, the narrator saved this report concerning Joseph's demand for the situation (43:1ff.) when Joseph's demand and Israel's tender paternal love come into gripping conflict. Red[JE] removed 42:37 from its context in J because he needed this verse as a response to Reuben's suggestion in 42:37 (E). **1** This general element, the precondition for the whole narrative, forcefully interrupts the family narrative. **3** הָאִישׁ refers to the unknown. Concerning בִּלְתִּי with a nominal clause see §163c. **6** According to our sense for language הַעוֹד introduces an indirect question (§150i n. 3). The brothers' whole conversation with Joseph is not recounted here (contra Wellhausen; cf. the source analysis of Gen 42), but only the second portion concerning Benjamin. Joseph asked about their background then on the pretext of seeing whether they had evil intentions. **7** Concerning נֵדַע see §107t; concerning יֹאמַר see §107k.

8-10 *Judah's noble suggestion* (‖ 42:37 E). **8** Since Jacob is so concerned for Benjamin, Judah has reason for referring to the fact that they also have small children which must starve if he delays. **9b** Regarding the construction see §159n,o. **10** Judah's statement is a (naive) exhortation. כִּי עַתָּה appears in the apodosis as in 31:42. The notion that they have already delayed for a long time demonstrates the narrator's efforts to extend the action in the hearer's imagination. V 10b means, "Then we would already have the second journey successfully behind us" (Winckler, <448> *Forschungen* 3:460).

11-13 *Israel reluctantly acquiesces.* As an experienced man, he knows the wonders a small gift at the right time can accomplish and he recommends to his sons that they take such a gift with them. The narrator took up this motif in order more clearly to distinguish the two encounters with Joseph. They brought no gift on the first; in the second it plays a specific role. The gift also demonstrates how respect for Joseph has grown in the meanwhile. It is common for one to appear before someone more powerful with a gift (33:11; 1 Sam 10:27; 1 Kgs 5:1). The gifts mentioned here, intended to please the eminent Egyptian, will be products of the land of Canaan that are rare and costly in Egypt (cf. 37:25). **11** The meaning of the word זִמְרָה (καρποί) is clear from the context. The origin of the word is dubious. It is hardly related to זִמְרָה, string sound, song. דְּבַשׁ is honey or (like Arabic *dibs*) condensed grape syrup (also an export product from Palestine in Ezek 27:17). בָּטְנִים is probably the nuts of the *pistacia vera*, a favorite snack. שְׁקֵדִים are almonds. Regarding צֳרִי וְלֹאת לֹט see the comments on 37:25. V **12** presumes that the brothers have also told about the rediscovered money. This, too, must have been in the brothers' unpreserved report at the end of the first journey. וְכֶסֶף מִשְׁנֶה means a second sum (cf. Gesenius-Buhl[14], s.v. מִשְׁנֶה). It means substantially the same as כֶּסֶף אַחֵר (v 22). מִשְׁנֶה is appositional (§131e). Contrariwise, משנה-כסף (v 15) means "twice as much money" (§131q). **14a** E. This blessing with which the father dismisses his sons concludes the speech in which Jacob permits them to travel with Benjamin and is therefore part of Jacob's response to 42:37. "And . . . Benjamin!" Poor Jacob's last statement is especially touching. אֵל שַׁדַּי does not occur elsewhere in E and may stem from editors. אֲחִיכֶם אַחֵר resembles אֲחִיכֶםאֶחָד (42:19). **14b** The sad resignation with which Jacob dismisses his sons differs markedly from the hopeful blessing in v 14a E. Consequently, v 14b will not be from E. שָׁכֹלְתִּי is a pausal form (§29u). Regarding the perfect see §106o. There is a nice contrast between this passionate speech and the calm tone of the account which continues in vv 15ff.

II. The Encounter in Joseph's House 43:15-34 J (E)

The narrator distinguished the two encounters with Joseph as much as possible in order to avoid the boredom of repetition. The first time, Joseph confuses his brothers by treating them harshly, the second time by being very cordial to them and even inviting them into his house. This second encounter takes place, then, in Joseph's home, while the first takes place in his office. The narrator separated this narrative also <449> into two scenes: At first the brothers are in the house (vv 17-23) without Joseph, who has something to do (vv 17-25), then Joseph joins them (vv 26-34).

15-16 *Transition.* If Joseph were to see Benjamin already, the point of the touching scene (vv 29-30) would be precluded. אֶת־בִּנְיָמִן is the addition of a person who wanted to establish Joseph's cordiality toward his brothers which was actually intended to confuse them. One should read אֹתָם. Hospitality toward business acquaintances is often practiced in the Orient and also by us. The fact, however, that the brothers are supposed to dine with the high-ranking minister and that he even has an animal slaughtered for them is a high, excessive honor. Concerning טְבֹחַ see §65b. The presumption is that the Egyptians eat their main meal at midday.

17-25 *First scene.* The unusual cordiality which the brothers could in no wise expect causes them, as Joseph had wished, new anxiety. The narrator considers this element poignant. It resembles the notion that Joseph falls prey to the hatred of his brothers because of his father's preference and the notion that the favor of his Egyptian lord brings him into a situation which lands him in prison. Narrators in this style enjoy reporting such rare consequences. In the context of the whole, the brothers' anxiety is especially important. Joseph's anxiety is requited in this fashion (42:21). Consequently, the narrators do not weary of reporting the brothers distress in ever new variations. The narrator took up this element here all the more happily since it offered him such a good opportunity to repeat once again the matter of the money in the sacks in a new situation. **18** הַשָּׁב is an intentionally ambiguous expression. The brothers fear the loss of the money will be recouped from them and their donkeys. Such treatment of the thief is common in Israel (Exod 22:2), and things will not have been much different in Egypt. This is, after all, the nature of the matter. וּלְהִתְנַפֵּל עָלֵינוּ is a variant for the preceding (Ball, Kautzsch[3]). **19** They begin to speak as soon as they enter the door. **20-22** They excuse themselves before they are accused. All this demonstrates their anxiety. **21** Compare 42:27. The money is weighed. There were no coins yet (cf. Benzinger[2], 196ff.). **23a** This anxiety, however, proves to be unfounded—a surprising turn of events. The caretaker's answer is only comprehensible if he is aware of Joseph's intentions (similarly in 44:10). The reference to the foreign god is hardly Egyptian, but it seems natural to the Israelite narrator who knows of only one God. **23b** E. **25** <450> They arrange the gift and set it up already so one can see how large and expensive it is. LXX reads יֹאכַל (Dillmann; Kittel dubiously).

    26-34 *Second scene in Joseph's house.* **26a** Concerning וַיָּבִיאוּ (in Baer), the (consonantal) א with mappiq, see §14d. הַבַּיְתָה[2] has probably entered the text erroneously (Holzinger, et al.). **26b** "They fell to the ground before him" (‖ v 28) may stem from E. There is no further discussion of the gift or how Joseph received it. The motif is dropped. It is even more remarkable that the money found in the sack is not mentioned to Joseph (cf. above p. 423). The accusation that they may be spies is not made again in the second encounter either. In the old, tight, legend style, such dropped motifs do not occur. In this point, the old style is more skillful than the more detailed style. **27** That Joseph first asks about his father is a touching feature: he is a good son (cf. 43:7 J and 45:3 E). **28** They fall down before him in acknowledgment of the great honor the high lord has shown them by his question about their fathers' well-being. The legend here and elsewhere emphasizes Joseph's superiority to his brothers and how submissive they are. Sam and LXX insert וַיֹּאמֶר בָּרוּךְ הָאִישׁ הַהוּא לֵאלֹהִים after v 28a and transfrom the prostration before Joseph into a prostration before God. Judaism considers it apostasy to prostrate oneself before a human (cf. Esth 3:2ff.). **29-31** Joseph sees Benjamin. This scene, how the brothers see one another after such a long separation, makes a particularly tender impression. **29** Joseph guesses that Benjamin stands before him (הֲ with a positive response, §150e). He does not know him. In the narrator's opinion, Benjamin can only have been a very small child when Joseph was stolen. Benjamin is—this is presumed (בְּנִי)—much younger than Joseph. Concerning יָחְנְךָ see §67n. **30** Regarding Joseph's tears see the variant 42:24. Even the cousin rejoices and cries for joy when he meets his cousin abroad (29:11). Why should the brother not cry when he sees his only brother once again in a foreign country! Here no eye would be dry among the ancient hearers. The brothers' punishment is not yet complete, however. Instead, the worst is yet to come. Therefore, Joseph does not yet reveal himself. This psychological depiction—how "his bowels burn," how he involuntarily breaks out in tears, how he quickly withdraws and cries in quiet and thus finds the strength to control himself—this whole portrayal is a minor museum piece. Such psychological portrayals require a highly developed ability for psychological observation. One does not yet find such in the oldest legends. Sam reads עַל־אֶחָיו (Ball; cf. 1 Kgs 3:26). 32 As the superior, Joseph eats alone. <451> But the brothers and the Egyptians also eat separately (concerning this Egyptian practice, cf. Exod 8:22; according to Herodotus 2:41, no Egyptian used the utensils of a Greek; Dillmann). This element is superfluous for the course of the action. The narrator employed it because his hearers like to hear unusual Egyptian practices. This element interests us for the history of religion. In ancient times, Israel must have been much more open-minded in its (religious) table practices than later. It was amazed at that time at this Egyptian reticence which it later practiced itself. At any rate, the reference is not to separate tables—the Egyptians do not sit around a table at banquets as we do (cf. the figures in Erman 338-39, 344-45)—but, since sitting is first mentioned in v 33 and food service in v 32, to separate seats. תוֹעֵבָה is a technical term for that which is religiously (morally and esthetically) abominable, forbidden. One should read למצרים (Ball; Holzinger; et al.). 33 The purpose of the table order is to frighten the brothers: they must believe in magic! What sort of man knows their ages although they have not told him? This is the kind of situation that otherwise plays out between a person and a god who has appeared unawares. The assumption is that the brothers are ranked according to their ages. If they recognized Joseph, the brothers would find this table order natural. 34 A third comment about the way they ate, perhaps from E? Joseph honors Benjamin (according to ancient practice) by multiple portions (cf. comments on 18:6ff.). One concerned with custom and decorum, however, will not eat all of this. The number five recurs in the Joseph narrative (45:22; 47:2 [41:34; 47:24]; cf. also Isa 19:18). "One could conclude from this that, at least in the opinion of the Hebrews, the number five played a role with the Egyptians" (Meinhold, *Sabbat*, 19; concerning the [not very frequent] number five in the O.T., cf. Meinhold, loc. cit.; concerning the number five among the Babylonians, cf. KAT[3], see index, s.v. *ḥamuštu*; according to Winckler, *Gesch. Isr.* 2:60, the number five in the Joseph narrative is supposed to signify the five epagomenae). In this first scene showing the brothers with Joseph once again, then, Joseph was extremely cordial. In the following, he adopts the reverse attitude. He has them imprisoned as thieves. Thus, the narrator distinguished the two from one another as clearly as possible. The narrator intentionally reports at the end of the first scene that the brothers finally, when they drink, are in good spirits (concerning שכר cf. comments on 9:21). They forgot all distress. The torment Joseph prepares for them now will plunge them all the more deeply. "In the abrupt, yet well-grounded alternation of events and attitudes, the narrator once again demonstrates his mastery" (Kautzsch[3]).

III. The Concealed Cup 44

1ff. The narrator now once again introduces the motif of the concealed valuables in a beautiful variation. The first time it was only money and in all the sacks, now it is Joseph's cup and in Benjamin's sack. Thus the conflict comes <452> to a head. Now the fate of Benjamin, the youngest so beloved and carefully protected by his father, comes into question. A later reader did not appreciate this delightful intensification and thus added v 1b and וְאֵת כֶּסֶף שִׁבְרוֹ (v 2) from 42:25. But the point of the following account consists precisely in the fact that Benjamin is the only guilty party (Holzinger;

Kautzsch[3]). Joseph gives them grain, as much as they can carry, thus more than they deserve by rights, as a sign of his special favor. Their guilt will seem all the greater when they are caught as thieves. As in Gen 42, Joseph's thoughts and intentions are not given here either. At first glance, his behavior seems contradictory. We do not know until the decisive moment what he plans to do with his brothers. This corresponds to his high status. It is seemly for the superior to conceal his thoughts. At the same time, however, the hearer is held until the last in increasing suspense.

4 Neither the name of the city nor of the king are mentioned—fairy-tale style. Concerning the syntax of לֹא הִרְחִיקוּ see §156f. LXX (Vulg, Pesh) reads ἵνα τί ἐκλέψατέ μου τὸ κόνδυ τὸ ἀργυροῦν after v 4 (Holzinger, et al.). This makes the text smoother, but not better (Dillmann, Ball, Ehrlich). Instead, the brothers are treated as captured thieves who need not be told what they have stolen. One may observe that the brothers themselves do not seem quite to know what is involved (v 8). Joseph will have chosen an accusation which seems very plausible. Such travelers are not to be trusted in the matter of personal property. **5** Here the crime is particularly serious because they have used a meal, to which they were so benevolently invited by a high lord, for theft and were so unashamed as to steal his cup—surely an especially costly piece. And now it turns out—here horror and dismay is supposed to fall over the brothers—it is even his magic cup! The narrator, very reticent on this ticklish point, does not make it clear whether Joseph really used this cup for giving oracles or only pretends to do so. At any rate, his brothers are supposed to believe it. They are supposed to have the impression, after all they have experienced with him (43:33 [42:25ff]) that he is skilled in mysteries (v 14; cf. also the comments on 45:6). We may associate what has been reported about Joseph's wondrous dreams, dream interpretations, and his demonic wisdom (41:38) with this element. Unusually, the narrators do not associate these elements, which, taken together, would produce a picture of Joseph as a great inspired man and magician. Instead, they appear in isolation and, in part, rather insignificantly. Neither 42:28 nor 43:33 say that his brothers consider Joseph a magician so that 44:15 appears to us to be wholly unprepared. The narrator could also have utilized the brothers' fear of the magician quite differently. An earlier form of these accounts will have probably portrayed this side of Joseph straightforwardly and clearly as a main point. These things receded, however, in a later period which did not want to deal with magic. Since magic bloomed in Egypt and the narrative takes place in Egypt, one may ask whether perhaps an Egyptian magical legend underlies it (cf. above p. 386). Oracle giving from a cup, κυλικομαντεία, also attested elsewhere in antiquity, consisted of observing the particles of gold, silver, etc, thrown into a cup filled with water. The Babylonian *barû* priests predicted from the behavior of oil poured into a cup filled with water (cf. Hunger, <453> *Becherwahrsagung bei den Babyloniern* [1903]). The notion that one employs such a magical ability specifically for the purpose of recovering stolen goods (v 15) is surely a rather common and very comprehensible element in antiquity. Why did not Joseph go after his brothers himself? The narrator would respond, "that would not be seemly for such an eminent man." His actual reason for this, however, is so that he can separate the action into two scenes: (1) the brothers before the caretaker outside the city (vv 6-12), preliminary scene, and (2) the brothers' before Joseph in his house (vv 13ff), main scene.

6-12 *Outside the city.* **7** The clause with לָמָּה contains a "respectful disapproval" (cf. Exod 5:15; 32:12; 1 Sam 24:10; Ehrlich). **8** This reference to prior events is supposed to demonstrate their integrity. Here the narrator has woven together the two variants of the same motif. For כֶּסֶף[1] Sam and LXX read הַכֶּסֶף (Ball, Holzinger, et al.). **9** For יָמֻת in the apodosis see §112ii. The voluntary offer of punishment and, indeed, specifically of the death penalty for the thief also occurs in 31:32. For our sense of justice, the penalty remarkably applies not only to the criminal, but also to the others. Israelite antiquity, however, was accustomed to co-atonement on the part of the whole group in such especially heinous cases. The brothers suggest such an at least unusually severe penalty because they feel completely innocent (likewise in 31:32). **10** The caretaker states his agreement, softened but significantly, apparently according to Joseph's instructions (cf. comments on 43:23). The narrator had the opportunity here to recount how the death penalty hung over Benjamin's head. He could have significantly sharpened the conflict. He refrained from doing so, however. He wants to shake us, not horrify us. He feels that the frightful death penalty would not fit the rest of the narrative. Joseph cannot even seem to have planned this for his beloved brother—a sign of true, simple skill. **12** Although the caretaker knows where the cup is concealed, he first searches all the other sacks. This element is supposed to extend the action and heighten suspense. We are to imagine how the brothers exhale in relief ten times and are already sure of their sacks when the cup is found, after all—in Benjamin's sack. David's anointing is similar (1 Sam 16:6ff.). Instead of the perfects, one will better read with Ball and others the inf. absolutes הָהֵל כַּלֵּה (§113h). V **13** intentionally emphasizes very sharply the extreme despair of the brothers, lasting throughout the whole subsequent scene (cf. comments on 42:21ff.).

14-34 *Main scene, before Joseph.* **14** Joseph, sure of the outcome, waited on them. This clear indication of foreknowledge could also have horrified the brothers. <454> **16-17** Wellhausen (*Composition*[3], 58) strikes יְהוּדָה in v 16 as a false explicative and reads וַיֹּאמְרוּ. In this way, the subsequent escalation is more apparent. The speech shows that the brothers are thoroughly shattered. "God found our guilt." When in misfortune, the ancient feels himself under God's wrath and guilty. Then he looses composure and self-control: no one is right over against God. This misfortune, too, must therefore be caused—in the brothers' opinion—by their guilt, even though they are convinced that Benjamin is no thief, and even though they do not know what sin they have committed. They do not think of a specific sin (such as the sin against Joseph) here, however (contra 42:21ff. E). Skillfully the narrator varies the penalty that could be imposed on the brothers. They make the most severe suggestion themselves, before the cup is found: the thief should die, the others should become slaves (v 9). The caretaker makes a milder suggestion (v 10) which Joseph also insists upon (v 17): only Benjamin shall become a slave. Here Joseph intentionally separates their fate and Benjamin's in order to torment them most severely. He knows, after all, that they cannot return without Benjamin. Then, quite broken, they make a third suggestion. They will all become slaves (v 16). Finally, Judah makes even a fourth suggestion: he, alone, will remain behind as a slave (vv 32-34). It is customary to say at this point that the brothers behaved in a more brotherly fashion toward Benjamin than toward Joseph and that this very improvement was Joseph's ultimate intention. These are modern intrusions, however. The brothers hold fast to this suggestion that they themselves will pay, as slaves, with the thief because they could not appear before their old father without Benjamin. This suggestion shows, not that they have improved, but that they are now completely broken. One may observe, further, that the brothers' behavior does not tip the scales with Joseph, but the calming speech of the noble Judah does. Joseph's means of punishing his brothers is an example of fine narrative art: Joseph does not treat them roughly; he does nothing to them physically. Instead, he torments them much more severely and finely by torturing them in their deepest emotions: in their sense of responsibility for the youngest and in their sympathy for their dying father. **16** Sam and LXX read והאלהים (Kautzsch[3]).

18-34 Judah's speech prepares for the climax. Similar scenes are 43:1-10 (J) and 42:29-34 (E). Judah's long speech repeats everything that has transpired as far as Benjamin is concerned. The narrator wants to illuminate the case from all sides. Characteristically for his art, he does not do so through an explicit discussion of the pertinent issues, but is only able to do so through such an account. This grand, passionate speech, a masterpiece of Hebrew rhetoric once again depicting all the motivations of the acting persons, is a mighty surge the narrator makes now immediately prior to the final turn of events. Jacob's grand speech in 31:36ff. is quite parallel. Judah's speech consists of two parts: (1) the passage in vv 18-31, whose point is to grippingly portray the prospect that the old Jacob must go to his grave with a sorrowful heart and (2) Judah's noble suggestion in vv 32-34. Thus, the hearer's emotions <455> are moved mightily. We feel the brothers' total despair and recognize that Joseph can no longer remain harsh. In tone, Judah's speech is submissive ("our father, your servant," "my lord," etc.). After all, they are now totally dependent upon the man's favor. In the details, this speech is not a completely faithful rendition of what has been narrated. There are abbreviations and also supplementations (vv 21b, 27-28): the narrators did not refer back to what they had written on such occasions (cf. introduction ¶3.20). **18** "Indeed, you are like Pharaoh" means, I am well aware to whom I speak. Concerning כְ . . . כְ see §161c.

20 אָחִיו מֵת—He cannot yet speak the truth. The narrator does not hold this minor lie of necessity against him. **21** "That I keep my eye on him" means "take him under my care" (cf. Jer 39:12; 40:4; Psa 33:18; 34:14). Judah cleverly explains Joseph's wish to see Benjamin as a sign of his goodwill for him (Driver). **22b** Regarding the syntax see §159g. **30** "To whose soul his soul is bound" means "whom he loves as himself" (1 Sam 18:1), "at whose death he will die himself." The expression—but only the expression—may derive from the belief that a person's life can be bound to an object whose destruction must be accompanied by his death (cf. the Egyptian fairy tale of the brothers, v. d. Leyen 115:6, 8 and the Greek legend of Meleagros). **31** Sam, LXX, Pesh, and Vulg read הַנַּעַר אִתָּנוּ (Ball, Holzinger, et al.). **34** Concerning פֶּן see §152w. Now Joseph hears of his father's distress and sees his brother's honor. Thus <456> he is persuaded. This reversal in Joseph's attitude, upon which all that follows depends, is very well founded artistically. This description will delight the reader as long as Genesis is read. If so many academics pass by such beauty because of rigid scholarship, we may take comfort that the children and the artists, even without scholarship, will feel what the narrator wanted here.

68. The Disclosure 45:1-24 EJ

Source analysis. Two strands appear in the following. Twice Joseph discloses himself to his brothers ("I am Joseph," v 31 ‖ v 4b). Twice he commands them to tell Jacob of his high position (v 9 ‖ v 13). The command to his brothers to bring Jacob to Egypt is given several times (vv 13, 18, 19). According to v 1 Joseph intentionally arranged it so that none of the Egyptians learn of his relationship to the foreigners. Thus this relationship is entirely new to the Pharaoh in 47:1ff.; 46:31ff. Pharaoh must even be informed of the dwelling place of the men and the purpose of their coming (46:31; 47:3). According to vv 2, 16, in contrast, Joseph cried so loudly in the recognition scene that the news reached Pharaoh's court. Subsequently, Pharaoh himself arranged the brothers' resettlement (vv 17, 18; concerning v 19, see below). According to v 10aα Jacob is to abide in the land of Goshen, according to v 10aβ, in contrast, near Joseph, thus not far from the royal court. If the two are supposed to mean the same thing (Eerdmans, 68), one would expect the second, more general designation before the first. The same two designations occur in the Exodus narrative (cf. Meyer, *Israeliten*, 35, 42-43). Furthermore, one report mentions wagons Joseph gives his brothers for the move (vv 19, 27; 46:5). This seems to be the same report that often emphasizes that Jacob brought all his belongings with him (vv 10b, 11b; 46:1aα, 32; 47:1). The other, in contrast, seems to have mentioned only donkeys, their own (v 17) and some given them (v 23), on the assumption that a great deal could not be brought with them when they moved (v 20).

The details of the source analysis are very difficult. The sources seem to have been thoroughly combined. The following indications, essentially following Dillmann and Wellhausen, are to a degree, therefore, only an attempt.

V 1a is from J (cf. 43:31). This assignment is confirmed by the fact that 46:31ff.; 47:1ff., where Pharaoh does not yet know of Joseph's brothers, also stem from J. Consequently, the other report, vv 2, 16-18, is from E. V 1b seems to parallel v 1a and will belong to E because of הִתְוֹדַע (Num 12:6). V 4b (Joseph was sold, 37:28) is from J. Therefore v 3 (‖ v 4b) is from E. This assignment is also confirmed by the fact that Joseph inquires about whether his father lives, whereas he has already learned this in J (43:28). The most important idea in the whole J passage is that Joseph is persuaded by regard for the pain he does his father, thus that he knows that his father lives. V 4a could belong to either source. In J it would be a precautionary measure of Joseph as in v 1a, in E an encouragement of the brothers in contrast to their horror in v 3b. V 5aα (J עָצֵב וַ) parallels v 5aβ (E; cf. 31:35). V 5aγ is J (Joseph's sale). V 5b is E because of אלהים. V 6 seems to continue v 5b, and is thus from E. Yet, the expression חָרִישׁ וְקָצִיר (cf. Exod 34:21) would speak for J (Procksch). V 7 stems entirely from E (cf. אלהים and to הַחֲיוֹת, 50:20). Yet the verse seems to be redundant (Dillmann). Consequently one may attribute v 7aβ to J. V 8 is E because of הָאֱלֹהִים. It may be overloaded. V 9 belongs to E because of אלהים. The fact that only J mentions the land of Goshen (46:28-29, 34; 47:1, 4, 6, 27; 50:8; Exod 8:18; 9:26) points to J for v 10aα. V 10aβ parallels v 10aα, <457> and is thus from E. In contrast, v 10b, perhaps from אַתָּה on, seems to be from J ("sheep, cattle, and all belongings," cf. esp. 46:32; 47:1). V 11a is from E because of 47:12; 50:21. V 11b may be from J (all belongings). V 12 is indeterminate. V 13 is J (‖ v 9 E). V 14 is J: the diction resembles 46:29. V 15 is E (נִשֵּׁק לְ as in 32:1). Vv 16-18 are E (cf. above; to v 16b, cf. 41:37; 34:18). The packing of the animals in v 17 has already taken place according to J (44:13). Also, J uses עָמַס (44:13), whereas E has טָעַן here. V 19 is yet another command to bring Jacob (‖ vv 17, 18), and is thus from J (cf. also the verbatim repetition in 46:5b, J). These words cannot have been Pharaoh's command in J (in J, he only learns of the coming of the brothers in 47:1ff.), but must be Joseph's speech reworked by R^{JE}. Consequently, צִוָּה אֹתָם (see the comments on the passage) will be a redactional parenthesis and אֲבִיכֶם should be emended to אָבִי. V 20 is to be attributed to E as the continuation of v 18. The diction is somewhat verbose, but the verse need not be a gloss for this reason. V 21aα comes too soon and is probably a gloss (Dillmann). V 21aβ, "Joseph gave them wagons," is J. "According to Pharaoh's command" stems from the redactor as does "Pharaoh" in 46:5 (cf. 45:27, according to which Joseph sent the wagons). The rest, vv 21b-24, may be attributed to E: צֵדָה (v 21; cf. 42:25, according to J, the brothers were already underway and will, therefore, already have provisions); v 22 is a remote variant of 43:34 J; בָּר (v 23, 24b), "is belated after v 24" (Procksch) and thus seems to belong to J. Procksch differs somewhat. He attributes vv 1b, 3, 5aβ,b, 7a, 8, 9a, 13, 15, 16-18, 20, 21aβ, 24b to E. The details may be disputed. But v 2 must belong to E, because, even according to Procksch, Pharaoh learns of the matter only after the resettlement of the brothers, and the "wagons" in vv 19 and 27 may not be separated from those in v 21.

1 Now, finally, after such a long climb, the narrative has reached the climax. The account now returns to Joseph. Like us, he has long since been touched. Only in regard to the Egyptians standing around has he held himself back (v 1a, the continuation of 43:31b). Now, however, he is so overcome by the feelings flooding him that he can no longer control himself. He decides to send all the Egyptians away. Now follow the decisive words which mark the turning point of the whole narrative, "I am Joseph!" (v 4). To this point, the account is J. Characteristic of the Israelite popular spirit, Joseph does not forget clever calculation in the moment of highest emotion. He fears that it would not please Pharaoh if he were to bring foreigners into Egypt in the time of famine. Therefore, he pursues the matter secretly at first in order to surprise Pharaoh with a fait accompli (Holzinger). This is according to J. E narrates here in a less refined manner. According to E, there was indeed (accidentally) no foreign witness to Joseph's revelation, but he cried so loudly that the matter soon reached Pharaoh, whose free grace then permitted the sons of Jacob to resettle (vv 2, 16-18). **2** One may read כָּל־מִצְרַיִם with Kittel, following LXX mss. Vv bα and bβ are probably only manuscript variants (Sievers 2:354). V 2 is intended to prepare for vv 16-18 (contra Holzinger). **3** Touchingly, Joseph immediately asks whether his father is alive. In J he has known about this for a long time already (43:27; cf. above). This implies that the punishment of the brothers and the persuasion of Joseph must have been fundamentally different in E than in J. In horror at seeing Joseph, whom they once wanted to kill, they are stunned. This provides the basis for the brothers' silence in this scene. The same speechlessness of the brothers occurs in J. This silence is very conspicuous in J in contrast to their immediately preceding verbosity. But this corresponds to the <458> narrative style: in this and, to a degree, in the following scenes, too, everything depends on Joseph's behavior and words. The brothers' actions are insignificant for the continued action. Therefore, they become silent now, just as in the Paradise narrative man and wife fall silent before Yahweh's curse (cf. introduction ¶3.13).

4 Concerning אֲשֶׁר אֹתִי see §138d. **5** Joseph acts extremely magnanimously when, far from reproaching them for what they did to him, he even comforts them, "Do not grieve so!" (cf. v 24). He may think that they have been sufficiently punished. But his mild attitude is particularly motivated by another consideration. He has already decided to bring his relatives to Egypt and to care for them there in the famine. How would he be in the position, however, to preserve their lives so if he had not come to Egypt as a result of their crime? Thus he perceives in all the confusion the hand of God who sent him ahead to deliver the whole family! Thus, the scales are supposed to fall from our eyes, too. Here is the finger of God (similarly in 50:20)! The narrator (E) expresses one of the basic notions of the Joseph narrative. One should note this profound concept of divine "providence." Here religious sensitivity seeks God no longer in an isolated event which by nature stands out among usual, normal matters (in a "wonder," in an externally visible or audible divine epiphany). Instead, one finds God's hand in an event which is per se very natural. Dismayed and shaken, one sees the purposefulness of the event and recognizes in it the hand of God who secretly so orders things that they must serve his purposes. Here, therefore, we observe a religious sensitivity that is not "ancient," but "modern." A massive gulf is fixed between the Joseph narrative's doctrine of providence and, say, the account of the three men with Abraham or even of the struggle at Penuel. 6 One may note that Joseph pronounces an oracle without further explanation. The brothers must, therefore, already know from their own experiences with Joseph that such oracles can be expected of him. זֶה occurs here with a temporal designation as in 31:38. 7 The object of לְהַחֲיוֹת seems to be missing. Or should one read פְּלֵיטָה with Sam, LXX, and Pesh (Ball, Kittel, et al.; the latter option is reflected in Gunkel's translation)?

8 The title "father of the king" as the highest title in the realm also occurs in Add Esth 3:13 and 9:12; 1 Macc 11:32. Here אָב may be the Hebraization of the Egyptian *abu*, "lord high steward" (Erman, 155-56; Heyes, *Bibel u. Äg.*, 171; Holzinger following Brugsch). 9 כֹּה אָמַר is the standard introduction of messages; thus it is common in the prophets who consider themselves Yahweh's messengers. Joseph wants them to hurry because he longs for his father. If they delay, he may die in the meanwhile <459> (v 13). 10 The notion that the Canaanite slave who has attained high status in Egypt brings his relatives to him and cares for them with state goods will be a realistic feature. Similar elements concerning Jews in foreign civil service favoring Jews occur in Esth 8:1-2; Tob 1:21-22; 2:10. The Hebrew narrators report this in praise of Joseph. Despite the wrong done him he has not forgotten faithfulness to his paternal household. The strangers who bear the cost probably think differently about the Hebrew's tenacious family feelings. This still echoes clearly in J, where Joseph sees to the matter secretly. Goshen, LXX Γέσεμ Ἀραβίας, Egyptian *Kesem*, is the *Wadi Tûmîlât*, a narrow valley between the Nile and the salt marshes watered by a Nile canal, a rich pasture land (cf. Erman, 49; Dillmann; Spiegelberg, *Aufenthalt Israels in Ägypten*, 21-22, with a map). This land is Israel's dwelling place in Egypt according to J. 11 חוּרַשׁ should be pronounced in this way, not as though from יָרַשׁ, but as a hophal of רוּשׁ (Ehrlich). V 12 is supposed to allay the potential mistrust of the brothers who could see the suggestion to resettle as a new torment. "You see yourselves that I say it." 15b Thus, his brothers finally gain the courage to speak confidentially with him. This is the counterpart to v 3b (Holzinger).

16-24 *Pharaoh's permission for the resettlement and Joseph's gifts.* 16 Pharaoh so favored Joseph—the patriotic hearers are glad to hear this—that everyone rejoices with him. 18 The "fat" is the best. The Hebrew likes to drink sweet drinks and eat fat. The Israelite legend proudly recounts that Jacob received the best in the whole land of Pharaoh. This statement in E is less realistic and an intensification in contrast to J according to which they received Goshen. **19** וְאַתָּה צֻוֵּיתָה is difficult. It is easier to read with Kittel and Kautzsch[3] following LXX and Vulg צַוֵּה אֹתָם or with Ehrlich עֲלָה is a cargo wagon in contrast to מֶרְכָּבָה, the battle or luxury wagon (cf. Erman, *Ägypten*, 650-51). Such wagons are considered a witness to Egyptian culture and as an especially impressive gift of Pharaoh for the resettlement here. **21-23** Joseph's gifts are (1) for the brothers—provisions for the trip and changes of clothing (i.e., especially beautiful <460> garments such as those worn at feasts) and (2) for his father—ten donkeys with Egyptian valuables (objects such as those produced by the highly famed "wisdom" of Egypt) and ten jennies with grain, as well as provisions for the journey. These are extraordinarily rich gifts, then! **23** Concerning כָּזֹאת see §102g. **24** אַל־תִּרְגְּזוּ means "Have no fear" that I could continue to be angry. Others understand it to mean "Do not be agitated about my (Joseph's) high position or about your guilt."

69. Jacob Journeys to Egypt and Remains in Goshen
45:25-28; 46:1-5, 28-34; 47:1-5a, 6b, 12, 27a JE

Structure. The climax of the Joseph narrative has already been passed in the preceding. In the old style, the narrative would now be abruptly broken off. This extensive style differs. An account that rose so gradually to a climax cannot suddenly fall off, but must slowly and calmly fade out. Consequently, an additional series of pieces follow now: Jacob journeys to Egypt and abides in Goshen (45:25ff.); Jacob blesses Joseph's children and dies (47:29ff.); Jacob's burial (50:2ff.) and Joseph's death, the conclusion of the account (50:23ff.). All this is a continuous thread. Insertions deal with how Joseph made all Egypt Pharaoh's servants (47:13-26) and with Jacob's blessing on the twelve tribes, a poem (Gen 49).

Source criticism of the narrative of Jacob's journey to Egypt. Sections from P often interrupt the JE narrative. The following belongs to J. When the father sees the wagons (cf. 45:19) and is then convinced that Joseph lives, he decides immediately to move to Egypt (45:27aγ,δ, 28; יִשְׂרָאֵל v 28). The sons load him and his family on the wagons, and he sets out (46:5b, 1aα; best in this sequence; cf. the name "Israel," the wagons, the points of contact with 45:19). The continuation is 46:28-34, Joseph's meeting with Israel: this passage is a unit. It belongs to J because of Israel (vv 29, 30), Goshen (vv 28, 29, 34), and Judah (v 28). V 30 refers back to 45:28 (J): הַפַּעַם (v 30). V 32b refers to "all belongings" as does 46:1aα. The immediate continuation of this passage is 47:1-5a, 6b, 27a: Joseph carries out what he promised in 46:31-34 (in detail, cf. Israel, v 27a, Goshen, vv 1, 4, 6b, 27a; regarding the list "sheep, cattle, and all belongings," v 1, cf. 46:32). Other verbal similarities link the passages (e.g., "permit your servants to remain in the land of Goshen," v 4; "they may remain in the land of Goshen," v 6b; "thus Israel remained in the land of Goshen," v 27a). The whole J unit is present without a gap from 45:28 onward. The divine revelation in Beer-sheba (46:1b-5a) stems from E: אלהים (v 2), אֵל (v 3), and Jacob (vv 2, 5a). The divine revelation in a night vision and the beginning of the conversation in v 2b are characteristic of E. Whereas Israel decided immediately to move to Egypt according to J (45:28), he has misgivings here (46:3). Gen 47:12 also belongs to E (כִּלְכֵּל as in 45:11a), as does the beginning of the passage (45:25-27aα,b, to אֲלֵהֶם: and v 27b—Jacob vv 25, 27b). V 26b belongs with v 27b. V 26a alludes to v 8. One may take v 27aα,b as the protasis of v 27b and as a parallel for v 27aγ,δ (J). Accordingly, E is rather well preserved at the beginning. There is only a gap between 45:27b and 46:1b. On the other hand, only one comment from E (47:12) is present concerning the encounter with Joseph and the further course of events. From 46:5a one gains the impression that Jacob dwelt in Beer-sheba until then (cf. above pp. 382, 388, 391). Therefore, v 1aβ seems to be an addition from the final redactor who wanted to associate this information from E with the assumption of (R^J and) P that Jacob lived in Hebron (cf. 37:14b). <461>

45:25-28 *Jacob learns that Joseph lives.* At first he does not want to believe it and remains indifferent and apathetic. It is indeed too incredible. He is convinced by their extensive account, however, that it is true. Then he becomes lively. This is E, a well-founded portrayal of the inner life of the old man. Even more characteristic is Israel's statement in J (v 28), "Enough!" He refuses any further discussion and delay. "Joseph lives. I want to go and see him before I die." The father's heart does not ask about Joseph's status and gifts. Instead, it is happy that he lives (similarly 46:30). Israel's statement is also impressive because of its brevity. The narrator attains his effects also by leaving some of the statements as brief as they were in the old style and extending others. Similar brief statements appear in 46:30; 45:3a; 37:33; 18:5b. "Before I die"—here, too, Israel is guided by thoughts of his approaching death, this time to hurry. For our sensitivities it is conspicuous that the brothers do not tell of their crime against Joseph. Here, the narrator allowed significant niceties to go unattended. In the Joseph account, not all motives given in the situation are developed equally.

46:1aβ-5a *The divine epiphany at Beer-sheba E.* Jacob—this is the assumption—is afraid of the journey. Why do not hear why. It must have been clear in the context of E. He probably fears that Joseph may still be angry with his brothers (cf. 50:15ff.). In this painful uncertainty, he sacrifices at the holy place (זֶבַח, a sacrifice with a sacred meal; cf. comments on 8:20). We discern his intention from the context. He wants thereby to gain information from God. Concerning the fact that one brings sacrifice in order to "summon" God and to receive an oracle, see Num 23:1ff.; 1 Kgs 3:4ff. The same practice is quite common in Babylonia (cf. Zimmern, *Beiträge*, 96ff.). Others take the clause with 45:27a and understand the sacrifice as a thanksgiving sacrifice. Yet the two concepts can coexist (Dillmann). The god of the site at Beer-sheba is called "the God of Isaac" (vv 1, 3). Accordingly, the narrator presupposes a narrative here according to which Isaac consecrated this site to God. J reports this narrative in Gen 26. The E variant presupposed here concerning the same event is not preserved for us (with the possible exception of 26:2aβ,b; cf. above p. 294). Such references by one account to another do not occur in the old legends and always indicate the late origin of a passage (cf. introduction, ¶3.6). This account of Jacob's vision in Beer-sheba will, therefore, have been shaped on the pattern of the older account of Isaac's vision in Beer-sheba. Once, in a famine, God commanded Isaac—it seems—not to go to Egypt (26:2); now he commands Jacob the contrary. The account at hand is, therefore, not a "cult legend." It does not seek to establish the sacredness of the place. Instead, it presumes it. It is a free composition on the basis of an older cultic legend. It is very noteworthy that the narrator does not recall Abraham, who, according to another E account, is supposed to have established Beer-sheba <462> (21:22ff.). We have an E strand before us, therefore, which did not contain this Abraham narrative, but had an Isaac narrative instead. **2** For וַיֹּאמֶר it may be better to read וַיֵּרָא. A later hand exchanged לְיִשְׂרָאֵל with לְיַעֲקֹב (Dillmann, et al.). The plural בְּמַרְאֹת is conspicuous (cf. §124e). One should read בְּמַרְאַת following LXX (Kittel, Kautzsch[3]).

3-4 The revelation begins with the name of the god (cf. comments on 17:1). Concerning רְדָה (v 3) see §69m. The form is characteristic of E (cf. Holzinger, *Hexateuch*, 190). "I will go with you" (v 4): The notion that the god accompanies the traveler on his way does not seem obvious to the ancient as it does to us. Instead, since the god is somehow bound to a place and a land, it is a special mercy (cf. 24:7; 28:15; 31:3). The relationship between vv 3 and 4 is, "Do not fear the journey, for I will go with you myself, and protect you." This relationship is disturbed by v 3bβ (Kautzsch-Socin). A later reader found God's promise to Jacob too insignificant. If the statement were authentic, it would stand after v 4. Similar additions appear in 13:14ff.; 22:15ff.; 26:24; 28:14. "I will bring you back" in a coffin. This announces Jacob's burial in Canaan. גַּם־עָלֹה as in 31:15 (E) is a qal inf. with a hiphil (§113w). "Joseph will lay his hand on your eyes" is a tender expression for "close your eyes." It is a special comfort to the ancient that the most beloved hand, that of the flourishing son, does him this last loving service (the same motif in Goethe's "Euphrosyne"). The OT does not mention closing the eyes elsewhere, but the Mishnah does and it was common practice in antiquity (cf. Dillmann, *Torge, Seelenglaube*, 175ff.). **5** יעקב[2] is a later addition. One should imagine that cattle pull the wagons. פַּרְעֹה is an explicative inserted by the redactor. According to J, Joseph sent the wagons (45:27). LXXA reads Ἰωσηφ.

46:28-30 *Israel's meeting with Joseph.* **28b** Israel sends Judah, Joseph's most faithful brother, ahead. לְהֹורֹת means "in order to show," so that he (Joseph) may give directions before him (Jacob) to Goshen. The expression is difficult. Sam and Pesh read לְהֵרָאֹות, niph. inf. (cf. v 29), "so that he (Joseph) should appear before him (Jacob) in Goshen." This, too, is difficult. **29** Joseph honors his father by going to meet him. By coming to meet him in a magnificent chariot, he also shows him at first glance the high honor he enjoys in Egypt. The scene when father and son are reunited, moves the hearer to tears.

46:31-34 Joseph instructs his brothers for their audience with the Pharaoh. The following account is to show how Joseph arranged it so his relatives obtained the land of Goshen as a dwelling place. The fact that he goes to such effort for Goshen can probably be explained by the fact that Goshen is on the border where it would be possible for his brothers to leave Egypt again if they want. Here, then, the legend looks ahead <463> to the exodus narrative. It was later possible for Israel to escape Egypt precisely because they dwelt near the border. The calculations of the farsighted Joseph were fulfilled at that time. The fact that Goshen is regarded here as the best land is hardly likely since, according to subsequent statements, it is supposed to be primarily grassland. But Pharaoh will not so easily grant this border province to the foreigners, Joseph fears. Then, Joseph remembers at the right time that Goshen is pastureland, especially well suited for sheep. Pharaoh's own flocks pasture there (47:6b). Thus Joseph gets the clever idea to present his relatives to Pharaoh as herdsman, especially as shepherds. Now since Joseph explicitly instructs his brothers to acknowledge this profession, this cannot have been the simple truth. It must have been untrue or partially true (cf. Eerdmans 2:42, 71-72). It is difficult to accept the notion that the men would be unable to answer such a simple question because of confusion in the presence of the royal majesty so that Joseph gave them the proper response in advance (contra Spiegelberg, *Aufenthalt Israels in Ägypten*, 22n.1). The secret purpose of the answer they are to give is also explicitly reported in v 34. What, however, was the actual profession of Israel and his sons according to this narrator? One will respond, "In his opinion, they reared cattle, camels, and donkeys and probably farmed." Joseph's lie did not seem to the narrator to be a disgrace, but wisdom. In this way he glorifies the clever man who was honorable toward his family (cf. comments on 12:11ff.). Joseph's plan is somewhat more complicated in v 34bβ: according to it, he also considers the fact that the Egyptians abhor shepherds and that they will therefore allow them to dwell at the border. This Egyptian abhorrence of shepherds is not currently attested. We only know that herders of cattle were despised in Egypt and dwelt in the northern marshes (Erman, 583). The clause, v 34bβ, which seems to appear too late, may be a secondary addition (Holzinger). **31** וְאֶל־בֵּית אָבִיו, missing in LXX mss, has been introduced from v 31b. One confers on such matters with men, but not with the women and children, too. "I will go up." One goes up to kings and princes (who dwell up in the royal citadel).

32 כִּי־אַנְשֵׁי מִקְנֶה הָיוּ is not a misplaced variant for אַנְשֵׁי מִקְנֶה הָיוּ (v 34). **33** Concerning מַעֲשֵׂיכֶם, a sing. or a plural, see §93ss. **34** "We have been shepherds from our youth, as were our fathers." Thus, Pharaoh should think that these men are useful for nothing else. Hebr mss, Sam, Targ. Onq, Pesh, and Vulg read רֹעֵי (Ball, Holzinger, et al.). Gen 47:3 should read the same according to Hebr mss, Sam, LXX mss, Targ. Onq, Pesh, and Vulg.

47:1-5a, 6b *The audience.* We are not supposed to hear the scene without private enjoyment. Pharaoh may be a mighty king, but it would serve him well to be somewhat more clever. He allows the wool to be pulled over his eyes in the most desirable way. The notion that Pharaoh himself decides the residence of the people and personally deals with them is fairy-tale-like. **1** Thus, Joseph very cleverly arranged it so that the brothers are already in Goshen before Pharaoh learns of it. He did not tell Pharaoh that he intentionally sent them. <464> He should rather believe that they are there by chance. Thus it is probable that he will let them stay there. **2** Sam (LXX) reads לָקַח עִמּוֹ (Ball, Holzinger, et al.). **3-4** For אָחִיו (v 3), Sam, LXX mss, Pesh, and Targ. Jon have אֲחֵי יוֹסֵף (Ball, Holzinger, et al.). The double beginning, "they said to Pharaoh," contradicts a rule of Hebrew style (cf. comments on 19:9). A speech has probably fallen out between the two introductions, "Pharaoh said, 'Why have you come here?'" (so also Ball). The brothers' response corresponds to Joseph's instructions. They very wisely do not betray to Pharaoh that Joseph called them to Egypt, and they declare to him that they are nothing other than shepherds who came to Egypt only because of the sheep. One sees that they have understood Joseph. These are—the narrator thinks—the ancestors of the twelve tribes of Israel; and so they remained. In **5, 6** passages from J and P have been interwoven in the current Hebrew text. LXX still read them in distinction from one another (cf. further below). Pharaoh not only permitted them to settle in Goshen, but, in order to show favor to his minister, he wants to make the brothers royal chief shepherds. Here the narrator is delightfully amused: Pharaoh is magnanimous and—somewhat stupid. The modern reader may be amazed or even offended that such a touching scene as the previous is following by a humorous one. One should remember, however, that such alterations of touching and humorous motifs occur in many literatures. Such is human nature: we are not in a position to bear such emotion for too long. Instead, we are thankful to the author who permits us to laugh once again after all the tears. For the conspicuous וְיָשֶׂם־בָּם Ball follows Sam and reads הָיֹשׁ בָּם; Ehrlich reads כִּי־יָשׂ־בָם.

12, 27a *Jacob and his sons remain in Egypt.* Concerning כִּלְכֵּל (v 12) with a double accusative see §117cc. "According to the number of children" means according to the size of each household.

70. Joseph Subjects Egypt to Pharaoh's Taxation 47:13-26 J

The position of the passage in the composition of the Joseph narrative. The piece quite perceptibly interrupts the narrative of Joseph's relationship to his brothers. After Jacob's arrival in Egypt we expect the account of Jacob's death immediately (cf. 45:28 and 46:30; cf. further, comments on 47:29ff. and p. 381). After Pharaoh's permission "they may remain in Goshen" (47:6b), we immediately expect the account "so they remained in Goshen" (47:27a). Whereas the passage (vv 13-26) is only disruptive here, it would fit wonderfully in 41:55-56. These words, identical in content to 47:13, are, in fact, the exposition of 47:14-26. Accordingly, this passage is to be considered the originally intended continuation of Gen 41 (Dillmann, etc.). In the Joseph narrative, the narrator has fused two main strands: <465> (1) Joseph's fortunes in Egypt (Gen 39; 40; 41) and (2) Joseph's relations with his family (Gen 37; 42-47:12; 47:27-50). The passage in 47:13-26 belongs, in theme, to the first main strand. Its current position in the midst of the accounts of the second thread is not natural or original. This is also apparent in the mention of Canaan (vv 13, 14, 15) intended to join this passage to the current context a bit better, but which does not fit well into the passage itself which otherwise only treats Egyptian matters (Holzinger, Driver, Cheyne, et al.). The passage has been removed from its old position and placed here for chronological reasons: it treats the second year of the famine (v 18), while Gen 42 (cf. 45:6) begins already with the first year. Yet it is also distinct, as Haller (146) correctly emphasizes, from the accounts of the main thread because of its political interests and its relatively precise knowledge of the property situation in Egypt; the main accounts emphasize the personal elements more.

The passage contains an etiological legend. The Hebrew who comes to Egypt is amazed at the agrarian circumstances there which diverge so widely from the situation in his own land. While Canaan has a free peasantry and the king is only the first landowner in the land, the property in Egypt is almost entirely state owned. The farmers must, however—so we may assume according to our account—pay a fifth, in Hebrew terms an extraordinarily high levy. Only the priests (and, according to Diodorus, *Bibl. hist.* 1:73-74, the warriors) own private property (concerning the social situation of the New Kingdom, cf. Erman, 188; see a theory concerning the origin of these unusual agrarian circumstances in Erman, 152-53). The Hebrew who observes these things has doubts about it. What mighty power must Pharaoh have in his land in relation to the limited power of the king of Israel! What a wise minister must that ancient Pharaoh have had to have been able to subject the whole land to taxation! Now national pride—a very prominent Israelite character trait since the ancient times—maintains that our Joseph was this wise minister. This contention, thus, sprang from the same source as the later contentions that Joseph was the creator of Lake Moeris, that Abraham taught the Egyptians astronomy, that Moses was the actual founder of all culture in Egypt, and that Plato borrowed from Moses (cf. Schürer, *Geschichte des jüdischen Volkes*[3] 3:354-55). Thus, we are supposed to read the following account with delight at the wisdom of our people. The notion, however, that the policy of a minister—who utilized the land's distress to reduce the people to serfdom, and who treats natives so harshly while favoring his own foreign kindred—that such a policy could have yet another less praiseworthy side has gone unnoticed by the old narrator. He does not consider the "ruin of the land and people" (Reuß), but only the growth of Pharaoh's power. The whole passage emphasizes that everything Joseph does is to Pharaoh's advantage. We must guard against importing modern attitudes and either finding Joseph's policy "altogether shameful" (Holzinger) or, conversely, maintaining that he was "no less [concerned] with the interests of the land than of the king" (Franz Delitzsch). It has been observed above (pp. 385-86) that the narrative may trace back to an Egyptian account.

Arrangement. I. In the first year Joseph obtains all the money (vv 13, 14) and all the flocks (vv 15-17) for Pharaoh. II. In the second year he buys (the people and) the land of the Egyptians (vv 18-22) and subjects them to the payment of the fifth portion (vv 23-26).

Source criticism. The determination of the sources is associated with that in Gen 41. The theory was expressed above (p. 416) that 41:55, 56, the exposition of this passage, belongs to J and 41:34b, a comment concerning the fifth, a variant of this passage, to E. Accordingly, the passage stems from J. This is further suggested by <466> וְנִהְיֶה וְלֹא נָמוּת (v 19 as in 42:2; 43:8 [J]), יָדֹת "parts" (v 24 as in 43:34 [J]), מִקְנֵה הַצֹּאן וּמִקְנֵה הַבָּקָר (v 17 as in 26:14 [J]), מָצָא חֵן בְּעֵינֵי (v 25, common in J [Dillmann]). Holzinger assumes that a dual strand is also present here: v 23 reprises vv 20f.; v 24 makes a somewhat different statement than vv 20-21; the awkward style also indicates composition from several sources. He finds two parallel accounts: (1) vv 19aβ,ba*, 23a, 25, 20, 21—for grain (לֶחֶם), the Egyptians sell their property and persons and (2) vv 19bβ,γ, 23b, 24, 26a—the Egyptians plead for seed so that they do not die and their fields go wild. But this source analysis is objectionable: Holzinger overlooks the arrangement whereby the author wants to speak here (1) of the purchase of the fields (and the people), vv 20-22 and (2) of the levy placed upon them, vv 23-26. Vv 23ff., therefore, do not reprise v 20, but continue it. וַיִּקֶן (v 20) means "then he bought" and הֵן קָנִיתִי (v 23) means "hereby I have now purchased." The statement in v 24 is none other than in v 20. Instead, v 24 states what has been placed on the Egyptians because of the purchase made (v 20). "Cereal grain" and "seed," both are mentioned in the account, are not contradictory in general terms. Both are necessary for people and fields. Procksch wants to separate vv 13b, 14, 20, 21, 22 out of J's report for E. But v 14 is the necessary precondition for v 15, and vv 20-22 are linked with vv 19, 23 by the words קָנָה (מָכַר) אֲדָמָה (vv 19, 20, 22bis, 23). Sievers (2:358-59), following Holzinger in principle, attributes vv 13-15, 20, 21b, 22 to his "Jβ", the other (except for a few additions) to his "Jδ": the first recounts only the sale of the land; the second, the sale of the cattle, the personal property, and the payment of the fifth. In contrast, in addition to what has already been observed in response to Holzinger and Procksch, it is also true that vv 15, 19 belong together as לָמָּה נָמוּת demonstrates. On the other hand, it is correct that the style of the passage is not smooth. The zeugma in v 19 is not merely difficult for our feeling for language (yet, cf. also 43:18). V 24b seems to be glossed. The unnecessary repetitions in vv 20aα,γ are conspicuous. One may also attempt to see whether one can simplify the style by assuming interpolations. The sale of the persons may be additional and the original text may have only spoken of the sale of the fields, as vv 22, 26 seem to indicate. (This analysis is provisionally reflected in Gunkel's translation.) One must admit that the unity of the text is significantly improved in this manner.

13-17 In the famine, all the money and cattle of the Egyptian's comes into Pharaoh's possession. **13, 14** In the course of a year (!), Joseph takes in all the money from Egypt and the whole world so that nothing else remains: a fairy tale. וַיְלַקֵּט (v 13) from להה only occurs here. Sam reads וַיְכַל (cf. 19:11; Ball). LXX reads ἐχέλιπεν (= וַיִּכֶל?; cf. 41:30). Concerning בַשֶּׁבֶר (v 14), "for the grain," see §119p. The money goes into Pharaoh's treasury. **15-17** Furthermore, all the cattle come into Pharaoh's possession. This too is fairy-tale-like. How did people plow? What did Pharaoh do with all the cattle? The legend does not consider the notion that, in the end, there were still enough valuable objects in Egypt besides money and cattle <467> to be sold or pawned. Sam (LXX) reads הכסף (vv 15b, 16 as in vv 15a, 18; Ball, Kautzsch[3]). **16** לָכֶם לֶחֶם is preferable (with Sam, LXX, and Vulg; Ball, Spurrell, et al.). Concerning מִקְנֵיכֶם see §93ss.

18-22 All the farmland becomes Pharaoh's property. "The second year," of course, is the second of the seven years of famine. Consequently, the impoverishment of Egypt went very quickly in the narrator's opinion. This, too, is extremely naive. The notion that the Egyptians request seed (v 19) does not point to the last year of the famine (contra Holzinger). Naturally, people sow every year. **18** Concerning the singular אֲדֹנִי see the comments on 23:6. Ball misses a word such as בָא before אֶל־אֲדֹנִי. **19** Joseph is much too clever to volunteer such a proposal. Instead, he waits until, in despair, the Egyptians suggest it themselves. The Egyptians think that if they retain their fields, people and farmland are lost. Only if they sell the fields can both parties be delivered. בַלֶּחֶם may also be additional since it conflicts with "give seed" (cf. also v 24). In this case, the first part of the whole will speak of "bread," the second, from v 19 onward, where the author wants to lead to the acquisition of the fields and to the payment of the fifth, speaks of the seed. **21a** Procksch translates: "He had the people pass by cities to be registered" for the purpose of an appropriate division of the grain in the cities equipped with granaries (41:35, 48). This is linguistically (אֹתוֹ) and substantively impossible. הֶעֱבִיד אֹתוֹ לַעֲבָדִים should be read following Sam and LXX (Vulg) with Dillmann, Ball, et al. Regarding the construction see Jer 17:4. **22** Concerning וְאָכְלוּ see §112l. The comment that the priests receive annual grants from the king should not be considered unhistorical (contra Holzinger). King Ramses II, for example, granted the temples 185,000 sacks of grain annually (cf. Erman, 188). It is also historical that there were large temple fields in addition to the royal domains in Egypt (cf. Erman, 403ff., et al.).

23-26 *The institution of the fifth.* **24** בַתְּבוּאֹת means "with the inbringing" or "at the harvests" with a partitive ב (see §119m; cf. 2 Sam 19:44; 2 Kgs 11:7). Dillmann and Kittel want to omit the preposition b with LXX or to read מִן instead. The omission of וּלְאָכְלְכֶם וְלַאֲשֶׁר בְּבָתֵּיכֶם is to be recommended in the interest of the style and unity of the whole (cf. comments on v 19). וְלֶאֱכֹל לְטַפְּכֶם, omitted by LXX, is awkward and is surely a gloss (Dillmann, Holzinger, et al.). Similar large levies, indeed even larger, are not <468> unheard of in antiquity and even today in the Orient (cf. Dillmann). **25** The Egyptians, duped, agree readily and praise Joseph's mercy—to the pleasure of the narrator. הֶחֱיִתָנוּ is the opposite of נָמוּת (v 19). **26** For לַחֹמֶשׁ it is better to read לְחַמֵּשׁ rearranged with LXX in the order לְחַמֵּשׁ לְפַרְעֹה (Holzinger, Kittel, et al.). According to Ball, both words are glosses.

27a See above p. 442.

71. Jacob's Final Testament
47:29-31; 48:1, 2, 7-22; 49:33ab; 50:1 JE

The whole Joseph narrative presupposes that Jacob is near death (37:35; 42:39; 43:27-28; 44:22-29, 31; 45:9, 13, 28; 46:30). In order to see Joseph once more before he dies, he came to Egypt (45:28). Now that he has seen him, he is ready to die (46:30). Inherent in the account, then, is the notion that Jacob's journey to Egypt will be followed immediately by his death. This situation has been obscured by 47:13-26 which has been interpolated in the current form of the text. This account of Jacob's death is not an independent narrative, but only an extended conclusion. The narrators fill the piece with lively details by having Jacob give final instructions (a novelistic motif to prepare for the account of his burial in 50:2ff.) and by recounting his blessing on Ephraim and Manasseh (an etiological feature).

Source criticism. The following points to two strands: 48:1-2 mark an entirely new beginning after 47:29-31. In 47:29-31, Israel and Joseph already discuss Israel's grave, whereas Joseph first learns in 48:1 that Jacob is ill and could die. According to 47:29, Joseph is called to his father; according to 48:1 he comes voluntarily on the news of his illness. According to v 10a, Israel can no longer see, but according to vv 8a, 11, he "sees" Joseph and Joseph's sons. Twice Joseph brings his sons to Jacob וַיַּגֵּשׁ אֵלָיו (v 10b ‖ v 13). "Then Joseph brought the two" (v 13) refers back to "bring them to me" (v 9b), disregarding the intervening vv 10-12. Vv 17-19 immediately continue vv 13, 14. Vv 17-19 further explain the action in vv 13, 14. The intervening vv 15-16 disrupt this relationship. Vv 13, 14 express the preference for Ephraim over Manasseh by an action; v 20, in contrast, expresses it by a statement. The following belong to J: 47:29-31 (Israel vv 29, 31; אִם־נָא מָצָאתִי חֵן בְּעֵינֶיךָ v 29; "place you hand under my thigh" v 29 as in 24:2), 48:2b (Israel; מִטָּה as in 47:31), vv 9b, 10a (preparation for vv 13-15), vv 13-15 (Israel vv 13, 14; צָעִיר v 14; the action in vv 13-15 parallels the statement in v 20 E), vv 17-19 (the continuation of vv 13-15), וַיְבָרֲכֵם בַּיּוֹם הַהוּא from v 20aα (J must have contained the statement, since the preceding reports the gesture of blessing but not the blessing itself; the statement would be perceptibly disruptive in E; cf. below), 49:33aβ (מִטָּה as in 47:31; 48:2), and 50:2. The following belong to E: 48:1, 2a (a new beginning after 47:29-31; Jacob v 2a), 8 (he "sees" v 8a, while, according to vv 10a, 13, 14, 17-19 J, he "cannot see"; יִשְׂרָאֵל in v 8a is a false explicative; v 8b is the question to which v 9 responds, v 9 (אֱלֹהִים), vv 10b, 11, 12 (these verses do not belong to the context of J, cf. above); וַיַּגֵּשׁ v 10b ‖ v 13 J; he "sees" v 11; the form רְאֹה; אֱלֹהִים v 11; Joseph prostrates himself v 12, while according to J, he stands before Jacob's bed with his children; he prostrates himself in order to receive the blessing, the continuation, then, is the blessing itself, vv 15-16; יִשְׂרָאֵל in v 11 is a false explicative), vv 15, 16 (הָאֱלֹהִים v 15), v 20 from בְּךָ יְבָרֵךְ onward (אֱלֹהִים; the words of the blessing immediately continue v 16; v 20b is necessary to elucidate v 20a; in J, where vv 13-15 are already explained

by vv 17-19, <469> it would be superfluous), v 21 (אֱלֹהִים; יִשְׂרָאֵל is a false explicative).
Concerning v 22 see the commentary. This source analysis follows Dillmann. The recognition that two recensions are involved here stems from Budde (ZAW 3:61). Eerdmans
(69) declares vv 8-22 a "coherent unit" despite the inherent difficulties. Sievers (2:360)
divides 47:27–48:22 among "not less then nine" sources.

The assignment of v 7 to a source is a special problem. The statement currently
stands entirely without context (Dillmann). Bruston's (ZAW 7:207-208) hypothesis that
Jacob's wish to be buried in Rachel's grave originally may have been linked to this mention of her grave is very illuminating. It is capricious, however, for Bruston and Ball to
insert the verse in the J unit after 47:29 and to read בִּקְבֻרָתָהּ after v 30. How is the
verse in question supposed to have reached its present position? Dillmann's attempt to
attribute the verse to P as the introduction to 49:29abff. is similarly unfortunate. There,
too, the verse is awkward. Why does Jacob speak of Rachel's grave if he himself wants
to be buried, not with Rachel, but with his fathers in the cave of Machpelah? Budde's
complicated hypothesis (ZAW 3:56ff.) is also unlikely. According to it, the verse was
originally a redactional addition to 49:29-32 whose current position can be explained as
the result of a displacement of 49:29-32 which originally stood after 48:3-6. The notion
that this verse derives from a redactor should exclude the possibility that the idea in the
background is tender and deep (cf. the exegesis). Thus the simple solution remains that
it belongs to E. In this view, it fits its current position exquisitely. The account of J also
divides into two parts: (1) the instructions concerning the grave (47:29-31) and (2) the
blessing. The same is true in E: (1) the wish to lie near Rachel and (2) the blessing (vv
8ff.). A similar situation also prevails in P.

The account varies the motif we know from Gen 24 and 27: the testament of the
dying one. The same is also true in the subsequent section (50:24-25). It is a particularly
beautiful scene: the old father who wants now to die after having seen the fortune of his
favorite son. Past and future come into contact here. He, himself, looks back on his long
life (v 15), on the love of his youth (v 7), he remembers his father and grandfather (47:30;
48:15), and his last wish is to rest beside Rachel in the grave (48:7). Before the dying
man, however, stand his young grandchildren, the fresh shoots of the old tribe, the representatives of Israel's future. The old man kisses and blesses them. As an inheritance, he
gives them God's blessing which helped him and the patriarchs in all times of need. Men
die, but God lives from generation to generation. The dying man catches a glimpse of his
tribe's future. He sees how the firstborn will yield to the younger. He predicts that his
family will not always remain in Egypt. The loving and pious tones are joined by the
mysterious sound of wondrous presentiment. Thus, this scene appears beautifully at the
end of the patriarchal legend. The old clan dies away, but a new future dawns and God
remains the same.

47:29-31; 48:1, 2, 7 *Joseph visits the dying Jacob. The place of burial.* **47:29-31** *The
J recension.* The ancient places greatest value on the place of his grave (cf. comments on
Gen 23, p. 269). To be buried in a foreign land is regarded a great misfortune. Thus,
Jacob, too, wants by no means to be buried in Egypt (cf. 50:25), but in Canaan in the
family crypt. He requires of Joseph no small thing, a difficult and dangerous journey even
for someone of his high status (cf. 50:4). Therefore, he places Joseph under oath. <470>
For us moderns, such a dying wish and the transport of corpses is still well known. Con-

cerning the gesture accompanying the oath, see the comment on 24:2. וְשָׁכַבְתִּי (v 30) should probably be taken as the apodosis. Regarding the idiom, see Deut 31:16; 1 Kgs 2:10. "In their burial place" (v 30) and "in my grave I dug for myself" (50:5 J) are contradictory. Therefore, Wellhausen (*Composition*[3], 60) suspects the text of J in 47:30 has been altered in reference to the Cave of Machpelah in P. When Joseph swears, Jacob lays his head on the pillow in prayer thanking God that he has fulfilled this last wish. The narrator probably explicitly reports the הִשְׁתַּחֲוָה on the bed because it seems to him to be a particularly remarkable situation. Normally, one does this on the ground, but Israel is no longer in a situation to do so because of his age. A similar scene occurs in 1 Kgs 1:47. Holzinger theorizes that a divine image was placed at the head of the bed (cf. 1 Sam 19:13). This is possible. Cheyne reads עַל-עֶרֶשׂ הַמִּטָּה (cf. עֶרֶשׂ יְצוּעִי Psa 132:3). The reason Israel regains his strength is missing between 47:31 and 48:2b in J. He hears from Joseph that he has brought his two sons along. This news revives him. The spirit comes upon the dying man so that he may bless his grandchildren. V 9b then follows v 2b in J.

48:1, 2, 7 *Joseph's visit with Jacob and the burial place according to E.* **48:1, 2** וַיֹּאמֶר means "they say" and וַיַּגֵּד "they report." It may be better to read וַיֹּאמֶר (or, following LXX and Pesh, וַיֹּאמֶר; cf. Josh 2:2; Ehrlich) and וַיַּגֵּד (§144d n. 2). LXX adds וַיָּבֹא אֶל-יַעֲקֹב (Ball, Procksch; cf. v 2; 11:31; 12:5). V 7 is a fragment from E (cf. above): The wish to lie beside Rachel in death, taken up still by R[JE], is omitted because it contradicts 47:30 J (and 49:29-32 P). This wish is very understandable to modern sensibilities. It is more tender than Israel's wish in J to lie in his own grave. It is much more tender in this account than in J (cf. v 10b "he kissed and embraced them"). Jacob's whole life is filled with love for Rachel, a love that caused him so much distress and pain. First, he had to serve many years for her, then she bore him no sons for a long period, and she died giving birth to the second child. Then he transferred his love for her to her sons. But how much sorrow have Joseph and Benjamin caused him! Now, when he has both sons again, and he is about to die, his final wish is to sleep the long sleep beside his beloved. This charming element is, however, too tender to be original. The fact that the old tradition did not know it can be seen in the fact that one speaks of "Rachel's grave" (1 Sam 10:2). Only the later account maintains that Jacob rests there too. The words are an allusion to, in part a verbatim repetition of, 35:16-20. "Paddan" occurs only here. P says "Paddan-aram," which Sam, LXX, and Pesh also have here. עָלַי means "to my sorrow." Sam and LXX add to רָחֵל the term אִמֶּךָ. It can hardly be omitted (Ball, Ehrlich). For אֶפְרָת Sam reads אֶפְרָתָה (Ball). הוּא בֵּית לֶחֶם is an insertion as in 35:19.

8-20 *Jacob's blessing on Ephraim and Manasseh. An etiological <471> legend.* Joseph's sons are famed in Israel for their rich land, bravery, and numbers. They are the true bearers of the history of northern Israel. The legend explains this "blessing" on them as the blessing with which dying Jacob blessed them above all other tribes. The account presumes that Manasseh, although the firstborn, has diminished before the younger Ephraim, the leading tribe of the northern kingdom (Isa 7:9; 9:8). Thus, it presumes a relationship similar to the one between Jacob and Esau and perhaps also between Perez and Zerah. The legend explains this historical relationship by the fact that the patriarch was, indeed, brought the firstborn, who stood at his right, but that the old man crossed his arms and placed his right hand on the head of the younger! This account shows us clearly how naively the sufficient basis for the explanation of contemporary ethnic circumstances was regarded in such ancient blessings. E (v 20) is similar, but less naive. **8, 9** The assumption is that Jacob does not yet know his grandchildren. Just arrived in Egypt, he now sees the children for the first time (v 11). P's chronology (47:28) differs. Regarding קֶהֶם־נָא see §58g. Regarding וַאברכֵם see §60d. **10a** In J, this is the precondition for vv 13, 14, 17-19, that is, because Jacob is blind, Joseph believes at first that his father errs. The motif of the blindness of the one blessing also occurs in 27:1 (cf. also 1 Kgs 14:4). According to v **10bα** the E text must have referred to the old man taking his grandchildren on his knee since, in v 12, Joseph takes them down again. Originally, this reference to the boys sitting on his knees may have signified their adoption by their grandfather. וַיִּקְרָא בָהֶם שְׁמִי (v 16) points to this understanding (cf. Stade, ZAW 6:144). The same idea also occurs in P (48:5). The account of such an adoption is supposed to explain the fact that the sons of Joseph are not counted as clans of the tribe of Joseph, as still occurs in older sources (49:22; Deut 33:13; Judg 1:23; etc.), but as independent tribes. We already hear this reckoning of the two as tribes in the song of Deborah. In the E recension before us, this juristic sense has faded, and the scene remains merely a beautiful, tender image. Joseph's sons are envisioned as small children. **11** This, too, is a moving statement: thanks to God who granted him such a beautiful conclusion to his life exceeding his request and ability to comprehend. The narrator introduced such a statement with joy. After we have suffered with the old Jacob, we are supposed to realize that God dried his tears and transformed his sorrow into joy. **12** Joseph takes the children from Jacob's knees so that they may receive the blessing standing or kneeling.

13, 14, 17-19 *The blessing in J.* The gesture of blessing is the laying on of hands (elsewhere the gesture of dedication, Num 27:18, of transferal of the spirit, Deut 34:9; etc.; cf. Benzinger[2], 380). The oldest concept of this rite as a gesture of blessing, that a mysterious power is transmitted through the hand, is still quite evident here. The good right hand (35:18) transmits the superior, the left, the inferior blessing. To וַיְשַׁ (v 13), LXX, Pesh, and Vulg add אֹתָם (cf. v 10; Ball; Sievers 2:361; et al.). **14** שִׂכֵּל is a verbal circumstantial clause (§156d). "For Manasseh was the firstborn" is disruptive here, is absent in LXX mss, and is probably a gloss on v 17a. <472> **19** The repetition, "I know well, my son, I know well," is nice. Slowly and solemnly Israel speaks these words. His blind eyes see into the future. "The small one will become greater" is a play on words. וַיְבָרֲכֵם בַּיּוֹם הַהוּא concludes the account in J (cf. the similar passage, 15:18). J does not report the blessings themselves since their content is already clear from the preceding.

15, 16, 20 *The blessing in E.* **15** For אֶת־יוֹסֵף LXX (Vulg) reads אֹתָם (Ball; Kittel). It would better suit what follows, but not v 12b. Joseph is blessed in his children. For the multiplication of divine names in solemn appeals see the parallels Psa 80:2; 50:1. In such a case, the polytheist names all the gods he worships (for the Babylonian practice, see Jastrow, *Rel. Bab. u. Ass.* 1:101, 166, 203, 291), the ancient monotheist mentions all the names of God he knows. The addition of attributes is also preferred in oaths and the like in order to strengthen the power of the invoked divine name (cf. Heitmüller, 250ff., 334ff.). Here the words serve to express confidence in assistance (cf. comments on 24:12; 32;10). The threefold repetition is preferred in solemn appeals, effectual oaths, magical acts, and the like, not only in ancient Israel, but also in Babylonia and elsewhere (cf. Josh 22:22; Psa 50:1; Isa 6:3; the threefold curse of Canaan, Gen 9:25ff.; and, especially, the tripartite Aaronic blessing, Num 6:24ff.; cf. Stade, ZAW 26:124ff.; for Babylonia, cf. Hehn, *Siebenzahl u. Sabbat*, 63ff., where several tripartite Babylonian blessings are cited [65], one of which recalls the Aaronic blessing; "that which is said and done three times is considered complete and finished, especially effective and powerful, unalterable and mysterious," Stade, ZAW 26:125). In polytheism, one calls upon three different gods in solemn acts, oaths, or the like (Usener, *Rhein. Museum* 58: 17ff.), just as it is a widespread human tendency to imagine the deity in the form of trinity (34-35). The monotheistic adaptation of a polytheistic blessing practice is present here. "The God before whom my fathers walked"—the context would better accommodate אֲשֶׁר הִתְהַלֵּךְ לִפְנֵי אֲבֹתַי, "the God who walked before my fathers (on their pilgrimages, in order to prepare the way for them)." The text has probably been altered because of religious reticence (as in 24:20; similarly in 18:22). The expression רָעָה seems to have been a technical term in Israel (cf. the divine name "Shepherd of Israel," Psa 80:2; יִשְׂרָאֵל שֹׁמֵר "watchman of Israel," Psa 121:4; cf. further God's promise to Jacob at Bethel where the expression שָׁמַר stands in both sources, 28:15, 20, and the divine name "shepherd of Israel," 49:24; cf. comments on the passage). The expression רָעָה is conspicuous because a shepherd does not herd a single sheep but a flock. One may, therefore, probably assume that these expressions first referred to the people Israel and were then applied to the patriarch. **16** The mention "of the angel" beside "God" can be explained as the result of the effort to mention all the divine beings concerned. God and the angel are, as always, distinguished as lord and servant. The servant stands appropriately in second position. The words וְיִקָּרֵא בָהֶם שְׁמִי were probably originally an adoption formula. In the current context of E, where וְשֵׁם אֲבֹתַי אַבְרָהָם וְיִצְחָק follows, they only mean that the tribes, although born in Egypt of an Egyptian mother, should not forget that they are Israelites. <473> **20** Regarding blessings of this nature by the name of a famed bearer of blessing, see the comments on 12:3. LXX, Pesh, and Vulg read יְבָרֵךְ. LXX reads בָּכֶם (Budde, ZAW 3:59; Ball; et al.). The context in E requires בָּם.

21, 22 *The conclusion to Jacob's statement in E.* **21** This prediction of the future return to Canaan (also in 50:24) is distinct from the other predictions, even in this passage, in that it is not etiological in origin. It only serves to create an appropriate connection between the Joseph narrative and the subsequent Exodus narrative and is thus, by nature, of later origins. **22** The favored son receives "a shoulder" more than the other, that is, in addition to the portion of his brother. Clearly this is supposed to allude to the possession of שְׁכֶם, Shechem. The possession of the city of Shechem is considered extraordinary here. Shechem must have been the leading city in central Palestine in the earliest period (Josh 24:1; Judg 9:1ff.; 1 Kgs 12:1). Shechem, the chief city, must have been granted to the chief tribe, Joseph. But what is the true sense of this intentionally ambivalent, prophetically mysterious clause? Moderns understand שְׁכֶם to mean "mountain range," which it never meant. One must remain with the meaning "shoulder": Jacob pretends that, as he, the head of the household, divides the pieces among his sons in a זֶבַח, he gives the favored son a shoulder piece in addition to his portion (cf. 1 Sam 1:4-5). The abruptness of this clause is extremely well suited to the oracular style known to us elsewhere. At the same time, however, the statement presumes that the inheritance has just been divided among Jacob's sons and that Joseph receives an additional special portion. Accordingly, the verse does not belong in the current context. Additionally, such a division of the inheritance seems only conceivable if Jacob is in Canaan. The verse seems not to know about the migration to Egypt, then (Meyer, *Israeliten*, 414-15). The allusion to a war in which Jacob conquered Shechem is also very conspicuous in relation to the other Joseph narratives in which Jacob is a private individual whose thoughts are far removed from battle and war. The verse stems from another context unknown to us. It shares the "Amorites" with E (Holzinger, *Hexateuch*, 182). The statement has a "poetic flavor" but is not, apparently, metrical. The significance of this statement and its relationship to 33:19 (E), according to which Jacob purchases property near Shechem, are disputed. In our understanding, already presented above (pp. 356, 360-61), three traditions are involved which originally had no relation to one another. The tradition in 33:19 involves a sacred field near Shechem, <474> the other two involve the city of Shechem itself. The Dinah legend recounts an attack on Shechem which did not make the Jacob tribes lords of the city, however. Gen 48:22, in contrast, speaks of the final possession of the city by conquest. The two are different events. Only a final narrator, combining the traditions, imperfectly wove two of them, Gen 33:19 and 48:22, together in Josh 24:32. The legend to which 48:22 alludes is probably an echo of the Abimelech narrative (cf. above p. 361). "The transformation of Shechem into the virtual capital city of Israel," an event which in actual history belongs in the "period of the Judges," "is traced back here to the primordial period and the ancestor of the people" (Meyer, *Israeliten*, 415). Concerning אֶחָד see §130g. **49:33aβ** Characteristically for this narrative style, the various circumstances of Israel are manifested by the bed. In thanksgiving he falls on his bed (47:31); to bless he sits up in it (48:2b); in death he stretches out on it. The redactor recounts the death itself, following P.

72. Jacob's Blessing 49:1-28a J[b]

1. The poem intends, as the introduction (v 2) states, to transmit the statements of Jacob the patriarch to his sons, that is, concerning the tribes of Israel. The sayings contain, then, as R[J] correctly understood in v 1, prophecies and, indeed, a few of them have the form of the "blessing" (wishes; vv 4, 7, 10ff., 17, 25-26). The very closely related "blessing of Moses" (Deut 33), as well as the blessing and curse of Balaam (Num 23ff.), of Noah (Gen 9), and of Isaac (Gen 27), belong to the same genre (cf. also the curses in the Paradise narrative, Gen 3, etc.). All these passages have poetic form and are pseudonymous. They are descriptions of the author's present in the mouth of a patriarch: *vaticinia ex eventu* by poets. Similar secondary prophecies occur elsewhere in antiquity (examples in Reuß, *A.T.* 3:310) and in modern literature (e.g., Shakespeare's prophecy of Queen Elizabeth in "Henry VIII," V.2, Michael Beer's prophecy about Napolean I in "Streunsee" [esp. characteristic] and very many moderns in reference to the events of 1870). The precondition of this blessing is that in ancient Israel the patriarchs (especially when very near death) could make effectual pronouncements. Normal words are not involved here, but those that are miraculous, effective, and productive. Such wonderwords naively explain current circumstances: in those days science and poetry were still intertwined (cf. above p. 81). Such "blessings" were originally part of a legend that tells how this statement came about and are consequently only comprehensible in the context of such an account (i.e., Noah's blessing, Isaac's, etc.). But, gradually, these "blessings" developed into an independent genre. The sayings of Balaam are already almost independent of the Balaam

legend. The blessings of Jacob and of Moses no longer have a close relationship to any individual legend and belong, by nature, more in a collection of songs than in a book of legends. At the same time, these "blessings" differ significantly in scope from the older ones that appear in the context of an account. The older blessings are rather brief, the later much longer. Further, the oldest blessings, because they are part of a national legend, are of popular origins. The later ones, however, as extensive poems, are the products of literary poetry. The content of these blessings also indicates that they should be assigned to two different time periods: the words of Noah and Isaac originally deal with pre-Israelite circumstances, <475> and are, thus, very old tradition in Israel. The blessings of Jacob, Moses, and Balaam speak of historical Israel and are, thus, much younger. Accordingly, we may imagine the development of this genre as follows: in many ancient national legends the blessing played a significant role. This style was adopted in a later time by poets and utilized for larger independent poems. The theme of this new genre was Israel's majesty and power, the fame of the people blessed by God. The unusual poetic device is that an old man of God speaks words in which he wishes for all this. The basic attitude is inspiration and these poems are also meant to inspire. The hearer should delight to see how the ancient words are now so gloriously fulfilled. Here, then, is where Israel's nationalism expresses itself most forcefully. Yet Israelite patriotism in the earliest period was strong enough to find details worthy of reproach in Israel, too: thus Gen 49:14-15 reproaches Issachar (and Zebulon?). The patriarch cursed even Reuben, Simeon, and Levi (49:3-4, 5-7). In contrast, a later period with its stress on nationalism could no longer bear reproach and curse. Deut 33 knows only praise and blessing. The style of this genre requires that all these words have been fulfilled in the time of the poet (p. 81). Yet, later poets have also interpolated patriotic wishes which inspired them and their time. There are few of these interpolations in Gen 49 (cf. vv 16, 10ff.), in contrast to several in Deut 33 (cf. vv 6, 7, 11, 20). This, too, indicates that Deut 33 is younger than Gen 49.

2. The form of the passage is remarkably similar to the style of the oracle especially as we know it from the prophets (cf. "Israelitische Literatur," in *Kultur der Gegenward* I/7, 85). The two, the wish for and the announcement of the future, are by nature closely related and in Hebrew are often impossible or difficult to distinguish from one another. The blessing-poets will have imitated the forms the men of God in their times employed. As imitations of the artistic form of the oracle, these poems are all the more valuable to us for the history of this genre because they are the oldest such Israelite literature we possess. The saying concerning the Messiah is clearly a proper prophecy. The chief, consistent characteristic of the oracle style, including here, is the mysterious idiom. The oracle received by the men of God in obscure circumstances, when they perceive the ineffable, cannot be precisely rendered in prose. Prophetic speech is enigmatic speech. As a classic example of this enigmatic style, one may compare the wonderful description of David in Num 24:17ff. Therefore, these legends avoid mentioning names from the patriarch's future. Thus, we do not learn who shoots his arrow at Joseph, who Benjamin plunders, whom Issachar serves, whom Simeon and Levi treated so roguishly, and, above all, who "the coming one" is to whom Judah must yield dominion, etc. Most of these allusions were very clear to the poet's contemporaries; for us, however, they are sometimes very difficult. At any rate, before one attempts an explanation, one may at least initially acknowledge that the poet intentionally speaks ἐν μυστηρίῳ. Another means

for veiling descriptions, employed especially often in Gen 49, is to allude to the intended referent by an image only. The fact that these images are often taken from the life of wild animals is indicative of the state of culture in the period when humans are still familiar with the animals of the field and admire some of them very much. Further noteworthy for Gen 49 are the many wordplays on the names: the profoundly insightful eyes of the man of God perceives in the name an oracle on the fate of the bearer. All this also characterizes the oldest prophetic style.

3. The chief difference between these blessing poems and prophetic style consists in the fact that they essentially describe their present. This is also apparent in their form: the "prophetic perfect" is absent from Gen 49 and the imperfects are <476> mostly to be translated with the English present. In fact, the poet even recounts a few things that have already happened prior to his time (vv 6b, 9, 15, 23-24). This should be taken together with the fact that Gen 49 manifests conspicuous, even verbal points of contact with the passage in the Song of Deborah where the poet lists the tribes of Israel with praise and reproach (Judg 5:14ff.). We will have to explain both (according to Greßmann's oral communication) as evidence that there was a literature of praise and reproach sayings concerning the tribes. Such sayings poems will apparently have been publicly recited when a common military undertaking or a grand worship festival united several tribes. The poets of Gen 49 and Judges adopted this style. The poet of Gen 49 created a poem from sayings concerning all twelve tribes and clothed them as the partriarch's blessing.

4. Gen 49 is most closely related to Deut 33, also an old man's blessing on the tribes. Characteristic for both poems is the structure which divides the whole into individual, loosely combined sayings. Each tribe has a saying beginning with the name of the tribe. Description, even narrative (v 21) also intermingles in the blessing. The two poems even agree in wording (cf. the saying about Joseph). The two poems thus represent a particular variety of the genre: the union of the blessing form with description of the tribe's present in individual sayings. Is the poet of Gen 49 the inventor of this variety and the poet of Deut 33 his imitator? This is indeed possible, but there could have been a whole series of such poems. The length of the individual sayings in Gen 49 varies greatly. Five of them are only one line in length, the sayings concerning Judah and Joseph nine each. This great variety will hardly have been original. One may assume that such sayings were originally rather brief (just as the earliest Hebrew poetry had very small units, cf. "Israelitische Literatur," pp. 53-54) and later, according to a law which becomes apparent elsewhere in Hebrew literature (cf. introduction ¶3.20), were sometimes expanded. This is also indicated by the fact that almost all the longer sayings of Gen 49 are conceivable as expansions of the first line. The statement concerning Dan falls clearly into two originally independent sayings. The passage concerning Judah contains three markedly distinct portions (vv 8, 9, 10ff.). The arrangement of the tribes is according to age and agrees on the whole with 29:31ff., but diverges in the details.

5. The age of the sayings poem and of Gen 49. The sayings of Gen 49 belong to various eras. The saying concerning Judah clearly presupposes that Judah rules the other tribes. The context of the song shows how Judah acquired the birthright. This points to the time of David or Solomon. The sayings concerning Issachar, Dan, and Benjamin, however, are better explained against the time before the development of the Israelite state. The Song of Deborah already presupposes the saying concerning Zebulon. The sayings concerning Reuben and concerning Simeon and Levi also deal with ancient matters. Yet

one notes that the Reuben saying no longer knows the actual events but only the legend about them. The description of Joseph does not necessarily point to the period of the divided monarchy, as is usually assumed. Regarding the details, see below. To explain this multiple situation, one must remember the origin of the genre: sayings such as those taken up in Gen 49 were sung by Israel's singers since ancient times and exist in many recensions in Israel. This is also clear from the fact that a few plays on words underlying the sayings of Gen 49 are now missing (cf. comments on vv 13, 15, 20). The tribal identity of the singers will also have influenced the variety of such recensions. The saying concerning Joseph which so glorifies this tribe may have originated in Joseph itself. The age of such sayings poetry is evidenced by points of contact with the Song of Deborah and results from the nature of the matter. The development of a form of poetry which speaks particularly concerning <477> every tribe can only be explained in relation to a time when the tribes, individually, led separate lives, thus before the rise of the united state. The collection and revision of Gen 49 before us will stem from a Judaean pen and from the time of Judah's dominion over Israel. No saying points with certainty to the time of the divided monarchy. The advanced age of the poem is also apparent in its moral viewpoints—it glorifies the life of Benjamin who lives by murder and theft—and in its religion—the poem is far removed from the "prophetic" ideals of a later time. Yahweh is Israel's helper who accompanies Israel in wars and blesses Israel with fertility. The Messiah luxuriates in wine and milk and has little to do with the prophetic ideal of a just ruler. "Any assessment of the religious situation is missing" (Dillmann). The militant spirit of the sayings (vv 8-9, 17, 23-24, 27), which distinguishes them very markedly from the peaceful spirit of the patriarchal narratives, suits the oldest historical legends and historical accounts of Israel (Haller, 121). The esthetic features of the song show how old it is. It breathes the rhythm and power of the old heroic period. At that time, poetry had not yet (as in most Psalms) shied away from true life. Instead, one still attempted to see reality and poetry together. The language of the poem with its many rare expressions is also very ancient (cf. Dillmann, 453). Next to Judg 5, Gen 49 is the most important chapter in the OT for the earliest history of the tribes. The poem consists almost entirely of "dual trimeters" (cf. Sievers 1:404ff.; 2:152ff., 361ff.). Exceptions are the isolated trimeters (vv 18, 27a) and quadrameters (vv 7b, 8aα). V 22 is probably a heptameter. Concerning vv 13, 24b see the exegesis. The text is very corrupt in places. Dillmann (456) has an extensive bibliography.

6. Source. The poem, itself very old, was, however, only inserted into the patriarchal legends at a late date (cf. pp. 380-81). In fact, it seems to have belonged first to the book of J. The close relationship between 49:3-4 and 35:22 supports this conclusion.

7. Zimmern (ZA 7:161ff.), following earlier scholars on the basis of the many animal metaphors, has presented, although with great caution, the ingenious theory that the tribes correspond to the twelve signs of the zodiac. Others have expanded and adapted the hypothesis (cf. Jeremias ATAO[2], 395ff., with bibliography; and Winckler, *Forschungen* 3:465ff.). Since, however, there is no metaphor in reference to a few of the tribes, since a few of the animals mentioned are not known to us to be represented in the zodiac, and since the sequence of the tribes does not completely correspond to those in the zodiac, this hypothesis cannot be demonstrated (cf. also Ball, 114ff.). Eerdmans (2:50n.1) has demonstrated the caprice of Jeremias' proposal. The way divergent results can be obtained in this

manner can be seen from a comparison of Jeremias and Winckler. "Others will find (still) other traces" (Jeremias, ATAO², 395). This may well be.

49:1b-28a *Jacob's blessing.* **1b** The words do not have poetic form and thus stem, like the concluding verse, from the hand of the one who inserted the poem here, that is, probably from R^J. בְּאַחֲרִית הַיָּמִים is a term from prophetic eschatology, "the farthest future the prophet can see at all" (Dillmann), the time spoken of by the greatest eschatological prophecy (Isa 2:2; Mic 4:1; Jer 23:20; 30:24; Ezek 38:16; Dan 10:14 [Sir 48:24]). From Jacob's standpoint, David's time is the "end of days." The same expression, also in imitation of prophetic style, occurs in Num 24:14; Deut 4:30; 31:29. The contention that Ezekiel first coined the phrase which was interpolated here (Stade, *Bibl. Theol.*, 295, following Staerk, ZAW 11:247ff.), is tendentious and entirely undemonstrable. <478> **2** *The introduction of the poem.* The folk singer and also the prophet begin with such a summons to hear (Isa 1:10; 28:14; 32:9; 34:1; Jer 7:2; Deut 32:1; etc.). The other "independent" legends also have major or minor introductions. The dual וְשִׁמְעוּ is conspicuous; the first is probably an addition (Sievers 1:405; 2:362).

3, 4 *Saying about Reuben.* Reuben is addressed, as are Judah and Joseph later. The other sayings are in the third person. Direct address occurs in especially passionate passages, also in prophetic style. The firstborn is begotten by the father's full strength (Deut 21:17; Psa 78:51) and is thus the strongest among his brothers. According to the ancient Hebrew perspective, the strongest, however, is, at the same time, the wildest, most passionate. In this very way, Reuben demonstrated and forfeited his firstborn status. Therefore יֶתֶר . . . אַל־תּוֹתַר . . . יֶתֶר belong together—an ingenious play on words. The verse division disrupts this context. יֶתֶר (advantage) and פַּחַז (insolence) are examples of the abstract for the concrete—a powerful idiom. The Rabbis point שְׂאֵת as שְׂאֵת, a qal inf. > נשׂא, although the intransitive meaning of נשׂא, following which this passage is often translated "height," is not attested with certainty (cf. *Schöpfung und Chaos*, 33n.2). One should read שָׂאֹה. שָׂאֹה is a term referring to the arrogant, destructive roaring of the sea and of Leviathan (cf. *Schöpfung und Chaos*, 84, 97) or perhaps שָׂאָה, "storm, thunderstorm" (Kittel). עז (in pause עָז) here means "wildness, passion" (cf. עַז ‖ עָרִיץ, Isa 25:3). עַז describes, for example, the lion (Judg 14:14), death (Cant 8:6), and most often the passion of love (Can 8:6). פָּחַז means "to be careless, impudent, shameless, frivolous." The usual meaning assumed for this passage, "to bubble over," is not attested. Accordingly, כַּמַּיִם seems corrupt. Concerning תּוֹתַר see §53n. It may be that תּוּתַר (niphal) should be read with the Pesh (Ball, etc.). The third, long line expressly states what the second vaguely suggested. Reuben's passion had no regard even for his father's bed: an allusion to the legend of Reuben's intercourse with Bilhah (35:22). Regarding מִשְׁכְּבֵי, plural, see §124b. The conclusion, "Then you desecrated; he mounted my bed," is hardly in order. The change of persons (§144p) is conspicuous. After the forceful beginning, אָז ("at that time, therefore," Jer 22:15; Psa 40:8; 56:10; Gesenius¹⁴), one expects something new and not a parallel to the preceding. A curse is missing from the context. One may read הִלַּלְתִּי and perhaps יְצוּעִי with LXX: the father deplored the criminal association and "desecrated" his own bed. A similar motif occurs in Schiller's "Braut von Messina": "And in the wrath of horrible curses, the patriarch shed terrible seed on the sinful marriage bed." Or one may translate with Ehrlich, "Therefore I desecrated, that is, took away the honor (Ezek 28:16; Lam 2:2), from him who mounted my bed." LXX reads "then you desecrated the bed you mounted" (עָלִיתָ with Pesh, Targ. Onq, and Targ. Jon), for which one can adduce 1 Chron 5:1. Reuben, always mentioned as the first in the genealogical system (p. 323), also once the leader of the tribes of Israel, must have later seriously declined (Deut 33:6). Apparently, it was gradually consumed in battles with the Moabites (and Ammonites; Meyer, *Israeliten*, 531).

5-7 *Concerning Simeon and Levi.* **5** Simeon and Levi are called "brothers." There is, therefore, <479> a tradition in the background according to which the two are full brothers. The same tradition appears in 34:25 (cf. above pp. 358, 365). "Brothers" also means "colleagues, equals" (Prov 18:9; Job 30:29). מכרתיהם is usually, although without support, explained as a kind of weapon. Ball thinks more correctly of מִכְרָה "pit" from כרה "to dig" (cf. מִכְרֶה "pit" Zeph 2:9). כלי is equivalent to כִּילַי, "wily." One may read כְּלִי וְהָמָס מְכֹרֹתֵיהֶם, "cunning (literally: cunningly) and violence are their pits," with which they trap people. Regarding the combination of the adjective and the substantive see טֹוב וָחֶסֶד (Psa 23:6). Regarding this unusual combination of the abstract and the concrete see Amos 3:10, "They heap up injustice and violence in their palaces." Digging pits is a common image for deceit. Sam, Targ. Onq, and LXX read כלו. Ball and Kittel cautiously propose כִּלּוּ הֲמַס מְכֹרֹתָם (מְכֹרֹתֵיהֶם), "they carry out their evil attacks (?)," following (LXX) VetLat. The phrase alludes, at any rate, to the Shechem-Dinah narrative, also treated in the following material. Concerning these allusions see above p. 359. Deut 33 (cf. vv 2-5, 8, 9 [Exod 32:26], 16, 21) contains a whole series of allusions to the legend. This, too, probably signifies later origins. **6-7** Appalled, Jacob denies any association with this crime. The ancestor's words express Israel's common judgment. קָהָל ‖ סֹוד is the assembly of the people for the purpose of settling a matter (Stade, *Bibl. Theol.*, 147-48). It is better to pronounce כְּבֹדִי following LXX and in analogy to Babylonian כְּבֵדִי, "my liver" (so also in Psa 7:6; 16:9, and perhaps also in 30:13; 57:9; 108:2; cf. recently Freiherrn v. Gall, *Herrlichkeit Gottes*, 7-8; the liver is the seat of the psyche, cf. Lam 2:11). Since כָּבֵד is masculine, one should read יֵחַד (according to Sam יחר) with Ball. אִישׁ and שֹׁור are collectives. The anticlimax is unusual for our sensibilities (Meyer, *Israeliten*, 412n.2). רָצֹון means "malice" (Esth 9:5). The old Israelite is not sentimental in war and executes the "ban" without reservation. How Simeon and Levi must have raged! "I will scatter them." Jacob himself scatters them by this very curse. "Jacob" and "Israel" are the people here and thus anachronistic. Of particular importance in this saying is the fact that according to it Levi was originally a tribe like the others. We hear nothing of its priesthood. On the other hand, it is by no means excluded here (contra Holzinger). The description of Levi, from our perspective very profane, does not at all render it impossible that priestly traditions were nurtured in it since those old priests were certainly not "spiritual" (in our sense). The blessing of Moses says nothing of Simeon and speaks of Levi only as the tribe of priests—a clear indication of a later time.

8-12 *Concerning Judah.* The situation in the poem is as follows. After Reuben has lost his birthright, and Simeon and Levi have lost their independence, Judah obtained the dominion over his brothers. This situation is not explicitly stated, but only indicated by the structure. The clear demarcations at the end of each section hinder a clearer organization of the whole. This unusually flawed interrelationship, namely, that the lesser demarcations are too strong and the organization of the <480> whole is not clear enough, was always the weakness of Hebrew literature. The following section is a dithyramb. In order to comprehend all the emotion expressed in it, one may imagine it performed at a Judaean folk festival. The earth echoes with the hearers' cries of jubilation! The piece is also extremely significant historically: we learn from it of Judah's enthusiasm raised to new heights by David—an enthusiasm like that of our people in 1870. The passage concerning Judah first of all praises its glorious present, then its even more glorious future. **8** Regarding the emphasis on the suffix in אַתָּה see §135e. יוֹדוּךְ alludes to the name יְהוּדָה. The same etymology, but in reference to the praise of God, occurs in 29:35. יָדְךָ is also a play on this name. His enemies (Philistia, Edom, Ammon, the Aramaeans) flee before him, but he still grabs them by the neck. The tribes of Israel acknowledge him as lord. V **9** describes Judah's growth in poetic style. Once a גּוּר אַרְיֵה, then elevated through much booty (עָלָה "to grow up" Ezek 19:3), the old lion now lies sated in his lair. No one quarrels with him! V **9b** = Num 24:9a.

   10 *The eternity of his dominion.* His regime will endure until the coming one arrives at the end of days. The scepter (שֵׁבֶט, essentially the equivalent of מְחֹקֵק) is a long staff, perhaps adorned with emblems, which the ruler holds between his feet when sitting. The poet does not say over whom Judah rules (regarding this mysterious style see above p. 451), but it becomes clear from the context (v 8): over the conquered enemies and over his brothers. V **10b** is, as is almost universally acknowledged today, "Messianic," that is, to be understood in relation to the ruler of the end time. Only "an ideal date" can be portrayed here (Wellhausen, *Composition*[3], 323) and וְלוֹ demonstrates that the foregoing discusses a specific personality (Sellin, *Schiloh-Weissagung*, 5). This alone clearly indicates that this coming one is only alluded to from afar. The Messiah is also discussed in this oracular style (cf. Isa 9; Mic 5). The prediction of the future king is a great, divine secret which may not be expressed in broad daylight (cf. "Israeltische Literatur," 85). It follows, however, that the hearers, if they are supposed to have understood these words, must have been familiar with the eschatological expectation. In this passage we have its earliest attestation. עַד־כִּי does not mean that Judah's dominion ceases with the Messiah, but that it is only then truly secured (cf. Psa 112:8). בּוֹא refers to the appearance of the Messiah in Ezek 21:32; Deut 33:7, too. Despite all the efforts of the centuries, שִׁילֹה has still not been interpreted with certainty. The formerly preferred translations, "Until he (Judah) comes to Shiloh (city in Ephraim where the ark was located and Eli was priest)," or similarly, are now as good as abandoned. The interpretation recently suggested by Ehrlich and W. Schröder (ZAW 19:186ff.), "Until Shelah (Judah's son, 38:5) comes," is supposed to mean, according to Schröder, "Until Judah dies and the son inherits from the father." But may one attribute such foolish sophistry even to a glossator (the clause is supposed to be an interpolation)? Hebr mss, Sam, LXX, Pesh, Theod, Targ. Onq, and Targ. Jon read שֶׁלֹה = שֶׁלֹה = אֲשֶׁר לוֹ (regarding שֶׁ = אֲשֶׁר see ¶36, in old texts, Judg 5:7; Gen 6:3; regarding לֹה = לוֹ see §91e) which should be interpreted, perhaps, to mean "Until the one comes to whom it (scepter and staff) belongs." עַד־בֹּא אֲשֶׁר־לוֹ הַמִּשְׁפָּט (Ezek 21:32) may be comparable (so recently Driver, Kittel, <481> and Kautzsch[3]). Admittedly, one misses the subject of the relative clause in this interpretation. Wellhausen's (*Gesch. Isr.* 1:375) suggestion that וְלוֹ may be a gloss on שֶׁלֹה or vice versa is a sin against poetical structure. Others think of שֶׁלֹו, which following שִׁלְיָה, "afterbirth," would mean "his newborn son," or, better, conjecture following Mic 5:1; Jer 30:21; Zech

9:9-10, מָשְׁלוֹ, "his ruler," or שְׁאִילוֹ, "his chosen one." It may be simplest to read שָׁלוֹ, "the peaceful." The root שׁלה and its derivatives mean "to live happily in carefree calm." This is the most beautiful wish of the peaceful citizen and, at the same time, the ideal of an idyllic commonwealth (‖ צלח, בטח, שָׁלוֹם, שָׁאַן). Good fortune and pleasure, plentiful nourishment and wealth accompany this idea. The opposite is bickering and strife, destruction, and sudden catastrophe. Such a word would be extremely well-suited as the mysterious name of the Prince of Peace (Greßmann, *Ursprung der isr.-jüd. Eschatologie*, 286ff.) and would also fit well into the context here as a contrast to the prior forceful dominion of Judah and as a transition to vv 11-12 which describe the good fortune of the coming one. Bibliography: Posnanski, *Schiloh* (1904; dealing with exegesis in antiquity and the Middle Ages); Dillmann, 463-64; Ball, 109-10; Sellin, *Schiloh-Weissagung*; etc. Modern scholars (Wellhausen, *Composition*³, 323-24; Stade, *Gesch. Isr.* 1:159n.5; *Bibl. Theologie*, 213-14; Holzinger; Kautzsch³; etc.; most recently Marti, ZAW 29:137-38, who very prosaicly relates the statement to Nebuchadnezzar) want to remove the verse as an interpolation, W. Schröder (ZAW 29: 195-96), contrary to the poetical structure of v 10bα, because it disrupts the unit. But its relationship to the preceding and the following is outstanding since v 10a requires a phrase such as "forever" and vv 11-12 continues to describe the Messiah (Sellin, *Schiloh-Weissagung*, 9).

The assumption that this passage is an interpolation is also tendentious. Most moderns are of the opinion that the (writing) "prophets" first created Israel's eschatology, and, consequently, strike this verse because it contradicts this basic conviction. The author does not share this conviction. He believes, rather, that one can only understand the prophets if one assumes that they were already aware of an eschatology they adopted, resisted, transformed (cf. *Zum religionsgeschichtlichen Verständnis des NT*, 21ff.; "Israelitische Literatur," 68; "Endhoffnung der Psalmisten," *Christl. Welt* [1903] cols. 1130ff.; Greßmann, *Ursprung der isr.-jüd. Eschatologie*, 147, 160, 245ff.; etc.). Deut 33:7a, "Hear, Yahweh, Judah's pleas and bring him (mysteriously: the great king for whom Israel pleas) to his people," seems to presume a similar prophecy. Concerning יקהת see §20h. LXX, Vulg, and Pesh translate "expectation, hope" (= תִּקְוָה Isa 42:4; cf. Dillmann). The hope for world dominion belongs to the image of the Messiah (Mic 5:3; Zech 9:10; Isa 11:10; Psa 2; 72:8ff.; 110) and fits the context. Precisely because the nations obey him, the Messiah lives in undisturbed good fortune (שָׁלוֹ). This hope will hardly have developed in the Israelite countryside where the actual circumstances could not have brought even the greatest visionary to it. Instead, it will be the product of a people who ruled a large territory. The enthusiasm of the Davidic period, however—we may assume—will have given Israelite patriots the courage to apply such an audacious expectation to Israel and Judah (cf. *Ausgewählte Psalmen*², 19-20; Greßmann, *Ursprung der isr.-jüd. Eschatologie*, 253-54, 265.).

11, 12 *The plenty of wine and milk in that time.* V **11** links directly by means of a participle, and thus continues the description of the Messiah (so, following earlier predecessors, Greßmann, *Ursprung der jüd.-isr. Eschatologie*, 287-88; Sellin, *Schiloh-Weissagung*, 7-8). That ruler luxuriates in the most glorious pleasures, in wine and milk. The abundance of milk and wine also characterizes the <482> eschaton elsewhere (Greßmann, 208ff.). Isa 7:15 also presumes the notion that the Messiah himself (as a child) enjoys this plenty. That the ruler of the eschaton is understood as living such a life of luxury is thoroughly consistent with the image of an Oriental king and demonstrates the very advanced age of this description. At the time in Israel, wine was valued as a gift of God, too (cf. comments on Gen 5:29). Of course, the idea is that the subjects will also benefit then. It is also easily understood that the "donkey" is mentioned as the king's mount: the horse first came to Israel under David and Solomon and always remained the mount for war. The Messiah's donkey also occurs in Zech 9:9. In this understanding, the words of vv 10-12 are a single unit. Others relate vv 11-12 to Judah and understood the verses as a description of the present. The details: in the land of the Messiah there is so much wine he hitches his donkey to the vines (which one otherwise anxiously guards against animals) and he can wash his clothes in wine. Both are very strong—for our tastes too strong—hyperboles (Deut 33:24; Job 29:6 are similar). Regarding אסרי and בני (v 11), as well as חכלילי (v 12), see §90k,l. Regarding עירה (from עַיִר) see §93v. The participle (§116p) is continued by the perfect כִּבֵּס (§116x). The blood of grapes is an image for red wine also known to the ancient Arabs (G. Jacob, *Altarab. Parallelen zum A.T.*, 6; *Beduinenleben²*, 102). For סוּתֹה Sam reads כסיתו. 12 Wine makes the eyes sparkle (Prov 23:29-30). Dripping with milk, the teeth shine white. This demonstrates the ancient Israelite ideal of beauty: sparkling eyes and white teeth shine forth from the (yellow or reddish) face. חַכְלִיל certainly does not mean "cloudy," for that would be a blemish. Greßmann (*Ursprung der isr.-jüd. Eschatologie*, 288 no. 1) compares כחל, "to make up one's eyes," whereby they become fiery and brilliant. לְבֶן is from the absolute state לָבֵן (§93dd).

13 *Concerning Zebulon.* The first clause describes Zebulon's location on the Great (Mediterranean) Sea. An older recension will have read יובל זְבוּלֻן for יִשְׁכֹּן in allusion to the names (cf. 30:20). The Song of Deborah (Judg 5:7) reads אֲשֶׁר יָשַׁב לְחוֹף יַמִּים. The saying which, as the play on words shows, originally referred to Zebulon, has been reinterpreted in reference to Asher. The Song of Deborah is secondary here, therefore (see further above p. 452). In the second clause, the repetition of לְחוֹף violates the style of Hebrew poetry. The first clause is assured by Judg 5:17. According to Ball one may read וַיְהִי חֹבֵל so that the saying would contain a reproach. וַיַרְכָתוֹ עַל-צִידֹן (Hebr mss, Sam, LXX, Pesh, Targ. Onq, Targ. Jon, and Vulg עַד-צִידֹן) as a foot with two accents does not fit the rhythm and its prose does not suit the style. It is, therefore, probably an explanatory addition (Ball; Sievers 2:362). Concerning Zebulon's territory see Sanda, *Mitt. Vorderas. Gesellsch.* (1902) 2:39ff.

14, 15 *Concerning Issachar.* Issachar has enough strength, but prefers calm and comfort. In order to be able to enjoy its beautiful land (lower Galilee and the plain of Jezreel) and calm, it forsook honor and submitted itself to foreign servitude (i.e., to the Canaanite, Phoenician cities). So goes the acid reproach. These are probably the circumstances of the premonarchical times. In the background stands the <483> explanation of the name Issachar (= אִישׁ שָׂכָר, "day laborer"), no longer clearly evident in the present text. **14** Sam reads גֵרִים, but "donkey of the foreigner" is hardly tolerable. The same expression, בֵּין הַמִּשְׁפְּתָיִם, occurs in reference to Issachar in Judg 5:16. Issachar is compared to the animal grazing comfortably on a familiar pasture. For טֹוב Sam reads מְנוּחָה. טובה. מְנוּחָה is a term for sedentary as opposed to nomadic life (cf. Deut 12:9; Psa 95:11). Issachar plays a brilliant role in the Song of Deborah. It is difficult to say whether this saying falls to an earlier or later time than Judg 5.

16-18 *Two sayings concerning Dan. Dan's struggle for its independence (v 16), Dan the viper (v 17), and a short fervent prayer (v 18).* **16** The tribe of Dan includes only a few men (Judg 18:11) and struggles mightily. The poet wishes that it may preserve its independence and jurisdiction (cf. Luther, ZAW 21:15; Meyer, *Israeliten*, 505, 526). Here, too, is a play on words: דָּן יָדִין. עַמּוֹ are Dan's own people, not Israel. **16** The second saying has no connection to the preceding. It may have originally been a variant reflecting the same situation of the tribe. שְׁפִיפֹן is probably the viper, the horned adder, a small, very dangerous species of snake. The small viper can bite the horse and, if the hose rears up in pain, cause the rider to fall. May Dan so ward off its mighty enemies! It is probably no accident that horses are mentioned in the metaphor. Dan must fight against steed and rider. Concerning עקבי see §20h. V **18** seems, if not a gloss (so most recently Ball, Kautzsch[3]), to suit v 16 better than v 17. The statement is in the style of the Psalms (Psa 119:81, 123, 166, 174). The presumed circumstances point to the time prior to the monarchy here, too. Dan fights quite alone. Combined Israel only has good wishes for it. On the other hand, the Dan's position among the northern tribes already presumes Dan's settlement in the North.

19 *Gad.* The brief saying has three plays on words, and is, thus, especially ingenious in Hebrew terms. For עָקֵב מֵאָשֵׁר: one should read עֲקֵבָם: אָשֵׁר with LXX mss, VetLat (Pesh, Vulg; as do many modern scholars). ידונו and יגד derive from the root גדד (König, *Lehrgebäude d. hebr. Sprache* 1:356). The war parties which Gad disturbs are desert nomads seeking to follow Israel into the fertile land, specifically the Ammonites, but also Moabites and Aramaeans.

20 *Asher* dwells on fertile ground (Deut 33:24). This text, too, is probably based on a play on words: אָשֵׁר = "fortunate." Its produce reaches even princely tables, such as those of the Phoenician kings (Ezek 27:17).

21 The saying concerning *Naphtali* cannot be explained with certainty. Either, "N. is a far-reaching terebinth (LXX אֵילָה) which grows beautiful bows (אִמְרֵי)," or, better, <484> since the other tribes, if compared to anything, are compared to animals, "N. is an agile (unfettered, free-roaming, Job 39:5) hind, which gives birth to beautiful lambs (אִמְרֵי)." Both occurrences of הַנֹּתֵן should preferably be read as the feminine הַנֹּתֶנֶת. The image is not entirely transparent in either occurrence. The translation of the second element, "who makes pleasing speech," is far removed from the first.

22-26 *Praise for Joseph, next to the saying concerning Judah, the most extensive saying.* The poem is partisan toward Judah, but takes pains to do justice to Joseph, too. Several sections may be distinguished: (1) Joseph as a bull (?), v 22; (2) Joseph's way against the archers, vv 23, 24a; (3) divine assistance, vv 24b, 25aα,b and blessings, vv 25aβ-26. The text is severely corrupt at points and is probably irrecoverable for the most part. V **22** is partially untranslatable (Meyer, *Israeliten*, 282n.3). One usually interprets, "A young (בֵּן, construct state; Dillmann, etc.) grapevine (פֹּרָת = פֹּרִיָּה §80g), a young grapevine at a well; tendrils climb up (sing. §145k) the wall" (Dillmann and also Kautzsch[3]). But this meaning of בָּנוֹ is assumed only here and צער means "to stride into," not "to climb." פרת is a wordplay on the old name אֶפְרָת (the derivative אֶפְרָתִי = Ephraimite), and is thus assured, but it is better interpreted as = פָּרָה, "cow," just as שׁוֹר (v 22b) seems to be the equivalent of שׁוֹר, "cattle," and just as Joseph is also compared to cattle (שׁוֹר) in Deut 33:17. Thus, there is an animal image here, too (cf. comments on v 21; cf. Zimmern, ZA [1892], 164ff.). LXX reads υἱός ηὐξημένος Ἰωσήφ, υἱὸς ηὐξημένος μου ζηλωτός (LXX thinks of עין, "to envy"), υἱός μου νεώτατος (Sam בני צעירי) πρὸς μὲ ἀνάστρεψον (= עלי שוב; Sam עלי שור).

23, 24a *Joseph's battle against the archers.* **23** וְרֹבּוּ (regarding the form, see §67m) should at least read וַיָּרֹבּוּ (Kittel). Sam and LXX read וַיְרִיבָהוּ (Ball, Holzinger, et al.); or should one perhaps think of the root רבה? V **24a** is usually translated "yet unshaken he holds his bow, and his hands moved agilely" (so Kautzsch[3]). But this meaning of ישׁב is dubious. According to Smend (*Weisheit des Jesus Sirach*, 373-74) אֵיתָן does not mean "perennial," but "strong." זְרֹעֵי אָדָיו is difficult. V 23 is also puzzling since the bow is in Joseph's hand and not in those of the "archers." But the connection to v 24b in this translation is virtually impossible (Meyer, *Israeliten*, 282n.3, 283n.1; Sievers 2:362).

V **24b** requires Joseph's enemies to have been already defeated. LXX reads καὶ συνετρίβη μετὰ κράτους τὰ τόξα αὐτῶν, καὶ ἐξελύθα τὰ νεῦρα βραχιόνων χειρὸς (χειρῶν) αὐτῶν. Two variants, נידי and ידם, seem to have been combined. Accordingly, one may read, "But their bows (קשׁתם) were broken (וַתִּשָׁבֵר) by a mighty one (to this point following Ball) and the desires of their arms are shattered (וַיִּפֹּצְצוּ נִידֵי זְרֹעָם, poal of פצץ; cf. VetLat, Vulg, and Pesh). The decisive issue for dating the poem is how one explains these "archers." Are they the desert nomads who crossed the fords of the Jordan and terrorized Israelite farmers during the "Judges period," for example, the Midianites, against whom Gideon—who could even be "the mighty one"—went to battle (Dillmann)? Or are they the Aramaeans of Damascus who made life difficult in the northern kingdom (Wellhausen, *Composition*[3], 323; Stade, *Gesch. Isr.* 1:165; etc.)? Joseph's territory, concentrated in the Transjordan, was not actually impacted, however, by the Aramaic movements <485> and archery is characteristic, not of the Aramaeans, but of the nomads (21:20). Finally, the saying in no way presumes a unified northern Israel (whose chief representative would be Joseph), but speaks of circumstances which concern the tribe of Joseph, alone. Accordingly, we are pointed to the time before the unified state and must think of attacks by nomads.

24b, 25aα,b *The divine assistance by which Joseph's enemies are annihilated.* The following material connects well, given the passive meaning of the verbs in v 24a. Concerning the solemn concentration of divine names see the comments on 48:15. **24b** מִידֵי means "by the (helping) hands." Concerning מן with passive verbs see Gesenius[14] מן, 1g; §121f. אביר יעקב (Isa 1:24; 49:26; 60:16; Psa 132:2, 5) is an ancient divine name; it probably means "Bull of Jacob," and thus echoes an animal symbol (Stade, *Bibl. Theologie*, 121; the rabbis point אֲבִיר, without dagesh in contrast to the usual אַבִּיר, in order to distance any pagan notion, cf. Hoffmann, ZAW 3:124). מִשָּׁם, "from there" (so also Kautzsch[3]) is senseless (Meyer, *Israeliten* 283n.4; Targ. Onq and Pesh read מִשֵּׁם). Deliverance and help comes from God's "name," especially in war (cf. Psa 20:2, 8; 44:6; 54:3; 89:25; 118:10ff.; 124:8; Prov 18:10; 1 Sam 17:45; 2 Chron 14:10), for God, solemnly summoned by his name, hears and appears. For this reason, "name" is associated with "might" and "hand" (cf. 1 Kgs 8:42; Psa 54:3; Jer 16:21; Mic 5:3; cf. Giesebrecht, *A.T.liche Schätzung des Gottesnames*, 41ff.; Heitmüller, 34ff.). "Guardian of Israel's rock" can hardly be right (Ball) and is also metrically difficult (Sievers 1:406-407). The simplest assumption is probably that the older and later objectionable divine name "Rock of Israel" was replaced by the name "Guardian of Israel" which became common later, and that the two variants were combined in the text. "Rock of Israel" (like צור ישראל, Isa 30:29) may have been a cultic name in Bethel (Meyer, *Israeliten*, 284) and would, therefore, be well-suited for Joseph. "Shepherd of Israel" occurs in Psa 80:2 and "Guardian of Israel" occurs in Psa 121:4. Dillmann, Ball, and Kittel treat other conjectures. **25aα** וְיַעְזְרֶךָ means "so may he help you." **25aβ** Hebr mss, Sam, LXX, and Pesh read וְאֵל, as do many old and modern commentators. **25aγ,δ,b** The blessings parallel Deut 33:13-16. Grammatically, the word בִּרְכֹת could be taken as the accusative of יברכך (so Dillmann) or as the subj. of חהיין (v 26). Such lists of all "that the heart desires" sound quite wondrous to the Israelite ear. Heaven is to bless Joseph with rain and dew, the flood beneath with springs and wells (7:11). The Hebrew wants, then, water, much water, water above and below. This wish is characteristic for its climate. In the expression רבץ "to store," one hears echoes of the fact that תְהוֹם was once a monstrous animal (cf. above p. 105). This association of the highest and the deepest is clever by Hebrew standards. Sievers (1:496-97) theorizes that רֹבֵצֶת has found its way here from the parallel passage (Deut 33:13). This would make the scansion simpler. Kittel cautiously suggests the reading מִתָּחַת. The second wish is fertility for people and animals—that the womb bear children, that the breasts give milk to nourish them! One notes the divine epiphany. God blesses through fertility.

26 "The blessings of your father were greater <486> (exceeded, excelled) the blessings of the ancient mountains" (LXX reads הַרְרֵי עַד, cf. Deut 33:15; Hab 3:6 ‖ גִּבְעֹת עוֹלָם). But this makes no sense, destroys balance and parallelism, and should not be repeated (so with Meyer, *Israeliten*, 283n.2 contra Driver and Kautzsch³). One may perhaps suggest בִּרְכֹת אָב אַךְ גֶּבֶר וְעוּל. In the parallel, first the women, and now the men are blessed. For תַּאֲוַת it is better to read simply תְּבוּאֹת (as in Deut 33:14; Olshausen; Cheyne). The blessings are supposed to come on Joseph's head (Deut 33:16; תְּבוֹאֶנָה). The expression (also in Prov 10:6; 11:26) can probably be explained by the fact that one lays one's hand on the head to bless. Joseph is called the נָזִיר among his brothers. We do not quite know what a נָזִיר was in the ancient period. Yet, we can conclude from the story of Samson, the only Nazirite we know, that the נָזִיר was the Israelite champion and partisan who single-handedly fought Yahweh's wars (cf. Sellin, *Beiträge* II/1:131ff.; Schwally, *Heiliger Krieg*, 62-63, 101ff.; Stade, *Bibl. Theol.*, 133). Applied to Joseph, it would mean that he battled Israel's common enemies single-handedly; he was Israel's champion. The Nazirite wears consecrated hair. Consequently, Nazirite and "crown" are associated here. This is a clear sign that the old meaning of נָזִיר is to be accepted here, and not the later, weakened "consecrated, noble, prince" (Lam 4:7). This image, too, does not necessarily point to Joseph's monarchy, but is better understood against the "Judges period." Joseph already led the northern Israelite tribes during the entry into Canaan. The piece about Joseph is a unit in the understanding suggested here. The suggestions that vv 24b-26 (Fripp, ZAW 11: 262ff.), or vv 24b-26a (Sievers 2:362), or vv 24b, 25a (Meyer, *Israeliten*, 283) are insertions, or that vv 25-26 is borrowed from Deut 33:13ff. (Kautzsch³) are unnecessary.

27 *Concerning Benjamin.* Benjamin is glorified as a ravening (יִטְרָף pausal form, §29u) wolf. If he begins to eat in the morning, he has only eaten enough by evening to be ready to share. Benjamin was famed for robbing, probably the caravans that passed through his territory. Highway robbery was no shame for earliest Israel, but a heroic profession. Several of Israel's greatest heroes were sometime robbers. Remarkably, the saying contains two allusions to Saul's kingship.

28a,bα (up to אֲבִיהֶם). The subscription of R^J.

73. Jacob's Burial.
Conclusion of the Joseph Account 50:2-11, 14-26 JE

Source criticism. The two negotiations between Joseph and his brothers (vv 15-21, 24, 25) stem from E (Dillmann): אלהים (vv 19, 20, 24, 25); שׂטם (v 15 as in 27:41 E); לִפְנֵי מוֹתוֹ (v 16 as in 27:7, 10 E); הֲתַחַת אֱלֹהִים (v 19 as in 30:2 E); v 20 alludes to 45:5b, 7b E; כִּלְכֵּל (v 21 as in 45:11; 47:12 E); יֻלַּד עַל־בִּרְכַּיִם (v 23 as in 30:3 E); and the prediction of the Exodus (vv 24, 25 as in 48:21 E). Holzinger and Procksch also assume a dual strand here, but the text can be understood as a unified composition. Two sources are employed in the story of Joseph's burial. This is most evident in v 10, where the funeral lament for Jacob is recounted twice: "and they held a lament there" ‖ "and he arranged a mourning ceremony." Thus, two places for the lament are also mentioned: Goren-atad (v 10aα) and Abel-mizraim (v 11). V 10b (אֵבֶל) prepares for the latter verse (so far in agreement with Kautzsch-Socin, Kautzsch³). <487> Joseph's escort seems to be mentioned twice also (vv 7, 8 ‖ 9). According to one report, Joseph's brothers were present at the burial (vv 8, 14). Contrariwise, v 9, according to which Joseph was accompanied by knights, does not seem to assume the brothers' participation. Vv 15ff. E confirms this assumption. According to this passage, Joseph's brothers first learn in v 15 that their father has died and they meet Joseph for the first time after Jacob's death in vv 18ff. If they had already made the whole, long journey with him and buried their father together, they would have already seen how Joseph was disposed against them (contra Eerdmans, 70). Accordingly, one obtains for J the journey of Joseph and his brothers (vv 7, 8) and their return (vv 14, 22a). V 22b (‖ v 26a) may also belong to J. V 9 belongs to E. "Goshen" further indicates that v 8 stems from J. Vv 7, 8 seem to be overfilled. As the points of contact in wording show, vv 4-6 belong with vv 7, 14. אִם־נָא מָצָאתִי חֵן בְּעֵינֵיכֶם (v 4), דִּבֶּר בְּאָזְנֵי (v 4 as in 44:18), and the allusion to Joseph's oath (vv 5, 6; 47:29-31, J) also demonstrate that these verses belong to J. Similarly, one will attribute vv 1-3 to J because of יִשְׂרָאֵל in v 2. The seventy days of weeping (v 3) contradict the forty days of embalming and probably also the seven days of mourning (v 11). It seems most advisable, then, to assign vv 3b, 4aα, 10a to E and vv 10, 11 (הַכְּנַעֲנִי) and 26 (וַיַּחַנְטוּ אֹתוֹ) to J. בְּגֹרֶן הָאָטָד (v 11) is the addition of R^{JE} who wanted to equate the two names (Kautzsch-Socin; Procksch; Kautzsch³; Sievers 2:364). Procksch analyzes somewhat differently. He attributes vv 2a, 3a to E from the outset. But the "embalming" by the "physicians" (vv 2a, 2b, 3a and v 26—the latter, according to Procksch from E) belongs to the same source.

50:1 Cf. p. 450.

50:2-11, 14 *Jacob's burial.* The account has the purpose of combining two different traditions: on the one hand, the Joseph legend recounts that Jacob died in Egypt; on the other hand, however, there was an apparently older tradition which located the grave he dug for himself (v 5) in Canaan and which also maintained, of course, that he died in Canaan. The narrators harmonize. Jacob did, in fact, die in Egypt, but on his express wish, he was buried in Canaan through Joseph's faithfulness. This mourning at such a distance, therefore, evidences how little the old tradition had to do with Jacob's migration to Egypt (Meyer, *Israeliten*, 281). **2** The embalming is a specifically Egyptian element, of which the Joseph narrative contains many. The hearer is pleased at these foreign practices. The embalming was necessary here so that the corpse could survive the long transport. Is אֶת־הָרֹפְאִים an addition (Sievers 2:363)? **3a** This duration of the preparation of the mummy is also reported as a remarkable, even amazing foreign practice. How carefully must the Egyptians treat the corpse if they take forty days! As of yet, these forty days are not yet attested from Egyptian reports (cf. Erman, 431). **3b** The seventy days of weeping are to show how highly Joseph respected his father. Diodorus (*Bibl. hist.* I.72) mentions seventy-two days as the mourning period for the Egyptian king. The usual period of mourning in Israel (1 Sam 31:13; 1 Chron 10:12; Judith 16:24; Sir 22:12), as also in Babylonia (Hehn, *Siebenzahl und Sabbat*, 42), is seven days or only one or two days (Sir 38:17), in special cases a month (Num 20:29; Deut 21:13; 34:8). Concerning the mourning rites of the Egyptians see Erman, 431ff. **4** Joseph does not want to make this request of Pharaoh personally. Instead, he desires the intercession <488> of the court since his wish could be falsely interpreted: the departure from the land could easily seem to be an attempt at treason (therefore, the explicit statement וְאָשׁוּבָה). The idea may also stand in the background that Joseph, as a mourner unclean, could not appear before Pharaoh himself. LXX reads דַּבְּרוּ־נָא עָלַי (Sievers 2:363). V **5a** is a brief reprise of 47:29ff. Yet, one must also consider the possibility that v 5a is a fragment from the E report. מֵת הִנֵּה אָנֹכִי (as in 48:21; 50:24 [E]), the oath to bring the corpse to Canaan (as in 50:25), would support this conclusion. Between vv 5 and 6 a clause concerning the fact that the courtiers say this to Pharaoh is omitted as understood. Similarly, in prophetic style, when Yahweh commissions the prophet to do something, the execution of the command is often not recounted (Isa 7:3; 8:1; 22:15; 38:4-5). The courtiers speak to Pharaoh as though Joseph himself were speaking; Pharaoh speaks as though Joseph stood before him. This is authentic Hebrew idiom (Ehrlich).

7, 8 The list of the great entourage (like the wagons and the knights **9** E) is to honor Joseph and Jacob. The narrator (especially in v 7b) bit off a mouth full (the זִקְנִים of the royal house as in 2 Sam 12:17). The description of the exceedingly solemn weeping which even the Canaanites notice in vv **10, 11** has the same purpose. Mourning rites are often portrayed in Egyptian graves (e.g., Erman, *Ägypten*, 432-33). V 11 offers an etymological feature. The name Abel-mizraim (i.e., "pasture of the Egyptians") is explained as *'ebel miṣraim*, "sorrow of the Egyptians." The place is so called because the Egyptians mourned Jacob there. The location of both places is unknown. The current text does not suggest that Jacob's grave was at the same place. But, at any rate, it must have been quite nearby. If the source analysis proposed is correct, then Goren-atad [EVV "threshing floor of Atad"] is to be sought near Rachel's grave in the vicinity of Ephrath (cf. comments on 48:7). Eusebius (Lagarde, *Onom. sacra*², 85:15ff. [p. 121]; Klostermann, 8) maintains that the location is Bethagla, now *'Ain Ḥagla*, south of Jericho (cf. Buhl, *Palästina*, 180). This is hardly likely. Accordingly, Abel-mizraim must have been located "beyond the Jordan" (v 11), perhaps near Penuel and Mahanaim. This region, located not far from the Jordan, can indeed be included in "Canaan" (vv 5, 11) in the broader sense. When the two names Abel-mizraim and Goren-atad stood together in the book, they were naturally equated. Consequently, "beyond the Jordan" (v 10) was added (Kautzsch-Socin; Procksch; Sievers

2:364). The name "Abel-mizraim" (with a genitive modifier because there are many "Abels" in Palestine; several places with this name also occur in the Egyptian lists; Meyer, *Israeliten*, 280n.1) is interesting. The name should probably be seen as a final remnant from the period of Egyptian dominion in Canaan <489> (cf. the German "Schwedenschanze"). שָׁמָּה (Sam and Pesh שָׁמוֹ) is supposed to refer to גֹּרֶן. The original text must have read שֵׁם הַמָּקוֹם or the like. JE's report of the burial itself is not preserved in favor of P's. V **14b** is absent in LXX mss, "laboriously connected" (Holzinger), probably an addition (Sievers 2:364).

15-21 *Another variation concerning the motif of Joseph's relationship with his brothers.* This motif is so enchanting to the narrator that he takes it up once again in order to show the form this relationship took after Jacob's death. The narrator gladly emphasizes once again that the brothers were afraid (cf. comments on 42:22ff.; 44:13; etc.). They think that Joseph's cordiality toward them was only based on consideration for their father and would now transform into an even more frightful wrath. Further, the narrator utilizes the opportunity to report how they confess their crime and ask for forgiveness (v 17). E had not yet said this previously (Gen 45) and probably intentionally reserved it for this scene. The brothers' fear of Joseph even after Jacob's death is indicative of the narrator's whole understanding: if he had primarily wanted to portray the brothers' improvement, he would have added how a new, positive relationship now developed between Joseph and his brothers. But there is no mention of this. Instead, he emphasizes once again the brothers' fear of Joseph and their guilty consciences. The account is divided into several scenes: (1) a conversation among the brothers (v 15), (2) then the brothers' embassy to Joseph—at first, they do not dare to go to him personally; they appeal to their fathers' final wish (E will have mentioned this previously; it is probably not understood as a lie, but as a "supplementation") and to their common God; the latter is very characteristic: a common cult binds people together most strongly, more than even brotherhood (vv 16, 17), 3) when Joseph seems touched, they come themselves. Now the narrator takes up the main motif once again: they prostrate themselves before him and offer themselves as his servants (the same in J, 44:16). This is once again the situation Joseph had envisioned in the dream. Thus the end refers back to the beginning. But Joseph once again demonstrates his nobility: he refrains from revenge. God, himself, has judged! "Am I in God's place?" (30:2) does not mean that judgment and punishment are God's alone. Instead, it means, "I am not in a position to thwart God's plans; God's plans now are salvation and deliverance." And, once more, he expresses the basic ideas of the narrative. They meant it for evil, but according to God's plan, it has turned out for good (cf. 45:5-7). It is certainly an accomplishment that the author rises to express such ideas. But one should note that he finds, not an abstract statement, but a very concrete one. The abstract statement, the belief that God can weave even human beings' sins into his mysterious fabric, would surely have been entirely inaccessible to him. **16** For וַיְצַוּוּ LXX and Pesh read וַיִּגְּשׁוּ. Ball, Holzinger (cautiously), and Procksh prefer the LXX reading. It seems, however, to be only a correction. **20** Sam, LXX, Pesh, and Vulg read וְהָאֱלֹהִים (Ball). "The great <490> people" is Jacob's family (45:7). The old narrative hardly intends the Egyptians. **21** The presumption here and in v 20 is that the famine still continues.

22-26 *Joseph's age and death.* **22a** J continues v 14. If attributed to E, the statement would make no sense. **22b** According to the Egyptian idea, 110 years are the limits of the human life span (cf. Stern, *Zeitschr. f. äg. Spr. u. Alt.* [1873]:75-76). A ripe old age: God favored him. **23-26** Joseph's death, a harmonious, pleasant conclusion. **23** Joseph is able to see his great-grandchildren; he sees his family blossom before he goes to the grave: a beautiful death. לְאֶפְרַיִם corresponds to לְאָמוֹ in 44:20. LXX, Vulg, Pesh, Targ. Onq, and Targ. Jon read "great-grandchildren." Instead of בְּנֵי שִׁלֵּשִׁים "great-great-grandchildren," one should probably read with Sam בָּנִים שׁ (Ball, Spurrell) since Machir's sons are also his great-grandchildren. Machir's sons were born on Joseph's knees. In the earliest understanding, this would mean that Joseph adopted them (cf. Stade, ZAW 6:145ff.). Machir is actually listed among the tribes of Israel in Judg 5:14 so that Machir's sons (i.e., the clans) could have been considered Joseph's sons in another system. Thus the legend creates a substitute for Joseph since Jacob adopted Manasseh and Ephraim (Meyer, *Israeliten*, 516). Concerning the tribe of Machir see Meyer, *Israeliten*, 516-17. For עַל־בִּרְכֵי Sam reads the weakened בִּימֵי, preferred by Holzinger and Kautzsch[3].

24, 25 *Joseph's final wish.* Here the motif of Jacob's testament (47:29-31; 48:21) is repeated and transformed: Joseph, too, predicts the exodus and the entry into Canaan which God promised the fathers. This allusion to the earlier accounts would stand very suitably here, at the end of the patriarchal legends, but it derives from the redactor (Dillmann: the diction is formulaic and recurs frequently, Exod 6:8; 33:1; Num 32:11; Deut 1:8; etc.; cf. Staerk, *Studien* 1:23). **24** Sam and LXX read והאלהים. **25** Here, too, the dying one requires an oath, not that he be brought immediately to Canaan, but that, one day, he be taken along. This is a small variation. The origin of this element will be the same as in the Jacob parallel. Joseph's grave was located in Canaan, specifically near Shechem (Josh 24:32). Consequently, the author feels obligated to show how Joseph's bones came from Egypt to Shechem. Joseph's wish is carried out (Exod 13:19; Josh 24:32). Concerning יִפְקֹד, an imperf. in a conditional clause, see §159c. Hebr mss, Sam, LXX, Pesh, Vulg, and Ball read אֶתְכֶם + מִזֶּה following Exod 13:19.

26 *Joseph's death.* וַיִּישֶׂם may be a passive (§73f). Sam, Kittel, and Kautzsch[3] read וַיּוּשַׂם; LXX, Pesh, Targ. Onq, and Ball read וַיָּשִׂימוּ. Concerning "the coffin" see §126r. Such wooden or stone sarcophagi, coffins, have been preserved. Sarcophagi are specifically Egyptian, unknown to the Hebrews (Benzinger[2], 127) and the ancient Arabs (Jacob, *Beduinenleben*[2], 139). The gradual ebbing of the account and the preparation for the subsequent Exodus narrative is beautiful. <491>

74. Account of Jacob (Joseph) in P
37:2 . . . 41:46a . . . 46:6, 7[8-27]; 47:5*, 6, 7-11 . . . 27b, 28; 48:3-6; 49:1a, 28b-33aα,b; 50:12, 13

Just as the Jacob narratives appear under the subscription "genealogy of Isaac" (p. 371), so now the Joseph narratives of P are treated under the superscription "genealogy of Jacob." Concerning the reason for this shift see p. 371. This superscription is tolerable because Jacob dies only at the end of the Joseph narratives.

Of the whole, the conclusion, Jacob's migration to Egypt, his testament, death, and burial are almost the only portions preserved for us. Only two comments concerning Joseph's experiences are preserved. R[JE,P] held primarily to JE here, then, just as in the Jacob narratives (cf. p. 371). This will be attributable to the fact that the Joseph narrative in P was very scanty. P had no interest in Joseph's adventures in Egypt and no ear for the tender, touching tone which resounds in these narratives.

As in the Abraham and Jacob narratives (cf. pp. 257, 371), P generally follows the tradition of J here, too. Jacob blesses all of his sons (49:28b; cf. 49:1-27 [J]); Jacob is buried by all his sons (49:29-32; 50:12f.; cf. 50:8 [J]). On the other hand, traditions from E can also be heard. Jacob remains in the best land of Egypt (47:6, 11; cf. 45:18, 20 [E]); Jacob adopts Ephraim and Manasseh (48:5f.; cf. v 16 [E]).

37:2 . . . 41:46a Only this fragment of P concerning Joseph's experiences in Egypt is transmitted. P is indicated by the superscription, אֵלֶּה תֹלְדוֹת, and the two numbers. Gen 37:2 belongs entirely to P. These clauses were originally intended to introduce an account of Joseph's abduction to Egypt which is clearly distinct form the J and E recension. According to it, not all the brothers (as in J and E) but only the sons of Bilhah and Zilpah sinned against Joseph. This is apparently an intentional alteration by P, who shifts the crime to the subordinate ancestors of the secondary tribes. The brothers' anger with Joseph is also given a different basis. Here they are angry with him because he informs on them to their father. E has the dreams at this point, J the sleeved garment. Furthermore, the information that Joseph was accustomed to tending the flocks together with his brothers cannot be accommodated to J and E according to whom he only went to them once as an exception (vv 13, 14). וְהוּא נַעַר אֶת־ makes no sense. One may read וְהוּא נֹעַר עַל, "he became angry about," namely, about their evil (cf. hithp. Job 17:8) or perhaps וְהוּא רֹעֶה, "and he had dealings with." In the narrator's opinion, Joseph's "tattling" is not intended to cast aspersions on Joseph. Concerning anarthrous רָעָה see §126z. **41:46a** The pedantic addition מֶלֶךְ־מִצְרַיִם characterizes P (Holzinger). "He appeared before him," that is, in his service (Gesenius[14], s.v. עמד 2d).

. . . 46:6, 7 *Jacob's move to Egypt.* רְכָשׁ, רְכוּשׁ, the grand expansiveness of the lists, and the parallels to 12:5; 31:18; 36:6 point to P. **6** Concerning מִקְנֵיהֶם see §93ss. <492>

46:8-27 *List of the seventy souls.* According to the tradition (Deut 10:22; Exod 1:1ff.), seventy souls came to Egypt. The number seventy (seventy-two) is also considered elsewhere the number of the chief clans of Israel (cf. the seventy elders, Exod 24:19; Num 11:16), of the nations (cf. above, p. 155), or of the epochs of the world (cf. above pp. 260-61). According to Hehn (*Siebenzahl und Sabbat*, 89-90) the number is of astronomical origins. The year of 360 (350) days fall into 72 (70) sections of five days each (cf. A. Jeremias, ATAO[2], 62; idem, *Babylonisches im N.T.*, 93). In spirit and diction (פַּדַּן אֲרָם v15; נֶפֶשׁ v 15, etc.; יָצְאֵי יְרֵכוֹ v 26), the piece is very close to P. P itself was satisfied with a general statement (Exod 1:1-5). P also speaks immediately previously (46:7) of Jacob's daughters and granddaughters, while the list only knows of one daughter (v 15) and one granddaughter (v 17). Thus, the passage likely derives from a later pen related to P (cf. Wellhausen, *Composition*[3], 51). The piece has it own history, as Dillmann has shown. Originally, Er and Onan were included among the children of Leah. In contrast, Dinah was omitted. Thus the sons of Leah total thirty-three. The other numbers are sixteen plus fourteen plus seven. The total number seventy, then, is the number of Jacob's children, not including Jacob, himself. The same is also true of Exod 1:4. A later hand first omitted Joseph and his sons from the accounting, since they did not come to Egypt with Jacob, and, in contrast, included Jacob. Similarly, Er and Onan (as already deceased) are also stricken from the accounting and Dinah was inserted. Thus, the number of the children of Leah amounts to thirty-two, those who immigrated with Jacob, sixty-six, and all Jacob's children total sixty-nine. This calculation contains the subtlety that the children of Leah (32) are twice as many as those of Zilpah (16), and those of Rachel (14) are twice as many as those of Bilhah (7). This editor is the source, then, of the following additions: יַעֲקֹב וּבָנָיו (v 8; but according to the preceding, it should be only the sons of Israel), v 12bα (the same clause in Num 26:19), וְאֵת דִּינָה בִּתּוֹ (v 15aγ, very awkward), וּבְנוֹתָיו (v 15b), שְׁשִׁים וָשֵׁשׁ (v 26), and v 27 through מִצְרַיְמָה. The (syntactically harsh) clause אֲשֶׁר through אֹן (v 20) is probably an addition. There are also many variations in the parallel lists (Exod 6:14-16; Num 26; 1 Chron 2-8). The information preserved here concerning the clans of Israel is, in part, of very dubious value. Reuben and Simeon, for example, had long since disappeared at that time and the great number of the clans of Benjamin is hardly historical. The author also knows only what we ourselves know about Judah (cf. Meyer, *Israeliten*, 299-300).

A list of Jacob's sons seems to have fallen out after v 8 (cf. 25:13; 35:33; Num 3:20).

9-15 *Leah's children*. **9** *Clans of Reuben* (Meyer, *Israeliten*, 532). חֲנוֹךְ (4:17; 5:18-24) is a clan in Midian (25:4). פַּלּוּא also appears in Num 26:8-9. חֶצְרוֹן is one of Judah's grandchildren (v 12). כַּרְמִי is a Judaean name (Josh 7:1). According to Steuernagel (*Isr. Stämme*, 18), the two clans of Hezron and Carmi are sometimes linked with Judah, sometimes with Reuben. **10** *Clans of Simeon* (cf. Meyer, 411n.2). יְמוּאֵל also appears in Exod 6:15; נְמוּאֵל in Num 26:12; 1 Chron 4:24. אֹהַד is missing in Num and Chron; it may be an error for צֹהַר (Kittel). For יָכִין 1 Chron 4:24 has יָרִיב. צֹהַר also appears in Exod 6:15. זֶרַח appears in Num 26:13; 1 Chron 4:24. צֹחַר is the father of the Hittite Ephron (23:8; 25:9). The "son of the Canaanite woman" is, therefore, it seems, a well-known figure. **12** *Clans* <493> *of Judah* (cf. Meyer, 432-33, 406). חֶצְרֹן is a city in Judah (Josh 15:25). For חמול Sam reads חמואל. **13** *Clans of Issachar* (cf. Meyer, 537). תּוֹלָע, Puah's son, is a judge from Issachar in Shamir (Judg 10:1). As an appellative it means "purple snail," "purple thing." The name of this "judge," his father, and his city seem to be taken from the clan names. פֻּוָּה also appears in Num 26:23. Sam, Pesh, and 1 Chron 7:1 read פוּאָה (Judg 10:1). According to Lagarde (*Mitteilungen* 3:281-82) it means "seaweed" (φῦκος, used to die wool). For עוב LXX, Sam, Num 26:24, 1 Chron 7:1, and qere read יָשׁוּב (Ball, Kittel). Steuernagel (13) and Meyer (537) associate שמרון with שָׁמִיר "in the mountains of Ephraim" (Judg 10:1) and שֹׁמְרוֹן, Samaria. **14b** *Clans of Zebulon* (cf. Meyer, 538). אֵילוֹן is a judge (Judg 12:11; Steuernagel, 14). **15** The redactor included Jacob himself here in order to obtain the number 33.

16-18 *Zilpah's sons*. **16** *Clans of Gad* (cf. Meyer, 532). For צְפִיוֹן Sam reads צפון, LXX Σαφων, and Num 26:15 צְפוֹן (cf. צְפוֹנִי Num 26:15). צָפוֹן (Josh 13:27; Judg 12:1) is a city east of Jordan. For אֶצְבֹּן Sam and Pesh read אצבעון; Num 26:16 has אָזְנִי. For אֲרוֹדִי Num 26:17 has אָרוֹד. **17** *Clans of Asher* (cf. Meyer, 541). יִשְׁוָה apppears here and in 1 Chron 7:30 and is absent from Num 26:44. Is it a variant for יִשְׁוִי (Holzinger)? The clan name בְּרִיעָה also occurs in Ephraim (1 Chron 7:23) and in Benjamin (1 Chron 8:13ff.). חֶבֶר and מִיכָאֵל (*sic*) also appear in 1 Chron 8:16-17 as a Benjamite clan, a situation explained by Steuernagel (30-31) in terms of Asher's old relationship with Ephraim and Benjamin. To חֶבֶר compare the *Habiri* of the Amarna correspondence.

Concerning מַלְכִּיאֵל, the southern Palestinian chief Milkili, see the Amarna correspondence again (bibliography in Gesenius[14]).

19-22 *Sons of Rachel.* **20** One may supplement וַיִּוָּלֵד in the current text with בָּנִים, perhaps. LXX also adds, following Num 26:29, 35-36, the sons and grandchildren of Manasseh and Ephraim, in all five souls. **21** *Clans of Benjamin* (cf. A. W. Hogg, *Jewish Quarterly Review* 11:102ff. (unavailable to me); Meyer, 431-32, 524). Only Becher and Gera are historically attested. בֶּכֶר is missing in 1 Chron 8:1 and is mentioned in Num 26:35 as Ephraim's son. (Saul, 1 Sam 9? and) Sheba, who rebelled against David (2 Sam 20:1) stem(s) from this clan. גֵּרָא is missing in Num 26:38; in 1 Chron 8:3, 5 it refers to a son of בֶּלַע. Ehud (Judg 3:15) and Shimei (2 Sam 16:5) stem from Gera. נַעֲמָן is a son of בֶּלַע in Num 26:40 and 1 Chron 8:4. For אֵהִי וָרֹאשׁ מֻפִּים Num 26:38-39 has אֲחִירָם and שְׁפוּפָם, 1 Chron 8:1 has אַחְרַח, and 1 Chron 8:5 has שְׁפוּפָן. For חֻפִּים Num 26:39 has חוּפָם and 1 Chron 8:5 has חוּרָם, a son of בֶּלַע. In Num 26:40 אַרְדְּ is a son of בֶּלַע; it is probably the equivalent of אַדָּר in 1 Chron 8:3. LXX mentions only βαλα, Χοβωρ (= בֶּכֶר) and Ασβηλ as Benjamin's sons, Γηρα, Νοεμαν, Αγχεις, Ρως, Μαμφειν, and Οφιμιν as Bala's sons, and Αραδ as Gera's son. Num 26:38-40 offers a third presentation (cf. above). The notion that Benjamin went to Egypt with ten sons is a harsh contrast to the Joseph narrative where Benjamin is a small boy. LXX, however, presents an even harsher contrast. According to it, he even has grandchildren. **22** For יֶלֶד Hebr mss, Sam, LXX, and Pesh have עֶלְדָּה (cf. v 20).

23-25 *Sons of Bilhah.* **23** *Tribe of Dan* (cf. Meyer, 430, 499n.1). וּבְנֵי appears, although only one name follows (cf. 36:25). For חֻשִׁים Num 26:42 has שׁוּחָם. 1 Chron 7:12 <494> lists חֻשִׁם under Benjamin. **24** *Clans of Naphtali* (cf. Meyer, 540). For שִׁלֵּם (as in Num 26:49) Sam and 1 Chron 7:13 read שַׁלּוּם.

26, 27 *Concluding totals.* **27** For יֶלֶד (cf. v 22; 35:26) Hebr mss, Sam, LXX, Pesh, Targ. Onq, VetLat, and Vulg read יֻלְּדוּ. LXX has five more souls for Joseph (cf. above), one less for Benjamin, includes Jacob in the total and arrives at seventy-five (so also Acts 7:14).

47:5*, 6a, 7-11 . . . 27b *Jacob in Egypt.* The current Hebrew text is smoothed. LXX mss still have the older text: 47:1-4, 5a (without לֵאמֹר), 6b (from J), yielding ἦλθον δὲ εἰς Αἴγυπτον πρὸς Ἰωσὴφ Ἰακὼβ καὶ οἱ υἱοὶ αὐτοί; καὶ ἤκουσεν Φαραω βασιλευς Αιγυπτου (= Hebr וַיִּשְׁמַע מִצְרַיְמָה אֶל-יוֹסֵף וּבָנָיו וְיַעֲקֹב וַיָּבֹאוּ פַּרְעֹה מֶלֶךְ מִצְרַיִם), it then continues with vv 5, 6a, 7ff. The fact that a source other than J speaks here is indicated by the doublets, particularly evident in the LXX text, and a few differences. There five of the brothers are presented to Pharaoh, here Jacob himself is. There Pharaoh sends them to Goshen, here Joseph sends them to the land of Ramses. The diction indicates that this source is P: יְמֵי שְׁנֵי חַיַּי (vv 8-9; cf. 25:7), מְגוּרִים (v 9), אֲחֻזָּה (v 11, very common in P), and the age given in v 9. In v 27b נֵאחֲזוּ and פָּרָה וְרָבָה speak for P. In this scene P follows the presentation of the J tradition. But, naturally, he did not adopt the roguish tone of the old legend. His portrayal is uniform in contrast to the vital portrayal of J, but it, nevertheless, has solemn dignity. Like a man of God, Jacob appears with a blessing before the king and he parts with a blessing once again. Pharaoh, however, is astonished to hear of his advanced age which was far exceeded by those of his fathers (Isaac 180, Abraham 175 years). This is a rather nicely conceived way to introduce Jacob's impressive age. **9** The statement "my life has been sorrowful" indicates that P must have previously recounted the distress he endured with Laban and the pain he suffered because of Joseph. **11** "The land of Ramses" is probably equivalent to Goshen (now *Wâdi Tûmîlât*, cf. p. 437). The capital city is "Ramses" (Exod 1:11) to be found in the vicinity of *Tell-el-kebîr* (cf. Gesenius[14]). The city of Ramses was built by king Ramses II to guard against the Cheta (Hittites; cf. Erman, 49-50, 78-79). According to J, Goshen is not the best land in Egypt, but a pastureland. <495>

47:28; 48:3-6; 49:1a, 28b-33aα,b; 50:12, 13 *Jacob's bequest, death, and burial.* The chronological information in 47:28 points to P as do the reference in 48:3-4 to 35:6a, 11, 12; the expressions אֵל שַׁדַּי (v 3), הִפְרְה וְהִרְבָּה (v 4), קְהַל עַמִּים (v 4), "your seed after you" (v 4), אֲחֻזַּת עוֹלָם (v 4), הוֹלִיד and מוֹלֶדֶת "descendants" (v 6), קְרָא אֶל (49:1a), the reference back to the Gen 23 Machpelah narrative in 49:29-33 and 50:13, as well as the expressions אֵיַוַח־קֶבֶר (v 40), נֶאֱסַף אֶל־עַמָּיו (v 29, 33), and גָּוַע (v 33). **47:28** The information concerning the age, such as P usually offers immediately before the report concerning the patriarch's death (9:28-29; 11:32; 23:1; 25:7; 35:28). Hebr mss and Sam read וַיִּהְיוּ (cf. 9:29; 11:32; 23:1 35:28; Ball; Kittel). שְׁנֵי חַיָּיו is a variant for יְמֵי יַעֲקֹב (quite similar to 23:1). The simpler יְמֵי is to be preferred on analogy with 9:29; 11:32; 35:28 (cf. Kautzsch[3]).

48:3-6 *Adoption of Ephraim and Manasseh in accord with the E tradition (cf. v 16).* This tradition interests P because it has significance for constitutional law. Jacob remembers the revelation at Luz because, on the force of this revelation, these instructions for his family also have significance for the people Israel and the land of Canaan. The sequence Ephraim-Manasseh is a remnant of the old tradition (v 20) if it does not derive from the redactor (Dillmann). Elsewhere, Manasseh usually occupies first position in P (Num 26:28ff.; 34:23-24; etc. contrast Num 1:10). **6** Those born later are considered sons of Ephraim or Manasseh. Such sons of Joseph do not appear elsewhere.

49:1a, 28bβ *Jacob blesses his sons, a remnant of the tradition of 49:1-28 J.* קְרָא אֶל appears in P (28:1). "Jacob called his sons and blessed them" resembles 28:1 "Isaac called Jacob and blessed him." V **28bβ** does not belong to J because every son does not receive a blessing there. אֲשֶׁר is absent in Hebr mss, Sam, LXX, Pesh, and Vulg. It is probably an error for אִישׁ (Franz Delitzsch, Ball, etc.).

49:29-32 *Jacob's instructions concerning his burial.* The sequence, summons, blessing, command, also occurs in 28:1. Dillmann (449) postulates that the original sequence may have been 49:1a (summons of the sons), 28bβ (blessing), 29aα ("he gave them a command"), 48:3-7 (adoption), and 49:29ff. (burial). According to Budde (ZAW 3:68), the sequence in P was 48:3-6 (brief transition), 49:29-32; 48:7; 49:33. Bruston (ZAW 8:203) wants to place the adoption after 49:32. In the event one should undertake to rearrange the text, the latter proposal is preferable. It is, however, not entirely necessary. **29** אֶל־עַמִּי, otherwise consistently a plural, should therefore probably be read עַמִּי (Ball, Holzinger, etc.). In **29-32** the text has been disrupted by interpolated variants: אֶת־הַשָּׂדֶה (v 30; as in 50:13) is the addition of a reader for whom the text was not precise enough (§138b n.1). A later reader then expanded it in v 32 (missing in the Vulg). Vv 29b and 30aα are also variants. Similarly, the relative clause in 50:13, which separates עַל־פְּנֵי מַמְרֵא from its proper context, is an addition to which אֶת־הַשָּׂדֶה was then added. **31** The fact that Rachel is not mentioned among the ancestors who rest at Machpelah <496> may be a remnant of tradition (one should consider that Rachel's grave is located very near to Jerusalem), but it can also be a redactional correction (Budde, ZAW 3:82ff.).

    49:33aα,b; 50:12, 13 *Jacob's death and burial.* Quite characteristically for P, only Jacob's sons, no Egyptians, bury Jacob. Concerning 50:13 see the comments on 49:29-32.

Indexes

Biblical Passages

<498>

Hebrew Words

Genesis
by Hermann Gunkel
translated by Mark E. Biddle

Mercer University Press, 6316 Peake Road, Macon, Georgia 31210-3960.
Isbn 0-86554-517-0. Catalog and warehouse pick number: MUP/H400.
Text and interior design, composition, and layout by Edmon L. Rowell, Jr.
Cover and dust jacket design and layout by Smyth & Helwys Publishing.
Dust jacket illustration: *The Birth/Creation of Adam*, Sistine Chapel fresco
    by Michelangelo Buonarotti (1475–1564).
Camera-ready pages composed on a Gateway 2000
    via dos WordPerfect 5.1 and WordPerfect for Windows 5.1/5.2
        and printed on a LaserMaster 1000.
Text fonts: TimesNewRomanPS 10/12; ATECH Hebrew and Greek.
    Display font: TimesNewRomanPS bf.
Printed and bound by Braun-Brumfield Inc., Ann Arbor, Michigan 48106,
    via offset lithography on 50# Natural Hi-Bulk ppi 400.
Smyth sewn and cased into Arrestox C 11400 (gray) cloth,
    one-hit foil stamping on spine and c. 4 with gold foil S19.
Dust jacket printed four-color process, and film laminated.

[June 1997]

050997elr